A Descriptive Bibliography of the Works of Emanuel Swedenborg

A Descriptive Bibliography of the Works of Emanuel Swedenborg 1688–1772

VOLUME TWO

Edited and compiled by
NORMAN RYDER

The Swedenborg Society
20-21 Bloomsbury Way
London WC1A 2TH

2012

Edited and compiled by Norman Ryder

Published by:
The Swedenborg Society
Swedenborg House
20-21 Bloomsbury Way
London WC1A 2TH

Typeset at Swedenborg House
Book design: Stephen McNeilly
Printed and bound in Great Britain at
T J International, Padstow

ISBN 978-0-85448-175-0
British Library Cataloguing-in-Publication Data
A catalogue record for this book is available
from the British Library

GENERAL OUTLINE OF CONTENTS

CONTENTS OF VOLUME TWO

INTRODUCTION

The principles adopted in the compilation of the *Bibliography* are to be found in my Introduction to Volume 1, and I invite those who use Volume 2 to reacquaint themselves with what I stated there.

My thanks are due to the earliest readers of Volume 1 for their encouraging comments. I am grateful to the editors of *Things Heard and Seen* [1] and of *The Annual Journal of the New Church Historical Society* [2] who have published respectively my addresses to the Swedenborg Publishers Conference in June 2010 and the Swedenborg Society's Road Show in Manchester in April 2011.

The Contents of Volume 2

This volume describes the editions and versions of the works which Swedenborg composed from 1743 to 1755. In this period he moved more and more from his scientific and philosophical interests into the religious preoccupations to which he devoted the remainder of his life.

This is illustrated in his letter to Anders Johan von Höpken dated 10 April 1760, accompanying his gift of Jan Swammerdam's *Biblia Naturae*:

> Den boken tienar mig hädanefter intet ehra till nytta, emedan jag wendt mina tanckar ifrän Naturalia till Spiritualia. <This book will be of no use to me hereafter for I have turned my thoughts from natural things to spiritual.> [3]

The composition of the works described in this volume also shows how Swedenborg retained his interest in and sense of responsibility for serving his country in the House of Nobles of the Swedish Diet, as he would continue to do even until 1761.

Special problems in publishing Volume 2

From the start of my work on the *Bibliography* I knew that we would face a major problem in regard to versions of Swedenborg's works translated into languages other than those of Western Europe, especially those whose character sets are syllabic, not alphabetical. [4]

I thank the Swedenborg Society for obtaining the services of professional linguists so that we are able to provide quasi-facsimile transcriptions of the title information of such volumes, as indicated in my Introduction to Volume 1. [5] In addition, transcriptions of Japanese characters have been provided by Mika Shibata, and transcriptions of Georgian and Malayalam characters have been provided by the translators of the works concerned.

We meet the first examples of versions in such languages in Volume 2: versions in Greek, Slavonic languages in Cyrillic alphabets, and Gujarati, Japanese, and Korean.

Ongoing research

In my Introduction to Volume 1 (pp xvi-xvii, xxviii) I noted the use of the *Bibliography* to researchers into the history of printing and publishing. While preparing Volume 2 my attention was drawn to the archives preserved at North of England New Church House in Manchester. This body originated in 1782 as 'The Society of Gentlemen'. [6] The archives include a ledger with entries dated from 1782 to 1800, which record the names of booksellers trading in London, Manchester, Sheffield, Bristol, Bolton, Edinburgh, Liverpool, Birmingham, and Hull, who placed orders for the Society's publications in this period.

In my address 'The Stories in the Book(s)', referred to above, [7] I described how publishers used to name on the title page of a book the booksellers who had placed prepublication orders for copies of it, and how on occasion different booksellers would be named on a limited number of copies of an issue. A comparison of the information recorded in the ledger with surviving copies of the books which they had purchased may shed light on this and other practices of booksellers and publishers.

The flow of new editions and versions

The continuing efforts of Swedenborgian publishers worldwide are to be welcomed; and we have recorded recently issued editions and versions of the works described in this volume as far as it has been possible for us to do so.

As the flow of new editions and versions of Swedenborg's works continues, the *Bibliography* will never be complete. Our long-term aim is to make the *Bibliography* available online, updating its contents as the new publications are produced. Meanwhile, users of the *Bibliography* are invited to register with the Swedenborg Society to receive regular supplements describing additions to the volumes published in previous years.

Conclusion

Since publication of Volume 1 in 2010 most of my work has been conducted at home. I thank my wife Pamela, my 'engine', for her patience and forbearance over the many hours which I have spent in my study as I have continued to compile and edit my descriptions of the contents of the veritable cornucopia of Swedenborg's works old and new.

I have continued to benefit from the assistance of librarians and scholars in Europe and the United States. Above all, I am indebted to Stephen McNeilly and James Wilson who never fail to meet my requests for information. James, in particular, deals with my pleas to incorporate amendments to my text, no matter how late in the process of typesetting I make them: how he manages to maintain his equanimity I cannot imagine. I affirm my debt to them for their continuing support and encouragement

The author of the Book of Ecclesiastes was correct when he wrote, 'Of the making of many books there is no end,' but not in his conclusion to the verse. [8]

Norman Ryder
Chester July 2012

ENDNOTES

1 *Things Heard and Seen* Newsletter of the Swedenborg Society, no 32 Summer 2010, pp 36-40: 'The Story of the Book(s)'.

2 *The Annual Journal of the New Church Historical Society for the Year 2012,* pp 87-94: 'The Stories in the Book(s)'.

3 Quoted in my editorial introduction to 50/01 *On Influx. Bybel der Natuure* by Jan

Swammerdam (1637-1680) was translated into Latin and published in 1737-1738 by Herman Boerhaave (1668-1737) as *Biblia Naturae sive Historia Insectorum* (The Book of Nature, or The History of Insects).

4 Volume 1, pp xxvi-xxvii.

5 Volume 1, p xxv.

6 The Society of Gentlemen: its full title was 'The Society of Gentlemen formed for the express purpose of printing and publishing the Theological Works of Emanuel Swedenborg, now translated into English, and other writings which inculcate the true Christian Life and doctrines'. See D K and M McCallum, *New Church House and its origins 1782-1982* published by The North of England New Church House, Manchester, March 1982.

7 See note 2.

8 Ecclesiastes 12:12.

LISTS OF ABBREVIATIONS

1. Abbreviations for languages

Ar Arabic
Be Bengali
Bg Bulgarian
Br Braille
BrEn English Braille
BrDu Dutch Braille
Bu Burmese
Ch Chinese
Cr Croatian
Cz Czech
Da Danish
Du Dutch
En English
EnSh English Shorthand, Isaac Pitman's character set
Es Esperanto
Fi Finnish
Fr French
Ge German
Gg Georgian
Gk Greek
Gu Gujarati
Hi Hindi
Hu Hungarian
Ic Icelandic
Il Ilukano, a language of the Philippines
It Italian
Ja Japanese
Ko Korean
La Latin
LaDu Latin Dutch bilingual edition
LaEn Latin English bilingual edition
LaEnJa Latin, English, and Japanese texts or versions in the same volume
LaFr Latin French bilingual edition
LaKo Latin Korean bilingual edition
LaSw Latin Swedish bilingual edition
La&Sw Latin and Swedish texts in the same volume
La&Sw&En Latin, Swedish, and English texts or versions in the same volume
Lv Latvian <formerly termed 'Lettish'>
Ma Malayalam
Ne Nepali
No Norwegian
Nu Nupe, a language of Nigeria

Pl	Polish	Ta	Tamil
Pt	Portuguese	Ts	Tswana, a language of Southern Africa
Ro	Romanian		
Ru	Russian	Ua	Ukrainian
Se	Serbian	Ur	Urdu
SeCr	Serbo-Croatian	We	Welsh
So	Sotho	Yo	Yoruba
Sw	Swedish	Zu	Zulu

2. Abbreviations for the names of countries and of libraries and institutions

UK **The United Kingdom of Great Britain and Northern Ireland**

SOC	The Swedenborg Society, London
BL	The British Library, London
BOD	The Bodleian Library, Oxford
CAM	The University, Cambridge
CHE	Chester Society of the New Church
CHT	Chetham's Library, Manchester
CON	The General Conference of the New Church, London
CRS	The former Camden Road Society of the New Church
FIT	FitzWilliam College, Cambridge
GUI	The Guildhall, London
LINN	The Linnean Society, London
LON	University College, London
MER	Merton College, Oxford
NCC	New Church College, Radcliffe, Manchester
NCH	New Church House, Manchester
PUR	Purley Chase Centre, Mancetter, Atherstone
RSO	The Royal Society for the Advancement of Scientific Knowledge, London
RYL	John Rylands University Library of Manchester
WIL	Dr Williams's Library, London
WOR	Worcester, College, Oxford
NR	Personal collection of Norman Ryder

Europe

CZE **Czech Republic**

LM	Lenka Máchová
PM	Petra Maříková

DEN **Denmark**

RLD	Det Kongelige Bibliotek <The Royal Library>, Copenhagen

FRA	**France**	
	BNF	Bibliothèque nationale de France, Paris
GER	**Germany**	
	BAV	Landesbibliothek, Bavaria
	BER	Landesbibliothek, Berlin
	DNF	Deutsche Nationalbibliothek <National Library of Germany>, Frankfurt/Main
	FRE	Technische Universität Bergakademie Freiburg <Freiburg School of Mining>
	FUB	Universitätsbibliothek Freiburg im Breisgau
	GRE	Greifswald Universitätsbibliothek
	GSU	Niedersächsische Staats- und Universitätsbibliothek, Göttingen
	HAM	Universitätsbibliothek, Hamburg
	HEI	Universitätsbibliothek, Heidelburg
	KAR	Gewerbebücherei des Landesgewerbeamtes Baden-Württemberg, Karlsruhe
	REG	Staatliche Bibliothek, Regensburg
	VER	Swedenborg Verlag, Moos-Weiler
	WLB	Württembergische Landesbibliothek, Stuttgart
HUN	**Hungary**	
	KSE	Könyvtár Szabó Ervin, Pesch, Budapest
	KTA	Könyvtára Theologiai Akademia, Debrecen
IRE	**Ireland**	
	TRI	Trinity College, Dublin
LAT	**Latvia**	
	RIG	Latvijas Nacionala Biblioteka <Latvian National Library>, Riga
NET	**Netherlands**	
	BOE	Swedenborg Boekhuis, Breda / Baarle Herzog / Baarle Nassau
	GEN	Swedenborg Genootschap <Swedenborg Society>, The Hague
	KB	Koninklijke Bibliotheek <Royal Library> The Hague
	THY	Bibliotheek van Joannes Thysius <Thysian Library>, Leyden
POL	**Poland**	
	BNW	Biblioteka Naradowa <National Library>, Warsaw
	BUW	Biblioteka Uniwersytecka w Warszie <University Library>, Warsaw
	GDA	Biblioteka Gdansk Polska Academia Nauk <Library of the Polish Academy of Sciences>, Biblioteka Glówna Uniwersytetu Gdanskiego <University Library>, Gdansk
	JAG	Biblioteka Jagiellońska <Jagiellonian Library>, Cracow
	LUB	Biblioteka Uniwersytet Lubelski <Catholic University Library>, Lublin
	POZ	Biblioteka Raczynskiego <Raczynski Library>, Poznan

RUS **Russia**

RAS Российская Академия Наук <Russian Academy of Sciences>, St Petersburg

SPA **Spain**

MAD Hemeroteca Municipal de Madrid <Municipal Library of Madrid>

SAL Archivo de la Guerra Civil <Archive of the Civil War>, Salamanca

SWE **Sweden**

ROY Kungliga Biblioteket <The National Library of Sweden>, Stockholm

COM Board of Commerce, Stockholm

GDA Göteborg Domkapitlets Arkiv <Gothenburg Cathedral Archives>

GEN Stockholm Society of the General Church of the New Jerusalem

GGY Gymnasium-Biblioteket <Senior High School Library>, Göteborg

GSB Göteborgs Stadsbiblioteket <Gothenburg City Library>

GUB Göteborgs Universitets Biblioteket <University Library>, Gothenburg

HNK Swedenborgs Biblioteket Herrens Nya Kyrka <The Swedenborg Library, the Lord's New Church>, Stockholm

KVA Kungl Vetenskapsakademien <The Royal Swedish Academy of Sciences>, Stockholm

LIN Stifts-Biblioteket <Diocesan Library>, Linköping

LUN Universitets Biblioteket <University Library>, Lund

NBS Nykyrkliga Bokförlaget, Stockholm

NRO National Records Office <includes Archives of the Board of Mines>, Stockholm

RIA Riksarkivet <The State Archives of Sweden>, Stockholm

SKA Stifts-Biblioteket <Diocesan Library>, Skara

SUB Universitets Biblioteket <University Library>, Stockholm

UPP Universitets Biblioteket <University Library>, Uppsala

VIS Stifts-Biblioteket <Diocesan Library>, Visby

SWI **Switzerland**

LAU La Nouvelle Église, Lausanne

ZÜR Swedenborg Centrum, Zürich

UKR **Ukraine**

DNE Swedenborg Centre, Dnepropetrovsk

North and South America

USA **The United States of America**

ANC The Swedenborg Library, Academy of the New Church, Bryn Athyn PA

	CGR	The Library of Congress, Washington DC
	FOU	The Swedenborg Foundation, West Chester PA
	JPC	John Pitcairn Archives, Bryn Athyn PA
	MNC	Massachusetts New Church Union, Boston MA
	NOV	The Lord's New Church which is Nova Hierosolyma, Bryn Athyn PA
	NYC	Columbia University, New York
	PRI	Princeton University NJ
	SHS	The Swedenborgian House of Studies, Berkeley CA
	SSA	Swedenborg Scientific Association, Bryn Athyn PA
BRA	**Brazil**	
	RIO	Rio de Janeiro Society of the New Church

Rest of the World

AUS	**Australia**	
	SYD	The New Church Enquiry Centre, North Ryde, Sydney NSW
NZ	**New Zealand**	
	WEL	Alexander Turnbull Library, Wellington
MAU	**Mauritius**	
	CUR	La Nouvelle Église, Curepipe
	PLO	La Nouvelle Église, Port Louis
SA	**South Africa**	
	MMC	Mooki Memorial College, Orlando, Soweto

3. Abbreviations for the names of American States

AL	Alabama
CA	California
CT	Connecticut
DC	District of Columbia
IL	Illinois
IN	Indiana
MA	Massachusetts
MD	Maryland
ME	Maine
MN	Michigan
MT	Montana
NJ	New Jersey
NY	New York
OH	Ohio
PA	Pennsylvania
SC	South Carolina
TN	Tennessee

4. Symbols and general abbreviations

< >	indicates editorial insertions in transcribed title matter, and editorial notes elsewhere
<< >>	indicates title matter which has not been transcribed but has been recorded or deduced from other sources
ACSD	The Academy Collection of Swedenborg Documents, in the Swedenborg Library, Bryn Athyn PA
ast(s)	asterisk(s)
BAPB	Bryn Athyn Post-Bibliography, in the Swedenborg Library, Bryn Athyn PA, and the Swedenborg Society, London
c	circa
ch	chapter(s)
d	died
edn	edition
eg	for example
et seq	and following
f, ff	following
ibid	the same place
ie	that is
ISBN	International Standard Book Number
ISSN	International Standard Serial Number
jnr	junior
mf	microfilm
mm	millimetre(s)
MS, MSS	manuscript, manuscripts
n, no(s)	number, paragraph number
nd	no date
NR	Norman Ryder, in references to the printers' ornaments described in Appendix A
O	Original <MS>
orn	ornament
p, pp	page, pages
snr	senior
vol, vols	volume, volumes
wf	wrong font

5. Paper formats and sizes

a. The technical terms used to describe the number of leaves into which the sheets have been folded.

folio		folded once, making 2 leaves/4 pages to a section
4to	quarto	folded twice with the second fold at right angles to the first, making 4 leaves/8 pages

6mo	sixmo	folded six times to make 6 leaves/12 pages
8vo	octavo	folded three times with the second and third folds at right angles to the previous fold, making 8 leaves/16 pages
12mo	duodecimo	folded in a number of ways, making 12 leaves/24 pages
16mo	sextodecimo	folded in a number of ways, making 16 leaves/32 pages
24mo	vicesimo-quarto	folded in a number of ways, making 24 leaves/48 pages
32mo	tricesimo-secundo	folded in a number of ways, making 32 leaves/64 pages

b. The sheets of paper used in printing are of various sizes, and the technical terms for them are based on their measurement in inches. In modern printed books these terms are not given. The terms are also used to indicate the sizes of notebooks prepared for manuscript drafts.

The principal sizes are as follows:

double royal	40 x 25 inches
double demy	35.5 x 22.5 inches
double large post	33 x 21 inches
double crown	30 x 20 inches
double foolscap	27 x 17 inches
imperial	30 x 22 inches
super or large royal	27 x 20 inches
royal	25 x 20 inches
medium	24 x 19 inches
demy	22.5 x 17.5 inches
large post	21 x 16.5 inches
crown	20 x 15 inches
post	19 x 15.5 inches
foolscap	17 x 13.5 inches
pott	15 x 12 inches

For example: a sheet of demy paper folded once is termed demy folio, and makes 2 leaves/4 pages c 17 x 11 inches

a sheet of demy paper folded twice is termed demy 4to, and makes 4 leaves/8 pages c 11 x 8.5 inches

The principal metric sizes are as follows:

A3	297 x 420 mm
A4	210 x 297 mm
A5	148 x 210 mm

A GLOSSARY OF BIBLIOGRAPHICAL TERMS

author's colophon:	a colophon in a MS, distinguished by the absence of any mention of printing
brace:	a piece of type used to indicate where a single line of type is changed into 2 or more lines
catchword:	a word printed below the last line of a page (aligned to the right margin) which is the first word of the succeeding page, as a guide for the binder
codex:	a manuscript volume
colophon:	an inscription at the end of a text giving the name of the printer and the date and place of printing
device:	a cast, carved, or engraved piece of type used by the printer or publisher as a distinguishing mark of his work, as a kind of trademark, also termed a logo
factotum:	an ornamental block with a hollow centre into which a piece of type or a printer's ornament can be inserted
font:	a complete set of one size of one design of type
forme:	type pages locked in the metal frame or chase of a printing machine ready for printing
gathering:	the group of leaves which results from the folding of a whole sheet, part of a sheet, or more than one sheet to form the sewing unit of a book
gothic, or black letter:	a group of types distinct from roman and italic
half title:	a leaf which usually precedes the title leaf and bears a short form of the title
impression:	all copies printed from the same type at any one time, eg '3rd impression of the 2nd edition'
imprint:	a statement which records the names of those associated with the printing, publishing, and selling of the book; now usually on the title leaf, it may also be found at the end of the book; see also 'colophon'

issue:	printed sheets of an impression to which new matter has been added or of which the arrangement is different from the book when first printed
italic:	type in which the letters slope to the right
leaf:	2 pages, one on the recto of a leaf and one on the verso; a leaf can be missing from a copy, a page cannot be
ornament:	carved wood or engraved metal pieces of type used to embellish the printed text
prepublication state:	copies of a book containing faulty printing discovered before distribution for sale, but accidentally distributed and not returned to the publisher
recto:	the right-hand page of an open book; the other side of the leaf is the verso
reissue:	original sheets of an impression issued for sale at a later date and differentiated in some way such as having a different paperback binding
roman:	ordinary, upright printed type
rule:	a strip of type-high metal used to print a line, either continuous or patterned; rules may also be used to provide a frame containing all or part of the matter printed on a title page
running head:	a line of type at the top of a page above the text
section title:	a leaf or page preceding a sub-section or part of a book
signature:	the series of letters which are found, normally below the last line of text, on at least the first page of each gathering, in books printed up to the end of the 20th century, though not usually printed in books nowadays
state:	otherwise identical copies of an edition in which changes were made before it was placed on sale; these changes can range from corrections made when errors have been discovered before all copies were printed (considered to be of the same issue) to the composition of a different title page for a specified bookseller for whom a specific number of copies have been printed
title page:	the recto of an early leaf in a book, on which is printed the official title of the book; also printed may be the names of the author/editor/translator and printer/publisher, and the place and date of publication; in modern books, important detail of this nature is printed on the verso
turned letters:	individual type letters placed upside down or sideways in the forme; they are treated as misprints and are noted at the end of the transcript

variants:	differences between copies which might be supposed to be identical, such as variant title pages and textual variants
version:	a translation from one language to another
verso:	the left-hand page of an open book; the other side of the leaf is the recto
wrong font:	individual type letters taken from a different font, treated as misprints and noted at the end of the transcript

Section C:
Bibliographical Descriptions, 1743-1755

43/01 The Generative Organs Hyde CXVIII

The autograph MS forms a major part of Codex 53 in the Library of the Royal Swedish Academy of Sciences, Stockholm.

Swedenborg marked the leaves of the MS 'llll-yyyy, aaaa-kkkk', as far as p 24. The first 22 chapters, written on c 85 leaves, are no longer extant.

In *De Sensu Communi* <44/01/La O/1> Swedenborg wrote on p 80, 'In caeteris vide excerpta mea priora' <For further details see my earlier excerpts> (at the end of the article *De Aure et Sensu Auditus*), and on p 92, 'Vide etiam priora excerpta' <See also the earlier excerpts> (at the beginning of the article *De Coloribus*, part of *De Oculo et Visu*). The excerpts referred to are those in chapters 25 and 26 of the present work, which were both uncompleted.

LATIN

Editions:

La O MS
La 1 J F I Tafel, editor

43/01/La O/1 1743 Hyde 406, 3000

<<ANATOMIA CORPORIS: DE PERIOSTEO, MAMMIS, MEMBRIS GENITALIBUS, DEQUE ORGANIS QUINQUE SENSUUM AGUNT.>>

double foolscap oblong 8vo <330 x 102 mm>

text: cap 23 De Periosteo, pp 2a-4b.
cap 24 De Mammis, pp 5a-10b.
cap 25 De Aure et Auditu <uncompleted>, pp 10b-24b.
<cap 26 De Oculo et Visu> <uncompleted>, pp 25a-44b.
cap 27 Arteriae spermaticae, pp 45a-47b.
cap 28 De Testiculis, epididymidibus, pp 48a-57a.
cap 29 De Scroto, pp 57b-59b.
cap 30 De Vasis deferentibus, pp 60a-62b.
cap 31 De Vesiculis seminalibus, pp 63a-71a.
cap 32 De Prostatis, pp 71b-75a.
cap 33 De Urethra, pp 75a-78b.
cap 34 De Pene et corporibus cavernosis, pp 79a-86b.
cap 35 De Semine virili, pp 87a-90b.
cap 36 De Membris genitalibus mulierum externis, pp 91a-96a.
cap 37 De Utero, pp 96b-97b, 98b-105a; p 98a blank.

cap 38 De Ovariis, pp 105b-106b.
cap 39 De Tubis Fallopianis, pp 106b-110b.
cap 40 De Utero <plura>, pp 111a-117a.
cap 41 De Placenta uterina, pp 117b-124b.
cap 42 De Chorio, Amnio et hujus liquore, pp 125a-129b.
cap 43 De Funiculo umbilicali, pp 130a-134a.
cap 44 De Statu embryonis, ejusque inchoamentis, communiter, pp 134b-137b.

An unpublished copy has been recorded as follows.

1 SWE: KVA A MS transcript of the text of cap 25-26 made by G Ekelöf.

MS not seen; description deduced from La O/2 and Hyde 406.

SWE: KVA

43/01/La 1/1 **1849** Hyde 410

EMAN. SWEDENBORGII, | SACRAE REGIAE MAJESTATIS REGNIQUE SUECIAE | COLLEGII METALLICI ASSESSORIS, | REGNUM ANIMALE | ANATOMICE, PHYSICE ET PHILOSOPHICE | PERLUSTRATUM. | CUJUS | SUPPLEMENTUM | SIVE | PARTIS SEXTAE | SECTIO PRIMA | DE PERIOSTEO ET DE MAMMIS | AGIT. | <short rule> | E CHIROGRAPHO EJUS | IN BIBLIOTHECA REGIAE ACADEMIAE HOLMIENSIS | ASSERVATO | NUNC PRIMUM EDIDIT | Dr. JO. FR. IM. TAFEL, | PHILOSOPHIAE PROFESSOR ET REGIAE BIBLIOTHECAE UNIVERSITATIS | TUBINGENSIS PRAEFECTUS. | <multiple rule> | TUBINGAE | CURAM ADMINISTRAT **„Verlagsexpedition;"** | LONDINI, | WILLIAM NEWBERY, 6, KING STREET, HOLBORN; | H. BALLIERE, 219. REGENT STREET. | 1849. <*stet* BALLIERE>

2nd title page: EMAN. SWEDENBORGII, | SACRAE REGIAE MAJESTATIS REGNIQUE SUECIAE | COLLEGII METALLICI ASSESSORIS, | OPUSCULUM | DE PERIOSTEO ET DE MAMMIS. | <short rule> | E CHIROGRAPHO EJUS | IN BIBLIOTHECA REGIAE ACADEMIAE HOLMIENSIS | ASSERVATO | NUNC PRIMUM EDIDIT | Dr. JO. FR. IM. TAFEL, | PHILOSOPHIAE PROFESSOR ET REGIAE BIBLIOTHECAE UNIVERSITATIS | TUBINGENSIS PRAEFECTUS. | <multiple rule> | TUBINGAE | CURAM ADMINISTRAT **„Verlagsexpedition;"** | LONDINI, | WILLIAM NEWBERY, 6, KING STREET, HOLBORN; | H. BALLIERE, 219. REGENT STREET. | 1849. <*stet* BALLIERE>

8vo

title leaves, 4 pp; text cap 23-24, pp 1-23; Notae criticae editoris, pp 24-26.

UK: SOC, CON, NCC, NR; GER: GSU; NET: GEN

43/01/La 1/2 **1849** Hyde 411

EMAN. SWEDENBORGII, | SACRAE REGIAE MAJESTATIS REGNIQUE SUECIAE | COLLEGII METALLICI ASSESSORIS, | REGNUM ANIMALE | ANATOMICE, PHYSICE ET PHILOSOPHICE | PERLUSTRATUM. | CUJUS | SUPPLEMENTUM | SIVE | PARTIS SEXTAE | SECTIO SECUNDA | DE GENERATIONE, DE PARTIBUS GENITALIBUS | UTRIUSQUE SEXUS, ET DE FORMATIONE | FOETUS IN UTERO | AGIT. | <short rule>| E CHIROGRAPHO EJUS | IN BIBLIOTHECA REGIAE ACADEMIAE HOLMIENSIS | ASSERVATO | NUNC PRIMUM EDIDIT | Dr. JO. FR. IM. TAFEL, | PHILOSOPHIAE PROFESSOR ET REGIAE BIBLIOTHECAE UNIVERSITATIS | TUBINGENSIS PRAEFECTUS. | <multiple rule> | TUBINGAE | CURAM ADMINISTRAT **„Verlagsexpedition;"** | LONDINI, | WILLIAM NEWBERY, 6, KING STREET, HOLBORN; | H. BALLIERE, 219. REGENT STREET. | 1849. <*stet* BALLIERE>

2nd title page: EMAN. SWEDENBORGII, | SACRAE REGIAE MAJESTATIS REGNIQUE SUECIAE | COLLEGII METALLICI ASSESSORIS, | OPUSCULUM | DE GENERATIONE, DE PARTIBUS GENITALIBUS | UTRIUSQUE SEXUS, ET DE FORMATIONE | FOETUS IN UTERO. | <short rule> | E CHIROGRAPHO EJUS | IN BIBLIOTHECA REGIAE ACADEMIAE HOLMIENSIS | ASSERVATO | NUNC PRIMUM EDIDIT | Dr. JO. FR. IM. TAFEL, | PHILOSOPHIAE PROFESSOR ET REGIAE BIBLIOTHECAE UNIVERSITATIS | TUBINGENSIS PRAEFECTUS. | <multiple rule> | TUBINGAE |

CURAM ADMINISTRAT „Verlagsexpedition;" | LONDINI, | WILLIAM NEWBERY, 6, KING STREET, HOLBORN; | H. BALLIERE, 219. REGENT STREET. | 1849. <*stet* BALLIERE>
8vo
title leaves, 4 pp; Praefatiuncula editoris, pp V-VIII; text cap 27-44, pp 1-217; Notae criticae editoris, pp 218-231; Errata, p 232.
UK: soc, ncc, nr; NET: gen

43/01/La O/2, **D** La 1869/1 **1869** Hyde 408, 3034
25. | De Aure et auditu.
<26. | De Oculo et visu.>
folio
title and text, pp 108-176.
Reproduction of parts of La O/1, published in photolithographed edition, vol 6 <*Supplementum Regni Animalis* **D** La 1869/1 = Hyde 3034> Stockholm.
Unpublished copies have been recorded as follows.
1 UK: soc & USA: anc, shs A reproduction on microfilm 16 or 17, Bryn Athyn pa.
UK: soc, bl, cht, con, ncc, nch, ryl; GER: gsu; NET: gen; SWE: roy, kva, lun, upp; USA: anc, fou, shs; AUS: syd

43/01/La O/3, **D** La 1928/2 **1928** Hyde 408/2, 3038/26
25. | De Aure et auditu.
folio
titles and text: De Aure et audito, pp 10b-24b; <De Oculo et visu.> pp 25a-44b.
Photographic reproduction of the text of cap 25-26 in La O/1, published in *Autographa Editio Photostata* vol 5 <**D** La 1928/2 = Hyde 3038/26> Bryn Athyn pa.
Unpublished copies have been recorded as follows.
1 UK: soc & USA: anc, shs A reproduction on microfilm 21 made in 1962, Bryn Athyn pa.
UK: soc; USA: anc

43/01/La O/4, **D** La 1928/2 **1928** Hyde 406/1, 3038/26
<untitled>
folio
text: cap 23, pp 2a-4b; cap 24, pp 5a-10b; cap 27-44, pp 45a-137b.
Photographic reproduction of the text of cap 23-24, 27-44 of La O/1, in *Autographa Editio Photostata* vol 5 <**D** La 1928/2 = Hyde 3038/26> Bryn Athyn pa.
Unpublished copies have been recorded as follows.
1 UK: soc & USA: anc, shs A reproduction on microfilm 21 made in 1962, Bryn Athyn pa.
UK: soc; USA: anc

ENGLISH

Translators:
En 1 J J G Wilkinson
En 2 A Acton
En 3 E E Iungerich

43/01/En 1/1 **1852** Hyde 412
THE | GENERATIVE ORGANS, | CONSIDERED | ANATOMICALLY, PHYSICALLY AND PHILOSOPHICALLY. | A POSTHUMOUS WORK | OF | EMANUEL SWEDENBORG, | LATE MEMBER

OF THE HOUSE OF NOBLES IN THE ROYAL DIET OF SWEDEN, ASSESSOR OF THE ROYAL | METALLIC COLLEGE OF SWEDEN, FELLOW OF THE ROYAL ACADEMY OF SCIENCES OF UPSALA, | AND OF THE ROYAL ACADEMY OF SCIENCES OF STOCKHOLM, CORRESPONDING MEMBER | OF THE IMPERIAL ACADEMY OF SCIENCES OF ST. PETERSBURG. | TRANSLATED FROM THE LATIN | BY | JAMES JOHN GARTH WILKINSON, | MEMBER OF THE ROYAL COLLEGE OF SURGEONS OF ENGLAND, ONE OF THE SURGEONS TO THE | HAHNEMANN HOSPITAL, AND AUTHOR OF "THE HUMAN BODY AND ITS CONNEXION WITH MAN." | <short rule> | LONDON: | WILLIAM NEWBERY, 6, KING STREET, HOLBORN. | 1852.
verso: *Published by the Swedenborg Association.*
half title: THE GENERATIVE ORGANS.
verso: LONDON: | PRINTED BY WALTON AND MITCHELL, | WARDOUR ST., OXFORD ST.
section title: PART 1. | THE MALE GENERATIVE ORGANS.
2nd section title: PART II. | THE FEMALE GENERATIVE ORGANS.
3rd section title: THE MAMMÆ.
4th section title: THE PERIOSTEUM.
8vo
half title and title leaves, 4 pp; Advertisement, pp vii-x; Index <i.e. Contents>, p xi; section title leaf, pp xiii-xiv; text n 1-105, pp 1-139; 2nd section title leaf, pp 141-142; text n 106-289, pp 143-291; 3rd section title leaf, pp 293-294; text n 1-23, pp 295-313; 4th section title leaf, pp 315-316; text n 1-6, pp 317-327.
Printed at the expense of Joseph Senior. The 'Advertisement' is an introduction by the translator.
UK: soc, nr; NET: gen; SWE: gsb, upp

43/01/En 2/1 **1912** Hyde 412/1

The Animal Kingdom | CONSIDERED | ANATOMICALLY, PHYSICALLY AND | PHILOSOPHICALLY | BY | EMANUEL SWEDENBORG | <short rule> | PARTS 4 AND 5 | THE ORGANS OF GENERATION, AND THE FORMATION | OF THE FOETUS IN THE WOMB | AFTER WHICH FOLLOW CHAPTERS ON | THE BREASTS AND THE PERIOSTEUM | TRANSLATED FROM THE LATIN AND EDITED BY | ALFRED ACTON | <short rule> | BOERICKE & TAFEL, | PHILADELPHIA, | 1912
section title: THE | ORGANS OF GENERATION | THE MALE ORGANS
2nd section title: THE FEMALE ORGANS | AND | THE FORMATION OF THE FETUS IN THE WOMB
3rd section title: APPENDIX
4th section title: THE BREASTS
5th section title THE PERIOSTEUM
6th section title: INDEXES, ETC.
8vo
title leaf, 2 pp; Contents, p 3; Editor's preface, pp 5-15; section title leaf p 17-18; text n 1-176, pp 19-166; 2nd section title leaf, pp 167-168; text n 177-365, pp 169-326; 3rd section title leaf, pp 327-328; text Appendix: from the works of Martin Schurig, pp 329-333; 4th section title leaf, pp 335-336; text n 1-24, pp 337-356; 5th section title leaf, pp 357-358; text n 1-11, pp 359-370; 6th section title leaf, pp 371-372; Index of subjects, pp 373-391; Index of authors, pp 392-395; Key to paragraphs, pp 396-397; Corrections to the Latin text <La 1/1>, p 398; Plates I-X.
The Key to paragraphs compares the numbering in La 1/1, En 1/1, and En 2/1.
UK: soc, nr; NET: gen; SWE: upp; USA: anc

43/01/En 3/1 **1924** Hyde 412/1a

<<THE EAR AND HEARING; THE EYE AND SIGHT>>
title and text of chapters 25-26 of La 0/1 = Hyde 406, pp 67-164.
Translated by E E Iungerich, typewritten MS entitled *Various Philosophical and Physiological Studies* Chapters 7-8.

Document not seen; description recorded from catalogue of USA: ANC.
USA: ANC

43/01/En 2/2 **1928** Hyde 412/2

The Animal Kingdom | CONSIDERED | ANATOMICALLY, PHYSICALLY AND | PHILOSOPHICALLY | BY | EMANUEL SWEDENBORG | <short rule> | PARTS 4 AND 5 | THE ORGANS OF GENERATION, AND THE FORMATION | OF THE FOETUS IN THE WOMB | AFTER WHICH FOLLOW CHAPTERS ON | THE BREASTS AND THE PERIOSTEUM | TRANSLATED FROM THE LATIN AND EDITED BY | ALFRED ACTON, M.A., D.TH. | SECOND EDITION. | <short rule> | ACADEMY OF THE NEW CHURCH | BRYN ATHYN, PA. | 1928
section title: THE | ORGANS OF GENERATION | THE MALE ORGANS
2nd section title: THE FEMALE ORGANS | AND | THE FORMATION OF THE FETUS IN THE WOMB
3rd section title: APPENDIX
4th section title: THE BREASTS
5th section title: THE PERIOSTEUM
6th section title: INDEXES, ETC.
8vo
title leaf, 2 pp; Contents, p 3; Editor's preface, pp 5-15; section title leaf, pp 17-18; text n 1-176, pp 19-166; 2nd section title leaf, pp 167-168; text n 177-365, pp 169-326; 3rd section title leaf, pp 327-328; text Appendix: from the works of Martin Schurig, pp 329-333; 4th section title leaf, pp 335-336; text n 1-24, pp 337-356; 5th section title leaf, pp 357-358; text n 1-11, pp 359-370; 6th section title leaf, pp 371-372; Index of subjects, pp 373-391; Index of authors, pp 392-395; Key to paragraphs, pp 396-397; Corrections to the Latin text <La 1/1>, p 398; Plates I-X.
Reprint of En 2/1.
UK: SOC; NET: GEN; SWE: ROY; USA: ANC

43/01/En 2/3 **1955** Hyde 412/–

<<The Animal Kingdom | CONSIDERED | ANATOMICALLY, PHYSICALLY AND | PHILOSOPHICALLY | BY | EMANUEL SWEDENBORG | <short rule> | PARTS 4 AND 5 | THE ORGANS OF GENERATION, AND THE FORMATION | OF THE FOETUS IN THE WOMB | AFTER WHICH FOLLOW CHAPTERS ON | THE BREASTS AND THE PERIOSTEUM | TRANSLATED FROM THE LATIN AND EDITED BY | ALFRED ACTON | <short rule> | BOERICKE & TAFEL, | PHILADELPHIA, | 1912>>
section title: <<THE | ORGANS OF GENERATION | THE MALE ORGANS>>
2nd section title: <<THE FEMALE ORGANS | AND | THE FORMATION OF THE FETUS IN THE WOMB>>
3rd section title: <<APPENDIX>>
4th section title: <<THE BREASTS>>
5th section title: <<THE PERIOSTEUM>>
6th section title: <<INDEXES, ETC.>>
8vo
title leaf, 2 pp; Contents, p 3; Editor's preface, pp 5-15; section title leaf p 17-18; text n 1-176, pp 19-166; 2nd section title leaf, pp 167-168; text n 177-365, pp 169-326; 3rd section title leaf, pp 327-328; text Appendix: from the works of Martin Schurig, pp 329-333; 4th section title leaf, pp 335-336; text n 1-24, pp 337-356; 5th section title leaf, pp 357-358; text n 1-11, pp 359-370; 6th section title leaf, pp 371-372; Index of subjects, pp 373-391; Index of authors, pp 392-395; Key to paragraphs, pp 396-397; Corrections to the Latin text <La 1/1>, p 398; Plates I-X.
Photo-offset reprint of En 2/1, published by the Swedenborg Scientific Association, Bryn Athyn PA.
Copy not seen; description deduced from En 2/1 and 2/4.

43/01/En 1/2 **2003** Hyde 412/3

THE | GENERATIVE ORGANS, | CONSIDERED | ANATOMICALLY, PHYSICALLY AND PHILOSOPHICALLY. | A POSTHUMOUS WORK | OF | EMANUEL SWEDENBORG, | LATE MEMBER OF THE HOUSE OF NOBLES IN THE ROYAL DIET OF SWEDEN, ASSESSOR OF THE ROYAL | METALLIC COLLEGE OF SWEDEN, FELLOW OF THE ROYAL ACADEMY OF SCIENCES OF UPSALA, | AND OF THE ROYAL ACADEMY OF SCIENCES OF STOCKHOLM, CORRESPONDING MEMBER | OF THE IMPERIAL ACADEMY OF SCIENCES OF ST. PETERSBURG. | TRANSLATED FROM THE LATIN | BY | JAMES JOHN GARTH WILKINSON, | MEMBER OF THE ROYAL COLLEGE OF SURGEONS OF ENGLAND, ONE OF THE SURGEONS TO THE | HAHNEMANN HOSPITAL, AND AUTHOR OF "THE HUMAN BODY AND ITS CONNEXION WITH MAN." | Fredonia Books | Amsterdam, The Netherlands

verso: The Generative Organs, Considered Anatomically, | Physically and Philosophically | by | Emanuel Swedenborg | ISBN: 1-4101-0171-1 | Copyright © 2003 by Fredonia Books | Reprinted from the 1852 edition | Fredonia Books | Amsterdam, The Netherlands | http://www.fredoniabooks.com | All rights reserved, including the right to reproduce this book, or portions thereof, in any form.

half title: EMANUEL SWEDENBORG | THE | GENERATIVE ORGANS | CONSIDERED | ANATOMICALLY, PHYSICALLY AND PHILOSOPHICALLY

2nd half title: THE GENERATIVE ORGANS

section title: PART I. | THE MALE GENERATIVE ORGANS

2nd section title: PART II. | THE FEMALE GENERATIVE ORGANS

3rd section title title: THE MAMMÆ

4th section title: THE PERIOSTEUM

8vo

1st and 2nd half title and title leaves, 6 pp; Advertisement, pp VII-X; Index, p XI; section title leaf, pp XIII-XIV; text n 1-105, pp 1-139; 2nd section title leaf, pp 141-142; text n 106-289, pp 143-291; 3rd section title leaf, pp 293-294; text n 1-23, pp 295-313; 4th section title leaf, pp 315-316; text n 1-6, pp 317-327.

Photographic replica reprint of En 1/1 = Hyde 412, published by Fredonia Books, Amsterdam. Printed in the United Kingdom by Lightning Source UK Ltd.

UK: soc

43/01/En 1/3 **2004** Hyde 412/4

THE | GENERATIVE ORGANS, | CONSIDERED | ANATOMICALLY, PHYSICALLY AND PHILOSOPHICALLY. | A POSTHUMOUS WORK | OF | EMANUEL SWEDENBORG, | LATE MEMBER OF THE HOUSE OF NOBLES IN THE ROYAL DIET OF SWEDEN, ASSESSOR OF THE ROYAL | METALLIC COLLEGE OF SWEDEN, FELLOW OF THE ROYAL ACADEMY OF SCIENCES OF UPSALA, | AND OF THE ROYAL ACADEMY OF SCIENCES OF STOCKHOLM, CORRESPONDING MEMBER | OF THE IMPERIAL ACADEMY OF SCIENCES OF ST. PETERSBURG. | TRANSLATED FROM THE LATIN | BY | JAMES JOHN GARTH WILKINSON, | MEMBER OF THE ROYAL COLLEGE OF SURGEONS OF ENGLAND, ONE OF THE SURGEONS TO THE | HAHNEMANN HOSPITAL, AND AUTHOR OF "THE HUMAN BODY AND ITS CONNEXION WITH MAN." | LONDON: | WILLIAM NEWBERY, 6, KING STREET, HOLBORN. | 1852.

verso *Published by the Swedenborg Association*.

section title: PART I. | THE MALE GENERATIVE ORGANS.

2nd section title: PART II. | THE FEMALE GENERATIVE ORGANS.

3rd section title: THE MAMMÆ.

4th section title: THE PERIOSTEUM.

8vo

title leaf, 2 pp; Advertisement, pp vii-x; Index, p xi; section title leaf, pp xiii-xiv; text n 1-105, pp 1-139; 2nd section title leaf, pp 141-142; text n 106-289, pp 143-291; 3rd section title leaf, pp 293-

294; text n 1-23, pp 295-313; 4th section title leaf, pp 315-316; text n 1-6, pp 317-327.
Photographic replica reprint of En 1/1 = Hyde 412, published by Kessinger Publishing, Whitefish MT. Printed in the United States of America.

UK: SOC

43/01/En 2/4 **2009** Hyde 412/5

The Animal Kingdom | CONSIDERED | ANATOMICALLY, PHYSICALLY, AND | PHILOSOPHICALLY | BY | EMANUEL SWEDENBORG | <short rule> | PARTS FOUR AND FIVE | THE ORGANS OF GENERATION AND THE FORMATION OF THE FOETUS | AFTER WHICH FOLLOW CHAPTERS ON | THE BREASTS AND THE PERIOSTEUM | TRANSLATED FROM THE LATIN AND EDITED BY | ALFRED ACTON | <short rule> | BOERICKE & TAFEL, | PHILADELPHIA | 1912 | Reproduced by Photo-offset | SWEDENBORG SCIENTIFIC ASSOCIATION | 1955

verso: © 2009 by Swedenborg Scientific Association | All rights reserved | A. Acton translation published by Boericke & Tafel, Philadel- | phia 1912 | Reprinted 1928, Academy of the New Church, Bryn Athyn, | PA | ISBN-13:978-0-915221-86-8 | Four-volume set with *The Soul's Domain* (vols. I & II), and *The* | *Five Senses* | ISBN-13: 978-0-915221-87-5 | Swedenborg Scientific Association | P.O. Box 757, Bryn Athyn, PA 19009 | Email:ssacontact@verizon.net | www.swedenborg-philosophy.org | Printed in the United States of America

half title: THE ORGANS | OF | GENERATION

section title: THE | ORGANS OF GENERATION | THE MALE ORGANS

2nd section title: THE FEMALE ORGANS | AND | THE FORMATION OF THE FETUS IN THE WOMB

3rd section title: APPENDIX

4th section title: THE BREASTS

5th section title: THE PERIOSTEUM

6th section title: INDEXES, ETC.

8vo

half title and title leaves, 4 pp; Contents, p 3; Editor's preface, pp 5-15; section title leaf, pp 17-18; text n 1-176, pp 19-166; 2nd section title leaf, pp 167-168; text n 177-365, pp 169-326; 3rd section title leaf, pp 327-328; text Appendix: from the works of Martin Schurig, pp 329-333; 4th section title leaf, pp 335-336; text n 1-24, pp 337-356; 5th section title leaf, pp 357-358; text n 1-11, pp 359-370; 6th section title leaf, pp 371-372; Index of subjects, pp 373-391; Index of authors, pp 392-395; Key to paragraphs, pp 396-397; Corrections to the Latin text <La 1/1>, p 398; Plates I-X.
Photographic replica reprint of En 2/2 by Fidlar Doubleday, U.S.A., published with a new title leaf by the Swedenborg Scientific Association, Bryn Athyn PA.

UK: SOC; USA: ANC

ENGLISH EXTRACTS

X 43/01/En 1887/1, **D** En 1887/1 **1887** Hyde 412, 3132

6. FROM THE WORK ENTITLED: "GENERATIVE ORGANS."

8vo

title and text n 683u, pp 294-296.
The text is drawn from En 1/1, n 32, published by R L Tafel in *The Brain* 2 <40/09/En 1/1 = Hyde 412> London.

UK: SOC, CON, NCC, NR; NET: GEN, KB; SWE: UPP; USA: ANC, SHS; AUS: SYD

X 43/01/En 1958/1, **E:b** En 1958/4 **1958** Hyde 3336/25iv

<untitled>

4to

text, pp 682-684.

Translated and edited by A Acton, published in *The Life of Emanuel Swedenborg* 4 <**E:b** En 1958/4 = Hyde 3336/25iv> Bryn Athyn PA.
UK: SOC, NCC; USA: ANC

X 43/01/En 1994/1, **D** En 1994/2 **1994** Hyde 412/–, 3132/–
<<6. FROM THE WORK ENTITLED: "GENERATIVE ORGANS.">>
8vo
title and text n 683u, pp 294-296.
Photographic replica reprint of X En 1887/1 = Hyde 412, published in *The Brain* 2 <**D** En 1994/2> by Gryphon Editions, Birmingham AL.
Copy not seen; description deduced from X En 1887/1 and publisher's advertisement.

X 43/01/En 2005/1, **D** En 2005/2 **2005** Hyde 412/–, 3132/1
6. FROM THE WORK ENTITLED: "GENERATIVE ORGANS."
8vo
title and text n 683u, pp 294-296.
Photographic replica reprint of X En 1887/1, published in *The Brain* 2 <**D** En 2005/2> by The Swedenborg Scientific Association, Bryn Athyn PA.
UK: SOC; USA: ANC

43/02 Quotations from Works by Schurigius and Leeuwenhoek Hyde CXVIII

The autograph MS forms part of Codex 53 in the Library of the Royal Swedish Academy of Sciences, Stockholm.

LATIN

43/02/La O/1 **1743** Hyde 407

<< <Ex Martini Schurigii> >>
<<Ex Anton: a Leeuwenhoek>>
double foolscap oblong 8vo <330 x 102 mm>
title and text <Schurigius>, pp 138a-143a;
title and text <Leeuwenhoek>, pp 143a-148b.
MS not seen; description deduced from La O/2.

SWE: KVA

43/02/La O/2, D La 1869/2 **1869** Hyde 409, 3034

Ex Anton: a Leeuwenhoek
folio
title and text, pp 177-184.
Reproduction of part of La O/1, published in photolithographed edition, vol 6 <*Supplementum Regni Animalis* **D** La 1869/2 = Hyde 3034> Stockholm.
Unpublished copies have been recorded as follows.

1 UK: SOC & USA: ANC, SHS A reproduction on microfilm 16 or 17, Bryn Athyn PA.

UK: SOC, BL, CHT, CON, NCC, NCH, RYL; GER: GSU; NET: GEN; SWE: ROY, KVA, LUN, UPP; USA: ANC, FOU, SHS; AUS: SYD

43/02/La O/3, D La 1928/2 **1928** Hyde 409/1, 3038/26

Ex Anton: a Leeuwenhoek
folio
title and text, pp 138a-148b.
Photographic reproduction of La O/2, published in *Autographa Editio Photostata* vol 5 <**D** La 1928/2 = Hyde 3038/26> Bryn Athyn PA.
Unpublished copies have been recorded as follows.

1 UK: SOC & USA: ANC, SHS A reproduction on microfilm 21 made in 1962, Bryn Athyn PA.

UK: SOC; USA: ANC

ENGLISH

43/02/En 1/1 **<1924>** Hyde —

<<Emanuel Swedenborg | Excerpts from Leeuwenhoek and Swammerdam | translated by E E Iungerich>>

Typed MS, in USA: ANC.

Document not seen; description recorded from catalogue of USA: ANC.

USA: ANC

ENGLISH EXTRACTS

X 43/02/En 1912/1 **1912** Hyde 412/1

FROM THE WORKS OF MARTIN SCHURIG

8vo

title and text n 1-13, pp 329-333.

Translated by A Acton, published in *The Animal Kingdom ... Parts 4 and 5* <43/01/En 2/1 = Hyde 412/1> Philadelphia.

UK: SOC, NR; USA: ANC

X 43/02/En 1928/1 **1928** Hyde 412/2

FROM THE WORKS OF MARTIN SCHURIG

8vo

title and text n 1-13, pp 329-333.

Reprint of X En 1912/1, published in *The Animal Kingdom ... Parts 4 and 5* 2nd edition <43/01/En 2/2 = Hyde 412/2> Bryn Athyn PA.

UK: SOC; USA: ANC

X 43/02/En 1955/1 **1955** Hyde 412/3

<<FROM THE WORKS OF MARTIN SCHURIG>>

8vo

title and text n 1-13, pp 329-333.

Reprint of X En 1912/1, published in *The Animal Kingdom ... Parts FOUR and FIVE* <43/01/En 2/3 = Hyde 412/3> Bryn Athyn PA.

Copy not seen; description deduced from X En 1912/1 and X En 2009/1.

X 43/02/En 2009/1 **2009** Hyde 412/6

FROM THE WORKS OF MARTIN SCHURIG

8vo

title and text n 1-13, pp 329-333.

Photographic replica reprint of X En 1912/1 by Fidlar Doubleday, USA, published in *The Organs of Generation* <43/01/En 2/4 = Hyde 412/6> by the Swedenborg Scientific Association, Bryn Athyn PA.

UK: SOC; USA: ANC

43/03 Swedenborg's Journal of Dreams Hyde CXXIII

The autograph MS is in the Royal Library, Stockholm. It is bound in parchment with the title 'Swedenborgs Drömmar 1744' on the spine. The latest date, 21 December 1744, is recorded in a memorandum on p 107.

On p 1 are the words, 'Manuscript af Em. Svedenborg, funnit i afl. professoren och lectoren i Westarås R. Scheringssons boksamling, af́ L. B. Borberg' <A manuscript by Em. Swedenborg, found by L B Borberg in the library of the late R Scheringsson, Professor and Schoolmaster in Westerås>. Scheringsson died in 1849 aged 90 years; in October 1858 the MS was purchased by the Royal Library.

SWEDISH

Editions:

- Sw O MS
- Sw 1 G E Klemming, editor
- Sw 2 A Kahl and J A Sevén, editors
- Sw 3 K Barr, editor
- Sw 4 P E Wahlund, editor
- Sw 5 E Wahlund, editor
- Sw 6 L Bergquist, editor

43/03/Sw O/1 **1743** Hyde 428

<< <untitled> >>

foolscap broad 8vo <159 x 102 mm>

note <given above>, 1 p; text, 21 July to 20 August 1743, pp 2-6; 4 pp torn out; 16 pp blank; 1 to 11 December 1743, pp 7-8; 24 March to 27 October 1744, pp 9-98; 16 pp blank; additional note, p 101; 2 pp blank; memoranda of financial transactions in 1743 and 1744, pp 104-107; note in Latin, p 108.

Copy not seen; description deduced from Sw O/2.

SWE: ROY

43/03/Sw 1/1 **1859** Hyde 429, 2689

SVEDENBORGS | DRÖMMAR | 1744 | JEMTE ANDRA HANS ANTECKNINGAR | <short rule> | EFTER ORIGINAL-HANDSKRIFTER | MEDDELADE | AF | G. E. KLEMMING. | Ita provisum est a

Domino, ut phantasiæ | iis appareant prorsus sicut realiter forent. | *Diarium Spirituale* 4360. | <short orn rule> | N:o ~~ *Herr Bibliotekar Ahlstrand.*
imprint: Stockholm. 1859. P. A. Nordstedt & Söner, Kongl. Boktryckare.
8vo
title leaf, 2 pp; Dedication addressed to J F I Tafel and J J G Wilkinson, 2 pp; Förord, 2 pp; text, pp 1-64; Bihang <Appendix>, pp 65-79; Anmärckningar <Notes>, pp 80-84; imprint, p 84; facsimile of a page from the MS, inserted facing p 84.
99 copies were printed, and each copy of the edition was numbered at the foot of the title page.
On pp 65-72 the editor published the Swedish text of paragraphs from *Experientiae Spirituales* <47/05>: n 4679[a], 4787, 5763, 6027, 6035, and the closing Memoranda; on pp 73-77 he published 69/13/La 1/1 with the title *Om Hästens betydelse och om Hieroglypherna. Efter originalet i Engeströmska biblioteket*; and on pp 77-78 he printed Swedenborg's letter to SWE: KVA dated 10 September 1766.
UK: SOC, CON; DEN: RLD; GER: WLB; SWE: ROY, GEN, GSB; USA: SHS

43/03/Sw 2/1 1860 Hyde 430

Swedenborgs | Drömmar | 1744 | JEMTE ANDRA HANS ANTECKNINGAR. | <short rule> | EFTER ORIGINAL-HANDSKRIFTER. | Ita provisum est a Domino, ut phantasiæ | iis appareant prorsus sicut realiter forent. | *Diarium Spirituale* 4360. | <short orn rule>
verso: *Denna märkliga urkund var ursprungligen icke | ämnad för en större allmänhet, och meddelades derför | endast åt några få upplyste tänkande och för ämnet | intresserade. Sedan den numera blifvit öfversatt på | Engelska, Franska och Tyska språken, finnes intet skäl | att neka originalet en större offentlighet i SWEDENBORGS | fäderneslαnd; hvarför nu ett oförändradt aftryck af Hr | KLEMMINGS upplaga, med hans tillstånd och öfverlåtande | af förlagsrätten, utgifves tillgängligt i bokhandeln.* | <short wavy rule> | *Från original-upplagan införes följande intyg, såsom | gällande äfven för detta aftryck: | På begäran af hr kongl. v. bibliothekarien Klem- | ming har jag jemfört följande sifor 1—64 med original- | handskriften af Swedenborgs egen hand, och intygar | härmed aftryckets fullkomliga trohet, så vidt det varit | möjligt att utreda de ofta svårtydda skriftdragen. | Stockholm den 4 Juni 1859. | F. A. Dahlgren.* | <short wavy rule> | *(Original-upplagans förord igenfinnes i början af | de föregående Reflexionerna.)* | <short wavy rule>
8vo
title leaf, 2 pp; text, pp 1-64; Bihang <Appendix>, pp 65-79; Anmärckningar <Notes>, pp 80-84; Reflexioner <Observations>, pp 85-94.
Edited from Sw 1/1 by A Kahl and J A Sevén, in an edition of 500 copies. The unsigned 'Reflexioner' was written by Anna Fredrika Ehrenborg, who published the work in *Reflexioner öfver de nyligen uppdagade Swedenborgs Drömmar 1744, hvilka derjemte oförandrade bifogas* Stockholm, Tryckt Hos J. & A. Riis, 1860. The *Reflexioner* was also published separately
UK: SOC, CON; NET: GEN; SWE: GEN, GSB

43/03/Sw 2/2 1860 Hyde 430

<<Swedenborgs | Drömmar | 1744 | JEMTE ANDRA HANS ANTECKNINGAR. | <short rule> | EFTER ORIGINAL-HANDSKRIFTER. | Ita provisum est a Domino, ut phantasiæ | iis appareant prorsus sicut realiter forent. | *Diarium Spirituale* 4360. | <short orn rule> >>
verso: <<Denna märkliga urkund var ursprungligen icke | ämnad för en större allmänhet, och meddelades derför | endast åt några få upplyste tänkande och för ämnet | intresserade. Sedan den numera blifvit öfversatt på | Engelska, Franska och Tyska språken, finnes intet skäl | att neka originalet en större offentlighet i SWEDENBORGS | fädernesland; hvarför nu ett oförändradt aftryck af Hr | KLEMMINGS upplaga, med hans tillstånd och öfverlåtande | af förlagsrätten, utgifves tillgängligt i bokhandeln. | <short wavy rule> | *Från original-upplagan införes följande intyg,*

såsom | *gällande äfven för detta aftryck:* | *På begäran af hr kongl. v. bibliothekarien Klem-* | *ming har jag jemfört följande sifor 1–64 med original-* | *handskriften af Swedenborgs egen hand, och intygar* | *härmed aftryckets fullkomliga trohet, så vidt det varit* | *möjligt att utreda de ofta svårtydda skriftdragen.* | *Stockholm den 4 Juni 1859.* | *F. A. Dahlgren.* | <short wavy rule> | *(Original-upplagans förord igenfinnes i början af* | *de föregående Reflexionerna.)* | <short wavy rule> >>
8vo
title leaf, 2 pp; text, pp 1-64; Bihang <Appendix>, pp 65-79; Anmärckningar <notes>, pp 80-84; Reflexioner <Observations>, pp 85-94.
The same as Sw 2/1, published in *Strödda uppsatser rörande Swedenborgs Drömmar 1744* Christianstad.
Copy not seen; description deduced from Sw 2/1 and Hyde 430.

43/03/Sw O/2, **D** La&Sw 1916/1 **1916** Hyde 428/1, 3038/18

<untitled>
folio
text, pp 590-618.
Reproduction of Sw O/1, published in phototyped edition, vol 18 <*Miscellanea Theologica* **D** La 1916/13 = Hyde 3038/18> Stockholm.
Unpublished copies have been recorded as follows.
1 UK: SOC & USA: ANC, SHS A reproduction on microfilm 12 made in 1962, Bryn Athyn PA.
UK: SOC, BL, BOD, CAM, CON, LON, NCC, NCH, RYL, WIL; NET: GEN; SWE: ROY, KVA, LUN, UPP; USA: ANC, FOU, SHS; AUS: SYD; NZ: WEL

43/03/Sw 3/1 **1924** Hyde 430/1

SWEDENBORGS | DRÖMMAR | *Emanuel Swedenborgs dagbok* | *1743–1744* | utgiven och kommenterad med förklarande | noter samt med bibliografiska och | biografiska essayer | av | KNUT BARR | <publisher's logo 12 x 19 mm> | STOCKHOLM | <short rule> | P. A. Norstedt & Söners | Förlag
verso: *Av denna bok* | *är tryckt en bibliofilupplaga i* | *50 numrerade exemplar* | STOCKHOLM 1924 | KUNGL. BOKTRYCKERIET. P. A. NORSTEDT & SÖNER | 241112
half title: *Knut Barr* | SWEDENBORGS DRÖMMAR
frontispiece facing title leaf
section title: I. | SWEDENBORGS DRÖMMAR
2nd section title: II. | DRÖMDAGBOKEN
3rd section title: III. | UR SWEDENBORGS LIV OCH VERK
8vo
half title leaf, frontispiece, and title leaf, 6 pp; Tillägnan <Dedication> by Knut Barr, pp 5-6; section title leaf, pp 7-8; Photographic reproduction of a page from Sw O/1, p 9; text, pp 11-92; plate, 2 pp; 2nd section title leaf, pp 95-96; Drömdagboken <An account of the MS and its publication>, pp 97-117; 3rd section title leaf, pp 119-120; Ur Swedenborgs liv och verk <A biography of Swedenborg>, pp 121-174; Innehåll <Contents>, p 175; Rättelser <Corrections>, on a slip pasted at the back of the book.
The frontispiece is a copy of a portrait of Swedenborg described as 'Oljemålning av Per Krafft d. ä. Gripsholm' <Oil painting by Per Krafft the elder. Gripsholm Castle, Stockholm>.
UK: SOC; NET: GEN; SWE: ROY, GEN, GSB; USA: ANC

43/03/Sw 4/1 **1952** Hyde 430/2

EMANUEL SWEDENBORG | DRÖMBOKEN | JOURNALANTECKNINGAR | 1743–44 | STOCKHOLM

| WAHLSTRÖM & WIDSTRAND
verso: *Ronzo Boktryckeri AB* | *Stockholm 1952*
half title: WAHLSTRÖM & WIDSTRANDS KULTURBIBLIOTEK | URVAL REDAKTION: PER ERIK WAHLUND | VOLYM IV | *Emanuel Swedenborg: Drömboken*
8vo
half title and title leaves, 4 pp; Inledning <Introduction, by Per Erik Wahlund>, pp 5-8; text, pp 9-70; Anmärkningar <Notes>, pp 71-78.
ISSN 99-1551755-6
UK: SOC; SWE: ROY, GEN, GSB; USA: ANC

43/03/Sw 5/1 **1964** Hyde 430/3
Emanuel Swedenborg | Drömboken | Journalanteckningar 1743-44 | redigerade och kommenterade av Per Erik Wahlund | Wahlström & Widstrand Stockholm 1964
half title: W&Wserien 69 Drömboken
verso: © Wahlström & Widstrand 1964 | Omslag av Per Åhlin | W&Wserien typografi har utformats av Vidar Forsberg | Drömboken publicerades första gången 1859 av G. E. Klemming | Föreliggande utgåva ingår som nr 69 i W&Wserien hösten 1964 | Tryckt hos Victor Pettersons Bokindustri AB | Stockholm 1964 | <publishers' logo 21 x 21 mm> WE&Wserien
8vo
half title and title leaves, 4 pp; Inledning <Introduction, by Per Erik Wahlund>, pp 5-10; text, pp 11-80; Anmärckningar <Notes>, pp 81-98; advertisement, 2 pp.
UK: SOC; SWE: ROY, GSB; USA: ANC

43/03/Sw 6/1 **1988** Hyde 430/4
LARS BERGQUIST | SWEDENBORGS | DRÖMBOK | GLÄDJEN | OCH DET STORA | KVALET | NORSTEDTS
verso: *Lars Bergquist* | Arronax' minnen 1975 | Annas smak 1977 | Spegelskrift 1978 | Per Brahes undergång och bärgning 1980 | Isvandring med Nordenskiöld 1981 | René Char: Strånghet i ett mandelregn, tolkning 1982 | Boken utges med stöd av Långmanska Fonden och | Skandinaviska Swedenborgssällskapet | ISBN 91-1-871162-6 | © Lars Bergquist 1988 | Norstedts Förlag, Stockholm | Omslag: Rolf Hernegran | Stockholm 1988. Norstedts Tryckeri 67-587
half title: Naar En forsker objektivt efter Udødeligheden, en Anden | sætter | Uendelighedens Lidenskab ind paa Uvisheden: hvor er der saa | meest Sandhed, og hvo meest Vished? | Kierkegaard: Afsluttende uvidenskabelig Efterskrift
section title: Dagboken
8vo
half title and title leaves, 4 pp; Innehåll <Contents>, p 5; Inledning <Introduction>, pp 7-70; section title leaf, pp 71-72; text, pp 73-296; Noter <Editorial notes>, pp 297-311; Litteraturförteckning <Bibliography>, pp 312-316; Personregister <Index of people>, pp 317-320; Efterskrift <Postscript>, p 321.
Edited by L Bergqvist, published by Norstedts Förlag, Stockholm, with the support of the Längmanska Foundation and the Scandinavian Swedenborg Society. Book cover design by Rolf Hernegran.
GER: WLB; NET: GEN; SWE: GEN, GSB

43/03/Sw 5/2 **1995** Hyde —
<<Emanuel Swedenborg | Drömboken | Journalanteckningar 1743-44 | redigerade och kommenterade av Per Erik Wahlund | Wahlström & Widstrand Stockholm 1995>>
8vo

half title and title leaves, 4 pp; Inledning <Introduction, by Per Erik Wahlund>, pp 5-10; text, pp 11-80; Anmärckningar <Notes>, pp 81-98; advertisement, 2 pp.
Reprint of Sw 5/1. Copy not seen; description deduced from Sw 5/1 and catalogue of GER: WLB.
GER: WLB

ENGLISH

Translators:
En 1 J J G Wilkinson
En 2 R L Tafel
En 3 C Th Odhner
En 4 C Th Odhner
En 5 A H Stroh
En 6 A Hallengren

43/03/En 1/1 <pre 1860> Hyde 431

<MS version> Swedenborg's | Dreams | 1744 | With some other of his Pieces: | Edited | from the Original Manuscripts | by | G. E. Klemming. | Translated into English.
copy broad 8vo <199 x 118 mm>
title, 1 p; Dedication, 1 p; Preface, etc., 1 p; text, 156 pp; Appendix, 23 pp.
<typescript version> SWEDENBORG'S | DREAMS | 1744 | WITH SOME OTHER OF | HIS PIECES: | EDITED | From the Original manuscripts By | G. E. Klmming. | Translated into English. | This copy is taken from a book bound in black and which | on the leaf before the title-page bears the inscription: | "This book is the property of The Swedenborgian Society. | Thomas Watson." *<stet* Swedenborgian>
4to folded in half <330 x 178 mm>
title, 1 p; Dedication, p 1; Preface, pp 2-4; text, pp 5-82; Note concerning Antony and John Gill from Hultman on Peter Hultman's account, p 83; Extracts from *Spiritual Diary* <47/05>, pp 83-92; Memorandum from 1771, pp 92-93; a reference to 'Of the signification of the Horse, and of the Hieroglyphics. From the original in the Engeström Library', p 93; List of spiritual treasures, p 95.
Translated by J J G Wilkinson; MS in UK: SOC <Archives B/55>. In *Emanuel Swedenborg: a Biographical Sketch* <Hyde 3302, published in 1886> in a note on p 251 Wilkinson stated that he translated the *Drömmar* from its Old Swedish for the Revd Augustus Clissold and that the accuracy of the version was avouched by F L Cöster of the Swedish Consulate.
UK: SOC

43/03/En 1/2 1859 Hyde 431/a

<MS version> <no title page>
4to <254 x 203 mm>
Translator's preface <signed D H and dated Sept 10, 1849, emended to 1859>, 4 pp; Dedication to J F I Tafel and J J G Wilkinson, p 1; Editor's preface, pp 1-3; Translator's remarks, p 3; text, pp 4-68. Written on one side of each page, with some notes to the text on the reverse of pp 3, 5, 7, 9, 11, 13, 17, 19, 23, 25, 27, 29, 31, 37, 39, 41, 49, 51, 53, 59, 65.
<typescript version> An English translation of | SWEDENBORG'S DREAMS | by | Dirkink-Holmfeldt.
foolscap <330 x 203 mm>
title, 1 p; Translator's preface <signed D H and dated Septbr 10, 1859>, pp 1-3; Dedication to J F I Tafel and J J G Wilkinson, p 4; Editor's preface, pp 4-6; Translator's remarks, pp 6-7; text, pp 7-85. This may be the original of the version described as En 1/3, purporting to be a new translation by

C Dirckinck-Holmfeldt. <UK: SOC Archives B/56>
A typed MS described as 'An English translation of Swedenborg's Dreams, by Dirkink-Holmfeldt 1859 (?)' is in USA: ANC, reference Sw123 fE1859.2.
UK: SOC; USA: ANC

43/03/En 1/3 **1861-1862** Hyde 432
FRAGMENT OF SWEDENBORG'S DIARY, | 1743-1744. | <short rule> | EDITED BY G. E. KLEMMING, ROYAL LIBRARIAN OF | STOCKHOLM. | <short rule>
large 8vo
title and editor's introduction, p 40; Swedish editor's dedication, p 40; Swedish editor's preface, with note by F A Dahlgren, pp 40-41; text: **1861** pp 41, 62, 82, 102, 122, 141-142, 162, 182, 202, 220-222, 238; **1862** pp 22, 42, 62, 81-82, 102, 121-122, 141-142.
Published in *The Dawn: A Journal of Social and Religious Progress* London. Footnotes credited to 'Baron Holmfeldt/Holmfield' are to be found in **1861** pp 41, **1862** pp 22, 81, 82 of this version, which was an unauthorized copy made from En 1/1.
In En 1/8 = Hyde 433/2b, p xiii, W R Woofenden states that this is a pirated and abridged version of J J G Wilkinson's translation, which claimed to be the work of a Baron Holmfeld of Denmark.
The matter is also discussed by R L Tafel in *Documents* 2:1 <**E:b** En 1877/1 = Hyde 3275> p 136.
UK: SOC, CON, NR

43/03/En 1/4 **1863-1864 <?>** Hyde —
<<FRAGMENT OF SWEDENBORG'S DIARY, | 1743-1744. | <short rule> | EDITED BY G. E. KLEMMING, ROYAL LIBRARIAN OF | STOCKHOLM. | <short rule> >>
Reprinted from En 1/3, published in *The Crisis* LaPorte IN.
In En 1/8 = Hyde 433/2b, p xiii, W R Woofenden refers to this reprint.
Copy not seen; description deduced from En 1/3.

43/03/En 2/1, **E:b** En 1877/1 **1877** Hyde 433, 3275
SWEDENBORG'S JOURNAL OF TRAVEL | IN 1743.
title and text, 21 July to 20 August 1743, pp 131-133.
SWEDENBORG'S SPIRITUAL EXPERIENCE | IN 1743.
title, p 134; text, 1 to 11 December 1743, pp 147-149.
SWEDENBORG'S SPIRITUAL EXPERIENCE | IN 1744.
title and text, 24 March to 27 October 1744, pp 149-219; memoranda, p 219.
royal 8vo
Translated by R L Tafel, published in *Documents* 2:1 <**E:b** En 1877/1 = Hyde 3275> London.
UK: SOC, CON, NCC, NCH, PUR, WIL, NR; GER: GSU; NET: GEN; SWE: SUB, UPP; USA: ANC; AUS: SYD

43/03/En 2/2, **E:b** En 1890/1 **1890** Hyde 3275/a
SWEDENBORG'S JOURNAL OF TRAVEL | IN 1743.
title and text, 21 July to 20 August 1743, pp 131-133.
SWEDENBORG'S SPIRITUAL EXPERIENCE | IN 1743.
title, p 134; text, 1 to 11 December 1743, pp 147-149.
SWEDENBORG'S SPIRITUAL EXPERIENCE | IN 1744.
title and text, 24 March to 27 October 1744, pp 149-219; memoranda, p 219.
royal 8vo
Reprint of En 2/1, published in *Documents* 2 <**E:b** En 1890/1 = Hyde 3275/a> London.
UK: SOC, BL; SWE: UPP

43/03/En 3/1 **1915** Hyde 433/1

SWEDENBORG'S DIARY AND DREAMS. | 1743-1744.

8vo

title and text n [1-286], pp 251-263, 315-329, 389-410, 449-457, 514-526, 579-587.

Translated and edited by C Th Odhner, published in *New Church Life* Bryn Athyn PA.

UK: SOC, NCC; USA: ANC

43/03/En 4/1 **1918** Hyde 433/2

EMANUEL SWEDENBORG'S | JOURNAL OF DREAMS | AND | SPIRITUAL EXPERIENCES | IN THE YEAR SEVENTEEN HUN- | DRED AND FORTY-FOUR. TRANS- | LATED FROM THE SWEDISH BY | REV. C. TH. ODHNER. | <type orn 12 x 12 mm> | THE ACADEMY BOOK ROOM | BRYN ATHYN, PENNSYLVANIA | NINETEEN EIGHTEEN

8vo

title leaf, 2 pp; Translator's introduction, pp 3-7; text n [1-286], pp 9-102; Index, pp 103-108.

The translator added many footnotes and cross-references.

UK: SOC, NR; NET: GEN; USA: ANC

43/03/En 5/1 **no date** Hyde 433/3

Third Journal, for 1743-1744.

4to

title and text n 390-630, pp 209-308.

Translated and edited by A H Stroh, in the archives of USA: ANC <Ar 2001>.

The file also contains 33/02/En 2/1 = Hyde 253/1, 37/01/En 2/1 = Hyde 267/1, and an Index to all three works, compiled by Stroh in 1917.

n 627 <headed [May ?] 11th x 12th.> is translated into Latin.

An unpublished copy is recorded as follows.

1 UK: SOC A photocopied facsimile.

USA: ANC

43/03/En 1/5 **1974-1975** Hyde —

SWEDENBORG'S JOURNAL OF DREAMS | 1743-1744 | <orn 17 x 39 mm> | Edited from the original Swedish | by G. E. Klemming | Translated into English (in 1860) | by J. J. G. Wilkinson | Now for the first time edited for the press | by William Ross Woofenden

8vo

1974 January: title leaf, pp 11-12; Preface to the 1859 Swedish edition, pp 13, 15-16; facsimile of p 57 of Swedenborg's original MS, p 14; Preface to this edition, pp 17-18; Facsimile of title page of Sw 1/1, p 19; text n [1-56], pp 21-36; **1974** June: n [57-128], pp 3-24; **1975** January: n [129-214], pp 3-26; **1975** June: n [215-286], pp 3-25.

Published in *Studia Swedenborgiana* Newton MA.

UK: SOC, NR; USA: SHS

43/03/En 1/6 **1977** Hyde 433/5

SWEDENBORG'S JOURNAL OF DREAMS | 1743-1744 | <orn 15 x 35 mm> | Edited from the original Swedish | by G. E. Klemming | Translated into English (in 1860) | by J. J. G. Wilkinson | Edited by William Ross Woofenden | 1977 | Swedenborg Foundation, Inc. | New York, N. Y.

verso: SWEDENBORG'S JOURNAL OF DREAMS | *First published in Swedish, Stockholm, 1859* | ISBN 0-87785-157-3 | Library of Congress Catalog Card Number 77-70221 | *Cover design by Bill Heustis* | Printed in the United States of America | Swedenborg Foundation, Inc. | 139 East 23rd Street | New York, N.Y. 10010

half title: <portrait of Swedenborg>
176 x 110 mm, perfect bound
half title and title leaves, 4 pp; Editor's preface, pp i-iv; 'Swedenborg's Journey Within' by Wilson Van Dusen, pp v-xxiii; text n [1-286], pp 1-91; Index, pp 93-97; catalogue, 3 pp.
The text was reprinted from En 1/5.
UK: PUR, NR; NET: GEN; USA: ANC

43/03/En 1/7 **1986** Hyde 433/7
Swedenborg's | Journal of Dreams | 1743 – 1744 | Commentary by Wilson Van Dusen | Edited from the original Swedish by G.E. Klemming | Translated into English in 1860 by J.J.G. Wilkinson | Edited by William Ross Woofenden | 1986 | Swedenborg Foundation, Inc. | New York, N.Y.
verso: SWEDENBORG'S JOURNAL OF DREAMS | *First published in Swedish, Stockholm, 1859* | ISBN 0-87785-133-6 | Library of Congress Catalog Card Number 86-70341 | Cover Calligraphy by Bettie Hall | Cover and Book Design by John N. Tierney | Printed in the United States of America | Swedenborg Foundation, Inc. | 139 East 23rd Street | New York, N.Y. 10010
8vo, perfect bound
title leaf, 2 pp; Dedication, 1 p; Contents leaf, 2 pp; History of this Journal and acknowledgments, 3 pp; Chapter 1, Introduction, pp 1-9; Chapter 2, The Journal <the dreams and their interpretation>, n [1-286], pp 10-165; Chapter 3, Summing it up, pp 166-194; Bibliography, pp 195-196.
UK: SOC, NR; NET: GEN

43/03/En 1/8 **1989** Hyde 433/2b
SWEDENBORG'S | JOURNAL OF DREAMS | 1743-1744 | Emanuel Swedenborg | Edited from the original Swedish | by *G. E. Klemming* | Translated into English, 1860, | by *J. J. G. Wilkinson* | Edited by *William Ross Woofenden* | With an Introduction | by *Wilson Van Dusen,* | Second Edition, 1989 | Swedenborg Scientific Association | Bryn Athyn, PA | Swedenborg Society | London, England
verso: © Copyright 1989 Swedenborg Scientific Association | Library of Congress Cataloging-in-Publication Data | Swedenborg, Emanuel, 1688-1772. | [Drömboken. English] | Swedenborg's journal of dreams, 1743-1744 / Emanuel Swedenborg; | edited from the original Swedish by G.E. Klemming; translated into | English 1860 by J.J.G. Wilkinson; edited by William Ross Woofenden; | with an introduction by Wilson Van Dusen. — 2nd ed. | p. cm. | Translation of: Drömboken. | Includes bibliographical references. | ISBN 0-915221-67-5 | 1. Swedenborg, Emanuel, 1688-1772—Diaries. 2. Mys- | tics—Sweden—Diaries—Early works to 1800. 3. Dreams—Early works | to 1800. | I. Klemming, G. E. II. Woofenden, William Ross. III. Title. IV. Title: | Journal of dreams, 1743-1744. | BX8712.D994 1989 | 289.4' 092 —dc20 | [B] 89-39612 | <short rule> | British Library Cataloging in Publication Data | Swedenborg, Emanuel, 1688-1772 | Swedenborg's Journal of dreams 1743-1744. — 2nd ed. | 1. Dreams — Biographies | I. Title. II. Klemming, G. E. III. Woofenden, William Ross, 1921 - | IV. Swedenborg Society. V. Swedenborg's drommar, 1744. English | 135.3092 | ISBN 0-85448-109-5
half title: SWEDENBORG'S | JOURNAL OF DREAMS | 1743-1744
8vo
half title and title leaves, 4 pp; Dedication, p v; Preface to the 2nd edition, pp vii-ix; Preface to the 1977 edition <En 1/6 = Hyde 433/5>, pp x-xiv; W Van Dusen 'Swedenborg's Journey Within', pp xv-xxxvi; text n [1]-[286], pp 1-113; Index, pp 115-120.
UK: SOC, PUR, NR; GER: WLB; USA: ANC

43/03/En 2/3, **E:b** En 2000/1 **2000** Hyde —
<<SWEDENBORG'S JOURNAL OF TRAVEL | IN 1743.>>

title and text, 21 July to 20 August 1743, pp 131-133.
<<SWEDENBORG'S SPIRITUAL EXPERIENCE | IN 1743.>>
title, p 134; text, 1 to 11 December 1743, pp 147-149.
<<SWEDENBORG'S SPIRITUAL EXPERIENCE | IN 1744.>>
title and text, 24 March to 27 October 1744, pp 149-219; memoranda, p 219.
8vo
Photographic replica reprint of En 2/1, published in *Documents* 2:1 <**E:b** En 2000/1> by Adamant Media Corporation, New York.
Copy not seen; description deduced from En 2/3 and publisher's advertisement.

43/03/En 6/1 **2001** Hyde 433/9
SWEDENBORG'S | DREAM DIARY | Lars Bergquist | TRANSLATED BY | Anders Hallengren | <logo 19 x 14 mm> | SWEDENBORG FOUNDATION PUBLISHERS | WEST CHESTER, PENNSYLVANIA
verso: ©2001 by the Swedenborg Foundation | The original Swedish edition appeared in 1989 as | *Swedenborgs drömbok: Glädjen och det stora kvalet,* | published by Norstedts Förlag, Stockholm. | All rights reserved. No part of this publication may be | reproduced or transmitted in any form or by any means, electronic | or mechanical, including photocopying, recording, or any | information storage or retrieval system, without prior | permission from the publisher. | Swedenborg Studies is a scholarly series published by the | Swedenborg Foundation. The primary purpose of the series is to | make materials available for understanding the life and thought | of Emanuel Swedenborg (1688-1772) and the impact his thought | has had on others. The Foundation undertakes to publish original | studies and English translations of such studies and to republish | primary sources that are otherwise difficult to access. | Proposals should be sent to: | Senior Editor, Swedenborg Studies | Swedenborg Foundation | 320 North Church Street | West Chester, Pennsylvania | 19380 | Library of Congress Cataloging-in-Publication Data | Bergquist, Lars, 1930- | [Swedenborgs drömbok. English] | Swedenborg's dream diary / Lars Bergquist; | translated by Anders Hallengren. | p. cm. — (Swedenborg studies; 11) | Includes bibliographical references and index. | ISBN 0-87785-198-0 (hc) — 0-87785-199-9 (pbk.) | 1. Swedenborg, Emanuel, 1688-1772. Drèmboken. | 2. Swedenborg, Emanuel, 1688-1772—Diaries. | 3. Mystics—Sweden—Diaries. | 4. Dreams—Early works to 1800. | I. Hallengren, Anders, 1950- . II. Title. III. Series | BX8712.D9949 B4713 2001 | 289'.4'092 —dc21 | [B] 00-049247 | Edited by Mary Lou Bertucci | Designed by Alice Hyvonen, Philadelphia, Pennsylvania | Set in Wiess, Frutiger, and Footlight by Sans Serif, Inc. | Printed in the United States of America.
half title: SWEDENBORG'S | DREAM DIARY | <orn 15 x 10 mm> | SWEDENBORG STUDIES | NO. 11 | MONOGRAPHS | OF THE | SWEDENBORG FOUNDATION
section title: PART ONE | *An Introduction* | <orn 15 x 10 mm>
2nd section title: PART TWO | *The Dream Diary* | <orn 15 x 10 mm> | WITH COMMENTARY BY | LARS BERGQUIST
large 8vo
half title and title leaves, 4 pp; Contents, pp V-VI; Acknowledgments, p VII; section title leaf, pp 1-2; text, pp 3-70; Notes, pp 70-75; 2nd section title leaf, pp 77-78; text n 1-287, pp 79-324; Notes, pp 325-348; Bibliography, pp 349-358; Index, pp 359-371.
UK: SOC, PUR, NR; NET: KB; SWE: ROY

43/03/En 2/4, **E:b** En 2004/2 **2004** Hyde —
SWEDENBORG'S JOURNAL OF TRAVEL | IN 1743.
title and text, 21 July to 20 August 1743, pp 131-133.
SWEDENBORG'S SPIRITUAL EXPERIENCE | IN 1743.
title, p 134; text, 1 to 11 December 1743, pp 147-149.
SWEDENBORG'S SPIRITUAL EXPERIENCE | IN 1744.

title and text, 24 March to 27 October 1744, pp 149-219; memoranda, p 219.
8vo
Photographic replica reprint of En 2/1, published in *Documents* 2:1 <**E:b** En 2004/2> by Kessinger Publishing, Whitefish MT.
UK: NR

ENGLISH EXTRACTS

X 43/03/En 1861/1 **1861** Hyde —
FROM AN UNPUBLISHED DIARY OF SWEDENBORG, | LATELY FOUND. 1743-1744.
large 8vo
title and text, p 20.
Published in *The Dawn* London.
Portions of the paragraphs numbered <in editions from 1918 onwards> 71, 74, 87-89. No translator is named; and the wording is not exactly the same as the version printed later in this journal in 1861 and 1862 <see En 1/3>.
UK: SOC, CON, NR

X 43/03/1867/1 **1867** Hyde 3320
<untitled>
8vo
text: 21 July to 20 August 1743, pp 198-200; 24 March to 20 May 1744, pp 201-219; 11 June to 27 October 1744, pp 233-241; final entry, p 241.
Edited with comments interspersed by William White, published in *Emanuel Swedenborg: his life and writings* <Hyde 3320> London.
On p 197 White recorded: "The Baron Constant Dirckinck Holmfeld of Copenhagen has very kindly made for me a translation into English of the rough and difficult Swedish of '*The Dreams*.'" In *Documents* 2:1, p 136 <**E:b** En 1877/1 = Hyde 3275> R L Tafel stated that he had compared J J G Wilkinson's MS translation <En 1/1> with the one published in *The Dawn* <En 1/3 = Hyde 432> and concluded that though the latter was provided with notes by Holmfeld it had been copied inaccurately from the former.
UK: SOC, NR

X 43/03/En 1868/1 **1868** Hyde 3320
<untitled>
8vo
text: 21 July 1743, pp 120-121; 24 March to 20 May 1744, pp 121-127; 1 July to 27 October 1744, pp 134-137; final entry, p 137.
Edited with comments interspersed by William White, published in *Life of Emanuel Swedenborg* second revised edition <Hyde 3320> London. The passages are not quoted in full.
UK: SOC, NR

X 43/03/En 1952/1 **1952** Hyde 3336/24
A number of passages are quoted and paraphrased, though not in chronological order, on pp 184-193 in C S Odhner *The Swedenborg Epic* <Hyde 3336/24> New York.
UK: SOC, CON, NCC, NR; NET: GEN; USA: ANC

X 43/03/En 1958/1, **E:b** En 1958/4 **1958** Hyde 3336/25iv
<untitled>
4to

text, pp 705-710, 714-717, 719-722, 729, 731, 733-741, 743-768, 772-777, 781, 783, 786, 795, 797, 803, 805-823, 825.
Translated and edited by A Acton, published in *The Life of Emanuel Swedenborg* 4 <**E:b** En 1958/4 = Hyde 3336/25iv> Bryn Athyn PA.
UK: SOC, NCC; USA: ANC

X 43/01/En 1981/1 **1981** Hyde 3336/24–
Reprinted from X En 1952/1, published in *The Swedenborg Epic* <Hyde 3336/24–> London.
UK: SOC, NR; NET: GEN; USA: ANC

DANISH

43/03/Da 1/1 **1999** Hyde —
Emanuel Swedenborg | Drømmebogen | På dansk ved Jette Frantzen | FilosofiBiblioteket | Hans Reitzels Forlag
verso: *Drømmebogen* er oversat fra svensk | af Jette Frantzen efter „Drömboken", | redigeret og kommenteret af Per Erik Wahlund | © Wahlström & Widstrand 1964 | og for den danske udgave | © Hans Reitzels Forlag A/S, København 1999 | Forlagsredaktion: Asger Schnack | Omslag: Michael Jensen | Bogen er sat med Times hos Satsform, Aabyhøj | og trykt hos Narayana Press, Gylling | Printed in Denmark 1999 | ISBN 87-412-2800-6 | Originaludgaven blez første gang offentliggjort | i 1859 af G.E. Klemming | Kopiering fra denne bog er *kun* tilladt i oversens- | stemmelse med overenskomst mellem Undervis- | ningsministeriet og Copy-Dan. Enhver anden ud- | nyttelse er uden forlagets skriftlige samtykke for- | budt efter ophavsretsloven. Undtaget herfra er korte | uddrag til brug i anmeldelser. | Hans Reitzels Forlag · København 62 · 1150 København K
half title, verso: <publisher's information>
8vo
half title and title leaves, 4 pp; Indhold <Contents>, 1 p; Forord <Preface>, pp 1-7; text, pp 15-90; Noter <Notes>, p 92.
Translated by Jette Frantzen; edited by Per Erik Wahlund.
The contents are listed as follows: Forord af Per Erik Wahlund, p 7; Drømmebogen, p 15; Noter, p 92.
DEN: RLD; SWE: ROY

DUTCH

43/03/Du 1/1 **2011** Hyde 433/16
Swedenborgs Droomdagboek | Buitengewoon verslag | over de transformatie | van een wetenschapper | in een ziener. [1743/'44]
A3 folded to A4
Editie 75: Introduction, p 1; title and text n 1-156, pp 4-20; editie 76: title and text n 157-186, pp 2-16.
Translated by Henk Weevers, published in *Swedenborgiana* Baarle Nassau. The paragraph numbering follows that introduced by C Th Odhner in En 4/1 = Hyde 3336/24.
UK: SOC, NR; NET: BOE, GEN, KB; USA: ANC

DUTCH EXTRACTS

X 43/03/Du 2002/1 **2002** Hyde —
<untitled>
A3 folded to A4
Translated by G Janssens from X En 1952/1, published as 'Swedenborg Epos Hofdstuk 23' in *Swedenborgiana* Editie 45 pp 2-8, Baarle Nassau.
UK: SOC, NR; NET: BOE, GEN, KB; USA: ANC

X 43/03/Du 2011/1 **2011** Hyde —
Swedenborgs Droomdagboek.
A3 folded to A4
title and text, pp 3-9.
A translation by Henk Weevers of portions of *Emanuel Swesdenborg's Journal of Dreams* with commentary by Wilson Van Dusen <43/03/En 1/7 = Hyde 433/7> , published in *Swedenborgiana* Editie 74, Baarle Nassau.
UK: SOC, NR; NET: BOE, GEN, KB; USA: ANC

FRENCH

43/03/Fr 1/1 **1979** Hyde 433/6
EMMANUEL SWEDENBORG | *le livre des rêves* | <rule> | (Drömboken) | *Journal des années 1743-1744* | présenté et traduit par Régis Boyer | <type orn 7 x 7 mm> | PANDORA/LE MILIEU
verso: © Pandora Editions, 1979 | ISBN 2-86371-006-0
half title: LE LIVRES DES RÉVES <*stet* LIVRES>
8vo
blank leaf; half title and title leaves, 4 pp; L'Itinéraire spirituel de Swedenborg <signed Régis Boyer 2 Mars 1977>, pp 7-42; text, pp 43-156.
The editor's notes follow at the end of each 'Dream Diary' entry.
UK: SOC; SWE: ROY

43/03/Fr 1/2 **1985** Hyde 433/–
<<LE LIVRE DES RÊVES: Journal des années 1743-1744 Emanuel Swedenborg. (Dromboken) Journal ... présenté et traduit par Régis Boyer. Berg International. 1985. Paris.>>
8vo
title leaf, 2 pp; Preliminary material, ... ; text, 120 pp; Colophon, p 121.
Revised edition of Fr 1/1. ISBN 2-900269-37-7.
Copy not seen; description deduced from catalogue of SWE: ROY.
SWE: ROY

FRENCH EXTRACTS

X 43/03/Fr nd/1 **no date** Hyde 433/4
<untitled>
MS translation of entries dated 1744 April 2x3, 3x4, 4x5, 5x6, March 25x26, 30x31, 6 pp. <UK: SOC Archives A/125>
Translated by A Harlé, accompanied by a slip written by M Matter which is dated 3 Mai 1863.
UK: SOC

GERMAN

Translators:
Ge 1 I Meyer-Lüne
Ge 2 F Prochaska

43/03/Ge 1/1 **1925** Hyde 433/–
<<*EMANUEL SWEDENBORGS | TRAUMTAGEBUCH | aus dem Jahre 1744 | Nach dem druck der handschrift von 1859 | aus dem schwedischen übersetzt | von | ILSE MEYER-LÜNE. | Ausgabe der | HAMBURGER HANDDRUCKE. | Hamburg 1925* >>

4to
title leaf, 2 pp; <quotation from Swedenborg's *Spiritual Diary*>, 1 p; Ein Vorstück <A preliminary statement>, pp 1-4; text, pp 5-102; Nachwort <Postscript>, pp 103-106; Publisher's note, p 107.
Translated by Ilse Meyer-Lüne.
The colophon states that this edition of The Dream Diary of Emanuel Swedenborg of 1744 has been printed as the sixth book by the Hamburger Handdrucke <Hamburg Hand Press>, Printer: The workshop Lerchenfeld for the Buchbund Hamburg <League of the Book Hamburg>. The setting and layout was done by Johannes Schulz. The print on the hand press was made by Karl Runki. The type is the bold italic one by the Type-Foundry Genzsch & Heye. Edition 150 copies. A small number of proof copies were provided to public libraries. This copy is numbered 168.
Unpublished copies have been recorded as follows.
1 GER: WLB A photographic reproduction on microfiche, made from the copy in GER: BER.
2 UK: SOC A copy made from <1>.
GER: BER, HAM; SWE: ROY

43/03/Ge 2/1 **1978** Hyde 433/–
Emanuel Swedenborg | TRAUMTAGEBUCH | 1743—1744 | *Aus dem Schwedischen übersetzt* | *von* | *Felix Prochaska* | SWEDENBORG VERLAG ZÜRICH
verso: Aus dem Schwedischen übersetzt von Hofrat Feliz Prochaska † | © 1978 by Swedenborg Verlag Zürich | Gesamtherstellung: Swedenborg Verlag Zürich | ISBN-Nr. 3-85927-037-0
half title: EMANUEL SWEDENBORG • TRAUMTAGEBUCH 1743–1744
A5 perfect bound
half title and title leaves, 4 pp; Die Reise nach innen <The Journey within>, pp 1-2; Translator's foreword to this edition, pp 3-6; text, pp 7-73; Anmerckungen <Notes>, pp 75-87; Werbung <advertisement>, pp 89-90.
The ISBN was changed later to 3-85927-042-7.
Die Reise nach innen is a translation of an extract from *The Presence of Other Worlds* by Wilson van Dusen.
UK: SOC; SWI: ZÜR

43/03/Ge 2/2 **1987** Hyde 433/–
<<Emanuel Swedenborg | TRAUMTAGEBUCH | 1743—1744 | *Aus dem Schwedischen übersetzt* | *von* | *Felix Prochaska* | SWEDENBORG VERLAG ZÜRICH>>
verso: <<Aus dem Schwedischen übersetzt von Hofrat Feliz Prochaska † | © 1987 by Swedenborg Verlag Zürich | Gesamtherstellung: Swedenborg Verlag Zürich | ISBN-3-85927-042-7>>
half title: <<EMANUEL SWEDENBORG • TRAUMTAGEBUCH 1743–1744>>
A5 perfect bound
half title and title leaves, 4 pp; Translator's foreword to this edition, pp 1-6; text, pp 7-73; Anmerckungen <Notes>, pp 75-87; Werbung <advertisement>, pp 89-90.
Photographic reprint of Ge 2/1.
Copy not seen; description deduced from Ge 2/1 and publisher's information.

GERMAN EXTRACTS

X 43/03/Ge 1924 **1924** Hyde —
Swedenborg's Träume. | Ein Beitrag zur Phänomenologie seiner Mystik. | Von | Hans W. Gruhle.
small 4to
title and text, pp 273-320.
Extracts taken from a translation by Ilse Meyer-Lüne <cp Ge 1/1>, edited by H W Gruhle in *Psychologische Forschung: Zeitschrift für Psychologie und ihre Grenzwissenschaften* Berlin,

Göttingen, Heidelberg.
The portions selected are interspersed with a commentary by the editor.
An unpublished copy is recorded as follows.

1 UK: SOC A photocopied facsimile of the article provided by GER: WLB.

GER: WLB

GREEK EXTRACTS

X 43/03/Gk 1992/1 **1992** Hyde 993/–

ΕΜΑΝΟΥΕΛ ΣΒΕΝΤΕΝΜΠΟΓΚ | ΤΟ ΒΙΒΛΙΟ | ΤΩΝ ΟΝΕΙΡΩΝ | ΕΠΙΛΟΓΗ – ΜΕΤΑΦΡΑΣΗ – ΕΙΣΑΓΩΓΗ – ΣΧΟΛΙΑ | ΜΑΡΓΑΡΙΤΑ ΜΕΛΜΠΕΡΓΚ | ΚΕΔΡΟΣ
verso: © *Μαργαρίτα Μέλμπεργκ, 1992* | *Εχδόσεις Κέδρος, Α. Ε., 1992*
half title: ΤΟ ΒΙΒΛΙΟ | ΤΩΝ ΟΝΕΙΡΩΝ
section title: ΤΑ ΟΝΕΙΡΑ* | * *Τα τέσσερα πρώτα όνειρα είναι από σκόρπιες σημειώσεις από* | *το πρώτο μέρος του Βιβλίου των Ονείρων.*
8vo
title leaf, 2 pp; Περιεχόμενα <Contents>, 1 p; text: Σημείωμα της μεταφραστριας <Remarks of the translator>, pp 9-10; Προλογος για την ελληνιχή έχδοςη <Prologue to the Greek edition>, pp 11-18; Χρονολόγιο <Chronology of Swedenborg's life and work, compared with contemporary events>, pp 19-29; Η ζωή και το έργο του <Swedenborg's life and work>, pp 31-49; Το έργο του Σβέντενμπορκ πηγή επιδράσεων <Swedenborg's influence on others>, pp 51-59; Το Βιβλίο των Ονείρων <The Book of Dreams>, pp 61-74; Η γλώσσα των ονείρων <The language of dreams>, p 75-78; section title leaf, pp 79-80; Τα όνειρα <The dreams – extracts from 43/03>, pp 81-152; imprint, p 155.
Edited and translated by Margarita Melmberg <b 1951>. Published by Κέδρος, Athens. ISBN 960-04-0631-6.
The extracts translated in this version are the records of the dreams which Swedenborg experienced in 1744, dated by him to March 24/25, 30/31; April 1/2, 3/4, 6/7, 8/9, 10/11, 13/14, 14/15, 15/16, 17/18, 22/23, 23/24, 24/25, 25/26; April 30/May 1; May 5/6; June 11/12, 15/16, 20/21, 26/27; July 3/4, 9/10, 14/15, 24/25, 39/30; July 31/August 1; August 4/5, 8/9, 27/28; September 1/2, 16, 18/19, 21, 29/30; October 3 to 6, 9/10, 10/11, 19/20, 26/27.

SWE: ROY

ITALIAN

43/03/It 1/1 **1982** Hyde 433/–

<<EMMANUEL SWEDENBORG | IL LIBRO DEI SOGNI | Presentazione Dii Michelangelo Coviello | IL MELOGRANO>>
verso: <<Titolo originale: *Le livre des réves* | Copertina di Giuliano Vittori | Traduzione di Franco Montesanti | © *1981 Il Melograno - Edizioni A.B E,T.E. S.p.A.* | *Via Prenestina, 685 - Roma - Tel. 221841*>>
8vo
title leaf, 2 pp; Tema di Michelangelo Coviello, pp 5-6; text, pp 7-107.
Translated by Michelangelo Coviello. ISBN 88-7047-019-6.
Copy not seen; description deduced from information provided by SWE: ROY.

SWE: ROY

JAPANESE

Translators:

Ja 1 Imamura Kōichi
Ja 2 Yasayuki Suzuki

43/03/Ja 1/1 **1983** Hyde 433/–

<< <4 columns of characters, with a rule border 122 x 26 mm, in which the 2nd and 4th columns are printed as part of the vertical borders, with 6 characters printed horizontally as part of the bottom of the border> <1:> □生命の正体を探るもう一つの科学シリーズ□ <2:> 今村光一 訳・解説 <3:> 巨大霊能者の秘密 <4:> スウェデンボルグの夢日記 1743.7.21 - 1744.10.27 叢文社版>>
verso: <<*The Journal of Dreams* | *by* | *Emanuel Swedenborg*>>
frontispiece <portrait of Swedenborg>
8vo
title leaf, 2 pp; frontispiece; text, 203 pp; 4 plates.
Translated by Imamura Kōichi from an English version, published in the series 'Seimei no shōtai wo saguru mō hitotsu no kagaku shirīzu', Tokyo. ISBN 4-7947-0071-7.
Copy not seen; description deduced from catalogue entry and photocopies provided by SWE: ROY.
In the catalogue of SWE: ROY title information is transliterated as follows: Kyodai renōsha no himitsu; Suedenborugu no yumenikki; Imamura Kōichi yaku-kaisetsu. Tokyo: Sōbun-sha Shōwa 57 (58).
SWE: ROY

43/03/Ja 2/1 **1995** Hyde 433/–

title page: <superimposed on a picture of a woman about to enter a doorway, printed within an elliptical label> スウェーデンボルグの | *SWEDENBORG'S JOURNAL OF DREAMES 1743-1744* | 夢日記 | エマヌエル・スウェーデンボルグ | 鈴木泰之 訳 | <below the elliptical label> たま出版 <*stet* DREAMES>
half title: SWEDENBORG'S | JOURNAL OF DREAMES | 1743~1744 | Emanuel Swedenborg | Edited from the original Swedish | by G. E. Klemming | Translated into English, 1860, | by J. J. G. Wilkinson | Edited by William Ross Woofenden | With an Introduction | by Wilson Van Dusen, | Second Edition, 1989 | Swedenborg Scientific Association | Bryn Athyn, PA | Swedenborg Society | London, England | Translated and published by permission of | the Swedenborg Scientific Association <*stet* DREAMES>
frontispiece <portrait of Swedenborg>
8vo
half title and title leaves, 4 pp; frontispiece, 1 p; Contents, pp 2-3; text, pp 4-237; Index, p 238; publishing information, p 239; advertisement, p 240.
Translated by Yasuyuki Suzuki, published by Tama Publishing Company, Tokyo. ISBN 4-88481-367-7 C0014. An edition of 500 copies was printed.
UK: SOC

POLISH

43/03/Pl 1/1 **1996** Hyde 433/–

<<Dziennik Snów: 1743-1744 | Emanuel Swedenborg; przeł., przedmową i przypisami opatrzył Mariusz Kalinowski; posł. Bolesław Andrzejewski.>>
8vo
title leaf, preface, text, and footnotes, 127 pp; 1 p; 2 illustrations.
Translated and edited by Mariusz Kalinowski, assisted by Bolesław Andrzejewski; published by Dom Wydawniczy REBIS, Poznan 1996. Series title: Spotkania z Mistrzem <Meetings with Masters>. ISBN 8371202636.
Copy not seen; description deduced from catalogue of POL: BNW.
POL: BNW

ROMANIAN

43/03/Ro 1/1 **1995** Hyde 433/8

EMANUEL SWEDENBORG | CARTEA | DE VISE | Traducere din suedeză, prezentare şi note de | GABRIELA MELINESCU | Cu un portret al autorlui de | JORGE LUIS BORGES

verso: Coperta: ANA-MARIA ORBAN | Lector: ILEANA MĂLĂNCIOIU | Redactor: DENISA COMĂNESCU | Publicarea acestui volum | a fost sprijinită de | Svenska Institutet, Stockholm. | EMANUEL SWEDENBORG | *Drömboken* | Wahlström & Widstrand | Stockholm, 1964 | Toate drepturile asupra prezentei versiuni româneşti | aparţin Editurii UNIVERS, | 79739, Bucureşti, Piata Presei Libere nr. 1 | ISBN: 973-34-0326-1

half title: EMANUEL SWEDENBORG | CARTEA DE VISE | <type orn 17 x 10 mm> | EDITURA UNIVERS | Bucureşti, 19-95

verso: <frontispiece, portrait of Swedenborg>

half title and title leaves, 4 pp; Dedication, p 5; facsimile of a page from Sw O/1, p 6; Introductory essay by J L Borges, pp 7-19; Translator's introduction, pp 20-28; text, pp 29-157; Cuprins <Contents>, p 159; bibliographical information, p 160.

Translated from Sw 5/1 by Gabriela Melinescu.

UK: SOC, NR; SWE: ROY; USA: ANC

RUSSIAN EXTRACTS

X 43/03/Ru 1999/1 **1999** Hyde 3390/13

A number of passages are quoted and paraphrased, though not in chronological order, on pp 162-175 in V A Maliavin's translation of C S Odhner *The Swedenborg Epic* Moscow, ISBN 6-8213-0038-X.

UK: SOC

X 43/03/Ru 2003/1 **2003** Hyde —

A reprint of X Ru 1999/1, on pp 120-130 of a volume compiled and edited by V A Maliavin entitled Однер Зигстедт Змануэль Сведенборг Избранное <The Epic Emanuel Swedenborg Selected Works> Moscow, **D** Ru 2003/1 = Hyde 3158/6; ISBN 5-17-019737-3 (AST) and 5-271-06825-0 (Astrel).

UK: SOC

43/04 Swammerdam's *Books of Nature* Hyde CXIX

The autograph MS forms part of Codex 53 in the Library of the Royal Swedish Academy of Sciences, Stockholm. Swedenborg's analysis of Swammerdam's *Biblia Naturae*, published in Leyden in 1737, follows the conclusion of 43/01/La O/1, which ends on the page on which the present work begins.

LATIN

43/04/La O/1 1743 Hyde 413
<<Johannis Swammerdamii Biblia Naturæ>>
foolscap long 4to <330 x 102 mm>
text: Pars prior, pp 142b-151a.
De scorpione, Tom: I, p 151a.
De Cochlea operculari, Tom: I, pp 151b-157a.
De Cochlea hortensi, p 157a.
De Cochlea domestica sive nuda, pp 157b-158a.
De Cochlea mirabili, vivipara, chrystallina, pp 158a-158b.
De Cancello, pp 159a-160a.
De Scorpione aquatico volanti, pp 160a-160b.
De Hemerobio, ephemero, sive diaria, pp 160b-162b.
De Scarabaeo nasicorni, p 162b.
De Cosse, houtwurm, seu verme scarabaei, pp 162b-166b.
De Culice, pp 166b-167a.
De Apibus, pp 167a-169a, 170a-175a; p 169b blank.
De Hydrocantharo, p 175b.
De Papilione diurno vulgari coloribus distincto, pp 176a-178b.
De Verme, e quo musca azÿlus, pp 179a-180b.
De Acaro, verme et musca, pp 180b-181a.
De Ranis et gÿrinis ranarum, pp 181b-185b.
De Sepia pisce, pp 185b-189a.
De 4 ordinibus mutationum, p 189a.
De Sanguine, p 189a; p 189b blank.
MS not seen; description deduced from La O/2.
SWE: KVA

43/04/La O/2, **D** La 1869/2 **1869** Hyde 414, 3034
Johannis Swammerdamii Biblia Naturæ
folio
title and text, pp 184-264.
Reproduction of La O/1, published in photolithographed edition, vol 6 <*Supplementum Regni Animalis* **D** La 1869/2 = Hyde 3034> Stockholm.
Unpublished copies have been recorded as follows.
1 UK: SOC & USA: ANC, SHS A reproduction on microfilm 16 or 17, Bryn Athyn PA.
UK: SOC, BL, CHT, CON, NCC, NCH, RYL; GER: GSU; NET: GEN; SWE: ROY, KVA, LUN, UPP; USA: ANC, FOU, SHS; AUS: SYD

43/04/La O/3, **D** La 1927/1 **1928** Hyde 414/1, 3038/26
Johannis Swammerdamii Biblia Naturæ
folio
title and text, pp 143-189.
Photographic reproduction of La O/2, published in *Autographa Editio Photostata* vol 5 <*de Periosteo et Mammis etc* **D** La 1927/1 = Hyde 3038/26> Bryn Athyn PA.
Unpublished copies have been recorded as follows.
1 UK: SOC & USA: ANC, SHS A reproduction on microfilm 21 made in 1962, Bryn Athyn PA.
UK: SOC; USA: ANC

ENGLISH EXTRACTS

X 43/04/En 1923/1 **1923** Hyde 414/2
THE GOVERNMENT OF BEES.
8vo
title and text, pp 141-146.
Translated by E E Iungerich, published in *The New Philosophy* Philadelphia, following an article entitled 'The propagation of bees', pp 122-135.
UK: SOC; USA: ANC

X 43/04/En 1958/1, **E:b** En 1958/4 **1958** Hyde 3336/25iv
<untitled>
4to
text, pp 690-693.
Translated and edited by A Acton, published in *The Life of Emanuel Swedenborg* 4 <**E:b** En 1958/4 = Hyde 3336/25iv> Bryn Athyn PA.
UK: SOC, NCC; USA: ANC

44/01 The Five Senses Hyde CXX

The autograph MS forms part of Codex 58 in the Library of the Royal Swedish Academy of Sciences, Stockholm. Swedenborg numbered the pages 1-197; later, a Librarian of the Academy numbered the leaves 2a-92b, 100a-101b. In describing La O/1, the leaf numbers are given first, and Swedenborg's page numbers are given in parentheses.

At the close of the article *Continuatio de regulis harmonicis seu musicis* on p 187, Swedenborg wrote, 'Vide somnium 1-2 Juli' <See the dream between 1 and 2 July>. This reference is to 43/03/Sw O/1 <n 211>; at the date given Swedenborg wrote what he perceived to be the significance of what he had learned about sensation.

On p 1, above the word 'Prologus' Swedenborg wrote the number 4, indicating a change in his plan for *Regnum Animale* in which the extended scheme included the subject of this MS at chapter 6. The 'Prologus' explains the reason for this change and why the present subject was now given precedence over *De Generatione* <43/01>, which had been planned for chapters 4 and 5.

LATIN

Editions:

La O MS
La 1 J F I Tafel, editor

44/01/La O/1 1744 Hyde 415, 3004

<<De Sensu communi, ejusque Influxu in animam, et hujus reactione.>>
pott folio <318 x 191 mm>
text: I. Prologus n 1-6, pp 2a-2b (1-2).
II. De Carotidum truncis communibus n 1-7, pp 3a-4a (3-5).
De Ramo communi carotidis externae n 1-6, pp 4b-5a (6-7).
De Reliquis ramis carotidis externae n 1-6, pp 6a-7a (9-11).
III. De Sensu in genere n 1-13, pp 7b-10a (12-17).
De Sensu gustus, seu lingua, pp 10a-10b (17-18).
De Sensu gustus, ejusque sensorio, in genere et in specie n 1-2 <deleted>, p 11a (19).
De Sensu gustus, in genere et in specie, n 1-7, pp 11b-17a (20-31).
De Olfactu n 1-11, pp 17b-23a (32-43).
De sensu tactus, seu cuticulis, n 1-16 and 11-16, pp 23a-31b (44-60).
De Aure, et sensu auditus, n 1-23, 23-25, 25-26, 26, 26-27, 29-30, pp 32a-41a and 51a (61-75, 76-80, and 99); p 51a is to be read with p 39a.
De Cochlea n 1-10, pp 41b-43a (80-83).

De Oculo et visu n 1-12, pp 43b-46a (84-89).
De Lumine et coloribus n 1-5, pp 46a-47b (89-92).
De Coloribus n 1-3, pp 47b-49a (92-95).
De Externis partibus oculis n 1-11, pp 49a-50b (95-98).
De Musculis oculi n 1-3, pp 51a-52b (100-102).
De Tunicis oculi n 1-4, pp 52b-55a (102-107).
De Humoribus oculi, et retina, n 1-3, pp 55a-55b (107-108).
De Humoribus et visu, pp 56a-62a (109-121).
Experimenta physica ex Desaguille n 1-9, pp 62b-63a (122-123).
Optica n 1-3, pp 63a-64b (123-126).
De Ideis visu et tactu, p 65a (127); p 65b (128) blank.
De Sensibus, seu sensatione in genere. Epilogus n 1-6, 1-11, 13-37, pp 66a-73a (129-144).
De Veritatibus n 1-10, pp 73a-74b (144-147).
Ulterius haec probe notanda, magis sedulo explorata n 1-5, pp 74b-76a (147-150).
In summa, Expositio generalis. De Sensatione et affectione, pp 76a-80b (150-159).
Continuatio ex regulis harmonicis seu musicis, pp 81a-94b (160-187).
Intellectus vero et ejus operatio, pp 94b-98b (187-195).
Conclusio, p 99a (196); p 92b (197) blank.

Index de sensu communi, ejusque influxu in animam, et hujus re-actione; [Iteratum de veritatibus; Ulterius et accuratius; Continuatio ex regulis musicis; Ulterius; et Intellectus et ejus operatio], pp 100a-101b <written in double columns>.

Unpublished copies have been recorded as follows.

1 SWE: KVA A MS transcript made by G Ekelöf.

2 USA: SSA A MS transcript of 'Experimenta physica ex Desaguille'. <Archives envelope F>

MS not seen; description deduced from La O/3.

SWE: KVA

44/01/La 1/1 — 1848 — Hyde 417

EMAN. SWEDENBORGII, | SACRAE REGIAE MAJESTATIS REGNIQUE SUECIAE | COLLEGII METALLICI ASSESSORIS | REGNUM ANIMALE | ANATOMICE, PHYSICE ET PHILOSOPHICE | PERLUSTRATUM. | CUJUS | PARS QUARTA | DE | CAROTIDIBUS, DE SENSU OLFACTUS, AUDITUS ET VISUS, | DE SENSATIONE ET AFFECTIONE IN GENERE, AC DE | INTELLECTU ET EJUS OPERATIONE | AGIT. | <short rule> | E CHIROGRAPHO EJUS | IN BIBLIOTHECA REGIAE ACADEMIAE HOLMIENSIS | ASSERVATO | NUNC PRIMUM EDIDIT | Dr JO. FR. IM. TAFEL, | PHILOSOPHIAE PROFESSOR ET REGIAE BIBLIOTHECAE UNIVERSITATIS | TUBINGENSIS PRAEFECTUS. | <multiple rule> | TUBINGAE | CURAM ADMINISTRAT „Verlagsexpedition;" | LONDINI, | WILLIAM NEWBERY, 6, KING STREET, HOLBORN; | H. BALLIERE, 219. REGENT STREET. | 1848. <*stet* BALLIERE>

8vo

title leaf, 2 pp; text: <pp 1-7, 32-43, 61-121, 129-196 of La O/1>, pp 1-227; <Index leaves 100a-101b of La O/1>, pp 227-234; Notae criticae editoris, pp 235-251; Errata, p 252; diagram, p 253.

The missing portions were omitted by the direction of the Swedenborg Association, London, at whose expense the work was printed.

UK: SOC, NCC, NR; GER: GSU

44/01/La O/2, D La 1869/2 — 1869 — Hyde 416, 3034

De Sensu gustus, seu Lingua.
De Sensu tactus seu cuticulis.
Experimenta Physica ex Desaguille.
folio

text <pp 17-31, 44-60, 122-127 of La O/1>, pp 26-40, 41-57, 102-107.
Reproduction of parts of La O/1, published in photolithographed edition, vol 6 <*Supplementum Regni Animalis* **D** La 1869/2 = Hyde 3034> Stockholm. The editor gives no reasons for reproducing only this portion of the autograph MS; he may have done so because the remainder of La O/1 had been printed in La 1/1.
Unpublished copies have been recorded as follows.

1 USA: ANC A typed transcript of 'Experimeneta physica ex Desaguille' in 15 pp, made by A H Stroh. <Archives envelope F>

2 A MS transcript of 'De Sensu Gustus, seu Lingua' by E E Iungerich. <Current whereabouts unknown>

3 UK: SOC & USA: ANC, SHS A reproduction on microfilm 16 or 17 made in 1962, Bryn Athyn PA.

UK: SOC, BL, CHT, CON, NCC, NCH, RYL; GER: GSU; NET: GEN; SWE: ROY, KVA, LUN, UPP; USA: ANC, FOU, SHS; AUS: SYD

44/01/La O/3, **D** La 1927/2 **1927** Hyde 416/1, 3038/31
<untitled>
folio
title and text, pp 1-197.
Photographic reproduction of La O/1, published in *Autographa Editio Photostata* vol 10 <*De Sensibus, etc.* **D** La 1927/2 = Hyde 3038/31> Bryn Athyn PA.
Unpublished copies have been recorded as follows.

1 UK: SOC & USA: ANC, SHS A reproduction on microfilm 21 or 22 made in 1962, Bryn Athyn PA.

UK: SOC; USA: ANC

ENGLISH

44/01/En 1/1 **1900-1912** Hyde 419
ON THE SENSES. | PART FOUR OF "THE ANIMAL KINGDOM" | BY EMANUEL SWEDENBORG.
8vo
title and text: **1900** ch I 'Prologue', pp 129-133; **1901** ch II, pp 1-8; n 36-51, pp 33-40; n 52-66, pp 105-113; **1902** n 67-81, pp 1-10; n 82-88, pp 145-151; **1903** n 89-96, pp 1-7; n 97-111, pp 109-114; **1904** n 112-125, pp 1-6; n 126-135, pp 109-112; **1905** n 136-149, pp 149-153; n 150-172, pp 185-192; **1906** n 173-183, pp 97-102; **1907** n 184-203, pp 129-134; n 204-211, pp 161-163; n 212-267, pp 237-251; **1908** n 268-359, pp 8-22; n 360-372, pp 47-50; n 373-391, pp 94-110; n 392-402, pp 124-134; **1909** n 403-417, pp 15-26; n 418-425, pp 44-54; n 426-430, pp 99-104; n 431-446, pp 126-136; **1910** n 447-463, pp 23-32; n 464-494, pp 34-50; n 495-533, pp 110-124; n 534-568, pp 137-156; **1911** n 569-596, pp 5-19; n 597-624, pp 34-50; n 625-641, pp 101-111; 'Touch, or the Cuticular Sense', pp 141-154; **1912** 'Touch, or the Cuticular Sense' continued, pp 5-23; 'The sense of Taste, or the Tongue', pp 67-76, 114-126.
Translated by E S Price from La 1/1, published in *The New Philosophy* Lancaster PA.

UK: SOC, NCC; USA: ANC

44/01/En 1/2 **1914** Hyde 419/1
THE FIVE SENSES | BY | EMANUEL SWEDENBORG.| Being the first draft of a treatise intended as a part of the | Animal Kingdom series, and parts of which were | elaborated by the author and published as | THE ANIMAL KINGDOM | PART III | <short rule> | TRANSLATED FROM THE LATIN | BY | ENOCH S. PRICE, A.M. | <short rule> | PHILADELPHIA, PA. | SWEDENBORG SCIENTIFIC ASSOCIATION | 1914
8vo
title leaf, 2 pp; Table of contents, p iii; Translator's preface, pp iv-v; Bibliographical note, pp vi-viii; text n 1-749, pp 1-338.

Reprint of En 1/1. Edited and translated by E S Price from La 1/1. The two portions of text entitled 'De sensu gustus' and 'De sensu tactus' omitted from La 1/1 were transcribed from La 0/1 by E E Iungerich, edited and translated by E S Price, and published as n 642-749 on pp 283-338; according to their place in La 0/1 they would appear between n 66 and 67 and n 96 and 97 respectively.
The Index was prepared by W H Alden and revised by A Acton. E S Price had prepared a long word index to the work, and his MS is preserved in USA: ANC.

UK: SOC; NET: GEN; USA: ANC

44/01/En 1/3 **1976** Hyde 419/2

THE FIVE SENSES | BY | EMANUEL SWEDENBORG.| Being the first draft of a treatise intended as a part of the | Animal Kingdom series, and parts of which were | elaborated by the author and published as | THE ANIMAL KINGDOM | PART III | <short rule> | TRANSLATED FROM THE LATIN | BY | ENOCH S. PRICE, A.M. | <short rule> | PHILADELPHIA, PA. | SWEDENBORG SCIENTIFIC ASSOCIATION | 1914
verso: Reprinted in 1976 400 copies | Swedenborg Scientific Association | Bryn Athyn, Pennsylvania
section title: INDEXES
8vo
title leaf, 2 pp; Table of contents, p iii; Translator's preface, pp iv-v; Bibliographical note, pp vi-viii; text n 1-749, pp 1-338; 1 blank leaf; section title leaf, pp 339-340; Subject index, pp 341-378; Index of authors cited, p 379; Corrigenda, pp 379-380; advertisement, p 381.
Photographic replica reprint of En 1/2 with the addition of the section title leaf and the material on pp 341-381.

UK: SOC, NR; USA: ANC

44/01/En 1/4 **2006** Hyde 419/3

THE FIVE SENSES | BY | EMANUEL SWEDENBORG| Being the first draft of a treatise intended as a part of the | Animal Kingdom series, and parts of which were | elaborated by the author and published as | THE ANIMAL KINGDOM | PART III | TRANSLATED FROM THE LATIN | BY | ENOCH S. PRICE, A.M. | Philadelphia, PA. | Swedenborg Scientific Association | 1914
verso: © 2006 by Swedenborg Scientific Association | all rights reserved | First Latin edition by J.F. Immanuel Tafel published in Tübingen | and London, 1848 | English translation by Rev. Enoch S. Price published by Swedenborg | Scientific Association, 1914 | Reprinted, 1976 | Reprinted, 2006 | Library of Congress Cataloging-in-Publication Data | Swedenborg, Emanuel, 1688-1772. | [Regnum animale. Part 3., English] | The five senses: being the first draft of a treatise intended as part of the Animal | kingdom series, and parts of which were elaborated by the author and published as the | Animal kingdom Part III / by Emanuel Swedenborg; translated from the Latin by Enoch S. | Price. | p. cm. | Includes bibliographical references and index. | ISBN 0-915221-78-0 (pbk.: alk. paper) | 1. Senses and sensation- -Early works to 1800. I. Title. | QP431.S94 2006 | 612.8--dc22 | ISBN-10: 0-915221-78-0 | ISBN-13: 978-0-915221-78-3 | Three-volume set with *The Soul's Domain* | ISBN-10: 0-915221-80-2 | ISBN-13: 078-0-915221-80-6 | Swedenborg Scientific Association | P.O. Box 757, Bryn Athyn, PA 19009 | Email: ssa@comcast.net | www.swedenborg-philosophy.org | Printed in the United States of America
half title: THE FIVE SENSES
8vo
half title and title leaves, 4 pp; Table of contents, p v; Translator's preface, pp vii-viii; Bibliographical note, pp ix-xi; text n 1-749, pp 1-368; Index of subjects, pp 369-411; Index of authors cited, pp 413-414; advertisement, p 415.
Photographic replica reprint of En 1/3 = Hyde 419/2 by Fidlar Doubleday, U.S.A.

UK: SOC; USA: ANC

ENGLISH EXTRACTS

X 44/01/En 1854/1 **1854** Hyde 420
MENTAL PHILOSOPHY, OR THE INTELLECT AND ITS | OPERATIONS. | *(From Swedenborg's Manuscripts, not hitherto translated.)*
8vo
title and text, pp 255-261, 317-325.
Translated by J H Smithson from La 1/1, published in *The Intellectual Repository* London.
UK: SOC, BL, CHT, CON, NCC, NR; USA: ANC

X 44/01/En 1882/1, **D** En 1882/3 **1882** Hyde 421, 3131
A. *THE COMMON TRUNKS OF THE CAROTIDS.*
8vo
title and text n 400a-400h, pp 387-392 <pp 3-5 of La 0/1>.
Edited and translated by R L Tafel, published in *The Brain* 1 <**D** En 1882/3 = Hyde 3131> London.
UK: SOC, CON, NCC, NR; NET: GEN, KB; SWE: UPP; USA: ANC, SHS; AUS: SYD

X 44/01/En 1887/1, **D** En 1887/1 **1887** Hyde 422, 3132
5. FROM THE WORK ENTITLED: "THE SENSES AND SENSATION | IN GENERAL."
8vo
title and text n 683s-t, pp 293-294.
Translated by R L Tafel, published in *The Brain* 2 <**D** En 1887/1 = Hyde 3132> London.
UK: SOC, CON, NCC, NR; NET: GEN, KB; SWE: UPP; USA: ANC, SHS; AUS: SYD

X 44/01/En 1934/1, **D** En 1934/1 **1934** Hyde 421/1, 3131/1
A. *THE COMMON TRUNKS OF THE CAROTIDS.*
8vo
title and text n 400a-400h <pp 3-5 of La 0/1>, pp 387-392.
Reprint of X En 1882/1, published in *The Brain* 1 <**D** En 1934/1 = Hyde 3131> London.
UK: SOC; NET: KB; USA: SHS

X 44/01/En 1958/1, **E:b** En 1958/4 **1958** Hyde 3336/25iv
<untitled>
4to
text, pp 778-784, 788-797.
Translated and edited by A Acton, published in *The Life of Emanuel Swedenborg* 4 <**E:b** En 1958/4 = Hyde 3336/25iv> Bryn Athyn PA.
UK: SOC, NCC; USA: ANC

X 44/01/En 1994/1, **D** En 1994/1 **1994** Hyde 421/–, 3131/–
<<A. *THE COMMON TRUNKS OF THE CAROTIDS.*>>
8vo
title and text n 400a-400h, pp 387-392 <pp 3-5 of La 0/1>.
Photographic replica reprint of X En 1882/1 = Hyde 421, published in *The Brain* 1 <**D** En 1994/1> by Gryphon Editions, Birmingham AL.
Copy not seen; description deduced from X En 1882/1 and publisher's advertisement.

X 44/01/En 1994/2, **D** En 1994/2 **1994** Hyde 422/–, 3132/–
<<*5. FROM THE WORK ENTITLED: "THE SENSES AND SENSATION | IN GENERAL."*>>

8vo
title and text n 683s-t, pp 293-294.
Photographic replica reprint of X En 1887/1 = Hyde 422, published in *The Brain* 2 <**D** En 1994/2> by Gryphon Editions, Birmingham AL.
Copy not seen; description deduced from X En 1887/1 and publisher's advertisement.

X 44/01/En 2005/1, **D** En 2005/1 **2005** Hyde 421/2, 3131/2
A. *THE COMMON TRUNKS OF THE CAROTIDS.*
8vo
title and text n 400a-400h <pp 3-5 of La O/1>, pp 387-392.
Photographic replica reprint of X En 1882/1, published in *The Brain* 1 <**D** En 2005/1 = Hyde 3131/2> by The Swedenborg Scientific Association, Bryn Athyn PA.
UK: SOC, NR; USA: ANC

X 44/01/En 2005/2, **D** En 2005/2 **2005** Hyde 422/2, 3131/2
5. FROM THE WORK ENTITLED: "THE SENSES AND SENSATION | IN GENERAL."
8vo
title and text n 683s-t, pp 293-294.
Photographic replica reprint of X En 1882/1, published in *The Brain* 1 <**D** En 2005/2> published by The Swedenborg Scientific Association, Bryn Athyn PA.
UK: SOC, NR; USA: ANC

44/02 Quotations from a Work by Cassebohm Hyde CXX

The autograph MS forms part of Codex 58 in the Library of the Royal Swedish Academy of Sciences, Stockholm. Written in the same Codex as 44/01, though paged separately by Swedenborg, this was probably intended to have been used as a supplement to the chapter *De Aure, et Sensu Auditus* in the final version of the work on the senses. The quotations were taken from *De Aure Humano* by J F Cassebohm, published in Halle in 1735.

LATIN

44/02/La O/1 1744 Hyde 418

<<De Aure Humana ex Joh: Friderico Cassebom. Tract I <II et III> >>
pott folio <318 x 191 mm>
title and text, pp 126a-131a (i-xi); p 131b blank.
MS not seen; description deduced from La O/2.
SWE: KVA

44/02/La O/2, **D** La 1927/2 1927 Hyde 418/1, 3038/31

De Aure Humana. ex Joh: Friderico Cassebom | Tract I.
folio
title and text, pp 126a-131a.
Photographic reproduction of La O/1, published in *Autographa Editio Photostata* vol 10 <*De Sensibus, etc.* **D** La 1927/2 = Hyde 3038/31> Bryn Athyn PA.
Unpublished copies have been recorded as follows.
1 UK: SOC & USA: ANC, SHS A reproduction on microfilm 22 made in 1962, Bryn Athyn PA.
UK: SOC; USA: ANC

44/03 The Brain 2 Hyde CXXI

The autograph MS forms the major part of Codex 58 in the Library of the Royal Swedish Academy of Sciences, Stockholm. Swedenborg numbered the pages 198-241, continuing from his numbering of 44/01/La O/1; later, a Librarian of the Academy numbered the leaves 2a-123b. In describing La O/1, the leaf numbers are given first, and Swedenborg's pages numbers are given in parentheses.

From Swedenborg's pagination it is fair to assume that he wrote this treatise immediately after 44/01. Further, in *Drömmar* <43/03/Sw O/1>, 3-4 July 1744, he wrote after his statement that he had finished writing the work on the senses, 'Och at jag nu kommer til andra dehlen som år Cerebrum.' <And that now I come to the next part, which is the Cerebrum.>

In Swedenborg's final scheme for *Regnum Animale* <44/01/La 1/1 = Hyde 436>, while 'the organs of the external senses' were to be treated of as part VI, 'the cerebrum and the internal sensoria' were to constitute part VII; and he composed the material in this order.

It appears that he finished the draft by 1 August, for at that date in *Drömmar* we read, 'Som betyder mitt arbete jag nu begynt, den senare det om Cerebro.' <This signifies the work I have now begun; the past was that on the Cerebrum.>

References which Swedenborg added to the MS indicate that he had intended to draw material for the planned work from his other MSS in which he had dealt with the same subject material; see, for example, on p 202 of the MS his note that the anatomical authorities quoted on p 73 of chapter I were to be inserted here.

LATIN

44/03/La O/1 1744 Hyde 423

<< <untitled> >>

pott folio <318 x 191 mm>

text: Praefatio ad Partem de Cerebro: sed praemissum immediate Capiti Primo, n 1-7, pp 102a-104a (198-202).

Caput Imum. De Cerebro, ejus fabrica et motu, de functione in genere <heading only>. Praemittenda est experientia Cap: VII p: LXXIII, in prima projectione: etiam de motu fortassis in C: I, ut et de substantia corticali et medullari in genere alibi in scriptis et editis; obs. jussus sum, p 104a (202).

De Cerebro n 1-7, pp 104a-104b (202-203).

De Cerebri fabrica: vide Caput VII nostrae prioris projectionis, p 104b (203).

De Cerebri motu: vide Caput Im nostrae prioris projectionis, p 104b (203).

De functione Cerebri n 1-<4> <deleted>, pp 104b-105a (203-204).

Cap: II. De Cranio et ejus ossibus <heading only>, p 105a (204).

Cap: III. De Dura Matre, et ejus productionibus: et sic porro <heading only>, p 105a (204).

De fabrica Cerebri n 1-5 <deleted>, p 105b (205).
De fabrica Cerebri n 1-4, 4-7, pp 106a-107a (206-208).
<De> Motu: vide mea <heading only>, p 107b (209).
De functionibus Cerebri in genere n 1-15, pp 107b-110b (209-215).
Hic ordo in functionibus Cerebri designandis, observandus, nam instructior et de iis factus sum, n 1-22, pp 110b-113b (215-221).
<Quomodo anima agit in suum corpus, et hoc vicissim reagit in animam> n 1-3, pp 113b-114b (221-223).
<In the margin of n 3 Swedenborg wrote, 'Observanda, quod haec non inserenda sint in Capite seu These, nam praematurum est; Ad reservanda. Ita videar mandatum in eum.' <It is to be observed that this paragraph must not be inserted in the chapter or thesis, for it is premature; it is to be reserved. It seems to me that I have been commanded so.>
Catena et vinculum usuum n 1-18, pp 114b-119a (223-232).
In compendium redacta, pp 119a-119b (232-233).
<Cap. IV:> De dura matre n 1-11, pp 120a-123b (234-241); 3 pp blank, and 1 p with a memorandum.

Unpublished copies have been recorded as follows.

1 SWE: KVA A MS transcript made by G Ekelöf.

2 USA: ANC A MS transcript made by B G Briscoe.

MS not seen; description deduced from La O/2.

SWE: KVA

44/03/La O/2, **D** La 1869/2 **1869** Hyde 424, 3034
<untitled>
folio
text <as La O/1, without the final memorandum>, pp 58-101.
Reproduction of La O/1, published in photolithographed edition, vol 6 <*Supplementum Regni Animalis* **D** La 1869/2 = Hyde 3034> Stockholm.
Unpublished copies have been recorded as follows.

1 UK: SOC & USA: ANC, SHS A reproduction on microfilm 16 or 17 made in 1962, Bryn Athyn PA.

UK: SOC, BL, CHT, CON, NCC, NCH, RYL; GER: GSU; NET: GEN; SWE: ROY, KVA, LUN, UPP; USA: ANC, FOU, SHS; AUS: SYD

44/03/La O/3, **D** La 1927/2 **1927** Hyde 424/1, 3038/31
<untitled>
folio
text, pp 198-241.
Photographic reproduction of La O/1, published in *Autographa Editio Photostata* vol 10 <*De Sensibus, etc.* **D** La 1927/2 = Hyde 3038/31> Bryn Athyn PA.
Unpublished copies have been recorded as follows.

1 UK: SOC & USA: ANC, SHS A reproduction on microfilm 21 made in 1962, Bryn Athyn PA.

UK: SOC; USA: ANC

ENGLISH EXTRACTS

X 44/03/En 1882/1, **D** En 1882/3 **1882** Hyde 425, 3131
INTRODUCTION.

A. *THE CEREBRUM.*

C. *THE MOTION OF THE CEREBRUM.* <from Codex 51, chapter 1, n 41-60>

D. *THE FUNCTIONS OF THE CEREBRUM IN GENERAL.*
F. *THE CHAIN AND BOND OF USES.*
G. *A SUMMARY*
I. | THE CEREBRUM, ITS SUBSTANCES AND MEMBERS IN GENERAL. <from Codex 55, chapter 7>
II. | THE FUNCTIONS OF THE BRAIN IN GENERAL.
III.| SUPPLEMENT TO SUB-SECTION ON THE SOUL.
<ANALYSES.> | II.

8vo
titles and text: Introduction: n 1-7, pp 1-8 <La O/2 pp 58-62>;
A. n 26-40, pp 38-44 <La O/2 pp 66-68>;
C. n 41-60, pp 44-56;
D. n 60-83, pp 56-66 <La O/2 pp 75-82>;
F. n 84-104, pp 67-82 <La O/2 pp 83-92>;
G. n 104, pp 82-83 <La O/2, pp 92-93>;
I. n 104a-k, pp 84-90 <44/04/La O/1>;
II. n 104l-y, pp 91-101 <La O/2, pp 69-75>;
III. n 104z, pp 101-102 <La O/2, p 83>;
<ANALYSES.> II. n 258-286, pp 247-262 <La O/2, pp 94-101>.
Edited and translated by R L Tafel from 44/03/La O/2 and 40/04/La O/2, published in *The Brain* 1 <**D** En 1882/3 = Hyde 3131> London.
UK: SOC, CON, NCC, NR; NET: GEN, KB; SWE: UPP; USA: ANC, SHS; AUS: SYD

X 44/03/En 1925/1 **1925** Hyde 425/1
<<THE FUNCTION OF THE CEREBRUM; THE FABRIC OF THE CEREBRUM>>
title and text, pp 1-4.
Typescript translation from La O/2 made by E E Iungerich.
Document not seen; description recorded from Hyde 425/1.
USA: ANC

X 44/03/En 1934/1, **D** En 1934/1 **1934** Hyde 425/–, 3131/1
INTRODUCTION.
A. *THE CEREBRUM.*
C. *THE MOTION OF THE CEREBRUM.* <from Codex 51, chapter 1, n 41-60>
D. *THE FUNCTIONS OF THE CEREBRUM IN GENERAL.*
F. *THE CHAIN AND BOND OF USES.*
G. *A SUMMARY*
I. | THE CEREBRUM, ITS SUBSTANCES AND MEMBERS IN GENERAL. <from Codex 55, chapter 7>
II. | THE FUNCTIONS OF THE BRAIN IN GENERAL.
III. | SUPPLEMENT TO SUB-SECTION ON THE SOUL.
<ANALYSES.> II.

8vo
titles and text: pp 1-8, 38-44, 44-56, 56-66, 67-83, 84-90, 91-101, 101-102, 247-262.
Reprint of X En 1882/1, published in *The Brain* 1 <**D** En 1934/1 = Hyde 3131/1> London.
UK: SOC; NET: KB; USA: SHS

X 44/03/En 1958/1, **E:b** En 1958/4 **1958** Hyde 3336/25iv
<untitled>

4to
text, pp 674-677.
Translated and edited by A Acton, published in *The Life of Emanuel Swedenborg* 4 <**E:b** En 1958/4 = Hyde 3336/25iv> Bryn Athyn PA.
UK: SOC, NCC; USA: ANC

X 44/03/En 1994/1, **D** En 1994/1 **1994** Hyde 425/–, 3131/–
<<INTRODUCTION.
A. *THE CEREBRUM.*
C. *THE MOTION OF THE CEREBRUM.* <from Codex 51, chapter 1, n 41-60>
D. *THE FUNCTIONS OF THE CEREBRUM IN GENERAL.*
F. *THE CHAIN AND BOND OF USES.*
G. *A SUMMARY*
I. | THE CEREBRUM, ITS SUBSTANCES AND MEMBERS IN GENERAL. <from Codex 55, chapter 7>
II. | THE FUNCTIONS OF THE BRAIN IN GENERAL.
III.| SUPPLEMENT TO SUB-SECTION ON THE SOUL.
<ANALYSES.> | II.>>
8vo
titles and text: pp 1-8, 38-44, 44-56, 56-66, 67-83, 84-90, 91-101, 101-102, 247-262.
Photographic replica reprint of X En 1882/1, published in *The Brain* 1 <**D** En 1994/1> by Gryphon Editions, Birmingham AL.
Copy not seen; description deduced from X En 1882/1 and publisher's advertisement.

X 44/03/En 2005/1, **D** En 2005/1 **2005** Hyde 425/2, 3131/2
INTRODUCTION.
A. *THE CEREBRUM.*
C. *THE MOTION OF THE CEREBRUM.* <from Codex 51, chapter 1, n 41-60>
D. *THE FUNCTIONS OF THE CEREBRUM IN GENERAL.*
F. *THE CHAIN AND BOND OF USES.*
G. *A SUMMARY*
I. | THE CEREBRUM, ITS SUBSTANCES AND MEMBERS IN GENERAL. <from Codex 55, chapter 7>
II. | THE FUNCTIONS OF THE BRAIN IN GENERAL.
III. | SUPPLEMENT TO SUB-SECTION ON THE SOUL.
<ANALYSES.> | II.
8vo
titles and text: pp 1-8, 38-44, 44-56, 56-66, 67-83, 84-90, 91-101, 101-102, 247-262.
Photographic replica reprint of X En 1882/1 = Hyde 425, published in *The Brain* 1 <**D** En 2005/1 = Hyde 3131/2> by The Swedenborg Scientific Association, Bryn Athyn PA.
UK: SOC; USA: ANC, SSA

44/04 Muscles of the Face and the Abdomen Hyde CXXII

The autograph MS forms part of Codex 58 in the Library of the Royal Swedish Academy of Sciences, Stockholm. Swedenborg numbered the leaves 1-7; later, a Librarian of the Academy renumbered the leaves 132a-138b, and these numbers are given in the description of La O/1. The MS was probably written about the same time as 44/03. See 39/01, in which Swedenborg copied extracts from authorities on the muscles in general, ending the MS with the words, 'Sed de his alibi.' <But concerning these things, elsewhere.>

LATIN

44/04/La O/1 **1744** Hyde 426
<< <untitled> >>
pott folio <318 x 191 mm>
text: De Musculis faciei n 1-10, pp 132a-133a.
Musculi mediae regionis faciei n 1-7, pp 133a-133b.
Musculi inservientes naso n 1-6, pp 134a-134b.
Musculi auris externae n 1, p 134b.
De Musculis qui labrum superius movent n 1-3, pp 134b-135a.
Musculi regionis infimae faciei n 1-4, p 135a.
De Affectionibus animi in vultu effigiatis n 1-7, p 135b.
Musculi maxillae inferioris n 1-5, p 136a.
Musculi qui movent caput super vertebras n 1-4, pp 136b-137a.
De Musculis adbominis <deleted>, p 137a; p 137b blank.
De Musculis adbominis, p 138a.
Usus n 1-3, p 138b.
An unpublished copy has been recorded as follows.
1 SWE: KVA A MS transcript made by G Ekelöf.
MS not seen; description deduced from La O/2.
SWE: KVA

44/04/La O/2, **D** La 1869/2 **1869** Hyde 427, 3034
<untitled>
folio
text, pp 13-25.
Reproduction of La O/1, published in photolithographed edition, vol 6 <*Supplementum Regni*

Animalis **D** La 1869/2 = Hyde 3034> Stockholm.
Unpublished copies have been recorded as follows.
1 UK: SOC & USA: ANC, SHS A reproduction on microfilm 16 or 17, Bryn Athyn PA.
UK: SOC, BL, CHT, CON, NCC, NCH, RYL; GER: GSU; NET: GEN; SWE: ROY, KVA, LUN, UPP; USA: ANC, FOU, SHS; AUS: SYD

44/04/La 0/3, **D** La 1927/2 **1927** Hyde 427/1, 3038/31
De Musculis Faciei
De | Musculis abdominis
folio
titles and text, 11 pp.
Reproduction of La 0/1, published in *Autographa Editio Photostata* vol 10 <*De Sensibus, etc.* Hyde 3038/31> Bryn Athyn PA.
Unpublished copies have been recorded as follows.
1 UK: SOC & USA: ANC, SHS A reproduction on microfilm 22 made in 1962, Bryn Athyn PA.
UK: SOC; USA: ANC

ENGLISH

44/04/En 1/1 **1924** Hyde 427/2
<<THE MUSCLES>>
text: chapter 24, pp 23-48.
Typewritten MS translation by E E Iungerich, in *Various Philosophical and Physiological Studies*.
Document not seen; description recorded from Hyde 427/2.
USA: ANC

44/05 The Soul's Domain, Parts 1 and 2 Hyde CXXIV

This, with Part 3 <45/01>, was the last of the series of works on the natural sciences which Swedenborg completed before he began his works of biblical exposition and spiritual revelation.

He was in The Hague from 25 April to 13 May 1744, when he departed for London. Though he probably saw the commencement of printing Part 1, we may infer from the number of printing mistakes in the 2 volumes that he did not see Parts 1 and 2 through the press — see the 'Monitum' at the end of Part 2 which lists the many typographical errors in them. Part 1 was published about June or July. Reviews and notices of Parts 1 and 2 appeared as follows:

Bibliothèque Raisonnée Amsterdam 1744, pp 155-168 <see Fr 1744/1 below>;
Neue Zeitungen von Gelehrten Sachen Leipzig 1744, pp 706-707;
Commercium Litterarium 1744, p 296;
Nova Acta Eruditorum Leipzig 1747, pp 507-514, noted in *Neue Zeitungen* September 1747;
Journal des Sçavans 1746, pp 541-542.

Translations of these reviews are to be found in *The New Philosophy* Bryn Athyn PA, 1932, pp 111-120; 1933, pp 141-150, 180; 2010, pp 1017-1040.

Codex 36 in the Library of the Royal Swedish Academy of Sciences, Stockholm, includes pages on which Swedenborg made several drafts for the title page and chapter headings of the work.

The *Index Rerum Totius* printed in Part 1 gives the scheme which Swedenborg envisaged for the whole of his psychological studies under the title *Regnum Animale*. The scheme is as follows, with references added here to indicate the portions of Swedenborg's works and MSS which he intended to use for this purpose:

I. De Visceribus Abdominis <44/05 = Hyde 436, IV-VXI>
II. De Visceribus Thoracis <44/05 = Hyde 437, III-IV>
III. De Corde, Arteriis, Venis, et Sanguine <40/01 = Hyde 288>
IV. De Membris Genitalibus Virorum <43/01 = Hyde 406, ch 27-35>
V. De Membris Genitalibus Mulierum; et de Formatione Foetus in Utero <43/01 = Hyde 406, ch 36-44>
VI. De Organis Sensuum Externorum <44/01 = Hyde 415; 43/01 = Hyde 406, ch 25, 26; 42/01 = Hyde 384, ch XV>
VII. De Cerebro, et Sensoriis Internis <44/03 = Hyde 423>
VIII. De Cerebello, Medulla Oblongata et Spinali <40/09 = Hyde 318>
IX. De Substantia corticali, et de medullari cerebri: deque fibra nervea; at motrice corporis. Tum de spiritu animali <40/01 = Hyde 289; 40/09 = Hyde 318; 41/08 = Hyde 359>
X. De Organismo motu animalis
XI. De affectionibus corporis, seu de morbis, cum primis capitis aut cerebri <40/09 = Hyde 318>

XII. Introductio ad Psychologiam rationalem: seu doctrina formarum, ordinis et graduum; ut et serierum et societatis, influxuum, correspondentiarum, atque repraesentationum, tum modificationum <40/01 = Hyde 288; 41/06 = Hyde 352; 42/01 = Hyde 384>
XIII. De Actione, sensu externo; et interno, imaginatione, memoria <41/11 = Hyde 374; 42/01 = Hyde 384>
XIV. De Affectionibus, et aegritudinibus animi <42/01 = Hyde 384>
XV. De Intellectu, seu de cogitatione, et voluntate; de instinctu; de affectionibus mentis rationalis <42/01 = Hyde 384>
XVI. De Anima, ejusque statu in corpore, commercio, affectione, immortalitate; deque ejus statu post vitam corporis <42/01 = Hyde 384>
XVII. Concordantia systematum de Anima, ejusque natura et commercio <42/01 = Hyde 384>

LATIN

Editions:
La O MS
La 1 1st edition

44/05/La O/1 1744 Hyde —
<< <untitled> >>
pott long 4to <314 x 92 mm>
drafts of title page and chapter headings, pp <349-353, 355-357> in Codex 36.
MS not seen; description described from La O/2.
SWE: KVA

44/05/La 1/1 1744 Hyde 436
EMANUELIS SWEDENBORGII, | SACRÆ REGIÆ MAJESTATIS REGNI- | QUE SUECIÆ COLLEGII METAL- | LICI ASSESSORIS | REGNUM ANIMALE | ANATOMICE, PHYSICE ET PHILOSOPHICE | PERLUSTRATUM. | CUJUS | *PARS PRIMA.* | DE | VISCERIBUS ABDOMINIS | SEU DE | ORGANIS REGIONIS INFERIORIS | AGIT. | <orn> | *HAGÆ COMITUM,* | Apud ADRIANUM BLYVENBURGIUM, | MDCCXLIV.
title page: NR 219; p <iii>: line orn as head-piece NR 220; p <iv>: tail-piece NR 221; p 1: line orn as head-piece NR 222; line orn NR 223; initial NIhil N^6 NR 224; p 11: line orn as head-piece NR 225; initial VIscera V^6 NR 226; p 24: line orn as head-piece NR 231; initial USus U^5 NR 228; p 45: tail-piece NR 229; p 46: line orn as head-piece NR 230; initial IN I^6 NR 231; p 55: line orn as head-piece NR 225; initial COntinuus C^5 NR 232; p 69: tail-piece NR 233; p 70: line orn as head-piece NR 230; initial CLar. C^6 NR 232; p 76: tail-piece NR 233; p 77: line orn as head-piece NR 225; initial PHarynx P^6 NR 234; p 89: tail-piece NR 235; p 90: line orn as head-piece NR 227; initial CLar. C^6 NR 232; p 100: tail-piece NR 220; p 101: line orn as head-piece NR 225; initial VEntriculus V^5 NR 226; p 116: line orn as head-piece NR 227; initial CLar. C^6 NR 232; p 128: tail-piece NR 221; p 129: line orn as head-piece NR 225; initial PArtes P^5 NR 234; p 153: line orn as head-piece NR 227; initial CLar. C^6 NR 232; p 158: tail-piece NR 235; p 159: line orn as head-piece NR 225; initial CLar. C^5 NR 232; p 173: line orn as head-piece NR 227; initial CLar. C^6 NR 232; p 175: tail-piece NR 221; p 176: line orn as head-piece NR 225; initial SAnguis S^5 NR 360; p 184: tail-piece NR 235; p 185: line orn as head-piece NR 227; initial ORdine O^6 NR 237; p 193: tail-piece NR 221; p 194: line orn as head-piece NR 225; initial MIrificissimos M^5 NR 238; p 208: tail-piece NR 239; p 209: line orn as head-piece NR 227; initial CLar. C^6 NR 232; p 219: line orn as head-piece NR 225; initial HEpar H^5 NR 240; p 252: tail-piece NR 221; p 253: line orn as head-piece NR 241; initial CLar. C^6 NR 232; p 256: tail-piece NR 235; p 257:

line orn as head-piece NR 225; initial PAncreatis P^5 NR 234; p 271: tail-piece NR 239; p 272: line orn as head-piece NR 227; initial CLar. C^6 NR 232; p 279: tail-piece NR 221; p 280: line orn as head-piece NR 225; initial QUicquid Q^5 NR 242; p 300: tail-piece NR 235; p 301: line orn as head-piece NR 227; initial CLar. C^6 NR 232; p 307: tail-piece NR 221; p 308: line orn as head-piece NR 225; initial QUid Q^5 NR 242; p 324: tail-piece NR 235; p 325: line orn as head-piece NR 227; initial CLar. C^6 NR 232; p 329: tail-piece NR 221; p 330: line orn as head-piece NR 225; initial PRimae P^5 NR 234; p 344: tail-piece NR 259; p 345: line orn as head-piece NR 227; initial CLar. C^6 NR 232; p 354: tail-piece NR 221; p 355: line orn as head-piece NR 225; initial AOrta A^5 NR 243; p 379: tail-piece NR 221; p 380: line orn as head-piece NR 227; CLar. C^6 NR 232; p 384: tail-piece NR 235; p 385: line orn as head-piece NR 225; initial SIngula S^5 NR 236; p 400: line orn as head-piece NR 227; initial CLar. C^6 NR 232; p 404: tail-piece NR 221; p 405: line orn as head-piece NR 225; initial COrpus C^5 NR 232; p 421: line orn as head-piece NR 212; p 423: tail-piece NR 235; p 424: line orn as head-piece NR 225; initial CIrca C^5 NR 232; p 438: tail-piece NR 235

4to

title leaf, 2 pp; Index rerum totius operis, 2 pp;

text: Prologus n 1-23, pp 1-10.

Cap. I. De Lingua n 24-49, pp 11-45.
Cap. II. De Labris, ore, palato, et glandulis salivalibus n 50-72, pp 46-69.
Cap. III. De Pharynge et oesophago, et eorum glandulis n 73-86, pp 70-89.
Cap. IV. De Ventriculo, et ejus orificiis n 87-106, pp 90-115.
Cap. V. De Intestinis n 107-140, pp 116-152.
Cap. VI. De Mesenterio, et vasis lacteis n 141-157, pp 153-172.
Cap. VII. De Ductu thoracico, et vasis lymphaticis n 158-170, pp 173-184.
Cap. VIII. De Glandulis in genere n 171-190, pp 185-208.
Cap. IX. De Hepate, et vesica fellis n 191-218, pp 209-252.
Cap. X. De Pancreate n 219-234, pp 253-271.
Cap. XI. De Liene n 235-249, pp 272-300.
Cap. XII. De Omento n 250-265, pp 301-324.
Cap. XIII. De Renibus succenturiatis n 266-277, pp 325-344.
Cap. XIV. De Renibus et ureteribus n 266, 217-228, 230-234, pp 345-379.
Cap. XV. De Vesica urinaria n 235-247, pp 380-399.
Cap. XVI. De Peritonaeo n 248-265, pp 400-423.
Epilogus n 266-274, pp 424-438. <p 266 and 283 are misprinted as 466 and 383; on p 137 a second para is numbered as 128; paragraphs 90, 92, 93, 196, 197 are unnumbered; on p 302 para 252 is unnumbered; on p 403 para 251 is unnumbered>

After Cap. XIII Swedenborg reverted to n 216 <misprinted as 266>, and then continued from n 217-228; after this he omitted n 229 and then proceeded from n 230 to the end of n 274. The effect is that n 217-228 and 230-274 occur twice in the series. It is possible that after writing Cap. XIV he considered repositioning it; if he envisaged placing it before Cap. XIII, he may have altered the first number in the MS to 266, although he continued with n 217. Finally, when he decided to leave Cap. XIV where it is, he omitted to renumber the paragraphs accordingly.

It is possible that originally he expected to terminate the work with Cap. XII and the Epilogue <which also begins with n 266>. Having then inserted Cap. XIII-XVI, he did not rectify the duplication of the paragraph numbers.

A copy in UK: SOC has marginalia written by S T Coleridge. A copy in SWE: ROY is inscribed 'Bibliothecae Upsaliensis a. 1746'. Swedenborg's own copy is in SWE: KVA. The Journal Book of the Royal Society, London <volume 18, pp 250-251>, records that Swedenborg had presented a copy to the Society.

UK: SOC, CON, NCC, RSO; SWE: ROY, KVA; USA: ANC

44/05/La 1/2 **1744** Hyde 437

EMANUELIS SWEDENBORGII, | SACRÆ REGIÆ MAJESTATIS REGNI- | QUE SUECIÆ COLLEGII METAL- | LICI ASSESSORIS | REGNUM ANIMALE | ANATOMICE, PHYSICE ET PHILOSOPHICE | PERLUSTRATUM. | CUJUS | *PARS SECUNDA.* | DE | VISCERIBUS THORACIS | SEU DE | ORGANIS REGIONIS SUPERORIS | AGIT. | <orn> | *HAGÆ COMITUM,* | Apud ADRIANUM BLYVENBURGIUM, | MDCCXLIV.

title page: NR 219; p 1: line orn as head-piece NR 244; line orn NR 245; initial CLar. C⁶ NR 232; p 7: tail-piece NR 219; p 8: line orn as head-piece NR 225; initial SIcut S⁵ NR 236; p 30: tail-piece NR 219; p 31: line orn as head-piece NR 244; initial CLar. C⁶ NR 232; p 36: line orn as head-piece NR 225; initial LARYNX L⁵ NR 246; p 67: tail-piece NR 235; p 68: line orn as head-piece NR 244; initial CLar. C⁶ NR 232; p 72: tail-piece NR 221; p 73: line orn as head-piece NR 225; initial SIcut S⁵ NR 236; p 94: line orn as head-piece NR 244; initial CLar. C⁶ NR 232; p 107: line orn as head-piece NR 225; initial FOrmae F⁵ NR 247; p 164: tail-piece NR 219; p 165: line orn as head-piece NR 248; initial CLar. C⁶ NR 232; p 172: tail-piece NR 221; p 173: line orn as head-piece NR 225; initial SI S⁵ NR 236; p 206: tail-piece NR 221; p 207: line orn as head-piece NR 244; initial CLar. C⁶ NR 232; p 209: line orn as head-piece NR 225; initial UBicunque U⁵ NR 228; p 227: tail-piece NR 249; p 228: line orn as head-piece NR 244; initial CLar. C⁶ NR 232; p 232: tail-piece NR 250; p 233: line orn as head-piece NR 225; initial DIAPHRAGMA D⁵ NR 251; p 256: tail-piece NR 250; p 257: line orn as head-piece NR 225; initial PUlmones P⁵ NR 234; p 285: tail-piece NR 252

4to

title leaf, 2 pp;

text: Cap. I. De Naso et uvula n 275-291, pp 1-30.
Cap. II. De Larynge et epiglottide n 292-306, pp 31-67.
Cap. III. De Trachea arteria n 307-322, pp 68-93.
Cap. IV. De Pulmonibus n 307, 324-348, pp 94-164.
Cap. V. De Pleura, mediastino, et pericardio n 349-367, pp 165-206.
Cap. VI. De Thymo n 368-379, pp 207-227.
Cap. VII. De Diaphragmate n 380-393, 228-256.
Epilogus n 394-404, pp 257-285.
Capita rerum, 1 p.
Monitum <explaining the many typographical errors>, 2 pp. <para nos 277, 278, 279, 288, 323 misprinted as 276, 277, 278, 238, 307; n 381 omitted at start of para>.

A copy in UK: SOC has marginalia written by S T Coleridge. A copy in SWE: ROY is inscribed 'Bibliothecae Upsaliensis a. 1746'. Swedenborg's own copy is in SWE: KVA. The Journal Book of the Royal Society, London <vol 18, pp 250-251>, records that Swedenborg had presented a copy to the Society.

UK: SOC, CON, NCC, RSO; SWE: ROY, KVA; USA: ANC

44/05/La 0/2, **D** La 1869/2 **1869** Hyde 3034

<untitled>

folio

text, pp 349-353, 354-357.

Reproduction of La 0/1, published in photolithographed edition, vol 6 <*Supplementum Regni Animalis* **D** La 1869/2 = Hyde 3034> Stockholm.

Unpublished copies have been recorded as follows.

1 UK: SOC & USA: ANC, SHS A reproduction on microfilm 16 or 17, Bryn Athyn PA.

UK: SOC, BL, CHT, CON, NCC, NCH, RYL; GER: GSU; NET: GEN; SWE: ROY, KVA, LUN, UPP; USA: ANC, FOU, SHS; AUS: SYD

44/05/La O/3, **D** La 1929/1 **1929** Hyde 3038/24
<untitled>
folio
text, 4 pp.
Photographic reproduction of La O/1, published in *Autographa Editio Photostata* vol 3 <*Indices Anatomicae* **D** La 1927/1 = Hyde 3038/24> Bryn Athyn PA.
Unpublished copies have been recorded as follows.
1 UK: SOC & USA: ANC, SHS A reproduction on microfilm 21 made in 1962, Bryn Athyn PA.
UK: SOC; USA: ANC

ENGLISH

Translators:
En 1 J J G Wilkinson
En 2 A H Stroh and C E Doering

44/05/En 1/1 **1843** Hyde 439
THE | ANIMAL KINGDOM, | CONSIDERED | ANATOMICALLY, PHYSICALLY, AND PHILOSOPHICALLY. | BY | EMANUEL SWEDENBORG, | LATE MEMBER OF THE HOUSE OF NOBLES IN THE ROYAL DIET OF SWEDEN, | ASSESSOR OF THE ROYAL METALLIC COLLEGE OF SWEDEN, | FELLOW OF THE ROYAL ACADEMY OF SCIENCES OF UPSALA, AND OF THE ROYAL ACADEMY | OF SCIENCES OF STOCKHOLM, | CORRESPONDING MEMBER OF THE IMPERIAL ACADEMY OF SCIENCES OF ST. PETERSBURG. | TRANSLATED FROM THE LATIN | BY | JAMES JOHN GARTH WILKINSON, | MEMBER OF THE ROYAL COLLEGE OF SURGEONS, LONDON. | PART I. | THE VISCERA OF THE ABDOMEN, OR THE ORGANS OF THE INFERIOR | REGION. | LONDON: | W. NEWBERY, CHENIES STREET, BEDFORD SQUARE; | H. BAILLIÈRE, 219, REGENT STREET; | OTIS CLAPP, SCHOOL STREET, BOSTON, UNITED STATES. | <short rule> | 1843.
verso: "EO PROVECTI SUMUS, UT HODIE AURIS ET OCULI SENSATIONEM VALDE | SUPRA SEIPSAM, AUT SUPRA NATURALE SUUM ACUMEN, PER ARTIFICIALIA | ORGANA EXALTARE SCIAMUS: JAM SUPEREST, UT ETIAM MENTEM, SEU AUDI- | TUM ET VISUM RATIONALEM."— SWEDENBORG, ŒCONOMIA REGNI ANIMALIS, | TR. II., N. 207. | "COGITATIO EX OCULO OCCLUDIT INTELLECTUM, AT COGITATIO EX INTEL- | LECTU APERIT OCULUM."— SWEDENBORG, SAPIENTIA ANGELICA DE DIVINO AMORE, N. 46.
half title: THE ANIMAL KINGDOM.
revised title page issued with En 1/2: THE | ANIMAL KINGDOM, | CONSIDERED | ANATOMICALLY, PHYSICALLY, AND PHILOSOPHICALLY. | BY | EMANUEL SWEDENBORG, | LATE MEMBER OF THE HOUSE OF NOBLES IN THE ROYAL DIET OF SWEDEN, | ASSESSOR OF THE ROYAL METALLIC COLLEGE OF SWEDEN, | FELLOW OF THE ROYAL ACADEMY OF SCIENCES OF UPSALA, AND OF THE ROYAL ACADEMY OF SCIENCES | OF STOCKHOLM, | CORRESPONDING MEMBER OF THE IMPERIAL ACADEMY OF SCIENCES OF ST. PETERSBURG. | TRANSLATED FROM THE LATIN | BY | JAMES JOHN GARTH WILKINSON, | MEMBER OF THE ROYAL COLLEGE OF SURGEONS, LONDON. | VOLUME I. | LONDON: | W. NEWBERY, 6, KING STREET, HOLBORN; | H. BAILLIÈRE, 219, REGENT STREET; | OTIS CLAPP, SCHOOL STREET, BOSTON, UNITED STATES. | <short rule> | 1843.
half title <provided with En 1/2>: THE | ANIMAL KINGDOM, | CONSIDERED | ANATOMICALLY, PHYSICALLY, AND PHILOSOPHICALLY. | PART I. | THE VISCERA OF THE ABDOMEN, OR THE ORGANS OF THE | INFERIOR REGION.
8vo
half title and title leaves, 4 pp; Contents of Part I, p v; Translator's preface to Part I, pp vii-xiv;

Swedenborg's Index of contents of the whole work, pp xv-xvi; text n 1-334, pp 1-526; advertisement, 1 p.
A note headed 'Directions to the Binder' was issued with En 1/2, specifying: 'In re-binding the Animal Kingdom particular attention is requested as to the sheets placed at the end of this volume, *but forming part of the* FIRST *volume*, which are to be arranged in the following order:- The Title Page and Table of Contents to Vol. I, in place of the former. The "Introductory remarks by the Translator" (three sheets and one leaf), to be placed after "Translator's Preface to Part I." (page xiv.); after which the leaf headed "The Author's Index of Contents to the whole Work," and then the Half-title to Part I.'
Printed by Walton and Mitchell, Wardour Street, London.
The volume was reviewed in *The Monthly Review* London, June 1844; and this review was commented upon in *The Intellectual Repository* London, 1844, pp 263-268.
UK: SOC, NR; NET: GEN; SWE: UPP; USA: ANC

44/05/En 1/2 **1844** Hyde 440

THE | ANIMAL KINGDOM, | CONSIDERED | ANATOMICALLY, PHYSICALLY, AND PHILOSOPHICALLY. | BY | EMANUEL SWEDENBORG, | LATE MEMBER OF THE HOUSE OF NOBLES IN THE ROYAL DIET OF SWEDEN, | ASSESSOR OF THE ROYAL METALLIC COLLEGE OF SWEDEN, | FELLOW OF THE ROYAL ACADEMY OF SCIENCES OF UPSALA, AND OF THE ROYAL ACADEMY OF SCIENCES | OF STOCKHOLM, | CORRESPONDING MEMBER OF THE IMPERIAL ACADEMY OF SCIENCES OF ST. PETERSBURG. | TRANSLATED FROM THE LATIN | BY | JAMES JOHN GARTH WILKINSON, | MEMBER OF THE ROYAL COLLEGE OF SURGEONS OF LONDON. | VOLUME II. | LONDON: | W. NEWBERY, 6, KING STREET, HOLBORN; | H. BAILLIÈRE, 219, REGENT STREET; | OTIS CLAPP, SCHOOL STREET, BOSTON, UNITED STATES. | <short rule> | 1844.
verso: "EO PROVECTI SUMUS, UT HODIE AURIS ET OCULI SENSATIONEM VALDE | SUPRA SEIPSAM, AUT SUPRA NATURALE SUUM ACUMEN, PER ARTIFICIALIA | ORGANA EXALTARE SCIAMUS: JAM SUPEREST, UT ETIAM MENTEM, SEU AUDI- | TUM ET VISUM RATIONALEM."— SWEDENBORG, ŒCONOMIA REGNI ANIMALIS, | TR. II., N. 207. | "COGITATIO EX OCULO OCCLUDIT INTELLECTUM, AT COGITATIO EX INTEL- | LECTU APERIT OCULUM."— SWEDENBORG, SAPIENTIA ANGELICA DE DIVINO AMORE, N. 46.
half title: THE ANIMAL KINGDOM.
section title: THE ANIMAL KINGDOM, | CONSIDERED | ANATOMICALLY, PHYSICALLY, AND PHILOSOPHICALLY. | PART II. | THE VISCERA OF THE THORAX, OR THE ORGANS OF THE | SUPERIOR REGION.
2nd section title: THE | ANIMAL KINGDOM, | CONSIDERED | ANATOMICALLY, PHYSICALLY, AND PHILOSOPHICALLY. | PART III. | THE SKIN, THE SENSES OF TOUCH AND TASTE, AND | ORGANIC FORMS GENERALLY.
8vo
half title and title leaves, 4 pp; Contents of volume II, p v; Translator's preface to Parts II and III, pp vii-viii; section title leaf, pp ix-x; text Part II, n 335-466, pp 1-366; 2nd section title leaf, pp 367-368; text Part III, n 467-596, pp 369-593 <45/01/En 1/1>; Index of authors, pp 595-598; Bibliographical notices, pp 599-608; Index of subjects, pp 609-652; Appendix, pp 653-658; Corrections in the work, p 658.
The Appendix is entitled, 'An Account of Swedenborg's Physiological Manuscripts in the Library of the Royal Academy of Sciences of Stockholm. By Dr J E Svedbom, Librarian to the Royal Academy of Sciences Stockholm, PhD, AM.' It is a continuation of the similar account printed as an Appendix to *The Economy of the Animal Kingdom* vol 2 <40/01/En 1/2 = Hyde 294> pp 423-426, dated July 1845.
The volume was reviewed in *The Forceps* 16 November 1844; and extracts from this review were printed in *The Intellectual Repository* London, 1845, pp 73-75.
UK: SOC, NR; NET: GEN; SWE: UPP; USA: ANC

44/05/En 1/3 **1850** Hyde 441

THE | ANIMAL KINGDOM, | CONSIDERED | ANATOMICALLY, PHYSICALLY, AND PHILOSOPHICALLY. | BY | EMANUEL SWEDENBORG, | LATE MEMBER OF THE HOUSE OF NOBLES IN THE ROYAL DIET OF SWEDEN, | ASSESSOR OF THE ROYAL METALLIC COLLEGE OF SWEDEN, | FELLOW OF THE ROYAL ACADEMY OF SCIENCES OF UPSALA, AND OF THE ROYAL ACADEMY OF SCIENCES | OF STOCKHOLM, | CORRESPONDING MEMBER OF THE IMPERIAL ACADEMY OF SCIENCES OF ST. PETERSBURG. | TRANSLATED FROM THE LATIN | BY | JAMES JOHN GARTH WILKINSON, | MEMBER OF THE ROYAL COLLEGE OF SURGEONS OF LONDON | VOLUME I. | ST. CLAIRSVILLE, OHIO: | PUBLISHED BY J. H. WILLIAMS. | <short rule> | 1850.
verso: "EO PROVECTI SUMUS, UT HODIE AURIS ET OCULI SENSATIONEM VALDE SUPRA | SEIPSAM, AUT SUPRA NATURALE SUUM ACUMEN, PER ARTIFICIALIA ORGANA EX- | ALTARE SCIAMUS: JAM SUPEREST, UT ETIAM MENTEM, SEU AUDITUM ET VISUM | RATIONALEM."—SWEDENBORG, ŒCONOMIA REGNI ANIMALIS, TR. II., N. 207. | "COGITATIO EX OCULO OCCLUDIT INTELLECTUM, AT COGITATIO EX INTELLECTU | APERIT OCULUM."—SWEDENBORG, SAPIENTIA ANGELICA DE DIVINO AMORE, N. 46.
8vo
title leaf, 2 pp; portrait; Translator's preface to Part I, pp III-VII; Swedenborg's index of contents of the whole work, p VII; text: Part I n 1-334, pp 9-324; Introductory remarks by the translator, pp 325-352; Translator's preface to Parts II and III, p 355; text: Part II n 335-466, pp 357-575; Part III n 467-596 <45/01/En 1/2>, pp 576-705; Bibliographical notices, pp 706-714; Index of subjects, pp 714-753; Appendix, pp 753-758; Contents of Parts I, II, III, 1 p.
The Appendix <pp 753-758> is an account by J E Svedbom of Swedenborg's physiological MSS in SWE: KVA.
The work was stereotyped and published by J H Williams, who bore the whole cost of doing so. The edition is said to have been reprinted in 1851; but no copy seen by Hyde bore that date. He concluded that the title page of vol II may have been dated 1851; but the copies in UK: SOC and USA: ANC lack a title page to vol II.
UK: SOC; USA: ANC

44/05/En 1/4 **1858** Hyde 442

THE | ANIMAL KINGDOM, | CONSIDERED | ANATOMICALLY, PHYSICALLY, AND PHILOSOPHICALLY. | BY | EMANUEL SWEDENBORG, | LATE MEMBER OF THE HOUSE OF NOBLES IN THE ROYAL DIET OF SWEDEN, | ASSESSOR OF THE ROYAL METALLIC COLLEGE OF SWEDEN, | FELLOW OF THE ROYAL ACADEMY OF SCIENCES OF UPSALA, AND OF THE ROYAL ACADEMY | OF SCIENCES OF STOCKHOLM, | CORRESPONDING MEMBER OF THE IMPERIAL ACADEMY OF SCIENCES OF ST. PETERSBURG. | TRANSLATED FROM THE LATIN | BY | JAMES JOHN GARTH WILKINSON, | MEMBER OF THE ROYAL COLLEGE OF SURGEONS OF LONDON. | VOLUME I. | CINCINNATI: | E. MENDENHALL. | BOSTON,—OTIS CLAPP. | .... | 1858.
verso: "EO PROVECTI SUMUS, UT HODIE AURIS ET OCULI SENSATIONEM VALDE SUPRA | SEIPSAM, AUT SUPRA NATURALE SUUM ACUMEN, PER ARTIFICIALIA ORGANA EX- | ALTARE SCIAMUS: JAM SUPEREST, UT ETIAM MENTEM, SEU AUDITUM ET VISUM | RATIONALEM."—SWEDENBORG, ŒCONOMIA REGNI ANIMALIS, | TR. II., N. 207. | "COGITATIO EX OCULO OCCLUDIT INTELLECTUM, AT COGITATIO EX INTELLECTU | APERIT OCULUM."—SWEDENBORG, SAPIENTIA ANGELICA DE DIVINO AMORE, N. 46.
8vo
title leaf, 2 pp; portrait; Contents of vol I, p II; Translator's preface to Part I, pp III-VII; Swedenborg's index of contents of the whole work, p VII; text: n 1-334, pp 9-324; Introductory remarks by the translator, pp 325-352.
The same as En 1/2 with a new title page.
UK: SOC; NET: GEN

44/05/En 1/5 **1858** Hyde 443

THE | ANIMAL KINGDOM, | CONSIDERED | ANATOMICALLY, PHYSICALLY, AND PHILOSOPHICALLY. | BY | EMANUEL SWEDENBORG, | LATE MEMBER OF THE HOUSE OF NOBLES IN THE ROYAL DIET OF SWEDEN, | ASSESSOR OF THE ROYAL METALLIC COLLEGE OF SWEDEN, | FELLOW OF THE ROYAL ACADEMY OF SCIENCES OF UPSALA, AND OF THE ROYAL ACADEMY | OF SCIENCES OF STOCKHOLM, | CORRESPONDING MEMBER OF THE IMPERIAL ACADEMY OF SCIENCES OF ST. PETERSBURG. | TRANSLATED FROM THE LATIN | BY | JAMES JOHN GARTH WILKINSON, | MEMBER OF THE ROYAL COLLEGE OF SURGEONS OF LONDON. | VOLUME II. | CINCINNATI: | E. MENDENHALL. | BOSTON,—OTIS CLAPP. | .... | 1858.

8vo

title leaf, pp 353-354; Contents of vol II, p 355; Translator's preface to Parts II and III, p 356; text: Part II n 335-466, pp 357-575; Part III n 467-596, pp 576-705 <45/01/En 1/3>; Bibliographical notices, pp 706-714; Index of subjects, pp 714-753; Appendix, pp 753-758.

The same as En 1/3 = Hyde 441 with a new title page.

UK: SOC; NET: GEN

44/05/En 2/1 **no date** Hyde 443/1

<<The Animal Kingdom>>

Translated by A H Stroh and C E Doering. MS in USA: ANC <Archives Ar 2001>.

The Archives of USA: SSA <envelope J> contain a batch of notes regarding a revision of the translation of part of vol I, made by Stroh and Doering.

Document not seen; description deduced from USA: ANC records.

USA: ANC

44/05/En 1/6 **1960** Hyde 443/–

THE | ANIMAL KINGDOM, | CONSIDERED | ANATOMICALLY, PHYSICALLY. AND PHILOSOPHICALLY. | BY | EMANUEL SWEDENBORG, | LATE MEMBER OF THE HOUSE OF NOBLES IN THE ROYAL DIET OF SWEDEN, | ASSESSOR OF THE ROYAL METALLIC COLLEGE OF SWEDEN, | FELLOW OF THE ROYAL ACADEMY OF SCIENCES OF UPSALA, AND OF THE ROYAL ACADEMY OF SCIENCES | OF STOCKHOLM, | CORRESPONDING MEMBER OF THE IMPERIAL ACADEMY OF SCIENCES OF ST. PETERSBURG. | TRANSLATED FROM THE LATIN | BY | JAMES JOHN GARTH WILKINSON, | MEMBER OF THE ROYAL COLLEGE OF SURGEONS OF LONDON. | VOLUME I. | LONDON: | W. NEWBERY, 6, KING STREET, HOLBORN; | H. BAILLIÈRE, 219, REGENT STREET. | OTIS CLAPP, SCHOOL STREET, BOSTON, UNITED STATES. | <short rule> | 1843. | Reproduced by Photo Offset | SWEDENBORG SCIENTIFIC ASSOCIATION | 1960

verso: "EO PROVECTI SUMUS, UT HODIE AURIS ET OCULI SENSATIONEM VALDE | SUPRA SEIPSAM, AUT SUPRA NATURALE SUUM ACUMEN, PER ARTIFICIALIA | ORGANA EXALTARE SCIAMUS: JAM SUPEREST, UT ETIAM MENTEM, SEU AUDI- | TUM ET VISUM RATIONALEM."—SWEDENBORG, ŒCONOMIA REGNI ANIMALIS, | TR. II., N. 207. | "COGITATIO EX OCULO OCCLUDIT INTELLECTUM, AT COGITATIO EX INTEL- | LECTU APERIT OCULUM."—SWEDENBORG, SAPIENTIA ANGELICA DE DIVINO AMORE, N. 46.

8vo

title leaf, 2 pp; portrait; Translator's preface to Part I, pp iii-vii; Swedenborg's index of contents of the whole work, p vii; Text: Part I n 1-334, pp 9-324; Introductory remarks by the translator, pp 325-352.

Reprint of En 1/1.

USA: ANC; AUS: SYD

44/05/En 1/7 **1960** Hyde 443/–

THE | ANIMAL KINGDOM, | CONSIDERED | ANATOMICALLY, PHYSICALLY, AND

PHILOSOPHICALLY. | BY | EMANUEL SWEDENBORG, | LATE MEMBER OF THE HOUSE OF NOBLES IN THE ROYAL DIET OF SWEDEN, | ASSESSOR OF THE ROYAL METALLIC COLLEGE OF SWEDEN, | FELLOW OF THE ROYAL ACADEMY OF SCIENCES OF UPSALA, AND OF THE ROYAL ACADEMY OF SCIENCES | OF STOCKHOLM, | CORRESPONDING MEMBER OF THE IMPERIAL ACADEMY OF SCIENCES OF ST. PETERSBURG. | TRANSLATED FROM THE LATIN | BY | JAMES JOHN GARTH WILKINSON, | MEMBER OF THE ROYAL COLLEGE OF SURGEONS OF LONDON. | VOLUME II. | ----
verso: "EO PROVECTI SUMUS, UT HODIE AURIS ET OCULI SENSATIONEM VALDE | SUPRA SEIPSAM, AUT SUPRA NATURALE SUUM ACUMEN, PER ARTIFICIALIA | ORGANA EXALTARE SCIAMUS: JAM SUPEREST, UT ETIAM MENTEM, SEU AUDI- | TUM ET VISUM RATIONALEM."—SWEDENBORG, ŒCONOMIA REGNI ANIMALIS, | TR. II., N. 207. | "COGITATIO EX OCULO OCCLUDIT INTELLECTUM, AT COGITATIO EX INTEL- | LECTU APERIT OCULUM."—SWEDENBORG, SAPIENTIA ANGELICA DE DIVINO AMORE, N. 46.
half title: THE ANIMAL KINGDOM.
section title: THE ANIMAL KINGDOM, | CONSIDERED | ANATOMICALLY, PHYSICALLY, AND PHILOSOPHICALLY. | PART II. | THE VISCERA OF THE THORAX, OR THE ORGANS OF THE | SUPERIOR REGION.
2nd section title: THE ANIMAL KINGDOM, | CONSIDERED | ANATOMICALLY, PHYSICALLY, AND PHILOSOPHICALLY. | PART III. | THE SKIN, THE SENSES OF TOUCH AND TASTE, AND | ORGANIC FORMS GENERALLY.
8vo
half title and title leaves, 4 pp; Contents of volume II, p v; Translator's preface to Parts II and III, pp vii-viii; section title leaf, pp ix-x; text Part II, n 335-466, pp 1-366; 2nd section title leaf, pp 367-368; text Part III, n 467-596, pp 369-593 <45/01/En 1/4>; Index of authors, pp 595-598; Bibliographical notices, pp 599-608; Index of subjects, pp 609-652; Appendix, pp 653-658; Corrections in the work, p 658.
Reprint of En 1/2.
USA: ANC; AUS: SYD

44/05/En 1/8 **2004** Hyde 443/–
<<THE | ANIMAL KINGDOM, | CONSIDERED | ANATOMICALLY, PHYSICALLY, AND PHILOSOPHICALLY. | BY | EMANUEL SWEDENBORG, | LATE MEMBER OF THE HOUSE OF NOBLES IN THE ROYAL DIET OF SWEDEN, | ASSESSOR OF THE ROYAL METALLIC COLLEGE OF SWEDEN, | FELLOW OF THE ROYAL ACADEMY OF SCIENCES OF UPSALA, AND OF THE ROYAL ACADEMY OF SCIENCES | OF STOCKHOLM, | CORRESPONDING MEMBER OF THE IMPERIAL ACADEMY OF SCIENCES OF ST. PETERSBURG. | TRANSLATED FROM THE LATIN | BY | JAMES JOHN GARTH WILKINSON, | MEMBER OF THE ROYAL COLLEGE OF SURGEONS OF LONDON. | VOLUME II. | LONDON: | W. NEWBERY, 6, KING STREET, HOLBORN; | H. BAILLIÈRE, 219, REGENT STREET; | OTIS CLAPP, SCHOOL STREET, BOSTON, UNITED STATES. | <short rule> | 1844.>>
verso: <<"EO PROVECTI SUMUS, UT HODIE AURIS ET OCULI SENSATIONEM VALDE | SUPRA SEIPSAM, AUT SUPRA NATURALE SUUM ACUMEN, PER ARTIFICIALIA | ORGANA EXALTARE SCIAMUS: JAM SUPEREST, UT ETIAM MENTEM, SEU AUDI- | TUM ET VISUM RATIONALEM."—SWEDENBORG, ŒCONOMIA REGNI ANIMALIS, | TR. II., N. 207. | "COGITATIO EX OCULO OCCLUDIT INTELLECTUM, AT COGITATIO EX INTEL- | LECTU APERIT OCULUM."—SWEDENBORG, SAPIENTIA ANGELICA DE DIVINO AMORE, N. 46.>>
half title: <<THE ANIMAL KINGDOM.>>
section title: <<THE ANIMAL KINGDOM, | CONSIDERED | ANATOMICALLY, PHYSICALLY, AND PHILOSOPHICALLY. | PART II. | THE VISCERA OF THE THORAX, OR THE ORGANS OF THE | SUPERIOR REGION.>>

2nd section title: <<THE | ANIMAL KINGDOM, | CONSIDERED | ANATOMICALLY, PHYSICALLY, AND PHILOSOPHICALLY. | PART III. | THE SKIN, THE SENSES OF TOUCH AND TASTE, AND | ORGANIC FORMS GENERALLY.>>
8vo
half title and title leaves, 4 pp; Contents of volume II, p v; Translator's preface to Parts II and III, pp vii-viii; section title leaf, pp ix-x; text Part II, n 335-466, pp 1-366; 2nd section title leaf, pp 367-368; text Part III, n 467-596, pp 369-593 <45/01/En 1/1>; Index of authors, pp 595-598; Bibliographical notices, pp 599-608; Index of subjects, pp 609-652; Appendix, pp 653-658; Corrections in the work, p 658.
Photographic replica reprint of En 1/2, published by Kessinger Publishing, Whitefish MT.
Copy not seen; description deduced from En 1/2 and publisher's advertisement.

44/05/En 1/9 **2006** Hyde 439/1

THE | ANIMAL KINGDOM, | CONSIDERED | ANATOMICALLY, PHYSICALLY, AND PHILOSOPHICALLY. | BY | EMANUEL SWEDENBORG, | LATE MEMBER OF THE HOUSE OF NOBLES IN THE ROYAL DIET OF SWEDEN, | ASSESSOR OF THE ROYAL METALLIC COLLEGE OF SWEDEN, | FELLOW OF THE ROYAL ACADEMY OF SCIENCES OF UPSALA, AND OF THE ROYAL ACADEMY OF SCIENCES | OF STOCKHOLM, | CORRESPONDING MEMBER OF THE IMPERIAL ACADEMY OF SCIENCES OF ST. PETERSBURG. | TRANSLATED FROM THE LATIN | BY | JAMES JOHN GARTH WILKINSON, | MEMBER OF THE ROYAL COLLEGE OF SURGEONS OF LONDON. | VOLUME I. | LONDON: | W. NEWBERY, 6, KING STREET, HOLBORN; | H. BAILLIÈRE, 219, REGENT STREET. | OTIS CLAPP, SCHOOL STREET, BOSTON, UNITED STATES. | <short rule> | 1843. | Reproduced by Photo Offset | SWEDENBORG SCIENTIFIC ASSOCIATION | 1960
verso: © 2006 by Swedenborg Scientific Association | All rights reserved | "EO PROVECTI SUMUS, UT HODIE AURIS ET OCULI SENSATIONEM VALDE SUPRA SEIPSAM, | AUT SUPRA NATURALE SUUM ACUMEN, PER ARTIFICIALIA ORGANA EXALTARE SCIAMUS: JAM | SUPEREST, UT ETIAM MENTEM, SEU AUDITUM ET VISUM RATIONALEM."—SWEDENBORG, | ŒCONOMIA REGNI ANIMALIS, TR. II., N. 207. | "COGITATIO EX OCULO OCCLUDIT INTELLECTUM, AT COGITATIO EX INTELLECTU APERIT | OCULUM."—SWEDENBORG, SAPIENTIA ANGELICA DE DIVINO AMORE, N. 46. | ISBN-10: 0-915221-79-9 | ISBN-13: 978-0-915221-79-0 | Two-volume set | Reprinted 1960 as *The Animal Kingdom* | Reprinted 2006 as *The Soul's Domain* | Swedenborg Scientific Association | P.O. Box 757, Bryn Athyn PA 19009 | Email: ssa@comcast.net | www.swedenborg-philosophy.org | Printed in the United States of America
half title: THE | SOUL'S DOMAIN | Formerly titled *The Animal Kingdom;* see back cover
section title: THE | ANIMAL KINGDOM, | CONSIDERED | ANATOMICALLY, PHYSICALLY, AND PHILOSOPHICALLY. | PART I. | THE VISCERA OF THE ABDOMEN, OR THE ORGANS OF THE | INFERIOR REGION.
8vo
half title and title leaves, 4 pp; Contents of volume I, p III; Preface to 1960 photo offset edition, pp V-VI; Translator's preface to Part I, pp vii-xix; Section title leaf, pp xv-xvi; text n 1-334, pp 1-526.
Photographic replica reprint of *The Animal Kingdom* vol 1 <En 1/1> by Fidlar Doubleday U.S.A., published by the Swedenborg Scientific Association
UK: SOC; USA: ANC

44/05/En 1/10 **2006** Hyde 440/1

THE | ANIMAL KINGDOM, | CONSIDERED | ANATOMICALLY, PHYSICALLY, AND PHILOSOPHICALLY. | BY | EMANUEL SWEDENBORG, | LATE MEMBER OF THE HOUSE OF NOBLES IN THE ROYAL DIET OF SWEDEN, | ASSESSOR OF THE ROYAL METALLIC COLLEGE OF SWEDEN, | FELLOW OF THE ROYAL ACADEMY OF SCIENCES OF UPSALA, AND OF THE ROYAL ACADEMY OF SCIENCES | OF STOCKHOLM, | CORRESPONDING MEMBER OF THE IMPERIAL ACADEMY OF SCIENCES OF

ST. PETERSBURG. | TRANSLATED FROM THE LATIN | BY | JAMES JOHN GARTH WILKINSON, | MEMBER OF THE ROYAL COLLEGE OF SURGEONS OF LONDON. | VOLUME II. | LONDON: | W. NEWBERY, 6, KING STREET, HOLBORN; | H. BAILLIÈRE, 219, REGENT STREET. | OTIS CLAPP, SCHOOL STREET, BOSTON, UNITED STATES. | <short rule> | 1844.
verso: © 2006 by Swedenborg Scientific Association | All rights reserved | "EO PROVECTI SUMUS, UT HODIE AURIS ET OCULI SENSATIONEM VALDE SUPRA SEIPSAM, | AUT SUPRA NATURALE SUUM ACUMEN, PER ARTIFICIALIA ORGANA EXALTARE SCIAMUS: JAM | SUPEREST, UT ETIAM MENTEM, SEU AUDITUM ET VISUM RATIONALEM."—SWEDENBORG, | ŒCONOMIA REGNI ANIMALIS, TR. II., N. 207. | "COGITATIO EX OCULO OCCLUDIT INTELLECTUM, AT COGITATIO EX INTELLECTU APERIT | OCULUM."—SWEDENBORG, SAPIENTIA ANGELICA DE DIVINO AMORE, N. 46. | ISBN-10: 0-915221-79-9 | ISBN-13: 978-0-915221-79-0 | Two-volume set | Reprinted 1960 as *The Animal Kingdom* | Reprinted 2006 as *The Soul's Domain* | Swedenborg Scientific Association | P.O. Box 757, Bryn Athyn PA 19009 | Email: ssa@comcast.net | www.swedenborg-philosophy.org | Printed in the United States of America
half title: THE | SOUL'S DOMAIN* | Formerly titled *The Animal Kingdom;* see back cover
section title: THE | ANIMAL KINGDOM, | CONSIDERED | ANATOMICALLY, PHYSICALLY, AND PHILOSOPHICALLY. | PART II. | THE VISCERA OF THE THORAX, OR THE ORGANS OF THE | SUPERIOR REGION
2nd section title: THE | ANIMAL KINGDOM, | CONSIDERED | ANATOMICALLY, PHYSICALLY, AND PHILOSOPHICALLY. | PART II. | THE SKIN, THE SENSES OF TOUCH AND TASTE, AND | ORGANIC FORMS GENERALLY.
8vo
half title and title leaves, 4 pp; Contents of volume II, p v; Translator's preface to parts II and III, pp vii-viii; section title leaf, p ix; text n 335-466, pp 1-366; 2nd section title leaf, pp 367-368; text n 467-596, pp 369-593; Index of authors, pp 595-598; Bibliographical notices, pp 599-608; Index of subjects, pp 609-658; Corrections in the work, p 658.
Photographic replica reprint of *The Animal Kingdom* vol 2 <En 1/2> by Fidlar Doubleday U.S.A., published by the Swedenborg Scientific Association.
UK: SOC; USA: ANC

ENGLISH EXTRACTS

X 44/05/En 1825/1 **1825** Hyde 444
PREFACE TO THE FIRST PART OF THE REGNUM ANIMALE | OF THE HON. E. SWEDENBORG.
8vo
title and text n 1-23, pp 342-349, 447-458.
Translated by J Clowes, published in *The Intellectual Repository* London.
UK: SOC, BL, CHT, CON, NCC, NR; USA: ANC

X 44/05/En 1825/2 **1825** Hyde 445
EXTRACT FROM THE EPILOGUE TO THE SECOND PART OF | THE REGNUM ANIMALE OF E. S.
8vo
title and text <n 394-404>, pp 521-532.
Translated by J Clowes, published in *The Intellectual Repository* London.
UK: SOC, BL, CHT, CON, NCC, NR; USA: ANC

X 44/05/En 1834/1 **1834** Hyde 446
SWEDENBORG'S ANIMAL KINGDOM
8vo
title and text: n 32-39, 71, 422-424, 470-472, pp 345-349, 372-374, 419-422.

Translated by Luther Clark, published in *The New Jerusalem Magazine* Boston MA.
UK: SOC, CON, NCC; USA: ANC

X 44/05/En 1835/1 **1835** Hyde 447
SWEDENBORG'S "ANIMAL KINGDOM."
8vo
title and text Part II n 394-395, 396-404, 330-333, pp 45-47, 129-131, 152-155, 430-433.
n 394-395, 330-333 translated by L Clark, and n 396-404 reprinted from X En 1825/2, published in *The New Jerusalem Magazine* Boston MA.
UK: SOC, CON, NCC; USA: ANC

X 44/05/En 1835/2 **1835** Hyde 448
CONCERNING THE LUNGS. CONCERNING THE CUTIS.
8vo
title and text Part II n 334-336, 338, pp 15-17; n 439, 445, 447, 451-452, 454-455, 457-458, pp 46-49.
Translated by L Clark, published in *The New Jerusalem Magazine* Boston MA.
UK: SOC, CON, NCC; USA: ANC

X 44/05/En 1838/1 **1838** Hyde 449
Preface to Swedenborg's Regnum Animale, | *Part I. Published in* 1744.
large 8vo
text, pp 274-276, 290-292.
Translated by Edwin A Attlee, published in *The Precursor* Cincinnati OH.
UK: SOC, NR

X 44/05/En 1839/1 **1839** Hyde 450
ANALYSIS OF THE TONGUE.
large 8vo
title and text n 32-43, pp 374-377, 385-389.
Translated by E A Attlee, published in *The Precursor* Cincinnati OH.
UK: SOC, NR

X 44/05/En 1839/2 **1839** Hyde 451
EXTRACTS FROM THE ANIMAL KINGDOM.
8vo
title and text Part I n 239, 247, 252-257, 266-270, 272, 274, pp 67-68, 91-95, 136-138, 178-179.
Translated by L Clark, published in *The New Jerusalem Magazine* Boston MA.
UK: SOC, CON, NCC; USA: ANC

X 44/05/En 1842/1 **1842** Hyde 452
TRANSLATION FROM SWEDENBORG'S | REGNUM ANIMALE.
8vo
title and text Part I cap I n 32-49, cap II n 59-72, cap III n 79-86, cap IV n 94-106, cap V n 124-140, cap VI n 147-157, cap VII n 162-170, cap VIII n 171, 178-190, cap IX n 200-218, cap X n 225-234, cap XI n 239-249, cap XII n 256-265, cap XIII n 271-277, cap XIV n 284-295, pp 93-96, 101-104, 110-111, 118-119, 132-135, 149-151, 157, 173-175, 189-192, 197-199, 214-216, 221-223, 270-272, 277-279.
Translated by J J G Wilkinson, published in *The New Church Advocate* London.
UK: SOC, CON, NR

X 44/05/En 1842/2 **1842** Hyde 453
<<Swedenborg on the Intestines>>
8vo
title and text n 124-140, pp 717-721.
Translated by 'Medicus Londinensis' ie J J G Wilkinson, published in *The London Medical Gazette.*
Copy not seen; description deduced from X En 1842/3 and Hyde 453.

X 44/05/En 1842/3 **1842** Hyde 453
SWEDENBORG ON THE INTESTINES
8vo
title and text n 124-140, pp 99-105.
Reprint of X En 1842/2, published in *The New Jerusalem Magazine* Boston MA.
UK: soc, con, ncc; USA: anc

X 44/05/En 1842/4 **1842** Hyde 454
[From the New Church Advocate.] | TRANSLATION FROM SWEDENBORG'S REGNUM ANIMALE. | CHAP. II. | ON THE LIPS, MOUTH, PALATE AND SALIVARY GLANDS.
8vo
title and text n 59-72, pp 145-151.
Reprinted from X En 1842/1, published in *The New Jerusalem Magazine* Boston MA.
UK: soc, con, ncc; USA: anc

X 44/05/En 1843/1 **1843** Hyde 453
<<SWEDENBORG ON THE INTESTINES>>
title and text, p 193.
Reprint of X En 1842/1, published in *The Boston Medical and Surgical Journal* Boston MA.
Copy not seen; description deduced from X En 1842/1 and Hyde 453.

X 44/05/En 1844/1 **1844** Hyde 455
SWEDENBORG'S ANIMAL KINGDOM.
8vo
title, p 94; Swedenborg's 'Index of Contents of the whole work', pp 94-95; text of Prologue 1-13, 14-23, pp 95-100, 148-152.
Quoted from En 1/1, published in *The New Jerusalem Magazine* Boston MA.
UK: soc, con, ncc; USA: anc

X 44/05/En 1862/1 **1862** Hyde 456
Swedenborg's Introduction | TO HIS WORK | ON THE ANIMAL KINGDOM.
title and text n 1-23, pp i-xvii; Contents of the whole work, pp xvii-xviii.
Published by J Spurgin in *The True Characteristics of Emanuel Swedenborg* London. <UK: soc Archives S4/92>
UK: soc

X 44/05/En 1882/1, **D** En 1882/3 **1882** Hyde 457, 3131
THE LUNGS AND THEIR MOTION.
8vo
title and text n 1-19, pp 778-794.
Reprinted from En 1/1 <n 392-410, pp 138-211>, published in *The Brain* 1 <**D** En 1882/3 = Hyde 3131> London.
UK: soc, con, ncc, nr; NET: gen, kb; SWE: upp; USA: anc; AUS: syd

X 44/05/En 1932/1 **1932** Hyde —
Regnum Animale ...
8vo
title and text, pp 112-120.
Translation by A Acton of X Fr 1744/1, published in *The New Philosophy* Lancaster PA.
UK: SOC, NCC, NR; USA: ANC

X 44/05/En 1934/1, **D** En 1934/1 **1934** Hyde 457/–, 3131/1
THE LUNGS AND THEIR MOTION.
8vo
title and text n 1-19, pp 778-794.
Reprint of X En 1882/1, published in *The Brain* 1 <**D** En 1934/1 = Hyde 3131/1> London.
UK: SOC; NET: KB; USA: SHS

X 44/05/En 1947/1 **1947** Hyde —
THE TONGUE | Adapted from Swedenborg's *Animal Kingdom* | BY DONALD. G. GLADISH, M.D. | in Collaboration with ALFRED ACTON
8vo
title and text, pp 121-128; plate facing p 122.
Published in *The New Philosophy* Lancaster and Bryn Athyn PA.
UK: SOC, NCC; USA: ANC

X 44/05/En 1948/1 **1948** Hyde —
THE LIPS, MOUTH, PALATE, AND SALIVARY GLANDS | Adapted from Swedenborg's *Animal Kingdom* | BY DONALD. G. GLADISH, M.D.
8vo
title and text, pp 147-154; plate facing p 148.
Published in *The New Philosophy* Lancaster and Bryn Athyn PA.
UK: SOC, NCC; USA: ANC

X 44/05/En 1949/1 **1949** Hyde —
THE PHARYNX AND ESOPHAGUS | Adapted from Swedenborg's *Animal Kingdom* | BY DONALD G. GLADISH, M.D.
8vo
title and text, pp 289-295; 2 plates between pp 290 and 291.
Published in *The New Philosophy* Lancaster and Bryn Athyn PA.
UK: SOC, NCC; USA: ANC

X 44/05/En 1949/2 **1949** Hyde —
THE STOMACH | Adapted from Swedenborg's *Animal Kingdom* | BY DONALD G. GLADISH, M.D.
8vo
title and text, pp 330-336; 2 plates between pp 330 and 331.
Published in *The New Philosophy* Lancaster and Bryn Athyn PA.
UK: SOC, NCC; USA: ANC

X 44/05/En 1949/3 **1949** Hyde —
THE INTESTINES | Adapted from Swedenborg's *Animal Kingdom* | BY DONALD G. GLADISH, M.D.
8vo
title and text, pp 369-381; plate <reproduced from Flint's *Human Physiology*> facing p 370.

Published in *The New Philosophy* Lancaster and Bryn Athyn PA.
UK: SOC, NCC; USA: ANC

X 44/05/En 1950/1 **1950** Hyde —
THE MESENTERY AND THE LACTEALS | Adapted from Swedenborg's *Animal Kingdom* | BY DONALD G. GLADISH, M.D.
8vo
title and text, pp 13-22; 2 plates between pp 14 and 15.
Published in *The New Philosophy* Lancaster and Bryn Athyn PA.
UK: SOC, NCC; USA: ANC

X 44/05/En 1950/2 **1950** Hyde —
THE THORACIC DUCT AND THE LYMPHATICS | Adapted from Swedenborg's *Animal Kingdom* | BY DONALD G. GLADISH, M.D.
8vo
title and text, pp 109-114; plate facing p 109.
Published in *The New Philosophy* Lancaster and Bryn Athyn PA.
UK: SOC, NCC; USA: ANC

X 44/05/En 1951/1 **1951** Hyde —
ON THE GLANDS GENERALLY | Adapted from Swedenborg's *Animal Kingdom* | BY DONALD G. GLADISH, M.D.
8vo
title and text, pp 151-161; plate facing p 152.
Published in *The New Philosophy* Lancaster and Bryn Athyn PA.
UK: SOC, NCC; USA: ANC

X 44/05/En 1951/2 **1951** Hyde —
THE LIVER AND THE GALL BLADDER | Adapted from Swedenborg's *Animal Kingdom* | BY DONALD G. GLADISH, M.D.
8vo
title and text, pp 221-228, 252-260; 2 plates facing pp 252 and 254.
Published in *The New Philosophy* Lancaster and Bryn Athyn PA.
UK: SOC, NCC; USA: ANC

X 44/05/En 1952/1 **1952** Hyde —
THE PANCREAS | Adapted from Swedenborg's *Animal Kingdom* | BY DONALD G. GLADISH, M.D.
8vo
title and text, pp 298-305; plate facing p 298.
Published in *The New Philosophy* Lancaster and Bryn Athyn PA.
UK: SOC, NCC; USA: ANC

X 44/05/En 1953/1 **1953** Hyde —
THE SPLEEN | Adapted from Swedenborg's *Animal Kingdom* | BY DONALD G. GLADISH, M.D.
8vo
title and text, pp 23-30; plate facing p 24.
Published in *The New Philosophy* Lancaster and Bryn Athyn PA.
UK: SOC, NCC; USA: ANC

X 44/05/En 1954/1 **1954** Hyde 457/a
PROLOGUE TO SWEDENBORG'S | ANIMAL KINGDOM
8vo
title and text n 1-23, pp 229-242.
Reprinted from X En 1844/1, published in *The New Philosophy* Lancaster and Bryn Athyn PA.
UK: soc, ncc; USA: anc

X 44/05/En 1958/1, **E:b** En 1958/4 **1958** Hyde 3336/25iv
<untitled>
4to
text of the Prologue, p 686; other portions, pp 711-716, 722-726, 743, 778, 809, 810.
Translated and edited by A Acton, published in *The Life of Emanuel Swedenborg* 4 <**E:b** En 1958/4 = Hyde 3336/25iv> Bryn Athyn PA.
UK: soc, ncc; USA: anc

X 44/05/En 1994/1, **D** En 1994/1 **1994** Hyde 457/–, 3131/–
<<*THE LUNGS AND THEIR MOTION.*>>
8vo
title and text n 1-19, pp 778-794.
Photographic replica reprint of X En 1882/1 = Hyde 457, published in *The Brain* 1 <**D** En 1994/1> by Gryphon Editions, Birmingham AL.
Copy not seen; description deduced from X En 1882/1 and publisher's advertisement.

X 44/05/En 2005/1, **D** En 2005/1 **2005** Hyde 457/–, 3131/–
THE LUNGS AND THEIR MOTION.
8vo
title and text n 1-19, pp 778-794.
Photographic replica reprint of X En 1882/1, published in *The Brain* 1 <**D** En 2005/1 = Hyde 3131/2>, The Swedenborg Scientific Association, Bryn Athyn PA.
UK: soc, ncc, nr; USA: anc

FRENCH

44/05/Fr 1/1 **1787** Hyde 3431, 443/a
Emmanuel Swedenborg. | Le Regne Animal | éclairei | anatomiquement, Physiquement, | et philosophiquement; | <short rule> | 1e Partie, | sur les viscères de l'abdomen, | ou | sur les organes de la Région inférieure. | <short rule> | traduction en françois, sur l'édition latine impri- | mée à lahaye en 1744. J. P. M. | 1787. | à die 27^{a} mensis Maii ad 20^{am} mens. Septemb.
small 4to
title leaf, 2 pp; text n 1-274, pp 1-844.
MS translation made by J P Moët, in vol marked '33'. The MS was purchased by J A Tulk from Moët's widow. <UK: soc Archives B/110>
UK: soc

FRENCH EXTRACTS

X 44/05/Fr 1744/1 **1744** Hyde —
<<Regnum Animale ...>>
title, quotations from the text, and a review of the whole volume, pp 155-168.

Anonymous review published in *Bibliothèque Raisonnée*. <see X En 1932/1 above>.
Copy not seen; description recorded from X En 1932/1.
UK: SOC; USA: ANC

44/06 Index to *The Soul's Domain*, Parts 1 and 2 Hyde CXXIV

The autograph MS forms part of Codex 38 in the Library of the Royal Swedish Academy of Sciences, Stockholm. Swedenborg compiled this Index after Parts 1 and 2 of the work had been printed, as indicated by its references to the printed pages.

LATIN

44/06/La O/1 **1744** Hyde 434

<<Index Partis Primæ et Secundæ Regni Ani- | malis, de Visceribus Abdominis et Thoracis.>>
pott long 4to <321 x 95 mm>
title and text A to V, pp 9-61; p 62 and 2 unnumbered pp are blank.
MS not seen; description deduced from La O/2.
SWE: KVA

44/06/La O/2, **D** La 1869/1 **1869** Hyde 435, 3034

Index Partis Primæ et Secundæ Regni Ani- | malis, de Visceribus Abdominis et Thoracis.
folio
titles and text, pp XI-XXXVII.
Reproduction of La O/1, published in photolithographed edition, vol 6 <*Supplementum Regni Animalis* **D** La 1869/1 = Hyde 3034> Stockholm.
Unpublished copies have been recorded as follows.
1 UK: SOC & USA: ANC, SHS A reproduction on microfilm 16 or 17, Bryn Athyn PA.
UK: SOC, BL, CHT, CON, NCC, NCH, RYL; GER: GSU; NET: GEN; SWE: ROY, KVA, LUN, UPP; USA: ANC, FOU, SHS; AUS: SYD

44/06/La O/3, **D** La 1929/1 **1929** Hyde 435/1, 3038/24

Index Partis Primæ et Secundæ Regni Ani- | malis, de Visceribus Abdominis et Thoracis
folio
title and text <written in 2 columns>, 27 pp.
Photographic reproduction of La O/1, published in *Autographa Editio Photostata* vol 3 <*Indices Anatomicae, et De Messia* **D** La 1929/1 = Hyde 3038/24> Bryn Athyn PA.
Unpublished copies have been recorded as follows.
1 UK: SOC & USA: ANC, SHS A reproduction on microfilm 22 made in 1962, Bryn Athyn PA.
UK: SOC; USA: ANC

45/01 The Soul's Domain, Part 3 Hyde CXXIV

A number of entries in Swedenborg's *Journal of Dreams* <43/03> indicate when he was writing the MS of the present work. He referred to completion of the section 'on organic forms in general' in n 243 <29-30 September 1744>, and to 'sensory impressions' in n 262 <9-10 October>. On 26-27 October he indicated symbolically that he must discontinue the work <n 277, 278>: his practice of analysing and summarizing the findings of other anatomists is seen in a dream as 'small wares' or 'trash' <Swedish *kram*>, upon which he should no longer draw.

It appears that he had been giving the MS to the printer in sections. Though he wrote no more of the MS, he gave the last sections written to the printer, and the work was published quickly enough for him to present a copy to the Royal Society, London, at its meeting on 28 February 1745 <The Society's Journal Book vol 18, pp 369, 374>. The unnamed publishers of La 1/1 were probably J Nourse and R Manby, judging by a comparison with type fonts and printer's ornaments used in 45/02/La 1/1 and 1/2.

LATIN

45/01/La 1/1 1745 Hyde 438

EMANUELIS SWEDENBORGII, | SACRÆ REG. MAJESTATIS REGNIQUE SUECIÆ | COLLEGII METALLICI ASSESSORIS | REGNUM ANIMALE | ANATOMICE, PHYSICE, ET PHILOSOPHICE | PERLUSTRATUM; | CUJUS | *PARS TERTIA*. | DE | CUTE, SENSU TACTUS, & GUSTUS; | ET DE | FORMIS ORGANIS IN GENERE, | AGIT. | <rule> | <orn> | <2 rules> | *LONDINI.* | MDCCXLV.

title page: NR 253; p 1: line orn as head-piece NR 254; initial DE D^5 NR 255; p 2: tail-piece NR 256; p 3: line orn as head-piece NR 257; initial CL. C^5 NR 258; p 9: tail-piece NR 259; p 10: line orn as head-piece NR 260; initial HOMO, H^5 NR 261; p 115: tail-piece NR 262; p 116: line orn as head-piece NR 263; p 144: tail-piece NR 264; p 145: line orn as head-piece NR 265; initial IN I^6 NR 266; p 148: tail-piece NR 267; p 169: tail-piece NR 256

4to

title leaf, 2 pp; text: Prologus n 405-407, pp 1-2.

Cap. I. De Cute, et sensu tactus n 408-469, pp 3-68.

De Formis organicis in genere n 470-486, pp 69-115.

De Sensu et sensorio; tactus, in specie n 487-506, pp 116-139.

De Usu tactus n 507-512, pp 139-144.

Cap. II. De Sensu gustus n 513-535, pp 145-169.

In the running head on p 105 GENERE is misprinted GERERE; page nos 108 and 139 are misprinted 110 and 136; para n 421 is misprinted as 431, 437 as 427, 472 as 172, 514 as 524, and

515 as 5L5; there is no paragraph numbered 459.
Swedenborg's copy is in the Library of SWE: kva.
UK: soc, con; SWE: kva; USA: anc

ENGLISH

45/01/En 1/1 **1844** Hyde 440
THE | ANIMAL KINGDOM, | CONSIDERED | ANATOMICALLY, PHYSICALLY, AND PHILOSOPHICALLY. | PART III. | THE SKIN, THE SENSES OF TOUCH AND TASTE, AND | ORGANIC FORMS GENERALLY.
8vo
title leaf, pp 367-368; text: Prologue n 467-469, pp 369-371; Chapter 1 n 470-573, pp 372-561; Chapter 2, n 574-596, pp 562-593.
Published with Part II in *The Animal Kingdom* 2 <44/05/En 1/2 = Hyde 440> London.
Translated by J J G Wilkinson, with the co-operation of John D Spurgin; published by the Swedenborg Association.
UK: soc, nr; USA: anc

45/01/En 1/2 **1850** Hyde 441
THE ANIMAL KINGDOM. | PART III.
8vo
title and text of Prologue n 467-469, pp 576-577; Chapter 1 n 470-573, pp 577-687; Chapter 2, n 574-596, pp 687-705.
Published in *The Animal Kingdom* 2 <44/05/En 1/3 = Hyde 441> St Clairsville oh, stereotyped from 44/05/En 1/1,2 = Hyde 439, 440.
UK: soc; USA: anc

45/01/En 1/3 **1858** Hyde 443
THE ANIMAL KINGDOM. | PART III.
8vo
title and text of Prologue n 467-469, pp 576-577; Chapter 1 n 470-573, pp 577-687; Chapter 2, n 574-596, pp 687-705.
Reprinted from En 1/1, published with Part II in *The Animal Kingdom* 2 <44/05/En 1/5 = Hyde 443> Cincinnati oh and Boston ma.
UK: soc

45/01/En 1/4 **1960** Hyde —
<<THE | ANIMAL KINGDOM, | CONSIDERED | ANATOMICALLY, PHYSICALLY, AND PHILOSOPHICALLY. | PART III. | THE SKIN, THE SENSES OF TOUCH AND TASTE, AND | ORGANIC FORMS GENERALLY.>>
8vo
title leaf, pp 367-368; text: Prologue n 467-469, pp 369-371; Chapter 1 n 470-573, pp 372-561; Chapter 2 n 574-596, pp 562-593.
Published in *The Animal Kingdom* 2 <44/05/En 1/7>, reprinted from En 1/3 = Hyde 443, Bryn Athyn pa.
Copy not seen; description deduced from En 1/5.
USA: anc

45/01/En 1/5 **2007** Hyde —
THE | ANIMAL KINGDOM, | CONSIDERED | ANATOMICALLY, PHYSICALLY, AND PHILOSOPHICALLY. | PART III. | THE SKIN, THE SENSES OF TOUCH AND TASTE, AND | ORGANIC FORMS GENERALLY.

8vo
title leaf, pp 367-368; text: Prologue n 467-469, pp 369-371; Chapter 1 n 470-573, pp 372-561; Chapter 2 n 574-596, pp 562-593.
Photographic replica reprint of En 1/4 by Fidlar Doubleday, U.S.A., published in *The Soul's Domain* Swedenborg Scientific Association, Bryn Athyn PA.
UK: SOC; USA: SSA

ENGLISH EXTRACTS

X 45/01/En 1834/1 **1834** Hyde 446
SWEDENBORG'S "ANIMAL KINGDOM."
8vo
title and text n 32-39, 71, pp 345-349; n 422-424, pp 372-374; n 470-472, pp 419-422.
Translated by Luther Clark, published in *The New Jerusalem Magazine* Boston MA.
UK: SOC, CON, NCC; USA: ANC

X 45/01/En 1835/1 **1835** Hyde 448
CONCERNING THE CUTIS. | [Translated from Swedenborg's Animal Kingdom.]
8vo
title and text n 439, 445, 447, 451-452, 454-455, 457-458, pp 46-49.
Translated by L Clark, published in *The New Jerusalem Magazine* Boston MA.
UK: SOC, CON, NCC; USA: ANC

X 45/01/En 1949/1 **1949** Hyde —
EXPERIENCE
8vo
title and text, p 303.
Extracted from Part 2, p 347 note, published in *The New Philosophy* Lancaster and Bryn Athyn PA.
UK: SOC, NCC; USA: ANC

45/02 The Worship and Love of God, Parts 1, 2, 3 Hyde CXXV

When Swedenborg stopped writing *Regnum Animale* <44/05> at the end of October 1744, he had already begun to compose this work. The first mention of it is to be found in *Journal of Dreams* n 250, 6-7 October 1744 <43/03>: 'Elliest berettades något om min bok, man sade at den wore en Liber divinus de Dei cultu et amore.' <Furthermore something was told about my book. It was said that it would be a divine book on the worship and love of God.> On 26-27 October he recorded, 'Sades mig förr at d 27 oct: skulle komma igen. då jag tog mig före cultum et amorem Dei.' <I had been told that 27 October would return: then I undertook The Worship and Love of God.>

He was then in London, where he stayed until the middle of 1745. <Hyde was mistaken when he stated that Swedenborg was in Sweden in October 1744; see Hyde 458.>

On 28 February 1745 Swedenborg presented a copy of the newly published volume 1 of *De Cultu et Amore Dei* to the Royal Society, London <Journal Book vol 18, p 369>. The unnamed publishers of La 1/1 and 1/3 were probably J Nourse and R Manby, judging by a comparison of type fonts and printer's ornaments with those used in La 1/2.

G A Beyer included entries from vols 1 and 2 in his *Index Initialis in Opera Swedenborgii Theologica* published in 1779 <Hyde 3166>.

LATIN

Editions:

La O MS
La 1 1st edition
La 2 R Hindmarsh, editor
La 3 T M Gorman, editor

45/02/La O/1 1744 Hyde 461/a
<<Fragmentum Partis III:ae>>
4to
1 leaf; verso blank.
Described by A H Stroh and G Ekelöf in *An Abridged Chronological List* 1910, p 38 <Hyde 3276/1>.
MS not seen; description recorded from Hyde 3276/1.
SWE: ROY

45/02/La 0/2 **1744** Hyde 461

<< <untitled> >>

double foolscap broad 4to <337 x 206 mm>

text: n <117>-131, pp 7a-16b; p 7b blank.

draft of cap. II-IV, pp 17a-17b.

draft of cap. III, pp 19a-19b.

The autograph MS forms part of Codex 51.

MS not seen; description recorded from La 0/4 and Hyde 461.

SWE: KVA

45/02/La 1/1 **1745** Hyde 458, 3155

PARS PRIMA | DE | CULTU | ET | AMORE DEI; | Ubi agitur | DE | Telluris Ortu, Paradiso & Vivario, | TUM DE | Primogeniti seu Adami Nativitate, | Infantia, & Amore, | AB | EMAN. SWEDENBORG. | <rule> | <orn> | <2 spaced rules> | *LONDINI.* | <short rule> | MDCCXLV.

title page: orn NR 268; p 1: line orn as head-piece NR 269; initial CUM C^5 NR 270; p 2: initial CIRCUM C^6 NR 271; p 13: initial TELLUS T^4 NR 272; p 27: tail-piece NR 256; p 28: line orn as head-piece NR 273; initial TELLUS T^5 NR 274; p 120: tail-piece NR 262

4to

title leaf, 2 pp; text n 1-86, pp 1-120.

Part 1 was published early in 1745. Swedenborg's copy of parts 1 and 2 constitute Codex 68 in SWE: KVA; part 1 has his notes in the margins throughout.

The Revd William Hill's copy is in UK: SOC. A copy with marginalia by S T Coleridge was in the Library of James Speirs in 1906 <Hyde>; these annotations were printed in *The Monthly Magazine* vol 5, London, 1841, pp 614-616, from which they were reprinted in *The New Jerusalem Magazine* Boston MA, 1841, pp 474-476.

UK: SOC, NCC, NR; DEN: RLD; SWE: KVA; SWI: LAU

45/02/La 1/2 **1745** Hyde 459

PARS SECUNDA | DE | CULTU | ET | AMORE DEI; | Ubi agitur | DE | Conjugio Primogeniti seu Adami, | ET INIBI DE | Anima, Mente Intellectuali, Statu Inte- | gritatis, & Imagine Dei. | AB | EMAN. SWEDENBORG. | <2 spaced rules> | *LONDINI:* | Apud JOH. NOURSE, & RICHARD MANBY. | <short rule> | MDCCXLV.

p 1: line orn as head-piece NR 275; initial LUCUS L^5 NR 276

8vo

title leaf, 2 pp; text n 87-110, pp 1-24; advertisement of *De Cultu et Amore Dei*, *Regnum Animale*, and *Oeconomia Regni Animalis*, 2 pp.

The Revd William Hill's copy is in UK: SOC. A copy with marginalia by S T Coleridge was in the Library of James Speirs in 1906 <Hyde>; these annotations were printed in *The Monthly Magazine* vol 5, London 1841, pp 614-616, from which they were reprinted in *The New Jerusalem Magazine* Boston MA 1841, pp 474-476.

UK: SOC, CON; SWE: KVA

45/02/La 1/3 **1745** Hyde 460

<< <orn> | PARS TERTIA, | DE | VITA CONJUGII PARIS | PRIMOGENITI.>>

p 1: head-piece NR 277; initial CUM C^5 NR 270

4to

title and text n 111-125, pp 1-10, 12-16; p 11 blank; a page of text which is not found in n 122.

The printer's proof sheets, of which the first sheet is bound in Codex 68. The remainder forms part of Codex 51 in SWE: KVA.

Copy not seen; description deduced from La 1/6 = Hyde 464.
SWE: KVA

45/02/La 0/3 **1745** Hyde 461
<< <untitled> >>
double foolscap broad 4to <337 x 206 mm>
text: n <117>-131, pp 7a-16b; p 7b blank.
draft of cap. II-VI, pp 17a-17b.
draft of n 128 <deleted>, pp 18a-18b.
draft of cap. III, pp 19a-19b.
Swedenborg's MS of part 3, forming part of Codex 51. Throughout the MS from pp 8-16b, the text has the following running heads: Pars Tertia. and De Vita Conjugii Paris Primogeniti.
An unpublished copy has been recorded as follows.
1 UK: SOC A transcript made by F F Coulson in 1968. <Archives A/199>
MS not seen; description deduced from La 0/4 = Hyde 465.
SWE: KVA

45/02/La 2/1 **1791** Hyde 466
PARS SECUNDA, | DE | CULTU | ET | AMORE DEI; | Ubi agitur | DE | Conjugio Primogeniti seu Adami, | ET INIBI DE | Anima, Mente Intellectuali, Statu Inte- | gritatis, & Imagine Dei. | AB | EMAN. SWEDENBORG. | <2 spaced rules> | *LONDINI:* | E Prelo ROBERTI HINDMARSH, Typographi REGIÆ CELSITUDINIS | GEORGII GALLORUM PRINCIPIS. | MDCCXCI.
4to
title leaf, 2 pp; text n 87-110, pp 3-26; advertisement, 2 pp.
UK: SOC, NCC

45/02/La 1/4, **D** La 1870/2 **1870** Hyde 462, 3035
PARS PRIMA | DE | CULTU | ET | AMORE DEI, | Ubi agitur | DE | Telluris Ortu, Paradiso & Vivario | TUM DE | Primogeniti seu Adami Nativitate, | Infantia, & Amore, | AB | EMAN. SWEDENBORG. | <rule> | <orn 22 x 33 mm > | <2 spaced rules> | *LONDINI.* | <short rule> | MDCCXLV.
folio
title page, p 1; text: Introductio n 1-2, p 2; n 3-86, pp 3-70.
Reproduction of Swedenborg's copy of La 1/1 from Codex 51, published in photolithographed edition, vol 7 <*De Cultu et Amore Dei* **D** La 1870/2 = Hyde 3035> Stockholm.
In this edition the 4to pages of the original edition have been converted into folios; the footnotes to chapter 1 have been repositioned after n 15 <pp 6-8>, n 21 <pp 11-12>, n 28 <pp 16-17>, n 38 <pp 21-22>, n 56 <pp 34-40>, n 86 <pp 63-70>.
Unpublished copies have been recorded as follows.
1 UK: SOC & USA: ANC, SHS A reproduction on microfilm 17, Bryn Athyn PA.
2 UK: SOC A transcript made by F F Coulson in 1968 of Swedenborg's annotations. <Archives A/199>
3 UK: SOC A transcript of Swedenborg's annotations made by R A Gill in 1970. <Archives A/199>
UK: SOC, BL, CHT, CON, NCC, NCH, RYL; GER: GSU; NET: GEN; SWE: ROY, KVA, LUN, UPP; USA: ANC, FOU, SHS; AUS: SYD

45/02/La 1/5, **D** La 1870/2 **1870** Hyde 463, 3035
PARS SECUNDA | DE | CULTU | ET | AMORE DEI; | Ubi agitur | DE | Conjugio Primogeniti seu Adami, | ET INIBI DE | Anima, Mente Intellectuali, Statu Inte- | gritatis, & Imagine Dei. | AB |

EMAN. SWEDENBORG. | <2 spaced rules> | *LONDINI:* | Apud JOH. NOURSE, & RICHARD MANBY. | <short rule> | MDCCXLV.
folio
title leaf, pp 71-72; text n 87-110, pp 73-86.
Reproduction of Swedenborg's copy of La 1/2 from Codex 51, published in photolithographed edition, vol 7 <*De Cultu et Amore Dei* **D** La 1870/2 = Hyde 3035> Stockholm.
In this edition the quarto pages of the original edition have been converted into folios; the footnotes have been repositioned after n 110, on pp 85-86.
Unpublished copies have been recorded as follows.

1 UK: SOC & USA: ANC, SHS A reproduction on microfilm 17, Bryn Athyn PA.

UK: SOC, BL, CHT, CON, NCC, NCH, RYL; GER: GSU; NET: GEN; SWE: ROY, KVA, LUN, UPP; USA: ANC, FOU, SHS; AUS: SYD

45/02/La 1/6, D La 1870/2 — 1870 — Hyde 464, 3035

<orn> | PARS TERTIA, | DE | VITA CONJUGI PARIS | PRIMOGENITI.
folio
title and text n 111-119, pp 87-91.
Reproduction of La 1/3, published in photolithographed edition, vol 7 <*De Cultu et Amore Dei* **D** La 1870/2 = Hyde 3035> Stockholm.
Unpublished copies have been recorded as follows.

1 UK: SOC & USA: ANC, SHS A reproduction on microfilm 17, Bryn Athyn PA.

2 UK: SOC A typed transcript made in 1970 by J M Sutton. <Archives A/199>

UK: SOC, BL, CHT, CON, NCC, NCH, RYL; GER: GSU; NET: GEN; SWE: ROY, KVA, LUN, UPP; USA: ANC, FOU, SHS; AUS: SYD

45/02/La 0/4, D La 1870/2 — 1870 — Hyde 465, 3035

<untitled>
folio
title and text n 120-131, pp 92-108; Sciagraphia Partis Tertiae, pp 109-110; Fragmenta Varia, pp 111-114.
Reproduction of La 0/3, published in photolithographed edition, vol 7 <*De Cultu et Amore Dei* **D** La 1870/2 = Hyde 3035> Stockholm. On facing pages throughout from pp 92-108, the text has the following running heads: Pars Tertia. and De Vita Conjugii Paris Primogeniti.
Unpublished copies have been recorded as follows.

1 USA: ANC A transcript made by A Acton c 1913 of n 120-121 and rough drafts of some of these and continuation.

2 UK: SOC & USA: ANC, SHS A reproduction on microfilm 17, Bryn Athyn PA.

3 UK: SOC A transcript made by F F Coulson in 1968. <Archives A/199>

UK: SOC, BL, CHT, CON, NCC, NCH, RYL; GER: GSU; NET: GEN; SWE: ROY, KVA, LUN, UPP; USA: ANC, FOU, SHS; AUS: SYD

45/02/La 3/1 — 1883 — Hyde 467

PARS PRIMA | DE | CULTU ET AMORE DEI; | UBI AGITUR DE TELLURIS ORTU, | PARADISO, & VIVARIO, | TUM DE | PRIMOGENITI SEU ADAMI NATIVITATE, | INFANTIA, & AMORE, | AB | EMAN. SWEDENBORG. | AD FIDEM EDITIONIS PRINCIPIS 1745 LONDINI EXCUSÆ | DENUO EDIDIT | THO. MURRAY GORMAN, M.A. | E COLL. HERT. OXON. | *LONDINI:* | APUD KEGAN PAUL, TRENCH, ET SOC. | MDCCCLXXXIII.
verso: CHISWICK PRESS: EXCUDEBANT C. WHITTINGHAM ET SOC., | LONDINI
half title: <orn 5 x 43 mm> | DE CULTU ET AMORE DEI. | <orn 5 x 13 mm>

section title: *PARS SECUNDA* | DE | CULTU ET AMORE DEI; | UBI AGITUR DE | CONJUGIO PRIMOGENITI | SEU ADAMI, | ET INIBI DE | ANIMA, MENTE INTELLECTUALI, STATU | INTEGRITATIS, & IMAGINE DEI. | AB | EMAN. SWEDENBORG. | <short rule> | *LONDINI:* | MDCCCLXXXII. <*stet* MDCCCLXXXII.>
imprint: CHISWICK PRESS:- EXCUDEBANT C. WHITTINGHAM ET SOC., | LONDINI.
small 8vo
half title and title leaves, 4 pp; text: Introductio n 1-2, pp v-vii; n 3-86, pp 1-184; section title leaf, 2 pp; n 87-110, pp 1-39; advertisement, p 41; imprint, p 42.
Parts 1 and 2. n 1-86 and 87-110; edited by Thomas Murray Gorman, published by Kegan Paul, Trench, et Soc., London.
UK: SOC, CON, NR; NET: GEN, KB; SWE: GSB

45/02/La 0/5 **1896** Hyde —
[Outline of *De Cultu et Amore Dei.*]
8vo
title and text, p 186.
A summary of the subject of the whole work, printed from La 0/1, published in *New Church Life* Bryn Athyn PA, with the following introductory description, 'On a loose sheet, preserved in the Royal Library in Stockholm, the following note is found, referring, undoubtedly, to the work on the *Worship and Love of God:*'.
UK: SOC, NCC; USA: ANC

45/02/La 1/7 **1930** Hyde 465/1, 3038/33
PARS PRIMA | DE | CULTU | ET | AMORE DEI; | Ubi agitur | DE | Telluris Ortu, Paradiso & Vivario, | TUM DE | Primogeniti seu Adami Nativitate, | Infantia, & Amore, | AB | EMAN. SWEDENBORG. | <rule> | <orn 22 x 33 mm> | <2 spaced rules> | *LONDINI.* | <short rule> | MDCCXLV.
folio
title leaf, 2 pp; text n 1-86, pp 1-120.
Photographic reproduction of La 1/1 from Codex 68, published in *Autographa Editio Photostata* vol 25 <*De Cultu et Amore Dei* Hyde 3038/33> Bryn Athyn PA.
Unpublished copies have been recorded as follows.
1 UK: SOC & USA: ANC, SHS A reproduction on microfilm 22 made in 1962, Bryn Athyn PA.
UK: SOC; USA: ANC

45/02/La 0/7 **1930** Hyde 465/2, 3038/25
<untitled>
folio
printed title and text of n 111-118, pp 1-8; MS text of n 118-131, pp 7a-19b; MS draft of n 128 <crossed out>, 2 pp; draft MS material, 4 pp.
Photographic reproduction of La 1/3 and 0/3 from Codex 51, published in *Autographa Editio Photostata* vol 12 <*De Cultu et Amore Dei* Hyde 3038/25> Bryn Athyn PA.
Unpublished copies have been recorded as follows.
1 UK: SOC & USA: ANC, SHS A reproduction on microfilm 22 made in 1962, Bryn Athyn PA.
UK: SOC; USA: ANC

LATIN EXTRACTS

X 45/02/La 1841/1 **1841** Hyde 289
COLERIDGE'S VIEW OF SWEDENBORG. | *Passages from the Œconomia Regni Animalis, and de Cultu et* | *Amore Dei, of Swedenborg. With Original Comments thereon.* | *By the late*

Samuel Taylor Coleridge.
8vo
title and text, pp 607-609. <on *Oeconomia*, pp 600-607>
Published in *The Monthly Magazine* London; quotations of the Latin text, with a transcript of Coleridge's annotations in English, followed by the comments of the editor <initialled 'C. R.'>.
UK: BL

X 45/02/La 1841/2 **1841** Hyde 289
COLERIDGE'S VIEW OF SWEDENBORG. | *Passages from the Œconomia Regni Animalis, and de Cultu et | Amore Dei, of Swedenborg. With Original Comments thereon. | By the late Samuel Taylor Coleridge.*
8vo
title and text, pp 474-476. <on *Oeconomia*, pp 468-474>
Reprint of X 1841/1, published in *The New Jerusalem Magazine* Boston MA.
UK: SOC, CON, NCC

LATIN/ENGLISH EXTRACTS

X 45/02/LaEn 1954/1, **D** X En 1954/1 **1954** Hyde —
COLERIDGE'S ANNOTATIONS TO SWEDENBORG'S DE CULTU | ET AMORE DEI (THE WORSHIP AND LOVE OF GOD)
8vo
title and text <quoted from *The New Jerusalem Magazine* Boston MA, 1841 pp 468 ff> pp 11, 12, 16, 22 of La 1/1 in Latin and English with Coleridge's comments, pp 231-234.
Compiled by L M Edmisten in his dissertation entitled *Coleridge's Commentary on Swedenborg* <**D** X En 1954/1>, published in the series '20th Century Academic Theses' 1992, Ann Arbor MI.
UK: NCC; AUS: SYD

X 45/02/LaEn 2004/1 **2004** Hyde —
A DRAMA OF CREATION | <orn 5 mm diameter> | Sources and Influences | in Swedenborg's | *Worship and Love of God* | INGE JONSSON | *translated by* | Matilda McCarthy | <publisher's logo> | Swedenborg Foundation Publishers
verso: © 2004 by Inge Jonsson | All rights reserved. No part of the publication may be reproduced or transmitted | in any form or by any means, electronic or mechanical, including photocopying, | recording, or any information storage or retrieval system, without prior | permission from the publisher. | Swedenborg Studies is a scholarly series published by the Swedenborg Foundation. | The primary purpose of the series is to make materials available for understanding | the life and thought of Emanuel Swedenborg (1688-1772) and the impact his | thought has had on others. The Foundation undertakes to publish original | studies and English translations of such studies and to republish primary | sources that are otherwise difficult to access. Proposals should be sent to: | Senior Editor, Swedenborg Studies, Swedenborg Foundation, 320 North | Church Street, West Chester, Pennsylvania 19380. | Library of Congress Cataloging-in-Publication Data | Jonsson, Inge. | A drama of creation: sources and influences in Swedenborg's | Worship and love of God / Inge Jonsson; translator, Matilda | McCarthy. | p. cm. — (Swedenborg studies) | Includes bibliographical references and index. | ISBN 0-87785-315-0 | 1. Swedenborg, Emanuel, 1688-1772. De cultu et amore Dei. | 2. Creation — Early works to 1800. 3. Adam (Biblical figure) | 4. Eve (Biblical figure) I. Title. II. Series. | BX8712.W79J59 2004 | 231.7'65—dc22 | 2004014766 | *Credits*: The Scripture quotations contained herein are from the New Revised Standard Version Bible, copyright © 1989 by the Division of Christian | Education of the National Council of Churches of Christ in the | U.S.A., and are used by permission. All rights reserved. | All quotations from Ovid's

Metamorphoses are taken from | *Metamorphoses*, translated by Rolfe Humphries (Bloomington, Ind.: | Indiana University Press, 1955. 1983) and are used by permission. | Excerpt from "The Birds: An English Version" from *ARISTOPHANES:* | *Four Comedies* by Dudley Fitts, copyright © 1957 by Harcourt, Inc. and renewed | 1985 by Cornelia Fitts, Daniel H. Fitts, and Deborah W. Fitts, reprinted by | permission of the publisher. CAUTION: *All rights, including professional,* | *amateur, motion picture, recitation, lecturing, performance, public reading,* | *radio broadcasting, and television are strictly reserved.* | Inquiries on all rights should be addressed to Harcourt, Inc., | Permissions Department, Orlando FL 32887-6777. | *Cover:* "The Formation of Eve" by Gustav Doré from | *The Doré Bible Illustrations* (Mineola, NY: Dover Publications, 1974). | Front cover design by Karen Connor. | Edited by Mary Lou Bertucci | Designed by Sans Serif, Inc., Saline, Michigan | Set in Sabon by Sans Serif, Inc. | Printed in the United States of America
half title: A DRAMA OF CREATION | <orn 5 mm diameter> | Swedenborg Studies / No. 16 | Monographs of the Swedenborg Foundation
8vo
The text contains extracts from n 2, 9, 14, 17-20, 26, 33, 43-44, 48-49, 55, 67-69, 74, 77, 82, 91, 105-106, 122, and from a loose page of the MS, on pp 53, 69-70, 74, 82, 86-88, 97-98, 106, 122, 145, 147, 150, 181-182, 184, 189-192, 195-196, 231, 239, 241, and 259.
UK: SOC

ENGLISH

Translators:

En 1 R Hindmarsh
En 2 S and H Osbaldiston
En 3 J Clowes
En 4 A H Stroh and F Sewall
En 5 A Acton

45/02/En 1/1 **1790-1791** Hyde 468

A TREATISE *on the* ORIGIN *of the* EARTH, *on* PARADISE, | *and the* ANIMALS *therein; also concerning the* BIRTH, | INFANCY, *and* LOVE *of the* FIRST-BEGOTTEN, *or* | ADAM. Translated from the Latin of the Hon. | EMANUEL SWEDENBORG.
8vo
title, Translator's preface, text n 1-4, 5-6, 7-11, **1790** pp 377-381, 421-424, 445-451; n 12-17, 18-23, 24-27, 28-32, 33-40, 41-44, **1791** pp 19-25, 71-78, 124-132, 167-173, 213-221, 249-257.
Probably translated by Robert Hindmarsh, published in *The New Magazine of Knowledge* London.
UK: SOC, CON, NCC, NR

45/02/En 2/1 **1795** Hyde 246

In 1795 W Cowherd published 34/01/En 1/1; on the final page he announced his plan to publish English versions of several of Swedenborg's philosophical works. The final statement reads:

> 4. De Cultu et Amore Dei, or Of the Worship and Love of God. The first Part treats of the Origin of the Earth, of Paradise, of the Birth, Infancy, and Love of the first Man, or Adam. London, 1744, in 4to. The second part treats of the Marriage of the first Man, of the Soul, of the intellectual Spirit, of the State of Integrity, and of the Image of God. London, 1745, in 4to. This Work is now in translating by the two OSBALDISTONS, mentioned as translators of part of the Prodromus; and is proposed to be printed in the course of the present year.

As far as is known, the proposed version was not published.

45/02/En 1/2 **1799** Hyde 469
ON THE WORSHIP AND LOVE OF GOD. | *BY EMANUEL SWEDENBORG.*
small 8vo
Editor's introduction, p 40; title and text n 1-2, 3-6, 7-8, pp 41-43, 83-86, 127-132.
Reprinted from En 1/1 in *The Aurora* London.
As indicated on p 165 of this periodical, these paragraphs were reissued with a title page to accompany further instalments of the version published with later issues of *The Aurora*.
UK: soc, con, ncc, nr; AUS: syd

45/02/En 1/3 **1801** Hyde 470
ON THE | WORSHIP | AND | LOVE OF GOD; | TRANSLATED FROM | THE ORIGINAL LATIN | OF | *EMANUEL SWEDENBORG.* | <short orn rule> | *LONDON:* | PRINTED AT THE AURORA PRESS, | BY J. HODSON, | NO. 15, CROSS-STREET, HATTON-GARDEN. | <short double rule> | 1801.
imprint: <short orn rule> | *LONDON:* | PRINTED AT THE AURORA PRESS, | BY J. HODSON, | NO. 15, CROSS-STREET, HATTON-GARDEN. | <short double rule> | 1801.
12mo
title leaf, 2 pp; text n 1-2, pp i-iv; n 3-110, pp 3-251; imprint, p 251.
n 1-44 reprinted from En 1/1; originally issued with *The Aurora* <En 1/2> in detachable instalments. Part Two <n 87 ff> has no separate title page.
UK: soc, nr; AUS: syd

45/02/En 1/4 **1812** Hyde 471
A TREATISE ON THE CREATION OF THE EARTH. | [*Translated from the Latin.*]
8vo
title and text n 1-4, 5-6, 7-11, 12-17, 18-23, 24 <23 printed>-27, 28-32, 33-40, 41-42, 43-44, pp 14-17, 71-73, 119-124, 164-168, 218-223, 256-262, 311-316, 345-351, 456-459, 508-510.
Reprinted from En 1/1, published in *The Halcyon Luminary* Boston ma.
UK: soc, cht, con, nr

45/02/En 3/1 **1816** Hyde 472
Part the First, | ON | THE WORSHIP | AND LOVE OF GOD; | TREATING OF | THE BIRTH OF THE EARTH, | OF PARADISE, | AND OF LIVING CREATURES, | ALSO OF | THE NATIVITY, THE INFANCY, AND THE LOVE OF | THE FIRST-BEGOTTEN, OR ADAM. | <short double rule> | Translated from the original Latin | OF | *EMANUEL SWEDENBORG.* | <short double rule> | **Manchester:** | PRINTED BY F. DAVIS, 5, HANGING DITCH. | Sold by Messrs. Clarke, in the Market-place, Manchester; and in London, | by E. Hodson, Cross-street, Hatton Garden; T. Goyder, 8, | Charles-street, Westminster; and may be had of all | other Booksellers. | <short wavy rule> | 1816.
section title: **Part the Second,** | CONCERNING | THE WORSHIP | AND LOVE OF GOD; | TREATING OF | THE MARRIAGE OF THE FIRST-BEGOTTEN, | OR ADAM, | AND, IN CONNECTION WITH IT, | OF THE SOUL, | THE INTELLECTUAL MIND, THE STATE | OF INTEGRITY, | AND | **The Image of God,** | BY | *EMANUEL SWEDENBORG.*
8vo
title leaf, 2 pp; Preface by the translator, pp iii-xxi; advertisement <a glossary> by the translator, pp xxiii-xxv; text n 1-86, pp 1-237; section title leaf, pp 239-240; text n 87-110, pp 241-291.
Translated by J Clowes; an edition of 250 copies was published by the Society for Printing, Publishing, and Circulating the Writings of Swedenborg, Manchester.
UK: soc, nr; SWE: upp; AUS: syd

45/02/En 3/2 **1828** Hyde 473

PART THE FIRST, | ON THE | WORSHIP AND LOVE | OF | GOD; | TREATING OF THE | BIRTH OF THE EARTH, OF PARADISE, | AND OF | LIVING CREATURES, | ALSO OF | THE NATIVITY, THE INFANCY, AND THE LOVE | OF THE | FIRST-BEGOTTEN, OR ADAM. | <short wavy rule > | TRANSLATED FROM THE ORIGINAL LATIN | OF | EMANUEL SWEDENBORG. | <short wavy rule> | SECOND EDITION. | <short rule> | *LONDON:* | PRINTED AND PUBLISHED BY J. S. HODSON, | 15, *Cross Street, Hatton Garden;* | AND SOLD BY T. GOYDER, DARTMOUTH STREET, WESTMINSTER; W. SIMPKIN AND R. | MARSHALL, STATIONERS' HALL COURT, LUDGATE STREET; AND BY | W. AND W. CLARKE, MANCHESTER. | <short rule> | 1828.

half title: ON | THE WORSHIP AND LOVE | OF | *GOD*.

section title: PART THE SECOND, CONCERNING THE WORSHIP AND LOVE OF GOD: TREATING OF THE MARRIAGE OF THE FIRSTBEGOTTEN, OR ADAM, AND, IN CONNECTION WITH IT, OF THE SOUL, THE INTELLECTUAL MIND, THE STATE OF INTEGRITY AND THE IMAGE OF GOD, by Emanuel Swedenborg.

8vo

half title and title leaves, 4 pp; Preface by the translator, pp v-xviii; advertisement, pp xix-xxi; text n 1-86, pp 1-171; advertisement, 1 p; section title leaf, pp 173-174; text n 87-110, pp 175-210.

Reprinted from En 3/1.

UK: SOC; AUS: SYD

45/02/En 3/3 **1832** Hyde 474

ON THE | WORSHIP AND LOVE | OF | GOD; | TREATING OF THE | BIRTH OF THE EARTH, OF PARADISE, | AND OF | LIVING CREATURES, | ALSO OF | THE NATIVITY, THE INFANCY, AND THE LOVE | OF THE | FIRST-BEGOTTEN, OR ADAM. | <short rule> | TRANSLATED FROM THE ORIGINAL LATIN | OF EMANUEL SWEDENBORG. | <short rule> | FIRST AMERICAN FROM SECOND LONDON EDITION. | <short orn rule> | BOSTON: | PUBLISHED BY JOHN ALLEN, | No. 11, School Street. | <short rule> | 1832.

section title: PART THE SECOND. | CONCERNING THE | WORSHIP AND LOVE | OF | GOD; | TREATING OF THE | MARRIAGE OF THE FIRST-BEGOTTEN, OR ADAM, | AND, IN CONNEXION WITH IT | OF THE SOUL, | THE INTELLECTUAL MIND, THE STATE OF INTEGRITY, | AND THE IMAGE OF GOD. | BY EMANUEL SWEDENBORG.

verso: ADVERTISEMENT. | THE Treatise which follows is evidently a continuation of | the foregoing one, though published by the Author as a dis- | tinct work. It is therefore thought proper to give it the dis- | tinct title in the translation which the Author has given it in | the original.

12mo

title leaf, 2 pp; advertisement to the American edition, 2 pp; Advertisement <ie, editorial note>, pp v-vii; text n 1-86, pp 1-174; section title leaf, pp 175-176; text n 87-110, pp 177-213.

Reprinted from En 3/2.

UK: SOC

45/02/En 3/4 **1864** Hyde 475

ON THE | WORSHIP AND LOVE OF GOD; | TREATING OF THE | BIRTH OF THE EARTH, OF PARADISE, | AND OF | LIVING CREATURES; | ALSO OF | The Nativity, the Infancy, and the Love | OF THE | FIRST-BEGOTTEN, OR ADAM. | TRANSLATED FROM THE ORIGINAL LATIN OF | EMANUEL SWEDENBORG. | <short rule> | Second American Edition. | <short rule> | BOSTON: | PUBLISHED BY T. H. CARTER & COMPANY, | No. 21, BROMFIELD STREET. | 1864.

verso: BOSTON: | PRINTED BY CHARLES H. CROSBY, | 5 & 7 Water Street.

section title: PART THE SECOND. | <short rule> | CONCERNING THE | WORSHIP AND LOVE OF GOD; | TREATING OF THE | MARRIAGE OF THE FIRST-BEGOTTEN, OR ADAM, | AND, IN

CONNECTION WITH IT, | OF THE SOUL, | **The Intellectual Mind, the State of Integrity,** | AND | THE IMAGE OF GOD. | <short rule> | BY | EMANUEL SWEDENBORG.
small 8vo
title leaf, 2 pp; advertisement to the American edition, p 3; advertisement <glossary>, pp v-vii; text n 1-86, pp 9-198; section title page, p 199; advertisement <editorial note>, p 200; text n 87-110, pp 201-240.
Reprinted from En 3/3.
UK: SOC, NR

45/02/En 3/5 **1885** Hyde 476

ON THE | WORSHIP AND LOVE OF GOD; | TREATING OF THE BIRTH OF THE EARTH, | PARADISE, AND THE ABODE OF | LIVING CREATURES; | ALSO OF | THE NATIVITY, INFANCY, AND LOVE | OF THE FIRST-BEGOTTEN, | OR ADAM. | TRANSLATED FROM THE ORIGINAL LATIN OF | EMANUEL SWEDENBORG. | *NEW EDITION.* | LONDON: | KEGAN PAUL, TRENCH, AND CO. | 1885.
verso: CHISWICK PRESS: C. WHITTINGHAM AND CO., TOOKS COURT, | CHANCERY LANE.
half title: THE | WORSHIP AND LOVE | OF | GOD.
section title: *PART THE SECOND.* | <short rule> | CONCERNING THE | WORSHIP AND LOVE OF GOD; | TREATING OF THE | MARRIAGE OF THE FIRST-BEGOTTEN, OR ADAM, | AND, IN CONNECTION WITH IT, | OF THE SOUL, | **The Intellectual Mind, the State of Integrity,** | AND | THE IMAGE OF GOD. | <short rule> | BY | EMANUEL SWEDENBORG.
verso: ADVERTISEMENT. | The Treatise which follows is evidently a con- | tinuation of the foregoing one, though published | by the Author as a distinct work. It is therefore | thought proper to give it the distinct title in the | translation which the author has given it in the | original.—[TR.]
announcement facing the half title: <within a rule border 81 x 81 mm> DE CULTU ET AMORE DEI; | AB EMAN. SWEDENBORG. | Ad fidem editionis principis 1745 Londini excusae | denuo edidit | THO. MURRAY GORMAN, M.A., | E. COLL. HERT. OXON. | <short rule> | LONDINI: | APUD KEGAN, PAUL, TRENCH ET SOC. | MDCCCLXXXIII.
imprint: <rule> | CHISWICK PRESS:- C. WHITTINGHAM AND CO., TOOKS COURT, | CHANCERY LANE.
small 8vo
announcement, half title, and title leaves, 6 pp; Editor's address to the reader, pp v-xxxi; Translator's preface, pp xxxiii-xlix; advertisement <glossary>, pp l-lii; text n 1-86, p liii-lv, 1-206; section title leaf, pp 207-208; text n 87-110, pp 209-253; imprint, p 253.
Reprinted with a few alterations from En 3/2, edited by T M Gorman.
UK: SOC, NR; NET: GEN, KB; SWE: ROY, UPP; AUS: SYD

45/02/En 4/1 **1914** Hyde 476/1

THE | WORSHIP AND LOVE OF GOD | BY | EMANUEL SWEDENBORG | ORIGINALLY PUBLISHED AT LONDON IN 1745 | IN THREE PARTS.| A REVISED AND COMPLETED TRANSLATION INCLUDING THE | THIRD PART NOW FIRST PUBLISHED AND TRANSLATED | INTO ENGLISH FROM THE LATIN MANUSCRIPT | OF THE AUTHOR | BY | ALFRED H. STROH, A.M. | AND | FRANK SEWALL, A.M., D.D. | <short rule> | BOSTON | PUBLISHED BY THE TRUSTEES OF LYDIA S. ROTCH | MASSACHUSETTS NEW-CHURCH UNION | 134 BOWDOIN STREET | 1914.
section title: THE | WORSHIP AND LOVE OF GOD | BY | EMANUEL SWEDENBORG | PART THE SECOND | TREATING OF THE | MARRIAGE OF THE FIRST-BORN, OR ADAM | AND, IN CONNECTION WITH IT, | OF THE SOUL, THE INTELLECTUAL MIND, THE STATE | OF INTEGRITY, AND THE IMAGE OF GOD | <short rule> | ORIGINALLY PUBLISHED AT LONDON IN 1745 | <short rule> | BOSTON | PUBLISHED BY THE TRUSTEES OF LYDIA S. ROTCH | MASSACHUSETTS NEW-CHURCH UNION | 134 BOWDOIN STREET | 1914

2nd section title: THE | WORSHIP AND LOVE OF GOD | BY | EMANUEL SWEDENBORG | PART THE THIRD | TREATING OF THE | MARRIED LIFE OF THE FIRST-BORN PAIR, | AND, IN CONNECTION WITH IT, | OF THE SUN OF LIFE, | THE SPIRITUAL AND NATURAL BORDERS | AND | THE DEGREES OF THE MIND AND OF FORMS | NOW FIRST TRANSCRIBED AND TRANSLATED FROM THE ORIGINAL | MANUSCRIPT OF THE AUTHOR BY ALFRED H. STROH, M.A. | <short rule> ORIGINALLY PUBLISHED AT LONDON IN 1745 | <short rule> | BOSTON | PUBLISHED BY THE TRUSTEES OF LYDIA S. ROTCH | MASSACHUSETTS NEW-CHURCH UNION | 134 BOWDOIN STREET | 1914
small 8vo
title leaf, 2 pp; Preface of the translators, pp iii-iv; Contents, 1 p; text n 1-86, pp 5-204; section title leaf, pp 205-206; n 87-110, pp 207-246; 2nd section title leaf, pp 247-248; n 111-131, pp 249-278; Appendix, n 112, 133, pp 279-281; Editorial observations <by F Sewall>, pp 283-288; Index, pp 289-292.
UK: SOC; NET: GEN; USA: ANC

45/02/En 5/1 **1924** Hyde 476/3

<<On the Worship and Love of God, by Emanuel Swedenborg. Part 3, concerning the married life of the first born pair. Translated from the photolithographed MS by Dr. A. Acton [1924].>>
title and text, 44 pp.
Typewritten MS.
Document not seen; description recorded from BAPB p 53.
USA: ANC

45/02/En 4/2 **1925** Hyde 476/2

THE | WORSHIP AND LOVE OF GOD | BY | EMANUEL SWEDENBORG | ORIGINALLY PUBLISHED AT LONDON IN 1745 | IN THREE PARTS | A REVISED AND CORRECTED TRANSLATION INCLUDING THE | THIRD PART NOW FIRST PUBLISHED AND TRANSLATED | INTO ENGLISH FROM THE LATIN MANUSCRIPT | OF THE AUTHOR | BY | ALFRED H. STROH, A.M. | AND | FRANK SEWALL, A.M., D.D. | <short rule> | BOSTON | PUBLISHED BY THE TRUSTEES OF LYDIA S. ROTCH | MASSACHUSETTS NEW-CHURCH UNION | 134 BOWDOIN STREET | 1925.
section title: THE | WORSHIP AND LOVE OF GOD | BY | EMANUEL SWEDENBORG | PART THE SECOND | TREATING OF THE | MARRIAGE OF THE FIRST-BORN, OR ADAM | AND, IN CONNECTION WITH IT, | OF THE SOUL, THE INTELLECTUAL MIND, THE STATE | OF INTEGRITY, AND THE IMAGE OF GOD | <short rule> | ORIGINALLY PUBLISHED AT LONDON IN 1745 | <short rule> | BOSTON | PUBLISHED BY THE TRUSTEES OF LYDIA S. ROTCH | MASSACHUSETTS NEW-CHURCH UNION | 134 BOWDOIN STREET | 1925
2nd section title: THE | WORSHIP AND LOVE OF GOD | BY | EMANUEL SWEDENBORG | PART THE THIRD | TREATING OF THE | MARRIED LIFE OF THE FIRST-BORN PAIR, | AND, IN CONNECTION WITH IT, | OF THE SUN OF LIFE, | THE SPIRITUAL AND NATURAL BORDERS | AND | THE DEGREES OF THE MIND AND OF FORMS | NOW FIRST TRANSCRIBED AND TRANSLATED FROM THE ORIGINAL | MANUSCRIPT OF THE AUTHOR BY ALFRED H. STROH, M.A. | <short rule> ORIGINALLY PUBLISHED AT LONDON IN 1745 | <short rule> | BOSTON | PUBLISHED BY THE TRUSTEES OF LYDIA S. ROTCH | MASSACHUSETTS NEW-CHURCH UNION | 134 BOWDOIN STREET | 1925
small 8vo
title leaf, 2 pp; Preface of the translators, pp iii-iv; Contents, 1 p; text n 1-86, pp 5-204; section title leaf, pp 205-206; n 87-110, pp 207-246; 2nd section title leaf, pp 247-248; n 111-131, pp 249-278; Appendix, n 112, 133, pp 279-281; Editorial observations <by F Sewall>, pp 283-288; Index, pp 289-292.
Reprint of En 4/1.
NET: GEN; SWE: ROY; USA: ANC

45/02/En 4/3 **1956** Hyde 476/4

THE | WORSHIP AND LOVE OF GOD | BY | EMANUEL SWEDENBORG | ORIGINALLY PUBLISHED AT LONDON IN 1745 | IN THREE PARTS | A REVISED AND COMPLETED TRANSLATION INCLUDING THE | THIRD PART NOW FIRST PUBLISHED AND TRANSLATED | INTO ENGLISH FROM THE LATIN MANUSCRIPT | OF THE AUTHOR | BY | ALFRED H. STROH, A.M. | AND | FRANK SEWALL, A.M., D.D. | <short rule> | BOSTON | PUBLISHED BY THE TRUSTEES OF LYDIA S. ROTCH | MASSACHUSETTS NEW-CHURCH UNION | 134 BOWDOIN STREET | 1956

section title: THE WORSHIP AND LOVE OF GOD | BY | EMANUEL SWEDENBORG | PART THE FIRST | TREATING OF | THE ORIGIN OF THE EARTH, PARADISE, AND THE | ABODE OF LIVING CREATURES, | ALSO OF THE | BIRTH, INFANCY, AND LOVE | OF THE | FIRST-BORN OR ADAM | <short rule> | ORIGINALLY PUBLISHED AT LONDON IN 1745 | <short rule> | BOSTON | PUBLISHED BY THE TRUSTEES OF LYDIA S. ROTCH | MASSACHUSETTS NEW-CHURCH UNION | 134 BOWDOIN STREET

2nd section title: THE WORSHIP AND LOVE OF GOD | BY | EMANUEL SWEDENBORG | PART THE SECOND | TREATING OF THE | MARRIAGE OF THE FIRST-BORN, OR ADAM | AND, IN CONNECTION WITH IT, | OF THE SOUL, THE INTELLECTUAL MIND, THE STATE | OF INTEGRITY, AND THE IMAGE OF GOD | <short rule> | ORIGINALLY PUBLISHED AT LONDON IN 1745 | <short rule> | BOSTON | PUBLISHED BY THE TRUSTEES OF LYDIA S. ROTCH | MASSACHUSETTS NEW-CHURCH UNION | 134 BOWDOIN STREET

3rd section title: THE WORSHIP AND LOVE OF GOD | BY | EMANUEL SWEDENBORG | PART THE THIRD | TREATING OF THE | MARRIED LIFE OF THE FIRST-BORN PAIR, | AND, IN CONNECTION WITH IT, | OF THE SUN OF LIFE, | THE SPIRITUAL AND NATURAL BORDERS | AND | THE DEGREES OF THE MIND AND OF FORMS | NOW FIRST TRANSCRIBED AND TRANSLATED FROM THE ORIGINAL | MANUSCRIPT OF THE AUTHOR BY ALFRED H. STROH, M.A. | <short rule> | ORIGINALLY PUBLISHED AT LONDON IN 1745 | <short rule> | BOSTON | PUBLISHED BY THE TRUSTEES OF LYDIA S. ROTCH | MASSACHUSETTS NEW-CHURCH UNION | 134 BOWDOIN STREET

small 8vo

title leaf, 2 pp; Preface of the translators, pp iii-iv; Contents, 2 pp; text n 1-2, pp 5-7; section title leaf, 2 pp; text n 3-86, pp 9-204; 2nd section title leaf, pp 205-206; text n 87-110, pp 207-246; 3rd section title leaf, pp 247-248; text n 111-131, pp 249-278; Appendix n [112, 133], pp 279-281; Observations on the character and purpose of this work, signed by F Sewall, pp 283-288; Index, pp 289-292.

The appendix is described as being fragments of what seems to be a continuance of the work in MS, transcribed and translated by A Acton.

UK: SOC, NR; NET: GEN; USA: ANC; AUS: SYD

45/02/En 4/4 **1996** Hyde 476/5

THE | WORSHIP AND LOVE OF GOD | by | EMANUEL SWEDENBORG | IN THREE PARTS | TRANSLATED BY | ALFRED H. STROH | and | FRANK SEWALL | <short rule> | THE SWEDENBORG FOUNDATION THE SWEDENBORG SOCIETY | WEST CHESTER, PENNSYLVANIA LONDON, ENGLAND | 1996

verso: Published by | The Swedenborg Foundation and The Swedenborg Society | 320 North Church Street Swedenborg House | West Chester, Pennsylvania 20-21 Bloomsbury Way | 19380 London WC1A 2TH. England | *De Cultu et Amore Dei*, first published in Latin, London, 1745 | First English translation, by R. Hindmarsh, London, 1790-1791 | First U.S. edition, translated by A. H. Stroh and F. Sewall, Boston, 1914 | Fourth printing, 1997 | Library of Congress Cataloging-in-Publication Data | Swedenborg, Emanuel, 1688-1772 | [De Cultu et Amore Dei. English] | The worship and love of God / by Emanuel Swedenborg | / translated by Alfred H. Stroh and Frank Sewall. | p. cm. | Originally published: Boston: | Massachusetts New-Church Union, 1914. |

Includes index. | ISBN 0-87785-297-9 (casebound) | 1. Creation—Early works to 1800. 2. Adam (biblical figure). | 3. Eve (biblical figure). I. Stroh, Alfred Henry, 1878-1922. | II. Sewall, Frank, 1837-1915. III. Title. | BX8712.W7 1996 | 231.7'65—dc20 96-25694 | CIP | Printed in the United States of America
half title: THE | WORSHIP AND LOVE OF GOD
section title: THE | WORSHIP AND LOVE OF GOD
small 8vo
half title and title leaves, 4 pp; Preface of the translators, pp iii-iv; Contents, 1 p; text n 1-2, pp 5-6; section title leaf, 2 pp; statement of the subject of Part One, 2 pp; text n 3-86, pp 9-204; statement of the subject of Part Two, pp 205-206; text n 87-110; pp 207-246; statement of the subject of Part Three, pp 247-248; text n 111-131, pp 249-278; Appendix n [112, 133], pp 279-281; Observations on the character and purpose of this work, signed by F Sewall, pp 283-288; Index, pp 289-292.
The appendix is described as being fragments of what seems to be a continuance of the work in MS, transcribed and translated by A Acton.
Reprint of En 4/3.
UK: SOC, NR; SWE: ROY; USA: ANC

45/02/En 3/6 **2004** Hyde 476/—
<<ON THE | WORSHIP AND LOVE OF GOD; | TREATING OF THE | BIRTH OF THE EARTH, OF PARADISE, | AND OF | LIVING CREATURES; | ALSO OF | **The Nativity, the Infancy, and the Love** | OF THE | FIRST-BEGOTTEN, OR ADAM. | TRANSLATED FROM THE ORIGINAL LATIN OF | EMANUEL SWEDENBORG. | <short rule> | **Second American Edition.** | <short rule> | BOSTON: | PUBLISHED BY T. H. CARTER & COMPANY, | No. 21, BROMFIELD STREET. | 1864.>>
verso: BOSTON: | PRINTED BY CHARLES H. CROSBY, | 5 & 7 Water Street.
section title: <<PART THE SECOND. | <short rule> | CONCERNING THE | WORSHIP AND LOVE OF GOD; | TREATING OF THE | MARRIAGE OF THE FIRST-BEGOTTEN, OR ADAM, | AND, IN CONNECTION WITH IT, | OF THE SOUL, | **The Intellectual Mind, the State of Integrity,** | AND | THE IMAGE OF GOD. | <short rule> | BY | EMANUEL SWEDENBORG.>>
small 8vo
title leaf, 2 pp; advertisement to the American edition, p 3; advertisement <glossary>, pp v-vii; text n 1-86, pp 9-198; section title page, p 199; advertisement <editorial note>, p 200; text n 87-110, pp 201-240.
Photographic replica reprint of En 3/4 = Hyde 475, published by Kessinger Publishing, Whitefish MT. Published in the United States.
Copy not seen; description deduced from En 3/4 and **E:b** En 2004/1.

ENGLISH EXTRACTS

X 45/02/En 1886/1 **1886** Hyde 3302
THE FIRMAMENT OF THE NATURAL UNIVERSES.
small 8vo
title and text, pp 292-295; editorial comment, p 295.
Published in *Emanuel Swedenborg A Biographical Sketch* by J J G Wilkinson, London <Hyde 3302>, 2nd edition of En 1849/1.
UK: SOC, NR

X 45/02/En 1923/1 **1923** Hyde —
Swedenborg's Hobby
8vo
title and text, p 72.

Quotation from the Introduction, in an article by Cyriel Ljungberg Odhner <later Sigstedt>, published in *New Church Life* Bryn Athyn PA.
UK: SOC, NCC; USA: ANC

X 45/02/En 1957/1 **1957** Hyde —
<untitled>
8vo
text, pp 65-66.
Translation by A Acton of the text printed in La 0/5, in an article entitled 'The Worship and Love of God: Part III', published in *New Church Life* Bryn Athyn PA.
UK: SOC, NCC, NR; USA: ANC

X 45/02/En 1958/1, **E:b** En 1958/4 **1958** Hyde 3336/25iv
<untitled>
4to
text, pp 826-827.
Translated by A Acton, published in *The Life of Emanuel Swedenborg* 4 <**E:b** En 1958/4 = Hyde 3336/25iv> Bryn Athyn PA.
UK: SOC, NCC; USA: ANC

FRENCH

Translators:
Fr 1 J P Moët
Fr 2 L Paillard

45/02/Fr 1/1 **1780-1785** Hyde 476/a, 3432
Emmanuel Swedenborg. | Le Premier-né, | ou | la naisaance, l'enfance et | l'amour d'Adam; | avec les notes; 1e Partie. | <short rule> | 1780. | <short rule> | Intrà Sacrum et Saxum inveniuntur Regnum | Dei et Sanctitudo ejus. | J. P. M.... | Imprimé à Londres, en latin, 3n 1745. in-4⁰ de culto et a- | more Dei.
medium broad 8vo <219 x 140 mm>
title leaf, 2 pp; text: Part I n 1-86, pp 1-149; Notes, pp 1-68.
Translated by J P Moët, from whose widow the MS was purchased by J A Tulk. <UK: SOC Archives B/65/1>
UK: SOC

45/02/Fr 1/2 **1785** Hyde 476/a, 3432
Le Premier-né, | ou | du culte et de l'amour de | Dieu, où il s'agit du Mariage du | Premier-né ou Adam; et où il | est traité de l'ame, de l'entende- | ment intellectuel, de l'Etat d'inté- | grité. et de l'image de Dieu; | avec les Notes; 2e Partie. | <rule> | 1785. | <rule>
title leaf, 2 pp; text: Part II n 87-110, pp 1-44; Notes, pp 1-5.
Translated by J P Moët, from whose widow the MS was purchased by J A Tulk. <UK: SOC Archives B/65/2>
UK: SOC

45/02/Fr 2/1 **post 1828** Hyde 476/b
Première partie | sur | le Culte et l'amour | de | Dieu; | Traitant de la naissance | de la Terre du Paradis, | et | des Créatures vivantes, | ainsi que de | la nativité, l'Enfance | et | l'amour du premier

| Engendré, ou d'Adam. | <wavy line> | Traduit (en anglais) du latin orig[al]. | de | Emanuel Swédenborg | <wavy line> | Seconde Edition. | <wavy line> | à Londre. | Imprimé et publié par J. S. Hodson | Cross Street 15 Hatton Garden | 1828.
210 x 127 mm
title and text, 525 pp.
MS translation in the handwriting of Lucien Paillard, made from En 2/2. <UK: SOC Archives B/41>
UK: SOC

GERMAN EXTRACTS

X 45/02/Ge 1949/1, D Ge 1949/1 **1949** Hyde 478/2, 3263/1
1. | Gottes=Anbetung und Gottes=Liebe | De Cultu et Amore Dei | London 1745
8vo
title leaf, pp 37-38; text n 1-2, 29-43, 87-90, 99-115, pp 39-78.
Translated by I Meyer-Lünen from X Sw 1925/1, published in *Ausgewählte religiöse Schriften* edited by E Benz and R F Merkel, Marburg/Lahn.
UK: SOC; SWI: ZÜR

SWEDISH

Translators:
- Sw 1 A A Afzelius
- Sw 2 B E Boyesen and A H Stroh
- Sw 3 R Jonsson

45/02/Sw 1/1 **1816** Hyde 477
<<OM GUDSDYRKAN OCH KÄRLEK. 1816.>>
8vo
text n 1-27, pp 1-48.
The three printed sheets of the text are in SWE: ROY, and the above title is on a printed label pasted on the back of the cover, where the following note is written: 'Ofver. af De Cultu et Amore Dei gjord af A. A. Afzelius. Endast 3 ark tryckta; hos Deleen, 1816.' <A translation of De Cultu et Amore Dei made by A A Afzelius. Only three sheets printed, by Deleen, 1816> A A Afzelius, n 1-27.
Copy not seen; description deduced from Hyde 477 and catalogue of SWE: ROY.
SWE: ROY

45/02/Sw 2/1 **1902-1903** Hyde 478
<<Om Gudsdyrkan och Kärleken till Gud. Första delen: jordens uppkomst, paradiset och lefvande varelsers boning; äfvensom den förstföddes eller Adams födelse, barndom och kärlek. Andra delen: den förstföddes eller Adams bröllop; äfvensom själen, det förnuftiga sinnet, renhetstill ståndet och Guds afbild. Tredje delen: det förstfödda parets äkta förbund; äfvensom lifvets sol, de andliga och naturliga zonerna, och om sinnets och formers grader. Af Emanuel Swedenborg. Öfversatt från den latinska urskriften af Joseph E. Boyesen och Alfred H. Stroh. Stockholm: Nya Tryckeri-Aktiebolaget.>>
8vo
title: **1902** p 19; Förord, p 20; title to Part 1, p 21; text n 1-15, pp 22-26, 53-57; **1903** pp 33-35, 69-71, 92-93.
Published in *Nya Kyrkans Härold* Stockholm, and said by Hyde to have been continued in later issues of the journal.
Copy not seen; description recorded from Hyde 478.
USA: ANC

45/02/Sw 3/1 **1961** Hyde 478/1

EMANUEL SWEDENBORG | Om Guds dyrkan | och kärleken till Gud | (DE CULTU ET AMORE DEI) | NATUR OCH KULTUR | STOCKHOLM
verso: *Till svenska av* | RITVA JONSSON | *Inledning av* | INGE JONSSON | Printed in Sweden | Rydahls Boktryckeri AB | Stockholm 1961
half title: *Levande litteratur* | NATUR OCH KULTUR KLASSIKERSERIE
section title: I | *Första delen, som handlar* | *om jordens uppkomst, paradiset och* | *levande varelsers boning samt om den förstföddes* | *eller Adams födelse, barndom* | *och kärlek.*
2nd section title: II | *Andra delen, vilken handlar* | *om den förstföddes eller Adams giftermål* | *och därigenom om själen, det intellektuella förnuftet,* | *oskuldens tillstånd och Guds avbild.*
3rd section title: III | *Tredje delen* | *Om det förstfödda oparets* | *äktenskapliga liv*
4th section title: NOTER
8vo
half title and title leaves, 4 pp; Innehall <Contents>, pp 5-6; Inledning <Introduction>, pp 7-22; Översättarens förord <Translator's foreword>, pp 23-24; section title leaf, pp 25-26; text n 1-86, pp 27-140; 2nd section title leaf, pp 141-142; n 87-110, pp 143-172; 3rd title leaf, pp 173-174; n 111-131, pp 175-194; 4th section title leaf, pp 195-196; Noter, pp 197-261.
UK: SOC; SWE: ROY, GSB; USA: ANC

45/02/Sw 3/2 **1997** Hyde 478/–

<<EMANUEL SWEDENBORG | Om Guds dyrkan | och kärleken till Gud | (DE CULTU ET AMORE DEI) | NATUR OCH KULTUR | STOCKHOLM>>
verso: <<*Till svenska av* | RITVA JONSSON | *Inledning av* | INGE JONSSON | Printed in Sweden | Rydahls Boktryckeri AB | Stockholm 1961>>
half title: <<*Levande litteratur* | NATUR OCH KULTUR KLASSIKERSERIE>>
section title: <<I | *Första delen, som handlar* | *om jordens uppkomst, paradiset och* | *levande varelsers boning samt om den förstföddes* | *eller Adams födelse, barndom* | *och kärlek.*>>
2nd section title: <<II | *Andra delen, vilken handlar* | *om den förstföddes eller Adams giftermål* | *och därigenom om själen, det intellektuella förnuftet,* | *oskuldens tillstånd och Guds avbild.*>>
3rd section title: <<III | *Tredje delen* | *Om det förstfödda oparets* | *äktenskapliga liv*>>
4th section title: <<NOTER>>
8vo
half title and title leaves, 4 pp; Innehall <Contents>, pp 5-6; Inledning <Introduction>, pp 7-22; Översättarens förord <Translator's foreword>, pp 23-24; section title leaf, pp 25-26; text n 1-86, pp 27-140; 2nd section title leaf, pp 141-142; n 87-110, pp 143-172; 3rd title leaf, pp 173-174; n 111-131, pp 175-194; 4th section title leaf, pp 195-196; Noter, pp 197-261.
A reprint of Sw 3/1. ISBN 9789127063297.
Copy not seen; description deduced from Sw 3/1 and catalogue of SWE: GSB.
SWE: GSB

SWEDISH EXTRACTS

X 45/02/Sw 1771/1 1771 Hyde 477/a, 3276/1

<<Öfversättning | Forsta delen | om | Dyrkan och Kärlek | hvaruti handles | om | Jordenes uprinnelse, Paradiset. och | Djur-Cården | såsom och om | Förstfödingens eller Adams Födelse Barndom och Kä#rlek. | af Eman. Swedenborg utgifven, och trykt i London 1745. 4.o, af Christ. Johansen öfversätt pa Tunafors 1771.>>
folio
title, 1 p; text n 1-28, 19 pp.

MS in SWE: ROY; see A H Stroh and G Ekelöf *Abridged Chronological List* p 38 <Hyde 3276/1>.
MS not seen; description deduced from ACSD n 1482.11.
SWE: ROY

X 45/02/Sw 1925/1, **D** Sw 1925/1 **1925** Hyde 478/–, 3270/–

UR | OM GUDS DYRKAN OCH KÄRLEKEN TILL GUD. | DE CULTU ET AMORE DEI.
8vo
section title leaf, pp 1-2; text n 1-2, 29-43, 87-90, 99-115, pp 3-38.
Translated by H Bergstedt, published in *Emanuel Swedenborg Religiosa Skrifter i Urval* Stockholm, Hugo Gebers Förlag.
SWE: ROY, HNK

X 45/02/Sw 1938/1, **D** Sw 1938/1 **1938** Hyde 478/–, 3270/1

UR | OM GUDS DYRKAN OCH KÄRLEKEN TILL GUD | DE CULTU ET AMORE DEI | I – 37828. *Emanuel Swedenborg.*
8vo
title leaf, pp 1-2; text n 1-2, 29-43, 87-90, 99-115, pp 3-37.
Reprinted from X Sw 1925/1, published in *Emanuel Swedenborg Religiosa Skrifter i Urval* Stockholm, Hugo Gebers Förlag <**D** Sw 1938/1 = Hyde 3270/1>.
UK: SOC, NR; SWE: ROY, GSB

X 45/02/Sw 1998/1 **1998** Hyde —

DET STORA VÄRLDSÄGGET | ett ovatorium | efter E. Swedenborgs skapelsdrama | "De cultu et amore Dei" | *manus:* Maria af Malmborg | *musik:* Björn Linnman | Copyright Maria af Malmborg & Linnman Producktion 1998
A4
title leaf, 2 pp; Performance details, 1 p; Libretto, pp 1-26.
The 'ovatorium' was performed in September-October 1998 in Kopparlunden, Västeras, Sweden, as a co-production between Teater Västmanland and Musik i Västmanland, with the Mariachoir of Västeras Cathedral and Västeras Sinfonietta. The dramatization is based on the Swedish translation of *De Cultu et Amor Dei* made by Ritva Jonsson <Sw 4/1>.
In UK: SOC, the copy of the libretto is accompanied by a compact disc recording of a performance, a compact disc containing photographs of the performance, and a copy of the performance programme.
UK: SOC

45/03 Concerning the Messiah about to Come Hyde CXXVII

The autograph MS forms part of Codex 38 in the Library of the Royal Swedish Academy of Sciences, Stockholm.

The work is mainly a compilation of passages from the Old and New Testaments and the Apocrypha, all of which Swedenborg took from Sebastian Castellio's Latin version published in London in 1726 in four duodecimo volumes. The order in which he used them (and the order in which he wrote the quotations in each section of the text) was:

vol 3 Isaiah, Jeremiah, Baruch <including the Letter of Jeremiah>, Ezekiel to Malachi;
vol 2 Psalms;
vol 1 Genesis to Ezra <1 Esdras>, 2-4 Esdras, Tobit, Judith, Esther to Song of Solomon, Wisdom of Solomon, Ecclesiasticus;
vol 4 New Testament.

A Acton judged that Swedenborg wrote the work between mid-April and mid-July 1745, while he was resident in London <45/03/En 1/1 p vi>; but this does not explain the date of the memorandum which Swedenborg wrote on p 127 of Codex 38:

'Nov: 17, 1745, begynta här tilskriva.
Herre Jesu Christe led mig til och på the wägen en som Tu wil at jag wandra skal.
Sancti eritis, dabimini Spiritu Dei et Christi, et perseverabitis in justitia, hoc erit regni Dei testimonium.'

<November 17, 1745, I began to write. Lord Jesus Christ, lead me to and on the way on which You will that I shall walk. Be holy; be gifted with the Spirit of God and Christ; and persevere in righteousness. This will be the testimony of the Kingdom of God.>

Acton believed that the memorandum refers to the composition of *The Historical Word* <45/05 = Hyde CXXVIII>, in n 475 and 1003 of which Swedenborg gives date references which indicate mid-November as the time when he began to write it. As *The History of Creation* <45/04 = Hyde CXXVI> and volume 1 of *The Historical Word* constitute Codex 59, we have no explanation as to why Swedenborg wrote this memorandum in Codex 38.

LATIN

45/03/La 0/1 1745 Hyde 481

<<*Varii Loci | in Scriptura Sacra | de Messiah Venturo in Mundum, | de Babylone cet.*>>
pott long 4to <321 x 95 mm>
text: De regno Dei quae est Venire n 1-4, p 1.
De Messia venturo in mundum n 1-67, pp 63-64, 65-70; between pp 64 and 65 there are 3 pp blank.

12 memoranda concerning the kingdom of God, p 70.
Ex Apocalypsi n 1-5, p 71.
5 memoranda concerning the kingdom of God, p 72; 8 pp blank.
De Messia itera venturo ut reducat Judaeos n 1-94, pp 73-92.
De regno Dei n 1-210, pp 93-120, 121; p 122 blank.
Ex Novo Testamento, p 120.
De Babylone n 1-10, pp 123, 125-126.
Several memoranda concerning the Tree of Knowledge, Wisdom, and Moses, p 124.
Other memoranda, p 127; 1 p blank.

pp 2-61 of the Codex contain *Index to Regnum Animale* 1 and 2 <44/06>.
Copy not seen; description deduced from La O/2.

SWE: KVA

45/03/La O/2, **D** La 1870/2 **1870** Hyde 482, 3036

VI. | Varii Loci | in Scriptura Sacra | de Messiah Venturo in Mundum, | de Babylone cet.
folio
title, 1 p; Nota editoris, 1 p; text, pp 1-32.
Reproduction of La O/1, published in photolithographed edition, vol 8 <*Miscellanea Theologica* **D** La 1870/2 = Hyde 3036> Stockholm.
In this edition the pages are printed in double columns.
Unpublished copies have been recorded as follows.

1 USA: ANC A bound typed transcript, made and edited by B G Briscoe and corrected by A Acton. <Hyde 482/2>

2 UK: SOC & USA: ANC, SHS A reproduction on microfilm 12, Bryn Athyn PA.

UK: SOC, BL, CHT, CON, NCC, NCH, RYL; GER: GSU; NET: GEN; SWE: ROY, KVA, LUN, UPP; USA: ANC, FOU, SHS; AUS: SYD

45/03/La O/3, **D** La 1929/1 **1929** Hyde 482/1, 3038/24

Varii Loci | in Scriptura Sacra | de Messiah Venturo in Mundum, | de Babylone cet.
folio
title and text, 127 pp.
Photographic reproduction of La O/1, published in *Autographa Editio Photostata* vol 3 <*Indices Anatomicae et de Messia* **D** La 1929/1 = Hyde 3038/24> Bryn Athyn PA.
Unpublished copies have been recorded as follows.

1 UK: SOC & USA: ANC, SHS A reproduction on microfilm 22 made in 1962, Bryn Athyn PA.

UK: SOC; USA: ANC

ENGLISH

45/03/En 1/1 **1949** Hyde 482/3

CONCERNING | THE MESSIAH ABOUT TO COME | AND CONCERNING | THE KINGDOM OF GOD | AND | THE LAST JUDGMENT | A POSTHUMOUS WORK | BY | EMANUEL SWEDENBORG | Now for the first time translated and edited from a phototyped copy | of the original manuscript preserved in the Royal | Academy of Sciences, Sweden | BY | ALFRED ACTON, M.A., D.Th. | DEAN OF THE THEOLOGICAL SCHOOL OF | THE ACADEMY OF THE NEW CHURCH | ACADEMY OF THE NEW CHURCH | BRYN ATHYN, PA. | 1949
8vo
title leaf, 2 pp; Translator's preface, pp iii-vii; Contents, p ix; text Sections I- XIV, pp 1-105; Index to Swedenborg's notes in the text, p 106; Index to Bible passages, pp 107-112.

UK: SOC, NR; NET: GEN; USA: ANC; AUS: SYD

45/04 The History of Creation Hyde CXXVI

The autograph MS forms the first part of Codex 59 in the Library of the Royal Swedish Academy of Sciences, Stockholm.

With reference to the phrase 'In Nomine Dei' in the title of the work I note the abbreviations with which the titles of three much earlier works begin: 18/01 and 18/02, 'I. H. N.' <for 'I Herrans Namn' *In the Lord's Name*>; and 19/01, 'I. N. D.' <for 'In Nomine Dei *or* Domini' *In God's* or *the Lord's Name*>. See also *Journal of Dreams* <43/03> n 278, where Swedenborg wrote on 27 October 1744 'detta betyder alt det arbete jag nu för hender tager i Gudz namn' <this refers to all the work upon which I now enter in God's name>.

LATIN

Editions:

La 0 MS
La 1 J F I Tafel, editor

45/04/La 0/1 1745 Hyde 479

<<In Nomine Domini | Historia Creationis a Mose Tradita | Ex Smidio et ex Castellione.>> <In the Name of the Lord! The History of Creation related by Moses. From the versions of Schmidius and Castellio>
pott folio <311 x 194 mm>
text of Matthew 6:33, Comparatio Regni Deo n 1-5, and 2 sentences concerning 'Via veritatis', p 1.
title, and text of Genesis Cap. I, pp 3-7.
Cap. II, pp 8-11.
Cap. III, pp 11-18.
Copy not seen; description deduced from La 0/3.
SWE: KVA

45/04/La 1/1, D La 1847/1, 1848/1 1847 Hyde 480, 3039

IN NOMINE DOMINI. | HISTORIA CREATIONIS A MOSE | TRADITA.
8vo
title and text, pp 1-25; text of Matthew 6:33, Comparatio Regni Deo n 1-5, 2 sentences concerning 'Via veritatis', p 844.
Edited by J F I Tafel, published in *Adversaria* <D La 1847/1, 1848/1 = Hyde 3039, 3040> Tübingen, title and text, vol 1, part 1; other matter, vol 2, part 1.
UK: SOC, NR; GER: GSU; NET: GEN, KB; USA: ANC

45/04/La O/2 **no date** Hyde 479/a
In Nomine Domini | Historia Creationis a Mose Tradita | Ex Smidio et ex Castellione.
2 photolithographed copies of part of the work. <UK: SOC Archives A/42>
UK: SOC

45/04/La O/3, **D** La 1916/4 **1916** Hyde 479/1, 3038/7
In Nomine Domini | Historia Creationis a Mose Tradita | Ex Smidio et ex Castellione.
folio
title and text, pp 7-22.
Reproduction of La O/1, published in phototyped edition, vol 7 <*Explicationes in Verbum seu Adversaria* vol 1 **D** La 1916/4 = Hyde 3038/7>, Stockholm.
Proof sheets bound by the Academy of the New Church, in USA: ANC.
Unpublished copies have been recorded as follows.
1 UK: SOC & USA: ANC, SHS A reproduction on microfilm 1, Bryn Athyn PA.
UK: SOC, BL, BOD, CAM, CON, NCC, RYL, WIL; DEN: RLD; NET: GEN, KB; SWE: ROY, KVA, UPP; USA: ANC, FOU, SHS; AUS: SYD; NZ: WEL

ENGLISH

45/04/En 1/1 **1910-1911** Hyde 480/1
THE HISTORY OF CREATION AS GIVEN BY MOSES. | BY EMANUEL SWEDENBORG. | GENESIS.
8vo
title and text: **1910** n 1-10, pp 754-762, n 11-22, pp 829-837; **1911** n 23-42, pp 89-102.
Translated by A Acton, published in *New Church Life* Bryn Athyn PA.
UK: SOC, NCC; USA: ANC

45/04/En 1/2 **1911** Hyde 480/2
<<THE HISTORY OF CREATION | AS GIVEN BY MOSES>>
8vo
title leaf, pp 1-2; Editor's preface, pp 3-9; text n 1-42, pp 11-44; Translator's notes, pp 45-56.
Translated and edited by A Acton; published by the Academy of the New Church, Bryn Athyn PA.
Copy not seen; description deduced from catalogue of USA: ANC, En 1/4, and a study by W E Closterman.
USA: ANC

45/04/En 1/3 **1928** Hyde 480/3
THE HISTORY OF CREATION | AS GIVEN BY MOSES | A POSTHUMOUS WORK | OF | EMANUEL SWEDENBORG | Translated from the Latin | BY | ALFRED ACTON, M.A., D.Th. | DEAN OF THE THEOLOGICAL SCHOOL OF | THE ACADEMY OF THE NEW CHURCH | *SECOND EDITION REVISED* | ACADEMY OF THE NEW CHURCH | BRYN ATHYN, PA. | 1928
verso: LANCASTER PRESS, INC. | LANCASTER, PA.
8vo
title leaf, 2 pp; text n 1-42, pp 3-30.
2nd revised edition of En 1/2.
UK: SOC; USA: ANC

45/04/En 1/4 **1928** Hyde 480/4, 488/1
IN THE NAME OF THE LORD | THE HISTORY OF CREATION | AS GIVEN BY MOSES
half title: THE HISTORY OF CREATION
verso: MATTH. VI:33 | *Seek ye first the kingdom of the heavens and its righteousness,* | *and all*

these things (which are recounted), *shall be added unto* | *you.* | Comparison of the kingdom of God: | 1. With the human body from inmosts to outmosts; and there- | fore concerning that society wherein the Messiah is the | Soul, and which shall form one body as one man. | 2. With the kindred in the house of Abraham and Nahor. | 3. With the land of Canaan and its bordering countries. | 4. With the Paradise of Eden. | 5. With a marriage and a feast. | [*For the above comparisons, see (1) n. 596* seq. *(2) n. 567-68.* | *(3) n. 477* seq. *(4) n. 498* seq., *879* seq. *(5) n. 568.*] | Men are men only so far as they walk in the way of truth. | But so far as they turn aside therefrom, they approach to the na- | ture of a beast.

8vo

half title, pp 1-2; title and text n 1-42, pp 3-30.

Reprint of En 1/3, published in *The Word of the Old Testament Explained* 1 <45/05/En 2/1 = Hyde 488/1> Bryn Athyn PA.

UK: SOC, NR; NET: GEN; SWE: ROY; USA: ANC; AUS: SYD

45/05 The Word Explained, Parts 1, 2, 3 Hyde CXXVIII

The autograph MSS of Parts 1, 2, 3 respectively form the major part of Codex 59 and Codices 60 and 61 in the Library of the Royal Swedish Academy of Sciences, Stockholm. Each Part has its own paragraph numbering sequence beginning with '1'. The first 18 pp of Codex 59 contain *The History of Creation* <45/04>, the text of the present work following immediately on pp 19 ff.

Date references in n 475 and 1003 of Part 1 indicate that Swedenborg began to compose the work in the autumn of 1745. Note also the memorandum dated 17 November 1745 in Codex 38, quoted in the description of 45/03, which A Acton believed to be a reference to the writing of the present work.

At intervals throughout the text of each Part Swedenborg recorded a number of his spiritual experiences which have now been recognized as the beginnings of what he later wrote as *Experientiae Spirituales* <47/05>. Although he did not number these paragraphs in a separate series, he distinguished them clearly from the text of *The Historical Word*, by indenting them in the MS, by annotations such as 'num haec inserenda sunt, postea videbitur' <whether these should be inserted will be seen later> in Part 1 n 317e, and by the heading 'Experientia', for example in Part 1 n 541.

In Parts 2 and 3 there are some references to passages written at the end of the volume, though the Codices no longer contain the pages on which Swedenborg had written such passages; see for example Part 2 n 59, 'Confer ... ad calcem hujus tomi scripta sunt et dictata.' <Consult the things which have been written and dictated at the end of the present volume> As Swedenborg included the subjects of such passages in his *Index to the Spiritual Diary* <47/05/La 0/4-7>, it appears that when he prepared this Index he removed the pages from Codices 60, 61 although they have not been preserved with the MSS of *Experientiae Spirituales*.

With references to A Acton's translation of Parts 1-3 of this work, recorded below as En 2/1-7, I note that he prepared and published a volume of Indices to these and 47/02, which he entitled *The Word of the Old Testament Explained ... Indices* <Hyde 488/9>, published by the Academy of the New Church, Bryn Athyn PA, 1951. It contains Indices of subjects, authors, and Bible passages, with several Appendices.

LATIN

Editions:

La 0 MSS
La 1 J F I Tafel, editor

45/05/La O/1 **1745** Hyde 483

<< <untitled> >>

pott folio <318 x 194 mm>

text: Preliminary note, p 19; Genesis 1:1-35:15 n 1-1713, pp 19-707; pp 432, 651, 690, 708-733 blank.
Contents under 102 headings, pp 734-739; pp 740-742 blank.
Memoranda on the inside of the back cover.

The words 'EXPLICATIO IN VERBUM HISTORICUM VET. TEXT.' are written on the spine of the parchment binding of the volume, which is now designated as Codex 59.

MS not seen; description deduced from La O/4, Hyde 483, and a description by A Acton in *An Introduction to the Word Explained* Bryn Athyn PA, 1927 pp 2-3.

SWE: KVA

45/05/La O/2 **1746** Hyde 484

<<Tom: II>>

pott folio <318 x 197 mm>

text: Alphabetical register, on the inside of the front cover.
Tom: II, p 1; p 2 blank.
Genesis 35:16-50:26 n 1-1515, pp 3-382; pp 383-384 blank.
Exodus 1:1-14:28 n 1516-2476, pp 385-590; 3 pp blank.
Memoranda on the inside of the back cover.

The words 'EXPLICATIO IN VERBUM HISTORICUM VET. TEXT.' are written on the spine of the parchment binding of the volume, which is now designated as Codex 60.

MS not seen; description deduced from La O/5, Hyde 484, and a description by A Acton in *An Introduction to the Word Explained* Bryn Athyn PA, 1927 pp 2-3.

SWE: KVA

45/05/La O/3 **1746** Hyde 485

<< <untitled> >>

pott folio <318 x 203 mm>

Memoranda on the inside of the front cover; 2 pp blank.
De loquela Coelestium, p 3.
Cur populus Jud: toties in deserto tentatus est, p 4.

text: Exodus 14:29-36:5 n 1-4450, pp 5-354.
Joshua 1-24 n 4451-4636, pp 355-377.
Judges 1-8, 11, 13, 18-21 n 4637-4649, 4670-4856, pp 377-386.
Ruth 2 n 4857-4860, p 386.
1 Samuel 1-4, 6-14, 16-19, 25-28, 30-31 n 4861-5039, pp 387-400.
2 Samuel 1-3, 22-23 n 5040-5180, pp 400-406.
1 Kings 6-8, 10-11, 13, 17-19 n 5181-5315, pp 407-411.
2 Kings 19, 23 n 5316-5396, pp 411-415.
1 Chronicles 21-22, 28 n 5397-5401, p 416.
2 Chronicles 5-6, 18 n 5402-5409, pp 416-418.
Exodus 40:30-38 and parts of Leviticus 1-27 n 5410-6496, pp 419-487.
parts of Numbers 1-36 n 6497-7648, pp 488-643.
parts of Deuteronomy 1, 4, 14, 16-18, 20-25, 31-34 n 7649-7762, pp 644-666; 2 pp blank.
Memoranda pasted on the inside of the back cover.

Dates are given in two places in the MS: n 5396, 13 August 1746 old style; n 6317, 22 July 1746.
The words 'EXPLICATIO IN VERBUM HISTORICUM VET. TEXT.' are written on the spine of the

parchment binding of the volume, which is now designated as Codex 61.
See En 2/6, *Notes by the Translator*, for a discussion of Swedenborg's treatment of Joshua to 2 Chronicles in this Part of the work.
MS not seen; description deduced from La 0/6, Hyde 485, and a description by A Acton in *An Introduction to the Word Explained* Bryn Athyn PA, 1927 pp 2-3.
SWE: KVA

45/05/La 1/1 **1840** Hyde 3046, 3048

<<EMAN. SWEDENBORGII | ADVERSARIA | IN LIBROS VETERIS TESTAMENTI HISTORICOS. | EX OPERIBUS | EJUS POSTHUMIS IN BIBLIOTHECA REGIAE ACADEMIAE | HOLMIENSIS ASSERVATIS | NUNC PRIMUM EDIDIT ET NOTIS ILLUSTRAVIT | D[r] JOH. FRID. IMMAN. TAFEL, | REGIAE UNIVERSITATIS TUBINGENSIS BIBLIOTHECARIUS. | <short rule> | FASCICULUS I. | TUBINGÆ, IN BIBLIOPOLIO ZU - GUTTENBERG. | 1840.>>
8vo
verso: <editorial note>
title leaf, 2 pp; text n 5410-6476, pp 1-96.
A review of this fascicle, by J H Smithson, appeared in *The Intellectual Repository* pp 380-387 London 1840, with extracts described below as X En 1840/1.
Copy not seen; description deduced from La 1/4 and Hyde 3048.

45/05/La 1/2 **1841** Hyde 3046

<<EMAN. SWEDENBORGII | ADVERSARIA | IN LIBROS VETERIS TESTAMENTI HISTORICOS. | EX OPERIBUS | EJUS POSTHUMIS IN BIBLIOTHECA REGIAE ACADEMIAE | HOLMIENSIS ASSERVATIS | NUNC PRIMUM EDIDIT EDIDIT ET NOTIS ILLUSTRAVIT | D[r] JOH. FRID. IMMAN. TAFEL, | REGIAE UNIVERSITATIS TUBINGENSIS BIBLIOTHECARIUS. | FASCICULUS II. | TUBINGÆ, IN BIBLIOPOLIO ZU - GUTTENBERG. | 1841.>>
8vo
title leaf, 2 pp; text n 6477-7202, pp 97-192.
Copy not seen; description deduced from La 1/4 and Hyde 3048.
NET: KB

45/05/La 1/3 **1842** Hyde 488, 3045, 3048

EMAN. SWEDENBORGII | ADVERSARIA | IN LIBROS VETERIS TESTAMENTI. | EX OPERIBUS | EJUS POSTHUMIS IN BIBLIOTHECA REGIAE ACADEMIAE | HOLMIENSIS ASSERVATIS | NUNC PRIMUM EDIDIT | D[r] JO. FR. IM. TAFEL, | REGIAE UNIVERSITATIS TUBINGENSIS BIBLIOTHECARIUS. | <short rule> | PARS SECUNDA, | CONTINENS | JOSUAM, JUDICES, RUTH, SAMUELEM, REGES | ET CHRONICA. | <multiple rule> | TUBINGÆ, IN BIBLIOPOLIO ZU - GUTTENBERG. | 1842.
8vo
title leaf, 2 pp; text: Joshua 1-24 n 4451-4636, pp 1-30; Judges 1-21 n 4637-4856, pp 31-49; Ruth 2 n 4757, 4858-4860, p 50; 1 Samuel 1-4, 6-14, 16-120, 24-28, 30-31 n 4861-5039, pp 51-70; 2 Samuel 1-3, 22-23 n 5040-5180, pp 70-81; 1 Kings 6-11, 13, 17-19 n 5181-5315, pp 82-97; 2 Kings 19, 23 n 5316-5395, pp 97-105; 1 Chronicles 21-22, 28 n 5397-5401, pp 106-107; 2 Chronicles 5-6, 18 n 5402-5405, pp 107-108; Observanda n 5407-5409, pp 108-109; Notae criticae editoris, pp 110-121; Errata, p 121.
Published in Hyde 3045. Part 2 was printed from a copy made by an amanuensis in Stockholm; having subsequently compared this with the autograph MS, Tafel published a correction of the many errors of the printed version; these critical notes are in *Adversariorum Supplementum* pp 1-60, part of *Adversaria ... Partis Primae Volumen Sextum* <Hyde 3048>.
UK: SOC, NCC, NR; NET: GEN, KB; USA: ANC

45/05/La 1/4 **1842** Hyde 488, 3046, 3048

EMAN. SWEDENBORGII | ADVERSARIA | IN LIBROS VETERIS TESTAMENTI. | EX OPERIBUS | EJUS POSTHUMIS IN BIBLIOTHECA REGIAE ACADEMIAE | HOLMIENSIS ASSERVATIS | NUNC PRIMUM EDIDIT | D[r] JO. FR. IM. TAFEL, | REGIAE UNIVERSITATIS TUBINGENSIS BIBLIOTHECARIUS. | <short rule> | PARS TERTIA, | CONTINENS | LEVITICUM, NUMEROS ET DEUTERONIUM. | <multiple rule> | TUBINGAE | IN BIBLIOPOLIO ZU - GUTTENBERG. | 1842.

8vo

title leaf, 2 pp; text: Exposition of Exodus 40:30-38 n 5410-5420, pp 1-3; and of parts of Leviticus 1-27 n 5421-6496, pp 3-98; of Numbers 1-36 n 6497-7648, pp 99-330; of Deuteronomy 1, 4, 14, 16-18, 20-25, 32-34 n 7649-7762, pp 331-367; Notae criticae editoris, pp 368-386; Erratum, p 386.

45/05/La 1/1, 2 published in one volume with the remainder of the volume <Hyde 3046>. Part 3 was printed from a copy made by an amanuensis in Stockholm; having subsequently compared this with the autograph MS, Tafel published a correction of the many errors of the printed version; these critical notes are in *Adversariorum Supplementum* pp 1-60, part of *Adversaria ... Partis Primae Volumen Sextum* <Hyde 3048>.

UK: SOC, NCC, NR; NET: GEN, KB; USA: ANC

45/05/La 1/5 **1846** Hyde 930, 3049, 3057

EMAN. SWEDENBORGII | ADVERSARIA | IN | LIBROS VETERIS TESTAMENTI. | E CHIROGRAPHO EJUS | IN BIBLIOTHECA REGIAE ACADEMIAE HOLMIENSIS | ASSERVATO | NUNC PRIMUM EDIDIT | D[r] JO. FR. IM. TAFEL, | REGIAE BIBLIOTHECAE UNIVERSITATIS TUBINGENSIS PRAEFECTUS. | <short rule> | PARTIS QUINTAE VOLUMEN PRIMUM | CONTINENS | PARTEM PRIMAM INDICIS ADVERSARIORUM, ET DIARII | SPIRITUALIS PARTIS I, 1. 2. II. ET IV. | ABDOMEN – LIBER. | <multiple rule> | TUBINGAE | CURAM ADMINISTRAT „Verlagsexpedition." | LONDINI, | WILLIAM NEWBERY, CHENIES STREET, | BEDFORD-SQUARE. | 1846.

8vo

title leaf, 2 pp; text <Abdomen- Liber>, pp 1-512.

Also published as *Diarium Spirituale* volume I of part V <47/05/La 1/8 = Hyde 930, 3057>.

UK: SOC, CON, NCC, NR; GER: GSU; NET: GEN, KB; USA: ANC

45/05/La 1/6 **1847** Hyde 931, 3050, 3058

EMAN. SWEDENBORGII | ADVERSARIA | IN | LIBROS VETERIS TESTAMENTI. | E CHIROGRAPHO EJUS | IN BIBLIOTHECA REGIAE ACADEMIAE HOLMIENSIS | ASSERVATO | NUNC PRIMUM EDIDIT | D[r] JO. FR. IM. TAFEL, | REGIAE BIBLIOTHECAE UNIVERSITATIS TUBINGENSIS PRAEFECTUS. | <short rule> | PARTIS QUINTAE VOLUMEN PRIMUM | CONTINENS | PARTEM SECUNDAM INDICIS ADVERSARIORUM, ET DIARII | SPIRITUALIS PARTIS I, 1. 2. II. ET IV. | LIBERTAS–ZELUS. | <multiple rule> | TUBINGAE | CURAM ADMINISTRAT „Verlagsexpedition." | LONDINI, | WILLIAM NEWBERY, CHENIES STREET, | BEDFORD-SQUARE. | 1847.

8vo

title leaf, 2 pp; text <Libertas-Zelus>, pp 1-466; Notae criticae editoris, pp 467-491; <Editorial memorandum concerning the following supplementary entries>, p 492; Supplementum editoris, pp 493-518; Errata et additamenta, p 518.

The supplementary entries are continuations concerning 'Amor', 'Cerebrum', 'Ecclesia', 'Fides', 'Hypocrita', and 'Verbum' stated by Tafel to be written in 'quintus autographi tomus hujus partis quintae'.

Also published as *Diarium Spirituale* volume II of part V <57/05/La 1/9 = Hyde 931, 3058>.

UK: SOC, CON, NCC, NR; GER: GSU; NET: GEN, KB; USA: ANC

45/05/La 1/7 **1847** Hyde 486, 3039, 3048

EMAN. SWEDENBORGII | ADVERSARIA | IN | LIBROS VETERIS TESTAMENTI. | E CHIROGRAPHO

EJUS | IN BIBLIOTHECA REGIAE ACADEMIAE HOLMIENSIS | ASSERVATO | NUNC PRIMUM EDIDIT | Dr. JO. FR. IM. TAFEL, | REGIAE BIBLIOTHECAE UNIVERSITATIS TUBINGENSIS PRAEFECTUS. | <short rule> | PARTIS PRIMÆ VOLUMEN PRIMUM, | CONTINENS | EXPLICATIONEM GENESEOS CAP. I AD CAP. XXIX, | VERS. 30. SEU INDE A N.1-680. | <multiple rule> | TUBINGAE | CURAM ADMINISTRAT „Verlagsexpedition;" | LONDINI, | WILLIAM NEWBERY, 6, KING STREET, | HOLBORN. | 1847.
8vo
title leaf, 2 pp; text: Preliminary note, p 25; Genesis 1-29:30 n 1-680, pp 25-437.
Published in Hyde 3039. Additional critical notes were published by Tafel in *Adversariorum Supplementum* pp 90-91, as part of *Adversaria ... Partis Primae Volumen Sextum* <Hyde 3048>.
UK: SOC, NCC, NR; NET: KB; USA: ANC

45/05/La 1/8 **1848** Hyde 486, 3040, 3048
EMAN. SWEDENBORGII | ADVERSARIA | IN | LIBROS VETERIS TESTAMENTI. | E CHIROGRAPHO EJUS | IN BIBLIOTHECA REGIAE ACADEMIAE HOLMIENSIS | ASSERVATO | NUNC PRIMUM EDIDIT | Dr. JO. FR. IM. TAFEL, | REGIAE BIBLIOTHECAE UNIVERSITATIS TUBINGENSIS PRAEFECTUS. | <short rule> | PARTIS PRIMÆ VOLUMEN SECUNDUM, | CONTINENS | EXPLICATIONEM GENESEOS CAP. XXIX, VERS. 31— | CAP. XXXV, VERS. 14, SIVE N°. 681—1713. | <multiple rule> | TUBINGAE | CURAM ADMINISTRAT „Verlagsexpedition;" | LONDINI, | WILLIAM NEWBERY, 6, KING STREET, | HOLBORN. | 1848.
8vo
title leaf, pp 439-440; text: Genesis 29:31-35:14 n 681-1713, pp 441-835; Contenta n 1-102, pp 836-843; <Memoranda>, pp 843-844; Notae criticae editoris, pp 845-876; Errata, p 876; advertisement, 2 pp.
Published in Hyde 3040. Additional critical notes were published by Tafel in *Adversariorum Supplementum* pp 90-91, as part of *Adversaria ... Partis Primae Volumen Sextum* <Hyde 3048>.
UK: SOC, NCC, NR; NET: KB; USA: ANC

45/05/La 1/9 **1851** Hyde 487, 3041, 3048
EMAN. SWEDENBORGII | ADVERSARIA | IN | LIBROS VETERIS TESTAMENTI: | E CHIROGRAPHO EJUS | IN BIBLIOTHECA REGIAE ACADEMIAE HOLMIENSIS | ASSERVATO | NUNC PRIMUM EDIDIT | Dr. JO. FR. IM. TAFEL, | PHILOSOPHIAE PROFESSOR REGIUS, ET REGIAE BIBLIOTHECAE UNIVER- | SITATIS TUBINGENSIS PRAEFECTUS. | <short rule> | PARTIS PRIMÆ VOLUMEN TERTIUM, | CONTINENS | EXPLICATIONEM GENESEOS CAP. XXXV, VERS. 16— | CAP. XLVII, VERS. 26. SIVE N°. 1—1066. | <multiple rule> | TUBINGAE | CURAM ADMINISTRAT „Verlagsexpedition." | 1851.
8vo
title leaf, 2 pp; text: Genesis 35:16-47:26 n 1-1066, pp 1-309; Notae criticae editoris, pp 310-326; Errata, p 326.
Published in Hyde 3041. Additional critical notes were published by Tafel in *Adversariorum Supplementum* p 91.
UK: SOC, NCC, NR; NET: KB; USA: ANC

45/05/La 1/10 **1852** Hyde 487, 3042, 3048
EMAN. SWEDENBORGII | ADVERSARIA | IN | LIBROS VETERIS TESTAMENTI. | E CHIROGRAPHO EJUS | IN BIBLIOTHECA REGIAE ACADEMIAE HOLMIENSIS | ASSERVATO | NUNC PRIMUM EDIDIT | Dr. JO. FR. IM. TAFEL, | PHILOSOPHIAE PROFESSOR REGIUS, REGIAE BIBLIOTHECAE UNIVER- | SITATIS TUBINGENSIS PRAEFECTUS, ET SOCIETATIS HISTORICO-THEOLO- | GICAE

LIPSIENSIS SOCIUS ORDINARIUS. | <short rule> | PARTIS PRIMÆ VOLUMEN QUARTUM, | CONTINENS | EXPLICATIONEM GENESEOS CAP. XLVII, VERS. 27. ad | EXODI CAP. XIV, VERS. 28. SIVE N°. 1067—2476. | <multiple rule> | TUBINGAE | CURAM ADMINISTRAT **„Verlagsexpedition."** | 1852.

8vo

title leaf, 2 pp; text: Observationes n 1067-1077, pp 1-4; Genesis 47:27-26 n 1078-1515, pp 4-123; Exodus 1:1-14:28 n 1516-2476, pp 124-347; Memoranda, pp 348-349; Notae criticae editoris, pp 350-364; Errata, p 364; advertisement, 2 pp.

Published in Hyde 3042. Additional critical notes were published by Tafel in *Adversariorum Supplementum* pp 96-101, as part of *Adversaria ... Partis Primae Volumen Sextum* <Hyde 3048>.

UK: soc, nr; NET: kb; USA: anc

45/05/La 1/11 **1853** Hyde 488, 3043, 3048

EMAN. SWEDENBORGII | ADVERSARIA | IN | LIBROS VETERIS TESTAMENTI. | E CHIROGRAPHO EJUS | IN BIBLIOTHECA REGIAE ACADEMIAE HOLMIENSIS | ASSERVATO | NUNC PRIMUM EDIDIT | Dr. JO. FR. IM. TAFEL, | PHILOSOPHIAE PROFESSOR REGIUS, REGIAE BIBLIOTHECAE UNIVER- | SITATIS TUBINGENSIS PRAEFECTUS, ET SOCIETATIS HISTORICO-THEOLO- | GICAE LIPSIENSIS SOCIUS ORDINARIUS. | <short rule> | PARTIS PRIMÆ VOLUMEN QUINTUM, | CONTINENS | EXPLICATIONEM EXODI CAP. XIV, VERS. 29. USQUE AD | CAP. XXVIII, VERS. 43. SIVE TOM: III. N°. 1—2037. | <multiple rule> | TUBINGAE | CURAM ADMINISTRAT **„Verlagsexpedition."** | 1853.

8vo

title leaf, 2 pp; text: De Loquela coelestium, p 1; Preliminary notes, pp 1-2; Exodus 14:29-28:43 n 1-2037, pp 3-282; Notae criticae editoris, pp 283-293; Errata, p 293.

Published in Hyde 3043. Additional critical notes were published by Tafel in *Adversariorum Supplementum* pp 101-104, as part of *Adversaria ... Partis Primae Volumen Sextum* <Hyde 3048>.

UK: soc, ncc, nr; NET: kb; USA: anc

45/05/La 1/12 **1854** Hyde 488, 3044, 3048

EMAN. SWEDENBORGII | ADVERSARIA| IN | LIBROS VETERIS TESTAMENTI. | E CHIROGRAPHO EJUS | IN BIBLIOTHECA REGIAE ACADEMIAE HOLMIENSIS | ASSERVATO | NUNC PRIMUM EDIDIT | Dr. JO. FR. IM. TAFEL, | PHILOSOPHIAE PROFESSOR REGIUS, REGIAE BIBLIOTHECAE UNIVERSI- | TATIS TUBINGENSIS PRAEFECTUS, ET SOCIETATIS HISTORICO-THEOLO- | GICAE LIPSIENSIS SOCIUS ORDINARIUS. | <short rule> | PARTIS PRIMÆ VOLUMEN SEXTUM, | IDQUE ULTIMUM. | CONTINENS | EXPLICATIONEM EXODI CAP. XXIX, USQUE AD CAP. | XXXVI, VERS. 5. SIVE TOM: III. N°. 2038—4450. | <multiple rule> | TUBINGAE | CURAM ADMINISTRAT **„Verlagsexpedition;"** | 1854.

8vo

title leaf, 2 pp; text: Exodus 29:1-36:5 n 2038-4449, pp 1-263; Observandum n 4450, p 263; Notae criticae editoris, pp 264-274; Errata, p 274.

Published in Hyde 3044. Additional critical notes were published by Tafel in *Adversariorum Supplementum* pp 101-104, as part of *Adversaria ... Partis Primae Volumen Sextum* <Hyde 3048>.

UK: soc, ncc, nr; NET: kb; USA: anc

45/05/La 0/4, **D** La 1916/4 **1916** Hyde 483/1, 3038/7

<untitled>

folio
text, pp 23-725.
Reproduction of La O/1, published in phototyped edition, vol 7 <*Explicationes in Verbum seu Adversaria* vol 1 <**D** La 1916/4 = Hyde 3038/7>, Stockholm.
Unpublished copies have been recorded as follows.

1 UK: soc & USA: anc, shs A reproduction on microfilm 1, Bryn Athyn pa.

UK: soc, bl, bod, cam, con, ncc, ryl, wil; DEN: rld; NET: gen, kb; SWE: roy, kva, upp; USA: anc, fou, shs; AUS: syd; NZ: wel

45/05/La O/5 **1916** Hyde 484/1, 3038/8
<TOM. II>
folio
title and text, pp 2-601.
Reproduction of La O/1, published in phototyped edition, vol 8 <*Explicationes in Verbum seu Adversaria* vol 2 <**D** La 1916/5 = Hyde 3038/8>, Stockholm.
Unpublished copies have been recorded as follows.

1 UK: soc & USA: anc, shs A reproduction on microfilms 1 and 2, Bryn Athyn pa.

UK: soc, bl, bod, cam, con, ncc, ryl, wil; DEN: rld; NET: gen, kb; SWE: roy, kva, upp; USA: anc, fou, shs; AUS: syd; NZ: wel

45/05/La O/6, **D** La 1916/5 **1916** Hyde 485/1, 3038/9
<untitled>
folio
text, pp 1-681.
Reproduction of La O/1, published in phototyped edition, vol 9 <*Explicationes in Verbum seu Adversaria* vol 3 <**D** La 1916/5 = Hyde 3038/9>, Stockholm.
Unpublished copies have been recorded as follows.

1 UK: soc & USA: anc, shs A reproduction on microfilm 2, Bryn Athyn pa.

UK: soc, bl, bod, cam, con, ncc, ryl, wil; DEN: rld; NET: gen, kb; SWE: roy, kva, upp; USA: anc, fou, shs; AUS: syd; NZ: wel

LATIN EXTRACTS

X 45/05/La 1983/1, 47/05/La 2/1 **1983** Hyde 517/1
[Paragraphi ex *Explicationis in Verbum Veteris Testamenti* Tomo I ...]
[Paragraphi ex *Explicationis in Verbum Veteris Testamenti* Tomo II ...]
[Paragraphi ex *Explicationis in Verbum Veteris Testamenti* Tomo III ...]
8vo
title and text n [1a-34a], pp 1-26 <n 317, 459, 475, 541, 943, 967, 1003, 1144, 1147-1150, 1214-1215, 1268-1269, 1352-1353, 1366, 1395-1396, 1409, 1461, 1469-1470, 1511, 1526-1530, 1644-1646, 1649, 1656, 1694-1695, 1711-1712 of La O/1>.
title and text n [35a-100a], pp 27-66 <n 52-54, 58-59, 87-88, 134-135, 143-145, 180-184, 217, 356-357, 410-411, 514, 529-530, 560-561, 686-687, 836-839, 926-927, 1075-1077, 1091, 1132-1133, 1281-1282, 1284-1285, 1344, 1353, 1425-1426, 1432-1435, 1461-1462, 1478-1479, 1482-1485, 1557-1558, 1602-1605, 1654, 1660, 1675-1676, 1681-1685, 1760-1763, 1779, 1792, 1813, 1819-1820, 1860-1861, 1865, 1883-1884, 1956-1957, 1974, 1979-1980, 1999-2001, 2054-2055 of La O/2>.
title and text <unnumbered paragraph>, p 67; n [101a-369a], pp 68-183 <n 22-23, 43-44, 86-87, 135, 138, 144-145, 167, 208-209, 278-279, 336-337, 355-356, 612-613, 659-660, 677-681, 707-708, 746-748, 810-811, 865-866, 868-869, 1100-1101, 1128-1129, 1201-1203, 1138[a]-1141[a],

1145[a]-1146[a], 1148[a]-1151[a], 1164[a]-1165[a], 1175[a]-1177[a], 1210[a]-1211[a], 1220[a]-1221[a], 1248-1250, 1261-1263, 1287-1288, 1398-1399, 1625-1626, 1631-1632, 1659-1660, 1729-1730, 1829-1830, 1887-1888, 1902-1903, 2039-2040, 2052-2057, 2065-2066, 2085-2086, 2091-2092, 2120-2121, 2170-2171, 2217-2221, 2230-2231, 2287-2288, 2292-2293, 2296-2297, 2308, 2350-2351, 2360-2361, 2370, 2390, 2442-2443, 2456-2458, 2471-2472, 2476-2480, 2486-2488, 2492-2493, 2631-2632, 2653-2655, 2732, 2758-2759, 2767-2768, 2999, 3102-3103, 3143-3149, 3171-3173, 3340, 3372-3388, 3399-3403, 3435-3439, 3443-3444, 3447-3448, 3495-3497, 3518-3519, 3524-3527, 3535-3543, 3583-3584, 3646, 3762-3765, 3771-3772, 3782-3784, 3808-3809, 3892-3895, 3903-3909, 3959, 3962-3963, 4104-4105, 4159-4160, 4162-4163, 4170-4171, 4183-4185, 4191-4193, 4226-4228, 4250-4252, 4296-4297, 4326-4331, 4339-4345, 4417-4419, 4443-4445, 4454-4455, 4510-4514, 4531-4532, 4535-4536, 4570-4571, 4632, 4641-4642, 4648-4649, 4680-4684, 4700-4701, 4728-4729, 4736-4737, 4784-4786, 4795-4797, 4801-4802, 4806-4807, 4812-4813, 4815-4817, 5015-5016, 5019-5025, 5189-5193, 5204-5205, 5224-5228, 5365, 5393-5396, 5404-5406, 5419-5420, 5444-5446, 5481, 5540-5541, 5557-5558, 5618-5620, 6181-6183, 6292-6293, 6348-6350, 6371-6373, 6392-6393, 6464-6467, 6544-6545, 6665-6666, 6795-6796, 6925, 6957-6966, 6979-6981, 7011-7012, 7166-7167, 7185-7187, 7194-7195, 7268-7269, 7287-7289, 7298-7301, 7359-7362, 7364-7365, 7440-7441, 7482-7485, 7508-7509, 7528-7529, 7534-7536, 7543-7544, 7565-7567, 7571-7572, 7611-7612, 7690-7691, 7693-7694, 7704-7705 of La O/3>.
Edited by John Durban Odhner, published in *Experientiae Spirituales* 1 <47/05/La 2/1 = Hyde 517/1> Bryn Athyn PA.
UK: SOC, NR; NET: GEN; USA: ANC

LATIN/ENGLISH EXTRACTS

X 45/05/LaEn 1841/1 **1841** Hyde 489, 475, 1003
"Extract from Swedenborg's unpublished Adversaria on | Genesis and Exodus:–
8vo
title and text, pp 24-26.
Latin text provided by A Kahl, translated by J J G Wilkinson, published in The Thirty-second Annual Report of the Swedenborg Society.
UK: SOC

ENGLISH

Translators:
En 1 E Gould
En 2 A Acton

45/05/En 1/1 **pre 1907** Hyde —
The New Church Magazine London, 1907 p 239, reports that just before his death in 1907 the Revd Edwin Gould was engaged in making a translation of *Adversaria*. In *An Introduction to the Word Explained* Bryn Athyn PA, 1927 p 16, A Acton noted that the portion translated was n 1-2828.

45/05/En 2/1 **1928** Hyde 488/1
THE WORD | OF THE | OLD TESTAMENT EXPLAINED | A POSTHUMOUS WORK | BY | EMANUEL SWEDENBORG | Now for the first time translated from a phototyped copy of the original | manuscript preserved in the Royal Academy of Sciences, Sweden | BY | ALFRED ACTON, M.A., D.Th. | DEAN OF THE THEOLOGICAL SCHOOL OF | THE ACADEMY OF THE NEW CHURCH | VOLUME I | ACADEMY OF THE NEW CHURCH | BRYN ATHYN, PA. | 1928

verso: LANCASTER PRESS, INC. | LANCASTER, PA.
half title: THE WORD OF THE OLD | TESTAMENT EXPLAINED
section title: THE WORD EXPLAINED | THE HISTORICAL WORD
verso: JOSHUA 1:7, 8 | *Only be thou strong and very courageous, that thou mayest ob- | serve to do according to all the law which Moses my servant com- | manded thee; turn not thou from it to the right hand or to the left, | that thou mayest act with prudence in all things whithersoever thou | goest. This book of the law shall not depart out of thy mouth; but thou shalt meditate therein day and night that thou mayest | observe to do according to all that is written therein; for then thou | shalt make thy way prosperous and then thou shalt act with pru- | dence.* (See n. 5580.) | [The above is inserted here in accordance with a suggestion written by the | author on the inside of the front cover page of Codex 61. His words are: | "Perhaps the words in Joshua, chapter 1, verses 7 and 8, should precede the | explanation of Genesis and Exodus." Then follows a brief explanation of | these verses, which was afterwards crossed off and the words "Respecting | these words, confer n. 4464 [our n. 5880]" substituted. The same suggestion | is made on the inside of the back cover, where we read: "The words in Joshua, | chapter 1, verses 7 and 8, should perhaps precede the explanation of Genesis | or of Exodus, or of both. The explanation may be seen in n. 4464." In this | quotation from Joshua, Swedenborg used Schmidius' version.]
8vo
half title and title leaves, 4 pp; General table of contents, p 5; Swedenborg's table of contents, pp vii-li; section title leaf, pp 31-32; text: Genesis 1:1-28:22 and n 1-541, pp 33-462.
The title and text of *The History of Creation* <45/04/En 1/4 = Hyde 480/4> are to be found on pp 1-30 of this volume.
See also A Acton *An Introduction to The Word Explained* <Hyde 3336/11> Bryn Athyn PA, 1927, for his study of the history and composition of the manuscript of the present work.
UK: SOC, NR; NET: GEN; USA: ANC

45/05/En 2/2 **1929** Hyde 488/2
THE WORD | OF THE | OLD TESTAMENT EXPLAINED | A POSTHUMOUS WORK | BY | EMANUEL SWEDENBORG | Now for the first time translated from a phototyped copy of the original | manuscript preserved in the Royal Academy of Sciences, Sweden | BY | ALFRED ACTON, M.A., D.Th. | DEAN OF THE THEOLOGICAL SCHOOL OF | THE ACADEMY OF THE NEW CHURCH | VOLUME II | ACADEMY OF THE NEW CHURCH | BRYN ATHYN, PA. | 1929
verso: JOSHUA 1:7, 8 | *Only be thou strong and very courageous, that | thou mayest observe to do according to all the law | which Moses my servant commanded thee; turn not | thou from it to the right hand or to the left, that thou | mayest act with prudence in all things whithersoever | thou goest. This book of the law shall not depart | out of thy mouth; but thou shalt meditate therein | day and night that thou mayest observe to do ac- | cording to all that is written therein; for then thou | shalt make thy way prosperous and then thou shalt | act with prudence.* | LANCASTER PRESS, INC. | LANCASTER, PA.
half title: THE WORD OF THE OLD | TESTAMENT EXPLAINED
8vo
half title and title leaves, 4 pp; text: Genesis 29:1-34:20 and n 542-[1649a], pp 1-549.
UK: SOC, NR; NET: GEN; SWE: ROY; USA: ANC

45/05/En 2/3 **1934** Hyde 488/3
THE WORD | OF THE | OLD TESTAMENT EXPLAINED | A POSTHUMOUS WORK | BY | EMANUEL SWEDENBORG | Now for the first time translated from a phototyped copy of the original | manuscript preserved in the Royal Academy of Sciences, Sweden | BY | ALFRED ACTON, M.A., D.Th. | DEAN OF THE THEOLOGICAL SCHOOL OF | THE ACADEMY OF THE NEW CHURCH | VOLUME III | ACADEMY OF THE NEW CHURCH | BRYN ATHYN, PA. | 1934

verso: JOSHUA 1:7, 8 | *Only be thou strong and very courageous, that* | *thou mayest observe to do according to all the law* | *which Moses my servant commanded thee; turn not* | *thou from it to the right hand or to the left, that thou* | *mayest act with prudence in all things whithersoever* | *thou goest. This book of the law shall not depart* | *out of thy mouth; but thou shalt meditate therein* | *day and night that thou mayest observe to do ac-* | *cording to all that is written therein; for then thou* | *shalt make thy way prosperous and then thou shalt* | *act with prudence.* | LANCASTER PRESS, INC. | LANCASTER, PA.
half title: THE WORD OF THE OLD | TESTAMENT EXPLAINED
8vo
half title and title leaves, 4 pp; text: Genesis 35-50:26 and n 1650-3193, pp 1-579.
Part 2 of the work <La O/2> begins with the text of Genesis 35:16 and n 1; Acton renumbered the paragraphs of parts 2 and 3 to make one consecutive sequence following Part 1 — that is, n 1 of Part 2 is here given as n 1714. The volume and paragraph numbers of the MS are indicated at the foot of each page of the English text from here onwards.
UK: SOC, NR; NET: GEN; SWE: ROY; USA: ANC

45/05/En 2/4 **1936** Hyde 488/4
THE WORD | OF THE | OLD TESTAMENT EXPLAINED | A POSTHUMOUS WORK | BY | EMANUEL SWEDENBORG | Now for the first time translated from a phototyped copy of the original | manuscript preserved in the Royal Academy of Sciences, Sweden | BY | ALFRED ACTON, M.A., D.Th. | DEAN OF THE THEOLOGICAL SCHOOL OF | THE ACADEMY OF THE NEW CHURCH | VOLUME IV | ACADEMY OF THE NEW CHURCH | BRYN ATHYN, PA. | 1936
verso: JOSHUA 1:7, 8 | *Only be thou strong and very courageous, that* | *thou mayest observe to do according to all the law* | *which Moses my servant commanded thee; turn not* | *thou from it to the right hand or to the left, that* | *thou mayest act with prudence in all things whither-* | *soever* | *thou goest. This book of the law shall not* | *depart out of thy mouth; but thou shalt meditate* | *therein day and night that thou mayest observe to do* | *according to all that is written therein; for then thou* | *shalt make thy way prosperous and then thou shalt* | *act with prudence.* | (See n. 5880.) | [The above is inserted here in accordance with a sug- | gestion written by the author on the inside of the front cover | page of Codex 61. His words are: "Perhaps the words in | Joshua, chapter 1, verses 7 and 8, should precede the expla- | tion of Genesis and Exodus." Then follows a brief explana- | tion of these verses, which was afterwards crossed off and | the words "Respecting these words, confer n. 4464 [our | n. 5880]" substituted. The same suggestion is made on the | inside of the back cover, where we read: "The words in| Joshua, chapter 1, verses 7 and 8, should perhaps precede the | explanation of Genesis or of Exodus, or of both. The ex- | planation may be seen in n. 4464." In this quotation from | Joshua, Swedenborg used Schmidius' version.] | <short rule> | LANCASTER PRESS, INC. | LANCASTER, PA.
half title: THE WORD OF THE OLD | TESTAMENT EXPLAINED
8vo
half title and title leaves, 4 pp; text: Exodus 1-22 and n 3194-4558, pp 1-553.
See La O/2-3: n 3194-4001 are Part 2 n 1516-2476; n 4002-4005 are a translation of memoranda on pp 3-4 of Codex 60; n 4006-4558 are Part 3 n 1-1055. The volume and paragraph numbers of the MS are indicated at the foot of each page of the English text.
UK: SOC, NR; NET: GEN; SWE: ROY; USA: ANC

45/05/En 2/5 **1941** Hyde 488/5
THE WORD | OF THE | OLD TESTAMENT EXPLAINED | A POSTHUMOUS WORK | BY | EMANUEL SWEDENBORG | Now for the first time translated from a phototyped copy of the original | manuscript preserved in the Royal Academy of Sciences, Sweden | BY | ALFRED ACTON, M.A., D.Th. | DEAN OF THE THEOLOGICAL SCHOOL OF | THE ACADEMY OF THE NEW CHURCH | VOLUME V

| ACADEMY OF THE NEW CHURCH | BRYN ATHYN, PA. | 1941
verso: JOSHUA 1:7, 8 | *Only be thou strong and very courageous, that | thou mayest observe to do according to all the law | which Moses my servant commanded thee; turn not | thou from it to the right hand or to the left, that | thou mayest act with prudence in all things whither- | soever | thou goest. This book of the law shall not | depart out of thy mouth; but thou shalt meditate | therein day and night that thou mayest observe to do | according to all that is written therein; for then thou | shalt make thy way prosperous and then thou shalt | act with prudence.* | (See n. 5880.) | [The above is inserted here in accordance with a sug- | gestion written by the author on the inside of the front cover | page of Codex 61. His words are: "Perhaps the words in | Joshua, chapter 1, verses 7 and 8, should precede the explana- | tion of Genesis and Exodus." Then follows a brief explana- | tion of these verses, which was afterwards crossed off and | the words "Respecting these words, confer n. 4464 [our | n. 5880]" substituted. The same suggestion is made on the | inside of the back cover, where we read: "The words in| Joshua, chapter 1, verses 7 and 8, should perhaps precede the | explanation of Genesis or of Exodus, or of both. The ex- | planation may be seen in n. 4464." In this quotation from | Joshua, Swedenborg used Schmidius' version.] | <short rule> | LANCASTER PRESS, INC. | LANCASTER, PA.
half title: THE WORD OF THE OLD | TESTAMENT EXPLAINED
8vo
half title and title leaves, 4 pp; text: Exodus 23:1 to 36:5 and n 4559-5872, pp 1-499; Translator's note, pp 499-500. See La 0/3: n 4559-5872 are Part 3 n 1056-4450. The volume and paragraph numbers of the MS are indicated at the foot of each page of the English text.
UK: SOC, NR; NET: GEN; SWE: ROY; USA: ANC

45/05/En 2/6 **1942** Hyde 488/6
THE WORD | OF THE | OLD TESTAMENT EXPLAINED | A POSTHUMOUS WORK | BY | EMANUEL SWEDENBORG | Now for the first time translated from a phototyped copy of the original | manuscript preserved in the Royal Academy of Sciences, Sweden | BY | ALFRED ACTON, M.A., D.Th. | DEAN OF THE THEOLOGICAL SCHOOL OF | THE ACADEMY OF THE NEW CHURCH | VOLUME VI | ACADEMY OF THE NEW CHURCH | BRYN ATHYN, PA. | 1942
verso: <Note by the translator> | <short rule> | LANCASTER PRESS, INC., LANCASTER, PA.
half title: THE WORD OF THE OLD | TESTAMENT EXPLAINED
8vo
half title and title leaves, 4 pp; text: Joshua 1-24 and n 5873-5994, pp 1-71; Judges 1-21 and n 5995-6076, pp 71-117; Ruth 1-4 and n 6077-6078, pp 117-121; 1 Samuel 1-31 and n 6079- 6166, pp 122-174; 2 Samuel 1-24 and n 6167-6243, pp 175-203; 1 Kings 1-22 and n 6244-6309, pp 204-243; 2 Kings 1-25 and n 6310-6328, pp 243-270; 1 Chronicles 21, 22, 28 and n 6329-6333, pp 270-274; 2 Chronicles 5-6, 18 and n 6334-6339, pp 274-280. See La 0/3: the text is Part 3 n 4451-5409. The translator's note on the verso of the title leaf is repeated here as follows, since it includes comment upon Swedenborg's method of composition of the work.

NOTE BY THE TRANSLATOR After finishing his explanation of Genesis and Exodus, and before continuing with the remaining books of the Pentateuch in their order, the Author made a preliminary study of the books of Joshua to II Chronicles, writing down explanations here and there. Thus, these explanations differ in their scope from those of Genesis and Exodus; for, while the latter cover each chapter verse by verse, the former cover only certain verses, or deal with a chapter only as a whole, and frequently omit one or more chapters. This indicates that they were written as notes preparatory to a more detailed explanation, to be taken up after the completion of the Pentateuch. It is this preliminary study that constitutes volume VI of *The Word Explained*.

In view of the above, it has been somewhat of a problem to decide as to how much of the Scripture text shall be premised to the explanations. To introduce the entire text of each chapter would be a work of superfluity. To introduce merely the text specifically explained would be to omit the necessary context. Furthermore, the Author sometimes refers to his underscoring of words in the text of Schmidius' Latin translation of the Bible, even when he does not explain these words (see n 5904, 5961, 5962, 5972, 6308), and it is manifest that the reader should know where these underscorings are. In passing, it may be noted that they appear to indicate the words and phrases on which Swedenborg intended specially to dwell when writing his detailed commentary.

These considerations have led to the determination to include only such portions of the Scripture text as fall under one or more of the following heads: Verses or parts of verses (1) explained or referred to in the present volume; (2) underscored by the Author in his Schmidius' Bible; (3) necessary to supply the due context. The above, however, does not apply to the books of the Chronicles.

The present volume differs from other volumes of the work in the use of italics. In the other volumes, italics are used to designate the words or phrases of the text under consideration, as they are taken up for particular explanation; these words or phrases are not underscored in the Author's text. In the present volume, with the exception of clauses enclosed in brackets, italics are used exclusively to designate words or phrases underscored by the Author himself, the italics in the chapter citations preceding the explanations indicating the Author's underscorings in his copy of Schmidius' Latin translation of the Bible.

UK: SOC, NR; NET: GEN; SWE: ROY; USA: ANC

45/05/En 2/7 **1945** Hyde 488/7

THE WORD | OF THE | OLD TESTAMENT EXPLAINED | A POSTHUMOUS WORK | BY | EMANUEL SWEDENBORG | Now for the first time translated from a phototyped copy of the original | manuscript preserved in the Royal Academy of Sciences, Sweden | BY | ALFRED ACTON, M.A., D.Th. | DEAN OF THE THEOLOGICAL SCHOOL OF | THE ACADEMY OF THE NEW CHURCH | VOLUME VII | ACADEMY OF THE NEW CHURCH | BRYN ATHYN, PA. | 1945

half title: THE WORD OF THE OLD | TESTAMENT EXPLAINED

8vo

half title and title leaves, 4 pp; text: Exodus 40:30-38 and n 6340, p 1; parts of Leviticus 1-27 and n 6341-6710, pp 1-175; parts of Numbers 1-10 and n 6711-6984, pp 176-288; Exposition of Psalm 132 n 6985, pp 288-293; parts of Numbers 11-36 and n 6986-7462, pp 293-544; parts of Deuteronomy 1, 4, 14, 16-18, 20-25, 31-34 and n 7463-7566, pp 545-609. See La 0/3: the text is Part 3 n 5410-7766.

Volume 8 of this version is described as 47/02/En 1/1 = Hyde 488/8.

UK: SOC, NR; NET: GEN; SWE: ROY; USA: ANC

ENGLISH EXTRACTS

X 45/05/En 1840/1 **1840** Hyde —

<untitled>

8vo

text n 5410-5412, 5445-5448, 5480-5483, 5494-5495, 5529, pp 385-387.

Translated and edited by J H Smithson, in a review of La 1/1 published in *The Intellectual Repository* London.

UK: SOC, BL, CHT, CON, NCC, NR; USA: ANC

X 45/05/En 1841/1 **1841** Hyde 490

SWEDENBORG'S ADVERSARIA ON NUMBERS. | THE LAWS OF THE NAZARITESHIP EXPLAINED. | CHAP. VI. FROM 6767—6885.

8vo
title and text, pp 145-155; Editor's note, pp 155-156.
Translated and edited by J H Smithson, published in *The Intellectual Repository* London.
UK: SOC, BL, CHT, CON, NCC, NR; USA: ANC

X 45/05/En 1841/2 **1841** Hyde 490
SWEDENBORG'S ADVERSARIA ON NUMBERS. | CHAP. XVI. FROM 7147 TO 7222.
8vo
title and text n 7147-7177, pp 241-250.
Translated and edited by J H Smithson, published in *The Intellectual Repository* London.
UK: SOC, BL, CHT, CON, NCC, NR; USA: ANC

X 45/05/En 1841/3 **1841** Hyde 490
SWEDENBORG'S NOTES ON NUMBERS. | CHAP. XI. FROM 7178-7222. | (*Continued from p.* 250.)
8vo
title and text, pp 337-346.
Translated and edited by J H Smithson, published in *The Intellectual Repository* London.
UK: SOC, BL, CHT, CON, NCC, NR; USA: ANC

X 45/05/En 1841/4 **1841** Hyde 490
SWEDENBORG'S NOTES ON NUMBERS. | CHAP. XXII. FROM 7527 TO 7551. | (*Continued from p.* 346.)
8vo
title and text, pp 513-521.
Translated and edited by J H Smithson, published in *The Intellectual Repository* London.
UK: SOC, BL, CHT, CON, NCC, NR; USA: ANC

X 45/05/En 1841/5 **1841** Hyde —
BALAAM'S ASS.
8vo
title, p 313; text of Numbers 33:21-35, p 314; text n 7534-7536, 7545-7548 <numbered 7352-7353, 7361-7364 in En 2/7>, pp 314-316.
Passages from 45/05, translated from X Fr 1841/1 by R de Charms, published in *The New Churchman* Philadelphia. The paragraphs quoted here are followed by a long quotation from 59/02 n 140.2,4.
UK: SOC

X 45/05/ En 1842/1 **1842** Hyde 490
SWEDENBORG'S NOTES ON NUMBERS. | CHAP. 23, FROM 7552 TO 7567. | (*Continued from former vol. p.* 521.)
8vo
title and text, pp 41-45.
Translated and edited by J H Smithson, published in *The Intellectual Repository* London.
UK: SOC, BL, CHT, CON, NCC, NR; USA: ANC

X 45/05/ En 1842/2 **1842** Hyde 490
SWEDENBORG'S NOTES ON NUMBERS. | CHAP. 24. THE HISTORY OF BALAAM AND BALAK. | (*Concluded from p.* 45.)
8vo

title and text n 7568-7589, pp 121-128.
Translated and edited by J H Smithson, published in *The Intellectual Repository* London.
UK: SOC, BL, CHT, CON, NCC, NR; USA: ANC

X 45/05/En 1848/1 **1848-1849** Hyde 491
COMMENTARIES | ON SOME OF THE | BOOKS OF THE OLD TESTAMENT, | BY | EMANUEL SWEDENBORG. | FROM HIS POSTHUMOUS WORKS PRESERVED IN THE LIBRARY OF THE ROYAL | ACADEMY OF STOCKHOLM. EDITED IN THE ORIGINAL LATIN, | BY | DR. JNO. FR. IM. TAFEL: | PROFESSOR OF PHILOSOPHY, & LIBRARIAN OF THE ROYAL UNIVERSITY, TUBINGEN, | NOW FIRST TRANSLATED | BY | ELIHU RICH. | <short rule> | WITH THE ADDITION OF ILLUSTRATIVE NOTES, AND AN APPENDIX, TREATING | OF THE RELATION BETWEEN THE LEVITICAL INSTITUTES, TOGETHER WITH | OTHER REMAINS OF ANTIQUITY, AND THE CHRISTIAN CHURCH. | BY THE TRANSLATOR. | <short rule> | LONDON: | E. RICH, 108, HATTON GARDEN. | THE OFFICE OF THE NEW CHURCH QUARTERLY REVIEW: | AND DEPOSITORY OF THE SOCIETY FOR THE DIFFUSION | OF NEW CHURCH LITERATURE. | 1849.
verso: *"All appearances, discourses, and events in the Historical por- | tions of the Word, are representative; but what they represent | does not appear unless the Historical expressions are regarded | as objects, like objects of sight, which suggest matter and occasion | of thinking concerning things more sublime."* | SWEDENBORG'S ARCANA CŒLESTIA, n. 2143.
8vo
title leaf, 2 pp; Advertisement by the translator, pp 3-4; Translator's introductory notes, pp 5-8; text: Exodus 40:34-38 n 5410-5420, pp 9-12; Leviticus 1-10 and n 5421-5514 <incomplete>, pp 13-64.
Issued in four quarterly instalments of 16 pp each attached to the parts of *The New Church Quarterly Review* London. The first instalment was issued with part 4 in 1848; the others with parts 1-3 in 1849.
UK: CON, NR

X 45/05/En 1852/1 **1852** Hyde 492
THE TRUE STRUCTURE OF MAN'S NATURE. | EXTRACT FROM SWEDENBORG'S "ADVERSARIA"— NOW FIRST TRANSLATED.
8vo
title and text n I-III, pp 515-516.
Translated by G Bush, published in *The New Church Repository* New York.
UK: SOC, CON

X 45/05/En 1914/1 **1914-1927** Hyde 492/2
ADVERSARIA. | BY EMANUEL SWEDENBORG.
8vo
title and text n 3879-3881, 3894-3896, 3994, 4003-4007, 4107, 6499-6500, 423-430, 628-668, 475, 541, 941, 943, 1351-1353, 130-150, 2871-2886, 1893-1897, 916-932, 933-949, 950-967, 968-997, 998-1019, 505-511, 1511, 1526-1530, 1432-1435, 1602-1605, 1675-1676, 1854-1866, 288-294, 533-535, **1914** pp 752-754; **1918** pp 721-727; **1919** pp 79-94; **1921** pp 385-390; **1922** pp 497-505; **1924** pp 321-329, 513-518, 591-597, 671-677, 722-729; **1925** pp 13-21; **1926** pp 1-7, 65-71; **1927** pp 129-132.
Translated and edited by A Acton, published in *New Church Life* Bryn Athyn PA.
UK: SOC, NCC; USA: ANC

X 45/05/En 1958/1, **E:b** En 1958/4 **1958** Hyde 3336/25iv
<untitled>
4to

text, pp 710-711, 713.
Translated and edited by A Acton, published in *The Life of Emanuel Swedenborg* 4 <**E:b** En 1958/4 = Hyde 3336/25iv> Bryn Athyn PA.
UK: SOC, NCC; USA: ANC

X 45/05/En 1998/1 **1998** Hyde 492/3, 523/2
[Paragraphs from *The Word of the Old Testament Explained*, Tome I ...]
[Paragraphs from *The Word of the Old Testament Explained*, Tome II ...]
[Paragraphs from *The Word of the Old Testament Explained*, Tome II ...]
8vo
title and text n [1a-34a], pp 1-24 <n 317, 459, 475, 541, 943, 967, 1003, 1144, 1147-1150, 1214-1215, 1268-1269, 1352-1353, 1366, 1395-1396, 1409, 1461, 1469-1470, 1511, 1526-1530, 1644-1646, 1649, 1656, 1694-1695, 1711-1712 of La O/1>.
title and text n [35a-100a], pp 25-62 <n 52-54, 58-59, 87-88, 134-135, 143-145, 180-184, 217, 356-357, 410-411, 514, 529-530, 560-561, 686-687, 836-839, 926-927, 1075-1077, 1091, 1132-1133, 1281-1282, 1284-1285, 1344, 1353, 1425-1426, 1432-1435, 1461-1462, 1478-1479, 1482-1485, 1557-1558, 1602-1605, 1654, 1660, 1675-1676, 1681-1685, 1760-1763, 1779, 1792, 1813, 1819-1820, 1860-1861, 1865, 1883-1884, 1956-1957, 1974, 1979-1980, 1999-2001, 2054-2055 of La O/2>.
title and text n 4005 <unnumbered in autograph MS>, p 63; n [101a-369a], pp 64-171 <n 22-23, 43-44, 86-87, 135, 138, 144-145, 167, 208-209, 278-279, 336-337, 355-356, 612-613, 659-660, 677-681, 707-708, 746-748, 810-811, 865-866, 868-869, 1100-1101, 1128-1129, 1201-1203, 1138[a]-1141[a], 1145[a]-1146[a], 1148[a]-1151[a], 1164[a]-1165[a], 1175[a]-1177[a], 1210[a]-1211[a], 1220[a]-1221[a], 1248-1250, 1261-1263, 1287-1288, 1398-1399, 1625-1626, 1631-1632, 1659-1660, 1729-1730, 1829-1830, 1887-1888, 1902-1903, 2039-2040, 2052-2057, 2065-2066, 2085-2086, 2091-2092, 2120-2121, 2170-2171, 2217-2221, 2230-2231, 2287-2288, 2292-2293, 2296-2297, 2308, 2350-2351, 2360-2361, 2370, 2390, 2442-2443, 2456-2458, 2471-2472, 2476-2480, 2486-2488, 2492-2493, 2631-2632, 2653-2655, 2732, 2758-2759, 2767-2768, 2999, 3102-3103, 3143-3149, 3171-3173, 3340, 3372-3388, 3399-3403, 3435-3439, 3443-3444, 3447-3448, 3495-3497, 3518-3519, 3524-3527, 3535-3543, 3583-3584, 3646, 3762-3765, 3771-3772, 3782-3784, 3808-3809, 3892-3895, 3903-3909, 3959, 3962-3963, 4104-4105, 4159-4160, 4162-4163, 4170-4171, 4183-4185, 4191-4193, 4226-4228, 4250-4252, 4296-4297, 4326-4331, 4339-4345, 4417-4419, 4443-4445, 4454-4455, 4510-4514, 4531-4532, 4535-4536, 4570-4571, 4632, 4641-4642, 4648-4649, 4680-4684, 4700-4701, 4728-4729, 4736-4737, 4784-4786, 4795-4797, 4801-4802, 4806-4807, 4812-4813, 4815-4817, 5015-5016, 5019-5025, 5189-5193, 5204-5205, 5224-5228, 5365, 5393-5396, 5404-5406, 5419-5420, 5444-5446, 5481, 5540-5541, 5557-5558, 5618-5620, 6181-6183, 6292-6293, 6348-6350, 6371-6373, 6392-6393, 6464-6467, 6544-6545, 6665-6666, 6795-6796, 6925, 6957-6966, 6979-6981, 7011-7012, 7166-7167, 7185-7187, 7194-7195, 7268-7269, 7287-7289, 7298-7301, 7359-7362, 7364-7365, 7440-7441, 7482-7485, 7508-7509, 7528-7529, 7534-7536, 7543-7544, 7565-7567, 7571-7572, 7611-7612, 7690-7691, 7693-7694, 7704-7705 of La O/3>.
Edited and translated by John Durban Odhner, published in *Spiritual Experiences* vol 1 <47/05/En 6/1 = Hyde 523/2> Bryn Athyn PA.
UK: SOC, PUR, NR; SWE: ROY; USA: ANC

DUTCH EXTRACTS

X 45/05/Du 1940/1 **1940** Hyde 492/—
DE ZEGENING EN HET ONZEVADER | *Uittreksel uit „Het Woord Ontvouwd"* | *Numeri, n. 6887—6930*

8vo
title and text n 6887-6930, pp 93-97.
Published in *De Hemelsche Leer* The Hague.
UK: SOC; NET: GEN; USA: ANC

X 45/05/Du 1941/1 **1941** Hyde 492/–
UIT DE ONTVOUWING VOOR HET HISTORISCHE WOORD
8vo
title and text n 1298, pp 91-92.
Published in *De Hemelsche Leer* The Hague.
UK: SOC; NET: GEN; USA: ANC

X 45/05/Du 1941/2 **1942** Hyde 492/–
UIT DE ONTVOUWING VOOR HET HISTORISCHE | WOORD
8vo
title and text , 596-611, pp 198-203.
Published in *De Hemelsche Leer* The Hague.
UK: SOC; NET: GEN; USA: ANC

FRENCH EXTRACTS

X 45/05/Fr 1841/1 **1841** Hyde —
L'Anesse de Balaam. | (NOMBR. XXII, 21-35.)
8vo
title, p 65; text of Numbers 22:21-35, pp 66-67; text of n 7534-7536, 7545-7548 <numbered 7352-7353, 7361-7364 in En 2/7>, pp 67-69; text of parts of 59/02 n 140.
Translated and edited by A Harlé, published in *La Nouvelle Jérusalem* St Amand (Cher).
UK: SOC

GERMAN EXTRACTS

X 45/05/Ge 1896/1 **1896-1899** Hyde 493, 486
<<Swedenborg's *Adversaria*>>
4to
title and text n 915-922, 942, 924-941, 944-1018, 1039-1050, 1019, 1051-1055, 1059, 1069, 1070, 1147, 1144, 1147-1150, 1212-1215, 1244-1269, 1271, 1280, 1293, 1317, 1351, 1353, 1396-1398, 1409, 1461, 1469, 1470, **1896** p 91; **1897** pp 7, 14-15, 37-38, 44-45, 54, 59, 68-69, 83, 91; **1898** pp 4, 12-13, 61-62, 83; **1899** pp 3, 35, 35<b>, 51, 59, 67, 75, 83.
Translated by L H Tafel from La 1/8 = Hyde 486, published in *Neukirchenblatt* Berlin, Canada.
Copy not seen; description recorded from Hyde 493.

X 45/05/Ge 1899/1 **1899-1901** Hyde 494, 487
<<Swedenborg's *Adversaria*>>
4to
title and text n 59, 87-88, 134-135, 138, 180-184, 356, 357, 514, 518-525, 687, 734-736, 836-839, 1075-1077, 1280-1285, 1434, 1435, 1478-1480, 1482-1485, 1558, 1602-1603, 1605, 1654, **1899** p 91; **1900** pp 6, 19, 43, 59, 67, 75, 83, 91; **1901** pp 3, 11, 19.
Translated by L H Tafel from La 1/7, 8, published in *Neukirchenblatt* Berlin, Canada, and Lancaster PA.
Copy not seen; description recorded from Hyde 494.

X 45/05/Ge 1900/1 **1900-1907** Hyde 495, 488

<<Swedenborg's *Adversaria*>>

4to

title and text n 144-146, 209, 336, 337, 677-683, 864, 865, 1101, 1128, 1129, 1141-1145, 1138-1140, 1141, 1145, 1146, 1164-1166, 1396, 1831, 1886-1892, 1894-1903, 1914-1936, 2039-2044, 2046, 2047, 2049, 2052, 2053, 2056, 2057-2060, 2065, 2066, 2083-2102, 2121, 2471-2474, 2476-2480, 2492, 2493, 2632, 2653-2655, 2719-2737, 2740-2759, 2766-2768, 2771-2773, 2996-3000, 3101-3103, 3148, 3149, 3173, 3183, 3185-3188, 3375-3388, 3399-3413, 3433-3439, 3441-3444, 3447, 3448, 3450, 3451, 3491-3498, 3500-3535, 3631-3649, 3764-3774, **1900** pp 19, 35, 54, 67, 75, 83, 91; **1901** pp 3, 11, 19, 43, 51, 59, 67, 83, 91; **1902** pp 3, 11, 19, 37, 45, 53, 69, 84-85, 93; **1903** pp 19, 27, 35. <Remainder not recorded by Hyde or A Acton>

Translated by L H Tafel from La 1/9, 10, published in *Neukirchenblatt* Berlin, Canada, and Lancaster PA. In *An Introduction to the Word Explained* Bryn Athyn PA, 1928 p 16, A Acton recorded that this translation continued until L H Tafel's death in 1907, and that he had published 140 paragraphs from La 1/1-2, 50 paragraphs from La 1/3, and more than 1300 paragraphs from La 1/4 including n 3803-4765.

Copy not seen; description deduced from Hyde 495 and 488.

46/01 Biblical Index of the Historical Books of the Old Testament Hyde CXXIX

The autograph MSS, bound in their original parchment covers, form Codices 40 and 41 in the Library of the Royal Swedish Academy of Sciences, Stockholm. The words INDEX BIBLICUS are written on the spine of the cover of each Codex.

The Index includes the historical books from Joshua to 2 Kings. Whereas Hyde judged that the MSS were compiled while 45/05/La 0/3 was being written, A Acton proposed that Swedenborg began to write it in the middle of August 1745 before composing 45/04 <*Historia Creationis a Mose tradita*> and 45/05; see Preface to *Concerning the Messiah about to Come* <45/03/En 1/1> p vi. I have followed Hyde in my dating of the commencement of the work.

LATIN

Editions:

La 0 MSS
La 1 J F I Tafel, editor

46/01/La 0/1 1745 Hyde 496

<< <untitled> >>

pott long 4to <314 x 95 mm>

Codex 40: 2 pp blank; text: A, pp 1-28; B, pp 1-6; C, pp 1-28; D, pp 1-14; E, pp 1-12; F, pp 1-18; G, pp 1-8; H, pp 1-6; I and J, pp 1-18; L, pp 1-14; M, pp 1-24; N, pp 1-8; O, pp 1-10; P, pp 1-32; Q, pp 1-4; R, pp 1-14; S, pp 1-36; T, pp 1-26; U and V, pp 1-31 and on the pages of Z, pp 1, 2, 3-5; Z, pp 1, 2; Alphabetical index, inside of the back cover.

In this Codex the subjects are arranged alphabetically.

An unpublished copy has been recorded as follows.

1 A memorial notice to A H Searle in *The New Church Magazine* London, 1914 p 96, stated that 'he did valuable work in collating and copying the text of the *Index Biblicus* for the Swedenborg Society', adding '– a task he has left not quite finished'. The whereabouts of this transcript are unknown.

MS not seen; description deduced from La 0/3, Hyde 496, and a study by W E Closterman.

SWE: KVA

46/01/La O/2 **1746** Hyde 496

<< <untitled> >>

pott long 4to <302 x 95 mm>

Codex 41: text, pp 1-372; pp 1, 3, 5, 20, 27, 32, 58, 61, 102, 107, 115, 121, 131, 143, 164, 169, 181-182, 197-198, 201, 220-221, 229, 233, 237-239, 249, 259, 264-265, 274, 280-281, 296-297, 305, 327, 334, 340, 345, 362-363, and 367 are all blank; notes of reference on the inside of the back cover.

In this Codex the various entries are not arranged alphabetically, although they form a continuation of the entries in La O/1.

An unpublished copy has been recorded as follows.

1 A memorial notice to A H Searle in *The New Church Magazine* London, 1914 p 96, stated that 'he did valuable work in collating and copying the text of the *Index Biblicus* for the Swedenborg Society.' adding '– a task he has left not quite finished'. The whereabouts of this transcript are unknown.

MS not seen; description deduced from La O/3, Hyde 496, and a study by W E Closterman.

SWE: KVA

46/01/La 1/1-1/3, 47/06/La 1/1 **1859, 1860, 1863** Hyde 497, 3066-3068

La 1/1: EMANUELIS SWEDENBORGII | INDEX BIBLICUS | SIVE | THESAURUS BIBLIORUM | EMBLEMATICUS ET ALLEGORICUS. | ... | VOLUMEN PRIMUM. | ... | 1859.

La 1/2: EMANUELIS SWEDENBORGII | INDEX BIBLICUS | SIVE | THESAURUS BIBLIORUM | EMBLEMATICUS ET ALLEGORICUS. | ... | VOLUMEN SECUNDUM. | ... | 1860.

La 1/3: EMANUELIS SWEDENBORGII | INDEX BIBLICUS | SIVE | THESAURUS BIBLIORUM | EMBLEMATICUS ET ALLEGORICUS. | ... | VOLUMEN TERTIUM. | ... | 1863.

8vo

vol I: title leaf, 2 pp; Praefatiuncula editoris, 2 pp; text, pp 1-476.

vol II: title leaf, 2 pp; catalogue, pp 1-6; text, pp 1-480.

vol III: title leaf, 2 pp; text, pp 1-576.

The text of La O/1, O/2 amalgamated by the editor, J F I Tafel, with the text of 47/06/La O/1 <Codex 4>, 47/07/La O/1 <Codex 39>, 48/01/La O/1 <Codex 5>, and extracts from Swedenborg's later works, especially *Arcana Coelestia* <49/01/La O/11> and *Apocalypsis Explicata* <59/02/La O/1>: see 'Praefatiuncula editoris'. Published as *Index Biblicus* vol 1-3, Tübingen <Hyde 3066-3068>.

UK: SOC, CON, NR; DEN: RLD; GER: GSU; NET: GEN; SWE: GSB; USA: ANC

46/01/La O/3, **D** La 1916/2 **1916** Hyde 496/1, 3038/4

EMANUELIS SWEDENBORGII | INDEX BIBLICUS | <short rule> | AD AUTOGRAPHI SIMILITUDINEM IN BIBLIOTHECA REGIAE ACADEMIAE SCIENTIARUM | SUECICAE ADSERVATI, OPE ARTIS PHOTOTYPOGRAPHICAE DELINEATI, EDITUS JUSSU | SOCIETATIS SWEDENBORGIANAE LONDINENSIS | <short orn rule> | VOL. I. | <type orn 15 x 37 mm> | HOLMIAE | EX OFFICINA PHOTOTYPOGRAPHICA LAGRELIUS & WESTPHAL | MCMXVI.

half title: EMANUELIS SWEDENBORGII | AUTOGRAPHA | <short rule> | TOMUS IV.

folio

half title and title leaves, 4 pp; Prooemium, 1 p <verso blank>; Indicis Biblici vol I Contenta, 1 p <verso blank>; reproduction of La O/1, O/2 <Codices 40, 41> and 47/03/La O/2 <Codex 6>, pp 1-174, 177-354, 356-719.

Unpublished copies have been recorded as follows.

1 UK: SOC & USA: ANC, SHS A reproduction on microfilms 2 and/or 3, Bryn Athyn PA.

UK: SOC, BL, BOD, CAM, CON, LON, NCC, RYL; DEN: RLD; NET: GEN, KB; SWE: ROY, KVA, UPP; USA: ANC, FOU, SHS; AUS: SYD; NZ: WEL

47/01 Gad and Asher Hyde CXXX

The autograph MS is in the Library of the Swedenborg Society <A/140>, to which it was presented by the Bath Society of the New Church in April 1947. Its provenance is traced back to the Revd Samuel Dean, by whom it was given to J N Cossham <1778-1846> of Bristol, who recorded that it was fixed to the back of a frontispiece portrait of Swedenborg printed in a copy of the first English edition of *Heaven and Hell* <58/02/En 1/1>. Cossham gave the volume to the Revd J W Barnes <1794-1877> of Bristol, after whose death it passed into the care of the Bath Society of the New Church.

The document relates to the distinction of the heavens, and correlatively to the signification of Gad and Asher in Genesis 49. At the close of the text Swedenborg wrote a note, dated 8 February 1747, 'quo die de benedictionibus filiorum Jacobi, Genes: Cap: XLIX, aliquod in margine annotare licuit.' <on which day it was permitted me to note in the margin something concerning the blessings of the sons of Jacob, Genesis XLIX> This refers to his annotations to Genesis 49:19-20 in his copy of the Schmidius Bible version, 1696 <47/04 = Hyde CXXXIII>, where his comments are similar to the contents of the present MS and refer further to Numbers 32 and to 45/05/La 0/3, tome III n 7634, where Gad is treated of in connection with the allocation of his inheritance in Canaan. At the head of the same page in this Bible Swedenborg later wrote 'de Gade et Aschere, vide Experient: Tom. III, ad finem' <Concerning Gad and Asher, see Experiences, vol. III, at the end>.

In the lost part of *Experientiae Spirituales* <47/05>, n 28 and 29 dealt with the same subject, as indicated by the entries in the Index of this work.

LATIN

Editions:

La 0 MS
La 1 J D Odhner, editor

47/01/La 0/1 1747 Hyde 498
<untitled>
single sheet <177 x 172 mm>
text, 1 p.
Unpublished copies have been recorded as follows.

1 UK: SOC A MS transcript made by R L Tafel. <Archives A/140, Hyde 498>
2 UK: SOC A MS transcript made by J G Dufty c 1930; Dufty Documents file 503.
3 USA: ANC A transcript in ACSD, also reproduced on microfilm 32 made in 1962, Bryn Athyn PA.

UK: SOC

47/01/La 0/2 **1910** Hyde 498/–
<untitled>
single sheet <22 x 17 mm>
Reprint of La 0/1, published in *The New Church Magazine* prefixed to p 169, London; also issued separately.
UK: SOC, CON, NCC, NR; USA: ANC

47/01/La 1/1 **1983** Hyde 517/1, 3077/6
[BATHAE FRAGMENTUM]
8vo
title and text, pp 213-214.
Edited by J D Odhner, published in *Experientiae Spirituales* 1, Bryn Athyn PA <47/05/La 2/1 = Hyde 3077/6>.
UK: SOC, NR; NET: GEN; USA: ANC

LATIN/ENGLISH

Editons:
LaEn 1 A H Searle, editor
LaEn 2 W Harbutt, editor
LaEn 3 A W Acton, editor

47/01/LaEn 1/1 **1910** Hyde —
<untitled>
8vo
text: Latin, pp 179-180; English, p 180.
Transcribed, edited, and translated by A H Searle, with a transcript and translation of Swedenborg's note in the margin of his Schmidius Bible <47/04/La 0/1> at Genesis 49:9, 20. A facsimile reproduction of La 0/1 faces p 169.
Published in *The New Church Magazine* London.
UK: SOC, CON, NCC; USA: ANC

47/01/LaEn 2/1 **1910** Hyde 498/1
Latin: <untitled>
single sheet <27 x 22 mm>
Reproduction of La 0/1 by photolithography.
English: *Translation of the Swedenborg MS.*
23 x 20 mm
Reprint of En 1/1 with slight changes.
Published by W Harbutt for private circulation in *Particulars concerning a Fragment of a Missing Swedenborg MS* Bath.
The booklet is made up as follows.
title page; reproduction of La 0/1, 1 p; reprint of the title page of 58/02/En 1/1 in which the MS had been pasted, 1 p; reprint of statements by J N Cossham and J W Barnes concerning the provenance of the MS, 1 p; reprint of En 1/1, 1 p; notes by C Higham concerning the MS, 2 pp.
A copy of the booklet in UK: SOC is preserved as Archives D/46.
UK: SOC

47/01/LaEn 3/1 **1962** Hyde 523/1

English: THE "BATH FRAGMENT"
Latin: <untitled>
8vo
English title and text, p 4; facsimile reproduction of the Latin MS, with editorial notes, p 5; transcript of the Latin MS, p 417.
Translated and edited by A W Acton, published in *The Spiritual Diary* 1 <47/05/En 5/1 = Hyde 523/1> London.
UK: SOC, CON, NCC, NR; NET: GEN; SWE: UPP; USA: ANC

47/01/LaEn 3/2 **1977** Hyde 523/–

English: <<THE "BATH FRAGMENT">>
Latin: << <untitled> >>
8vo
English title and text, p 4; facsimile reproduction of the Latin MS, with editorial notes, p 5; transcript of the Latin MS, p 417.
Photographic reprint of LaEn 3/1, published in *The Spiritual Diary* 1 <47/05/En 5/2 = Hyde 523/–> Bryn Athyn PA.
Copy not seen; description deduced from LaEn 3/1.
USA: ANC, FOU

ENGLISH

Translators:
En 1 R L Tafel
En 2 J Hyde
En 3 J D Odhner
En 4 A W Acton

47/01/En 1/1 **no date** Hyde 498

<untitled>
23 x 18 mm
text, 1 page.
Translation by R L Tafel <UK: SOC Archives A/140>.
UK: SOC

47/01/En 2/1 **1907** Hyde —

A FRAGMENT OF THE LOST PART OF THE "SPIRITUAL | DIARY."
8vo
title and text, pp 442-443.
Translated and edited by J Hyde, published in *The New Church Review* Boston MA. The editorial notes are on pp 441-442 and 443-444.
An unpublished MS draft is recorded as follows.
1 UK: SOC Translation with editorial notes, in Dufty Documents file 503.
UK: SOC

47/01/En 1/2, **D** En 1914/1 **1914** Hyde 498/2, 3118/2

GAD AND ASHER. | <short rule>
8vo

title and text, p 604.
Translation by R L Tafel, revised by J Whitehead, published in *Posthumous Theological Works* 1 <**D** En 1914/1 = Hyde 3118/2> New York. An editorial note following the text states that the MS translation described in En 1/1 is not in the handwriting of R L Tafel.
UK: SOC, NR; NET: GEN; USA: ANC, SHS

47/01/En 1/3, **D** En 1928/2 **1928** Hyde 498/3, 3118/4
GAD AND ASHER | <short rule>
8vo
title and text, p 604.
Reprint of En 1/2, published in *Posthumous Theological Works* 1 <**D** En 1928/2 = Hyde 3118/4> New York.
UK: SOC; NET: GEN; USA: ANC, SHS

47/01/En 1/4, **D** En 1947/1 **1947** Hyde 498/–, 3118/–
GAD AND ASHER | <short rule>
8vo
title and text, p 604.
Reprint of En 1/3, published in *Posthumous Theological Works* 1 <**D** En 1947/1 = Hyde 3118/–> New York.
USA: SHS

47/01/En 1/5, **D** En 1951/1 **1951** Hyde 498/–, 3118/–
GAD AND ASHER | <short rule>
8vo
title and text, p 604.
The same as En 1/4, published in *Posthumous Theological Works* 1 <**D** En 1951/1 = Hyde 3118/–> New York.
USA: ANC, SHS

47/01/En 1/6, **D** En 1954/1 **1954** Hyde 498/–, 3118/–
GAD AND ASHER.
8vo
title and text, p 604.
The same as En 1/5, published in *Posthumous Theological Works* 1 <**D** En 1954/1 = Hyde 3118/–> New York.
USA: SHS

47/01/En 1/7, **D** En 1956/1 **1956** Hyde 498/–, 3118/–
GAD AND ASHER.
8vo
title and text, p 604.
The same as En 1/6, published in *Posthumous Theological Works* 1 <**D** En 1956/1 = Hyde 3118/–> New York.
USA: ANC

47/01/En 1/8, **D** En 1961/1 **1961** Hyde 498/–, 3118/–
GAD AND ASHER.

8vo
title and text, p 604.
The same as En 1/7, published in *Posthumous Theological Works* 1 <**D** En 1961/1 = Hyde 3118/–> New York.
SWE: UPP

47/01/En 1/9, **D** En 1969/1 **1969** Hyde 498/–, 3118/–
GAD AND ASHER.
8vo
title and text, p 604.
The same as En 1/8, published in *Posthumous Theological Works* 1 <**D** En 1969/1 = Hyde 3118/–> New York.
AUS: SYD; SA: MMC

47/01/En 1/10, **D** En 1972/1 **1972** Hyde 498/–, 3118/–
GAD AND ASHER.
8vo
title and text, p 604.
The same as En 1/9, published in *Posthumous Theological Works* 1 <**D** En 1972/1 = Hyde 3118/–> New York.
USA: ANC

47/01/En 1/11, **D** En 1978/1 **1978** Hyde 498/–, 3118/–
GAD AND ASHER.
8vo
title and text, p 604.
The same as En 1/10, published in *Posthumous Theological Works* 1 <**D** En 1978/1 = Hyde 3118/–> New York.
USA: SHS

47/01/En 1/12, **D** En 1996/3 **1996** Hyde 498/4, 3118/8
<within a rule border 161 x 102 mm> Gad | and | Asher | <short rule> | 1747
8vo
title leaf, pp 609-610; text, pp 611-612.
Reprinted from En 1/3 = Hyde 498/–, with minor textual revisions by W R Woofenden, published in *Posthumous Theological Works* 2 <**D** En 1996/3 = Hyde 3118/8> West Chester PA.
UK: SOC, NR; USA: ANC, SHS

47/01/En 3/1 **1998** Hyde 523/–
[THE "BATH FRAGMENT":]
8vo
title and text, pp 196-197.
Translated by J D Odhner, published in *Spiritual Experiences* 1 <47/05/En 6/1 = Hyde 523/–> Bryn Athyn PA.
UK: SOC, PUR, NR; SWE: ROY; USA: ANC

47/01/En 4/1 **2002** Hyde 523/–
The 'Bath fragment'
8vo

title and text, pp 3-4.
Translated by A W Acton <reprinted from LaEn 2/1>, published in *The Spiritual Diary* 1 <47/05/ En 5/3 = Hyde 523/–> London.
UK: SOC, CON, NCC, PUR, NR; NET: GEN; SWE: ROY; USA: ANC

47/02 Isaiah and Jeremiah Explained Hyde CXXXI

The autograph MS, bound in its original parchment cover, forms Codex 62 in the Library of the Royal Swedish Academy of Sciences, Stockholm.

In 4 places Swedenborg dated his descriptions of spiritual experiences after commenting on these verses:

Isaiah 41:20—7 November 1746, old style;
Jeremiah 7:12—20, 21 November 1746, old style;
Jeremiah 23:18—23 February 1747, old style;
Jeremiah 50:13—9 February 1747.

While composing this work he compiled an Index <see 47/03/La 0/1 = Hyde 501>, which has the date 7 August 1747 in the Latin note written on page 1a.

LATIN

Editions:

La 0 MS
La 1 J F I Tafel, editor

47/02/La 0/1 **1747** Hyde 499

<< <untitled> >>
pott folio <311 x 197 mm>
text: Memorandum, 1 p; 3 pp blank.
Esajas propheta 1-38, 40-66, pp 1-55, 57-60, 60-77; p no 56 omitted, and p no 60 repeated.
Jeremias 1-32, 50, pp 78-106.
Threni, crossed out, p 107; remainder of the Codex, 630 pp, blank.
The title 'Esajas et Jeremias Explicata' is written on the spine of the cover.
MS not seen; description deduced from La 0/2 and Hyde 499.
SWE: KVA

47/02/La 1/1 **1843** Hyde 500, 3048

EMAN. SWEDENBORGII | ADVERSARIA | IN | LIBROS VETERIS TESTAMENTI. | EX OPERIBUS | EJUS POSTHUMIS IN BIBLIOTHECA REGIAE ACADEMIAE | HOLMIENSIS ASSERVATIS | NUNC PRIMUM EDIDIT | Dr. JO. FR. IM. TAFEL, | REGIAE BIBLIOTHECAE UNIVERSITATIS TUBINGENSIS PRAEFECTUS. | <short rule> | PARS QUARTA, | CONTINENS | JESAJAM ET JEREMIAM. | <multiple

rule> | STUTTGARDIAE | APUD EBNER ET SEUBERT. | 1843.
8vo
title leaf, 2 pp; memorandum, p 1; text: Esajas Propheta, pp 1-162; Jeremias, pp 163-225; Notae criticae editoris, pp 226-251; Corrigenda, p 252; advertisement, 2 pp.
UK: SOC, NR; NET: GEN, KB; USA: ANC

47/02/La 0/2, **D** La 1916/5 **1916** Hyde 499/1, 3038/9
<untitled>
folio
title and text, pp 682-799.
Reproduction of La 0/1, published in phototyped edition, vol 9 <*Explicationes in Verbum seu Adversaria* vol 2, **D** La 1916/5 = Hyde 3038/9> Stockholm.
Unpublished copies have been recorded as follows.
1 UK: SOC & USA: ANC, SHS A reproduction on microfilm 2, Bryn Athyn PA.
UK: SOC, BL, BOD, CAM, CON, LON, NCC, RYL, WIL; DEN: RLD; NET: GEN, KB; SWE: ROY, KVA, UPP; USA: ANC, FOU, SHS; AUS: SYD; NZ: WEL

ENGLISH

47/02/En 1/1 **1948** Hyde 488/8
THE WORD | OF THE | OLD TESTAMENT EXPLAINED | A POSTHUMOUS WORK | BY | EMANUEL SWEDENBORG | Now for the first time translated from a phototyped copy of the original | manuscript preserved in the Royal Academy of Sciences, Sweden | BY | ALFRED ACTON, M.A., D.Th. | DEAN OF THE THEOLOGICAL SCHOOL OF | THE ACADEMY OF THE NEW CHURCH | VOLUME VIII | ACADEMY OF THE NEW CHURCH | BRYN ATHYN, PA. | 1948
half title: THE WORD OF THE OLD | TESTAMENT EXPLAINED
section title: APPENDIX
8vo
half title and title leaves, 4 pp; text: Isaiah 1-38, 40-66, n 7567-8051, pp 1-296; Jeremiah 1-32, 49:34-36, 50, n 8052-8263, pp 297-417; Lamentations 1, summary exposition, p 417; Appendix: section title leaf, pp 419-420; text, pp 421-441.
Edited and translated by A Acton, published as a continuation of vol 1-7 <45/05/En 2/1-7 = Hyde 488/1-7> Bryn Athyn PA. On p 421 Acton states that he translated the Appendix from a phototype edition <La 0/2>.
UK: SOC, NR; NET: GEN; SWE: ROY; USA: ANC

47/03 Biblical Index of Isaiah and parts of Jeremiah and Genesis Hyde CXXXII

The autograph MS, bound in its original parchment cover, forms Codex 6 in the Library of the Royal Swedish Academy of Sciences, Stockholm.

The entries in this Index give not only the passages quoted from the Bible but also the correspondences or spiritual sense of them. Those relating to Isaiah and Jeremiah were copied by Swedenborg in Codices 4 and 39 <see 47/06/La O/1 and 47/07/La O/1>. Swedenborg appears to have compiled the Index while writing *Esajas et Jeremias Explicata* <47/02/La O/1>. Genesis is indexed as far as chapter 15.

The Swedish memoranda on p 89a relate to matters written to Peter Hultman, Swedenborg's banker. The Latin note written on p 1a reads '1747, d: 7 Aug: st: vet: mutatio status in me, in cœleste Regnum, in imagine' <On 7 August 1747, old style, a change of state in me, into the celestial kingdom, in an image>.

LATIN

47/03/La O/1 **1747** Hyde 501

<< <untitled> >>

pott long folio <397 x 159 mm>

text: Three memoranda, on the inside of the front cover.
Notes in Latin and Swedish, dated 7 August 1747, p 1a.
Note in Swedish, dated November 1747, p 1b.
Index <all crossed out except p 89a>, pp 2a-181b, of which 43 pp are blank.
Memoranda in Swedish, p 89a.
Register of the entry-headings in alphabetical order and the pages, on the inside of the back cover.

MS not seen; description deduced from La O/2 = Hyde 501/1.

SWE: KVA

47/03/La O/2, **D** La 1916/2 **1916** Hyde 501/1, 3038/4

<untitled>

folio

text, pp 1a-89a.

Reproduction of La O/1, published in phototyped edition, vol 4 <*Index Biblicus* vol 1, **D** La

1916/2 = Hyde 3038/4> Stockholm.
Unpublished copies have been recorded as follows.

1 UK: SOC & USA: ANC, SHS A reproduction on microfilm 3, Bryn Athyn PA.

UK: SOC, BL, BOD, CAM, CON, LON, NCC, RYL, WIL; DEN: RLD; NET: GEN, KB; SWE: ROY, KVA, UPP; USA: ANC, FOU, SHS; AUS: SYD; NZ: WEL

LATIN EXTRACTS

X 47/03/La 1870/1, **D** La 1870/5 **1870** Hyde 501, 3038

<untitled>

folio

text of two of the memoranda on the inside of the front cover of the MS, and the Latin note on p 1a, p 1164.

Reproduction of these parts of La O/1, published in photolithographed edition, vol 10 <*Apocalypsis Explicata* vol 2, **D** La 1870/5 = Hyde 3038> Stockholm.

Unpublished copies have been recorded as follows.

1 UK: SOC & USA: ANC, SHS A reproduction on microfilm 11, Bryn Athyn PA.

UK: SOC, BL, CHT, CON, NCC, NCH, RYL; GER: GSU; NET: GEN; SWE: ROY, KVA, UPP; USA: ANC, SHS; AUS: SYD

47/04 Marginal Notes in the Schmidius Bible Hyde CXXXIII

Swedenborg's annotated copy of the Schmidius version of the Bible, published in 1696 in 2 volumes, forms Codices 89 and 90 in the Library of the Royal Swedish Academy of Sciences, Stockholm.

The annotations were written at varying times, and they were neither written consecutively from beginning to end nor in any regular order of sequence. It would appear however that, in general, the order of annotation was as follows: the Prophets, Genesis and the other historical books, Psalms, and the Book of Revelation; then some further notes on Exodus, Numbers, and Deuteronomy. <See the description of 47/06 for an example of Swedenborg's sequential system in indexing biblical books.>

That Swedenborg began his annotations of this Bible version at least when he was nearing the end of Codex 62 <47/02/La O/1>, see that MS at Jeremiah 18:18, where we read 'de iis vide annotata in margine' <concerning these matters see the annotations in the margin>. The annotation referred to is at Jeremiah 18:18 in the margin of the present work.

The Indices recorded as 47/06/La O/1 and 47/07/La O/1 are referred to in annotations in the present work; for example, the Bible at Daniel 5:28 is annotated 'vide Media et Persia in collect: vide not: ad reliquiae' <See 'Media' and 'Persia' in the Index; see notes at 'reliquiae'>. The annotations to Ezekiel occur in chapters 1-12, 24-25, and 43-48; at 24:16-20 are the words 'cum scribens, 1747, 25 — st. v.' <when writing on 25 — 1747, old style>; the name of the month was lost when Swedenborg trimmed the margin of this page, but September appears to be the month which he had written.

Swedenborg continued to use and annotate this Bible for almost twenty years. For example, see p 241, Deuteronomy 32, where he wrote, 'n: 4832, expl: quod sit falsum mali' <n 4832, explanation that it is the falsity of evil>, which is a reference to *Arcana Coelestia* n 4832, where the falsity of evil is explained in connection with Deuteronomy 32:5, 19, 20, 23, 24, 28, 32-35; this volume of *Arcana Coelestia* <49/02> was published in 1752. See also Revelation 12:8 and 19:6, where Swedenborg referred to *Apocalypsis Revelata* n 535 and 641, 615 <66/01/La 1/1>.

There are six annotations which are not in Swedenborg's handwriting. Five of these are in Latin and are very brief: at Genesis 4:14; Leviticus 16:14; Isaiah 3:1 and 57:1; and Matthew 22:11. The sixth, at Revelation 1, is much longer and is in German. It appears that they were written by a previous owner of the two volumes.

In a number of places Swedenborg referred to other Bible versions which he used. See Hosea 12:4, where he underlined 'potenter pugnavit' and noted 'Beza — principem se gessit'. In the margin of Isaiah 2:22 he wrote 'Trem. III', indicating that in the Latin version made by Immanuel Tremellius the chapter-break is numbered differently; a number of similar variations are also noted.

Swedenborg also owned a copy of the two-volume 1740 edition of the Schmidius Bible, in which E Van der Hooght's Massoretic Hebrew text and the Schmidius Latin version were printed in parallel columns. His copy is in the Library of the Royal Swedish Academy of Sciences <Codices 73 and 64>. His use of this and other Bible versions is discussed in articles in the following journals:

A Nordenskjöld 'On the Different Editions of the Bible made use of by Emanuel Swedenborg' *The New-Jerusalem Magazine* London 1790, pp 87 ff.

J Hyde 'Swedenborg's Bibles' *The New Church Magazine* London 1901, pp 348 ff, 388 ff, 439 ff, 488 ff.

S D Cole 'Swedenborg's Hebrew Bible' *The New Philosophy* Bryn Athyn PA 1977, pp 28-33.

LATIN

Editions:

La O MS annotations in printed volumes
La 1 A Acton, editor

47/04/La O/1 1747 Hyde 502

<<BIBLIA SACRA | SIVE | TESTAMENTUM | VETUS ET NOVUM | EX | LINGUIS ORIGINALIBUS | IN | LINGUAM LATINAM | TRANSLATUM, | ADDITIS CAPITUM SUMMARIIS | ET PARTITIONIBUS, | à | SEBASTIANO SCHMIDT, SS.TH.D. | Argent. Universitat. Prof. Sen. Convent. Eccl. Præside, | & Cap. Thom. Præposito. | *CUM PRIVILEGIIS,* | <orn 40 x 36 mm> | *ARGENTORATI,* | Sumptibus JOH. FRIDERICI SPOOR, Bibliop. | <short rule> | M DC XCVI.>>
small 4to
Engraved portrait of Schmidius and illustration, 4 pp; Praefatio, 14 pp <only the last 2 leaves preserved; last p blank>;
text: Genesis, with Swedenborg's marginal annotations, pp 1-16, 59-62; pp 17-58 and 63 lost.
Exodus, with marginal annotations, pp 105-114; pp 64-104 lost.
Leviticus, with very few notes, pp 114-136, 139-142; pp 137-138 and 143-151 lost.
Numbers, with occasional references, pp 161-202; pp 151-160 lost.
Deuteronomy, with very few references, pp 202-208, 241-244; pp 209-240 lost.
Joshua and Judges, with a few references, pp 245-304.
Ruth, without annotations, pp 305-309.
1 and 2 Samuel, with a few references, pp 309-382.
1 and 2 Kings, with very few references, pp 382-457 <309-384 in La O/3>.
1 and 2 Chronicles, with a few brief notes, pp 458-536.
Ezra to Job, pp 537-607.
Psalms, with a few notes, pp 608-687 <385-464 in La O/3>.
Proverbs, pp 687-712.
Ecclesiastes and Song of Solomon, with occasional notes, pp 712-726 <465-479 in La O/3>.
Isaiah to Amos, with marginal annotations, pp 727-939 <480-702 in La O/3>.
Obadiah to Malachi, without notes, pp 940-982 <703-735 in La O/3>.
Apocrypha, title and pp 1-176.
This volume forms Codex 89. The title leaf is missing.
An unpublished copy has been recorded as follows.

1 E E Iungerich recorded that he had assembled a transcript of the marginal notes, composed of drafts of the notes in Daniel, Genesis and Exodus, other portions of the marginal notes made by Collegiate students at Bryn Athyn PA, and the notes in Samuel and Chronicles with the notes and memoranda written on the covers of La O/2 deciphered by H Lj Odhner <47/04/En 1/1 = Hyde 504/1, p 5>. The whereabouts of this compilation is unknown.

Copy not seen; description deduced from La O/3.
SWE: KVA

47/04/La O/2 **1747** Hyde 503

<<NOVI TESTAMENTI | JESU CHRISTI | VERSIO LATINA.>>
small 4to
Memorandum, on the inside of the front cover.
title and text of the Gospels, with occasional notes, pp 1-138 <736-873 in La O/3>.
Acts and Epistles, pp 138-289.
Revelation, with a few notes, pp 290-308 <874-892 in La O/3>.
Errata, 4 pp.
Memorandum and Index of books, on the inside of the back cover.
This volume forms Codex 90.
Copy not seen; description deduced from La O/3.
SWE: KVA

47/04/La O/3 **1872** Hyde 504

BIBLIA SACRA, | SIVE | **Testamentum Vetus et Novum** | EX LINGUIS ORIGINALIBUS | IN | LINGUAM LATINAM | TRANSLATUM, | À | SEBASTIANO SCHMIDT. | ARGENTORATI, | MDCXCVI. | <short rule> | AD FIDEM EXEMPLARIS ANNOTATIONIBUS EMANUELIS SVEDENBORGII MANU SCRIPTIS LOCUPLETATI, | QUOD HOLMIÆ IN BIBLIOTHECA REGIÆ ACADEMIÆ SCIENTIARUM ASSERVATUR, | OPE LUMINUM SOLIS DESCRIPTUM ET DELINEATUM | EDIDIT | RUDOLPHUS LEONARDUS TAFEL. | HOLMIÆ. | EX OFFICINA SOCIETATIS PHOTO-LITHOGRAPHICÆ. | 1872.
half title: BIBLIA SACRA, | **Cum Annotationibus Svedenborgii.**
4to
half title and title leaves, 4 pp; Praefatiuncula editoris, p <1>; facsimile of the title page of the Schmidius version, reproduced from another copy, p <3>; text with Swedenborg's annotations: Genesis to Ruth, 1 and 2 Kings, Psalms, Ecclesiastes, Song of Songs, Isaiah to Malachi, Matthew to John, Revelation, pp 1-892.
Photolithographic reproduction of La O/1 and 2, with the pages missing from Codex 89 <La O/1> reproduced from another copy of the original version. The books not containing an internal sense <except Ruth, Ecclesiastes, and Song of Songs> were not reproduced, and 1 and 2 Samuel were omitted by an error on the part of the printer. The whole volume was repaged consecutively. See the listing of the contents of La O/1 and 2 for a comparison of the two sets of page numbers. The verso of p 735 is blank, and the pagination of the New Testament begins with p 736 on the recto of the facing leaf.
The reproduction was made at the expense of Theodore Muellensiefen.
UK SOC, CON, NCC, NR; GER: WLB; NET: GEN; SWE: UPP; USA: ANC

47/04/La 1/1 **1955** Hyde 504/3

EMANUELIS SWEDENBORGII | ANNOTATIONES | in margine | BIBLIAE SACRAE | a SEBASTIANO SCHMIDT Translatae | ex Exemplari Photolithographo Transcriptae | ab | ALFRED ACTON | ---- oOo ---- | Vol. I | (Genesis-Isaiah) | ---- oOo ---- | una cum Indice Anglice | scripto ac eodem congesto | 1955
verso: THE ANNOTATIONS | written in the Margin of | SEBASTIANI SCHMIDII | BIBLIA SACRA | by | EMANUEL SWEDENBORG | Transcribed and Edited | by | ALFRED ACTON | Together with an Index compiled | by the Editor
American 4to loose-leaf pages
title leaf, 2 pp; Contenta, 3 pp; Preface, pp i-viii; Praeliminaria, pp a, b; Praemissum, p 1; text: Genesis I-XVI, pp 2-29; XLVI-L, pp 30-41; Exodus XXXIV-XL, pp 42-48; Leviticus I, III-XI, XIII-XVI, XVIII, pp 49-57; Numeri VI-XVIII, XX-XXVII, XXXII-XXV, pp 58-72; Deuteronomium I-IV, pp 73; XXXII-XXXIV, pp 73-74; Joshua I-XXIV, pp 75-101; Judicum I-XXI, pp 102-116; Ruth, p 117-118;

I Samuelis I-XXII, XXIV-XXXI, pp 119, 119a-v; II Samuelis I-IX, XI-XXIV, pp 119v-ee; I Regum I-XXII, pp 119ee, 120; II Regum I-VI, VIII-XXV, pp 143-171; I Chronicles V-VIII, XVI-XVII, XXI-XXII, pp 172, 172a-b; II Chronicles XXXIV, XXXV, pp 172b-c; Job IX:7, p 172c; Psalmi VIII-IX, XI, XIV, XVIII-XIX, XXX-XXXI, XXXV, XLIV, XLVIII, LI-LIV, LVI, LXVI, LXVIII, LXII-LXXIV, LXXVI, LXXVIII-LXXIX, XXC-XXCI, XXCIII-XXCV, XXCIX-XC, XCV, XCVII-XCIX, CII, CIV-CVII, CX, CXIV-CXV, CXVIII-CXIX, CXXI-CXII, CXXII, CXXV, CXXIX-CXXXVII, CXLII, CXLVI-CXLVIII, pp 173-190; Ecclesiastes I-XII, pp 191-199; Canticum Canticorum I, pp 200; Isaiah I-XIII, XVI-XIX, XXI-XXII, XXIV-XXXIV, XXXVII, XL-XLIV, XLVI, LIII-LVII, LIX-LXI, LXIII, pp 201-240.
On p 5, E E Iungerich records that he assembled a transcription of the marginal notes, composed of drafts of the notes in Daniel, Genesis and Exodus, other portions of the marginal notes made by Collegiate students at Bryn Athyn PA, and the notes in Samuel and Chronicles with the notes and memoranda on the covers of La O/2 deciphered by H Lj Odhner.
Typed MS in USA: ANC; a photographic copy of this MS is in UK: SOC. <Archives A/197, 196>
UK: SOC; USA: ANC

47/04/La 1/2 **1955** Hyde 504/3

EMANUELIS SWEDENBORGII | ANNOTATIONES | in margine | BIBLIAE SACRAE | a SEBASTIANO SCHMIDT Translatae | ex Exemplari Photolithographo Transcriptae | ab | ALFRED ACTON | -----ooo----- | Vol. II | (Jeremiah-Apocalypse) | -----ooo----- | una cum Indice Anglice | scripto ac eodem congesto | 1955
American 4to loose-leaf pages
title leaf, 2 pp; text: Jeremias V, VIII, XIII-XIV, XIX-XXIII, XXXV-XXXVI, XL-XLIV, XLVIII-LII, pp 241-278; Threnorum I-V, pp 279-285; Ezechielis I-XII, XXIV, XXV, XLIII-XLVIII, pp 286-333; Danijelis II-V, VII-XII, pp 334-355; Hoseae I-XIV, pp 356-391; Joel I-IV, pp 392-404; Amos I-VII, pp 405-423; Jonah IV:11, p 424; Michah II:12, 13; V:6-9; VI:1, p 424; Habakuk L:13, p 425; Zephaniah III:10, p 425; Haggai II:9, p 426; Sachariae IX:6, 9, 16, p 426; Malachiae I:2; II:11, p 426; Matthew I-V, VII-XX, XXII-XXVI, XVIII, pp 427-439; Marcus I-IV, VI, VIII-X, XII-XVI, pp 440-444; Lucas I-XXII, XXIV, pp 445-453; Joannes I-XVII, XIX-XXI, pp 454-466; Apocalypse I-XXII, pp 467-481; Memoranda, p 482; Indices: Classified Index, pp 483-516; Index of Bible passages, pp 517-520; Works referred to, pp 521-522.
Typed MS in USA: ANC; a photographic copy of this MS is in UK: SOC. <Archives A/197, 196>
UK: SOC; USA: ANC

47/04/La 0/4 **2005** Hyde504/4

BIBLIA SACRA, | SIVE | **Testamentum Vetus et Novum** | EX LINGUIS ORIGINALIBUS | IN | LINGUAM LATINAM | TRANSLATUM, | À | SEBASTIANO SCHMIDT. | ARGENTORATI, | MDCXCVI. | <short rule> | AD FIDEM EXEMPLARIS ANNOTATIONIBUS EMANUELIS SVEDENBORGII MANU SCRIPTIS LOCUPLETATI, | QUOD HOLMIÆ IN BIBLIOTHECA REGIÆ ACADEMIÆ SCIENTIARUM ASSERVATUR, | OPE LUMINUM SOLIS DESCRIPTUM ET DELINEATUM | EDIDIT | RUDOLPHUS LEONARDUS TAFEL. | HOLMIÆ. | EX OFFICINA SOCIETATIS PHOTO-LITHOGRAPHICÆ. | 1872. | [VOLUME I 2005 EDITION]
verso: © by The Academy of the New Church, Bryn Athyn, Pennsylvania | All rights reserved | Printed in the United States of America | ISBN 0-910557-65-9
half title: BIBLIA SACRA, | **Cum Annotationibus Svedenborgii.**
4to
half title and title leaves, 4 pp; Praefatiuncula editoris, p <1>; Preface to the 2005 edition, p <2>; facsimile reproduction of notes on the front flyleaves, pp <3-4>; facsimile of the title page of the Schmidius version, p <5>; text with Swedenborg's annotations: Genesis to Ruth, pp 1-309; 1 and 2 Samuel, pp 309-382; 1 and 2 Kings, pp 382, 310-384; 1 Chronicles 4:30-43, 5:1-8:21, 16:5-43, 17:1-19a, 21:30-22:19a, 34:13-35:18a, Job 8:21-9:35, pp 463, 465, 467-468, 478-479, 484, 533-534, 582.

Photographic replica reprint from La 0/3, published by The Academy of the New Church, Bryn Athyn PA. The pagination from p 1 begins on the verso of p <5>.
This reprint includes material which was not included in La 0/3: the two books of Samuel, notes from the front and back flyleaves, a piece of Chronicles, and Job. Photocopies of this material were obtained from Codices 89 and 90 in SWE: KVA, and are in USA: ANC, and they have added notes by Stephen D Cole.
UK: SOC, NCC, NR; NET: GEN; USA: ANC

47/04/La 0/5 **2005** Hyde 504/5
BIBLIA SACRA, | SIVE | **Testamentum Vetus et Novum** | EX LINGUIS ORIGINALIBUS | IN | LINGUAM LATINAM | TRANSLATUM, | À | SEBASTIANO SCHMIDT. | ARGENTORATI, | MDCXCVI. | <short rule> | AD FIDEM EXEMPLARIS ANNOTATIONIBUS EMANUELIS SVEDENBORGII MANU SCRIPTIS LOCUPLETATI, | QUOD HOLMIÆ IN BIBLIOTHECA REGIÆ ACADEMIÆ SCIENTIARUM ASSERVATUR, | OPE LUMINUM SOLIS DESCRIPTUM ET DELINEATUM | EDIDIT | RUDOLPHUS LEONARDUS TAFEL. | HOLMIÆ. | EX OFFICINA SOCIETATIS PHOTO-LITHOGRAPHICÆ. | 1872. | [VOLUME II 2005 EDITION]
verso: © by The Academy of the New Church, Bryn Athyn, Pennsylvania | All rights reserved | Printed in the United States of America | ISBN 0-910557-65-9
half title: BIBLIA SACRA, | **Cum Annotationibus Svedenborgii.**
4to
half title and title leaves, 4 pp; text with Swedenborg's annotations: Psalms, Ecclesiastes, Song of Songs, Isaiah to Malachi, Matthew to John, Revelation, pp 385-892; Errata, 4 pp; Facsimile reproduction of notes on the flyleaf, 1 p.
Photographic replica reprint from La 0/3, published by The Academy of the New Church, Bryn Athyn PA. The verso of p 735 is blank, and the pagination of the New Testament begins with p 736 on the recto of the facing leaf.
UK: SOC, NCC, NR; NET: GEN; USA: ANC

LATIN EXTRACTS

X 47/04/La 1910/1 **1910** Hyde —
<<Notes on Samuel>>
Transcribed by A H Stroh, recorded in *A Chronological List of Swedenborgiana* Part 1, n 153. Document not seen; description recorded from this listing.
USA: ANC

X 47/04/La 1988/1 **1988** Hyde —
<untitled>
A4 perfect bound
text of p 1 <Genesis 1:1-16> between pp 64 and 65.
Photolithographic facsimile made from La 0/3, published in *Emanuel Swedenborg 1688–1772 Naturforscher und Kundiger der Überwelt* <**D** Ge 1988/1> Stuttgart.
UK: SOC, NR; GER: WLB; NET: KB; SWE: UPP; SWI: ZÜR; USA: ANC

ENGLISH

47/04/En 1/1 **1917** Hyde 504/1
The | Schmidius Marginalia | together with | The Expository Material | of | The Index Biblicus | by | EMANUEL SWEDENBORG | <coat of arms of the publisher 26 x 21 mm> | Bryn Athyn, Pa. | ACADEMY OF THE NEW CHURCH | 1917

8vo
title leaf, 2 pp; Preface, pp 3-6; Explanation of orthographic signs in the volume, p 7; text: Detached notes, p 8; Genesis to Judges, 1 and 2 Samuel, 1 and 2 Kings, 1 Chronicles, Esther, Job, Psalms, Ecclesiastes, Song of Solomon, Isaiah to Micah, Habbakuk <*stet*> to Malachi, Matthew to John, Revelation, pp 9-631.
The marginal annotations in the Schmidius Bible <La 0/1, 0/2> were translated by E E Iungerich from transcriptions made by him and those listed at La 0/4. Interspersed with these annotations, he included a translation of the expository material in Codices 4 and 39 of *Index Biblicus* <47/06, 47/07>.

UK: soc, con, nr; NET: gen; SWE: roy; USA: anc

47/05 The Spiritual Diary Hyde CXXXVII, CXXXIX, CXL, CLXXIV, CXLI, CLXXV

The autograph MSS, forming the Codices listed below, are in the Library of the Royal Swedish Academy of Sciences, Stockholm.

The Latin editions of this work have been known for many years by the descriptive titles *Diarium Spirituale* and *Memorabilia*, although Swedenborg did not use these titles for any of the material. His title for the work has proved to be *Experientiae Spirituales*. He used it first in the margin of his Schmidius Bible <47/04> on p 62 in the upper left corner, above the running head. Here he wrote, 'De Gade et Aschere, vide Experient: Tom: III ad finem' <Concerning Gad and Asher, see Experiences, vol 3 at the end>. In another note, found in Codex 6 <47/03> on p 1a, Swedenborg jotted down a list of things to be done prior to his departure to London about November 1748. Here he wrote, 'Taga ut exp: sp: och se<n> legg dem ehop' <To take the spiritual experiences and join them together>. His intention at that time seems to have been to rewrite the indented items recorded in *The Historical Word* <45/05> and the 149 paragraphs of *Experientiae Spirituales* which are no longer extant, and to group them with the material in the Codices described above which he had already begun to write.

On 23 August 1748 he wrote in n 2894 of Codex 2, 'sicut omnia quae in tribus his libris, et alioquin, scripta sunt ... usque experientiae sunt' <So everything written in these three books and elsewhere ... are nevertheless experiences>. See J D Odhner's examination and explanation of these matters in 47/05/La 2/1, pp iv-ix.

The index Codices <42-45 and 110> contain no date references; and the dates when Swedenborg began to use each of them may be determined only from internal evidence and from his practice in indexing other works. It appears likely that he would have begun to index Codex 2, the first surviving MS in this group, after he had written a substantial portion of it. I therefore suggest that Swedenborg began to write Codex 42 <the first of the Index Codices> during the year 1748. He would have started to use Codices 43 to 45 piecemeal, as he filled up the spaces which he had allocated in Codex 42; I have dated the commencement of these three Codices arbitrarily also to 1748, so that their contents may be described in sequence with those of Codex 42. Swedenborg's first entries in Codex 110 are likely to have been written in 1749, as he used it to index Codex 111 and the second section of Codex 3.

The Codex containing n 1 to 148 is no longer extant, though Swedenborg indexed its contents in Codex 42.

Codex 2: The paragraphs are numbered from 149 to 170 and 178 to 3427. The first date in the

Codex, 9 October 1747 old style, is recorded in n 149, and the last, 24 October 1748, in n 3422. <Hyde CXXXVII>

Codex 3, pp 1-151: The paragraphs are numbered from 3428 to 4544. The earliest date in the Codex, 2 October 1748, is recorded in n 3440, and the last, 15 September 1749, in n 4389. Note that the date in n 3422 is 24 October 1748; J D Odhner seemed to suggest that Swedenborg added some of the date-references when indexing the paragraphs in which they occur, rather than when he recorded the experiences. <Hyde CXXXIX>

Codex 111: The paragraphs are numbered from 4545 to 4655 and 4657 to 4715, followed by 71 articles not given numbers by Swedenborg. I date the beginning of this Codex to 1749, following on from Codex 3 above. The only date recorded, 19 November 1751, occurs in the penultimate unnumbered article, on the last page in the Codex. In the final article, Swedenborg wrote, 'Cum scriberem de Bethlechem, unde Messias, n. 4593,' <When I was writing about Bethlehem, from where the Messiah came, n 4593> a reference to *Arcana Coelestia* vol 4, written and published in 1752: this and other out-of-sequence date references suggest that Swedenborg returned to his record of his spiritual experiences and expanded the entries at times. <Hyde CXL>

Codex 42: The first of the Index Codices, in which Swedenborg allocated pages to each letter of the alphabet, paginating each group of pages separately. The entries run from *Abdomen* to *Zelus*. <Hyde CXLI>

Codex 43: The second Index Codex, in which Swedenborg numbered the pages 63 to 439 but did not arrange the entries alphabetically. Some references are given on the inside of the back cover. <Hyde CXLI>

Codex 44: The third Index Codex, paginated 440 to 816 but not arranged alphabetically. <Hyde CXLI>

Codex 45: The fourth Index Codex, paginated 817-1194 but not arranged alphabetically. <Hyde CXLI>

Codex 3, pp 152 to 501: The paragraphs are numbered from 4545 to 6096, followed by unnumbered entries, 33 blank pages; and a memorandum in Swedish. The first date recorded, 11 January 1752, is found in n 4550, and the last, 29 April 1765, in an unnumbered paragraph on p 500. <Hyde CLXXIV>

Codex 110: The fifth Index Codex, compiled from Codices 111 and 3 <second section>, not arranged alphabetically; paginated from 1 to 276, though several pages are blank, and pp 158-260 have been removed. A memorandum on p 261 is not in Swedenborg's handwriting. Pages 272 to 276 contain an alphabetical index of the contents. <Hyde CLXXXV>

LATIN

Editions:

La O MSS
La 1 J F I Tafel, editor
La 2 J D Odhner, editor

47/05/La O/1 1747 Hyde 513

<< <untitled> >>
pott long folio <400 x 152 mm>
text: 2 pp blank.

Zea, Zelus, p 1 <numbered by Swedenborg p 64>; this leaf is marked Z at the top.
Zona and n 149-151, p 2 <65>.
n 152-170, pp 3-9 <66-72>.

n 178-205, pp 10-16 <73-79>.
Memorandum, *Quomodo in primitivo Ecclesia loquuti sint variis linguis*, p 17 <201>.
n 972-206, pp 18-191 <not paginated by Swedenborg>: written from p 191 backward; p 192 blank.
n 973-3427, pp 193-565 <not paginated by Swedenborg>; pp 333-566 blank.

The MS forms Codex 2; it was brought to England in 1787 by C B Wadström, and not returned to SWE: KVA until 1870.

Unpublished copies have been recorded as follows.

1 UK: SOC A MS transcript of n 149-199 made by W Spence <d 1792>, pp 1-19. <Archives A/45, 10a; Hyde 529>

2 UK: SOC A MS transcript of parts of La O/1 made by P B Chastanier, in a volume labelled on the spine 'Excerpta e Diario E. Swedenborgii. vol. I. MSS. Chastanier'. The copying of part 1 was finished on 17 December 1790; the second part was begun on 24 December 1790 and finished on 27 March 1791; copy broad 4to <254 x 219 mm> text: n 973-2908, pp 77-492; n 209-3427, pp 1-125; Index vel tabula, 24 pp. The first 76 pp of part 1 are missing. <Archives A/29; Hyde 514>

3 UK: SOC A MS transcript of part of La O/1 made by P B Chastanier, in a volume labelled on the spine 'Excerpta e Diario E. Swedenborgii. vol. II. MSS. Chastanier'. It was begun on 28 March 1791; large post 6mo <219 x 191 mm> text: Memoranda, pp 1-2; n 3428-4544, pp 2-284. <Archives A/29; Hyde 897>

MS not seen; description deduced from 2nd title page in La O/10 and Hyde 513.

SWE: KVA

47/05/La O/2 **1748** Hyde 896

<< <untitled> >>

leaf 1, demy long 4to <397 x 140 mm>; remainder, foolscap long folio <410 x 165 mm>

text: Memoranda, pp 1-2.
n 3428-4544, pp 3-42 and 41-151.

The MS forms part of Codex 3; for the remainder of the Codex, see La O/9 = Hyde 2163; it was brought to England in 1788 by C B Wadström, and not returned to SWE: KVA until about 1845, by which time it had been rebound, and lettered on the spine 'Swedenborgii Diarium, MS., vol II, pars I'.

MS not seen; description deduced from La O/11 and Hyde 896.

SWE: KVA

47/05/La O/3 **1748** Hyde 926

<< <untitled> >>

pott long 4to <318 x 95 mm>

text: 1 p blank and 1 p Memoranda.
A, pp 1-12; B, pp 1-5; C, pp 1-21; D, pp 1-10; E, pp 1-6; F, pp 1-14; G, pp 1-4; H, pp 1-3; I/J, pp 1-11; p 12 blank; L, pp 1-10; M, pp 1-18; N, pp 1-6; O, pp 1-5; P, pp 1-20; Q, pp 1-2; R, pp 1-8; S, pp 1-22; T, pp 1-7; U/V, pp 1-16; 1 p blank; Z, p 1.
Additional entries, pp 1-62; pp 2, 25, 26, 37, 40, 52, 58, 61 blank.

The MS forms Codex 42.

MS not seen; description deduced from La O/12 and Hyde 926.

SWE: KVA

47/05/La O/4 **1748** Hyde 927

<< <untitled> >>

pott long 4to <318 x 95 mm>
text, in continuation of La O/3, not alphabetically arranged, pp 440-816.
The following pages are blank: 63-64, 81-82, 93-94, 104, 108, 118, 123-124, 128, 132, 135-136, 154, 177-178, 180, 198, 204, 206, 208, 215-216, 218-220, 226, 235-236, 239-240, 242, 248-250, 252, 254, 263-264, 268-270, 272, 276, 278, 282-284, 286, 297-298, 300, 302, 305-306, 308, 310, 312, 322, 326, 330, 336, 340, 342-344, 346, 348, 350-352, 354, 356-358, 360, 363-366, 370-372, 374, 380-382, 386, 392-394, 397-398, 402-404, 408-411, 413-415, 420-421, 423, 427-429, 433, 435, 437, 439.
The MS forms Codex 43.
MS not seen; description deduced from La O/12 and Hyde 927.
SWE: KVA

47/05/La O/5 **1748** Hyde 928
<< <untitled> >>
pott long 4to <318 x 95 mm>
text, in continuation of La O/4, not alphabetically arranged, pp 440-816.
The following pages are blank: 440-441, 453, 456-457, 460-463, 465, 467, 469, 471, 474-475, 478-481, 483, 485, 487-489, 493-497, 503, 505, 507, 513, 515-517, 523, 533, 535, 537, 539, 541, 546-547, 552-553, 556-557, 560-561, 566-567, 569, 573, 575, 577, 579, 582-583, 586-587, 589, 591-593, 596-599, 605-607, 613, 615, 617-619, 622-625, 627, 629, 631, 635-637, 639, 641, 645-646, 649, 651, 671, 679, 685-687, 689, 696-699, 702-703, 705, 709, 711-713, 717, 719, 721, 725-727, 729, 735, 737-739, 741-743, 745, 748-751, 756-757, 759, 769, 771, 776-777, 779, 782-783, 790-791, 794, 798, 800, 804, 810-812, 815-816.
Some references are written on the inside of the back cover.
The MS forms Codex 44.
MS not seen; description deduced from La O/12 and Hyde 928.
SWE: KVA

47/05/La O/6 **1748** Hyde 929
<< <untitled> >>
pott long 4to <318 x 95 mm>
text, in continuation of La O/5, not alphabetically arranged, pp 817-1194.
The following pages are blank: 817-818, 821-822, 824, 827-828, 831-834, 836-838, 842, 844-849, 851, 853, 855, 857, 860-861, 863-867, 869, 872-873, 875-879, 882-883, 886-887, 889, 891-893, 895, 897, 899, 902-904, 907-908, 910-912, 923-924, 926, 928, 930, 932-934, 938, 940, 942-944, 952-954, 959-960, 962, 964, 974, 976-978, 980, 990, 994, 996, 998, 1016, 1022, 1032, 1038-1040, 1045-1046, 1051-1052, 1056, 1064-1066, 1068-1070, 1076, 1078-1080, 1089-1092, 1101-1102, 1108-1112, 1117-1118, 1121-1124, 1128, 1132-1134, 1139-1142, 1146-1148, 1151-1156, 1158-1162, 1168-1170, 1172-1176, 1180-1184, 1187-1188, 1191-1194.
Some references are written on the inside of the back cover.
The MS forms Codex 45.
MS not seen; description deduced from La O/12 and Hyde 929.
SWE: KVA

47/05/La O/7 **1749** Hyde 915
<< <untitled> >>
pott 6mo <162 x 102 mm>
text: n 4545-4655, 4657-4715, and 71 unnumbered articles, pp 1-134.
It will be noted that Swedenborg repeated the numeration 4545 to 4715 in the second part of Codex

3 <see La O/9 = Hyde 2163> when he recommenced the recording of his experiences at a later date. The MS forms Codex 111, originally numbered as Codex 95 <see Tafel *Documents* 2:2, p 874, **E:b** En 1877/2 = Hyde 3274>; it was brought to England by C B Wadström in 1788, and not returned to SWE: KVA until 1842.

On the flyleaf the following memorandum is written: 'This original book is to Mr. Spence's disposition in order to find out the faults in the amanuensis' copy, which I intreat Mr. Spence for the sake of truth not to forget before it is printed, in order that truth may be so exactly done as it is possible in this wicked world.' The copy referred to was made by P B Chastanier <see below>, and his copy bears evidence of Spence's examination, and his testimony to its accuracy.

An unpublished copy has been recorded as follows.

> 1 UK: SOC A MS transcript made by P B Chastanier, in a volume labelled on the spine 'Excerpta e Diario E. Swedenborgii. vol. I. MSS. Chastanier'. It was begun on 24 February 1789 and finished on 21 March 1789; Chastanier rearranged the contents so that subjects are grouped together. copy broad 4to <254 x 219 mm> text: n 4545-4655, 4657-4715, and 71 unnumbered articles, pp 1-75; Table of contents <appended by M Sibly to Chastanier's transcript>, pp 1-37. <Archives A/29; Hyde 916>

MS not seen; description deduced from La O/11.

SWE: KVA

47/05/La O/8 — 1749 — Hyde 2193

<< <untitled> >>

pott folio <314 x 184 mm>

Note not written by Swedenborg <see below>, p 1.

text, not arranged alphabetically, pp 2-19, 21-42, 44-52, 54-102, 104-126, 128-155; pp 20, 43, 53, 103, 127, 156-157 are blank; pp 158-260 have been removed.

Memorandum, not written by Swedenborg <see below>, p 261; pp 265-271 blank.

Alphabetical index of contents, written with three columns on a page, pp 272-276.

The MS forms Codex 110, originally numbered as Codex 63 <see Tafel *Documents* 2:2, p 862, **E:b** En 1877/2 = Hyde 3274>; it was brought to England in 1788 by C B Wadström, and not returned to SWE: KVA until 1842.

The note on p 1 reads, 'Hic codex est index generalis de diurnali Swedenborg spiritualium experientiarum in mundo spirituali.' <This Codex is a general index of the Swedenborg diary of spiritual experiences in the spiritual world.>

The memorandum on p 261 reads, 'This paper cut out here is on account to give room for more paper in the bog, because it was not wrote upon it a single-word.' The word *bog* <'book'> seems to indicate that the writer was a Dane.

MS not seen; description deduced from La O/12 and Hyde 2193.

SWE: KVA

47/05/La O/9 — 1752 — Hyde 2163

<< <untitled> >>

foolscap long folio <410 x 165 mm>

text: n 4545-5001, pp 152-166, 165-170, 169-228, 227-234, 233-256.

n 5002-6096, pp 257-488.

De Conjugio et adulterio varia, 82 unnumbered sections, pp 489-501; 33 pp blank.

Memoranda in Swedish, 1 p.

It will be noted that Swedenborg had previously used the numeration 4545 to 5001 when recording his experiences in Codex 111 <see La O/7 = Hyde 915>.

The MS forms part of Codex 3; for the remainder of the Codex, see La O/2 = Hyde 896; it was brought to England in 1788 by C B Wadström, and not returned to SWE: KVA until about 1845, by

which time it had been rebound, and lettered on the spine 'Swedenborgii Diarium, MS., vol II, pars II'.
To the end are attached 9 sheets of paper, ruled 'for cash', on the 2nd page of which are some notes written by M Sibly.
There are references in the text to *Arcana Coelestia*: in n 4620 to n 5893, published in 1753; in n 4630 to the appendices to Genesis 27 to 42, published in 1752 and 1753; and in 5192 to n 10604, published in 1756. In n 5600 there are references to *De Nova Hierosolyma et ejus Doctrina Coelestia*, published in 1758; and in n 5946 there are references to *De Coelo et de Inferno*, *De Ultimo Judicio*, *De Telluribus in Universo*, *De Equo Albo*, and *De Nova Hierosolyma et ejus Doctrina Coelestia*, all published in 1758. Among the *Varia de Conjugio* there is a reference to *Apocalypsis Revelata* n 543, published in 1766. From these details it may be inferred that Swedenborg had laid the Codex aside for a number of years. The subjects dealt with in n 6096 <headed *De Amore Conjugiali*> and in *De Conjugio et adulterio varia* do not contain any record of Swedenborg's experiences in the spiritual world.
An unpublished copy has been recorded as follows.

1 UK: SOC A MS transcript of part of La O/9 made by P B Chastanier, in a volume labelled on the spine 'Excerpta e Diario E. Swedenborgii. vol. II. MSS. Chastanier; the copy finished abruptly in n 5589 <there is no date in this part of the transcript to indicate when it was written; but it appears from *The New Magazine of Knowledge* vol 2, London 1791 p 293, that the copying was continuing in July 1791>; large post 6mo <219 x 191 mm> text: n 4545-5589, pp 284-599; Index rerum, pp 1-37. <Archives A/29; Hyde 2164>

MS not seen; description deduced from La O/11 and Hyde 2163.
SWE: KVA

47/05/La 1/1 **1843** Hyde 899, 3053

EMAN. SWEDENBORGII | DIARII SPIRITUALIS | PARS SECUNDA. | <short rule> | E CHIROGRAPHO EJUS IN BIBLIOTHECA REGIAE | ACADEMIAE HOLMIENSIS ASSERVATO | NUNC PRIMUM EDIDIT | Dr. JO. FR. IM. TAFEL, | REGIAE BIBLIOTHECAE UNIVERSITATIS TUBINGENSIS PRAEFECTUS. | <multiple rule> | LONDINI, | APUD WILLIAM NEWBERY, CHENIES STREET, | BEDFORD - SQUARE. | STUTTGARDIAE | APUD EBNER ET SEUBERT. | 1843.
8vo
title leaf, 2 pp; text: <Memoranda,> pp 1-2; n 3428-4544, pp 2-372; Notae criticae editoris, pp 373-398; Emendanda, p 398.
An unpublished copy has been recorded as follows.

1 UK: SOC A MS transcript made by H Wrightson, begun in November 1852 and completed on 22 February 1853; small post broad 4to <238 x 191 mm> text: n 3428-4544, 327 pp. <Archives A/95j, 96/a,b,c; Hyde 898>

UK: SOC, CON, NCC, NR; GER: GSU; NET: GEN, KB; USA: ANC, FOU

47/05/La 1/2 **1843** Hyde 918, 3056

EMAN. SWEDENBORGII | DIARII SPIRITUALIS | PARS QUARTA | SIVE | DIARIUM MINUS. | E CHIROGRAPHO EJUS NUNC PRIMUM EDIDIT | Dr. JO. FR. IM. TAFEL, | BIBLIOTHECAE REGIAE UNIVERSITATIS TUBINGENSIS PRAEFECTUS. | <multiple rule> | LONDINI, | APUD WILLIAM NEWBERY, CHENIES STREET, | BEDFORD-SQUARE. | STUTGARDIAE | APUD EBNER ET SEUBERT. | 1843.
8vo
title leaf, 2 pp; Lectori benevolo s. p. d. editor, pp IV-X; text: n 4545-4655, 4657-4715, and 71 unnumbered articles, pp 1-84; Notae criticae editoris, pp 85-95; A note concerning P B Chastanier's transcript of the autograph MS, p 95; Emendanda, pp 96-97; Contenta, pp 98-102.

Only the title of n 4679, and not the Swedish text, is printed in this edition.
An unpublished copy has been recorded as follows.

1 UK: SOC A MS transcript made by H Wrightson, completed on 2 September 1853; small post broad 4to <238 x 191 mm> text: n 4545-4657-4715, and 71 unnumbered articles, 73 pp. <Archives A/96d; Hyde 917>

UK: SOC, CON, NCC, NR; GER: GSU; NET: GEN, KB; USA: ANC, FOU

47/05/La 1/3 1844 Hyde 517, 3051

EMAN. SWEDENBORGII | DIARII SPIRITUALIS | PARTIS PRIMAE | VOLUMEN PRIMUM. | <short rule> | E CHIROGRAPHO EJUS IN BIBLIOTHECA REGIAE | ACADEMIAE HOLMIENSIS ASSERVATO | NUNC PRIMUM EDIDIT | Dr. JO. FR. IM. TAFEL, | REGIAE BIBLIOTHECAE UNIVERSITATIS TUBINGENSIS PRAEFECTUS. | <multiple rule> | TUBINGAE | CURAM ADMINISTRAT **„Verlagsexpedition."** | LONDINI, | APUD WILLIAM NEWBERY, CHENIES STREET, | BEDFORD - SQUARE. | 1844.

8vo

title leaf, 2 pp; Praefatio editoris, pp II-XIV; text: articles headed 'Zea', 'Zelus', 'Zona', p 1; n 149-1538, pp 1-424; Notae criticae editoris, pp 425-449; Errata et emendanda, p 450.
An unpublished copy has been recorded as follows.

1 UK: SOC A MS transcript made by H Wrightson, begun on 10 September 1850; small post broad 4to <238 x 191 mm> text: n 149-1538, 379 pp. <Archives A/95a-f; Hyde 515>

UK: SOC, CON, NCC, NR; GER: GSU; NET: GEN, KB; USA: ANC, FOU

47/05/La 1/4 1844 Hyde 2166, 3054

EMAN. SWEDENBORGII | DIARII SPIRITUALIS | PARTIS TERTIAE | VOLUMEN PRIMUM. | <short rule> | E CHIROGRAPHO EJUS IN BIBLIOTHECA REGIAE | ACADEMIAE HOLMIENSIS ASSERVATO | NUNC PRIMUM EDIDIT | Dr. JO. FR. IM. TAFEL, | REGIAE BIBLIOTHECAE UNIVERSITATIS TUBINGENSIS PRAEFECTUS. | <multiple rule> | LONDINI, | APUD WILLIAM NEWBERY, CHENIES STREET, | BEDFORD - SQUARE. | STUTTGARDIAE | APUD EBNER ET SEUBERT. | 1844.

8vo

title leaf, 2 pp; text: n 4545-5659, pp 1-379; Notae criticae editoris, pp 380-407; Errata, p 408.
An unpublished copy has been recorded as follows.

1 UK: SOC A MS transcript made by H Wrightson, begun on 22 February 1853; small post broad 4to <238 x 191 mm> text: n 4545-5659. <Archives A/96c,d?; Hyde 2165>

UK: SOC, CON, NCC, NR; GER: GSU; NET: GEN, KB; USA: ANC, FOU

47/05/La 1/5 1844 Hyde 2167, 3055

EMAN. SWEDENBORGII | DIARII SPIRITUALIS | PARTIS TERTIAE | VOLUMEN SECUNDUM. | <short rule> | E CHIROGRAPHO EJUS IN BIBLIOTHECA REGIAE | ACADEMIAE HOLMIENSIS ASSERVATO | NUNC PRIMUM EDIDIT | Dr. JO. FR. IM. TAFEL, | REGIAE BIBLIOTHECAE UNIVERSITATIS TUBINGENSIS PRAEFECTUS. | <multiple rule> | LONDINI, | APUD WILLIAM NEWBERY, CHENIES STREET, | BEDFORD - SQUARE. | STUTTGARDIAE | APUD EBNER ET SEUBERT. | 1844.

8vo

title leaf, 2 pp; text: n 5660-6096, pp 1-198; unnumbered paragraphs, pp 198-223; Notae criticae editoris, pp 224-241; Errata, p 242.
The Swedish text of n 4787, 5763, 6027, 6035, and the closing memoranda are omitted in this edition.
An unpublished copy has been recorded as follows.

1 UK: soc A MS transcript made by H Wrightson, completed on 13 March 1853; small post broad 4to <238 x 191 mm> text: n 5660 to the end. <Archives A/96c,d; Hyde 2165>

UK: soc, con, ncc, nr; GER: gsu; NET: gen, kb; USA: anc, fou

47/05/La 1/6 **1845** Hyde 518, 3052

EMAN. SWEDENBORGII | DIARII SPIRITUALIS | PARTIS PRIMAE | VOLUMEN SECUNDUM. | <short rule> | E CHIROGRAPHO EJUS IN BIBLIOTHECA REGIAE | ACADEMIAE HOLMIENSIS ASSERVATO | NUNC PRIMUM EDIDIT | Dr JO. FR. IM. TAFEL, | REGIAE BIBLIOTHECAE UNIVERSITATIS TUBINGENSIS PRAEFECTUS. | <multiple rule> | TUBINGAE | CURAM ADMINISTRAT „Verlagsexpedition." | LONDINI, | WILLIAM NEWBERY, CHENIES STREET, | BEDFORD - SQUARE. | 1845.

8vo

title leaf, 2 pp; text: n 1539-3427, pp 1-545; Notae criticae editoris, pp 546-576; Errata, p 576.

An unpublished copy has been recorded as follows.

1 UK: soc A MS transcript made by H Wrightson, completed in November 1852; small post broad 4to <238 x 191 mm> text: n 1539-3427, 531 pp. <Archives A/95f-j; Hyde 515>

UK: soc, con, ncc, nr; GER: gsu; NET: gen, kb; USA: anc, fou

47/05/La 1/7 **1845** Hyde 2194, 3059

EMAN. SWEDENBORGII | DIARII SPIRITUALIS | PARS SEXTA | CONTINENS | INDICEM PARTIUM II — IV. | <short rule> | E CHIROGRAPHO EJUS IN BIBLIOTHECA REGIAE | ACADEMIAE HOLMIENSIS ASSERVATO | NUNC PRIMUM EDIDIT | Dr JO. FR. I. TAFEL, | REGIAE BIBLIOTHECAE UNIVERSITATIS TUBINGENSIS PRAEFECTUS. | <multiple rule> | TUBINGAE | CURAM ADMINISTRAT „Verlagsexpedition." | LONDINI, | WILLIAM NEWBERY, CHENIES STREET, | BEDFORD - SQUARE. | 1845.

8vo

title leaf, 2 pp; text: <Adulterium-Zonae,> pp 1-137; Contents, pp 138-144; Notae criticae editoris, pp 145-150; Erratum, p 150.

UK: soc, con, ncc, nr; GER: gsu; NET: gen, kb; USA: anc, fou

47/05/La 1/8 **1846** Hyde 930, 3049, 3057

EMAN. SWEDENBORGII | DIARII SPIRITUALIS | PARTIS QUINTAE VOLUMEM PRIMUM, | CONTINENS | INDICEM PARTIUM I, 1. 2. II. IV. | UT ET | ADVERSARIORUM IN LIBROS VET. TESTAMENTI. | *ABDOMEN — LIBER*. | <short rule> | E CHIROGRAPHO EJUS IN BIBLIOTHECA REGIAE | ACADEMIAE HOLMIENSIS ASSERVATO | NUNC PRIMUM EDIDIT | Dr JO. FR. IM. TAFEL, | REGIAE BIBLIOTHECAE UNIVERSITATIS TUBINGENSIS PRAEFECTUS. | <multiple rule> | TUBINGAE | CURAM ADMINISTRAT „Verlagsexpedition." | LONDINI, | WILLIAM NEWBERY, CHENIES STREET, | BEDFORD - SQUARE. | 1846. <*stet* VOLUMEM>

2nd title: EMAN. SWEDENBORGII | ADVERSARIA | IN LIBROS VETERISTESTAMENTI. | E CHIROGRAPHO EJUS | IN BIBLIOTHECA REGIAE ACADEMIAE HOLMIENSIS | ASSERVATO | NUNC PRIMUM EDIDIT | Dr JO. FR. IM. TAFEL, | REGIAE BIBLIOTHECAE UNIVERSITATIS TUBINGENSIS PRAEFECTUS. | <short rule> | PARTIS QUINTAE VOLUMEN PRIMUM | CONTINENS | PARTEM PRIMAM INDICIS ADVERSARIORUM, ET DIARII | SPIRITUALIS PARTIS I, 1. 2. II. ET IV. | ABDOMEN — LIBER. | <multiple rule> | TUBINGAE | CURAM ADMINISTRAT „Verlagsexpedition." | LONDINI, | WILLIAM NEWBERY, CHENIES STREET, | BEDFORD - SQUARE. | 1846.

8vo

title leaves, 4 pp; text: <Abdomen-Liber,> pp 1-512.

Also issued as *Adversaria* volume I of part V <45/05/La 1/5 = Hyde 3049>.
UK: soc, con, ncc, nr; GER: gsu; NET: gen, kb; USA: anc, fou

47/05/La 1/9 **1847** Hyde 931, 3050, 3058

EMAN. SWEDENBORGII | DIARII SPIRITUALIS | PARTIS QUINTAE VOLUMEM SECUNDUM, | CONTINENS | PARTEM SECUNDAM INDICIS PARTIUM I, 1. 2. II. IV. | NEC NON | ADVERSARIORUM IN LIBROS VET. TESTAMENTI. | *LIBERTAS — ZELUS.* | <short rule> | E CHIROGRAPHO EJUS IN BIBLIOTHECA REGIAE | ACADEMIAE HOLMIENSIS ASSERVATO | NUNC PRIMUM EDIDIT | D[r]. JO. FR. IM. TAFEL, | REGIAE BIBLIOTHECAE UNIVERSITATIS TUBINGENSIS PRAEFECTUS. | <multiple rule> | TUBINGAE | CURAM ADMINISTRAT „Verlagsexpedition;" | LONDINI, | WILLIAM NEWBERY, 6, KING STREET, | HOLBORN. | 1847. <*stet* VOLUMEM>
2nd title: EMAN. SWEDENBORGII | ADVERSARIA | IN | LIBROS VETERIS TESTAMENTI. | E CHIROGRAPHO EJUS IN BIBLIOTHECA REGIAE | ACADEMIAE HOLMIENSIS ASSERVATO | NUNC PRIMUM EDIDIT | D[r]. JO. FR. IM. TAFEL, | REGIAE BIBLIOTHECAE UNIVERSITATIS TUBINGENSIS PRAEFECTUS. | <short rule> | PARTIS QUINTAE VOLUMEN SECUNDUM, | CONTINENS | PARTEM SECUNDAM INDICIS ADVERSARIORUM, NEC | NON DIARII SPIRITUALIS PARTIS I, 1. 2. II. ET IV. | LIBERTAS — ZELUS. | <multiple rule> | TUBINGAE | CURAM ADMINISTRAT „Verlagsexpedition;" | LONDINI, | WILLIAM NEWBERY, 6, KING STREET, | HOLBORN. | 1847.
8vo
title leaves, 4 pp; text: <Libertas-Zelus,> pp 1-466; Notae criticae editoris, pp 467-491; Editorial memorandum concerning the following supplementary entries, p 492; Supplementum editoris, pp 493-518; Errata et additamenta, p 518.
The supplementary entries are continuations concerning 'Amor', 'Cerebrum', 'Ecclesia', 'Fides', 'Hypocrita', and 'Verbum' stated by Tafel to be written in 'quintus autographi tomus hujus partis quintae'.
Also issued as *Adversaria* volume II of part V <45/05/La 1/6 = Hyde 3050>.
UK: soc, con, ncc, nr; GER: gsu; NET: gen, kb; USA: anc, fou

47/05/La 0/10 **1901** Hyde 516, 3038/1

EMANUELIS SWEDENBORGII | MEMORABILIA | SEU | DIARIUM SPIRITUALE | AB ANNO 1747 AD ANNUM 1765 | AD AUTOGRAPHI SIMILITUDINEM IN BIBLIOTHECA REGIAE ACADEMIAE SCIEN- | TIARUM SUECANAE ASSERVATI, OPE PHOTOTYPOGRAPHIAE DELINEATUM, | JUSSU CONVENTIONIS GENERALIS NOVAE HIEROSOLYMAE, ATQUE | ACADEMIAE NOVAE ECCLESIAE, IN AMERICA SEPTEN- | TRIONALI, EDITUM, SOCIETATE SWEDENBORGI- | ANA, LONDINI, OPERAM CONFERENTE. | <short orn rule> | VOL. I. | <orn 25 x 47 mm> | HOLMIA | EX OFFICINA LITHOGRAPHIAE WARNER SILFVERSPARRE | 1901.
2nd title page: EMANUEL SWEDENBORG'S | MEMORABILIA | OR | SPIRITUAL DIARY | FROM THE YEAR 1747 TO THE YEAR 1765 | A FACSIMILE OF THE ORIGINAL MANUSCRIPT REPRODUCED | BY MEANS OF PHOTO-TYPOGRAPHY | VOL. I. | PUBLISHED BY ORDER OF | THE GENERAL CONVENTION OF THE NEW JERUSALEM | AND | THE ACADEMY OF THE NEW CHURCH | IN THE UNITED STATES OF AMERICA | WITH THE COÖPERATION OF | THE SWEDENBORG SOCIETY, LONDON. | <orn 16 x 32 mm> | STOCKHOLM | WARNER SILFVERSARRES NYA GRAFISKA AKTIEBOLAG | 1901.
folio
title leaves, 4 pp; Historical note by C Th Odhner, 2 pp; Praefatiuncula, 2 pp; text: Zea, Zelus, p 1; Zona, p 1; n 149-3427, pp 1-565.
Photographic reproduction of La 0/1, published in phototyped edition, vol 1 <*Memorabilia seu Diarium Spirituale* vol 1, Hyde 3038/1> Stockholm. Produced under the supervision of J E Boyesen.

Unpublished copies have been recorded as follows.
1 UK: SOC & USA: ANC, SHS A reproduction on microfilm 4, Bryn Athyn PA.
UK: SOC, BL, CON, NCC, RYL; DEN: RLD; NET: GEN, KB; SWE: ROY, KVA, UPP; USA: ANC, FOU, SHS; AUS: SYD

47/05/La O/11, **D** La 1905/1 **1905** Hyde 896/1, 915/1, 2163/1, 3038/2

EMANUELIS SWEDENBORGII | MEMORABILIA | SEU | DIARIUM SPIRITUALE | AB ANNO 1747 AD ANNUM 1765 | AD AUTOGRAPHI SIMILITUDINEM IN BIBLIOTHECA REGIAE ACADEMIAE SCIEN- | TIARUM SUECANAE ASSERVATI, OPE PHOTOTYPOGRAPHIAE DELINEATUM, | JUSSU CONVENTIONIS GENERALIS NOVAE HIEROSOLYMAE, ATQUE | ACADEMIAE NOVAE ECCLESIAE, IN AMERICA SEPTEN- | TRIONALI, EDITUM, SOCIETATE SWEDENBORGI- | ANA, LONDINI, OPERAM CONFERENTE. | <short orn rule> | VOL. II. | <orn 25 x 47 mm> | HOLMIA | EX OFFICINA LITHOGRAPHIAE WARNER SILFVERSPARRE | 1905.
folio
title leaf, 2 pp; Praefatiuncula, 2 pp; text n 3428-4544, pp 1-152; n 4545-4655, 4657-4715, 71 unnumbered articles, pp 1-515; 3 blank pp; text n 4545m-<4792m>, pp 1-35.
Photographic reproduction of La O/2, 7, 9, published in phototyped edition, vol 2 <*Memorabilia seu Diarium Spirituale* vol 2, Hyde 3038/2> Stockholm.
Unpublished copies have been recorded as follows.
1 UK: SOC & USA: ANC, SHS A reproduction on microfilm 4, Bryn Athyn PA.
UK: SOC, BL, CON, NCC, RYL; DEN: RLD; NET: GEN, KB; SWE: ROY, KVA, UPP; USA: ANC, FOU, SHS; AUS: SYD

47/05/La O/12, **D** La 1905/2 **1905** Hyde 926/1, 927/1, 928/1, 929/1, 2193/1, 3038/3

EMANUELIS SWEDENBORGII | MEMORABILIA | SEU | DIARIUM SPIRITUALE | AB ANNO 1747 AD ANNUM 1765 | AD AUTOGRAPHI SIMILITUDINEM IN BIBLIOTHECA REGIAE ACADEMIAE SCIEN- | TIARUM SUECANAE ASSERVATI, OPE PHOTOTYPOGRAPHIAE DELINEATUM, | JUSSU CONVENTIONIS GENERALIS NOVAE HIEROSOLYMAE, ATQUE | ACADEMIAE NOVAE ECCLESIAE, IN AMERICA SEPTEN- | TRIONALI, EDITUM, SOCIETATE SWEDENBORGI- | ANA, LONDINI, OPERAM CONFERENTE. | <short orn rule> | VOL. III. | <orn 25 x 47 mm> | HOLMIA | EX OFFICINA LITHOGRAPHIAE LAGRELIUS & WESTPHAL | 1905.
folio
title leaf, 2 pp; Praefatiuncula, 2 pp; text, pp 1-691.
Photographic reproduction of La O/3, 4, 5, 6, 8, published in phototyped edition, vol 3 <*Memorabilia seu Diarium Spirituale* vol 3, Hyde 3038/3> Stockholm.
Unpublished copies have been recorded as follows.
1 UK: SOC & USA: ANC, SHS A reproduction on microfilms 5 and 6, Bryn Athyn PA.
UK: SOC, BL, CON, NCC, RYL; DEN: RLD; NET: GEN, KB; SWE: ROY, KVA, UPP; USA: ANC, FOU, SHS; AUS: SYD

47/05/La 2/1 **1983** Hyde 517/1, 3077/6

[Emanuelis Swedenborgii Diarium, | ubi memorantur] | EXPERIENTIAE SPIRITUALES | [intra annos 1745 ad 1765] | [VOLUMEN PRIMUM, | continens materias liminares | undecunque sumptas, ut et | paragraphos numeratas ex | *Indice Biblico* extractas] | Academy of the New Church | Bryn Athyn, Pa., U.S.A. | 1983
verso: in servitio Domini | primum Tubingae 1843-60 a Dr. Johann Friedrich Immanuel | Tafel excusae, nunc denuo certius ex propiori comparatione | auctoris autographi editae a Dr. John Durban Odhner | Copyright © 1982 by the Academy of the New Church | Library of Congress Catalog Card | No. 82-72768 | Academy of the New Church, Publisher | P.O. Box 278, Bryn Athyn, Pa. 19009 | Printed in the United States of America by the | General Church Press | First edition 200 copies | ISBN 0-910557-01-2 (Volume I, cloth) | ISBN 0-910557-00-4 (6 Volume set)

half title: EXPERIENTIAE SPIRITUALES
8vo
half title, 2 pp; title leaf, pp i-ii; Preface to the second Latin edition, pp iii-xxviii; Preface to the first volume, pp xxix-xxxviii; Typographica, p xxxix; Sigla et compendia, p xl; text: The indented paragraphs from 45/05/La O/1-3, n [1a]-[369a], pp 1-183; The indented paragraphs from 47/02/ La O/1, n [370a]-[403a], pp 184-205; A reconstruction of the contents of the lost paragraphs of *Experientae Spirituales* <here numbered n 1-148⅓>, pp 206-248; Three memoranda from 47/02/La O/1, n [148¼], [148⅕], [148⅙], p 249; n 149-205, pp 251-280; n 206-972½, pp 281-573.
47/01/La 1/1 is printed on pp 213-214.
UK: soc, nr; NET: gen; USA: anc

47/05/La 2/2 1989 Hyde 3077/7

[Emanuelis Swedenborgii Diarium, | ubi memorantur] | EXPERIENTIAE SPIRITUALES | [intra annos 1745 ad 1765] | [VOLUMEN SECUNDUM, | continens paragraphos a 973 ad 3427 numeratas] | Academy of the New Church | Bryn Athyn, Pa., U.S.A. | 1989
verso: in servitio Domini | primum Tubingae 1843-60 a Dr. Johann Friedrich Immanuel | Tafel excusae, nunc denuo certius ex propiori comparatione | auctoris autographi editae a Dr. John Durban Odhner | Copyright © 1989 by the Academy of the New Church | Library of Congress Cataloging-in-Publication Data | (Revised for vol 2) | Swedenborg, Emanuel, 1688-1772. | (Emanuelis Swedenborgii Diarium, ubi memorantur) | Experientiae spirituales (intra annos 1745 ad 1765) | Text in Latin; pref. in English. | Constitutes the 2nd Latin ed. of: Diarium spirituale. | Limited edition of 200 copies. | Includes bibliographical references. | Contents: v. primum. Continens materias liminares | undecunque sumptas, ut et paragraphos numeratas ex | Indice Biblico extractas: 1a-403a, 1-972½ — v. secundum. | Continens paragraphos a 973 ad 3427 numeratas. | 1. Spiritual life—Early works to 1800. 2. Swedenborg, Emanuel, 1688-1772 —Diaries. 3. Swedenborgians— | Sweden—Diaries—Early works to 1800. I. Title: Diarium, | ubi memorantur Experientiae spirituales intra annos 1745 ad | 1765. II. Title: Experientiae spirituales. III. Title. | BX8712.S6 1983 289.4'092 82-72768 | ISBN 0-910557-00-4 (set) | ISBN 0-910557-02-0 (v2)
half title: EXPERIENTIAE SPIRITUALES
8vo
half title and title leaves, pp i-iv; Preface to the second volume, pp v-xi; Sigla et compendia, p xii; text, n 973-3427, pp 1-761.
UK: soc, nr; NET: gen; USA: anc

47/05/La 2/3 1991 Hyde 3077/8

[Emanuelis Swedenborgii Diarium, | ubi memorantur] | EXPERIENTIAE SPIRITUALES | [intra annos 1745 ad 1765] | [VOLUMEN TERTIUM, | continens paragraphos a | 3428 ad 4544, dein | 4545[a] ad [4832a] | sive Diarii Minoris] | a John Durban Odhner editae | Academy of the New Church | Bryn Athyn, Pa., U.S.A. | 1991
verso: in servitio Domini | primum Tubingae 1843-60 a Dr. Johann Friedrich Immanuel | Tafel excusae, nunc denuo certius ex propiori comparatione | auctoris autographi editae a Dr. John Durban Odhner | Copyright © 1991 by the Academy of the New Church | Library of Congress Cataloging-in-Publication Data | (Revised for vol. 3) | Swedenborg, Emanuel, 1688-1772. | (Emanuelis Swedenborgii Diarium, ubi memorantur) | Experientiae spirituales (intra annos 1745 ad 1765). | Vol. 3 — edited by John Durban Odhner | Text in Latin; pref. in English. | Constitutes the 2nd Latin ed. of: Diarium Spirituale. | Limited edition of 200 copies. | Includes bibliographical references. | Contents: v. primum. Continens materias liminares | undecunque sumptas, ut et paragraphos numeratas ex Indice Biblico | extractas: 1a-403a, 1-972 — v. secundum. Continens

paragraphos | a 973 ad 3427 numeratas. — v. tertium. Continens paragraphos a | 3428 ad 4544, dein 4545[a] ad [4832a] sive Diarii minoris. | 1. Spiritual life—Early works to 1800. 2. Swedenborg, | Emanuel, 1688-1772—Diaries. 3. Swedenborgians—Sweden | —Diaries—Early works to 1800. I. Odhner, John D. II. Title. III. | Title: Diarium, ubi memorantur Experientiae spirituales intra annos | 1745 ad 1765. IV. Title: Experientiae spirituales. | BX8712.S6 1983 289.4'092 82-72768 | ISBN 0-910557-00-4 (set) | ISBN 0-910557-03-9 (v3)]
half title: EXPERIENTIAE SPIRITUALES
8vo
half title and title leaves, pp i-iv; Preface to the third volume, pp v-ix; Sigla et compendia, p x; text: n [3427 ½-⅙], pp 1-2; n 3428-4544, pp 2-421; n 4545[a]-4715[a] *<Diarium Minus>*, pp 422-469; n [4716a]-[4832a], pp 469-516.
UK: soc, nr; NET: gen; USA: anc

47/05/La 2/4 1993 Hyde 3077/9
[Emanuelis Swedenborgii Diarium, | ubi memorantur] | EXPERIENTIAE SPIRITUALES | [intra annos 1745 ad 1765] | [VOLUMEN QUARTUM, | continens paragraphos | a 4445 ad [6110½] | numeratas] | a John Durban Odhner editae | Academy of the New Church | Bryn Athyn, Pa., U.S.A. | 1993
verso: in servitio Domini | primum Tubingae 1843-60 a Dr. Johann Friedrich Immanuel | Tafel excusae, nunc denuo certius ex propiori comparatione | auctoris autographi editae a Dr. John Durban Odhner | Copyright © 1993 by the Academy of the New Church | Library of Congress Cataloging-in-Publication Data | (Revised for volume 4) | Swedenborg, Emanuel, 1688-1772. | (Emanuelis Swedenborgii Diarium, ubi memorantur) | Experientiae spirituales (intra annos 1745 ad 1765). | Text in Latin; pref. in English. | Constitutes the 2nd Latin ed. of: Diarium Spirituale. | Limited edition of 200 copies. | Includes bibliographical references. | Contents: v. primum. Continens materias liminares | undecunque sumptas, ut et paragraphos numeratas ex Indice Biblico | extractas: 1a-403a, 1-972½ — —v. quartum. Continens | paragraphos a 4545 ad [6110½] numeratas. | 1. Spiritual life—Early works to 1800. | 2. Swedenborg, Emanuel, 1688-1772—Diaries. | 3. Swedenborgians—Sweden—Diaries—Early works to | 1800. I. Diarium, ubi memorantur Experientiae spirituales intra | annos 1745 ad 1765. II. Experientiae spirituales. III. Title. | BX8712.S6 1983 289.4'092 82-72768 | ISBN 0-9105557-00-4 (set) | ISBN 0-910557-04-7 (v.4)
half title: EXPERIENTIAE SPIRITUALES
8vo
half title and title leaves, pp i-iv; Preface to the fourth volume, pp v-ix; Sigla et compendia, p x; text: n 4545-6096, [6097]-[6110 ½], pp 1-678.
n [6110 ½] is in Swedish; a Latin translation of it is given in a footnote on pp 677-678.
UK: soc, nr; NET: gen; USA: anc

47/05/La 2/5 1995 Hyde 3077/10
[Emanuelis Swedenborgii Diarium, | ubi memorantur] | EXPERIENTIAE SPIRITUALES | [intra annos 1745 ad 1765] | [VOLUMEN QUINTUM, | continens Indicem I | ab ABDOMEN ad MYSTERIA] | a John Durban Odhner editae | Academy of the New Church | Bryn Athyn, Pa., U.S.A. | 1995
verso: in servitio Domini | primum Tubingae 1843-60 a Dr. Johann Friedrich Immanuel | Tafel excusae, nunc denuo certius ex propiori comparatione | auctoris autographi editae a Dr. John Durban Odhner | Copyright © 1995 by the Academy of the New Church | Library of Congress Cataloging-in-Publication Data | (Revised for volume 5) | Swedenborg, Emanuel, 1688-1772. | (Emanuelis Swedenborgii Diarium, ubi memorantur) | Experientiae spirituales (intra annos 1745 ad 1765). | Text in Latin; pref. in English. | Constitutes the 2nd Latin ed. of: Diarium spirituale. | Limited edition of 200 copies. | Includes bibliographical references. | Contents: v.

primum. Continens materias liminares | undecunque sumptas, ut et paragraphos numeratas ex Indice Biblico | extractas: 1a-403a, 1-972½ — —v. quintum. Continens | indicem I ab ABDOMEN ad MYSTERIA. | 1. Spiritual life—Early works to 1800. Swedenborg, | Emanuel, 1688-1772—Diaries. | 2. Swedenborgians—Sweden—Diaries—Early works to | 1800. I. Diarium ubi memorantur Experientiae spirituales intra | annos 1745 ad 1765. II. Experientiae spirituales. III. Title. | BX8712.S6 1983 289.4'092 [B] 82-72768 | ISBN 0-910557-00-4 (set) | ISBN 0-910557-05-5 (v. 5)
half title: EXPERIENTIAE SPIRITUALES
8vo
half title and title leaves, pp i-iv; Preface to the fifth volume, p v; Sigla et compendia, p vi; text: Index to n 1a-403a and 1-4644a, Abdomen-Mysteria, pp 1-623.
UK: soc, nr; NET: gen; USA: anc

47/05/La 2/6 **1997** Hyde 3077/11
[Emanuelis Swedenborgii Diarium, | ubi memorantur] | EXPERIENTIAE SPIRITUALES | [intra annos 1745 ad 1765] | [VOLUMEN SEXTUM, | continens Indicem I | ab NARES ad ZELUS, | Indicem II, et Appendicem] | a John Durban Odhner editae | Academy of the New Church | Bryn Athyn, Pa., U.S.A. | 1997
verso: in servitio Domini | primum Tubingae 1843-60 a Dr. Johann Friedrich Immanuel | Tafel excusae, nunc denuo certius ex propiori comparatione | auctoris autographi editae a Dr. John Durban Odhner | Copyright © 1997 by the Academy of the New Church | Library of Congress Cataloging-in-Publication Data | (Revised for vol 6) | Swedenborg, Emanuel, 1688-1772. | (Emanuelis Swedenborgii Diarium, ubi memorantur) | Experientiae spirituales (intra annos 1745 ad 1765). | Text in Latin; pref. in English. | Constitutes the 2nd Latin ed. of: Diarium spirituale. | Limited edition of 200 copies. | Includes bibliographical references. | Contents: v. primum. Continens materias liminares | undecunque sumptas, ut et paragraphos numeratas ex Indice | Biblico extractas: 1a-403a, 1-972½ — v. sextum. Continens | indicem I ab NARES ad ZELUS, indicem II, et appendicem. | 1. Spiritual life—Early works to 1800. 2. Swedenborg, | Emanuel, 1688-1772—Diaries. | 3. Swedenborgians—Sweden— | Diaries—Early works to 1800. I. Diarium, ubi memorantur | Experientiae spirituales intra annos 1745 ad 1765. | II. Experientiae spirituales. III. Title. | BX8712.S6 1983 289.4'092 [B] 82-72768 | ISBN 0-910557-00-4 (set) | ISBN 0-910557-06-3 (v. 6)
half title: EXPERIENTIAE SPIRITUALES
8vo
half title and title leaves, pp i-iv; Preface to the sixth volume, p v-vii; Sigla et compendia, p viii; text: Index to n 1a-403a and 1-4644a, pp 1-353; Index to n 3428-6110½, pp 354-494; Appendices: Contents, p 1; Appendix A: text: Supplement to Index I compiled by J F I Tafel <entries headed 'Amor', 'Cerebrum', 'Ecclesia', 'Fides', 'Hypocrita', 'Verbum', see La 1/9>, pp 3-25; Appendix B: text, Address by J D Odhner to the Scandinavian Swedenborg Society, 29 January 1986, pp 27-39; Appendix C: A chronological list of literature on Swedenborg's Latin, pp 41-42; Appendix D: Astrological symbols used by Swedenborg in the text of the current work, p 43; Appendix E: Transcript and translation of Swedenborg's marginal annotations to his copy of the Schmidius Bible referred to in n 29 <the 'Bath fragment', 47/01>, pp 45-54.
UK: soc, nr; NET: gen; SWE: roy; USA: anc

LATIN EXTRACTS

X 47/05/La nd/1 **no date** Hyde 530, 903, 2172
<<Excerpta ex Memorabilibus manuscriptis Emanuelis Swedenborgii, ex autographis in Bibliotheca Academiae Scientiarum Stockholmiensis descripta.>>

foolscap broad 4to <216 x 171 mm>
text n 202, 805, 807, 780, 781, 767-773, 385, 302, 1165, 1212, 1950-1955, 2040-2041, 2523, 2147-2149, 2821, 2909, 2951, 3191, 4418, 4396-4397, 4543, 5999, <6107>, 4693-4700, 4707-4708, 4717, 4722, 6064, 6071, 5960, 4830, 5099, 5492-5495, 4811-4812, 5228, 5883-5885, 5897, 5900, 5962, 6016, 6028, 6033, 6036, 6044, 6066, 6009, 6019, 6087, 6033-6034, 4704, 4741-4743, 4745-4746, 4748-4752, 4754, 4900, pp 1-40.
A transcript, formerly possessed by the Exegetic-Philanthropical Society, Stockholm, which was in the possession of J Hyde in 1906. Its present whereabouts are unknown. It appears to have been compiled with a view to collecting the references to Swedish people made by Swedenborg in the text of the work.
Document not seen; description recorded from Hyde 530, 903, 2172.

X 47/05/La 1846/1 **1846** Hyde 1645, 3060
Supplementum ad Eman. Swedenborgii Diarium | continens | Literas ac delineationes scripturae | assimilatas, et arte lithographica expressas
8vo
title and text on pp numbered N. 1 to N. 26.
Edited by J F I Tafel, published in *Eman. Swedenborgii Diarii Spirituales Pars Septima continens Appendicem* <Hyde 3060> Tübingen and London.
Diagrams sketched by Swedenborg in the MS of *Experientiae Spirituales* are reproduced as follows.
N. 6, n 5249; N. 7, n 5278; N. 8, n 5290; N. 9, n 5303; N. 10, n 5317, 5466, 5467; N. 14, n 5946.
The Swedish original of n 6027 is reproduced on N. 14-21.
UK: SOC, CON, NCC, NR; GER: GSU, WLB; NET: GEN; USA: ANC

X 47/05/La 1920/1 **1920** Hyde 1631/1
26 | 4626 De Charitate et fide
8vo
Facsimile reproduction of La O/7 = Hyde 915, n 4626[a], printed on frontispiece to 62/01/Sw 2/1 = Hyde 1631/1.
UK: SOC; SWE: GUB

X 47/05/La 1988/1, **D** Ge 1988/1 **1988** Hyde —
Visionsskizzen | Swedenborgs
Handschrift aus | seinem Notizbuch
A4 perfect bound
text, p 110.
Facsimile reproduction of pp numbered N. 10, 11, 6, 7, 8, and 9 in X 47/05/La 1846/1 = Hyde 1645, 3060.
text, p 165.
Published in *Emanuel Swedenborg 1688–1772 Naturforscher und Kundiger der Überwelt* <**D** Ge 1988/1> Stuttgart.
UK: SOC, NR; GER: WLB; NET: KB; SWE: UPP; SWI: ZÜR; USA: ANC

X 47/05/La 1998/1 **1998** Hyde —
26 | 4626 De Charitate et fide
8vo
Facsimile reproduction of La O/7 = Hyde 915, n 4626[a], printed on frontispiece to 62/01/Sw 2/2 = Hyde 1631/–.
UK: SOC; SWE: ROY, HNK

LATIN/ENGLISH EXTRACTS

X 47/05/LaEn 1828/1 **1828** Hyde 531

EXTRACTS FROM THE MANUSCRIPT DIARY OF E. SWEDENBORG.

8vo

English title and text n 2040-2041, p 291; n 5670-5672, pp 292-293.

Latin text n 2040-2041 <misprinted as 2140, 2141>, pp 291-292; n 5670-5672, p 293.

Translated by M Sibly and published in *The Intellectual Repository* London. In 1828 no Latin text had been published, but it appears that Sibly had access to the transcript made by P B Chastanier <Hyde 514; see La O/1>. This is confirmed from the fact that La O/9 = Hyde 2163, also a transcript by Chastanier, has an attached page bearing notes written by Sibly.

UK: SOC, BL, CHT, CON, NCC, NR; USA: ANC

X 47/05/LaEn 1840/1 **1840** Hyde 532

Diary of Memorable Things

8vo

Latin text n 1166, p 410.

English title, p 410; text n 1166, p 411.

Translated by M Sibly and published in *The Intellectual Repository* London. In 1840 no Latin text had been published, but it appears that Sibly had access to the transcript made by P B Chastanier. <Hyde 514; see La O/1>.

UK: SOC, BL, CHT, CON, NCC, NR; USA: ANC

X 47/05/LaEn 1849/1 **1849** Hyde —

<untitled>

8vo

text n 3959, p 130.

Edited and translated by G Bush, published in *The New Church Repository* New York, in an article entitled 'Swedenborg, Aristotle and the Antipodes'.

UK: SOC, NR

X 47/05/LaEn 1849/2 **1849** Hyde —

ON A PASSAGE IN THE SPIRITUAL DIARY.

8vo

title and text n 4459, pp 559-560.

Edited and translated by 'Amicus', published in *The New Church Repository* New York, in a letter to the editor.

UK: SOC, NR

LATIN/SWEDISH EXTRACTS

X 47/05/LaSw 1790/1 **1790** Hyde 34259a, 3500

<untitled>

foolscap folded in half

text: Latin transcriptions, pp 1-136; Swedish translations, 36 unnumbered pages; 4 pp blank; Index, 4 pp.

The 'Index' lists in page order the titles of the paragraphs transcribed.

The MS is in UK: CON <Archives A/18>, and is in the handwriting of A Nordenskjöld, with occasional notes and translations in English written by J A Tulk, and also comparisons of the part copied in Latin by Nordenskjöld with Dr Ekenstam's copies.

On the flyleaf is written: 'J. A. Tulk, 1790. The gift of Mr. Augustus Nordenskjold.'
On p 134 is written the following 'Remark': 'The following are copied from three small manuscript books brought from Sweden by Dr. Fabian Wilhelm Ekenstam (1814). The originals, or most of them, in the handwriting of E. S., including his diary, are in the possession of Mr. Sibley, who purchased them of Mr. Chastanier, through Mr. Dawes for two guineas. These original manuscripts were brought from the Royal Library in Stockholm by Mr. Wadstrom, who was responsible for their safe return, as well as for the mpt copy of the Apoc. Explicata. All these manuscripts, therefore, are strictly the property of the above Royal Library. Mr. Wadstrom wrote me from Paris to procure them from B. Chastanier, and return them to Sweden, which B. C. refused. J. A. Tulk, 15th Feby., 1814.' <*stet* Sibley>
UK: CON

ENGLISH

Translators:
- En 1 John Henry Smithson
- En 2 George Bush
- En 3 G Bush and J H Smithson
- En 4 James Frederick Buss
- En 5 William H Acton and A Wynne Acton
- En 6 John Durban Odhner

The first proposals to print *Diarium Spirituale* in English were issued by the London Universal Society for the Promotion of the New Jerusalem Church in 1791, in a syllabus of 8 pages, entitled 'PROPOSALS *for Printing by Subscription*, Emanuel Swedenborg's SPIRITUAL DIARY; *or a Collection of his Experiences and Aphorisms, from the year* 1746 to 1764.—*carefully classed under proper Heads, and faithfully translated from his Manuscripts, in order to preserve, as much as possible, whatever flowed from his inspired pen, and to assist the sincere lovers of spiritual and celestial truths with fresh supplies for their confirmation therein; by a society of gentlemen. Ut ædificentur muri Hierosolymæ*, Psalm LI. 18. 1791.' The translation was to have been made by P B Chastanier, who held the MSS at this time. The proposals were accompanied by extracts as specimens of the work <see X 47/05/En 1791/3 = Hyde 534>, and were advertised in *The New Jerusalem Magazine* London, in the Appendix, p 304, published in 1791.

47/05/En 1/1 **1846** Hyde 519, 932, 3120
THE | SPIRITUAL DIARY | OF | EMANUEL SWEDENBORG; OR, | A BRIEF RECORD, DURING TWENTY YEARS, | OF HIS SUPERNATURAL EXPERIENCE. | LATELY PUBLISHED FROM THE LATIN MANUSCRIPTS OF THE AUTHOR, BY | DR. J. F. I. TAFEL, OF THE ROYAL UNIVERSITY OF TÜBINGEN. | Translated from the Original | BY J. H. SMITHSON. | <short rule> | VOL. I. | <short rule> | LONDON: | NEWBERY, 6, KING STREET, HOLBORN; | HODSON, CLIFFORD'S INN PASSAGE, FLEET STREET. | MANCHESTER: KENWORTHY, CATEATON STREET. | 1846.
verso: MANCHESTER: | CAVE AND SEVER, PRINTERS, ST. ANN'S STREET.
half title: <double rule> | THE SPIRITUAL DIARY | OF | EMANUEL SWEDENBORG. | <double rule>
8vo
half title and title leaves, 4 pp; Preface, pp v-xv; text n 149-170, 178-1538, pp 1-456; Appendix, pp i-iv; Errata et emendanda, p iv.
Partly reprinted from X En 1844/1 and 1845/1 = Hyde 536 and 537. The Appendix contains a reconstruction of some of the headings of n 1-148 <Hyde 932>, deduced from the volume of the

Latin edition of the Index to the work which had been published in 1846 <La 1/8 = Hyde 930>.
UK: SOC, CON; NET: GEN; SWE: ROY; USA: FOU

47/05/En 2/1 **1849** Hyde 900, 3125

THE | SPIRITUAL DIARY | OF | EMANUEL SWEDENBORG; | OR | A BRIEF RECORD, DURING TWENTY YEARS, OF HIS | SUPERNATURAL EXPERIENCE. | PUBLISHED FROM THE LATIN MANUSCRIPTS OF THE AUTHOR BY J. F. I. TAFEL, | OF THE ROYAL UNIVERSITY OF TUBINGEN. | TRANSLATED FROM THE ORIGINAL | BY GEORGE BUSH. | <short wavy rule> | VOL. III. | <short wavy rule> | NEW-YORK: | PUBLISHED BY LEWIS C. BUSH, 16 HOWARD STREET. | BOSTON: OTIS CLAPP, 23 SCHOOL STREET. | LONDON: J. S. HODSON AND W. NEWBERY. | <short rule> | 1849.
verso: <short rule> | J. P. PRALL *Printer*, 9 Spruce Street, N. Y.
half title: <double rule> | THE SPIRITUAL DIARY | OF | EMANUEL SWEDENBORG. | <double rule>
8vo
half title and title leaves, 4 pp; text: 3 unnumbered articles, n 3428-4544, pp 1-300; Addendum <the Latin text of n 3453>, p 300.
The body of the text contains no English translation of n 3453.
UK: SOC, CON, NR

47/05/En 1/2 **1850** Hyde 520, 933, 3121

THE | SPIRITUAL DIARY | OF | EMANUEL SWEDENBORG; | OR | A BRIEF RECORD, DURING TWENTY YEARS, OF HIS | SUPERNATURAL EXPERIENCE. | PUBLISHED FROM THE LATIN MANUSCRIPTS OF THE AUTHOR BY J. F. I. TAFEL, | OF THE ROYAL UNIVERSITY OF TUBINGEN. | TRANSLATED FROM THE ORIGINAL | BY J. H. SMITHSON. | <short wavy rule> | VOL. I. | <short wavy rule> | NEW-YORK: | PUBLISHED BY LEWIS C. BUSH, 16 HOWARD STREET. | BOSTON: OTIS CLAPP, 23 SCHOOL STREET. | LONDON: J. S. HODSON AND W. NEWBERY. | <short rule> | 1850.
verso: <short rule> | J. P. PRALL *Printer*, 9 Spruce Street, N. Y.
half title: <double rule> | THE SPIRITUAL DIARY | OF | EMANUEL SWEDENBORG. | <double rule>
8vo
half title and title leaves, 4 pp; Advertisement <editorial note by G Bush>, p v; Preface by J H Smithson, dated September 1846, pp vii-xiv; text, n 149-170, 178-1538, pp 15-370; Appendix, pp 371-379.
The Appendix contains a reconstruction of some of the headings of n 1-148, expanded by G Bush from the one made by J H Smithson in En 1/1, using the second volume of the Latin edition which had been published in 1847 <La 1/9 = Hyde 933>.
UK: SOC, CON, NR

47/05/En 2/2 **1871** Hyde 521, 3123

THE | SPIRITUAL DIARY | OF | EMANUEL SWEDENBORG; | OR, | A BRIEF RECORD OF HIS SUPERNATURAL | EXPERIENCE. | FROM MARCH 19 TO JUNE 22, 1748. | <short rule> | *Translated from the Original,* | BY GEORGE BUSH, | LATE PROF. OF HEB. AND ORIENT. LIT. IN N. Y. CITY UNIVERSITY. | <short rule> | EDITED BY | SAMUEL BESWICK. | PART I. VOL. II. | BOSTON: | HENRY H. AND T. W. CARTER. | 1871.
verso: Entered according to Act of Congress, in the year 1871, by | HENRY H. & T. W. CARTER, | In the Office of the Librarian of Congress, at Washington. | John C. Regan & Co., Electrotypers and Stereotypers, | 65 Congress Street, Boston.
small 8vo
title leaf, 2 pp; Preface, pp iii-iv; Introduction, pp v-x; text n 1539-2381, pp 1- 230.
UK: SOC; SWE: UPP

47/05/En 2/3 **1872** Hyde 522, 3124

THE | SPIRITUAL DIARY | OF | EMANUEL SWEDENBORG; | OR, | A BRIEF RECORD OF HIS SUPERNATURAL | EXPERIENCE. | FROM MARCH 19 TO JUNE 22, 1748. | <short rule> | *Translated from the Original,* | BY GEORGE BUSH, | LATE PROF. OF HEB. AND ORIENT. LIT. IN N. Y. CITY UNIVERSITY. | <short rule> | EDITED BY | SAMUEL BESWICK. | PART II. VOL. II. | BOSTON: | CARTER AND PETTEE, | 1872.
small 8vo
title leaf, 2 pp; text n 2382-3427, pp 1- 330.
UK: SOC; SWE: UPP

47/05/En 3/1 **1883** Hyde 523, 934, 3122

THE | SPIRITUAL DIARY | OF | EMANUEL SWEDENBORG | *BEING THE RECORD DURING TWENTY YEARS OF* | *HIS SUPERNATURAL EXPERIENCE* | TRANSLATED BY | PROFESSOR GEORGE BUSH, M.A. | AND THE | REV. JOHN H. SMITHSON | *IN FIVE VOLUMES* | VOLUME I. | NUMBERS 1 TO 1538 | JAMES SPEIRS | 36 BLOOMSBURY STREET, LONDON. | 1883
half title: THE SPIRITUAL DIARY | OF | EMANUEL SWEDENBORG
imprint: <short rule> | MUIR, PATERSON AND BRODIE, PRINTERS, EDINBURGH.
8vo
half title and title leaves, 4 pp; Translators' preface, pp iii-xii; text n 149-170, 178-1538, pp 1-472; imprint, p 472.
Reprinted from En 1/1 = Hyde 519, with some alterations to the preface; n 1-148 are reprinted from La 1/9 = Hyde 933.
UK: SOC, NR; NET: GEN; SWE: ROY, UPP

47/05/En 3/2 **1883** Hyde 524, 3126

THE | SPIRITUAL DIARY | OF | EMANUEL SWEDENBORG | *BEING THE RECORD DURING TWENTY YEARS OF* | *HIS SUPERNATURAL EXPERIENCE* | TRANSLATED BY | PROFESSOR GEORGE BUSH, M.A. | AND THE | REV. JOHN H. SMITHSON | *IN FIVE VOLUMES* | VOLUME II. | NUMBERS 1539 TO 3240 | JAMES SPEIRS | 36 BLOOMSBURY STREET, LONDON. | 1883
half title: THE SPIRITUAL DIARY | OF | EMANUEL SWEDENBORG
imprint: <short rule> | JAMES MUIR, PRINTER, EDINBURGH.
8vo
half title and title leaves, 4 pp; text n 1539-3240, pp 1-492; imprint, p 492.
Reprinted from En 2/2 and 3 = Hyde 521 and 522.
UK: SOC, NR; NET: GEN; SWE: ROY, UPP

47/05/En 3/3 **1883** Hyde 525, 901, 3127

THE | SPIRITUAL DIARY | OF | EMANUEL SWEDENBORG | *BEING THE RECORD DURING TWENTY YEARS OF* | *HIS SUPERNATURAL EXPERIENCE* | TRANSLATED BY | PROFESSOR GEORGE BUSH, M.A. | AND THE | REV. JOHN H. SMITHSON | *IN FIVE VOLUMES* | VOLUME III. | NUMBERS 3241 TO 4544 | JAMES SPEIRS | 36 BLOOMSBURY STREET, LONDON. | 1883
half title: THE SPIRITUAL DIARY | OF | EMANUEL SWEDENBORG
8vo
half title and title leaves, 4 pp; text n 3241-4544, pp 1-448.
Reprinted from En 2/3 and 3/3 = Hyde 521 and 901.
UK: SOC, NR; NET: GEN; SWE: ROY, UPP; AUS: SYD

47/05/En 2/4 **1886** Hyde 525/a, 3124/a

THE | SPIRITUAL DIARY | OF | EMANUEL SWEDENBORG; | OR, | A BRIEF RECORD OF HIS

SUPERNATURAL | EXPERIENCE. | FROM MARCH 19 TO JUNE 22, 1748. | *TRANSLATED FROM THE ORIGINAL | BY* | GEORGE BUSH, | LATE PROFESSOR OF HEBREW AND ORIENTAL LITERATURE | IN NEW YORK CITY UNIVERSITY. | *EDITED BY* | SAMUEL BESWICK. | PARTS I. AND II. VOLUME. II. | <short rule> | BOSTON: T. H. CARTER. | For sale at the Rooms of the MASS. New Church Union, 169 Tremont St., | and at 20 Cooper Union, New York. | 1886.
verso: Entered according to Act of Congress, in the year 1871, by | HENRY H. & T. W. CARTER, | In the Office of the Librarian of Congress, at Washington.
small 8vo
title leaf, 2 pp; Preface, pp iii-iv; Introduction, pp v-x; text: n 1539-2381, pp 1-230; n 2382-3427, pp 1-330. Reprint of En 2/2, 3 = Hyde 312, 3124.
UK: SOC; USA: ANC

47/05/En 4/1 **1889** Hyde 919, 2168, 3128
THE | SPIRITUAL DIARY | OF | EMANUEL SWEDENBORG | *BEING THE RECORD DURING TWENTY YEARS OF | HIS SUPERNATURAL EXPERIENCE* | TRANSLATED BY | PROFESSOR GEORGE BUSH, M.A. | AND THE | REV. JAMES F. BUSS | *IN FIVE VOLUMES* | VOLUME IV. | NUMBERS 4545 TO 5659 | INCLUDING THE PORTION USUALLY KNOWN AS THE "SMALLER DIARY" | JAMES SPEIRS | 36 BLOOMSBURY STREET, LONDON. | 1889
half title: THE SPIRITUAL DIARY | OF | EMANUEL SWEDENBORG
imprint: MORRISON AND GIBB, PRINTERS, EDINBURGH.
8vo
half title and title leaves, 4 pp; Editor's preface by J F Buss, pp v-xxv; Table of contents, pp xxvii-xxxvii; text: n 4545m-4715m, [4716m]-[4792m], pp 1-91; n 4545-5659, pp 91-494; imprint, p 494.
The paragraphs in which La 0/7 = Hyde 915 are translated are denoted by the suffix "m"; those which Swedenborg did not number are here numbered [4716m] to [4792m].
n [4545m]-[4792m] and 4545-5401 were translated by G Bush and revised by J F Buss; n 5402-5659 were translated by J F Buss.
UK: SOC, NR; NET: GEN; SWE: ROY, UPP; AUS: SYD

47/05/En 4/2 **1902** Hyde 2169, 3129
THE | SPIRITUAL DIARY | OF | EMANUEL SWEDENBORG | *BEING THE RECORD DURING TWENTY YEARS OF | HIS SUPERNATURAL EXPERIENCE* | TRANSLATED BY THE | REV. JAMES F. BUSS | *IN FIVE VOLUMES* | VOLUME V. | NUMBERS 5660 TO THE END | AND INDEX TO THE WHOLE WORK | JAMES SPEIRS | 36 BLOOMSBURY STREET, LONDON. | 1902
half title: THE SPIRITUAL DIARY | OF | EMANUEL SWEDENBORG
imprint: <short rule> | *Robert R. Sutherland, Printer, Edinburgh.*
8vo
half title and title leaves, 4 pp; Translator's preface, pp v-xvi; Contents, pp xvii-xxii; text: n 5660-6096, [6097]-[6110], pp 1-234; Index, pp 235-391; Key to the two systems of numbering paragraphs of the 'Smaller Diary' <La 0/7> in the *Swedenborg Concordance* compiled by J F Potts and in vol IV of the present version, pp 392-393; imprint, p 393; catalogue, 2 pp.
UK: SOC, NR; NET: GEN; SWE: ROY, UPP; AUS: SYD

47/05/En 4/3 **1960** Hyde 2169/1, 3129/1
THE | SPIRITUAL DIARY | OF | EMANUEL SWEDENBORG | *BEING THE RECORD DURING TWENTY YEARS OF | HIS SUPERNATURAL EXPERIENCE* | TRANSLATED BY THE | REV. JAMES F. BUSS | *IN FIVE VOLUMES* | VOLUME V. | NUMBERS 5660 TO THE END | AND INDEX TO THE WHOLE WORK | JAMES SPEIRS | 1 BLOOMSBURY STREET, LONDON | 1902

half title: THE SPIRITUAL DIARY | OF | EMANUEL SWEDENBORG
8vo
half title and title leaves, 4 pp; Translator's preface, pp v-xvi; Contents, pp xvii-xxii; text n 5660-6096, [6097]-[6110], pp 1-234; Index, pp 235-391; Key to the two systems of numbering paragraphs of the 'Smaller Diary' <La 0/7> in the *Swedenborg Concordance* compiled by J F Potts and in vol IV of the present version, pp 392-393; catalogue, 2 pp.
Xerographed edition. An authorized reprint of En 4/2, produced by microfilm-Xerox by University Microfilms, Inc., Ann Arbor MI.
UK: soc

47/05/En 5/1 **1962** Hyde 523/1, 934/1, 3122/1
THE | SPIRITUAL DIARY | Records and Notes made by | EMANUEL SWEDENBORG | between 1745 and 1765 | from his experiences in the spiritual world | PUBLISHED POSTHUMOUSLY | SWEDENBORG SOCIETY (INCORPORATED) | 20-21 Bloomsbury Way | London, W.C.1 | 1962
verso: *Printed in England by Eyre and Spottiswoode Limited,* | *Her Majesty's Printers at The Thanet Press*
8vo
title leaf, 2 pp; Contents, p i; General preface, pp iii-viii; Special preface to vol 1, pp ix-xii; Reconstruction, from the Index, of the 'missing' n 1-148, pp 1-3, 6-19; translation of the 'Bath Fragment' <47/01>, p 4, and photographic reproduction of the MS , with editorial notes, inserted between pp 4 and 5; text: translation of three unnumbered paragraphs found at the beginning of Codex 6, p 20; n 153-171, 178-199, 152, 200-205, 149-151, 206-1538, pp 21-397; List of amended readings of the Latin text, pp 399-412; Notes and comments on the Latin text, pp 413-415; List of Swedish words and phrases found in the text, p 416; transcript of the 'Bath fragment', p 417; Transcript of the three unnumbered paragraphs found at the beginning of Codex 6, p 418; Notes on the conjugations of Hebrew verbs found after n 192 in the MS, pp 419-420; Information concerning the dates and order of writing of the 'missing numbers', compiled by F F Coulson from *The Word Explained* <45/05>, pp 421-423; Index of words and subjects, pp 425-448.
The translation was first made in draft by W H Acton; after his death it was finalized by A W Acton with F F Coulson as his consultant. The amended readings of the Latin text were based on work done by A Acton, C Vinet, and W H Acton.
UK: soc, con, ncc, pur, nr; NET: gen; SWE: upp; USA: anc; AUS: syd

47/05/En 3/4 **1962** Hyde 523/–
<<THE | SPIRITUAL DIARY | OF | EMANUEL SWEDENBORG | *BEING THE RECORD DURING TWENTY YEARS OF* | *HIS SUPERNATURAL EXPERIENCE* | TRANSLATED BY | PROFESSOR GEORGE BUSH, M.A. | AND THE | REV. JOHN H. SMITHSON | *IN FIVE VOLUMES* | VOLUME I. | NUMBERS 1 TO 1538 | ...>>
half title: <<THE SPIRITUAL DIARY | OF | EMANUEL SWEDENBORG>>
8vo
half title and title leaves, 4 pp; Translators' preface, pp iii-xii; text n 149-170, 178-1538, pp 1-472.
Photo offset reprint of En 3/1 = Hyde 523, 934 by University Microfilms, Inc., Arbor MI.
Copy not seen; description deduced from En 3/1.
SWE: upp

47/05/En 3/5 **1962** Hyde 524/–
<<THE | SPIRITUAL DIARY | OF | EMANUEL SWEDENBORG | *BEING THE RECORD DURING TWENTY YEARS OF* | *HIS SUPERNATURAL EXPERIENCE* | TRANSLATED BY | PROFESSOR GEORGE BUSH, M.A. | AND THE | REV. JOHN H. SMITHSON | *IN FIVE VOLUMES* | VOLUME II. |

NUMBERS 1539 TO 3240 | ...>>
half title: <<THE SPIRITUAL DIARY | OF | EMANUEL SWEDENBORG>>
8vo
half title and title leaves, 4 pp; text n 1539-3240, pp 1-492.
Photo offset reprint of En 3/2 = Hyde 524 by University Microfilms, Inc., Ann Arbor MI.
Copy not seen; description deduced from En 3/2.
SWE: UPP

47/05/En 3/6 **1962** Hyde 525/–
<<THE | SPIRITUAL DIARY | OF | EMANUEL SWEDENBORG | *BEING THE RECORD DURING TWENTY YEARS OF* | *HIS SUPERNATURAL EXPERIENCE* | TRANSLATED BY | PROFESSOR GEORGE BUSH, M.A. | AND THE | REV. JOHN H. SMITHSON | *IN FIVE VOLUMES* | VOLUME III. | NUMBERS 3241 TO 4544 | ...>>
half title: <<THE SPIRITUAL DIARY | OF | EMANUEL SWEDENBORG>>
8vo
half title and title leaves, 4 pp; text n 3241-4544, pp 1-448.
Photo offset reprint of En 3/3 = Hyde 525 by University Microfilms, Inc., Ann Arbor MI.
Copy not seen; description deduced from En 3/3.
SWE: UPP

47/05/En 4/4 **1962** Hyde 919/–, 2168/–, 3128/–
<<THE | SPIRITUAL DIARY | OF | EMANUEL SWEDENBORG | *BEING THE RECORD DURING TWENTY YEARS OF* | *HIS SUPERNATURAL EXPERIENCE* | TRANSLATED BY | PROFESSOR GEORGE BUSH, M.A. | AND THE | REV. JAMES F. BUSS | *IN FIVE VOLUMES* | VOLUME IV. | NUMBERS 4545 TO 5659 | INCLUDING THE PORTION USUALLY KNOWN AS THE "SMALLER DIARY" | ...>>
half title: <<THE SPIRITUAL DIARY | OF | EMANUEL SWEDENBORG>>
8vo
half title and title leaves, 4 pp; Editor's preface by J F Buss, pp v-xxv; Table of contents, pp xxvii-xxxvii; text n 4545m-4715m, [4716m]-[4792m], pp 1-91; n 4545-5659, pp 91-494.
Photo offset reprint of En 4/1 = Hyde 919, 2168 by University Microfilms, Inc., Ann Arbor MI.
Copy not seen; description deduced from En 4/1.
SWE: UPP

47/05/En 4/5 **1962** Hyde 2169/–, 3129/–
<<THE | SPIRITUAL DIARY | OF | EMANUEL SWEDENBORG | *BEING THE RECORD DURING TWENTY YEARS OF* | *HIS SUPERNATURAL EXPERIENCE* | TRANSLATED BY | < THE | SPIRITUAL DIARY | OF | EMANUEL SWEDENBORG | *BEING THE RECORD DURING TWENTY YEARS OF* | *HIS SUPERNATURAL EXPERIENCE* | TRANSLATED BY | THE REV. JAMES F. BUSH | *IN FIVE VOLUMES* | VOLUME V. | NUMBERS 5660 TO THE END AND INDEX TO THE WHOLE WORK | ...>>
half title: <<THE SPIRITUAL DIARY | OF | EMANUEL SWEDENBORG>>
8vo
half title and title leaves, 4 pp; Translator's preface, pp v-xvi; Contents, pp xvii-xxii; text n 5660-6096, [6097]-[6110], pp 1-234; Index, pp 235-391; Key to the two systems of numbering paragraphs of the 'Smaller Diary' <La O/7> in the *Swedenborg Concordance* compiled by J F Potts and in vol IV of the present version, pp 392-393.
Photo offset reprint of En 4/2 = Hyde 2169 by University Microfilms, Inc., Ann Arbor MI.
Copy not seen; description deduced from En 4/2.
SWE: UPP

47/05/En 5/2 **1977** Hyde 523/–

<<THE | SPIRITUAL DIARY | Records and Notes made by | EMANUEL SWEDENBORG | between 1745 and 1765 | from his experiences in the spiritual world | PUBLISHED POSTHUMOUSLY | SWEDENBORG FOUNDATION, INC. | NEW YORK | * * * | THE ACADEMY OF THE NEW CHURCH | BRYN ATHYN, PENNSYLVANIA>>

verso: <<First published in Latin, Stuttgart and Tubingen, 1843-1845 | First English translation Volume I published in England, 1846 | First English translation Volume I published in U.S.A., 1850 | Fourth printing this edition Volume II-V U.S.A., 1978 | ISBN: 0—87785—081—X | *Library of Congress Catalog Number 77-93540* | Printed in the United States of America>>

half title: <<THE SPIRITUAL DIARY | OF | EMANUEL SWEDENBORG>>

8vo

title leaf, 2 pp; Contents, p i; General preface, pp iii-viii; Special preface to vol 1, pp ix-xii; Reconstruction, from the Index, of the 'missing' n 1-148, pp 1-3, 6-19; translation of the 'Bath Fragment' <47/01>, p 4, and photographic reproduction of the MS, with editorial notes, inserted between pp 4 and 5; text: translation of three unnumbered paragraphs found at the beginning of Codex 6, p 20; n 153-171, 178-199, 152, 200-205, 149-151, 206-1538, pp 21-397; List of amended readings of the Latin text, pp 399-412; Notes and comments on the Latin text, pp 413-415; List of Swedish words and phrases found in the text, p 416; transcript of the 'Bath fragment', p 417; transcript of the three unnumbered paragraphs found at the beginning of Codex 6, p 418; Notes on the conjugations of Hebrew verbs found after n 192 in the MS, pp 419-420; Information concerning the dates and order of writing of the 'missing numbers', compiled by F F Coulson from *The Word Explained*, pp 421-423; Index of words and subjects, pp 425-448.

Photographic reprint of En 5/1.

Copy not seen; description deduced from En 5/1.

USA: ANC, FOU

47/05/En 3/7 **1978** Hyde 524/–, 3126/–

THE | SPIRITUAL DIARY | OF | EMANUEL SWEDENBORG | *BEING THE RECORD DURING TWENTY YEARS OF* | *HIS SUPERNATURAL EXPERIENCE* | TRANSLATED BY | GEORGE BUSH | AND | JOHN H. SMITHSON | *IN FIVE VOLUMES* | VOLUME II. | NUMBERS 1539 TO 3240 | SWEDENBORG FOUNDATION, INC. | NEW YORK | * * * | THE ACADEMY OF THE NEW CHURCH | BRYN ATHYN, PENNSYLVANIA

verso: First published in Latin, Stuttgart and Tubingen, 1843-1845 | First English translation Volume I published in England, 1846 | First English translation Volume I published in U.S.A., 1850 | Fourth printing this edition Volume II-V U.S.A., 1978 | ISBN: 0—87785—081—X | *Library of Congress Catalog Number 77-93540* | Printed in the United States of America

half title: THE SPIRITUAL DIARY | OF | EMANUEL SWEDENBORG

imprint: <short rule> | JAMES MUIR, PRINTER, EDINBURGH.

8vo

half title and title leaves, 4 pp; text n 1539-3240, pp 1-492; imprint, p 492.

Photographic reprint of En 3/2 = Hyde 524, 3126.

USA: ANC, FOU

47/05/En 3/8 **1978** Hyde 525/–, 901/–, 3127/–

THE | SPIRITUAL DIARY | OF | EMANUEL SWEDENBORG | *BEING THE RECORD DURING TWENTY YEARS OF* | *HIS SUPERNATURAL EXPERIENCE* | TRANSLATED BY | GEORGE BUSH | AND | JOHN H. SMITHSON | *IN FIVE VOLUMES* | VOLUME III. | NUMBERS 3241 TO 4544 | SWEDENBORG FOUNDATION, INC. | NEW YORK | * * * | THE ACADEMY OF THE NEW CHURCH | BRYN ATHYN, PENNSYLVANIA

verso: First published in Latin, Stuttgart and Tubingen, 1843-1845 | First English translation Volume I published in England, 1846 | First English translation Volume I published in U.S.A., 1850 | Fourth printing this edition Volume II-V U.S.A., 1978 | ISBN: 0—87785—081—X | *Library of Congress Catalog Number 77-93540* | Printed in the United States of America
half title: THE SPIRITUAL DIARY | OF | EMANUEL SWEDENBORG
8vo
half title and title leaves, 4 pp; text n 3241-4544, pp 1-448.
Photographic reprint of En 3/3 = Hyde 525, 901.
USA: ANC, FOU

47/05/En 4/6 1978 Hyde 919/–, 2168/–, 3128/–

THE | SPIRITUAL DIARY | OF | EMANUEL SWEDENBORG | *BEING THE RECORD DURING TWENTY YEARS OF* | *HIS SUPERNATURAL EXPERIENCE* | TRANSLATED BY | GEORGE BUSH | AND | JAMES F. BUSS | *IN FIVE VOLUMES* | VOLUME IV. | NUMBERS 4545 TO 5659 | INCLUDING THE PORTION USUALLY KNOWN AS THE "SMALLER DIARY" | SWEDENBORG FOUNDATION, INC. | NEW YORK | * * * | THE ACADEMY OF THE NEW CHURCH | BRYN ATHYN, PENNSYLVANIA
verso: First published in Latin, Stuttgart and Tubingen, 1843-1845 | First English translation Volume I published in England, 1846 | First English translation Volume I published in U.S.A., 1850 | Fourth printing this edition Volume II-V U.S.A., 1978 | ISBN: 0—87785—081—X | *Library of Congress Catalog Number 77-93540* | Printed in the United States of America
half title: THE SPIRITUAL DIARY | OF | EMANUEL SWEDENBORG
imprint: MORRISON AND GIBB, PRINTERS, EDINBURGH.
8vo
half title and title leaves, 4 pp; Editor's preface by J F Buss, pp v-xxv; Table of contents, pp xxvii-xxxvii; text n 4545m-4715m, [4716m]-[4792m], pp 1-91; n 4545-5659, pp 91-494; imprint, p 494.
Reprint of En 4/1 = Hyde 919, 2168.
USA: ANC, FOU

47/05/En 4/7 1978 Hyde 2169/–, 3129/–

<<THE | SPIRITUAL DIARY | OF | EMANUEL SWEDENBORG | *BEING THE RECORD DURING TWENTY YEARS OF* | *HIS SUPERNATURAL EXPERIENCE* | TRANSLATED BY | JAMES F. BUSS | *IN FIVE VOLUMES* | VOLUME V. | NUMBERS 5660 TO THE END | SWEDENBORG FOUNDATION, INC. | NEW YORK | * * * | THE ACADEMY OF THE NEW CHURCH | BRYN ATHYN, PENNSYLVANIA>>
verso: <<First published in Latin, Stuttgart and Tubingen, 1843-1845 | First English translation Volume I published in England, 1846 | First English translation Volume I published in U.S.A., 1850 | Fourth printing this edition Volume II-V U.S.A., 1978 | ISBN: 0—87785—081—X | *Library of Congress Catalog Number 77-93540* | Printed in the United States of America>>
half title: <<THE SPIRITUAL DIARY | OF | EMANUEL SWEDENBORG>>
imprint: << <short rule> | *Robert R. Sutherland, Printer, Edinburgh.*>>
8vo
half title and title leaves, 4 pp; Translator's preface, pp v-xvi; Contents, pp xvii-xxii; text n 5660-6096, [6097]-[6110], pp 1-234; Index, pp 235-391; Key to the two systems of numbering the paragraphs of the 'Smaller Diary' <La O/7> in the *Swedenborg Concordance* compiled by J F Potts and in vol IV of the present version, pp 392-393; imprint, p 393.
Photographic reprint of En 4/2 = Hyde 2169.
Copy not seen; description deduced from En 4/2.
USA: ANC, FOU

47/05/En 6/1 **1998** Hyde 3122/2

Emanuel Swedenborg's Diary, | recounting | SPIRITUAL EXPERIENCES | during the years 1745 to 1765 | FIRST VOLUME | including indented paragraphs from | *The Word Explained*, and numbered paragraphs | from *The Bible Index* | General Church of the New Jerusalem | Bryn Athyn, Pennsylvania | 1998

verso: Copyright © 1998 by The General Church of the New | Jerusalem. | Library of Congress Cataloging-in-Publication Data | Swedenborg, Emanuel, 1688-1772. | [Diarium spirituale. English.] | Emanuel Swedenborg's diary, recounting Spiritual | experiences during the years 1745-1765. | p. cm. | Includes bibliographical references and index. | ISBN 0-945003-17-x (set). -- ISBN 0-945003-11-0 (v. 1: alk. paper) | 1. Swedenborg, Emanuel, 1688-1772--Diaries. 2. Swe- | denborgians–Sweden–Diaries. 3. Spiritual life. I. Title. | BX8712.S71998 | 289' .4'092--dc21 98-42631 | [B] CIP | First edition 1000 copies | Some of the Scripture quotations in this translation are | from *The New King James Version*, © 1979, 1980, 1982, | Thomas Nelson, Inc.

half title: SPIRITUAL EXPERIENCES

8vo

half title and title leaves, 4 pp; Translator's preface, pp i-x; text: n [1a]-[34a] <from *The Word of the Old Testament Explained* Tome I>, pp 1-24; n [35a]-[100a] <from *The Word of the Old Testament Explained* Tome II>, pp 25-62; n [101a]-[369a] <from *The Word of the Old Testament Explained* Tome III>, pp 63-171; n [370a]-[403a] <from *The Word of the Old Testament Explained* Tome IV>, pp 172-192; n 1-148⅓ <from Index to *Spiritual Experiences* and the 'Bath Fragment' 47/01>, pp 193-212; n [148¼]-[148⅙] <from *The Bible Index of Isaiah and Jeremiah*>, p 213; n 149-205 <extracted from *The Bible Index of Isaiah and Jeremiah*>, pp 214-243; n 206-972½ <extracted from *The Bible Index of the Prophetical Books*>, pp 244-530.

Translated by J D Odhner, with J S Rose, K P Nemitz, C C Odhner, S Shotwell, and R Longstaff as consultants.

UK: SOC, PUR, NR; SWE: ROY; USA: ANC

47/05/En 6/2 **1999** Hyde —

Emanuel Swedenborg's Diary, | recounting | SPIRITUAL EXPERIENCES | during the years 1745 to 1765 | SECOND VOLUME | containing paragraphs numbered | from 973 to 3427 | General Church of the New Jerusalem | Bryn Athyn, Pennsylvania | 1999

verso: Copyright © 1999 by The General Church of the New | Jerusalem. | Library of Congress Cataloging-in-Publication Data | Swedenborg, Emanuel, 1688-1772. | [Diarium spirituale. English.] | Emanuel Swedenborg's diary, recounting Spiritual | experiences during the years 1745-1765. | p. cm. | Includes bibliographical references and index. | ISBN 0-945003-17-x (set). -- ISBN 0-945003-12-9 (v. 2 | : alk. paper) | 1. Swedenborg, Emanuel, 1688-1772--Diaries. 2. Swe- | denborgians--Sweden--Diaries. 3. Spiritual life. I. Title. | BX8712.S71998 | 289' .4'092--dc21 98-42631 | [B] CIP | First edition 1000 copies | Translated by J. Durban Odhner | Some of the Scripture quotations in this translation are | from *The New King James Version*, © 1979, 1980, 1982, | Thomas Nelson, Inc.

half title: SPIRITUAL EXPERIENCES

8vo

half title and title leaves, 4 pp; Translator's preface, 1 p; text n 973-3427, pp 1-748.

Translated by J D Odhner, with K P Nemitz, C C Odhner, and R Longstaff as consultants.

UK: PUR, NR; SWE: ROY; USA: ANC

47/05/En 6/3 **2002** Hyde —

Emanuel Swedenborg's Diary, | recounting | SPIRITUAL EXPERIENCES | during the years 1745 to 1765 | THIRD VOLUME | containing paragraphs numbered | from 3427½ to 4832a | General

Church of the New Jerusalem | Bryn Athyn, Pennsylvania | 2002
verso: Copyright © 2002 by The General Church of the New | Jerusalem. | Library of Congress Cataloging-in-Publication Data | Swedenborg, Emanuel, 1688-1772. | [Diarium spirituale. English.] | Emanuel Swedenborg's diary, recounting Spiritual | experiences during the years 1745-1765. | p. cm. | Includes bibliographical references and index. | ISBN 0-945003-17-x (set). —ISBN 0-945003-13-7 (v.3 | : alk. paper) | 1. Swedenborg, Emanuel, 1688-1772--Diaries. 2. Swe- | denborgians--Sweden--Diaries. 3. Spiritual life. I. Title. | BX8712.S71998 | 289' .4'092--dc21 98-42631 | [B] CIP | First edition 1000 copies | Translated by J. Durban Odhner | Some of the Scripture quotations in this translation are | from *The New King James Version*, © 1979, 1980, 1982, | Thomas Nelson, Inc.
half title: SPIRITUAL EXPERIENCES
8vo
half title and title leaves, 4 pp; Translator's preface, pp i-ii; text n [3427½]-4544, pp 1-410; n 4545[a]-[4832a] <part of La 0/9, formerly called *The Minor Diary*>, pp 411-505.
Translated by J D Odhner, with K P Nemitz, C C Odhner, and R Longstaff as consultants.
UK: PUR, NR; NET: GEN; SWE: ROY; USA: ANC

47/05/En 5/3 **2002** Hyde 3122/1a

The Spiritual Diary | Records and Notes made by Emanuel Swedenborg | between 1746 and 1765 from his | Experiences in the Spiritual World | Volume one containing sections 1-1538 | Published Posthumously | <orn 12 x 26 mm> | The Swedenborg Society | 20-21 Bloomsbury Way | London WC1A 2TH | 2002
verso: ACKNOWLEDGEMENTS | The introductory essay, by Jorge Luis Borges, is translated from the Spanish by | Catherine Rodriguez-Nieto. Reprinted from *Emanuel Swedenborg: A Continuing Vision*, | ed. by Robin Larsen et al. (New York: Swedenborg Foundation, 1983), 349-353 with the | permission of the Swedenborg Foundation. | Many thanks to Emma Keast, Heather Ferguson and Paul McNeilly for their careful | reading of the text. Thanks also to Sasha Levy-Andersson for his help in | preparing this edition. | Volume one reprinted from the 1977 edition. | Translated by W H Acton and A W Acton, Consultant F F Coulson. | © 2002 The Swedenborg Society. | Published by: | The Swedenborg Society | Swedenborg House | 20-21 Bloomsbury Way | London WC1A 2TH | Book Design: Stephen McNeilly | Typeset at Swedenborg House. | Printed and bound in Great Britain | at Biddles. | ISBN 0 85448 132 X | British Library Cataloguing-in-Publication Data. | A Catalogue record for this book is available | from the British Library
half title: The Spiritual Diary | <short rule>
section title: Introductory Essay | <short rule> | Jorge Luis Borges
2nd section title: The Spiritual Diary | <short rule> | Emanuel Swedenborg
large 8vo
half title and title leaves, 4 pp; Preliminary note to the text by S McNeilly, pp v-vi; Table of contents, pp vii-xxxiv; section title leaf, pp xxxv-xxxvi; 'Testimony to the Invisible' by J L Borges, pp xxxvii-xlvi; 2nd section title leaf, pp xlvii-xlviii; text: n 1-148b, pp 1-15; 3 unnumbered paragraphs from Codex 6, p 16; n 153-171, 178-199, 152, 200-205, 149-151, 206-1538, pp 17-446.
Reprint of the text of En 5/2.
The book *Emanuel Swedenborg: A Continuing Vision* referred to on the verso of the title leaf was published in 1988.
UK: SOC, CON, NCC, PUR, NR; NET: GEN; SWE: ROY; USA: ANC

47/05/En 3/9 **2002** Hyde 3126/1

The Spiritual Diary | Records and Notes made by Emanuel Swedenborg | between 1746 and 1765 from his | Experiences in the Spiritual World | Volume two containing sections 1539-3240 | Published Posthumously | <orn 9 x 20 mm> | The Swedenborg Society | 20-21 Bloomsbury Way

| London WC1A 2TH | 2002
verso: ACKNOWLEDGEMENTS | Many thanks to Emma Keast, Paul McNeilly and Heather Ferguson for their | careful reading of the text. Thanks also to Sasha Levy-Andersson for his help in | preparing this edition. | Volume two reprinted from the 1978 edition published by the | Swedenborg Foundation. | Translated by George Bush and John H Smithson. | © 2002 The Swedenborg Society. | Published by: | The Swedenborg Society | Swedenborg House | 20-21 Bloomsbury Way | London WC1A 2TH | Book Design: Stephen McNeilly | Typeset at Swedenborg House. | Printed and bound in Great Britain | at Biddles. | ISBN 0 85448 133 8 | British Library Cataloguing-in-Publication Data. | A Catalogue record for this book is available | from the British Library
half title: The Spiritual Diary | <short rule>
section title: The Spiritual Diary | <short rule> | Emanuel Swedenborg
large 8vo
half title and title leaves, 4 pp; Table of contents, pp v-xxxvi; section title leaf, pp xxxvii-xxxviii; text n 1539-3240, pp 1-494.
Reprint of the text of En 3/5.
UK: soc, pur, nr; SWE: roy

47/05/En 3/10 **2003** Hyde 3127/1
The Spiritual Diary | Records and Notes made by Emanuel Swedenborg | between 1746 and 1765 from his | Experiences in the Spiritual World | Volume three containing sections 3241-4544 | Published Posthumously | <orn 9 x 20 mm> | The Swedenborg Society | 20-21 Bloomsbury Way | London WC1A 2TH | 2003
verso: ACKNOWLEDGEMENTS | Many thanks to Emma Keast, Paul McNeilly and Victoria Gordon for their | careful reading of the text. Thanks also to Sasha Levy-Andersson for his help in | preparing this edition. | Volume three reprinted from the 1978 edition published by the | Swedenborg Foundation. | Translated by George Bush and John H Smithson. | © 2003 The Swedenborg Society. | Published by: | The Swedenborg Society | Swedenborg House | 20-21 Bloomsbury Way | London WC1A 2TH | Book Design: Stephen McNeilly | Typeset at Swedenborg House. | Printed and bound in Great Britain | at Biddles. | ISBN 0 85448 135 4 | British Library Cataloguing-in-Publication Data. | A Catalogue record for this book is available | from the British Library
half title: The Spiritual Diary | <short rule>
section title: The Spiritual Diary | <short rule> | Emanuel Swedenborg
large 8vo
half title and title leaves, 4 pp; Table of contents, pp v-xxvi; section title leaf, pp xxvii-xxviii; text n 3241-4544, pp 1-451.
Reprint of En 3/6.
UK: soc, pur, nr; SWE: roy

47/05/En 4/8 **2004** Hyde 919/–, 3128/–
<<THE | SPIRITUAL DIARY | OF | EMANUEL SWEDENBORG | *BEING THE RECORD DURING TWENTY YEARS OF* | *HIS SUPERNATURAL EXPERIENCE* | TRANSLATED BY | PROFESSOR GEORGE BUSH, M.A. | AND THE | REV. JAMES F. BUSS | *IN FIVE VOLUMES* | VOLUME IV. | NUMBERS 4545 TO 5659 | INCLUDING THE PORTION USUALLY KNOWN AS THE "SMALLER DIARY" | JAMES SPEIRS | 36 BLOOMSBURY STREET, LONDON. | 1889>>
half title: <<THE SPIRITUAL DIARY | OF | EMANUEL SWEDENBORG>>
imprint: <<MORRISON AND GIBB, PRINTERS, EDINBURGH.>>
8vo
half title and title leaves, 4 pp; Editor's preface by J F Buss, pp v-xxv; Table of contents, pp xxvii-xxxvii; text: n 4545m-4715m, [4716m]-[4792m], pp 1-91; n 4545-5659, pp 91-494; imprint, p 494.

Photographic replica reprint of En 4/1, published by Kessinger Publishing, Whitefish MT.
Copy not seen; description deduced from En 4/1 and publisher's advertisement.

47/05/En 4/9 **2004** Hyde 2169/–, 3129/–
THE | SPIRITUAL DIARY | OF | EMANUEL SWEDENBORG | *BEING THE RECORD DURING TWENTY YEARS OF* | *HIS SUPERNATURAL EXPERIENCE* | TRANSLATED BY THE | REV. JAMES F. BUSS | *IN FIVE VOLUMES* | VOLUME V. | NUMBERS 5660 TO THE END | AND INDEX TO THE WHOLE WORK | JAMES SPEIRS | 36 BLOOMSBURY STREET, LONDON. | 1902
verso: <within a double rule border 141 x 113 mm, publisher's advertisement>
imprint: Printed in the United States | 1488861.voooo1B/8/A | <bar code> | 9 780766 143012
8vo
title leaf, 2 pp; Translator's preface, pp v-xvi; Contents, pp xvii-xxii; text n 5660-6096, [6097]-[6110], pp 1-234; Index, pp 235-391; Key to the two systems of numbering paragraphs of the 'Smaller Diary' <La 0/7> in the *Swedenborg Concordance* compiled by J F Potts and in vol IV of the present version, pp 392-393; imprint, p 394.
Photographic replica reprint of En 4/2, published by Kessinger Publishing, Whitefish MT.

47/05/En 4/10 **2008** Hyde 919/– , 2168/–, 3128/–
EMANUEL SWEDENBORG | SPIRITUAL DIARY | VOLUME IV | Translated by | George Bush and James F. Bush | <publisher's logo 9 x 8 mm> | BIBLIOBAZAAR
half title: SPIRITUAL DIARY
verso: Copyright © 2008 Bibliobazaar | All rights reserved
section title: SPIRITUAL DIARY
imprint: Printed in the United States | 148793LV00004B/1/A | <bar code> | 9 780559 061967
8vo
half title and title leaves, 4 pp; section title leaf, 2 pp; text <n 4545-5659, omitting the paragraph numbers>, pp 1-470. Footnotes gathered at the end of each section, the final group being on pp 471-478; imprint, 1 p.
A digitally scanned and freshly typeset print-on-demand version of En 4/1, omitting the 'Minor Diary' paragraphs 4545-4792, published by Bibliobazaar, Charleston SC.

ENGLISH EXTRACTS

X 47/05/En 1790/1 **1790** Hyde 2174
Passages extracted from the Manuscripts of E. SWEDENBORG.
8vo
title and text n <5793-5797>, pp 215-217.
Translated by P B Chastanier, published in *The New Jerusalem Magazine* London.
UK: SOC, CON, NCC, NR

X 47/05/En 1790/2 **1790** Hyde 2174
<untitled>
8vo
text n 5601, pp 242-243.
Translated by P B Chastanier, published in *The New Jerusalem Magazine* London.
UK: SOC, CON, NCC, NR

X 47/05/En 1790/3 **1790** Hyde 2174
Extracts from the manuscript journal of memorable relations, | Vol. II. N° 6011.
Concerning Deceit. Vol. II. N° 6053.

8vo
title and text, p 246.
Translated by P B Chastanier, published in *The New Jerusalem Magazine* London.
UK: SOC, CON, NCC, NR

X 47/05/En 1790/4 **1790** Hyde 921
In what manner it is to be understood, that as the Tree falls so | it remains. Translated from the manuscripts of Emanuel | Swedenborg.
8vo
title and text n <4645m-4646m>, p 251.
Translated by P B Chastanier, published in *The New Jerusalem Magazine* London.
The suffix 'm' indicates that these paragraphs were written in La 0/7; see the note in En 4/1.
UK: SOC, CON, NCC, NR

X 47/05/En 1791/1 **1791** Hyde 533
Important and useful extracts from the manuscripts of Emanuel | Swedenborg, *in a letter from* B. C. *to his friend* C. B. W.
8vo
title and text n <2993>, <2955>, pp 277-278.
Translated by P B Chastanier, published in the Appendix to *The New Jerusalem Magazine* London. In the title 'C. B. W.' refers to Carl Bernhard Wadström.
UK: SOC, CON, NCC, NR

X 47/05/En 1791/2 **1791** Hyde 904
<untitled>
8vo
text n <3427>, 4037-4039, <4322>, pp 297-299.
Translated by P B Chastanier, published in the Appendix to *The New Jerusalem Magazine* London.
UK: SOC, CON, NCC, NR

X 47/05/En 1791/3 **1791** Hyde 534
PROPOSALS | FOR PRINTING BY SUBSCRIPTION, | *Emanuel Swedenborg*'s | SPIRITUAL DIARY; | OR, | A COLLECTION OF | HIS EXPERIENCES AND APHORISMS, | FROM THE YEAR 1746, TO 1764. | Carefully classed under proper Heads, and faithfully translated | from his MANUSCRIPTS, in order to preserve, as much as | possible, whatever flowed from his inspired Pen, and to assist | the Sincere Lovers of SPIRITUAL and CELESTIAL TRUTH with | fresh Supplies for their Confirmation therein. | BY A SOCIETY OF GENTLEMEN. | <short orn rule> | *Ut ædificentur Muri Hierosolymæ.* | PSALM LI. 18. | <short orn rule> | M,DCC,XCI.
8vo
title, p 1; Proposal, pp 2-4, 8; text n 3114-3116, 2793-2794, 2993, pp 5-7.
Text translated by P B Chastanier. The prospectus is advertised in the Appendix to *The New Jerusalem Magazine* London 1791 on p 304.
UK: SOC

X 47/05/En 1791/4 **1791** Hyde 905
ON REGENERATION. | *Extracted from* EMANUEL SWEDENBORG'*s MS.* Spiritual | Diary, *n.* 3654.
8vo
title and text, pp 292-293.

Translated by P B Chastanier, published in *The New Magazine of Knowledge* London.
UK: SOC, CON, NCC, NR

X 47/05/En 1791/5 **1791** Hyde 905, 2175
<untitled>
8vo
text n 4206, 5002-5003, pp 348-350.
Translated by P B Chastanier, published in *The New Magazine of Knowledge* London.
UK: SOC, CON, NCC, NR

X 47/05/En 1791/6 **1791** Hyde 2175
<untitled>
8vo
text n 4824, p 391.
Translated by P B Chastanier, published in *The New Magazine of Knowledge* London.
UK: SOC, CON, NCC, NR

X 47/05/En 1791/7 **1791** Hyde 905
How many shall receive what is written by me.
8vo
title and text n 4422, pp 406-407.
Translated by P B Chastanier, published in *The New Magazine of Knowledge* London.
UK: SOC, CON, NCC, NR

X 47/05/En 1791/8 **1791** Hyde 2175
<untitled>
8vo
text n 5151, pp 445-446.
Translated by P B Chastanier, published in *The New Magazine of Knowledge* London.
UK: SOC, CON, NCC, NR

X 47/05/En 1792/1 **1792** Hyde 906
Punishments even of the damned are real Mercies.
8vo
title and text n 4421, pp 83-84.
Translated by P B Chastanier, published in *The New Jerusalem Journal* London.
UK: SOC, CON, NCC, NR

X 47/05/En 1792/2 **1792** Hyde 535
Concerning the YEAR 1757.
8vo
title and text, p 92.
Translated by P B Chastanier, published in *The New Jerusalem Journal* London.
In the MS, in both the paragraph title and the text, Swedenborg wrote '1657' not '1757'.
UK: SOC, CON, NCC, NR

X 47/05/En 1792/3 **1792** Hyde 907
Concerning Amendment in the other Life. | From EMANUEL SWEDENBORG's Spiritual Diary.
8vo

title and text n 4037-4039, pp 237-239.
Translated by R Hindmarsh, published in *The New Jerusalem Journal* London.
UK: SOC, CON, NCC, NR

X 47/05/En 1792/4 **1792** Hyde 908
CONCERNING LOVE. | *Extracted from Emanuel Swedenborg's Diary.*
8vo
title and text n 4046, pp 383-384.
Translated by P B Chastanier, published in *The New Jerusalem Journal* London.
UK: SOC, CON, NCC, NR

X 47/05/En 1799/1 **1799** Hyde —
OF THE HELLS OF REVENGE. | *Taken out of Emanuel Swedenborg's Spiritual Diary.*
8vo
title and text n 5096-5098, pp 38-39.
Translated by P B Chastanier, published in *The Aurora* London.
UK: SOC, BL, CON, NR

X 47/05/En 1799/2 **1799** Hyde 909
CONCERNING PERSUASIONS.
8vo
title and text n 4050-4052, pp 81-82.
Translated by P B Chastanier, published in *The Aurora* London.
UK: SOC, BL, CON, NR

X 47/05/En 1799/3 **1799** Hyde 922, 921
That as the tree falls, so it remains—in what manner it is | to be understood. | *Extracted from the Manuscripts of E. S.*
8vo
title and text n <4645m-4646m>, pp 239-241.
Reprinted from X En 1790/4 = Hyde 921, published in *The Aurora* London.
UK: SOC, BL, CON, NR

X 47/05/En 1806/1 **1806** Hyde 2176
SOME EXTRACTS | FROM THE | *Manuscript Memorabilia of Emanuel Swedenborg,* | CONCERNING | THE NEW CHURCH IN AFRICA, &c.
small 8vo
title and text n 4773-4777, 4779-4780, 4783, 5518, 5809, 5919, 5946, pp 31-39.
Translated by M Sibly, appended to *A Sermon on the Nature and Quality of the New Church* London. <UK: SOC Archives S4/61>
UK: SOC

X 47/05/En 1826/1 **1826** Hyde 2177
EXTRACTS | *From the Manuscripts of E. S. concerning the commencement* | *of the New Church, in different parts of the world; but more* | *especially in Africa, with some observations thereon relative to* | *Africa; with the view to colonizing, for the purpose of opening* | *a communication with the interior.*
8vo
title and text 4770 <part>, 4774 <part>, 4777 <part>, 5518, 5946-5947 <parts>, 4780, pp 331-334.

Translated by M Sibly, published in *The New Jerusalem Magazine* London.
An 'Outline map of Africa' is printed on p 330, to accompany the description given by Swedenborg in n 4777.
UK: SOC, BL, CON, NCC, NR

X 47/05/En 1827/1 **1827** Hyde 2178
OF SIR ISAAC NEWTON.
8vo
title and text n <6064>, pp 47-48.
Translated by M Sibly, published in *The New Jerusalem Magazine* London.
UK: SOC, BL, CON, NCC, NR

X 47/05/En 1830/1 **1830** Hyde 2179, 2178
Extract from the Manuscript Diary of Swedenborg. | OF SIR ISAAC NEWTON.
8vo
title and text n <6064>, pp 20-21.
Reprinted from X 1827/1 = Hyde 2178, published in *The New Jerusalem Magazine* Boston MA.
UK: SOC, CON, NCC; USA: ANC

X 47/05/En 1837/1 **1837** Hyde 2180
EXTRACT FROM THE MSS. OF E. SWEDENBORG.
8vo
title and text n 5660-5667, pp 341-342.
Translated by M Sibly, published in *The Intellectual Repository* London.
UK: SOC, BL, CHT, CON, NCC, NR; USA: ANC

X 47/05/En 1843/1 **1843** Hyde 910, 923
EXTRACTS FROM SWEDENBORG'S SPIRITUAL DIARY.
8vo
title and text n 4630, 4637, 4046, 4545-4547, 4553-4560, 4562-4625, 4578-4579, pp 255-260.
Translated by J H Smithson, published in *The Intellectual Repository* London.
UK: SOC, BL, CHT, CON, NCC, NR; USA: ANC

X 47/05/En 1843/2 **1843** Hyde 910, 923
EXTRACTS FROM SWEDENBORG'S SPIRITUAL DIARY.
8vo
title and text n 4610-4614, 4645-4646, 4037-4039, 4628-4629, 4648-4650, <4724>, <4726>, <4734>, 4697, pp 294-301.
Translated by J H Smithson, published in *The Intellectual Repository* London.
UK: SOC, BL, CHT, CON, NCC, NR; USA: ANC

X 47/05/En 1843/3 **1843** Hyde 910, 923
EXTRACTS FROM SWEDENBORG'S SPIRITUAL DIARY.
8vo
title and text n <4737m>, <4741m>, <4745m>, <4756m>, <4773m>, <4788m>, 3910, 4651, 4644-4646, pp 337-342.
Translated by J H Smithson, published in *The Intellectual Repository* London.
UK: SOC, BL, CHT, CON, NCC, NR; USA: ANC

X 47/05/En 1843/4 **1843** Hyde 2181
EXTRACTS FROM SWEDENBORG'S SPIRITUAL DIARY. | (*Now first translated from the original Latin.*)
8vo
title and text n 4757-4759, 4561, 4564, pp 380-384.
Translated by J H Smithson, published in *The Intellectual Repository* London.
UK: SOC, BL, CHT, CON, NCC, NR; USA: ANC

X 47/05/En 1843/5 **1843** Hyde 910
EXTRACTS FROM SWEDENBORG'S SPIRITUAL DIARY. | (*Now first translated from the original Latin.*)
8vo
title and text n 3569-3571, 3590, 3615, 3618-3619, 3622-3623, 4056, 4155, 4165, 4113, pp 460-464.
Translated by J H Smithson, published in *The Intellectual Repository* London.
UK: SOC, BL, CHT, CON, NCC, NR; USA: ANC

X 47/05/En 1844/1 **1844** Hyde 911, 2182
EXTRACTS FROM SWEDENBORG'S SPIRITUAL DIARY. | (*Now first translated from the original Latin.*)
8vo
title and text n 4375, 4421, <4433>, <5099>, 4935, 4568-4569, 5187-5190, 5151, pp 15-20.
Translated by J H Smithson, published in *The Intellectual Repository* London.
UK: SOC, BL, CHT, CON, NCC, NR; USA: ANC

X 47/05/En 1844/2 **1844** Hyde 912
EXTRACTS FROM SWEDENBORG'S SPIRITUAL DIARY. | (From the Intellectual Repository.)
8vo
title and text n 4037-4039, 4046, pp 157-159, 185.
Reprinted from X 1843/2 = Hyde 910, published in *The New Jerusalem Magazine* Boston MA.
UK: SOC, CON, NCC; USA: ANC

X 47/05/En 1844/3 **1844** Hyde 924, 923
EXTRACTS FROM SWEDENBORG'S SPIRITUAL DIARY. | (From the Intellectual Repository.)
8vo
title and text n 4630, 4637, 4046, 4545-4547, 4553-4560, 4622-4625, 4578-4579, pp 184-188.
Reprinted from X 1843/2 = Hyde 910, published in *The New Jerusalem Magazine* Boston MA.
UK: SOC, CON, NCC; USA: ANC

X 47/05/En 1844/4 **1844** Hyde 2182
EXTRACTS FROM SWEDENBORG'S SPIRITUAL DIARY. | (*Now first translated from the original Latin.*)
8vo
title and text n 5700-5710, pp 57-61.
Translated by J H Smithson, published in *The Intellectual Repository* London.
UK: SOC, BL, CHT, CON, NCC, NR; USA: ANC

X 47/05/En 1844/5 **1844** Hyde 2182
EXTRACTS FROM SWEDENBORG'S SPIRITUAL DIARY. | (*Now first translated from the original Latin.*)

8vo
title and text n 4829, 5240-5242, 5244-5246, 5248, pp 96-100.
Translated by J H Smithson, published in *The Intellectual Repository* London.
UK: SOC, BL, CHT, CON, NCC, NR; USA: ANC

X 47/05/1844/6 **1844** Hyde 536
EXTRACTS FROM SWEDENBORG'S SPIRITUAL DIARY. | (*Now first translated from the original Latin.*)
8vo
title and text n 149, 159, 158, 191, 205-206, 210-213, 245, 251-252, 254, 258, pp 207-214.
Translated by J H Smithson, published in *The Intellectual Repository* London.
UK: SOC, BL, CHT, CON, NCC, NR; USA: ANC

X 47/05/En 1844/7 **1844** Hyde 2183, 2182
SWEDENBORG'S SPIRITUAL DIARY.
8vo
title and text n 5240-5242, 5244-5246, 5248, 4548, 4551, pp 356-359, 498-499.
Reprinted from X 1844/5 = Hyde 2182, published in *The New Jerusalem Magazine* Boston MA.
UK: SOC, CON, NCC; USA: ANC

X 47/05/En 1844/8 **1844** Hyde 2182
EXTRACTS FROM SWEDENBORG'S SPIRITUAL DIARY. | (*Now first translated from the original Latin.*)
8vo
title and text n 4548, 4551, 4560, 4593, 4616-4618, pp 253-257.
Translated by J H Smithson, published in *The Intellectual Repository* London.
UK: SOC, BL, CHT, CON, NCC, NR; USA: ANC

X 47/05/En 1844/9 **1844** Hyde 536
EXTRACTS FROM SWEDENBORG'S SPIRITUAL DIARY. | (*Now first translated from the original Latin.*)
8vo
title and text n 249-250, 322, 384-385, 431, 457, 592, 693, 780-781, pp 308-312.
Translated by J H Smithson, published in *The Intellectual Repository* London.
UK: SOC, BL, CHT, CON, NCC, NR; USA: ANC

X 47/05/En 1845/1 **1845** Hyde 537, 2184
EXTRACTS FROM SWEDENBORG'S SPIRITUAL DIARY.
8vo
title and text n 4716, 4711-4713, 2652-2654, 2626-2627, 2841, 2906-2907, 2514-2516, pp 321-326.
Translated by J H Smithson, published in *The Intellectual Repository* London.
UK: SOC, BL, CHT, CON, NCC, NR; USA: ANC

X 47/05/En 1845/2 **1845** Hyde —
EXTRACTS FROM SWEDENBORG'S SPIRITUAL DIARY.
8vo
title and text n 798-807, 885-888, 2470-2471, pp 401-405.

Translated by J H Smithson, published in *The Intellectual Repository* London.
UK: SOC, BL, CHT, CON, NCC, NR; USA: ANC

X 47/05/En 1845/3 **1845** Hyde 2185
EXTRACT FROM SWEDENBORG'S SPIRITUAL DIARY.
8vo
title and text n 4560, pp 37-38.
Reprinted from X 1844/5 = Hyde 2182, published in *The New Jerusalem Magazine* Boston MA.
UK: SOC, CON, NCC; USA: ANC

X 47/05/En 1846/1 **1846** Hyde 538
EXTRACTS FROM SWEDENBORG'S SPIRITUAL DIARY.
8vo
title and text n 2299-2301, 2422, pp 142-144.
Translated by J H Smithson, published in *The Intellectual Repository* London.
UK: SOC, BL, CHT, CON, NCC, NR; USA: ANC

X 47/05/En 1846/2 **1846** Hyde 538
EXTRACTS FROM SWEDENBORG'S SPIRITUAL DIARY.
8vo
title and text n 2688-2689, pp 226-227.
Translated by J H Smithson, published in *The Intellectual Repository* London.
UK: SOC, BL, CHT, CON, NCC, NR; USA: ANC

X 47/05/En 1846/3 **1846** Hyde 538
EXTRACTS FROM SWEDENBORG'S SPIRITUAL DIARY.
8vo
title and text n 1950-1955, 1139-1141, pp 330-333.
Translated by J H Smithson, published in *The Intellectual Repository* London.
UK: SOC, BL, CHT, CON, NCC, NR; USA: ANC

X 47/05/En 1846/4 **1846** Hyde 538
EXTRACTS FROM SWEDENBORG'S SPIRITUAL DIARY.
8vo
title and text n 1589-1592, 1627-1635, pp 377-381.
Translated by J H Smithson, published in *The Intellectual Repository* London.
UK: SOC, BL, CHT, CON, NCC, NR; USA: ANC

X 47/05/En 1846/5 **1846** Hyde 932, 3120
The missing paragraphs of the Spiritual Diary.
8vo
title and text n 48, 64, 65, 91, 124, 137, 53, 54, 69, 98, 143, 86, 110, 141, 26, 129, 139, 31, 92-93, 27, 39-40, 101-102, 20, 171, 72, 73, 77, 122, 140, 146, 42, 112-113, 10, 82, 21, 51, 94, 58, 4, 79, 133, 148⅓, 77, 33, 127, 132, 15-16, 10, 25, 62, 82-85, 82-86, 93, 118, 128, 83, 84, 36, 18, 47-48, 50, 58, 68, 104, pp i-iii.
Compiled and translated by J H Smithson, published in the Appendix to *The Spiritual Diary of Emanuel Swedenborg* vol 1 <En 1/1 = Hyde 3120>, London. A reconstruction of some of the headings of n 1-148 <Hyde 932>, deduced from the volume of the Latin edition of the Index to the work, which had been published in 1846 <La 1/8 = Hyde 930>.
UK: SOC, CON; NET: GEN; SWE: ROY; USA: FOU

X 1847/En 1847/1 **1847** Hyde 539

EXTRACTS FROM SWEDENBORG'S SPIRITUAL DIARY.
8vo
title and text n 1643-1644, pp 109-110.
Translated by J H Smithson, published in *The Intellectual Repository* London.
UK: SOC, BL, CHT, CON, NCC, NR; USA: ANC

X 1847/En 1847/2 **1847** Hyde 2186

THE CAUSES WHY MEN, IN THE CHRISTIAN WORLD, | HAVE NOT BELIEVED IN THE RESURRECTION IM- | MEDIATELY AFTER DEATH. | *(From Swedenborg's Diary.)*
ON THE LIFE OF CHARITY IN MAN. | *(From Swedenborg's Diary.)*
8vo
text n 5752, 5881, pp 142-143.
Translated by J H Smithson, published in *The Intellectual Repository* London.
UK: SOC, BL, CHT, CON, NCC, NR; USA: ANC

X 47/05/En 1847/3 **1847** Hyde 538

THAT THE HEBREW LANGUAGE IS SO CON- | STITUTED, THAT NOTHING THEREIN IS ARTIFCIAL, | AS [INSTANCED] IN THE CASE OF SPIRITS WHEN | SPEAKING. | *(From the Spiritual Diary of Swedenborg.)* <*stet* ARTIFCIAL>
(CONCERNING THE HEBREW LANGUAGE.) | *(From Swedenborg's Spiritual Diary.)*
8vo
titles and text n 2631, 2414, pp 225-227; Editorial comment, pp 227-228.
Translated by J H Smithson, published in *The Intellectual Repository* London.
UK: SOC, BL, CHT, CON, NCC, NR; USA: ANC

X 47/05/En 1847/4 **1847** Hyde 538

(CONCERNING THE FOUR DEGREES [CONSTITUENT] OF | [A PLENARY] FAITH.) | *(From Swedenborg's Spiritual Diary.)*
(That the angels experience much sweetness in the perception that they do | not [even] think from themselves.)
8vo
title and text n 2947, 2870-2871, pp 262-263.
Translated by J H Smithson, published in *The Intellectual Repository* London.
UK: SOC, BL, CHT, CON, NCC, NR; USA: ANC

X 47/05/En 1847/5 **1847** Hyde 538

(THAT EVIL SPIRITS ARE [THEMSELVES] TO BLAME | FOR WHATEVER EVIL BEFALLS THEM.) | *(From Swedenborg's Diary.)*
8vo
title and text n 3037-3039, pp 336-337.
Translated by J H Smithson, published in *The Intellectual Repository* London.
UK: SOC, BL, CHT, CON, NCC, NR; USA: ANC

X 47/05/En 1847/6 **1847** Hyde 538

THOSE WHO WITHIN THEMSELVES CONDEMN OTHERS, | WHILST WITH THEIR LIPS THEY DISSEMBLE. | *(From Swedenborg's Spiritual Diary.)*
THAT EVIL IS NOT IMPUTED TO THE ONE WHO IS IN | FAITH TOWARDS THE LORD; NOR IS THE GOOD | WHICH SUCH A ONE DOETH, ATTRIBUTED TO | HIMSELF. | *(From Swedenborg's*

Spiritual Diary.)
8vo
titles and text n 3169-3171, 2944-2946, pp 423-425.
Translated by J H Smithson, published in *The Intellectual Repository* London.
UK: SOC, BL, CHT, CON, NCC, NR; USA: ANC

X 47/05/En 1848/1 **1848** Hyde 913
EXTRACTS FROM SWEDENBORG'S SPIRITUAL DIARY. | NOW FIRST TRANSLATED FROM THE ORIGINAL LATIN.
8vo
title and text n 3998, 4096, 4099, 4102-4103, pp 61-62.
Translated by G Bush, published in *The New Church Repository* New York.
UK: SOC, CON, NR

X 47/05/En 1848/2 **1848** Hyde —
How Swedenborg's state, in this intercourse with spirits, dif- | fered from that of other men.
8vo
title and text n 3963, 3464, 2955, pp 81-82, 86-87, 93-94.
Translated by G Bush, published in *The New Church Repository* New York, in an article entitled 'Swedenborg's claim to intercourse with the spiritual world'.
UK: SOC, CON, NR

X 47/05/En 1848/3 **1848** Hyde 913
EXTRACTS FROM SWEDENBORG'S SPIRITUAL DIARY. | NOW FIRST TRANSLATED FROM THE ORIGINAL LATIN.
8vo
title and text n 4104-4105, 4107-4110, 4113, 4016-4017, 4021-4023, 4046, 4048, 4055, pp 123-127.
Translated by G Bush, published in *The New Church Repository* New York.
UK: SOC, CON, NR

X 47/05/En 1848/4 **1848** Hyde 913
EXTRACTS FROM SWEDENBORG'S SPIRITUAL DIARY. | NOW FIRST TRANSLATED FROM THE ORIGINAL LATIN.
8vo
title and text n 4057-4059, 4000-4010, 4013-4015, pp 171-176.
Translated by G Bush, published in *The New Church Repository* New York.
UK: SOC, CON, NR

X 47/05/En 1848/5 **1848** Hyde 913
EXTRACTS FROM SWEDENBORG'S SPIRITUAL DIARY. | NOW FIRST TRANSLATED FROM THE ORIGINAL LATIN.
8vo
title and text n 4173, 4175, 4179, 4184-4186, 4189, 4192-4193, 4195, 4200-4201, pp 313-316.
Translated by G Bush, published in *The New Church Repository* New York.
UK: SOC, CON, NR

X 47/05/En 1848/6 **1848** Hyde —
Concerning Dippel.
8vo

title and text n 3485-3487, pp 377-378.
Translated by G Bush, published in *The New Church Repository* New York, in an article entitled 'Swedenborg's account of Dippel'.
UK: SOC, CON, NR

X 47/05/En 1848/7 **1848** Hyde 540
ON THE GOVERNMENT OF THE UNIVERSE. | *(From Swedenborg's Spiritual Diary.)*
IN THE UNIVERSE NO EFFECT CAN EXIST WITHOUT | A PASSIVE AND AN ACTIVE, THUS WITHOUT A | MARRIAGE. | *(From Swedenborg's Spiritual Diary.)*
8vo
titles and text n 2713-2717, 2722-2724, pp 304-306.
Translated by G Bush, published in *The New Church Repository* New York.
UK: SOC, CON, NR

X 47/05/En 1848/8 **1848** Hyde 913
EXTRACTS FROM SWEDENBORG'S SPIRITUAL DIARY. | NOW FIRST TRANSLATED FROM THE ORIGINAL LATIN.
8vo
title and text n 4150, 4154, 4156, 4159-4162, pp 483-486.
Translated by G Bush, published in *The New Church Repository* New York.
UK: SOC, CON, NR

X 47/05/En 1848/9 **1848** Hyde 913
EXTRACTS FROM SWEDENBORG'S SPIRITUAL DIARY. | NOW FIRST TRANSLATED FROM THE ORIGINAL LATIN.
8vo
title and text n 3972-3973, 4067, 4077, 4260-4262, pp 570-572.
Translated by G Bush, published in *The New Church Repository* New York.
UK: SOC, CON, NR

X 47/05/En 1848/10 **1848** Hyde —
THE CORRESPONDENCE OF BREAD IN THE HOLY SUPPER.
8vo
title and text n 2626-2627, pp 572-573.
Translated by G Bush, published in *The New Church Repository* New York.
UK: SOC, CON, NR

X 47/05/En 1848/11 **1848** Hyde —
<untitled>
8vo
text n 3894, 6096, pp 616, 617.
Translated by G Bush, published in *The New Church Repository* New York, in an article entitled 'Witchcraft'.
UK: SOC, CON, NR

X 47/05/En 1848/12 **1848** Hyde 913
EXTRACTS FROM SWEDENBORG'S SPIRITUAL DIARY. | (NOW FIRST TRANSLATED FROM THE ORIGINAL LATIN.)
8vo

title and text n 3976, 3990-3991, 4019-4020, 4313-4316, 4324-4325, pp 630-634.
Translated by G Bush, published in *The New Church Repository* New York.
UK: SOC, CON, NR

X 47/05/En 1848/13 **1848** Hyde 913
EXTRACTS FROM SWEDENBORG'S SPIRITUAL DIARY. | NOW FIRST TRANSLATED FROM THE ORIGINAL LATIN.
8vo
title and text n 4114-4120, 4123, 4125, 4136, pp 694-697.
Translated by G Bush, published in *The New Church Repository* New York.
UK: SOC, CON, NR

X 47/05/En 1848/14 **1848** Hyde 913
EXTRACTS FROM SWEDENBORG'S SPIRITUAL DIARY. | NOW FIRST TRANSLATED FROM THE ORIGINAL LATIN.
8vo
title and text n 4121-4122, 4130-4132, pp 760-762.
Translated by G Bush, published in *The New Church Repository* New York.
UK: SOC, CON, NR

X 47/05/En 1849/1 **1849** Hyde 2187
(From Swedenborg's Spiritual Diary, now first translated.)
8vo
title and text n 5933, 6075, 6080, 6072, pp 134-136.
Translated by J H Smithson, published in *The Intellectual Repository* London.
UK: SOC, BL, CHT, CON, NCC, NR; USA: ANC

X 47/05/En 1849/2 **1849** Hyde 2187
(From Swedenborg's Spiritual Diary, now first translated.)
8vo
title and text n 5552-5553, 5570, pp 187-188.
Translated by J H Smithson, published in *The Intellectual Repository* London.
UK: SOC, BL, CHT, CON, NCC, NR; USA: ANC

X 47/05/En 1849/3 **1849** Hyde 541
EXTRACTS FROM SWEDENBORG'S SPIRITUAL DIARY.
8vo
title and text n 2301, pp 560-561.
Translated by G Bush, published in *The New Church Repository* New York.
UK: SOC, CON, NR

X 47/05/En 1850/1 **1850** Hyde 933, 3121
THE MISSING NUMBERS OF THE SPIRITUAL DIARY.
8vo
title and text n 1-148 with editorial introduction and postscript, pp 371-379.
Reprinted, with additions compiled by G Bush, from X En 1846/5, published in the appendix to *The Spiritual Diary of Emanuel Swedenborg* 1 <En 1/2 = Hyde 3121> New York.
UK: SOC, CON, NR

X 47/05/En 1851/1 **1851** Hyde 542
EXTRACTS FROM SWEDENBORG'S SPIRITUAL DIARY. | *(Not hitherto translated.)*
8vo
title and text n 2019, 1910-1912, 1790, 2947, pp 25-27.
Translated by J H Smithson, published in *The Intellectual Repository* London.
UK: SOC, BL, CHT, CON, NCC, NR; USA: ANC

X 47/05/En 1851/2 **1851** Hyde 542
EXTRACTS FROM SWEDENBORG'S SPIRITUAL DIARY. | *(Not hitherto translated.)*
8vo
title and text n 2947, pp 111-112.
Translated by J H Smithson, published in *The Intellectual Repository* London.
UK: SOC, BL, CHT, CON, NCC, NR; USA: ANC

X 47/05/En 1851/3 **1851** Hyde 542
EXTRACTS FROM SWEDENBORG'S SPIRITUAL DIARY. | *(Not hitherto translated.)*
8vo
title and text n 3169-3171, pp 264-265.
Translated by J H Smithson, published in *The Intellectual Repository* London.
UK: SOC, BL, CHT, CON, NCC, NR; USA: ANC

X 47/05/En 1851/4 **1851** Hyde 542
EXTRACTS FROM SWEDENBORG'S SPIRITUAL DIARY. | *(Not hitherto translated.)*
8vo
title and text n 3178-3179, 2592, 2563, pp 308-310.
Translated by J H Smithson, published in *The Intellectual Repository* London.
UK: SOC, BL, CHT, CON, NCC, NR; USA: ANC

X 47/05/En 1853/1 **1853** Hyde 543
EXTRACTS | FROM SWEDENBORG'S SPIRITUAL DIARY.
8vo
title, Editorial note, and text n 1539-1625, 1627-1673, 1672½, 1672¼, 1673-1698, pp 31-34, 71-74, 135-139, 179-181, 267-271, 319-322, 363-366, 419-423, 462-464, 508-510, 562-567.
Translated by G Bush, published in *The New Church Repository* New York.
UK: SOC, CON, NR

X 47/05/En 1853/2 **1853** Hyde 2188
THE HUMAN SOUL; INFLUX; THE VARIOUS KINDS OF | MENTAL LIGHT; AND THE SENSUAL MAN. | *(From Swedenborg's "Spiritual Diary," not hitherto translated.)*
8vo
title and text n 4627, pp 138-143.
Translated by J H Smithson, published in *The Intellectual Repository* London.
UK: SOC, BL, CHT, CON, NCC, NR; USA: ANC

X 47/05/En 1854/1 **1854** Hyde 544
EXTRACTS | FROM SWEDENBORG'S SPIRITUAL DIARY.
8vo
title and text n 1699-1731, 1731-1776, 1778-1812, 1819-1826, pp 32-34, 71-74, 134-136, 281-283, 308-312, 359-362, 404-406, 454-458, 500-503, 546-548.

Translated by G Bush, published in *The New Church Repository* New York.
UK: SOC, CON, NR

X 47/05/En 1854/2 **1854** Hyde 2189
THE RUSSIAN PEOPLE. | *(From Swedenborg's "Spiritual Diary," not hitherto translated.)*
8vo
Editorial introduction, pp 65-66; text n 5452-5456, pp 66-67; n 5952, in a footnote to p 66; n 5949, p 67; n 5963, pp 67-68; editorial conclusion, pp 68-70.
Edited and translated by J H Smithson, published in *The Intellectual Repository* London.
UK: SOC, BL, CHT, CON, NCC, NR; USA: ANC

X 47/05/En 1854/3 **1854** Hyde 914
COMPARISONS BETWEEN THE STATES OF CERTAIN | CHRSTIANS AND THE STATES OF MAHOMETANS. | *(From Swedenborg's "Spiritual Diary," not hitherto translated.)*
8vo
Editorial introduction, pp 227-228; text n <3494>, p 228; editorial conclusion, pp 228-229.
Edited and translated by J H Smithson, published in *The Intellectual Repository* London.
UK: SOC, BL, CHT, CON, NCC, NR; USA: ANC

X 47/05/En 1855/1 **1855** Hyde 545
EXTRACTS | FROM SWEDENBORG'S SPIRITUAL DIARY.
8vo
title and text n 1827-1939, pp 33-35, 85-87, 120-123, 182-184, 230-233, 279-281, 378-380, 423-425, 526-528, 550-552.
Translated by G Bush, published in *The New Church Repository* New York.
UK: SOC, CON, NR

X 47/05/En 1856/1 **1856** Hyde 546
EXTRACTS | FROM SWEDENBORG'S SPIRITUAL DIARY.
8vo
title and text n 1940-1974, 1978-2022, 2024-2061, pp 15-17, 79-82, 115-117, 164-167, 222-224, 275-278, 322-326, 509-511, 594-596, 656-657.
Translated by G Bush, published in *The New Church Repository* New York.
UK: SOC, CON, NR

X 47/05/En 1856/2 **1856** Hyde 547
EXTRACTS | FROM SWEDENBORG'S SPIRITUAL DIARY.
8vo
title and text n 2021-2061, pp 34-38, 221-223, 306-308, 368-369.
Reprinted from X 1856/1, published in *The New Church Herald* Philadelphia.
UK: SOC

X 47/05/En 1857/1 **1857** Hyde 2190
EXTRACT FROM SWEDENBORG. | *(Not hitherto translated.)*
8vo
titles and text n 5752, 5720, pp 131-132.
Translated by J H Smithson, published in *The Intellectual Repository* London.
UK: SOC, BL, CHT, CON, NCC, NR; USA: ANC

X 47/05/En 1858/1 **1858** Hyde 2191
ON THE CONJUNCTION OF MAN WITH HEAVEN:- | ITS SIGNS. | *(From Swedenborg's Spiritual Diary, not hitherto translated.)*
Concerning those who are in Good and not in Truths.
8vo
titles and text n 5933, 5925, pp 74-76.
Translated by J H Smithson, published in *The Intellectual Repository* London.
UK: SOC, BL, CHT, CON, NCC, NR; USA: ANC

X 47/05/En 1861/1 **1861** Hyde 548
EXTRACTS FROM SWEDENBORG'S SPIRITUAL DIARY. | (Not hitherto Translated.)
8vo
title and text n 2420, 2450, 2459, 2592, pp 367-368, 415.
Translated by J H Smithson, published in *The Intellectual Repository* London.
UK: SOC, BL, CHT, CON, NCC, NR; USA: ANC

X 47/05/En 1861/2 **1861** Hyde 2192
THE NEW CHURCH IN AFRICA. | EXTRACTS FROM SWEDENBORG'S SPIRITUAL DIARY.
8vo
title and text n 4773-4777, 4779-4780, 4783, 5518, 5809, 5919, 5946, pp 17-21.
Reprinted from Hyde 2176, published in *The New Jerusalem Magazine* Boston MA.
UK: SOC, CON, NCC; USA: ANC

X 47/05/En 1877/1, **E:b** En 1877/2 **1877** Hyde 3276
PRIVATE MEMORANDA.
royal 8vo
title, editorial notes, and text, pp 748-750.
Memoranda written on the last page on the MS, and on an unspecified flyleaf, translated and edited by R L Tafel, published in *Documents* 2:2 <**E:b** En 1877/2 = Hyde 3276> London.
UK: SOC, CON, NCC, PUR, WIL, NR; GER: GSU; NET: GEN; SWE: SUB, UPP; USA: ANC; AUS: SYD

X 47/05/En 1883/1 **1883** Hyde 934, 3122
<untitled>
8vo
text n 1-148, pp 1-10.
Reprinted from X 1850/1, published in *The Spiritual Diary of Emanuel Swedenborg* 1 <En 3/1 = Hyde 3122> London.
UK: SOC, NR; NET: GEN; SWE: ROY, UPP

X 47/05/En 1890/1, **E:b** En 1890/2 **1890** Hyde 3276
PRIVATE MEMORANDA.
royal 8vo
title, editorial notes, and text, pp 748-750.
The same as X En 1877/1, published in *Documents* 3 <**E:b** En 1890/2 = Hyde 3276> London.
UK: SOC, BL; SWE: UPP

X 47/05/En 1958/1, **E:b** En 1958/4 **1958** Hyde 3336/25iv
<untitled>
4to

text, pp 728, 734-735, 768, 811-814.
Translated and edited by A Acton, published in *The Life of Emanuel Swedenborg* 4 <**E:b** En 1958/4, Hyde 3336/25iv> Bryn Athyn PA.
UK: SOC, NCC; USA: ANC

X 47/05/En 1962/1 **1962** Hyde 523/–, 3122/1
<untitled>
8vo
text n 1-148, pp 1-19.
A reconstruction of the 'missing' numbers, compiled from the Index, translated by W H Acton and A W Acton, published in *The Spiritual Diary* vol 1 <En 5/1 = Hyde 523/1> London.
UK: SOC, CON, NCC, NR; NET: GEN; SWE: UPP; USA: ANC

X 47/05/En 1977/1 **1977** Hyde 934/2, 3122/2
<untitled>
8vo
text n 1-148, pp 1-19.
Reprint of X En 1962/1 = Hyde 934/1, published in En 5/2 = Hyde 3122/1, by the Swedenborg Foundation, New York.
USA: ANC, FOU

X 47/05/En 2000/1, **E:b** En 2000/2 **2000** Hyde 3276/–
<<PRIVATE MEMORANDA.>>
8vo
title, editorial notes, and text, pp 748-750.
Photographic replica reprint of X En 1877/1, published in *Documents* 2:2 <**E:b** En 2000/2> by Adamant Media Corporation, New York.
Copy not seen; description deduced from X En 1877/1 and publisher's advertisement.

X 47/05/En 2002/1 **2002** Hyde 934/3, 3122/3
<untitled>
large 8vo
text n 1-148, pp 1-15.
Reprint of X En 1977/1 = Hyde 934/2, published in En 5/3 = Hyde 3122/2, by the Swedenborg Society.
UK: SOC, CON, NR; SWE: ROY

X 47/05/En 2004/1, **E:b** En 2004/3 **2004** Hyde 3276/–
PRIVATE MEMORANDA.
8vo
title, editorial notes, and text, pp 748-750.
Photographic replica reprint of X En 1877/1, published in *Documents* 2:2 <**E:b** En 2004/3> by Kessinger Publishing, Whitefish MT.
UK: NR

DANISH

47/05/Da 1/1 **1983-1987** Hyde —
<<DEN ANDELIGE DAGBOG | af | Emanuel Swedenborg>>
A4 folded to A5

title and text n 1-818, 334 pp.
Translated by G Boolsen, published in *Nykirkeligt Tidsskrift* no 4 1983 to no 3 1987, Copenhagen; offset litho printed.
Copy not seen; description deduced from Da 1/2 = Hyde 2171/1.

47/05/Da 1/2 **1983** Hyde 3144/1, 2171/1
DEN ÅNDELIGE DAGBOG | af | Emanuel Swedenborg | indeholdende | Optegnelser og Notater | om hans erfaringer i den åndelige verden | årene 1746 - 1765 | Første Bind | NYKIRKELIGT TIDSSKRIFT Tryk, København 1983
A4 folded to A5
title leaf, 2 pp; Indledning <Introduction>, pp i-v; Information concerning the 'missing numbers' <reprinted from En 5/1, pp 421-423>, pp vi-viii; reproduction from La 1/3 <p 1>, p ix; reproduction from La 2/1 <pp v-vii>, pp x-xii; text n 1-818, pp 1-48, 53-334; reproduction from En 5/1 <pp 419-420> and notes concerning the Hebrew language, pp 51-52.
Reprint of Da 1/1; offset litho printed.
UK: SOC; DEN: RLD

47/05/Da 1/3 **1987** Hyde 3144/2, 2171/2
DEN ÅNDELIG DAGBOG | af | Emanuel Swedenborg | Indeholdende | Optegnelser og notater | om hans erfaringer i den åndelige verden | årene 1746 - 1765 | Andet Bind | NYKIRKELIGT TIDSSKRIFT Tryk, København 1987
A4 folded to A5
title leaf, 2 pp; text n 819-1824, pp 1-338.
Translated by G Boolsen; offset litho printed.
UK: SOC; DEN: RLD

47/05/Da 1/4 **1990** Hyde 3144/3, 2171/3
DEN ÅNDELIG DAGBOG | af | Emanuel Swedenborg | Indeholdende | Optegnelser og notater | om hans erfaringer i den åndelige verden | årene 1746 - 1765 | Oversat fra latin | af | Gudmund Boolsen | Tredje Bind | NYKIRKELIGT TIDSSKRIFT Tryk, København 1990
verso: DEN ÅNDELIGE DAGBOG udgives også i Nykirkeligt Tidsskrift | ISSN 0903-1847 (Kvartalsvis). | Hidtil er udkommet af Den Åndelige Dagbog: | 1.bind (Nr.1-818) Nykirkeligt Tidsskrift Nr.4,1983-Nr.3,1987 | 2.bind (Nr.819-1824) " " Nr.4,1987-Nr.4,1988 | 3.bind (Nr.1825-2779) " " Nr.1,1989-Nr.1,1990
A4 folded to A5
title leaf, 2 pp; text n 1825-2779, pp 1-338.
Translated by G Boolsen; offset litho printed.
UK: SOC; DEN: RLD

47/05/Da 1/5 **1991** Hyde 3144/4, 2171/4
DEN ÅNDELIGE DAGBOG | af | Emanuel Swedenborg | Indeholdende | Optegnelser og notater | om hans erfaringer i den åndelige verden | årene 1746 - 1765 | Oversat fra latin | af | Gudmund Boolsen | Fjerde Bind | *SWEDENBORG BOGLADE* | Valby Langgade 39, 1.th. | 2500 Valby, Tlf. 31 16 94 66 | NYKIRKELIGT TIDSSKRIFT Tryk, København 1991
verso: DEN ÅNDELIGE DAGBOG udgives også i Nykirkeligt Tidsskrift | ISSN 0903-1847 (Kvartalsvis). | Hidtil er udkommet af Den Åndelige Dagbog: | 1.bind (Nr.1-818) Nykirkeligt Tidsskrift Nr.4,1983-Nr.3,1987 | 2.bind (Nr.819-1824) " " Nr.4,1987-Nr.4,1988 | 3.bind (Nr.1825-2779) " " Nr.1,1989-Nr.1,1990
A4 folded to A5

title leaf, 2 pp; text n 2780-3592, pp 1-338.
Translated by G Boolsen; offset litho printed.
UK: SOC; DEN: RLD

47/05/Da 1/6 **1992** Hyde 3144/5, 2171/5

DEN ÅNDELIGE DAGBOG | af | Emanuel Swedenborg | Indeholdende | Optegnelser og notater | om hans erfaringer i den åndelige verden | årene 1746 - 1765 | Oversat fra latin | af | Gudmund Boolsen | Femte Bind | Swedenborg Boglade | Valby Langgade 39 | 2500 Valby | NYKIRKELIGT TIDSSKRIFT Tryk, København 1992
verso: DEN ÅNDELIGE DAGBOG udgives også i Nykirkeligt Tidsskrift | ISSN 0903-1847 (Kvartalsvis). | Hidtil er udkommet af den Åndelige Dagbog: 1. bind (Nr.1-818) Nykirkeligt Tidsskrift Nr.4,1983-Nr.3,1987 | 2. bind (Nr.819-1824) " " Nr.4,1987-Nr.4,1988 | 3. bind (Nr.1825-2779) " " Nr.1,1989-Nr.1,1990 | 4. bind (Nr.2780-3592) " " Nr.2.1990-Nr.2,1991 | SWEDENBORG BOGLADE | Valby Langgade 39, 1. th. | 2500 Valby, tlf. 31 16 94 66
A4 folded to A5
title leaf, 2 pp; text n 3593-4379, pp 1-338.
Translated by G Boolsen; offset litho printed.
UK: SOC; DEN: RLD

47/05/Da 1/7 **1993** Hyde 3144/6, 2171/6

DEN ÅNDELIGE DAGBOG | af | Emanuel Swedenborg | Indeholdende | Optegnelser og notater | om hans erfaringer i den åndelige verden | årene 1746 - 1765 | Oversat fra latin | af | Gudmund Boolsen | Sjette Bind | SWEDENBORG BOGLADE | Valby Langgade 39, 1.th. | 2500 Valby, Tlf. 31 16 94 66 | NYKIRKELIGT TIDSSKRIFT Tryk, København 1993
verso: DEN ÅNDELIGE DAGBOG udgives også i Nykirkeligt Tidsskrift | ISSN 0903-1847 (Kvartalsvis). | Hidtil er udkommet af den Åndelige Dagbog: 1. bind (Nr.1-818) Nykirkeligt Tidsskrift Nr.4,1983-Nr.3,1987 | 2. bind (Nr.819-1824) " " Nr.4,1987-Nr.4,1988 | 3. bind (Nr.1825-2779) " " Nr.1,1989-Nr.1,1990 | 4. bind (Nr.2780-3592) " " Nr.2.1990-Nr.2,1991 | 5. bind (Nr.3593-4379) " " Nr.3,1991-Nr.3,1992 | SWEDENBORG BOGLADE | Valby Langgade 39, 1. th. | 2500 Valby, tlf. 31 16 94 66
A4 folded to A5
title leaf, 2 pp; text n 4380-4812, pp 1-338.
Translated by G Boolsen; offset litho printed.
UK: SOC; DEN: RLD

47/05/Da 1/8 **1995** Hyde 3144/7, 2171/7

DEN ÅNDELIG DAGBOG | af | Emanuel Swedenborg | Indeholdende | Optegnelser og notater | om hans erfaringer i den åndelige verden | årene 1746 - 1765 | Oversat fra latin | af | Gudmund Boolsen | Syvende Bind | Swedenborg Boglade | Valby Langgade 39, | 2500 Valby | NYKIRKELIGT TIDSSKRIFT Tryk, København 1995
verso: DEN ÅNDELIGE DAGBOG udgives også i Nykirkeligt Tidsskrift | ISSN 0903-1847 (Kvartalsvis). | Hidtil er udkommet af den Åndelige Dagbog: 1. bind (Nr.1-818) Nykirkeligt Tidsskrift Nr.4,1983-Nr.3,1987 | 2. bind (Nr.819-1824) " " Nr.4,1987-Nr.4,1988 | 3. bind (Nr.1825-2779) " " Nr.1,1989-Nr.1,1990 | 4. bind (Nr.2780-3592) " " Nr.2.1990-Nr.2,1991 | 5. bind (Nr.3593-4379) " " Nr.3,1991-Nr.3,1992 | 6. bind (Nr.4380-4812) " " Nr.4.1992-Nr.4,1993 | SWEDENBORG BOGLADE | Valby Langgade 39, 1. th. | 2500 Valby, tlf. 31 16 94 66
A4 folded to A5
title leaf, 2 pp; text n 4813-5695, pp 1-358.
Translated by G Boolsen; offset litho printed.
UK: SOC; DEN: RLD

47/05/Da 1/9 **1995** Hyde 3144/8, 2171/8

DEN ÅNDELIGE DAGBOG | af | Emanuel Swedenborg | Indeholdende | Optegnelser og notater | om hans erfaringer i den åndelige verden | årene 1746 - 1765 | Oversat fra latin | af | Gudmund Boolsen | Ottende Bind | SWEDENBORG BOGLADE | Valby Langgade 39, 1.th. | 2500 Valby, Tlf. 31 16 94 66 | NYKIRKELIGT TIDSSKRIFT Tryk, København 1995

verso: DEN ÅNDELIGE DAGBOG udgives også i Nykirkeligt Tidsskrift | ISSN 0903-1847 (Kvartalsvis). | Hidtil er udkommet af den Åndelige Dagbog: 1. bind (Nr.1-818) Nykirkeligt Tidsskrift Nr.4,1983-Nr.3,1987 | 2. bind (Nr.819-1824) " " Nr.4,1987-Nr.4,1988 | 3. bind (Nr.1825-2779) " " Nr.1,1989-Nr.1,1990 | 4. bind (Nr.2780-3592) " " Nr.2.1990-Nr.2,1991 | 5. bind (Nr.3593-4379) " " Nr.3,1991-Nr.3,1992 | 6. bind (Nr.4380-4812) " " Nr.4,1992-Nr.4,1993 | 7. bind (Nr.4813-5695) " " Nr.1,1994-Nr.1,1995 | 8. og sidste bind (Nr. 5696 - 6110) forventes; | Nykirkeligt Tidsskrift, Nr.2, 1995 - Nr.2, 1996 | SWEDENBORG BOGLADE | Valby Langgade 39, 1. th. | 2500 Valby, tlf. 31 16 94 66

A4 folded to A5

title leaf, 2 pp; text n 5696-[6110½], pp 1-283; Register <Index>, pp 284-340; Indsættes <Passages to be inserted in vols 3, 4, 5>, pp 341-342; Rettelser til Tegninger, p 342; Rettelser <Corrections to be made in vols 1, 2, 3, 7, and 8>, pp 345-346; Henvisninger til den Hellige Skrift <Index to Bible passages cited>, pp 347-352; Reproduction of pages from En 4/2 <pp 392-393> comparing alternative systems of numbering paragraphs 4729-4792; Efterskrift <Postscript signed G. B.>, p 354.

Translated by G Boolsen; offset litho printed.

UK: SOC; DEN: RLD

DUTCH

Translators:

Du 1 A Zelling
Du 2 H Weevers

47/05/Du 1/1 **1971** Hyde 3129/2a

OPMERKENSWAARDIGE | LEVENDE | ONDERVINDINGEN | *BAND I* | <orn> | <double rule> | *UITGEGEVEN VOOR HET* | SWEDENBORG GENOOTSCHAP | DOOR | MARTINUS NIJHOFF | *'S-GRAVENHAGE:* | 1971

verso: „Dat onze Heiland mij heft toegestaan | dit te ondervinden, is niet een persoonlijke | aangelegenheid, maar terwille van een | subliem belang, hetwelk het eeuwige | welzijn van alle Christenen betreft". | *Brief aan den Koning* | *van Zweden, 10 Mei, 1770.* | Documents, deel VII, pag. 373-377. | Deze titel verrijst als het ware uit het Manuscript zelf, want daarin is voortdurend sprake van *Onder-* | *vindingen*, voorts van *Levende Ondervindingen*, en, nog nadrukkelijker, van *Opmerkenswaardige* | *Levende Ondervindingen* (Vivae Experientiae, observatione dignae); hetgeen de voorkeur verdient | boven „Gedenkwaardigheden" of „Geestelijk Dagboek", bewijze den brief aan den Koning van | Zweden. „Levende Ondervindingen" will zeggen: ondervonden aan den levenden lijve. <*stet* VII>

8vo

title leaf, 2 pp; text: n 149-1756, pp 3-560.

The printer's ornament on the title page is a reproduction of NR 340.

Translated by A Zelling.

The editorial note on the verso of the title leaf explains the title which Zelling gave to his version: 'This title arises as it were from the Manuscript itself, for therein is continuously spoken of Experiences, and then of Living Experiences, and still more expressly of Noteworthy Living Experiences (Vivae Experientiae observatione dignae); which is preferable to "Memorabilia" or "Spiritual Diary," as the letter to the King of Sweden confirms. "Living Experiences" means, experienced by one's living body.' The text of the letter to the King of Sweden was written by Swedenborg on 10 May 1770, see R L Tafel *Documents* 2:1, pp 373-377 <**E:b** En 1877/1 = Hyde 3275> London.

UK: SOC; NET: GEN

47/05/Du 1/2 **1972** Hyde 3129/2b

OPMERKENSWAARDIGE | LEVENDE | ONDERVINDINGEN | *BAND II* | <orn> | <double rule> | *UITGEGEVEN VOOR HET* | SWEDENBORG GENOOTSCHAP | DOOR | MARTINUS NIJHOFF | *'S-GRAVENHAGE:* | 1972

verso: „Dat onze Heiland mij heft toegestaan | dit te ondervinden, is niet een persoonlijke | aangelegenheid, maar terwille van een | subliem belang, hetwelk het eeuwige | welzijn van alle Christenen betreft". | *Brief aan den Koning* | *van Zweden, 10 Mei, 1770.* | Documents, deel VII, pag. 373-377. | ...vidi, audivi, sensi ... | *„ik heb gezien, gehoord, gevoeld"* | Hemelse Verborgenheden nr. 68 | <orn> <*stet* VII>

8vo

title leaf, 2 pp; text n 1757-3425, pp 563-1135.

Translated by A Zelling.

The printer's ornament on the title page is a reproduction of NR 340, and the ornament on the verso is a reproduction of NR 336.

UK: SOC; NET: GEN

47/05/Du 1/3 **1973** Hyde 3129/2c

OPMERKENSWAARDIGE | LEVENDE | ONDERVINDINGEN | *BAND III* | <orn> | <double rule> | *UITGEGEVEN VOOR HET* | *'S-GRAVENHAGE* | SWEDENBORG GENOOTSCHAP | 1973

verso: „Dat onze Heiland mij heft toegestaan | dit te ondervinden, is niet een persoonlijke | aangelegenheid, maar terwille van een | subliem belang, hetwelk het eeuwige | welzijn van alle Christenen betreft". | *Brief aan den Koning* | *van Zweden, 10 Mei, 1770.* | Documents, deel VII, pag. 373-377. | ...vidi, audivi, sensi ... | *„ik heb gezien, gehoord, gevoeld"* | Hemelse Verborgenheden nr. 68 | <orn> <*stet* VII>

8vo

title leaf, 2 pp; text n 3426-4544, pp 1139-1595; n 4545-4792 = Minor Diary, pp 1595-1698; n 4545-4678, pp 1698-1775.

Translated by A Zelling.

The printer's ornament on the title page is a reproduction of NR 340, and the ornament on the verso is a reproduction of NR 336.

UK: SOC; NET: GEN

47/05/Du 1/4 **1973** Hyde 3129/2d

OPMERKENSWAARDIGE | LEVENDE | ONDERVINDINGEN | *BAND IV* | <orn> | <double rule> | *'S-GRAVENHAGE* | SWEDENBORG GENOOTSCHAP | 1973

verso: „Dat onze Heiland mij heft toegestaan | dit te ondervinden, is niet een persoonlijke | aangelegenheid, maar terwille van een | subliem belang, hetwelk het eeuwige | welzijn van alle Christenen betreft". | *Brief aan den Koning* | *van Zweden, 10 Mei, 1770.* | Documents, deel VII, pag. 373-377. | ... vidi, audivi, sensi ... | *„ik heb gezien, gehoord, gevoeld"* | Hemelse Verborgenheden nr. 68 | <orn> <*stet* VII>

8vo

title leaf, 2 pp; text n 4679-6110, pp 1777-2433; Anhangsel I, een elftal schetsen die ion het manuscript voorkwamen <a reproduction of the diagrams which Swedenborg sketched in his

MS>, pp 2435-2442; Anhangsel II, een reconstructie van de ontbrekende eerste 148 nrs. op basis van door Swedenborg zelf samengestelde indexen <a reconstruction of the contents of n 1-148, compiled from Swedenborg's index to the work>, pp 2443-2458.
Translated by A Zelling.
The printer's ornament on the title page is a reproduction of nr 340, and the ornament on the verso is a reproduction of nr 336.
UK: soc; NET: gen

47/05/Du 2/1 **2009-2010** Hyde —
OPMERKENSWAARDIGE | LEVENDE | ONDERVINDINGEN
A3 folded to A4
title and text: **2009** n 149-171, 172-178, 179-190, editie 67 pp 3-11; n 191-203, pp 22-24; n 203-241, editie 68 pp 14-23; n 242-261, editie 69 pp 2-6; **2010** n 262-287, editie 70 pp 2-6; n 288-314, editie 71 pp 7-12.
Paragraph n 178 of Swedenborg's MS is numbered as n 172-178, with no indication that his MS does not contain n 172-177.
Translated by Henk Weevers, published in *Swedenborgiana* Baarle Nassau.
UK: soc, nr; NET: boe, gen, kb; USA: anc

DUTCH EXTRACTS

X 47/05/Du 1927/1, **D** Du 1927/1 **1927** Hyde 1515/7, 2373/2
UIT DE MEMORABILIA | EEN EN ANDER OVER HUWELIJK EN ECHTBREUCK
HET HUWELIJK | TUSSCHEN DE KEIZERIN VAN RUSLAND | EN DE LA GARDIE
OP WELKE WIJZE MEISJES IN HET ANDERE LEVEN | EN IN DEN HEMEL WORDEN OPGEVOED
DE OPVOEDING DER KINDEREN
small 8vo
title and text n [6110], pp 97-118; text n 6027, pp 119-123; text n 5660-5667, pp 124-125; text n 5668, p 126.
Published by the Swedenborg Genootschap, The Hague, in *Het Huwelijk (De Conjugio)* <66/06/ Du 1/1, **D** Du 1927/1 = Hyde 2373/2>. Some parts of n 6027 have been omitted.
UK: soc, nr; GER: wlb; NET: gen; USA: anc

X 47/05/Du 1933/1 **1933** Hyde 2192/1–
UIT DE MEMORABILIA | *Over geesten die de innerlijke en de meer vaar het binnenste | gelegen dingen des Woords niet willen hooren en toclaten*
8vo
title and text n 1139-1145½, pp 350-352.
Published in *De Hemelsche Leer* The Hague.
UK: soc, con; NET: gen; USA: anc

GERMAN

Translators:
Ge 1 W Pfirsch
Ge 2 H Grob

47/05/Ge 1/1 **1902** Hyde 526
Emanuel Swedenborg's | Geistiges Tagebuch | — oder — | kurze Aufzeichnungen seiner

geistigen Erfahrungen während eines | Zeitraums von zwanzig Jahren. | <short rule> | Veröffentlicht aus der lateinischen Handschrift des Verfassers von | Dr. J. F. I. Tafel, Universitätsbibliothekar in Tübingen. | <short rule> | Aus der Urschrift übersetzt | — von — | Prof. W. Pfirsch. | <short rule> | Erster Band. | <short rule> | Im Verlag des | Deutschen Missions-Vereins der Neuen Kirche in Amerika, | 1011 Arch Straße, Philadelphia, Pa. | 1902.
large 8vo
title leaf, 2 pp; Vorrede des Herausgebers des lateinischen Textes <Preface of the publisher of the Latin edition>, pp i-vi; Anmerkungen zu der Vorrede <Notes on the preface>, pp vi-ix; Vorwort <Foreword>, pp x-xiv; text n 1-1538, pp 1-366.
Translated at the expense of J G Mittnacht, and revised by L H Tafel.
UK: SOC; NET: GEN; SWE: ROY

47/05/Ge 1/2 **1986** Hyde 526/1
Emanuel Swedenborgs | Geistiges Tagebuch | Erste Niederschrift seiner visionären Erlebnisse während | eines Zeitraums von zwanzig Jahren | Aus der von Dr. I. Tafel | herausgegebenen lateinischen Handschrift | übersetzt von Prof. W. Pfirsch | Band I | Faksimile-Nachdruck der Ausgabe von 1902 | Swedenborg Verlag Zürich
verso: © 1986 copyright des Faksimile-Nachdrucks | der 1. Auflage von 1902, Philadelphia, Pa. | Swedenborg Verlag Zürich | ISBN 3-85927-037.0
half title: SWEDENBORG • GEISTIGES TAGEBUCH
8vo
half title and title leaves, 4 pp; Vorrede des Herausgebers des lateinischen Textes <Preface of the Latin editor>, pp i-vi; Anmerkungen zu der Vorrede <Notes on the preface>, pp vi-ix; Vorwort <Foreword>, pp x-xiv; text n 1-1538, pp 1-366; Werbung <advertisement>, pp 367-368.
Facsimile reprint of Ge 1/1.
GER: WLB; SWI: ZÜR; USA: ANC

47/05/Ge 1/3 **1991** Hyde 526/2
Emanuel Swedenborgs | Geistiges Tagebuch | Erste Niederschrift seiner visionären Erlebnisse während | eines Zeitraumes von zwanzig Jahren | Aus der von Dr. I. Tafel | herausgegebenen lateinischen Handschrift | übersetzt von Prof. W. Pfirsch | Band 1 | Faksimile-Nachdruck der Ausgabe von 1902 | Swedenborg Verlag Zürich
verso: © 1986 copyright des Faksimile-Nachdrucks | der 1. Auflage von 1902, Philadelphia, Pa. | Swedenborg Verlag Zürich | ISBN 3-85927-037.0
half title: SWEDENBORG • GEISTIGES TAGEBUCH
8vo
half title and title leaves, 4pp; Vorrede des Herausgebers des lateinischen Textes <Preface of the Latin editor>, pp i-vi; Anmerkungen zu der Vorrede <Notes on the preface>, pp vi-ix; Vorwort <Foreword>, pp x-xiv; text n 1-1538, pp 1-366; Werbung <advertisement>, pp 367-368.
Facsimile reprint of Ge 1/1. Cover designed by J Horn.
GER: VER

47/05/Ge 1/4 **2010** Hyde 3129/3a
Emanuel Swedenborg | Das Geistige Tagebuch | Erste Niederschrift seiner visionären Erlebnisse während | eines Zeitraumes von zwanzig Jahren | Aus der von Dr. Immanuel Tafel | herausgegebenen lateinischen Handschrift übersetzt von | Prof. W. Pfirsch | Band I | 1 bis 1538 | Swedenborg Verlag Zürich
verso: Auflage 2010 | © Swedenborg Verlag Zürich 2010 | ISBN 978-3-85927-085-5 = Band 1-7 | ISBN 978-3-85927-086-2 = Band 1

half title: Emanuel Swedenborg Das Geistige Tagebuch | Band 1 | nunc | <orn 2 x 112 mm> | licet
8vo
half title and title leaves, 4pp; Ein par Worte zu dieser Ausgabe <A note concrerning this edition>, pp 3-4; Vorrede des Herausgebers des lateinischen Textes <Preface of the Latin editor>, pp 3-4; Vorwort des Herausgebers <Publisher's preface>, pp 5-17; Vorwort des deutschen Übersetzers, Prof. W. Pfirsch <Translator's foreword>, pp 17-24; text n 1-1538, pp 25-588; GT Band 1 Inhaltsverzeichnis <Table of contents of volume 1>, pp 589-622.
Reprint of Ge 1/3 in Antiquaschrift.
GER: VER, WLB; SWI: ZÜR

47/05/Ge 2/1 **2010** Hyde 3129/3b
Emanuel Swedenborg | Das Geistige Tagebuch | Erste Niederschrift seiner visionären Erlebnisse während | eines Zeitraumes von zwanzig Jahren | Aus der von Dr. Immanuel Tafel | herausgegebenen lateinischen Ausgabe übersetzt von | Heinz Grob | Band 2 | 1539 bis 3427 | Swedenborg Verlag Zürich
verso: <Publisher's explanation that this section of the text was translated by H Grob in 2009> | Auflage 2010 | © Swedenborg Verlag Zürich 2010 | ISBN 978-3-85927-085-5 = Band 1-7 | ISBN 978-3-85927-087-9 = Band 2
half title: Emanuel Swedenborg Das Geistige Tagebuch | Band 2 | nunc | <orn 2 x 112 mm> | licet
8vo
half title and title leaves, 4pp; text n 1539-3427, pp 5-659; GT Band 2 Inhaltsverzeichnis <Table of contents of volume 2>, pp 661-697.
GER: VER, WLB; SWI: ZÜR

47/05/ Ge 1/5 **2010** Hyde 3129/3c
Emanuel Swedenborg | Das Geistige Tagebuch | Erste Niederschrift seiner visionären Erlebnisse während | eines Zeitraumes von zwanzig Jahren | Aus der von Dr. Immanuel Tafel | herausgegebenen lateinischen Handschrift übersetzt von | Prof. W. Pfirsch | Band 3 | 3428 bis 4544 | Swedenborg Verlag Zürich
verso: Auflage 2010 | ISBN 978-3-85927-085-5 = Band 1-7 | ISBN 978-3-85927-088-6 = Band 3
half title: Emanuel Swedenborg Das Geistige Tagebuch | Band 3 | nunc | <orn 2 x 112 mm> | licet
8vo
half title and title leaves, 4pp; text n 3428-4544, pp 5-518; Inhaltsverzeichnis GT Band 3 <Table of contents of volume 3>, pp 519-540.
GER: VER, WLB; SWI: ZÜR

47/05/Ge 1/6 **2010** Hyde 3129/3d
Emanuel Swedenborg | Das Geistige Tagebuch | Erste Niederschrift seiner visionären Erlebnisse während | eines Zeitraumes von zwanzig Jahren | Aus der von Dr. Immanuel Tafel | herausgegebenen lateinischen Handschrift übersetzt von | Prof. W. Pfirsch | Band 4 | Das kleine Tagebuch | 4545 bis 4792 | und die Fortsetzung von Band 3 | 4545 bis 5659 | Swedenborg Verlag Zürich
verso: Auflage 2010 | © Swedenborg Verlag Zürich 2010 | ISBN 978-3-85927-085-5 = Band 1-7 | ISBN 978-3-85927-089-3 = Band 4
half title: Emanuel Swedenborg Das Geistige Tagebuch | Band 4 | nunc | <orn 2 x 112 mm> | licet
8vo
half title and title leaves, 4pp; Vorrede des Dr. Tafel <Dr Tafel's foreword>, pp 5-10; text n 4545-

4715 and unnumbered paragraphs, pp 10-124; and Fortsetzung <Continuation> of Band 3 n 4545-5659, pp 125-644; Inhaltsverzeichnung GT 4. Band <Table of contents of volume 4>, pp 645-668.
GER: VER, WLB; SWI: ZÜR

47/05/Ge 1/7 **2010** Hyde 3129/e
Emanuel Swedenborg | Das Geistige Tagebuch | Erste Niederschrift seiner visionären Erlebnisse während | eines Zeitraumes von zwanzig Jahren | Aus der von Dr. Immanuel Tafel | herausgegebenen lateinischen Handschrift übersetzt von | Prof. W. Pfirsch | Band 5 | 5660 bis 6110 | Anhang | und kleines A-Z Register | oder kleiner Index | Swedenborg Verlag Zürich
verso: Auflage 2010 | © Swedenborg Verlag Zürich 2010 | ISBN 978-3-85927-085-5 = Band 1-7 | ISBN 978-3-85927-090-8 = Band 5
half title: Emanuel Swedenborg Das Geistige Tagebuch | Band 5 | nunc | <orn 2 x 112 mm> | licet
8vo
half title and title leaves, 4pp; text n 5660-6110, pp 5-308; Anhang zum Geistigen Tagebuch VII Teil, Abteilung 4, pp 309-372; Anhang zu dem Geistigen Tagebuch verfaßt Achatius Kahl <Appendix to the Spiritual Diary, composed by A Kahl>, pp 373-422; Kleineres A-Z Register oder Index zum Geistigen Tagebuch sowie auch zu den Adversarien, pp 423-593; Inhaltsverzeichnis GT Band 5 <Table of contents of volume 5>, pp 595-609.
GER: VER, WLB; SWI: ZÜR

47/05/Ge 1/8 **2010** Hyde 3129/3f
Emanuel Swedenborg | Das Geistige Tagebuch | Erste Niederschrift seiner visionären Erlebnisse während | eines Zeitraumes von zwanzig Jahren | Aus der von Dr. Immanuel Tafel | herausgegebenen lateinischen Handschrift übersetzt von | Prof. W. Pfirsch | Band 6 | Großer Index | A bis j | Swedenborg Verlag Zürich <*stet* A bis j>
verso: Auflage 2010 | © Swedenborg Verlag Zürich 2010 | ISBN 978-3-85927-085-5 = Band 1-7 | ISBN 978-3-85927-091-6 = Band 6
half title: Emanuel Swedenborg Das Geistige Tagebuch | Band 6 | nunc | <orn 2 x 112 mm> | licet
8vo
half title and title leaves, 4pp; Vorwort des Herausgebers <Publisher's preface>, p 5; text of Großer Index <Larger Index> Aas-Jupitergeister, pp 6-555.
GER: VER, WLB; SWI: ZÜR

47/05/Ge 1/9 **2010** Hyde 3129/3g
Emanuel Swedenborg | Das Geistige Tagebuch | Erste Niederschrift seiner visionären Erlebnisse während | eines Zeitraumes von zwanzig Jahren | Aus der von Dr. Immanuel Tafel | herausgegebenen lateinischen Handschrift übersetzt von | Prof. W. Pfirsch | Band 7 | Großer Index | K bis Z | Swedenborg Verlag Zürich
verso: Auflage 2010 | © Swedenborg Verlag Zürich 2010 | ISBN 978-3-85927-085-5 = Band 1-7 | ISBN 978-3-85927-092-7 = Band 7
half title: Emanuel Swedenborg Das Geistige Tagebuch | Band 7 | nunc | <orn 2 x 112 mm> | licet
8vo
half title and title leaves, 4pp; text of Großer Index <Larger Index> Kain-Zwölf, pp 5-557; Ergänzung <Supplement> des Dr Tafel zu den Worten: Liebe, Hirn, Kirche, Glaube Heuchler Wort, pp 557-587.
GER: VER, WLB; SWI: ZÜR

47/05/Ge 1/10 **2011** Hyde 526/–

Emanuel Swedenborg | Das Geistige Tagebuch | Erste Niederschrift seiner visionären Erlebnisse während | eines Zeitraumes von zwanzig Jahren | Aus der von Dr. Immanuel Tafel | herausgegebenen lateinischen Handschrift übersetzt von | Prof. W. Pfirsch | Band I | 1 bis 1538 | Neue Überarbeitung 2011 | von | Heinz Grob | Swedenborg Verlag Zürich
verso: Dieses ist eine Überarbeitung | von Heinz Grob | des 1. Bandes Geistiges Tagebuch | der Übersetzung von Prof. Pfirsch | Auflage 2011 | © Swedenborg Verlag Zürich 2011| ISBN 978-3-85927-093-0
half title: Emanuel Swedenborg Das Geistige Tagebuch | Band 1 | nunc | <orn 2 x 112 mm> | licet
8vo
half title and title leaves, 4 pp; Vorrede des Herausgebers des lateinischen Textes <Foreword of the editor of the Latin text>, pp 5-16; Vorwort des Übersetzers Prof. W. Pfirsch <Translator's foreword>, pp 17-23; text n 1-1538, pp 25-554; Inhaltsverzeichnis des 1. Bandes <Table of contents of volume 1>, pp 555-587.
Neue moderne Überarbeitung (zeitgemäßes Deutsch) von Heinz Grob 2008 <New modern revision in current German, prepared by Heinz Grob in 2008>.
GER: VER; SWI: ZÜR

GERMAN EXTRACTS

X 47/05/Ge 1949/1, **D** Ge 1949/1 **1949** Hyde 2192/1a, 3263/1

5. | **Das geistiche Tagebuch** | Diarium Spirituale | **von Swedenborg selbst „Denkwürdigkeiten"** | (Memorabilia) **gennant** | 1747—1763
8vo
title leaf, pp 235-236; text n 5012-5014, 5034-5039, 5041-5058, 5322-5336, 5711-5716, 5718-5719, 5721, 5742-5746, 5758-5764, 5767, 5765-5766⅓, 5768-5769, 5786-5792¼, 5814-5816, 5819-5820, 5871, 5875, 6020, pp 237-270 <n 5034 misprinted as 5014>.
Translated by I Meyer-Lünen from X Sw 1925/1, published in *Ausgewählte religiöse Schriften* edited by E Benz and R F Merkel <**D** Sw 1925/1 = Hyde 3270/–>, Marburg/Lahn.
UK: SOC; SWI: ZÜR

JAPANESE

47/05/Ja 1/1 **1980** Hyde 528/a

<within a rule border 151 x 113 mm, divided into 3 panels by 2 rules 151 mm> <1:> イマヌエルスエデンボルグ著　柳瀬芳意　訳 <2:> 霊界日記　ー遺稿　第一巻 | ー著者の一七四六年(五八才)から一七六五年(七七才)に至る二十年間に霊 | 界における経験を基として執筆されたものー <3:> 静思社
section title leaf: 霊界日記
8vo
title leaf, 2 pp; Preface, pp 1-3; section title leaf, pp 1-2; text n 1-692, pp 1-372; publishing information, below which is printed 3316—790201—4012, p 373.
Volume 1, translated by Y Yanase from En 5/1 <= Hyde 523/1>, published in Tokyo, Seishi-sha, Shōwa 55-59.
In the catalogue of SWE: ROY title page information is transliterated as follows: Reikai nikki ko / Emanueru Suedenborugu cho; Yanese Yoshii yaku. Tokyō: Seishi-sha, Showa 55-59 [1980-84].
UK: SOC; SWE: ROY; USA: ANC, SHS

47/05/Ja 1/2 **1981** Hyde 528/b

<within a rule border 155 x 115 mm, divided into 3 panels by 2 rules 155 mm> <1:> イマヌエル

スエデンボルグ著　柳瀬芳意　訳 <2:> 霊界日記　ー遺稿　第二巻 | ー著者の一七四六年(五八歳)から一七六五年(七七歳)に至る二十年間に霊 | 界における経験を基として執筆されたものー <3:> 静思社
section title leaf: 霊界日記
8vo
title leaf, 2 pp; Preface, pp 1-2; text n 693-1538, pp 3-360; publishing information, p 361.
Volume 2, translated by Y Yanase, from En 5/1 and 3/1, published in Tokyo, Seishi-sha, Shōwa 55-59.
UK: SOC; SWE: ROY; USA: ANC, SHS

47/05/Ja 1/3 **1982-1983** Hyde 528/c
<< <within a rule border 155 x 115 mm, divided into 3 panels by 2 rules 155 mm> <1:> イマヌエル　スエデンボルグ著　柳瀬芳意　訳 <2:> 霊界日記　ー遺稿　第三巻 | ー著者の一七四六年(五八歳)から一七六五年(七七歳)に至る二十年間 | に霊界における経験を基として執筆されたものー <3:> 静思社>>
section title leaf: <<霊界日記>>
8vo
title leaf, 2 pp; Preface, pp 1-4; section title leaf, 2 pp; text n 1539-2450, pp 1-421; publisher's information, 3 pp.
Volume 3, translated by Y Yanase from En 3/2, published in Tokyo, Seishi-sha, Shōwa 55-59.
SWE: ROY; USA: ANC, SHS

47/05/Ja 1/4 **1982-1983** Hyde 528/d
<< <within a rule border 155 x 115 mm, divided into 3 panels by 2 rules 151 mm> <1:> イマヌエル　スエデンボルグ著　柳瀬芳意　訳 <2:> 霊界日記　ー遺稿　第四巻 | ー著者の一七四六年(五八歳)から一七六五年(七七歳)に至る二十年間 | に霊界における経験を基として執筆されたものー <3:> 静思社>>
section title leaf: <<霊界日記>>
8vo
title leaf, 2 pp; Preface, pp 1-2; section title leaf, 2 pp; text 2451-3240, pp 1-407; publisher's information, 15 pp.
Volume 4, translated by Y Yanase from En 3/2, published in Tokyo, Seishi-sha, Shōwa 55-59.
SWE: ROY; USA: ANC, SHS

47/05/Ja 1/5 **1983** Hyde 528/5
<within a rule border 151 x 115 mm, divided into 3 panels by 2 rules 151 mm> <1:> イマヌエル　スエデンボルグ著　柳瀬芳意　訳 <2:> 霊界日記　ー遺稿　第五巻 | ー著者の一七四六年(五八歳)から一七六五年(七七歳)に至る二十年間 | に霊界における経験を基として執筆されたものー <3:> 静思社
section title leaf: 霊界日記
8vo
title leaf, 2 pp; Preface, pp 1-2; section title leaf, 2 pp; text n 3241-3916, pp 1-374; publishing information, below which is printed 3316–790201–4012, p 375.
Volume 5, translated by Y Yanase from En 3/3, published in Tokyo, Seishi-sha, Shōwa 55-59.
UK: SOC; SWE: ROY; USA: ANC, SHS

47/05/Ja 1/6 **1983** Hyde 528/e
<< <within a rule border 151 x 115 mm, divided into 3 panels by 2 rules 155 mm> <1:> イマヌエル　スエデンボルグ著　柳瀬芳意　訳 <2:> 霊界日記　ー遺稿　第六巻 | ー著者の一七四

六年(五八歳)から一七六五年(七七歳)に至る二十年間 | に霊界における経験を基として執筆されたものー <3:> 静思社>>
section title leaf: <<霊界日記>>
8vo
title leaf, 2 pp; section title leaf, 2 pp; text n 3917-4544, pp 1-378; publisher's information, 2 pp.
Volume 6, translated by Y Yanase, published in Tokyo, Seishi-sha, Shōwa 55-59.
SWE: ROY; USA: SHS

47/05/Ja 1/7 **1983** Hyde 528/e
<< <within a rule border 155 x 115 mm, divided into 3 panels by 2 rules 155 mm> <1:> イマヌエル　スエデンボルグ著　柳瀬芳意　訳 <2:> 霊界日記　ー遺稿　第七巻 | ー著者の一七四六年(五八歳)から一七六五年(七七歳)に至る二十年間 | に霊界における経験を基として執筆されたものー <3:> 静思社>>
section title leaf: <<霊界日記>>
8vo
title leaf, 2 pp; section title leaf, 2 pp; text n 4545-4792 <Minor Diary>, pp 1-155; n 4545-4906, pp 156-419; publisher's information, 2 pp.
Volume 7, translated by Y Yanase, published in Tokyo, Seishi-sha, Shōwa 55-59.
SWE: ROY; USA: SHS

47/05/Ja 1/8 **1983** Hyde 528/e
<< <within a rule border 155 x 115 mm, divided into 3 panels by 2 rules 155 mm> <1:> イマヌエル　スエデンボルグ著　柳瀬芳意　訳 <2:> 霊界日記　ー遺稿　第八巻 | ー著者の一七四六年(五八歳)から一七六五年(七七歳)に至る二十年間 | に霊界における経験を基として執筆されたものー <3:> 静思社>>
section title leaf: <<霊界日記>>
8vo
title leaf, 2 pp; section title leaf, 2 pp; text n 4907-5659, pp 1-315; publisher's information, 1 p.
Volume 8, translated by Y Yanase, published in Tokyo, Seishi-sha, Shōwa 55-59.
SWE: ROY; USA: SHS

47/05/Ja 1/9 **1983** Hyde 528/e
<< <within a rule border 155 x 115 mm, divided into 3 panels by 2 rules 155 mm> <1:> イマヌエル　スエデンボルグ著　柳瀬芳意　訳 <2:> 霊界日記　ー遺稿　第九巻 | ー著者の一七四六年(五八歳)から一七六五年(七七歳)に至る二十年間 | に霊界における経験を基として執筆されたものー <3:> 静思社>>
section title leaf: <<霊界日記>>
8vo
title leaf, 2 pp; section title leaf, 2 pp; text n 5660-6110, pp 1-386; publisher's information, 2 pp.
Volume 9, translated by Y Yanase, published in Tokyo, Seishi-sha, Shōwa 55-59.
SWE: ROY; USA: SHS

JAPANESE EXTRACTS

X 47/05/Ja 2001/1 **2001?** Hyde —
A volume containing extracts from *Spiritual Experiences,* edited and translated by Professor Kazuo Takahasi, was referred to in the Newsletter of Swedenborg Publishers International, Bryn Athyn PA, Fall 2003.

KOREAN EXTRACTS

X 47/05/Ko 2003/1 **2003** Hyde —

A volume containing extracts from *Spiritual Experiences*, translated from X Ja 2001/1, to be published by the Arcana Press, Tokyo, in November 2003, was referred to in the Newsletter of Swedenborg Publishers International, Bryn Athyn PA, Fall 2003.

SERBO-CROATIAN EXTRACTS

X 47/05/SeCr 1986/1 **1986** Hyde 2192/2

<untitled>

Extracts from *Spiritual Experiences* translated by Ivana Milankova, published in *Knijuzeuna Rec* June 1986. <UK: SOC Archives L/425>

UK: SOC

SWEDISH

47/05/Sw 1/1 **no date** Hyde 527, 3159

<<Emanuel Swedenborgs Större Dagbok, Eller Minnesvärdigheter. Emanuel Swedenborgs Andeliga Dägbok, första delens förra afdelning. Utur dess handskrift, förvarad uti Kongl: Universitets Biblioteket i Upsala. Nu först utgifven af Dr. Jo, Fr. Im. Tafel, Kongl. Universitets Biibliotekarie i Tübingen. Öfversättning. Tybingen, 1844. [Till Svenska öfversatt af A. F. Winnberg, Kyrkoherde i Frostviken i Jemland.]>>

foolscap broad 4to <210 x 169 mm>

Inledning <Introduction>, pp 1-19; Utgifvarens företal <Publisher's statement>, pp 1-12; text n 1-1538, pp 13-674.

Part 1, section 1 of the MS, which in 1906 was in Nykyrkliga Bokförlaget, Stockholm; its present whereabouts are unknown. A copy of the MS is held in SWE: UPP.

MS not seen; description recorded from Hyde 527.

47/05/Sw 1/2 **no date** Hyde 528, 3159

<<EMANUEL SWEDENBORGS STÖRRE DAGBOK, ELLER MINNESVÄRDIGHETER.| Första delens andra volum.>>

foolscap broad 4to <210 x 169 mm>

text n 1539-3427, pp 1-1047.

Translated by A F Winnberg; Part 1, section 2 of the MS, which in 1906 was in Nykyrkliga Bokförlaget, Stockholm; its present whereabouts are unknown. A copy of the MS is held in SWE: UPP.

MS not seen; description recorded from Hyde 528.

47/05/Sw 1/3 **no date** Hyde 902, 3159

<<Emanuel Swedenborgs Andeliga Dägbok, eller samling af Minnesvärdigheter. Andra delen.>>

foolscap broad 4to <210 x 169 mm>

text n 3428-4544, pp 1-781.

Translated by A F Winnberg; Part 2 of the MS, which in 1906 was in Nykyrkliga Bokförlaget, Stockholm; its present whereabouts are unknown. A copy of the MS is held in SWE: UPP.

MS not seen; description recorded from Hyde 902.

47/05/Sw 1/4 **no date** Hyde 920, 3159

<<Emanuel Swedenborgs Mindea Dagbök, eller samling af Minnesvärdigheter.>>

foolscap broad 4to <210 x 169 mm>

Utgifvarens företal <Publisher's statement>, pp 1-16; text n 4545-4655, 4657-4715, and 71

unnumbered articles, pp 17-210.
Translated by A F Winnberg; Part 4 of the MS, which in 1906 was in Nykyrkliga Bokförlaget, Stockholm; its present whereabouts are unknown. A copy of the MS is held in SWE: UPP.
MS not seen; description recorded from Hyde 920.

47/05/Sw 1/5 **no date** Hyde 2170, 3159
<<Emanuel Swedenborgs Större Dagbök. Tredje delen, förra afdelningen.>>
foolscap broad 4to <210 x 169 mm>
text n 4545-5659, pp 1-858.
Translated by A F Winnberg; Part 3, section 1 of the MS, which in 1906 was in Nykyrkliga Bokförlaget, Stockholm; its present whereabouts are unknown. A copy of the MS is held in SWE: UPP.
MS not seen; description recorded from Hyde 2170.

47/05/Sw 1/6 **no date** Hyde 2171, 3159
<<Emanuel Swedenborgs Större Dagbök, Eller Minnesvärdigheter. Tredje delens andra afdelninn.>>
foolscap broad 4to <210 x 169 mm>
text n 5660-6096, etc, pp 1-485.
Translated by A F Winnberg; Part 3, section 2 of the MS, which in 1906 was in Nykyrkliga Bokförlaget, Stockholm; its present whereabouts are unknown. A copy of the MS is held in SWE: UPP.
MS not seen; description recorded from Hyde 2171.

SWEDISH EXTRACTS

X 47/05/Sw 1846/1 **1846** Hyde 1645, 3060
<untitled>
8vo
facsimile of the text of n 6027, reproduced on pages numbered N. 14-21.
Edited by J F I Tafel, published in *Diarii Spiritualis Pars Septima continens Appendicem, una cum autoris imagine et tabulis lithographicis ad chirographi similitudinem expressis* <Hyde 3060> Tübingen and London.
UK: SOC, CON, NCC, NR; GER: GSU; NET: GEN; USA: ANC

X 47/05/Sw 1859/1 **1859** Hyde 429
Bihang <Appendix>
8vo
title and text n 4679m, 4787 part, 5763, 6027, 6035 part, closing memorabilia <written on the last page of the MS>, pp 65-72.
Published by G E Klemming, in *Svedenborgs Drömmar 1744* <43/03/Sw 1/1 = Hyde 429>.
UK: SOC, CON; USA: SHS

X 47/05/Sw 1860/1 **1860** Hyde 430
Bihang <Appendix>
8vo
title and text n 4679m, 4787 part, 5763, 6027, 6035 part, closing memorabilia <written on the last page of the MS>, pp 65-72.
Published by A Kahl and J A Sevén, in *Svedenborgs Drömmar 1744* <43/03/Sw 2/1 = Hyde 430>.
UK: SOC, CON; USA: SHS

X 47/05/Sw 1925/1, **D** Sw 1925/1 **1925** Hyde 430/–, 3270/–
UR ANDLIGA DAGBOKEN | DIARIUM SPIRITUALE | AV SWEDENBORG SJÄLV KALLAD | MÄRKVÄRDIGHETER | MEMORABILIA
8vo
section title leaf, pp 199-200; text n 5012-5014, 5034, 5058, 5322-5336, 5711-5716, 5718-5719, 5721, 5742-5750, 5758-5764, 5767, 5765-5766, 5768-5769, 5786, 5789-5792, 5812-5816, 5819-5821, 5781, 5875, 6020, pp 201-233.
Translated by G Bergstedt, published by Hugo Gebers Förlag in *Religiösa Skrifter i Urval* <**D** Sw 1925/1 = Hyde 3270/–> Stockholm.
SWE: ROY, HNK

X 47/05/Sw 1932/1 **1932-1936** Hyde 430/–
Ur «Swedenborgs andliga dagboken»
4to and small 4to
title and text: **1932** n 5547-5553, pp 60-61; n 3590, 4096, 2894, 4267, 397, 2120, 2922, 6107, 4385, 4388, pp 84-87; **1933** n 609, 4752m, 2486, 3542-3545, 3561, 832-835, 3590, 335, 722, pp 19-21; n 4791m, 2234-2235, 2209, 6094, pp 28-29; n 4259, 4313, 4425-4426, 4821-4822, pp 36-37; n 434, 2591, 4410, 4418, pp 44-45; n 4439, 1996-1998, 4730-4731, 4729, 3623, pp 52-53; n 4224, 2913, 4422, 4652m, 4177, p 61; n 3480-3484, pp 84-85; **1934** n 488, 2583, 2826-2827, p 5; n 4645m, p 13; n 3115, 5571, 3064-3065, 3028, 3622, pp 21-22; n 269, p 29; n 1959, 1961, pp 58-59; n 3308, 1960, 3427, 5700, 5705, p 68; n 5705, 5002-5003, p 76; **1935** n 2260-2261, 2873, p 7; n 2874-2875, 2919, 2879, 150, 4792m, 5227, 170, 3474, pp 13-15; n 3474-3475, 856, 655-657, pp 21-22; n 6064, 6077, 3485-3487, 5960, 5959, pp 29-30; n 3292, 4340, 1981-1982, 2097, p 38; n 4781m-4786m, 4101, pp 46-47; n 4103, 4094, p 61; n 5907, 4697m, 4693m, 3753, 3604, 3636, pp 79-80; n 4323, 689, 2895, 3538, 3959-3961, 4018, pp 84-86; **1936** n 338, 4720, p 6; n 4732-4733, 5956, 2019, 498, pp 12-13; n 3537, 152, pp 29-30; n 2014, 3892, 1966, 400, 2756-2757, 2040-2041, 4181-4182, pp 46-48; n 5645, 595, 557, 6102, 6029, 6059, 5172-5176, 6049, 6058, 4271, 3878, 4772, pp 53-56; n 4701-4703, 4829, pp 61-62; n 6021, p 86.
Published in *Nya Kyrkans Budskap* Stockholm. The translator is identified only by the initials 'I.H.'.
UK: CON

47/06 Biblical Index of the Prophetical Books of the Old Testament, etc. Hyde CXXXIV

The autograph MS, bound in parchment, forms Codex 4 in the Library of the Royal Swedish Academy of Sciences, Stockholm. On the spine of the codex, these words are written: INDEX BIBLICUM | VET. TEST | TOM. I. II.

Swedenborg copied the entries relating to Isaiah and Jeremiah which he had written in Codex 6 <47/03/La O/1> into this MS. To these he added references from his Schmidius Bible <47/04/La O/1, O/2> on Jeremiah and Ezekiel <as far as chapter 21>, and then entries from this Bible on Psalms, Job, Revelation, Exodus, Leviticus, Numbers, and Deuteronomy.

Under the heading *Mare* he wrote <among others> the following entry: 'Venit tumultus non celeusma seu ovatio montium, tumultus pro deturbatione infidelium a coelo ultimo, quod assimilabis tumultui maris, de quo vide quid visum 1747, d. 9 Oct. Ovatio montium pro ovatione ex amore sui, Ezech: VII, 7.' <A tumult comes, not the cry or ovation of the mountains: tumult stands for a casting down of the unfaithful from the ultimate heaven, which may be likened to a tumult of the sea, concerning which see what appeared on 9 October 1747 <old style>; an ovation of the mountains stands for an ovation from the love of self, Ezek. 7:7.> See *Experientiae Spirituales* <47/05> n 243, where Swedenborg recounted his spiritual experience in connection with a roaring sea. It is clear that these entries in the *Biblical Index* and *Spiritual Experiences* were made at about the same time. The latter entry is undated, but it appears between two memoranda which are dated: n 242, 6 November 1747, and n 244, 12 November 1747; it appears therefore that '9 Oct.' written here in the *Biblical Index* is a slip of the pen for '9 Nov.'

LATIN

Editions:

La O MS
La 1 J F I Tafel, editor

47/06/La O/1 1747 Hyde 505

<< <untitled> >>
double foolscap long 4to <406 x 159 mm>
text: Memoranda, p 1b.
Doctrina charitatis, p 2a.
Index, with the pages allocated for each letter numbered separately, pp 2b-236b; 1 p blank.

Register of the pages occupied by the Index, p 237a; pp 237b-238a blank.
Memoranda, p 238b.
Various entries, not alphabetically arranged, in continuation of the *Biblical Index* by way of addenda, paged by Swedenborg 1-200, but numbered in pencil also as pp 239a-337b; 30 pp blank.

MS not seen; description deduced from La O/2.
SWE: KVA

47/06/La 1/1, 46/01/La 1/1-1/3 — **1859, 1860, 1863** — Hyde 506, 3066-3068

EMANUELIS SWEDENBORGII | INDEX BIBLICUS | SIVE | THESAURUS BIBLIORUM | EMBLEMATICUS ET ALLEGORICUS. | ... | VOLUMEN PRIMUM. | ... | 1859.
EMANUELIS SWEDENBORGII | INDEX BIBLICUS | SIVE | THESAURUS BIBLIORUM | EMBLEMATICUS ET ALLEGORICUS. | ... | VOLUMEN SECUNDUM. | ... | 1860.
EMANUELIS SWEDENBORGII | INDEX BIBLICUS | SIVE | THESAURUS BIBLIORUM | EMBLEMATICUS ET ALLEGORICUS. | ... | VOLUMEN TERTIUM. | ... | 1863.
8vo
vol I: title leaf, 2 pp; Praefatiuncula editoris, 2 pp; text, pp 1-476.
vol II: title leaf, 2 pp; catalogue, pp 1-6, text, pp 1-480.
vol III: title leaf, 2 pp; text, pp 1-576.
The text of La O/1 amalgamated by the editor, J F I Tafel, with the text of 46/01/La 1/1-1/3 <Codices 40 and 41>, 47/07/La O/1 <Codex 39>, 48/01/La O/1 <Codex 5>, and extracts from Swedenborg's later works, especially *Arcana Coelestia* <49/01/La O/1> and *Apocalypsis Explicata* <59/02/La O2/1> <see 'Praefatiuncula editoris'>. Published as *Index Biblicus* vol 1-3, Tübingen <46/01/La 1/1 = Hyde 3066-3068>.
UK: SOC, NR; DEN: RLD; GER: GSU; NET: GEN; SWE: GSB; USA: ANC

47/06/La 1/2 — **1868** — Hyde 507, 3069

EMANUELIS SWEDENBORGII | INDEX BIBLICUS | SIVE | THESAURUS BIBLIORUM | EMBLEMATICUS ET ALLEGORICUS. | <short rule> | E CHIROGRAPHO EJUS | IN BIBLIOTHECA REGIÆ ACADEMIÆ HOLMIENSIS | ASSERVATO | NUNC PRIMUM EDIDIT | ACHATIUS KAHL, | THEOLOGIÆ ET PHILOSOPHIÆ DOCTOR, ARCHIDIACONUS TEMPLI | LUNDENSIS, PASTOR ET PRÆPOSITUS ECCLESIARUM ST. RÅBY | ET BJELLERUP, MEMBRUM DE STELLA POLARI. | VOLUMEN QUARTUM. | Debilis — Zona. | <short orn rule> | LUNDÆ, | EX OFFICINA LUNDBERGIANA; | LONDINI, | "THE DEPOT OF THE SWEDENBORG SOCIETY, | 36, BLOOMSBURY STREET, OXFORD STREET." | 1868.
8vo
title leaf, 2 pp; Praefatiuncula editoris, pp III-IV; text: Debilis to Zona, pp 1-1060.
From 'Debilis' to 'Hortus' <pp 1-260>, Kahl rearranged the references in the order of the books of the Bible; but from 'Hostis' to 'Zona' <pp 260-1060> he followed the order in which Swedenborg had written them in the MS, that is, from Isaiah to Deuteronomy.
UK: SOC, CON, NR; NET: GEN; SWE: GSB; USA: ANC

47/06/La O/2 — **1916** — Hyde 505/1, 3038/5

EMANUELIS SWEDENBORGII | INDEX BIBLICUS | AD AUTOGRAPHI SIMILITUDINEM IN BIBLIOTHECA REGIAE ACADEMIAE SCIENTIARUM | SUECICAE ADSERVATI, OPE ARTIS PHOTOTYPOGRAPHICAE DELINEATI, EDITUS JUSSU | SOCIETATIS SWEDENBORGIANAE LONDINENSIS | <short orn rule> | VOL. II. | <orn 15 x 37 mm> | HOLMIAE | EX OFFICINA PHOTOTYPOGRAPHICA LAGRELIUS & WESTPHAL | MCMXVI.

half title: EMANUELIS SWEDENBORGII | AUTOGRAPHA | <short rule> | TOMUS V.
folio
half title and title leaves, 4 pp; Contenta, 1 p; blank page; text, pp 2-675.
Reproduction of La O/1, published in phototyped edition, vol 5 <*Index Biblicus* vol 2, Hyde 3038/5> Stockholm.
Unpublished copies have been recorded as follows.

1 UK: SOC & USA: ANC, SHS A reproduction on microfilm 3, Bryn Athyn PA.

UK: SOC, BL, BOD, CAM, CON, LON, NCC, RYL, WIL; DEN: RLD; NET: GEN, KB; SWE: ROY, UPP; USA: ANC, FOU, SHS; AUS: SYD; NZ: WEL

ENGLISH

47/06/En 1/1 **1917** Hyde 507/1

The | Schmidius Marginalia | together with | The Expository Material | of | The Index Biblicus | by | EMANUEL SWEDENBORG | <coat of arms of the publisher 26 x 21 mm> | Bryn Athyn, Pa. | ACADEMY OF THE NEW CHURCH | 1917
8vo
title leaf, 2 pp; Preface, pp 3-6; Explanation of orthographic signs in the volume, p 7; text: Detached notes, p 8; Genesis to Judges, 1 and 2 Samuel, 1 and 2 Kings, 1 Chronicles, Esther, Job, Psalms, Ecclesiastes, Song of Solomon, Isaiah to Micah, Habakkuk to Malachi, Matthew to John, Revelation, pp 9-631.
The marginal annotations in the Schmidius Bible <47/04/La O/1, O/2> were translated by E E Iungerich from transcriptions made by him and others. Interspersed with these annotations, he included a translation of the expository material in Codices 4 <47/06> and 39 <47/07> of *Index Biblicus*.

UK: SOC, NR; USA: ANC

47/07 Names of Men, Lands, Kingdoms, and Cities Hyde CXXXV

The autograph MS, bound in its original parchment cover, with *Index Bibl. Nom. Propriorum* written on the spine, forms Codex 39 in the Library of the Royal Swedish Academy of Sciences, Stockholm.

Swedenborg compiled this Index while composing the works described as 46/01/La 0/1, 47/03/La 0/1, 47/06/La 0/1, and 48/01/La 0/1; it also includes references to the Schmidius marginalia <see 47/04/La 0/1> as far as Amos. The entries in this Index were made in the same order as those Indices: that is, Joshua to 2 Kings, Isaiah, a portion of Jeremiah, Genesis 1 to 15, the remainder of Jeremiah, Lamentations to Malachi, the prophetical sections of the Historical Books, Psalms, Job, Revelation, Exodus to Deuteronomy, Matthew, John, Luke, and Mark.

LATIN

Editions:

La 0 MS
La 1 J F I Tafel and R L Tafel, editors

47/07/La 0/1 — 1747 — Hyde 508
<<Nomina Virorum, Terrarum, Regnorum, Urbium>>
pott long 4to <318 x 95 mm>
text: <Praefatiuncula,> p 7a.
Note relating to p 1a, p 7b.
Index, arranged alphabetically, pp 8a-139b; pp 53a, 135a, 140a and b, blank.
Memorandum on the inside of the back cover.
MS not seen; description deduced from La 0/2.
SWE: KVA

47/07/La 1/1, 46/01/La 1/1-3 — **1859, 1860, 1863** — Hyde 509, 3066-3068
EMANUELIS SWEDENBORGII | INDEX BIBLICUS | SIVE | THESAURUS BIBLIORUM | EMBLEMATICUS ET ALLEGORICUS. | ... | VOLUMEN PRIMUM. | ... | 1859.
EMANUELIS SWEDENBORGII | INDEX BIBLICUS | SIVE | THESAURUS BIBLIORUM | EMBLEMATICUS ET ALLEGORICUS. | ... | VOLUMEN SECUNDUM. | ... | 1860.
EMANUELIS SWEDENBORGII | INDEX BIBLICUS | SIVE | THESAURUS BIBLIORUM | EMBLEMATICUS ET ALLEGORICUS. | ... | VOLUMEN TERTIUM. | ... | 1863.

8vo
vol I: title leaf, 2 pp; Praefatiuncula editoris, 2 pp; text, pp 1-476.
vol II: title leaf, 2 pp; catalogue, pp 1-6, text, pp 1-480.
vol III: title leaf, 2 pp; text, pp 1-576.
The text of La 0/1 amalgamated by the editor, J F I Tafel, with the text of 46/01/La 0/1, 2 <Codices 40 and 41>, 47/06/La 0/1 <Codex 4>, 48/01/La 0/1 <Codex 5>, and extracts from Swedenborg's later works, especially *Arcana Coelestia* <49/01/La 0/1> and *Apocalypsis Explicata* <59/02/La 02/1> <see 'Praefatiuncula editoris'>, published as *Index Biblicus* vol 1-3, Tübingen <46/01/La 1/1-3 = Hyde 3066-3068>.
UK: SOC, NR; DEN: RLD; GER: GSU; NET: GEN; SWE: GSB; USA: ANC

47/07/La 1/2, 46/01/La 1/1 **1873** Hyde 510, 3070
SUPPLEMENTUM | VOLUMINIS QUARTI | INDICIS BIBLICI | EMANUELIS SWEDENBORGII, | CONTNENS | NOMINA VIRORUM, TERRARUM, URBIUM. | <short rule> | EX CHIROGRAPHO EJUS | IN BIBLIOTHECA REGIAE ACADEMIAE HOLMIENSIS ASSERVATO, | NUNC PRIMUM EDIDIT | RUDOLPHUS LEONARDUS TAFEL. | <short rule> | LONDINII: | SWEDENBORG SOCIETY, 36 BLOOMSBURY STREET. | 1873.
imprint: Lipsiae, Typis Guil. Drugulini.
8vo
title leaf, 2 pp; Autoris praefatiuncula, pp III-IV; text: *Damascus – Zoan Aegypti*, pp 5-37; Notae criticae editoris, pp I-VII; imprint, p VII.
UK: SOC, NR; DEN: RLD; GER: GSU; NET: GEN; SWE: GSB; USA: ANC

47/07/La 0/2 **1916** Hyde 508/1, 3038/6
Nomina Virorum, Terrarum, Regnorum, Urbium
folio
title leaf, pp 1-2; text, pp 511-646.
Reproduction of La 0/1, published in phototyped edition, vol 6 <*Index Biblicus* vol 3, Hyde 3038/6> Stockholm.
Unpublished copies have been recorded as follows.
1 UK: SOC & USA: ANC, SHS A reproduction on microfilms 3 and 4, Bryn Athyn PA.
UK: SOC, BL, BOD, CAM, CON, LON, NCC, RYL, WIL; DEN: RLD; NET: GEN, KB; SWE: ROY, UPP; USA: ANC, FOU, SHS; AUS: SYD; NZ: WEL

ENGLISH EXTRACTS

X 47/07/En 1917/1 **1917** Hyde 510/1
The | Schmidius Marginalia | together with | The Expository Material | of | The Index Biblicus | by | EMANUEL SWEDENBORG | <coat of arms of the publisher 26 x 21 mm> | Bryn Athyn, Pa. | ACADEMY OF THE NEW CHURCH | 1917
8vo
title leaf, 2 pp; Preface, pp 3-6; Explanation of orthographic signs in the volume, p 7; text: Detached notes, p 8; Genesis to Judges, 1 and 2 Samuel, 1 and 2 Kings, 1 Chronicles, Esther, Job, Psalms, Ecclesiastes, Song of Solomon, Isaiah to Micah, Habakkuk to Malachi, Matthew to John, Revelation, pp 9-631.
The marginal annotations in the Schmidius Bible <47/04/La 0/1, 2> were translated by E E Iungerich from transcriptions made by him and others. Interspersed with these annotations, he included a translation of the expository material in Codices 4 <47/06> and 39 <47/07> of *Index Biblicus*.
UK: SOC, NR; USA: ANC

48/01 Biblical Index of the New Testament Hyde CXXXVI

The autograph MS, bound in its original parchment cover, forms the major part of Codex 5 in the Library of the Royal Swedish Academy of Sciences, Stockholm.

Only the four Gospels are indexed in this MS, and the references are entered in the order Matthew, John, Luke, and Mark. Swedenborg indexed the proper names from the Gospels <in the order just given> in Codex 39 <47/07/La O/1> after he had entered the references from other books of the Bible, which indicates that the present Index was the last to be compiled. The year 1748 is deduced as the date of compilation, though no dates are mentioned in the text.

LATIN

Editions:

La O MS
La 1 J F I Tafel, editor

48/01/La O/1 **1748** Hyde 511
<< <untitled> >>
double foolscap 4to <406 x 152 mm>
text: Memorandum on the inside of the front cover.
Index, with each letter paged separately, 486 pp, of which 8 pp are blank.
Memorandum on the inside of the back cover.
MS not seen; description deduced from La O/2.
SWE: KVA

48/01/La 1/1, 46/01/La 1/1 **1859, 1860, 1863** Hyde 512, 3066-3068
EMANUELIS SWEDENBORGII | INDEX BIBLICUS | SIVE | THESAURUS BIBLIORUM | EMBLEMATICUS ET ALLEGORICUS. | ... | VOLUMEN PRIMUM. | ... | 1859.
EMANUELIS SWEDENBORGII | INDEX BIBLICUS | SIVE | THESAURUS BIBLIORUM | EMBLEMATICUS ET ALLEGORICUS. | ... | VOLUMEN SECUNDUM. | ... | 1860.
EMANUELIS SWEDENBORGII | INDEX BIBLICUS | SIVE | THESAURUS BIBLIORUM | EMBLEMATICUS ET ALLEGORICUS. | ... | VOLUMEN TERTIUM. | ... | 1863.
8vo
vol I: title leaf, 2 pp; Praefatiuncula editoris, 2 pp; text, pp 1-476.
vol II: title leaf, 2 pp; catalogue, pp 1-6, text, pp 1-480.

vol III: title leaf, 2 pp; text, pp 1-576.
The text of La O/1 amalgamated by the editor, J F I Tafel, with the text of 46/01/La O/1, 0/2 <Codices 40 and 41>, 47/06/La O/1 <Codex 4>, 47/07/La O/1 <Codex 39>, and extracts from Swedenborg's later works, especially *Arcana Coelestia* <49/01/La O/1> and *Apocalypsis Explicata* <59/02/La O2/1> <see 'Praefatiuncula editoris'>, published as *Index Biblicus* vol 1-3, Tübingen <46/01/La 1/1 = Hyde 3066-3068>.

UK: SOC, NR; DEN: RLD; GER: GSU; NET: GEN; SWE: GSB; USA: ANC

48/01/La O/2 **1916** Hyde 511/1, 3038/6

<untitled>
folio
title and text, pp 2-471, 474-475.
Reproduction of La O/1, published in phototyped edition, vol 6 <*Index Biblicus* vol 3, Hyde 3038/6> Stockholm.
Unpublished copies have been recorded as follows.

1 UK: SOC & USA: ANC, SHS A reproduction on microfilm 4, Bryn Athyn PA.

UK: SOC, BL, BOD, CAM, CON, LON, NCC, RYL, WIL; DEN: RLD; NET: GEN, KB; SWE: ROY, UPP; USA: ANC, FOU, SHS; AUS: SYD; NZ: WEL

48/02 The Greek Religion Hyde CXXXVI

The work forms the last four pages of Codex 5 in the Library of the Royal Swedish Academy of Sciences, Stockholm.

The text consists of 22 unnumbered paragraphs <of which the last and the penultimate are probably Swedenborg's own comments and conclusions>, and it has been suggested that he extracted and translated the remainder from an unknown French work. I note that Swedenborg owned a copy of *Voyage du Tour du Monde* by Gemelli Careri, translated into French by 'L. M. N.' and published in Paris in 1719, and that he quoted paragraphs concerning the Mahommedan Religion from pp 387-392 of volume 1 in his Codex 36 under the heading *Correspondentiae et Repraesentationes* <see 41/06>.

In his theological writings, Swedenborg refers only three times to the Greek Orthodox Church and its doctrines: see *Summaria Expositio* n 18 <69/09> and *Vera Christiana Religio* n 153, 647.3 <71/02>.

LATIN

48/02/La 0/1 1748 Hyde 511

<<Religio Græca.>>

double foolscap 4to <406 x 152 mm>

title and text, 4 unnumbered pp containing 22 unnumbered paragraphs.

MS not seen; description deduced from La 0/2.

SWE: KVA

48/02/La 0/2 1916 Hyde 511/1, 3038/6

Religio Græca.

folio

title and text, pp 471-473.

Reproduction of La 0/1, published in phototyped edition, vol 6 <*Index Biblicus* vol 3, Hyde 3038/6> Stockholm.

Unpublished copies have been recorded as follows.

1 UK: SOC & USA: ANC, SHS A reproduction on microfilm 4, Bryn Athyn PA.

UK: SOC, BL, BOD, CAM, CON, LON, NCC, RYL, WIL; DEN: RLD; NET: GEN, KB; SWE: ROY, UPP; USA: ANC, FOU, SHS; AUS: SYD; NZ: WEL

ENGLISH

48/02/En 1/1 1922 Hyde 512/1,2

THE GREEK RELIGION.
8vo
title and text n 1-22, pp 165-178; editorial notes, pp 138-140.
Translated and edited by A Acton, published in *The New Philosophy* Lancaster PA.
A copy reprinted from the journal, printed on one side of the page only, is in USA: ANC.
UK: SOC, NCC; USA: ANC

49/01 Arcana Caelestia Hyde CXXXVIII

The autograph MSS are to be found in Codices 8-10, 15-26, and 80 in the Library of the Royal Swedish Academy of Sciences, Stockholm, and are described below in the entries numbered La O/1-16. They form Swedenborg's first drafts of the work from Genesis chapter 16 onwards. The fair copy MSS sent to the printer are no longer extant.

LATIN

Editions:

- La O MSS
- La 1 1st edition
- La 2 proposed edition, editor not named
- La 3 J F I Tafel, editor
- La 4 editor unnamed, probably S H Worcester
- La 5 P H Johnson and others, editors

49/01/La 1/1 1749 Hyde 565, 3435

Arcana Cœlestia | QUÆ IN | *SCRIPTURA SACRA*, | SEU | *VERBO DOMINI* | SUNT, DETECTA: | Hic Primum quæ in | *GENESI.* | Una cum Mirabilibus | Quæ visa sunt | In Mundo Spirituum, & in Cœlo Angelorum. | <2 spaced rules> | PARS PRIMA. | <2 spaced rules> | MDCCXLIX.
verso: MATTH. VI: 33. | *Quærite primo Regnum Dei, & Justitiam ejus,* | *& omnia adjicientur vobis.*
leaf <2a>: asts as line orn NR 212; p 1: head-piece NR 278; p 2: line orn NR 279; p 5: line orn NR 280; p 23: line orn NR 281; p 26: line orn NR 279; p 28: line orn NR 282; p 40: asts as line orn NR 212; p 41: line orn NR 283; p 49: line orn NR 284; p 52: line orn NR 280; p 53: line orn NR 282; p 63: asts as line orn NR 212; p 64: line orn NR 281; p 74: asts as line orn NR 212; p 76: line orn NR 282; p 84: line orn NR 281; p 87: line orn NR 284; p 90: line orn NR 285; p 120: line orn NR 282; p 122: tail-piece NR 286; p 126: line orn NR 283; p 128: line orn NR 285; p 143: line orn NR 282; p 146: tail-piece NR 286; p 150: line orn NR 279; p 151: line orn NR 284; p 166: asts as line orn NR 212; p 168: line orn NR 281; p 193: line orn NR 282; p 195: tail-piece NR 287; p 198: line orn NR 283; p 199: asts as line orns 3 times NR 212; p 200: asts as line orns twice NR 212; p 201: line orn NR 281; p 237: line orn NR 284; p 247: line orn NR 283; asts as line orn NR 212; p 248: asts as line orns twice NR 212; p 249: line orn NR 281; p 292: line orn NR 288; p 296: tail-piece NR 289; p 303: line orn NR 283; p 304: asts as line orn NR 212; p 305: asts as line orn NR 212; p 306: line orn NR 281; p 367: line orn NR 279; p 369: tail-piece NR 287; p 374: line orn NR 283; p 376: line orn NR 282; p 414: line orn NR 279; p 417: tail-piece NR 290; p 420: line orn NR 283; p 422: line orn NR

282; p 451: line orn NR 288; p 453: tail-piece NR 290; p 458: line orn NR 283; p 460: line orn NR 282; p 492: line orn NR 281; p 500: line orn NR 283; p 502: line orn NR 279; p 530: line orn NR 288; p 534: tail-piece NR 287; p 541: line orn NR 280; p 543: line orn NR 281; p 581: line orn NR 283; p 586: line orn NR 288; p 588: line orn NR 279; p 624: line orn NR 283; p 628: asts as line orn NR 212; p 630: tail-piece NR 289
4to
title leaf, 2 pp; Swedenborg's list of subjects, 2 pp; text: n I-V, 6-1885, pp 1-630. <paragraph n II is misprinted as 'I'>
Published in London by John Lewis, 1 Paternoster Row, and printed by John Hart, Poppins Court, Fleet Street, London, though neither are named in the book <see *The Intellectual Repository* London 1836, p 30>. The book was also sold by Mr Nourse at the Lamb, opposite Katharine Street, in the Strand, and by Mr Ware, at the Bible, on Ludgate Hill. The price, unbound, was six shillings per volume. The cost of printing volumes 1 and 2 was £200 each, and the entire proceeds from the sale of the work were given to the Society for the Propagation of the Gospel in Foreign Parts. <**E:b** En 1841/1 = Hyde 3271, p 98>
A set of the 8 volumes of the first edition in UK: CON <formerly owned by C B Bragg> has the royal arms of Sweden on the front cover of each volume. A copy in USA: FOU has notes said to have been written by Swedenborg. Copies in UK: SOC were owned by Sir Charles Mordaunt, Sir Hildebrand Jacob, and John Flaxman; a set also has the words 'Emanuelis Swedenborgii' printed <at a later date> at the head of the title page. A set in UK: SOC was once owned by P B Chastanier, and has his annotations in the margins. A set in USA: ANC <formerly in USA: JPC) has on the flyleaf the erased signature and date 'Augustus Nordenskiöld 1777'. Thomas Hartley bequeathed his set to The Society for Promoting the Heavenly Doctrines of the New Jerusalem Church; its present whereabouts are unknown <*The New Church Magazine* London 1917, p 513>.
UK: SOC, CON, NCC, NR; DEN: RLD; GER: WLB; SWE: GGY; USA: ANC, FOU, SHS

49/01/La O/1 **1749-1750** Hyde 550

<<Arcana Cœlestia, | quæ in | Scriptura Sacra seu | Verbo Domini | sunt, detecta. | Sequuntur quæ in | Genesi: | hic in ejus quæ in | Capita Decimo Sexto | cum mirabilibus | quæ visa sunt | in mundo spirituum et cœlo angelorum. | I. | <2 lines 92 and 88 mm> | MDCCXLIX.>>
The size of the paper varies, but it is generally 369 x 102 mm.
title and text of Praefatio, Genesis 16-21, and n 1886-2759, 2 blank pp and pp 1-458.
The MS forms Codex 10. Each chapter has a separate title page, as issued from the press in six parts <see volume 2 below>. Parts I-III <ie n 1886-2309> are dated 1749, and parts IV-VI <n 2310-2759> are dated 1750.
The MS is prepared for the printer with instructions as to type, etc., which with the dates on the MS places its composition immediately before the date of printing.
MS not seen; description deduced from La O/17.
SWE: KVA

49/01/La 1/2 **1750** Hyde 566

Arcana Cœlestia, | QUÆ IN | *SCRIPTURA SACRA*, | SEU | *VERBO DOMINI* | SUNT, DETECTA: | Sequuntur quæ in | *GENESI* | Hic quæ in | *Capite Decimo Sexto:* | Una cum Mirabilibus | Quæ visa sunt | In Mundo Spirituum, & Cœlo Angelorum. | I. | <2 spaced rules> | MDCCL.
verso: MATTH. VI: 33. | *Quærite primo Regnum Dei, & Justitiam ejus,* | *& omnia adjicientur vobis.*
p 3: line orn as head-piece NR 291; p 5: head-piece NR 292; p 8: line orn as head-piece NR 283; p 9: line orn NR 280; p 39: line orn NR 282
4to
title leaf, 2 pp; text: Praefatio, 2 pp; n 1886-1983, pp 5-44; Errata, p 44.

This part of volume 2 was sold at eight pence each copy. <**E:b** En 1841/1 = Hyde 3271, p 99>
DEN: RLD

49/01/La 1/3 **1750** Hyde 567

Arcana Cœlestia, | QUÆ IN | *SCRIPTURA SACRA*, | SEU | *VERBO DOMINI* | SUNT, DETECTA: | Hic quæ in | *GENESI* | *Capite Decimo Septimo:* | Una cum Mirabilibus | Quæ visa & audita sunt | In Mundo Spirituum, & Cœlo Angelorum; | Hic ad finem, quæ de | Ultimo Judicio. | II. | <2 spaced rules> | MDCCL.

p 3: head-piece NR 293; p 4: line orn NR 281; p 7: line orn NR 284; p 57: line orn NR 281; p 64: tail-piece NR 289

verso: MATTH. VI: 33. | *Quærite primo Regnum Dei, & Justitiam ejus,* | *& omnia adjicientur vobis.*

4to

title leaf, 2 pp; text: n 1984-2134, pp 3-64.

This part of volume 2 was sold at nine pence each copy. <**E:b** En 1841/1 = Hyde 3271, p 99>

An unpublished copy has been recorded as follows.

1 UK: SOC A MS transcript of extracts by an unknown copyist. <Archives A/34>

DEN: RLD

49/01/La 1/4 **1750** Hyde 568

Arcana Cœlestia, | QUÆ IN | *SCRIPTURA SACRA*, | SEU | *VERBO DOMINI* | SUNT, DETECTA: | Hic quæ in | *GENESI* | *Capite Decimo Octavo:* | Una cum Mirabilibus | Quæ visa & audita sunt | In Mundo Spirituum, & Cœlo Angelorum; | Hic ad finem, quæ de | Statu Infantum in altera vita. | III. | <2 spaced rules> | MDCCL.

p 3: line orn as head-piece NR 294; p 4: tail-piece NR 287; p 5: head-piece NR 278; p 7: line orn NR 284; p 10: line orn NR 282; p 69: line orn NR 283

verso: MATTH. VI: 33. | *Quærite primo Regnum Dei, & Justitiam ejus,* | *& omnia adjicientur vobis.*

4to

title leaf, 2 pp; text: Praefatio, 2 pp; n 2135-2309, pp 5-75.

This part of volume 2 was sold at nine pence each copy.

An unpublished copy has been recorded as follows.

1 UK: SOC A MS transcript of extracts by an unknown copyist. <Archives A/34>

DEN: RLD

49/01/La 1/5 **1750** Hyde 569

Arcana Cœlestia, | QUÆ IN | *SCRIPTURA SACRA*, | SEU | *VERBO DOMINI* | SUNT, DETECTA: | Hic quæ in | *GENESI* | *Capite Decimo Nono:* | Una cum Mirabilibus, | Quæ visa & audita sunt | In Mundo Spirituum, & Cœlo Angelorum; | Hic ad finem, quæ de | Memoria remanente hominis post mortem, & reminiscentia | eorum, quæ egerat in vita corporis. | IV. | <2 spaced rules> | MDCCL.

p 3: head-piece NR 293; p 5: line orn NR 284; p 8: line orn NR 295; p 76: line orn NR 296

4to

title leaf, 2 pp; text: n 2310-2494, pp 3-83; Errata in Parte Secunda, section I, p 83.

This part of volume 2 was sold at nine pence each copy.

An unpublished copy has been recorded as follows.

1 UK: SOC A MS transcript of extracts by an unknown copyist. <Archives A/34>

49/01/La 1/6 **1750** Hyde 570

Arcana Cœlestia, | QUÆ IN | *SCRIPTURA SACRA*, | SEU | *VERBO DOMINI* | SUNT, DETECTA: | Hic quæ in | *GENESI* | *Capite Vigesimo:* | Una cum Mirabilibus, | Quæ visa & audita sunt | In

Mundo Spirituum, & Cœlo Angelorum; | Hic ad finem, quæ de | Gentium & Populorum, qui extra Ecclesiam nati sunt, | statu & sorte in altera vita. | V. | <2 spaced rules> | MDCCL.
p 3: head-piece NR 292; p 5: line orn NR 281; p 7: line orn NR 282; p 53: line orn NR 296; p 59: tail-piece NR 297
4to
title leaf, 2 pp; text: n 2495-2605, pp 3-59.
This part of volume 2 was sold at nine pence each copy.
DEN: RLD

49/01/La 1/7 1750 Hyde 571

Arcana Cœlestia, | QUÆ IN | *SCRIPTURA SACRA*, | SEU | *VERBO DOMINI* | SUNT, DETECTA: | Hic quæ in | *GENESI* | *Capite Vigesimo Primo:* | Una cum Mirabilibus, | Quæ visa & audita sunt | In Mundo Spirituum, & Cœlo Angelorum; | Hic ad finem | De Conjugiis, quomodo considerantur in Cœlo, & de | Adulteriis. | VI. | <2 spaced rules> | MDCCL.
p 3: head-piece NR 298; p 6: line orn NR 282; asts as line orn NR 212; p 7: asts as line orn NR 212; p 8: line orn NR 281; p 26: asts as line orn NR 212; p 62: line orn NR 282
4to
title leaf, 2 pp; text: n 2606-2759, pp 3-71.
This part of volume 2 was sold at nine pence each copy.
DEN: RLD

49/01/La 1/8 1750 Hyde 566-571

<<ARCANA CŒLESTIA, quæ in Scriptura Sacra, seu Verbo Domini sunt, detecta. ... I-VI.>>
4to
The six chapters described above as La 1/2-7 were also sold together as the second volume of the entire work, with no overall title page.
A volume in USA: FOU has a note in Swedish, written by Swedenborg, on the page facing the back cover, which states, '50 arch latin, och 56¼ arch engelska, tilsamans 106¼ arch. För uti copie 636 pag: om 1½ arch copie giör 1 arch tryck.' <50 sheets Latin, and 56¼ sheets English, together 106¼ sheets. In the copy 636 pages: 1½ sheets of the copy makes one printed sheet>
A copy in USA: ANC (formerly in USA: JPC) has on the flyleaf the erased signature of Augustus Nordenskjöld dated 1777.
UK: SOC, CON, NCC, NR; DEN: RLD; SWE: GGY; USA: ANC, FOU, SHS

49/01/La O/2 1751 Hyde 551

<<Genes. | Cap: XXII | n: 2760 ad 2893.>>
small post broad 4to <235 x 187 mm>
Præfatio, 2 pp <the text on the verso is crossed out>; text of Genesis ch 22 and n 2760-2887, pp 1a-26a; p 26b blank; n 2870-2873 crossed out, and n [2874]-2893 written out afresh, pp 25a-26b.
The MS forms Codex 80. With Codices 9 and 15 it forms La 1/9 = Hyde 572. The MS has Swedenborg's instructions for the printer.
Unpublished copies have been recorded as follows.
1 UK: SOC & USA: ANC, SHS A reproduction on microfilm 6, Bryn Athyn PA.
MS not seen; description deduced from La O/17.
SWE: KVA

49/01/La O/3 1751 Hyde 552

<<Genes. | Cap: XXIII: | n: 2894-3003.
Genes: | Cap: XXIV. | n: 3004 ad 3227.>>

Genesis 23 and the fair copy of Genesis 24 are written on large post long 4to paper <406 x 133 mm>; the first draft of Genesis 24 is written on paper measuring 352 x 95 mm.
text: Genesis ch 23 n 2894-2986, pp 1a-17a;

De representationibus et correspondentibus n 2987-3003, pp 18a-19b;

Genesis ch 24, first draft of consecutive text and general explanation, deleted, 12 pp; the same, n 3004-3212, pp 1a-34b;

Continuatio de representationibus et correspondentibus n 3213-3220, pp 34b-36a.

The MS forms Codex 9. With Codices 80 and 15 it forms La 1/9 = Hyde 572.
Unpublished copies have been recorded as follows.

1 UK: SOC & USA: ANC, SHS A reproduction on microfilm 6, Bryn Athyn PA.

MS not seen; description deduced from La 0/17.

SWE: KVA

49/01/La 0/4 — 1751 — Hyde 549

<<ARCANA CŒLESTIA, quæ in Scripture Sacra, seu Verbo Domini sunt, detecta.>>
copy long 4to <406 x 133 mm>
text of Genesis 26-32, pp 1-44; text of Genesis 24, pp 45-50; text of De libero hominis n 2872-2875 <n 2874-2875 crossed out and paged 24, see Hyde 551>, pp 51-52; text of Genesis 35-43, pp 53-94; p 74 blank.
The MS forms Codex 8. The text contains only the consecutive translation and general explanation of the chapters in Genesis. It appears to be a first draft of material in Codices 15 and 16 <La 0/5, 0/6>.
Unpublished copies have been recorded as follows.

1 UK: SOC & USA: ANC, SHS A reproduction on microfilm 6, Bryn Athyn PA.

MS not seen; description deduced from La 0/17.

SWE: KVA

49/01/La 0/5 — 1751 — Hyde 553

<<Genes. | Caput XXV: | n: 3228 ad 3352
Geneseos | Caput Vigesimum Sextum
Geneseos | Caput Vigesimum Septimum
Geneseos | Caput Vigesimum Octavum
Libri Geneseos | Caput Vigesimum Nonum
Libri Geneseos | Caput Trigesimum>>
foolscap long 4to <327 x 98 mm>
text of Genesis 25 and n 3228-3352, 8 pp and pp 1a-39b; Genesis 26 and n 3353-3485, pp 1a-38a; Genesis 27 and n 3486-3649, pp 1a-34a; Genesis 28 and n 3650-3750, pp 1a-40b; Genesis 29 and n 3751-3896, pp 1a-45a; Genesis 30 n 3897-4055, pp 1a-42a.
The MS forms Codex 15. With Codices 80 and 9 it forms La 1/9 = Hyde 572.
Unpublished copies have been recorded as follows.

1 UK: SOC & USA: ANC, SHS A reproduction on microfilm 6, Bryn Athyn PA.

MS not seen; description deduced from La 0/18.

SWE: KVA

49/01/La 1/9 — 1751 — Hyde 572

Arcana Cœlestia, | QUÆ IN | *SCRIPTURA SACRA*, | SEU | *VERBO DOMINI* | SUNT, DETECTA: | Hic quæ in | *GENESI* | Una cum Mirabilibus, | Quæ visa sunt | In Mundo Spirituum, & Cœlo Angelorum. | <2 spaced rules> | PARS TERTIA. | <rule> | MDCCLI.
p 3: head-piece NR 299; p 4: tail-piece NR 300; p 5: head-piece NR 292; p 10: line orn NR 284; p

12: line orn NR 295; p 72: line orn NR 282; p 82: line orn NR 295; p 84: line orn NR 284; p 118: line orn NR 295; p 126: line orn NR 282; p 130: line orn NR 284; p 206: line orn NR 284; p 211: tail-piece NR 289; p 213: line orn NR 295; p 214 twice: asts as line orn NR 212; p 215: line orn NR 282; p 228: asts as line orn NR 212; p 235: asts as line orn NR 212; p 250: asts as line orn NR 212; p 273: line orn NR 282; p 279: tail-piece NR 287; p 283: line orn NR 295; p 285: asts as line orn NR 212; p 286: line orn NR 284; p 336: line orn NR 282; p 343: tail-piece NR 286; p 347: line orn NR 284; p 350: line orn NR 281; p 401: line orn NR 295; p 416: line orn NR 281; p 417: asts as line orn NR 212; p 418: line orn NR 282; p 475: line orn NR 301; p 484: line orn NR 301; p 486: line orn NR 302; p 556: line orn NR 301; p 563: tail-piece NR 303; p 571: line orn NR 304; p 572: asts as line orn NR 212; p 574: line orn NR 302; p 609: asts as line orn NR 212; p 636: line orn NR 305; p 643: tail-piece NR 306
4to
title leaf, 2 pp; text: Praefatio, 2 pp; n 2760-4055, pp 5-643.
pp 242-247 are bound out of order; p 498 is numbered 298.
A copy in USA: ANC (formerly in USA: JPC) has on the flyleaf the erased signature of Augustus Nordenskjöld dated 1777.
An unpublished copy of extracts has been recorded as follows.

1 UK: SOC A MS transcript by an unknown copyist. <Archives A/34>

UK: SOC, CON, NCC; SWE: GGY; USA: ANC, FOU, SHS

49/01/La O/6 1752 Hyde 554

<<Arcana Cœlestia | quæ in| Scriptura Sacra | seu | Verbo Domini | sunt, detecta: | hic quæ in | Genesi | una cum Mirabilibus | quæ visa sunt | in Mundo Spirituum, et in Cœlo Angelorum. | <2 lines 67 and 66 mm> | Pars Quarta | MDCCLII.>>
foolscap long 4to <330 x 102 mm>
text: n 4056-4228, pp 1a-34b; n 4229-4331, pp 1a-49b; n 4332-4421, pp 1a-28a; n 4422-4534, pp 1a-51a; n 4535-4634, pp 1a-42a; n 4635-4660, pp 1a-10b.
The MS forms Codex 16, and with Codex 17 forms La 1/10 = Hyde 573.
Unpublished copies have been recorded as follows.

1 UK: SOC & USA: ANC, SHS A reproduction on microfilms 6 and 7, Bryn Athyn PA.

MS not seen; description deduced from La O/18.

SWE: KVA

49/01/La O/7 1752 Hyde 555

<<Geneseos | Caput Trigesimum Septimum
Geneseos | Caput Trigesimum Octavum
Geneseos | Caput Trigesimum Nonum
Geneseos | Caput Quadragesimum.>>
foolscap long 4to <340 x 102 mm>
text: n 4661-4806, pp 1a-54b; n 4807-4953, pp 1a-46a; n 4954-5062, pp 1a-33a; n 5063-5190, pp 1a-53a.
The MS forms Codex 17, and with Codex 16 forms La 1/10 = Hyde 573.
In this Codex, Genesis ch 40, p 53a, there is a first draft of a letter in English, to the printer, John Lewis, and on p 53b there is a more perfect copy of the same, which reads, 'The copies of the Vth Part, I am send<ing> to Master Hart, because he has my money to pay the postage, thence you can have them. You have not yet approved my account, though it was exactly forwarded upon yours, and not yet answered upon the <surety> to pay the 80 p: at the end of the three years, though it was according to your accompt; your promise was in 2 or 3 years. As soon as this IV Part is finished I plaise to send 2 *of the remaining sheets,* well empacked to Master Lindegren.' The words italicized here were crossed out by Swedenborg.

Unpublished copies have been recorded as follows.
1 UK: SOC & USA: ANC, SHS A reproduction on microfilm 7, Bryn Athyn PA.
MS not seen; description deduced from La 0/18.
SWE: KVA

49/01/La 1/10 1752 Hyde 573

Arcana Cœlestia | QUÆ IN | *SCRIPTURA SACRA* | SEU | *VERBO DOMINI* | SUNT, DETECTA; | HIC QUÆ IN | *GENESI:* | Una cum Mirabilibus | Quæ visa sunt | In Mundo Spirituum, & Cœlo Angelorum. | <2 spaced rules> | PARS QUARTA. | <2 spaced rules> | MDCCLII.
p 3: head-piece NR 307; p 7: line orn NR 308; p 10: line orn NR 309; p 71: line orn NR 310; p 77: tail-piece NR 311; p 80: line orn NR 308; p 81: asts as line orn NR 212; p 82: line orn NR 309; p 101: asts as line orn NR 212; p 132: line orn NR 310; p 141: tail-piece NR 306; p 146: line orn NR 308; p 147: line orn NR 309; p 172: line orn NR 310; p 179: tail-piece NR 311; p 183: line orn NR 308; p 185: line orn NR 309; p 226: line orn NR 310; p 235: line orn NR 308; p 237: line orn NR 309; p 277: line orn NR 312; p 284: tail-piece NR 311; p 288: line orn NR 308; p 291: line orn NR 309; p 296: line orn NR 312; p 303: line orn NR 308; p 306: line orn NR 309; p 371: line orn NR 312; p 378: tail-piece NR 311; p 381: line orn NR 308; p 383: line orn NR 309; p 434: line orn NR 312; p 443: line orn NR 308; p 445: line orn NR 309; p 481: line orn NR 312; p 491: line orn NR 308; p 493: line orn NR 309; p 551: line orn NR 312; p 559: tail-piece NR 306
4to
title leaf, 2 pp; text: n 4056-5190, pp 3-559.
A copy in USA: ANC (formerly in USA: JPC) has on the flyleaf the erased signature of Augustus Nordenskjöld dated 1777.
UK: SOC, CON, NCC; SWE: GGY; USA: ANC, FOU, SHS

49/01/La 0/8 1753 Hyde 556

<<Arcana Cœlestia | quæ in | Scriptura Sacra | seu | Verbo Domini, | sunt, detecta, | hic quæ in | Genesi. | una cum mirabilibus, quæ visa sunt | in Mundo Spirituum, et in Cœlo Angelorum. | <2 lines 73 and 57 mm> | Pars quinta | <2 lines 64 and 63 mm> | MDCCLII | <line 83 mm> >>
foolscap long 4to <330 x 102 mm>
text: n 5191-5396, pp 1a-87b; n 5396-5573, pp 1a-50a; n 5574-5727, pp 1a-56a; n 5728-5866, pp 1a-30b.
The MS forms Codex 18, and with Codex 19 forms La 1/11 = Hyde 574.
In this Codex, chapter 41, there is a first draft of a letter in English, asking that John Lewis be instructed to send examples of the printed pages to the author <see Plate 2 in the Appendix Volume, La 5/9>.
Unpublished copies have been recorded as follows.
1 UK: SOC & USA: ANC, SHS A reproduction on microfilm 7, Bryn Athyn PA.
MS not seen; description deduced from La 0/18.
SWE: KVA

49/01/La 0/9 1753 Hyde 557

<<Caput XLV Genes:
Cap: XLVI: Genes:
Caput XLVIII
Caput XLIX Genes:
Cap: L: Genes:>>
foolscap long 4to <327 x 102 mm>
text: Genesis ch 45 n 5867-5993, pp 1a-45a; Genesis ch 46 n 5994-6058, pp 1a-26b; Genesis ch

48 n 6216-6327, pp 1a-32a; Genesis ch 49 n 6328-6496, pp 1a-62a; Genesis ch 50 n 6497-6626, pp 1a-33b.
The MS forms Codex 19, and with Codex 18 forms La 1/11 = Hyde 574.
Unpublished copies have been recorded as follows.

1 UK: SOC & USA: ANC, SHS A reproduction on microfilm 7, Bryn Athyn PA.

MS not seen; description deduced from La 0/18.

SWE: KVA

49/01/La 1/11 1753 Hyde 574

Arcana Cœlestia | QUÆ IN | *SCRIPTURA SACRA*, | SEU | *VERBO DOMINI* | SUNT, DETECTA: | Hic quæ in | *GENESI*. | Una cum Mirabilibus, | Quæ visa sunt | IN | Mundo Spirituum & Cœlo Angelorum. | <2 spaced rules> | PARS QUINTA. | <2 spaced rules> | MDCCLIII.
verso: MATTH. VI: 33, | *Quærite primo Regnum Dei, et Justitiam ejus,* | *et omnia adjicientur vobis.*
p 3: head-piece NR 313; p 7: line orn NR 309; p 90: line orn NR 312; p 99: tail-piece NR 311; p 102: line orn NR 314; p 145: line orn NR 308; p 154: line orn NR 309; p 202: line orn NR 308; p 209: tail-piece NR 311; p 212: line orn NR 309; p 241: line orn NR 308; p 248: tail-piece NR 311; p 251: line orn NR 309; p 292: line orn NR 308; p 299: tail-piece NR 311; p 302: line orn NR 309; p 324: line orn NR 308; p 328: tail-piece NR 311; p 331: line orn NR 309; p 372: line orn NR 308; p 383: tail-piece NR 311; p 386: line orn NR 310; p 415: line orn NR 308; p 423: tail-piece NR 311; pp 426, 485: line orn NR 309; p 497: line orn NR 310; p 525: line orn NR 309; p 535: tail-piece NR 306
4to
title leaf, 2 pp; text: n 5191-6626, pp 3-535.
A copy in USA: ANC (formerly in USA: JPC) has on the flyleaf the erased signature of Augustus Nordenskjöld dated 1777.

UK: SOC, CON, NCC; SWE: GGY; USA: ANC, FOU, SHS

49/01/La 0/10 1753 Hyde 558

<<Exod: | Caput Decimum Sextum.
Exod: Cap: 1.
Exodi | Caput Secundum.
Exodi | Caput Tertium
Sensus Internus Capitis | III Exodi.
Caput IV.
Exodi | Caput Quintum.
Exodi | Caput Sextum
Caput VII.
Exodi | Caput Octavum.>>
foolscap long 4to <330 x 102 mm>
Exodus 16 n 8387-8395, pp 1a-2b; Exodus ch 1 n 6627-6702, pp 1a-23a; Exodus ch 2 n 6703-6817, n 1a-33a; Exodus ch 3 Sensus Internus vv 1-22 and text of n 6933-6938, pp 1a-39a; Exodus ch 4 n 6933-7079, pp 1a- 21b; Exodus ch 5 n 7080-7177, pp 1a-21b; Exodus ch 6 n 7178-7254, pp 1a-18a; Exodus ch 7 n 7255-7365, pp 1a-29b; Exodus ch 8 n 7366-7487, pp 1a-30b.
The MS forms Codex 20, and with Codex 21 and chapter 15 of Codex 22 forms La 1/12 = Hyde 575. Exodus 16 and n 8387-8395 are misplaced; they should have been bound with Codex 22; see Hyde 560.
Unpublished copies have been recorded as follows.

1 UK: SOC & USA: ANC, SHS A reproduction on microfilms 7 and 8, Bryn Athyn PA.

MS not seen; description deduced from La 0/19.

SWE: KVA

49/01/La 0/11 **1753** Hyde 559

<<Exodi | Caput Nonum
Exodi | Caput Decimum
Geneseos | Caput Undecimum
Exodi | Caput Duodecimum
Exodi | Caput Decimum Tertium
Exodi | Caput Decimum Quartum>>
foolscap long 4to <330 x 95 mm>
text: Exodus ch 9 n 7488-7622, pp 1a-37a; Exodus ch 10 n 7623-7751, pp 1a-28a; Exodus ch 11 n 7752-7813, pp 1a-18b; Exodus ch 12 n 7814-8032, pp 1a-58b; Exodus ch 13 n 8033-8119, pp 1a-24a; Exodus ch 14 n 8120-8251, pp 1a-38a.
The MS forms Codex 21, and with Codex 20 and chapter 15 of Codex 22 forms La 1/12 = Hyde 575.
Unpublished copies have been recorded as follows.
1 UK: SOC & USA: ANC, SHS A reproduction on microfilm 8, Bryn Athyn PA.
MS not seen; description deduced from La 0/19.
SWE: KVA

49/01/La 0/12 **1753** Hyde 560

<<Arcana Cœlestia | quæ in | Scriptura Sacra | seu | Verbo Domini | sunt, detecta, | hic quæ in | Exodo | una cum mirabilibus | quæ visa sunt | in Mundo Spirituum et in Cælo | Angelorum. | <2 lines> | Pars Secunda | <2 lines> | MDCCLIV.
Exodi | Caput Decimum Quintum.
Libri Exodi | Caput Decimum Sextum
Exodi | Caput Decimum Septimum
Exodi | Caput Decimum Octa- | vum
Exodi | Caput Decimum Nonum
Exodi | Caput Vigesimum>>
foolscap long 4to <330 x 95 mm>
text: Exodus ch 15 n 8252-8386, pp 1a-45a; Exodus ch 16 n 8387-8547, pp 3a-49b; Exodus ch 17 n 8548-8634, pp 1a-31b; Exodus ch 18 n 8635-8741, pp 1a-31b; Exodus ch 19 n 8742-8852, pp 1a-38a; Exodus ch 20 n 8853-8941 <unfinished>, pp 1a-60b.
The MS forms Codex 22; Codices 20 and 21, and chapter 15 of Codex 22, form La 1/12 = Hyde 575. The title and that part of Exodus 16 which is bound in Codex 20 <viz. pp 1a-2b, Hyde 558> should be in this MS.
Unpublished copies have been recorded as follows.
1 UK: SOC & USA: ANC, SHS A reproduction on microfilm 8, Bryn Athyn PA.
MS not seen; description deduced from La 0/19.
SWE: KVA

49/01/La 1/12 **1753** Hyde 575

Arcana Cœlestia, | QUÆ IN | *SCRIPTURA SACRA*, | SEU | *VERBO DOMINI* | SUNT, DETECTA: | Hic quæ in | *EXODO,* | Una cum Mirabilibus | Quæ visa sunt | In Mundo Spirituum, & Cœlo Angelorum. | <2 spaced rules> | PARS PRIMA. | <2 spaced rules> | MDCLIII. <*stet* MDCLIII>
p 3: head-piece NR 278; p 5: line orn NR 282; p 6: line orn NR 295; p 28: line orn NR 281; p 33: line orn NR 280; p 35: line orn NR 284; p 66: line orn NR 279; p 70: line orn NR 281; p 72: line orn NR 280; p 106: line orn NR 282; p 110: tail-piece NR 315; p 112: line orn NR 284; pp 115, 160: line orn NR 295; p 165: line orn NR 279; p 167: line orn NR 281; p 191: line orn NR 309; p 194: tail-piece NR 306; p 196: line orn NR 309; pp 198, 217: line orn NR 308; p 219: tail-piece NR 306; p 221: line orn NR 309; pp 224, 253: line orn NR 309; p 256[b]: tail-piece NR 306; p 259[b]: line orn NR 310; p 261:

line orn NR 308; p 289: line orn NR 309; p 293: line orn NR 310; p 296: line orn NR 308; p 332: line orn NR 310; p 333: tail-piece NR 311; p 335: line orn NR 309; p 337: line orn NR 308; p 367: line orn NR 309; p 370: tail-piece NR 306; p 372[b]: line orn NR 310; p 374: line orn NR 308; p 386: line orn NR 309; p 390: tail-piece NR 306; p 392: line orn NR 310; pp 396, 454: line orn as head-piece NR 308; p 457: tail-piece NR 306; pp 459, 461: line orn NR 310; pp 481, 485: line orn NR 309; p 487: NR 308; p 524: line orn NR 309; p 527: tail-piece NR 311; p 529: line orn NR 309; p 531: line orn NR 310; p 577: line orn NR 309
4to
title leaf, 2 pp; text: n 6627-8386, pp 3-580.
On p 580 are the words 'Finis Partis Septimae' instead of 'Finis Partis Sextae'; and there are other indications that the volume was issued in 2 parts, divided at p 256.
A copy in USA: ANC (formerly in USA: JPC) has on the flyleaf the erased signature of Augustus Nordenskjöld dated 1777.
UK: SOC, CON, NCC; SWE: GGY; USA: ANC, FOU, SHS

49/01/La 0/13 1754 Hyde 561
<<Exodi | Caput Vigesimum Primum
Exodi | Caput Vigesimum Se- | cundum
Exodi | Caput Vigesimum Tertium>>
foolscap long 4to <343 x 95 mm>
text: Exodus ch 21 n 8958-9111, pp 1a-84a; Exodus ch 22 n 9112-9238, pp 1a-72a; Exodus ch 23 n 9239-9362, pp 1a-85b.
The MS forms Codex 23. Codices 20 <chapter 16, pp 1a-2b>, 22 <chapters 16-20>, 23, and 24 <chapter 24> <Hyde 559, 560-562> together form La 1/13 = Hyde 576.
Unpublished copies have been recorded as follows.
1 UK: SOC & USA: ANC, SHS A reproduction on microfilm 8, Bryn Athyn PA.
MS not seen; description deduced from La 0/19.
SWE: KVA

49/01/La 0/14 1754 Hyde 562
<<Exodi | Caput Vigesimum ~~Tertium~~ Quartum>>
foolscap long 4to <340 x 102 mm>
text: Exodus ch 24 n 9363-9442, pp 1a-73a; <Exodus ch 25> n 9456-9576 <unfinished>, pp 3a-54b; <Exodus ch 26> n 9592-9692, pp 3a-41b; <Exodus ch 27> n 9713-9784 <unfinished>, pp 3a-30b.
The MS forms Codex 24. Codices 20 <chapter 16, pp 1a-2b>, 22 <chapters 16-20>, 23, and 24 <chapter 24> <Hyde 558, 560-562> together form La 1/13 = Hyde 576.
Unpublished copies have been recorded as follows.
1 UK: SOC & USA: ANC, SHS A reproduction on microfilm 8, Bryn Athyn PA.
MS not seen; description deduced from La 0/20.
SWE: KVA

49/01/La 1/13 1754 Hyde 576
Arcana Cœlestia, | QUÆ IN | *SCRIPTURA SACRA*, | SEU | *VERBO DOMINI* | SUNT, DETECTA: | Hic quæ in | *EXODO*, | Una cum Mirabilibus | Quæ visa sunt | In Mundo Spirituum, & Cœlo Angelorum. | <2 spaced rules> | PARS SECUNDA. | <2 spaced rules> | MDCCLIV.
p 3: head-piece NR 316; p 5: line orn NR 282; p 7: line orn NR 295; p 52: line orn NR 281; p 56: line orn NR 295; p 57: line orn NR 282; p 84: line orn NR 317; p 86: tail-piece NR 318; p 88: line orn NR 319; p 90: line orn NR 320; p 118: line orn NR 309; p 120: tail-piece NR 306; p 124: line orn NR 309; p

156: line orn NR 310; p 158: tail-piece NR 311; pp 160, 162: line orn NR 309; p 217: line orn NR 321; p 218: tail-piece 311; p 221: line orn NR 323; p 223: line orn NR 317; p 293: line orn NR 309; p 298: line orn NR 305; p 300: line orn NR 308; p 368: line orn NR 309; p 369: tail-piece NR 311; p 372: line orn NR 310; p 374: line orn NR 305; p 453: line orn NR 309; p 457: line orn NR 310; p 459: line orn NR 309; p 518: line orn NR 323; p 521: tail-piece NR 306
4to
title leaf, 2 pp; text: n 8387-9442, pp 3-521.
A copy in USA: ANC (formerly in USA: JPC) has on the flyleaf the erased signature of Augustus Nordenskjöld dated 1777.
UK: SOC, CON, NCC; SWE: GGY; USA: ANC, FOU, SHS

49/01/La O/15 **1756** Hyde 563
<< <untitled> >>
foolscap long 4to <343 x 102 mm>
text: <Exodus ch 28> n 9804-9965, pp 3a-108b; <Exodus ch 29> n 9985-10158, pp 3a-118b.
The MS forms Codex 25. Codices 24 <chapters 25-27>, 25, and 26 <Hyde 562-564> together form La 1/14 = Hyde 577.
Unpublished copies have been recorded as follows.
1 UK: SOC & USA: ANC, SHS A reproduction on microfilms 8 and 9, Bryn Athyn PA.
MS not seen; description deduced from La O/20.
SWE: KVA

49/01/La O/16 **1756** Hyde 564
<<Caput XXX
Exodi | Caput Trigesimum Sextum
Exodi | Caput Trigesimum Septimum
Exodi | Caput Trigesimum Octavum
Exodi | Caput Trigesimum Nonum
Exodi | Caput Quadragesimum>>
foolscap long 4to <337 x 95 mm>
text: Exodus ch 30 n 10176-10307 <unfinished>, pp 3a-94b; <Exodus ch 31> n 10327-10372 <unfinished>, pp 3a-22b; <Exodus ch 32> n 10395-10509 <unfinished>, pp 3a-36b; <Exodus ch 33> n 10524-10584 <unfinished>, pp 5a-30b; <Exodus ch 34> n 10598-10708, pp 3a-41b; <Exodus ch 35> n 10726-10739, pp 5a-8b; Exodus ch 36 n 10740-10759, pp 9a-13b; Exodus ch 37 n 10760-10772, pp 14a-16b; Exodus ch 38 n 10773-10788, pp 17a-21a; Exodus ch 39 n 10769-10814, pp 21b-26b; Exodus ch 40 n 10815-10837, pp 27a-30b.
The MS forms Codex 26. Codices 24 <chapters 25-27>, 25, and 26 <Hyde 562-564> together form La 1/14 = Hyde 577.
Unpublished copies have been recorded as follows.
1 UK: SOC & USA: ANC, SHS A reproduction on microfilm 9, Bryn Athyn PA.
MS not seen; description deduced from La O/20.
SWE: KVA

49/01/La 1/14 **1756** Hyde 577
Arcana Cœlestia, | QUÆ IN | *SCRIPTURA SACRA,* | SEU | *VERBO DOMINI* | SUNT, DETECTA: | Hic quæ in | *EXODO,* | Una cum Mirabilibus | Quæ visa sunt | In Mundo Spirituum, & Cœlo Angelorum. | <2 spaced rules> | PARS TERTIA. | <2 spaced rules> | MDCCLVI.
p 3: head-piece NR 293; p 7: line orn NR 319; p 55: line orn NR 324; p 56: tail-piece NR 325; p 58: line orn NR 326; p 60: line orn NR 319; p 100: line orn NR 301; p 101: tail-piece NR 327; p 103: line orn NR

328; p 105: line orn NR 280; p 133: line orn NR 284; p 134: tail-piece NR 287; p 136: line orn NR 319; p 139: line orn NR 324; p 244: line orn NR 280; p 246: tail-piece NR 289; p 248: line orn NR 301; p 251: line orn NR 328; p 371: line orn NR 329; p 373: tail-piece NR 330; p 375: line orn NR 284; p 378: line orn NR 326; p 471: line orn NR 328; p 472: tail-piece NR 289; p 474: line orn NR 301; p 475: line orn NR 319; p 498: line orn NR 328; p 501: line orn NR 280; p 504: line orn NR 326; p 555: line orn NR 301; p 557: line orn NR 328; p 559: line orn NR 331; p 595: line orn NR 281; p 598: NR 319; p 601: line orn NR 280; p 646: line orn NR 326; p 648: tail-piece NR 287; p 650: line orn NR 331; p 652: line orn NR 281; p 655: line orn NR 328; p 663: line orn NR 301; p 666: tail-piece NR 289; p 668: line orn NR 284; p 670: line orn NR 281; p 672: line orn NR 326; p 674: line orn NR 280; p 676: tail-piece NR 332; p 679: line orn NR 328; p 682: line orn NR 319; p 686: tail-piece NR 297; p 691: line orn NR 301; p 694: line orn NR 281; p 695: tail-piece NR 297
4to
title leaf, 2 pp; text: n 9443-10837, pp 3-695.
There is a manuscript transcript of this volume, made by M Sibly <started 21 August 1827, finished 17 June 1829> in UK: NCC.
A copy in USA: ANC (formerly in USA: JPC) has on the flyleaf the erased signature of Augustus Nordenskjöld dated 1777.
UK: SOC, CON, NCC; SWE: GGY; USA: ANC, FOU, SHS

49/01/La 2/1 **1819** Hyde 577 note

In 1819 H Hodson issued a proposal to re-publish *Arcana Cœlestia*, in Latin, in London. The work was to appear in six demy 4to volumes; the price to subscribers was to be 10 guineas, and to non-subscribers 12½ guineas. The edition was not however issued. The prospectus in which the proposal was made was appended to the April-June number of *The Intellectual Repository* London 1819. In UK: SOC a copy is bound in a book by J C Hill *The chief obstacles that prevent the blessings of peace* Birmingham. <Archives S4/184>

49/01/La 3/1 **1833** Hyde 578; see also 3436

ARCANA COELESTIA | QUAE IN | SCRIPTURA SACRA | SEU | *VERBO DOMINI* | SUNT, DETECTA: | HIC PRIMUM QUAE IN | *GENESI.* | UNA CUM MIRABILIBUS | QUAE VISA SUNT | IN MUNDO SPIRITUUM ET IN COELO ANGELORUM. | <short rule> | OPUS | EMANUELIS SWEDENBORG. | <short orn rule> | AD FIDEM EDITIONIS PRINCIPIS 1749 ss. LONDINI | EXCUSAE DENUO CASTIGATIUS EDIDIT | Dr. JO. FR. IM. TAFEL. | <short rule> | PARTIS PRIMAE | VOL. I. | <multiple rule> | PROSTAT | TUBINGAE | IN BIBLIOPOLIO ZU-GUTTENBERG. | 1833.
verso: MATTH. VI: 33. | *Quaerite primo Regnum Dei, et Justitiam ejus, et omnia* | *adjicientur vobis.*
8vo
title leaf, 2 pp; text: Contents, 2 pp, n I-V, 6-946, pp 1-397; Notae criticae editoris, pp 398-404; Errata, p 404.
R Hindmarsh supplied J F I Tafel with many of the critical notes to this edition <La 3/1-13 = Hyde 578-590>.
The whole edition was printed on both fine and common paper.
UK: SOC, CON, NCC, NR; DEN: RLD; NET: GEN, KB; SWE: UPP; USA: ANC, FOU, SHS

49/01/La 3/2 **1834** Hyde 579

ARCANA COELESTIA | QUAE IN | SCRIPTURA SACRA | SEU | *VERBO DOMINI* | SUNT, DETECTA: | HIC PRIMUM QUAE IN | *GENESI.* | UNA CUM MIRABILIBUS | QUAE VISA SUNT | IN MUNDO SPIRITUUM ET IN COELO ANGELORUM. | <short rule> | OPUS | EMANUELIS SWEDENBORG. | <short orn rule> | AD FIDEM EDIT. PRINCIP. 1749 ss. LONDINI EXCUSAE | DENUO CASTIGATIUS

EDIDIT | Dr JO. FR. IM. TAFEL. | <short rule> | PARTIS PRIMAE | VOL. II. | <multiple rule> | PROSTAT | TUBINGAE | IN BIBLIOPOLIO ZU-GUTTENBERG. | 1834.
8vo
title leaf, 2 pp; text: n 947-1885, pp 405-860; Errata, p 860; Notae criticae editoris, pp 861-866.
UK: soc, con, ncc, nr; DEN: rld; NET: gen, kb; SWE: upp; USA: anc, fou, shs

49/01/La 3/3 **1835** **Hyde 580**
ARCANA COELESTIA | QUAE IN | SCRIPTURA SACRA | SEU | *VERBO DOMINI* | SUNT, DETECTA: | HIC QUAE IN | *GENESI.* | UNA CUM MIRABILIBUS | QUAE VISA SUNT | IN MUNDO SPIRITUUM ET IN COELO ANGELORUM. | <short rule> | OPUS | EMANUELIS SWEDENBORG. | <short orn rule> | AD FIDEM EDIT. PRINCIP. 1749 ss. LONDINI EXCUSAE | DENUO CASTIGATIUS EDIDIT | Dr JO. FR. IM. TAFEL. | <short rule> | PARS SECUNDA, | SEU TOTIUS OPERIS VOL. III. | <multiple rule> | PROSTAT | TUBINGAE | IN BIBLIOPOLIO ZU-GUTTENBERG. | 1835.
verso: MATTH. VI: 33. | Quaerite primo Regni Dei, et Justitiam ejus, et omnia | adjicientur vobis.
8vo
title leaf, 2 pp; text: Praefatio, n 1886-2759, pp 1-509; Errata, p 509; Notae criticae editoris, pp 510-522; Index operum Swedenborgii theologicorum, pp 523-526.
UK: soc, con, ncc, nr; DEN: rld; NET: gen, kb; SWE: upp; USA: anc, fou, shs

49/01/La 3/4 **1836** **Hyde 581**
ARCANA COELESTIA | QUAE IN | SCRIPTURA SACRA | SEU | *VERBO DOMINI* | SUNT, DETECTA: | HIC QUAE IN | *GENESI* | UNA CUM MIRABILIBUS | QUAE VISA SUNT | IN MUNDO SPIRITUUM ET IN COELO ANGELORUM. | <short rule> | OPUS | EMANUELIS SWEDENBORG. | <short orn rule> | AD FIDEM EDIT. PRINCIP. 1749 ss. LONDINI EXCUSAE | DENUO CASTIGATIUS EDIDIT | Dr JO. FR. IM. TAFEL. | <short rule> | PARTIS TERTIAE | VOL. I. | SEU TOTIUS OPERIS VOL. IV. | <multiple rule> | PROSTAT | TUBINGAE | IN BIBLIOPOLIO ZU-GUTTENBERG. | 1836.
8vo
title leaf, 2 pp; text: Praefatio, n 2760-3352, pp III-IV, 1-374; Errata, p 374; Notae criticae editoris, pp 375-386; Index editionum principum maximam partem rariorum quas Libraria Zu-Guttenberg emturientibus offert, 2 pp.
UK: soc, con, ncc, nr; DEN: rld; NET: gen, kb; SWE: upp; USA: anc, fou, shs

49/01/La 3/5 **1838** **Hyde 582**
ARCANA COELESTIA | QUAE IN | SCRIPTURA SACRA | SEU | *VERBO DOMINI* | SUNT, DETECTA: | HIC QUAE IN | *GENESI* | UNA CUM MIRABILIBUS | QUAE VISA SUNT | IN MUNDO SPIRITUUM ET IN COELO ANGELORUM. | <short rule> | OPUS | EMANUELIS SWEDENBORG. | <short orn rule> | AD FIDEM EDIT. PRINCIP. 1749 ss. LONDINI EXCUSAE | DENUO CASTIGATIUS EDIDIT | Dr JO. FR. IM. TAFEL. | <short rule> | PARTIS TERTIAE | VOL. II. | SEU TOTIUS OPERIS VOL. V. | <multiple rule> | PROSTAT | TUBINGAE | IN BIBLIOPOLIO ZU-GUTTENBERG. | 1838.
8vo
title leaf, 2 pp; text: n 3353-4055, pp 389-875; Notae criticae editoris, pp 876-890; Errata, p 890.
UK: soc, con, ncc, nr; DEN: rld; NET: gen, kb; SWE: upp; USA: anc, fou, shs

49/01/La 3/6 **1838** **Hyde 583, 2596**
ARCANA COELESTIA | QUAE IN | SCRIPTURA SACRA | SEU | *VERBO DOMINI* | SUNT, DETECTA: | HIC QUAE IN | *GENESI* | UNA CUM MIRABILIBUS | QUAE VISA SUNT | IN MUNDO SPIRITUUM ET IN COELO ANGELORUM. | <short rule> | OPUS | EMANUELIS SWEDENBORG. | <short orn rule> | AD FIDEM EDIT. PRINCIP. 1749 ss. LONDINI EXCUSAE | DENUO CASTIGATIUS EDIDIT | Dr JO. FR. IM. TAFEL. | <short rule> | PARTIS QUARTAE | VOL. I. | SEU TOTIUS OPERIS VOL. VI. |

<multiple rule> | PROSTAT | TUBINGAE | IN BIBLIOPOLIO ZU-GUTTENBERG. | 1838.
8vo
title leaf, 2 pp; title leaf and text of 69/12/La 2/1 = Hyde 2596, pp 1-6; Lectiones variantes, p 6; text of *Arcana Coelestia* n 4056-4634, pp 1-378; Errata, p 378; Notae criticae editoris, pp 379-392.
UK: SOC, CON, NCC, NR; DEN: RLD; NET: GEN, KB; SWE: UPP; USA: ANC, FOU, SHS

49/01/La 3/7 **1839** Hyde 584
ARCANA COELESTIA | QUAE IN | SCRIPTURA SACRA | SEU | *VERBO DOMINI* | SUNT, DETECTA: | HIC QUAE IN | *GENESI* | UNA CUM MIRABILIBUS | QUAE VISA SUNT | IN MUNDO SPIRITUUM ET IN COELO ANGELORUM. | <short rule> | OPUS | EMANUELIS SWEDENBORG. | <short orn rule> | AD FIDEM EDIT. PRINCIP. 1749 ss. LONDINI EXCUSAE | DENUO CASTIGATIUS EDIDIT | D^r^ JO. FR. IM. TAFEL. | <short rule> | PARTIS QUARTAE | VOL. II. | SEU TOTIUS OPERIS VOL. VII. | <multiple rule> | PROSTAT | TUBINGAE | IN BIBLIOPOLIO ZU-GUTTENBERG. | 1839.
8vo
title leaf, 2 pp; text: n 4635-5190, pp 395-764; Notae criticae editoris, pp 765-776; Errata, p 776.
UK: SOC, CON, NCC, NR; DEN: RLD; NET: GEN, KB; SWE: UPP; USA: ANC, FOU, SHS

49/01/La 3/8 **1839** Hyde 585
ARCANA COELESTIA | QUAE IN | SCRIPTURA SACRA, | SEU | *VERBO DOMINI* | SUNT, DETECTA: | HIC QUAE IN | *GENESI.* | UNA CUM MIRABILIBUS, | QUAE VISA SUNT | IN MUNDO SPIRITUUM ET IN COELO ANGELORUM. | <short rule> | OPUS | EMANUELIS SWEDENBORG. | <short orn rule> | AD FIDEM EDIT. PRINCIP. 1749 ss. LONDINI EXCUSAE | DENUO CASTIGATIUS EDIDIT | D^r^ JO. FR. IM. TAFEL. | <short rule> | PARS QUINTA | SEU TOTIUS OPERIS VOL. VIII. | <multiple rule> | PROSTAT | TUBINGAE | IN BIBLIOPOLIO ZU-GUTTENBERG. | 1839.
8vo
title leaf, 2 pp; text: n 5191-6626, pp 1-718; Errata, p 718; Notae criticae editoris, pp 719-750.
UK: SOC, CON, NCC, NR; DEN: RLD; NET: GEN, KB; SWE: UPP; USA: ANC, FOU, SHS

49/01/La 3/9 **1840** Hyde 586
ARCANA COELESTIA, | QUAE IN | SCRIPTURA SACRA, | SEU | *VERBO DOMINI* | SUNT, DETECTA: | HIC QUAE IN | *EXODO,* | UNA CUM MIRABILIBUS | QUAE VISA SUNT | IN MUNDO SPIRITUUM, ET IN COELO ANGELORUM. | <short rule> | OPUS | EMANUELIS SWEDENBORG. | <short orn rule> | AD FIDEM EDIT. PRINCIP. 1749 ss. LONDINI EXCUSAE | DENUO CASTIGATIUS EDIDIT | D^r^ JO. FR. IM. TAFEL. | <short rule> | PARTIS PRIMAE | VOL. I. | SEU TOTIUS OPERIS VOL. IX. | <multiple rule> | PROSTAT | TUBINGAE | IN BIBLIOPOLIO ZU-GUTTENBERG. | 1840.
8vo
title leaf, 2 pp; text: n 6627-7487, pp 1-386; Notae criticae editoris, pp 387-402; Errata, p 402.
UK: SOC, CON, NCC, NR; DEN: RLD; NET: GEN, KB; SWE: UPP; USA: ANC, FOU, SHS

49/01/La 3/10 **1840** Hyde 587
ARCANA COELESTIA, | QUAE IN | SCRIPTURA SACRA, | SEU | *VERBO DOMINI* | SUNT, DETECTA: | HIC QUAE IN | *EXODO,* | UNA CUM MIRABILIBUS | QUAE VISA SUNT | IN MUNDO SPIRITUUM, ET IN COELO ANGELORUM. | <short rule> | OPUS | EMANUELIS SWEDENBORG. | <short orn rule> | AD FIDEM EDIT. PRINCIP. 1749 ss. LONDINI EXCUSAE | DENUO CASTIGATIUS EDIDIT | D^r^ JO. FR. IM. TAFEL. | <short rule> | PARTIS PRIMAE | VOL. II. | SEU TOTIUS OPERIS VOL. X. | <multiple rule> | PROSTAT | TUBINGAE | IN BIBLIOPOLIO ZU-GUTTENBERG. | 1840.
8vo

title leaf, 2 pp; text: n 7488-8386, pp 405-791; Notae criticae editoris, pp 792-810; Errata et emendanda, p 810.

UK: SOC, CON, NCC, NR; DEN: RLD; NET: GEN, KB; SWE: UPP; USA: ANC, FOU, SHS

49/01/La 3/11 **1841** Hyde 588

ARCANA COELESTIA, | QUAE IN | SCRIPTURA SACRA, | SEU | *VERBO DOMINI* | SUNT, DETECTA: | HIC QUAE IN | *EXODO*, | UNA CUM MIRABILIBUS | QUAE VISA SUNT | IN MUNDO SPIRITUUM, ET IN COELO ANGELORUM. | <short rule> | OPUS | EMANUELIS SWEDENBORG. | <short orn rule> | AD FIDEM EDIT. PRINCIP. 1749 ss. LONDINI EXCUSAE | DENUO CASTIGATIUS EDIDIT | D[r] JO. FR. IM. TAFEL. | <short rule> | PARS SECUNDA. | SEU TOTIUS OPERIS VOL. XI. | <multiple rule> | PROSTAT | TUBINGAE | IN BIBLIOPOLIO ZU-GUTTENBERG. | 1841.

8vo

title leaf, 2 pp; text: n 8387-9442, pp 1-713; Notae criticae editoris, pp 714-752; Errata et emendanda, p 752; catalogue, 2 pp.

UK: SOC, CON, NCC, NR; DEN: RLD; NET: GEN, KB; SWE: UPP; USA: ANC, FOU, SHS

49/01/La 3/12 **1841** Hyde 589

ARCANA COELESTIA, | QUAE IN | SCRIPTURA SACRA, | SEU | *VERBO DOMINI* | SUNT, DETECTA: | HIC QUAE IN | *EXODO*, | UNA CUM MIRABILIBUS | QUAE VISA SUNT | IN MUNDO SPIRITUUM, ET IN COELO ANGELORUM. | <short rule> | OPUS | EMANUELIS SWEDENBORG. | <short orn rule> | AD FIDEM EDIT. PRINCIP. 1749 ss. LONDINI EXCUSAE | DENUO CASTIGATIUS EDIDIT | D[r] JO. FR. IM. TAFEL. | <short rule> | PARS TERTIAE | VOL. I. | SEU TOTIUS OPERIS VOL. XII. | <multiple rule> | PROSTAT | TUBINGAE | IN BIBLIOPOLIO ZU-GUTTENBERG. | 1841.

8vo

title leaf, 2 pp; text: n 9443-9973, pp 1-335; Notae criticae editoris, pp 336-352; advertisement, 2 pp.

UK: SOC, CON, NCC, NR; DEN: RLD; NET: GEN, KB; SWE: UPP; USA: ANC, FOU, SHS

49/01/La 3/13 **1842** Hyde 590

ARCANA COELESTIA, | QUAE IN | SCRIPTURA SACRA, | SEU | *VERBO DOMINI* | SUNT, DETECTA: | HIC QUAE IN | *EXODO*, | UNA CUM MIRABILIBUS | QUAE VISA SUNT | IN MUNDO SPIRITUUM, ET IN COELO ANGELORUM. | <short rule> | OPUS | EMANUELIS SWEDENBORG. | <short orn rule> | AD FIDEM EDIT. PRINCIP. 1749 ss. LONDINI EXCUSAE | DENUO CASTIGATIUS EDIDIT | D[r] JO. FR. IM. TAFEL. | <short rule> | PARS TERTIAE | VOL. II. | SEU TOTIUS OPERIS VOL. XIII. | <multiple rule> | PROSTAT | TUBINGAE | IN BIBLIOPOLIO ZU-GUTTENBERG. | 1842.

8vo

title leaf, 2 pp; text: n 9974-10837, pp 355-964; Notae criticae editoris, pp 965-987; Corrigenda, p 987; Announcement concerning publication of *Diarium Spirituale*, *Adversaria*, *De Commercio Animae et Corporis*, and *Sapientia Angelica de Divino Amore et de Divina Sapientia*, 1 p; Erklärung <Statement>, 2 pp; catalogue, 2 pp.

UK: SOC, CON, NCC, NR; DEN: RLD; NET: GEN, KB; SWE: UPP; USA: ANC, FOU, SHS

49/01/La 4/1 **1910** Hyde —

The Annual Report of the American Swedenborg Printing and Publishing Society, New York, stated that work had been suspended on the new Latin edition of *Arcana Coelestia*, promised in an earlier report. <*New Church Life* Bryn Athyn PA, 1910 pp 438-439>

49/01/La 0/17 **1916** Hyde 3038/10, 549/1, 550/1, 551/1, 552/1

EMANUELIS SWEDENBORGII | ARCANA COELESTIA | <short rule> | AD AUTOGRAPHI

SIMILITUDINEM IN BIBLIOTHECA REGIAE ACADEMIAE SCIENTIARUM | SUECICAE ADSERVATI, OPE ARTIS PHOTOTYPOGRAPHICAE DELINEATI, EDITA JUSSU | CONVENTUS GENERALIS AMERICANI NOVAE HIEROSOLYMAE | SOCIETATIS AMERICANAE PRO SCRIPTIS EDENDIS SWEDENBORGII | ACADEMIAE NOVAE ECCLESIAE AMERICANAE | CONCILII GENERALIS NOVAE ECCLESIAE BRITANNICAE | CUSTODUM CURATELAE ROTCHIANAE AMERICANAE | ET | SOCIETATIS SWEDENBORGIANAE LONDINENSIS | <short orn rule> | VOL. I. | <orn 15 x 37 mm> | HOLMIAE | EX OFFICINA PHOTOTYPOGRAPHICA LAGRELIUS & WESTPHAL | MCMXVI.
half title: EMANUELIS SWEDENBORGII | AUTOGRAPHA | <short rule> | TOMUS X.
folio
half title and title leaves, 4 pp; Prooemium, 2 pp; Contenta, 1 p; p 1 blank;
Codex 8: inside of front cover and first blank pp of MS, pp 2-5; text, pp 5-94; last blank pp and inside of back cover of MS, pp 95-97; back and front covers of Codex, pp 98-99.
Codex 10: first blank pp of MS, pp 102-103; text, pp 103-339; inside of back cover, p 339; back and front covers of Codex, pp 340-341.
Codex 80: inside of front cover, p 344; title page, p 345; first blank p of MS, p 346; text, pp 347-404; inside of back cover, p 405; back and front covers of Codex, pp 406-407.
Codex 9: inside of front cover, p 410; first blank pp of MS, pp 411-412; title page, p 413; blank p of MS, p 414; text, pp 415-541; blank p and inside of back cover, pp 542-543; back and front covers of Codex, pp 544-545.
Reproduction of Codices 8, 10, 80, 9, published in phototyped edition, vol 10 <*Arcana Coelestia* vol 1, Hyde 3038/10> Stockholm.
On p 104 is Swedenborg's quotation of Matthew 6:33 <Quaerite primo Regnum Dei, et Justititiam | ejus, et omnia adjicientur vobis.> with a note 'Double Pica Italique.'
On p 487 is Swedenborg's note of the costs for a small building, perhaps his summer house.
Unpublished copies have been recorded as follows.

1 UK: soc & USA: anc, shs A reproduction on microfilm 6, Bryn Athyn pa

UK: soc, bl, bod, cam, con, lon, ncc, ryl, wil; DEN: rld; NET: gen, kb; SWE: roy, upp; USA: anc, fou, shs; AUS: syd; NZ: wel

49/01/La O/18 **1916** Hyde 3038/11, 553/1, 554/1, 555/1, 556/1, 557/1

EMANUELIS SWEDENBORGII | ARCANA COELESTIA | <short rule> | AD AUTOGRAPHI SIMILITUDINEM IN BIBLIOTHECA REGIAE ACADEMIAE SCIENTIARUM | SUECICAE ADSERVATI, OPE ARTIS PHOTOTYPOGRAPHICAE DELINEATI, EDITA JUSSU | CONVENTUS GENERALIS AMERICANI NOVAE HIEROSOLYMAE | SOCIETATIS AMERICANAE PRO SCRIPTIS EDENDIS SWEDENBORGII | ACADEMIAE NOVAE ECCLESIAE AMERICANAE | CONCILII GENERALIS NOVAE ECCLESIAE BRITANNICAE | CUSTODUM CURATELAE ROTCHIANAE AMERICANAE | ET | SOCIETATIS SWEDENBORGIANAE LONDINENSIS | <short orn rule> | VOL. II. | <orn 15 x 37 mm> | HOLMIAE | EX OFFICINA PHOTOTYPOGRAPHICA LAGRELIUS & WESTPHAL | MCMXVI.
half title: EMANUELIS SWEDENBORGII | AUTOGRAPHA | <short rule> | TOMUS XI.
folio
half title and title leaves, 4 pp; Contenta, 1 p.
Codex 15: inside of front cover of MS, p 2; first blank pp of MS, pp 2, 3, 4; title page, p 3; text, pp 4-255; last blank pp of MS, p 256; title page and inside of back cover of MS, p 257; back and front covers of Codex, pp 258-259.
Codex 16: inside of front cover and title page, p 262; first blank p of MS, p 263; text, pp 263-484; inside of back cover, p 484; back and front covers of Codex, pp 485-486.
Codex 17: inside of front cover, p 488; text, pp 488-688; title page and inside of back cover, p 489; back and front covers of Codex, pp 690-691.
Codex 18: inside of front cover and title page, p 694; text, p 694-927; inside of back cover, p 927;

back and front covers of Codex, pp 928-929.
Codex 19: inside of front cover, p 932; text, pp 932-1146; inside of back cover, p 1146; back and front covers of Codex, pp 1148-1149.
Reproduction of Codices 15, 16, 17, 18, 19, published in phototyped edition, vol 11 <*Arcana Coelestia* vol 2, Hyde 3038/10> Stockholm.
On pp 688-689 is Swedenborg's draft of a letter to J Lewis; and on p 773 he drafted a note to J Hart. The latter note is reproduced as Autograph Plate 2 in La 5/9 = Hyde 590/9.
Unpublished copies have been recorded as follows.

1 UK: soc & USA: anc, shs A reproduction on microfilms 6 and 7, Bryn Athyn pa.

UK: soc, bl, bod, cam, con, lon, ncc, ryl, wil; DEN: rld; NET: gen, kb; SWE: roy, upp; USA: anc, fou, shs; AUS: syd; NZ: wel

49/01/La 0/19 **1916** Hyde 3038/12, 558/1, 559/1, 560/1, 561/1

EMANUELIS SWEDENBORGII | ARCANA COELESTIA | <short rule> | AD AUTOGRAPHI SIMILITUDINEM IN BIBLIOTHECA REGIAE ACADEMIAE SCIENTIARUM | SUECICAE ADSERVATI, OPE ARTIS PHOTOTYPOGRAPHICAE DELINEATI, EDITA JUSSU | CONVENTUS GENERALIS AMERICANI NOVAE HIEROSOLYMAE | SOCIETATIS AMERICANAE PRO SCRIPTIS EDENDIS SWEDENBORGII | ACADEMIAE NOVAE ECCLESIAE AMERICANAE | CONCILII GENERALIS NOVAE ECCLESIAE BRITANNICAE | CUSTODUM CURATELAE ROTCHIANAE AMERICANAE | ET | SOCIETATIS SWEDENBORGIANAE LONDINENSIS | <short orn rule> | VOL. III. | <orn 15 x 37 mm> | HOLMIAE | EX OFFICINA PHOTOTYPOGRAPHICA LAGRELIUS & WESTPHAL | MCMXVI.
half title: EMANUELIS SWEDENBORGII | AUTOGRAPHA | <short rule> | TOMUS XII.
folio
half title and title leaves, 4 pp; Contenta, 1 p.
Codex 20: inside of front cover, p 2; text, pp 2-261; title page and inside of back cover, p 262; back and front covers, pp 263-264.
Codex 21: inside of front cover, p 266; text, pp 266-487; title page and inside of back cover, p 488; back and front covers of Codex, pp 489-490.
Codex 22: inside of front cover, p 492; text, p 492-756; inside of back cover, p 756; back and front covers of Codex, pp 757-758.
Codex 23: inside of front cover, p 760; text, pp 761-1012; blank page and inside of back cover, p 1013; back and front covers of codex, pp 1014-1015.
Reproduction of Codices 20, 21, 22, 23, published in phototyped edition, vol 12 <*Arcana Coelestia* vol 3, Hyde 3038/10> Stockholm.
Unpublished copies have been recorded as follows.

1 UK: soc & USA: anc, shs A reproduction on microfilms 7 and 8, Bryn Athyn pa.

UK: soc, bl, bod, cam, con, lon, ncc, ryl, wil; DEN: rld; NET: gen, kb; SWE: roy, upp; USA: anc, fou, shs; AUS: syd; NZ: wel

49/01/La 0/20 **1916** Hyde 3038/13, 562/1, 563/1, 564/1

EMANUELIS SWEDENBORGII | ARCANA COELESTIA | <short rule> | AD AUTOGRAPHI SIMILITUDINEM IN BIBLIOTHECA REGIAE ACADEMIAE SCIENTIARUM | SUECICAE ADSERVATI, OPE ARTIS PHOTOTYPOGRAPHICAE DELINEATI, EDITA JUSSU | CONVENTUS GENERALIS AMERICANI NOVAE HIEROSOLYMAE | SOCIETATIS AMERICANAE PRO SCRIPTIS EDENDIS SWEDENBORGII | ACADEMIAE NOVAE ECCLESIAE AMERICANAE | CONCILII GENERALIS NOVAE ECCLESIAE BRITANNICAE | CUSTODUM CURATELAE ROTCHIANAE AMERICANAE | ET | SOCIETATIS SWEDENBORGIANAE LONDINENSIS | <short orn rule> | VOL. IV. | <orn 15 x 37

mm> | HOLMIAE | EX OFFICINA PHOTOTYPOGRAPHICA LAGRELIUS & WESTPHAL | MCMXVI.
half title: EMANUELIS SWEDENBORGII | AUTOGRAPHA | <short rule> | TOMUS III.
folio
half title and title leaves, 4 pp; Contenta, 1 p.
Codex 24: inside of front cover, p 2; text, pp 2-204; inside of back cover, p 204; back and front covers of Codex, pp 205-206.
Codex 25: inside of front cover, p 208; text, pp 208-446; brief notes in Swedish and inside of back cover, p 447; back and front covers of Codex, pp 448-449.
Codex 26: inside of front cover, p 452; text, pp 452-708; inside of back cover, p 708; back and front covers of Codex, pp 709-710.
Reproduction of Codices 24, 25, 26, published in phototyped edition, vol 13 <*Arcana Coelestia* vol 4, Hyde 3038/10> Stockholm.
Unpublished copies have been recorded as follows.

1 UK: SOC & USA: ANC, SHS A reproduction on microfilms 7 and 8, Bryn Athyn PA.

UK: SOC, BL, BOD, CAM, CON, LON, NCC, RYL, WIL; DEN: RLD; NET: GEN, KB; SWE: ROY, UPP; USA: ANC, FOU, SHS; AUS: SYD; NZ: WEL

49/01/La 5/1 1949 Hyde 590/1

ARCANA CAELESTIA | quae in SCRIPTURA SACRA | seu VERBO DOMINI sunt | detecta: nempe quae in | GENESI ET EXODO | una cum mirabilibus quae | visa sunt in Mundo | Spirituum et in Caelo | Angelorum | AB | EMANUELE SWEDENBORG | TOMUS I | CONTINENS | GENESEOS cap. i-xv. (n.-1-1885) | EDITIO TERTIA | Londinii 1949 <*stet* (n.-1-1885)>
verso: FIRST EDITION 1749-1756 | SECOND EDITION 1833-1842 | THIRD EDITION 1949- | The Swedenborg Society | was established in 1810 to | keep in print the works of | Emanuel Swedenborg | This third Latin edition of the "Arcana Caelestia", the | first work to be printed containing the Divine Revelation | of the truths of the Second Advent, has been edited by | Rev. P. H. Johnson, B.A., B.Sc. | The Editor's notes are in English, his Preface in both English and Latin | SWEDENBORG SOCIETY (INC.), | 20/21 BLOOMSBURY WAY, | LONDON | 1949
8vo
title leaf, 2 pp; Praefatio, pp v-viii; Sigla et compendia, pp ix-x; List of abbreviations, signs, etc, pp x-xi; Preface, p 1-4; Swedenborg's summary of the contents of the volume, pp 5-6; text: n I-V, 6-1885, pp 7-784; Minor corrections, pp 785-786.

UK: SOC, CON, NCC, NR; NET: GEN, KB; SWE: ROY, UPP; USA: ANC, SHS; AUS: SYD

49/01/La 5/2 1952 Hyde 590/2

ARCANA CAELESTIA | quae in SCRIPTURA SACRA | seu VERBO DOMINI sunt | detecta: nempe quae in | GENESI ET EXODO | una cum mirabilibus quae | visa sunt in Mundo | Spirituum et in Caelo | Angelorum | AB | EMANUELE SWEDENBORG | TOMUS II | CONTINENS | GENESEOS cap. XVI-XXI (n.1886—2759) | EDITIO TERTIA | Londinii 1952
verso: FIRST EDITION 1749-1756 | SECOND EDITION 1833-1842 | THIRD EDITION 1949- | The Swedenborg Society | was established in 1810 to | keep in print the works of | Emanuel Swedenborg | This third Latin edition of the "Arcana Caelestia", the | first work to be printed containing the Divine Revelation | of the truths of the Second Advent, has been edited by | Rev. P. H. Johnson, B.A., B.Sc. | The Editor's notes are in English, his Preface in both English and Latin | SWEDENBORG SOCIETY (INC.), | 20/21 BLOOMSBURY WAY, | LONDON | 1952
section title, verso <facing p 1>: *Matthaeus* vi 33 | QUAERITE PRIMO REGNUM DEI, ET JUSTITIAM EJUS, | ET OMNIA ADJICIENTUR VOBIS.
8vo
title leaf, 2 pp; Sigla et compendia, pp iii-iv; List of abbreviations, signs, etc, pp iv-v; Errata in Volume I, p vi; section title, p viii; text: Praefatio <ab auctore>, pp 1-2; n 1886-2759, pp 3-490;

Minor corrections, pp 491-492.
UK: SOC, CON, NCC, NR; NET: GEN, KB; SWE: ROY, UPP; USA: ANC, SHS; AUS: SYD

49/01/La 5/3 **1953** Hyde 590/3

ARCANA CAELESTIA | quae in SCRIPTURA SACRA | seu VERBO DOMINI sunt | detecta: nempe quae in | GENESI ET EXODO | una cum mirabilibus quae | visa sunt in Mundo | Spirituum et in Caelo | Angelorum | AB | EMANUELE SWEDENBORG | TOMUS III | CONTINENS | GENESEOS cap. XXII-XXX (n. 2760—4055) | EDITIO TERTIA | Londinii 1953
verso: FIRST EDITION 1749-1756 | SECOND EDITION 1833-1842 | THIRD EDITION 1949- | The Swedenborg Society | was established in 1810 to | keep in print the works of | Emanuel Swedenborg | This third Latin edition of the "Arcana Caelestia", the | first work to be printed containing the Divine Revelation | of the truths of the Second Advent, has been edited by | Rev. P. H. Johnson, B.A., B.Sc. | The Editor's notes are in English, his Preface in both English and Latin | SWEDENBORG SOCIETY | 20/21 BLOOMSBURY WAY | LONDON | 1953
section title, verso <facing p 1>: *Matthaeus* vi 33 | QUAERITE PRIMO REGNUM DEI, ET JUSTITIAM EJUS, | ET OMNIA ADJICIENTUR VOBIS.
8vo
title leaf, 2 pp; Sigla et compendia, pp iii-iv; List of abbreviations, signs, etc, pp iv-vi; section title, p viii; text: Praefatio <ab auctore>, p 1; n 2760-4055, pp 3-840; Minor corrections, pp 841-844.
UK: SOC, CON, NCC, NR; NET: GEN, KB; SWE: ROY, UPP; USA: ANC, SHS; AUS: SYD

49/01/La 5/4 **1956** Hyde 590/4

ARCANA CAELESTIA | quae in SCRIPTURA SACRA | seu VERBO DOMINI sunt | detecta: nempe quae in | GENESI ET EXODO | una cum mirabilibus quae | visa sunt in Mundo | Spirituum et in Caelo | Angelorum | AB | EMANUELE SWEDENBORG | TOMUS IV | CONTINENS | GENESEOS cap. XXXI-XL (n. 4056-5190) | EDITIO TERTIA | Londinii 1956
verso: FIRST EDITION 1749-1756 | SECOND EDITION 1833-1842 | THIRD EDITION 1949- | The Swedenborg Society | was established in 1810 to | keep in print the works of | Emanuel Swedenborg | This third Latin edition of the "Arcana Caelestia", the | first work to be printed containing the Divine Revelation | of the truths of the Second Advent, has been edited by | Rev. P. H. Johnson, B.A., B.Sc. | The Editor's notes are in English, | his Preface in both English and Latin | SWEDENBORG SOCIETY (INC.) | 20/21 BLOOMSBURY WAY | LONDON | 1956
section title: ARCANA CAELESTIA
verso: *Matthaeus* vi 33 | QUAERITE PRIMO REGNUM DEI, ET JUSTITIAM EJUS, | ET OMNIA ADJICIENTUR VOBIS.
8vo
title leaf, 2 pp; Sigla et compendia, pp v-vi; List of abbreviations, signs, etc, pp vi-vii; section title leaf, 2 pp; text: n 4056-5190, pp 1-735; Minor corrections, pp 737-739.
Printed by The Thanet Press, Margate.
UK: SOC, CON, NCC, NR; NET: GEN, KB; SWE: ROY, UPP; USA: ANC, SHS; AUS: SYD

49/01/La 1/17 **1960** Hyde 565/1

Arcana Cœlestia | QUÆ IN | *SCRIPTURA SACRA*, | SEU | *VERBO DOMINI* | SUNT, DETECTA: | Hic Primum quæ in | *GENESI*. | Una cum Mirabilibus | Quæ visa sunt | In Mundo Spirituum, & in Cœlo Angelorum. | <2 spaced rules> | PARS PRIMA. | <2 spaced rules> | MDCCXLIX.
verso: MATTH. VI: 33. | *Quærite primo Regnum Dei, & Justitiam ejus,* | *& omni adjicientur vobis.*
4to

blank leaf and title leaf, 4 pp; Swedenborg's list of contents, 2 pp; text: n I-V, 6-1885, pp 1-630; blank leaf.
Reprint of La 1/1 = Hyde 565 by offset phototypography; published by The Lord's New Church which is Nova Hierosolyma, Bryn Athyn PA. Reviewed in *New Church Life* Bryn Athyn PA, 1960 p 340.
UK: soc, con, ncc, nr; NET: gen, kb; SWE: roy, upp; USA: anc, shs; AUS: syd

49/01/La 5/5 **1961** Hyde 590/5
ARCANA CAELESTIA | quae in SCRIPTURA SACRA | seu VERBO DOMINI sunt | detecta: nempe quae in | GENESI ET EXODO | una cum mirabilibus quae | visa sunt in Mundo | Spirituum et in Caelo | Angelorum | AB | EMANUELE SWEDENBORG | TOMUS V | CONTINENS | GENESEOS cap. XLI-L (n. 5191-6626) | EDITIO TERTIA | Londinii 1961
verso: FIRST EDITION 1749-1756 | SECOND EDITION 1833-1842 | THIRD EDITION 1949 | The Swedenborg Society | was established in 1810 to | keep in print the works of | Emanuel Swedenborg | This third Latin edition of the "Arcana Caelestia", the | first work to be printed containing the Divine Revelation | of the truths of the Second Advent, has been edited by | Rev. P. H. Johnson, B.A., B.Sc., and after his death by | Rev. E. C. Mongredien. | The Editor's notes are in English, | his Preface in both English and Latin | SWEDENBORG SOCIETY (INC.) | 20/21 BLOOMSBURY WAY | 1961 <*stet* 1949>
half title: ARCANA CAELESTIA
verso: *Printed in England by Eyre & Spottiswoode Limited | Her Majesty's Printers, at The Thanet Press*
section title: *Matthaeus* vi 33 | QUAERITE PRIMO REGNUM DEI, ET JUSTITIAM | EJUS, ET OMNIA ADJICIETUR VOBIS
8vo
half title and title leaves, 4 pp; Sigla et compendia, pp v-vi; List of abbreviations, signs, etc, pp vi-vii; section title leaf, pp 1-2; text: n 5191-6626, pp 3-714; Minor corrections, pp 715-720.
UK: soc, con, ncc, nr; NET: gen, kb; SWE: roy, upp; USA: anc, shs; AUS: syd

49/01/La 5/6 **1968** Hyde 590/6
ARCANA CAELESTIA | quae in SCRIPTURA SACRA | seu VERBO DOMINI sunt | detecta: nempe quae in | GENESI ET EXODO | una cum mirabilibus quae | visa sunt in Mundo | Spirituum et in Caelo | Angelorum | AB | EMANUELE SWEDENBORG | TOMUS VI | CONTINENS | EXODI cap. I-XV (n. 6627-8386) | EDITIO TERTIA | Londinii 1968
verso: FIRST EDITION 1749-1756 | SECOND EDITION 1833-1842 | THIRD EDITION 1949- | The Swedenborg Society | was established in 1810 to | keep in print the works of | Emanuel Swedenborg | Volumes I-IV of this third Latin edition of the "Arcana | Caelestia" were edited by the late Rev. P. H. Johnson, | B.A., B.Sc., assisted by the late Rev. E. C. Mongredien. | Volume V was edited by the Rev. E. C. Mongredien assisted | by the Rev. Erik Sandström, B.Th., and Volume VI has | been edited | by the Rev. John E. Elliott, B.A., B.D., the | Rev. Norman Ryder, and the Rev. Erik Sandström. The | Rev. P. H. Johnson had also examined and made notes on | the whole of Volumes V-VIII, and the Rev. E. C. Mon- | gredien was preparing Volume VI when ill-health compelled him to retire from the work. | The Editors' notes are in English, their | Prefaces in both English and Latin | THE SWEDENBORG SOCIETY | 20/21 BLOOMSBURY WAY | LONDON | 1968
half title: ARCANA CAELESTIA
verso: *Printed in England by Eyre & Spottiswoode Ltd | Her Majesty's Printers, at The Thanet Press*
section title: *Matthew* vi 33 | QUAERITE PRIMO REGNUM DEI, ET JUSTITIAM EJUS, | ET OMNIA ADJICIENTUR VOBIS
8vo

half title and title leaves, 4 pp; Praefatio, pp v-vii; Sigla et compendia, pp viii-ix; Preface, pp x-xii; List of abbreviations, signs, etc, pp xiii-xiv; section title leaf, pp xv-xvi; text: n 6627-8386, pp 1-811; Minor corrections, pp 813-822.

UK: SOC, CON, NCC, NR; NET: GEN, KB; SWE: ROY, UPP; USA: ANC, SHS; AUS: SYD

49/01/La 5/7 1971 Hyde 590/7

ARCANA CAELESTIA | quae in SCRIPTURA SACRA | seu VERBO DOMINI sunt | detecta: nempe quae in | GENESI ET EXODO | una cum mirabilibus quae | visa sunt in Mundo | Spirituum et in Caelo | Angelorum | AB | EMANUELE SWEDENBORG | TOMUS VII | CONTINENS | EXODI cap. XVI-XXIV (n. 8387-9442) | EDITIO TERTIA | Londinii 1971

verso: FIRST EDITION 1749-1756 | SECOND EDITION 1833-1842 | THIRD EDITION 1949- | The Swedenborg Society | was established in 1810 to | keep in print the works of | Emanuel Swedenborg | Volumes I-IV of this third Latin edition of the "Arcana | Caelestia" were edited by the late Rev. P. H. Johnson, B.A., B.Sc., assisted by the late Rev. E. C. Mongredien. | Volume V was edited by the Rev. E. C. Mongredien assisted | by the Rev. Erik Sandström, B.Th., Volume VI was edited | by the Rev. John E. Elliott, B.A., B.D., the Rev. Norman | Ryder, and the Rev. Erik Sandström, and Volume VII has | been edited by | the Rev. John Elliott, assisted by the | Rev. Norman Ryder. The Rev. P. H. Johnson had also | examined and made notes on the whole of Volumes V-VIII, | and the Rev. E. C. Mongredien was preparing Volume VI | when ill-health compelled him to retire from the work. | The Editors' notes are in English, their | Prefaces in both English and Latin | THE SWEDENBORG SOCIETY | 20/21 BLOOMSBURY WAY | LONDON | 1971

half title: ARCANA CAELESTIA

verso: *Printed in England by Eyre & Spottiswoode Ltd* | *Her Majesty's Printers, Thanet Press, Margate*

section title: *Matthaeus* vi 33 | QUAERITE PRIMO REGNUM DEI, ET JUSTITIAM EJUS, | ET OMNIA ADJICIENTUR VOBIS

8vo

half title and title leaves, 4 pp; Sigla et compendia, pp v-vi; List of abbreviations, signs, etc, pp vii-viii; section title leaf, pp ix-x; text: n 8387-9442, pp 1-754; Minor corrections, pp 755-768.

UK: SOC, CON, NCC, NR; NET: GEN, KB; SWE: ROY, UPP; USA: ANC, SHS; AUS: SYD

49/01/La 5/8 1973 Hyde 590/8

ARCANA CAELESTIA | quae in SCRIPTURA SACRA | seu VERBO DOMINI sunt | detecta: nempe quae in | GENESI ET EXODO | una cum mirabilibus quae | visa sunt in Mundo | Spirituum et in Caelo | Angelorum | AB | EMANUELE SWEDENBORG | TOMUS VIII | CONTINENS | EXODI cap. XXV-XL (n. 9443-10,837) | EDITIO TERTIA | Londinii 1973

verso: FIRST EDITION 1749-1756 | SECOND EDITION 1833-1842 | THIRD EDITION 1949-1973 | The Swedenborg Society | was established in 1810 to | keep in print the works of | Emanuel Swedenborg | Volumes I-IV of this third Latin edition of the "Arcana | Caelestia" were edited by the late Rev. P. H. Johnson, B.A., B.Sc., assisted by the late Rev. E. C. Mongredien. | Volume V was edited by the Rev. E. C. Mongredien assisted | by the Rev. Erik Sandström, B.Th., Volume VI was edited | by the Rev. John E. Elliott, B.A., B.D., the Rev. Norman | Ryder, and the Rev. Erik Sandström, and Volumes VII, | VIII, and the Appendix Volume, have been edited by | the Rev. John Elliott, assisted by the Rev. Norman | Ryder. The Rev. P. H. Johnson had also examined and | made notes on the whole of Volumes V-VIII, and the | Rev. E. C. Mongredien was preparing Volume VI when | ill-health compelled him to retire from the work. | The Editors' notes are in English, their | Prefaces in both English and Latin | THE SWEDENBORG SOCIETY | 20/21 BLOOMSBURY WAY | LONDON | 1973

half title: ARCANA CAELESTIA

verso: *Printed in England by Eyre & Spottiswoode Ltd* | *Her Majesty's Printers, Thanet Press, Margate*

section title: *Matthaeus* vi 33 | QUAERITE PRIMO REGNUM DEI, ET JUSTITIAM EJUS, | ET OMNIA ADJICIENTUR VOBIS
8vo
half title and title leaves, 4 pp; Sigla et compendia, pp v-vi; List of abbreviations, signs, etc, pp vii-viii; 2 preliminary notes, p ix; section title leaf, pp xi-xii; text: n 9443-10837, pp 1-1033; Minor corrections, pp 1035-1048.
UK: soc, con, ncc, nr; NET: gen, kb; SWE: roy, upp; USA: anc, shs; AUS: syd

49/01/La 5/9 **1973** Hyde 590/9
AN APPENDIX | TO | ARCANA CAELESTIA | THE SWEDENBORG SOCIETY | 20/21 BLOOMSBURY WAY | LONDON | 1973
imprint: *Printed in England by Eyre & Spottiswoode Ltd | Her Majesty's Printer's, Thanet Press, Margate* <*stet* Printer's>
8vo
title leaf, 2 pp; Contents, p 3; Editor's preface, pp 5-6; Abbreviations, p 7; Matters promised in footnotes <to the 3rd edition, La 5/1-8>, pp 9-22; 2 additional notes, pp 23-24; Title pages to the 1st edition, p 25 and 13 unnumbered leaves; Variant readings in the drafts of these title pages, pp 27-28; List of words of which the spellings were altered in the 3rd edition, pp 29-32; Other changes, p 33; Additional matters found in the Autograph, pp 35-53; Notes concerning the Autograph, pp 57-58; Note concerning the 2nd edition, p 59; imprint, p 60; Photographic reproductions of pages of the Autograph placed in a pocket in the back of the book.
UK: soc, con, ncc, nr; NET: gen, kb; SWE: roy, upp; USA: anc, shs; AUS: syd

LATIN EXTRACTS

X 49/01/La 1949/1 **1949** Hyde —
REVELATION | THROUGH THE AGES | BY | PHILIP H. JOHNSON, B.A., B.Sc. | *A brochure to mark the occasion of | the publication of the Third Latin Edition of |* **Arcana Caelestia** | BY EMANUEL SWEDENBORG | *and of the Two Hundredth Anniversary of the | publication of the First Edition* | SWEDENBORG SOCIETY (INC) | 20 Bloomsbury Way, London | 1949
verso: MADE AND PRINTED IN GREAT BRITAIN BY | W. S. COWELL LTD, BUTTER MARKET, IPSWICH
4to trimmed and folded in half
title leaf, 2 pp; text, pp 3-24; 8 pages of photographs between pp 12 and 13.
The photographs include the following: 3 photographs on the centrefold are reproductions of the title pages of La 1/1, La 3/1, and La 5/1; they are followed by a reproduction of a page of La 0/17 <n 2859 (part)-2862 (part)>, and a reproduction of the title page of En 1/1.
UK: soc, nr; USA: shs

X 49/01/La 1956/1 **1956** Hyde —
<<REVELATION | THROUGH THE AGES | BY | PHILIP H. JOHNSON, B.A., B.Sc. | *A brochure to mark the occasion of | the publication of the Third Latin Edition of |* **Arcana Caelestia** | BY EMANUEL SWEDENBORG | *and of the Two Hundredth Anniversary of the | publication of the First Edition* | SWEDENBORG SOCIETY (INC) | 20 Bloomsbury Way, London | 1949>>
verso: <<MADE AND PRINTED IN GREAT BRITAIN BY | W. S. COWELL LTD, BUTTER MARKET, IPSWICH>>
4to trimmed and folded in half
title leaf, 2 pp; text, pp 3-24; 8 pages of photographs between pp 12 and 13.
A reprint of X La 1949/1 in an edition of 5,000 copies.
Copy not seen; description deduced from X La 1949/1 and annual report of UK: soc.

X 49/01/La 1999/1 **1999** Hyde —

Arcana Cœlestia | QUÆ IN | *SCRIPTURA SACRA*, | SEU | *VERBO DOMINI* | SUNT, DETECTA: | Hic Primum quæ in | *GENESI.* | Una cum Mirabilibus | Quæ visa sunt | In Mundo Spirituum, & in Cœlo Angelorum. | <2 spaced rules> | PARS PRIMA. | <2 spaced rules> | MDCCXLIX.

A3 folded to A4

Reduced facsimile reproduction of the title page of La 1/1, published in a brochure to mark the completion of the translation of the whole work by J E Elliott <En 5/1-12>. Reduced facsimile reproductions of orn NR 278 and 289 were printed on pp 1 and 3 respectively; and a facsimile of p 436 of *The London Magazine* for September 1749, containing John Lewis's advertisement for 49/01/La 1/1, was reproduced on p 6.

UK: NR

LATIN/ENGLISH EXTRACTS

X 49/01/LaEn 1943/1 **1943** Hyde 868/4

Latin=English Edition | DE MIRACULIS | et quod hodie circa finem saeculi nulla | exspectanda | MIRACLES AND SIGNS | and that they are not to be expected at this time | when the end of the age is near | Extracted from Vol. X of the Phototype Edition | of the manuscripts of Emanuel Swedenborg, and | now printed and published for the first time, | together with a translation into English | Translated and edited | by | REV. P. H. JOHNSON, B.A., B.Sc. | SWEDENBORG SOCIETY (Inc.) | 20/21 Bloomsbury Way, London, W.C. 1 | 1943

8vo

title page, p 1; Editor's foreword, pp 2-3; Latin text n 1-18, pp 4, 6, 8, 10, 12, 14, 16, 18, 20, 22, 24, 26; English text n 1-18, pp 5, 7, 9, 11, 13, 15, 17, 19, 21, 23, 25, 27.

The original text is to be found in Codex 80 <La 0/2>, where the paragraphs are numbered 2870-2887; however, Swedenborg later replaced this section with one entitled *de Libero hominis* <see n 2870-2893 in La 1/9, etc.>.

In his Foreword the editor acknowledged receipt of the assistance of E A Sutton.

UK: SOC, CON, NR

X 49/01/LaEn 1947/1 **1947** Hyde 868/5

Latin=English Edition | DE MIRACULIS | et quod hodie circa finem saeculi nulla | exspectanda | MIRACLES | They are not to be expected at this time | when the end of the age is near | Extracted from Vol. X of the Phototype Edition | of the manuscripts of Emanuel Swedenborg, and | now printed and published for the first time, | together with a translation into English | Translated and edited | by | REV. P. H. JOHNSON, B.A., B.Sc. | SWEDENBORG SOCIETY (Inc.) | 20/21 Bloomsbury Way, London, W.C. 1 | 1943. Revised 1947

8vo

title page, p 1; Editor's foreword, pp 2-3; Latin text n 1-18, pp 4, 6, 8, 10, 12, 14, 16, 18, 20, 22, 24, 26; English text n 1-18, pp 5, 7, 9, 11, 13, 15, 17, 19, 21, 23, 25, 27.

In his Foreword the editor acknowledged receipt of the assistance of E C Mongredien and E A Sutton.

UK: SOC, CON, NR; NET: GEN, KB; USA; ANC, SHS; AUS: SYD

ENGLISH

Translators:

En 1 John Marchant
En 2 John Clowes and later revisers
En 3 George Harrison

En 4 Arthur Hodson Searle vols 1–7, 9
Lewis Alexander Slight vol 8
James Speirs vol 10
Rudolph Leonard Tafel vol 11
unnamed vol 12
En 5 John Faulkner Potts and later revisers
En 6 Philip Henry Johnson
En 7 John Edward Elliott
En 8 Lisa Hyatt Cooper

49/01/En 1/1 **1750** Hyde 619

ARCANA CÆLESTIA: | OR, | Heavenly Secrets, | Which are in the | SACRED SCRIPTURE, | OR, | WORD OF THE LORD, | LAID OPEN: | These which follow are in | GENESIS: | Here those contained in the | Sixteenth Chapter. | Together with the | WONDERFUL THINGS | That have been seen in the | World of Spirits, and in the Heaven of Angels. | I. | <2 spaced rules> | M DCC L. | [Price Eight-pence.]
verso: MATT. VI. 33. | *Seek ye first the Kingdom of God, and his* | *Righteousness, and all these Things shall be* | *added unto you.*
p 3: line orn as head-piece NR 291; p 5: tail-piece NR 287; p 6: head-piece NR 292; pp 9, 11: line orn NR 281; p 45: line orn NR 282; p 52: tail-piece NR 297
4to
title leaf 2 pp; text: Swedenborg's preface, pp 3-5; Genesis 16 and n 1886-1983, pp 6-52.
Translated by John Marchant, and published by John Lewis, 1 Paternoster Row, London, at Swedenborg's expense.
An unpublished copy has been recorded as follows.
1 NET: GEN A photocopied reproduction.
UK: SOC; USA: ANC

49/01/En 1/2 **1750** Hyde 620

ARCANA CÆLESTIA: | OR, | Heavenly Secrets, | Which are in the | SACRED SCRIPTURE, | OR, | WORD OF THE LORD, | LAID OPEN: | Here, those which are in the | Seventeenth Chapter | OF | GENESIS. | Together with the | WONDERFUL THINGS | Which have been seen and heard in the | World of Spirits, and Heaven of Angels. | At the Conclusion, is a Discovery of such Things as relate | to the LAST JUDGMENT. | II. | <2 spaced rules> | M DCC L. | [Price Nine-pence.]
verso: MATT. VI. 33. | *Seek first the Kingdom of God, and his Righ-* | *teousness, and all these Things shall be added* | *unto you.*
p 3: head-piece NR 293; pp 5, 7: line orn NR 281; line 7: line orn NR 279; p 64: line orn NR 284
4to
title leaf 2 pp; text of Genesis 17 and n 1984-2134, pp 3-72.
Translated by John Marchant, and published by John Lewis, 1 Paternoster Row, London, at Swedenborg's expense.
Unpublished copies have been recorded as follows.
1 UK: SOC & USA: ANC, SHS Reproduction on microfilm 78 made in 1967, Bryn Athyn PA.
2 NET: GEN A photocopied reproduction.
UK: SOC

49/01/En 1/3 **1750** Hyde 621

ARCANA CÆLESTIA: | OR, | Heavenly Secrets, | Which are in the | SACRED SCRIPTURE, | OR, | WORD OF THE LORD, | LAID OPEN: | Here, those which are in the | Eighteenth Chapter | OF | GENESIS. | Together with the | WONDERFUL THINGS | Which have been seen and heard in the |

World of Spirits, and Heaven of Angels: | Here, at the End, such Things as concern the STATE of | INFANTS after DEATH. | III. | <2 spaced rules> | M DCC L. | [Price Nine-pence.]
verso: MATT. VI. 33. | *Seek ye first the Kingdom of God, and his Righ- | teousness, and all these Things shall be added | unto you.*
p 3: line orn as head-piece NR 291; p 4: tail-piece NR 287; p 5: head-piece NR 292; p 7: line orn NR 284; p 78: line orn NR 309
4to
title leaf 2 pp; text: Swedenborg's preface, pp 3-4; Genesis 18 and n 2135-2308, pp 5-84.
Translated by John Marchant, and published by John Lewis, 1 Paternoster Row, London, at Swedenborg's expense.
An unpublished copy has been recorded as follows.
1 NET: GEN A photocopied reproduction.
UK: SOC

49/01/En 1/4 **1750** Hyde 622
ARCANA CÆLESTIA: | OR, | Heavenly Secrets, | Which are in the | SACRED SCRIPTURE, | OR, | WORD OF THE LORD, | LAID OPEN: | Here, those which are in the | Nineteenth Chapter | OF | GENESIS. | Together with the | WONDERFUL THINGS | Which have been seen and heard in the | World of Spirits, and Heaven of Angels: | Here, at the End, such Things as relate to the Memory | of Man remaining after Death, and the Recollection | of those Things which he had acted in the Life of the Body. | IV. | <rule> | M DCC L. | [Price Nine-pence.]
p 3: head-piece NR 293; p 5: line orn NR 281; p 9: line orn NR 280; p 88: line orn NR 309
4to
title leaf 2 pp; text of Genesis 19 and n 2310-2494, pp 3-95.
Translated by John Marchant, and published by John Lewis, 1 Paternoster Row, London, at Swedenborg's expense.
An unpublished copy has been recorded as follows.
1 NET: GEN A photocopied reproduction.
UK: SOC

49/01/En 1/5 **1750** Hyde 623
ARCANA CÆLESTIA: | OR, | Heavenly Secrets, | Which are in the | SACRED SCRIPTURE, | OR, | WORD of the LORD, | LAID OPEN: | Here, those which are in the | Twentieth Chapter | OF | GENESIS. | Together with the | WONDERFUL THINGS | Which have been seen and heard in the | World of Spirits, and Heaven of Angels: | Here at the End, such Things as relate to the State and | Condition of Nations and people, in the other Life, | who were born without the Church. | V. | <rule> | M DCC L | [Price Nine-pence.]
p 3: head-piece NR 298; pp 5, 7: line orn NR 283; p 6: line orn NR 281; p 59: line orn NR 309; p 66: tail-piece NR 297
4to
title leaf, 2 pp; text of Genesis 20 and n 2495-2605, pp 3-66.
Translated by John Marchant, and published by John Lewis, 1 Paternoster Row, London, at Swedenborg's expense.
An unpublished copy has been recorded as follows.
1 NET: GEN A photocopied reproduction.
UK: SOC

49/01/En 1/6 **1750** Hyde 624
ARCANA CÆLESTIA: | OR, | Heavenly Secrets, | Which are in the | SACRED SCRIPTURE, | OR, |

WORD OF THE LORD, | LAID OPEN: | Here, those which are in the | Twenty-First Chapter | OF | GENESIS. | Together with the | WONDERFUL THINGS | Which have been seen and heard in the | World of Spirits, and Heaven of Angels: | Here at the End, concerning Marriages, how they are | consider'd in Heaven, and of Adulteries. | VI. | <rule> | M DCC L. | [Price Nine-pence.]
p 3: head-piece NR 293; p 6: line orn NR 281; p 8: line orn NR 283; pp 28, 61: asts as line orn NR 212; p 69: line orn NR 309; p 80: tail-piece NR 287
4to
title leaf 2 pp; text of Genesis 21 and n 2606-2759, pp 3-80.
Translated by John Marchant, and published by John Lewis, 1 Paternoster Row, London, at Swedenborg's expense.
An unpublished copy has been recorded as follows.
1 NET: GEN A photocopied reproduction.
UK: SOC, BOD

49/01/En 1/7 **1750** Hyde 619-624

The above six chapters are also found bound together in one 4to volume.
The copy in UK: SOC formerly belonged to J Clowes and C A Tulk. The copy in UK: CON does not contain chapter 5.

49/01/En 2/1 **1783** Hyde 591

ARCANA COELESTIA: | OR | HEAVENLY MYSTERIES | CONTAINED IN THE | SACRED SCRIPTURES, | OR | WORD OF THE LORD, | MANIFESTED AND LAID OPEN; | BEGINNING WITH THE BOOK OF | *GENESIS.* | INTERSPERSED WITH | RELATIONS OF WONDERFUL THINGS | SEEN | IN THE | WORLD OF SPIRITS AND THE HEAVEN OF ANGELS. | NOW FIRST TRANSLATED FROM THE ORIGINAL LATIN OF | *EMANUEL SWEDENBORG,* | BY A SOCIETY OF GENTLEMEN. | <rule> | VOLUME THE FIRST. | <double rule> | *LONDON*: | Printed for the said SOCIETY: And to be had of Mr. BUCKLAND, Bookseller, | in Pater-noster-row; Messrs DENIS and Son, No. 2, New-Bridge-Street, | Black-Friars; R. HAWES, Bookseller and Printer, No. 40, Dorset-Street, | Spitalfields; and Mr. CLARKE, Bookseller at Manchester. | M DCC LXXXIII.
verso: Matt. vi.33. | *Seek ye first the Kingdom of God and his | Righteousness, and all Things shall be | added unto you.*
frontispiece: <within an elliptical orn frame 122 x 100 mm, portrait bust of Swedenborg, under which is printed> *Anno ætatis 80. | Eman^{l}. Swedenborg, | SERVANT of the LORD. | Born at Stockholm Jan. 29th. 1688, died in London March 29th. | Battersby sculp:*
8vo
frontispiece; title leaf, 2 pp; Translator's preface, pp iii-xv; text of Genesis 1-9 and n 1-1113, pp 1-556.
Translated by J Clowes, an edition of 500 copies was printed for the Society for Printing, Publishing, and Circulating the Writings of Swedenborg, Manchester, whose Report for 1802 (p 1) and M Sibly *History of the New Church* (p 52) state that the volume was printed in 1782. The volume was issued in 12 parts at sixpence each, and was the Society's first publication.
A copy in UK: SOC does not have the frontispiece.
P B Chastanier's copy of this volume was in USA: MNC in 1906.
UK: SOC; USA: ANC

49/01/En 2/2 **1784** Hyde 592

ARCANA COELESTIA: | OR | HEAVENLY MYSTERIES | CONTAINED IN THE | SACRED SCRIPTURES, | OR | WORD OF THE LORD, | MANIFESTED AND LAID OPEN; | BEGINNING WITH THE BOOK OF | *GENESIS.* | INTERSPERSED WITH | RELATIONS OF WONDERFUL THINGS | SEEN IN THE | World

of Spirits and the Heaven of Angels. | NOW FIRST TRANSLATED FROM THE ORIGINAL LATIN | OF | *EMANUEL SWEDENBORG,* | BY A SOCIETY OF GENTLEMEN. | <rule> | VOL. I. | <double rule> | *LONDON:* | Printed by R. HINDMARSH, No. 32, Clerkenwell-Close; | And Sold by T. EVANS, and J. BUCKLAND, Paternoster-Row; J. DENIS, | New Bridge-Street, Fleet-Street; I. CLARKE, and I. HASLINGDEN, | Manchester; and by all other Booksellers in Town and Country. | M.DCC.LXXXIV.
verso: Matt. vi.33. | *Seek ye first the Kingdom of GOD and it's* | *Righteousness, and all Things shall be* | *added unto you.*
8vo
frontispiece; title leaf, 2 pp; Translator's preface, pp iii-xv; text of Genesis 1-9 and n 1-1113, pp 1-556.
The frontispiece is a portrait of Swedenborg, labelled 'Battersby sculp.'
Reprint of 49/01/En 2/1 = Hyde 591, with a fresh title page. Sibly records this as the second appearance of the volume <*History of the New Church* p 53>. A copy in UK: CON was formerly in the possession of J Hindmarsh.
UK: SOC, CON, NCC; NET: GEN; USA: ANC, SHS; AUS: SYD

49/01/En 2/3 **1784** Hyde 625
ARCANA COELESTIA: | OR | HEAVENLY MYSTERIES | CONTAINED IN THE | SACRED SCRIPTURES, | OR | WORD OF THE LORD, | MANIFESTED AND LAID OPEN; | BEGINNING WITH THE BOOK OF | *GENESIS.* | INTERSPERSED WITH | RELATIONS OF WONDERFUL THINGS | SEEN IN THE | World of Spirits and the Heaven of Angels. | NOW FIRST TRANSLATED FROM THE ORIGINAL LATIN | OF | *EMANUEL SWEDENBORG,* | BY A SOCIETY OF GENTLEMEN. | <rule> | VOL. II. | <double rule> | *LONDON:* | Printed by R. HINDMARSH, No. 32, Clerkenwell-Close; | And Sold by T. EVANS and T. BUCKLAND, Paternoster-Row; J. DENIS | and SON, New Bridge-Street, Fleet-Street; I. CLARKE and I. HAS- | LINGDEN, Manchester; T. MILLS, Bristol; S. HAZARD, Bath; and by | all other Booksellers in Town and Country. | M.DCC.LXXXIV.
verso: Matt. vi.33. | *Seek ye first the Kingdom of GOD and his* | *Righteousness, and all Things shall be* | *added unto you.*
8vo
title leaf, 2 pp; text of Genesis 10-17 and n 1114-2134, pp 1-261, 265-570.
Between pp 261 and 265 are 2 pp of advertisements, which begin with the following statement: 'The Public are respectfully informed, that the Second Part of this Volume will be given as soon as it can be prepared for the Press, and that it will contain Five other Chapters to complete it for Binding, viz. the 14th, 15th, 16th, 17th, and 18th of Genesis.'
Translated by J Clowes, an edition of 500 copies was printed for the Society for Printing, Publishing, and Circulating the Writings of Swedenborg, Manchester. It was issued in two parts, the first in 1784 and the second in 1785.
A copy in UK: CON was formerly in the possession of J Hindmarsh.
UK: SOC, CON, NCC; NET: GEN; USA: ANC, SHS; AUS: SYD

49/01/En 2/4 **1788** Hyde 644
ARCANA COELESTIA: | OR | HEAVENLY MYSTERIES | CONTAINED IN THE | SACRED SCRIPTURES, | OR | WORD OF THE LORD, | MANIFESTED AND LAID OPEN; | BEGINNING WITH THE BOOK OF | *GENESIS.* | INTERSPERSED WITH | RELATIONS OF WONDERFUL THINGS | SEEN IN THE | World of Spirits and the Heaven of Angels. | NOW FIRST TRANSLATED FROM THE ORIGINAL LATIN | OF | *EMANUEL SWEDENBORG.* | By a SOCIETY of GENTLEMEN. | <rule> | VOL. III. | <double rule> | *LONDON:* | Printed and Sold by R. HINDMARSH, | PRINTER TO HIS ROYAL HIGHNESS THE PRINCE OF WALES, | No. 32, Clerkenwell-Close: | Sold also by J. BUCKLAND, Paternoster-Row; J. DENIS, New Bridge-Street, | Fleet-Street; T. MILLS, Bristol; I. and W. CLARKE, Manchester; and all | other Booksellers in Town and Country. | MDCCLXXXVIII.

verso: Matt. vi:33 | *Seek ye first the Kingdom of GOD and his* | *Righteousness, and all Things shall be* | *added unto you.*
8vo
title leaf, 2 pp; text of Swedenborg's preface, Genesis 18-22, and n 2135-2893, pp 1-528.
Translated by J Clowes, an edition of 400 copies was printed for the Society for Printing, Publishing, and Circulating the Writings of Swedenborg, Manchester, in the year 1787.
A copy in UK: con was formerly in the possession of J Hindmarsh.
UK: soc, con, ncc; NET: gen; USA: anc, shs; AUS: syd

49/01/En 2/5 **1789** Hyde 662
ARCANA COELESTIA: | OR | HEAVENLY MYSTERIES | CONTAINED IN THE | SACRED SCRIPTURES, | OR | WORD OF THE LORD, | MANIFESTED AND LAID OPEN; | BEGINNING WITH THE BOOK OF | *GENESIS.* | INTERSPERSED WITH | RELATIONS OF WONDERFUL THINGS | SEEN IN THE | World of Spirits and the Heaven of Angels. | NOW FIRST TRANSLATED FROM THE ORIGINAL LATIN | OF | *EMANUEL SWEDENBORG.* | By a SOCIETY of GENTLEMEN. | <rule> | VOL. IV. | <double rule> | *LONDON:* | Printed and Sold by R. HINDMARSH, | PRINTER TO HIS ROYAL HIGHNESS THE PRINCE OF WALES, | No. 32, Clerkenwell-Close. | Sold also by J. DENIS, New Bridge-Street; I. and W. CLARKE, Manchester; | and by all other Booksellers in Town and Country. | M.DCC.LXXXIX.
verso: Matt. vi:33 | *Seek ye first the Kingdom of GOD and his* | *Righteousness, and all Things shall be* | *added unto you.*
8vo
title leaf, 2 pp; text of Genesis 23-27 and n 2894-3649, pp 3-485; catalogue 2 pp.
Translated by J Clowes, an edition of 400 copies was printed for the Society for Printing, Publishing, and Circulating the Writings of Swedenborg, Manchester.
A copy in UK: con was formerly in the possession of J Hindmarsh.
UK: soc, con, ncc; NET: gen; USA: anc, shs

49/01/En 2/6 **1792** Hyde 679
ARCANA COELESTIA: | OR | HEAVENLY MYSTERIES | CONTAINED IN THE | SACRED SCRIPTURES, | OR | WORD OF THE LORD, | MANIFESTED AND LAID OPEN; | BEGINNING WITH THE BOOK OF | *GENESIS.* | INTERSPERSED WITH | RELATIONS OF WONDERFUL THINGS | SEEN IN THE | World of Spirits and the Heaven of Angels. | NOW FIRST TRANSLATED FROM THE ORIGINAL LATIN | OF | *EMANUEL SWEDENBORG.* | By a SOCIETY OF GENTLEMEN. | <rule> | VOL. V. | <double rule> | *LONDON:* | Printed and Sold by R. HINDMARSH, | PRINTER TO HIS ROYAL HIGHNESS THE PRINCE OF WALES, | No. 32, Clerkenwell-Close. | Sold also by I. and W. CLARKE, Manchester; and by all other Booksellers | in Town and Country. | M.DCC.XCII.
verso: Matt. vi.33. | *Seek ye first the Kingdom of GOD and his* | *Righteousness, and all Things shall be* | *added unto you.*
8vo
title leaf, 2 pp; text of Genesis 28-31 and n 3650-4228, pp 3-451; catalogue, 1 p.
Translated by J Clowes, an edition of 400 copies was printed for the Society for Printing, Publishing, and Circulating the Writings of Swedenborg, Manchester.
UK: soc, con, ncc; NET: gen; USA: anc, fou, shs

49/01/En 2/7 **1794** Hyde 593
ARCANA COELESTIA: | OR | HEAVENLY MYSTERIES, | CONTAINED IN THE | SACRED SCRIPTURES, | OR | *WORD OF THE LORD,* | MANIFESTED AND LAID OPEN; | BEGINNING WITH THE BOOK OF | GENESIS. | <short rule> | INTERSPERSED WITH | RELATIONS OF WONDERFUL THINGS | SEEN IN THE | World of Spirits and the Heaven of Angels. | TRANSLATED FROM THE ORIGINAL

LATIN OF | <short orn rule> | EMANUEL SWEDENBORG | <short orn rule> | VOL. I. | <double rule> | PRINTED AT THE Apollo Press IN BOSTON, | NO. 9, DOCK-SQUARE. | <short rule> | MDCCXCIV.
verso: Matthew vi. 33. | *Seek ye first the kingdom of GOD and it's righteousness,* | *and all things shall be added unto you.*
8vo
title leaf, 2 pp; Translator's preface, pp 3-16; text of Genesis 1-9 and n 1-319, pp 17-130.
Reprint of En 2/2 = Hyde 592 at the expense of Revd William Hill, and published in monthly numbers. No more were printed.
The copy in UK: soc contains only n 1-66.
UK: soc; USA: anc, shs

49/01/En 2/8 — 1795 — Hyde 697

ARCANA CŒLESTIA: | OR | HEAVENLY MYSTERIES | CONTAINED IN THE | SACRED SCRIPTURES, | OR | WORD OF THE LORD, | MANIFESTED AND LAID OPEN; | BEGINNING WITH THE BOOK OF | *GENESIS.* | INTERSPERSED WITH | RELATIONS OF WONDERFUL THINGS | SEEN IN THE | World of Spirits and the Heaven of Angels. | NOW FIRST TRANSLATED FROM THE ORIGINAL LATIN | OF | *EMANUEL SWEDENBORG.* | By a SOCIETY of GENTLEMEN. | <rule> | VOL. VI. | <double rule> | *LONDON:* | PRINTED AND SOLD BY R. HINDMARSH, | PRINTER TO HIS ROYAL HIGHNESS THE PRINCE OF WALES, | *OLD-BAILEY.* | Sold also by I. and W. CLARKE, Manchester; and by all other Booksellers | in Town and Country. | M.DCC.XCV.
verso: Matt. vi: 33 | *Seek ye first the Kingdom of GOD and his* | *Righteousness, and all Things shall be* | *added unto you.*
8vo
title leaf, 2 pp; text of Genesis 32-38 and n 4229-4953, pp 3-545; catalogue 2 pp.
Translated by J Clowes, an edition of 400 copies was printed for the Society for Printing, Publishing, and Circulating the Writings of Swedenborg, Manchester. Hyde states that a slip attached apologizes for the delay in publishing; this slip is absent from the copy in UK: con.
A copy in UK: con was formerly in the possession of J Hindmarsh.
UK: soc, con, ncc; NET: gen; USA: anc, fou, shs

49/01/En 2/9 — 1797 — Hyde 713

ARCANA CŒLESTIA: | OR | HEAVENLY MYSTERIES | CONTAINED IN THE | SACRED SCRIPTURES, | OR | WORD OF THE LORD, | MANIFESTED AND LAID OPEN; | BEGINNING WITH THE BOOK OF | *GENESIS.* | INTERSPERSED WITH | RELATIONS OF WONDERFUL THINGS | SEEN IN THE | World of Spirits and the Heaven of Angels. | NOW FIRST TRANSLATED FROM THE ORIGINAL LATIN | OF | *EMANUEL SWEDENBORG.* | By a SOCIETY of GENTLEMEN. | <rule> | VOL. VII. | <double rule> | *LONDON:* | PRINTED AND SOLD BY R. HINDMARSH, | PRINTER TO HIS ROYAL HIGHNESS THE PRINCE OF WALES, | *OLD-BAILEY.* | Sold also by I. and W. CLARKE, Manchester; and by all other Booksellers | in Town and Country. | M.DCC.XCVII.
verso: Matt. vi:33 | *Seek ye first the Kingdom of GOD and his* | *Righteousness, and all Things shall be* | *added unto you.*
8vo
title leaf, 2 pp; an 'advertisement' concerning the translation of the term 'Divinum Humanum' is inserted in some copies between the title leaf and the text, 2 pp; text of Genesis 39-43 and n 4954-5727, pp 3-500.
Translated by J Clowes, an edition of 400 was printed in 1796 for the Society for Printing, Publishing, and Circulating the Writings of Swedenborg, Manchester.
A copy in UK: con was formerly in the possession of J Hindmarsh.
UK: soc, con, ncc; NET: gen; USA: anc, fou, shs

49/01/En 2/10 **1799** Hyde 729

ARCANA CŒLESTIA: | OR | HEAVENLY MYSTERIES | CONTAINED IN THE | SACRED SCRIPTURES, | OR | WORD OF THE LORD, | MANIFESTED AND LAID OPEN; | BEGINNING WITH THE BOOK OF | *GENESIS.* | INTERSPERSED WITH | RELATIONS OF WONDERFUL THINGS | SEEN IN THE | World of Spirits and the Heaven of Angels. | NOW FIRST TRANSLATED FROM THE ORIGINAL LATIN | OF | *EMANUEL SWEDENBORG.* | By a SOCIETY of GENTLEMEN. | <rule> | VOL. VIII. | <double rule> | *LONDON:* | PRINTED UNDER THE INSPECTION OF R. HINDMARSH, | LATE PRINTER TO HIS ROYAL HIGHNESS THE PRINCE OF WALES: | And Sold by W. BAYNES, No. 54, Paternoster-Row; | By I. and W. CLARKE, Manchester; and by all other Booksellers | in Town and Country. | M.DCC.XCIX.

verso: Matt. vi:33 | *Seek ye first the Kingdom of GOD and his* | *Righteousness, and all Things shall be* | *added unto you.*

8vo

title leaf, 2 pp; text of Genesis 44-50 and n 5728-6626, pp 3-497; advertisement, 2 pp.

Translated by J Clowes; an edition of 400 copies was printed for the Society for Printing, Publishing, and Circulating the Writings of Swedenborg, Manchester.

A copy in UK: CON was formerly in the possession of J Hindmarsh.

UK: SOC, CON, NCC; NET: GEN; USA: ANC, FOU, SHS

49/01/En 2/11 **1800** Hyde 746

ARCANA CŒLESTIA: | OR | HEAVENLY MYSTERIES | CONTAINED IN | THE SACRED SCRIPTURES, | OR | WORD OF THE LORD, | MANIFESTED AND LAID OPEN; | BEGINNING WITH | *THE BOOK OF GENESIS.* | INTERSPERSED WITH | RELATIONS OF WONDERFUL THINGS | SEEN IN | THE WORLD OF SPIRITS AND THE HEAVEN OF ANGELS. | Now first translated from the original Latin of | *EMANUEL SWEDENBORG.* | BY A SOCIETY OF GENTLEMEN. | <short double rule> | VOL. IX. | <short double rule> | *LONDON:* | PRINTED BY. J. HODSON, | AND SOLD AT THE AURORA PUBLISHING OFFICE, NO. 15, CROSS- | STREET, HATTON-GARDEN. | ALSO BY J. AND W. CLARKE, MANCHESTER, AND ALL OTHER | BOOKSELLERS. | <short double rule> | 1800.

verso: Matt. vi.33. | *Seek ye first the Kingdom of GOD and his* | *Righteousness, and all things shall be* | *added unto you.*

half title <in some copies following title leaf>: *ARCANA CŒLESTIA:* | OR | *HEAVENLY MYSTERIES* | CONTAINED IN | THE SACRED SCRIPTURES, | OR | WORD OF THE LORD, | MANIFESTED AND LAID OPEN. | <short orn rule> | Vol. IX. | Part I.-Price 4s. 6d | <double rule>

verso: <advertisements>

8vo

half title and title leaves, 4 pp; text of Exodus 1-12 and n 6627-8032, pp 1-629; advertisement, 1 p.

Translated by J Clowes. Printed at the expense of Dr James Hodson. It was issued in two parts: I, pp 1-303 (n 6627-7254); II, pp 305-629 (n 7255-8032).

A copy in UK: CON was formerly in the possession of J Hindmarsh.

UK: SOC, CON, NCC; NET: GEN; USA: ANC, FOU, SHS

49/01/En 2/12 **1800, 1803** Hyde 760

ARCANA CŒLESTIA:| OR | HEAVENLY MYSTERIES | CONTAINED IN | THE SACRED SCRIPTURES, | OR | WORD OF THE LORD, | MANIFESTED AND LAID OPEN; | BEGINNING WITH | *THE BOOK OF GENESIS.* | INTERSPERSED WITH | RELATIONS OF WONDERFUL THINGS | SEEN IN | THE WORLD OF SPIRITS AND THE HEAVEN OF ANGELS. | Now first translated from the original Latin of | *EMANUEL SWEDENBORG.* | BY A SOCIETY OF GENTLEMEN. | <short double rule> | VOL. X. | <short double rule> | *LONDON:* | PRINTED BY J. HODSON, | AND SOLD AT THE AURORA PUBLISHING-OFFICE, NO. 15, CROSS- | STREET, HATTON-GARDEN; | ALSO BY J. AND W. CLARKE,

MANCHESTER, AND ALL OTHER | BOOKSELLERS. | <short double rule> | 1800.
verso: Matt. vi.33. | *Seek ye first the Kingdom of GOD and his* | *Righteousness, and all things shall be* | *added unto you.*
8vo
title leaf, 2 pp; text of Exodus 13-21 and n 8033-9111, pp 3-592. After p 298, the following 30 pages bear the numbers 269-298, then the remaining pages of the volume are numbered 299-562; n 7841 is printed as 1741.
Translated by J Clowes, an edition of 500 copies was printed for the Society for Printing, Publishing, and Circulating the Writings of Swedenborg, Manchester. Issued in two parts: I, pp 1-292 (n 8033-8634), printed in 1800; II, pp 293-298,269-562 (n 8635-9111), printed in 1803. Some copies have title page of part I dated 1801.
A copy in UK: CON <with the title page dated 1801> was formerly in the possession of J Hindmarsh.
UK: SOC, CON, NCC; NET: GEN; USA: ANC, FOU, SHS

49/01/En 2/13 **1802** Hyde 594

ARCANA CŒLESTIA : | OR | HEAVENLY MYSTERIES | CONTAINED IN | THE SACRED SCRIPTURES, | OR | WORD OF THE LORD, | MANIFESTED AND LAID OPEN; | BEGINNING WITH | *THE BOOK OF GENESIS.* | INTERSPERSED WITH | RELATIONS OF WONDERFUL THINGS | SEEN IN | THE WORLD OF SPIRITS AND THE HEAVEN OF ANGELS. | Now first translated from the original Latin of | *EMANUEL SWEDENBORG.* | BY A SOCIETY OF GENTLEMEN | <short double rule> | VOL. I. | <short double rule> | *LONDON:* | PRINTED BY J. HODSON, | AND SOLD AT THE AURORA PUBLISHING-OFFICE, NO. 15, CROSS- | STREET, HATTON-GARDEN; | ALSO BY J. AND W. CLARKE, MANCHESTER, AND ALL OTHER | BOOKSELLERS. | <short double rule> | 1802.
verso: Matt. vi. 33. | *Seek ye first the Kingdom of GOD and his* | *Righteousness, and all things shall be* | *added unto you.*
8vo
title leaf, 2 pp; Translator's preface, pp iii-xv; text of Genesis 1-9 and n 1-1113, pp 1-540; advertisement, 2 pp.
Reprint of En 2/2 = Hyde 592.
UK: SOC; USA: ANC, FOU, SHS

49/01/En 2/14 **1802** Hyde 626

ARCANA CŒLESTIA: | OR | HEAVENLY MYSTERIES | CONTAINED IN | THE SACRED SCRIPTURES, | OR | WORD OF THE LORD, | MANIFESTED AND LAID OPEN; | BEGINNING WITH | *THE BOOK OF GENESIS.* | INTERSPERSED WITH | RELATIONS OF WONDERFUL THINGS | SEEN IN | THE WORLD OF SPIRITS AND THE HEAVEN OF ANGELS. | Now first translated from the original Latin of | *EMANUEL SWEDENBORG.* | BY A SOCIETY OF GENTLEMEN. | <short double rule> | VOL. II. | <short double rule> | *LONDON:* | PRINTED BY J. & E. HODSON, | AND SOLD AT THE AURORA PUBLISHING-OFFICE, NO, 15, CROSS- | STREET, HATTON-GARDEN; | ALSO BY J. AND W. CLARKE, MANCHESTER, AND ALL OTHER | BOOKSELLERS. | <short double rule> | 1802.
verso: Matt. vi: 33. | *Seek ye first the Kingdom of GOD and* | *his Righteousness, and all Things shall* | *be added unto you.*
8vo
title leaf, 2 pp; text of Genesis 10-17 and n 1114-2134, pp 3-524.
Reprint of En 2/3 = Hyde 625.
UK: SOC, CON, NCC; USA: ANC, SHS

49/01/En 2/15 **1803** Hyde 645

ARCANA CŒLESTIA: | OR | HEAVENLY MYSTERIES | CONTAINED IN | THE SACRED SCRIPTURES,

| OR | WORD OF THE LORD, | MANIFESTED AND LAID OPEN; | BEGINNING WITH | *THE BOOK OF GENESIS:* | INTERSPERSED WITH | RELATIONS OF WONDERFUL THINGS | SEEN IN | THE WORLD OF SPIRITS AND THE HEAVEN OF ANGELS. | Now first translated from the original Latin of | *EMANUEL SWEDENBORG.* | BY A SOCIETY OF GENTLEMEN. | <short double rule> | VOL. III. | <short double rule> | *LONDON:* | PRINTED BY J. & E. HODSON, | AND SOLD AT THE AURORA PUBLISHING-OFFICE, NO. 15, CROSS- | STREET, HATTON-GARDEN. | ALSO BY J. AND W. CLARKE, MANCHESTER, AND ALL OTHER | BOOKSELLERS. | <short double rule> | 1803.
verso: Matt. vi. 33. | *Seek ye first the Kingdom of GOD and His | Righteousness, and all things shall be | added unto you.*
8vo
title leaf, 2 pp; Swedenborg's preface and text of Genesis 18-22 and n 2135-2893, pp 3-506; catalogue, pp 1-8.
Reprint of En 2/4 = Hyde 644.
UK: soc, con, ncc; USA: anc, shs

49/01/En 2/16 **1803, 1805** Hyde 775
ARCANA CŒLESTIA: | OR | HEAVENLY MYSTERIES | CONTAINED IN | THE SACRED SCRIPTURES, | OR | WORD OF THE LORD, | MANIFESTED AND LAID OPEN; | BEGINNING WITH | *THE BOOK OF GENESIS:* | INTERSPERSED WITH | RELATIONS OF WONDERFUL THINGS | SEEN IN | THE WORLD OF SPIRITS AND THE HEAVEN OF ANGELS. | Now first translated from the original Latin of | *EMANUEL SWEDENBORG.* | BY A SOCIETY OF GENTLEMEN. | <short double rule> | VOL. XI. | <short double rule> | *LONDON:* | PRINTED BY J. & E. HODSON, | AND SOLD AT THE AURORA PUBLISHING-OFFICE, NO. 15, CROSS- | STREET, HATTON-GARDEN. | ALSO BY J. AND W. CLARKE, MANCHESTER, AND ALL OTHER | BOOKSELLERS. | <short double rule> | 1803.
verso: Matt. vi. 33. | *Seek ye first the Kingdom of GOD and his | Righteousness, and all things shall be | added unto you.*
8vo
title leaf, 2 pp; text of Exodus 22-28 and n 9112-9973, pp 3-655; advertisement, 1 p; p 307 is misnumbered 107.
Translated by J Clowes, an edition of 500 copies was printed for the Society for Printing, Publishing, and Circulating the Writings of Swedenborg, Manchester. It was issued in two parts: I, n 9112 to the text of Exodus 25, pp 1-320, in 1803; II, n 9455-9973, pp 321-655, in 1805.
A copy in UK: con was formerly in the possession of J Hindmarsh.
UK: soc, con, ncc; NET: gen; USA: anc, fou, shs

49/01/En 2/17 **1806** Hyde 784
ARCANA CŒLESTIA: | OR | HEAVENLY MYSTERIES | CONTAINED IN | THE SACRED SCRIPTURES, | OR | WORD OF THE LORD, | MANIFESTED AND LAID OPEN; | BEGINNING WITH | *THE BOOK OF GENESIS:* | INTERSPERSED WITH | RELATIONS OF WONDERFUL THINGS | SEEN IN | THE WORLD OF SPIRITS AND THE HEAVEN OF ANGELS. | Now first translated from the original Latin of | *EMANUEL SWEDENBORG.* | BY A SOCIETY OF GENTLEMEN. | <short double rule> | VOL. XII. | <short double rule> | *LONDON:* | PRINTED BY J. & E. HODSON, | AND SOLD AT THE AURORA PUBLISHING-OFFICE, NO. 15, CROSS- | STREET, HATTON-GARDEN. | ALSO BY J. AND W. CLARKE, MANCHESTER, AND ALL OTHER | BOOKSELLERS. | <short double rule> | 1806.
verso: Matt. vi. 33. | *Seek ye first the Kingdom of GOD and his | Righteousness, and all things shall be | added unto you.*
8vo
title leaf, 2 pp; text of Exodus 29-40 and n 9974-10837, pp 3-630; 'The Translator's Prayer on finishing the Translation of the Arcana Cœlestia', pp 631-632; Errata in Arcana Coelestia, vol I-XII, pp 1-5; catalogue, pp 6-8.

Translated by J Clowes, an edition of 500 copies was printed for the Society for Printing, Publishing, and Circulating the Writings of Swedenborg, Manchester. It was issued in two parts in 1806.
A copy in UK: con was formerly in the possession of J Hindmarsh.
UK: soc, con, ncc; NET: gen; USA: anc, fou, shs

49/01/En 2/18 **1807** Hyde 663
ARCANA CŒLESTIA: | OR | HEAVENLY MYSTERIES | CONTAINED IN | THE SACRED SCRIPTURES, | OR | WORD OF THE LORD, | MANIFESTED AND LAID OPEN; | BEGINNING WITH | *THE BOOK OF GENESIS:* | INTERSPERSED WITH | RELATIONS OF WONDERFUL THINGS | SEEN IN | THE WORLD OF SPIRITS AND THE HEAVEN OF ANGELS. | Translated from the original Latin of | *EMANUEL SWEDENBORG.* | <short double rule> | VOL. IV. | <short double rule> | *LONDON:* | PRINTED BY J. AND E. HODSON, | AND SOLD AT THE AURORA PUBLISHING-OFFICE, NO. 15, CROSS- | STREET, HATTON-GARDEN. | ALSO BY MESSRS. CLARKE AND CO. MANCHESTER, AND ALL OTHER | BOOKSELLERS. | <short double rule> | 1807.
verso: Matt. vi. 33. | *Seek ye first the Kingdom of GOD and his* | *Righteousness, and all things shall be* | *added unto you.*
8vo
title leaf, 2 pp; text of Genesis 23-27 and n 2894-3649, pp 3-487; advertisement, 1 p.
Reprint of En 2/5 = Hyde 662.
UK: soc; USA: anc, shs

49/01/En 2/19 **1808** Hyde 680
ARCANA CŒLESTIA: | OR | HEAVENLY MYSTERIES | CONTAINED IN | THE SACRED SCRIPTURES, | OR | WORD OF THE LORD, | MANIFESTED AND LAID OPEN; | BEGINNING WITH | *THE BOOK OF GENESIS.* | INTERSPERSED WITH | RELATIONS OF WONDERFUL THINGS | SEEN IN | THE WORLD OF SPIRITS AND THE HEAVEN OF ANGELS. | Now first translated from the original Latin of | *EMANUEL SWEDENBORG.* | BY A SOCIETY OF GENTLEMEN. | <short double rule> | VOL. V. | <short double rule> | SECOND EDITION. | *LONDON:* | Printed by J. & E. HODSON, Cross Street, Hatton Garden, | AND SOLD BY LONGMAN, HURST, REES AND ORME, | PATERNOSTER-ROW. | ALSO BY J. AND W. CLARKE, MANCHESTER, AND ALL OTHER | BOOKSELLERS. | <short double rule> | 1808.
verso: Matt. vi. 33. | *Seek ye first the Kingdom of GOD and his* | *Righteousness, and all things shall be* | *added unto you.*
8vo
title leaf, 2 pp; text of Genesis 28-31 and n 3650-4228, pp 3-460.
Reprint of En 2/6 = Hyde 679.
UK: soc; USA: anc, fou, shs

49/01/En 2/20 **1812** Hyde 714
ARCANA CŒLESTIA; | OR | HEAVENLY MYSTERIES | CONTAINED IN | THE SACRED SCRIPTURES, | OR | WORD OF THE LORD, | MANIFESTED AND LAID OPEN; | BEGINNING WITH | *THE BOOK OF GENESIS.* | INTERSPERSED WITH | RELATIONS OF WONDERFUL THINGS | SEEN IN | THE WORLD OF SPIRITS AND THE HEAVEN OF ANGELS. | Now first translated from the original Latin of | *EMANUEL SWEDENBORG.* | BY A SOCIETY OF GENTLEMEN. | <short double rule> | VOL. VII. | <short double rule> | SECOND EDITION. | *MANCHESTER:* | Printed by J. Gleave, 196, Deansgate; | And Sold by J. and E. Hodson, Cross Street, Hatton Garden, | and Mr. Sibley, 35, Goswell Street, London; | Messrs. Clarkes', Manchester, and all | other Booksellers. | <short double rule> | 1812. <*stet* Sibley>
verso: Matt. vi. 33. | *Seek ye first the Kingdom of GOD and* | *his Righteousness, and all Things* | *shall be added unto you.*

8vo
title leaf, 2 pp; advertisement concerning the translation of the term 'humanum', 2 pp; text of Genesis 39-43 and n 4954-5727, pp 5-508.
An edition of 500 copies reprinted from En 2/9 = Hyde 713.
UK: SOC, CON, NCC; USA: ANC, SHS

49/01/En 2/21 **1812** Hyde 730

ARCANA CŒLESTIA; | OR | HEAVENLY MYSTERIES | CONTAINED IN | THE SACRED SCRIPTURES, | OR | WORD OF THE LORD, | MANIFESTED AND LAID OPEN; | BEGINNING WITH | *THE BOOK OF GENESIS.* | INTERSPERSED WITH | RELATIONS OF WONDERFUL THINGS | SEEN IN | THE WORLD OF SPIRITS AND THE HEAVEN OF ANGELS. | Now first translated from the original Latin of | *EMANUEL SWEDENBORG.* | BY A SOCIETY OF GENTLEMEN. | <short double rule> | VOL. VIII. | <short double rule> | SECOND EDITION. | *MANCHESTER :* | PRINTED BY J. GLEAVE, DEANSGATE, | AND SOLD BY MR. T. KELLY, NO. 52, PATERNOSTER-ROW, | LONDON; | MESSRS. CLARKES', MANCHESTER, AND ALL OTHER | BOOKSELLERS. | <short double rule> | 1812.
verso: Matt. vi. 33. | *Seek ye first the Kingdom of GOD and* | *his Righteousness, and all things* | *shall be added unto you.*
8vo
title leaf, 2 pp; text of Genesis 44-50 and n 5728-6626, pp 3-449; advertisement, 2 pp.
Reprint of En 2/10 = Hyde 729.
UK: SOC, CON, NCC; USA: ANC, SHS

49/01/En 2/22 **1816** Hyde 698

ARCANA CŒLESTIA; | OR | *HEAVENLY MYSTERIES* | CONTAINED IN | The sacred Scriptures, or Word of the Lord, | MANIFESTED AND LAID OPEN; | BEGINNING WITH | THE BOOK OF GENESIS. | INTERSPERSED WITH | RELATIONS OF WONDERFUL THINGS | SEEN IN | *The World of Spirits and the Heaven of Angels.* | Now first translated from the original Latin of | *EMANUEL SWEDENBORG.* | BY A SOCIETY OF GENTLEMEN. | <short double rule> | VOL. VI. | <short double rule> | SECOND EDITION. | <short double rule> | **Manchester:** | *Printed by J. Gleave, 196, Deansgate;* | And Sold by Messrs. Clarke, Manchester; and in London by E. Hodson, | Cross Street, Hatton Garden; T. Goyder, 8, Charles Street, | Westminster; and may be had of all other Booksellers. | <short rule> | 1816.
verso: Matt.:vi. 33. | *Seek ye first the Kingdom of GOD and* | *his Righteousness, and all Things* | *shall be added unto you.*
imprint: Printed by J. Gleave, 196, Deansgate, Manchester.
8vo
title leaf, 2 p; text of Genesis 32-38 and n 4229-4953, pp 3-508; imprint, p 508
Reprint of En 2/8 = Hyde 697; an edition of 500 copies was printed.
UK: SOC, CON; SWE: UPP; USA: ANC, SHS

49/01/En 2/23 **1819** Hyde 761

ARCANA CŒLESTIA: | OR | HEAVENLY MYSTERIES | CONTAINED IN | *THE SACRED SCRIPTURES,* | OR | WORD OF THE LORD, | MANIFESTED AND LAID OPEN; | BEGINNING WITH | *THE BOOK OF GENESIS.* | INTERSPERSED WITH | RELATIONS OF WONDERFUL THINGS | *Seen in the World of Spirits and the Heaven of Angels.* | Now first Translated from the Original Latin of | *EMANUEL SWEDENBORG.* | BY A SOCIETY OF GENTLEMEN. | *SECOND EDITION.* | <short rule> | VOL. X. | <short rule> | MANCHESTER: | Printed by W. D. VAREY, Red Lion-street, St. Ann's Square; | SOLD BY MESSRS. CLARKES, MARKET-PLACE, MANCHESTER. | AND IN LONDON, | BY H. HODSON,

CROSS-STREET, HATTON-GARDEN; | T. GOYDER, 8, CHARLES-STREET, WESTMINSTER; AND OTHER | BOOKSELLERS. | 1819.
verso: Matt. vi. 33. | *Seek ye first the Kingdom of GOD and his* | *Righteousness, and all things shall be* | *added unto you.*
imprint: W. D. VAREY, Printer, Red Lion-street, | St. Ann's Square, Manchester.
8vo
title leaf, 2 pp; text of Exodus 13-21 and n 8033-9111, pp 3-590; imprint, p 590.
Reprint of En 2/12 = Hyde 760.
UK: soc, con; USA: anc

49/01/En 2/24 **1820** Hyde 776
ARCANA CŒLESTIA: | OR | HEAVENLY MYSTERIES | CONTAINED IN | THE SACRED SCRIPTURES, | OR | *WORD OF THE LORD*, | MANIFESTED AND LAID OPEN; | BEGINNING WITH | *THE BOOK OF GENESIS:* | INTERSPERSED WITH | RELATIONS OF WONDERFUL THINGS | SEEN IN | THE WORLD OF SPIRITS AND THE HEAVEN OF ANGELS. | Now first Translated from the Original Latin of | *EMANUEL SWEDENBORG.* | BY A SOCIETY OF GENTLEMEN. | *SECOND EDITION.* | <short double rule> | VOL. XI. | <short double rule> | MANCHESTER: | Printed by W. D. VAREY, Red Lion-street, St. Ann's-square. | SOLD BY MESSRS. CLARKES, MARKET-PLACE, MANCHESTER. | AND IN LONDON, | BY H. HODSON, CROSS-STREET, HATTON-GARDEN; | T. GOYDER, 8, CHARLES STREET, WESTMINSTER ; AND OTHER | BOOKSELLERS. | <short rule> | 1820.
verso: Matt. vi.33. | *Seek ye first the Kingdom of GOD and His Righteousness,* | *and all things shall be added unto you.*
8vo
title leaf, 2 pp; text of Exodus 22-28 and n 9112-9973, pp 3-655.
Reprint of En 2/16 = Hyde 775.
UK: soc <incomplete copy, n 9112-9468 part>; USA: anc

49/01/En 2/25 **1820** Hyde 785
ARCANA CŒLESTIA: | OR | HEAVENLY MYSTERIES | CONTAINED IN | THE SACRED SCRIPTURES, | OR | *WORD OF THE LORD,* | MANIFESTED AND LAID OPEN; | BEGINNING WITH | *THE BOOK OF GENESIS:* | INTERSPERSED WITH | RELATIONS OF WONDERFUL THINGS | SEEN IN THE WORLD OF SPIRITS AND THE HEAVEN OF ANGELS. | Now first Translated from the Original Latin of | *EMANUEL SWEDENBORG.* | BY A SOCIETY OF GENTLEMEN. | *SECOND EDITION.* | <short double rule> | VOL. XII. | <short double rule> | MANCHESTER: | Printed by W. D. VAREY, Red Lion-street, St. Ann's-square. | SOLD BY MESSRS. CLARKES, MARKET-PLACE, MANCHESTER. | AND IN LONDON, | BY H. HODSON, CROSS-STREET, HATTON-GARDEN; | T. GOYDER, 8, CHARLES-STREET, WESTMINSTER; AND OTHER | BOOKSELLERS. | <short rule> | 1820.
verso: Matt. vi. 33. | *Seek ye first the Kingdom of GOD and His* | *Righteousness, and all things shall be* | *added unto you.*
8vo
title leaf, 2 pp; text of Exodus 29-40 and n 9974-10837, pp 3-630; Translator's prayer, pp 631-632; Errata in vols 1-11, pp 1-6.
Reprint of En 2/17 = Hyde 784.
UK: soc; USA: anc

49/01/En 2/26 **1823** Hyde 595
ARCANA CŒLESTIA: OR | HEAVENLY MYSTERIES | CONTAINED IN THE | SACRED SCRIPTURES, | OR | WORD OF THE LORD, | MANIFESTED AND LAID OPEN; | BEGINNING WITH | THE BOOK OF GENESIS. | INTERSPERSED WITH | Relations of Wonderful Things, | SEEN IN THE | WORLD

OF SPIRITS, AND THE HEAVEN OF ANGELS. | <short double rule> | TRANSLATED FROM THE ORIGINAL LATIN OF | *EMANUEL SWEDENBORG.* | <short double rule> | FIRST AMERICAN EDITION. | <short double rule> | VOLUME I. | <short double rule> | **New=York:** | PRINTED AND PUBLISHED BY SAMUEL WOODWORTH, EDITOR AND PUBLISHER | OF THE NEW-JERUSALEM MISSIONARY. | <short dotted rule> | 1823.
verso: <short double rule> | Seek ye, *first*, the Kingdom of GOD, and His | Righteousness, and all things shall be added unto | you. *Matt.* vi. 33. | <short double rule>
8vo
title leaf, 2 pp; Translator's preface, pp 3-10; text of Genesis 1:1 to 3:20 and n 1-287 <unfinished>, pp 11-96.
Reprinted from En 2/13 = Hyde 594, in 12 monthly parts with *The New Jerusalem Missionary* vol 1, New York 1823-1824; no more was printed.
UK: SOC; USA: ANC, SHS

49/01/En 2/27 **1825** Hyde 596
ARCANA CŒLESTIA : | OR | HEAVENLY MYSTERIES, | CONTAINED IN | *THE SACRED SCRIPTURES,* | OR | WORD OF THE LORD, | MANIFESTED AND LAID OPEN: | BEGINNING WITH THE BOOK OF GENESIS. | INTERSPERSED WITH | *RELATIONS OF WONDERFUL THINGS* | SEEN | IN THE WORLD OF SPIRITS AND THE HEAVEN OF ANGELS. | <short double rule> | Translated from the Original Latin of | EMANUEL SWEDENBORG. | *First published at London in* 1749. | <short double rule> | VOL I. | <short wavy rule> | LONDON : | Printed and Sold for the Society for Printing and Publishing the Writings of | Emanuel Swedenborg, Instituted in London, in the Year 1810, | By J. S. HODSON, 15, Cross Street, Hatton Garden; | Sold also by T. Goyder, 415, Strand; and J. and W. Clarke, Manchester: | *And may be had of all Booksellers in Town and Country.* | <short rule> | 1825.
verso: Matthew vi. 33. | *Seek ye first the Kingdom of God and his* | *Righteousness, and all things shall be* | *added unto you.*
8vo
title leaf, 2 pp; Translator's preface, pp iii-xvi; text of Genesis 1-9 and n 1-1113, pp 1-536.
Reprint of En 2/2 = Hyde 592.
UK: SOC; USA: ANC

49/01/En 2/28 **1831** Hyde 627
ARCANA CŒLESTIA: | OR | HEAVENLY MYSTERIES | CONTAINED IN | *THE SACRED SCRIPTURES,* | OR | WORD OF THE LORD, | MANIFESTED AND LAID OPEN: | BEGINNING WITH THE BOOK OF GENESIS. | INTERSPERSED WITH | *RELATIONS OF WONDERFUL THINGS* | SEEN | IN THE WORLD OF SPIRITS AND THE HEAVEN OF ANGELS. | <short double rule> | TRANSLATED FROM THE LATIN OF | EMANUEL SWEDENBORG. | <short double rule> | VOL. II. | THIRD EDITION. | <short wavy rule> | LONDON: | PUBLISHED BY J. S. HODSON, CROSS STREET, HATTON GARDEN: | SOLD ALSO BY W. SIMPKIN AND R. MARSHALL, STATIONERS' HALL COURT, | LUDGATE STREET; T. GOYDER, DARTMOUTH STREET, WESTMINSTER; | AND W. CLARKE, MANCHESTER. | <short rule> | 1831.
verso: *This Work is printed at the expense of, and published for,* | "THE SOCIETY FOR PRINTING AND PUBLISHING THE | WRITINGS OF THE HON. EMANUEL SWEDENBORG, INSTI- | TUTED IN LONDON IN THE YEAR 1810."
imprint: J. S. HODSON, Printer, 15, Cross Street, Hatton Garden, London.
8vo
title leaf, 2 pp; advertisement <note concerning the formatting of Swedenborg's references to other parts of *Arcana Coelestia*>, 1 p; text of Genesis 10-17 and n 1114-2134, pp 3-547; imprint, p 548.
Version revised by S Noble; printed by J S Hodson.
UK: SOC, CON; USA: ANC

49/01/En 2/29 **1832** Hyde 646

ARCANA CŒLESTIA: | OR | HEAVENLY MYSTERIES | CONTAINED IN | *THE SACRED SCRIPTURES,* | OR | WORD OF THE LORD, | MANIFESTED AND LAID OPEN; | BEGINNING WITH THE BOOK OF GENESIS. | INTERSPERSED WITH | *RELATIONS OF WONDERFUL THINGS,* | SEEN | IN THE WORLD OF SPIRITS AND THE HEAVEN OF ANGELS. | <short double rule> | TRANSLATED FROM THE LATIN OF | EMANUEL SWEDENBORG. | <short double rule> | VOL. III. | THIRD EDITION. | <short wavy rule> | LONDON: | PUBLISHED BY J. S. HODSON, CROSS-STREET, HATTON GARDEN: | SOLD ALSO BY W. SIMKIN AND R. MARSHALL, STATIONERS' HALL COURT, | LUDGATE-STREET; T. GOYDER, DARTMOUTH-STREET, WESTMINSTER; | W. CLARKE, SWAIN AND DEWHURST, AND EDWARD BAYLIS, | MANCHESTER. | <short rule> | 1832. <*stet* SIMKIN>

verso: *This Work is printed at the expense of, and published for,* "THE | SOCIETY FOR PRINTING AND PUBLISHING THE WRITINGS OF THE | HON. EMANUEL SWEDENBORG, INSTITUTED IN MANCHESTER." | T. SOWLER, PRINTER, 4, ST. ANN'S-SQUARE, MANCHESTER.

8vo

title leaf, 2 pp; text: Swedenborg's preface, pp 3-4, text of Genesis 18-22 and n 2135-2893, pp 5-503. Reprinted from En 2/15 = Hyde 646.

UK: soc, con; USA: anc

49/01/En 2/30 **1834** Hyde 747

ARCANA CŒLESTIA: | OR | HEAVENLY MYSTERIES | CONTAINED IN | *THE SACRED SCRIPTURES,* | OR | WORD OF THE LORD, | MANIFESTED AND LAID OPEN: | BEGINNING WITH THE BOOK OF GENESIS. | INTERSPERSED WITH | *RELATIONS OF WONDERFUL THINGS* | SEEN | IN THE WORLD OF SPIRITS AND THE HEAVEN OF ANGELS. | <short double rule> | TRANSLATED FROM THE ORIGINAL LATIN OF | EMANUEL SWEDENBORG, | *Late Member of the House of Nobles in the Royal Diet of Sweden,* | *Assessor of the Royal Board of Mines,* | *Fellow of the Royal Society of Upsala, and of the Royal Academy of Sciences of Stockholm* | *And Corresponding Member of the Academy of Sciences* | *of St. Petersburg.* | <short double rule> | VOL. IX. | THIRD EDITION. | <short wavy rule> | LONDON: | PUBLISHED BY J. S. HODSON, CROSS STREET, HATTON GARDEN; | SOLD ALSO BY W. SIMPKIN AND R. MARSHALL, STATIONERS' HALL COURT; AND | IN MANCHESTER, BY W. AND R. CLARKE, E. BAYLIS, BANCKS AND CO.; | AND BY ALL OTHER BOOKSELLERS IN TOWN AND COUNTRY. | <short rule> | 1834.

verso: Matt. vi. 33. | *Seek ye first the Kingdom of GOD and his* | *Righteousness, and all Things shall be added* | *unto you.*

half title: ARCANA CŒLESTIA : | OR | HEAVENLY MYSTERIES | CONTAINED IN | *THE SACRED SCRIPTURES,* | OR | WORD OF THE LORD, | MANIFESTED AND LAID OPEN. | <short rule> | VOL IX. | <short rule> | *This Work is printed at the expense of, and published for,* | "THE SOCIETY INSTITUTED IN MANCHESTER IN THE | YEAR 1782, FOR PRINTING, PUBLISHING, AND CIRCULAT- | ING THE THEOLOGICAL WRITINGS OF THE HON. EMANUEL | SWEDENBORG, &C."

imprint: Printed by J. S. Hodson, Cross Street, Hatton Garden.

8vo

half title and title leaves, 4 pp; text of Exodus 1-12 and n 6627-8032, pp 1-628; imprint, p 628. Reprinted by J S Hodson from En 2/11 = Hyde 746. This is not the third edition of the present volume, but the ninth volume of the third edition of the whole work.

UK: soc, con; USA: anc

49/01/En 2/31 **1837** Hyde 597

ARCANA CŒLESTIA. | <short double rule> | THE | HEAVENLY ARCANA | WHICH ARE CONTAINED IN | THE HOLY SCRIPTURES OR WORD | OF THE LORD | UNFOLDED, | BEGINNING WITH THE

BOOK OF GENESIS. | TOGETHER WITH | WONDERFUL THINGS SEEN IN THE WORLD OF SPIRITS | AND IN THE HEAVEN OF ANGELS. | <short double rule> | BY | EMANUEL SWEDENBORG, | *Late Member of the House of Nobles in the Royal Diet of Sweden,* | *Assessor of the Royal Board of Mines,* | *Fellow of the Royal Society of Upsala, and of the Royal Academy of Sciences of Stockholm,* | *and Corresponding Member of the Academy of Sciences* | *of St. Petersburg.* | <short double rule> | VOL. I. | <short double rule> | LONDON: | PUBLISHED BY JAMES S. HODSON, | 112, FLEET STREET. | <short rule> | 1837.
verso: Matthew vi. 33. | *Seek ye first the Kingdom of GOD and his Righteousness,* | *and all these things shall be added unto you.*
half title: ARCANA CŒLESTIA.
verso: *This work is printed at the expense of, and published for,* | "THE SOCIETY FOR PRINTING AND PUBLISHING THE | WRITINGS OF EMANUEL SWEDENBORG, INSTITUTED IN | LONDON IN THE YEAR 1810." | <short rule> | London: Printed by J. S. Hodson, 15, Cross Street, Hatton Garden.
imprint: J. S. Hodson, Printer, Cross Street, Hatton Garden.
8vo
half title and title leaves, 4 pp; Translator's preface, pp v-xvi; text of Genesis 1-9 and n 1-1113, pp 1-518; imprint, p 518.
Revised by J Spurgin. Some copies have 2 pp of advertisements after the text.
UK: SOC, CON; SWE: UPP; USA: ANC, SHS

49/01/En 2/32 1837 Hyde 598

HEAVENLY ARCANA, | WHICH ARE IN THE | SACRED SCRIPTURE OR WORD OF THE LORD, | LAID OPEN. | TOGETHER WITH WONDERFUL THINGS | WHICH WERE SEEN IN THE | WORLD OF SPIRITS AND IN THE HEAVEN OF ANGELS. | GENESIS. | <short rule> | BY EMANUEL SWEDENBORG. | <short rule> | ORIGINALLY PUBLISHED IN LATIN, AT LONDON, A. D. MDCCXLIX. | VOL I. | <short rule> | BOSTON: | PUBLISHED FOR THE NEW CHURCH PRINTING SOCIETY, | BY OTIS CLAPP, NO. 121 WASHINGTON STREET. | MDCCCXXXVII.
verso: MATTHEW VI. 33. | *Seek ye first the Kingdom of God, and His Righteousness, and* | *all things shall be added unto you.*
half title: HEAVENLY ARCANA.
verso: <short dotted rule> | FREEMAN AND BOLLES, | Printers.....Washington Street.
8vo
half title and title leaves, 4 pp; Contents, pp v-viii; text of Genesis 1-9 and n 1-1113, pp 1-504.
Revised by Luther Clark MD. An edition of 1,250 copies was printed.
UK: SOC; USA: SHS

49/01/En 2/33 1838 Hyde 628

HEAVENLY ARCANA, | WHICH ARE IN THE | SACRED SCRIPTURE OR WORD OF THE LORD, | LAID OPEN. | TOGETHER WITH WONDERFUL THINGS | WHICH WERE SEEN IN THE | WORLD OF SPIRITS AND IN THE HEAVEN OF ANGELS. | GENESIS. | <short rule> | BY EMANUEL SWEDENBORG. | <short rule> | ORIGINALLY PUBLISHED IN LATIN, AT LONDON, A. D. MDCCXLIX. | VOL. II. | <short rule> | BOSTON: | PUBLISHED FOR THE NEW CHURCH PRINTING SOCIETY, | BY OTIS CLAPP, NO. 121 WASHINGTON STREET. | MDCCCXXXVIII.
verso: MATTHEW VI. 33. | *Seek ye first the Kingdom of God, and His Righteousness, and* | *all things shall be added unto you.*
half title: HEAVENLY ARCANA.
verso: <short rule> | FREEMAN AND BOLLES, | Printers.....Washington Street.
8vo
half title and title leaves, 4 pp; text of Genesis 10-17 and n 1114-2134, pp 1-507.
UK: SOC; USA: SHS

49/01/En 2/34 **1839** Hyde 647

<<HEAVENLY ARCANA, | WHICH ARE IN THE | SACRED SCRIPTURE OR WORD OF THE LORD, | LAID OPEN. | TOGETHER WITH WONDERFUL THINGS | WHICH WERE SEEN IN THE WORLD OF SPIRITS AND IN THE HEAVEN OF ANGELS. | GENESIS. | <short rule> | BY EMANUEL SWEDENBORG. | <short rule> | ORIGINALLY PUBLISHED IN LATIN, AT LONDON, A. D. MDCCLI. | VOL. III. | <short rule> | BOSTON: | PUBLISHED FOR THE NEW CHURCH PRINTING SOCIETY, | BY OTIS CLAPP, NO. 121, WASHINGTON STREET. | MDCCCXXXIX.>>

verso: <<MATTHEW VI. 33. | *Seek ye first the Kingdom of God, and His Righteousness, and | all things shall be added unto you.*>>

half title: <<HEAVENLY ARCANA.>>

verso: << <short dotted rule> | FREEMAN AND BOLLES, | Printers.....Washington Street.>>

8vo

half title and title leaves, 4 pp; text of Swedenborg's preface, pp vii-viii; text of Genesis 18-22 and n 2135-2893, pp 1-484.

Revised by L Clark; an edition of 1,250 copies was printed.

Copy not seen; description deduced from En 2/32.

USA: ANC, SHS

49/01/En 2/35 **1840** Hyde 664

ARCANA CŒLESTIA. | <short double rule> | THE | HEAVENLY ARCANA | WHICH ARE CONTAINED IN | THE HOLY SCRIPTURES OR WORD | OF THE LORD | UNFOLDED, | BEGINNING WITH THE BOOK OF GENESIS. | TOGETHER WITH | WONDERFUL THINGS SEEN IN THE WORLD OF SPIRITS | AND IN THE | HEAVEN OF ANGELS. | <short double rule> | BY | EMANUEL SWEDENBORG. | <short double rule> | VOL IV. | <short double rule> | LONDON: | JAMES S. HODSON 112, FLEET STREET; | WILLIAM NEWBERY, CHENIES STREET, BEDFORD SQUARE; | EDWARD BAYLIS, MANCHESTER. | 1840.

verso: Matthew vi. 33. | *Seek ye first the Kingdom of GOD and His Righteousness,* | *and all these things shall be added unto you.*

half title: ARCANA CŒLESTIA.

verso: *This work is printed at the expense of, and published for,* | "THE SOCIETY FOR PRINTING AND PUBLISHING THE | WRITINGS OF EMANUEL SWEDENBORG, INSTITUTED IN | LONDON IN THE YEAR 1810." | <short rule> | PRINTED BY WALTON AND MITCHELL, WARDOUR STREET OXFORD STREET.

8vo

half title and title leaves, 4 pp; text of Genesis 23-27 and n 2894-3649, pp 5-427.

Reprint of En 2/18 = Hyde 663, supervised by J Spurgin; an edition of 1,000 copies was printed.

Also found with a variant title page: ARCANA CŒLESTIA. | <short double rule> | THE | HEAVENLY ARCANA | CONTAINED IN | THE HOLY SCRIPTURES, OR WORD | OF THE LORD, | UNFOLDED, | BEGINNING WITH THE BOOK OF GENESIS : | TOGETHER WITH | WONDERFUL THINGS SEEN IN THE WORLD OF SPIRITS | AND IN THE HEAVEN OF ANGELS. | <short double rule> | BY | EMANUEL SWEDENBORG. | <short double rule> | VOL IV. | <short double rule> | LONDON : | WILLIAM NEWBERY, 6, KING STREET, HOLBORN. | <short rule> | 1840.

verso: Matthew vi. 33. | *Seek ye first the Kingdom of GOD and His Righteousness, and* | *all these things shall be added unto you.*

A copy of this variant state is in UK: SOC.

UK: CON; DEN: RLD; SWE: UPP; USA: ANC

49/01/En 2/36 **1840** Hyde 681

ARCANA CŒLESTIA. | <short double rule> | THE | HEAVENLY ARCANA | WHICH ARE CONTAINED

IN | THE HOLY SCRIPTURES OR WORD | OF THE LORD | UNFOLDED, | BEGINNING WITH THE BOOK OF GENESIS. | TOGETHER WITH | WONDERFUL THINGS SEEN IN THE WORLD OF SPIRITS | AND IN THE HEAVEN OF ANGELS. | <short double rule> | BY | EMANUEL SWEDENBORG. | <short double rule> | VOL V. | <short double rule> | LONDON: | JAMES S. HODSON, 112, FLEET STREET; | WILLIAM NEWBERY, CHENIES STREET, BEDFORD SQUARE; | EDWARD BAYLIS, MANCHESTER. | 1840.
verso: Matthew vi. 33. | *Seek ye first the Kingdom of GOD and His Righteousness,* | *and all these things shall be added unto you.*
half title: ARCANA CŒLESTIA.
verso: *This work is printed at the expense of, and published for,* | "THE SOCIETY FOR PRINTING AND PUBLISHING THE | WRITINGS OF EMANUEL SWEDENBORG, INSTITUTED IN | LONDON IN THE YEAR 1810." | <rule> | PRINTED BY WALTON AND MITCHELL, WARDOUR STREET, OXFORD STREET.
imprint: PRINTED BY WALTON AND MITCHELL, WARDOUR STREET, OXFORD STREET.
8vo
half title and title leaves, 4 pp; text of Genesis 28-31 and n 3650-4228, pp 5-390; imprint, p 390.
Reprint of En 2/19 = Hyde 680, supervised by J J G Wilkinson; an edition of 1,000 copies was printed.
Also found with a variant title page: ARCANA CŒLESTIA. | <short double rule> | THE | HEAVENLY ARCANA | CONTAINED IN | THE HOLY SCRIPTURES, OR WORD | OF THE LORD, | UNFOLDED, | BEGINNING WITH THE BOOK OF GENESIS : | TOGETHER WITH | WONDERFUL THINGS SEEN IN THE WORLD OF SPIRITS | AND IN THE HEAVEN OF ANGELS. | <short double rule> | BY | EMANUEL SWEDENBORG. | <short double rule> | VOL V. | <short double rule> | LONDON : | WILLIAM NEWBERY, 6, KING STREET, HOLBORN. | <short rule> | 1840.
verso: Matthew vi. 33. | *Seek ye first the Kingdom of GOD and His Righteousness, and* | *all these things shall be added unto you.*
A copy of this variant state is in UK: soc.
UK: con; DEN: rld; SWE: upp; USA: anc

49/01/En 2/37 **1840** Hyde 777
ARCANA CŒLESTIA. | <short double rule> | THE | HEAVENLY ARCANA | WHICH ARE CONTAINED IN | THE HOLY SCRIPTURES OR WORD | OF THE LORD | UNFOLDED, | BEGINNING WITH THE BOOK OF GENESIS. | TOGETHER WITH | WONDERFUL THINGS SEEN IN THE WORLD OF SPIRITS | AND IN THE HEAVEN OF ANGELS. | <short double rule>. | BY | EMANUEL SWEDENBORG. | <short double rule> | VOL XI. | <short double rule> | LONDON: | JAMES S. HODSON 112, FLEET STREET; | WILLIAM NEWBERY, CHENIES STREET, BEDFORD SQUARE; | EDWARD BAYLIS, MANCHESTER. | 1840.
verso: Matthew vi. 33. | *Seek ye first the Kingdom of GOD and His Righteousness,* | *and all these things shall be added unto you.*
half title: ARCANA CŒLESTIA.
verso: *This work is printed at the expense of, and published for,* | "THE SOCIETY FOR PRINTING AND PUBLISHING THE | WRITINGS OF EMANUEL SWEDENBORG, INSTITUTED IN | LONDON IN THE YEAR 1810." | <rule> | PRINTED BY WALTON AND MITCHELL, WARDOUR STREET, OXFORD STREET.
imprint: PRINTED BY WALTON AND MITCHELL, WARDOUR STREET, OXFORD STREET.
8vo
half title and title leaves, 4 pp; text of Exodus 22-28 and n 9112-9973, pp 5-607; imprint, p 607; Editorial note, p 608.
Revised by J J G Wilkinson and T P Lloyd; an edition of 1,000 copies was printed.
Also found with a variant title page: Also found with a variant title page: ARCANA CŒLESTIA. |

<short double rule> | THE | HEAVENLY ARCANA | CONTAINED IN | THE HOLY SCRIPTURES, OR WORD | OF THE LORD, | UNFOLDED, | BEGINNING WITH THE BOOK OF GENESIS : | TOGETHER WITH | WONDERFUL THINGS SEEN IN THE WORLD OF SPIRITS | AND IN THE HEAVEN OF ANGELS. | <short double rule> | BY | EMANUEL SWEDENBORG. | <short double rule> | VOL XI. | <short double rule> | LONDON : | WILLIAM NEWBERY, 6, KING STREET, HOLBORN. | <short rule> | 1840.
verso: Matthew vi. 33. | *Seek ye first the Kingdom of GOD and His Righteousness, and | all these things shall be added unto you.*
A copy of this variant state is in UK: SOC.
UK: CON; DEN: RLD; USA: ANC

49/01/En 2/38 **1840** Hyde 786
ARCANA CŒLESTIA. | <short double rule> | THE | HEAVENLY ARCANA | WHICH ARE CONTAINED IN | THE HOLY SCRIPTURES OR WORD | OF THE LORD | UNFOLDED, | BEGINNING WITH THE BOOK OF GENESIS. | TOGETHER WITH | WONDERFUL THINGS SEEN IN THE WORLD OF SPIRITS | AND IN THE HEAVEN OF ANGELS. | <short double rule> | BY | EMANUEL SWEDENBORG. | <short double rule> | VOL XII. | <short double rule> | LONDON: | JAMES S. HODSON, 112, FLEET STREET; | WILLIAM NEWBERY, CHENIES STREET, BEDFORD SQUARE; | EDWARD BAYLIS, MANCHESTER. | 1840.
verso: Matthew vi. 33. | *Seek ye first the Kingdom of GOD and His Righteousness, | and all these things shall be added unto you.*
half title: ARCANA CŒLESTIA.
verso: *This Work is printed at the expense of, and published for,* | "THE SOCIETY FOR PRINTING AND PUBLISHING THE | WRITINGS OF EMANUEL SWEDENBORG, INSTITUTED IN | LONDON IN THE YEAR 1810." | <short rule> | PRINTED BY WALTON AND MITCHELL, WARDOUR STREET, OXFORD STREET.
imprint: PRINTED BY WALTON AND MITCHELL, WARDOUR STREET, OXFORD STREET.
8vo
half title and title leaves, 4 pp; text of Exodus 29-40 and n 9974-10837, pp 5-569; Translator's prayer, pp 571-572; imprint, p 572.
Revised by J J G Wilkinson; an edition of 1,000 copies was printed.
Also found with a variant title page: Also found with a variant title page: ARCANA CŒLESTIA. | <short double rule> | THE | HEAVENLY ARCANA | CONTAINED IN | THE HOLY SCRIPTURES, OR WORD | OF THE LORD, | UNFOLDED, | BEGINNING WITH THE BOOK OF GENESIS : | TOGETHER WITH | WONDERFUL THINGS SEEN IN THE WORLD OF SPIRITS | AND IN THE HEAVEN OF ANGELS. | <short double rule> | BY | EMANUEL SWEDENBORG. | <short double rule> | VOL XII. | <short double rule> | LONDON : | WILLIAM NEWBERY, 6, KING STREET, HOLBORN. | <short rule> | 1840.
verso: Matthew vi. 33. | *Seek ye first the Kingdom of GOD and His Righteousness, and | all these things shall be added unto you.*
Copies of this variant state are in UK: SOC, PUR.
UK: CON; DEN: RLD; SWE: UPP; USA: ANC

49/01/En 2/39 **1840** Hyde 665
HEAVENLY ARCANA, | WHICH ARE IN THE | SACRED SCRIPTURE OR WORD OF THE LORD, | LAID OPEN. | TOGETHER WITH WONDERFUL THINGS | WHICH WERE SEEN IN THE | WORLD OF SPIRITS AND IN THE HEAVEN OF ANGELS. GENESIS. | <short rule> | BY EMANUEL SWEDENBORG. | <short rule> | ORIGINALLY PUBLISHED IN LATIN, AT LONDON, A. D. MDCCLI. | VOL. IV. | <short rule> | BOSTON: | PUBLISHED FOR THE NEW CHURCH PRINTING SOCIETY, | BY OTIS CLAPP, NO. 121 WASHINGTON STREET. | MDCCCXL.

verso: MATTHEW VI. 33. | *Seek ye first the Kingdom of God, and His Righteousness, and | all things shall be added unto you.*
half title: HEAVENLY ARCANA.
verso: <short rule> | FREEMAN AND BOLLES. | Printers......Washington Street.
8vo
half title and title leaves, 4 pp; text of Genesis 23-27 and n 2894-3649, pp 1-451.
Reprinted, with some alterations, from En 2/18 = Hyde 663; an edition of 1,250 copies was printed.
UK: soc; USA: anc, shs

49/01/En 2/40 **1843** Hyde 682
HEAVENLY ARCANA, | WHICH ARE IN THE | SACRED SCRIPTURE OR WORD OF THE LORD, | LAID OPEN. | TOGETHER WITH WONDERFUL THINGS | WHICH WERE SEEN IN THE | WORLD OF SPIRITS AND IN THE HEAVEN OF ANGELS. | GENESIS. | <short rule> | BY EMANUEL SWEDENBORG. | <short rule> | ORIGINALLY PUBLISHED IN LATIN, AT LONDON, A. D. MDCCLI. | VOL. V. | <short rule> | BOSTON: | PUBLISHED FOR THE PROPRIETORS, | BY OTIS CLAPP, NO. 12 SCHOOL STREET. | MDCCXLIII.
verso: MATTHEW VI. 33. | *Seek ye first the Kingdom of God, and His Righteousness, and | all things shall be added unto you.*
half title: HEAVENLY ARCANA.
verso: <short rule> | FREEMAN AND BOLLES, | Printers......Washington Street.
8vo
half title and title leaves, 4 pp; advertisement, 2 pp; text of Genesis 28-31 and n 3650-4228, pp 1-425.
Reprinted, with slight alterations, from En 2/36 = Hyde 681, and published by private enterprise.
UK: soc; USA: anc, shs

49/01/En 2/41 **1843** Hyde 699
HEAVENLY ARCANA, | WHICH ARE IN THE | SACRED SCRIPTURE OR WORD OF THE LORD, | LAID OPEN. | TOGETHER WITH WONDERFUL THINGS | WHICH WERE SEEN IN THE | WORLD OF SPIRITS AND IN THE HEAVEN OF ANGELS. | GENESIS. | <short rule> | BY EMANUEL SWEDENBORG. | <short rule> | ORIGINALLY PUBLISHED IN LATIN, AT LONDON, A. D. MDCCLI. | VOL. VI. | <short rule> | BOSTON: | PUBLISHED FOR THE PROPRIETORS, | BY OTIS CLAPP, NO. 12 SCHOOL STREET. | MDCCCXLIII.
verso: MATTHEW VI. 33. | *Seek ye first the Kingdom of God, and His Righteousness, and | all things shall be added unto you.*
half title: HEAVENLY ARCANA.
verso: BOSTON: | PRINTED BY FREEMAN AND BOLLES, | WASHINGTON STREET.
8vo
half title and title leaves, 4 pp; text of Genesis 32-38 and n 4229-4953, pp 1-490.
Reprinted, with slight alterations, from En 2/22 = Hyde 698, and published by private enterprise.
UK: soc; USA: anc, shs

49/01/En 2/42 **1843** Hyde 715
HEAVENLY ARCANA, | WHICH ARE IN THE | SACRED SCRIPTURE OR WORD OF THE LORD, | LAID OPEN. | TOGETHER WITH WONDERFUL THINGS | WHICH WERE SEEN IN THE | WORLD OF SPIRITS AND IN THE HEAVEN OF ANGELS. | GENESIS. | <short rule> | BY EMANUEL SWEDENBORG. | <short rule> | ORIGINALLY PUBLISHED IN LATIN, AT LONDON, A. D. MDCCLII-III. | VOL. VII. | <short rule> | BOSTON: | PUBLISHED FOR THE PROPRIETORS, | BY OTIS CLAPP, NO. 12 SCHOOL STREET. | MDCCCXLIII.
verso: BOSTON: | PRINTED BY FREEMAN AND BOLLES, | WASHINGTON STREET.

half title: HEAVENLY ARCANA.
verso: MATTHEW VI. 33. | *Seek ye first the Kingdom of God, and His Righteousness, and | all things shall be added unto you.*
8vo
half title and title leaves, 4 pp; text of Genesis 39-43 and n 4954-5727, pp 1-452; catalogue, 2 pp.
Reprinted, with slight alterations, from En 2/20 = Hyde 714, and published by private enterprise.
UK: soc; USA: anc, fou, shs

49/01/En 2/43 **1844** Hyde 731
HEAVENLY ARCANA, | WHICH ARE IN THE | SACRED SCRIPTURE OR WORD OF THE LORD, | LAID OPEN. | TOGETHER WITH WONDERFUL THINGS | WHICH WERE SEEN IN THE | WORLD OF SPIRITS AND IN THE HEAVEN OF ANGELS. | GENESIS. | <short rule> | BY EMANUEL SWEDENBORG. | <short rule> | ORIGINALLY PUBLISHED IN LATIN, AT LONDON, A. D. MDCCLIII. | VOL. VIII. | <short rule> | BOSTON: | PUBLISHED FOR THE PROPRIETORS, | BY OTIS CLAPP, NO. 12 SCHOOL STREET. | MDCCCXLIV.
verso: BOSTON: | PRINTED BY FREEMAN AND BOLLES, | WASHINGTON STREET.
half title: HEAVENLY ARCANA.
verso: MATTHEW VI. 33. | *Seek ye first the Kingdom of God, and His Righteousness, and | all things shall be added unto you.*
8vo
half title and title leaves, 4 pp; text of Genesis 44-50 and n 5728-6626, pp 1-438.
Reprinted, with slight alterations, from En 2/21 = Hyde 730, and published by private enterprise.
UK: soc; USA: anc, fou, shs

49/01/En 2/44 **1845** Hyde 648
ARCANA CŒLESTIA. | <short double rule> | THE | HEAVENLY ARCANA | CONTAINED IN | THE HOLY SCRIPTURES, OR WORD | OF THE LORD, | UNFOLDED, | BEGINNING WITH THE BOOK OF GENESIS: | TOGETHER WITH | WONDERFUL THINGS SEEN IN THE WORLD OF SPIRITS | AND IN THE HEAVEN OF ANGELS. | <short double rule> | BY | EMANUEL SWEDENBORG. | <short double rule> | VOL. III. | <short double rule> | LONDON: | WILLIAM NEWBERY, 6, KING STREET, HOLBORN. | <short rule>
verso MATTHEW vi. 33. | *Seek ye first the Kingdom of GOD and His Righteousness, and | all these things shall be added unto you.*
8vo
title leaf, 2 pp; text of Swedenborg's preface, Genesis 18-22, and n 2135-2893, pp 3-503.
The same as En 2/29 = Hyde 646, issued with a fresh title page, about 1845.
UK: soc; DEN: rld; SWE: upp; USA: anc, shs

49/01/En 2/45 **1845** Hyde 748
ARCANA CŒLESTIA. | <short double rule> | THE | HEAVENLY ARCANA | CONTAINED IN | THE HOLY SCRIPTURES, OR WORD | OF THE LORD, | UNFOLDED, | BEGINNING WITH THE BOOK OF GENESIS: | TOGETHER WITH | WONDERFUL THINGS SEEN IN THE WORLD OF SPIRITS | AND IN THE HEAVEN OF ANGELS. | <short double rule> | BY | EMANUEL SWEDENBORG. | <short double rule> | VOL. IX. | <short double rule> | LONDON: | WILLIAM NEWBERY, 6, KING STREET, HOLBORN. | <short rule>
verso: MATTHEW vi. 33. | *Seek ye first the Kingdom of GOD and His Righteousness, and | all these things shall be added unto you.*
8vo
title leaf, 2 pp; text of Exodus 1-12 and n 6627-8032, pp 1-628.

The same as En 2/30 = Hyde 747, issued with a fresh title page in 1845.
UK: soc; DEN: RLD; SWE: UPP; USA: ANC, SHS

49/01/En 2/46 **1845** Hyde 749

HEAVENLY ARCANA, | WHICH ARE IN THE | SACRED SCRIPTURE OR WORD OF THE LORD, | LAID OPEN. | TOGETHER WITH WONDERFUL THINGS | WHICH WERE SEEN IN THE | WORLD OF SPIRITS AND IN THE HEAVEN OF ANGELS. | EXODUS. | <short rule> | BY EMANUEL SWEDENBORG. | <short rule> | ORIGINALLY PUBLISHED IN LATIN, AT LONDON, A. D. MDCCLIII. | VOL. IX. | <short rule> | BOSTON: | PUBLISHED FOR THE PROPRIETORS, | BY OTIS CLAPP, NO. 12, SCHOOL STREET. | MDCCCXLV.
verso: BOSTON: | PRINTED BY FREEMAN AND BOLLES, | WASHINGTON STREET.
half title: HEAVENLY ARCANA.
verso: MATTHEW VI. 33. | *Seek ye first the Kingdom of God, and His Righteousness, and | all things shall be added unto you.*
8vo
half title and title leaves, 4 pp; text of Exodus 1-12 and n 6627-8032, pp 1-588.
Reprinted, with slight alterations, from En 2/45 = Hyde 748, and published by private enterprise.
UK: soc; USA: ANC, FOU, SHS

49/01/En 2/47 **1846** Hyde 762

HEAVENLY ARCANA, | WHICH ARE IN THE | SACRED SCRIPTURE OR WORD OF THE LORD, | LAID OPEN. | TOGETHER WITH WONDERFUL THINGS | WHICH WERE SEEN IN THE | WORLD OF SPIRITS AND IN THE HEAVEN OF ANGELS. | EXODUS. | <short rule> | BY EMANUEL SWEDENBORG. | <short rule> | ORIGINALLY PUBLISHED IN LATIN, AT LONDON, A. D. MDCCLIV. | VOL. X. | <short rule> | BOSTON: | PUBLISHED FOR THE PROPRIETORS, | BY OTIS CLAPP, NO. 12, SCHOOL STREET. | MDCCCXLVI.
half title: HEAVENLY ARCANA.
verso: MATTHEW VI. 33. | *Seek ye first the Kingdom of God, and His Righteousness, and | all things shall be added unto you.*
8vo
half title and title leaves, 4 pp; text of Exodus 13-21 and n 8033-9111, pp 1-552.
Reprinted, with slight alterations, from En 2/23 = Hyde 761, and published by private enterprise.
UK: soc; USA: ANC, FOU, SHS

49/01/En 2/48 **1846** Hyde 778

HEAVENLY ARCANA, | WHICH ARE IN THE | SACRED SCRIPTURE OR WORD OF THE LORD, | LAID OPEN. | TOGETHER WITH WONDERFUL THINGS | WHICH WERE SEEN IN THE | WORLD OF SPIRITS AND IN THE HEAVEN OF ANGELS. | EXODUS. | <short rule> | BY EMANUEL SWEDENBORG. | <short rule> | ORIGINALLY PUBLISHED IN LATIN, AT LONDON, A. D. MDCCLIV. | VOL. XI. | <short rule> | BOSTON: | PUBLISHED FOR THE PROPRIETORS, | BY OTIS CLAPP, NO. 12, SCHOOL STREET. | MDCCCXLVI.
verso: MATTHEW VI. 33. | *Seek ye first the Kingdom of God, and His Righteousness, and | all things shall be added unto you.*
half title: HEAVENLY ARCANA.
8vo
half title and title leaves, 4 pp; text of Exodus 22-28 and n 9112-9973, pp 1-627.
Reprinted, with slight alterations, from En 2/37 = Hyde 777, and published by private enterprise.
UK: soc; USA: ANC, FOU, SHS

49/01/En 2/49 **1846** Hyde 732

ARCANA CŒLESTIA. | <short double rule> | THE | HEAVENLY ARCANA | WHICH ARE CONTAINED IN | THE SACRED SCRIPTURES, OR WORD | OF THE LORD, | UNFOLDED, | BEGINNING WITH THE BOOK OF GENESIS. | TOGETHER WITH | WONDERFUL THINGS SEEN IN THE WORLD OF SPIRITS | AND IN THE HEAVEN OF ANGELS. | <short double rule> | BY EMANUEL SWEDENBORG. | <short double rule> | VOL. VIII. | <short double rule> | LONDON: | WILLIAM NEWBERY, 6, KING STREET, HOLBORN. | 1846.
verso: MATTHEW VI. 33. | *Seek ye first the Kingdom of God, and His Righteousness, and* | *all things shall be added unto you.*
8vo
title leaf, 2 pp; text of Genesis 44-50 and n 5728-6626, pp 5-407.
Revised by J K Bragge; an edition of 1,000 copies was printed.
UK: soc, con; DEN: rld; SWE: upp; USA: anc, shs

49/01/En 2/50 **1847** Hyde 599

ARCANA CŒLESTIA. | <short wavy rule> | THE | HEAVENLY ARCANA | WHICH ARE CONTAINED IN | THE HOLY SCRIPTURES OR WORD OF THE LORD | UNFOLDED; | BEGINNING WITH THE BOOK OF GENESIS. | TOGETHER WITH | WONDERFUL THINGS | SEEN IN THE WORLD OF SPIRITS AND IN THE HEAVEN OF | ANGELS. | <short rule> | BY EMANUEL SWEDENBORG, | *Late Member of the House of Nobles in the Royal Diet of Sweden,* | *Assessor of the Royal Board of Mines,* | *Fellow of the Royal Society of Upsala, and of the Royal Academy of Sciences at Stockholm.* | *And Corresponding Member of the Academy of Sciences of St. Petersburg.* | <short rule> | VOL. I. | <short double rule> | NEW YORK: | PUBLISHED FOR THE PROPRIETOR BY | JOHN ALLEN, No. 139 NASSAU STREET, | AND OTIS CLAPP, No. 12 SCHOOL STREET, BOSTON | 1847.
verso: <double rule> | Matthew vi. 33. | *Seek ye first the Kingdom of GOD and his Righteousness,* | *and all these things shall be added unto you.* | <double rule> | <short wavy rule> | STEREOTYPED AND PRINTED BY | JOHN DOUGLAS, 106 FULTON STREET, NEW YORK.
half title: ARCANA CŒLESTIA.
8vo
half title and title leaves, 4 pp; advertisement, 1 p; Contents, in general, pp vii-x; text of Swedenborg's preface, Genesis 1-9, and n 1-1113, pp 11-504.
Reprinted from En 2/31 = Hyde 597, with a few alterations and a reversion to Swedenborg's Bible text, and stereotyped.
UK: soc; USA: anc

49/01/En 2/51 **1847** Hyde 700

ARCANA CŒLESTIA. | <short double rule> | THE | HEAVENLY ARCANA | CONTAINED IN | THE HOLY SCRIPTURES, OR WORD | OF THE LORD, | UNFOLDED, | BEGINNING WITH THE BOOK OF GENESIS: | TOGETHER WITH | WONDERFUL THINGS SEEN IN THE WORLD OF SPIRITS | AND IN THE HEAVEN OF ANGELS. | <short double rule> | BY | EMANUEL SWEDENBORG. | <short double rule> | VOL. VI. | <short double rule> | LONDON: | WILLIAM NEWBERY, 6, KING STREET, HOLBORN. | 1847.
verso: Matthew vi. 33. | *Seek ye first the Kingdom of GOD and His Righteousness, and* | *all these things shall be added unto you.*
8vo
half title and title leaves, 4 pp; text of Genesis 32-38 and n 4229-4953, pp 5-456.
Revised by C E Strutt and J K Bragge; an edition of 1,000 copies was printed.
UK: soc, con; DEN: rld; USA: anc

49/01/En 2/52 **1847** Hyde 716

ARCANA CŒLESTIA. | <short double rule> | THE | HEAVENLY ARCANA | CONTAINED IN | THE HOLY SCRIPTURES, OR WORD | OF THE LORD, | UNFOLDED, | BEGINNING WITH THE BOOK OF GENESIS: | TOGETHER WITH | WONDERFUL THINGS SEEN IN THE WORLD OF SPIRITS | AND IN THE HEAVEN OF ANGELS. | <short double rule> | BY | EMANUEL SWEDENBORG. | <short double rule> | VOL. VII. | <short double rule> | LONDON: | WILLIAM NEWBERY, 6, KING STREET, HOLBORN. | 1847.

verso: Matt. vi. 33. | *Seek ye first the Kingdom of GOD and His Righteousness, and | all these things shall be added unto you.*

8vo

title leaf, 2 pp; text of Genesis 39-43 and n 4954-5727, pp 5-413.

Revised by H Butter and J K Bragge.

UK: soc, con; DEN: rld; SWE: upp; USA: anc

49/01/En 2/53 **1847** Hyde 787

HEAVENLY ARCANA, | WHICH ARE IN THE | SACRED SCRIPTURE OR WORD OF THE LORD, | LAID OPEN. | TOGETHER WITH WONDERFUL THINGS | WHICH WERE SEEN IN THE | WORLD OF SPIRITS AND IN THE HEAVEN OF ANGELS. | EXODUS. | <short rule> | BY EMANUEL SWEDENBORG. | <short rule> | ORIGINALLY PUBLISHED IN LATIN, AT LONDON, A. D. MDCCLVI. | VOL. XII. | <short rule> | BOSTON: | PUBLISHED FOR THE PROPRIETORS, | BY OTIS CLAPP, NO. 12, SCHOOL STREET. | MDCCCXLVII.

verso: BOSTON: | PRINTED BY FREEMAN AND BOLLES, | DEVONSHIRE STREET.

half title: HEAVENLY ARCANA.

verso: MATTHEW VI. 33. | *Seek ye first the Kingdom of God, and His Righteousness, and | all things shall be added unto you.*

8vo

half title and title leaves, 4 pp; text of Exodus 29-40 and n 9974-10837, pp 1-584.

Reprinted, with slight alterations, from En 2/28 = Hyde 786, and published by private enterprise.

UK: soc; USA: anc, fou

49/01/En 2/54 **1848** Hyde 600

ARCANA CŒLESTIA. | <short double rule> | THE | HEAVENLY ARCANA | CONTAINED IN | THE HOLY SCRIPTURES, OR WORD | OF THE LORD, | UNFOLDED, | BEGINNING WITH THE BOOK OF GENESIS: | TOGETHER WITH | WONDERFUL THINGS SEEN IN THE WORLD OF SPIRITS | AND IN THE HEAVEN OF ANGELS. | <short double rule> | BY | EMANUEL SWEDENBORG. | <short double rule> | VOL. I. | <short double rule> | LONDON: | WILLIAM NEWBERY, 6, KING STREET, HOLBORN. | 1848.

verso: Matthew vi. 33. | *Seek ye first the Kingdom of GOD and his Righteousness, and | all these things shall be added unto you.*

half title: ARCANA CŒLESTIA.

verso: *This work is printed at the expense of, and published for,* | "THE SOCIETY FOR PRINTING AND PUBLISHING THE | WRITINGS OF EMANUEL SWDENBORG, INSTITUTED IN | LONDON IN THE YEAR 1810." | <rule> | LONDON: | PRINTED BY WALTON AND MITCHELL, WARDOUR STREET, OXFORD STREET.

8vo

half title and title leaves, 4 pp; Translator's preface to the first English edition, pp v-xvi; text of Genesis 1-9 and n 1-1113, pp 1-457.

A reprint of En 2/31 = Hyde 597, under the supervision of Henry Bateman.

UK: soc, con; DEN: rld; USA: anc

49/01/En 2/55 **1848** Hyde 629

ARCANA CŒLESTIA. | <short double rule > | THE | HEAVENLY ARCANA | CONTAINED IN | THE HOLY SCRIPTURES, OR WORD | OF THE LORD, | UNFOLDED, | BEGINNING WITH THE BOOK OF GENESIS: | TOGETHER WITH | WONDERFUL THINGS SEEN IN THE WORLD OF SPIRITS | AND IN THE HEAVEN OF ANGELS. | <short double rule> | BY | EMANUEL SWEDENBORG. | <short double rule> | VOL. II. | <short double rule> | LONDON: | WILLIAM NEWBERY, 6, KING STREET, HOLBORN. | 1848.

verso: Matthew vi. 33. | *Seek ye first the Kingdom of GOD and His Righteousness, and* | *all these things shall be added unto you.*

8vo

title leaf, 4 pp; text of Genesis 10-17 and n 1114-2134, pp 1-486.

A reprint, with slight alterations, of En 2/28 = Hyde 627; an edition of 1,250 copies was printed.

UK: SOC, CON; DEN: RLD; SWE: UPP; USA: ANC

49/01/En 2/56 **1851** Hyde 763

ARCANA CŒLESTIA. | <short double rule> | THE | HEAVENLY ARCANA | CONTAINED IN | THE HOLY SCRIPTURE, OR WORD | OF THE LORD, | UNFOLDED, | BEGINNING WITH THE BOOK OF GENESIS: | TOGETHER WITH | WONDERFUL THINGS SEEN IN THE WORLD OF SPIRITS | AND IN THE | HEAVEN OF ANGELS. | <short double rule> | BY | EMANUEL SWEDENBORG. | <short double rule> | VOL. X. | <short double rule> | LONDON: | WILLIAM NEWBERY, 6, KING STREET, HOLBORN. | 1851.

half title: ARCANA CŒLESTIA.

verso: *This work is printed at the expense of, and published for,* | "THE SOCIETY FOR PRINTING AND PUBLISHING THE | WRITINGS OF EMANUEL SWEDENBORG, INSTITUTED IN | LONDON IN THE YEAR 1810." | <rule> | LONDON: | PRINTED BY WALTON AND MITCHELL, WARDOUR STREET, OXFORD STREET.

8vo

half title and title leaves, 4 pp; text of Exodus 13-21 and n 8033-9111, pp 3-517.

Revised by H Butter; an edition of 1,000 copies was printed.

UK: SOC, CON; DEN: RLD; SWE: UPP; USA: ANC

49/01/En 2/57 **1852** Hyde 649

ARCANA CŒLESTIA. | <short rule> | THE | HEAVENLY MYSTERIES | CONTAINED IN | THE HOLY SCRIPTURE, OR WORD | OF THE LORD, | UNFOLDED, | IN AN EXPOSITION OF GENESIS AND EXODUS. | TOGETHER WITH A RELATION OF | WONDERFUL THINGS SEEN IN THE WORLD OF SPIRITS AND IN THE | HEAVEN OF ANGELS. | <short double rule> | BY EMANUEL SWEDENBORG. | <short double rule> | BEING A TRANSLATION OF HIS WORK ENTITLED | "ARCANA CŒLESTIA quæ in Scriptura Sacra, seu Verbo Domini sunt, detecta: hic primum | quæ in Genesi. Una cum Mirabilibus quæ visa sunt in Mundo Spirituum et in | Cœlo Angelorum." Londoni, 1749-1756. | IN TWELVE VOLUMES. | VOL. III. | GENESIS, CHAP. XVIII. TO XXII. | LONDON: | PUBLISHED BY THE SWEDENBORG SOCIETY, | (INSTITUTED 1810,) | 36, BLOOMSBURY STREET, OXFORD STREET. | EDIT. OF 1852.

verso: Matt. vi. 33. | *Seek ye first the Kingdom of GOD and his Righteousness, and* | *all these things shall be added unto you.*

half title: ARCANA CŒLESTIA.

verso: *This work is printed at the expense of, and published for,* | "THE SOCIETY FOR PRINTING AND PUBLISHING THE | WRITINGS OF EMANUEL SWEDENBORG, INSTITUTED IN | LONDON IN THE YEAR 1810." | <rule> | PRINTED BY WALTON AND MITCHELL, WARDOUR STREET, OXFORD STREET.

8vo
half title and title leaves, 4 pp; text of Swedenborg's preface, Genesis 18-22 and n 2135-2893, pp 3-457.
A reprint of En 2/29 = Hyde 646, supervised by F de Soyres; an edition of 1,000 copies was printed.
UK: SOC, BL, CON; USA: ANC

49/01/En 2/58 **1853** **Hyde 601**
<<ARCANA CŒLESTIA. | <short wavy rule> | THE | HEAVENLY ARCANA | WHICH ARE CONTAINED IN | THE HOLY SCRIPTURES OR WORD OF THE LORD | UNFOLDED; | BEGINNING WITH THE BOOK OF GENESIS. | TOGETHER WITH | WONDERFUL THINGS | SEEN IN THE WORLD OF SPIRITS AND IN THE HEAVEN OF | ANGELS. | <short rule> | BY EMANUEL SWEDENBORG, | *Late Member of the House of Nobles in the Royal Diet of Sweden,* | *Assessor of the Royal Board of Mines,* | *Fellow of the Royal Society of Upsala, and of the Royal Academy of Sciences at Stockholm.* | *And Corresponding Member of the Academy of Sciences of St. Petersburg.* | <short rule> | VOL. I. | <short double rule> | BOSTON: | PUBLISHED BY OTIS CLAPP, | 23 SCHOOL STREET. | 1853.>>
verso: << <double rule> | Matthew vi. 33. | *Seek ye first the Kingdom of GOD and his Righteousness,* | *and all these things shall be added unto you.* | <double rule> | <short wavy rule> | STEREOTYPED AND PRINTED BY | JOHN DOUGLAS, 106 FULTON STREET, NEW YORK.>>
half title: <<ARCANA CŒLESTIA.>>
8vo
half title and title leaves, 4 pp; advertisement, 1 p; Contents, pp vii-x; text of Genesis 1-9 and n 1-1113, pp 11-504.
The same as En 2/50 = Hyde 599.
Copy not seen; description deduced from En 2/50.
USA: ANC, SHS

49/01/En 2/59 **1853** **Hyde 602**
ARCANA COELESTIA. | <short rule> | THE | HEAVENLY ARCANA | CONTAINED IN | THE HOLY SCRIPTURES OR WORD OF THE LORD | UNFOLDED, | BEGINNING WITH THE BOOK OF GENESIS: | TOGETHER WITH | WONDERFUL THINGS SEEN IN THE WORLD OF SPIRITS | AND IN THE HEAVEN OF ANGELS. | <short rule> | *Translated from the Latin of* | EMANUEL SWEDENBORG, *Servant of the Lord Jesus Christ.* | <short rule> | VOL. I. | NEW YORK: | AMERICAN SWEDENBORG PRINTING AND PUBLISHING SOCIETY, | GENERAL DEPOT 139 NASSAU-STREET. | 1853.
verso: *Published by* THE AMERICAN SWEDENBORG PRINTING AND PUBLISHING | SOCIETY, *organized for the purpose of Stereotyping, Printing, and* | *Publishing Uniform Editions of the Theological Writings of* EMANUEL | SWEDENBORG, *and incorporated in the State of New York* A. D. 1850. | STEREOTYPED BY | RICHARD C. VALENTINE, | NEW YORK. | <short wavy rule> | C. A. ALVORD, Printer | 29 Gold-street.
half title: ARCANA CŒLESTIA.
8vo
half title and title leaves, 4 pp; text of Genesis 1-11 and n 1-1382, pp 1-568.
Reprinted from En 2/54, 55 = Hyde 600, 629, stereotyped; an edition of 500 copies was printed.
UK: SOC; USA: ANC, SHS

49/01/En 2/60 **1854** **Hyde 630**
ARCANA COELESTIA. | <short rule> | THE | HEAVENLY ARCANA | CONTAINED IN | THE HOLY SCRIPTURES OR WORD OF THE LORD | UNFOLDED, | BEGINNING WITH THE BOOK OF GENESIS: | TOGETHER WITH | WONDERFUL THINGS SEEN IN THE WORLD OF SPIRITS | AND IN THE

HEAVEN OF ANGELS. | <short rule> | *Translated from the Latin of* | EMANUEL SWEDENBORG, *Servant of the Lord Jesus Christ.* | <short rule> | VOL. II. | NEW YORK: | AMERICAN SWEDENBORG PRINTING AND PUBLISHING SOCIETY, | BIBLE HOUSE, ASTOR PLACE, ROOM NO. 47. | 1854.
verso: *Published by* THE AMERICAN SWEDENBORG PRINTING AND PUBLISHING | SOCIETY, *organized for the purpose of Stereotyping, Printing, and* | *Publishing Uniform Editions of the Theological Writings of* EMANUEL | SWEDENBORG, *and incorporated in the State of New York* A. D. 1850
half title: ARCANA CŒLESTIA.
8vo
half title and title leaves, 4 pp; text of Genesis 12-19 and n 1383-2494, pp 5-576.
A reprint from En 2/55, 57 = Hyde 629, 649, stereotyped; an edition of 500 copies was printed.
UK: SOC; USA: ANC, SHS

49/01/En 2/61 **1854** Hyde 650

ARCANA COELESTIA. | <short rule> | THE | HEAVENLY ARCANA | CONTAINED IN | THE HOLY SCRIPTURES OR WORD OF THE LORD | UNFOLDED, | BEGINNING WITH THE BOOK OF GENESIS: | TOGETHER WITH | WONDERFUL THINGS SEEN IN THE WORLD OF SPIRITS | AND IN THE HEAVEN OF ANGELS. | <short rule> | *Translated from the Latin of* | EMANUEL SWEDENBORG, | *Servant of the Lord Jesus Christ.* | <short rule> | VOL. III. | NEW YORK: | AMERICAN SWEDENBORG PRINTING AND PUBLISHING SOCIETY, | BIBLE HOUSE, ASTOR PLACE, ROOM NO. 47. | 1854.
verso: *Published by* THE AMERICAN SWEDENBORG PRINTING AND PUBLISHING | SOCIETY, *organized for the purpose of Stereotyping, Printing, and* | *Publishing Uniform Editions of the Theological Writings of* EMANUEL | SWEDENBORG, *and incorporated in the State of New York* A. D. 1850.
half title: ARCANA CŒLESTIA. | STEREOTYPED BY | RICHARD C. VALENTINE, | NEW YORK. | <short wavy rule>
8vo
half title and title leaves, 4 pp; text of Genesis 20-25 and n 2495-3352, pp 5-515.
A reprint from En 2/57, 35 = Hyde 649, 664, stereotyped.
UK: SOC; USA: ANC, SHS

49/01/En 2/62 **1854** Hyde 666

ARCANA COELESTIA. | THE | HEAVENLY ARCANA | CONTAINED IN | THE HOLY SCRIPTURES OR WORD OF THE LORD | UNFOLDED, | BEGINNING WITH THE BOOK OF GENESIS: | TOGETHER WITH | WONDERFUL THINGS SEEN IN THE WORLD OF SPIRITS | AND IN THE HEAVEN OF ANGELS. | <short rule> | *Translated from the Latin of* | EMANUEL SWEDENBORG, | *Servant of the Lord Jesus Christ.* | <short rule> | VOL. IV. | NEW YORK: | AMERICAN SWEDENBORG PRINTING AND PUBLISHING SOCIETY, | BIBLE HOUSE, ASTOR PLACE, ROOM NO. 47. | 1854.
verso: *Published by* THE AMERICAN SWEDENBORG PRINTING AND PUBLISHING | SOCIETY, *organized for the purpose of Stereotyping, Printing, and* | *Publishing Uniform Editions of the Theological Writings of* EMANUEL | SWEDENBORG, *and incorporated in the State of New York* A. D. 1850.
half title: ARCANA CŒLESTIA.
8vo
half title and title leaves, 4 pp; text of Genesis 26-31 and n 3353-4228, pp 5-557.
A reprint from En 2/35, 36 = Hyde 664, 681.
UK: SOC; USA: ANC, SHS

49/01/En 2/63 1855 Hyde 603

ARCANA CŒLESTIA. | <short rule> | THE | HEAVENLY MYSTERIES | CONTAINED IN | THE HOLY SCRIPTURE, OR WORD | OF THE LORD, | UNFOLDED, | IN AN EXPOSITION OF GENESIS AND EXODUS. | TOGETHER WITH A RELATION OF | WONDERFUL THINGS SEEN IN THE WORLD OF SPIRITS AND IN THE | HEAVEN OF ANGELS. | <short double rule> | BY EMANUEL SWEDENBORG. | <short double rule> | BEING A TRANSLATION OF HIS WORK ENTITLED | "ARCANA CŒLESTIA quæ in Scriptura Sacra, seu Verbo Domini sunt, detecta: hic primum | quæ in Genesis. Una cum Mirabilibus quæ visa sunt in Mundo Spirituum et in | Cœlo Angelorum." Londini, 1749–1756. | IN TWELVE VOLUMES. | VOL. I. | GENESIS, CHAP. I. TO CHAP. IX. | LONDON: | PUBLISHED BY THE SWEDENBORG SOCIETY, | (INSTITUTED 1810,) | 36, BLOOMSBURY STREET, OXFORD STREET. | EDIT. OF 1848.

verso: Matthew vi. 33. | *Seek ye first the kingdom of God and His Righteousness,* | *and all these things shall be added unto you.*

half title: ARCANA CŒLESTIA.

verso: *This work is printed at the expense of, and published for,* | "THE SOCIETY FOR PRINTING AND PUBLISHING THE | WRITINGS OF EMANUEL SWEDENBORG, INSTITUTED IN | LONDON IN THE YEAR 1810." | <rule> | PRINTED BY WALTON AND MITCHELL, WARDOUR STREET, OXFORD STREET.

8vo

half title and title leaves, 4 pp; Translator's preface, pp v-xvi; text of Genesis 1-9 and n 1-1113, pp 1-457.

The same as En 2/54 = Hyde 600, issued with a new title page in 1855.

UK: soc; USA: anc, shs

49/01/En 2/64 1855 Hyde 631

ARCANA CŒLESTIA. | <short rule> | THE | HEAVENLY MYSTERIES | CONTAINED IN | THE HOLY SCRIPTURE, OR WORD | OF THE LORD, | UNFOLDED, | IN AN EXPOSITION OF GENESIS AND EXODUS. | TOGETHER WITH A RELATION OF | WONDERFUL THINGS SEEN IN THE WORLD OF SPIRITS AND IN THE | HEAVEN OF ANGELS. | <short double rule> | BY EMANUEL SWEDENBORG. | <short double rule> | BEING A TRANSLATION OF HIS WORK ENTITLED | "ARCANA CŒLESTIA quæ in Scriptura Sacra, seu Verbo Domini sunt, detecta: hic primum | quæ in Genesis. Una cum Mirabilibus quæ visa sunt in Mundo Spirituum et in | Cœlo Angelorum." Londini, 1749–1756. | IN TWELVE VOLUMES. | VOL. II. | GENESIS, CHAP. X. TO CHAP. XVII. | LONDON: | PUBLISHED BY THE SWEDENBORG SOCIETY, | (INSTITUTED 1810,) | 36, BLOOMSBURY STREET, OXFORD STREET. | EDIT. OF 1848.

verso: Matthew vi. 33. | *Seek ye first the kingdom of God and His Righteousness,* | *and all these things shall be added unto you.*

half title: ARCANA CŒLESTIA.

verso: *This work is printed at the expense of, and published for,* | "THE SOCIETY FOR PRINTING AND PUBLISHING THE | WRITINGS OF EMANUEL SWEDENBORG, INSTITUTED IN | LONDON IN THE YEAR 1810." | <rule> | PRINTED BY WALTON AND MITCHELL, WARDOUR STREET, OXFORD STREET.

8vo

half title and title leaves, 4 pp; text of Genesis 10-17 and n 1114-2134, pp 5-486.

En 2/55 = Hyde 629, issued with a fresh title page in 1855.

UK: soc, con; USA: anc, shs

49/01/En 2/65 1855 Hyde 651

ARCANA CŒLESTIA. | <short rule> | THE | HEAVENLY MYSTERIES | CONTAINED IN | THE HOLY SCRIPTURE, OR WORD | OF THE LORD, | UNFOLDED, | IN AN EXPOSITION OF GENESIS AND

EXODUS. | TOGETHER WITH A RELATION OF | WONDERFUL THINGS SEEN IN THE WORLD OF SPIRITS AND IN THE | HEAVEN OF ANGELS. | <short double rule> | BY EMANUEL SWEDENBORG. | <short double rule> | BEING A TRANSLATION OF HIS WORK ENTITLED | "ARCANA CŒLESTIA quæ in Scriptura Sacra, seu Verbo Domini sunt, detecta: hic primum | quæ in Genesis. Una cum Mirabilibus quæ visa sunt in Mundo Spirituum et in | Cœlo Angelorum." Londini, 1749–1756. | IN TWELVE VOLUMES. | VOL. III. | GENESIS, CHAP. XVIII. TO CHAP. XXII. | LONDON: | PUBLISHED BY THE SWEDENBORG SOCIETY, | (INSTITUTED 1810,) | 36, BLOOMSBURY STREET, OXFORD STREET. | EDIT. OF 1852.
verso: Matthew vi. 33. | *Seek ye first the kingdom of God and His Righteousness, | and all these things shall be added unto you.*
half title: ARCANA CŒLESTIA.
verso: *This work is printed at the expense of, and published for,* | "THE SOCIETY FOR PRINTING AND PUBLISHING THE | WRITINGS OF EMANUEL SWEDENBORG, INSTITUTED IN | LONDON IN THE YEAR 1810." | <rule> | PRINTED BY WALTON AND MITCHELL, WARDOUR STREET, OXFORD STREET.
8vo
half title and title leaves, 4 pp; text of Swedenborg's preface, pp 5-6; text of Genesis 18-22 and n 2135-2893, pp 7-457.
En 2/57 = Hyde 649, issued with a fresh title page in 1855.
UK: soc, con; USA: anc, shs

49/01/En 2/66 **1855** Hyde 667

ARCANA CŒLESTIA. | <short rule> | THE | HEAVENLY MYSTERIES | CONTAINED IN | THE HOLY SCRIPTURE, OR WORD | OF THE LORD, | UNFOLDED, | IN AN EXPOSITION OF GENESIS AND EXODUS. | TOGETHER WITH A RELATION OF | WONDERFUL THINGS SEEN IN THE WORLD OF SPIRITS AND IN THE | HEAVEN OF ANGELS. | <short double rule> | BY EMANUEL SWEDENBORG. | <short double rule> | BEING A TRANSLATION OF HIS WORK ENTITLED | "ARCANA CŒLESTIA quæ in Scriptura Sacra, seu Verbo Domini sunt, detecta: hic primum | quæ in Genesis. Una cum Mirabilibus quæ visa sunt in Mundo Spirituum et in | Cœlo Angelorum." Londini, 1749–1756. | IN TWELVE VOLUMES. | VOL. IV. | GENESIS, CHAP. XXIII. TO CHAP. XXVII. | LONDON: | PUBLISHED BY THE SWEDENBORG SOCIETY, | (INSTITUTED 1810,) | 36, BLOOMSBURY STREET, OXFORD STREET. | EDIT. OF 1840.
verso: Matthew vi. 33. | *Seek ye first the kingdom of God and His Righteousness, | and all these things shall be added unto you.*
half title: ARCANA CŒLESTIA.
verso: *This work is printed at the expense of, and published for,* | "THE SOCIETY FOR PRINTING AND PUBLISHING THE | WRITINGS OF EMANUEL SWEDENBORG, INSTITUTED IN | LONDON IN THE YEAR 1810." | <rule> | PRINTED BY WALTON AND MITCHELL, WARDOUR STREET, OXFORD STREET.
8vo
half title and title leaves, 4 pp; text of Genesis 23-27 and n 2894-3649, pp 5-427.
En 2/35 = Hyde 664, issued with a fresh title page in 1855.
UK: soc, con; USA: anc, shs

49/01/En 2/67 **1855** Hyde 683

ARCANA CŒLESTIA. | <short rule> | THE | HEAVENLY MYSTERIES | CONTAINED IN | THE HOLY SCRIPTURE, OR WORD | OF THE LORD, | UNFOLDED, | IN AN EXPOSITION OF GENESIS AND EXODUS. | TOGETHER WITH A RELATION OF | WONDERFUL THINGS SEEN IN THE WORLD OF SPIRITS AND IN THE | HEAVEN OF ANGELS. | <short double rule> | BY EMANUEL SWEDENBORG. | <short double rule> | BEING A TRANSLATION OF HIS WORK ENTITLED | "ARCANA CŒLESTIA

quæ in Scriptura Sacra, seu Verbo Domini sunt, detecta: hic primum | quæ in Genesis. Una cum Mirabilibus quæ visa sunt in Mundo Spirituum et in | Cœlo Angelorum." Londini, 1749–1756. | IN TWELVE VOLUMES. | VOL. V. | GENESIS, CHAP. XXVIII. TO CHAP. XXXI. | LONDON: | PUBLISHED BY THE SWEDENBORG SOCIETY, | (INSTITUTED 1810,) | 36, BLOOMSBURY STREET, OXFORD STREET. | EDIT. OF 1840.
verso: Matthew vi. 33. | *Seek ye first the kingdom of God and His Righteousness, | and all these things shall be added unto you.*
half title: ARCANA CŒLESTIA.
verso: *This work is printed at the expense of, and published for,* | "THE SOCIETY FOR PRINTING AND PUBLISHING THE | WRITINGS OF EMANUEL SWEDENBORG, INSTITUTED IN | LONDON IN THE YEAR 1810." | <rule> | PRINTED BY WALTON AND MITCHELL, WARDOUR STREET, OXFORD STREET.
8vo
half title and title leaves, 4 pp; text of Genesis 28-31 and n 3650-4228, pp 5-390.
En 2/36 = Hyde 681, issued with a fresh title page in 1855.
UK: SOC, CON; USA: ANC, SHS

49/01/En 2/68 1855 Hyde 701

ARCANA CŒLESTIA. | <short rule> | THE | HEAVENLY MYSTERIES | CONTAINED IN | THE HOLY SCRIPTURE, OR WORD | OF THE LORD, | UNFOLDED, | IN AN EXPOSITION OF GENESIS AND EXODUS. | TOGETHER WITH A RELATION OF | WONDERFUL THINGS SEEN IN THE WORLD OF SPIRITS AND IN THE | HEAVEN OF ANGELS. | <short double rule> | BY EMANUEL SWEDENBORG. | <short double rule> | BEING A TRANSLATION OF HIS WORK ENTITLED | "ARCANA CŒLESTIA quæ in Scriptura Sacra, seu Verbo Domini sunt, detecta: hic primum | quæ in Genesis. Una cum Mirabilibus quæ visa sunt in Mundo Spirituum et in | Cœlo Angelorum." Londini, 1749–1756. | IN TWELVE VOLUMES. | VOL. VI. | GENESIS, CHAP. XXXII. TO CHAP. XXXVIII. | LONDON: | PUBLISHED BY THE SWEDENBORG SOCIETY, | (INSTITUTED 1810,) | 36, BLOOMSBURY STREET, OXFORD STREET. | EDIT. OF 1847.
verso: Matthew vi. 33. | *Seek ye first the kingdom of God and His Righteousness, | and all these things shall be added unto you.*
half title: ARCANA CŒLESTIA.
verso: *This work is printed at the expense of, and pubished for,* | "THE SOCIETY FOR PRINTING AND PUBLISHING THE | WRITINGS OF EMANUEL SWEDENBORG, INSTITUTED IN | LONDON IN THE YEAR 1810." | <rule> | PRINTED BY WALTON AND MITCHELL, WARDOUR STREET, OXFORD STREET.
8vo
half title and title leaves, 4 pp; text of Genesis 32-38 and n 4229-4953, pp 5-456.
En 2/51 = Hyde 700, issued with a fresh title page in 1855.
UK: SOC, CON; USA: ANC, SHS

49/01/En 2/69 1855 Hyde 717

ARCANA CŒLESTIA. | <short rule> | THE | HEAVENLY MYSTERIES | CONTAINED IN | THE HOLY SCRIPTURE, OR WORD | OF THE LORD, | UNFOLDED, | IN AN EXPOSITION OF GENESIS AND EXODUS. | TOGETHER WITH A RELATION OF | WONDERFUL THINGS SEEN IN THE WORLD OF SPIRITS AND IN THE | HEAVEN OF ANGELS. | <short double rule> | BY EMANUEL SWEDENBORG. | <short double rule> | BEING A TRANSLATION OF HIS WORK ENTITLED | "ARCANA CŒLESTIA quæ in Scriptura Sacra, seu Verbo Domini sunt, detecta: hic primum | quæ in Genesis. Una cum Mirabilibus quæ visa sunt in Mundo Spirituum et in | Cœlo Angelorum." Londini, 1749–1756. | IN TWELVE VOLUMES. | VOL. VII. | GENESIS, CHAP. XXXIX. TO CHAP. XLIII. | LONDON: | PUBLISHED BY THE SWEDENBORG SOCIETY, | (INSTITUTED 1810,) | 36, BLOOMSBURY STREET, OXFORD

STREET. | EDIT. OF 1847.
verso: Matthew vi. 33. | *Seek ye first the kingdom of God and His Righteousness,* | *and all these things shall be added unto you.*
half title: ARCANA CŒLESTIA.
verso: *This work is printed at the expense of, and published for,* | "THE SOCIETY FOR PRINTING AND PUBLISHING THE | WRITINGS OF EMANUEL SWEDENBORG, INSTITUTED IN | LONDON IN THE YEAR 1810." | <rule> | PRINTED BY WALTON AND MITCHELL, WARDOUR STREET, OXFORD STREET.
8vo
half title and title leaves, 4 pp; text of Genesis 39-43 and n 4954-5727, pp 5-413.
En 2/52 = Hyde 716, issued with a fresh title page in 1855.
UK: SOC, CON; USA: ANC, SHS

49/01/En 2/70 **1855** Hyde 733

ARCANA CŒLESTIA. | <short rule> | THE | HEAVENLY MYSTERIES | CONTAINED IN | THE HOLY SCRIPTURE, OR WORD | OF THE LORD, | UNFOLDED, | IN AN EXPOSITION OF GENESIS AND EXODUS. | TOGETHER WITH A RELATION OF | WONDERFUL THINGS SEEN IN THE WORLD OF SPIRITS AND IN THE | HEAVEN OF ANGELS. | <short double rule> | BY EMANUEL SWEDENBORG. | <short double rule> | BEING A TRANSLATION OF HIS WORK ENTITLED | "ARCANA CŒLESTIA quæ in Scriptura Sacra, seu Verbo Domini sunt, detecta: hic primum | quæ in Genesis. Una cum Mirabilibus quæ visa sunt in Mundo Spirituum et in | Cœlo Angelorum." Londini, 1749–1756. | IN TWELVE VOLUMES. | VOL. VIII. | GENESIS, CHAP. XLIV. TO CHAP. L. | LONDON: | PUBLISHED BY THE SWEDENBORG SOCIETY, | (INSTITUTED 1810,) | 36, BLOOMSBURY STREET, OXFORD STREET. | EDIT. OF 1846.
verso: Matthew vi. 33. | *Seek ye first the kingdom of God and His Righteousness,* | *and all these things shall be added unto you.*
half title: ARCANA CŒLESTIA.
verso: *This work is printed at the expense of, and published for,* | "THE SOCIETY FOR PRINTING AND PUBLISHING THE | WRITINGS OF EMANUEL SWEDENBORG, INSTITUTED IN | LONDON IN THE YEAR 1810." | <rule> | PRINTED BY WALTON AND MITCHELL, WARDOUR STREET, OXFORD STREET.
8vo
half title and title leaves, 4 pp; text of Genesis 44-50 and n 5728-6626, pp 5-407.
En 2/49 = Hyde 732, issued with a fresh title page in 1855.
UK: SOC, CON; USA: ANC, SHS

49/01/En 2/71 **1855** Hyde 764

ARCANA CŒLESTIA. | <short rule> | THE | HEAVENLY MYSTERIES | CONTAINED IN | THE HOLY SCRIPTURE, OR WORD | OF THE LORD, | UNFOLDED, | IN AN EXPOSITION OF GENESIS AND EXODUS. | TOGETHER WITH A RELATION OF | WONDERFUL THINGS SEEN IN THE WORLD OF SPIRITS AND IN THE | HEAVEN OF ANGELS. | <short double rule> | BY EMANUEL SWEDENBORG. | <short double rule> | BEING A TRANSLATION OF HIS WORK ENTITLED | "ARCANA CŒLESTIA quæ in Scriptura Sacra, seu Verbo Domini sunt, detecta: hic primum | quæ in Genesi. Una cum Mirabilibus quæ visa sunt in Mundo Spirituum et in | Cœlo Angelorum." Londini, 1749–1756. | IN TWELVE VOLUMES. | VOL. X. | EXODUS, CHAP. XIII. TO CHAP. XXI. | LONDON: | PUBLISHED BY THE SWEDENBORG SOCIETY, | (INSTITUTED 1810,) | 36, BLOOMSBURY STREET, OXFORD STREET. | EDIT. OF 1851.
verso: Matthew vi. 33. | *Seek ye first the kingdom of God and His Righteousness,* | *and all these things shall be added unto you.*
half title: ARCANA CŒLESTIA.

verso: *This work is printed at the expense of, and published for,* | "THE SOCIETY FOR PRINTING AND PUBLISHING THE | WRITINGS OF EMANUEL SWEDENBORG, INSTITUTED IN | LONDON IN THE YEAR 1810." | <rule> | LONDON: | PRINTED BY WALTON AND MITCHELL, WARDOUR STREET, OXFORD STREET.
8vo
half title and title leaves, 4 pp; text of Exodus 13-21 and n 8033-9111, pp 5-517.
En 2/56 = Hyde 763, issued with a fresh title page in 1855.
UK: SOC, CON; USA: ANC, SHS

49/01/En 2/72 **1855** Hyde 779
ARCANA CŒLESTIA. | <short rule> | THE | HEAVENLY MYSTERIES | CONTAINED IN | THE HOLY SCRIPTURE, OR WORD | OF THE LORD, | UNFOLDED, | IN AN EXPOSITION OF GENESIS AND EXODUS. | TOGETHER WITH A RELATION OF | WONDERFUL THINGS SEEN IN THE WORLD OF SPIRITS AND IN THE | HEAVEN OF ANGELS. | <short double rule> | BY EMANUEL SWEDENBORG. | <short double rule> | BEING A TRANSLATION OF HIS WORK ENTITLED | "ARCANA CŒLESTIA quæ in Scriptura Sacra, seu Verbo Domini sunt, detecta: hic primum | quæ in Genesis. Una cum Mirabilibus quæ visa sunt in Mundo Spirituum et in | Cœlo Angelorum." Londini, 1749—1756. | IN TWELVE VOLUMES. | VOL. XI. | EXODUS, CHAP. XXII. TO CHAP. XXVIII. | LONDON: | PUBLISHED BY THE SWEDENBORG SOCIETY, | (INSTITUTED 1810,) | 36, BLOOMSBURY STREET, OXFORD STREET. | EDIT. OF 1840.
verso: Matthew vi. 33. | *Seek ye first the kingdom of God and His Righteousness,* | *and all these things shall be added unto you.*
half title: ARCANA CŒLESTIA.
verso: *This work is printed at the expense of, and published for,* | "THE SOCIETY FOR PRINTING AND PUBLISHING THE | WRITINGS OF EMANUEL SWEDENBORG, INSTITUTED IN | LONDON IN THE YEAR 1810." | <rule> | PRINTED BY WALTON AND MITCHELL, WARDOUR STREET, OXFORD STREET.
8vo
half title and title leaves, 4 pp; text of Exodus 22-28 and n 9112-9973, pp 5-607; Editorial note, 1 p.
En 2/37 = Hyde 777, issued with a fresh title page in 1855.
UK: SOC, CON; USA: ANC, SHS

49/01/En 2/73 **1855** Hyde 788
ARCANA CŒLESTIA. | <short rule> | THE | HEAVENLY MYSTERIES | CONTAINED IN | THE HOLY SCRIPTURE, OR WORD | OF THE LORD, | UNFOLDED, | IN AN EXPOSITION OF GENESIS AND EXODUS. | TOGETHER WITH A RELATION OF | WONDERFUL THINGS SEEN IN THE WORLD OF SPIRITS AND IN THE | HEAVEN OF ANGELS. | <short double rule> | BY EMANUEL SWEDENBORG. | <short double rule> | BEING A TRANSLATION OF HIS WORK ENTITLED | "ARCANA CŒLESTIA quæ in Scriptura Sacra, seu Verbo Domini sunt, detecta: hic primum | quæ in Genesis. Una cum Mirabilibus quæ visa sunt in Mundo Spirituum et in | Cœlo Angelorum." Londini, 1749—1756. | IN TWELVE VOLUMES. | VOL. XII. | EXODUS, CHAP. XXIX. TO CHAP. XL. | LONDON: | PUBLISHED BY THE SWEDENBORG SOCIETY, | (INSTITUTED 1810,) | 36, BLOOMSBURY STREET, OXFORD STREET. | EDIT. OF 1840.
verso: Matthew vi. 33. | *Seek ye first the kingdom of God and His Righteousness,* | *and all these things shall be added unto you.*
half title: ARCANA CŒLESTIA.
verso: *This work is printed at the expense of, and published for,* | "THE SOCIETY FOR PRINTING AND PUBLISHING THE | WRITINGS OF EMANUEL SWEDENBORG, INSTITUTED IN | LONDON IN THE YEAR 1810." | <rule> | PRINTED BY WALTON AND MITCHELL, WARDOUR STREET, OXFORD STREET.

8vo
half title and title leaves, 4 pp; text of Exodus 29-40 and n 9974-10837, pp 5-569.
En 2/38 = Hyde 786, issued with a fresh title page in 1855.
UK: SOC, CON; USA: ANC, SHS

49/01/En 2/74 **1855** Hyde 684
ARCANA CŒLESTIA. | <short rule> | THE | HEAVENLY ARCANA. | CONTAINED IN | THE HOLY SCRIPTURES OR WORD OF THE LORD | UNFOLDED, | BEGINNING WITH THE BOOK OF GENESIS: | TOGETHER WITH | WONDERFUL THINGS SEEN IN THE WORLD OF SPIRITS | AND IN THE HEAVEN OF ANGELS. | <short rule> | *Translated from the Latin of* | EMANUEL SWEDENBORG, | *Servant of the Lord Jesus Christ.* | <short rule> | VOL. V. | NEW YORK: | AMERICAN SWEDENBORG PRINTING AND PUBLISHING SOCIETY, | BIBLE HOUSE, ASTOR PLACE, ROOM NO. 47. | 1855.
verso: *Published by* THE AMERICAN SWEDENBORG PRINTING AND PUBLISHING | SOCIETY, *organized for the purpose of Stereotyping, Printing, and* | *Publishing Uniform Editions of the Theological Writings of* EMANUEL | SWEDENBORG, *and incorporated in the State of New York* A.D. 1850.
half title: ARCANA CŒLESTIA.
8vo
half title and title leaves, 4 pp; text of Genesis 32-40 and n 4229-5190, pp 5-607.
Reprinted from En 2/51, 52 = Hyde 700, 716.
USA: ANC, SHS

49/01/En 2/75 **1856** Hyde 702
ARCANA CŒLESTIA. | <short rule> | THE | HEAVENLY ARCANA | CONTAINED IN | THE HOLY SCRIPTURES OR WORD OF THE LORD | UNFOLDED, | BEGINNING WITH THE BOOK OF GENESIS: | TOGETHER WITH | WONDERFUL THINGS SEEN IN THE WORLD OF SPIRITS | AND IN THE HEAVEN OF ANGELS. | <short rule> | *Translated from the Latin of* | EMANUEL SWEDENBORG, | *Servant of the Lord Jesus Christ.* | <short rule> | VOL. VI. | NEW YORK: | AMERICAN SWEDENBORG PRINTING AND PUBLISHING SOCIETY, | BIBLE HOUSE, ASTOR PLACE, ROOM NO. 47. | 1856.
verso: *Published by* THE AMERICAN SWEDENBORG PRINTING AND PUBLISHING | SOCIETY, *organized for the purpose of Stereotyping, Printing, and* | *Publishing Uniform Editions of the Theological Writings of* EMANUEL | SWEDENBORG, *and incorporated in the State of New York* A.D. 1850.
half title: ARCANA CŒLESTIA.
8vo
half title and title leaves, 4 pp; text of Genesis 41-49 and n 5191-6496, pp 5-624.
Reprinted from En 2/51, 52 = Hyde 700, 716.
USA: ANC

49/01/En 2/76 **1856** Hyde 718
ARCANA CŒLESTIA. | <short rule> | THE | HEAVENLY ARCANA | CONTAINED IN | THE HOLY SCRIPTURES OR WORD OF THE LORD | UNFOLDED, | BEGINNING WITH THE BOOK OF GENESIS: | TOGETHER WITH | WONDERFUL THINGS SEEN IN THE WORLD OF SPIRITS | AND IN THE HEAVEN OF ANGELS. | <short rule> | *Translated from the Latin of* | EMANUEL SWEDENBORG, | *Servant of the Lord Jesus Christ.* | <short rule> | VOL. VII. | NEW YORK: | AMERICAN SWEDENBORG PRINTING AND PUBLISHING SOCIETY, | BIBLE HOUSE, ASTOR PLACE, ROOM NO. 47. | 1856.

verso: *Published by* THE AMERICAN SWEDENBORG PRINTING AND PUBLISHING | SOCIETY, *organized for the purpose of Stereotyping, Printing, and* | *Publishing Uniform Editions of the Theological Writings of* EMANUEL | SWEDENBORG, *and incorporated in the State of New York* A.D. 1850.
half title: ARCANA CŒLESTIA.
8vo
half title and title leaves, 4 pp; text of Genesis 50, Exodus 1-12, and n 6497-8032, pp 5-627.
Reprinted from En 2/49, 78 = Hyde 732, 750.
USA: ANC, SHS

49/01/En 2/77 **1856** Hyde 734
ARCANA CŒLESTIA. | <short rule> | THE | HEAVENLY ARCANA | CONTAINED IN | THE HOLY SCRIPTURES OR WORD OF THE LORD | UNFOLDED, | BEGINNING WITH THE BOOK OF GENESIS: | TOGETHER WITH | WONDERFUL THINGS SEEN IN THE WORLD OF SPIRITS | AND IN THE HEAVEN OF ANGELS. | <short rule> | *Translated from the Latin of* | EMANUEL SWEDENBORG, | *Servant of the Lord Jesus Christ.* | <short rule> | VOL. VIII. | NEW YORK: | AMERICAN SWEDENBORG PRINTING AND PUBLISHING SOCIETY, | BIBLE HOUSE, ASTOR PLACE, ROOM NO. 47. | 1856.
verso: *Published by* THE AMERICAN SWEDENBORG PRINTING AND PUBLISHING | SOCIETY, *organized for the purpose of Stereotyping, Printing, and* | *Publishing Uniform Editions of the Theological Writings of* EMANUEL | SWEDENBORG, *and incorporated in the State of New York* A.D. 1850.
half title: ARCANA CŒLESTIA.
8vo
half title and title leaves, 4 pp; text of Exodus 13-21 and n 8033-9111, pp 5-543.
Reprinted from En 2/51, 52 = Hyde 700, 716.
USA: ANC, SHS

49/01/En 2/78 **1856** Hyde 750
ARCANA CŒLESTIA. | <short rule> | THE | HEAVENLY MYSTERIES | CONTAINED IN | THE HOLY SCRIPTURE, OR WORD | OF THE LORD, | UNFOLDED, | IN AN EXPOSITION OF GENESIS AND EXODUS. | TOGETHER WITH A RELATION OF | WONDERFUL THINGS SEEN IN THE WORLD OF SPIRITS AND IN THE | HEAVEN OF ANGELS. | <short double rule> | BY EMANUEL SWEDENBORG. | <short double rule> | BEING A TRANSLATION OF HIS WORK ENTITLED | "ARCANA CŒLESTIA quæ in Scriptura Sacra, seu Verbo Domini sunt, detecta: hic quæ in | Exodo. Una cum Mirabilibus quæ visa sunt in Mundo Spirituum et in | Cœlo Angelorum." Londini, 1749–1756. | IN TWELVE VOLUMES. | VOL. IX. | EXODUS, CHAP. I. TO CHAP. XII. | LONDON: | PUBLISHED BY THE SWEDENBORG SOCIETY, | (INSTITUTED 1810,) | 36 BLOOMSBURY STREET, OXFORD STREET. | 1856.
verso: Matthew vi. 33. | *Seek ye first the kingdom of God and His Righteousness,* | *and all these things shall be added unto you.* | <short rule> | BELL AND BAIN, PRINTERS, GLASGOW.
8vo
title leaf, 2 pp; text of Exodus 1-12 and n 6627-8032, pp 1-527.
Revised by W Bruce; an edition of 1,000 copies was printed.
UK: SOC, CON; USA: ANC, SHS

49/01/En 2/79 **1857** Hyde 652
ARCANA CŒLESTIA. | <short rule> | THE | HEAVENLY ARCANA | CONTAINED IN | THE HOLY SCRIPTURES OR WORD OF THE LORD | UNFOLDED, | BEGINNING WITH THE BOOK OF

GENESIS: | TOGETHER WITH | WONDERFUL THINGS SEEN IN THE WORLD OF SPIRITS | AND IN THE HEAVEN OF ANGELS. | <short rule> | *Translated from the Latin of* | EMANUEL SWEDENBORG, | *Servant of the Lord Jesus Christ.* | <short rule> | VOL. III | NEW YORK: | AMERICAN SWEDENBORG PRINTING AND PUBLISHING SOCIETY, | BIBLE HOUSE, ASTOR PLACE, ROOM NO. 47. | 1857.
verso: *Published by* THE AMERICAN SWEDENBORG PRINTING AND PUBLISHING | SOCIETY, *organized for the purpose of Stereotyping, Printing, and* | *Publishing Uniform Editions of the Theological Writings of* EMANUEL | SWEDENBORG, *and incorporated in the State of New York* A.D. 1850 | STEREOTYPED BY | RICHARD C. VALENTINE. | NEW YORK. | <short wavy rule>
half title: ARCANA CŒLESTIA.
8vo
half title and title leaves, 4 pp; text of Genesis 20-25 and n 2495-3352, pp 5-515.
Reprint of En 2/61 = Hyde 650.
USA: ANC

49/01/En 2/80 1857 Hyde 751

ARCANA CŒLESTIA. | <short rule> | THE | HEAVENLY ARCANA | CONTAINED IN | THE HOLY SCRIPTURES OR WORD OF THE LORD | UNFOLDED, | BEGINNING WITH THE BOOK OF GENESIS: | TOGETHER WITH | WONDERFUL THINGS SEEN IN THE WORLD OF SPIRITS | AND IN THE HEAVEN OF ANGELS. | <short rule> | *Translated from the Latin of* | EMANUEL SWEDENBORG, | *Servant of the Lord Jesus Christ.* | <short rule> | VOL. IX | NEW YORK: | AMERICAN SWEDENBORG PRINTING AND PUBLISHING SOCIETY. | BIBLE HOUSE, ASTOR PLACE, ROOM NO. 47. | 1857.
verso: Published by THE AMERICAN SWEDENBORG PRINTING AND PUBLISHING | SOCIETY, *organized for the purpose of Stereotyping, Printing, and* | *Publishing Uniform Editions of the Theological Writings of* EMANUEL | SWEDENBORG, *and incorporated in the State of New York* A.D. 1850.
half title, following title leaf: ARCANA CŒLESTIA.
verso: <short double rule> | NOTE. | *In this Volume, the numbers referring to passages have been revised* | *and corrected; but where the correct number could not be discovered,* | *the erroneous one is retained, and distinguished by an asterisk.* | <short double rule>
8vo
title and half title leaves, 4 pp; text of Exodus 22-28 and n 9112-9973, pp 5-607.
Reprint of En 2/37 = Hyde 777.
USA: ANC

49/01/En 2/81 1857 Hyde 765

ARCANA CŒLESTIA. | <short rule> | THE | HEAVENLY ARCANA | CONTAINED IN | THE HOLY SCRIPTURES OR WORD OF THE LORD | UNFOLDED, | BEGINNING WITH THE BOOK OF GENESIS: | TOGETHER WITH | WONDERFUL THINGS SEEN IN THE WORLD OF SPIRITS | AND IN THE HEAVEN OF ANGELS. | <short rule> | *Translated from the Latin of* | EMANUEL SWEDENBORG, | *Servant of the Lord Jesus Christ.* | <short rule> | VOL. X. | NEW YORK: | AMERICAN SWEDENBORG PRINTING AND PUBLISHING SOCIETY. | BIBLE HOUSE, ASTOR PLACE, ROOM NO. 47. | 1857.
verso: *Published by* THE AMERICAN SWEDENBORG PRINTING AND PUBLISHING | SOCIETY, *organized for the purpose of Stereotyping, Printing, and* | *Publishing Uniform Editions of the Theological Writings of* EMANUEL | SWEDENBORG, *and incorporated in the State of New York* A.D. 1850
half title: ARCANA CŒLESTIA.
verso: <short double rule> | NOTE. | *In this Volume, the numbers referring to passages have been revised* | *and corrected; but where the correct number could not be discovered,* | *the*

erroneous one is retained, and distinguished by an asterisk. | <short double rule>
8vo
half title and title leaves, 4 pp; text of Exodus 29-40 and n 9974-10837, pp 5-569.
Reprint of En 2/38 = Hyde 786.
USA: ANC

49/01/En 3/1 **1857** Hyde 604
THE | HEAVENLY SECRETS | WHICH ARE IN | THE HOLY SCRIPTURE, | OR | WORD OF THE LORD, | UNCOVERED. | FIRST, WHAT ARE IN | GENESIS. | TOGETHER WITH THE WONDERS | WHICH HAVE BEEN SEEN | IN THE WORLD OF SPIRITS, AND IN THE HEAVEN OF ANGELS. | <short rule> | MATTHEW vi. 33. | "Seek ye first the kingdom of God, and the justice thereof, and all things will be added to you." | <short rule> | TRANSLATED FROM THE ORIGINAL LATIN, PUBLISHED IN LONDON, | FROM 1749 TO 1756.
half title: A | NEW TRANSLATION | OF SOME PART OF | SWEDENBORG'S THEOLOGICAL WORKS. | VOL. I. | LONDON: | WILLIAM WHITE, 36 BLOOMSBURY STREET. | M.DCCC.LVII.
verso: LONDON: | PRINTED BY MITCHELL AND SON, | WARDOUR STREET (W.)
8vo
half title and title leaves, 4 pp; Translator's preface, pp iii-vi; text of Genesis 1-9 and n 1-1113 <but with the paragraph numbers omitted>, pp 1-590.
Translated by George Harrison.
UK: SOC, CON, NCC; SWE: UPP; USA: ANC, SHS

49/01/En 3/2 **1858** Hyde 632
THE | HEAVENLY SECRETS | WHICH ARE IN | THE HOLY SCRIPTURE, | OR | WORD OF THE LORD, | UNCOVERED. | FIRST, WHAT ARE IN | GENESIS. | TOGETHER WITH THE WONDERS | WHICH HAVE BEEN SEEN | IN THE WORLD OF SPIRITS, AND IN THE HEAVEN OF ANGELS. | <short rule> | MATTHEW vi.33. | "Seek ye first the kingdom of God, and the justice thereof, and all things will be added to you." | <short rule> | TRANSLATED FROM THE ORIGINAL LATIN, PUBLISHED IN LONDON, | FROM 1749 TO 1756.
half title: A | NEW TRANSLATION | OF SOME PART OF | SWEDENBORG'S THEOLOGICAL WORKS. | VOL. II. | LONDON: | WILLIAM WHITE, 36 BLOOMSBURY STREET. | M.DCCC.LVIII.
verso: LONDON: | PRINTED BY MITCHELL AND SON, | WARDOUR STREET (W.)
8vo
title and half title leaves, 4 pp; text of Genesis 10-17 and n 1114-2134 <but with the paragraph numbers omitted>, pp 1-582. Some copies have 1 p listing errors in volume 1.
Translated by George Harrison.
UK: SOC, CON, NCC; SWE: UPP; USA: ANC, SHS

49/01/En 3/3 **1858** Hyde 653
THE | HEAVENLY SECRETS | WHICH ARE IN | THE HOLY SCRIPTURE, | OR | WORD OF THE LORD, | UNCOVERED. | FIRST, WHAT ARE IN | GENESIS. | TOGETHER WITH THE WONDERS | WHICH HAVE BEEN SEEN | IN THE WORLD OF SPIRITS, AND IN THE HEAVEN OF ANGELS. | <short rule> | MATTHEW vi.33. | "Seek ye first the kingdom of God, and the justice thereof, and all things will be added to you." | <short rule> | TRANSLATED FROM THE ORIGINAL LATIN, PUBLISHED IN LONDON, | FROM 1749 TO 1756.
half title: A | NEW TRANSLATION | OF SOME PART OF | SWEDENBORG'S THEOLOGICAL WORKS. | VOL. III. | LONDON: | WILLIAM WHITE, 36 BLOOMSBURY STREET. | M.DCCC.LVIII.
verso: LONDON: | MITCHELL AND SON, | WARDOUR STREET (W.)
8vo

title and half title, 4 pp; text of Genesis 18-22 and n 2135-2893 <but with the paragraph numbers omitted>, pp 1-555; p 555 has a list of errors to be found in volume 2.
Translated by George Harrison.
UK: soc, con, ncc; SWE: upp; USA: anc, shs

49/01/En 3/4 **1858** Hyde 668

THE | HEAVENLY SECRETS | WHICH ARE IN | THE HOLY SCRIPTURE, | OR | WORD OF THE LORD, | UNCOVERED. | HERE, WHAT ARE IN | GENESIS. | TOGETHER WITH THE WONDERS | WHICH HAVE BEEN SEEN | IN THE WORLD OF SPIRITS, AND IN THE HEAVEN OF ANGELS. | <short rule> | MATTHEW vi.33. | "Seek ye first the kingdom of God, and the justice thereof, and all things will be added to you." | <short rule> | TRANSLATED FROM THE ORIGINAL LATIN, PUBLISHED IN LONDON, | FROM 1749 TO 1756.
verso: LONDON: | PRINTED BY MITCHELL AND SON | WARDOUR STREET (W.)
half title: A | NEW TRANSLATION | OF SOME PART OF | SWEDENBORG'S THEOLOGICAL WORKS | VOL. IV. | LONDON: | WILLIAM WHITE,| 36 BLOOMSBURY STREET. | M.DCCC.LVIII.
8vo
title and half title leaves, 4 pp; text of Genesis 23-27 and n 2894-3649 <but with the paragraph numbers omitted>, pp 1-520; p 520 has a list of errors to be found in volumes 2 and 3.
Translated by George Harrison.
UK: soc, con, ncc; SWE: upp; USA: anc, shs

49/01/En 3/5 **1858** Hyde 685

THE | HEAVENLY SECRETS | WHICH ARE IN | THE HOLY SCRIPTURE, | OR | WORD OF THE LORD, | UNCOVERED. | HERE, WHAT ARE IN | GENESIS. | TOGETHER WITH THE WONDERS | WHICH HAVE BEEN SEEN | IN THE WORLD OF SPIRITS, AND IN THE HEAVEN OF ANGELS. | <short rule> | MATTHEW vi.33. | "Seek ye first the kingdom of God, and the justice thereof, and all things will be added to you." | <short rule> | TRANSLATED FROM THE ORIGINAL LATIN, PUBLISHED IN LONDON, | FROM 1749 TO 1756.
verso: LONDON: | PRINTED BY MITCHELL AND SON | WARDOUR STREET (W.)
half title: A | NEW TRANSLATION | OF SOME PART OF | SWEDENBORG'S THEOLOGICAL WORKS. | VOL. V. | LONDON: | WILLIAM WHITE, 36 BLOOMSBURY STREET. | M.DCCC.LVIII.
8vo
title and half title leaves, 4 pp; text of Genesis 28-31 and n 3650-4228 <but with the paragraph numbers omitted>, pp 1-492. A slip listing errors in volumes 3 and 4 is pasted in before p 1.
Translated by George Harrison.
UK: soc, con, ncc; SWE: upp; USA: anc, shs

49/01/En 3/6 **1858** Hyde 703

THE | HEAVENLY SECRETS | WHICH ARE IN | THE HOLY SCRIPTURE, | OR | WORD OF THE LORD, | UNCOVERED. | HERE, WHAT ARE IN | GENESIS. | TOGETHER WITH THE WONDERS | WHICH HAVE BEEN SEEN | IN THE WORLD OF SPIRITS, AND IN THE HEAVEN OF ANGELS. | <short rule> | MATTHEW vi.33. | "Seek ye first the kingdom of God, and the justice thereof, and all things will be added to you." | <short rule> | TRANSLATED FROM THE ORIGINAL LATIN, PUBLISHED IN LONDON, | FROM 1749 TO 1756.
verso: LONDON: | PRINTED BY MITCHELL AND SON | WARDOUR STREET (W.)
half title: A | NEW TRANSLATION | OF SOME PART OF | SWEDENBORG'S THEOLOGICAL WORKS. | VOL. VI. | LONDON: | WILLIAM WHITE, 36 BLOOMSBURY STREET. | M.DCCC.LVIII.
8vo

title and half title leaves, 4 pp; text of Genesis 32-38 and n 4229-4953 <but with the paragraph numbers omitted>, pp 1-570; p 570 has a list of errors in volume 5.
Translated by George Harrison.
UK: SOC, CON, NCC; SWE: UPP; USA: ANC, SHS

49/01/En 3/7 **1858** Hyde 719

THE | HEAVENLY SECRETS | WHICH ARE IN | THE HOLY SCRIPTURE, | OR | WORD OF THE LORD, | UNCOVERED. | HERE, WHAT ARE IN | GENESIS. | TOGETHER WITH THE WONDERS | WHICH HAVE BEEN SEEN | IN THE WORLD OF SPIRITS, AND IN THE HEAVEN OF ANGELS. | <short rule> | MATTHEW vi. 33. | "Seek ye first the kingdom of God, and the justice thereof, and all things will be added to you." | <short rule> | TRANSLATED FROM THE ORIGINAL LATIN, PUBLISHED IN LONDON, | FROM 1749 TO 1756.
verso: LONDON: | PRINTED BY MITCHELL AND SON | WARDOUR STREET (W.)
half title: A | NEW TRANSLATION | OF SOME PART OF | SWEDENBORG'S THEOLOGICAL WORKS. | VOL. VII. | LONDON: | WILLIAM WHITE, 36 BLOOMSBURY STREET. | M.DCCC.LVIII.
8vo
title and half title leaves, 4 pp; text of Genesis 39-43 and n 4954-5727 <but with the paragraph numbers omitted>, pp 1-523; p 523 has a list of errors in volume 6.
Translated by George Harrison.
UK: SOC, CON, NCC; SWE: UPP; USA: ANC, SHS

49/01/En 3/8 **1859** Hyde 735

THE | HEAVENLY SECRETS | WHICH ARE IN | THE HOLY SCRIPTURE, | OR | WORD OF THE LORD, | UNCOVERED. | HERE, WHAT ARE IN | GENESIS. | TOGETHER WITH THE WONDERS | WHICH HAVE BEEN SEEN | IN THE WORLD OF SPIRITS, AND IN THE HEAVEN OF ANGELS. | <short rule> | MATTHEW 6:33. | "Seek ye first the kingdom of God, and the justice thereof, and all things will be added to you." | <short rule> | TRANSLATED FROM THE ORIGINAL LATIN, PUBLISHED IN LONDON, | FROM 1749 TO 1756.
verso: LONDON: | PRINTED BY MITCHELL AND SON, | WARDOUR STREET (W.)
half title: A | NEW TRANSLATION | OF SOME PART OF | SWEDENBORG'S THEOLOGICAL WORKS. | VOL. VIII. | LONDON: | WILLIAM WHITE, 36 BLOOMSBURY STREET. | M.DCCC.LIX.
8vo
title and half title leaves, 4 pp; text of Genesis 44-50 and n 5728-6626 <but with the paragraph numbers omitted>, pp 1-502; errors in volume 7, 1 p.
Translated by George Harrison.
UK: SOC, CON, NCC; SWE: UPP; USA: ANC, SHS

49/01/En 3/9 **1859** Hyde 752

THE | HEAVENLY SECRETS | WHICH ARE IN | THE HOLY SCRIPTURE, | OR | WORD OF THE LORD, | UNCOVERED. | HERE, WHAT ARE IN | EXODUS. | TOGETHER WITH THE WONDERS | WHICH HAVE BEEN SEEN | IN THE WORLD OF SPIRITS, AND IN THE HEAVEN OF ANGELS. | <short rule> | MATTHEW vi.33. | "Seek ye first the kingdom of God, and the justice thereof, and all things will be added to you." | <short rule> | TRANSLATED FROM THE ORIGINAL LATIN, PUBLISHED IN LONDON, | FROM 1749 TO 1756.
verso: LONDON: | PRINTED BY MITCHELL AND SON, | WARDOUR STREET (W.)
half title: A | NEW TRANSLATION | OF SOME PART OF | SWEDENBORG'S THEOLOGICAL WORKS. | VOL. IX. | LONDON: | WILLIAM WHITE, 36 BLOOMSBURY STREET. | M.DCCC.LIX.
8vo
title and half title leaves, 4 pp; text of Exodus 1-12 and n 6627-8032 <but with the paragraph

numbers omitted>, pp 1-688; a slip listing errors in volume 8 is pasted in after p 688.
Translated by George Harrison.
UK: SOC, CON, NCC; SWE: UPP; USA: ANC, SHS

49/01/En 3/10 **1859** Hyde 766

THE | HEAVENLY SECRETS | WHICH ARE IN | THE HOLY SCRIPTURE, | OR | WORD OF THE LORD, | UNCOVERED. | HERE, WHAT ARE IN | EXODUS. | TOGETHER WITH THE WONDERS | WHICH HAVE BEEN SEEN | IN THE WORLD OF SPIRITS, AND IN THE HEAVEN OF ANGELS. | <short rule> | MATTHEW vi.33. | "Seek ye first the kingdom of God, and the justice thereof, and all things will be added to you." | <short rule> | TRANSLATED FROM THE ORIGINAL LATIN, PUBLISHED IN LONDON, | FROM 1749 TO 1756.
verso: LONDON: | PRINTED BY MITCHELL AND SON, | WARDOUR STREET (W.)
half title: A | NEW TRANSLATION | OF SOME PART OF | SWEDENBORG'S THEOLOGICAL WORKS. | VOL. X. | LONDON: | WILLIAM WHITE, 36 BLOOMSBURY STREET. | M.DCCC.LIX.
8vo
title and half title leaves, 4 pp; text of Exodus 13-21 and n 8033-9111 <but with the paragraph numbers omitted>, pp 1-648; a slip listing errors in volume 9 is pasted in after p 648.
Translated by George Harrison.
UK: SOC, CON, NCC; SWE: UPP; USA: ANC, SHS

49/01/En 2/82 **1859** Hyde 686

<<ARCANA CŒLESTIA. | <short rule> | THE | HEAVENLY ARCANA | CONTAINED IN THE HOLY SCRIPTURES OR WORD OF THE LORD | UNFOLDED, | BEGINNING WITH THE BOOK OF GENESIS: | TOGETHER WITH | WONDERFUL THINGS SEEN IN THE WORLD OF SPIRITS | AND IN THE HEAVEN OF ANGELS. | <short rule> | *Translated from the Latin of* | EMANUEL SWEDENBORG, *Servant of the Lord Jesus Christ.* | <short rule> | VOL. V. | NEW YORK: | AMERICAN SWEDENBORG PRINTING AND PUBLISHING SOCIETY. | BIBLE HOUSE, ASTOR PLACE, ROOM NO. 47. | 1859.>>
verso: << <short double rule> | *Published by* THE AMERICAN SWEDENBORG PRINTING AND PUBLISHING | SOCIETY, *organized for the purpose of Stereotyping, Printing, and* | *Publishing Uniform Editions of the Theological Writings of* EMANUEL | SWEDENBORG, *and incorporated in the State of New York* A.D. 1850>>
half title: <<ARCANA CŒLESTIA>>
verso: << <short double rule> | NOTE. | *In this Volume, the numbers referring to passages have been revised* | *and corrected; but where the correct number could not be discovered,* | *the erroneous one is retained, and distinguished by an asterisk.* | <short double rule> >>
8vo
half title and title leaves, 4 pp; text of Genesis 32-40 and n 4229-5190, pp 5-607.
The same as En 2/74 = Hyde 684.
Copy not seen; description deduced from En 2/81.
USA: ANC

49/01/En 3/11 **1860** Hyde 780

THE | HEAVENLY SECRETS | WHICH ARE IN | THE HOLY SCRIPTURE, | OR | WORD OF THE LORD, | UNCOVERED. | HERE, WHAT ARE IN | EXODUS. | TOGETHER WITH THE WONDERS | WHICH HAVE BEEN SEEN | IN THE WORLD OF SPIRITS, AND IN THE HEAVEN OF ANGELS. | <short rule> | MATTHEW vi.33. | "Seek ye first the kingdom of God, and the justice thereof, and all things will be added to you." | <short rule> | TRANSLATED FROM THE ORIGINAL LATIN, PUBLISHED IN LONDON, | FROM 1749 TO 1756.

verso: LONDON: | PRINTED BY MITCHELL AND SON, | WARDOUR STREET (W.)
half title: A | NEW TRANSLATION | OF SOME PART OF | SWEDENBORG'S THEOLOGICAL WORKS. | VOL. XI. | LONDON: | WILLIAM WHITE, 36 BLOOMSBURY STREET. | M.DCCC.LX.
8vo
title and half title leaves, 4 pp; text of Exodus 22-28 and n 9112-9973 <but with the paragraph numbers omitted>, pp 1-724; a list of the errors in volume 10 is printed on p 724.
Translated by George Harrison.
UK: SOC, CON, NCC; SWE: UPP; USA: ANC, SHS

49/01/En 3/12 **1860** Hyde 789

THE | HEAVENLY SECRETS | WHICH ARE IN | THE HOLY SCRIPTURE, | OR | WORD OF THE LORD, | UNCOVERED. | HERE, WHAT ARE IN | EXODUS. | TOGETHER WITH THE WONDERS | WHICH HAVE BEEN SEEN | IN THE WORLD OF SPIRITS, AND IN THE HEAVEN OF ANGELS. | <short rule> | MATTHEW vi.33. | "Seek ye first the kingdom of God, and the justice thereof, and all things will be added to you." | <short rule> | TRANSLATED FROM THE ORIGINAL LATIN, PUBLISHED IN LONDON, | FROM 1749 TO 1756.
half title: A | NEW TRANSLATION | OF SOME PART OF | SWEDENBORG'S THEOLOGICAL WORKS. | VOL. XII. | LONDON: | WILLIAM WHITE, 36 BLOOMSBURY STREET. | M.DCCC.LX.
verso: LONDON: | PRINTED BY MITCHELL AND SON, | WARDOUR STREET (W.)
8vo
title and half title leaves, 4 pp; text of Exodus 29-40 and n 9974-10837 <but with the paragraph numbers omitted>, pp 1-669; a list of errors in volume 11 is printed on the verso of p 669.
Translated by George Harrison.
UK: SOC, CON, NCC; SWE: UPP; USA: ANC, SHS

49/01/En 2/83 **1862** Hyde 605

ARCANA CŒLESTIA. | <short rule> | THE | HEAVENLY MYSTERIES | CONTAINED IN | THE HOLY SCRIPTURE, OR WORD OF THE LORD, | UNFOLDED, | IN AN EXPOSITION OF GENESIS AND EXODUS: | TOGETHER WITH A RELATION OF | WONDERFUL THINGS SEEN IN THE WORLD OF SPIRITS AND | IN THE HEAVEN OF ANGELS. | <short double rule> | BY EMANUEL SWEDENBORG. | <short double rule> | BEING A TRANSLATION OF HIS WORK ENTITLED | "ARCANA CŒLESTIA QUÆ IN SCRIPTURA SACRA, SEU VERBO DOMINI SUNT, DETECTA; HIC | PRIMUM QUÆ IN GENESI. UNA CUM MIRABILIBUS QUÆ VISA SUNT IN MUNDO SPIRITUUM | ET IN CŒLO ANGELORUM. LONDINI, 1742-1756." | IN TWELVE VOLUMES. | VOLUME I. | GENESIS, CHAPTER I TO CHAPTER IX. | LONDON: | PUBLISHED BY THE SWEDENBORG SOCIETY, | (INSTITUTED 1810,) | 36 BLOOMSBURY STREET, OXFORD STREET, W.C. | 1861.
verso: Matthew vi. 33. | *Seek ye first the kingdom of God and his righteousness,* | *and all these things shall be added unto you.*
half title: ARCANA CŒLESTIA.
verso: *This Work is printed at the expense of, and published for,* | "THE SOCIETY FOR PRINTING AND PUBLISHING THE | WRITINGS OF EMANUEL SWEDENBORG, INSTITUTED IN | LONDON IN THE YEAR 1810." | <short rule> | LONDON: MITCHELL AND SON, PRINTERS, WARDOUR STREET, W.
8vo
half title and title leaves, 4 pp; Translator's preface, pp v-xvi; text of Genesis 1-9 and n 1-1113, pp 1-457; Errata, 1 p; advertisement, 2 pp.
Revised by S Warren. An edition of 1,000 copies, which was printed in 1862.
UK: SOC; SWI: LAU; USA: ANC, SHS

49/01/En 2/84 **1862** **Hyde 606**

<<ARCANA CŒLESTIA. | <short rule> | THE | HEAVENLY ARCANA | CONTAINED IN | THE HOLY SCRIPTURES OR WORD OF THE LORD | UNFOLDED, | BEGINNING WITH THE BOOK OF GENESIS: | TOGETHER WITH | WONDERFUL THINGS SEEN IN THE WORLD OF SPIRITS | AND IN THE HEAVEN OF ANGELS. | <short rule> | *Translated from the Latin of* | EMANUEL SWEDENBORG, | *Servant of the Lord Jesus Christ.* | VOL. I. | NEW YORK: | AMERICAN SWEDENBORG PRINTING AND PUBLISHING SOCIETY. | 1862.>>

verso: <<*Published by* THE AMERICAN SWEDENBORG PRINTING AND PUBLISHING | SOCIETY, *organized for the purpose of Stereotyping, Printing, and* | *Publishing Uniform Editions of the Theological Writings of* EMANUEL | SWEDENBORG, *and incorporated in the State of New York* A.D. 1850>>

half title: <<ARCANA CŒLESTIA>>

8vo

half title and title leaves, 4 pp; text of Genesis 1-11 and n 1-1382, pp 1-568.

The same as En 2/59 = Hyde 602; an edition of 500 copies was printed.

Copy not seen; description deduced from En 2/132.

USA: ANC, SHS

49/01/En 2/85 **1862** **Hyde 720**

<<ARCANA CŒLESTIA. | <short rule> | THE | HEAVENLY ARCANA | CONTAINED IN THE HOLY SCRIPTURES OR WORD OF THE LORD | UNFOLDED, | BEGINNING WITH THE BOOK OF GENESIS: | TOGETHER WITH | WONDERFUL THINGS SEEN IN THE WORLD OF SPIRITS | AND IN THE HEAVEN OF ANGELS. | <short rule> | *Translated from the Latin of* | EMANUEL SWEDENBORG, *Servant of the Lord Jesus Christ.* | VOL. VII. | NEW YORK: | AMERICAN SWEDENBORG PRINTING AND PUBLISHING SOCIETY. | 1862.>>

verso: <<*Published by* THE AMERICAN SWEDENBORG PRINTING AND PUBLISHING | SOCIETY, *organized for the purpose of Stereotyping, Printing, and* | *Publishing Uniform Editions of the Theological Writings of* EMANUEL | SWEDENBORG, *and incorporated in the State of New York* A.D. 1850>>

half title: <<ARCANA CŒLESTIA>>

8vo

half title and title leaves, 4 pp; text of Genesis 50, Exodus 1-12, and n 6497-8032, pp 5-627.

The same as En 2/76 = Hyde 718.

Copy not seen; description deduced from En 2/76.

USA: ANC, SHS

49/01/En 2/86 **1862** **Hyde 736**

<<ARCANA CŒLESTIA. | <short rule> | THE | HEAVENLY ARCANA | CONTAINED IN | THE HOLY SCRIPTURES OR WORD OF THE LORD | UNFOLDED, | BEGINNING WITH THE BOOK OF GENESIS: | TOGETHER WITH | WONDERFUL THINGS SEEN IN THE WORLD OF SPIRITS | AND IN THE HEAVEN OF ANGELS. | *Translated from the Latin of* | EMANUEL SWEDENBORG, | *Servant of the Lord Jesus Christ.* | VOL. VIII. | NEW YORK: | AMERICAN SWEDENBORG PRINTING AND PUBLISHING SOCIETY. | 1862.>>

verso: <<*Published by* THE AMERICAN SWEDENBORG PRINTING AND PUBLISHING | SOCIETY, *organized for the purpose of Stereotyping, Printing, and* | *Publishing Uniform Editions of the Theological Writings of* EMANUEL | SWEDENBORG, *and incorporated in the State of New York* A.D. 1850>>

half title: <<ARCANA CŒLESTIA>>

8vo

half title and title leaves, 4 pp; text of Exodus 13-21 and n 8033-9111, pp 5-543.
The same as En 2/77 = Hyde 734.
Copy not seen; description deduced from En 2/77.
USA: ANC, SHS

49/01/En 2/87 **1863** Hyde 633

ARCANA CŒLESTIA. | <short rule> | THE | HEAVENLY MYSTERIES | CONTAINED IN | THE HOLY SCRIPTURE, OR WORD OF THE LORD, | UNFOLDED, | IN AN EXPOSITION OF GENESIS AND EXODUS: | TOGETHER WITH A RELATION OF | WONDERFUL THINGS SEEN IN THE WORLD OF SPIRITS AND | IN THE HEAVEN OF ANGELS. | <short double rule> | BY EMANUEL SWEDENBORG. | <short double rule> | BEING A TRANSLATION OF HIS WORK ENTITLED | "ARCANA CŒLESTIA QUÆ IN SCRIPTURA SACRA, SEU VERBO DOMINI SUNT, DETECTA; HIC | PRIMUM QUÆ IN GENESI. UNA CUM MIRABILIBUS QUÆ VISA SUNT IN MUNDO SPIRITUUM | ET IN CŒLO ANGELORUM. LONDINI, 1742-1756." | IN TWELVE VOLUMES. | VOLUME II. | GENESIS, CHAPTER X TO CHAPTER XVII. | LONDON: | PUBLISHED BY THE SWEDENBORG SOCIETY, | (INSTITUTED 1810,) | 36 BLOOMSBURY STREET, OXFORD STREET, W.C. | 1861.
verso: Matthew vi. 33. | *Seek ye first the kingdom of God and His righteousness,* | *and all these things shall be added unto you.*
half title: ARCANA CŒLESTIA.
verso: *This Work is printed at the expense of, and published for,* | "THE SOCIETY FOR PRINTING AND PUBLISHING THE | WRITINGS OF EMANUEL SWEDENBORG, INSTITUTED IN | LONDON IN THE YEAR 1810." | <short rule> | LONDON: MITCHELL AND SON, PRINTERS, WARDOUR STREET, W.
8vo
half title and title leaves, 4 pp; text of Genesis 10-17 and n 1114-2134, pp 5-484.
A reprint from En 2/55 = Hyde 629, under the supervision of J Bayley; an edition of 1,000 copies was printed.
UK: SOC; SWI: LAU; USA: ANC, SHS

49/01/En 2/88 **1863** Hyde 654

ARCANA CŒLESTIA. | <short rule> | THE | HEAVENLY MYSTERIES | CONTAINED IN | THE HOLY SCRIPTURE, OR WORD OF THE LORD, | UNFOLDED, | IN AN EXPOSITION OF GENESIS AND EXODUS: | TOGETHER WITH A RELATION OF | WONDERFUL THINGS SEEN IN THE WORLD OF SPIRITS AND | IN THE HEAVEN OF ANGELS. | <short double rule> | BY EMANUEL SWEDENBORG. | <short double rule> | BEING A TRANSLATION OF HIS WORK ENTITLED | "ARCANA CŒLESTIA QUÆ IN SCRIPTURA SACRA, SEU VERBO DOMINI SUNT, DETECTA; HIC | PRIMUM QUÆ IN GENESI. UNA CUM MIRABILIBUS QUÆ VISA SUNT IN MUNDO SPIRITUUM | ET IN CŒLO ANGELORUM. LONDINI, 1749-1756." | IN TWELVE VOLUMES. | VOLUME III. | GENESIS, CHAPTER XVIII. TO CHAPTER XXII. | LONDON: | PUBLISHED BY THE SWEDENBORG SOCIETY, | (INSTITUTED 1810,) | 36 BLOOMSBURY STREET, OXFORD STREET, W.C. | 1863.
verso: Matthew vi. 33. | *Seek ye first the kingdom of God and His righteousness,* | *and all these things shall be added unto you.*
half title: ARCANA CŒLESTIA.
verso: *This Work is printed at the expense of, and published for,* | "THE SOCIETY FOR PRINTING AND PUBLISHING THE | WRITINGS OF EMANUEL SWEDENBORG, INSTITUTED IN | LONDON IN THE YEAR 1810." | <short rule> | LONDON: MITCHELL AND SON, PRINTERS, WARDOUR STREET, W.
8vo
half title and title leaves, 4 pp; text of Swedenborg's preface, Genesis 18-22, and n 2135-2893, pp 5-452.

A reprint of En 2/57 = Hyde 649, supervised by J Bayley; an edition of 1,000 copies was printed.
UK: soc; SWI: lau; USA: anc, shs

49/01/En 2/89 **1863** Hyde 669

ARCANA CŒLESTIA. | <short rule> | THE | HEAVENLY MYSTERIES | CONTAINED IN | THE HOLY SCRIPTURE, OR WORD OF THE LORD, | UNFOLDED, | IN AN EXPOSITION OF GENESIS AND EXODUS: | TOGETHER WITH A RELATION OF | WONDERFUL THINGS SEEN IN THE WORLD OF SPIRITS AND | IN THE HEAVEN OF ANGELS. | <short double rule> | BY EMANUEL SWEDENBORG. | <short double rule> | BEING A TRANSLATION OF HIS WORK ENTITLED | "ARCANA CŒLESTIA QUÆ IN SCRIPTURA SACRA, SEU VERBO DOMINI SUNT, DETECTA; HIC | PRIMUM QUÆ IN GENESI. UNA CUM MIRABILIBUS QUÆ VISA SUNT IN MUNDO SPIRITUUM | ET IN CŒLO ANGELORUM. LONDINI, 1749-1756." | IN TWELVE VOLUMES. | VOLUME IV. | GENESIS, CHAPTER XXIII. TO CHAPTER XXVII. | LONDON: | PUBLISHED BY THE SWEDENBORG SOCIETY, | (INSTITUTED 1810,) | 36 BLOOMSBURY STREET, OXFORD STREET, W.C. | 1863.
verso: Matthew vi. 33. | *Seek ye first the kingdom of God and His righteousness,* | *and all these things shall be added unto you.*
half title: ARCANA CŒLESTIA.
verso: *This Work is printed at the expense of, and published for,* | "THE SOCIETY FOR PRINTING AND PUBLISHING THE | WRITINGS OF EMANUEL SWEDENBORG, INSTITUTED IN | LONDON IN THE YEAR 1810." | <short rule> | LONDON: MITCHELL AND SON, PRINTERS, WARDOUR STREET, W.
8vo
half title and title leaves, 4 pp; text of Genesis 23-27 and n 2894-3649, pp 5-420.
A reprint of En 2/57 = Hyde 649, supervised by J Bayley; an edition of 1,000 copies was printed.
UK: soc; SWI: lau; USA: anc, shs

49/01/En 2/90 **1863** Hyde 687

ARCANA CŒLESTIA. | <short rule> | THE | HEAVENLY MYSTERIES | CONTAINED IN | THE HOLY SCRIPTURE, OR WORD OF THE LORD, | UNFOLDED, | IN AN EXPOSITION OF GENESIS AND EXODUS: | TOGETHER WITH A RELATION OF | WONDERFUL THINGS SEEN IN THE WORLD OF SPIRITS AND | IN THE HEAVEN OF ANGELS. | <short double rule> | BY EMANUEL SWEDENBORG. | <short double rule> | BEING A TRANSLATION OF HIS WORK ENTITLED | "ARCANA CŒLESTIA QUÆ IN SCRIPTURA SACRA, SEU VERBO DOMINI SUNT, DETECTA ; HIC | PRIMUM QUÆ IN GENESI. UNA CUM MIRABILIBUS QUÆ VISA SUNT IN MUNDO SPIRITUUM | ET IN CŒLO ANGELORUM. LONDINI, 1749-1756." | IN TWELVE VOLUMES. | VOLUME V | GENESIS, CHAPTER XXVIII. TO CHAPTER XXXI. | LONDON: | PUBLISHED BY THE SWEDENBORG SOCIETY, | (INSTITUTED 1810,) | 36 BLOOMSBURY STREET, OXFORD STREET, W.C. | 1863.
verso: Matthew vi. 33. | *Seek ye first the kingdom of God and His righteousness,* | *and all these things shall be added unto you.*
half title: ARCANA CŒLESTIA.
verso: *This Work is printed at the expense of, and published for,* | "THE SOCIETY FOR PRINTING AND PUBLISHING THE | WRITINGS OF EMANUEL SWEDENBORG, INSTITUTED IN | LONDON IN THE YEAR 1810." | <short rule> | LONDON: MITCHELL AND SON, PRINTERS, WARDOUR STREET, W.
8vo
half title and title leaves, 4 pp; text of Genesis 28-31 and n 3650-4228, pp 5-384.
A reprint of En 2/36 = Hyde 681, supervised by J Spurgin; an edition of 1,000 copies was printed.
UK: soc; SWI: lau; USA: anc, shs

49/01/En 2/91 **1863** Hyde 704

ARCANA CŒLESTIA. | <short rule> | THE | HEAVENLY MYSTERIES | CONTAINED IN | THE HOLY SCRIPTURE, OR WORD OF THE LORD, | UNFOLDED, | IN AN EXPOSITION OF GENESIS AND EXODUS: | TOGETHER WITH A RELATION OF | WONDERFUL THINGS SEEN IN THE WORLD OF SPIRITS AND | IN THE HEAVEN OF ANGELS. | <short double rule> | BY EMANUEL SWEDENBORG. | <short double rule> | BEING A TRANSLATION OF HIS WORK ENTITLED | "ARCANA CŒLESTIA QUÆ IN SCRIPTURA SACRA, SEU VERBO DOMINI SUNT, DETECTA ; HIC | PRIMUM QUÆ IN GENESI. UNA CUM MIRABILIBUS QUÆ VISA SUNT IN MUNDO SPIRITUUM | ET IN CŒLO ANGELORUM. LONDINI, 1749-1756." | IN TWELVE VOLUMES. | VOLUME VI. | GENESIS, CHAPTER XXXII. TO CHAPTER XXXVIII. | LONDON: | PUBLISHED BY THE SWEDENBORG SOCIETY, | (INSTITUTED 1810,) | 36 BLOOMSBURY STREET, OXFORD STREET, W.C. | 1863.
verso: Matthew vi. 33. | *Seek ye first the kingdom of God and His righteousness,* | *and all these things shall be added unto you.*
half title: ARCANA CŒLESTIA.
verso: *This Work is printed at the expense of, and published for,* | "THE SOCIETY FOR PRINTING AND PUBLISHING THE | WRITINGS OF EMANUEL SWEDENBORG, INSTITUTED IN | LONDON IN THE YEAR 1810." | <short rule> | LONDON: MITCHELL AND SON, PRINTERS, WARDOUR STREET, W.
8vo
half title and title leaves, 4 pp; text of Genesis 32-38 and n 4229-4953, pp 5-455.
A reprint of En 2/51 = Hyde 700; an edition of 1,010 copies was printed.
UK: soc; SWI: lau; USA: anc, shs

49/01/En 2/92 **1863** Hyde 721

ARCANA CŒLESTIA. | <short rule> | THE | HEAVENLY MYSTERIES | CONTAINED IN | THE HOLY SCRIPTURE, OR WORD OF THE LORD, | UNFOLDED, | IN AN EXPOSITION OF GENESIS AND EXODUS: | TOGETHER WITH A RELATION OF | WONDERFUL THINGS SEEN IN THE WORLD OF SPIRITS AND | IN THE HEAVEN OF ANGELS. | <short double rule> | BY EMANUEL SWEDENBORG. | <short double rule> | BEING A TRANSLATION OF HIS WORK ENTITLED | "ARCANA CŒLESTIA QUÆ IN SCRIPTURA SACRA, SEU VERBO DOMINI SUNT, DETECTA; HIC | PRIMUM QUÆ IN GENESI. UNA CUM MIRABILIBUS QUÆ VISA SUNT IN MUNDO SPIRITUUM | ET IN CŒLO ANGELORUM. LONDINI, 1749-1756." | IN TWELVE VOLUMES. | VOLUME VII. | GENESIS, CHAPTER XXXIX. TO CHAPTER XLIII. | LONDON: | PUBLISHED BY THE SWEDENBORG SOCIETY, | (INSTITUTED 1810,) | 36 BLOOMSBURY STREET, OXFORD STREET, W.C. | 1863.
verso: Matthew vi. 33. | *Seek ye first the kingdom of God and His righteousness,* | *and all these things shall be added unto you.*
half title: ARCANA CŒLESTIA.
verso: *This Work is printed at the expense of, and published for,* | "THE SOCIETY FOR PRINTING AND PUBLISHING THE | WRITINGS OF EMANUEL SWEDENBORG, INSTITUTED IN | LONDON IN THE YEAR 1810." | <short rule> | LONDON: MITCHELL AND SON, PRINTERS, WARDOUR STREET, W.
8vo
half title and title leaves, 4 pp; text of Genesis 39-43 and n 4954-5727, pp 5-412.
Reprinted from En 2/52 = Hyde 716; an edition of 1,014 copies was printed.
UK: soc; SWI: lau; USA: anc, shs

49/01/En 2/93 **1863** Hyde 737

ARCANA CŒLESTIA. | <short rule> | THE | HEAVENLY MYSTERIES | CONTAINED IN | THE HOLY SCRIPTURE, OR WORD OF THE LORD, | UNFOLDED, | IN AN EXPOSITION OF GENESIS

AND EXODUS: | TOGETHER WITH A RELATION OF | WONDERFUL THINGS SEEN IN THE WORLD OF SPIRITS AND | IN THE HEAVEN OF ANGELS. | <short double rule> | BY EMANUEL SWEDENBORG. | <short double rule> | BEING A TRANSLATION OF HIS WORK ENTITLED | "ARCANA CŒLESTIA QUÆ IN SCRIPTURA SACRA, SEU VERBO DOMINI SUNT, DETECTA; HIC | PRIMUM QUÆ IN GENESI. UNA CUM MIRABILIBUS QUÆ VISA SUNT IN MUNDO SPIRITUUM | ET IN CŒLO ANGELORUM. LONDINI, 1749–1756." | IN TWELVE VOLUMES. | VOLUME VIII. | GENESIS, CHAPTER XLIV. TO CHAPTER L. | LONDON: | PUBLISHED BY THE SWEDENBORG SOCIETY, | (INSTITUTED 1810,) | 36 BLOOMSBURY STREET, OXFORD STREET, W.C. | 1863.
verso: Matthew vi. 33. | *Seek ye first the kingdom of God and His righteousness,* | *and all these things shall be added unto you.*
half title: ARCANA CŒLESTIA.
verso: *This Work is printed at the expense of, and published for,* | "THE SOCIETY FOR PRINTING AND PUBLISHING THE | WRITINGS OF EMANUEL SWEDENBORG, INSTITUTED IN | LONDON IN THE YEAR 1810."
8vo
half title and title leaves, 4 pp; text of Genesis 44-50 and n 5728-6626, pp 5-406; advertisement, pp 1-2.
Reprinted from En 2/49 = Hyde 732; an edition of 1,010 copies was printed.
UK: SOC, BOD; SWI: LAU; USA: ANC, SHS

49/01/En 2/94 **1863** Hyde 781
ARCANA CŒLESTIA. | <short rule> | THE | HEAVENLY MYSTERIES | CONTAINED IN | THE HOLY SCRIPTURE, OR WORD OF THE LORD, | UNFOLDED, | IN AN EXPOSITION OF GENESIS AND EXODUS: | TOGETHER WITH A RELATION OF | WONDERFUL THINGS SEEN IN THE WORLD OF SPIRITS AND | IN THE HEAVEN OF ANGELS. | <short double rule> | BY EMANUEL SWEDENBORG. | <short double rule> | BEING A TRANSLATION OF HIS WORK ENTITLED | "ARCANA CŒLESTIA QUÆ IN SCRIPTURA SACRA, SEU VERBO DOMINI SUNT, DETECTA; HIC | PRIMUM QUÆ IN GENESI. UNA CUM MIRABILIBUS QUÆ VISA SUNT IN MUNDO SPIRITUUM | ET IN CŒLO ANGELORUM. LONDINI, 1749–1756." | IN TWELVE VOLUMES. | VOLUME XI. | EXODUS, CHAPTER XXII. TO CHAPTER XXVIII. | LONDON: | PUBLISHED BY THE SWEDENBORG SOCIETY, | (INSTITUTED 1810,) | 36 BLOOMSBURY STREET, OXFORD STREET, W.C. | 1863.
verso: Matthew vi. 33. | *Seek ye first the kingdom of God and His righteousness,* | *and all these things shall be added unto you.*
half title: ARCANA CŒLESTIA.
verso: *This Work is printed at the expense of, and published for,* | "THE SOCIETY FOR PRINTING AND PUBLISHING THE | WRITINGS OF EMANUEL SWEDENBORG, INSTITUTED IN | LONDON IN THE YEAR 1810." | <short rule> | MITCHELL AND SON, PRINTERS, WARDOUR STREET, W.
8vo
half title and title leaves, 4 pp; text of Exodus 22-28 and n 9112-9973, pp 5-603; note, 1 p; advertisement, pp 1-2.
Reprinted from En 2/37 = Hyde 777; an edition of 1,013 copies was printed.
UK: SOC; SWI: LAU; USA: ANC, SHS

49/01/En 2/95 **1863** Hyde 790
ARCANA CŒLESTIA. | <short rule> | THE | HEAVENLY MYSTERIES | CONTAINED IN | THE HOLY SCRIPTURE, OR WORD OF THE LORD, | UNFOLDED, | IN AN EXPOSITION OF GENESIS AND EXODUS: | TOGETHER WITH A RELATION OF | WONDERFUL THINGS SEEN IN THE WORLD OF SPIRITS AND | IN THE HEAVEN OF ANGELS. | <short double rule> | BY EMANUEL SWEDENBORG. | <short double rule> | BEING A TRANSLATION OF HIS WORK ENTITLED |

"ARCANA CŒLESTIA QUÆ IN SCRIPTURA SACRA, SEU VERBO DOMINI SUNT, DETECTA; HIC | PRIMUM QUÆ IN GENESI. UNA CUM MIRABILIBUS QUÆ VISA SUNT IN MUNDO SPIRITUUM | ET IN CŒLO ANGELORUM. LONDINI, 1749-1756." | IN TWELVE VOLUMES. | VOLUME XII. | EXODUS, CHAPTER XXIX. TO CHAPTER XL. | LONDON: | PUBLISHED BY THE SWEDENBORG SOCIETY, | (INSTITUTED 1810,) | 36 BLOOMSBURY STREET, OXFORD STREET, W.C. | 1863.
verso: Matthew vi. 33. | *Seek ye first the kingdom of God and His righteousness,* | *and all these things shall be added unto you.*
half title: ARCANA CŒLESTIA.
verso: This Work is printed at the expense of, and published by, | "THE SOCIETY FOR PRINTING AND PUBLISHING THE | WRITINGS OF EMANUEL SWEDENBORG, INSTITUTED IN | LONDON IN THE YEAR 1810." | <short rule> | LONDON: MITCHELL AND SON, PRINTERS, WARDOUR STREET, W.
8vo
half title and title leaves, 4 pp; text of Exodus 29-40 and n 9974-10837, pp 5-565; The translator's prayer on finishing the work, pp 567-568; advertisement, 2 pp.
Reprinted from En 2/38 = Hyde 786; an edition of 1,012 copies was printed.
UK: SOC; SWI: LAU; USA: ANC, SHS

49/01/En 2/96 **1863** Hyde 655
<<ARCANA CŒLESTIA. | <short rule> | THE | HEAVENLY ARCANA | CONTAINED IN | THE HOLY SCRIPTURES OR WORD OF THE LORD | UNFOLDED, | BEGINNING WITH THE BOOK OF GENESIS: | TOGETHER WITH | WONDERFUL THINGS SEEN IN THE WORLD OF SPIRITS | AND IN THE HEAVEN OF ANGELS. | <short rule> | *Translated from the Latin of* | EMANUEL SWEDENBORG, | *Servant of the Lord Jesus Christ.* | <short rule> | VOL. III. | NEW YORK: | AMERICAN SWEDENBORG PRINTING AND PUBLISHING SOCIETY. | 1863.>>
verso: <<*Published by* THE AMERICAN SWEDENBORG PRINTING AND PUBLISHING | SOCIETY, *organized for the purpose of Stereotyping, Printing, and* | *Publishing Uniform Editions of the Theological Writings of* EMANUEL | SWEDENBORG, *and incorporated in the State of New York* A. D. 1850>>
half title: <<ARCANA CŒLESTIA>>
8vo
half title and title leaves, 4 pp; text of Genesis 20-25 and n 2495-3352, pp 5-515.
The same as En 2/79 = Hyde 652.
Copy not seen; description deduced from En 2/124. See also En 2/61 = Hyde 650.
USA: ANC, SHS

49/01/En 2/97 **1863** Hyde 670
<<ARCANA CŒLESTIA. | <short rule> | THE HEAVENLY ARCANA | CONTAINED IN | THE HOLY SCRIPTURES OR WORD OF THE LORD | UNFOLDED, | BEGINNING WITH THE BOOK OF GENESIS: | TOGETHER WITH WONDERFUL THINGS SEEN IN THE WORLD OF SPIRITS | AND IN THE HEAVEN OF ANGELS. | <short rule> | *Translated from the Latin of* | EMANUEL SWEDENBORG, | *Servant of the Lord Jesus Christ.* | <short rule> | VOL. IV. | NEW YORK: | AMERICAN SWEDENBORG PRINTING AND PUBLISHING SOCIETY. | 1863.>>
verso: <<*Published by* THE AMERICAN SWEDENBORG PRINTING AND PUBLISHING | SOCIETY, *organized for the purpose of Stereotyping, Printing, and* | *Publishing Uniform Editions of the Theological Writings of* EMANUEL | SWEDENBORG, *and incorporated in the State of New York* A. D. 1850>>
half title: <<ARCANA CŒLESTIA>>
8vo
half title and title leaves, 4 pp; text of Genesis 26-31 and n 3353-4228, pp 5-557.

The same as En 2/62 = Hyde 666.
Copy not seen; description deduced from En 2/125.
USA: ANC, SHS

49/01/En 2/98 **1863** Hyde 688

<<ARCANA CŒLESTIA. | <short rule> | THE | HEAVENLY ARCANA | CONTAINED IN | THE HOLY SCRIPTURES OR WORD OF THE LORD | UNFOLDED, | BEGINNING WITH THE BOOK OF GENESIS: | TOGETHER WITH | WONDERFUL THINGS SEEN IN THE WORLD OF SPIRITS | AND IN THE HEAVEN OF ANGELS. | *Translated from the Latin of* | EMANUEL SWEDENBORG, | *Servant of the Lord Jesus Christ.* | VOL. V. | NEW YORK: AMERICAN SWEDENBORG PRINTING AND PUBLISHING SOCIETY. 1863.>>
verso: <<*Published by* THE AMERICAN SWEDENBORG PRINTING AND PUBLISHING | SOCIETY, *organized for the purpose of Stereotyping, Printing, and* | *Publishing Uniform Editions of the Theological Writings of* EMANUEL | SWEDENBORG, *and incorporated in the State of New York* A. D. 1850>>
half title: <<ARCANA CŒLESTIA>>
8vo
half title and title leaves, 4 pp; text of Genesis 32-40 and n 4229-5190, pp 5-607.
The same as En 2/82 = Hyde 686.
Copy not seen; description deduced from En 2/125 and 126.
USA: ANC, SHS

49/01/En 2/99 **1863** Hyde 705

<<ARCANA CŒLESTIA. | <short rule> | THE | HEAVENLY ARCANA | CONTAINED IN | THE HOLY SCRIPTURES OR WORD OF THE LORD | UNFOLDED, | BEGINNING WITH THE BOOK OF GENESIS: | TOGETHER WITH | WONDERFUL THINGS SEEN IN THE WORLD OF SPIRITS | AND IN THE HEAVEN OF ANGELS. | <short rule> | *Translated from the Latin of* | EMANUEL SWEDENBORG, | *Servant of the Lord Jesus Christ.* | <short rule> | VOL. VI. | NEW YORK: | AMERICAN SWEDENBORG PRINTING AND PUBLISHING SOCIETY. | 1863.>>
verso: <<*Published by* THE AMERICAN SWEDENBORG PRINTING AND PUBLISHING | SOCIETY, *organized for the purpose of Stereotyping, Printing, and* | *Publishing Uniform Editions of the Theological Writings of* EMANUEL | SWEDENBORG, *and incorporated in the State of New York* A. D. 1850>>
half title: <<ARCANA CŒLESTIA>>
8vo
half title and title leaves, 4 pp; text of Genesis 41-49 and n 5191-6496, pp 5-624.
The same as En 2/75 = Hyde 702.
Copy not seen; description deduced from En 2/126.
USA: ANC, SHS

49/01/En 2/100 **1863** Hyde 752/a

<<ARCANA CŒLESTIA. | <short rule> | THE | HEAVENLY ARCANA | CONTAINED IN | THE HOLY SCRIPTURES OR WORD OF THE LORD | UNFOLDED, | BEGINNING WITH THE BOOK OF GENESIS: | TOGETHER WITH | WONDERFUL THINGS SEEN IN THE WORLD OF SPIRITS | AND IN THE HEAVEN OF ANGELS. | <short rule> | *Translated from the Latin of* | EMANUEL SWEDENBORG, | *Servant of the Lord Jesus Christ.* | <short rule> | VOL. IX. | NEW YORK: | AMERICAN SWEDENBORG PRINTING AND PUBLISHING SOCIETY. | 1863.>>
verso: <<*Published by* THE AMERICAN SWEDENBORG PRINTING AND PUBLISHING | SOCIETY, *organized for the purpose of Stereotyping, Printing, and* | *Publishing Uniform Editions of*

the Theological Writings of EMANUEL | SWEDENBORG, *and incorporated in the State of New York* A. D. 1850>>
half title: <<ARCANA CŒLESTIA>>
8vo
half title and title leaves, 4 pp; text of Exodus 22-28 and n 9112-9973, pp 5-607.
Copy not seen; description deduced from En 2/128.
USA: ANC

49/01/En 2/101 **1863** Hyde 767
<<ARCANA CŒLESTIA. | <short rule> | THE | HEAVENLY ARCANA | CONTAINED IN | THE HOLY SCRIPTURES OR WORD OF THE LORD | UNFOLDED, | BEGINNING WITH THE BOOK OF GENESIS: | TOGETHER WITH WONDERFUL THINGS SEEN IN THE WORLD OF SPIRITS | AND IN THE HEAVEN OF ANGELS. | <short rule> | *Translated from the Latin of* | EMANUEL SWEDENBORG, *Servant of the Lord Jesus Christ.* | VOL. X. | NEW YORK: | AMERICAN SWEDENBORG PRINTING AND PUBLISHING SOCIETY. | 1863.>>
verso: <<*Published by* THE AMERICAN SWEDENBORG PRINTING AND PUBLISHING | SOCIETY, *organized for the purpose of Stereotyping, Printing, and* | *Publishing Uniform Editions of the Theological Writings of* EMANUEL | SWEDENBORG, *and incorporated in the State of New York* A.D. 1850>>
half title: <<ARCANA CŒLESTIA>>
8vo
half title and title leaves, 4 pp; text of Exodus 29-40 and n 9974-10837, pp 5-569.
The same as En 2/81 = Hyde 765.
Copy not seen; description deduced from En 2/81.
USA: ANC, SHS

49/01/En 2/102 **1864** Hyde 768
ARCANA CŒLESTIA. | <short rule> | THE | HEAVENLY MYSTERIES | CONTAINED IN | THE HOLY SCRIPTURE, OR WORD OF THE LORD, | UNFOLDED, | IN AN EXPOSITION OF GENESIS AND EXODUS: | TOGETHER WITH A RELATION OF | WONDERFUL THINGS SEEN IN THE WORLD OF SPIRITS AND | IN THE HEAVEN OF ANGELS. | <short double rule> | BY EMANUEL SWEDENBORG. | <short double rule> | BEING A TRANSLATION OF HIS WORK ENTITLED | "ARCANA CŒLESTIA QUÆ IN SCRIPTURA SACRA, SEU VERBO DOMINI SUNT, DETECTA; HIC | PRIMUM QUÆ IN GENESI. UNA CUM MIRABILIBUS QUÆ VISA SUNT IN MUNDO SPIRITUUM | ET IN CŒLO ANGELORUM. LONDINI, 1749-1756." | IN TWELVE VOLUMES. | VOLUME X. | EXODUS, CHAPTER XIII. TO CHAPTER XXI. | LONDON: | PUBLISHED BY THE SWEDENBORG SOCIETY, | (INSTITUTED 1810,) | 36 BLOOMSBURY STREET, OXFORD STREET, W.C. | 1864.
verso: Matthew vi. 33. | *Seek ye first the kingdom of God and His righteousness,* | *and all these things shall be added unto you.*
half title: ARCANA CŒLESTIA.
verso: *This Work is printed at the expense of, and published for,* | "THE SOCIETY FOR PRINTING AND PUBLISHING THE | WRITINGS OF EMANUEL SWEDENBORG, INSTITUTED IN | LONDON IN THE YEAR 1810." | <short rule> | MITCHELL AND SON, PRINTERS, WARDOUR STREET, W.
8vo
half title and title leaves, 4 pp; text of Exodus 13-21 and n 8033-9111, pp 5-514; catalogue, 2 pp.
Revised by S M Warren; an edition of 1,000 copies was printed.
UK: SOC; SWI: LAU; USA: ANC, SHS

49/01/En 2/103 **1865** Hyde 633/a

<<ARCANA COELESTIA. | <short rule> | THE | HEAVENLY ARCANA | CONTAINED IN THE HOLY SCRIPTURES OR WORD OF THE LORD | UNFOLDED, | BEGINNING WITH THE BOOK OF GENESIS: | TOGETHER WITH | WONDERFUL THINGS SEEN IN THE WORLD OF SPIRITS | AND IN THE HEAVEN OF ANGELS. | <short rule> | *Translated from the Latin of* | EMANUEL SWEDENBORG, | *Servant of the Lord Jesus Christ.* | <short rule> | VOL. II. | NEW YORK: AMERICAN SWEDENBORG PRINTING AND PUBLISHING SOCIETY. | 1865.>>

verso: <<*Published by* THE AMERICAN SWEDENBORG PRINTING AND PUBLISHING | SOCIETY, *organized for the purpose of Stereotyping, Printing, and* | *Publishing Uniform Editions of the Theological Writings of* EMANUEL | SWEDENBORG, *and incorporated in the State of New York* A.D. 1850>>

half title: <<ARCANA CŒLESTIA>>

8vo

half title and title leaves, 4 pp; text of Genesis 12-19 and n 1383-2494, pp 5-576.

Copy not seen; description deduced from En 2/60.

USA: ANC

49/01/En 2/104 **1865** Hyde 752/b

<<ARCANA COELESTIA. | <short rule> | THE | HEAVENLY ARCANA | CONTAINED IN | THE HOLY SCRIPTURES OR WORD OF THE LORD | UNFOLDED, | BEGINNING WITH THE BOOK OF GENESIS: | TOGETHER WITH | WONDERFUL THINGS SEEN IN THE WORLD OF SPIRITS | AND IN THE HEAVEN OF ANGELS. | <short rule> | *Translated from the Latin of* | EMANUEL SWEDENBORG, | *Servant of the Lord Jesus Christ.* | <short rule> | VOL. IX. | NEW YORK: | AMERICAN SWEDENBORG PRINTING AND PUBLISHING SOCIETY. | 1865.>>

verso: <<*Published by* THE AMERICAN SWEDENBORG PRINTING AND PUBLISHING | SOCIETY, *organized for the purpose of Stereotyping, Printing, and* | *Publishing Uniform Editions of the Theological Writings of* EMANUEL | SWEDENBORG, *and incorporated in the State of New York* A.D. 1850>>

half title: <<ARCANA CŒLESTIA>>

8vo

half title and title leaves, 4 pp; text of Exodus 22-28 and n 9112-9973, pp 5-607.

The same as En 2/100 = Hyde 752/a.

Copy not seen; description deduced from En 2/128.

USA: ANC

49/01/En 2/105 **1865** Hyde 768/a

<<ARCANA COELESTIA. | <short rule> | THE | HEAVENLY ARCANA | CONTAINED IN | THE HOLY SCRIPTURES OR WORD OF THE LORD | UNFOLDED, | BEGINNING WITH THE BOOK OF GENESIS: | TOGETHER WITH | WONDERFUL THINGS SEEN IN THE WORLD OF SPIRITS | AND IN THE HEAVEN OF ANGELS. | <short rule> | *Translated from the Latin of* | EMANUEL SWEDENBORG, | *Servant of the Lord Jesus Christ.* | <short rule> | VOL. X. | NEW YORK: | AMERICAN SWEDENBORG PRINTING AND PUBLISHING SOCIETY. | 1865.>>

verso: <<*Published by* THE AMERICAN SWEDENBORG PRINTING AND PUBLISHING | SOCIETY, *organized for the purpose of Stereotyping, Printing, and* | *Publishing Uniform Editions of the Theological Writings of* EMANUEL | SWEDENBORG, *and incorporated in the State of New York* A.D. 1850>>

half title: <<ARCANA CŒLESTIA>>

8vo

half title and title leaves, 4 pp; text of Exodus 29-40 and n 9974-10837, pp 5-569.

The same as En 2/101 = Hyde 767.
Copy not seen; description deduced from En 2/128.
USA: ANC

49/01/En 2/106 **1866** **Hyde 655/a**

<<ARCANA COELESTIA. | <short rule> | THE | HEAVENLY ARCANA | CONTAINED IN | THE HOLY SCRIPTURES OR WORD OF THE LORD | UNFOLDED, | BEGINNING WITH THE BOOK OF GENESIS: | TOGETHER WITH | WONDERFUL THINGS SEEN IN THE WORLD OF SPIRITS | AND IN THE HEAVEN OF ANGELS. | <short rule> | *Translated from the Latin of* | EMANUEL SWEDENBORG, | *Servant of the Lord Jesus Christ.* | <short rule> | VOL. III. | NEW YORK: | AMERICAN SWEDENBORG PRINTING AND PUBLISHING SOCIETY. | 1866.>>
verso: <<*Published by* THE AMERICAN SWEDENBORG PRINTING AND PUBLISHING | SOCIETY, *organized for the purpose of Stereotyping, Printing, and* | *Publishing Uniform Editions of the Theological Writings of* EMANUEL | SWEDENBORG, *and incorporated in the State of New York* A.D. 1850>>
half title: <<ARCANA CŒLESTIA>>
8vo
half title and title leaves, 4 pp; text of Genesis 20-25 and n 2495-3352, pp 5-515.
The same as En 2/96 = Hyde 655.
Copy not seen; description deduced from En 2/124.
USA: ANC

49/01/En 2/107 **1866** **Hyde 670/a**

<<ARCANA COELESTIA. | <short rule> | THE HEAVENLY ARCANA | CONTAINED IN | THE HOLY SCRIPTURES OR WORD OF THE LORD | UNFOLDED, | BEGINNING WITH THE BOOK OF GENESIS: | TOGETHER WITH | WONDERFUL THINGS SEEN IN THE WORLD OF SPIRITS | AND IN THE HEAVEN OF ANGELS. | <short rule> | *Translated from the Latin of* | EMANUEL SWEDENBORG, | *Servant of the Lord Jesus Christ.* | <short rule> | VOL. IV. | NEW YORK: | AMERICAN SWEDENBORG PRINTING AND PUBLISHING SOCIETY. | 1866.>>
verso: <<*Published by* THE AMERICAN SWEDENBORG PRINTING AND PUBLISHING | SOCIETY, *organized for the purpose of Stereotyping, Printing, and* | *Publishing Uniform Editions of the Theological Writings of* EMANUEL | SWEDENBORG, *and incorporated in the State of New York* A.D. 1850>>
half title: <<ARCANA CŒLESTIA>>
8vo
half title and title leaves, 4 pp; text of Genesis 26-31 and n 3353-4228, pp 5-557.
The same as En 2/97 = Hyde 670.
Copy not seen; description deduced from En 2/114.
USA: ANC

49/01/En 2/108 **1866** **Hyde 688/a**

<<ARCANA COELESTIA. | <short rule> | THE | HEAVENLY ARCANA | CONTAINED IN | THE HOLY SCRIPTURES OR WORD OF THE LORD | UNFOLDED, | BEGINNING WITH THE BOOK OF GENESIS: | TOGETHER WITH | WONDERFUL THINGS SEEN IN THE WORLD OF SPIRITS | AND IN THE HEAVEN OF ANGELS. | <short rule> | *Translated from the Latin of* | EMANUEL SWEDENBORG, | *Servant of the Lord Jesus Christ.* | <short rule> | VOL. V. | NEW YORK: | AMERICAN SWEDENBORG PRINTING AND PUBLISHING SOCIETY. | 1866.>>
verso: <<*Published by* THE AMERICAN SWEDENBORG PRINTING AND PUBLISHING | SOCIETY, *organized for the purpose of Stereotyping, Printing, and* | *Publishing Uniform Editions of*

the Theological Writings of EMANUEL | SWEDENBORG, *and incorporated in the State of New York* A.D. 1850>>
half title: <<ARCANA CŒLESTIA>>
8vo
half title and title leaves, 4 pp; text of Genesis 32-40 and n 4229-5190, pp 5-607.
The same as En 2/98 = Hyde 688.
Copy not seen; description deduced from En 2/124 and 126.
USA: ANC

49/01/En 2/109 **1866** Hyde 753
ARCANA CŒLESTIA | <short rule> | THE | HEAVENLY MYSTERIES | CONTAINED IN | THE HOLY SCRIPTURE, OR WORD OF THE LORD, | UNFOLDED, | IN AN EXPOSITION OF GENESIS AND EXODUS: | TOGETHER WITH A RELATION OF | WONDERFUL THINGS SEEN IN THE WORLD OF SPIRITS AND | IN THE HEAVEN OF ANGELS. | <short double rule> | BY EMANUEL SWEDENBORG | <short double rule> | BEING A TRANSLATION OF HIS WORK ENTITLED | "ARCANA CŒLESTIA QUÆ IN SCRIPTURA SACRA, SEU VERBO DOMINI SUNT, DETECTA; HIC | QUÆ IN EXODO. UNA CUM MIRABILIBUS QUÆ VISA SUNT IN MUNDO SPIRITUUM ET IN | CŒLO ANGELORUM. LONDINI, 1749-1756." | IN TWELVE VOLUMES. | VOLUME IX. | EXODUS, CHAPTER I. TO CHAPTER XII. | LONDON: | PUBLISHED BY THE SWEDENBORG SOCIETY, | (INSTITUTED 1810,) | 36 BLOOMSBURY STREET, OXFORD STREET, W.C.| 1866.
verso: Matthew vi. 33. | *Seek ye first the kingdom of God and His righteousness,* | *and all these things shall be added unto you.* | <short rule> | LONDON: MITCHELL AND HUGHES, PRINTERS, WARDOUR STREET, W.
half title: ARCANA CŒLESTIA.
8vo
half title and title leaves, 4 pp; text of Exodus 1-12 and n 6627-8032, pp 5-535.
Revised by J Bayley; an edition of 1,000 copies was printed.
UK: SOC, CON; SWI: LAU; USA: ANC, SHS

49/01/En 2/110 **1867** Hyde 606/a
<<ARCANA CŒLESTIA. | <short rule> | THE | HEAVENLY ARCANA | CONTAINED IN | THE HOLY SCRIPTURES OR WORD OF THE LORD | UNFOLDED, | BEGINNING WITH THE BOOK OF GENESIS: | TOGETHER WITH | WONDERFUL THINGS SEEN IN THE WORLD OF SPIRITS | AND IN THE HEAVEN OF ANGELS. | <short rule> | *Translated from the Latin of* | EMANUEL SWEDENBORG, | *Servant of the Lord Jesus Christ.* | <short rule> | VOL. I. | NEW YORK: | AMERICAN SWEDENBORG PRINTING AND PUBLISHING SOCIETY. | 1867.>>
verso: <<*Published by* THE AMERICAN SWEDENBORG PRINTING AND PUBLISHING | SOCIETY, *organized for the purpose of Stereotyping, Printing, and* | *Publishing Uniform Editions of the Theological Writings of* EMANUEL | SWEDENBORG, *and incorporated in the State of New York* A.D. 1850>>
half title: <<ARCANA CŒLESTIA.>>
8vo
half title and title leaves, 4 pp; text of Genesis 1-11 and n 1-1382, pp 1-568.
The same as En 2/84 = Hyde 606.
Copy not seen; description deduced from En 2/132.
USA: ANC

49/01/En 2/111 **1867** Hyde 721/a
<<ARCANA CŒLESTIA. | <short rule> | THE | HEAVENLY ARCANA | CONTAINED IN | THE

HOLY SCRIPTURES OR WORD OF THE LORD | UNFOLDED, | BEGINNING WITH THE BOOK OF GENESIS: | TOGETHER WITH | WONDERFUL THINGS SEEN IN THE WORLD OF SPIRITS | AND IN THE HEAVEN OF ANGELS. | <short rule> | *Translated from the Latin of* | EMANUEL SWEDENBORG, | *Servant of the Lord Jesus Christ.* | <short rule> | VOL. VII. | NEW YORK: | AMERICAN SWEDENBORG PRINTING AND PUBLISHING SOCIETY. | 1867.>>
verso: <<*Published by* THE AMERICAN SWEDENBORG PRINTING AND PUBLISHING | SOCIETY, *organized for the purpose of Stereotyping, Printing, and* | *Publishing Uniform Editions of the Theological Writings of* EMANUEL | SWEDENBORG, *and incorporated in the State of New York* A.D. 1850>>
half title: <<ARCANA CŒLESTIA.>>
8vo
half title and title leaves, 4 pp; text of Genesis 50, Exodus 1-12, and n 6497-8032, pp 5-627.
The same as En 2/85 = Hyde 720.
Copy not seen; description deduced from En 2/129 and 132.
USA: ANC

49/01/En 2/112 **1868** Hyde 634
<<ARCANA CŒLESTIA. | <short rule> | THE | HEAVENLY ARCANA | CONTAINED IN | THE HOLY SCRIPTURES OR WORD OF THE LORD | UNFOLDED, | BEGINNING WITH THE BOOK OF GENESIS: | TOGETHER WITH | WONDERFUL THINGS SEEN IN THE WORLD OF SPIRITS | AND IN THE HEAVEN OF ANGELS. | <short rule> | *Translated from the Latin of* | EMANUEL SWEDENBORG, | *Servant of the Lord Jesus Christ.* | <short rule> | VOL. II. | NEW YORK: | AMERICAN SWEDENBORG PRINTING AND PUBLISHING SOCIETY, | BIBLE HOUSE, ASTOR PLACE, ROOM NO. 47. | 1868.>>
verso: <<*Published by* THE AMERICAN SWEDENBORG PRINTING AND PUBLISHING | SOCIETY, *organized for the purpose of Stereotyping, Printing, and* | *Publishing Uniform Editions of the Theological Writings of* EMANUEL | SWEDENBORG, *and incorporated in the State of New York* A.D. 1850>>
half title: <<ARCANA CŒLESTIA.>>
8vo
half title and title leaves, 4 pp; text of Genesis 12-19 and n 1383-2494, pp 5-576.
The same as En 2/60 = Hyde 630; an edition of 500 copies was printed.
Copy not seen; description deduced from En 2/60.
USA: ANC

49/01/En 2/113 **1868** Hyde 656
<<ARCANA CŒLESTIA. | <short rule> | THE | HEAVENLY ARCANA | CONTAINED IN | THE HOLY SCRIPTURES OR WORD OF THE LORD | UNFOLDED, | BEGINNING WITH THE BOOK OF GENESIS: | TOGETHER WITH | WONDERFUL THINGS SEEN IN THE WORLD OF SPIRITS | AND IN THE HEAVEN OF ANGELS. | <short rule> | *Translated from the Latin of* | EMANUEL SWEDENBORG, | *Servant of the Lord Jesus Christ.* | <short rule> | VOL. III. | NEW YORK: | AMERICAN SWEDENBORG PRINTING AND PUBLISHING SOCIETY. | 1868.>>
verso: <<*Published by* THE AMERICAN SWEDENBORG PRINTING AND PUBLISHING | SOCIETY, *organized for the purpose of Stereotyping, Printing, and* | *Publishing Uniform Editions of the Theological Writings of* EMANUEL | SWEDENBORG, *and incorporated in the State of New York* A.D. 1850>>
half title: <<ARCANA CŒLESTIA.>>
8vo
half title and title leaves, 4 pp; text of Genesis 20-25 and n 2495-3352, pp 5-515.
The same as En 2/96 = Hyde 655.

Copy not seen; description deduced from En 2/96 and 124.
USA: ANC

49/01/En 2/114 **1868** Hyde 671

<<ARCANA CŒLESTIA. | <short rule> | THE | HEAVENLY ARCANA | CONTAINED IN | THE HOLY SCRIPTURES OR WORD OF THE LORD | UNFOLDED, | BEGINNING WITH THE BOOK OF GENESIS: | TOGETHER WITH | WONDERFUL THINGS SEEN IN THE WORLD OF SPIRITS | AND IN THE HEAVEN OF ANGELS. | <short rule> | *Translated from the Latin of* | EMANUEL SWEDENBORG, | *Servant of the Lord Jesus Christ.* | <short rule> | VOL. IV. | NEW YORK: | AMERICAN SWEDENBORG PRINTING AND PUBLISHING SOCIETY. | 1868.>>
verso: <<*Published by* THE AMERICAN SWEDENBORG PRINTING AND PUBLISHING | SOCIETY, *organized for the purpose of Stereotyping, Printing, and* | *Publishing Uniform Editions of the Theological Writings of* EMANUEL | SWEDENBORG, *and incorporated in the State of New York* A.D. 1850>>
half title: <<ARCANA CŒLESTIA.>>
8vo
half title and title leaves, 4 pp; text of Genesis 26-31 and n 3353-4228, pp 5-557.
The same as En 2/97 = Hyde 670.
Copy not seen; description deduced from En 2/97 and 125.
USA: ANC

49/01/En 2/115 **1868** Hyde 706

<<ARCANA CŒLESTIA. | <short rule> | THE | HEAVENLY ARCANA | CONTAINED IN | THE HOLY SCRIPTURES OR WORD OF THE LORD | UNFOLDED, | BEGINNING WITH THE BOOK OF GENESIS: | TOGETHER WITH | WONDERFUL THINGS SEEN IN THE WORLD OF SPIRITS | AND IN THE HEAVEN OF ANGELS. | <short rule> | *Translated from the Latin of* | EMANUEL SWEDENBORG, | *Servant of the Lord Jesus Christ.* | <short rule> | VOL. VI. | NEW YORK: | AMERICAN SWEDENBORG PRINTING AND PUBLISHING SOCIETY. | 1868.>>
verso: <<*Published by* THE AMERICAN SWEDENBORG PRINTING AND PUBLISHING | SOCIETY, *organized for the purpose of Stereotyping, Printing, and* | *Publishing Uniform Editions of the Theological Writings of* EMANUEL | SWEDENBORG, *and incorporated in the State of New York* A.D. 1850>>
half title: <<ARCANA CŒLESTIA.>>
8vo
half title and title leaves, 4 pp; text of Genesis 41-49 and n 5191-6496, p 5-624.
The same as En 2/99 = Hyde 705.
Copy not seen; description deduced from En 2/99 and 126.
USA: ANC

49/01/En 2/116 **1868** Hyde 738

<<ARCANA CŒLESTIA. | <short rule> | THE | HEAVENLY ARCANA | CONTAINED IN | THE HOLY SCRIPTURES OR WORD OF THE LORD | UNFOLDED, | BEGINNING WITH THE BOOK OF GENESIS: | TOGETHER WITH | WONDERFUL THINGS SEEN IN THE WORLD OF SPIRITS | AND IN THE HEAVEN OF ANGELS. | <short rule> | *Translated from the Latin of* | EMANUEL SWEDENBORG, | *Servant of the Lord Jesus Christ.* | <short rule> | VOL. VIII. | NEW YORK: | AMERICAN SWEDENBORG PRINTING AND PUBLISHING SOCIETY. | 1868.>>
verso: <<*Published by* THE AMERICAN SWEDENBORG PRINTING AND PUBLISHING | SOCIETY, *organized for the purpose of Stereotyping, Printing, and* | *Publishing Uniform Editions of the Theological Writings of* EMANUEL | SWEDENBORG, *and incorporated in the State of New York* A.D. 1850>>

half title: <<ARCANA CŒLESTIA.>>
8vo
half title and title leaves, 4 pp; text of Exodus 13-21 and n 8033-9111, pp 5-543.
The same as En 2/86 = Hyde 736.
Copy not seen; description deduced from En 2/86 and 127.
USA: ANC, SHS

49/01/En 2/117 **1868** Hyde 754

<<ARCANA CŒLESTIA. | <short rule> | THE | HEAVENLY ARCANA | CONTAINED IN | THE HOLY SCRIPTURES OR WORD OF THE LORD | UNFOLDED, | BEGINNING WITH THE BOOK OF GENESIS: | TOGETHER WITH | WONDERFUL THINGS SEEN IN THE WORLD OF SPIRITS | AND IN THE HEAVEN OF ANGELS. | <short rule> | *Translated from the Latin of* | EMANUEL SWEDENBORG, | *Servant of the Lord Jesus Christ.* | <short rule> | VOL. IX. | NEW YORK: | AMERICAN SWEDENBORG PRINTING AND PUBLISHING SOCIETY. | 1868.>>
verso: <<*Published by* THE AMERICAN SWEDENBORG PRINTING AND PUBLISHING | SOCIETY, *organized for the purpose of Stereotyping, Printing, and* | *Publishing Uniform Editions of the Theological Writings of* EMANUEL | SWEDENBORG, *and incorporated in the State of New York* A.D. 1850>>
half title: <<ARCANA CŒLESTIA.>>
8vo
half title and title leaves, 4 pp; text of Exodus 22-28 and n 9112-9973, pp 5-607.
The same as En 2/80 = Hyde 751.
Copy not seen; description deduced from En 2/80 and 128.
USA: ANC, SHS

49/01/En 2/118 **1868** Hyde 769

<<ARCANA CŒLESTIA. | <short rule> | THE | HEAVENLY ARCANA | CONTAINED IN | THE HOLY SCRIPTURES OR WORD OF THE LORD | UNFOLDED, | BEGINNING WITH THE BOOK OF GENESIS: | TOGETHER WITH | WONDERFUL THINGS SEEN IN THE WORLD OF SPIRITS | AND IN THE HEAVEN OF ANGELS. | <short rule> | *Translated from the Latin of* | EMANUEL SWEDENBORG, | *Servant of the Lord Jesus Christ.*| <short rule> | VOL. X. | NEW YORK: | AMERICAN SWEDENBORG PRINTING AND PUBLISHING SOCIETY. | 1868.>>
verso: <<*Published by* THE AMERICAN SWEDENBORG PRINTING AND PUBLISHING | SOCIETY, *organized for the purpose of Stereotyping, Printing, and* | *Publishing Uniform Editions of the Theological Writings of* EMANUEL | SWEDENBORG, *and incorporated in the State of New York* A.D. 1850>>
half title: <<ARCANA CŒLESTIA.>>
8vo
half title and title leaves, 4 pp; text of Exodus 22-28 and n 9974-10837, pp 5-569.
The same as En 2/101 = Hyde 767.
Copy not seen; description deduced from En 2/81.
USA: ANC, SHS

49/01/En 2/119 **1869** Hyde 607

<<ARCANA CŒLESTIA. | <short rule> | THE | HEAVENLY ARCANA | CONTAINED IN | THE HOLY SCRIPTURES OR WORD OF THE LORD | UNFOLDED, | BEGINNING WITH THE BOOK OF GENESIS: | TOGETHER WITH | WONDERFUL THINGS SEEN IN THE WORLD OF SPIRITS | AND IN THE HEAVEN OF ANGELS. | <short rule> | *Translated from the Latin of* | EMANUEL SWEDENBORG, | *Servant of the Lord Jesus Christ.* | <short rule> | VOL. I. | NEW YORK: | AMERICAN SWEDENBORG PRINTING AND PUBLISHING SOCIETY. | 1869.>>

verso: <<*Published by* THE AMERICAN SWEDENBORG PRINTING AND PUBLISHING | SOCIETY, *organized for the purpose of Stereotyping, Printing, and | Publishing Uniform Editions of the Theological Writings of* EMANUEL | SWEDENBORG, *and incorporated in the State of New York* A.D. 1850>>
half title: <<ARCANA CŒLESTIA.>>
8vo
half title and title leaves, 4 pp; text of Genesis 1-11 and n 1-1382, pp 1-568.
The same as En 2/84 = Hyde 606; an edition of 500 copies was printed.
Copy not seen; description deduced from En 2/124 and 132.
USA: ANC

49/01/En 2/120 **1869** Hyde 689
<<ARCANA CŒLESTIA. | <short rule> | THE | HEAVENLY ARCANA | CONTAINED IN | THE HOLY SCRIPTURES OR WORD OF THE LORD | UNFOLDED, | BEGINNING WITH THE BOOK OF GENESIS: | TOGETHER WITH | WONDERFUL THINGS SEEN IN THE WORLD OF SPIRITS | AND IN THE HEAVEN OF ANGELS. | <short rule> | *Translated from the Latin of* | EMANUEL SWEDENBORG, | *Servant of the Lord Jesus Christ.* | <short rule> | VOL. V. | NEW YORK: | AMERICAN SWEDENBORG PRINTING AND PUBLISHING SOCIETY. | 1869.>>
verso: <<*Published by* THE AMERICAN SWEDENBORG PRINTING AND PUBLISHING | SOCIETY, *organized for the purpose of Stereotyping, Printing, and | Publishing Uniform Editions of the Theological Writings of* EMANUEL | SWEDENBORG, *and incorporated in the State of New York* A.D. 1850>>
half title: <<ARCANA CŒLESTIA.>>
8vo
half title and title leaves, 4 pp; text of Genesis 32-40 and n 4229-5190, pp 5-607.
The same as En 2/98 = Hyde 688.
Copy not seen; description deduced from En 2/125 and 126.
USA: ANC, SHS

49/01/En 2/121 **1869** Hyde 722
<<ARCANA CŒLESTIA. | <short rule> | THE | HEAVENLY ARCANA | CONTAINED IN | THE HOLY SCRIPTURES OR WORD OF THE LORD | UNFOLDED, | BEGINNING WITH THE BOOK OF GENESIS: | TOGETHER WITH | WONDERFUL THINGS SEEN IN THE WORLD OF SPIRITS | AND IN THE HEAVEN OF ANGELS. | <short rule> | *Translated from the Latin of* | EMANUEL SWEDENBORG, | *Servant of the Lord Jesus Christ.* | <short rule> | VOL. VII. | NEW YORK: | AMERICAN SWEDENBORG PRINTING AND PUBLISHING SOCIETY. | 1869.>>
verso: <<*Published by* THE AMERICAN SWEDENBORG PRINTING AND PUBLISHING | SOCIETY, *organized for the purpose of Stereotyping, Printing, and | Publishing Uniform Editions of the Theological Writings of* EMANUEL | SWEDENBORG, *and incorporated in the State of New York* A.D. 1850>>
half title: <<ARCANA CŒLESTIA.>>
8vo
half title and title leaves, 4 pp; text of Genesis 50, Exodus 1-12, and n 6497-8032, pp 5-627.
The same as En 2/85 = Hyde 720.
Copy not seen; description deduced from En 2/76.
USA: ANC

49/01/En 2/122 **1870** Hyde 607/a
<<ARCANA CŒLESTIA. | <short rule> | THE | HEAVENLY ARCANA | CONTAINED IN | THE

HOLY SCRIPTURES OR WORD OF THE LORD | UNFOLDED, | BEGINNING WITH THE BOOK OF GENESIS: | TOGETHER WITH | WONDERFUL THINGS SEEN IN THE WORLD OF SPIRITS | AND IN THE HEAVEN OF ANGELS. | <short rule> | *Translated from the Latin of* | EMANUEL SWEDENBORG, | *Servant of the Lord Jesus Christ.* | <short rule> | VOL. I. | NEW YORK: | AMERICAN SWEDENBORG PRINTING AND PUBLISHING SOCIETY. | 1870.>>
verso: <<*Published by* THE AMERICAN SWEDENBORG PRINTING AND PUBLISHING | SOCIETY, *organized for the purpose of Stereotyping, Printing, and* | *Publishing Uniform Editions of the Theological Writings of* EMANUEL | SWEDENBORG, *and incorporated in the State of New York* A.D. 1850>>
half title: <<ARCANA CŒLESTIA.>>
8vo
half title and title leaves, 4 pp; text of Genesis 1-11 and n 1-1382, pp 1-568.
Copy not seen; description deduced from En 2/124 and 132.
USA: ANC

49/01/En 2/123 **1870** Hyde 635

<<ARCANA CŒLESTIA. | <short rule> | THE | HEAVENLY ARCANA | CONTAINED IN | THE HOLY SCRIPTURES OR WORD OF THE LORD | UNFOLDED, | BEGINNING WITH THE BOOK OF GENESIS: | TOGETHER WITH | WONDERFUL THINGS SEEN IN THE WORLD OF SPIRITS | AND IN THE HEAVEN OF ANGELS. | <short rule> | *Translated from the Latin of* | EMANUEL SWEDENBORG, | *Servant of the Lord Jesus Christ.* | <short rule> | VOL. II. | NEW YORK: | AMERICAN SWEDENBORG PRINTING AND PUBLISHING SOCIETY. | 1870.>>
verso: <<*Published by* THE AMERICAN SWEDENBORG PRINTING AND PUBLISHING | SOCIETY, *organized for the purpose of Stereotyping, Printing, and* | *Publishing Uniform Editions of the Theological Writings of* EMANUEL | SWEDENBORG, *and incorporated in the State of New York* A.D. 1850>>
half title: <<ARCANA CŒLESTIA.>>
8vo
half title and title leaves, 4 pp; text of Genesis 12-19 and n 1383-2494, pp 5-576.
The same as En 2/112 = Hyde 634; an edition of 500 copies was printed.
Copy not seen; description deduced from En 2/60.
USA: ANC, SHS

49/01/En 2/124 **1870** Hyde 656/a

ARCANA CŒLESTIA. | <short rule> | THE | HEAVENLY ARCANA | CONTAINED IN | THE HOLY SCRIPTURES OR WORD OF THE LORD | UNFOLDED, | BEGINNING WITH THE BOOK OF GENESIS: | TOGETHER WITH | WONDERFUL THINGS SEEN IN THE WORLD OF SPIRITS | AND IN THE HEAVEN OF ANGELS. | <short rule> | *Translated from the Latin of* | EMANUEL SWEDENBORG, | *Servant of the Lord Jesus Christ.* | <short rule> | VOL. III. | NEW YORK: | AMERICAN SWEDENBORG PRINTING AND PUBLISHING SOCIETY. | 1870.
verso: *Published by* THE AMERICAN SWEDENBORG PRINTING AND PUBLISHING | SOCIETY, *organized for the purpose of Stereotyping, Printing, and* | *Publishing Uniform Editions of the Theological Writings of* EMANUEL | SWEDENBORG, *and incorporated in the State of New York* A.D. 1850
half title: ARCANA CŒLESTIA.
8vo
half title and title leaves, 4 pp; text of Genesis 20-25 and n 2495-3352, pp 5-515.
Reprint of En 2/79 = Hyde 652.
USA: ANC, SHS

49/01/En 2/125 **1870** Hyde 672

<<ARCANA CŒLESTIA. | <short rule> | THE | HEAVENLY ARCANA | CONTAINED IN | THE HOLY SCRIPTURES OR WORD OF THE LORD | UNFOLDED, | BEGINNING WITH THE BOOK OF GENESIS: | TOGETHER WITH | WONDERFUL THINGS SEEN IN THE WORLD OF SPIRITS | AND IN THE HEAVEN OF ANGELS. | <short rule> | *Translated from the Latin of* | EMANUEL SWEDENBORG, | *Servant of the Lord Jesus Christ.* | <short rule> | VOL. IV. | NEW YORK: | AMERICAN SWEDENBORG PRINTING AND PUBLISHING SOCIETY. | 1870.>>

verso: <<*Published by* THE AMERICAN SWEDENBORG PRINTING AND PUBLISHING | SOCIETY, *organized for the purpose of Stereotyping, Printing, and* | *Publishing Uniform Editions of the Theological Writings of* EMANUEL | SWEDENBORG, *and incorporated in the State of New York* A.D. 1850>>

half title: <<ARCANA CŒLESTIA.>>

8vo

half title and title leaves, 4 pp; text of Genesis 26-31 and n 3353-4228, pp 5-557.

The same as En 2/114 = Hyde 671.

Copy not seen; description deduced from En 2/97.

USA: ANC, SHS

49/01/En 2/126 **1870** Hyde 707

ARCANA CŒLESTIA. | <short rule> | THE | HEAVENLY ARCANA | CONTAINED IN | THE HOLY SCRIPTURES OR WORD OF THE LORD | UNFOLDED, | BEGINNING WITH THE BOOK OF GENESIS: | TOGETHER WITH | WONDERFUL THINGS SEEN IN THE WORLD OF SPIRITS | AND IN THE HEAVEN OF ANGELS. | <short rule> | *Translated from the Latin of* | EMANUEL SWEDENBORG, | *Servant of the Lord Jesus Christ.* | <short rule> | VOL. VI. | NEW YORK: | AMERICAN SWEDENBORG PRINTING AND PUBLISHING SOCIETY. | 1870.

verso: *Published by* THE AMERICAN SWEDENBORG PRINTING AND PUBLISHING | SOCIETY, *organized for the purpose of Stereotyping, Printing, and* | *Publishing Uniform Editions of the Theological Writings of* EMANUEL | SWEDENBORG, *and incorporated in the State of New York* A.D. 1850

half title: ARCANA CŒLESTIA.

8vo

half title and title leaves, 4 pp; text of Genesis 41-49 and n 5191-6496, pp 5-624.

The same as En 2/115 = Hyde 706.

USA: ANC, SHS

49/01/En 2/127 **1870** Hyde 739

<<ARCANA CŒLESTIA. | <short rule> | THE | HEAVENLY ARCANA | CONTAINED IN | THE HOLY SCRIPTURES OR WORD OF THE LORD | UNFOLDED, | BEGINNING WITH THE BOOK OF GENESIS: | TOGETHER WITH | WONDERFUL THINGS SEEN IN THE WORLD OF SPIRITS | AND IN THE HEAVEN OF ANGELS. | <short rule> | *Translated from the Latin of* | EMANUEL SWEDENBORG, | *Servant of the Lord Jesus Christ.* | <short rule> | VOL. VIII. | NEW YORK: | AMERICAN SWEDENBORG PRINTING AND PUBLISHING SOCIETY. | 1870.>>

verso: <<*Published by* THE AMERICAN SWEDENBORG PRINTING AND PUBLISHING | SOCIETY, *organized for the purpose of Stereotyping, Printing, and* | *Publishing Uniform Editions of the Theological Writings of* EMANUEL | SWEDENBORG, *and incorporated in the State of New York* A.D. 1850>>

half title: <<ARCANA CŒLESTIA.>>

8vo

half title and title leaves, 4 pp; text of Exodus 13-21 and n 8033-9111, pp 5-543.

The same as En 2/116 = Hyde 738.
Copy not seen; description deduced from En 2/77 and 127.
USA: ANC, SHS

49/01/En 2/128 **1870** Hyde 755

ARCANA CŒLESTIA. | <short rule> | THE | HEAVENLY ARCANA | CONTAINED IN | THE HOLY SCRIPTURES OR WORD OF THE LORD | UNFOLDED, | BEGINNING WITH THE BOOK OF GENESIS: | TOGETHER WITH | WONDERFUL THINGS SEEN IN THE WORLD OF SPIRITS | AND IN THE HEAVEN OF ANGELS. | <short rule> | *Translated from the Latin of* | EMANUEL SWEDENBORG, | *Servant of the Lord Jesus Christ.* | <short rule> | VOL. IX. | NEW YORK: | AMERICAN SWEDENBORG PRINTING AND PUBLISHING SOCIETY. | 1870.
verso: *Published by* THE AMERICAN SWEDENBORG PRINTING AND PUBLISHING | SOCIETY, *organized for the purpose of Stereotyping, Printing, and* | *Publishing Uniform Editions of the Theological Writings of* EMANUEL | SWEDENBORG, *and incorporated in the State of New York* A.D. 1850
half title: ARCANA CŒLESTIA.
8vo
half title and title leaves, 4 pp; text of Exodus 22-28 and n 9112-9973, pp 5-607.
The same as En 2/117 = Hyde 754.
USA: ANC, SHS

49/01/En 2/129 **1870** Hyde 770

ARCANA CŒLESTIA. | <short rule> | THE | HEAVENLY ARCANA | CONTAINED IN | THE HOLY SCRIPTURES OR WORD OF THE LORD | UNFOLDED, | BEGINNING WITH THE BOOK OF GENESIS: | TOGETHER WITH | WONDERFUL THINGS SEEN IN THE WORLD OF SPIRITS | AND IN THE HEAVEN OF ANGELS. | <short rule> | *Translated from the Latin of* | EMANUEL SWEDENBORG, | *Servant of the Lord Jesus Christ.* | <short rule> | VOL. X. | NEW YORK: | AMERICAN SWEDENBORG PRINTING AND PUBLISHING SOCIETY. | 1870.
verso: *Published by* THE AMERICAN SWEDENBORG PRINTING AND PUBLISHING | SOCIETY, *organized for the purpose of Stereotyping, Printing, and* | *Publishing Uniform Editions of the Theological Writings of* EMANUEL | SWEDENBORG, *and incorporated in the State of New York* A.D. 1850
half title: ARCANA CŒLESTIA.
8vo
half title and title leaves, 4 pp; text of Exodus 29-40 and n 9974-10837, pp 5-569.
The same as En 2/118 = Hyde 769.
USA: ANC, SHS

49/01/En 2/130 **1871** Hyde 723

<<ARCANA CŒLESTIA. | <short rule> | THE | HEAVENLY ARCANA | CONTAINED IN | THE HOLY SCRIPTURES OR WORD OF THE LORD | UNFOLDED, | BEGINNING WITH THE BOOK OF GENESIS: | TOGETHER WITH | WONDERFUL THINGS SEEN IN THE WORLD OF SPIRITS | AND IN THE HEAVEN OF ANGELS. | <short rule> | *Translated from the Latin of* | EMANUEL SWEDENBORG, | *Servant of the Lord Jesus Christ.* | <short rule> | VOL. VII. | NEW YORK: | AMERICAN SWEDENBORG PRINTING AND PUBLISHING SOCIETY. | 1871.>>
verso: <<*Published by* THE AMERICAN SWEDENBORG PRINTING AND PUBLISHING | SOCIETY, *organized for the purpose of Stereotyping, Printing, and* | *Publishing Uniform Editions of the Theological Writings of* EMANUEL | SWEDENBORG, *and incorporated in the State of New York* A.D. 1850>>

half title: <<ARCANA CŒLESTIA.>>
8vo
half title and title leaves, 4 pp; text of Genesis 50, Exodus 1-12, and n 6497-8032.
The same as En 2/121 = Hyde 722.
Copy not seen; description deduced from En 2/76.
USA: ANC, SHS

49/01/En 2/131 — 1872 — Hyde 608

ARCANA CŒLESTIA | <short rule> | THE | HEAVENLY MYSTERIES | CONTAINED IN | THE HOLY SCRIPTURE, OR WORD OF THE LORD, | UNFOLDED: | BEING AN EXPOSITION OF GENESIS AND EXODUS; | TOGETHER WITH A RELATION OF | WONDERFUL THINGS SEEN IN THE WORLD OF SPIRITS AND | IN THE HEAVEN OF ANGELS. | <short double rule> | BY | EMANUEL SWEDENBORG. | <short double rule> | A TRANSLATION OF HIS WORK ENTITLED | "ARCANA CŒLESTIA QUÆ IN SCRIPTURA SACRA, SEU VERBO DOMINI SUNT, DETECTA; HIC | PRIMUM QUÆ IN GENESI. UNA CUM MIRABILIBUS QUÆ VISA SUNT IN MUNDO SPIRITUUM | ET IN CŒLO ANGELORUM. LONDINI, 1749-1756." | IN TWELVE VOLUMES. | VOLUME I. | GENESIS, CHAPTER I. TO CHAPTER IX. | LONDON: | PUBLISHED BY | THE SWEDENBORG SOCIETY, BRITISH AND FOREIGN, | (INSTITUTED 1810,) | 36 BLOOMSBURY STREET, OXFORD STREET, W.C. | 1872.
verso: Matthew vi. 33. | *Seek ye first the kingdom of God and his righteousness,* | *and all these things shall be added unto you.*
half title: ARCANA CŒLESTIA.
verso: LONDON: | MITCHELL AND HUGHES, PRINTERS, | 24 WARDOUR STREET, W.
8vo
half title and title leaves, 4 pp; Translator's preface, pp i-xv; text of Genesis 1-9 and n 1-1113, pp 1-458; Errata, 1 p.
The same as En 2/83 = Hyde 605; the printing was supervised by T M Gorman.
UK: CON; USA: ANC

49/01/En 2/132 — 1873 — Hyde 609

ARCANA CŒLESTIA. | <short rule> | THE | HEAVENLY ARCANA | CONTAINED IN | THE HOLY SCRIPTURES OR WORD OF THE LORD | UNFOLDED, | BEGINNING WITH THE BOOK OF GENESIS: | TOGETHER WITH | WONDERFUL THINGS SEEN IN THE WORLD OF SPIRITS | AND IN THE HEAVEN OF ANGELS. | <short rule> | *Translated from the Latin of* | EMANUEL SWEDENBORG, | *Servant of the Lord Jesus Christ.* | <short rule> | VOL. I. | NEW YORK: | AMERICAN SWEDENBORG PRINTING AND PUBLISHING SOCIETY. | 1873.
verso: *Published by* THE AMERICAN SWEDENBORG PRINTING AND PUBLISHING | SOCIETY, *organized for the purpose of Stereotyping, Printing, and* | *Publishing Uniform Editions of the Theological Writings of* EMANUEL | SWEDENBORG, *and incorporated in the State of New York* A.D. 1850
half title: ARCANA CŒLESTIA.
8vo
half title and title leaves, 4 pp; text of Genesis 1-11 and n 1-1382, pp 1-568.
The same as En 2/119 = Hyde 607; an edition of 500 copies was printed.
USA: ANC, SHS

49/01/En 2/133 — 1873 — Hyde 636

ARCANA CŒLESTIA. | <short rule> | THE | HEAVENLY ARCANA | CONTAINED IN | THE HOLY SCRIPTURES OR WORD OF THE LORD | UNFOLDED, | BEGINNING WITH THE BOOK OF

GENESIS: | TOGETHER WITH | WONDERFUL THINGS SEEN IN THE WORLD OF SPIRITS | AND IN THE HEAVEN OF ANGELS. | <short rule> | *Translated from the Latin of* | EMANUEL SWEDENBORG, | *Servant of the Lord Jesus Christ.* | <short rule> | VOL. II. | NEW YORK: | AMERICAN SWEDENBORG PRINTING AND PUBLISHING SOCIETY, BIBLE HOUSE, ASTOR PLACE, ROOM NO. 47. | 1873.
verso: *Published by* THE AMERICAN SWEDENBORG PRINTING AND PUBLISHING | SOCIETY, *organized for the purpose of Stereotyping, Printing, and* | *Publishing Uniform Editions of the Theological Writings of* EMANUEL | SWEDENBORG, *and incorporated in the State of New York* A.D. 1850
half title: ARCANA CŒLESTIA.
8vo
half title and title leaves, 4 pp; text of Genesis 12-19 and n 1383-2494, pp 5-576.
The same as En 2/123 = Hyde 635.
USA: ANC, SHS

49/01/En 2/134 **1873** Hyde 672/a

<<ARCANA CŒLESTIA. | <short rule> | THE | HEAVENLY ARCANA | CONTAINED IN | THE HOLY SCRIPTURES OR WORD OF THE LORD | UNFOLDED, | BEGINNING WITH THE BOOK OF GENESIS: | TOGETHER WITH | WONDERFUL THINGS SEEN IN THE WORLD OF SPIRITS | AND IN THE HEAVEN OF ANGELS. | <short rule> | *Translated from the Latin of* | EMANUEL SWEDENBORG, | *Servant of the Lord Jesus Christ.* | <short rule> | VOL. IV. | NEW YORK: | AMERICAN SWEDENBORG PRINTING AND PUBLISHING SOCIETY. | 1873.>>
verso: <<*Published by* THE AMERICAN SWEDENBORG PRINTING AND PUBLISHING | SOCIETY, *organized for the purpose of Stereotyping, Printing, and* | *Publishing Uniform Editions of the Theological Writings of* EMANUEL | SWEDENBORG, *and incorporated in the State of New York* A.D. 1850>>
half title: <<ARCANA CŒLESTIA.>>
8vo
half title and title leaves, 4 pp; text of Genesis 26-31 and n 3353-4228, pp 5-557.
Copy not seen; description deduced from En 2/97.
USA: ANC

49/01/En 2/135 **1873** Hyde 690

ARCANA CŒLESTIA. | <short rule> | THE | HEAVENLY ARCANA | CONTAINED IN | THE HOLY SCRIPTURES OR WORD OF THE LORD | UNFOLDED, | BEGINNING WITH THE BOOK OF GENESIS: | TOGETHER WITH | WONDERFUL THINGS SEEN IN THE WORLD OF SPIRITS | AND IN THE HEAVEN OF ANGELS. | <short rule> | *Translated from the Latin of* | EMANUEL SWEDENBORG, | *Servant of the Lord Jesus Christ.* | <short rule> | VOL. V. | NEW YORK: | AMERICAN SWEDENBORG PRINTING AND PUBLISHING SOCIETY. | 1873.
verso: *Published by* THE AMERICAN SWEDENBORG PRINTING AND PUBLISHING | SOCIETY, *organized for the purpose of Stereotyping, Printing, and* | *Publishing Uniform Editions of the Theological Writings of* EMANUEL | SWEDENBORG, *and incorporated in the State of New York* A.D. 1850
half title: ARCANA CŒLESTIA.
8vo
half title and title leaves, 4 pp; text of Genesis 32-40 and n 4229-5190, pp 5-607.
The same as En 2/120 = Hyde 689.
SWE: UPP; USA: ANC, SHS

49/01/En 2/136 **1873** Hyde 740

ARCANA CŒLESTIA. | <short rule> | THE | HEAVENLY ARCANA | CONTAINED IN | THE HOLY SCRIPTURES OR WORD OF THE LORD | UNFOLDED, | BEGINNING WITH THE BOOK OF GENESIS: | TOGETHER WITH | WONDERFUL THINGS SEEN IN THE WORLD OF SPIRITS | AND IN THE HEAVEN OF ANGELS. | <short rule> | *Translated from the Latin of* | EMANUEL SWEDENBORG, | *Servant of the Lord Jesus Christ.* | <short rule> | VOL. VIII. | NEW YORK: | AMERICAN SWEDENBORG PRINTING AND PUBLISHING SOCIETY. | 1873.
verso: *Published by* THE AMERICAN SWEDENBORG PRINTING AND PUBLISHING | SOCIETY, *organized for the purpose of Stereotyping, Printing, and* | *Publishing Uniform Editions of the Theological Writings of* EMANUEL | SWEDENBORG, *and incorporated in the State of New York* A.D. 1850
half title: ARCANA CŒLESTIA.
8vo
half title and title leaves, 4 pp; text of Exodus 13-21 and n 8033-9111, pp 5-543.
The same as En 2/127 = Hyde 739.
USA: SHS

49/01/En 2/137 **1874** Hyde 657

<<ARCANA CŒLESTIA. | <short rule> | THE | HEAVENLY ARCANA | CONTAINED IN | THE HOLY SCRIPTURES OR WORD OF THE LORD | UNFOLDED, | BEGINNING WITH THE BOOK OF GENESIS: | TOGETHER WITH | WONDERFUL THINGS SEEN IN THE WORLD OF SPIRITS | AND IN THE HEAVEN OF ANGELS. | <short rule> | *Translated from the Latin of* | EMANUEL SWEDENBORG, | *Servant of the Lord Jesus Christ.* | <short rule> | VOL. III. | NEW YORK: | AMERICAN SWEDENBORG PRINTING AND PUBLISHING SOCIETY. | 1874.>>
verso: <<*Published by* THE AMERICAN SWEDENBORG PRINTING AND PUBLISHING | SOCIETY, *organized for the purpose of Stereotyping, Printing, and* | *Publishing Uniform Editions of the Theological Writings of* EMANUEL | SWEDENBORG, *and incorporated in the State of New York* A.D. 1850>>
half title: <<ARCANA CŒLESTIA.>>
8vo
half title and title leaves, 4 pp; text of Genesis 20-25 and n 2495-3352, pp 5-515.
The same as En 2/113 = Hyde 656.
Copy not seen; description deduced from En 2/79.
USA: ANC, SHS

49/01/En 2/138 **1874** Hyde 673

ARCANA CŒLESTIA. | <short rule> | THE | HEAVENLY ARCANA | CONTAINED IN | THE HOLY SCRIPTURES OR WORD OF THE LORD | UNFOLDED, | BEGINNING WITH THE BOOK OF GENESIS: | TOGETHER WITH | WONDERFUL THINGS SEEN IN THE WORLD OF SPIRITS | AND IN THE HEAVEN OF ANGELS. | <short rule> | *Translated from the Latin of* | EMANUEL SWEDENBORG, | *Servant of the Lord Jesus Christ.* | <short rule> | VOL. IV. | NEW YORK: | AMERICAN SWEDENBORG PRINTING AND PUBLISHING SOCIETY. | 1874.
verso: *Published by* THE AMERICAN SWEDENBORG PRINTING AND PUBLISHING | SOCIETY, *organized for the purpose of Stereotyping, Printing, and* | *Publishing Uniform Editions of the Theological Writings of* EMANUEL | SWEDENBORG, *and incorporated in the State of New York* A.D. 1850
half title: ARCANA CŒLESTIA.
8vo
half title and title leaves, 4 pp; text of Genesis 26-31 and n 3353-4228, pp 5-557.

The same as En 2/125 = Hyde 672.
USA: ANC, SHS

49/01/En 2/139 **1875** Hyde 707/–
<<ARCANA CŒLESTIA. | <short rule> | THE | HEAVENLY ARCANA | CONTAINED IN | THE HOLY SCRIPTURES OR WORD OF THE LORD | UNFOLDED, | BEGINNING WITH THE BOOK OF GENESIS: | TOGETHER WITH | WONDERFUL THINGS SEEN IN THE WORLD OF SPIRITS | AND IN THE HEAVEN OF ANGELS. | <short rule> | *Translated from the Latin of* | EMANUEL SWEDENBORG, | *Servant of the Lord Jesus Christ.* | <short rule> | VOL. VI. | NEW YORK: | AMERICAN SWEDENBORG PRINTING AND PUBLISHING SOCIETY. | 1875.>>
verso: <<*Published by* THE AMERICAN SWEDENBORG PRINTING AND PUBLISHING | SOCIETY, *organized for the purpose of Stereotyping, Printing, and* | *Publishing Uniform Editions of the Theological Writings of* EMANUEL | SWEDENBORG, *and incorporated in the State of New York* A.D. 1850>>
half title: <<ARCANA CŒLESTIA.>>
8vo
half title and title leaves, 4 pp; text of Genesis 41-49 and n 5191-6496, pp 5-624.
Copy not seen; description deduced from En 2/126.
USA: ANC

49/01/En 2/140 **1875** Hyde 723/a
ARCANA CŒLESTIA. | <short rule> | THE | HEAVENLY ARCANA | CONTAINED IN | THE HOLY SCRIPTURES OR WORD OF THE LORD | UNFOLDED, | BEGINNING WITH THE BOOK OF GENESIS: | TOGETHER WITH | WONDERFUL THINGS SEEN IN THE WORLD OF SPIRITS | AND IN THE HEAVEN OF ANGELS. | <short rule> | *Translated from the Latin of* | EMANUEL SWEDENBORG, | *Servant of the Lord Jesus Christ.* | <short rule> | VOL. VII. | NEW YORK: | AMERICAN SWEDENBORG PRINTING AND PUBLISHING SOCIETY. | 1875.
verso: *Published by* THE AMERICAN SWEDENBORG PRINTING AND PUBLISHING | SOCIETY, *organized for the purpose of Stereotyping, Printing, and* | *Publishing Uniform Editions of the Theological Writings of* EMANUEL | SWEDENBORG, *and incorporated in the State of New York* A.D. 1850
half title: ARCANA CŒLESTIA.
8vo
half title and title leaves, 4 pp; text of Genesis 50, Exodus 1-12, and n 6497-8032, pp 5-627.
The same as En 2/130 = Hyde 723.
USA: ANC

49/01/En 2/141 **1877** Hyde 609/a
<<ARCANA CÆLESTIA. | <short rule> | THE | HEAVENLY ARCANA | CONTAINED IN | THE HOLY SCRIPTURES OR WORD OF THE LORD | UNFOLDED, | BEGINNING WITH THE BOOK OF GENESIS: | *TOGETHER WITH WONDERFUL THINGS SEEN IN THE WORLD OF* | *SPIRITS AND IN THE HEAVEN OF ANGELS* | TRANSLATED FROM THE LATIN OF | EMANUEL SWEDENBORG | *Servant of the Lord Jesus Christ.* | <short rule> | VOL. I. | <short rule> | NEW YORK | AMERICAN SWEDENBORG PRINTING AND PUBLISHING | SOCIETY | 1877.>>
verso: <<*Published by* THE AMERICAN SWEDENBORG PRINTING AND PUBLISHING | SOCIETY, *organized for the purpose of Stereotyping, Printing, and* | *Publishing Uniform Editions of the Theological Writings of* EMANUEL | SWEDENBORG, *and incorporated in the State of New York* A.D. 1850>>
half title: <<ARCANA CŒLESTIA>>

8vo
half title and title leaves, 4 pp; text of Genesis 1-11 and n 1-1382, pp 1-568.
Copy not seen; description deduced from En 2/124 and 132.
USA: ANC

49/01/En 2/142 1877 Hyde 657/a
<<ARCANA CÆLESTIA. | <short rule> | THE | HEAVENLY ARCANA | CONTAINED IN | THE HOLY SCRIPTURES OR WORD OF THE LORD | UNFOLDED, | BEGINNING WITH THE BOOK OF GENESIS: | *TOGETHER WITH WONDERFUL THINGS SEEN IN THE WORLD OF* | *SPIRITS AND IN THE HEAVEN OF ANGELS* | TRANSLATED FROM THE LATIN OF | EMANUEL SWEDENBORG | *Servant of the Lord Jesus Christ.* | <short rule> | VOL. III. | <short rule> | NEW YORK: | AMERICAN SWEDENBORG PRINTING AND PUBLISHING | SOCIETY | 1877.>>
verso: <<*Published by* THE AMERICAN SWEDENBORG PRINTING AND PUBLISHING | SOCIETY, *organized for the purpose of Stereotyping, Printing, and* | *Publishing Uniform Editions of the Theological Writings of* EMANUEL | SWEDENBORG, *and incorporated in the State of New York* A.D. 1850>>
half title: <<ARCANA CŒLESTIA>>
8vo
half title and title leaves, 4 pp; text of Genesis 20-25 and n 2495-3352, pp 5-515.
Copy not seen; description deduced from En 2/79.
USA: ANC

49/01/En 2/143 1877 Hyde 674
<<ARCANA CÆLESTIA. | <short rule> | THE | HEAVENLY ARCANA | CONTAINED IN | THE HOLY SCRIPTURES OR WORD OF THE LORD | UNFOLDED, | BEGINNING WITH THE BOOK OF GENESIS: | *TOGETHER WITH WONDERFUL THINGS SEEN IN THE WORLD OF* | *SPIRITS AND IN THE HEAVEN OF ANGELS* | TRANSLATED FROM THE LATIN OF | EMANUEL SWEDENBORG | *Servant of the Lord Jesus Christ.* | <short rule> | VOL. IV. | <short rule> | NEW YORK: | AMERICAN SWEDENBORG PRINTING AND PUBLISHING | SOCIETY | 1877.>>
verso: <<*Published by* THE AMERICAN SWEDENBORG PRINTING AND PUBLISHING | SOCIETY, *organized for the purpose of Stereotyping, Printing, and* | *Publishing Uniform Editions of the Theological Writings of* EMANUEL | SWEDENBORG, *and incorporated in the State of New York* A.D. 1850>>
half title: <<ARCANA CŒLESTIA>>
8vo
half title and title leaves, 4 pp; text of Genesis 26-31 and n 3353-4228, pp 5-557.
The same as En 2/138 = Hyde 673.
Copy not seen; description deduced from En 2/138 and 141.
USA: ANC

49/01/En 2/144 1877 Hyde 691
<<ARCANA CÆLESTIA. | <short rule> | THE | HEAVENLY ARCANA | CONTAINED IN | THE HOLY SCRIPTURES OR WORD OF THE LORD | UNFOLDED, | BEGINNING WITH THE BOOK OF GENESIS: | *TOGETHER WITH WONDERFUL THINGS SEEN IN THE WORLD OF* | *SPIRITS AND IN THE HEAVEN OF ANGELS* | TRANSLATED FROM THE LATIN OF | EMANUEL SWEDENBORG | *Servant of the Lord Jesus Christ.* | <short rule> | VOL. V | <short rule> | NEW YORK: | AMERICAN SWEDENBORG PRINTING AND PUBLISHING | SOCIETY | 1877.>>
verso: <<*Published by* THE AMERICAN SWEDENBORG PRINTING AND PUBLISHING | SOCIETY, *organized for the purpose of Stereotyping, Printing, and* | *Publishing Uniform Editions of*

the Theological Writings of EMANUEL | SWEDENBORG, *and incorporated in the State of New York* A.D. 1850>>
half title: <<ARCANA CŒLESTIA>>
8vo
half title and title leaves, 4 pp; text of Genesis 32-40 and n 4229-5190, pp 5-607.
The same as En 2/135 = Hyde 690.
Copy not seen; description deduced from En 2/135 and 141.
USA: ANC

49/01/En 2/145 **1877** Hyde 708
<<ARCANA CÆLESTIA. | <short rule> | THE | HEAVENLY ARCANA | CONTAINED IN | THE HOLY SCRIPTURES OR WORD OF THE LORD | UNFOLDED, | BEGINNING WITH THE BOOK OF GENESIS: | *TOGETHER WITH WONDERFUL THINGS SEEN IN THE WORLD OF | SPIRITS AND IN THE HEAVEN OF ANGELS* | TRANSLATED FROM THE LATIN OF | EMANUEL SWEDENBORG | *Servant of the Lord Jesus Christ.* | <short rule> | VOL. VI. | <short rule> | NEW YORK: | AMERICAN SWEDENBORG PRINTING AND PUBLISHING | SOCIETY | 1877.>>
verso: <<*Published by* THE AMERICAN SWEDENBORG PRINTING AND PUBLISHING | SOCIETY, *organized for the purpose of Stereotyping, Printing, and | Publishing Uniform Editions of the Theological Writings of* EMANUEL | SWEDENBORG, *and incorporated in the State of New York* A.D. 1850.>>
half title: <<ARCANA CŒLESTIA>>
8vo
half title and title leaves, 4 pp; text of Genesis 41-49 and n 5191-6496, pp 5-624.
Copy not seen; description deduced from En 2/126 and 141.
USA: ANC

49/01/En 2/146 **1877** Hyde 740/a
<<ARCANA CÆLESTIA. | <short rule> | THE | HEAVENLY ARCANA | CONTAINED IN | THE HOLY SCRIPTURES OR WORD OF THE LORD | UNFOLDED, | BEGINNING WITH THE BOOK OF GENESIS: | *TOGETHER WITH WONDERFUL THINGS SEEN IN THE WORLD OF | SPIRITS AND IN THE HEAVEN OF ANGELS* | TRANSLATED FROM THE LATIN OF | EMANUEL SWEDENBORG | *Servant of the Lord Jesus Christ.* | <short rule> | VOL. VIII. | <short rule> | NEW YORK: | AMERICAN SWEDENBORG PRINTING AND PUBLISHING | SOCIETY | 1877.>>
verso: <<*Published by* THE AMERICAN SWEDENBORG PRINTING AND PUBLISHING | SOCIETY, *organized for the purpose of Stereotyping, Printing, and | Publishing Uniform Editions of the Theological Writings of* EMANUEL | SWEDENBORG, *and incorporated in the State of New York* A.D. 1850>>
half title: <<ARCANA CŒLESTIA>>
8vo
half title and title leaves, 4 pp; text of Exodus 12-21 and n 8033-9111, pp 5-543.
Copy not seen; description deduced from En 2/127 and 141.
USA: ANC

49/01/En 2/147 **1877** Hyde 755/a
<<ARCANA CÆLESTIA. | <short rule> | THE | HEAVENLY ARCANA | CONTAINED IN | THE HOLY SCRIPTURES OR WORD OF THE LORD | UNFOLDED, | BEGINNING WITH THE BOOK OF GENESIS: | *TOGETHER WITH WONDERFUL THINGS SEEN IN THE WORLD OF | SPIRITS AND IN THE HEAVEN OF ANGELS* | TRANSLATED FROM THE LATIN OF | EMANUEL SWEDENBORG | *Servant of the Lord Jesus Christ.* | <short rule> | VOL. IX. | <short rule> | NEW YORK: |

AMERICAN SWEDENBORG PRINTING AND PUBLISHING | SOCIETY | 1877.>>
verso: <<*Published by* THE AMERICAN SWEDENBORG PRINTING AND PUBLISHING | SOCIETY, *organized for the purpose of Stereotyping, Printing, and | Publishing Uniform Editions of the Theological Writings of* EMANUEL | SWEDENBORG, *and incorporated in the State of New York* A.D. 1850>>
half title: <<ARCANA CŒLESTIA>>
8vo
half title and title leaves, 4 pp; text of Exodus 22-28 and n 9112-9973, pp 5-607.
Copy not seen; description deduced from En 2/128 and 141.
USA: ANC

49/01/En 2/148 **1878** Hyde 637
ARCANA CŒLESTIA | <short rule> | THE | HEAVENLY MYSTERIES | CONTAINED IN | THE HOLY SCRIPTURE, OR WORD OF THE LORD | UNFOLDED | IN AN EXPOSITION OF GENESIS AND EXODUS | TOGETHER WITH A RELATION OF | WONDERFUL THINGS SEEN IN THE WORLD OF SPIRITS AND | IN THE HEAVEN OF ANGELS | BY | EMANUEL SWEDENBORG | BEING A TRANSLATION OF HIS WORK ENTITLED | "ARCANA CŒLESTIA QUÆ IN SCRIPTURA SACRA, SEU VERBO DOMINI, SUNT DETECTA; HIC | PRIMUM QUÆ IN GENESI. UNA CUM MIRABILIBUS QUÆ VISA SUNT IN MUNDO SPIRITUUM | ET IN CŒLO ANGELORUM." LONDINI, 1749-1756. | IN TWELVE VOLUMES | VOLUME II. | GENESIS, CHAPTER X. TO CHAPTER XVII. | SWEDENBORG SOCIETY, BRITISH AND FOREIGN | (*INSTITUTED 1810*) | 36 BLOOMSBURY STREET, LONDON | 1878
verso: MATTHEW vi. 33. | *Seek ye first the kingdom of God and His righteousness, and all | these things shall be added unto you.*
half title: ARCANA CŒLESTIA
verso: MUIR AND PATERSON, PRINTERS, EDINBURGH
8vo
half title and title leaves, 4 pp; text of Genesis 10-17 and n 1114-2134, pp 1-464; advertisements, pp 1-4.
Revised by J Bayley; an edition of 1,074 copies was printed.
UK: SOC, CON; USA: ANC

49/01/En 2/149 **1878** Hyde 638
<<ARCANA CÆLESTIA. | <short rule> | THE | HEAVENLY ARCANA | CONTAINED IN | THE HOLY SCRIPTURES OR WORD OF THE LORD | UNFOLDED, | BEGINNING WITH THE BOOK OF GENESIS: | *TOGETHER WITH WONDERFUL THINGS SEEN IN THE WORLD OF | SPIRITS AND IN THE HEAVEN OF ANGELS* | TRANSLATED FROM THE LATIN OF | EMANUEL SWEDENBORG | *Servant of the Lord Jesus Christ.* | <short rule> | VOL. II. | <short rule> | NEW YORK: | AMERICAN SWEDENBORG PRINTING AND PUBLISHING | SOCIETY | 1878.>>
verso: <<*Published by* THE AMERICAN SWEDENBORG PRINTING AND PUBLISHING | SOCIETY, *organized for the purpose of Stereotyping, Printing, and | Publishing Uniform Editions of the Theological Writings of* EMANUEL | SWEDENBORG, *and incorporated in the State of New York* A.D. 1850>>
half title: <<ARCANA CŒLESTIA>>
8vo
half title and title leaves, 4 pp; text of Genesis 12-19 and n 1383-2494, pp 5-576.
The same as En 2/133 = Hyde 636. An edition of 500 copies was printed.
Copy not seen; description deduced from En 2/133 and 141.
USA: ANC

49/01/En 2/150 **1878** Hyde 724

<<ARCANA CÆLESTIA. | <short rule> | THE | HEAVENLY ARCANA | CONTAINED IN | THE HOLY SCRIPTURES OR WORD OF THE LORD | UNFOLDED, | BEGINNING WITH THE BOOK OF GENESIS: | *TOGETHER WITH WONDERFUL THINGS SEEN IN THE WORLD OF* | *SPIRITS AND IN THE HEAVEN OF ANGELS* | TRANSLATED FROM THE LATIN OF | EMANUEL SWEDENBORG | *Servant of the Lord Jesus Christ.* | <short rule> | VOL. VII. | <short rule> | NEW YORK: | AMERICAN SWEDENBORG PRINTING AND PUBLISHING | SOCIETY | 1878.>>
verso: <<*Published by* THE AMERICAN SWEDENBORG PRINTING AND PUBLISHING | SOCIETY, *organized for the purpose of Stereotyping, Printing, and* | *Publishing Uniform Editions of the Theological Writings of* EMANUEL | SWEDENBORG, *and incorporated in the State of New York* A.D. 1850>>
half title: <<ARCANA CŒLESTIA>>
8vo
half title and title leaves, 4 pp; text of Genesis 50, Exodus 1-11, and n 6497-8032, pp 5-627.
Copy not seen; description deduced from En 2/140 and 141.
USA: ANC

49/01/En 2/151 **1879** Hyde 675

ARCANA CŒLESTIA | <short rule> | THE | HEAVENLY MYSTERIES | CONTAINED IN | THE HOLY SCRIPTURE, OR WORD OF THE LORD | UNFOLDED | IN AN EXPOSITION OF GENESIS AND EXODUS | TOGETHER WITH A RELATION OF | WONDERFUL THINGS SEEN IN THE WORLD OF SPIRITS AND | IN THE HEAVEN OF ANGELS | BY | EMANUEL SWEDENBORG | BEING A TRANSLATION OF HIS WORK ENTITLED | "ARCANA CŒLESTIA QUÆ IN SCRIPTURA SACRA, SEU VERBO DOMINI SUNT, DETECTA; HIC | PRIMUM QUÆ IN GENESI. UNA CUM MIRABILIBUS QUÆ VISA SUNT IN MUNDO SPIRITUUM | ET IN CŒLO ANGELORUM." LONDINI, 1749-1756. | IN TWELVE VOLUMES | VOLUME IV. | GENESIS, CHAPTER XXIII. TO CHAPTER XXVII. | SWEDENBORG SOCIETY, BRITISH AND FOREIGN | (*INSTITUTED 1810*) | 36 BLOOMSBURY STREET, LONDON | 1879
verso: Matthew vi. 33. | *Seek ye first the kingdom of God and His righteousness,* | *and all these things shall be added unto you.*
half title: THE | HEAVENLY MYSTERIES.
imprint: LONDON: BRADBURY, AGNEW, & CO., PRINTERS, WHITEFRIARS.
8vo
half title and title leaves, 4 pp; text of Genesis 23-27 and n 2894-3649, pp 5-416; imprint, p 416.
A reprint from En 2/89 = Hyde 669; an edition of 1,000 copies was printed.
UK: SOC, CON; SWE: UPP; USA: ANC

49/01/En 2/152 **1879** Hyde 610

<<ARCANA CÆLESTIA. | <short rule> | THE | HEAVENLY ARCANA | CONTAINED IN | THE HOLY SCRIPTURES OR WORD OF THE LORD | UNFOLDED, | BEGINNING WITH THE BOOK OF GENESIS: | *TOGETHER WITH WONDERFUL THINGS SEEN IN THE WORLD OF* | *SPIRITS AND IN THE HEAVEN OF ANGELS* | TRANSLATED FROM THE LATIN OF | EMANUEL SWEDENBORG | *Servant of the Lord Jesus Christ.* | <short rule> | VOL. I | <short rule> | NEW YORK: | AMERICAN SWEDENBORG PRINTING AND PUBLISHING | SOCIETY | 1879.>>
verso: <<*Published by* THE AMERICAN SWEDENBORG PRINTING AND PUBLISHING | SOCIETY, *organized for the purpose of Stereotyping, Printing, and* | *Publishing Uniform Editions of the Theological Writings of* EMANUEL | SWEDENBORG, *and incorporated in the State of New York* A.D. 1850>>
half title: <<ARCANA CŒLESTIA>>

8vo
half title and title leaves, 4 pp; the Society's imprint, 1 p <verso blank>; text of Genesis 1-11 and n 1-1382, pp 1-568.
The same as En 2/132 = Hyde 609; an edition of 500 copies was printed.
Copy not seen; description deduced from En 2/124 and 141.
USA: ANC

49/01/En 2/153 **1879** Hyde 741

ARCANA CÆLESTIA. | <short rule> | THE | HEAVENLY ARCANA | CONTAINED IN | THE HOLY SCRIPTURES OR WORD OF THE LORD | UNFOLDED, | BEGINNING WITH THE BOOK OF GENESIS: | TOGETHER WITH | WONDERFUL THINGS SEEN IN THE WORLD OF SPIRITS | AND IN THE HEAVEN OF ANGELS. | <short rule> | *Translated from the Latin of* | EMANUEL SWEDENBORG, | *Servant of the Lord Jesus Christ.* | <short rule> | VOL. VIII. | NEW YORK: | AMERICAN SWEDENBORG PRINTING AND PUBLISHING SOCIETY. | <short rule> | 1879.
verso: *Published by* THE AMERICAN SWEDENBORG PRINTING AND PUBLISHING | SOCIETY, *organized for the purpose of Stereotyping, Printing, and* | *Publishing Uniform Editions of the Theological Writings of* EMANUEL | SWEDENBORG, *and incorporated in the State of New York* A. D. 1850.
half title: ARCANA CŒLESTIA.
8vo
half title and title leaves, 4 pp; text of Exodus 13-21 and n 8033-9111, pp 5-543.
The same as En 2/136 = Hyde 740.
UK: SOC

49/01/En 2/154 **1881** Hyde 692

ARCANA CŒLESTIA | <short rule> | THE | HEAVENLY MYSTERIES | CONTAINED IN | THE HOLY SCRIPTURE, OR WORD OF THE LORD, | UNFOLDED, | IN AN EXPOSITION OF GENESIS AND EXODUS: | TOGETHER WITH A RELATION OF | WONDERFUL THINGS SEEN IN THE WORLD OF SPIRITS AND | IN THE HEAVEN OF ANGELS. | BY | EMANUEL SWEDENBORG. | BEING A TRANSLATION OF HIS WORK ENTITLED | "ARCANA CŒLESTIA QUÆ IN SCRIPTURA SACRA, SEU VERBO DOMINI SUNT, DETECTA; HIC | PRIMUM QUÆ IN GENESI. UNA CUM MIRABILIBUS QUÆ VISA SUNT IN MUNDO SPIRITUUM | ET IN CŒLO ANGELORUM. LONDINI, 1749-1756." | IN TWELVE VOLUMES. | VOLUME V. | GENESIS, CHAPTER XXVIII. TO CHAPTER XXXI. | SWEDENBORG SOCIETY, BRITISH AND FOREIGN | (*INSTITUTED* 1810) | 36 BLOOMSBURY STREET, LONDON. | 1881
verso: Matthew vi. 33. | *Seek ye first the kingdom of God and His righteousness,* | *and all these things shall be added unto you.*
half title: THE | HEAVENLY MYSTERIES.
imprint: BRADBURY, AGNEW, & CO., PRINTERS, WHITEFRIARS.
8vo
half title and title leaves, 4 pp; text of Genesis 28-31 and n 3650-4228, pp 5-391; imprint, p 391.
Reprinted from En 2/90 = Hyde 687; an edition of 505 copies was printed.
UK: SOC, CON; SWE: UPP; USA: ANC

49/01/En 2/155 **1882** Hyde 611

ARCANA CÆLESTIA. | <short rule> | THE | HEAVENLY ARCANA | CONTAINED IN | THE HOLY SCRIPTURES OR WORD OF THE LORD | UNFOLDED | BEGINNING WITH THE BOOK OF GENESIS | *TOGETHER WITH WONDERFUL THINGS SEEN IN THE WORLD OF* | *SPIRITS AND IN THE HEAVEN OF ANGELS* | TRANSLATED FROM THE LATIN OF | EMANUEL SWEDENBORG |

Servant of the Lord Jesus Christ. | <short rule> | VOL. I. | <short rule> | NEW YORK: | AMERICAN SWEDENBORG PRINTING AND PUBLISHING | SOCIETY | 20 COOPER UNION | <short rule> | MDCCCLXXXII
half title: ARCANA CŒLESTIA.
8vo
half title and title leaves, 4 pp; the Society's imprint, 1 p <verso blank>; text of Genesis 1-11 and n 1-1382, pp 1-568.
The same as En 2/151 = Hyde 610; an edition of 500 copies was printed.
UK: SOC; USA: ANC, FOU

49/01/En 2/156 **1882** Hyde 639
ARCANA CÆLESTIA. | <short rule> | THE | HEAVENLY ARCANA | CONTAINED IN | THE HOLY SCRIPTURES OR WORD OF THE LORD | UNFOLDED, | BEGINNING WITH THE BOOK OF GENESIS: | *TOGETHER WITH WONDERFUL THINGS SEEN IN THE WORLD OF* | *SPIRITS AND IN THE HEAVEN OF ANGELS* | TRANSLATED FROM THE LATIN OF | EMANUEL SWEDENBORG | *Servant of the Lord Jesus Christ.* | <short rule> | VOL. II. | <short rule> | NEW YORK: | AMERICAN SWEDENBORG PRINTING AND PUBLISHING | SOCIETY | 1882.
verso: *Published by* THE AMERICAN SWEDENBORG PRINTING AND PUBLISHING | SOCIETY, *organized for the purpose of Stereotyping, Printing, and* | *Publishing Uniform Editions of the Theological Writings of* EMANUEL | SWEDENBORG, *and incorporated in the State of New York* A.D. 1850
half title: ARCANA CŒLESTIA
8vo
half title and title leaves, 4 pp; text of Genesis 12-19 and n 1383-2494, pp 5-576.
The same as En 2/148 = Hyde 638; an edition of 500 copies was printed.
UK: SOC; USA: ANC, FOU; SA: MMC

49/01/En 2/157 **1882** Hyde 658
ARCANA CÆLESTIA. | <short rule> | THE | HEAVENLY ARCANA | CONTAINED IN | THE HOLY SCRIPTURES OR WORD OF THE LORD | UNFOLDED, | BEGINNING WITH THE BOOK OF GENESIS: | *TOGETHER WITH WONDERFUL THINGS SEEN IN THE WORLD OF* | *SPIRITS AND IN THE HEAVEN OF ANGELS* | TRANSLATED FROM THE LATIN OF | EMANUEL SWEDENBORG | *Servant of the Lord Jesus Christ.* | <short rule> | VOL. III. | <short rule> | NEW YORK: | AMERICAN SWEDENBORG PRINTING AND PUBLISHING | SOCIETY | 1882.
verso: *Published by* THE AMERICAN SWEDENBORG PRINTING AND PUBLISHING | SOCIETY, *organized for the purpose of Stereotyping, Printing, and* | *Publishing Uniform Editions of the Theological Writings of* EMANUEL | SWEDENBORG, *and incorporated in the State of New York* A.D. 1850
half title: ARCANA CŒLESTIA
8vo
half title and title leaves, 4 pp; text of Genesis 20-25 and n 2495-3352, pp 5-515.
The same as En 2/137 = Hyde 657.
UK: SOC; SWE: UPP; USA: ANC, FOU; SA: MMC

49/01/En 2/158 **1882** Hyde 658/a
<<ARCANA CÆLESTIA. | <short rule> | THE | HEAVENLY ARCANA | CONTAINED IN | THE HOLY SCRIPTURES OR WORD OF THE LORD | UNFOLDED, | BEGINNING WITH THE BOOK OF GENESIS: | *TOGETHER WITH WONDERFUL THINGS SEEN IN THE WORLD OF* | *SPIRITS AND IN THE HEAVEN OF ANGELS* | TRANSLATED FROM THE LATIN OF | EMANUEL SWEDENBORG

| *Servant of the Lord Jesus Christ.* | <short rule> | VOL. III. | <short rule> | NEW YORK: | AMERICAN SWEDENBORG PRINTING AND PUBLISHING | SOCIETY | 1882.>>
verso: <<*Published by* THE AMERICAN SWEDENBORG PRINTING AND PUBLISHING | SOCIETY, *organized for the purpose of Stereotyping, Printing, and | Publishing Uniform Editions of the Theological Writings of* EMANUEL | SWEDENBORG, *and incorporated in the State of New York* A.D. 1850>>
half title: <<ARCANA CŒLESTIA>>
8vo
half title and title leaves, 4 pp; text of Genesis 20-25 and n 2495-3352, pp 5-515.
Copy not seen; description deduced from En 2/79 and 141.
USA: ANC

49/01/En 2/159 **1882** Hyde 676
ARCANA CÆLESTIA. | <short rule> | THE | HEAVENLY ARCANA | CONTAINED IN | THE HOLY SCRIPTURES OR WORD OF THE LORD | UNFOLDED | BEGINNING WITH THE BOOK OF GENESIS | *TOGETHER WITH WONDERFUL THINGS SEEN IN THE WORLD OF | SPIRITS AND IN THE HEAVEN OF ANGELS* | TRANSLATED FROM THE LATIN OF | EMANUEL SWEDENBORG | *Servant of the Lord Jesus Christ.* | <short rule> | VOL. IV | <short rule> | NEW YORK | AMERICAN SWEDENBORG PRINTING AND PUBLISHING | SOCIETY | 20 COOPER UNION | <short rule> | MDCCCLXXXII
verso: *Published by* THE AMERICAN SWEDENBORG PRINTING AND PUBLISHING | SOCIETY, *organized for the purpose of Stereotyping, Printing, and | Publishing Uniform Editions of the Theological Writings of* EMANUEL | SWEDENBORG, *and incorporated in the State of New York* A.D. 1850.
half title: ARCANA CŒLESTIA.
8vo
half title and title leaves, 4 pp; text of Genesis 26-31 and n 3353-4228, pp 5-557.
The same as En 2/142 = Hyde 674.
UK: SOC; USA: ANC, FOU; SA: MMC

49/01/En 2/160 **1882** Hyde 693
ARCANA CÆLESTIA. | <short rule> | THE | HEAVENLY ARCANA | CONTAINED IN | THE HOLY SCRIPTURES OR WORD OF THE LORD | UNFOLDED, | BEGINNING WITH THE BOOK OF GENESIS: | *TOGETHER WITH WONDERFUL THINGS SEEN IN THE WORLD OF | SPIRITS AND IN THE HEAVEN OF ANGELS* | TRANSLATED FROM THE LATIN OF | EMANUEL SWEDENBORG | *Servant of the Lord Jesus Christ.* | <short rule> | VOL. V. | <short rule> | NEW YORK: | AMERICAN SWEDENBORG PRINTING AND PUBLISHING | SOCIETY | 1882.
verso: *Published by* THE AMERICAN SWEDENBORG PRINTING AND PUBLISHING | SOCIETY, *organized for the purpose of Stereotyping, Printing, and | Publishing Uniform Editions of the Theological Writings of* EMANUEL | SWEDENBORG, *and incorporated in the State of New York* A.D. 1850
half title: ARCANA CŒLESTIA
8vo
half title and title leaves, 4 pp; text of Genesis 32-40 and n 4229-5190, pp 5-607.
The same as En 2/143 = Hyde 691.
UK: SOC; USA: ANC, FOU

49/01/En 2/161 **1882** Hyde 693/a
<<ARCANA CÆLESTIA. | <short rule> | THE | HEAVENLY ARCANA | CONTAINED IN | THE HOLY SCRIPTURES OR WORD OF THE LORD | UNFOLDED, | BEGINNING WITH THE BOOK OF

GENESIS: | *TOGETHER WITH WONDERFUL THINGS SEEN IN THE WORLD OF* | *SPIRITS AND IN THE HEAVEN OF ANGELS* | TRANSLATED FROM THE LATIN OF | EMANUEL SWEDENBORG | *Servant of the Lord Jesus Christ.* | <short rule> | VOL. V. | <short rule> | NEW YORK: | AMERICAN SWEDENBORG PRINTING AND PUBLISHING | SOCIETY | 3 WEST 29TH STREET. | 1882.>>
verso: <<*Published by* THE AMERICAN SWEDENBORG PRINTING AND PUBLISHING | SOCIETY, *organized for the purpose of Stereotyping, Printing, and* | *Publishing Uniform Editions of the Theological Writings of* EMANUEL | SWEDENBORG, *and incorporated in the State of New York* A.D. 1850>>
half title: <<ARCANA CŒLESTIA>>
8vo
half title and title leaves, 4 pp; text of Genesis 32-40 and n 4229-5190, pp 5-607.
Copy not seen; description deduced from En 2/135 and 141.
SWE: upp; USA: anc

49/01/En 2/162 **1882** Hyde 709
ARCANA CÆLESTIA. | <short rule> | THE | HEAVENLY ARCANA | CONTAINED IN | THE HOLY SCRIPTURES OR WORD OF THE LORD | UNFOLDED, | BEGINNING WITH THE BOOK OF GENESIS: | *TOGETHER WITH WONDERFUL THINGS SEEN IN THE WORLD OF* | *SPIRITS AND IN THE HEAVEN OF ANGELS* | TRANSLATED FROM THE LATIN OF | EMANUEL SWEDENBORG | *Servant of the Lord Jesus Christ.* | <short rule> | VOL. VI. | <short rule> | NEW YORK | AMERICAN SWEDENBORG PRINTING AND PUBLISHING | SOCIETY | 20 COOPER UNION | <short rule> | MDCCCLXXXII
verso: *Published by* THE AMERICAN SWEDENBORG PRINTING AND PUBLISHING | SOCIETY, *organized for the purpose of Stereotyping, Printing, and* | *Publishing Uniform Editions of the Theological Writings of* EMANUEL | SWEDENBORG, *and incorporated in the State of New York* A. D. 1850
half title: ARCANA CŒLESTIA
8vo
half title and title leaves, 4 pp; text of Genesis 41-49 and n 5191-6496, pp 5-624.
The same as En 2/144 = Hyde 708.
UK: soc; SWE: upp; USA: anc; SA: mmc

49/01/En 2/163 **1882** Hyde 709/a
<<ARCANA CÆLESTIA. | <short rule> | THE | HEAVENLY ARCANA | CONTAINED IN | THE HOLY SCRIPTURES OR WORD OF THE LORD | UNFOLDED, | BEGINNING WITH THE BOOK OF GENESIS: | *TOGETHER WITH WONDERFUL THINGS SEEN IN THE WORLD OF* | *SPIRITS AND IN THE HEAVEN OF ANGELS* | TRANSLATED FROM THE LATIN OF | EMANUEL SWEDENBORG | *Servant of the Lord Jesus Christ.* | <short rule> | VOL. VI. | <short rule> | NEW YORK: | AMERICAN SWEDENBORG PRINTING AND PUBLISHING | SOCIETY | 3 WEST 29TH STREET | 1882.>>
verso: <<*Published by* THE AMERICAN SWEDENBORG PRINTING AND PUBLISHING | SOCIETY, *organized for the purpose of Stereotyping, Printing, and* | *Publishing Uniform Editions of the Theological Writings of* EMANUEL | SWEDENBORG, *and incorporated in the State of New York* A.D. 1850>>
half title: <<ARCANA CŒLESTIA>>
8vo
half title and title leaves, 4 pp; text of Genesis 41-49 and n 5191-6496, pp 5-624.
Copy not seen; description deduced from En 2/162.
USA: anc, fou

49/01/En 2/164 **1882** Hyde 725

ARCANA CÆLESTIA | <short rule> | THE | HEAVENLY ARCANA | CONTAINED IN | THE HOLY SCRIPTURES OR WORD OF THE LORD | UNFOLDED | BEGINNING WITH THE BOOK OF GENESIS | *TOGETHER WITH WONDERFUL THINGS SEEN IN THE WORLD OF | SPIRITS AND IN THE HEAVEN OF ANGELS* | TRANSLATED FROM THE LATIN OF | EMANUEL SWEDENBORG | *Servant of the Lord Jesus Christ* | <short rule> | VOL. VII. | <short rule> | NEW YORK | AMERICAN SWEDENBORG PRINTING AND PUBLISHING | SOCIETY | 20 COOPER UNION | <short rule> | MDCCCLXXXII

verso: *Published by* THE AMERICAN SWEDENBORG PRINTING AND PUBLISHING | SOCIETY, *organized for the purpose of Stereotyping, Printing, and | Publishing Uniform Editions of the Theological Writings of* EMANUEL | SWEDENBORG, *and incorporated in the State of New York* A.D. 1850

half title: ARCANA CŒLESTIA

8vo

half title and title leaves, 4 pp; text of Genesis 50, Exodus 1-12, and n 6497-8032, pp 5-627.

The same as En 2/149 = Hyde 724.

UK: SOC; SWE: UPP; USA: ANC; SA: MMC

49/01/En 2/165 **1882** Hyde 725/a

<<ARCANA CÆLESTIA | <short rule> | THE | HEAVENLY ARCANA | CONTAINED IN | THE HOLY SCRIPTURES OR WORD OF THE LORD | UNFOLDED | BEGINNING WITH THE BOOK OF GENESIS | *TOGETHER WITH WONDERFUL THINGS SEEN IN THE WORLD OF | SPIRITS AND IN THE HEAVEN OF ANGELS* | TRANSLATED FROM THE LATIN OF | EMANUEL SWEDENBORG | *Servant of the Lord Jesus Christ* | <short rule> | VOL. VII. | <short rule> | NEW YORK | AMERICAN SWEDENBORG PRINTING AND PUBLISHING | SOCIETY | 20 COOPER UNION | <short rule> | MDCCCLXXXII>>

verso: <<*Published by The American Swedenborg Printing and Publishing Soci- | ety, organized for the purpose of Stereotyping, Printing and | Publishing Uniform Editions of the Theological Writings of | Emanuel Swedenborg, and incorporated in the State of New York, | A. D.*, 1850.>>

half title: <<ARCANA CŒLESTIA.>>

8vo

half title and title leaves, 4 pp; text of Genesis 50, Exodus 1-12, and n 6497-8032, pp 5-627.

Copy not seen; description deduced from En 2/162.

USA: ANC, FOU

49/01/En 2/166 **1882** Hyde 742

ARCANA CÆLESTIA | <short rule> | THE | HEAVENLY ARCANA | CONTAINED IN | THE HOLY SCRIPTURES OR WORD OF THE LORD | UNFOLDED | BEGINNING WITH THE BOOK OF GENESIS | *TOGETHER WITH WONDERFUL THINGS SEEN IN THE WORLD OF | SPIRITS AND IN THE HEAVEN OF ANGELS* | TRANSLATED FROM THE LATIN OF | EMANUEL SWEDENBORG | *Servant of the Lord Jesus Christ* | <short rule> | VOL. VIII. | <short rule> | NEW YORK | AMERICAN SWEDENBORG PRINTING AND PUBLISHING | SOCIETY | 20 COOPER UNION | <short rule> | MDCCCLXXXII

verso: *Published by The American Swedenborg Printing and Publishing Soci- | ety, organized for the purpose of Stereotyping, Printing and | Publishing Uniform Editions of the Theological Writings of | Emanuel Swedenborg, and incorporated in the State of New York, | A. D.,* 1850.

half title: ARCANA CŒLESTIA.

8vo

half title and title leaves, 4 pp; text of Exodus 13-21 and n 8033-9111, pp 5-543.
The same as En 2/152 = Hyde 741.
UK: soc; USA: anc

49/01/En 2/167 **1882** Hyde 742/a
<<ARCANA CÆLESTIA | <short rule> | THE | HEAVENLY ARCANA | CONTAINED IN | THE HOLY SCRIPTURES OR WORD OF THE LORD | UNFOLDED | BEGINNING WITH THE BOOK OF GENESIS | *TOGETHER WITH WONDERFUL THINGS SEEN IN THE WORLD OF* | *SPIRITS AND IN THE HEAVEN OF ANGELS* | TRANSLATED FROM THE LATIN OF | EMANUEL SWEDENBORG | *Servant of the Lord Jesus Christ* | <short rule> | VOL. VIII. | <short rule> | NEW YORK | AMERICAN SWEDENBORG PRINTING AND PUBLISHING | SOCIETY | 3 WEST 29TH STREET | <short rule> | MDCCCLXXXII>>
verso: <<*Published by The American Swedenborg Printing and Publishing Soci-* | *ety, organized for the purpose of Stereotyping, Printing and* | *Publishing Uniform Editions of the Theological Writings of* | *Emanuel Swedenborg, and incorporated in the State of New York,* | *A. D.,* 1850.>>
half title: <<ARCANA CŒLESTIA>>
8vo
half title and title leaves, 4 pp; text of Exodus 13-21 and n 8033-9111, pp 5-543.
Copy not seen; description deduced from En 2/162.
SWE: upp; USA: anc, fou

49/01/En 2/168 **1882** Hyde 756
ARCANA CÆLESTIA | <short rule> | THE | HEAVENLY ARCANA | CONTAINED IN | THE HOLY SCRIPTURES OR WORD OF THE LORD | UNFOLDED | BEGINNING WITH THE BOOK OF GENESIS | *TOGETHER WITH WONDERFUL THINGS SEEN IN THE WORLD OF* | *SPIRITS AND IN THE HEAVEN OF ANGELS* | TRANSLATED FROM THE LATIN OF | EMANUEL SWEDENBORG | *Servant of the Lord Jesus Christ* | <short rule> | VOL. IX. | <short rule> | NEW YORK | AMERICAN SWEDENBORG PRINTING AND PUBLISHING | SOCIETY | 20 COOPER UNION | <short rule> | MDCCCLXXXII
verso: *Published by The American Swedenborg Printing and Publishing Soci-* | *ety, organized for the purpose of Stereotyping, Printing and* | *Publishing Uniform Editions of the Theological Writings of* | *Emanuel Swedenborg, and incorporated in the State of New York,* | *A.D.,* 1850.
half title: ARCANA CŒLESTIA
8vo
half title and title leaves, 4 pp; text of Exodus 22-28 and n 9112-9973, pp 5-607.
The same En 2/128 = Hyde 755.
UK: soc; SWE: upp; USA: anc; SA: mmc

49/01/En 2/169 **1882** Hyde 756/a
ARCANA CÆLESTIA | <short rule> | THE | HEAVENLY ARCANA | CONTAINED IN | THE HOLY SCRIPTURES OR WORD OF THE LORD | UNFOLDED | BEGINNING WITH THE BOOK OF GENESIS | *TOGETHER WITH WONDERFUL THINGS SEEN IN THE WORLD OF* | *SPIRITS AND IN THE HEAVEN OF ANGELS* | TRANSLATED FROM THE LATIN OF | EMANUEL SWEDENBORG | *Servant of the Lord Jesus Christ* | <short rule> | VOL. IX. | <short rule> | NEW YORK | AMERICAN SWEDENBORG PRINTING AND PUBLISHING | SOCIETY | NO. 3 WEST TWENTY-NINTH STREET | <short rule> | MDCCCLXXXII
verso: *Published by The American Swedenborg Printing and Publishing Soci-* | *ety, organized for the purpose of Stereotyping, Printing and* | *Publishing Uniform Editions of the Theological Writings of* | *Emanuel Swedenborg, and incorporated in the State of New York,* | *A.D.,* 1850.
half title: ARCANA CŒLESTIA.

verso: <short double rule> | NOTE. | *In this Volume, the numbers referring to passages have been revised | and corrected; but where the correct number could not be discovered the erroneous one is retained, and distinguished by an asterisk.* | <short double rule>
8vo
half title and title leaves, 4 pp; text of Exodus 22-28 and n 9112-9973, pp 5-607.
UK: SOC; USA: ANC, FOU

49/01/En 2/170 **1882** Hyde 771
ARCANA CÆLESTIA | <short rule> | THE | HEAVENLY ARCANA | CONTAINED IN | THE HOLY SCRIPTURES OR WORD OF THE LORD | UNFOLDED | BEGINNING WITH THE BOOK OF GENESIS | TOGETHER WITH WONDERFUL THINGS SEEN IN THE WORLD OF | SPIRITS AND IN THE HEAVEN OF ANGELS | TRANSLATED FROM THE LATIN OF | EMANUEL SWEDENBORG, | *Servant of the Lord Jesus Christ.* | <short rule> | VOL. X. | NEW YORK | AMERICAN SWEDENBORG PRINTING AND PUBLISHING | SOCIETY | 20 COOPER UNION | <short rule> | MDCCCLXXXII
verso: *Published by* THE AMERICAN SWEDENBORG PRINTING AND PUBLISHING | SOCIETY, *organized for the purpose of Stereotyping, Printing and | Publishing Uniform Editions of the Theological Writings of* EMANUEL | SWEDENBORG, *and incorporated in the State of New York,* A. D.1850.
half title: ARCANA CŒLESTIA.
verso: <short rule> | NOTE. | *In this Volume, the numbers referring to passages have been revised | and corrected; but where the correct number could not be discovered | the erroneous one is retained, and distinguished by an asterisk.* | <short double rule>
8vo
half title and title leaves, 4 pp; text of Exodus 29-40 and n 9974-10837, pp 5-569.
The same as En 2/129 = Hyde 770.
UK: SOC; USA: ANC, FOU; SA: MMC

49/01/En 2/171 **1880-1885 ?** Hyde 612
ARCANA CŒLESTIA. | <short rule> | THE | HEAVENLY ARCANA | CONTAINED IN | THE HOLY SCRIPTURES OR WORD OF THE LORD | UNFOLDED, | BEGINNING WITH THE BOOK OF GENESIS: | TOGETHER WITH | WONDERFUL THINGS SEEN IN THE WORLD OF SPIRITS | AND IN THE HEAVEN OF ANGELS. | <short rule> | *Translated from the Latin of* | EMANUEL SWEDENBORG | *Servant of the Lord Jesus Christ.* | <short rule> | VOL I. | PHILADELPHIA: | CLAXTON, REMSEN & HAFFELFINGER, | 624, 626 & 628 MARKET STREET.
half title: ARCANA CŒLESTIA.
8vo
half title and title leaves, 4 pp; text of Genesis 1-11 and n 1-1382, pp 1-568.
The same as En 2/154 = Hyde 611. The date of issue is uncertain, but it is not later than 1885, though it may be before 1880.
USA: ANC

49/01/En 2/172 **1880-1885 ?** Hyde 640
ARCANA CŒLESTIA. | <short rule> | THE | HEAVENLY ARCANA | CONTAINED IN | THE HOLY SCRIPTURES OR WORD OF THE LORD | UNFOLDED, | BEGINNING WITH THE BOOK OF GENESIS: | TOGETHER WITH | WONDERFUL THINGS SEEN IN THE WORLD OF SPIRITS | AND IN THE HEAVEN OF ANGELS. | <short rule> | *Translated from the Latin of* | EMANUEL SWEDENBORG, | *Servant of the Lord Jesus Christ.* | <short rule> | VOL. II. | PHILADELPHIA: | CLAXTON, REMSEN & HAFFELFINGER, | 624, 626 & 628 MARKET STREET.
half title: ARCANA CŒLESTIA.

8vo
half title and title leaves, 4 pp; text of Genesis 12-19 and n 1383-2494, pp 5-576.
The same as En 2/155 = Hyde 639. The date of issue is uncertain, but it is not later than 1885, though it may be before 1880; see En 2/170 = Hyde 612.
USA: ANC

49/01/En 2/173 **1880-1885?** Hyde 659

ARCANA CŒLESTIA. | THE | HEAVENLY ARCANA | CONTAINED IN | THE HOLY SCRIPTURES OR WORD OF THE LORD | UNFOLDED, | BEGINNING WITH THE BOOK OF GENESIS: | TOGETHER WITH | WONDERFUL THINGS SEEN IN THE WORLD OF SPIRITS | AND IN THE HEAVEN OF ANGELS. | <short rule> | *Translated from the Latin of* | EMANUEL SWEDENBORG, | *Servant of the Lord Jesus Christ.* | VOL. III. | PHILADELPHIA: | CLAXTON, REMSEN & HAFFELFINGER | 624, 626 & 628 MARKET STREET.
half title: ARCANA CŒLESTIA.
8vo
half title and title leaves, 4 pp; text of Genesis 20-25 and n 2495-3352, pp 5-515.
The same as En 2/156 = Hyde 658. The date of issue is uncertain, but it is not later than 1885, though it may be before 1880; see En 2/170 = Hyde 612.
USA: ANC

49/01/En 2/174 **1880-1885?** Hyde 677

ARCANA CŒLESTIA. | THE | HEAVENLY ARCANA | CONTAINED IN | THE HOLY SCRIPTURES OR WORD OF THE LORD | UNFOLDED, | BEGINNING WITH THE BOOK OF GENESIS: | TOGETHER WITH | WONDERFUL THINGS SEEN IN THE WORLD OF SPIRITS | AND IN THE HEAVEN OF ANGELS. | <short rule> | *Translated from the Latin of* | EMANUEL SWEDENBORG, | *Servant of the Lord Jesus Christ.* | <short rule> | VOL. IV. | PHILADELPHIA: | CLAXTON, REMSEN & HAFFELFINGER, | 624, 626 & 628 MARKET STREET.
half title: ARCANA CŒLESTIA.
8vo
half title and title leaves, 4 pp; text of Genesis 26-31 and n 3353-4228, pp 5-557.
The same as En 2/158 = Hyde 676. The date of issue is uncertain, but it is not later than 1885, though it may be before 1880; see En 2/170 = Hyde 612. A copy seen by NR in Hay-on-Wye was dated 1894 on tp.
USA: ANC

49/01/En 2/175 **1880-1885?** Hyde 694

ARCANA CŒLESTIA. | THE | HEAVENLY ARCANA | CONTAINED IN THE HOLY SCRIPTURES OR WORD OF THE LORD | UNFOLDED | BEGINNING WITH THE BOOK OF GENESIS: | TOGETHER WITH | WONDERFUL THINGS SEEN IN THE WORLD OF SPIRITS | AND IN THE HEAVEN OF ANGELS. | <short rule> | *Translated from the Latin of* | EMANUEL SWEDENBORG, | *Servant of the Lord Jesus Christ.* | VOL. V. | <short rule> | PHILADELPHIA: | CLAXTON, REMSEN & HAFFELFINGER, | 624, 626 & 628 MARKET STREET.
half title: ARCANA CŒLESTIA.
8vo
half title and title leaves, 4 pp; text of Genesis 32-40 and n 4229-5190, pp 5-607.
The same as En 2/159 = Hyde 693. The date of issue is uncertain, but it is not later than 1885, though it may be before 1880; see En 2/170 = Hyde 612.
USA: ANC

49/01/En 2/176 **1880-1885 ?** Hyde 710

ARCANA CŒLESTIA. | <short rule> | THE | HEAVENLY ARCANA | CONTAINED IN | THE HOLY SCRIPTURES OR WORD OF THE LORD | UNFOLDED, | BEGINNING WITH THE BOOK OF GENESIS: | TOGETHER WITH | WONDERFUL THINGS SEEN IN THE WORLD OF SPIRITS | AND IN THE HEAVEN OF ANGELS. | <short rule> | *Translated from the Latin* of | EMANUEL SWEDENBORG, | *Servant of the Lord Jesus Christ.* | <short rule> | VOL. VI. | PHILADELPHIA: | CLAXTON, REMSEN & HAFFELFINGER, | 624, 626 & 628 MARKET STREET.
half title: ARCANA CŒLESTIA.
8vo
half title and title leaves, 4 pp; text of Genesis 41-49 and n 5191-6496, pp 5-624.
The same as En 2/161 = Hyde 709. The date of issue is uncertain, but it is not later than 1885, though it may be before 1880; see En 2/170 = Hyde 612.
USA: ANC

49/01/En 2/177 **1880-1885 ?** Hyde 726

ARCANA CŒLESTIA. | <short rule> | THE | HEAVENLY ARCANA | CONTAINED IN THE HOLY SCRIPTURES OR WORD OF THE LORD | UNFOLDED, | BEGINNING WITH THE BOOK OF GENESIS: | TOGETHER WITH WONDERFUL THINGS SEEN IN THE WORLD OF SPIRITS | AND IN THE HEAVEN OF ANGELS. | <short rule> | *Translated from the Latin of* | EMANUEL SWEDENBORG, | *Servant of the Lord Jesus Christ.* | <short rule> | VOL. VII. | PHILADELPHIA: | CLAXTON, REMSEN & HAFFELFINGER, | 624, 626 & 628 MARKET STREET.
half title: ARCANA CŒLESTIA.
8vo
half title and title leaves, 4 pp; text of Genesis 50, Exodus 1-12, and n 6497-8032, pp 5-627.
The same as En 2/163 = Hyde 725. The date of issue is uncertain, but it is not later than 1885, though it may be before 1880; see En 2/170 = Hyde 612.
USA: ANC

49/01/En 2/178 **1880-1885 ?** Hyde 743

ARCANA CŒLESTIA. | <short rule> | THE | HEAVENLY ARCANA | CONTAINED IN | THE HOLY SCRIPTURES OR WORD OF THE LORD | UNFOLDED, | BEGINNING WITH THE BOOK OF GENESIS: | TOGETHER WITH | WONDERFUL THINGS SEEN IN THE WORLD OF SPIRITS | AND IN THE HEAVEN OF ANGELS. | <short rule> | *Translated from the Latin of* | EMANUEL SWEDENBORG, | *Servant of the Lord Jesus Christ.* | VOL. VIII. | PHILADELPHIA: | CLAXTON, REMSEN & HAFFELFINGER, | 624, 626 & 628 MARKET STREET
half title: ARCANA CŒLESTIA.
8vo
half title and title leaves, 4 pp; text of Exodus 13-21 and n 8033-9111, pp 5-543.
The same as En 2/165 = Hyde 742. The date of issue is uncertain, but it is not later than 1885, though it may be before 1880; see En 2/170 = Hyde 612.
USA: ANC

49/01/En 2/179 **1880-1885 ?** Hyde 757

ARCANA CŒLESTIA. | <short rule> | THE | HEAVENLY ARCANA | CONTAINED IN THE HOLY SCRIPTURES OR WORD OF THE LORD | UNFOLDED, | BEGINNING WITH THE BOOK OF GENESIS: | TOGETHER WITH WONDERFUL THINGS SEEN IN THE WORLD OF SPIRITS | AND IN THE HEAVEN OF ANGELS. | <short rule> | *Translated from the Latin of* | EMANUEL SWEDENBORG, | *Servant of the Lord Jesus Christ.* | <short rule> | VOL. IX. | PHILADELPHIA: | CLAXTON, REMSEN & HAFFELFINGER, | 624, 626 & 628 MARKET STREET.

half title: ARCANA CŒLESTIA.
verso: <short double rule> | *In this Volume, the numbers referring to passages have been revised* | *and corrected; but where the correct number could not be discovered* | *the erroneous one is retained, and distinguished by an asterisk.* | <short double rule>
8vo
half title and title leaves, 4 pp; text of Exodus 22-28 and n 9112-9973, pp 5-607.
The same as En 2/167 = Hyde 756. The date of issue is uncertain, but it is not later than 1885, though it may be before 1880; see En 2/170 = Hyde 612.
USA: ANC

49/01/En 2/180 **1880-1885 ?** Hyde 772
ARCANA CŒLESTIA. | <short rule> | THE | HEAVENLY ARCANA | CONTAINED IN | THE HOLY SCRIPTURES OR WORD OF THE LORD | UNFOLDED, | BEGINNING WITH THE BOOK OF GENESIS: | TOGETHER WITH | WONDERFUL THINGS SEEN IN THE WORLD OF SPIRITS | AND IN THE HEAVEN OF ANGELS. | *Translated from the Latin of* | EMANUEL SWEDENBORG, | *Servant of the Lord Jesus Christ.* | <short rule> | VOL. X. | PHILADELPHIA: | CLAXTON, REMSEN & HAFFELFINGER, | 624, 626 & 628 MARKET STREET.
half title: ARCANA CŒLESTIA.
verso: <short double rule> | *In this Volume, the numbers referring to passages have been revised* | *and corrected; but where the correct number could not be discovered* | *the erroneous one is retained, and distinguished by an asterisk.* | <short double rule>
8vo
half title and title leaves, 4 pp; text of Exodus 29-40 and n 9974-10837, pp 5-569.
The same as En 2/169 = Hyde 771. The date of issue is uncertain, but it is not later than 1885, though it may be before 1880; see En 2/170 = Hyde 612.
USA: ANC

49/01/En 2/181 **1885** Hyde 791
ARCANA CŒLESTIA. | <short rule> | THE | HEAVENLY MYSTERIES | CONTAINED IN | THE HOLY SCRIPTURE, OR WORD OF THE LORD | UNFOLDED | IN AN EXPOSITION OF GENESIS AND EXODUS | TOGETHER WITH A RELATION OF | WONDERFUL THINGS SEEN IN THE WORLD OF SPIRITS AND | IN THE HEAVEN OF ANGELS | BY | EMANUEL SWEDENBORG | BEING A TRANSLATION OF HIS WORK ENTITLED | "ARCANA CŒLESTIA QUÆ IN SCRIPTURA SACRA SEU VERBO DOMINI SUNT, DETECTA; HIC | QUÆ IN EXODO. UNA CUM MIRABILIBUS QUÆ VISA SUNT IN MUNDO SPIRITUUM | ET IN CŒLO ANGELORUM. LONDINI, 1749-1756." | IN TWELVE VOLUMES | VOLUME XII. | EXODUS, CHAPTER XXIX. TO CHAPTER XL. | SWEDENBORG SOCIETY, BRITISH AND FOREIGN | (*INSTITUTED* 1810) | 36 BLOOMSBURY STREET, LONDON | 1885
verso: Matthew vi. 33. | *Seek ye first the kingdom of God and His righteousness,* | *and all these things shall be added unto you.* | LONDON: | BRADBURY, AGNEW, & CO., PRINTERS, WHITEFRIARS.
half title: ARCANA CŒLESTIA.
8vo
half title and title leaves, 4 pp; text of Exodus 29-40 and n 9974-10837, pp 5-563; The translator's prayer, pp 565-566.
Revised by W O'Mant; an edition of 1,000 copies was printed.
UK: SOC, CON; SWE: UPP; USA: ANC

49/01/En 4/1 **1889** Hyde 711
ARCANA CŒLESTIA | <short rule> | THE | HEAVENLY MYSTERIES | CONTAINED IN | THE HOLY SCRIPTURE, OR WORD OF THE LORD | UNFOLDED | IN AN EXPOSITION OF GENESIS AND EXODUS | TOGETHER WITH A RELATION OF | WONDERFUL THINGS SEEN IN THE WORLD

OF SPIRITS AND | IN THE HEAVEN OF ANGELS | BY | EMANUEL SWEDENBORG | BEING A TRANSLATION OF HIS WORK ENTITLED | "ARCANA CŒLESTIA QUÆ IN SCRIPTURA SACRA SEU VERBO DOMINI SUNT, DETECTA; | HIC QUÆ IN GENESI. UNA CUM MIRABILIBUS QUÆ VISA SUNT IN MUNDO | SPIRITUUM ET IN CŒLO ANGELORUM." LONDINI, 1749-1756. | *IN TWELVE VOLUMES* | VOLUME VI. | GENESIS, CHAPTER XXXII. TO CHAPTER XXXVIII. | THE SWEDENBORG SOCIETY | (INSTITUTED 1810) | 36 BLOOMSBURY STREET, LONDON | 1889
verso: *"Seek ye first the kingdom of God and His righteousness, | and all these things shall be added unto you."* | —MATTHEW vi. 33.
half title: ARCANA CŒLESTIA
imprint: MORRISON AND GIBB, PRINTERS, EDINBURGH.
8vo
half title and title leaves, 4 pp; text of Genesis 32-38 and n 4229-4953, pp 1-446; imprint, p 446; advertisements, 2 pp.
Revised by A H Searle; an edition of 1,080 copies was printed.
UK: SOC, CON; SWE: UPP; USA: ANC

49/01/En 4/2 **1889** Hyde 727
ARCANA CŒLESTIA | <short rule> | THE | HEAVENLY MYSTERIES | CONTAINED IN | THE HOLY SCRIPTURE, OR WORD OF THE LORD | UNFOLDED | IN AN EXPOSITION OF GENESIS AND EXODUS | TOGETHER WITH A RELATION OF | WONDERFUL THINGS SEEN IN THE WORLD OF SPIRITS AND | IN THE HEAVEN OF ANGELS | BY | EMANUEL SWEDENBORG | BEING A TRANSLATION OF HIS WORK ENTITLED | "ARCANA CŒLESTIA QUÆ IN SCRIPTURA SACRA SEU VERBO DOMINI SUNT, DETECTA; | HIC QUÆ IN GENESI. UNA CUM MIRABILIBUS QUÆ VISA SUNT IN MUNDO | SPIRITUUM ET IN CŒLO ANGELORUM." LONDINI, 1749-1756. | *IN TWELVE VOLUMES* | VOLUME VII. | GENESIS, CHAPTER XXXIX. TO CHAPTER XLIII. | THE SWEDENBORG SOCIETY | (INSTITUTED 1810) | 36 BLOOMSBURY STREET, LONDON | 1889
verso: *"Seek ye first the kingdom of God and His righteousness, | and all these things shall be added unto you."* | –MATTHEW vi. 33.
half title: ARCANA CŒLESTIA
imprint: MORRISON AND GIBB, PRINTERS, EDINBURGH.
8vo
half title and title leaves, 4 pp; text of Genesis 39-43 and n 4954-5727, pp 1-409; imprint, p 409; Erratum, p 410; advertisements, 2 pp.
Revised by A H Searle; an edition of 1,080 copies was printed.
UK: SOC, CON; SWE: UPP; USA: ANC

49/01/En 4/3 **1890** Hyde 660
ARCANA CŒLESTIA | <short rule> | THE | HEAVENLY MYSTERIES | CONTAINED IN | THE HOLY SCRIPTURE, OR WORD OF THE LORD | UNFOLDED | IN AN EXPOSITION OF GENESIS AND EXODUS | TOGETHER WITH A RELATION OF | WONDERFUL THINGS SEEN IN THE WORLD OF SPIRITS AND | IN THE HEAVEN OF ANGELS | BY | EMANUEL SWEDENBORG | BEING A TRANSLATION OF HIS WORK ENTITLED | "ARCANA CŒLESTIA QUÆ IN SCRIPTURA SACRA SEU VERBO DOMINI SUNT, DETECTA; | HIC QUÆ IN GENESI. UNA CUM MIRABILIBUS QUÆ VISA SUNT IN MUNDO | SPIRITUUM ET IN CŒLO ANGELORUM." LONDINI, 1749-1756. | *IN TWELVE VOLUMES* | VOLUME III. | GENESIS, CHAPTER XVIII. TO CHAPTER XXII. | THE SWEDENBORG SOCIETY | (INSTITUTED 1810) | 36 BLOOMSBURY STREET, LONDON | 1890
verso: *"Seek ye first the kingdom of God and His righteousness, | and all these things shall be added unto you."* | –MATTHEW vi. 33.
half title: ARCANA CŒLESTIA
imprint: MORRISON AND GIBB, PRINTERS, EDINBURGH.

8vo
half title and title leaves, 4 pp; text of Swedenborg's preface, Genesis 18-22, and n 2135-2893, pp 1-445; imprint, p 445; Erratum, p 446; advertisements, 2 pp.
Revised by A H Searle; an edition of 1,080 copies was printed.
UK: CON; SWE: UPP; USA: ANC

49/01/En 4/4 **1890** Hyde 744
ARCANA CŒLESTIA | <short rule> | THE | HEAVENLY MYSTERIES | CONTAINED IN | THE HOLY SCRIPTURE, OR WORD OF THE LORD | UNFOLDED | IN AN EXPOSITION OF GENESIS AND EXODUS | TOGETHER WITH A RELATION OF | WONDERFUL THINGS SEEN IN THE WORLD OF SPIRITS AND | IN THE HEAVEN OF ANGELS | BY | EMANUEL SWEDENBORG | BEING A TRANSLATION OF HIS WORK ENTITLED | "ARCANA CŒLESTIA QUÆ IN SCRIPTURA SACRA, SEU VERBO DOMINI SUNT, DETECTA; | HIC PRIMUM QUÆ IN GENESI. UNA CUM MIRABILIBUS QUÆ VISA SUNT IN MUNDO | SPIRITUUM ET IN CŒLO ANGELORUM." LONDINI, 1749-1756 | *IN TWELVE VOLUMES* | VOLUME VIII. | GENESIS, CHAPTER XLIV. TO CHAPTER L. | THE SWEDENBORG SOCIETY | (INSTITUTED 1810) | 36 BLOOMSBURY STREET, LONDON | 1890
verso: *"Seek ye first the kingdom of God, and His righteousness, | and all these things shall be added unto you."* | –MATTHEW vi. 33.
half title: ARCANA CŒLESTIA
imprint: EDINBURGH: ROBERT R. SUTHERLAND, PRINTER.
8vo
half title and title leaves, 4 pp; text n 5728-6626, pp 1-400; imprint, p 400.
Revised by L A Slight; an edition of 1,080 copies printed.
UK: SOC; SWE: UPP; USA: ANC

49/01/En 4/5 **1890** Hyde 782
THE | HEAVENLY ARCANA | CONTAINED IN | THE HOLY SCRIPTURE, OR WORD OF THE LORD | UNFOLDED | IN AN EXPOSITION OF GENESIS AND EXODUS | TOGETHER WITH THE | WONDERFUL THINGS SEEN IN THE WORLD OF SPIRITS AND | IN THE HEAVEN OF ANGELS | BY | EMANUEL SWEDENBORG | VOLUME XI. | SWEDENBORG SOCIETY, BRITISH AND FOREIGN | (INSTITUTED 1810) | 36 BLOOMSBURY STREET, LONDON | 1890
verso: *"Seek ye first the kingdom of God and His righteousness, | and all these things shall be added unto you."* | –MATTHEW vi. 33.
half title: THE HEAVENLY ARCANA
imprint: MORRISON AND GIBB, PRINTERS, EDINBURGH.
8vo
half title and title leaves, 4 pp; Translator's preface, pp v-vi; text of Exodus 22-28 and n 9112-9973, pp 1-620; imprint, p 620.
Translated by R L Tafel, with the assistance of J B Keene. An edition of 1,076 copies was printed.
UK: SOC, CON; SWE: UPP; USA: ANC

49/01/En 2/182 **1891** Hyde 613
ARCANA COELESTIA. | <short rule> | THE | HEAVENLY ARCANA | CONTAINED IN | THE HOLY SCRIPTURE, OR WORD OF THE LORD | UNFOLDED | IN AN EXPOSITION OF GENESIS AND EXODUS | TOGETHER WITH A RELATION OF | WONDERFUL THINGS SEEN IN THE WORLD OF SPIRITS AND | IN THE HEAVEN OF ANGELS | *FROM THE LATIN* | OF | EMANUEL SWEDENBORG | VOLUME I. | GENESIS, CHAPTER I. TO CHAPTER IX. | NOS. 1-1113. | THE SWEDENBORG SOCIETY | (INSTITUTED 1810) | 36 BLOOMSBURY STREET, LONDON | 1891.

verso: "*Seek ye first the kingdom of God and His righteousness,* | *and all these things shall be added unto you.*" | –MATTHEW vi. 33.
half title: ARCANA CŒLESTIA
8vo
half title and title leaves, 4 pp; Translator's preface, pp v-xiv; Contents, pp xv-xvi; text of Genesis 1-9 and n 1-1113, pp 1-464.
A reprint of En 2/83 = Hyde 605, supervised by J Speirs; an edition of 1,080 copies was printed.
UK: SOC; SWE: UPP; USA: ANC

49/01/En 2/183 **1892** Hyde 614
ARCANA COELESTIA | <short rule> | THE | HEAVENLY ARCANA | CONTAINED IN | THE HOLY SCRIPTURES OR WORD OF THE LORD | UNFOLDED | BEGINNING WITH THE BOOK OF GENESIS | *TOGETHER WITH WONDERFUL THINGS SEEN IN THE WORLD OF* | *SPIRITS AND THE HEAVEN OF ANGELS* | TRANSLATED FROM THE LATIN OF | EMANUEL SWEDENBORG | *Servant of the Lord Jesus Christ* | <short rule> | VOL. I | <short rule> | NEW YORK | AMERICAN SWEDENBORG PRINTING AND PUBLISHING | SOCIETY | NO 3 WEST TWENTY-NINTH STREET | <short rule> | MDCCCXCII
verso: MATTHEW VI. 33 | *Seek ye first the Kingdom of God and His Righteousness,* | *and all things shall be added unto you.*
imprint: *Published by The American Swedenborg Printing and Publishing Soci-* | *ety, organized for the purpose of Stereotyping, Printing and* | *Publishing Uniform Editions of the Theological Writings of* | *Emanuel Swedenborg, and incorporated in the State of New York* | *A.D., 1850.*
8vo
title leaf, 2 pp; the Society's imprint, 1 p <verso blank>; text of Genesis 1-11 and n 1-1382, pp 1-568.
The same as En 2/171 = Hyde 612; an edition of 500 copies was printed.
UK: SOC; SWE: UPP; USA: ANC

49/01/En 2/184 **1892** Hyde 615
THE HEAVENLY ARCANA | DISCLOSED | WHICH ARE IN THE SACRED SCRIPTURE | OR | WORD OF THE LORD | HERE, FIRST, THOSE WHICH ARE IN | GENESIS | TOGETHER WITH WONDERFUL THINGS SEEN IN THE | WORLD OF SPIRITS AND THE HEAVEN OF ANGELS | BY EMANUEL SWEDENBORG | ORIGINALLY PUBLISHED IN LATIN AT LONDON, A. D. 1749 | Rotch Edition | VOL. I. | NEW YORK | NEW-CHURCH BOARD OF PUBLICATION | 1892
verso: MATTHEW VI. 33. | Seek ye first the Kingdom of God and His Justice, and all things | shall be added unto you. | <short rule> | TYPOGRAPHY BY MASS. NEW-CHURCH UNION, BOSTON
small 8vo
title leaf, 2 pp; Note, 1 p; Contents, 1 p; text of Genesis 1-7 and n 1-823, pp 3-410.
Edited by J Worcester from a revision by S M Warren. For a later reprint, see En 2/191 = Hyde 616.
UK: SOC; SWE: UPP; USA: ANC

49/01/En 2/185 **1893** Hyde 641
THE HEAVENLY ARCANA | DISCLOSED | WHICH ARE IN THE SACRED SCRIPTURE | OR WORD OF THE LORD | HERE THOSE WHICH ARE IN | GENESIS | TOGETHER WITH WONDERFUL THINGS SEEN IN THE | WORLD OF SPIRITS AND THE HEAVEN OF ANGELS | BY EMANUEL SWEDENBORG | ORIGINALLY PUBLISHED IN LATIN AT LONDON, A. D. 1749. | Rotch Edition. | VOL. II. | NEW YORK | NEW-CHURCH BOARD OF PUBLICATION | 1893
verso: MATTHEW VI. 33. | Seek ye first the Kingdom of God and His Justice, and all things | shall be added unto you. | <short rule> | TYPOGRAPHY BY MASS. NEW-CHURCH UNION, BOSTON

small 8vo
title leaf, 2 pp; Note, 1 p; Contents, 1 p; text of Genesis 8-11 and n 824-1382, pp 3-369.
Edited by J Worcester, using a revision of chapters 10-12 by S M Warren; an edition of 500 copies was printed. For a later reprint, see En 2/195 = Hyde 642.
UK: SOC; SWE: UPP; USA: ANC

49/01/En 2/186 **1893** Hyde 661
THE HEAVENLY ARCANA | DISCLOSED | WHICH ARE IN THE SACRED SCRIPTURE | OR | WORD OF THE LORD | HERE, FIRST, THOSE WHICH ARE IN | GENESIS | TOGETHER WITH WONDERFUL THINGS SEEN IN THE | WORLD OF SPIRITS AND THE HEAVEN OF ANGELS | BY EMANUEL SWEDENBORG | ORIGINALLY PUBLISHED IN LATIN AT LONDON, A.D. 1749-1750. | Rotch Edition | VOL. III. | NEW YORK | NEW-CHURCH BOARD OF PUBLICATION | 1893
verso: MATTHEW VI. 33. | Seek ye first the Kingdom of God and His Justice, and all things | shall be added unto you. | <short rule> | TYPOGRAPHY BY MASS. NEW-CHURCH UNION, BOSTON
small 8vo
title leaf, 2 pp; Note, 1 p; Contents, 1 p; text of Genesis 12-16 and n 1383-1983, pp 3-391.
Edited by J Worcester, from a revision by S M Warren using a MS translation made by T B Hayward.
UK: SOC; SWE: UPP; USA: ANC; SA: MMC

49/01/En 2/187 **1893** Hyde 678
THE HEAVENLY ARCANA | DISCLOSED | WHICH ARE IN THE SACRED SCRIPTURE | OR | WORD OF THE LORD | HERE THOSE WHICH ARE IN | GENESIS | TOGETHER WITH WONDERFUL THINGS SEEN IN THE | WORLD OF SPIRITS AND THE HEAVEN OF ANGELS | BY EMANUEL SWEDENBORG | ORIGINALLY PUBLISHED IN LATIN AT LONDON, A. D. 1750 | Rotch Edition | VOL. IV. | NEW YORK | NEW-CHURCH BOARD OF PUBLICATION | 1893
verso: MATTHEW VI. 33. | Seek ye first the Kingdom of God and His Justice, and all things | shall be added unto you. | <short rule> | TYPOGRAPHY BY MASS. NEW-CHURCH UNION, BOSTON
small 8vo
title leaf, 2 pp; Note, 1 p; Contents, 1 p; text of Genesis 17-20 and n 1984-2605, pp 3-472.
Edited by J Worcester, from a revision by S M Warren using a MS translation made by T B Hayward.
UK: SOC; USA: ANC; SA: MMC

49/01/En 2/188 **1893** Hyde 695
THE HEAVENLY ARCANA | DISCLOSED | WHICH ARE IN THE SACRED SCRIPTURE | OR | WORD OF THE LORD | HERE THOSE WHICH ARE IN | GENESIS | TOGETHER WITH WONDERFUL THINGS SEEN IN THE | WORLD OF SPIRITS AND THE HEAVEN OF ANGELS | BY EMANUEL SWEDENBORG | ORIGINALLY PUBLISHED IN LATIN AT LONDON, A. D. 1750-1751 | Rotch Edition | VOL. V. | NEW YORK | NEW-CHURCH BOARD OF PUBLICATION | 1893
verso: MATTHEW VI. 33. | Seek ye first the Kingdom of God and His Justice, and all things | shall be added unto you. | <short rule> | TYPOGRAPHY BY MASS. NEW-CHURCH UNION, BOSTON
small 8vo
title leaf, 2 pp; Note, 1 p; Contents, 1 p; text of Genesis 21-24 and n 2606-3227, pp 3-482.
Edited by J Worcester, from a revision by S M Warren using a MS translation made by T B Hayward.
UK: SOC; SWE: UPP; USA: ANC; SA: MMC

49/01/En 4/6 **1893** Hyde 773
ARCANA CŒLESTIA | <short rule> | THE | HEAVENLY ARCANA | CONTAINED IN | THE HOLY SCRIPTURE, OR WORD OF THE LORD | UNFOLDED | IN AN EXPOSITION OF GENESIS AND EXODUS | TOGETHER WITH A RELATION OF | WONDERFUL THINGS SEEN IN THE WORLD OF

SPIRITS AND | IN THE HEAVEN OF ANGELS | *FROM THE LATIN* | OF | EMANUEL SWEDENBORG | VOLUME X. | EXODUS, CHAPTER XIII. TO CHAPTER XXI. | NOS. 8033-9111. | THE SWEDENBORG SOCIETY | (INSTITUTED 1810) | 36 BLOOMSBURY STREET, LONDON | 1893
verso: *"Seek ye first the kingdom of God and His righteousness,* | *and all these things shall be added unto you."* | —MATTHEW vi. 33.
half title: ARCANA CŒLESTIA
imprint: MORRISON AND GIBB, PRINTERS, EDINBURGH.
8vo
half title and title leaves, 4 pp; Prefatory note, p v; Contents, pp vii-viii; text of Exodus 13-21 and n 8033-9111, pp 1-518; imprint, p 518; advertisement, 2 pp.
Revised by James Speirs; an edition of 1,080 copies was printed.
UK: SOC; NET: GEN, KB; SWE: UPP; USA: ANC, SHS

49/01/En 2/189 **1894** Hyde 712
THE HEAVENLY ARCANA | DISCLOSED | WHICH ARE IN THE SACRED SCRIPTURE | OR WORD OF THE LORD | HERE THOSE WHICH ARE IN | GENESIS | TOGETHER WITH WONDERFUL THINGS SEEN IN THE | WORLD OF SPIRITS AND THE HEAVEN OF ANGELS | BY EMANUEL SWEDENBORG | ORIGINALLY PUBLISHED IN LATIN AT LONDON, A. D. 1751 | **Rotch Edition** | VOL. VI. | NEW YORK | NEW-CHURCH BOARD OF PUBLICATION | 1894
verso: MATTHEW VI. 33. | Seek ye first the Kingdom of God and His Justice, and all things | shall be added unto you. | <short rule> | TYPOGRAPHY BY MASS. NEW-CHURCH UNION, BOSTON
small 8vo
title leaf, 2 pp; Note, 1 p; Contents, 1 p; text of Genesis 25-27 and n 3228-3649, pp 7-347.
Edited by J Worcester, from a revision by S C Eby.
UK: SOC; USA: ANC; SA: MMC

49/01/En 2/190 **1895** Hyde 728
THE HEAVENLY ARCANA | DISCLOSED | WHICH ARE IN THE SACRED SCRIPTURE | OR | WORD OF THE LORD | HERE THOSE WHICH ARE IN | GENESIS | TOGETHER WITH WONDERFUL THINGS SEEN IN THE | WORLD OF SPIRITS AND THE HEAVEN OF ANGELS | BY EMANUEL SWEDENBORG | ORIGINALLY PUBLISHED IN LATIN AT LONDON, A. D. 1751-1752 | **Rotch Edition** | VOL. VII. | NEW YORK | NEW-CHURCH BOARD OF PUBLICATION | 1895
verso: MATTHEW VI. 33. | Seek ye first the Kingdom of God and His Justice, and all things | shall be added unto you. | <short rule> | TYPOGRAPHY BY MASS. NEW-CHURCH UNION, BOSTON
small 8vo
title leaf, 2 pp; Note, 1 p; Contents, 1 p; text of Genesis 28-31 and n 3650-4228, pp 7-539.
Edited by J Worcester, from a revision of chapters 28-29 by S C Eby and of chapters 30-31 by P B Cabell.
UK: SOC; SWE: UPP; USA: ANC; SA: MMC

49/01/En 4/7 **1895** Hyde 758
ARCANA CŒLESTIA | <short rule> | THE | HEAVENLY ARCANA | CONTAINED IN | THE HOLY SCRIPTURE, OR WORD OF THE LORD | UNFOLDED | IN AN EXPOSITION OF GENESIS AND EXODUS | TOGETHER WITH A RELATION OF | WONDERFUL THINGS SEEN IN THE WORLD OF SPIRITS AND | IN THE HEAVEN OF ANGELS | *FROM THE LATIN* | OF | EMANUEL SWEDENBORG | VOLUME IX. | EXODUS, CHAPTER I. TO CHAPTER XII. | NOS. 6627-8032 | THE SWEDENBORG SOCIETY | (INSTITUTED 1810) | 1 BLOOMSBURY STREET, LONDON | 1895
verso: *Seek ye first the kingdom of God, and His righteousness,* | *and all these things shall be added unto you."* | — MATTHEW vi. 33.
half title: ARCANA CŒLESTIA

imprint: ROBERT R. SUTHERLAND, PRINTER, EDINBURGH.
8vo
half title and title leaves, 4 pp; Translator's prefatory note, p v; Contents, p vii-viii; text of Exodus 1-12 and n 6627-8032 pp 1-581; Errata, p 582; imprint, p 582.
Translated by A H Searle. On p 47, the running header should read CHAPTER II.3; and on p 279 it should read CHAPTER VI.
UK: soc; NET: gen, kb; SWE: upp; USA: anc

49/01/En 2/191 **1896** Hyde 616
<<THE HEAVENLY ARCANA | DISCLOSED | WHICH ARE IN THE SACRED SCRIPTURE | OR | WORD OF THE LORD | HERE, FIRST, THOSE WHICH ARE IN | GENESIS | TOGETHER WITH WONDERFUL THINGS SEEN IN THE | WORLD OF SPIRITS AND THE HEAVEN OF ANGELS | BY EMANUEL SWEDENBORG | ORIGINALLY PUBLISHED IN LATIN AT LONDON, A. D. 1749 | **Rotch Edition** | VOL. I. | NEW YORK | NEW-CHURCH BOARD OF PUBLICATION | 1896>>
verso: <<MATTHEW VI. 33. | Seek ye first the Kingdom of God and His Justice, and all things | shall be added unto you. | <short rule> | TYPOGRAPHY BY MASS. NEW-CHURCH UNION, BOSTON>>
half title: <<ARCANA CŒLESTIA>>
small 8vo
half title and title leaves, 4 pp; Contents, 2 pp; text of Genesis 1-7 and n 1-823, pp 3-410.
The same as En 2/184 = Hyde 615.
Copy not seen; description deduced from En 2/184.
SWE: upp; USA: anc; SA: mmc

49/01/En 2/192 **1896** Hyde 642
<<THE HEAVENLY ARCANA | DISCLOSED | WHICH ARE IN THE SACRED SCRIPTURE | OR WORD OF THE LORD | HERE THOSE WHICH ARE IN | GENESIS | TOGETHER WITH WONDERFUL THINGS SEEN IN THE | WORLD OF SPIRITS AND THE HEAVEN OF ANGELS | BY EMANUEL SWEDENBORG | ORIGINALLY PUBLISHED IN LATIN AT LONDON, A. D. 1749. | **Rotch Edition.** | VOL. II. | NEW YORK | NEW-CHURCH BOARD OF PUBLICATION | 1896>>
verso: <<MATTHEW VI. 33. | Seek ye first the Kingdom of God and His Justice, and all things | shall be added unto you. | <short rule> | TYPOGRAPHY BY MASS. NEW-CHURCH UNION, BOSTON>>
half title: <<ARCANA CŒLESTIA>>
half title and title leaves, 4 pp; Contents, 2 pp; text of Genesis 8-11 and n 824-1382, pp 3-369.
The same as En 2/185; an edition of 500 copies was printed.
Copy not seen; description deduced from En 2/185 = Hyde 641.
USA: anc

49/01/En 4/8 **1896** Hyde 696
ARCANA CŒLESTIA | <short rule> | THE | HEAVENLY ARCANA | CONTAINED IN | THE HOLY SCRIPTURE, OR WORD OF THE LORD | UNFOLDED | IN AN EXPOSITION OF GENESIS AND EXODUS | TOGETHER WITH A RELATION OF | WONDERFUL THINGS SEEN IN THE WORLD OF SPIRITS AND | IN THE HEAVEN OF ANGELS | *FROM THE LATIN* | OF | EMANUEL SWEDENBORG | VOLUME V. | GENESIS, CHAPTER XXVIII. TO CHAPTER XXXI. | Nos. 3650-4228 | THE SWEDENBORG SOCIETY | (INSTITUTED 1810) | 1 BLOOMSBURY STREET, | LONDON | 1896
verso: "*Seek ye first the kingdom of God, and His righteousness,* | *and all these things shall be added unto you.*" | —MATTHEW vi. 33.
half title: ARCANA CŒLESTIA
imprint: ROBERT R. SUTHERLAND, PRINTER, EDINBURGH.
8vo

half title and title leaves, 4 pp; Prefatory note, p v; Contents, pp vii-viii; text of Genesis 28-31 and n 3650-4228, pp 1-397; imprint, p 397; catalogue, 2 pp.
Revised by A H Searle, with R L Tafel, S C Eby, and J Speirs as a consultative committee. An edition of 1,080 copies was printed.
UK: soc; NET: gen, kb; USA: anc

49/01/En 2/193 **1896** Hyde 745
THE HEAVENLY ARCANA | DISCLOSED | WHICH ARE IN THE SACRED SCRIPTURE | OR | WORD OF THE LORD | HERE THOSE WHICH ARE IN | GENESIS | TOGETHER WITH WONDERFUL THINGS SEEN IN THE | WORLD OF SPIRITS AND THE HEAVEN OF ANGELS | BY EMANUEL SWEDENBORG | ORIGINALLY PUBLISHED IN LATIN AT LONDON, A. D. 1752 | Rotch Edition | VOL. VIII. | NEW YORK | NEW-CHURCH BOARD OF PUBLICATION | 1896
verso: MATTHEW VI. 33. | Seek ye first the Kingdom of God and His Justice, and all things | shall be added unto you. | <short rule> | TYPOGRAPHY BY MASS. NEW-CHURCH UNION, BOSTON
small 8vo
title leaf, 2 pp; Note, 1 p; Contents 1 p; text of Genesis 31-36 and n 4229-4660, pp 7-384.
Edited by J Worcester using a MS translation by T B Hayward.
UK: soc; USA: anc; SA: mmc

49/01/En 2/194 **1897** Hyde 759
THE HEAVENLY ARCANA | DISCLOSED | WHICH ARE IN THE SACRED SCRIPTURE | OR WORD OF THE LORD | HERE THOSE WHICH ARE IN | GENESIS | TOGETHER WITH WONDERFUL THINGS SEEN IN THE | WORLD OF SPIRITS AND THE HEAVEN OF ANGELS | BY EMANUEL SWEDENBORG | ORIGINALLY PUBLISHED IN LATIN AT LONDON, A. D. 1752 | Rotch Edition | VOL. IX. | NEW YORK | NEW-CHURCH BOARD OF PUBLICATION | 1897
verso: MATTHEW VI. 33. | Seek ye first the Kingdom of God and His Justice, and all things | shall be added unto you. | <short rule> | TYPOGRAPHY BY MASS. NEW-CHURCH UNION, BOSTON
small 8vo
title leaf, 2 pp; Note, 1 p; Contents, 1 p; text of Genesis 37-40 and n 4661-5190, pp 7-458.
Edited by J Worcester from a revision by A L Kip.
UK: soc; SWE: upp; USA: anc; SA: mmc

49/01/En 2/195 **1897** Hyde 616, 642
THE HEAVENLY ARCANA | DISCLOSED | WHICH ARE IN THE SACRED SCRIPTURE | OR WORD OF THE LORD | HERE THOSE WHICH ARE IN | GENESIS | TOGETHER WITH WONDERFUL THINGS SEEN IN THE | WORLD OF SPIRITS AND THE HEAVEN OF ANGELS | BY EMANUEL SWEDENBORG | ORIGINALLY PUBLISHED IN LATIN AT LONDON, A. D. 1749. | Rotch Edition. | VOLS. I AND II. | NEW YORK | THE AMERICAN SWEDENBORG PRINTING AND PUBLISHING SOCIETY | 1896
verso: MATTHEW VI. 33. | Seek ye first the Kingdom of God and His Justice, and all things | shall be added unto you. | <short rule>
half title: ARCANA CŒLESTIA
small 8vo
half title and title leaves, 4 pp; Contents of Volume I, 2 pp; text of Genesis 1-7 and n 1-823, pp 3-410; Contents of Volume II, 2 pp; text of Genesis 8-11 and n 824-1382, pp 3-369.
Volumes 1 and 2 <En 2/191 and 192 = Hyde 616 and 642> were bound together and issued as 1 volume for distribution to the clergy and theological students, at the expense of J Ellis MD; an edition of 2,006 copies was printed for this purpose.
UK: soc; SWE: upp; USA: anc

49/01/En 2/196 **1898** Hyde 774

THE HEAVENLY ARCANA | DISCLOSED | WHICH ARE IN THE SACRED SCRIPTURE | OR WORD OF THE LORD | HERE THOSE WHICH ARE IN | GENESIS | TOGETHER WITH WONDERFUL THINGS SEEN IN THE | WORLD OF SPIRITS AND THE HEAVEN OF ANGELS | BY EMANUEL SWEDENBORG | ORIGINALLY PUBLISHED IN LATIN AT LONDON, A. D. 1753 | Rotch Edition | VOL. X. | BOSTON | MASSACHUSETTS NEW-CHURCH UNION | 1898

verso: MATTHEW VI. 33. | Seek ye first the Kingdom of God and His Justice, and all things | shall be added unto you.

half title: ARCANA CŒLESTIA

small 8vo

half title and title leaves, 4 pp; Note, 1 p; Contents, 1 p; text of Genesis 41-44 and n 5191-5866, pp 7-435.

Edited by J Worcester from a revision of chapters 41-43 by A L Kip and of chapter 44 by H W Wright.

UK: soc; SWE: upp; USA: anc; SA: mmc

49/01/En 2/197 **1899** Hyde 617

<<ARCANA CŒLESTIA. | <short rule> | THE | HEAVENLY ARCANA | CONTAINED IN | THE HOLY SCRIPTURE OR WORD OF THE LORD | UNFOLDED, | BEGINNING WITH THE BOOK OF GENESIS: | TOGETHER WITH | WONDERFUL THINGS SEEN IN THE WORLD OF SPIRITS | AND IN THE HEAVEN OF ANGELS. | <short rule> | *Translated from the Latin of* | EMANUEL SWEDENBORG, | *Servant of the Lord Jesus Christ.* | <short rule> | VOL. I. | NEW YORK: | AMERICAN SWEDENBORG PRINTING AND PUBLISHING SOCIETY, | NO. 3, WEST TWENTY-NINTH STREET. | <short rule> 1899.>>

verso: <<[INSCRIPTION BY THE AUTHOR.] | Seek ye first the Kingdom of God and His righteousness, and all these | things shall be added unto you (*Matt.* vi.33). | Published by The American Swedenborg Printing and Publishing Society, | organized for the purpose of Printing, Publishing, and Circulating uniform | editions of the Theological Writings of Emanuel Swedenborg for charitable | and missionary purposes. Incorporated in the State of New York, A.D. 1850.>>

half title: <<ARCANA CŒLESTIA>>

8vo

half title and title leaves, 4 pp; text of Genesis 1-11 and n 1-1382, pp 1-568.

The same as En 2/183 = Hyde 614; an edition of 500 copies was printed.

Copy not seen; description deduced from En 2/183.

USA: anc

49/01/En 2/198 **1899** Hyde 678/–

<<ARCANA CŒLESTIA | <short rule> | THE | HEAVENLY ARCANA | CONTAINED IN | THE HOLY SCRIPTURES OR WORD OF THE LORD | UNFOLDED, | BEGINNING WITH THE BOOK OF GENESIS: | TOGETHER WITH | WONDERFUL THINGS SEEN IN THE WORLD OF SPIRITS | AND THE HEAVEN OF ANGELS. | <short rule> | *Translated from the Latin of* | EMANUEL SWEDENBORG, | *Servant of the Lord Jesus Christ.* | <short rule> | VOL. IV. | NEW YORK: | AMERICAN SWEDENBORG PRINTING AND PUBLISHING SOCIETY. | <short rule> | 1899>>

verso: <<[INSCRIPTION BY THE AUTHOR.] | Seek ye first the Kingdom of God and His righteousness, and all these | things shall be added unto you (*Matt.* vi.33). | Published by The American Swedenborg Printing and Publishing Society, | organized for the purpose of Printing, Publishing, and Circulating uniform | editions of the Theological Writings of Emanuel Swedenborg for charitable | and missionary purposes. Incorporated in the State of New York, A.D. 1850.>>

half title: <<ARCANA CŒLESTIA>>

small 8vo
half title and title leaves, 4 pp; text of Genesis 26-31 and n 3353-4228, pp 5-557.
Copy not seen; description deduced from En 2/208 = Hyde 678/b.
USA: ANC

49/01/En 2/199 **1899** Hyde 774/–
<<ARCANA CŒLESTIA | <short rule> | THE | HEAVENLY ARCANA | CONTAINED IN | THE HOLY SCRIPTURES OR WORD OF THE LORD | UNFOLDED | BEGINNING WITH THE BOOK OF GENESIS | TOGETHER WITH | WONDERFUL THINGS SEEN IN THE WORLD OF SPIRITS | AND THE HEAVEN OF ANGELS | <short rule> | *Translated from the Latin of* | EMANUEL SWEDENBORG | *Servant of the Lord Jesus Christ* | <short rule> | VOL. X. | NEW YORK: | AMERICAN SWEDENBORG PRINTING AND PUBLISHING SOCIETY. | <short rule> | 1899>>
verso: <<[INSCRIPTION BY THE AUTHOR.] | Seek ye first the Kingdom of God and His righteousness, and all these | things shall be added unto you (*Matt.* vi.33). | Published by The American Swedenborg Printing and Publishing Society, | organized for the purpose of Printing, Publishing, and Circulating uniform | editions of the Theological Writings of Emanuel Swedenborg for charitable | and missionary purposes. Incorporated in the State of New York, A.D. 1850.>>
half title: <<ARCANA CŒLESTIA>>
small 8vo
half title and title leaves, 4 pp; text of Exodus 29-40 and n 9974-10837, pp 5-569.
Copy not seen; description deduced from En 2/170 = Hyde 771.
USA: ANC

49/01/En 2/200 **1899** Hyde 783
THE HEAVENLY ARCANA | DISCLOSED | WHICH ARE IN THE SACRED SCRIPTURE | OR | WORD OF THE LORD | HERE THOSE WHICH ARE IN | GENESIS | TOGETHER WITH WONDERFUL THINGS SEEN IN THE | WORLD OF SPIRITS AND THE HEAVEN OF ANGELS | BY EMANUEL SWEDENBORG | ORIGINALLY PUBLISHED IN LATIN AT LONDON, A. D. 1753. | Rotch Edition | VOL. XI. | BOSTON | MASSACHUSETTS NEW-CHURCH UNION | 1899
verso: MATTHEW VI. 33. | Seek ye first the Kingdom of God and His Justice, and all things | shall be added unto you.
small 8vo
title leaf, 2 pp; Note, 1 p; Contents, 1 p; text of Genesis 45-50 and n 5867-6626, pp 7-493.
Edited by J Worcester from a revision of ch 45-47 by H W Wright and of ch 48-50 by T F Wright.
UK: SOC; SWE: UPP; USA: ANC; SA: MMC

49/01/En 2/201 **1900** Hyde 792
THE HEAVENLY ARCANA | DISCLOSED | WHICH ARE IN THE SACRED SCRIPTURE | OR | WORD OF THE LORD | HERE THOSE WHICH ARE IN | EXODUS | TOGETHER WITH WONDERFUL THINGS SEEN IN THE | WORLD OF SPIRITS AND THE HEAVEN OF ANGELS | BY EMANUEL SWEDENBORG | ORIGINALLY PUBLISHED IN LATIN, AT LONDON, A. D. 1753 | Rotch Edition | VOL. XII. | BOSTON | MASSACHUSETTS NEW-CHURCH UNION | 1900
verso: MATTHEW VI. 33. | Seek ye first the Kingdom of God and His Justice, and all things | shall be added unto you.
small 8vo
title leaf, 2 pp; Note, 1 p; Contents, 1 p; text of Exodus 1-6 and n 6627-7254, pp 7-271.
Edited by J Worcester from a revision by T F Wright.
UK: SOC; SWE: UPP; USA: ANC; SA: MMC

49/01/En 4/9 **1901** Hyde 643

ARCANA CŒLESTIA. | <short rule> | THE | HEAVENLY ARCANA | CONTAINED IN | THE HOLY SCRIPTURE, OR WORD OF THE LORD | UNFOLDED | IN AN EXPOSITION OF GENESIS AND EXODUS | TOGETHER WITH A RELATION OF | WONDERFUL THINGS SEEN IN THE WORLD OF SPIRITS | AND IN THE HEAVEN OF ANGELS | *FROM THE LATIN* | OF | EMANUEL SWEDENBORG | VOLUME II. | GENESIS CHAPTER X. TO CHAPTER XVII. | Nos. 1114-2134 | THE SWEDENBORG SOCIETY | (INSTITUTED 1810) | 1 BLOOMSBURY STREET, LONDON | 1901

verso: "*Seek ye first the kingdom of God, and His righteousness,* | *and all these things shall be added unto you.*" | —MATTHEW vi. 33.

half title: ARCANA CŒLESTIA

imprint: *Robert R. Sutherland, Printer, Edinburgh.*

8vo

half title and title leaves, 4 pp; Prefatory note, p v; Contents, pp vii-viii; text of Genesis 10-17 and n 1114-2134, pp 1-482; imprint, p 482; catalogue, 2 pp.

Revised by A H Searle, with L A Slight and J Hyde as a consultative committee. An edition of 1,080 copies was printed.

UK: soc; NET: gen, kb; SWE: upp; USA: anc

49/01/En 2/202 **1902** Hyde 793

THE HEAVENLY ARCANA | DISCLOSED | WHICH ARE IN THE SACRED SCRIPTURE | OR | WORD OF THE LORD | HERE THOSE WHICH ARE IN | EXODUS | TOGETHER WITH WONDERFUL THINGS SEEN IN THE | WORLD OF SPIRITS AND THE HEAVEN OF ANGELS | BY EMANUEL SWEDENBORG | ORIGINALLY PUBLISHED IN LATIN AT LONDON, A. D. 1753 | Rotch Edition | VOL. XIII. | BOSTON | MASSACHUSETTS NEW-CHURCH UNION | 1902

verso: MATTHEW VI. 33. | Seek ye first the Kingdom of God and His Justice, and all things | shall be added unto you.

small 8vo

title leaf, 2 pp; Contents, 1 p; Note, 1 p; Contents, 1 p; text of Exodus 7-12 and n 7255-8032, pp 7-408.

Edited by B Worcester from a revision of chapters 7-10 by T F Wright and of chapters 11-12 by H W Wright.

UK: soc; SWE: upp; USA: anc; SA: mmc

49/01/En 2/203 **1902** Hyde 794

THE HEAVENLY ARCANA | DISCLOSED | WHICH ARE IN THE SACRED SCRIPTURE | OR | WORD OF THE LORD | HERE THOSE WHICH ARE IN | EXODUS | TOGETHER WITH WONDERFUL THINGS SEEN IN THE | WORLD OF SPIRITS AND THE HEAVEN OF ANGELS | BY EMANUEL SWEDENBORG | ORIGINALLY PUBLISHED IN LATIN AT LONDON, A. D. 1753-1754 | Rotch Edition | VOL. XIV. | BOSTON | MASSACHUSETTS NEW-CHURCH UNION | 1902

verso: MATTHEW VI. 33. | Seek ye first the Kingdom of God and His Justice, and all things | shall be added unto you.

small 8vo

title leaf, 2 pp; Note, 1 p; Contents, 1 p; text of Exodus 13-18 and n 8033-8741, pp 7-425.

Edited by B Worcester from a revision by H W Wright.

UK: soc; SWE: upp; USA: anc; SA: mmc

49/01/En 2/204 **1903** Hyde 794/A, 3440

THE HEAVENLY ARCANA | DISCLOSED | WHICH ARE IN THE SACRED SCRIPTURE | OR | WORD OF THE LORD | HERE THOSE WHICH ARE IN | EXODUS | TOGETHER WITH WONDERFUL THINGS SEEN IN THE | WORLD OF SPIRITS AND THE HEAVEN OF ANGELS | BY EMANUEL SWEDENBORG

| ORIGINALLY PUBLISHED IN LATIN AT LONDON, A. D. 1754 | Rotch Edition | VOL. XV. | BOSTON | MASSACHUSETTS NEW-CHURCH UNION | 1903
verso: MATTHEW VI. 33. | Seek ye first the Kingdom of God and His Justice, and all things | shall be added unto you.
small 8vo
title leaf, 2 pp; Note, 1 p; Contents, 1 p; text of Exodus 19-21 and n 8742-9111, pp 7-330.
Edited by B Worcester from a revision by H W Wright.
UK: soc; SWE: upp; USA: anc; SA: mmc

49/01/En 4/10 **1903** Hyde 618
ARCANA CŒLESTIA. | <short rule> | THE | HEAVENLY ARCANA | CONTAINED IN | THE HOLY SCRIPTURE, OR WORD OF THE LORD | UNFOLDED | IN AN EXPOSITION OF GENESIS AND EXODUS | TOGETHER WITH A RELATION OF | WONDERFUL THINGS SEEN IN THE WORLD OF SPIRITS | AND IN THE HEAVEN OF ANGELS | *FROM THE LATIN* | OF | EMANUEL SWEDENBORG | VOLUME I. | GENESIS, CHAPTER I. TO CHAPTER IX. | Nos. 1-1113. | THE SWEDENBORG SOCIETY | (INSTITUTED 1810) | 1 BLOOMSBURY STREET, LONDON | 1903
verso: *"Seek ye first the kingdom of God and His righteousness. | and all these things shall be added unto you."* | —MATTHEW vi. 33.
half title: ARCANA CŒLESTIA
imprint: TURNBULL AND SPEARS, PRINTERS, EDINBURGH.
8vo
half title and title leaves, 4 pp; Prefatory note, p v; Contents, pp vii-viii; text of Genesis 1-9 and n 1-1113, pp 1-489; Errata, p 490; imprint, p 490.
Revised by A H Searle, with L A Slight and J Hyde as a consultative committee. An edition of 1,000 copies was printed.
UK: soc; NET: gen, kb; SWE: upp; USA: anc

49/01/En 4/11 **1904** Hyde 678/a, 3439
ARCANA CŒLESTIA. | <short rule> | THE | HEAVENLY ARCANA | CONTAINED IN | THE HOLY SCRIPTURE OR | WORD OF THE LORD | UNFOLDED | IN AN EXPOSITION OF GENESIS AND EXODUS | TOGETHER WITH A RELATION OF | WONDERFUL THINGS SEEN IN THE WORLD OF SPIRITS AND | IN THE HEAVEN OF ANGELS | *FROM THE LATIN* | OF | EMANUEL SWEDENBORG | VOLUME IV. | GENESIS, CHAPTER XXIII. TO CHAPTER XXVII. | NOS. 2894-3649. | THE SWEDENBORG SOCIETY | (INSTITUTED 1810) | 1 BLOOMSBURY STREET, LONDON | 1904
verso: *"Seek ye first the kingdom of God and His righteousness, | and all these things shall be added unto you."* | —MATTHEW vi. 33.
imprint: PRINTED BY TURNBULL AND SPEARS, EDINBURGH.
8vo
title leaf, 2 pp; Prefatory note, p v; Contents, p vii; text of Genesis 23-27 and n 2894-3649, pp 1-435; imprint, p 436.
Revised by A H Searle, with J Hyde and I Tansley as a consultative committee. An edition of 1,000 copies was printed.
UK: soc; NET: gen, kb; SWE: upp; USA: anc, shs

49/01/En 2/205 **1904** Hyde 618/a
<<ARCANA CÆLESTIA | <short rule> | THE | HEAVENLY ARCANA | CONTAINED IN | THE HOLY SCRIPTURES OR WORD OF THE LORD | UNFOLDED | BEGINNING WITH THE BOOK OF GENESIS | *TOGETHER WITH WONDERFUL THINGS SEEN IN THE WORLD OF | SPIRITS AND IN THE HEAVEN OF ANGELS* | TRANSLATED FROM THE LATIN OF | EMANUEL SWEDENBORG, | *Servant of the Lord Jesus Christ.* | <short rule> | VOL. I. | <short rule> | NEW YORK | AMERICAN

SWEDENBORG PRINTING AND PUBLISHING | SOCIETY | NO. 3 WEST TWENTY-NINTH STREET. | <short rule> | 1904>>
verso: <<*Published by The American Swedenborg Printing and Publishing Soci- | ety, organized for the purpose of Stereotyping, Printing and | Publishing Uniform Editions of the Theological Writings of | Emanuel Swedenborg, and incorporated in the State of New York, | A.D.* 1850.>>
half title: <<ARCANA CŒLESTIA>>
8vo
half title and title leaves, 4 pp; text of Genesis 1-11 and n 1-1382, pp 1-568.
Copy not seen; description deduced from En 2/206 and catalogue of USA: ANC.
SWE: UPP; USA: ANC

49/01/En 2/206 **1904?** Hyde 643/a
ARCANA CÆLESTIA | <short rule> | THE | HEAVENLY ARCANA | CONTAINED IN | THE HOLY SCRIPTURES OR WORD OF THE LORD | UNFOLDED | BEGINNING WITH THE BOOK OF GENESIS | *TOGETHER WITH WONDERFUL THINGS SEEN IN THE WORLD OF | SPIRITS AND IN THE HEAVEN OF ANGELS* | TRANSLATED FROM THE LATIN OF | EMANUEL SWEDENBORG | *Servant of the Lord Jesus Christ* | <short rule> | VOL. II | <short rule> | NEW YORK | AMERICAN SWEDENBORG PRINTING AND PUBLISHING | SOCIETY | NO. 3 WEST TWENTY-NINTH STREET. | <short rule>
verso: *Published by The American Swedenborg Printing and Publishing Soci- | ety, organized for the purpose of Stereotyping, Printing and | Publishing Uniform Editions of the Theological Writings of | Emanuel Swedenborg, and incorporated in the State of New York, | A.D.* 1850.
half title: ARCANA CŒLESTIA
8vo
half title and title leaves, 4 pp; text of Genesis 12-19 and n 1383-2494, pp 5-576.
UK: SOC; SWE: UPP; USA: ANC

49/01/En 2/207 **1904?** Hyde 661/a
ARCANA CÆLESTIA | <short rule> | THE | HEAVENLY ARCANA | CONTAINED IN | THE HOLY SCRIPTURES OR WORD OF THE LORD | UNFOLDED | BEGINNING WITH THE BOOK OF GENESIS | *TOGETHER WITH WONDERFUL THINGS SEEN IN THE WORLD OF | SPIRITS AND IN THE HEAVEN OF ANGELS* | TRANSLATED FROM THE LATIN OF | EMANUEL SWEDENBORG | *Servant of the Lord Jesus Christ* | <short rule> | VOL. III. | <short rule> | NEW YORK | AMERICAN SWEDENBORG PRINTING AND PUBLISHING | SOCIETY | NO. 3 WEST TWENTY-NINTH STREET. | <short rule>
verso: *Published by The American Swedenborg Printing and Publishing Soci- | ety, organized for the purpose of Stereotyping, Printing and | Publishing Uniform Editions of the Theological Writings of | Emanuel Swedenborg, and incorporated in the State of New York,* | A.D. 1850.
half title: ARCANA CŒLESTIA
8vo
half title and title leaves, 4 pp; text of Genesis 20-25 and n 2495-3352, pp 5-515.
UK: SOC; USA: ANC

49/01/En 2/208 **1904?** Hyde 678/b
ARCANA CÆLESTIA | <short rule> | THE | HEAVENLY ARCANA | CONTAINED IN | THE HOLY SCRIPTURES OR WORD OF THE LORD | UNFOLDED | BEGINNING WITH THE BOOK OF GENESIS | *TOGETHER WITH WONDERFUL THINGS SEEN IN THE WORLD OF | SPIRITS AND IN THE HEAVEN OF ANGELS* | TRANSLATED FROM THE LATIN OF | EMANUEL SWEDENBORG | *Servant of the Lord Jesus Christ* | <short rule> | VOL. IV. | <short rule> | NEW YORK | AMERICAN

SWEDENBORG PRINTING AND PUBLISHING | SOCIETY | 3 WEST TWENTY-NINTH STREET. | <short rule>
verso: *Published by The American Swedenborg Printing and Publishing Soci- | ety, organized for the purpose of Stereotyping, Printing and | Publishing Uniform Editions of the Theological Writings of | Emanuel Swedenborg, and incorporated in the State of New York, | A.D.* 1850.
half title: ARCANA CŒLESTIA
8vo
half title and title leaves, 4 pp; text of Genesis 26-31 and n 3353-4228, pp 5-557.
UK: SOC; USA: ANC

49/01/En 2/209 **1904 ?** Hyde 745/a
ARCANA CÆLESTIA. | <short rule> | THE | HEAVENLY ARCANA | CONTAINED IN | THE HOLY SCRIPTURES OR WORD OF THE LORD | UNFOLDED | BEGINNING WITH THE BOOK OF GENESIS | *TOGETHER WITH WONDERFUL THINGS SEEN IN THE WORLD OF | SPIRITS AND IN THE HEAVEN OF ANGELS* | TRANSLATED FROM THE LATIN OF | EMANUEL SWEDENBORG | *Servant of the Lord Jesus Christ* | <short rule> | VOL. VIII. | <short rule> | NEW YORK | AMERICAN SWEDENBORG PRINTING AND PUBLISHING | SOCIETY | NO. 3 WEST TWENTY-NINTH STREET | <short rule>
verso: *Published by* THE AMERICAN SWEDENBORG PRINTING AND PUBLISHING | SOCIETY, *organized for the purpose of Stereotyping, Printing and | Publishing Uniform Editions of the Theological Writings of* EMANUEL | SWEDENBORG, *and incorporated in the State of New York* A. D. 1850.
half title: ARCANA CŒLESTIA
8vo
half title and title leaves, 4 pp; text of Exodus 13-21 and n 8033-9111, pp 5-543.
UK: SOC; USA: ANC

49/01/En 2/210 **1904 ?** Hyde 774/a
<<ARCANA CÆLESTIA. | <short rule> | THE | HEAVENLY ARCANA | CONTAINED IN | THE HOLY SCRIPTURES OR WORD OF THE LORD | UNFOLDED | BEGINNING WITH THE BOOK OF GENESIS | *TOGETHER WITH | WONDERFUL THINGS SEEN IN THE WORLD OF | SPIRITS AND IN THE HEAVEN OF ANGELS* | TRANSLATED FROM THE LATIN OF | EMANUEL SWEDENBORG | *Servant of the Lord Jesus Christ* | <short rule> | VOL. X. | <short rule> | NEW YORK | AMERICAN SWEDENBORG PRINTING AND PUBLISHING | SOCIETY | NO. 3 WEST TWENTY-NINTH STREET. | <short rule> >>
verso: <<*Published by* THE AMERICAN SWEDENBORG PRINTING AND PUBLISHING | SOCIETY, *organized for the purpose of Stereotyping, Printing and | Publishing Uniform Editions of the Theological Writings of* EMANUEL | SWEDENBORG, *and incorporated in the State of New York*, A. D. 1850.>>
half title: <<ARCANA CŒLESTIA>>
8vo
half title and title leaves, 4 pp; text of Exodus 29-40 and n 9974-10837, pp 5-569.
Copy not seen; description deduced from En 2/209 and catalogue of USA: ANC.
USA: ANC

49/01/En 2/211 **1905** Hyde 794/b
<<THE HEAVENLY ARCANA | DISCLOSED | WHICH ARE IN THE SACRED SCRIPTURE | OR | WORD OF THE LORD | HERE THOSE WHICH ARE IN | EXODUS | TOGETHER WITH WONDERFUL THINGS SEEN IN THE | WORLD OF SPIRITS AND THE HEAVEN OF ANGELS | BY EMANUEL SWEDENBORG | ORIGINALLY PUBLISHED IN LATIN AT LONDON, A. D. 1754 | **Rotch Edition** |

VOL. XVI. | BOSTON | MASSACHUSETTS NEW-CHURCH UNION | 1905>>
verso: <<MATTHEW VI. 33. | Seek ye first the Kingdom of God and His Justice, and all things | shall be added unto you.>>
half title: <<ARCANA CŒLESTIA>>
small 8vo
half title and title leaves, 4 pp; text of Exodus 22-24 and n 9112-9442, pp 1-420.
Edited by B Worcester from a revision by H W Wright.
Copy not seen; description deduced from En 2/203.
SWE: UPP; USA: ANC; SA: MMC

49/01/En 2/212 **1905** Hyde 794/1
<<THE HEAVENLY ARCANA | DISCLOSED | WHICH ARE IN THE SACRED SCRIPTURE | OR | WORD OF THE LORD | HERE THOSE WHICH ARE IN | EXODUS | TOGETHER WITH WONDERFUL THINGS SEEN IN THE | WORLD OF SPIRITS AND THE HEAVEN OF ANGELS | BY EMANUEL SWEDENBORG | ORIGINALLY PUBLISHED IN LATIN AT LONDON, A. D. 1756 | **Rotch Edition** | VOL. XVII. | BOSTON | MASSACHUSETTS NEW-CHURCH UNION | 1905>>
verso: <<MATTHEW VI. 33. | Seek ye first the Kingdom of God and His Justice, and all things | shall be added unto you.>>
half title: <<ARCANA CŒLESTIA>>
small 8vo
half title and title leaves, 4 pp; text of Exodus 25-28 and n 9443-9973, pp 1-447; Reviser's notes, p 448.
Edited by B Worcester from a revision by T F Wright.
Copy not seen; description deduced from En 2/203.
SWE: UPP; USA: ANC; SA: MMC

49/01/En 5/1 **1905** Hyde 618/b
<<ARCANA COELESTIA | THE | HEAVENLY ARCANA | CONTAINED IN THE HOLY SCRIPTURE OR WORD OF THE LORD | UNFOLDED | BEGINNING WITH THE BOOK OF GENESIS | TOGETHER WITH WONDERFUL THINGS SEEN IN THE WORLD OF | SPIRITS AND IN THE HEAVEN OF ANGELS | TRANSLATED FROM THE LATIN OF | EMANUEL SWEDENBORG | THOROUGHLY REVISED AND EDITED BY THE | REV. JOHN FAULKNER POTTS, B.A. LOND. | VOLUME I. | <short rule> | LIBRARY EDITION | <short rule> | NEW YORK | THE AMERICAN SWEDENBORG PRINTING AND PUBLISHING | SOCIETY | 3 WEST TWENTY-NINTH STREET | 1905>>
verso: <<[INSCRIPTION BY THE AUTHOR.] | Seek ye first the Kingdom of God and His righteousness, and all these | things shall be added unto you (*Matt.* vi.33). | Published by The American Swedenborg Printing and Publishing Society, | organized for the purpose of Printing, Publishing, and Circulating uniform | editions of the Theological Writings of Emanuel Swedenborg for charitable | and missionary purposes. Incorporated in the State of New York, A.D. 1850.>>
8vo
title leaf, 2 pp; text of Genesis 1-11 and n 1-1382, pp 1-568.
Copy not seen; description deduced from En 5/4 = Hyde 678/c.
SWE: UPP; USA: ANC, SHS

49/01/En 5/2 **1905** Hyde 643/b
<<ARCANA COELESTIA | THE | HEAVENLY ARCANA | CONTAINED IN THE HOLY SCRIPTURE OR WORD OF THE LORD | UNFOLDED | BEGINNING WITH THE BOOK OF GENESIS | TOGETHER WITH WONDERFUL THINGS SEEN IN THE WORLD OF | SPIRITS AND IN THE HEAVEN OF ANGELS | TRANSLATED FROM THE LATIN OF | EMANUEL SWEDENBORG | THOROUGHLY REVISED

AND EDITED BY THE | REV. JOHN FAULKNER POTTS, B.A. LOND. | VOLUME II. | <short rule> | LIBRARY EDITION | <short rule> | NEW YORK | THE AMERICAN SWEDENBORG PRINTING AND PUBLISHING | SOCIETY | 3 WEST TWENTY-NINTH STREET | 1905>>
verso: <<[INSCRIPTION BY THE AUTHOR.] | Seek ye first the Kingdom of God and His righteousness, and all these | things shall be added unto you (*Matt.* vi.33). | Published by The American Swedenborg Printing and Publishing Society, | organized for the purpose of Printing, Publishing, and Circulating uniform | editions of the Theological Writings of Emanuel Swedenborg for charitable | and missionary purposes. Incorporated in the State of New York, A.D. 1850.>>
8vo
title leaf, 2 pp; Swedenborg's table of contents, pp iii-iv; text of Genesis 12-19 and n 1383-2494, pp 5-582.
Copy not seen; description deduced from En 5/4 = Hyde 678/c.
SWE: UPP; USA: ANC, SHS

49/01/En 5/3 — **1906** — Hyde 661/b

ARCANA COELESTIA | THE | HEAVENLY ARCANA | CONTAINED IN THE HOLY SCRIPTURE OR WORD OF THE LORD | UNFOLDED | BEGINNING WITH THE BOOK OF GENESIS | TOGETHER WITH WONDERFUL THINGS SEEN IN THE WORLD OF | SPIRITS AND IN THE HEAVEN OF ANGELS | TRANSLATED FROM THE LATIN OF | EMANUEL SWEDENBORG | THOROUGHLY REVISED AND EDITED BY THE | REV. JOHN FAULKNER POTTS, B.A. LOND. | VOLUME III. | <short rule> | LIBRARY EDITION | <short rule> | NEW YORK | THE AMERICAN SWEDENBORG PRINTING AND PUBLISHING | SOCIETY | 3 WEST TWENTY-NINTH STREET | 1906
verso: [INSCRIPTION BY THE AUTHOR.] | Seek ye first the Kingdom of God and His righteousness, and all these | things shall be added unto you (*Matt.* vi. 33). | Published by The American Swedenborg Printing and Publishing Society, | organized for the purpose of Printing, Publishing, and Circulating uniform | editions of the Theological Writings of Emanuel Swedenborg for charitable | and missionary purposes. Incorporated in the State of New York, A.D. 1850.
8vo
title leaf, 2 pp; Contents, p iii; text of Genesis 18-22 and n 2135-2893, pp 1-558.
NET: GEN; USA: ANC, SHS

49/01/En 5/4 — **1906** — Hyde 678/c

ARCANA COELESTIA | THE | HEAVENLY ARCANA | CONTAINED IN THE HOLY SCRIPTURE OR WORD OF THE LORD | UNFOLDED | BEGINNING WITH THE BOOK OF GENESIS | TOGETHER WITH WONDERFUL THINGS SEEN IN THE WORLD OF | SPIRITS AND IN THE HEAVEN OF ANGELS | TRANSLATED FROM THE LATIN OF | EMANUEL SWEDENBORG | THOROUGHLY REVISED AND EDITED BY THE | REV. JOHN FAULKNER POTTS, B.A. LOND. | VOLUME IV. | <short rule> | LIBRARY EDITION | <short rule> | NEW YORK | THE AMERICAN SWEDENBORG PRINTING AND PUBLISHING | SOCIETY | 3 WEST TWENTY-NINTH STREET | 1906
verso: [INSCRIPTION BY THE AUTHOR.] | Seek ye first the Kingdom of God and His righteousness, and all these | things shall be added unto you (*Matt.* vi.33). | Published by The American Swedenborg Printing and Publishing Society, | organized for the purpose of Printing, Publishing, and Circulating uniform | editions of the Theological Writings of Emanuel Swedenborg for charitable | and missionary purposes. Incorporated in the State of New York, A.D. 1850.
8vo
title leaf, 2 pp; Table of contents, p iii; text of Genesis 23-27 and n 2894-3649, pp 1-525; Reviser's notes, pp 526-527.
UK: SOC; NET: GEN; SWI: LAU; USA: ANC, SHS

49/01/En 5/5 **1906** Hyde 696/b

ARCANA COELESTIA | THE | HEAVENLY ARCANA | CONTAINED IN THE HOLY SCRIPTURE OR WORD OF THE LORD | UNFOLDED | BEGINNING WITH THE BOOK OF GENESIS | TOGETHER WITH WONDERFUL THINGS SEEN IN THE WORLD OF | SPIRITS AND IN THE HEAVEN OF ANGELS | TRANSLATED FROM THE LATIN OF | EMANUEL SWEDENBORG | THOROUGHLY REVISED AND EDITED BY THE | REV. JOHN FAULKNER POTTS, B.A. LOND. | VOLUME V. | <short rule> | LIBRARY EDITION | <short rule> | NEW YORK | THE AMERICAN SWEDENBORG PRINTING AND PUBLISHING | SOCIETY | 3 WEST TWENTY-NINTH STREET | 1906
verso: [INSCRIPTION BY THE AUTHOR.] | Seek ye first the Kingdom of God and His righteousness, and all these | things shall be added unto you (*Matt.* vi.33). | Published by The American Swedenborg Printing and Publishing Society, organized for the purpose of Printing, Publishing, and Circulating uniform | editions of the Theological Writings of Emanuel Swedenborg for charitable | and missionary purposes. Incorporated in the State of New York, A.D. 1850.
8vo
title leaf, 2 pp; Table of contents, p iii; text of Genesis 28-31 and n 3650-4228, pp 1-490.
UK: soc; NET: gen; SWI: lau; USA: anc, shs

49/01/En 5/6 **1906** Hyde 712/b

ARCANA COELESTIA | THE | HEAVENLY ARCANA | CONTAINED IN THE HOLY SCRIPTURE OR WORD OF THE LORD | UNFOLDED | BEGINNING WITH THE BOOK OF GENESIS | TOGETHER WITH WONDERFUL THINGS SEEN IN THE WORLD OF | SPIRITS AND IN THE HEAVEN OF ANGELS | TRANSLATED FROM THE LATIN OF | EMANUEL SWEDENBORG | THOROUGHLY REVISED AND EDITED BY THE | REV. JOHN FAULKNER POTTS, B.A. LOND. | VOLUME VI. | <short rule> | LIBRARY EDITION | <short rule> | NEW YORK | THE AMERICAN SWEDENBORG PRINTING AND PUBLISHING | SOCIETY | 3 WEST TWENTY-NINTH STREET | 1906
verso: [INSCRIPTION BY THE AUTHOR.] | Seek ye first the Kingdom of God and His righteousness, and all these | things shall be added unto you (*Matt.* vi.33). | Published by The American Swedenborg Printing and Publishing Society, | organized for the purpose of Printing, Publishing, and Circulating uniform | editions of the Theological Writings of Emanuel Swedenborg for charitable | and missionary purposes. incorporated in the State of New York, A.D. 1850.
8vo
title leaf, 2 pp; Table of contents, p iii; text of Genesis 32-38 and n 4229-4953, pp 1-554.
UK: soc; NET: gen; SWI: lau; USA: anc, shs

49/01/En 2/213 **1906** Hyde 794/2

THE HEAVENLY ARCANA | DISCLOSED | WHICH ARE IN THE SACRED SCRIPTURE | OR | WORD OF THE LORD | HERE THOSE WHICH ARE IN | EXODUS | TOGETHER WITH WONDERFUL THINGS SEEN IN THE | WORLD OF SPIRITS AND THE HEAVEN OF ANGELS | BY EMANUEL SWEDENBORG | ORIGINALLY PUBLISHED IN LATIN AT LONDON, A. D. 1756 | Rotch Edition | VOL. XVIII. | BOSTON | MASSACHUSETTS NEW-CHURCH UNION | 1906
verso: MATTHEW VI. 33. | Seek ye first the Kingdom of God and His Justice, and all things | shall be added unto you.
small 8vo
title leaf, 2 pp; Note, 1 p; Contents, 1 p; text of Exodus 29-31 and n 9974-10317, pp 1-404.
Edited by B Worcester from a revision by T F Wright.
UK: soc; SWE: upp; USA: anc; SA: mmc

49/01/En 2/214 **1907** Hyde 794/3

THE HEAVENLY ARCANA | DISCLOSED | WHICH ARE IN THE SACRED SCRIPTURE | OR | WORD

OF THE LORD | HERE THOSE WHICH ARE IN | EXODUS | TOGETHER WITH WONDERFUL THINGS SEEN IN THE | WORLD OF SPIRITS AND THE HEAVEN OF ANGELS | BY EMANUEL SWEDENBORG | ORIGINALLY PUBLISHED IN LATIN AT LONDON, A. D. 1756 | Rotch Edition | VOL. XIX. | BOSTON | MASSACHUSETTS NEW-CHURCH UNION | 1907
verso: MATTHEW VI. 33. | Seek ye first the Kingdom of God and His Justice, and all things | shall be added unto you.
small 8vo
title leaf, 2 pp; Note, p 3; Contents, p 5; Note, p 6; text of Exodus 31-40 and n 10318-10837, pp 7-387.
UK: SOC; USA: ANC

49/01/En 2/215 **1907** Hyde 618/c

THE | HEAVENLY ARCANA | DISCLOSED | WHICH ARE IN THE SACRED SCRIPTURE | OR WORD OF THE LORD | HERE, FIRST, THOSE WHICH ARE IN | GENESIS | *TOGETHER WITH* | WONDERFUL THINGS SEEN IN THE | *WORLD OF SPIRITS* AND THE | *HEAVEN* | *OF ANGELS* | BY | EMANUEL SWEDENBORG | *First published in Latin, London*, 1749 | Rotch Edition | VOL. I. | BOSTON AND NEW YORK | HOUGHTON, MIFFLIN AND COMPANY | The Riverside Press, Cambridge | 1907
verso: MATTHEW VI. 33. | Seek ye first the Kingdom of God and His Justice, and all things | shall be added unto you.
half title: HEAVENLY ARCANA | VOL I
verso: <within a rule border 94 x 64 mm> 1907 Rotch Edition | OF | SWEDENBORG'S WORKS | VOLS. | 1-19 HEAVENLY ARCANA | 20 INDEX ARCANA | 21 HEAVEN AND HELL | 22 MISCELLANEOUS WORKS | FINAL JUDGMENT | WHITE HORSE | EARTHS IN THE UNIVERSE | SUMMARY EXPOSITION | 23 FOUR DOCTRINES | NEW JERUSALEM AND ITS HEAVENLY | DOCTRINES | 24 DIVINE LOVE AND WISDOM | INTERCOURSE BETWEEN THE SOUL | AND THE BODY | 25 DIVINE PROVIDENCE | 26-28 APOCALYPSE REVEALED | 29 MARRIAGE LOVE | 30-32 TRUE CHRISTIAN RELIGION
small 8vo
half title and title leaves, 4 pp; Note, 1 p; Contents, p 1; text of Genesis 1-7 and n 1-823, pp 3-410.
UK: SOC; NET: GEN; USA: ANC, SHS

49/01/En 2/216 **1907** Hyde 643/c

THE | HEAVENLY ARCANA | DISCLOSED | WHICH ARE IN THE SACRED SCRIPTURE | OR WORD OF THE LORD | HERE, THOSE WHICH ARE IN | GENESIS | *TOGETHER WITH* | WONDERFUL THINGS SEEN IN THE | *WORLD OF SPIRITS* AND *THE HEAVEN* | *OF ANGELS* | BY | EMANUEL SWEDENBORG | *First published in Latin, London*, 1749 | Rotch edition | VOL. II. | BOSTON AND NEW YORK | HOUGHTON, MIFFLIN AND COMPANY | The Riverside Press, Cambridge | 1907
verso: MATTHEW VI. 33. | Seek ye first the Kingdom of God and His Justice, and all things | shall be added unto you.
half title: HEAVENLY ARCANA | VOL II
verso: <within a rule border 94 x 63 mm> 1907 Rotch Edition | OF | SWEDENBORG'S WORKS | VOLS. | 1-19 HEAVENLY ARCANA | 20 INDEX ARCANA | 21 HEAVEN AND HELL | 22 MISCELLANEOUS WORKS | FINAL JUDGMENT | WHITE HORSE | EARTHS IN THE UNIVERSE | SUMMARY EXPOSITION | 23 FOUR DOCTRINES | NEW JERUSALEM AND ITS HEAVENLY | DOCTRINES | 24 DIVINE LOVE AND WISDOM | INTERCOURSE BETWEEN THE SOUL | AND THE BODY | 25 DIVINE PROVIDENCE | 26-28 APOCALYPSE REVEALED | 29 MARRIAGE LOVE | 30-32 TRUE CHRISTIAN RELIGION
small 8vo
half title and title leaves, 4 pp; Note, p 1; Contents, p 3; text of Genesis 8-11 and n 824-1382, pp 3-369.
UK: SOC; NET: GEN; USA: ANC, SHS

49/01/En 2/217 **1907** Hyde 661/c

THE | HEAVENLY ARCANA | DISCLOSED | WHICH ARE IN THE SACRED SCRIPTURE | OR WORD OF THE LORD | HERE, THOSE WHICH ARE IN | GENESIS | *TOGETHER WITH* | WONDERFUL THINGS SEEN IN THE | *WORLD OF SPIRITS* AND THE *HEAVEN* | *OF ANGELS* | BY | EMANUEL SWEDENBORG | *First published in Latin, London*, 1749-50 | Rotch Edition | VOL. III. | BOSTON AND NEW YORK | HOUGHTON, MIFFLIN AND COMPANY | The Riverside Press, Cambridge | 1907
verso: MATTHEW VI. 33. | Seek ye first the Kingdom of God and His Justice, and all things | shall be added unto you.
half title: HEAVENLY ARCANA | VOL. III
verso: <within a rule border 94 x 64 mm> 1907 Rotch Edition | OF | SWEDENBORG'S WORKS | VOLS. | 1-19 HEAVENLY ARCANA | 20 INDEX ARCANA | 21 HEAVEN AND HELL | 22 MISCELLANEOUS WORKS | FINAL JUDGMENT | WHITE HORSE | EARTHS IN THE UNIVERSE | SUMMARY EXPOSITION | 23 FOUR DOCTRINES | NEW JERUSALEM AND ITS HEAVENLY | DOCTRINES | 24 DIVINE LOVE AND WISDOM | INTERCOURSE BETWEEN THE SOUL | AND THE BODY | 25 DIVINE PROVIDENCE | 26-28 APOCALYPSE REVEALED | 29 MARRIAGE LOVE | 30-32 TRUE CHRISTIAN RELIGION
small 8vo
half title and title leaves, 4 pp; Note, 1 p; Contents, p 1; text of Genesis 12-16 and n 1383-1983, pp 3-391.
UK: SOC; NET: GEN; USA: ANC, SHS

49/01/En 2/218 **1907** Hyde 678/c

THE | HEAVENLY ARCANA | DISCLOSED | WHICH ARE IN THE SACRED SCRIPTURE | OR WORD OF THE LORD | HERE, THOSE WHICH ARE IN | GENESIS | *TOGETHER WITH* | WONDERFUL THINGS SEEN IN THE | *WORLD OF SPIRITS* | AND THE *HEAVEN* | *OF ANGELS* | BY | EMANUEL SWEDENBORG | *First published in Latin, London*, 1750 | Rotch Edition | VOL. IV | BOSTON AND NEW YORK | HOUGHTON, MIFFLIN AND COMPANY | The Riverside Press, Cambridge | 1907
verso: MATTHEW VI. 33. | Seek ye first the Kingdom of God and His Justice, and all things | shall be added unto you.
half title: HEAVENLY ARCANA | VOL. IV
verso: <within a rule border 94 x 63 mm> 1907 Rotch Edition | OF | SWEDENBORG'S WORKS | VOLS. | 1-19 HEAVENLY ARCANA | 20 INDEX ARCANA | 21 HEAVEN AND HELL | 22 MISCELLANEOUS WORKS | FINAL JUDGMENT | WHITE HORSE | EARTHS IN THE UNIVERSE | SUMMARY EXPOSITION | 23 FOUR DOCTRINES | NEW JERUSALEM AND ITS HEAVENLY | DOCTRINES | 24 DIVINE LOVE AND WISDOM | INTERCOURSE BETWEEN THE SOUL | AND THE BODY | 25 DIVINE PROVIDENCE | 26-28 APOCALYPSE REVEALED | 29 MARRIAGE LOVE | 30-32 TRUE CHRISTIAN RELIGION
small 8vo
half title and title leaves, 4 pp; Note, 1 p; Contents, p 1; text of Genesis 17-20 and n 1984-2605, pp 3-472.
UK: SOC; NET: GEN; USA: ANC; SA: MMC

49/01/En 2/219 **1907** Hyde 696/c

THE | HEAVENLY ARCANA | DISCLOSED | WHICH ARE IN THE SACRED SCRIPTURE | OR WORD OF THE LORD | HERE, THOSE WHICH ARE IN | GENESIS | *TOGETHER WITH* | WONDERFUL THINGS SEEN IN THE | *WORLD OF SPIRITS* AND THE *HEAVEN* | *OF ANGELS* | BY | EMANUEL SWEDENBORG | *First published in Latin, London*, 1750-51 | Rotch Edition | Vol. V | BOSTON AND NEW YORK | HOUGHTON, MIFFLIN AND COMPANY | The Riverside Press, Cambridge | 1907
verso: MATTHEW VI. 33. | Seek ye first the Kingdom of God and His Justice, and all things | shall be added unto you.

half title: HEAVENLY ARCANA | VOL V
verso: <within a rule border 94 x 63 mm> 1907 Rotch Edition | OF | SWEDENBORG'S WORKS | VOLS. | 1-19 HEAVENLY ARCANA | 20 INDEX ARCANA | 21 HEAVEN AND HELL | 22 MISCELLANEOUS WORKS | FINAL JUDGMENT | WHITE HORSE | EARTHS IN THE UNIVERSE | SUMMARY EXPOSITION | 23 FOUR DOCTRINES | NEW JERUSALEM AND ITS HEAVENLY | DOCTRINES | 24 DIVINE LOVE AND WISDOM | INTERCOURSE BETWEEN THE SOUL | AND THE BODY | 25 DIVINE PROVIDENCE | 26-28 APOCALYPSE REVEALED | 29 MARRIAGE LOVE | 30-32 TRUE CHRISTIAN RELIGION
small 8vo
half title and title leaves, 4 pp; Note, 1 p; Contents, p 1; text of Genesis 21-24 and n 2606-3227, pp 3-482.
UK: SOC; NET: GEN; USA: ANC; SA: MMC

49/01/En 2/220 **1907** Hyde 712/c
THE | HEAVENLY ARCANA | DISCLOSED | WHICH ARE IN THE SACRED SCRIPTURE | OR WORD OF THE LORD | HERE, THOSE WHICH ARE IN | GENESIS | *TOGETHER WITH* | WONDERFUL THINGS SEEN IN THE | *WORLD OF SPIRITS* | AND THE *HEAVEN OF ANGELS* | BY | EMANUEL SWEDENBORG | *First published in Latin, London*, 1751 | Rotch Edition | VOL. VI | BOSTON AND NEW YORK | HOUGHTON, MIFFLIN AND COMPANY | The Riverside Press, Cambridge | 1907
verso: MATTHEW VI. 33. | Seek ye first the Kingdom of God and His Justice, and all things | shall be added unto you.
half title: HEAVENLY ARCANA | VOL VI
verso: <within a rule border 94 x 63 mm> 1907 Rotch Edition | OF | SWEDENBORG'S WORKS | VOLS. | 1-19 HEAVENLY ARCANA | 20 INDEX ARCANA | 21 HEAVEN AND HELL | 22 MISCELLANEOUS WORKS | FINAL JUDGMENT | WHITE HORSE | EARTHS IN THE UNIVERSE | SUMMARY EXPOSITION | 23 FOUR DOCTRINES | NEW JERUSALEM AND ITS HEAVENLY | DOCTRINES | 24 DIVINE LOVE AND WISDOM | INTERCOURSE BETWEEN THE SOUL | AND THE BODY | 25 DIVINE PROVIDENCE | 26-28 APOCALYPSE REVEALED | 29 MARRIAGE LOVE | 30-32 TRUE CHRISTIAN RELIGION
small 8vo
half title and title leaves, 2 pp; Note, p 3; Contents, p 5; text of Genesis 25-27 and n 3228-649, pp 7-347.
UK: SOC; NET: GEN; USA: ANC; SA: MMC

49/01/En 2/221 **1907** Hyde 728/c
THE | HEAVENLY ARCANA | DISCLOSED | WHICH ARE IN THE SACRED SCRIPTURE | OR WORD OF THE LORD | HERE, THOSE WHICH ARE IN | GENESIS | *TOGETHER WITH* | WONDERFUL THINGS SEEN IN THE | *WORLD OF SPIRITS* AND THE *HEAVEN* | *OF ANGELS* | BY | EMANUEL SWEDENBORG | *First published in Latin, London*, 1751-52 | Rotch Edition | VOL. VII | BOSTON AND NEW YORK | HOUGHTON, MIFFLIN AND COMPANY | The Riverside Press, Cambridge | 1907
verso: MATTHEW VI. 33. | Seek ye first the Kingdom of God and His Justice, and all things | shall be added unto you.
half title: HEAVENLY ARCANA | VOL VII
verso: <within a rule border 94 x 64 mm> 1907 Rotch Edition | OF | SWEDENBORG'S WORKS | VOLS. | 1-19 HEAVENLY ARCANA | 20 INDEX ARCANA | 21 HEAVEN AND HELL | 22 MISCELLANEOUS WORKS | FINAL JUDGMENT | WHITE HORSE | EARTHS IN THE UNIVERSE | SUMMARY EXPOSITION | 23 FOUR DOCTRINES | NEW JERUSALEM AND ITS HEAVENLY | DOCTRINES | 24 DIVINE LOVE AND WISDOM | INTERCOURSE BETWEEN THE SOUL | AND THE BODY | 25 DIVINE PROVIDENCE | 26-28 APOCALYPSE REVEALED | 29 MARRIAGE LOVE | 30-32 TRUE CHRISTIAN RELIGION

small 8vo
half title and title leaves, 2 pp; Note, p 3; Contents, p 5; text of Genesis 28-31 and n 3650-4338, pp 7-539.
UK: SOC; NET: GEN; USA: ANC; SA: MMC

49/01/En 2/222 **1907** Hyde 745/c
THE | HEAVENLY ARCANA | DISCLOSED | WHICH ARE IN THE SACRED SCRIPTURE | OR WORD OF THE LORD | HERE, THOSE WHICH ARE IN | GENESIS | *TOGETHER WITH* | WONDERFUL THINGS SEEN IN THE | *WORLD OF SPIRITS* AND THE *HEAVEN* | *OF ANGELS* | BY | EMANUEL SWEDENBORG | *First published in Latin, London*, 1752 | Rotch Edition | VOL. VIII | BOSTON AND NEW YORK | HOUGHTON, MIFFLIN AND COMPANY | The Riverside Press, Cambridge | 1907
verso: MATTHEW VI. 33. | Seek ye first the Kingdom of God and His Justice, and all things | shall be added unto you.
half title: HEAVENLY ARCANA | VOL. VIII
verso: <within a rule border 94 x 63 mm> 1907 Rotch Edition | OF | SWEDENBORG'S WORKS | VOLS. | 1-19 HEAVENLY ARCANA | 20 INDEX ARCANA | 21 HEAVEN AND HELL | 22 MISCELLANEOUS WORKS | FINAL JUDGMENT | WHITE HORSE | EARTHS IN THE UNIVERSE | SUMMARY EXPOSITION | 23 FOUR DOCTRINES | NEW JERUSALEM AND ITS HEAVENLY | DOCTRINES | 24 DIVINE LOVE AND WISDOM | INTERCOURSE BETWEEN THE SOUL | AND THE BODY | 25 DIVINE PROVIDENCE | 26-28 APOCALYPSE REVEALED | 29 MARRIAGE LOVE | 30-32 TRUE CHRISTIAN RELIGION
small 8vo
half title and title leaves, 2 pp; Note, p 3; Contents, p 5; text of Genesis 31-36 and n 229-4660, pp 7-384.
UK: SOC; NET: GEN; USA: ANC; SA: MMC

49/01/En 2/223 **1907** Hyde 759/c
THE | HEAVENLY ARCANA | DISCLOSED | WHICH ARE IN THE SACRED SCRIPTURE | OR WORD OF THE LORD | HERE, THOSE WHICH ARE IN | GENESIS | *TOGETHER WITH* | WONDERFUL THINGS SEEN IN THE | *WORLD OF SPIRITS* AND THE *HEAVEN* | *OF ANGELS* | BY | EMANUEL SWEDENBORG | *First published in Latin, Londo*n, 1752 | Rotch Edition | VOL. IX. | BOSTON AND NEW YORK | HOUGHTON, MIFFLIN AND COMPANY | The Riverside Press, Cambridge | 1907
verso: MATTHEW VI. 33. | Seek ye first the Kingdom of God and His Justice, and all things | shall be added unto you.
half title: HEAVENLY ARCANA | VOL. IX
verso: <within a rule border 94 x 63 mm> 1907 Rotch Edition | OF | SWEDENBORG'S WORKS | VOLS. | 1-19 HEAVENLY ARCANA | 20 INDEX ARCANA | 21 HEAVEN AND HELL | 22 MISCELLANEOUS WORKS | FINAL JUDGMENT | WHITE HORSE | EARTHS IN THE UNIVERSE | SUMMARY EXPOSITION | 23 FOUR DOCTRINES | NEW JERUSALEM AND ITS HEAVENLY | DOCTRINES | 24 DIVINE LOVE AND WISDOM | INTERCOURSE BETWEEN THE SOUL | AND THE BODY | 25 DIVINE PROVIDENCE | 26-28 APOCALYPSE REVEALED | 29 MARRIAGE LOVE | 30-32 TRUE CHRISTIAN RELIGION
small 8vo
half title and title leaves, 2 pp; Note, p 3; Contents, p 5; text of Genesis 37-40 and n 4661-5190, pp 7-458.
UK: SOC; NET: GEN; USA: ANC; SA: MMC

49/01/En 2/224 **1907** Hyde 774/c
THE | HEAVENLY ARCANA | DISCLOSED | WHICH ARE IN THE SACRED SCRIPTURE | OR WORD

OF THE LORD | HERE, THOSE WHICH ARE IN | GENESIS | *TOGETHER WITH* | WONDERFUL THINGS SEEN IN THE | *WORLD OF SPIRITS* AND THE *HEAVEN* | *OF ANGELS* | BY | EMANUEL SWEDENBORG | *First published in Latin, London*, 1753 | Rotch Edition | VOL. X | BOSTON AND NEW YORK | HOUGHTON, MIFFLIN AND COMPANY | The Riverside Press, Cambridge | 1907
verso: MATTHEW VI. 33. | Seek ye first the Kingdom of God and His Justice, and all things | shall be added unto you.
half title: HEAVENLY ARCANA | VOL. X
verso: <within a rule border 94 x 63 mm> 1907 Rotch Edition | OF | SWEDENBORG'S WORKS | VOLS. | 1-19 HEAVENLY ARCANA | 20 INDEX ARCANA | 21 HEAVEN AND HELL | 22 MISCELLANEOUS WORKS | FINAL JUDGMENT | WHITE HORSE | EARTHS IN THE UNIVERSE | SUMMARY EXPOSITION | 23 FOUR DOCTRINES | NEW JERUSALEM AND ITS HEAVENLY | DOCTRINES | 24 DIVINE LOVE AND WISDOM | INTERCOURSE BETWEEN THE SOUL | AND THE BODY | 25 DIVINE PROVIDENCE | 26-28 APOCALYPSE REVEALED | 29 MARRIAGE LOVE | 30-32 TRUE CHRISTIAN RELIGION
small 8vo
half title and title leaves, 4 pp; Note, p 3; Contents, p 5; text of Genesis 41-44 and n 5191-5866, pp 7-435.
UK: soc; NET: gen; USA: anc

49/01/En 2/225 **1907** Hyde 783/a

THE | HEAVENLY ARCANA | DISCLOSED | WHICH ARE IN THE SACRED SCRIPTURE | OR WORD OF THE LORD | HERE, THOSE WHICH ARE IN | GENESIS | *TOGETHER WITH* | WONDERFUL THINGS SEEN IN THE | *WORLD OF SPIRITS* AND THE | *HEAVEN* | *OF ANGELS* | BY | EMANUEL SWEDENBORG | *First published in Latin, London*, 1753 | Rotch Edition | VOL. XI | BOSTON AND NEW YORK | HOUGHTON, MIFFLIN AND COMPANY | The Riverside Press, Cambridge | 1907
verso: MATTHEW VI. 33. | Seek ye first the Kingdom of God and His Justice, and all things | shall be added unto you.
half title: HEAVENLY ARCANA | VOL. XI
verso: <within a rule border 94 x 63 mm> 1907 Rotch Edition | OF | SWEDENBORG'S WORKS | VOLS. | 1-19 HEAVENLY ARCANA | 20 INDEX ARCANA | 21 HEAVEN AND HELL | 22 MISCELLANEOUS WORKS | FINAL JUDGMENT | WHITE HORSE | EARTHS IN THE UNIVERSE | SUMMARY EXPOSITION | 23 FOUR DOCTRINES | NEW JERUSALEM AND ITS HEAVENLY | DOCTRINES | 24 DIVINE LOVE AND WISDOM | INTERCOURSE BETWEEN THE SOUL | AND THE BODY | 25 DIVINE PROVIDENCE | 26-28 APOCALYPSE REVEALED | 29 MARRIAGE LOVE | 30-32 TRUE CHRISTIAN RELIGION
small 8vo
half title and title leaves, 2 pp; Note, p 3; Contents, p 5; text of Genesis 45-50 and n 5867-6626, pp 7-493.
UK: soc; NET: gen; USA: anc

49/01/En 2/226 **1907** Hyde 792/a

THE | HEAVENLY ARCANA | DISCLOSED | WHICH ARE IN THE SACRED SCRIPTURE | OR WORD OF THE LORD | HERE, THOSE WHICH ARE IN | EXODUS | *TOGETHER WITH* | WONDERFUL THINGS SEEN IN THE | *WORLD OF SPIRITS* AND THE *HEAVEN* | *OF ANGELS* | BY | EMANUEL SWEDENBORG | *First published in Latin, London*, 1753 | Rotch Edition | Vol. XII. BOSTON AND NEW YORK HOUGHTON, MIFFLIN AND COMPANY | The Riverside Press, Cambridge | 1907
verso: MATTHEW VI. 33. | Seek ye first the Kingdom of God and His Justice, and all things | shall be added unto you.
half title: HEAVENLY ARCANA | VOL. XII

verso: <within a rule border 94 x 64 mm> 1907 Rotch Edition | OF | SWEDENBORG'S WORKS | VOLS. | 1-19 HEAVENLY ARCANA | 20 INDEX ARCANA | 21 HEAVEN AND HELL | 22 MISCELLANEOUS WORKS | FINAL JUDGMENT | WHITE HORSE | EARTHS IN THE UNIVERSE | SUMMARY EXPOSITION | 23 FOUR DOCTRINES | NEW JERUSALEM AND ITS HEAVENLY | DOCTRINES | 24 DIVINE LOVE AND WISDOM | INTERCOURSE BETWEEN THE SOUL | AND THE BODY | 25 DIVINE PROVIDENCE | 26-28 APOCALYPSE REVEALED | 29 MARRIAGE LOVE | 30-32 TRUE CHRISTIAN RELIGION
small 8vo
half title and title leaves, 4 pp; Note, p 3; Contents, p 5; text of Exodus 1-6 and n 6627-7254, pp 3-371.
UK: SOC; NET: GEN; USA: ANC; SA: MMC

49/01/En 2/227 **1907** Hyde 793/a
THE | HEAVENLY ARCANA | DISCLOSED | WHICH ARE IN THE SACRED SCRIPTURE | OR WORD OF THE LORD | HERE, THOSE WHICH ARE IN | EXODUS | *TOGETHER WITH* | WONDERFUL THINGS SEEN IN THE | *WORLD OF SPIRITS* AND THE *HEAVEN* | *OF ANGELS* | BY | EMANUEL SWEDENBORG | *First published in Latin, London,* 1753 | Rotch Edition | VOL. XIII | BOSTON AND NEW YORK | HOUGHTON, MIFFLIN AND COMPANY | The Riverside Press, Cambridge | 1907
verso: MATTHEW VI. 33. | Seek ye first the Kingdom of God and His Justice, and all things | shall be added unto you.
half title: HEAVENLY ARCANA | VOL. XIII
verso: <within a rule border 94 x 64 mm> 1907 Rotch Edition | OF | SWEDENBORG'S WORKS | VOLS. | 1-19 HEAVENLY ARCANA | 20 INDEX ARCANA | 21 HEAVEN AND HELL | 22 MISCELLANEOUS WORKS | FINAL JUDGMENT | WHITE HORSE | EARTHS IN THE UNIVERSE | SUMMARY EXPOSITION | 23 FOUR DOCTRINES | NEW JERUSALEM AND ITS HEAVENLY | DOCTRINES | 24 DIVINE LOVE AND WISDOM | INTERCOURSE BETWEEN THE SOUL | AND THE BODY | 25 DIVINE PROVIDENCE | 26-28 APOCALYPSE REVEALED | 29 MARRIAGE LOVE | 30-32 TRUE CHRISTIAN RELIGION
small 8vo
half title and title leaves, 4 pp; Note, p 3; Contents, p 5; text of Exodus 7-12 and n 7255-8032, pp 7-408.
UK: SOC; NET: GEN; USA: ANC; SA: MMC

49/01/En 2/228 **1907** Hyde 794/aa
THE | HEAVENLY ARCANA | DISCLOSED | WHICH ARE IN THE SACRED SCRIPTURE | OR WORD OF THE LORD | HERE, THOSE WHICH ARE IN EXODUS | *TOGETHER WITH* | WONDERFUL THINGS SEEN IN THE | *WORLD OF SPIRITS* AND THE *HEAVEN* | *OF ANGELS* | BY | EMANUEL SWEDENBORG | *First published in Latin, London,* 1753-54 | Rotch Edition | VOL. XIV | BOSTON AND NEW YORK | HOUGHTON, MIFFLIN AND COMPANY | The Riverside Press, Cambridge | 1907
verso: MATTHEW VI. 33. | Seek ye first the Kingdom of God and His Justice, and all things | shall be added unto you.
half title: HEAVENLY ARCANA | VOL. XIV
verso: <within a rule border 94 x 64 mm> 1907 Rotch Edition | OF | SWEDENBORG'S WORKS | VOLS. | 1-19 HEAVENLY ARCANA | 20 INDEX ARCANA | 21 HEAVEN AND HELL | 22 MISCELLANEOUS WORKS | FINAL JUDGMENT | WHITE HORSE | EARTHS IN THE UNIVERSE | SUMMARY EXPOSITION | 23 FOUR DOCTRINES | NEW JERUSALEM AND ITS HEAVENLY | DOCTRINES | 24 DIVINE LOVE AND WISDOM | INTERCOURSE BETWEEN THE SOUL | AND THE BODY | 25 DIVINE PROVIDENCE | 26-28 APOCALYPSE REVEALED | 29 MARRIAGE LOVE | 30-32 TRUE CHRISTIAN RELIGION
small 8vo

half title and title leaves, 4 pp; Note, p 3; Contents, p 5; text of Exodus 13-18 and n 8033-8741, pp 7-425.

NET: GEN; USA: ANC

49/01/En 2/229 **1907** Hyde 794/aaa

THE | HEAVENLY ARCANA | DISCLOSED | WHICH ARE IN THE SACRED SCRIPTURE | OR WORD OF THE LORD | HERE, THOSE WHICH ARE IN | EXODUS | *TOGETHER WITH* | WONDERFUL THINGS SEEN IN THE | *WORLD OF SPIRITS* AND THE *HEAVEN* | *OF ANGELS* | BY | EMANUEL SWEDENBORG | *First published in Latin, London*, 1754 | Rotch Edition | VOL. XV | BOSTON AND NEW YORK | HOUGHTON, MIFFLIN AND COMPANY | The Riverside Press, Cambridge | 1907

verso: MATTHEW VI. 33. | Seek ye first the Kingdom of God and His Justice, and all things | shall be added unto you.

half title: HEAVENLY ARCANA | VOL. XV

verso: <within a rule border 94 x 63 mm> 1907 Rotch Edition | OF | SWEDENBORG'S WORKS | VOLS. | 1-19 HEAVENLY ARCANA | 20 INDEX ARCANA | 21 HEAVEN AND HELL | 22 MISCELLANEOUS WORKS | FINAL JUDGMENT | WHITE HORSE | EARTHS IN THE UNIVERSE | SUMMARY EXPOSITION | 23 FOUR DOCTRINES | NEW JERUSALEM AND ITS HEAVENLY | DOCTRINES | 24 DIVINE LOVE AND WISDOM | INTERCOURSE BETWEEN THE SOUL | AND THE BODY | 25 DIVINE PROVIDENCE | 26-28 APOCALYPSE REVEALED | 29 MARRIAGE LOVE | 30-32 TRUE CHRISTIAN RELIGION

small 8vo

half title and title leaves, 4 pp; Note, p 3; Contents, p 5; text of Exodus 19-21 and n 8742-9111, pp 7-330.

UK: SOC; NET: GEN; USA: ANC; SA: MMC

49/01/En 2/230 **1907** Hyde 794/bb

THE | HEAVENLY ARCANA | DISCLOSED | WHICH ARE IN THE SACRED SCRIPTURE | OR WORD OF THE LORD | HERE, THOSE WHICH ARE IN | EXODUS | *TOGETHER WITH* | WONDERFUL THINGS SEEN IN THE | *WORLD OF SPIRITS* AND THE *HEAVEN* | *OF ANGELS* | BY | EMANUEL SWEDENBORG | *First published in Latin, London*, 1754 | Rotch Edition | VOL. XVI | BOSTON AND NEW YORK | HOUGHTON, MIFFLIN AND COMPANY | The Riverside Press, Cambridge | 1907

verso: MATTHEW VI. 33. | Seek ye first the Kingdom of God and His Justice, and all things | shall be added unto you.

half title: HEAVENLY ARCANA CŒLESTIA | VOL. XVI

verso: <within a rule border 94 x 63 mm> 1907 Rotch Edition | OF | SWEDENBORG'S WORKS | VOLS. | 1-19 HEAVENLY ARCANA | 20 INDEX ARCANA | 21 HEAVEN AND HELL | 22 MISCELLANEOUS WORKS | FINAL JUDGMENT | WHITE HORSE | EARTHS IN THE UNIVERSE | SUMMARY EXPOSITION | 23 FOUR DOCTRINES | NEW JERUSALEM AND ITS HEAVENLY | DOCTRINES | 24 DIVINE LOVE AND WISDOM | INTERCOURSE BETWEEN THE SOUL | AND THE BODY | 25 DIVINE PROVIDENCE | 26-28 APOCALYPSE REVEALED | 29 MARRIAGE LOVE | 30-32 TRUE CHRISTIAN RELIGION

small 8vo

half title and title leaves, 4 pp; Note, p 3; Contents, p 5; text of Exodus 22-24 and n 9112-9442, pp 7-420.

UK: SOC; NET: GEN; USA: ANC; SA: MMC

49/01/En 2/231 **1907** Hyde 794/1a

THE | HEAVENLY ARCANA | DISCLOSED | WHICH ARE IN THE SACRED SCRIPTURE | OR WORD

OF THE LORD | HERE, THOSE WHICH ARE IN EXODUS | *TOGETHER WITH* | WONDERFUL THINGS SEEN IN THE | *WORLD OF SPIRITS* AND THE *HEAVEN* | *OF ANGELS* | BY | EMANUEL SWEDENBORG | *First published in Latin, London*, 1756 | Rotch Edition | VOL. XVII | BOSTON AND NEW YORK | HOUGHTON, MIFFLIN AND COMPANY | The Riverside Press, Cambridge | 1907
half title: HEAVENLY ARCANA | VOL. XVII
verso: <within a rule border 94 x 63 mm> 1907 Rotch Edition | OF | SWEDENBORG'S WORKS | VOLS. | 1-19 HEAVENLY ARCANA | 20 INDEX ARCANA | 21 HEAVEN AND HELL | 22 MISCELLANEOUS WORKS | FINAL JUDGMENT | WHITE HORSE | EARTHS IN THE UNIVERSE | SUMMARY EXPOSITION | 23 FOUR DOCTRINES | NEW JERUSALEM AND ITS HEAVENLY | DOCTRINES | 24 DIVINE LOVE AND WISDOM | INTERCOURSE BETWEEN THE SOUL | AND THE BODY | 25 DIVINE PROVIDENCE | 26-28 APOCALYPSE REVEALED | 29 MARRIAGE LOVE | 30-32 TRUE CHRISTIAN RELIGION
small 8vo
half title and title leaves, 4 pp; Note p 3; Contents, p 5; text of Exodus 25-28 and n 9443-9973, pp 7-447.

UK: soc; NET: gen; USA: anc; SA: mmc

49/01/En 2/232 **1907** Hyde 794/2a

THE | HEAVENLY ARCANA | DISCLOSED | WHICH ARE IN THE SACRED SCRIPTURE | OR WORD OF THE LORD | HERE, THOSE WHICH ARE IN | EXODUS | *TOGETHER WITH* | WONDERFUL THINGS SEEN IN THE | *WORLD OF SPIRITS* AND THE *HEAVEN* | *OF ANGELS* | BY | EMANUEL SWEDENBORG | *First published in Latin, London*, 1756 | Rotch Edition | VOL. XVIII | BOSTON AND NEW YORK | HOUGHTON, MIFFLIN AND COMPANY | The Riverside Press, Cambridge | 1907
verso: MATTHEW VI. 33. | Seek ye first the Kingdom of God and His justice, and all things | shall be added unto you.
half title: HEAVENLY ARCANA | VOL. XVIII
verso: <within a rule border 94 x 64 mm> 1907 Rotch Edition | OF | SWEDENBORG'S WORKS | VOLS. | 1-19 HEAVENLY ARCANA | 20 INDEX ARCANA | 21 HEAVEN AND HELL | 22 MISCELLANEOUS WORKS | FINAL JUDGMENT | WHITE HORSE | EARTHS IN THE UNIVERSE | SUMMARY EXPOSITION | 23 FOUR DOCTRINES | NEW JERUSALEM AND ITS HEAVENLY | DOCTRINES | 24 DIVINE LOVE AND WISDOM | INTERCOURSE BETWEEN THE SOUL | AND THE BODY | 25 DIVINE PROVIDENCE | 26-28 APOCALYPSE REVEALED | 29 MARRIAGE LOVE | 30-32 TRUE CHRISTIAN RELIGION
small 8vo
half title and title leaves, 4 pp; Note, p 3; Contents, p 5; text of Exodus 29-31 and n 9974-10317, pp 7-404.

UK: soc; NET: gen; USA: anc; SA: mmc

49/01/En 2/233 **1907** Hyde 794/3a

THE | HEAVENLY ARCANA | DISCLOSED | WHICH ARE IN THE SACRED SCRIPTURE | OR WORD OF THE LORD | HERE, THOSE WHICH ARE IN | EXODUS | *TOGETHER WITH* | WONDERFUL THINGS SEEN IN THE | *WORLD OF SPIRITS* AND THE *HEAVEN* | *OF ANGELS* | BY | EMANUEL SWEDENBORG | *First published in Latin, London*, 1756 | Rotch Edition | VOL. XIX. | BOSTON AND NEW YORK | HOUGHTON, MIFFLIN AND COMPANY | The Riverside Press, Cambridge | 1907
verso: MATTHEW VI. 33. | Seek ye first the Kingdom of God and His Justice, and all things | shall be added unto you.
half title: HEAVENLY ARCANA | VOL. XIX
verso: <within a rule border 94 x 63 mm> 1907 Rotch Edition | OF | SWEDENBORG'S WORKS | VOLS. | 1-19 HEAVENLY ARCANA | 20 INDEX ARCANA | 21 HEAVEN AND HELL | 22 MISCELLANEOUS WORKS | FINAL JUDGMENT | WHITE HORSE | EARTHS IN THE UNIVERSE | SUMMARY EXPOSITION

| 23 FOUR DOCTRINES | NEW JERUSALEM AND ITS HEAVENLY | DOCTRINES | 24 DIVINE LOVE AND WISDOM | INTERCOURSE BETWEEN THE SOUL | AND THE BODY | 25 DIVINE PROVIDENCE | 26-28 APOCALYPSE REVEALED | 29 MARRIAGE LOVE | 30-32 TRUE CHRISTIAN RELIGION
small 8vo
half title and title leaves, 4 pp; Note, p 3; Contents, p 5; Note, p 6; text of Exodus 31-40 and n 10318-10837, pp 7-387.
Edited by B Worcester from a revision by H W Wright.
UK: SOC; NET: GEN; USA: ANC

49/01/En 5/7 **1907** Hyde 728/b
ARCANA COELESTIA | THE | HEAVENLY ARCANA | CONTAINED IN THE HOLY SCRIPTURE OR WORD OF THE LORD | UNFOLDED | BEGINNING WITH THE BOOK OF GENESIS | TOGETHER WITH WONDERFUL THINGS SEEN IN THE WORLD OF | SPIRITS AND IN THE HEAVEN OF ANGELS | TRANSLATED FROM THE LATIN OF | EMANUEL SWEDENBORG | THOROUGHLY REVISED AND EDITED BY THE | REV. JOHN FAULKNER POTTS, B.A. LOND. | VOLUME VII. | <short rule> | LIBRARY EDITION | <short rule> | NEW YORK | THE AMERICAN SWEDENBORG PRINTING AND PUBLISHING | SOCIETY | 3 WEST TWENTY-NINTH STREET | 1907
<In some copies a label was later affixed over the last 5 lines:> IN 1928 THE CORPORATE NAME OF | The American Swedenborg Printing and Publishing Society | was changed to | SWEDENBORG FOUNDATION | INCORPORATED | NEW ADDRESS: 18 EAST 41st ST. NEW YORK
verso: [INSCRIPTION BY THE AUTHOR.] | Seek ye first the Kingdom of God and His righteousness, and all these | things shall be added unto you (*Matt.* vi. 33). | Published by The American Swedenborg Printing and Publishing Society, | organized for the purpose of Printing, Publishing, and Circulating uniform | editions of the Theological Writings of Emanuel Swedenborg for charitable | and missionary purposes. Incorporated in the State of New York, A.D. 1850.
8vo
title leaf, 2 pp; Table of contents, p iii; text of Genesis 39-43 and n 4954-5727, pp 1-516.
UK: SOC; NET: GEN; SWI: LAU; USA: ANC, SHS

49/01/En 5/8 **1908** Hyde 745/b
ARCANA COELESTIA | THE | HEAVENLY ARCANA | CONTAINED IN THE HOLY SCRIPTURE OR WORD OF THE LORD | UNFOLDED | BEGINNING WITH THE BOOK OF GENESIS | TOGETHER WITH WONDERFUL THINGS SEEN IN THE WORLD OF | SPIRITS AND IN THE HEAVEN OF ANGELS | TRANSLATED FROM THE LATIN OF | EMANUEL SWEDENBORG | THOROUGHLY REVISED AND EDITED BY THE | REV. JOHN FAULKNER POTTS, B.A. LOND. | VOLUME VIII. | <short rule> | LIBRARY EDITION | <short rule> | NEW YORK | THE AMERICAN SWEDENBORG PRINTING AND PUBLISHING | SOCIETY | 3 WEST TWENTY-NINTH STREET | 1908
<In some copies a label was later affixed over the last 5 lines:> IN 1928 THE CORPORATE NAME OF | The American Swedenborg Printing and Publishing Society | was changed to | SWEDENBORG FOUNDATION | INCORPORATED | NEW ADDRESS: 818 EAST 41st ST. NEW YORK
verso: [INSCRIPTION BY THE AUTHOR.] | Seek ye first the Kingdom of God and His righteousness, and all these | things shall be added unto you (*Matt.* vi. 33). | Published by The American Swedenborg Printing and Publishing Society, | organized for the purpose of Printing, Publishing, and Circulating uniform | editions of the Theological Writings of Emanuel Swedenborg for charitable | and missionary purposes. Incorporated in the State of New York, A.D. 1850.
8vo
title leaf, 2 pp; Table of contents, p iii; text of Genesis 44-50 and n 5728-6626, pp 1-502; Reviser's notes, pp 503-504.
UK: SOC; NET: GEN; SWI: LAU; USA: ANC, SHS

49/01/En 5/9 **1908** Hyde 759/b

ARCANA COELESTIA | THE | HEAVENLY ARCANA | CONTAINED IN THE HOLY SCRIPTURE OR WORD OF THE LORD | UNFOLDED | HERE THOSE WHICH ARE IN EXODUS | TOGETHER WITH WONDERFUL THINGS SEEN IN THE WORLD OF | SPIRITS AND IN THE HEAVEN OF ANGELS | TRANSLATED FROM THE LATIN OF | EMANUEL SWEDENBORG | THOROUGHLY REVISED AND EDITED BY THE | REV. JOHN FAULKNER POTTS, B.A. LOND. | VOLUME IX. | <short rule> | LIBRARY EDITION | <short rule> | NEW YORK | THE AMERICAN SWEDENBORG PRINTING AND PUBLISHING | SOCIETY | 3 WEST TWENTY-NINTH STREET | 1908
<in some copies a label was later affixed over the last 5 lines:> IN 1928 THE CORPORATE NAME OF | The American Swedenborg Printing and Publishing Society | was changed to | SWEDENBORG FOUNDATION | INCORPORATED | NEW ADDRESS: 818 EAST 41st ST. NEW YORK
verso: [INSCRIPTION BY THE AUTHOR.] | Seek ye first the Kingdom of God and His righteousness, and all these | things shall be added unto you (*Matt.* vi.33). | Published by The American Swedenborg Printing and Publishing Society, | organized for the purpose of Printing, Publishing, and Circulating uniform | editions of the Theological Writings of Emanuel Swedenborg for charitable | and missionary purposes. Incorporated in the State of New York, A.D. 1850.
8vo
title leaf, 2 pp; Table of contents, p iii; text of Exodus 1-12 and n 6627-8032, pp 1-685; Reviser's notes, pp 686.
UK: soc; NET: gen; SWI: lau; USA: anc, shs

49/01/En 5/10 **1909** Hyde 774/b

ARCANA COELESTIA | THE | HEAVENLY ARCANA | CONTAINED IN THE HOLY SCRIPTURE OR WORD OF THE LORD | UNFOLDED | HERE THOSE WHICH ARE IN EXODUS | TOGETHER WITH WONDERFUL THINGS SEEN IN THE WORLD OF | SPIRITS AND IN THE HEAVEN OF ANGELS | TRANSLATED FROM THE LATIN OF | EMANUEL SWEDENBORG | THOROUGHLY REVISED AND EDITED BY THE | REV. JOHN FAULKNER POTTS, B.A. LOND. | VOLUME X. | <short rule> | LIBRARY EDITION | <short rule> | NEW YORK | THE AMERICAN SWEDENBORG PRINTING AND PUBLISHING | SOCIETY | 3 WEST TWENTY-NINTH STREET | 1909
verso: [INSCRIPTION BY THE AUTHOR.] | Seek ye first the Kingdom of God and His righteousness, and all these | things shall be added unto you (*Matt.* vi.33). | Published by The American Swedenborg Printing and Publishing Society, | organized for the purpose of Printing, Publishing, and Circulating uniform | editions of the Theological Writings of Emanuel Swedenborg for charitable | and missionary purposes. Incorporated in the State of New York, A.D. 1850.
8vo
title leaf, 2 pp; Table of contents, p iii; text of Exodus 13-21 and n 8033-9111, pp 1-652.
UK: soc; NET: gen; SWI: lau; USA: anc

49/01/En 5/11 **1909** Hyde 618/1

ARCANA COELESTIA | THE | HEAVENLY ARCANA | CONTAINED IN THE HOLY SCRIPTURE OR WORD OF THE LORD | UNFOLDED | BEGINNING WITH THE BOOK OF GENESIS | TOGETHER WITH WONDERFUL THINGS SEEN IN THE WORLD OF | SPIRITS AND IN THE HEAVEN OF ANGELS | TRANSLATED FROM THE LATIN OF | EMANUEL SWEDENBORG | THOROUGHLY REVISED AND EDITED BY THE | REV. JOHN FAULKNER POTTS, B.A. LOND. | VOLUME I. | <short rule> | LIBRARY EDITION | <short rule> | NEW YORK | THE AMERICAN SWEDENBORG PRINTING AND PUBLISHING | SOCIETY | 3 WEST TWENTY-NINTH STREET | 1909
<in some copies a label was later affixed over the last 5 lines:> IN 1928 THE CORPORATE NAME OF | The American Swedenborg Printing and Publishing Society | was changed to | SWEDENBORG FOUNDATION | INCORPORATED | NEW ADDRESS: 818 EAST 41st ST. NEW YORK

verso: [INSCRIPTION BY THE AUTHOR.] | Seek ye first the Kingdom of God and His righteousness, and all these | things shall be added unto you (*Matt.* vi.33). | Published by The American Swedenborg Printing and Publishing Society, | organized for the purpose of Printing, Publishing, and Circulating uniform | editions of the Theological Writings of Emanuel Swedenborg for charitable | and missionary purposes. Incorporated in the State of New York, A.D. 1850.
8vo
title leaf, 2 pp; Prefatory notes, pp iii-vii; Table of contents, p viii; text of Genesis 1-9 and n 1-1113, pp 1-585.
UK: SOC; NET: GEN; SWI: LAU; USA: ANC

49/01/En 5/12 **1909** Hyde 618/2
ARCANA CÆLESTIA | <short rule> | THE | HEAVENLY ARCANA | CONTAINED IN | THE HOLY SCRIPTURES OR WORD OF THE LORD | UNFOLDED | BEGINNING WITH THE BOOK OF GENESIS | *TOGETHER WITH WONDERFUL THINGS SEEN IN THE WORLD OF | SPIRITS AND IN THE HEAVEN OF ANGELS* | TRANSLATED FROM THE LATIN OF | EMANUEL SWEDENBORG | *Servant of the Lord Jesus Christ* | <short rule> | VOL. I | <short rule> | NEW YORK | AMERICAN SWEDENBORG PRINTING AND PUBLISHING | SOCIETY | NO. 3 WEST TWENTY-NINTH STREET | <short rule> | 1909
verso: *Published by The American Swedenborg Printing and Publishing Soci- | ety, organized for the purpose of Stereotyping, Printing and | Publishing Uniform Editions of the Theological Writings of | Emanuel Swedenborg, and incorporated in the State of New York | A.D.*, 1850.
half title: ARCANA CŒLESTIA.
8vo
half title and title leaves, 4 pp; text of Genesis 1-11 and n 1-1382, pp 1-568.
UK: SOC; USA: ANC

49/01/En 5/13 **1909** Hyde 696/1
ARCANA CÆLESTIA | <short rule> | THE | HEAVENLY ARCANA | CONTAINED IN | THE HOLY SCRIPTURES OR WORD OF THE LORD | UNFOLDED | BEGINNING WITH THE BOOK OF GENESIS | *TOGETHER WITH WONDERFUL THINGS SEEN IN THE WORLD OF | SPIRITS AND IN THE HEAVEN OF ANGELS* | TRANSLATED FROM THE LATIN OF | EMANUEL SWEDENBORG | *Servant of the Lord Jesus Christ* | <short rule> | VOL. V | <short rule> | NEW YORK | AMERICAN SWEDENBORG PRINTING AND PUBLISHING | SOCIETY | <short rule> | 1909
verso: *Published by The American Swedenborg Printing and Publishing Soci- | ety, organized for the purpose of Stereotyping, Printing and | Publishing Uniform Editions of the Theological Writings of | Emanuel Swedenborg, and incorporated in the State of New York, | A.D.*, 1850.
half title: ARCANA CŒLESTIA
8vo
half title and title leaves, 4 pp; text of Genesis 32-40 and n 4229-5190, pp 5-607; Reviser's notes, p 608.
UK: SOC; USA: ANC, SHS

49/01/En 5/14 **1909** Hyde 712/1
ARCANA CÆLESTIA | <short rule> | THE | HEAVENLY ARCANA | CONTAINED IN | THE HOLY SCRIPTURES OR WORD OF THE LORD | UNFOLDED | BEGINNING WITH THE BOOK OF GENESIS | *TOGETHER WITH WONDERFUL THINGS SEEN IN THE WORLD OF | SPIRITS AND IN THE HEAVEN OF ANGELS* | TRANSLATED FROM THE LATIN OF | EMANUEL SWEDENBORG | *Servant of the Lord Jesus Christ* | <short rule> | VOL. VI | <short rule> | NEW YORK | AMERICAN SWEDENBORG PRINTING AND PUBLISHING | SOCIETY | NO. 3 WEST TWENTY-NINTH STREET. | <short rule> | 1909

verso: *Published by The American Swedenborg Printing and Publishing Soci- | ety, organized for the purpose of Stereotyping, Printing and | Publishing Uniform Editions of the Theological Writings of | Emanuel Swedenborg, and incorporated in the State of New York, | A.D.*, 1850.
half title: ARCANA CŒLESTIA.
8vo
half title and title leaves, 4 pp; text of Genesis 41-49 and n 5191-6456, pp 5-624.
UK: SOC; USA: ANC

49/01/En 5/15 **1909** Hyde 728/1
ARCANA CÆLESTIA | <short rule> | THE | HEAVENLY ARCANA | CONTAINED IN | THE HOLY SCRIPTURES OR WORD OF THE LORD | UNFOLDED | BEGINNING WITH THE BOOK OF GENESIS | *TOGETHER WITH WONDERFUL THINGS SEEN IN THE WORLD OF | SPIRITS AND IN THE HEAVEN OF ANGELS* | TRANSLATED FROM THE LATIN OF | EMANUEL SWEDENBORG | *Servant of the Lord Jesus Christ* | <short rule> | VOL. VII | <short rule> | NEW YORK | AMERICAN SWEDENBORG PRINTING AND PUBLISHING | SOCIETY | NO. 3 WEST TWENTY-NINTH STREET. | <short rule> | 1909
verso: *Published by The American Swedenborg Printing and Publishing Soci- | ety, organized for the purpose of Stereotyping, Printing and | Publishing Uniform Editions of the Theological Writings of | Emanuel Swedenborg, and incorporated in the State of New York, | A.D.*, 1850.
half title: ARCANA CŒLESTIA
8vo
half title and title leaves, 4 pp; text of Genesis 50, Exodus 1-12, and n 6497-8032, pp 5-627; Reviser's notes, p 628.
UK: SOC; USA: ANC, SHS

49/01/En 5/16 **1909** Hyde 759/1
ARCANA COELESTIA | THE | HEAVENLY ARCANA | CONTAINED IN THE HOLY SCRIPTURE OR WORD OF THE LORD | UNFOLDED | HERE THOSE WHICH ARE IN EXODUS | TOGETHER WITH WONDERFUL THINGS SEEN IN THE WORLD OF | SPIRITS AND IN THE HEAVEN OF ANGELS | TRANSLATED FROM THE LATIN OF | EMANUEL SWEDENBORG | THOROUGHLY REVISED AND EDITED BY THE | REV. JOHN FAULKNER POTTS, B.A. LOND. | VOLUME IX. | <short rule> | LIBRARY EDITION | <short rule> | NEW YORK | THE AMERICAN SWEDENBORG PRINTING AND PUBLISHING | SOCIETY | 3 WEST TWENTY-NINTH STREET | 1909
<In some copies a label was later affixed over the last 5 lines:> IN 1928 THE CORPORATE NAME OF | The American Swedenborg Printing and Publishing Society | was changed to | SWEDENBORG FOUNDATION | INCORPORATED | NEW ADDRESS: 18 EAST 41st ST. NEW YORK
verso: [INSCRIPTION BY THE AUTHOR.] | Seek ye first the Kingdom of God and His righteousness, and all these | things shall be added unto you (*Matt.* vi.33). | Published by The American Swedenborg Printing and Publishing Society, | organized for the purpose of Printing, Publishing, and Circulating uniform | editions of the Theological Writings of Emanuel Swedenborg for charitable | and missionary purposes. Incorporated in the State of New York, A.D. 1850.
8vo
title leaf, 2 pp; Table of contents, pp iii-iv; text of Exodus 22-28 and n 9112-9973, pp 1-607; Reviser's notes, p 608.
SWI: LAU; USA: ANC

49/01/En 5/17 **1909** Hyde 774/1
ARCANA CÆLESTIA | <short rule> | THE | HEAVENLY ARCANA | CONTAINED IN | THE HOLY SCRIPTURES OR WORD OF THE LORD | UNFOLDED | BEGINNING WITH THE BOOK OF

GENESIS | *TOGETHER WITH WONDERFUL THINGS SEEN IN THE WORLD OF* | *SPIRITS AND IN THE HEAVEN OF ANGELS* | TRANSLATED FROM THE LATIN OF | EMANUEL SWEDENBORG | *Servant of the Lord Jesus Christ* | <short rule> | VOL. X | <short rule> | NEW YORK | AMERICAN SWEDENBORG PRINTING AND PUBLISHING | SOCIETY | 3 WEST TWENTY-NINTH STREET. | <short rule> | 1909
verso: Published by THE AMERICAN SWEDENBORG PRINTING AND PUBLISHING | SOCIETY, *organized for the purpose of Stereotyping, Printing and* | *Publishing Uniform Editions of the Theological Writings of* EMANUEL | SWEDENBORG, *and incorporated in the State of New York* A.D. 1850.
half title: ARCANA CŒLESTIA.
8vo
half title and title leaves, 4 pp; text of Genesis 50, Exodus 1-12, and n 9974-10837, pp 5-569; Reviser's notes, p 570.
UK: soc; USA: anc, shs

49/01/En 5/18 1910 Hyde 643/1
ARCANA COELESTIA | THE | HEAVENLY ARCANA | CONTAINED IN THE HOLY SCRIPTURE OR WORD OF THE LORD | UNFOLDED | BEGINNING WITH THE BOOK OF GENESIS | TOGETHER WITH WONDERFUL THINGS SEEN IN THE WORLD OF | SPIRITS AND IN THE HEAVEN OF ANGELS | TRANSLATED FROM THE LATIN OF | EMANUEL SWEDENBORG | THOROUGHLY REVISED AND EDITED BY THE | REV. JOHN FAULKNER POTTS, B.A. LOND. | VOLUME II. | <short rule> | LIBRARY EDITION | <short rule> | NEW YORK | THE AMERICAN SWEDENBORG PRINTING AND PUBLISHING | SOCIETY | 3 WEST TWENTY-NINTH STREET | 1910
<In some copies a label was later affixed over the last 5 lines:> IN 1928 THE CORPORATE NAME OF | The American Swedenborg Printing and Publishing Society | was changed to | SWEDENBORG FOUNDATION | INCORPORATED | NEW ADDRESS: 818 EAST 41st ST. NEW YORK
verso: [INSCRIPTION BY THE AUTHOR.] | Seek ye first the Kingdom of God and His righteousness, and all these | things shall be added unto you (*Matt.* vi.33). | Published by The American Swedenborg Printing and Publishing Society, | organized for the purpose of Printing, Publishing, and Circulating uniform | editions of the Theological Writings of Emanuel Swedenborg for charitable | and missionary purposes. Incorporated in the State of New York, A.D. 1850.
8vo
title leaf, 2 pp; Swedenborg's table of contents, pp iii-iv; text of Genesis 10-17 and n 1114-2134, pp 1-582.
UK: soc; NET: gen; SWI: lau; USA: anc

49/01/En 5/19 1910 Hyde 783/b
ARCANA COELESTIA | THE | HEAVENLY ARCANA | CONTAINED IN THE HOLY SCRIPTURE OR WORD OF THE LORD | UNFOLDED | HERE THOSE WHICH ARE IN EXODUS | TOGETHER WITH WONDERFUL THINGS SEEN IN THE WORLD OF | SPIRITS AND IN THE HEAVEN OF ANGELS | TRANSLATED FROM THE LATIN OF | EMANUEL SWEDENBORG | THOROUGHLY REVISED AND EDITED BY THE | REV. JOHN FAULKNER POTTS, B.A. LOND. | VOLUME XI. | <short rule> | LIBRARY EDITION | <short rule> | NEW YORK | THE AMERICAN SWEDENBORG PRINTING AND PUBLISHING | SOCIETY | 3 WEST TWENTY-NINTH STREET | 1910
verso: [INSCRIPTION BY THE AUTHOR.] | Seek ye first the Kingdom of God and His righteousness, and all these | things shall be added unto you (*Matt.* vi.33). | Published by The American Swedenborg Printing and Publishing Society, | organized for the purpose of Printing, Publishing, and Circulating uniform | editions of the Theological Writings of Emanuel Swedenborg for charitable | and missionary purposes. Incorporated in the State of New York, A.D. 1850.
8vo

title leaf, 2 pp; Table of contents, p iii; text of Exodus 22-28 and n 9112-9973, pp 1-754.
UK: soc; NET: gen; SWI: lau; USA: anc, shs

49/01/En 5/20 **1910** Hyde 792/b

ARCANA COELESTIA | THE | HEAVENLY ARCANA | CONTAINED IN THE HOLY SCRIPTURE OR WORD OF THE LORD | UNFOLDED | HERE THOSE WHICH ARE IN EXODUS | TOGETHER WITH WONDERFUL THINGS SEEN IN THE WORLD OF | SPIRITS AND IN THE HEAVEN OF ANGELS | TRANSLATED FROM THE LATIN OF | EMANUEL SWEDENBORG | THOROUGHLY REVISED AND EDITED BY THE | REV. JOHN FAULKNER POTTS, B.A. LOND. | VOLUME XII. | <short rule> | LIBRARY EDITION | <short rule> | NEW YORK | THE AMERICAN SWEDENBORG PRINTING AND PUBLISHING | SOCIETY | 3 WEST TWENTY-NINTH STREET | 1910
verso: [INSCRIPTION BY THE AUTHOR.] | Seek ye first the Kingdom of God and His righteousness, and all these | things shall be added unto you (*Matt.* vi.33). | Published by The American Swedenborg Printing and Publishing Society, | organized for the purpose of Printing, Publishing, and Circulating uniform | editions of the Theological Writings of Emanuel Swedenborg for charitable | and missionary purposes. Incorporated in the State of New York, A.D. 1850.
8vo
title leaf, 2 pp; Reviser's note, 1 p; Contents, pp v-vi; text of Exodus 29-40 and n 9974-10837, pp 1-691; Reviser's notes, p 692.
UK: soc; NET: gen; USA: anc, shs

49/01/En 5/21 **1911** Hyde 618/3

<<ARCANA COELESTIA | THE | HEAVENLY ARCANA | CONTAINED IN THE HOLY SCRIPTURE OR WORD OF THE LORD | UNFOLDED | BEGINNING WITH THE BOOK OF GENESIS | TOGETHER WITH WONDERFUL THINGS SEEN IN THE WORLD OF | SPIRITS AND IN THE HEAVEN OF ANGELS | TRANSLATED FROM THE LATIN OF | EMANUEL SWEDENBORG | THOROUGHLY REVISED AND EDITED BY THE | REV. JOHN FAULKNER POTTS, B.A. LOND. | VOLUME I. | <short rule> | GIFT EDITION | <short rule> | NEW YORK | THE AMERICAN SWEDENBORG PRINTING AND PUBLISHING | SOCIETY | 3 WEST TWENTY-NINTH STREET | 1911>>
verso: <<[INSCRIPTION BY THE AUTHOR.] | Seek ye first the Kingdom of God and His righteousness, and all these | things shall be added unto you (*Matt.* vi.33). | Published by The American Swedenborg Printing and Publishing Society, | organized for the purpose of Printing, Publishing, and Circulating uniform | editions of the Theological Writings of Emanuel Swedenborg for charitable | and missionary purposes. Incorporated in the State of New York, A.D. 1850.>>
8vo
title leaf, 2 pp; text of Genesis 1-9 and n 1-1113, pp 1-568; text of Genesis 10-11 and n 1114-1382, pp 1-134; Reviser's notes, p 135.
Copy not seen; description deduced from En 5/11 and catalogue of USA: anc.
USA: anc

49/01/En 4/12 **1915** Hyde 783/1

ARCANA CŒLESTIA | <short rule> | THE | HEAVENLY ARCANA | CONTAINED IN | THE HOLY SCRIPTURE, OR | WORD OF THE LORD | UNFOLDED | IN AN EXPOSITION OF GENESIS AND EXODUS | TOGETHER WITH THE | WONDERFUL THINGS SEEN IN THE WORLD OF SPIRITS | AND IN THE HEAVEN OF ANGELS | BY | EMANUEL SWEDENBORG | VOLUME XI | THE SWEDENBORG SOCIETY | (INSTITUTED 1810) | 1 BLOOMSBURY STREET, LONDON | 1915
verso: *"Seek ye first the kingdom of God, and His righteousness,* | *and all these things shall be added unto you."* | —MATTHEW vi. 33.
half title: ARCANA CŒLESTIA

imprint: MADE AND PRINTED IN GREAT BRITAIN | BY THE CAMPFIELD PRESS, ST. ALBANS
8vo
half title and title leaves, 4 pp; Prefatory note, p v; Contents, pp vii-viii; text of Exodus 22-28 and n 9112-9973, pp 1-620; imprint, p 621.
Reprint of En 4/5.
UK: soc; NET: gen; USA: anc

49/01/En 4/13 **1915** Hyde 792/1

ARCANA CŒLESTIA | <short rule> | THE | HEAVENLY ARCANA | CONTAINED IN | THE HOLY SCRIPTURE OR | WORD OF THE LORD | UNFOLDED | IN AN EXPOSITION OF GENESIS AND EXODUS | TOGETHER WITH A RELATION OF | WONDERFUL THINGS SEEN IN THE WORLD OF SPIRITS | AND IN THE HEAVEN OF ANGELS | FROM THE LATIN OF | EMANUEL SWEDENBORG | VOLUME XII | EXODUS, CHAPTER XXIX TO CHAPTER XL | NOS. 9974-10837 | SWEDENBORG SOCIETY, BRITISH AND FOREIGN | (INSTITUTED 1810) | 1 BLOOMSBURY STREET, LONDON | 1915
verso: "*Seek ye first the kingdom of God and his righteousness,* | *and all these things shall be added unto you.*" | –MATTHEW vi. 33.
half title: ARCANA CŒLESTIA
imprint: PRINTED BY | TURNBULL AND SPEARS, EDINBURGH.
8vo
half title and title leaves, 4 pp; Prefatory note, p v; Contents, pp vii-ix; text of Exodus 29-40 and n 9974-10837, pp 1-569; imprint, p 570.
UK: soc; NET: gen; USA: anc

49/01/En 5/22 **1915** Hyde 618/4

ARCANA COELESTIA | THE | HEAVENLY ARCANA | CONTAINED IN THE HOLY SCRIPTURE OR WORD OF THE LORD | UNFOLDED | BEGINNING WITH THE BOOK OF GENESIS | TOGETHER WITH WONDERFUL THINGS SEEN IN THE WORLD OF | SPIRITS AND IN THE HEAVEN OF ANGELS | TRANSLATED FROM THE LATIN OF | EMANUEL SWEDENBORG | THOROUGHLY REVISED AND EDITED BY THE | REV. JOHN FAULKNER POTTS, B.A. LOND. | VOLUME I. | <short rule> | STANDARD EDITION | <short rule> | NEW YORK | THE AMERICAN SWEDENBORG PRINTING AND PUBLISHING | SOCIETY | 3 WEST TWENTY-NINTH STREET | 1915
verso: [INSCRIPTION BY THE AUTHOR.] | Seek ye first the Kingdom of God and His righteousness, and all these | things shall be added unto you (*Matt.* vi. 33). | Published by The American Swedenborg Printing and Publishing Society, | organized for the business and objects solely of printing, publishing and circu- | lating the Theological Works and Writings of Emanuel Swedenborg for charitable | and missionary purposes. Incorporated in the State of New York, A.D. 1850.
8vo
title leaf, 2 pp; Reviser's prefatory notes, pp iii-vi; Swedenborg's table of contents, pp vii-viii; text of Genesis 1-9 and n 1-1113, pp 1-585.
NET: gen; USA: anc

49/01/En 5/23 **1915** Hyde 643/2

ARCANA COELESTIA | THE | HEAVENLY ARCANA | CONTAINED IN THE HOLY SCRIPTURE OR WORD OF THE LORD | UNFOLDED | BEGINNING WITH THE BOOK OF GENESIS | TOGETHER WITH WONDERFUL THINGS SEEN IN THE WORLD OF | SPIRITS AND IN THE HEAVEN OF ANGELS | TRANSLATED FROM THE LATIN OF | EMANUEL SWEDENBORG | THOROUGHLY REVISED AND EDITED BY THE | REV. JOHN FAULKNER POTTS, B.A. LOND. | VOLUME II. | <short rule> | STANDARD EDITION | <short rule> | NEW YORK | THE AMERICAN SWEDENBORG PRINTING AND PUBLISHING | SOCIETY | 3 WEST TWENTY-NINTH STREET | 1915

verso: [INSCRIPTION BY THE AUTHOR.] | Seek ye first the Kingdom of God and His righteousness, and all these | things shall be added unto you (*Matt.* vi. 33). | Published by The American Swedenborg Printing and Publishing Society, | organized for the business and objects solely of printing, publishing and circu- | lating the Theological Works and Writings of Emanuel Swedenborg for charitable | and missionary purposes. Incorporated in the State of New York, A.D. 1850.
8vo
title leaf, 2 pp; Swedenborg's table of contents, pp iii-iv; text of Genesis 10-17 and n 1114-2134, pp 1-582.
NET: GEN; USA: ANC, SHS

49/01/En 5/24 **1915** Hyde 661/1
ARCANA COELESTIA | THE | HEAVENLY ARCANA | CONTAINED IN THE HOLY SCRIPTURE OR WORD OF THE LORD | UNFOLDED | BEGINNING WITH THE BOOK OF GENESIS | TOGETHER WITH WONDERFUL THINGS SEEN IN THE WORLD OF | SPIRITS AND IN THE HEAVEN OF ANGELS | TRANSLATED FROM THE LATIN OF | EMANUEL SWEDENBORG | THOROUGHLY REVISED AND EDITED BY THE | REV. JOHN FAULKNER POTTS, B.A. LOND. | VOLUME III. | <short rule> | STANDARD EDITION | <short rule> | NEW YORK | THE AMERICAN SWEDENBORG PRINTING AND PUBLISHING | SOCIETY | 3 WEST TWENTY-NINTH STREET | 1915
verso: [INSCRIPTION BY THE AUTHOR.] | Seek ye first the Kingdom of God and His righteousness, and all these | things shall be added unto you (*Matt.* vi. 33). | Published by The American Swedenborg Printing and Publishing Society, | organized for the business and objects solely of printing, publishing and circu- | lating the Theological Works and Writings of Emanuel Swedenborg for charitable | and missionary purposes. Incorporated in the State of New York, A.D. 1850.
8vo
title leaf, 2 pp; Table of contents, p iii; text of Swedenborg's preface, Genesis 18-23, and n 2135-2893, pp 1-558.
UK: SOC; NET: GEN; SWI: LAU; USA: ANC, SHS

49/01/En 5/25 **1915** Hyde 678/1
ARCANA COELESTIA | THE | HEAVENLY ARCANA | CONTAINED IN THE HOLY SCRIPTURE OR WORD OF THE LORD | UNFOLDED | BEGINNING WITH THE BOOK OF GENESIS | TOGETHER WITH WONDERFUL THINGS SEEN IN THE WORLD OF | SPIRITS AND IN THE HEAVEN OF ANGELS | TRANSLATED FROM THE LATIN OF | EMANUEL SWEDENBORG | THOROUGHLY REVISED AND EDITED BY THE | REV. JOHN FAULKNER POTTS, B.A. LOND. | VOLUME IV. | <short rule> | STANDARD EDITION | <short rule> | NEW YORK | THE AMERICAN SWEDENBORG PRINTING AND PUBLISHING | SOCIETY | 3 WEST TWENTY-NINTH STREET | 1915
verso: [INSCRIPTION BY THE AUTHOR.] | Seek ye first the Kingdom of God and His righteousness, and all these | things shall be added unto you (*Matt.* vi. 33). | Published by The American Swedenborg Printing and Publishing Society, | organized for the business and objects solely of printing, publishing and circu- | lating the Theological Works and Writings of Emanuel Swedenborg for charitable | and missionary purposes. Incorporated in the State of New York, A.D. 1850.
8vo
title leaf, 2 pp; Table of contents, p iii; text of Genesis 23-27 and n 2894-3649, pp 1-525; Editorial notes, pp 526-527.
NET: GEN; USA: ANC

49/01/En 5/26 **1915** Hyde 696/2
ARCANA COELESTIA | THE | HEAVENLY ARCANA | CONTAINED IN THE HOLY SCRIPTURE OR WORD OF THE LORD | UNFOLDED | BEGINNING WITH THE BOOK OF GENESIS | TOGETHER

WITH WONDERFUL THINGS SEEN IN THE WORLD OF | SPIRITS AND IN THE HEAVEN OF ANGELS | TRANSLATED FROM THE LATIN OF | EMANUEL SWEDENBORG | THOROUGHLY REVISED AND EDITED BY THE | REV. JOHN FAULKNER POTTS, B.A. LOND. | VOLUME V. | <short rule> | STANDARD EDITION | <short rule> | NEW YORK | AMERICAN SWEDENBORG PRINTING AND PUBLISHING | SOCIETY | 3 WEST TWENTY-NINTH STREET | 1915
<In some copies a label is affixed over the last 5 lines:> IN 1928 THE CORPORATE NAME OF | The American Swedenborg Printing and Publishing Society was changed to | SWEDENBORG FOUNDATION | INCORPORATED | NEW ADDRESS: 18 EAST 41st ST. NEW YORK
verso: [INSCRIPTION BY THE AUTHOR.] | Seek ye first the Kingdom of God and His righteousness, and all these | things shall be added unto you (*Matt.* vi. 33). | Published by The American Swedenborg Printing and Publishing Society, | organized for the business and objects solely of printing, publishing and circu- | lating the Theological Works and Writings of Emanuel Swedenborg for charitable | and missionary purposes. Incorporated in the State of New York, A.D. 1850.
8vo
title leaf, 2 pp; Table of contents, p iii; text of Genesis 28-31 and n 3650-4228, pp 1-490.
UK: SOC; NET: GEN; USA: ANC

49/01/En 5/27 **1915** Hyde 712/2
ARCANA COELESTIA | THE | HEAVENLY ARCANA | CONTAINED IN THE HOLY SCRIPTURE OR WORD OF THE LORD | UNFOLDED | BEGINNING WITH THE BOOK OF GENESIS | TOGETHER WITH WONDERFUL THINGS SEEN IN THE WORLD OF | SPIRITS AND IN THE HEAVEN OF ANGELS | TRANSLATED FROM THE LATIN OF | EMANUEL SWEDENBORG | THOROUGHLY REVISED AND EDITED BY THE | REV. JOHN FAULKNER POTTS, B.A. LOND. | VOLUME VI. | <short rule> | STANDARD EDITION | <short rule> | NEW YORK | THE AMERICAN SWEDENBORG PRINTING AND PUBLISHING | SOCIETY | 3 WEST TWENTY-NINTH STREET | 1915
verso: [INSCRIPTION BY THE AUTHOR.] | Seek ye first the Kingdom of God and His righteousness, and all these | things shall be added unto you (*Matt.* vi. 33). | Published by The American Swedenborg Printing and Publishing Society, | organized for the business and objects solely of printing, publishing and circu- | lating the Theological Works and Writings of Emanuel Swedenborg for charitable | and missionary purposes. Incorporated in the State of New York, A.D. 1850.
8vo
title leaf, 2 pp; Table of contents, p iii; text of Genesis 32-38 and n 4229-4953, pp 1-554.
NET: GEN; USA: ANC

49/01/En 5/28 **1915** Hyde 728/2
ARCANA COELESTIA | THE | HEAVENLY ARCANA | CONTAINED IN THE HOLY SCRIPTURE OR WORD OF THE LORD | UNFOLDED | BEGINNING WITH THE BOOK OF GENESIS | TOGETHER WITH WONDERFUL THINGS SEEN IN THE WORLD OF | SPIRITS AND IN THE HEAVEN OF ANGELS | TRANSLATED FROM THE LATIN OF | EMANUEL SWEDENBORG | THOROUGHLY REVISED AND EDITED BY THE | REV. JOHN FAULKNER POTTS, B.A. LOND. | VOLUME VII. | <short rule> | STANDARD EDITION | <short rule> | NEW YORK | THE AMERICAN SWEDENBORG PRINTING AND PUBLISHING | SOCIETY | 3 WEST TWENTY-NINTH STREET | 1915
verso: [INSCRIPTION BY THE AUTHOR.] | Seek ye first the Kingdom of God and His righteousness, and all these | things shall be added unto you (*Matt.* vi. 33). | Published by The American Swedenborg Printing and Publishing Society, | organized for the business and objects solely of printing, publishing and circu- | lating the Theological Works and Writings of Emanuel Swedenborg for charitable | and missionary purposes. Incorporated in the State of New York, A.D. 1850.
8vo
title leaf, 2 pp; Table of contents, p iii; text of Genesis 39-43 and n 4954-5727, pp 1-516.
NET: GEN; USA: ANC

49/01/En 5/29 **1915** Hyde 745/1

ARCANA COELESTIA | THE | HEAVENLY ARCANA | CONTAINED IN THE HOLY SCRIPTURE OR WORD OF THE LORD | UNFOLDED | BEGINNING WITH THE BOOK OF GENESIS | TOGETHER WITH WONDERFUL THINGS SEEN IN THE WORLD OF | SPIRITS AND IN THE HEAVEN OF ANGELS | TRANSLATED FROM THE LATIN OF | EMANUEL SWEDENBORG | THOROUGHLY REVISED AND EDITED BY THE | REV. JOHN FAULKNER POTTS, B.A. LOND. | VOLUME VIII. | <short rule> | STANDARD EDITION | <short rule> | NEW YORK | THE AMERICAN SWEDENBORG PRINTING AND PUBLISHING | SOCIETY | 3 WEST TWENTY-NINTH STREET | 1915

verso: INSCRIPTION BY THE AUTHOR.] | Seek ye first the Kingdom of God and His righteousness, and all these | things shall be added unto you (*Matt.* vi. 33). | Published by The American Swedenborg Printing and Publishing Society, | organized for the business and objects solely of printing, publishing and circu- | lating the Theological Works and Writings of Emanuel Swedenborg for charitable | and missionary purposes. Incorporated in the State of New York, A.D. 1850.

8vo

title leaf, 2 pp; Table of contents, p iii; text of Genesis 44-50 and n 5728-6626, pp 1-502; Editorial notes, pp 503-504.

NET: GEN; USA: ANC

49/01/En 5/30 **1915** Hyde 759/2

ARCANA COELESTIA | THE | HEAVENLY ARCANA | CONTAINED IN THE HOLY SCRIPTURE OR WORD OF THE LORD | UNFOLDED | HERE THOSE WHICH ARE IN EXODUS | TOGETHER WITH WONDERFUL THINGS SEEN IN THE WORLD OF | SPIRITS AND IN THE HEAVEN OF ANGELS | TRANSLATED FROM THE LATIN OF | EMANUEL SWEDENBORG | THOROUGHLY REVISED AND EDITED BY THE | REV. JOHN FAULKNER POTTS, B.A. LOND. | VOLUME IX. | <short rule> | STANDARD EDITION | <short rule> | NEW YORK | THE AMERICAN SWEDENBORG PRINTING AND PUBLISHING | SOCIETY | 3 WEST TWENTY-NINTH STREET | 1915

verso: [INSCRIPTION BY THE AUTHOR.] | Seek ye first the Kingdom of God and His righteousness, and all these | things shall be added unto you (*Matt.* vi. 33). | Published by The American Swedenborg Printing and Publishing Society, | organized for the business and objects solely of printing, publishing and circu- | lating the Theological Works and Writings of Emanuel Swedenborg for charitable | and missionary purposes. Incorporated in the State of New York, A.D. 1850.

8vo

title leaf, 2 pp; Table of contents, pp iii-iv; text of Exodus 1-12 and n 6627-8032, pp 1-685; Editorial notes, p 686.

NET: GEN; USA: ANC

49/01/En 5/31 **1915** Hyde 774/2

ARCANA COELESTIA | THE | HEAVENLY ARCANA | CONTAINED IN THE HOLY SCRIPTURE OR WORD OF THE LORD | UNFOLDED | HERE THOSE WHICH ARE IN EXODUS | TOGETHER WITH WONDERFUL THINGS SEEN IN THE WORLD OF | SPIRITS AND IN THE HEAVEN OF ANGELS | TRANSLATED FROM THE LATIN OF | EMANUEL SWEDENBORG | THOROUGHLY REVISED AND EDITED BY THE | REV. JOHN FAULKNER POTTS, B.A. LOND. | VOLUME X. | <short rule> | STANDARD EDITION | <short rule> | NEW YORK | THE AMERICAN SWEDENBORG PRINTING AND PUBLISHING | SOCIETY | 3 WEST TWENTY-NINTH STREET | 1915

verso: [INSCRIPTION BY THE AUTHOR.] | Seek ye first the Kingdom of God and His righteousness, and all these | things shall be added unto you (*Matt.* vi. 33). | Published by The American Swedenborg Printing and Publishing Society, | organized for the business and objects solely of printing, publishing and circu- | lating the Theological Works and Writings of Emanuel Swedenborg for charitable | and missionary purposes. Incorporated in the State of New York, A.D. 1850.

8vo
title leaf, 2 pp; Table of contents, p iii; text of Exodus 13-21 and n 8033-9111 pp 1-652.
UK: SOC; NET: GEN; USA: ANC

49/01/En 5/32 **1915** Hyde 783/2

ARCANA COELESTIA | THE | HEAVENLY ARCANA | CONTAINED IN THE HOLY SCRIPTURE OR WORD OF THE LORD | UNFOLDED | HERE THOSE WHICH ARE IN EXODUS | TOGETHER WITH WONDERFUL THINGS SEEN IN THE WORLD OF | SPIRITS AND IN THE HEAVEN OF ANGELS | TRANSLATED FROM THE LATIN OF | EMANUEL SWEDENBORG | THOROUGHLY REVISED AND EDITED BY THE | REV. JOHN FAULKNER POTTS, B.A. LOND. | VOLUME XI. | <short rule> | STANDARD EDITION | <short rule> | NEW YORK | THE AMERICAN SWEDENBORG PRINTING AND PUBLISHING | SOCIETY | 3 WEST TWENTY-NINTH STREET | 1915
verso: [INSCRIPTION BY THE AUTHOR.] | Seek ye first the Kingdom of God and His righteousness, and all these | things shall be added unto you (*Matt.* vi. 33). | Published by The American Swedenborg Printing and Publishing Society, | organized for the business and objects solely of printing, publishing and circu- | lating the Theological Works and Writings of Emanuel Swedenborg for charitable | and missionary purposes. Incorporated in the State of New York, A.D. 1850.
8vo
title leaf, 2 pp; Table of contents, p iii; text of Exodus 22-28 and n 9112-9973, pp 1-754.
NET: GEN, KB; USA: ANC

49/01/En 5/33 **1915** Hyde 792/2

ARCANA COELESTIA | THE | HEAVENLY ARCANA | CONTAINED IN THE HOLY SCRIPTURE OR WORD OF THE LORD | UNFOLDED | HERE THOSE WHICH ARE IN EXODUS | TOGETHER WITH WONDERFUL THINGS SEEN IN THE WORLD OF | SPIRITS AND IN THE HEAVEN OF ANGELS | TRANSLATED FROM THE LATIN OF | EMANUEL SWEDENBORG | THOROUGHLY REVISED AND EDITED BY THE | REV. JOHN FAULKNER POTTS, B.A. LOND. | VOLUME XII. | <short rule> | STANDARD EDITION | <short rule> | NEW YORK | THE AMERICAN SWEDENBORG PRINTING AND PUBLISHING | SOCIETY | 3 WEST TWENTY-NINTH STREET | 1915
verso: [INSCRIPTION BY THE AUTHOR.] | Seek ye first the Kingdom of God and His righteousness, and all these | things shall be added unto you (*Matt.* vi. 33). | Published by The American Swedenborg Printing and Publishing Society, | organized for the business and objects solely of printing, publishing and circu- | lating the Theological Works and Writings of Emanuel Swedenborg for charitable | and missionary purposes. Incorporated in the State of New York, A.D. 1850.
8vo
title leaf, 2 pp; Reviser's note, p iii; Reviser's table of contents of vol 12, pp v-vi; text of Exodus 29-40 and n 9974-10837, pp 1-691.
NET: GEN, KB; USA: ANC

49/01/En 4/14 **1916** Hyde 661/2

ARCANA CŒLESTIA | <short rule> | THE | HEAVENLY ARCANA | CONTAINED IN | THE HOLY SCRIPTURE OR | WORD OF THE LORD | UNFOLDED | IN AN EXPOSITION OF GENESIS AND EXODUS | TOGETHER WITH A RELATION OF | WONDERFUL THINGS SEEN IN THE WORLD OF SPIRITS | AND IN THE HEAVEN OF ANGELS | FROM THE LATIN OF | EMANUEL SWEDENBORG | VOLUME III | GENESIS, CHAPTER XVIII TO CHAPTER XXII | NOS. 2135-2893 | THE SWEDENBORG SOCIETY | (INSTITUTED 1810) | 1 BLOOMSBURY STREET, LONDON | 1916
verso: *"Seek ye first the kingdom of God and his righteousness,* | *and all these things shall be added unto you."* | –MATTHEW vi. 33.
half title: ARCANA CŒLESTIA

imprint: *Printed in Great Britain | by Turnbull and Spears, Edinburgh.*
8vo
half title and title leaves, 4 pp; Reviser's prefatory note, p v; Contents, pp vii-viii; text: Swedenborg's preface, pp 1-2; text of Genesis 18-22 and n 2135-2893, pp 3-455; imprint, p 456.
A revision by L Gilbey.
UK: SOC; NET: GEN, KB; USA: ANC

49/01/En 2/234 **1918** Hyde 696/–
THE | HEAVENLY ARCANA | DISCLOSED, | WHICH ARE IN THE SACRED SCRIPTURE, | OR WORD OF THE LORD: | HERE, FIRST, THOSE WHICH ARE IN | GENESIS; | *TOGETHER WITH* | WONDERFUL THINGS SEEN IN THE | *WORLD OF SPIRITS* AND | THE *HEAVEN OF ANGELS.* | BY | EMANUEL SWEDENBORG. | *Originally published in Latin at London*, A.D. 1750-51 | **Rotch Edition.** | Vol. V. | BOSTON: | MASSACHUSETTS NEW-CHURCH UNION. | 1918.
half title: ARCANA CŒLESTIA
small 8vo
half title and title leaves, 4 pp; text of Genesis 21-24 and n 2606-3227, pp 3-482.
SA: MMC

49/01/En 2/235 **1918** Hyde 759/–
THE | HEAVENLY ARCANA | DISCLOSED, | WHICH ARE IN THE SACRED SCRIPTURE, | OR WORD OF THE LORD: | HERE, FIRST, THOSE WHICH ARE IN | GENESIS; | *TOGETHER WITH* | WONDERFUL THINGS SEEN IN THE | *WORLD OF SPIRITS* AND | THE *HEAVEN OF ANGELS.* | BY | EMANUEL SWEDENBORG. | *Originally published in Latin at London*, A.D. 1752 | **Rotch Edition.** | Vol. IX. | BOSTON: MASSACHUSETTS NEW-CHURCH UNION. 1918.
half title: ARCANA CŒLESTIA
small 8vo
half title and title leaves, 4 pp; text of Genesis 37-40 and n 4661-5190, pp 3-458.
SA: MMC

49/01/En 5/34 **1919** Hyde 618/5
<<ARCANA COELESTIA | THE | HEAVENLY ARCANA | CONTAINED IN THE HOLY SCRIPTURE OR WORD OF THE LORD | UNFOLDED | BEGINNING WITH THE BOOK OF GENESIS | TOGETHER WITH WONDERFUL THINGS SEEN IN THE WORLD OF | SPIRITS AND IN THE HEAVEN OF ANGELS | TRANSLATED FROM THE LATIN OF | EMANUEL SWEDENBORG | THOROUGHLY REVISED AND EDITED BY THE | REV. JOHN FAULKNER POTTS, B.A. LOND. | VOLUME I. | <short rule> | LIBRARY EDITION | <short rule> | NEW YORK | THE AMERICAN SWEDENBORG PRINTING AND PUBLISHING | SOCIETY | 3 WEST TWENTY-NINTH STREET | 1919>>
verso: <<[INSCRIPTION BY THE AUTHOR.] | Seek ye first the Kingdom of God and His righteousness, and all these | things shall be added unto you (*Matt.* vi.33). | Published by The American Swedenborg Printing and Publishing Society, | organized for the purpose of Printing, Publishing, and Circulating uniform | editions of the Theological Writings of Emanuel Swedenborg for charitable | and missionary purposes. Incorporated in the State of New York, A.D. 1850.>>
8vo
title leaf, 2 pp; text of Genesis 1-9 and n 1-1113, pp 1-585.
Copy not seen; description deduced from En 5/22.
USA: ANC

49/01/En 5/35 **1920** Hyde 618/6
<<ARCANA COELESTIA | THE | HEAVENLY ARCANA | CONTAINED IN THE HOLY SCRIPTURE OR

WORD OF THE LORD | UNFOLDED | BEGINNING WITH THE BOOK OF GENESIS | TOGETHER WITH WONDERFUL THINGS SEEN IN THE WORLD OF | SPIRITS AND IN THE HEAVEN OF ANGELS | TRANSLATED FROM THE LATIN OF | EMANUEL SWEDENBORG | THOROUGHLY REVISED AND EDITED BY THE | REV. JOHN FAULKNER POTTS, B.A. LOND. | VOLUME I. | <short rule> | LIBRARY EDITION | <short rule> | NEW YORK | THE AMERICAN SWEDENBORG PRINTING AND PUBLISHING | SOCIETY | 3 WEST TWENTY-NINTH STREET | 1920>>
verso: <<[INSCRIPTION BY THE AUTHOR.] | Seek ye first the Kingdom of God and His righteousness, and all these | things shall be added unto you (*Matt.* vi.33). | Published by The American Swedenborg Printing and Publishing Society, | organized for the purpose of Printing, Publishing, and Circulating uniform | editions of the Theological Writings of Emanuel Swedenborg for charitable | and missionary purposes. Incorporated in the State of New York, A.D. 1850.>>
8vo
title leaf, 2 pp; text of Genesis 1-9 and n 1-1113, pp 1-585.
Copy not seen; description deduced from En 5/22.
USA: ANC

49/01/En 5/36 — 1922 — Hyde 712/3

ARCANA CŒLESTIA | <short rule> | HEAVENLY SECRETS | CONTAINED IN | THE HOLY SCRIPTURE OR | WORD OF THE LORD | DISCLOSED | HERE, THOSE IN GENESIS | TOGETHER WITH | WONDERFUL THINGS SEEN IN THE WORLD OF SPIRITS | AND IN THE HEAVEN OF ANGELS | BY | EMANUEL SWEDENBORG | BEING A TRANSLATION OF THE WORK ENTITLED ARCANA CŒLESTIA QUÆ | IN SCRIPTURA SACRA SEU VERBO DOMINI SUNT, DETECTA; HIC QUÆ IN | GENESI, UNA CUM MIRABILIBUS QUÆ VISA SUNT IN MUNDO SPIRITUUM | ET IN CŒLO ANGELORUM. LONDINI, 1749-1756 | VOLUME VI | GENESIS, CHAPTER XXXII TO CHAPTER XXXVIII | NOS. 4229-4953 | THE SWEDENBORG SOCIETY | (INSTITUTED 1810) | 1 BLOOMSBURY STREET, LONDON, W.C.1 | 1922
verso: "*Seek ye first the kingdom of God and his righteousness,* | *and all these things shall be added unto you.*" | –MATTHEW vi. 33.
half title: ARCANA CŒLESTIA
imprint: *Printed in Great Britain* | *by Turnbull & Spears, Edinburgh*
8vo
half title and title leaves, 4 pp; Reviser's prefatory note, p 5; Contents, pp vii-viii; text of Genesis 32-38 and n 4229-4953, p 1-455; imprint, p 456.
A revision by J R Rendell, with W A Presland and I Tansley as a consultative committee, of the version by J F Potts.
UK: SOC; NET: GEN, KB

49/01/En 4/15 — 1923 — Hyde 728/3

ARCANA CŒLESTIA | <short rule> | HEAVENLY ARCANA | CONTAINED IN | THE HOLY SCRIPTURE OR | WORD OF THE LORD | UNFOLDED IN AN EXPOSITION OF | GENESIS AND EXODUS | TOGETHER WITH | WONDERFUL THINGS SEEN IN THE WORLD OF SPIRITS | AND IN THE HEAVEN OF ANGELS | FROM THE LATIN OF | EMANUEL SWEDENBORG | IN TWELVE VOLUMES | VOLUME VII | GENESIS, CHAPTER XXXIX TO CHAPTER XLIII | NOS. 4954-5727 | THE SWEDENBORG SOCIETY | (INSTITUTED 1810) | 1 BLOOMSBURY STREET, LONDON, W.C.1 | 1923
verso: "*Seek ye first the kingdom of God and his righteousness,* | *and all these things shall be added unto you.*" | –MATTHEW vi. 33.
half title: ARCANA CŒLESTIA
imprint: *Printed in Great Britain* | *by Turnbull and Spears, Edinburgh.*
8vo

half title and title leaves, 4 pp; text of Genesis 39-43 and n 4954-5727, pp 1-409; imprint, p 410. Reprint of En 4/2 = Hyde 727.

UK: SOC; NET: GEN, KB

49/01/En 5/37 **1924** Hyde 643/3

ARCANA CŒLESTIA | <short rule> | HEAVENLY ARCANA | CONTAINED IN | THE HOLY SCRIPTURE OR | WORD OF THE LORD | DISCLOSED | HERE, BEGINNING WITH THOSE IN GENESIS | TOGETHER WITH | WONDERFUL THINGS SEEN IN THE WORLD OF SPIRITS | AND IN THE HEAVEN OF ANGELS | BY | EMANUEL SWEDENBORG | BEING A TRANSLATION OF THE WORK ENTITLED ARCANA CŒLESTIA QUÆ | IN SCRIPTURA SACRA SEU VERBUM DOMINI SUNT, DETECTA; HIC PRIMUM QUÆ IN | GENESI, UNA CUM MIRABILIBUS QUÆ VISA SUNT IN MUNDO | SPIRITUUM ET IN CŒLO ANGELORUM. LONDINI, 1749-1756 | VOLUME II | GENESIS, CHAPTER X TO CHAPTER XVII | NOS. 1114-2134 | THE SWEDENBORG SOCIETY | (INSTITUTED 1810) | 1 BLOOMSBURY STREET, LONDON, W.C.1 | 1924

verso: [INSCRIPTION BY THE AUTHOR] | *"Seek ye first the Kingdom of God, and his righteousness;* | *and all these things shall be added unto you."* | –MATTHEW vi. 33.

half title: ARCANA CŒLESTIA

imprint: *Printed in Great Britain* | *by Turnbull & Spears, Edinburgh*

8vo

half title and title leaves, 4 pp; Prefatory note, p v; Swedenborg's table of contents of volume II, p vii-viii; text of Genesis 10-17 and n 1114-2134, pp 1-471; imprint, p 472.

A revision by J R Rendell, with W A Presland and I Tansley as a consultative committee, based on the translation by J F Potts.

UK: SOC; NET: GEN

49/01/En 5/38 **1924** Hyde 745/2

ARCANA CŒLESTIA | <short rule> | HEAVENLY SECRETS | CONTAINED IN | THE HOLY SCRIPTURE OR | WORD OF THE LORD | DISCLOSED | HERE, THOSE IN GENESIS | TOGETHER WITH | WONDERFUL THINGS SEEN IN THE WORLD OF SPIRITS | AND IN THE HEAVEN OF ANGELS | BY | EMANUEL SWEDENBORG | BEING A TRANSLATION OF THE WORK ENTITLED ARCANA CŒLESTIA QUÆ | IN SCRIPTURA SACRA SEU VERBO DOMINI SUNT, DETECTA; HIC QUÆ IN | GENESI, UNA CUM MIRABILIBUS QUÆ VISA SUNT IN MUNDO SPIRITUUM | ET IN CŒLO ANGELORUM. LONDINI, 1749-1756 | VOLUME VIII | GENESIS, CHAPTER XLIV TO CHAPTER L | NOS. 5728-6626 | THE SWEDENBORG SOCIETY | (INSTITUTED 1810) | 1 BLOOMSBURY STREET, LONDON, W.C.1 | 1924

verso: *"Seek ye first the kingdom of God and his righteousness,* | *and all these things shall be added unto you"* | –Matthew vi. 33. | *Printed in Great Britain* | *by Turnbull & Spears, Edinburgh*

half title: ARCANA CŒLESTIA

8vo

half title and title leaves, 4 pp; Prefatory note, p v; Contents, pp vii-viii; text of Genesis 44-50 and n 5728-6626, pp 1-408.

A revision by I Tansley, with W A Presland and J R Presland as a consultative committee, based on the translation made by J F Potts.

UK: SOC; NET: GEN, KB

49/01/En 5/39 **1925** Hyde 618/6aa

ARCANA COELESTIA | THE | HEAVENLY ARCANA | CONTAINED IN THE HOLY SCRIPTURE OR WORD OF THE LORD | UNFOLDED | BEGINNING WITH THE BOOK OF GENESIS | TOGETHER WITH WONDERFUL THINGS SEEN IN THE WORLD OF | SPIRITS AND IN THE HEAVEN OF ANGELS

| TRANSLATED FROM THE LATIN OF | EMANUEL SWEDENBORG | THOROUGHLY REVISED AND EDITED BY THE | REV. JOHN FAULKNER POTTS, B.A. LOND. | VOLUME I. | <short rule> | STANDARD EDITION | <short rule> | NEW YORK | THE AMERICAN SWEDENBORG PRINTING AND PUBLISHING | SOCIETY | 16 EAST FORTY-FIRST STREET | 1925
verso: [INSCRIPTION BY THE AUTHOR.] | Seek ye first the Kingdom of God and His righteousness, and all these | things shall be added unto you (*Matt.* vi.33). | Published by The American Swedenborg Printing and Publishing Society, | organized for the business and objects solely of printing, publishing and circu- | lating the Theological Works and Writings of Emanuel Swedenborg for charitable | and missionary purposes. Incorporated in the State of New York, A.D. 1850.
8vo
title leaf, 2 pp; Reviser's prefatory notes, pp iii-vi; Swedenborg's table of contents, pp vii-viii; text of Genesis 1-9 and n 1-1113, pp 1-585.
UK: soc; USA: anc

49/01/En 5/40 1926 Hyde 618/6a
ARCANA CŒLESTIA | <short rule> | HEAVENLY ARCANA | CONTAINED IN | THE HOLY SCRIPTURE OR | WORD OF THE LORD | UNFOLDED | BEGINNING WITH THE BOOK OF GENESIS | TOGETHER WITH | WONDERFUL THINGS SEEN IN THE WORLD OF SPIRITS | AND IN THE HEAVEN OF ANGELS | BY | EMANUEL SWEDENBORG | BEING A TRANSLATION OF THE WORK ENTITLED ARCANA CŒLESTIA QUÆ | IN SCRIPTURA SACRA SEU VERBO DOMINI SUNT, DETECTA; HIC QUÆ IN | GENESI, UNA CUM MIRABILIBUS QUÆ VISA SUNT IN MUNDO SPIRITUUM | ET IN CŒLO ANGELORUM. LONDINI, 1749-1756 | VOLUME I | GENESIS, CHAPTER I TO CHAPTER IX | NOS. 1-1113 | THE SWEDENBORG SOCIETY (INCORPORATED) | SWEDENBORG HOUSE | 20 HART STREET, BLOOMSBURY SQUARE, LONDON, W.C.1 | 1926
verso: [INSCRIPTION BY THE AUTHOR] | "*Seek ye first the kingdom of God and His righteousness,* | *and all these things shall be added unto you.*" | –MATTHEW vi. 33. | *Printed in Great Britain* | *by Turnbull & Spears, Edinburgh*
half title: ARCANA CŒLESTIA
8vo
half title and title leaves, 4 pp; Reviser's prefatory note, p v; Swedenborg's table of contents, p vii; text of Genesis 1-9 and n 1-1113, pp 1-475.
A revision by J R Rendell, with W A Presland and I Tansley as a consultative committee, of the version by J F Potts.
UK: soc

49/01/En 5/41 1928 Hyde 643/3–
ARCANA COELESTIA | THE | HEAVENLY ARCANA | CONTAINED IN THE HOLY SCRIPTURE OR WORD OF THE LORD | UNFOLDED | BEGINNING WITH THE BOOK OF GENESIS | TOGETHER WITH WONDERFUL THINGS SEEN IN THE WORLD OF | SPIRITS AND IN THE HEAVEN OF ANGELS | TRANSLATED FROM THE LATIN OF | EMANUEL SWEDENBORG | THOROUGHLY REVISED AND EDITED BY THE | REV. JOHN FAULKNER POTTS, B.A. LOND. | VOLUME II. | <short rule> | STANDARD EDITION | <short rule> | 1928 | SWEDENBORG FOUNDATION | INCORPORATED | NEW YORK | <short rule> | Organized in 1850 as | The American Swedenborg Printing and Publishing Society
verso: [INSCRIPTION BY THE AUTHOR.] | Seek ye first the Kingdom of God and His righteousness, and all these | things shall be added unto you (*Matt.* vi. 33).
8vo
title leaf, 2 pp; Table of contents, pp iii-iv; text of Genesis 1-9 and n 1-1113, pp 1-582.
NET: gen

49/01/En 5/42 **1928** Hyde 661/2a

ARCANA COELESTIA | THE | HEAVENLY ARCANA | CONTAINED IN THE HOLY SCRIPTURE OR WORD OF THE LORD | UNFOLDED | BEGINNING WITH THE BOOK OF GENESIS | TOGETHER WITH WONDERFUL THINGS SEEN IN THE WORLD OF | SPIRITS AND IN THE HEAVEN OF ANGELS | TRANSLATED FROM THE LATIN OF | EMANUEL SWEDENBORG | THOROUGHLY REVISED AND EDITED BY THE | REV. JOHN FAULKNER POTTS, B.A. LOND. | VOLUME III. | <short rule> | STANDARD EDITION | <short rule> | 1928 | SWEDENBORG FOUNDATION | INCORPORATED | NEW YORK | <short rule> | Organized in 1850 as | The American Swedenborg Printing and Publishing Society

verso: [INSCRIPTION BY THE AUTHOR.] | Seek ye first the Kingdom of God and His righteousness, and all these | things shall be added unto you (*Matt.* vi. 33). | Manufactured in the U. S. A.

8vo

title leaf, 2 pp; Contents, p iii; text of Swedenborg's preface, Genesis 18-22, and n 2135-2893, pp 1-558.

UK: SOC; NET: GEN; SWE: ROY

49/01/En 5/43 **1929** Hyde 696/3

ARCANA CŒLESTIA | <short rule> | THE | HEAVENLY ARCANA | CONTAINED IN | THE HOLY SCRIPTURE OR | WORD OF THE LORD | UNFOLDED | IN AN EXPOSITION OF GENESIS AND EXODUS | TOGETHER WITH A RELATION OF | WONDERFUL THINGS SEEN IN THE WORLD OF SPIRITS | AND IN THE HEAVEN OF ANGELS | FROM THE LATIN OF | EMANUEL SWEDENBORG | VOLUME V | GENESIS, CHAPTER XXVIII TO CHAPTER XXXI | NOS. 3650-4228 | SWEDENBORG SOCIETY (INCORPORATED) | SWEDENBORG HOUSE | 20 HART STREET, BLOOMSBURY SQUARE | LONDON, W.C.1 | 1929

verso: *"Seek ye first the kingdom of God and His righteousness;* | *and all these things shall be added unto you."* | –MATTHEW vi. 33.

half title: ARCANA CŒLESTIA

8vo

half title and title leaves, 4 pp; Prefatory note, 1 p; Contents, 1 p; text of Genesis 28-31 and n 3650-4228, pp 1-395.

A revision by J R Rendell, with W A Presland and I Tansley as a consultative committee, of the version by J F Potts.

UK: SOC

49/01/En 5/44 **1932** Hyde 774/3

ARCANA CŒLESTIA | <short rule> | THE | HEAVENLY ARCANA | CONTAINED IN | THE HOLY SCRIPTURE OR | WORD OF THE LORD | DISCLOSED | IN THIS VOLUME THOSE IN EXODUS | CHAPTERS THIRTEEN TO TWENTY-ONE | TOGETHER WITH | WONDERFUL THINGS SEEN IN THE WORLD OF SPIRITS | AND IN THE HEAVEN OF ANGELS | FROM THE LATIN OF | EMANUEL SWEDENBORG | VOLUME X | NOS. 8033-9111 | SWEDENBORG SOCIETY (INCORPORATED) | SWEDENBORG HOUSE | 20 HART STREET, BLOOMSBURY SQUARE | LONDON, W.C.1 | 1932

verso: The issues of this volume, in an English demy 8vo | edition, by the Swedenborg Society have been:- | *First Edition* . . 1851 | *Second Edition* . 1864 | *Third Edition* . 1893 | *Fourth Edition* . 1932 | For other editions, see "A Bibliography of the Works | of Emanuel Swedenborg" No. 760 *et seq.* (JAMES HYDE). | *Printed in Great Britain* | *by Turnbull & Spears, Edinburgh*

half title: ARCANA CŒLESTIA

verso: *"Seek ye first the kingdom of God and His righteousness,* | *and all these things shall be added unto you."* | –MATTHEW vi. 33.

8vo

half title and title leaves, 4 pp; Prefatory note, p v; Contents, pp vii-viii; text of Exodus 13-21 and n 8033-9111, pp 1-534.
A revision made by W H Acton, assisted by J F Buss, based upon the translation by J F Potts published by the Swedenborg Foundation, New York.
UK: SOC; NET: GEN; USA: ANC

49/01/En 5/45 **1933** Hyde 618/6a/–
ARCANA COELESTIA | THE | HEAVENLY ARCANA | CONTAINED IN THE HOLY SCRIPTURE OR WORD OF THE LORD | UNFOLDED | BEGINNING WITH THE BOOK OF GENESIS | TOGETHER WITH WONDERFUL THINGS SEEN IN THE WORLD OF | SPIRITS AND IN THE HEAVEN OF ANGELS | TRANSLATED FROM THE LATIN OF | EMANUEL SWEDENBORG | THOROUGHLY REVISED AND EDITED BY THE | REV. JOHN FAULKNER POTTS, B.A. LOND. | VOLUME I. | <short rule> | STANDARD EDITION | <short rule> | 1933 | SWEDENBORG FOUNDATION | INCORPORATED | NEW YORK | <short rule> | Organized in 1850 as | The American Swedenborg Printing and Publishing | Society
verso: [INSCRIPTION BY THE AUTHOR.] | Seek ye first the Kingdom of God and His righteousness, and all these | things shall be added unto you (*Matt.* vi.33).
8vo
title leaf, 2 pp; Reviser's prefatory notes, pp iii-vi; Swedenborg's table of contents, pp vii-viii; text of Genesis 1-9 and n 1-1113, pp 1-585.
DEN: RLD; NET: GEN

49/01/En 5/46 **1934** Hyde 618/7
ARCANA CŒLESTIA | (THE HEAVENLY ARCANA) | WHICH ARE CONTAINED IN | THE HOLY SCRIPTURE OR | WORD OF THE LORD | DISCLOSED | FROM THE LATIN OF | EMANUEL SWEDENBORG | GENESIS, CHAPTERS I-VII | NOS. 1-823 | SWEDENBORG SOCIETY (INCORPORATED) | SWEDENBORG HOUSE | 20 HART STREET, LONDON, W.C. 1 | 1934
half title: <within a double rule border 72 x 72 mm> THEREFORE, when Heaven was opened | to me, I had first to learn the Hebrew | language, as well as the correspond- | ences, according to which the whole | Bible is composed, which led me to | read the Word of God over many | times; and, as God's Word is the | source whence all theology must be | derived, I was thereby enabled to | receive instruction from the Lord, | who is the Word. | SWEDENBORG | (*Letter to Dr. Beyer*).
verso: [INSCRIPTION BY THE AUTHOR] | "*Seek ye first the Kingdom of God, and* | *His righteousness; and all these things* | *shall be added unto you.*" | –MATTHEW vi. 33.
imprint: <short rule> | *Printed in Great Britain by The Campfield Press, St. Albans*
small 8vo
half title and title leaves, 4 pp; Prefatory note, pp 5-6; Contents, pp 7-8; text of Genesis 1-7 and n 1-823, pp 9-540; imprint, p 540.
A reprint of En 5/40 = Hyde 618/6a.
UK: SOC; NET: GEN; SWE: ROY

49/01/En 5/47 **1935** Hyde 618/7a
<<ARCANA CŒLESTIA | (THE HEAVENLY ARCANA) | WHICH ARE CONTAINED IN | THE HOLY SCRIPTURE OR | WORD OF THE LORD | DISCLOSED | FROM THE LATIN OF | EMANUEL SWEDENBORG | GENESIS, CHAPTERS I-VII | NOS. 1-823 | SWEDENBORG SOCIETY (INCORPORATED) | SWEDENBORG HOUSE | 20 HART STREET, LONDON, W.C. 1 | 1934>>
half title: << <within a double rule border 72 x 72 mm> THEREFORE, when Heaven was opened | to me, I had first to learn the Hebrew | language, as well as the correspond- | ences, according to

which the whole | Bible is composed, which led me to | read the Word of God over many | times; and, as God's Word is the | source whence all theology must be | derived, I was thereby enabled to | receive instruction from the Lord, | who is the Word. | SWEDENBORG | (*Letter to Dr. Beyer*).>>
verso: <<[INSCRIPTION BY THE AUTHOR] | "*Seek ye first the Kingdom of God, and* | *His righteousness; and all these things* | *shall be added unto you.*" | –MATTHEW vi. 33.>>
small 8vo
half title and title leaves, 4 pp; Prefatory note, pp 5-6; Contents, pp 7-8; text of Genesis 1-7 and n 1-823, pp 9-540; advertisement, pp 541-544.
A reprint of En 5/46 = Hyde 618/7 for sale in U.S.A. Printed by The Campfield Press, St Albans.
Copy not seen; description deduced from En 5/46.

49/01/En 5/48 **1936** Hyde 618/8
ARCANA CŒLESTIA | (THE HEAVENLY ARCANA) | WHICH ARE CONTAINED IN | THE HOLY SCRIPTURE OR | WORD OF THE LORD | DISCLOSED | FROM THE LATIN OF | EMANUEL SWEDENBORG | VOL. 1 | GENESIS, CHAPTERS I-VII | NOS. 1-823 | SWEDENBORG SOCIETY (INCORPORATED) | SWEDENBORG HOUSE | 20 HART STREET, LONDON, W.C. 1 | 1936
verso: POPULAR EDITION | First Issue, 1934 .. .. 5,000 copies | Reprint, 1935 .. .. .. 5,000 ,, | (For sale in America) | Reprint, 1936 .. .. .. 5,000 ,,
half title: <within a double rule border 72 x 72 mm> THEREFORE, when Heaven was opened | to me, I had first to learn the Hebrew | language, as well as the correspond- | ences, according to which the whole | Bible is composed, which led me to | read the Word of God over many | times; and, as God's Word is the | source whence all theology must be | derived, I was thereby enabled to | receive instruction from the Lord, | who is the Word. | SWEDENBORG | (*Letter to Dr. Beyer*).
verso: [INSCRIPTION BY THE AUTHOR] | "*Seek ye first the Kingdom of God, and* | *His righteousness; and all these things* | *shall be added unto you.*" | –MATTHEW vi. 33.
imprint: <rule> | *Printed in Great Britain by The Campfield Press, St. Albans*
small 8vo
half title and title leaves, 4 pp; Prefatory note, pp 5-6; Contents, pp 7-8; text of Genesis 1-7 and n 1-823, pp 9-540; advertisement, pp 541-544; imprint, p 544.
A reprint of En 5/46 = Hyde 618/7.
UK: SOC

49/01/En 4/16 **1936** Hyde 643/4
ARCANA CŒLESTIA | (HEAVENLY ARCANA) | WHICH ARE CONTAINED IN | THE HOLY SCRIPTURE OR | WORD OF THE LORD | DISCLOSED | FROM THE LATIN OF | EMANUEL SWEDENBORG | VOL. II | GENESIS, CHAPTERS VIII-XII | NOS. 824-1520 | SWEDENBORG SOCIETY (INCORPORATED) | SWEDENBORG HOUSE | 20 HART STREET, LONDON, W.C. 1 | 1936
half title: <within a double rule border 115 x 73 mm> <a quotation from *The Apocalypse Revealed* n 200.1>
imprint: <rule> | *Printed in Great Britain by The Campfield Press, St. Albans*
small 8vo
half title and title leaves, 4 pp; Reviser's prefatory note, pp 5-6; Contents, pp 7-8; text of Genesis 8-12 and n 824-1520, pp 9-565; advertisement, pp 566-568; imprint, p 568.
A revision prepared by L Gilbey.
UK: SOC; NET: GEN; USA: ANC

49/01/En 5/49 **1937** Hyde 678/1–
ARCANA COELESTIA | THE | HEAVENLY ARCANA | CONTAINED IN THE HOLY SCRIPTURE OR WORD OF THE LORD | UNFOLDED | BEGINNING WITH THE BOOK OF GENESIS | TOGETHER

WITH WONDERFUL THINGS SEEN IN THE WORLD OF | SPIRITS AND IN THE HEAVEN OF ANGELS | TRANSLATED FROM THE LATIN OF | EMANUEL SWEDENBORG | THOROUGHLY REVISED AND EDITED BY THE | REV. JOHN FAULKNER POTTS, B.A. LOND. | VOLUME IV. | <short rule> | STANDARD EDITION | <short rule> | SWEDENBORG FOUNDATION | INCORPORATED | NEW YORK | <short rule> | Organized in 1850 as | The American Swedenborg Printing and Publishing Society
verso: [INSCRIPTION BY THE AUTHOR.] | Seek ye first the Kingdom of God and His righteousness, and all these | things shall be added unto you (*Matt.* vi. 33).
8vo
title leaf, 2 pp; Table of contents, p iii; text of Genesis 23-27 and n 2894-3649, pp 1-525; Editorial notes, pp 526-527.
Reprint of En 5/25.
NET: GEN

49/01/En 5/50 **1938** Hyde 696/3–
ARCANA COELESTIA | THE | HEAVENLY ARCANA | CONTAINED IN THE HOLY SCRIPTURE OR WORD OF THE LORD | UNFOLDED | BEGINNING WITH THE BOOK OF GENESIS | TOGETHER WITH WONDERFUL THINGS SEEN IN THE WORLD OF | SPIRITS AND IN THE HEAVEN OF ANGELS | TRANSLATED FROM THE LATIN OF | EMANUEL SWEDENBORG | THOROUGHLY REVISED AND EDITED BY THE | REV. JOHN FAULKNER POTTS, B.A. LOND. | VOLUME V. | <short rule> | STANDARD EDITION | <short rule> | 1938 | SWEDENBORG FOUNDATION | INCORPORATED | NEW YORK | <short rule> | Organized in 1850 as | The American Swedenborg Printing and Publishing Society
verso: [INSCRIPTION BY THE AUTHOR.] | Seek ye first the Kingdom of God and His righteousness, and all these | things shall be added unto you (*Matt.* vi. 33).
8vo
title leaf, 2 pp; Reviser's table of contents of vol 5, p iii; text of Genesis 28-31 and n 3650-4228, pp 1- 490.
Reprint of En 5/26.
NET: GEN

49/01/En 5/51 **1938** Hyde 712/3–
ARCANA COELESTIA | THE | HEAVENLY ARCANA | CONTAINED IN THE HOLY SCRIPTURE OR WORD OF THE LORD | UNFOLDED | BEGINNING WITH THE BOOK OF GENESIS | TOGETHER WITH WONDERFUL THINGS SEEN IN THE WORLD OF | SPIRITS AND IN THE HEAVEN OF ANGELS | TRANSLATED FROM THE LATIN OF | EMANUEL SWEDENBORG | THOROUGHLY REVISED AND EDITED BY THE | REV. JOHN FAULKNER POTTS, B.A. LOND. | VOLUME VI. | <short rule> | STANDARD EDITION | <short rule> | 1938 | SWEDENBORG FOUNDATION | INCORPORATED | NEW YORK | <short rule> | Organized in 1850 as | The American Swedenborg Printing and Publishing Society
verso: [INSCRIPTION BY THE AUTHOR.] | Seek ye first the Kingdom of God and His righteousness, and all these | things shall be added unto you (*Matt.* vi. 33). | Published by the American Swedenborg Printing and Publishing Society, | organized for the business and objects solely of printing, publishing and circu- | lating the Theological Works and Writings of Emanuel Swedenborg for charitable | and missionary purposes. Incorporated in the State of New York, A.D. 1850.
8vo
title leaf, 2 pp; Reviser's table of contents of vol 6, p iii; text of Genesis 32-38 and n 4229-4953, pp 1-554.
Reprint of En 5/14.
NET: GEN

49/01/En 5/52 **1938** Hyde 728/3–

ARCANA COELESTIA | THE | HEAVENLY ARCANA | CONTAINED IN THE HOLY SCRIPTURE OR WORD OF THE LORD | UNFOLDED | BEGINNING WITH THE BOOK OF GENESIS | TOGETHER WITH WONDERFUL THINGS SEEN IN THE WORLD OF | SPIRITS AND IN THE HEAVEN OF ANGELS | TRANSLATED FROM THE LATIN OF | EMANUEL SWEDENBORG | THOROUGHLY REVISED AND EDITED BY THE | REV. JOHN FAULKNER POTTS, B.A. LOND. | VOLUME VII. | <short rule> | STANDARD EDITION | <short rule> | 1938 | SWEDENBORG FOUNDATION | INCORPORATED | NEW YORK | <short rule> | Organized in 1850 as The American Swedenborg Printing and Publishing Society

verso: [INSCRIPTION BY THE AUTHOR.] | Seek ye first the Kingdom of God and His righteousness, and all these | things shall be added unto you (*Matt.* vi. 33). | Published by The American Swedenborg Printing and Publishing Society, | organized for the business and objects solely of printing, publishing and circu- | lating the Theological Works and Writings of Emanuel Swedenborg for charitable | and missionary purposes. Incorporated in the State of New York, A.D. 1850.

8vo

title leaf, 2 pp; Table of contents, p iii; text of Genesis 39-43 and n 4954-5727, pp 1-516.

Reprint of En 5/28.

NET: GEN

49/01/En 5/53 **1938** Hyde 745/2–

ARCANA COELESTIA | THE | HEAVENLY ARCANA | CONTAINED IN THE HOLY SCRIPTURE OR WORD OF THE LORD | UNFOLDED | BEGINNING WITH THE BOOK OF GENESIS | TOGETHER WITH WONDERFUL THINGS SEEN IN THE WORLD OF | SPIRITS AND IN THE HEAVEN OF ANGELS | TRANSLATED FROM THE LATIN OF | EMANUEL SWEDENBORG | THOROUGHLY REVISED AND EDITED BY THE | REV. JOHN FAULKNER POTTS, B.A. LOND. | VOLUME VIII. | <short rule> | STANDARD EDITION | <short rule> | 1938 | SWEDENBORG FOUNDATION | INCORPORATED | NEW YORK | <short rule> | Organized in 1850 as | The American Swedenborg Printing and Publishing Society

verso: [INSCRIPTION BY THE AUTHOR.] | Seek ye first the Kingdom of God and His righteousness, and all these | things shall be added unto you (*Matt.* vi. 33). | Published by the American Swedenborg Printing and Publishing Society, | organized for the business and objects solely of printing, publishing and circu- | lating the Theological Works and Writings of Emanuel Swedenborg for charitable | and missionary purposes. Incorporated in the State of New York, A.D. 1850.

8vo

title leaf, 2 pp; Reviser's table of contents of vol 8, p iii; text of Genesis 44-50 and n 5728-6626, pp 1-502; Editorial notes, pp 503-504.

Reprint of En 5/29.

NET: GEN

49/01/En 5/54 **1938** Hyde 759/–

ARCANA COELESTIA | THE | HEAVENLY ARCANA | CONTAINED IN THE HOLY SCRIPTURE OR WORD OF THE LORD | UNFOLDED | HERE THOSE WHICH ARE IN EXODUS | TOGETHER WITH WONDERFUL THINGS SEEN IN THE WORLD OF | SPIRITS AND IN THE HEAVEN OF ANGELS | TRANSLATED FROM THE LATIN OF | EMANUEL SWEDENBORG | THOROUGHLY REVISED AND EDITED BY THE | REV. JOHN FAULKNER POTTS, B.A. LOND. | VOLUME IX. | <short rule> | STANDARD EDITION | <short rule> | 1938 | SWEDENBORG FOUNDATION | INCORPORATED | NEW YORK | <short rule> | Organized in 1850 as | The American Swedenborg Printing and Publishing Society

verso: [INSCRIPTION BY THE AUTHOR.] | Seek ye first the Kingdom of God and His righteousness, and all these | things shall be added unto you (*Matt.* vi. 33). | Published by the American Swedenborg

Printing and Publishing Society, | organized for the business and objects solely of printing, publishing and circu- | lating the Theological Works and Writings of Emanuel Swedenborg for charitable | and missionary purposes. Incorporated in the State of New York, A.D. 1850.
8vo
title leaf, 2 pp; Reviser's table of contents of vol 9, p iii; text of Exodus 1-13 and n 6627-8032, pp 1-685; Editorial notes, p 687.
Reprint of En 5/30.
NET: GEN

49/01/En 5/55 **1938** Hyde 774/3–
ARCANA COELESTIA | THE | HEAVENLY ARCANA | CONTAINED IN THE HOLY SCRIPTURE OR WORD OF THE LORD | UNFOLDED | HERE THOSE WHICH ARE IN EXODUS | TOGETHER WITH WONDERFUL THINGS SEEN IN THE WORLD OF | SPIRITS AND IN THE HEAVEN OF ANGELS | TRANSLATED FROM THE LATIN OF | EMANUEL SWEDENBORG | THOROUGHLY REVISED AND EDITED BY THE | REV. JOHN FAULKNER POTTS, B.A. LOND. | VOLUME X. | <short rule> | STANDARD EDITION | <short rule> | 1938 | SWEDENBORG FOUNDATION | INCORPORATED | NEW YORK | <short rule> | Organized in 1850 as | The American Swedenborg Printing and Publishing Society
verso: [INSCRIPTION BY THE AUTHOR.] | Seek ye first the Kingdom of God and His righteousness, and all these | things shall be added unto you (*Matt.* vi. 33). | Published by the American Swedenborg Printing and Publishing Society, | organized for the business and objects solely of printing, publishing and circu- | lating the Theological Works and Writings of Emanuel Swedenborg for charitable | and missionary purposes. Incorporated in the State of New York, A.D. 1850.
8vo
title leaf, 2 pp; Reviser's table of contents of vol 10, pp iii-iv; text of Exodus 14-21 and n 8033-9111, pp 1-652.
Reprint of En 5/31.
NET: GEN

49/01/En 5/56 **1938** Hyde 783/2–
ARCANA COELESTIA | THE | HEAVENLY ARCANA | CONTAINED IN THE HOLY SCRIPTURE OR WORD OF THE LORD | UNFOLDED | HERE THOSE WHICH ARE IN EXODUS | TOGETHER WITH WONDERFUL THINGS SEEN IN THE WORLD OF | SPIRITS AND IN THE HEAVEN OF ANGELS | TRANSLATED FROM THE LATIN OF | EMANUEL SWEDENBORG | THOROUGHLY REVISED AND EDITED BY THE | REV. JOHN FAULKNER POTTS, B.A. LOND. | VOLUME XI. | <short rule> | STANDARD EDITION | <short rule> | 1938 | SWEDENBORG FOUNDATION | INCORPORATED | NEW YORK | <short rule> | The American Swedenborg Printing and Publishing Society
verso: [INSCRIPTION BY THE AUTHOR.] | Seek ye first the Kingdom of God and His righteousness, and all these | things shall be added unto you (*Matt.* vi. 33). | Published by The American Swedenborg Printing and Publishing Society, | organized for the business and objects solely of printing, publishing and circu- | lating the Theological Works and Writings of Emanuel Swedenborg for charitable | and missionary purposes. Incorporated in the State of New York, A.D. 1850.
8vo
title leaf, 2 pp; Table of contents, p iii; text of Exodus 22-28 and n 9112-9973, pp 1-754.
Reprint of En 5/32.
NET: GEN

49/01/En 4/17 **1939** Hyde 661/3
ARCANA CŒLESTIA | (HEAVENLY ARCANA) | WHICH ARE CONTAINED IN | THE HOLY SCRIPTURE

OR | WORD OF THE LORD | DISCLOSED | FROM THE LATIN OF | EMANUEL SWEDENBORG | VOL. III | GENESIS, CHAPTERS XIII-XVII | NOS. 1521-2134 | SWEDENBORG SOCIETY (INCORPORATED) | SWEDENBORG HOUSE | 20/21 BLOOMSBURY WAY, LONDON, W.C. 1 | 1939
half title: ARCANA CŒLESTIA | GENESIS XIII-XVII
small 8vo
half title and title leaves, 4 pp; Reviser's prefatory note, pp 5-6; Definitions of terms, p 6; Contents, pp 7-8; text of Genesis 13-17 and n 1521-2134, pp 9-516; advertisements, 3 pp.
A revision by H Goyder Smith with C E Newall as consultant.
UK: SOC; NET: GEN; USA: ANC

49/01/En 5/57 **1940** Hyde 618/9
ARCANA CŒLESTIA | (THE HEAVENLY ARCANA) | WHICH ARE CONTAINED IN | THE HOLY SCRIPTURE OR | WORD OF THE LORD | DISCLOSED | FROM THE LATIN OF | EMANUEL SWEDENBORG | GENESIS, CHAPTERS I-VII | Nos. 1-823 | 1940 | SWEDENBORG FOUNDATION | INCORPORATED | 51 EAST FORTY-SECOND STREET | NEW YORK | Organized in 1850 as The American Swedenborg Printing and | Publishing Society
verso: [INSCRIPTION BY THE AUTHOR] | *"Seek ye first the Kingdom of God, and | His righteousness; and all these things | shall be added unto you."* | —MATTHEW vi. 33.
half title: <short rule> | *Made and Printed in Great Britain by The Campfield Press, St. Albans*
small 8vo
half title and title leaves, 4 pp; Prefatory note, pp 5-6; Contents, pp 7-8; text of Genesis 1-7 and n 1-823, pp 9-540; advertisement, pp 541-544.
A reprint of En 5/46 = Hyde 618/7, from plates lent by the Swedenborg Society.
UK: SOC

49/01/En 5/58 **1941** Hyde 618/–
ARCANA COELESTIA | THE | HEAVENLY ARCANA | CONTAINED IN THE HOLY SCRIPTURE OR WORD OF THE LORD | UNFOLDED | BEGINNING WITH THE BOOK OF GENESIS | TOGETHER WITH WONDERFUL THINGS SEEN IN THE WORLD OF | SPIRITS AND IN THE HEAVEN OF ANGELS | TRANSLATED FROM THE LATIN OF | EMANUEL SWEDENBORG | THOROUGHLY REVISED AND EDITED BY THE | REV. JOHN FAULKNER POTTS, B.A. LOND. | VOLUME I. | <short rule> | STANDARD EDITION | <short rule> | 1941 | SWEDENBORG FOUNDATION | INCORPORATED | NEW YORK | <short rule> | Organized in 1850 as | The American Swedenborg Printing and Publishing Society
verso: [INSCRIPTION BY THE AUTHOR.] | Seek ye first the Kingdom of God and His righteousness, and all these | things shall be added unto you (*Matt.* vi. 33).
8vo
title leaf, 2 pp; Prefatory notes by the reviser, pp iii-vi; Swedenborg's table of contents of vol 1, pp vii-viii; text of Genesis 1-11 and n 1-585.
Reprint of En 5/45, printed in U.S.A. by The Haddon Craftsmen Inc.
NET: GEN

49/01/En 5/59 **1941** Hyde 643/4–
ARCANA COELESTIA | THE | HEAVENLY ARCANA | CONTAINED IN THE HOLY SCRIPTURE OR WORD OF THE LORD | UNFOLDED | BEGINNING WITH THE BOOK OF GENESIS | TOGETHER WITH WONDERFUL THINGS SEEN IN THE WORLD OF | SPIRITS AND IN THE HEAVEN OF ANGELS | TRANSLATED FROM THE LATIN OF | EMANUEL SWEDENBORG | THOROUGHLY REVISED AND EDITED BY THE | REV. JOHN FAULKNER POTTS, B.A. LOND. | VOLUME II. | <short rule> | STANDARD EDITION | <short rule> | SWEDENBORG FOUNDATION | INCORPORATED

| NEW YORK | <short rule> | Organized in 1850 as | The American Swedenborg Printing and Publishing Society
verso: [INSCRIPTION BY THE AUTHOR.] | Seek ye first the Kingdom of God and His righteousness, and all these | things shall be added unto you (*Matt.* vi. 33).
8vo
title leaf, 2 pp; Table of contents, pp iii-iv; text of Genesis 10-17 and n 1114-2134, pp 1-582.
Reprint of En 5/41 = Hyde 643/–.
NET: GEN

49/01/En 5/60 **1946** Hyde 643/4–
ARCANA COELESTIA | THE | HEAVENLY ARCANA | CONTAINED IN THE HOLY SCRIPTURE OR WORD OF THE LORD | UNFOLDED | BEGINNING WITH THE BOOK OF GENESIS | TOGETHER WITH WONDERFUL THINGS SEEN IN THE WORLD OF | SPIRITS AND IN THE HEAVEN OF ANGELS | TRANSLATED FROM THE LATIN OF | EMANUEL SWEDENBORG | THOROUGHLY REVISED AND EDITED BY THE | REV. JOHN FAULKNER POTTS, B.A. LOND. | VOLUME II. | <short rule> | STANDARD EDITION | <short rule> | 1946 | SWEDENBORG FOUNDATION | INCORPORATED | NEW YORK | <short rule> | Organized in 1850 as | The American Swedenborg Printing and Publishing Society
verso: [INSCRIPTION BY THE AUTHOR.] | Seek ye first the Kingdom of God and His righteousness, and all these | things shall be added unto you (*Matt.* vi. 33).
8vo
title leaf, 2 pp; Swedenborg's table of contents of vol 2, pp iii-iv; text of Genesis 10-17 and n 1114-2134, pp 1-582.
Reprint of En 5/59.
NET: GEN

49/01/En 5/61 **1946** Hyde 678/–
ARCANA COELESTIA | THE | HEAVENLY ARCANA | CONTAINED IN THE HOLY SCRIPTURE OR WORD OF THE LORD | UNFOLDED | BEGINNING WITH THE BOOK OF GENESIS | TOGETHER WITH WONDERFUL THINGS SEEN IN THE WORLD OF | SPIRITS AND IN THE HEAVEN OF ANGELS | TRANSLATED FROM THE LATIN OF | EMANUEL SWEDENBORG | THOROUGHLY REVISED AND EDITED BY THE | REV. JOHN FAULKNER POTTS, B.A. LOND. | VOLUME IV. | <short rule> | STANDARD EDITION | <short rule> | 1946 | SWEDENBORG FOUNDATION | INCORPORATED | NEW YORK | <short rule> | Organized in 1850 as | The American Swedenborg Printing and Publishing Society
verso: [INSCRIPTION BY THE AUTHOR.] | Seek ye first the Kingdom of God and His righteousness, and all these | things shall be added unto you (*Matt.* vi. 33).
8vo
title leaf, 2 pp; Reviser's table of contents of vol 4, p iii; text of Genesis 23-27 and n 2894-3649, pp 1-525; Editorial notes, pp 526-527.
Reprint of En 5/49.
NET: GEN

49/01/En 5/62 **1946** Hyde 696/–
ARCANA COELESTIA | THE | HEAVENLY ARCANA | CONTAINED IN THE HOLY SCRIPTURE OR WORD OF THE LORD | UNFOLDED | BEGINNING WITH THE BOOK OF GENESIS | TOGETHER WITH WONDERFUL THINGS SEEN IN THE WORLD OF | SPIRITS AND IN THE HEAVEN OF ANGELS | TRANSLATED FROM THE LATIN OF | EMANUEL SWEDENBORG | THOROUGHLY REVISED AND EDITED BY THE | REV. JOHN FAULKNER POTTS, B.A. LOND. | VOLUME V. | <short rule>

| STANDARD EDITION | <short rule> | 1946 | SWEDENBORG FOUNDATION | INCORPORATED | NEW YORK | <short rule> | Organized in 1850 as | The American Swedenborg Printing and Publishing Society
verso: [INSCRIPTION BY THE AUTHOR.] | Seek ye first the Kingdom of God and His righteousness, and all these | things shall be added unto you (*Matt.* vi. 33).
8vo
title leaf, 2 pp; Reviser's table of contents of vol 5, p iii; text of Genesis 28-31 and n 3650-4228, pp 1- 490.
Reprint of En 5/50.
NET: GEN

49/01/En 6/1 **1949** Hyde 678/2
ARCANA CÆLESTIA | (THE HEAVENLY ARCANA) | WHICH ARE CONTAINED IN | THE HOLY SCRIPTURE OR | WORD OF THE LORD | DISCLOSED | FROM THE LATIN OF | EMANUEL SWEDENBORG | VOL. IV | GENESIS, CHAPTERS XVIII-XX | NOS. 2135-2605 | SWEDENBORG SOCIETY (INCORPORATED) | SWEDENBORG HOUSE | 20 BLOOMSBURY WAY, LONDON, W.C.1. | 1949
verso: POCKET EDITION | First Issue 1949
imprint: <rule> | *Printed in England by H. Sharp & Sons, Bath.*
small 8vo
title leaf, 2 pp; Translator's prefatory note, 2 pp; Contents, 1 p; text of Swedenborg's preface, 2 pp; text of Genesis 18-20 and n 2135-2605, pp 1-453; imprint, p 454.
Translated from La 5/1 by P H Johnson. Pocket edition.
UK: SOC, NR; NET: GEN; USA: ANC

49/01/En 5/63 **1949** Hyde 618/9–
ARCANA COELESTIA | THE | HEAVENLY ARCANA | CONTAINED IN THE HOLY SCRIPTURE OR WORD OF THE LORD | UNFOLDED | BEGINNING WITH THE BOOK OF GENESIS | TOGETHER WITH WONDERFUL THINGS SEEN IN THE WORLD OF | SPIRITS AND IN THE HEAVEN OF ANGELS | TRANSLATED FROM THE LATIN OF | EMANUEL SWEDENBORG | THOROUGHLY REVISED AND EDITED BY THE | REV. JOHN FAULKNER POTTS, B.A. LOND. | VOLUME I. | <short rule> | STANDARD EDITION | <short rule> | 1949 | SWEDENBORG FOUNDATION | INCORPORATED | NEW YORK | <short rule> | Organized in 1850 as | The American Swedenborg Printing and Publishing Society
verso: [INSCRIPTION BY THE AUTHOR.] | Seek ye first the Kingdom of God and His righteousness, and all these | things shall be added unto you (*Matt.* vi.33).
8vo
title leaf, 2 pp; Reviser's prefatory notes, pp iii-vi; Swedenborg's table of contents, pp vii-viii; text of Genesis 1-9 and n 1-1113, pp 1-585.
NET: GEN

49/01/En 5/64 **1949** Hyde 696/3–
ARCANA COELESTIA | THE | HEAVENLY ARCANA | CONTAINED IN THE HOLY SCRIPTURE OR WORD OF THE LORD | UNFOLDED | BEGINNING WITH THE BOOK OF GENESIS | TOGETHER WITH WONDERFUL THINGS SEEN IN THE WORLD OF | SPIRITS AND IN THE HEAVEN OF ANGELS | TRANSLATED FROM THE LATIN OF | EMANUEL SWEDENBORG | THOROUGHLY REVISED AND EDITED BY THE | REV. JOHN FAULKNER POTTS, B.A. LOND. | VOLUME V. | <short rule> | STANDARD EDITION | <short rule> | 1949 | SWEDENBORG FOUNDATION | INCORPORATED | NEW YORK | <short rule> | Organized in 1850 as | The American Swedenborg Printing and Publishing Society

<In some copies a label is affixed over the last 5 lines:> IN 1928 THE CORPORATE NAME OF | The American Swedenborg Printing and Publishing Society was changed to | SWEDENBORG FOUNDATION | INCORPORATED | NEW ADDRESS: 18 EAST 41st ST. NEW YORK
verso: [INSCRIPTION BY THE AUTHOR.] | Seek ye first the Kingdom of God and His righteousness, and all these | things shall be added unto you (*Matt.* vi. 33). | Printed in the United States of America
8vo
title leaf, 2 pp; Table of contents, p iii; text of Genesis 28-31 and n 3650-4228, pp 1-490.
NET: GEN

49/01/En 5/65 **1949** Hyde 712/3–
ARCANA COELESTIA | THE | HEAVENLY ARCANA | CONTAINED IN THE HOLY SCRIPTURE OR WORD OF THE LORD | UNFOLDED | BEGINNING WITH THE BOOK OF GENESIS | TOGETHER WITH WONDERFUL THINGS SEEN IN THE WORLD OF | SPIRITS AND IN THE HEAVEN OF ANGELS | TRANSLATED FROM THE LATIN OF | EMANUEL SWEDENBORG | THOROUGHLY REVISED AND EDITED BY THE | REV. JOHN FAULKNER POTTS, B.A. LOND. | VOLUME VI. | <short rule> | STANDARD EDITION | <short rule> | 1949 | SWEDENBORG FOUNDATION | INCORPORATED | NEW YORK | Organized in 1850 as | The American Swedenborg Printing and Publishing Society
verso: [INSCRIPTION BY THE AUTHOR.] | Seek ye first the Kingdom of God and His righteousness, and all these | things shall be added unto you (*Matt.* vi. 33). | Printed in the United States of America
8vo
title leaf, 2 pp; Table of contents, p iii; text of Genesis 32-38 and n 4229-4953, pp 1-554.
NET: GEN

49/01/En 5/66 **1949** Hyde 759/–
ARCANA COELESTIA | THE | HEAVENLY ARCANA | CONTAINED IN THE HOLY SCRIPTURE OR WORD OF THE LORD | UNFOLDED | HERE THOSE WHICH ARE IN EXODUS | TOGETHER WITH WONDERFUL THINGS SEEN IN THE WORLD OF | SPIRITS AND IN THE HEAVEN OF ANGELS | TRANSLATED FROM THE LATIN OF | EMANUEL SWEDENBORG | THOROUGHLY REVISED AND EDITED BY THE | REV. JOHN FAULKNER POTTS, B.A. LOND. | VOLUME IX. | <short rule> | LIBRARY EDITION | <short rule> | NEW YORK | THE AMERICAN SWEDENBORG PRINTING AND PUBLISHING | SOCIETY | 3 WEST TWENTY-NINTH STREET | 1949
verso: [INSCRIPTION BY THE AUTHOR.] | Seek ye first the Kingdom of God and His righteousness, and all these | things shall be added unto you (*Matt.* vi.33). | Published by The American Swedenborg Printing and Publishing Society, | organized for the purpose of Printing, Publishing, and Circulating uniform | editions of the Theological Writings of Emanuel Swedenborg for charitable | and missionary purposes. Incorporated in the State of New York, A.D. 1850.
8vo
title leaf, 2 pp; Table of contents, p iii; text of Exodus 1-12 and n 6627-8032, pp 1-685; Reviser's notes, p 686.
NET: GEN

49/01/En 5/67 **1949** Hyde 774/–
ARCANA COELESTIA | THE | HEAVENLY ARCANA | CONTAINED IN THE HOLY SCRIPTURE OR WORD OF THE LORD | UNFOLDED | HERE THOSE WHICH ARE IN EXODUS | TOGETHER WITH WONDERFUL THINGS SEEN IN THE WORLD OF | SPIRITS AND IN THE HEAVEN OF ANGELS | TRANSLATED FROM THE LATIN OF | EMANUEL SWEDENBORG | THOROUGHLY REVISED AND EDITED BY THE | REV. JOHN FAULKNER POTTS, B.A. LOND. | VOLUME X. | <short rule> | LIBRARY EDITION | <short rule> | NEW YORK | THE AMERICAN SWEDENBORG PRINTING AND PUBLISHING | SOCIETY | 3 WEST TWENTY-NINTH STREET | 1949

verso: [INSCRIPTION BY THE AUTHOR.] | Seek ye first the Kingdom of God and His righteousness, and all these | things shall be added unto you (*Matt.* vi.33). | Published by The American Swedenborg Printing and Publishing Society, | organized for the purpose of Printing, Publishing, and Circulating uniform | editions of the Theological Writings of Emanuel Swedenborg for charitable | and missionary purposes. Incorporated in the State of New York, A.D. 1850.
8vo
title leaf, 2 pp; Table of contents, p iii; text of Exodus 13-21 and n 8033-9111, pp 1-652.
USA: SHS

49/01/En 5/68 **1949** Hyde 783/3
ARCANA COELESTIA | THE | HEAVENLY ARCANA | CONTAINED IN THE HOLY SCRIPTURE OR WORD OF THE LORD | UNFOLDED | HERE THOSE WHICH ARE IN EXODUS | TOGETHER WITH WONDERFUL THINGS SEEN IN THE WORLD OF | SPIRITS AND IN THE HEAVEN OF ANGELS | TRANSLATED FROM THE LATIN OF | EMANUEL SWEDENBORG | THOROUGHLY REVISED AND EDITED BY THE | REV. JOHN FAULKNER POTTS, B.A. LOND. | VOLUME XI. | <short rule> | STANDARD EDITION | <short rule> | 1949 | SWEDENBORG FOUNDATION | INCORPORATED | NEW YORK | <short rule> | Organized in 1850 as | The American Swedenborg Printing and Publishing Society
verso: [INSCRIPTION BY THE AUTHOR.] | Seek ye first the Kingdom of God and His righteousness, and all these | things shall be added unto you (*Matt.* vi. 33.) | Printed in the United of States of America
8vo
title leaf, 2 pp; Contents, p iii; text of Exodus 22-28 and n 9112-9973, pp 1-754.
UK: SOC; USA: SHS

49/01/En 5/69 **1951** Hyde 643/–
ARCANA COELESTIA | THE | HEAVENLY ARCANA | CONTAINED IN THE HOLY SCRIPTURE OR WORD OF THE LORD | UNFOLDED | BEGINNING WITH THE BOOK OF GENESIS | TOGETHER WITH WONDERFUL THINGS SEEN IN THE WORLD OF | SPIRITS AND IN THE HEAVEN OF ANGELS | TRANSLATED FROM THE LATIN OF | EMANUEL SWEDENBORG | THOROUGHLY REVISED AND EDITED BY THE | REV. JOHN FAULKNER POTTS, B.A. LOND. | VOLUME II. | <short rule> | STANDARD EDITION | <short rule> | 1951 | SWEDENBORG FOUNDATION | INCORPORATED | NEW YORK | <short rule> | Organized in 1850 as | The American Swedenborg Printing and Publishing Society
verso: [INSCRIPTION BY THE AUTHOR.] | Seek ye first the Kingdom of God and His righteousness, and all these | things shall be added unto you (*Matt.* vi. 33.) | Printed in the United of States of America
8vo
title leaf, 2 pp; Swedenborg's table of contents, pp iii-iv; text of Genesis 10-17 and n 1114-2134, pp 1-582.
USA: SHS

49/01/En 5/70 **1951** Hyde 728/3–
ARCANA COELESTIA | THE | HEAVENLY ARCANA | CONTAINED IN THE HOLY SCRIPTURE OR WORD OF THE LORD | UNFOLDED | BEGINNING WITH THE BOOK OF GENESIS | TOGETHER WITH WONDERFUL THINGS SEEN IN THE WORLD OF | SPIRITS AND IN THE HEAVEN OF ANGELS | TRANSLATED FROM THE LATIN OF | EMANUEL SWEDENBORG | THOROUGHLY REVISED AND EDITED BY THE | REV. JOHN FAULKNER POTTS, B.A. LOND. | VOLUME VII. | <short rule> | STANDARD EDITION | <short rule> | 1951 | SWEDENBORG FOUNDATION | INCORPORATED | NEW YORK | <short rule> | Organized in 1850 as | The American Swedenborg Printing and Publishing Society

verso: [INSCRIPTION BY THE AUTHOR.] | Seek ye first the Kingdom of God and His righteousness, and all these | things shall be added unto you (*Matt.* vi. 33). | Published by The American Swedenborg Printing and Publishing Society, | organized for the business and objects solely of printing, publishing and circu- | lating the Theological Works and Writings of Emanuel Swedenborg for charitable | and missionary purposes. Incorporated in the State of New York, A.D. 1850.
8vo
title leaf, 2 pp; Table of contents, p iii; text of Genesis 39-43 and n 4954-5727, pp 1-516.
UK: soc; NET: GEN

49/01/En 5/71 **1951** Hyde 745/2–
ARCANA COELESTIA | THE | HEAVENLY ARCANA | CONTAINED IN THE HOLY SCRIPTURE OR WORD OF THE LORD | UNFOLDED | BEGINNING WITH THE BOOK OF GENESIS | TOGETHER WITH WONDERFUL THINGS SEEN IN THE WORLD OF | SPIRITS AND IN THE HEAVEN OF ANGELS | TRANSLATED FROM THE LATIN OF | EMANUEL SWEDENBORG | THOROUGHLY REVISED AND EDITED BY THE | REV. JOHN FAULKNER POTTS, B.A. LOND. | VOLUME VIII. | <short rule> | STANDARD EDITION | <short rule> | 1951 | SWEDENBORG FOUNDATION | INCORPORATED | NEW YORK | <short rule> | Organized in 1850 as | The American Swedenborg Printing and Publishing Society
verso: [INSCRIPTION BY THE AUTHOR.] | Seek ye first the Kingdom of God and His righteousness, and all these | things shall be added unto you (*Matt.* vi. 33). | Printed in the United States of America
8vo
title leaf, 2 pp; Table of contents, p iii; text of Genesis 44-50 and n 5728-6626, pp 1-502; Additional editorial notes, pp 503-504.
NET: GEN

49/01/En 5/72 **1951** Hyde 775/3–
ARCANA COELESTIA | THE | HEAVENLY ARCANA | CONTAINED IN THE HOLY SCRIPTURE OR WORD OF THE LORD | UNFOLDED | HERE THOSE WHICH ARE IN EXODUS | TOGETHER WITH WONDERFUL THINGS SEEN IN THE WORLD OF | SPIRITS AND IN THE HEAVEN OF ANGELS | TRANSLATED FROM THE LATIN OF | EMANUEL SWEDENBORG | THOROUGHLY REVISED AND EDITED BY THE | REV. JOHN FAULKNER POTTS, B.A. LOND. | VOLUME X. | <short rule> | STANDARD EDITION | <short rule> | 1951 | SWEDENBORG FOUNDATION | INCORPORATED | NEW YORK | <short rule> | Organized in 1850 as | The American Swedenborg Printing and Publishing Society
verso: [INSCRIPTION BY THE AUTHOR.] | Seek ye first the Kingdom of God and His righteousness, and all these | things shall be added unto you (*Matt.* vi. 33). | Published by The American Swedenborg Printing and Publishing Society, | organized for the business and objects solely of printing, publishing and circu- | lating the Theological Works and Writings of Emanuel Swedenborg for charitable | and missionary purposes. Incorporated in the State of New York, A.D. 1850.
8vo
title leaf, 2 pp; Table of contents, pp iii-iv; text of Exodus 13-21 and n 8033-9111, pp 1-652.
NET: GEN

49/01/En 5/73 **1951** Hyde 792/2–
ARCANA COELESTIA | THE | HEAVENLY ARCANA | CONTAINED IN THE HOLY SCRIPTURE OR WORD OF THE LORD | UNFOLDED | HERE THOSE WHICH ARE IN EXODUS | TOGETHER WITH WONDERFUL THINGS SEEN IN THE WORLD OF | SPIRITS AND IN THE HEAVEN OF ANGELS | TRANSLATED FROM THE LATIN OF | EMANUEL SWEDENBORG | THOROUGHLY REVISED AND EDITED BY THE | REV. JOHN FAULKNER POTTS, B.A. LOND. | VOLUME XII. | <short rule> |

STANDARD EDITION | <short rule> | 1951 | SWEDENBORG FOUNDATION | INCORPORATED | NEW YORK | Organized in 1850 as | the American Swedenborg Printing and Publishing Society
verso: [INSCRIPTION BY THE AUTHOR.] | Seek ye first the Kingdom of God and His righteousness, and all these | things shall be added unto you (*Matt.* vi. 33). | Printed in the United States of America
8vo
title leaf, 2 pp; Reviser's note, p iii; Reviser's table of contents of vol 12, pp v-vi; text of Exodus 29-40 and n 9974-10837, pp 1-691.
Reprint of En 5/33 = Hyde 792/2.
UK: SOC; NET: GEN

49/01/En 4/18 **1953** Hyde 661/–
<<*ARCANA CŒLESTIA* | <short rule> | THE | HEAVENLY ARCANA | CONTAINED IN | THE HOLY SCRIPTURE OR | WORD OF THE LORD | UNFOLDED | IN AN EXPOSITION OF GENESIS AND EXODUS | TOGETHER WITH THE | WONDERFUL THINGS SEEN IN THE WORLD OF SPIRITS | AND IN THE HEAVEN OF ANGELS | BY | EMANUEL SWEDENBORG | VOLUME III | THE SWEDENBORG SOCIETY (Inc.) | 20/21 BLOOMSBURY WAY, LONDON, W.C.1 | 1953>>
verso: <<"*Seek ye first the kingdom of God and his righteousness,* | *and all these things shall be added unto you.*" | –MATTHEW vi. 33.>>
half title: <<ARCANA CŒLESTIA>>
8vo
half title and title leaves, 4 pp; Reviser's prefatory note, p v; Contents, pp vii-viii; text: Swedenborg's preface, pp 1-2; text of Genesis 18-22 and n 2135-2893, pp 3-455.
An edition of 500 copies reprinted from the moulds of En 4/14 = Hyde 661/2.
Copy not seen; description deduced from En 4/14 and Annual Report for 1953 of UK: SOC.

49/01/En 4/19 **1953** Hyde 783/–
<<*ARCANA CŒLESTIA* | <short rule> | THE | HEAVENLY ARCANA | CONTAINED IN | THE HOLY SCRIPTURE OR | WORD OF THE LORD | UNFOLDED | IN AN EXPOSITION OF GENESIS AND EXODUS | TOGETHER WITH THE | WONDERFUL THINGS SEEN IN THE WORLD OF SPIRITS | AND IN THE HEAVEN OF ANGELS | BY | EMANUEL SWEDENBORG | VOLUME XI | THE SWEDENBORG SOCIETY (Inc.) | 20/21 BLOOMSBURY WAY, LONDON, W.C.1 | 1953>>
verso: <<"*Seek ye first the kingdom of God and his righteousness,* | *and all these things shall be added unto you.*" | –MATTHEW vi. 33.>>
half title: <<ARCANA CŒLESTIA>>
8vo
half title and title leaves, 4 pp; Prefatory note, p v; Contents, pp vii-viii; text of Exodus 22-28 and n 9112-9973, pp 1-620.
An edition of 500 copies reprinted from the moulds of En 4/12 = Hyde 783/1.
Copy not seen; description deduced from En 4/12 and Annual Report for 1953 of UK: SOC.

49/01/En 4/20 **1953** Hyde 792/3
ARCANA CŒLESTIA | <short rule> | THE | HEAVENLY ARCANA | CONTAINED IN | THE HOLY SCRIPTURE OR | WORD OF THE LORD | UNFOLDED | IN AN EXPOSITION OF GENESIS AND EXODUS | TOGETHER WITH A RELATION OF | WONDERFUL THINGS SEEN IN THE WORLD OF SPIRITS | AND IN THE HEAVEN OF ANGELS | FROM THE LATIN OF | EMANUEL SWEDENBORG | VOLUME XII | EXODUS, CHAPTER XXIX TO CHAPTER XL | NOS. 9974-10837 | THE SWEDENBORG SOCIETY (Inc.) | 20/21 BLOOMSBURY WAY, LONDON, W.C.1 | 1953
verso: "*Seek ye first the kingdom of God and his righteousness,* | *and all these things shall be added unto you.*" | –MATTHEW vi. 33.
half title: ARCANA CŒLESTIA

8vo
half title and title leaves, 4 pp; Prefatory note, p v; Contents, pp vii-ix; text of Exodus 29-40 and n 9974-10837, pp 1-569.
Reprint of En 4/13 = Hyde 792/1 with a different title page. Printed by The Campfield Press, St Albans.
UK: SOC; AUS: SYD

49/01/En 5/74 — 1953 — Hyde 618/10
ARCANA CŒLESTIA | (THE HEAVENLY ARCANA) | WHICH ARE CONTAINED IN | THE HOLY SCRIPTURE OR | WORD OF THE LORD | DISCLOSED | FROM THE LATIN OF | EMANUEL SWEDENBORG | VOL. I | GENESIS, CHAPTERS I-VII | Nos. 1-823 | SWEDENBORG SOCIETY (INCORPORATED) | SWEDENBORG HOUSE | 20 BLOOMSBURY WAY, LONDON, W.C. 1 | 1953
verso: POPULAR EDITION | First Issue, 1934 .. .. 5,000 copies | Reprint, 1935 .. .. .. 5,000 „ | (For sale in America) | Reprint, 1936 .. .. .. 5,000 „ | Reprint, 1953 .. .. .. 5,000 „
half title: <within a double rule border 71 x 71 mm> THEREFORE, when Heaven was opened | to me, I had first to learn the Hebrew | language, as well as the correspond- | ences, according to which the whole | Bible is composed, which led me to | read the Word of God over many | times; and, as God's Word is the | source whence all theology must be | derived, I was thereby enabled to | receive instruction from the Lord, | who is the Word. | SWEDENBORG | (*Letter to Dr. Beyer*).
verso: [INSCRIPTION BY THE AUTHOR] | "*Seek ye first the Kingdom of God, and | His righteousness; and all these things | shall be added unto you.*" | —MATTHEW vi. 33.
small 8vo
half title and title leaves, 4 pp; Prefatory note, pp 5-6; Contents, pp 7-8; text of Genesis 1-7 and n 1-823, pp 9-540; advertisement, pp 541-544.
A reprint, with modifications to the title page, from the plates of En 5/46 = Hyde 618/7.
UK: SOC

49/01/En 4/21 — 1954 — Hyde 728/4
ARCANA CŒLESTIA | <short rule> | HEAVENLY ARCANA | CONTAINED IN | THE HOLY SCRIPTURE OR | WORD OF THE LORD | UNFOLDED IN AN EXPOSITION OF | GENESIS AND EXODUS | TOGETHER WITH | WONDERFUL THINGS SEEN IN THE WORLD OF SPIRITS | AND IN THE HEAVEN OF ANGELS | FROM THE LATIN OF | EMANUEL SWEDENBORG | IN TWELVE VOLUMES | VOLUME VII | GENESIS, CHAPTER XXXIX TO CHAPTER XLIII | NOS. 4954-5727 | THE SWEDENBORG SOCIETY | (INSTITUTED 1810) | 1 BLOOMSBURY STREET, LONDON, W.C.1 | 1954
verso: "*Seek ye first the kingdom of God and his righteousness, | and all these things shall be added unto you.*" | —MATTHEW vi. 33.
half title: ARCANA CŒLESTIA
8vo
half title and title leaves, 4 pp; text of Genesis 39-43 and n 4954-5727, pp 1-409.
A reprint of En 4/15 = Hyde 728/3.
UK: SOC

49/01/En 4/22 — no date — Hyde 758/–
ARCANA CŒLESTIA | <short rule> | THE | HEAVENLY ARCANA | CONTAINED IN | THE HOLY SCRIPTURE, OR WORD OF THE LORD | UNFOLDED | IN AN EXPOSITION OF GENESIS AND EXODUS | TOGETHER WITH A RELATION OF | WONDERFUL THINGS SEEN IN THE WORLD OF SPIRITS AND | IN THE HEAVEN OF ANGELS | *FROM THE LATIN* | OF | EMANUEL SWEDENBORG | VOLUME IX. | EXODUS, CHAPTER I. TO CHAPTER XII. | NOS. 6627-8032 | THE SWEDENBORG SOCIETY | (INSTITUTED 1810) | 1 BLOOMSBURY STREET, LONDON

verso: *"Seek ye first the kingdom of God, and His righteousness,* | *and all these things shall be added unto you."* | –MATTHEW vi. 33.
half title: ARCANA CŒLESTIA
8vo
half title and title leaves, 4 pp; Translator's preface, p v; Contents, pp vii-viii; text of Exodus 1-12 and n 6627-8032 pp 1-581; Errata, p 582.
A photographic reprint of En 4/7 = Hyde 758 with a new title page, printed at The Campfield Press, St Albans. The errata noted on p 582 of En 4/7 were corrected in this edition, but not the incorrect running heads on pp 47, 279.

49/01/En 4/23 **1957** Hyde 678/–
<<*ARCANA CŒLESTIA*. | <short rule> | THE | HEAVENLY ARCANA | CONTAINED IN | THE HOLY SCRIPTURE OR | WORD OF THE LORD | UNFOLDED | IN AN EXPOSITION OF GENESIS AND EXODUS | TOGETHER WITH A RELATION OF | WONDERFUL THINGS SEEN IN THE WORLD OF SPIRITS AND | IN THE HEAVEN OF ANGELS | *FROM THE LATIN* | OF | EMANUEL SWEDENBORG | VOLUME IV. | GENESIS, CHAPTER XXIII. TO CHAPTER XXVII. | NOS. 2894-3649. | THE SWEDENBORG SOCIETY | (INSTITUTED 1810) | 1 BLOOMSBURY STREET, LONDON | 1957>>
verso:<<*"Seek ye first the kingdom of God and His righteousness,* | *and all these things shall be added unto you."* | –MATTHEW vi. 33.>>
8vo
title leaf, 2 pp; Prefatory note, p v; Contents, p vii; text of Genesis 23-27 and n 2894-3649, pp 1-435.
An edition of 500 copies reprinted from En 4/11 = Hyde 678/a.
Copy not seen; description deduced from En 4/11 and Annual Report for 1958 of UK: soc.

49/01/En 5/75 **1957** Hyde 712/–
<<*ARCANA CŒLESTIA* | <short rule> | HEAVENLY SECRETS | CONTAINED IN | THE HOLY SCRIPTURE OR | WORD OF THE LORD | DISCLOSED | HERE, THOSE IN GENESIS | TOGETHER WITH | WONDERFUL THINGS SEEN IN THE WORLD OF SPIRITS | AND IN THE HEAVEN OF ANGELS | BY | EMANUEL SWEDENBORG | VOLUME VI | GENESIS, CHAPTER XXXII TO CHAPTER XXXVIII | NOS. 4229-4953 | THE SWEDENBORG SOCIETY | (INSTITUTED 1810) | 1 BLOOMSBURY STREET, LONDON, W.C.1 | 1957>>
verso: <<*"Seek ye first the kingdom of God and his righteousness,* | *and all these things shall be added unto you."* | –MATTHEW vi. 33.>>
half title: <<ARCANA CŒLESTIA>>
8vo
half title and title leaves, 4 pp; Reviser's prefatory note, p 5; Contents, pp vii-viii; text of Genesis 32-38 and n 4229-4953, pp 1-455.
An edition of 500 copies reprinted from En 5/36 = Hyde 712/3.
Copy not seen; description deduced from En 5/36 and Annual Report for 1958 of UK: soc.

49/01/En 5/76 **1963** Hyde 618/–
ARCANA COELESTIA | THE | HEAVENLY ARCANA | CONTAINED IN THE HOLY SCRIPTURE OR WORD OF THE LORD | UNFOLDED | BEGINNING WITH THE BOOK OF GENESIS | TOGETHER WITH WONDERFUL THINGS SEEN IN THE WORLD OF | SPIRITS AND IN THE HEAVEN OF ANGELS | TRANSLATED FROM THE LATIN OF | EMANUEL SWEDENBORG | THOROUGHLY REVISED AND EDITED BY THE | REV. JOHN FAULKNER POTTS, B.A. LOND. | VOLUME I. | <short rule> | STANDARD EDITION | <short rule> | NEW YORK | THE AMERICAN SWEDENBORG PRINTING AND PUBLISHING | SOCIETY | 3 WEST TWENTY-NINTH STREET | 1963
verso: [INSCRIPTION BY THE AUTHOR.] | Seek ye first the Kingdom of God and His righteousness, and all these | things shall be added unto you (*Matt.* vi. 33). | Published by The American

Swedenborg Printing and Publishing Society, | organized for the business and objects solely of printing, publishing and circu- | lating the Theological Works and Writings of Emanuel Swedenborg for charitable | and missionary purposes. Incorporated in the State of New York, A.D. 1850.
8vo
title leaf, 2 pp; Table of contents, p iii; text of Genesis 1-9 and n 1-1113, pp 1-585.
SA: MMC

49/01/En 5/77 **1965** Hyde 618/–
<<ARCANA COELESTIA | THE | HEAVENLY ARCANA | CONTAINED IN THE HOLY SCRIPTURE OR WORD OF THE LORD | UNFOLDED | BEGINNING WITH THE BOOK OF GENESIS | TOGETHER WITH WONDERFUL THINGS SEEN IN THE WORLD OF | SPIRITS AND IN THE HEAVEN OF ANGELS | TRANSLATED FROM THE LATIN OF | EMANUEL SWEDENBORG | THOROUGHLY REVISED AND EDITED BY THE | REV. JOHN FAULKNER POTTS, B.A. LOND. | VOLUME I. | <short rule> | STANDARD EDITION | <short rule> | NEW YORK | SWEDENBORG FOUNDATION | INCORPORATED | 1965>>
verso: <<[INSCRIPTION BY THE AUTHOR.] | Seek ye first the Kingdom of God and His righteousness, and all these | things shall be added unto you (*Matt.* vi. 33). | Published by The American Swedenborg Printing and Publishing Society, | organized for the business and objects solely of printing, publishing and circu- | lating the Theological Works and Writings of Emanuel Swedenborg for charitable | and missionary purposes. Incorporated in the State of New York, A.D. 1850.>>
8vo
title leaf, 2 pp; Table of contents, p iii; text of Genesis 1-9 and n 1-1113, pp 1-585.
Copy not seen; description deduced from En 5/76.
SWE: ROY

49/01/En 4/24 **1966** Hyde 758/–
<<ARCANA CŒLESTIA | <short rule> | THE | HEAVENLY ARCANA | CONTAINED IN | THE HOLY SCRIPTURE, OR WORD OF THE LORD | UNFOLDED | IN AN EXPOSITION OF GENESIS AND EXODUS | TOGETHER WITH A RELATION OF | WONDERFUL THINGS SEEN IN THE WORLD OF SPIRITS AND | IN THE HEAVEN OF ANGELS | *FROM THE LATIN* | OF | EMANUEL SWEDENBORG | VOLUME IX. | EXODUS, CHAPTER I. TO CHAPTER XII. | NOS. 6627-8032 | THE SWEDENBORG SOCIETY | (INSTITUTED 1810) | 1 BLOOMSBURY STREET, LONDON>>
verso: <<*"Seek ye first the kingdom of God, and His righteousness, | and all these things shall be added unto you."* | –MATTHEW vi. 33.>>
half title: <<ARCANA CŒLESTIA>>
8vo
half title and title leaves, 4 pp; Translator's preface, p v; Contents, p vii-viii; text of Exodus 1-12 and n 6627-8032 pp 1-581; Errata, p 582.
Photolithographic reprint of En 4/20 in an edition of 500 copies.
Copy not seen; description deduced from En 4/20 and Annual Report for 1967 of UK: SOC.

49/01/En 5/78 **1967** Hyde 618/11
ARCANA CŒLESTIA | (THE HEAVENLY ARCANA) | WHICH ARE CONTAINED IN | THE HOLY SCRIPTURE OR | WORD OF THE LORD | DISCLOSED | FROM THE LATIN OF | EMANUEL SWEDENBORG | VOL. I | GENESIS, CHAPTER I TO VII | Nos. 1-823 | THE SWEDENBORG SOCIETY | 20/21 BLOOMSBURY WAY, LONDON, W.C.1. | 1967
verso: POCKET EDITION | First Issue, 1934 .. .. 5,000 copies | Reprint, 1935 .. .. .. 4,000 „ | (For sale in America) | Reprint, 1936 .. .. .. 5,000 „ | Reprint, 1953 .. .. .. 5,000 „ | Reprint, 1967 .. .. .. 5,000 „ | MADE AND PRINTED IN GREAT BRITAIN

half title: <within a double rule border 71 x 71 mm> THEREFORE, when Heaven was opened | to me, I had first to learn the Hebrew | language, as well as the correspond- | ences, according to which the whole | Bible is composed, which led me to | read the Word of God over many | times; and, as God's Word is the | source whence all theology must be | derived, I was thereby enabled to | receive instruction from the Lord, | who is the Word. | SWEDENBORG | (*Letter to Dr. Beyer*).
verso: [INSCRIPTION BY THE AUTHOR] | "*Seek ye first the Kingdom of God, and | His righteousness; and all these things | shall be added unto you.*" | –MATTHEW vi. 33.
8vo
half title and title leaves, 4 pp; Prefatory note, p 5-6; Swedenborg's table of contents, pp 7-8; text of Genesis 1-7 and n 1-823, pp 1-476.
A reprint of En 5/46 = Hyde 618/7.
UK: SOC; USA: ANC; AUS: SYD

49/01/En 5/79 **1967** Hyde 618/–
<<ARCANA COELESTIA | THE | HEAVENLY ARCANA | CONTAINED IN THE HOLY SCRIPTURE OR WORD OF THE LORD | UNFOLDED | BEGINNING WITH THE BOOK OF GENESIS | TOGETHER WITH WONDERFUL THINGS SEEN IN THE WORLD OF | SPIRITS AND IN THE HEAVEN OF ANGELS | TRANSLATED FROM THE LATIN OF | EMANUEL SWEDENBORG | THOROUGHLY REVISED AND EDITED BY THE | REV. JOHN FAULKNER POTTS, B.A. LOND. | VOLUME I. | <short rule> | STANDARD EDITION | <short rule> | NEW YORK | SWEDENBORG FOUNDATION | INCORPORATED | 1967>>
verso: <<[INSCRIPTION BY THE AUTHOR.] | Seek ye first the Kingdom of God and His righteousness, and all these | things shall be added unto you (*Matt.* vi. 33). | Published by The American Swedenborg Printing and Publishing Society, | organized for the business and objects solely of printing, publishing and circu- | lating the Theological Works and Writings of Emanuel Swedenborg for charitable | and missionary purposes. Incorporated in the State of New York, A.D. 1850.>>
8vo
title leaf, 2 pp; Table of contents, p iii; text of Genesis 1-9 and n 1-1113, pp 1-542.
Copy not seen; description deduced from En 5/76.
USA: ANC; AUS: SYD

49/01/En 5/80 **1967** Hyde 618/12
HEAVENLY SECRETS | (ARCANA COELESTIA) | WHICH ARE CONTAINED IN | THE HOLY SCRIPTURE OR | WORD OF THE LORD | DISCLOSED | FROM THE LATIN OF | EMANUEL SWEDENBORG | VOL. I. | GENESIS, CHAPTERS I-VII | Nos. 1-823 | 1967 | SWEDENBORG FOUNDATION (INCORPORATED) | 139 EAST 23 STREET | NEW YORK, NEW YORK
verso: First published in Latin, London 1749 | First English Translation published in London 1813 | First English Translation Published in USA in 1837 | 39th Printing in USA 1967 <*stet* 1813>
8vo
title leaf, 2 pp; Preface, pp 1-2; Introduction, pp 3-6; Contents, pp 7-8; text of Genesis 1-7 and n 1-823, pp 9-540; catalogue, pp 541-542.
The introduction is an extract from H Keller *My Religion*.
UK: SOC; USA: ANC

49/01/En 5/81 **1967** Hyde 643/–
ARCANA COELESTIA | THE | HEAVENLY ARCANA | CONTAINED IN THE HOLY SCRIPTURE OR WORD OF THE LORD | UNFOLDED | BEGINNING WITH THE BOOK OF GENESIS | TOGETHER WITH WONDERFUL THINGS SEEN IN THE WORLD OF | SPIRITS AND IN THE HEAVEN OF ANGELS | TRANSLATED FROM THE LATIN OF | EMANUEL SWEDENBORG | THOROUGHLY REVISED

AND EDITED BY THE | REV. JOHN FAULKNER POTTS, B.A. LOND. | VOLUME II. | <short rule> | STANDARD EDITION | <short rule> | NEW YORK | THE AMERICAN SWEDENBORG PRINTING AND PUBLISHING | SOCIETY | 3 WEST TWENTY-NINTH STREET | 1967
verso: [INSCRIPTION BY THE AUTHOR.] | Seek ye first the Kingdom of God and His righteousness, and all these | things shall be added unto you (*Matt.* vi. 33). | Published by The American Swedenborg Printing and Publishing Society, | organized for the business and objects solely of printing, publishing and circu- | lating the Theological Works and Writings of Emanuel Swedenborg for charitable | and missionary purposes. Incorporated in the State of New York, A.D. 1850.
8vo
title leaf, 2 pp; Table of contents, p iii; text of Genesis 10-17 and n 1114-2134, pp 1-582.
USA: ANC; SA: MMC

49/01/En 5/82 **1967** Hyde 661/–
ARCANA COELESTIA | THE | HEAVENLY ARCANA | CONTAINED IN THE HOLY SCRIPTURE OR WORD OF THE LORD | UNFOLDED | BEGINNING WITH THE BOOK OF GENESIS | TOGETHER WITH WONDERFUL THINGS SEEN IN THE WORLD OF | SPIRITS AND IN THE HEAVEN OF ANGELS | TRANSLATED FROM THE LATIN OF | EMANUEL SWEDENBORG | THOROUGHLY REVISED AND EDITED BY THE | REV. JOHN FAULKNER POTTS, B.A. LOND. | VOLUME III. | <short rule> | STANDARD EDITION | <short rule> | NEW YORK | THE AMERICAN SWEDENBORG PRINTING AND PUBLISHING | SOCIETY | 3 WEST TWENTY-NINTH STREET | 1967
verso: [INSCRIPTION BY THE AUTHOR.] | Seek ye first the Kingdom of God and His righteousness, and all these | things shall be added unto you (*Matt.* vi. 33). | Published by The American Swedenborg Printing and Publishing Society, | organized for the business and objects solely of printing, publishing and circu- | lating the Theological Works and Writings of Emanuel Swedenborg for charitable | and missionary purposes. Incorporated in the State of New York, A.D. 1850.
8vo
title leaf, 2 pp; Table of contents, p iii; text of Swedenborg's preface, Genesis 18-22, and n 2135-2893, pp 1-558.
USA: SHS; SA: MMC

49/01/En 5/83 **1967** Hyde 712/–
ARCANA COELESTIA | THE | HEAVENLY ARCANA | CONTAINED IN THE HOLY SCRIPTURE OR WORD OF THE LORD | UNFOLDED | BEGINNING WITH THE BOOK OF GENESIS | TOGETHER WITH WONDERFUL THINGS SEEN IN THE WORLD OF | SPIRITS AND IN THE HEAVEN OF ANGELS | TRANSLATED FROM THE LATIN OF | EMANUEL SWEDENBORG | THOROUGHLY REVISED AND EDITED BY THE | REV. JOHN FAULKNER POTTS, B.A. LOND. | VOLUME VI. | <short rule> | STANDARD EDITION | <short rule> | NEW YORK | THE AMERICAN SWEDENBORG PRINTING AND PUBLISHING | SOCIETY | 3 WEST TWENTY-NINTH STREET | 1967
verso: [INSCRIPTION BY THE AUTHOR.] | Seek ye first the Kingdom of God and His righteousness, and all these | things shall be added unto you (*Matt.* vi. 33). | Published by The American Swedenborg Printing and Publishing Society, | organized for the business and objects solely of printing, publishing and circu- | lating the Theological Works and Writings of Emanuel Swedenborg for charitable | and missionary purposes. Incorporated in the State of New York, A.D. 1850.
8vo
title leaf, 2 pp; Table of contents, p iii; text of Genesis 32-38 and n 4229-4953, pp 1-554.
USA: SHS; SA: MMC

49/01/En 5/84 **1968** Hyde 643/5
ARCANA CÆLESTIA | (HEAVENLY ARCANA) | WHICH ARE CONTAINED IN | THE HOLY SCRIPTURE OR | WORD OF THE LORD | DISCLOSED | FROM THE LATIN OF | EMANUEL SWEDENBORG |

Vol. II | GENESIS, CHAPTERS VIII-XII | Nos. 824-1520 | THE SWEDENBORG SOCIETY | 20/21 BLOOMSBURY WAY, LONDON, W.C.1 | 1968
verso: *Printed in Great Britain by | The Campfield Press, St. Albans*
half title: <within a double rule border 115 x 72 mm> <a quotation from *The Apocalypse Revealed* n 200.1>
small 8vo
half title and title leaves, 4 pp; Reviser's prefatory note, pp 5-6; Definitions of terms, p 6; Contents, pp 7-8; text of Genesis 8-12 and n 824-1520, pp 9-565; advertisement, pp 566-567.
Reprinted from En 5/85 = Hyde 643/5.
UK: soc

49/01/En 4/25 **1968** Hyde 661/4
ARCANA CÆLESTIA | (HEAVENLY ARCANA) | WHICH ARE CONTAINED IN | THE HOLY SCRIPTURE OR | WORD OF THE LORD | DISCLOSED | FROM THE LATIN OF | EMANUEL SWEDENBORG | Vol. III | GENESIS, CHAPTERS XIII-XVII | Nos. 1521-2134 | THE SWEDENBORG SOCIETY | 20/21 BLOOMSBURY WAY, LONDON, W.C.1 | 1968
verso: *Printed in Great Britain by | The Campfield Press, St. Albans*
half title: ARCANA CŒLESTIA | GENESIS XIII-XVII
small 8vo
half title and title leaves, 4 pp; Reviser's prefatory note, pp 5-6; Definitions of terms, p 6; Contents, pp 7-8; text of Genesis 13-17 and n 1521-2134, pp 9-516.
A reprint of En 4/14 = Hyde 661/3.
UK: soc

49/01/En 6/2 **1968** Hyde 678/3
ARCANA CÆLESTIA | (HEAVENLY ARCANA) | WHICH ARE CONTAINED IN | THE HOLY SCRIPTURE OR | WORD OF THE LORD | DISCLOSED | FROM THE LATIN OF | EMANUEL SWEDENBORG | Vol. IV | GENESIS, CHAPTERS XVIII-XX | Nos. 2135-2605 | THE SWEDENBORG SOCIETY | 20/21 BLOOMSBURY WAY, LONDON, W.C.1 | 1968
imprint: <rule> | *Printed in England by H. Sharp & Sons, Bath.*
small 8vo
title leaf, 2 pp; Reviser's prefatory note, 2 pp; blank page; Contents, 1 p; text of Swedenborg's preface, 2 pp; text of Genesis 18-20 and n 2135-2605, pp 1-453; imprint, p 454.
A reprint of En 6/1 = Hyde 678/2 with a fresh title page.
UK: soc

49/01/En 5/85 **1968** Hyde 678/–
ARCANA COELESTIA | THE | HEAVENLY ARCANA | CONTAINED IN THE HOLY SCRIPTURE OR WORD OF THE LORD | UNFOLDED | BEGINNING WITH THE BOOK OF GENESIS | TOGETHER WITH WONDERFUL THINGS SEEN IN THE WORLD OF | SPIRITS AND IN THE HEAVEN OF ANGELS | TRANSLATED FROM THE LATIN OF | EMANUEL SWEDENBORG | THOROUGHLY REVISED AND EDITED BY THE | REV. JOHN FAULKNER POTTS, B.A. LOND. | VOLUME IV. | <short rule> | STANDARD EDITION | <short rule> | NEW YORK | THE AMERICAN SWEDENBORG PRINTING AND PUBLISHING | SOCIETY | 3 WEST TWENTY-NINTH STREET | 1968
verso: [INSCRIPTION BY THE AUTHOR.] | Seek ye first the Kingdom of God and His righteousness, and all these | things shall be added unto you (*Matt.* vi. 33). | Published by The American Swedenborg Printing and Publishing Society, | organized for the business and objects solely of printing, publishing and circu- | lating the Theological Works and Writings of Emanuel Swedenborg for charitable | and missionary purposes. Incorporated in the State of New York, A.D. 1850.

8vo
title leaf, 2 pp; Table of contents, p iii; text of Genesis 23-27 and n 2894-3649, pp 1-527.
USA: SHS; SA: MMC

49/01/En 5/86 **1968** Hyde 696/–

ARCANA COELESTIA | THE | HEAVENLY ARCANA | CONTAINED IN THE HOLY SCRIPTURE OR WORD OF THE LORD | UNFOLDED | BEGINNING WITH THE BOOK OF GENESIS | TOGETHER WITH WONDERFUL THINGS SEEN IN THE WORLD OF | SPIRITS AND IN THE HEAVEN OF ANGELS | TRANSLATED FROM THE LATIN OF | EMANUEL SWEDENBORG | THOROUGHLY REVISED AND EDITED BY THE | REV. JOHN FAULKNER POTTS, B.A. LOND. | VOLUME V. | <short rule> | STANDARD EDITION | <short rule> | NEW YORK | AMERICAN SWEDENBORG PRINTING AND PUBLISHING | SOCIETY | 3 WEST TWENTY-NINTH STREET | 1968
verso: [INSCRIPTION BY THE AUTHOR.] | Seek ye first the Kingdom of God and His righteousness, and all these | things shall be added unto you (*Matt.* vi. 33). | Published by The American Swedenborg Printing and Publishing Society, | organized for the business and objects solely of printing, publishing and circu- | lating the Theological Works and Writings of Emanuel Swedenborg for charitable | and missionary purposes. Incorporated in the State of New York, A.D. 1850.
8vo
title leaf, 2 pp; Table of contents, p iii; text of Genesis 28-31 and n 3650-4228, pp 1-490.
USA: SHS; SA: MMC

49/01/En 5/87 **1969** Hyde 728/–

ARCANA COELESTIA | THE | HEAVENLY ARCANA | CONTAINED IN THE HOLY SCRIPTURE OR WORD OF THE LORD | UNFOLDED | BEGINNING WITH THE BOOK OF GENESIS | TOGETHER WITH WONDERFUL THINGS SEEN IN THE WORLD OF | SPIRITS AND IN THE HEAVEN OF ANGELS | TRANSLATED FROM THE LATIN OF | EMANUEL SWEDENBORG | THOROUGHLY REVISED AND EDITED BY THE | REV. JOHN FAULKNER POTTS, B.A. LOND. | VOLUME VII. | <short rule> | STANDARD EDITION | <short rule> | NEW YORK | THE AMERICAN SWEDENBORG PRINTING AND PUBLISHING | SOCIETY | 3 WEST TWENTY-NINTH STREET | 1969
verso: [INSCRIPTION BY THE AUTHOR.] | Seek ye first the Kingdom of God and His righteousness, and all these | things shall be added unto you (*Matt.* vi. 33). | Published by The American Swedenborg Printing and Publishing Society, | organized for the business and objects solely of printing, publishing and circu- | lating the Theological Works and Writings of Emanuel Swedenborg for charitable | and missionary purposes. Incorporated in the State of New York, A.D. 1850.
8vo
title leaf, 2 pp; Table of contents, p iii; text of Genesis 39-43 and n 4954-5727, pp 1-516.
USA: SHS; SA: MMC

49/01/En 5/88 **1970** Hyde 745/–

ARCANA COELESTIA | THE | HEAVENLY ARCANA | CONTAINED IN THE HOLY SCRIPTURE OR WORD OF THE LORD | UNFOLDED | BEGINNING WITH THE BOOK OF GENESIS | TOGETHER WITH WONDERFUL THINGS SEEN IN THE WORLD OF | SPIRITS AND IN THE HEAVEN OF ANGELS | TRANSLATED FROM THE LATIN OF | EMANUEL SWEDENBORG | THOROUGHLY REVISED AND EDITED BY THE | REV. JOHN FAULKNER POTTS, B.A. LOND. | VOLUME VIII. | <short rule> | STANDARD EDITION | <short rule> | NEW YORK | THE AMERICAN SWEDENBORG PRINTING AND PUBLISHING | SOCIETY | 3 WEST TWENTY-NINTH STREET | 1970
verso: [INSCRIPTION BY THE AUTHOR.] | Seek ye first the Kingdom of God and His righteousness, and all these | things shall be added unto you (*Matt.* vi. 33). | Published by The American Swedenborg Printing and Publishing Society, | organized for the business and objects solely of

printing, publishing and circu- | lating the Theological Works and Writings of Emanuel Swedenborg for charitable | and missionary purposes. Incorporated in the State of New York, A.D. 1850.
8vo
title leaf, 2 pp; Table of contents, p iii; text of Genesis 44-50 and n 5728-6626, pp 1-504.
USA: SHS; SA: MMC

49/01/En 5/89 **1970** Hyde 759/2
ARCANA COELESTIA | THE | HEAVENLY ARCANA | CONTAINED IN THE HOLY SCRIPTURE OR WORD OF THE LORD | UNFOLDED | HERE THOSE WHICH ARE IN EXODUS | TOGETHER WITH WONDERFUL THINGS SEEN IN THE WORLD OF | SPIRITS AND IN THE HEAVEN OF ANGELS | TRANSLATED FROM THE LATIN OF | EMANUEL SWEDENBORG | THOROUGHLY REVISED AND EDITED BY THE | REV. JOHN FAULKNER POTTS, B.A. LOND. | VOLUME IX. | <short rule> | STANDARD EDITION | <short rule> | NEW YORK | THE AMERICAN SWEDENBORG PRINTING AND PUBLISHING | SOCIETY | 3 WEST TWENTY-NINTH STREET | 1970
verso: [INSCRIPTION BY THE AUTHOR.] | Seek ye first the Kingdom of God and His righteousness, and all these | things shall be added unto you (*Matt.* vi. 33). | Published by The American Swedenborg Printing and Publishing Society, | organized for the business and objects solely of printing, publishing and circu- | lating the Theological Works and Writings of Emanuel Swedenborg for charitable | and missionary purposes. Incorporated in the State of New York, A.D. 1850.
8vo
title leaf, 2 pp; Table of contents, p iii; text of Exodus 1-12 and n 6627-8032, pp 1-685.
SA: MMC

49/01/En 5/90 **1970** Hyde 774/–
ARCANA COELESTIA | THE | HEAVENLY ARCANA | CONTAINED IN THE HOLY SCRIPTURE OR WORD OF THE LORD | UNFOLDED | HERE THOSE WHICH ARE IN EXODUS | TOGETHER WITH WONDERFUL THINGS SEEN IN THE WORLD OF | SPIRITS AND IN THE HEAVEN OF ANGELS | TRANSLATED FROM THE LATIN OF | EMANUEL SWEDENBORG | THOROUGHLY REVISED AND EDITED BY THE | REV. JOHN FAULKNER POTTS, B.A. LOND. | VOLUME X. | <short rule> | STANDARD EDITION | <short rule> | NEW YORK | THE AMERICAN SWEDENBORG PRINTING AND PUBLISHING | SOCIETY | 3 WEST TWENTY-NINTH STREET | 1970
verso: [INSCRIPTION BY THE AUTHOR.] | Seek ye first the Kingdom of God and His righteousness, and all these | things shall be added unto you (*Matt.* vi. 33). | Published by The American Swedenborg Printing and Publishing Society, | organized for the business and objects solely of printing, publishing and circu- | lating the Theological Works and Writings of Emanuel Swedenborg for charitable | and missionary purposes. Incorporated in the State of New York, A.D. 1850.
8vo
title leaf, 2 pp; Table of contents, p iii; text of Exodus 13-21 and n 8033-9111, pp 1-652.
USA: ANC; SA: MMC

49/01/En 5/91 **1970** Hyde 783/–
ARCANA COELESTIA | THE | HEAVENLY ARCANA | CONTAINED IN THE HOLY SCRIPTURE OR WORD OF THE LORD | UNFOLDED | HERE THOSE WHICH ARE IN EXODUS | TOGETHER WITH WONDERFUL THINGS SEEN IN THE WORLD OF | SPIRITS AND IN THE HEAVEN OF ANGELS | TRANSLATED FROM THE LATIN OF | EMANUEL SWEDENBORG | THOROUGHLY REVISED AND EDITED BY THE | REV. JOHN FAULKNER POTTS, B.A. LOND. | VOLUME XI. | <short rule> | STANDARD EDITION | <short rule> | NEW YORK | THE AMERICAN SWEDENBORG PRINTING AND PUBLISHING | SOCIETY | 3 WEST TWENTY-NINTH STREET | 1970
verso: [INSCRIPTION BY THE AUTHOR.] | Seek ye first the Kingdom of God and His righteousness,

and all these | things shall be added unto you (*Matt.* vi. 33). | Published by The American Swedenborg Printing and Publishing Society, | organized for the business and objects solely of printing, publishing and circu- | lating the Theological Works and Writings of Emanuel Swedenborg for charitable | and missionary purposes. Incorporated in the State of New York, A.D. 1850.
8vo
title leaf, 2 pp; Table of contents, p iii; text of Exodus 22-28 and n 9112-9973, pp 1-754.
USA: SHS; SA: MMC

49/01/En 5/92 **1971** Hyde 618/–
ARCANA COELESTIA | THE | HEAVENLY ARCANA | CONTAINED IN THE HOLY SCRIPTURE OR WORD OF THE LORD | UNFOLDED | BEGINNING WITH THE BOOK OF GENESIS | TOGETHER WITH WONDERFUL THINGS SEEN IN THE WORLD OF | SPIRITS AND IN THE HEAVEN OF ANGELS | TRANSLATED FROM THE LATIN OF | EMANUEL SWEDENBORG | THOROUGHLY REVISED AND EDITED BY THE | REV. JOHN FAULKNER POTTS, B.A. LOND. | VOLUME I. | <short rule> | STANDARD EDITION | <short rule> | NEW YORK | THE AMERICAN SWEDENBORG PRINTING AND PUBLISHING | SOCIETY | 3 WEST TWENTY-NINTH STREET | 1971
verso: [INSCRIPTION BY THE AUTHOR.] | Seek ye first the Kingdom of God and His righteousness, and all these | things shall be added unto you (*Matt.* vi. 33). | Published by The American Swedenborg Printing and Publishing Society, | organized for the business and objects solely of printing, publishing and circu- | lating the Theological Works and Writings of Emanuel Swedenborg for charitable | and missionary purposes. Incorporated in the State of New York, A.D. 1850.
8vo
title leaf, 2 pp; Table of contents, p iii; text of Genesis 1-9 and n 1-1113, pp 1-585.
SA: MMC

49/01/En 5/93 **1973** Hyde 618/–
<<ARCANA COELESTIA | THE | HEAVENLY ARCANA | CONTAINED IN THE HOLY SCRIPTURE OR WORD OF THE LORD | UNFOLDED | BEGINNING WITH THE BOOK OF GENESIS | TOGETHER WITH WONDERFUL THINGS SEEN IN THE WORLD OF | SPIRITS AND IN THE HEAVEN OF ANGELS | TRANSLATED FROM THE LATIN OF | EMANUEL SWEDENBORG | THOROUGHLY REVISED AND EDITED BY THE | REV. JOHN FAULKNER POTTS, B.A. LOND. | VOLUME I. | <short rule> | STANDARD EDITION | <short rule> | NEW YORK | THE AMERICAN SWEDENBORG PRINTING AND PUBLISHING | SOCIETY | 3 WEST TWENTY-NINTH STREET | 1973>>
verso: <<[INSCRIPTION BY THE AUTHOR.] | Seek ye first the Kingdom of God and His righteousness, and all these | things shall be added unto you (*Matt.* vi. 33). | Published by The American Swedenborg Printing and Publishing Society, | organized for the business and objects solely of printing, publishing and circu- | lating the Theological Works and Writings of Emanuel Swedenborg for charitable | and missionary purposes. Incorporated in the State of New York, A.D. 1850.>>
8vo
title leaf, 2 pp; Table of contents, p iii; text of Genesis 1-9 and n 1-1113, pp 1-585.
Copy not seen; description deduced from En 5/92 and catalogue of USA: SHS.
USA: SHS

49/01/En 4/26 **1973** Hyde 678/–
<<*ARCANA CŒLESTIA*. | <short rule> | THE | HEAVENLY ARCANA | CONTAINED IN | THE HOLY SCRIPTURE OR | WORD OF THE LORD | UNFOLDED | IN AN EXPOSITION OF GENESIS AND EXODUS | TOGETHER WITH A RELATION OF | WONDERFUL THINGS SEEN IN THE WORLD OF SPIRITS AND | IN THE HEAVEN OF ANGELS | *FROM THE LATIN* | OF | EMANUEL SWEDENBORG | VOLUME IV. | GENESIS, CHAPTER XXIII. TO CHAPTER XXVII. | NOS. 2894-3649. | THE

SWEDENBORG SOCIETY | (INSTITUTED 1810) | 1 BLOOMSBURY STREET, LONDON | 1957>>
verso: <<*"Seek ye first the kingdom of God and His righteousness,* | *and all these things shall be added unto you."* | —MATTHEW vi. 33.>>
8vo
title leaf, 2 pp; Prefatory note, p v; Contents, p vii; text of Genesis 23-27 and n 2894-3649, pp 1-435.
An edition of 500 copies reprinted from En 4/11 = Hyde 678/a.
Copy not seen; description deduced from En 4/11 and Annual Report for 1974 of UK: SOC.

49/01/En 5/94 **1980** Hyde 792/–
ARCANA COELESTIA | THE | HEAVENLY ARCANA | CONTAINED IN THE HOLY SCRIPTURE OR WORD OF THE LORD | UNFOLDED | HERE THOSE WHICH ARE IN EXODUS | TOGETHER WITH WONDERFUL THINGS SEEN IN THE WORLD OF | SPIRITS AND IN THE HEAVEN OF ANGELS | TRANSLATED FROM THE LATIN OF | EMANUEL SWEDENBORG | THOROUGHLY REVISED AND EDITED BY | JOHN FAULKNER POTTS | VOLUME XII. | <short rule> | *Standard Edition* | <short rule> | SWEDENBORG FOUNDATION | INCORPORATED | NEW YORK | <short rule> | Established in 1850
verso: First published in Latin, London, 1756 | First English translation published in U.S.A., 1847 | 2nd printing, 1980 | [INSCRIPTION BY THE AUTHOR.] | Seek ye first the Kingdom of God and His righteousness, and all these | things shall be added unto you (*Matt.* vi. 33). | ISBN: 0-87785-032-1 (Student), 12 Vol. set 087785-033-X | 0-87785-045-3 (Trade), 12 Vol. set 0-87785-046-1 | *Library of Congress Catalog Card Number 63 - 1828* | Manufactured in the United States of America
8vo
title leaf, 2 pp; Reviser's note, 1 p; Contents, pp v-vi; text of Exodus 29-40 and n 9974-10837, pp 1-691.
USA: SHS

49/01/En 5/95 **1981** Hyde 618/–
HEAVENLY SECRETS | (ARCANA CÆLESTIA) | WHICH ARE CONTAINED IN | THE HOLY SCRIPTURE OR | WORD OF THE LORD | DISCLOSED | FROM THE LATIN OF | EMANUEL SWEDENBORG | VOL. I. | GENESIS, CHAPTERS I-VII | Nos. 1-823 | SWEDENBORG FOUNDATION INCORPORATED | NEW YORK
verso: First published in Latin, London 1749 | First English Translation published in London 1813 | First English Translation Published in USA in 1837 | 44th Printing in USA 1981 | ISBN: 0-87785-053-4 | Library of Congress Catalog Card Number: 63—1828 | printed in the United States of America | Cover design by Virginia Smith | Swedenborg Foundation Inc. | 139 East 23rd Street | New York, New York 10010 <*stet* 1813>
8vo
title leaf, 2 pp; Preface, pp 1-2; Introduction, pp 3-6; Contents, pp 7-8; text of Genesis 1-7 and n 1-823, pp 9-540; catalogue, pp 541-542.
Reprint of En 5/46.
UK: SOC, PUR

49/01/En 5/96 **1982** Hyde 745/–
ARCANA COELESTIA | THE | HEAVENLY ARCANA | CONTAINED IN THE HOLY SCRIPTURE OR WORD OF THE LORD | UNFOLDED | BEGINNING WITH THE BOOK OF GENESIS | TOGETHER WITH WONDERFUL THINGS SEEN IN THE WORLD OF | SPIRITS AND IN THE HEAVEN OF ANGELS | TRANSLATED FROM THE LATIN OF | EMANUEL SWEDENBORG | REVISED AND EDITED BY | JOHN FAULKNER POTTS | VOLUME VIII. | <short rule> | *Standard Edition* | <short rule> | SWEDENBORG FOUNDATION | INCORPORATED | NEW YORK | <short rule> | Established in 1850
verso: First published in Latin, London, 1753 | First English translation published in U.S.A., 1844 |

38th printing, 1982 | [INSCRIPTION BY THE AUTHOR.] | Seek ye first the Kingdom of God and His righteousness, and all these | things shall be added unto you (*Matt.* vi. 33). | ISBN: 0-87785-028-3 (Student), 12 Vol. set 0-87785-033-X | 0-87785-041-0 (Trade), 12 Vol. set 0-87785-046-1 | *Library of Congress Catalog Card Number 63 - 1828* | Manufactured in the United States of America
8vo
title leaf, 2 pp; Contents, p iii; text of Genesis 44-50 and n 5728-6636, pp 1-502; Editor's notes, pp 503-504.

49/01/En 5/97 **1982** Hyde 774/–
ARCANA COELESTIA | THE | HEAVENLY ARCANA | CONTAINED IN THE HOLY SCRIPTURE OR WORD OF THE LORD | UNFOLDED | HERE THOSE WHICH ARE IN EXODUS | TOGETHER WITH WONDERFUL THINGS SEEN IN THE WORLD OF | SPIRITS AND IN THE HEAVEN OF ANGELS | TRANSLATED FROM THE LATIN OF | EMANUEL SWEDENBORG | REVISED AND EDITED BY | JOHN FAULKNER POTTS | VOLUME X. | <short rule> | *Standard Edition* | <short rule> | SWEDENBORG FOUNDATION | INCORPORATED | NEW YORK | <short rule> | Established in 1850
verso: First published in Latin, London, 1754 | First English translation published in U.S.A., 1846 | [INSCRIPTION BY THE AUTHOR.] | Seek ye first the Kingdom of God and His righteousness, and all these | things shall be added unto you (*Matt.* vi. 33). | ISBN: 0-87785-030-5 (Student), 12 Vol. set 0-87785-033-X | 0-87785-043-7 (Trade), 12 Vol. set 0-87785-046-1 | *Library of Congress Catalog Card Number 63 - 1828* | Manufactured in the United States of America
8vo
title leaf, 2 pp; Contents, p iii-iv; text of Exodus 13-21 and n 8033-9111, pp 1-652.

49/01/En 7/1 **1983** Hyde 618/13
EMANUEL SWEDENBORG | ARCANA CAELESTIA | <rule> | Principally a Revelation of the | inner or spiritual meaning of | Genesis and Exodus | VOLUME ONE | *Paragraphs 1-1113* | GENESIS 1 *Chapters 1-9* | TRANSLATED FROM | THE ORIGINAL LATIN BY | JOHN ELLIOTT | LONDON | THE SWEDENBORG SOCIETY | 1983
verso: Published by The Swedenborg Society | Swedenborg House, 20-21 Bloomsbury Way, London WC1A 2TH | © Swedenborg Society 1983 | Designed by James Butler MSIAD | Typeset in Palatino by | Goodfellow & Egan Phototypesetting Ltd, Cambridge | Printed and bound in Great Britain at the | University Press, Cambridge | ISBN 0 85448 088 9 Hard covers | ISBN 0 85448 089 7 Paperback
half title: ARCANA CAELESTIA
section title: THE BOOK | OF GENESIS | <rule>
8vo
half title and title leaves, 4 pp; Translator's introduction, pp v-xv; Chapters and paragraphs to volumes of the Latin and English editions, p xvi; translation of title page of La 1/1, p xvi; reproduction of title page of La 1/1, 1 p; text of Swedenborg's introductory note, p 1; section title leaf, pp 3-4; text of Genesis 1-9 and n 1-1113, pp 5-473; Word list, p 475.
UK: SOC, CON, NCC, PUR, NR; DEN: RLD; NET: GEN; POL: GDA; USA: ANC, SHS; AUS: SYD

49/01/En 7/2 **1984** Hyde 643/6
EMANUEL SWEDENBORG | ARCANA CAELESTIA | <rule> | Principally a Revelation of the | inner or spiritual meaning of | Genesis and Exodus | VOLUME TWO | *Paragraphs 1114-2134* | GENESIS *Chapters 10-17* | TRANSLATED FROM | THE ORIGINAL LATIN BY | JOHN ELLIOTT | LONDON | THE SWEDENBORG SOCIETY | 1984
verso: Published by The Swedenborg Society | Swedenborg House, 20-21 Bloomsbury Way, London WC1A 2TH | © Swedenborg Society 1984 | Designed by James Butler MSIAD | Typeset in Palatino by | Goodfellow & Egan Phototypesetting Ltd, Cambridge | Printed and bound in Great Britain at the

| University Press, Cambridge | ISBN 0 85448 090 0 Hard covers | ISBN 0 85448 091 9 Paperback
half title: ARCANA CAELESTIA
8vo
half title and title leaves, 4 pp; Translator's note, p v; Chapters and paragraphs to volumes of the Latin and English editions, p vii; text of Swedenborg's introductory note, continued <from vol 1>, p 1; text of Genesis 10-17 and n 1114-2134, pp 3-476; Word list, p 477; Errata in volume 1, p 479.
UK: SOC, CON, NCC, PUR, NR; DEN: RLD; NET: GEN; USA: ANC, SHS; AUS: SYD

49/01/En 7/3 **1985** Hyde 661/5
EMANUEL SWEDENBORG | ARCANA CAELESTIA | <rule> | Principally a Revelation of the | inner or spiritual meaning of | Genesis and Exodus | VOLUME THREE | *Paragraphs 2135-2893* | GENESIS *Chapters 18-22* | TRANSLATED FROM | THE ORIGINAL LATIN BY | JOHN ELLIOTT | LONDON | THE SWEDENBORG SOCIETY | 1985
verso: Published by The Swedenborg Society | Swedenborg House, 20-21 Bloomsbury Way, London WC1A 2TH | © Swedenborg Society 1985 | Designed by James Butler MSIAD | Typeset in Palatino by | Goodfellow & Egan Phototypesetting Ltd, Cambridge | Printed and bound in Great Britain at the | University Press, Cambridge | ISBN 0 85448 092 7 Hard covers | ISBN 0 85448 093 5 Paperback
half title: ARCANA CAELESTIA
8vo
half title and title leaves, 4 pp; Translator's notes, pp v-vi; Chapters and paragraphs to volumes of the Latin and English editions, p vii; text of Swedenborg's preface <to chapter 18>, pp 1-2; Genesis 18-22 and n 2135-2893, pp 3-456; Word list, p 457; Errata in volumes 1-2, p 459.
UK: SOC, CON, NCC, PUR, NR; DEN: RLD; NET: GEN; USA: ANC, SHS; AUS: SYD

49/01/En 5/98 **1985** Hyde 618/–
<<*Heavenly Secrets*: volume 1 of *Arcana Caelestia*>>
8vo
title leaf, 2 pp; Introduction and text of Genesis 1-9 and n 1-1113, pp 1-544.
Published by The Swedenborg Foundation in paperback. The introduction was written by Helen Keller. Listed by D B Eller in *Illuminating the World of the Spirit* p 126, Swedenborg Foundation, West Chester PA. ISBN 0-87785-190-5.
Copy not seen; description recorded from the above listing.
USA: FOU

49/01/En 7/4 **1986** Hyde 678/4
EMANUEL SWEDENBORG | ARCANA CAELESTIA | <rule> | Principally a Revelation of the | inner or spiritual meaning of | Genesis and Exodus | VOLUME FOUR | *Paragraphs 2894-3649* | GENESIS *Chapters 23-27* | TRANSLATED FROM | THE ORIGINAL LATIN BY | JOHN ELLIOTT | LONDON | THE SWEDENBORG SOCIETY | 1986
verso: Published by The Swedenborg Society | Swedenborg House, 20-21 Bloomsbury Way, London WC1A 2TH | © Swedenborg Society 1986 | Designed by James Butler MSIAD | Typeset in Palatino by | Goodfellow & Egan Phototypesetting Ltd, Cambridge | Printed and bound in Great Britain at the | University Press, Cambridge | ISBN 0 85448 094 3 Hard covers | ISBN 0 85448 095 1 Paperback
half title: ARCANA CAELESTIA
8vo
half title and title leaves, 4 pp; Translator's notes, p v; Chapters and paragraphs to volumes of the Latin and English editions, p vii; text of Genesis 23-27 and n 2894-3649, pp 1-417; Word list, p 419; Errata in volumes 1-3, p 421.
UK: SOC, CON, NCC, PUR, NR; DEN: RLD; NET: GEN; SWE: ROY; USA: ANC, SHS; AUS: SYD

49/01/En 7/5 **1987** Hyde 696/4

EMANUEL SWEDENBORG | ARCANA CAELESTIA | <rule> | Principally a Revelation of the | inner or spiritual meaning of | Genesis and Exodus | VOLUME FIVE | *Paragraphs 3650-422* | GENESIS *Chapters 28-31* | TRANSLATED FROM | THE ORIGINAL LATIN BY | JOHN ELLIOTT | LONDON | THE SWEDENBORG SOCIETY | 1987

verso: Published by The Swedenborg Society | Swedenborg House, 20-21 Bloomsbury Way, London WC1A 2TH | © Swedenborg Society 1987 | Designed by James Butler MSIAD | Typeset in Palatino by | Goodfellow & Egan Phototypesetting Ltd, Cambridge | Printed and bound in Great Britain at the | University Press, Cambridge | ISBN 0 85448 098 6 Hard covers | ISBN 0 85448 099 4 Paperback

half title: ARCANA CAELESTIA

8vo

half title and title leaves, 4 pp; Translator's notes, p v; Chapters and paragraphs to volumes of the Latin and English editions, p vii; text of Genesis 28-31 and n 3650-4228, pp 1-389; Word list, p 391; Errata in volumes 3-4, p 392.

UK: soc, con, ncc, pur, nr; DEN: rld; NET: gen; USA: anc, shs; AUS: syd

49/01/En 7/6 **1988** Hyde 712/4

EMANUEL SWEDENBORG | ARCANA CAELESTIA | <rule> | Principally a Revelation of the | inner or spiritual meaning of | Genesis and Exodus | VOLUME SIX | *Paragraphs 4229-4953* | GENESIS *Chapters 32-38* | TRANSLATED FROM | THE ORIGINAL LATIN BY | JOHN ELLIOTT | LONDON | THE SWEDENBORG SOCIETY | 1988

verso: Published by The Swedenborg Society | Swedenborg House, 20-21 Bloomsbury Way, London WC1A 2TH | © Swedenborg Society 1988 | Designed by James Butler MSIAD | Typeset in Palatino by | Goodfellow & Egan Phototypesetting Ltd, Cambridge | Printed and bound in Great Britain at the | University Press, Cambridge | ISBN 0 85448 106 0 Hard covers | ISBN 0 85448 107 9 Paperback

half title: ARCANA CAELESTIA

8vo

half title and title leaves, 4 pp; Translator's notes, p v; Chapters and paragraphs to volumes of the Latin and English editions, p vii; text of Genesis 32-38 and n 4229-4953, pp 1-457; Word list, p 459; Errata in volumes 3, 5, p 461.

UK: soc, con, ncc, pur, nr; DEN: rld; NET: gen; USA: anc, shs; AUS: syd

49/01/En 7/7 **1990** Hyde 728/5

EMANUEL SWEDENBORG | ARCANA CAELESTIA | <rule> | Principally a Revelation of the | inner or spiritual meaning of | Genesis and Exodus | VOLUME SEVEN | *Paragraphs 4954-5727* | GENESIS *Chapters 39-43* | TRANSLATED FROM | THE ORIGINAL LATIN BY | JOHN ELLIOTT | LONDON | THE SWEDENBORG SOCIETY | 1990

verso: Published by The Swedenborg Society | Swedenborg House, 20-21 Bloomsbury Way, London WC1A 2TH | © Swedenborg Society 1990 | Designed by James Butler MSIAD | Typeset in Palatino by | Goodfellow & Egan Phototypesetting Ltd, Cambridge | Printed and bound in Great Britain at the | University Press, Cambridge | ISBN 0 85448 110 9 Hard covers | ISBN 0 85448 111 7 Paperback

half title: ARCANA CAELESTIA

8vo

half title and title leaves, 4 pp; Translator's notes, pp v-vi; Chapters and paragraphs to volumes of the Latin and English editions, p vii; text of Genesis 39-43 and n 4954-5727, pp 1-436; Word list, p 437; Errata in volumes 1-2, 5-6, p 439.

UK: soc, con, ncc, pur, nr; DEN: rld; NET: gen; USA: anc, shs; AUS: syd

49/01/En 7/8 **1992** Hyde 745/3

EMANUEL SWEDENBORG | ARCANA CAELESTIA | <rule> | Principally a Revelation of the | inner or spiritual meaning of | Genesis and Exodus | VOLUME EIGHT | *Paragraphs 5728-6626* | GENESIS *Chapters 44-50* | TRANSLATED FROM | THE ORIGINAL LATIN BY | JOHN ELLIOTT | LONDON | THE SWEDENBORG SOCIETY | 1992

verso: Published by The Swedenborg Society | Swedenborg House, 20-21 Bloomsbury Way, London WC1A 2TH | © Swedenborg Society 1992 | Designed by James Butler MSIAD | Typeset in Palatino by | Goodfellow & Egan Phototypesetting Ltd, Cambridge | Printed and bound in Great Britain at the | University Press, Cambridge | ISBN 0 85448 113 3 Hard covers | ISBN 0 85448 114 1 Paperback

half title: ARCANA CAELESTIA

8vo

half title and title leaves, 4 pp; Translator's notes, p v; Chapters and paragraphs to volumes of the Latin and English editions, p vii; text of Genesis 44-50 and n 5728-6626, pp 1-410; Word list, p 411; Errata in volumes 1-2, 4-5, 7, p 413.

UK: SOC, CON, NCC, PUR, NR; DEN: RLD; NET: GEN; USA: ANC, SHS; AUS: SYD

49/01/En 7/9 **1993** Hyde 759/3

EMANUEL SWEDENBORG | ARCANA CAELESTIA | <rule> | Principally a Revelation of the | inner or spiritual meaning of | Genesis and Exodus | VOLUME NINE | *Paragraphs 6627-8032* | EXODUS *Chapters 1-12* | TRANSLATED FROM | THE ORIGINAL LATIN BY | JOHN ELLIOTT | LONDON | THE SWEDENBORG SOCIETY | 1993

verso: Published by The Swedenborg Society | Swedenborg House, 20-21 Bloomsbury Way, London WC1A 2TH | © Swedenborg Society 1993 | Designed by James Butler MSIAD | Typeset in Palatino by | Goodfellow & Egan Phototypesetting Ltd, Cambridge | Printed and bound in Great Britain at the | University Press, Cambridge | ISBN 0 85448 116 8 Hard covers | ISBN 0 85448 117 6 Paperback

half title: ARCANA CAELESTIA

section title: THE BOOK | OF EXODUS | <rule>

8vo

half title and title leaves, 4 pp; Translator's notes, p v; Chapters and paragraphs to volumes of the Latin and English editions, p vii; section title leaf, pp 1-2; text of Exodus 1-12 and n 6627-8032, pp 3-572; Word list, p 573; Errata in volumes 1-3, 6-8, p 575.

2,504 copies were bound in hard covers, and 1,535 in paper covers.

UK: SOC, CON, NCC, PUR, NR; DEN: RLD; NET: GEN; USA: ANC, SHS; AUS: SYD

49/01/En 7/10 **1995** Hyde 774/4

EMANUEL SWEDENBORG | ARCANA CAELESTIA | <rule> | Principally a Revelation of the | inner or spiritual meaning of | Genesis and Exodus | VOLUME TEN | *Paragraphs 8033-9111* | EXODUS *Chapters 13-21* | TRANSLATED FROM | THE ORIGINAL LATIN BY | JOHN ELLIOTT | LONDON | THE SWEDENBORG SOCIETY | 1995

verso: Published by The Swedenborg Society | Swedenborg House, 20-21 Bloomsbury Way, London WC1A 2TH | © Swedenborg Society 1995 | Designed by James Butler MSIAD | Typeset in Palatino by | Goodfellow & Egan Phototypesetting Ltd, Cambridge | Printed and bound in Great Britain at the | University Press, Cambridge | ISBN 0 85448 118 4 Hard covers | ISBN 0 85448 119 2 Paperback

half title: ARCANA CAELESTIA

section title: *Exodus continued* | <rule>

8vo

half title and title leaves, 4 pp; Translator's notes, p v; Chapters and paragraphs to volumes of the Latin and English editions, p vii; section title leaf, pp 1-2; text of Exodus 13-21 and n 8033-9111, pp 3-532; Word list, p 533; Errata in volumes 2-3, 6-9, p 535.

2,473 copies were bound in hard covers, and 1,547 copies in paper covers.
UK: SOC, CON, NCC, PUR, NR; DEN: RLD; NET: GEN; USA: ANC, SHS; AUS: SYD

49/01/En 5/99 **1995** Hyde 745/4

<within a rule border 167 x 101 mm>*Arcana* | *Coelestia* | <short rule> | *The heavenly arcana contained in the* | *Holy Scripture or Word of the Lord* | *unfolded, beginning with the book of Genesis* | <short rule> | EMANUEL SWEDENBORG | Volume 8 | (Numbers 5727-6626) | Translated from the original Latin by | John Clowes | Revised and Edited by | John Faulkner Potts | STANDARD EDITION | SWEDENBORG FOUNDATION | West Chester, Pennsylvania <*stet* 5727>
verso: © 1995 by the Swedenborg Foundation, Inc. | All rights reserved. No part of this publication may be reproduced or | transmitted in any form or by any means, electronic or mechanical, including | photocopying, recording, or any information storage or retrieval system, | without prior permission from the publisher. | First published in Latin, 8 volumes, London, 1749-1756 | First edition translated by J. Clowes, published in London, 1774-1806, | 12 volumes | First American printing, Boston, 1837-1847, 12 volumes, a revision based on | the translation of Clowes and his revisers | Second American printing, 1853-1857 | Third edition ("Rotch") published in New York and Boston, 1892-1908 | First Potts edition, 1905-1910 | Second Potts edition, 1995 | Printed in the United States of America | Library of Congress Cataloging-in-Publication Data | Swedenborg, Emanuel, 1688-1772.| Arcana coelestia = The heavenly arcana contained in the Holy Scripture or | Word of the Lord unfolded, beginning with the book of Genesis; translated | from original Latin by John Clowes; revised and edited by John Faulkner | Potts. -- Standard ed., 2nd Potts ed. | Contents: — v. 8. Numbers 5727-6626 | Translation of: Arcana coelestia quae in scriptura sacra sunt detecta. | 1. New Jerusalem Church—Doctrines. 2. Bible. O.T.—Genesis— | Commentaries. 3. Bible. O.T. —Exodus—Commentaries. I. Potts, John | Faulkner. II. Title. III. Title: Heavenly arcana contained in the Holy | Scripture or Word of the Lord unfolded, beginning with the book of Genesis. | BX8712.A8 1995 230'.94 94-36279 | ISBN 0-87785-252-9 (volume 8) | ISBN 0-87785-262-6 (12-volume set) | Typeset in Garamond by William Ross Woofenden | Designed by Joanna V. Hill | Printed and bound by BookCrafters, Inc. | For information contact: | Swedenborg Foundation | 320 North Church Street | West Chester, PA 19380 <*stet* 1774-1806; 5727>
half title: <within a rule border 167 x 101 mm> Arcana | Coelestia | <short rule> | Volume 8 | (Numbers 5727-6626) <*stet* 5727>
section title: <within a rule border 167 x 101 mm> Arcana | Coelestia | <short rule> | Volume 8 | (Numbers 5727-6626) <*stet* 5727>
8vo
half title and title leaves, 4 pp; Table of contents, p v; Editor's preface, pp vii-viii; section title leaf, pp ix-x; text of Genesis 44-50 and n 5728-6626, pp 1-561; Reviser's notes, pp 563-565.
A revision of the second Potts edition, scanned and reset with minor editorial changes by W R Woofenden.
UK: SOC; SWE: ROY; USA: SHS

49/01/En 5/100 **1995** Hyde 774/5

<within a rule border 167 x 101 mm> Arcana | Coelestia | <short rule> | *The heavenly arcana contained in the* | *Holy Scripture or Word of the Lord* | *unfolded, beginning with* | *the book of Genesis* | <short rule> | EMANUEL SWEDENBORG | Volume 10 | (Numbers 8033-9111) | Translated from the original Latin by | John Clowes | Revised and Edited by | John Faulkner Potts | STANDARD EDITION | SWEDENBORG FOUNDATION | West Chester, Pennsylvania
verso: © 1995 by the Swedenborg Foundation, Inc. | All rights reserved. No part of this publication may be reproduced or | transmitted in any form or by any means, electronic or mechanical, including | photocopying, recording, or any information storage or retrieval system, | without prior permission from the publisher. | First published in Latin, 8 volumes, London, 1749-1756

| First edition translated by J. Clowes, published in London, 1774-1806, | 12 volumes | First American printing, Boston, 1837-1847, 12 volumes, a revision based on | the translation of Clowes and his revisers | Second American printing, 1853-1857 | Third edition ("Rotch") published in New York and Boston, 1892-1908 | First Potts edition, 1905-1910 | Second Potts edition, 1995 | Printed in the United States of America | Library of Congress Cataloging-in-Publication Data | Swedenborg, Emanuel, 1688-1772. | Arcana coelestia = The heavenly arcana contained in the Holy Scripture or | Word of the Lord unfolded, beginning with the book of Genesis; translated | from original Latin by John Clowes; revised and edited by John Faulkner | Potts. -- Standard ed., 2nd Potts ed. | Contents: — v. 10. Numbers 8033-9111 | Translation of: Arcana coelestia quae in scriptura sacra sunt detecta. | 1. Bible. O.T.—Genesis—Commentaries. 2. Bible. O.T.—Exodus— | Commentaries. 3. New Jerusalem Church—Doctrines. I. Potts, John | Faulkner. II. Title. III. Title: Heavenly arcana contained in the Holy | Scripture or Word of the Lord unfolded, beginning with the book of Genesis. | BX8712.A8 1995 230'.94 94-36279 | ISBN 0-87785-256-1 (volume 10) | ISBN 0-87785-262-6 (12-volume set) | Typeset in Garamond by William Ross Woofenden | Designed by Joanna V. Hill | Printed and bound by BookCrafters, Inc. | For information contact: | Swedenborg Foundation | 320 North Church Street | West Chester, PA 19380 <*stet* 1774-1806>
half title: <within a rule border 167 x 101 mm> Arcana | Coelestia | <short rule> | Volume 10 | (Numbers 8033-9111)
section title: <within a rule border 167 x 101 mm> Arcana | Coelestia | <short rule> | Volume 10 | (Numbers 8033-9111)
8vo
half title and title leaves, 4 pp; Contents, pp iii-iv; Editor's preface, pp vii-viii; section title leaf, pp ix-x; text of Exodus 13-21 and n 8033-9111, pp 1-743; Critical notes, pp 745-746.
A revision of the second Potts edition, scanned and reset with minor editorial changes by W R Woofenden.
UK: SOC; USA: SHS

49/01/En 5/101 1997 Hyde 618/1a
<within a rule border 167 x 101 mm> Arcana | Coelestia | <short rule> | *The heavenly arcana contained in the* | *Holy Scripture or Word of the Lord* | *unfolded, beginning with* | *the book of Genesis* | <short rule> | EMANUEL SWEDENBORG | Volume 1 | (Numbers 1-1113) | Translated from the Original Latin by | John Clowes | Revised and Edited by | John Faulkner Potts | STANDARD EDITION | SWEDENBORG FOUNDATION | West Chester, Pennsylvania
verso: © 1995 by the Swedenborg Foundation, Inc. | All rights reserved. No part of this publication may be reproduced or | transmitted in any form or by any means, electronic or mechanical, including | photocopying, recording, or any information storage or retrieval system, | without prior permission from the publisher. | First published in Latin, 8 volumes, London, 1749-1756 | First edition translated by J. Clowes, published in London, 1774-1806, | 12 volumes | First American printing, Boston, 1837-1847, 12 volumes, a revision based on | the translation of Clowes and his revisers | Second American printing, 1853-1857 | Third edition ("Rotch") published in New York and Boston, 1892-1908 | First Potts edition, 1905-1910 | Second Potts edition, 1995-1998 | Printed in the United States of America | Library of Congress Cataloging-in-Publication Data | (CIP has been provided as follows for volumes 8 and 10): | Swedenborg, Emanuel, 1688-1772. | Arcana coelestia = The heavenly arcana contained in the Holy Scripture or | Word of the Lord unfolded, beginning with the book of Genesis; translated | from original Latin by John Clowes; revised and edited by John Faulkner Potts | —Standard ed., 2nd Potts ed. | Contents: — v. 1. Numbers 1-1113 | Translation of: Arcana coelestia quae in scriptura sacra sunt detecta. | 1.Bible. O.T. —Genesis—Commentaries. 2. Bible. O.T.—Exodus— | Commentaries. 3. New Jerusalem Church—Doctrines. I. Potts, John | Faulkner. II. Title. III. Title: Heavenly arcana contained in the Holy | Scripture or Word of the Lord unfolded, beginning with the book of Genesis. | BX8712.A8

1963 230'.94 94-36279 | ISBN 0-87785-213-8 (volume 1) | ISBN 0-87785-262-6 (12-volume set) | Typeset in Garamond by William Ross Woofenden | Designed by Joanna V. Hill | Printed and bound by BookCrafters, Inc. | For information contact: | Swedenborg Foundation | 320 North Church Street | West Chester, PA 19380 <*stet* 1774-1806>
half title: <within a rule border 167 x 101 mm> Arcana | Coelestia | <short rule> | Volume 1 | (Numbers 1-1113)
section title: <within a rule border 167 x 101 mm> | Arcana | Coelestia | <short rule> | Volume 1 | (Numbers 1-1113)
8vo
half title and title leaves, 4 pp; Contents, pp v-vi; Editor's preface, pp vii-viii; Reviser's preface, pp ix-xiii; section title leaf, pp xv-xvi; text of Genesis 1-9 and n 1-1113, pp 1-670; Critical notes, pp 671-673.
UK: SOC; USA: ANC, SHS

49/01/En 7/11 **1997** Hyde 783/4
EMANUEL SWEDENBORG | ARCANA CAELESTIA | <rule> | Principally a Revelation of the | inner or spiritual meaning of | Genesis and Exodus | VOLUME ELEVEN | *Paragraphs 9112-9973* | EXODUS *Chapters 22-28* | TRANSLATED FROM | THE ORIGINAL LATIN BY | JOHN ELLIOTT | LONDON | THE SWEDENBORG SOCIETY | 1997
verso: Published by The Swedenborg Society, Swedenborg House, 20-21 Bloomsbury Way, London WC1A 2TH | © Swedenborg Society 1997 | Designed by James Butler MSIAD | Typeset in Palatino by | Goodfellow & Egan Phototypesetting Ltd, Cambridge | Printed and bound in Great Britain at the | University Press, Cambridge | ISBN 0 85448 123 0 Hard covers | ISBN 0 85448 124 9 Paperback
half title: ARCANA CAELESTIA
8vo
half title and title leaves, 4 pp; Translator's notes, p v; Chapters and paragraphs to volumes of the Latin and English editions, p vii; text of Exodus 22-28 and n 9112-9973, pp 1-616; Word list, p 617; Errata in volumes 2-5, 7-10, pp 619-620.
UK: SOC, CON, NCC, PUR, NR; DEN: RLD; NET: GEN; SWE: ROY; USA: ANC, SHS; AUS: SYD

49/01/En 5/102 **1998** Hyde 643/7
<within a rule border 167 x 101 mm> Arcana | Coelestia | <short rule> | *The heavenly arcana contained in the | Holy Scripture or Word of the Lord | unfolded, beginning with | the book of Genesis* | <short rule> | EMANUEL SWEDENBORG | Volume 2 | (Numbers 1114-2134) | Translated from the Original Latin by | John Clowes | Revised and Edited by | John Faulkner Potts | STANDARD EDITION | SWEDENBORG FOUNDATION | West Chester, Pennsylvania
verso: © 1998 by the Swedenborg Foundation, Inc. | All rights reserved. No part of this publication may be reproduced or | transmitted in any form or by any means, electronic or mechanical, including | photocopying, recording, or any information storage or retrieval system, | without prior permission from the publisher. | First published in Latin, 8 volumes, London, 1749-1756 | First edition translated by J. Clowes, published in London, 1774-1806, | 12 volumes | First American printing, Boston, 1837-1847, 12 volumes, a revision based on | the translation of Clowes and his revisers | Second American printing, 1853-1857 | Third edition ("Rotch") published in New York and Boston, 1892-1908 | First Potts edition, 1905-1910 | Second Potts edition, 1995-1998 | Printed in the United States of America | Library of Congress Cataloging-in-Publication Data | (CIP has been provided as follows for volumes 8 and 10): | Swedenborg, Emanuel, 1688-1772. | Arcana coelestia = The heavenly arcana contained in the Holy Scripture or | Word of the Lord unfolded, beginning with the book of Genesis; translated | from original Latin by John Clowes; revised and edited by John Faulkner Potts. | —Standard ed., 2nd Potts ed. | Contents: —v. 2. Numbers 1114-2134 | Translation of: Arcana coelestia quae in scriptura sacra sunt detecta. | 1.Bible. O.T.—Genesis—Commentaries. 2. Bible. O.T.—Exodus— | Commentaries. 3. New Jerusalem

Church—Doctrines. I. Potts, John | Faulkner. II. Title. III. Title: Heavenly arcana contained in the Holy | Scripture or Word of the Lord unfolded, beginning with the book of Genesis. | BX8712.A8 1963 230'.94 94-36279 | ISBN 0-87785-215-4 (volume 2) | ISBN 0-87785-262-6 (12-volume set) | Typeset in Garamond by William Ross Woofenden | Designed by Joanna V. Hill | Printed and bound by BookCrafters, Inc. | For information contact: | Swedenborg Foundation | 320 North Church Street | West Chester, PA 19380 <*stet* 1774-1806>
half title: <within a rule border 167 x 101 mm> Arcana | Coelestia | <short rule> | Volume 2 | (Numbers 1114-2134)
section title: <within a rule border 167 x 101 mm> Arcana | Coelestia | <short rule> | Volume 2 | (Numbers 1114-2134)
8vo
half title and title leaves, 4 pp; Contents, pp v-vi; Editor's preface, pp vii-viii; section title leaf, pp ix-x; text of Genesis 10-17 and n 1114-2134, pp 1-674; Critical notes, pp 675-677.
A revision of the second Potts edition, scanned and reset with minor editorial changes by W R Woofenden.
UK: SOC; USA: ANC, SHS

49/01/En 5/103 **1998** Hyde 661/6
<within a rule border 167 x 101 mm> Arcana | Coelestia | <short rule> | *The heavenly arcana contained in the* | *Holy Scripture or Word of the Lord* | *unfolded, beginning with* | *the book of Genesis* | <short rule> | EMANUEL SWEDENBORG | Volume 3 | (Numbers 2135-2893) | Translated from the Original Latin by | John Clowes | Revised and Edited by | John Faulkner Potts | STANDARD EDITION | SWEDENBORG FOUNDATION | West Chester, Pennsylvania
verso: © 1998 by the Swedenborg Foundation, Inc. | All rights reserved. No part of this publication may be reproduced or | transmitted in any form or by any means, electronic or mechanical, including | photocopying, recording, or any information storage or retrieval system, | without prior permission from the publisher. | First published in Latin, 8 volumes, London, 1749-1756 | First edition translated by J. Clowes, published in London, 1774-1806, | 12 volumes | First American printing, Boston, 1837-1847, 12 volumes, a revision based on | the translation of Clowes and his revisers | Second American printing, 1853-1857 | Third edition ("Rotch") published in New York and Boston, 1892-1908 | First Potts edition, 1905-1910 | Second Potts edition, 1995-1998 | Printed in the United States of America | Library of Congress Cataloging-in-Publication Data | (CIP has been provided as follows for volumes 8 and 10): | Swedenborg, Emanuel, 1688-1772. | Arcana coelestia = The heavenly arcana contained in the Holy Scripture or | Word of the Lord unfolded, beginning with the book of Genesis; translated | from original Latin by John Clowes; revised and edited by John Faulkner Potts. | —Standard ed., 2nd Potts ed. | Contents: —v. 3. Numbers 2135-2893 | Translation of: Arcana coelestia quae in scriptura sacra sunt detecta. | 1. Bible. O.T.—Genesis— | Commentaries. 2. Bible. O.T.—Exodus—Commentaries. 3. New Jerusalem Church—Doctrines. I. Potts, John | Faulkner. II. Title. III. Title: Heavenly arcana contained in the Holy | Scripture or Word of the Lord unfolded, beginning with the book of Genesis. | BX8712.A8 1963 230'.94 94-36279 | ISBN 0-87785-217-0 (volume 3) | ISBN 0-87785-262-6 (12-volume set) | Typeset in Garamond by William Ross Woofenden | Designed by Joanna V. Hill | Printed and bound by BookCrafters, Inc. | For information contact: | Swedenborg Foundation | 320 North Church Street | West Chester, PA 19380 <*stet* 1774-1806>
half title: <within a rule border 167 x 101 mm> Arcana | Coelestia | <short rule> | Volume 3 | (Numbers 2135-2893)
section title: <within a rule border 167 x 101 mm> Arcana | Coelestia | <short rule> | Volume 3 | (Numbers 2135-2893)
8vo
half title and title leaves, 4 pp; Contents, pp v-vi; Editor's preface, pp vii-viii; section title leaf, pp

ix-x; text of Swedenborg's preface, Genesis 18-22, and n 2135-2893, pp 1-639; Critical notes, p 641. A revision of the second Potts edition, scanned and reset with minor editorial changes by W R Woofenden.

UK: SOC; USA: ANC, SHS

49/01/En 5/104 **1998** Hyde 678/5

<within a rule border 167 x 101 mm> Arcana | Coelestia | <short rule> | *The heavenly arcana contained in the* | *Holy Scripture or Word of the Lord* | *unfolded, beginning with* | *the book of Genesis* | <short rule> | EMANUEL SWEDENBORG | Volume 4 | (Numbers 2894-3649) | Translated from the Original Latin by | John Clowes | Revised and Edited by | John Faulkner Potts | STANDARD EDITION | SWEDENBORG FOUNDATION | West Chester, Pennsylvania

verso: © 1998 by the Swedenborg Foundation, Inc. | All rights reserved. No part of this publication may be reproduced or | transmitted in any form or by any means, electronic or mechanical, including | photocopying, recording, or any information storage or retrieval system, | without prior permission from the publisher. | First published in Latin, 8 volumes, London, 1749-1756 | First edition translated by J. Clowes, published in London, 1774-1806, | 12 volumes | First American printing, Boston, 1837-1847, 12 volumes, a revision based on | the translation of Clowes and his revisers | Second American printing, 1853-1857 | Third edition ("Rotch") published in New York and Boston, 1892-1908 | First Potts edition, 1905-1910 | Second Potts edition, 1995-1998 | Printed in the United States of America | Library of Congress Cataloging-in-Publication Data | (CIP has been provided as follows for volumes 8 and 10): | Swedenborg, Emanuel, 1688-1772. | Arcana coelestia = The heavenly arcana contained in the Holy Scripture or | Word of the Lord unfolded, beginning with the book of Genesis; translated | from original Latin by John Clowes; revised and edited by John Faulkner Potts. | —Standard ed., 2nd Potts ed. | Contents: — v. 4. Numbers 2894-3649 | Translation of: Arcana coelestia quae in scriptura sacra sunt detecta. | 1. Bible. O.T.—Genesis—Commentaries. 2. Bible. O.T.—Exodus—Commentaries. 3. New Jerusalem Church—Doctrines. I. Potts, John | Faulkner. II. Title. III. Title: Heavenly arcana contained in the Holy | Scripture or Word of the Lord unfolded, beginning with the book of Genesis. | BX8712.A8 1963 230'.94 94-36279 | ISBN 0-87785-219-7 (volume 4) | ISBN 0-87785-262-6 (12-volume set) | Typeset in Garamond by William Ross Woofenden | Designed by Joanna V. Hill | Printed and bound by BookCrafters, Inc. | For information contact: | Swedenborg Foundation | 320 North Church Street | West Chester, PA 19380 <*stet* 1774-1806>

half title: <within a rule border 167 x 101 mm> Arcana | Coelestia | <short rule> | Volume 4 | (Numbers 2894-3649)

section title: <within a rule border 167 x 101 mm> Arcana | Coelestia | <short rule> | Volume 4 | (Numbers 2894-3649)

8vo

half title and title leaves, 4 pp; Contents, pp v-vi; Editor's preface, pp vii-viii; section title leaf, pp ix-x; text of Genesis 23-27 and n 2894-3649, pp 1-603; Critical notes, pp 605-606.

A revision of the second Potts edition, scanned and reset with minor editorial changes by W R Woofenden.

UK: SOC; USA: ANC, SHS

49/01/En 5/105 **1998** Hyde 696/5

<within a rule border 166 x 101 mm> Arcana | Coelestia | <short rule> | *The heavenly arcana contained in the* | *Holy Scripture or Word of the Lord* | *unfolded, beginning with* | *the book of Genesis* | <short rule> | EMANUEL SWEDENBORG | Volume 5 | (Numbers 3650-4228) | Translated from the Original Latin by | John Clowes | Revised and Edited by | John Faulkner Potts | STANDARD EDITION | SWEDENBORG FOUNDATION | West Chester, Pennsylvania

verso: © 1998 by the Swedenborg Foundation, Inc. | All rights reserved. No part of this publication may be reproduced or | transmitted in any form or by any means, electronic or mechanical, including | photocopying, recording, or any information storage or retrieval system, | without prior permission from the publisher. | First published in Latin, 8 volumes, London, 1749-1756 | First edition translated by J. Clowes, published in London, 1774-1806, | 12 volumes | First American printing, Boston, 1837-1847, 12 volumes, a revision based on | the translation of Clowes and his revisers | Second American printing, 1853-1857 | Third edition ("Rotch") published in New York and Boston, 1892-1908 | First Potts edition, 1905-1910 | Second Potts edition, 1995-1998 | Printed in the United States of America | Library of Congress Cataloging-in-Publication Data | (CIP has been provided as follows for volumes 8 and 10): | Swedenborg, Emanuel, 1688-1772. | Arcana coelestia = The heavenly arcana contained in the Holy Scripture or | Word of the Lord unfolded, beginning with the book of Genesis; translated | from original Latin by John Clowes; revised and edited by John Faulkner Potts. | —Standard ed., 2nd Potts ed. | Contents: —v. 5. Numbers 3650-4228 | Translation of: Arcana coelestia quae in scriptura sacra sunt detecta. | 1. Bible. O.T.—Genesis— | Commentaries. 2. Bible. O.T.—Exodus—Commentaries. 3. New Jerusalem Church—Doctrines. I. Potts, John | Faulkner. II. Title. III. Title: Heavenly arcana contained in the Holy | Scripture or Word of the Lord unfolded, beginning with the book of Genesis. | BX8712.A8 1963 230'.94 94-36279 | ISBN 0-87785-221-9 (volume 5) | ISBN 0-87785-262-6 (12-volume set) | Typeset in Garamond by William Ross Woofenden | Designed by Joanna V. Hill | Printed and bound by BookCrafters, Inc. | For information contact: | Swedenborg Foundation | 320 North Church Street | West Chester, PA 19380 <*stet* 1774-1806>
half title: <within a rule border 167 x 101 mm> Arcana | Coelestia | <short rule> | Volume 5 | (Numbers 3650-4228)
section title: <within a rule border 167 x 101 mm> Arcana | Coelestia | <short rule> | Volume 5 | (Numbers 3650-4228)
8vo
half title and title leaves, 4 pp; Contents, p v; Editor's preface, pp vii-viii; section title leaf, pp ix-x; text of Genesis 28-31 and n 3650-4228, pp 1-560; Critical notes, pp 561-562.
A revision of the second Potts edition, scanned and reset with minor editorial changes by W R Woofenden.

UK: SOC; USA: ANC, SHS

49/01/En 5/106 **1998** Hyde 712/1a

<within a rule border 167 x 101 mm> Arcana | Coelestia | <short rule> | *The heavenly arcana contained in the* | *Holy Scripture or Word of the Lord* | *unfolded, beginning with* | *the book of Genesis* | <short rule> | EMANUEL SWEDENBORG | Volume 6 | (Numbers 4229-4953) | Translated from the Original Latin by | John Clowes | Revised and Edited by | John Faulkner Potts | STANDARD EDITION | SWEDENBORG FOUNDATION | West Chester, Pennsylvania
verso: © 1998 by the Swedenborg Foundation, Inc. | All rights reserved. No part of this publication may be reproduced or | transmitted in any form or by any means, electronic or mechanical, including | photocopying, recording, or any information storage or retrieval system, | without prior permission from the publisher. | First published in Latin, 8 volumes, London, 1749-1756 | First edition translated by J. Clowes, published in London, 1774-1806, | 12 volumes | First American printing, Boston, 1837-1847, 12 volumes, a revision based on | the translation of Clowes and his revisers | Second American printing, 1853-1857 | Third edition ("Rotch") published in New York and Boston, 1892-1908 | First Potts edition, 1905-1910 | Second Potts edition, 1995-1998 | Printed in the United States of America | Library of Congress Cataloging-in-Publication Data | (CIP has been provided as follows for volumes 8 and 10): | Swedenborg, Emanuel, 1688-1772. | Arcana coelestia = The heavenly arcana contained in the Holy Scripture or | Word of the Lord unfolded, beginning with the book of Genesis; translated | from original Latin by John Clowes; revised and

edited by John Faulkner Potts. | —Standard ed., 2nd Potts ed. | Contents: — v. 6. Numbers 4229-4953 | Translation of: Arcana coelestia quae in scriptura sacra sunt detecta. | 1. Bible. O.T.—Genesis—Commentaries. 2. Bible. O.T.—Exodus—Commentaries. 3. New Jerusalem Church—Doctrines. I. Potts, John | Faulkner. II. Title. III. Title: Heavenly arcana contained in the Holy | Scripture or Word of the Lord unfolded, beginning with the book of Genesis. | BX8712.A8 1963 230'.94 94-36279 | ISBN 0-87785-223-5 (volume 6) | ISBN 0-87785-262-6 (12-volume set) | Typeset in Garamond by William Ross Woofenden | Designed by Joanna V. Hill | Printed and bound by BookCrafters, Inc. | For information contact: | Swedenborg Foundation | 320 North Church Street | West Chester, PA 19380 <*stet* 1774-1806>
half title: <within a rule border 167 x 101 mm> Arcana | Coelestia | <short rule> | Volume 6 | (Numbers 4229-4953)
section title: <within a rule border 167 x 101 mm> Arcana | Coelestia | <short rule> | Volume 6 | (Numbers 4229-4953)
8vo
half title and title leaves, 4 pp; Contents, pp v-vi; Editor's preface, pp vii-viii; section title leaf, pp ix-x; text of Genesis 32-38 and n 4229-4953, pp 1-652; Critical notes, p 653.
A revision of the second Potts edition, scanned and reset with minor editorial changes by W R Woofenden.
UK: soc; USA: ANC, SHS

49/01/En 5/107 1998 Hyde 728/1a

<within a rule border 167 x 101 mm> Arcana | Coelestia | <short rule> | *The heavenly arcana contained in the* | *Holy Scripture or Word of the Lord* | *unfolded, beginning with* | *the book of Genesis* | <short rule> | EMANUEL SWEDENBORG | Volume 7 | (Numbers 4954-5727) | Translated from the Original Latin by | John Clowes | Revised and Edited by | John Faulkner Potts | STANDARD EDITION | SWEDENBORG FOUNDATION | West Chester, Pennsylvania
verso: © 1998 by the Swedenborg Foundation, Inc. | All rights reserved. No part of this publication may be reproduced or | transmitted in any form or by any means, electronic or mechanical, including | photocopying, recording, or any information storage or retrieval system, | without prior permission from the publisher. | First published in Latin, 8 volumes, London, 1749-1756 | First edition translated by J. Clowes, published in London, 1774-1806, | 12 volumes | First American printing, Boston, 1837-1847, 12 volumes, a revision based on | the translation of Clowes and his revisers | Second American printing, 1853-1857 | Third edition ("Rotch") published in New York and Boston, 1892-1908 | First Potts edition, 1905-1910 | Second Potts edition, 1995-1998 | Printed in the United States of America | Library of Congress Cataloging-in-Publication Data | (CIP has been provided as follows for volumes 8 and 10): | Swedenborg, Emanuel, 1688-1772. | Arcana coelestia = The heavenly arcana contained in the Holy Scripture or | Word of the Lord unfolded, beginning with the book of Genesis; translated | from original Latin by John Clowes; revised and edited by John Faulkner Potts. | —Standard ed., 2nd Potts ed. | Contents: —v. 7. Numbers 4954-5727 | Translation of: Arcana coelestia quae in scriptura sacra sunt detecta. | 1. Bible. O.T.—Genesis—Commentaries. 2. Bible. O.T.—Exodus—Commentaries. 3. New Jerusalem Church—Doctrines. I. Potts, John | Faulkner. II. Title. III. Title: Heavenly arcana contained in the Holy | Scripture or Word of the Lord unfolded, beginning with the book of Genesis. | BX8712.A8 1963 230'.94 94-36279 | ISBN 0-87785-250-2 (volume 7) | ISBN 0-87785-262-6 (12-volume set) | Typeset in Garamond by William Ross Woofenden | Designed by Joanna V. Hill | Printed and bound by BookCrafters, Inc. | For information contact: | Swedenborg Foundation | 320 North Church Street | West Chester, PA 19380 <*stet* 1774-1806>
half title: <within a rule border 167 x 101 mm> Arcana | Coelestia | <short rule> | Volume 7 | (Numbers 4954-5727)
section title: <within a rule border 167 x 101 mm> Arcana | Coelestia | <short rule> | Volume 7 | (Numbers 4954-5727)

8vo
half title and title leaves, 4 pp; Contents, p v; Editor's preface, pp vii-viii; section title leaf, pp ix-x; text of Genesis 39-43 and n 4954-5727, pp 1-593; Critical notes, p 595.
A revision of the second Potts edition, scanned and reset with minor editorial changes by W R Woofenden.
UK: SOC; USA: ANC, SHS

49/01/En 5/108 **1998** Hyde 759/b1
<within a rule border 167 x 101 mm> Arcana | Coelestia | <short rule> | *The heavenly arcana contained in the* | *Holy Scripture or Word of the Lord* | *unfolded, beginning with* | *the book of Genesis* | <short rule> | EMANUEL SWEDENBORG | Volume 9 | (Numbers 6627-8032) | Translated from the Original Latin by | John Clowes | Revised and Edited by | John Faulkner Potts | STANDARD EDITION | SWEDENBORG FOUNDATION | West Chester, Pennsylvania
verso: © 1998 by the Swedenborg Foundation, Inc. | All rights reserved. No part of this publication may be reproduced or | transmitted in any form or by any means, electronic or mechanical, including | photocopying, recording, or any information storage or retrieval system, | without prior permission from the publisher. | First published in Latin, 8 volumes, London, 1749-1756 | First edition translated by J. Clowes, published in London, 1774-1806, | 12 volumes | First American printing, Boston, 1837-1847, 12 volumes, a revision based on | the translation of Clowes and his revisers | Second American printing, 1853-1857 | Third edition ("Rotch") published in New York and Boston, 1892-1908 | First Potts edition, 1905-1910 | Second Potts edition, 1995-1998 | Printed in the United States of America | Library of Congress Cataloging-in-Publication Data | (CIP has been provided as follows for volumes 8 and 10): | Swedenborg, Emanuel, 1688-1772. | Arcana coelestia = The heavenly arcana contained in the Holy Scripture or | Word of the Lord unfolded, beginning with the book of Genesis; translated | from original Latin by John Clowes; revised and edited by John Faulkner Potts. | —Standard ed., 2nd Potts ed. | Contents: —v. 9. Numbers 6627-8032 | Translation of: Arcana coelestia quae in scriptura sacra sunt detecta. | 1. Bible. O.T.—Genesis— | Commentaries. 2. Bible. O.T.—Exodus— | Commentaries. 3. New Jerusalem Church—Doctrines. I. Potts, John | Faulkner. II. Title. III. Title: Heavenly arcana contained in the Holy | Scripture or Word of the Lord unfolded, beginning with the book of Genesis. | BX8712.A8 1963 230'.94 94-36279 | ISBN 0-87785-254-5 (volume 9) | ISBN 0-87785-262-6 (12-volume set) | Typeset in Garamond by William Ross Woofenden | Designed by Joanna V. Hill | Printed and bound by BookCrafters, Inc. | For information contact: | Swedenborg Foundation | 320 North Church Street | West Chester, PA 19380 <*stet* 1774-1806>
half title: <within a rule border 167 x 101 mm> Arcana | Coelestia | <short rule> | Volume 9 | (Numbers 6627-8032)
section title: <within a rule border 168 x 111 mm> Arcana | Coelestia | <short rule> | Volume 9 | (Numbers 6627-8032)
8vo
half title and title leaves, 4 pp; Contents, pp v-vi; Editor's preface, pp vii-viii; section title leaf, pp ix-x; text of Exodus 1-12 and n 6627-8032, pp 1-804; Critical notes, pp 805-807.
A revision of the second Potts edition, scanned and reset with minor editorial changes by W R Woofenden.
UK: SOC; USA: ANC, SHS

49/01/En 5/109 **1998** Hyde 783/2a
<within a rule border 166 x 101 mm> Arcana | Coelestia | <short rule> | *The heavenly arcana contained in the* | *Holy Scripture or Word of the Lord* | *unfolded, beginning with* | *the book of Genesis* | <short rule> | EMANUEL SWEDENBORG | Volume 11 | (Numbers 9112-9973) |

Translated from the Original Latin by | John Clowes | Revised and Edited by | John Faulkner Potts | STANDARD EDITION | SWEDENBORG FOUNDATION | West Chester, Pennsylvania
verso: © 1998 by the Swedenborg Foundation, Inc. | All rights reserved. No part of this publication may be reproduced or | transmitted in any form or by any means, electronic or mechanical, including | photocopying, recording, or any information storage or retrieval system, | without prior permission from the publisher. | First published in Latin, 8 volumes, London, 1749-1756 | First edition translated by J. Clowes, published in London, 1774-1806, | 12 volumes | First American printing, Boston, 1837-1847, 12 volumes, a revision based on | the translation of Clowes and his revisers | Second American printing, 1853-1857 | Third edition ("Rotch") published in New York and Boston, 1892-1908 | First Potts edition, 1905-1910 | Second Potts edition, 1995-1998 | Printed in the United States of America | Library of Congress Cataloging-in-Publication Data | (CIP has been provided as follows for volumes 8 and 10): | Swedenborg, Emanuel, 1688-1772. | Arcana coelestia = The heavenly arcana contained in the Holy Scripture or | Word of the Lord unfolded, beginning with the book of Genesis; translated | from original Latin by John Clowes; revised and edited by John Faulkner Potts. | —Standard ed., 2nd Potts ed. | Contents: —v.11. Numbers 9112-9973 | Translation of: Arcana coelestia quae in scriptura sacra sunt detecta. | 1. Bible. O.T.—Genesis— Commentaries. 2. Bible. O.T.—Exodus— | Commentaries. 3. New Jerusalem Church—Doctrines. I. Potts, John | Faulkner. II. Title. III. Title: Heavenly arcana contained in the Holy | Scripture or Word of the Lord unfolded, beginning with the book of Genesis. | BX8712.A8 1963 230'.94 94-36279 | ISBN 0-87785-258-8 (volume 11) | ISBN 0-87785-262-6 (12-volume set) | Typeset in Garamond by William Ross Woofenden | Designed by Joanna V. Hill | Printed and bound by BookCrafters, Inc. | For information contact: | Swedenborg Foundation | 320 North Church Street | West Chester, PA 19380 <*stet* 1774-1806>
half title: <within a rule border 167 x 101 mm> Arcana | Coelestia | <short rule> | Volume 11 | (Numbers 9112-9973)
section title: <within a rule border 168 x 111 mm> Arcana | Coelestia | <short rule> | Volume 11 | (Numbers 9112-9973)
8vo
half title and title leaves, 4 pp; Contents, pp v-vi; Editor's preface, pp vii-viii; section title leaf, pp ix-x; text of Exodus 22-28 and n 9112-9973, pp 1-880; Critical notes, pp 881-882.
A revision of the second Potts edition, scanned and reset with minor editorial changes by W R Woofenden.
UK: soc; USA: anc, shs

49/01/En 5/110 — 1998 — Hyde 792/2a

<within a rule border 167 x 101 mm> Arcana | Coelestia | <short rule> | *The heavenly arcana contained in the | Holy Scripture or Word of the Lord | unfolded, beginning with | the book of Genesis* | <short rule> | EMANUEL SWEDENBORG | Volume 12 | (Numbers 9974-10837) | Translated from the Original Latin by | John Clowes | Revised and Edited by | John Faulkner Potts | STANDARD EDITION | SWEDENBORG FOUNDATION | West Chester, Pennsylvania
verso: © 1998 by the Swedenborg Foundation, Inc. | All rights reserved. No part of this publication may be reproduced or | transmitted in any form or by any means, electronic or mechanical, including | photocopying, recording, or any information storage or retrieval system, | without prior permission from the publisher. | First published in Latin, 8 volumes, London, 1749-1756 | First edition translated by J. Clowes, published in London, 1774-1806, | 12 volumes | First American printing, Boston, 1837-1847, 12 volumes, a revision based on | the translation of Clowes and his revisers | Second American printing, 1853-1857 | Third edition ("Rotch") published in New York and Boston, 1892-1908 | First Potts edition, 1905-1910 | Second Potts edition, 1995-1998 | Printed in the United States of America | Library of Congress Cataloging-in-Publication Data | (CIP has

been provided as follows for volumes 8 and 10): | Swedenborg, Emanuel, 1688-1772. | Arcana coelestia = The heavenly arcana contained in the Holy Scripture or | Word of the Lord unfolded, beginning with the book of Genesis; translated | from original Latin by John Clowes; revised and edited by John Faulkner Potts. | —Standard ed., 2nd Potts ed. | Contents: —v. 12. Numbers 9974-10837 | Translation of: Arcana coelestia quae in scriptura sacra sunt detecta. | 1. Bible. O.T.—Genesis—Commentaries. 2. Bible. O.T.—Exodus— | Commentaries. 3. New Jerusalem Church—Doctrines. I. Potts, John | Faulkner. II. Title. III. Title: Heavenly arcana contained in the Holy | Scripture or Word of the Lord unfolded, beginning with the book of Genesis. | BX8712. A8 1963 230'.94 94-36279 | ISBN 0-87785-260-x (volume 12) | ISBN 0-87785-262-6 (12-volume set) | Typeset in Garamond by William Ross Woofenden | Designed by Joanna V. Hill | Printed and bound by BookCrafters, Inc. | For information contact: | Swedenborg Foundation | 320 North Church Street | West Chester, PA 19380 <*stet* 1774-1806>
half title: <within a rule border 167 x 101 mm> Arcana | Coelestia | <short rule> | Volume 12 | (Numbers 9974-10837)
section title: <within a rule border 168 x 111 mm> Arcana | Coelestia | <short rule> | Volume 12 | (Numbers 9974-10837)
8vo
half title and title leaves, 4 pp; Contents, pp v-vi; Editor's preface, pp vii-viii; section title leaf, pp ix-x; text of Exodus 29-40 n 9974-10837, pp 1-830; Critical notes, pp 831-832.
A revision of the second Potts edition, scanned and reset with minor editorial changes by W R Woofenden.
UK: soc; USA: anc, shs

49/01/En 7/12 **1999** Hyde 792/–
EMANUEL SWEDENBORG | ARCANA CAELESTIA | <rule> | Principally a Revelation of the | inner or spiritual meaning of | Genesis and Exodus | VOLUME TWELVE | *Paragraphs 9974-10837* | EXODUS *Chapters 29-40* | TRANSLATED FROM | THE ORIGINAL LATIN BY | JOHN ELLIOTT | LONDON | THE SWEDENBORG SOCIETY | 1999
verso: Published by The Swedenborg Society, | Swedenborg House, 20-21 Bloomsbury Way, London WC1A 2TH | © Swedenborg Society 1999 | Designed by James Butler MSIAD | Typeset in Palatino by | Goodfellow & Egan Phototypesetting Ltd, Cambridge | Printed and bound in Great Britain at the | University Press, Cambridge | ISBN 0 85448 127 3 Hard covers | ISBN 0 85448 128 1 Paperback
half title: ARCANA CAELESTIA
8vo
half title and title leaves, 4 pp; Translator's notes, p v; Chapters and paragraphs to volumes of the Latin and English editions, p vii; text n 9974-10837, pp 1-577; Word list, p 579; Errata in volumes 1-5, 7, 9-11, pp 581-582.
UK: soc, con, ncc, pur, nr; DEN: rld; NET: gen; USA: anc, shs; AUS: syd

49/01/En 2/236 **2000** Hyde 618/–
<<ARCANA CŒLESTIA. | <short double rule> | THE | HEAVENLY ARCANA | WHICH ARE CONTAINED IN | THE HOLY SCRIPTURES OR WORD | OF THE LORD | UNFOLDED, | BEGINNING WITH THE BOOK OF GENESIS. | TOGETHER WITH | WONDERFUL THINGS SEEN IN THE WORLD OF SPIRITS | AND IN THE HEAVEN OF ANGELS. | <short double rule> | BY | EMANUEL SWEDENBORG, | *Late Member of the House of Nobles in the Royal Diet of Sweden,* | *Assessor of the Royal Board of Mines,* | *Fellow of the Royal Society of Upsala, and of the Royal Academy of Sciences of Stockholm,* | *and Corresponding Member of the Academy of Sciences* | *of St. Petersburg.* | <short double rule> | VOL. I. | <short double rule> | LONDON: | PUBLISHED BY JAMES S. HODSON, | 112, FLEET STREET. | <short rule> | 1837.>>

verso: <<Matthew vi. 33. | *Seek ye first the Kingdom of GOD and his Righteousness,* | *and all these things shall be added unto you.*>>
half title: <<ARCANA CŒLESTIA.>>
verso: <<*This work is printed at the expense of, and published for,* | "THE SOCIETY FOR PRINTING AND PUBLISHING THE | WRITINGS OF EMANUEL SWEDENBORG, INSTITUTED IN | LONDON IN THE YEAR 1810." | <short rule> | London: Printed by J. S. Hodson, 15, Cross Street, Hatton Garden.>>
imprint: <<J. S. Hodson, Printer, Cross Street, Hatton Garden.>>
8vo
half title and title leaves, 4 pp; Translator's preface, pp v-xvi; text of Genesis 1-9 and n 1-1113, pp 1-518; imprint, p 518.
Photographic replica reprint of En 2/31 = Hyde 597, published by Adamant Media Corporation, New York. ISBN 9781402110108 hardback, 9781402183157 paperback.
Copy not seen; description deduced from En 2/31 and publisher's advertisement.

49/01/En 2/237 **2000** Hyde 643/–
<<ARCANA CŒLESTIA: | OR | HEAVENLY MYSTERIES | CONTAINED IN | *THE SACRED SCRIPTURES,* | OR | WORD OF THE LORD, | MANIFESTED AND LAID OPEN: | BEGINNING WITH THE BOOK OF GENESIS. | INTERSPERSED WITH | *RELATIONS OF WONDERFUL THINGS* | SEEN | IN THE WORLD OF SPIRITS AND THE HEAVEN OF ANGELS. | <short double rule> | TRANSLATED FROM THE LATIN OF | EMANUEL SWEDENBORG. | <short double rule> | VOL. II. | THIRD EDITION. | <short wavy rule> | LONDON: | PUBLISHED BY J. S. HODSON, CROSS STREET, HATTON GARDEN: | SOLD ALSO BY W. SIMPKIN AND R. MARSHALL, STATIONERS' HALL COURT, | LUDGATE STREET; T. GOYDER, DARTMOUTH STREET, WESTMINSTER; | AND W. CLARKE, MANCHESTER. | <short rule> | 1831.>>
verso: <<*This Work is printed at the expense of, and published for,* | "THE SOCIETY FOR PRINTING AND PUBLISHING THE | WRITINGS OF THE HON. EMANUEL SWEDENBORG, INSTI- | TUTED IN LONDON IN THE YEAR 1810.">>
imprint: <<J. S. HODSON, Printer, 15, Cross Street, Hatton Garden, London.>>
8vo
title leaf, 2 pp; advertisement <note concerning the formatting of Swedenborg's references to other parts of *Arcana Coelestia*>, 1 p; text of Genesis 10-17 and n 1114-2134, pp 3-547; imprint, p 548.
Photographic replica reprint of En 2/28 = Hyde 627, published by Adamant Media Corporation, New York. ISBN 9781402113871 hardback, 9781402183140 paperback.
Copy not seen; description deduced from En 2/28 and publisher's advertisement.

49/01/En 2/238 **2000** Hyde 661/–
<<ARCANA CŒLESTIA: | OR | HEAVENLY MYSTERIES | CONTAINED IN | *THE SACRED SCRIPTURES,* | OR | WORD OF THE LORD, | MANIFESTED AND LAID OPEN; | BEGINNING WITH THE BOOK OF GENESIS. | INTERSPERSED WITH | *RELATIONS OF WONDERFUL THINGS,* | SEEN | IN THE WORLD OF SPIRITS AND THE HEAVEN OF ANGELS. | <short double rule> | TRANSLATED FROM THE LATIN OF | EMANUEL SWEDENBORG. | <short double rule> | VOL. III. | THIRD EDITION. | <short wavy rule> | LONDON: | PUBLISHED BY J. S. HODSON, CROSS-STREET, HATTON GARDEN: | SOLD ALSO BY W. SIMKIN AND R. MARSHALL, STATIONERS' HALL COURT, | LUDGATE-STREET; T. GOYDER, DARTMOUTH-STREET, WESTMINSTER; | W. CLARKE, SWAIN AND DEWHURST, AND EDWARD BAYLIS, | MANCHESTER. | <short rule> | 1832.>> <*stet* SIMKIN>
verso: <<*This Work is printed at the expense of, and published for,* "THE | SOCIETY FOR PRINTING AND PUBLISHING THE WRITINGS OF THE | HON. EMANUEL SWEDENBORG, INSTITUTED IN MANCHESTER." | T. SOWLER, PRINTER, 4, ST. ANN'S-SQUARE, MANCHESTER.>>
8vo

title leaf, 2 pp; text: Swedenborg's preface, pp 3-4, text of Genesis 18-22 and n 2135-2893, pp 5-503.
Photographic replica reprint of En 2/29 = Hyde 646, published by Adamant Media Corporation, New York. ISBN 9781402126185 hardback, 9781402183133 paperback.
Copy not seen; description deduced from En 2/29 and publisher's advertisement.

49/01/En 2/239 **2000** Hyde 661/–
<<ARCANA CŒLESTIA. | <short double rule> | THE | HEAVENLY ARCANA | WHICH ARE CONTAINED IN | THE HOLY SCRIPTURES OR WORD | OF THE LORD | UNFOLDED, | BEGINNING WITH THE BOOK OF GENESIS. | TOGETHER WITH | WONDERFUL THINGS SEEN IN THE WORLD OF SPIRITS | AND IN THE | HEAVEN OF ANGELS. | <short double rule> | BY | EMANUEL SWEDENBORG. | <short double rule> | VOL IV. | <short double rule> | LONDON: | JAMES S. HODSON 112, FLEET STREET; | WILLIAM NEWBERY, CHENIES STREET, BEDFORD SQUARE; | EDWARD BAYLIS, MANCHESTER. | 1840.>>
verso: <<Matthew vi. 33. | *Seek ye first the Kingdom of GOD and His Righteousness, | and all these things shall be added unto you.*>>
half title: <<ARCANA CŒLESTIA.>>
verso: <<*This work is printed at the expense of, and published for,* | "THE SOCIETY FOR PRINTING AND PUBLISHING THE | WRITINGS OF EMANUEL SWEDENBORG, INSTITUTED IN | LONDON IN THE YEAR 1810." | <short rule> | PRINTED BY WALTON AND MITCHELL, WARDOUR STREET OXFORD STREET.>>
8vo
half title and title leaves, 4 pp; text of Genesis 23-27 and n 2894-3649, pp 5-427.
Photographic replica reprint of En 2/35 = Hyde 664, published by Adamant Media Corporation, New York. ISBN 9781421288857 hardback, 9781402183102 paperback.
Copy not seen; description deduced from En 2/35 and publisher's advertisement.

49/01/En 2/240 **2000** Hyde 696/–
<<ARCANA CŒLESTIA: | OR | HEAVENLY MYSTERIES | CONTAINED IN | THE SACRED SCRIPTURES, | OR | WORD OF THE LORD, | MANIFESTED AND LAID OPEN; | BEGINNING WITH | *THE BOOK OF GENESIS.* | INTERSPERSED WITH | RELATIONS OF WONDERFUL THINGS | SEEN IN | THE WORLD OF SPIRITS AND THE HEAVEN OF ANGELS. | Now first translated from the original Latin of | *EMANUEL SWEDENBORG.* | BY A SOCIETY OF GENTLEMEN. | <short double rule> | VOL. V. | <short double rule> | SECOND EDITION. | *LONDON:* | Printed by J. & E. HODSON, Cross Street, Hatton Garden, | AND SOLD BY LONGMAN, HURST, REES AND ORME, | PATERNOSTER-ROW. | ALSO BY J. AND W. CLARKE, MANCHESTER, AND ALL OTHER | BOOKSELLERS. | <short double rule> | 1808.>>
verso: <<Matt. vi. 33. | *Seek ye first the Kingdom of GOD and his* | *Righteousness, and all things shall be* | *added unto you.*>>
8vo
title leaf, 2 pp; text of Genesis 28-31 and n 3650-4228, pp 3-460.
Photographic replica reprint of En 2/19 = Hyde 680, published by Adamant Media Corporation, New York. ISBN 9781402126192 hardback, 9781402183058 paperback.
Copy not seen; description deduced from En 2/19 and publisher's advertisement.

49/01/En 2/241 **2000** Hyde 696/–
<<ARCANA CŒLESTIA; | OR | *HEAVENLY MYSTERIES* | CONTAINED IN | The sacred Scriptures, or Word of the Lord, | MANIFESTED AND LAID OPEN; | BEGINNING WITH | THE BOOK OF GENESIS. | INTERSPERSED WITH | RELATIONS OF WONDERFUL THINGS | SEEN IN | *The World of Spirits and the Heaven of Angels.* | Now first translated from the original Latin of | *EMANUEL*

SWEDENBORG. | BY A SOCIETY OF GENTLEMEN. | <short double rule> | VOL. VI. | <short double rule> | SECOND EDITION. | <short double rule> | Manchester: | *Printed by J. Gleave, 196, Deansgate;* And Sold by Messrs. Clarke, Manchester; and in London by E. Hodson, | Cross Street, Hatton Garden; T. Goyder, 8, Charles Street, | Westminster; and may be had of all other Booksellers. | <short rule> | 1816.>>
verso: <<Matt vi: 33. | *Seek ye first the Kingdom of GOD and* | *his Righteousness, and all Things* | *shall be added unto you.*>>
imprint: <<Printed by J. Gleave, 196, Deansgate, Manchester.>>
8vo
title leaf, 2 pp; text of Genesis 32-38 and n 4229-4953, pp 3-508; imprint, p 508.
Photographic replica reprint of En 2/22 = Hyde 698, published by Adamant Media Corporation, New York. ISBN 97814021288826 hardback, 9781402183065 paperback.
Copy not seen; description deduced from En 2/22 and publisher's advertisement.

49/01/En 2/242 **2000** Hyde 728/–
<<ARCANA CŒLESTIA; | OR | HEAVENLY MYSTERIES | CONTAINED IN | THE SACRED SCRIPTURES, | OR | WORD OF THE LORD, | MANIFESTED AND LAID OPEN; | BEGINNING WITH | *THE BOOK OF GENESIS.* | INTERSPERSED WITH | RELATIONS OF WONDERFUL THINGS | SEEN IN | THE WORLD OF SPIRITS AND THE HEAVEN OF ANGELS. | Now first translated from the original Latin of | *EMANUEL SWEDENBORG.* | BY A SOCIETY OF GENTLEMEN. | <short double rule> | VOL. VII. | <short double rule> | SECOND EDITION. | *MANCHESTER:* | Printed by J. Gleave, 196, Deansgate; | And Sold by J. and E. Hodson, Cross Street, Hatton Garden, | and Mr. Sibley, 35, Goswell Street, London; | Messrs. Clarkes', Manchester, and all | other Booksellers. | <short double rule> | 1812.>> <*stet* Sibley>
verso: <<Matt. vi. 33. | *Seek ye first the Kingdom of GOD and* | *his Righteousness, and all Things* | *shall be added unto you.*>>
imprint: <<Printed by J. Gleave, 196, Deansgate, Manchester.>>
8vo
title leaf, 2 pp; advertisement concerning the translation of the term 'humanum', 2 pp; text of Genesis 39-43 and n 4954-5727, pp 5-508; imprint, p 508.
Photographic replica reprint of En 2/20 = Hyde 714, published by Adamant Media Corporation, New York. ISBN 97814021262086 hardback, 9781402183041 paperback.
Copy not seen; description deduced from En 2/20 and publisher's advertisement.

49/01/En 2/243 **2000** Hyde 745/–
<<ARCANA CŒLESTIA; | OR | HEAVENLY MYSTERIES | CONTAINED IN | THE SACRED SCRIPTURES, | OR | WORD OF THE LORD, | MANIFESTED AND LAID OPEN; | BEGINNING WITH | *THE BOOK OF GENESIS.* | INTERSPERSED WITH | RELATIONS OF WONDERFUL THINGS | SEEN IN | THE WORLD OF SPIRITS AND THE HEAVEN OF ANGELS. | Now first translated from the original Latin of | *EMANUEL SWEDENBORG.* | BY A SOCIETY OF GENTLEMEN. | <short double rule> | VOL. VIII. | <short double rule> | SECOND EDITION. | *MANCHESTER :* | PRINTED BY J. GLEAVE, DEANSGATE, | AND SOLD BY MR. T. KELLY, NO. 52, PATERNOSTER-ROW, | LONDON; | MESSRS. CLARKES', MANCHESTER, AND ALL OTHER | BOOKSELLERS. | <short double rule> | 1812.>>
verso: <<Matt. vi. 33. | *Seek ye first the Kingdom of GOD and* | *his Righteousness, and all things* | *shall be added unto you.*>>
8vo
title leaf, 2 pp; text of Genesis 44-50 and n 5728-6626, pp 3-449; advertisement, 2 pp.
Photographic replica reprint of En 2/21 = Hyde 730, published by Adamant Media Corporation, New York. ISBN 9781402113840 hardback, 9781402183096 paperback.
Copy not seen; description deduced from En 2/21 and publisher's advertisement.

49/01/En 2/244 **2000** Hyde 759/–

<<ARCANA CŒLESTIA: | OR | HEAVENLY MYSTERIES | CONTAINED IN | *THE SACRED SCRIPTURES,* | OR | WORD OF THE LORD, | MANIFESTED AND LAID OPEN: | BEGINNING WITH THE BOOK OF GENESIS. | INTERSPERSED WITH | *RELATIONS OF WONDERFUL THINGS* | SEEN | IN THE WORLD OF SPIRITS AND THE HEAVEN OF ANGELS. | <short double rule> | TRANSLATED FROM THE ORIGINAL LATIN OF | EMANUEL SWEDENBORG, | *Late Member of the House of Nobles in the Royal Diet of Sweden,* | *Assessor of the Royal Board of Mines,* | *Fellow of the Royal Society of Upsala, and of the Royal Academy of Sciences of Stockholm* | *And Corresponding Member of the Academy of Sciences* | *of St. Petersburg.* | <short double rule> | VOL. IX. | THIRD EDITION. | <short wavy rule> | LONDON : | PUBLISHED BY J. S. HODSON, CROSS STREET, HATTON GARDEN; | SOLD ALSO BY W. SIMPKIN AND R. MARSHALL, STATIONERS' HALL COURT; AND | IN MANCHESTER, BY W. AND R. CLARKE, E. BAYLIS, BANCKS AND CO.; | AND BY ALL OTHER BOOKSELLERS IN TOWN AND COUNTRY. | <short rule> | 1834.>>

verso: <<Matt. vi. 33. | *Seek ye first the Kingdom of GOD and his* | *Righteousness, and all Things shall be added* | *unto you.*>>

half title: <<ARCANA CŒLESTIA : | OR | HEAVENLY MYSTERIES | CONTAINED IN | *THE SACRED SCRIPTURES,* | OR | WORD OF THE LORD, | MANIFESTED AND LAID OPEN. | <short rule> | VOL IX. | <short rule> | *This Work is printed at the expense of, and published for,* | "THE SOCIETY INSTITUTED IN MANCHESTER IN THE | YEAR 1782, FOR PRINTING, PUBLISHING, AND CIRCULAT- | ING THE THEOLOGICAL WRITINGS OF THE HON. EMANUEL | SWEDENBORG, &C.">>

imprint: <<Printed by J. S. Hodson, Cross Street, Hatton Garden.>>

8vo

half title and title leaves, 4 pp; text of Exodus 1-12 and n 6627-8032, pp 1-628; imprint, p 628.

Photographic replica reprint of En 2/30 = Hyde 747, published by Adamant Media Corporation, New York. ISBN 9781402113857 hardback, 9781402183119 paperback.

Copy not seen; description deduced from En 2/30 and publisher's advertisement.

49/01/En 2/245 **2000** Hyde 774/–

<<ARCANA CŒLESTIA: | OR | HEAVENLY MYSTERIES | CONTAINED IN | *THE SACRED SCRIPTURES,* | OR | WORD OF THE LORD, | MANIFESTED AND LAID OPEN; | BEGINNING WITH | *THE BOOK OF GENESIS.* | INTERSPERSED WITH | RELATIONS OF WONDERFUL THINGS | *Seen in the World of Spirits and the Heaven of Angels.* | Now first Translated from the Original Latin of | *EMANUEL SWEDENBORG.* | BY A SOCIETY OF GENTLEMEN. | *SECOND EDITION.* | <short rule> | VOL. X. | <short rule> | MANCHESTER: | Printed by W. D. VAREY, Red Lion-street, St. Ann's Square; | SOLD BY MESSRS. CLARKES, MARKET-PLACE, MANCHESTER. | AND IN LONDON, | BY H. HODSON, CROSS-STREET, HATTON-GARDEN; | T. GOYDER, 8, CHARLES-STREET, WESTMINSTER; AND OTHER | BOOKSELLERS. | 1819.>>

verso: <<Matt. vi. 33. | *Seek ye first the Kingdom of GOD and his* | *Righteousness, and all things shall be* | *added unto you.*>>

imprint: <<W. D. VAREY, Printer, Red Lion Street, | St. Ann's Square, Manchester.>>

8vo

title leaf, 2 pp; text of Exodus 13-21 and n 8033-9111, pp 3-590; imprint, p 590.

Photographic replica reprint of En 2/23 = Hyde 761, published by Adamant Media Corporation, New York. ISBN 9781421288864 hardback, 9781402183126 paperback.

Copy not seen; description deduced from En 2/23 and publisher's advertisement.

49/01/En 2/246 **2000** Hyde 783/–

<<ARCANA CŒLESTIA: | OR | HEAVENLY MYSTERIES | CONTAINED IN | THE SACRED SCRIPTURES, | OR | *WORD OF THE LORD,* | MANIFESTED AND LAID OPEN; | BEGINNING WITH | *THE BOOK*

OF GENESIS: | INTERSPERSED WITH | RELATIONS OF WONDERFUL THINGS | SEEN IN | THE WORLD OF SPIRITS AND THE HEAVEN OF ANGELS. | Now first Translated from the Original Latin of | *EMANUEL SWEDENBORG.* | BY A SOCIETY OF GENTLEMEN. | *SECOND EDITION.* | <short double rule> | VOL. XI. | <short double rule> | MANCHESTER : | Printed by W. D. VAREY, Red Lion-street, St. Ann's-square. | SOLD BY MESSRS. CLARKES, MARKET-PLACE, MANCHESTER. | AND IN LONDON, | BY H. HODSON, CROSS-STREET, HATTON-GARDEN; | T. GOYDER, 8, CHARLES STREET, WESTMINSTER; AND OTHER | BOOKSELLERS. | <short rule> | 1820.>>
verso: <<Matt. vi.33. | *Seek ye first the Kingdom of GOD and His Righteousness,* | *and all things shall be added unto you.*>>
8vo
title leaf, 2 pp; text of Exodus 22-28 and n 9112-9973, pp 3-655.
Photographic replica reprint of En 2/24 = Hyde 776, published by Adamant Media Corporation, New York. ISBN 9781421288840 hardback, 9781402183089 paperback.
Copy not seen; description deduced from En 2/24 and publisher's advertisement.

49/01/En 2/247 **2000** Hyde 792/–
<<ARCANA CŒLESTIA: | OR | HEAVENLY MYSTERIES | CONTAINED IN | THE SACRED SCRIPTURES, | OR | *WORD OF THE LORD,* | MANIFESTED AND LAID OPEN; | BEGINNING WITH | *THE BOOK OF GENESIS:* | INTERSPERSED WITH | RELATIONS OF WONDERFUL THINGS | SEEN IN THE WORLD OF SPIRITS AND THE HEAVEN OF ANGELS. | Now first Translated from the Original Latin of | *EMANUEL SWEDENBORG.* | BY A SOCIETY OF GENTLEMEN. | *SECOND EDITION.* | <short double rule> | VOL. XII. | <short double rule> | MANCHESTER: | Printed by W. D. VAREY, Red Lion-street, St. Ann's-square. | SOLD BY MESSRS. CLARKES, MARKET-PLACE, MANCHESTER. | AND IN LONDON, | BY H. HODSON, CROSS-STREET, HATTON-GARDEN; | T. GOYDER, 8, CHARLES-STREET, WESTMINSTER; AND OTHER | BOOKSELLERS. | <short rule> | 1820.>>
verso: <<Matt. vi. 33. | *Seek ye first the Kingdom of GOD and His* | *Righteousness, and all things shall be* | *added unto you.*>>
8vo
title leaf, 2 pp; text of Exodus 29-40 and n 9974-10837, pp 3-630; Translator's prayer, pp 631-632; Errata in vols 1-11, pp 1-6.
Photographic replica reprint of En 2/25 = Hyde 785, published by Adamant Media Corporation, New York. ISBN 9781421288833 hardback, 9781402183072 paperback.
Copy not seen; description deduced from En 2/25 and publisher's advertisement.

49/01/En 2/248 **2004** Hyde 618/–
<<ARCANA CŒLESTIA. | <short double rule> | THE | HEAVENLY ARCANA | WHICH ARE CONTAINED IN | THE HOLY SCRIPTURES OR WORD | OF THE LORD | UNFOLDED, | BEGINNING WITH THE BOOK OF GENESIS. | TOGETHER WITH | WONDERFUL THINGS SEEN IN THE WORLD OF SPIRITS | AND IN THE HEAVEN OF ANGELS. | <short double rule> | BY | EMANUEL SWEDENBORG, | *Late Member of the House of Nobles in the Royal Diet of Sweden,* | *Assessor of the Royal Board of Mines,* | *Fellow of the Royal Society of Upsala, and of the Royal Academy of Sciences of Stockholm,* | *and Corresponding Member of the Academy of Sciences* | *of St. Petersburg.* | <short double rule> | VOL. I. | <short double rule> | LONDON: | PUBLISHED BY JAMES S. HODSON, | 112, FLEET STREET. | <short rule> | 1837.>>
verso: <<Matthew vi. 33. | *Seek ye first the Kingdom of GOD and his Righteousness,* | *and all these things shall be added unto you.*>>
half title: <<ARCANA CŒLESTIA.>>
verso: <<*This work is printed at the expense of, and published for,* | "THE SOCIETY FOR PRINTING AND PUBLISHING THE | WRITINGS OF EMANUEL SWEDENBORG, INSTITUTED IN |

LONDON IN THE YEAR 1810." | <short rule> | London: Printed by J. S. Hodson, 15, Cross Street, Hatton Garden.>>
imprint: <<J. S. Hodson, Printer, Cross Street, Hatton Garden.>>
8vo
half title and title leaves, 4 pp; Translator's preface, pp v-xvi; text of Genesis 1-9 and n 1-1113, pp 1-518; imprint, p 518.
Photographic replica reprint of En 2/31 = Hyde 597, published by Kessinger Publishing, Whitefish MT. Printed in the United States.
Copy not seen; description deduced from En 2/31 and **E:b** En 2004/1.

49/01/En 2/249 **2004** Hyde 661/–
<<ARCANA CŒLESTIA: | OR | HEAVENLY MYSTERIES | CONTAINED IN | *THE SACRED SCRIPTURES,* | OR | WORD OF THE LORD, | MANIFESTED AND LAID OPEN; | BEGINNING WITH THE BOOK OF GENESIS. | INTERSPERSED WITH | *RELATIONS OF WONDERFUL THINGS,* | SEEN | IN THE WORLD OF SPIRITS AND THE HEAVEN OF ANGELS. | <short double rule> | TRANSLATED FROM THE LATIN OF | EMANUEL SWEDENBORG. | <short double rule> | VOL. III. | THIRD EDITION. | <short wavy rule> | LONDON: | PUBLISHED BY J. S. HODSON, CROSS-STREET, HATTON GARDEN: | SOLD ALSO BY W. SIMKIN AND R. MARSHALL, STATIONERS' HALL COURT, | LUDGATE-STREET; T. GOYDER, DARTMOUTH-STREET, WESTMINSTER; | W. CLARKE, SWAIN AND DEWHURST, AND EDWARD BAYLIS, | MANCHESTER. | <short rule> | 1832.>> <*stet* SIMKIN>
verso: <<*This Work is printed at the expense of, and published for,* "THE | SOCIETY FOR PRINTING AND PUBLISHING THE WRITINGS OF THE | HON. EMANUEL SWEDENBORG, INSTITUTED IN MANCHESTER." | T. SOWLER, PRINTER, 4, ST. ANN'S-SQUARE, MANCHESTER.>>
8vo
title leaf, 2 pp; text of Swedenborg's preface, pp 3-4, text of Genesis 18-22 and n 2135-2893, pp 5-503.
Photographic replica reprint of En 2/29 = Hyde 646, published by Kessinger Publishing, Whitefish MT. Printed in the United States.
Copy not seen; description deduced from En 2/29 and **E:b** En 2004/1.

49/01/En 2/250 **2004** Hyde 678/–
<<ARCANA CŒLESTIA. | <short rule> | THE | HEAVENLY ARCANA | WHICH ARE CONTAINED IN | THE HOLY SCRIPTURES OR WORD | OF THE LORD | UNFOLDED, | BEGINNING WITH THE BOOK OF GENESIS. | TOGETHER WITH | WONDERFUL THINGS SEEN IN THE WORLD OF SPIRITS | AND IN THE | HEAVEN OF ANGELS. | <short double rule> | BY | EMANUEL SWEDENBORG. | <short double rule> | VOL IV. | <short double rule> | LONDON: | JAMES S. HODSON 112, FLEET STREET; | WILLIAM NEWBERY, CHENIES STREET, BEDFORD SQUARE; | EDWARD BAYLIS, MANCHESTER. | 1840.>>
verso: <<Matthew vi. 33. | *Seek ye first the Kingdom of GOD and His Righteousness,* | *and all these things shall be added unto you.*>>
half title: <<ARCANA CŒLESTIA.>>
verso: <<*This work is printed at the expense of, and published for,* | "THE SOCIETY FOR PRINTING AND PUBLISHING THE | WRITINGS OF EMANUEL SWEDENBORG, INSTITUTED IN | LONDON IN THE YEAR 1810." | <short rule> | PRINTED BY WALTON AND MITCHELL, WARDOUR STREET OXFORD STREET.>>
8vo
half title and title leaves, 4 pp; text of Genesis 17-20 and n 2894-3649, pp 5-427.
Photographic replica reprint of En 2/35 = Hyde 664, published by Kessinger Publishing, Whitefish MT. Printed in the United States.
Copy not seen; description deduced from En 2/35 and **E:b** En 2004/1.

49/01/En 2/251 **2004** Hyde 696/–

<<ARCANA CŒLESTIA: | OR | HEAVENLY MYSTERIES | CONTAINED IN | THE SACRED SCRIPTURES, | OR | WORD OF THE LORD, | MANIFESTED AND LAID OPEN; | BEGINNING WITH | *THE BOOK OF GENESIS.* | INTERSPERSED WITH | RELATIONS OF WONDERFUL THINGS | SEEN IN | THE WORLD OF SPIRITS AND THE HEAVEN OF ANGELS. | Now first translated from the original Latin of | *EMANUEL SWEDENBORG.* | BY A SOCIETY OF GENTLEMEN. | <short double rule> | VOL. V. | <short double rule> | SECOND EDITION. | *LONDON:* | Printed by J. & E. HODSON, Cross Street, Hatton Garden, | AND SOLD BY LONGMAN, HURST, REES AND ORME, | PATERNOSTER-ROW. | ALSO BY J. AND W. CLARKE, MANCHESTER, AND ALL OTHER | BOOKSELLERS. | <short double rule> | 1808.>>

verso: <<Matt. vi. 33. | *Seek ye first the Kingdom of GOD and his* | *Righteousness, and all things shall be* | *added unto you.*>>

8vo

title leaf, 2 pp; text of Genesis 28-31 and n 3650-4228, pp 3-460.

Photographic replica reprint of En 2/18 = Hyde 663, published by Kessinger Publishing, Whitefish MT. Printed in the United States.

Copy not seen; description deduced from En 2/19 and **E:b** En 2004/1.

49/01/En 2/252 **2004** Hyde 712/–

<<ARCANA CŒLESTIA; | OR | *HEAVENLY MYSTERIES* | CONTAINED IN | The sacred Scriptures, or Word of the Lord, | MANIFESTED AND LAID OPEN; | BEGINNING WITH | THE BOOK OF GENESIS. | INTERSPERSED WITH | RELATIONS OF WONDERFUL THINGS | SEEN IN | *The World of Spirits and the Heaven of Angels.* | Now first translated from the original Latin of | *EMANUEL SWEDENBORG.* | BY A SOCIETY OF GENTLEMEN. | <short double rule> | VOL. VI. | <short double rule> | SECOND EDITION. | <short double rule> | Manchester: | *Printed by J. Gleave, 196, Deansgate;* And Sold by Messrs. Clarke, Manchester; and in London by E. Hodson, | Cross Street, Hatton Garden; T. Goyder, 8, Charles Street, | Westminster; and may be had of all other Booksellers. | <short rule> | 1816.>>

verso: <<Matt vi: 33. | *Seek ye first the Kingdom of GOD and* | *his Righteousness, and all Things* | *shall be added unto you.*>>

imprint: <<Printed by J. Gleave, 196, Deansgate, Manchester.>>

8vo

title leaf, 2 pp; text of Genesis 32-38 and n 4229-4953, pp 3-508; imprint, p 508.

Photographic replica reprint of En 2/22 = Hyde 698, published by Kessinger Publishing, Whitefish MT. Printed in the United States.

Copy not seen; description deduced from En 2/22 and **E:b** En 2004/1.

49/01/En 2/253 **2004** Hyde 745/–

<<ARCANA CŒLESTIA; | OR | HEAVENLY MYSTERIES | CONTAINED IN | THE SACRED SCRIPTURES, | OR | WORD OF THE LORD, | MANIFESTED AND LAID OPEN; | BEGINNING WITH | *THE BOOK OF GENESIS.* | INTERSPERSED WITH | RELATIONS OF WONDERFUL THINGS | SEEN IN | THE WORLD OF SPIRITS AND THE HEAVEN OF ANGELS. | Now first translated from the original Latin of | *EMANUEL SWEDENBORG.* | BY A SOCIETY OF GENTLEMEN. | <short double rule> | VOL. VIII. | <short double rule> | SECOND EDITION. | *MANCHESTER :* | PRINTED BY J. GLEAVE, DEANSGATE, | AND SOLD BY MR. T. KELLY, NO. 52, PATERNOSTER-ROW, | LONDON; | MESSRS. CLARKES', MANCHESTER, AND ALL OTHER | BOOKSELLERS. | <short double rule> | 1812.>>

verso: <<Matt. vi. 33. | *Seek ye first the Kingdom of GOD and* | *his Righteousness, and all things* | *shall be added unto you.*>>

8vo

title leaf, 2 pp; text of Genesis 44-50 and n 5728-6626, pp 3-449; advertisement, 2 pp.
Photographic replica reprint of En 2/21 = Hyde 730, published by Kessinger Publishing, Whitefish MT. Printed in the United States.
Copy not seen; description deduced from En 2/21 and **E:b** En 2004/1.

49/01/En 2/254 **2004** Hyde 759/–

<<ARCANA CŒLESTIA: | OR | HEAVENLY MYSTERIES | CONTAINED IN | *THE SACRED SCRIPTURES*, | OR | WORD OF THE LORD, | MANIFESTED AND LAID OPEN: | BEGINNING WITH THE BOOK OF GENESIS. | INTERSPERSED WITH | *RELATIONS OF WONDERFUL THINGS* | SEEN | IN THE WORLD OF SPIRITS AND THE HEAVEN OF ANGELS. | <short double rule> | TRANSLATED FROM THE ORIGINAL LATIN OF | EMANUEL SWEDENBORG, | *Late Member of the House of Nobles in the Royal Diet of Sweden,* | *Assessor of the Royal Board of Mines,* | *Fellow of the Royal Society of Upsala, and of the Royal Academy of Sciences of Stockholm* | *And Corresponding Member of the Academy of Sciences* | *of St. Petersburg.* | <short double rule> | VOL. IX. | THIRD EDITION. | <short wavy rule> | LONDON : | PUBLISHED BY J. S. HODSON, CROSS STREET, HATTON GARDEN; | SOLD ALSO BY W. SIMPKIN AND R. MARSHALL, STATIONERS' HALL COURT; AND | IN MANCHESTER, BY W. AND R. CLARKE, E. BAYLIS, BANCKS AND CO.; | AND BY ALL OTHER BOOKSELLERS IN TOWN AND COUNTRY. | <short rule> | 1834.>>
verso: <<Matt. vi. 33. | *Seek ye first the Kingdom of GOD and his* | *Righteousness, and all Things shall be added* | *unto you.*>>
half title: <<ARCANA CŒLESTIA : | OR | HEAVENLY MYSTERIES | CONTAINED IN | *THE SACRED SCRIPTURES*, | OR | WORD OF THE LORD, | MANIFESTED AND LAID OPEN. | <short rule> | VOL IX. | <short rule> | *This Work is printed at the expense of, and published for,* | "THE SOCIETY INSTITUTED IN MANCHESTER IN THE | YEAR 1782, FOR PRINTING, PUBLISHING, AND CIRCULAT- | ING THE THEOLOGICAL WRITINGS OF THE HON. EMANUEL | SWEDENBORG, &C.">>
imprint: <<Printed by J. S. Hodson, Cross Street, Hatton Garden.>>
8vo
half title and title leaves, 4 pp; text of Exodus 1-12 and n 6627-8032, pp 1-628; imprint, p 628.
Photographic replica reprint of En 2/30 = Hyde 747, published by Kessinger Publishing, Whitefish MT. Printed in the United States.
Copy not seen; description deduced from En 2/30 and **E:b** En 2004/1.

49/01/En 2/255 **2004** Hyde 774/–

<<ARCANA CŒLESTIA. | <short rule> | THE | HEAVENLY MYSTERIES | CONTAINED IN | THE HOLY SCRIPTURE, OR WORD OF THE LORD, | UNFOLDED, | IN AN EXPOSITION OF GENESIS AND EXODUS: | TOGETHER WITH A RELATION OF | WONDERFUL THINGS SEEN IN THE WORLD OF SPIRITS AND | IN THE HEAVEN OF ANGELS. | <short double rule> | BY EMANUEL SWEDENBORG. | <short double rule> | BEING A TRANSLATION OF HIS WORK ENTITLED | "ARCANA CŒLESTIA QUÆ IN SCRIPTURA SACRA, SEU VERBO DOMINI SUNT, DETECTA; HIC | PRIMUM QUÆ IN GENESI. UNA CUM MIRABILIBUS QUÆ VISA SUNT IN MUNDO SPIRITUUM | ET IN CŒLO ANGELORUM. LONDINI, 1749-1756." | IN TWELVE VOLUMES. | VOLUME X. | EXODUS, CHAPTER XIII. TO CHAPTER XXI. | LONDON: | PUBLISHED BY THE SWEDENBORG SOCIETY, | (INSTITUTED 1810,) | 36 BLOOMSBURY STREET, OXFORD STREET, W.C. | 1864.>>
verso: <<Matthew vi. 33. | *Seek ye first the kingdom of God and His righteousness,* | *and all these things shall be added unto you.*>>
half title: <<ARCANA CŒLESTIA.>>
verso: <<*This Work is printed at the expense of, and published for,* | "THE SOCIETY FOR PRINTING AND PUBLISHING THE | WRITINGS OF EMANUEL SWEDENBORG, INSTITUTED IN | LONDON IN THE YEAR 1810." | <short rule> | MITCHELL AND SON, PRINTERS, WARDOUR STREET, W.>>

8vo
half title and title leaves, 4 pp; text of Exodus 13-21 and n 8033-9111, pp 5-514.
Photographic replica reprint of En 2/102 = Hyde 768, published by Kessinger Publishing, Whitefish MT. Printed in the United States.
Copy not seen; description deduced from En 2/102 and **E:b** En 2004/1.

49/01/En 2/256 **2004** Hyde 783/–
<<ARCANA CŒLESTIA: | OR | HEAVENLY MYSTERIES | CONTAINED IN | THE SACRED SCRIPTURES, | OR | *WORD OF THE LORD,* | MANIFESTED AND LAID OPEN; | BEGINNING WITH | *THE BOOK OF GENESIS:* | INTERSPERSED WITH | RELATIONS OF WONDERFUL THINGS | SEEN IN | THE WORLD OF SPIRITS AND THE HEAVEN OF ANGELS. | Now first Translated from the Original Latin of | *EMANUEL SWEDENBORG.* | BY A SOCIETY OF GENTLEMEN. | *SECOND EDITION.* | <short double rule> | VOL. XI. | <short double rule> | MANCHESTER : | Printed by W. D. VAREY, Red Lion-street, St. Ann's-square. | SOLD BY MESSRS. CLARKES, MARKET-PLACE, MANCHESTER. | AND IN LONDON, | BY H. HODSON, CROSS-STREET, HATTON-GARDEN; | T. GOYDER, 8, CHARLES STREET, WESTMINSTER ; AND OTHER | BOOKSELLERS. | <short rule> | 1820.>>
verso: <<Matt. vi.33. | *Seek ye first the Kingdom of GOD and His Righteousness,* | *and all things shall be added unto you.*>>
8vo
title leaf, 2 pp; text of Exodus 22-28 and n 9112-9973, pp 3-655.
Photographic replica reprint of En 2/24 = Hyde 776, published by Kessinger Publishing, Whitefish MT. Printed in the United States.
Copy not seen; description deduced from En 2/24 and **E:b** En 2004/1.

49/01/En 2/257 **2004** Hyde 792/–
<<ARCANA CŒLESTIA: | OR | HEAVENLY MYSTERIES | CONTAINED IN | THE SACRED SCRIPTURES, | OR | *WORD OF THE LORD,* | MANIFESTED AND LAID OPEN; | BEGINNING WITH | *THE BOOK OF GENESIS:* | INTERSPERSED WITH | RELATIONS OF WONDERFUL THINGS | SEEN IN THE WORLD OF SPIRITS AND THE HEAVEN OF ANGELS. | Now first Translated from the Original Latin of | *EMANUEL SWEDENBORG.* | BY A SOCIETY OF GENTLEMEN. | *SECOND EDITION.* | <short double rule> | VOL. XII. | <short double rule> | MANCHESTER: | Printed by W. D. VAREY, Red Lion-street, St. Ann's-square. | SOLD BY MESSRS. CLARKES, MARKET-PLACE, MANCHESTER. | AND IN LONDON, | BY H. HODSON, CROSS-STREET, HATTON-GARDEN; | T. GOYDER, 8, CHARLES-STREET, WESTMINSTER; AND OTHER | BOOKSELLERS. | <short rule> | 1820.>>
verso: <<Matt. vi. 33. | *Seek ye first the Kingdom of GOD and His* | *Righteousness, and all things shall be* | *added unto you.*>>
8vo
title leaf, 2 pp; text of Exodus 29-40 and n 9974-10837, pp 3-630; Translator's prayer, pp 631-632; Errata in vols 1-11, pp 1-6.
Photographic replica reprint of En 2/25 = Hyde 785, published by Kessinger Publishing, Whitefish MT. Printed in the United States.
Copy not seen; description deduced from En 2/25 and **E:b** En 2004/1.

49/01/En 7/13 **2006** Hyde 618/–
EMANUEL SWEDENBORG | ARCANA CAELESTIA | <rule> | Principally a Revelation of the | inner or spiritual meaning of | Genesis and Exodus | VOLUME ONE | *Paragraphs 1-1113* | GENESIS 1 *Chapters 1-9* | TRANSLATED FROM | THE ORIGINAL LATIN BY | JOHN ELLIOTT | LONDON | THE SWEDENBORG SOCIETY | 1983
verso: Published by The Swedenborg Society | Swedenborg House, 20-21 Bloomsbury Way, London

WC1A 2TH | © Swedenborg Society 1983 | Designed by James Butler MSIAD | Typeset in Palatino by | Goodfellow & Egan Phototypesetting Ltd, Cambridge | Printed and bound in Great Britain at the | University Press, Cambridge | ISBN 0 85448 088 9 Hard covers | ISBN 0 85448 088 9 Hard covers | ISBN 0 85448 089 7 Paperback
half title: ARCANA CAELESTIA
section title: THE BOOK | OF GENESIS | <rule>
8vo
half title and title leaves, 4 pp; Translator's introduction, pp v-xv; Chapters and paragraphs to volumes of the Latin and English editions, p xvi; translation of title page of La 1/1, p xvi; reproduction of title page of La 1/1, 1 p; text of Swedenborg's introductory note, p 1; section title leaf, pp 3-4; text of Genesis 1-9 and n 1-1113, pp 5-473; Word list, p 475.
Sheets of En 7/1 reissued in a redesigned paperback binding.
UK: SOC

49/01/En 8/1 **2008** Hyde 618/14
<in black and red> A Disclosure of | SECRETS OF HEAVEN | Contained in | SACRED SCRIPTURE | or THE WORD OF THE LORD | Here First Those in | Genesis | *Together with Amazing Things Seen | in the World of Spirits & in the Heaven of Angels* | EMANUEL SWEDENBORG | Volume 1 | Translated from the Latin by Lisa Hyatt Cooper | With a Reader's Guide by William Ross Woofenden and Jonathan S. Rose | An Introduction by Wouter J. Hanegraaff | And Notes by Reuben P. Bell, Lisa Hyatt Cooper, George F. Dole, Robert H. Kirven, | James F. Lawrence, Grant H. Odhner, John L. Odhner, Jonathan S. Rose, | Stuart Shotwell, Richard Smoley, and Lee S. Woofenden | <2 spaced rules> | <orn NR 327> | <2 spaced rules> | SWEDENBORG FOUNDATION | *West Chester, Pennsylvania*
verso: © Copyright 2008 by the Swedenborg Foundation, Inc. All rights reserved. No part of this pub- | lication may be reproduced or transmitted in any form or by any means, electronic or mechani- | cal, including photocopying, recording, or any information storage or retrieval system, without | prior permission from the publisher. Printed in the United States of America. This book is | printed on acid-free paper that meets the ANSI Z39.48-1992 standard. | Originally published in Latin as *Arcana Coelestia*, London, 1749-1756. The present volume is | indicated in red type in the list below. | <The list is reproduced here as in the volume>

Volume number in this edition	Text treated	Volume number in the Latin first edition	Section numbers	ISBN (of hardcover except where noted)
<in red> 1	Genesis 1–8	1	§§1–946	978-0-87785-486-9 978-0-87785-504-0 (pb)
2	Genesis 9–15	1	§§947–1885	978-0-87785-487-6
3	Genesis 16–21	2 (in 6 fascicles)	§§1886–2759	978-0-87785-488-3
4	Genesis 22–26	3	§§2760–3485	978-0-87785-489-0
5	Genesis 27–30	3	§§3486–4055	978-0-87785-490-6
6	Genesis 31–35	4	§§4056–4634	978-0-87785-491-3
7	Genesis 36–40	4	§§4635–5190	978-0-87785-492-0
8	Genesis 41–44	5	§§5191–5866	978-0-87785-493-7
9	Genesis 45–50	5	§§5867–6626	978-0-87785-494-4
10	Exodus 1–8	6	§§6627–7487	978-0-87785-495-1
11	Exodus 9–15	6	§§7488–8386	978-0-87785-496-8
12	Exodus 16–21	7	§§8387–9111	978-0-87785-497-5
13	Exodus 22–24	7	§§9112–9442	978-0-87785-498-2
14	Exodus 25–29	8	§§9443–10166	978-0-87785-499-9
15	Exodus 30–40	8	§§10167–10837	978-0-87785-500-2 |

Library of Congress Cataloging-in-Publication Data | Swedenborg, Emanuel, 1688–1772. | [Arcana coelestia. English] | A disclosure of secrets of heaven contained in Sacred Scripture, or, The Word of the Lord: | here first those in Genesis, together with amazing things seen in the world of spirits and in the | heaven of angels / Emanuel Swedenborg; translated from the Latin by Lisa Hyatt Cooper; | with introductions by Wouter J. Hanegraaff and William Ross Woofenden; annotated by Lisa Hyatt Cooper and Richard Smoley. | p. cm. -- (The new century edition of the works of Emanuel Swedenborg) | Includes bibliographical references (v. 1, p.). | ISBN 978-0-87785-486-9 (hard cover) – ISBN 978-0-87785-504-0 (pbk.) | 1. New Jerusalem Church–Doctrines. 2. Bible. O.T. Genesis–Commentaries. | 3. Bible. O.T. Exodus–Commentaries. I. Cooper, Lisa Hyatt. II. Smoley, | Richard, 1956– III. Title. IV. Series: Swedenborg, Emanuel, 1688–1772. | Works. English. 2000. | BX8712.A8 2006 | 230´.94--dc22 | Senior copy editor, Alicia L. Dole. Cover design by Caroline Kline and Karen Connor. Text designed by Joanna V. Hill. Typesetting and diagrams by Alicia L. Dole. Index to prefaces, | reader's guide, introduction, and notes by Chara Cooper Daum, Alicia L. Dole, Kate Mertes, and | Chara M. Odhner. Ornaments from the first Latin edition, 1749. | Paperback cover image: NASA, C. R. O'Dell and S. K. Wong (Rice University) | Certain Scripture quotations so identified in the annotations are from the New Revised Standard | Version Bible, copyright © 1989 National Council of the Churches of Christ in the United States | of America. Used by permission. All rights reserved. | For information about the New Century Edition of the Works of Emanuel Swedenborg, contact | the Swedenborg Foundation, 320 North Church Street, West Chester, PA 19380 U.S.A.

half title: <in red> SECRETS | OF | HEAVEN

verso: The New Century Edition | of the Works of Emanuel Swedenborg | <short rule> | Jonathan S. Rose | Series Editor | Stuart Shotwell | Managing Editor | EDITORIAL COMMITTEE | Wendy E. Closterman | Lisa Hyatt Cooper | George F. Dole | Sylvia Shaw | Alice B. Skinner

section title: <in red> SECRETS | OF | HEAVEN

verso: First seek God's kingdom and its justice | and you will gain all. | – Matthew 6:33

2nd section title: <in red> Notes & Indexes

4to

half title and title leaves, 4 pp; Contents, pp V-VIII; Series editor's preface, pp 1-2; Translator's preface, pp 3-12; Works cited in the translator's preface, p 13; Selected list of editions of *Secrets of Heaven*, pp 14-15; A reader's guide to *Secrets of Heaven*, pp 17-59; Works cited in the reader's guide, pp 60-61; Introduction: 'Swedenborg's Magnum Opus', Wouter Hanegraaff, pp 63-118; Appendix: the structure of *Secrets of Heaven*, pp 119-124; Works cited in the introduction, pp 125-129; Short titles and other conventions used in this work, pp 131-139; section title leaf, pp 141-142; Swedenborg's table of contents, pp 143-144; text of Genesis 1-8 and n 1-946, pp 145-592; 2nd section title leaf, pp 593-594; Notes, pp 595-652; Works cited in the notes, pp 653-657; Index to prefaces, reader's guide, introduction, and notes, pp 659-672; Index to text of vol 1, pp 673-758; Biographical note concerning Swedenborg, p 759.

UK: SOC; USA: ANC, CGR, FOU, SHS

49/01/En 8/2 **2010** Hyde 618/15

SECRETS | OF | HEAVEN | *The Portable New Century Edition* | EMANUEL SWEDENBORG | Volume 1 | Translated from the Latin by Lisa Hyatt Cooper | <double rule> | <orn NR 327> | <double rule> | SWEDENBORG FOUNDATION | *West Chester, Pennsylvania*

verso: © Copyright 2010 by the Swedenborg Foundation, Inc. All rights reserved. No part of this pub- | lication may be reproduced or transmitted in any form or by any means, electronic or mechani- | cal, including photocopying, recording, or any information storage or retrieval system, without | prior permission from the publisher. Printed in the United States of America. This book is | printed on acid-free paper that meets the ANSI Z39.48-1992 standard. | Originally published in Latin as *Arcana Coelestia*, London, 1749-1756. Annotated editions of this | volume are available as follows: | <The list is reproduced here as in the volume>

Volume number in this edition	Text treated	Volume number in the Latin first edition	Section numbers	ISBN (of hardcover except where noted)
1	Genesis 1–8	1	§1–946	978-0-87785-486-9 978-0-87785-504-0 (pb)
2	Genesis 9–15	1	§§947–1885	978-0-87785-487-6
3	Genesis 16–21	2 (in 6 fascicles)	§§1886–2759	978-0-87785-488-3
4	Genesis 22–26	3	§§2760–3485	978-0-87785-489-0
5	Genesis 27–30	3	§§3486–4055	978-0-87785-490-6
6	Genesis 31–35	4	§§4056–4634	978-0-87785-491-3
7	Genesis 36–40	4	§§4635–5190	978-0-87785-492-0
8	Genesis 41–44	5	§§5191–5866	978-0-87785-493-7
9	Genesis 45–50	5	§§5867–6626	978-0-87785-494-4
10	Exodus 1–8	6	§§6627–7487	978-0-87785-495-1
11	Exodus 9–15	6	§§7488–8386	978-0-87785-496-8
12	Exodus 16–21	7	§§8387–9111	978-0-87785-497-5
13	Exodus 22–24	7	§§9112–9442	978-0-87785-498-2
14	Exodus 25–29	8	§§9443–10166	978-0-87785-499-9
15	Exodus 30–40	8	§§10167–10837	978-0-87785-500-2 |

Library of Congress Cataloging-in-Publication Data | Swedenborg, Emanuel, 1688-1772. | [Arcana coelestia. English] | Secrets of heaven / Emanuel Swedenborg; translated from the Latin by | Lisa Hyatt Cooper. — Portable New Century ed. | p. cm. | Includes bibliographical references and indexes. | ISBN 978-0-87785-408-1 (alk. paper) | 1. New Jerusalem Church—Doctrines. 2. Bible. O.T. Genesis—Commentaries—Early | works to 1800. 3. Bible. O.T. Exodus—Commentaries—Early works to 1800. 1. Title. | BX8712.A8 2010 | 230'.94--dc22 | 2009054171 | Senior copy editor, Alicia L. Dole. | Text designed by Joanna V. Hill. | Typesetting and diagrams by Alicia L. Dole. | Index to prefaces, reader's guide, introduction, and notes by Chara Cooper Daum, Alicia L. Dole, Kate Mertes, and Chara M. Odhner. | Ornaments from the first Latin edition, 1749. | Cover design by Karen Connor. | Certain Scripture quotations so identified in the annotations are from the New Revised Standard | Version Bible, copyright © 1989 National Council of the Churches of Christ in the United States | of America. Used by permission. All rights reserved. | For information about the New Century Edition of the Works of Emanuel Swedenborg, contact | the Swedenborg Foundation, 320 North Church Street, West Chester, PA 19380 U.S.A. | tel: 800-355-3222 • web: www.swedenborg.com • email: info@swedenborg.com

half title: SECRETS | OF | HEAVEN

section title: SECRETS | OF | HEAVEN

verso: First seek God's kingdom and its justice | and you will gain all. | —Matthew 6:33

8vo

half title and title leaves, 4 pp; Contents, pp V-VIII; Conventions used in this work, pp IX-XI; section title leaf, pp 1-2; Swedenborg's table of contents, pp 3-4; text of Genesis 1-8 and n 1-946, pp 5-452; Index, pp 453-538; Biographical note, p 539.

UK: soc; USA: anc, fou

49/01/En 8/3 **2012** **Hyde 643/8**

SECRETS | OF | HEAVEN | *The Portable New Century Edition* | EMANUEL SWEDENBORG | Volume 2 | Translated from the Latin by Lisa Hyatt Cooper | <double rule> | <orn NR 327> | <double rule> | SWEDENBORG FOUNDATION | *West Chester, Pennsylvania*

verso: © Copyright 2012 by the Swedenborg Foundation, Inc. All rights reserved. No part of this pub- | lication may be reproduced or transmitted in any form or by any means, electronic or mechani- | cal, including photocopying, recording, or any information storage or retrieval system, without | prior permission from the publisher. Printed in the United States of America. This book is | printed on acid-free paper that meets the ANSI Z39.48-1992 standard. | Originally published in Latin as *Arcana Coelestia*, London, 1749-1756. The volume contents of | this and the original Latin edition, along with ISBNs of the annotated version, are as follows: | <The list is reproduced here as in the volume>

Volume number in this edition	Text treated	Volume number in the Latin first edition	Section numbers	ISBN (of hardcover except where noted)
1	Genesis 1–8	1	§1–946	978-0-87785-486-9 978-0-87785-504-0 (pb)
2	Genesis 9–15	1	§§947–1885	978-0-87785-487-6
3	Genesis 16–21	2 (in 6 fascicles)	§§1886–2759	978-0-87785-488-3
4	Genesis 22–26	3	§§2760–3485	978-0-87785-489-0
5	Genesis 27–30	3	§§3486–4055	978-0-87785-490-6
6	Genesis 31–35	4	§§4056–4634	978-0-87785-491-3
7	Genesis 36–40	4	§§4635–5190	978-0-87785-492-0
8	Genesis 41–44	5	§§5191–5866	978-0-87785-493-7
9	Genesis 45–50	5	§§5867–6626	978-0-87785-494-4
10	Exodus 1–8	6	§§6627–7487	978-0-87785-495-1
11	Exodus 9–15	6	§§7488–8386	978-0-87785-496-8
12	Exodus 16–21	7	§§8387–9111	978-0-87785-497-5
13	Exodus 22–24	7	§§9112–9442	978-0-87785-498-2
14	Exodus 25–29	8	§§9443–10166	978-0-87785-499-9
15	Exodus 30–40	8	§§10167–10837	978-0-87785-500-2 |

The ISBN of this Portable New Century Edition *Secrets of Heaven* volume 2 is 978-0-87785-411-1. | (The ISBN in the Library of Congress data shown below is that of volume 1.) | Library of Congress Cataloging-in-Publication Data | Swedenborg, Emanuel, 1688-1772. | [Arcana coelestia. English] | Secrets of heaven / Emanuel Swedenborg; translated from the Latin by | Lisa Hyatt Cooper. — Portable New Century ed. | p. cm. | Includes bibliographical references and indexes. | ISBN 978-0-87785-408-1 (alk. paper) | 1. New Jerusalem Church—Doctrines. 2. Bible. O.T. Genesis—Commentaries—Early | works to 1800. 3. Bible. O.T. Exodus—Commentaries—Early | works to 1800. I. Title. | BX8712.A8 2010 | 230'.94—dc22 | 2009054171 | Senior copy editor, Alicia L. Dole | Text designed by Joanna V. Hill | Typesetting by Alicia L. Dole | Ornaments from the first Latin edition, 1749 | Cover design by Karen Connor | For information about the New Century Edition of the Works of Emanuel Swedenborg, contact | the Swedenborg Foundation, 320 North Church Street, West Chester, PA 19380 U.S.A. | Telephone: (610) 430-3222 • web: www.swedenborg.com • E-mail: info@swedenborg.com

half title: SECRETS | OF | HEAVEN

section title: SECRETS | OF | HEAVEN

8vo

half title and title leaves, 4 pp; Contents, pp V-VI; Conventions used in this work, pp VII-IX; section title leaf, pp 1-2; text of Genesis 9-15 and n 947-1885, pp 3-500; Biographical note, p 501.

Initial copies of this volume were issued in December 2011.

UK: SOC; USA: ANC, FOU

ENGLISH EXTRACTS

X 49/01/En 1792/1 **1792** Hyde 860

CONCERNING VASTATIONS. | [From the *Arcana Cœlestia*, n. 1106 to 1113.]

8vo

title and text, pp 260-263.

Translated, with footnotes added, by R Hindmarsh, published in *The New Jerusalem Journal* London.

UK: SOC, CHT, CON, NCC, NR

X 49/01/En 1792/2 **1792** Hyde 861

On Civil Government.

Doctrine of Charity and Faith.

8vo

title and text n 10814, pp 361-362, 367-370; title and text n 10815-10831, pp 371-378.

Translated, with footnotes added, by P B Chastanier, published in *The New Jerusalem Journal* London.

UK: SOC, CHT, CON, NCC, NR

X 49/01/En 1807/1 **1807** Hyde 3175

A | SUMMARY EXPOSITION | OF THE | INTERNAL SENSE | OF | THE BOOKS | OF | *GENESIS AND EXODUS*, | OF THE | GOSPEL ACCORDING TO MATTHEW, | And of the | REVELATIONS; | Extracted from the | *ARCANA COELESTIA* | OF | BARON SWEDENBORG, | From the | NEW TRANSLATION | Of the | *GOSPEL ACCORDING TO MATTHEW*, | And from the | APOCALYPSE REVEALED. | <short double rule> | *LONDON:* | PRINTED AND SOLD BY J. & E. HODSON, | CROSS-STREET, HATTON-GARDEN. | ALSO BY J. AND W. CLARKE, MANCHESTER, AND | ALL OTHER BOOKSELLERS. | <short rule> | 1807.

12mo

title leaf, 2 pp; advertisement, 2 pp; text, pp 1-171; catalogue, 1 p.

Reprinted from translations by J Clowes of *Arcana Coelestia* <49/01/En>, n 6, 73, 81, 131, 137, 190, 234, 241, 280, 286, 324, 337, 460, 468, 554, 560, 599, 605, 701, 705, 832, 838, 971, 979, 1130, 1140, 1279, 1283, 1401, 1403, 1535, 1540, 1651, 1659, 1778, 1783, 1890, 1985, 2136, 2312, 2496, 2498, 2610, 2667, 2671, 2719, 2764, 2901, 3012, 3230, 3257, 3362, 3490, 3636, 3758, 3759, 3902, 4061, 4232, 4336, 4337, 4125, 4536, 4639, 4665, 4811, 4960, 5072, 5191, 5306, 5398, 5574, 5728, 5867, 5994, 6059, 6216, 6328, 6497, 6634, 6713, 6825, 6939, 7087, 7183, 7264, 7378, 7495, 7628, 7763, 7822, 8038, 8125, 8258, 8395, 8554, 8641, 8748, 8859, 8970, 8791, 9123, 9246, 9370, 9455, 9592, 9710, 9804, 9985, <10175½,> 10326, 10893, 10523, 10598, 10725, 10750, 10767, 10782, 10807, 10832, and of *Matthew*, and by N Tucker of *Apocalypse Revealed* <66/01/En 1, 2 = Hyde 2200-2201>. <*stet* 8791>

UK: SOC, CON; SWE: UPP; USA: SHS

X 49/01/En 1809/1 **<1809>** Hyde —

A late esteemed Author makes the following | (among other) remarks on ECCLESIASTIC | and CIVIL GOVERNMENT.

8vo

title and text n 10790-10804, pp 28-31.

Edited by J C Hill, published in *The Chief Obstacles that prevent, and the means to obtain, the Blessings of Peace, clearly pointed out* Birmingham. The edition is undated, but the frontispiece refers to Horatio, Lord Nelson <d 1805>, Sir Ralph Abercrombie <d 1801>, Charles, 1st Marquess Cornwallis <d 1805>, and Sir John Moore <d 1809>. A copy of proposals made in 1819 to publish a new Latin edition of *Arcana Coelestia* <49/01/La 2/1> is bound in the copy in UK: SOC. <Archives S4/184>

UK: SOC

X 49/01/En 1820/1 **1820** Hyde 862

<<Genesis, chapter I explained, according to its internal or spiritual sense. By the Hon. Emanuel

Swedenborg, Servant of the Lord Jesus Christ. London: printed and published by H. Hodson, 15, Cross Street, Hatton Garden; and may be had of all other booksellers. 1820.>>
12mo
title leaf, 2 pp; 'To the Clergy of the United Kingdom', pp iii-xx; text, pp 1-45; catalogue, 2 pp.
Translated and edited by J Clowes.
Copy not seen; description recorded from Hyde 862 and catalogue of USA: ANC.
USA: ANC

X 49/01/En 1821/1 **1821** Hyde 863
THE | DOCTRINE | OF | CHARITY AND FAITH, | EXTRACTED FROM THE | ARCANA COELESTIA | OF THE | HON. EMANUEL SWEDENBORG, | AS IT STANDS | PREFIXED TO EVERY CHAPTER | OF HIS | EXPLICATION OF THE BOOK OF EXODUS. | <short orn rule> | BY A SOCIETY OF GENTLEMEN. | <short orn rule> | **Manchester:** | PRINTED AND SOLD BY J. GLEAVE, 191, DEANSGATE. | SOLD ALSO BY MESSRS. CLARKE, MARKET-PLACE; | AND IN LONDON, BY MRS. HODSON, CROSS-STREET, HATTON GARDEN; | THOMAS GOYDER, CHARLES-STREET, WESTMINSTER; | AND OTHER BOOKSELLERS. | <short rule> | 1821.
8vo
title leaf, 2 pp; Preface, pp iii-viii; Contents, pp ix-x; text, pp 1-90.
An edition of 500 copies printed by J Gleave for the Society for Printing, Publishing, and Circulating the Writings of Swedenborg, Manchester.
UK: SOC, NR; NET: GEN; USA: SHS

X 49/01/En 1829/1 **1829** Hyde 3184
<< <untitled> >>
small 8vo
text n 5377, 5711, pp 11-12.
Published in *New Jerusalem Tract* no 4 <X 58/02/En 1829/4>, by Adonis Howard, Boston MA.
Copy not seen; description deduced from **D** X En 1830/1 = Hyde 3184.

X 49/01/En 1829/2 **1829** Hyde 3184
<<From "*Arcana Cœlestia: or Heavenly Mysteries contained in the Sacred Scrip- | tures, or Word of the Lord, manifested and laid open: beginning with the Book | of Genesis. Interspersed with Relations of wonderful Things seen in the world | of Spirits and the Heaven of Angels:*" a work of Emanuel Swedenborg. | EXPLANATION OF GENESIS xiv. 5.>>
small 8vo
title and text n 1667, 1668, pp 10-12.
Published in *New Jerusalem Tract* no 6 <X 58/02/En 1829/6>, by Adonis Howard, Boston MA.
Copy not seen; description recorded from **D** X En 1830/1 = Hyde 3184.

X 49/01/En 1829/3 **1829** Hyde 864
<<The Doctrine of the New Jerusalem Church concerning Angels and Spirits attendant on Man, and concerning Influx, and the Commerce of the Soul with the Body. By Emanuel Swedenborg. Philadelphia: Published for gratuitous distribution. William Brown, Printer. | 1829.>>
12mo
title leaf, 2 pp; Advertisement, pp iii-iv; text n 5846-5993, 6053-6626, pp 1-80.
Edited by D Harrington.
Copy not seen; description recorded from Hyde 864.
USA: SHS

X 49/01/En 1830/1, **D** X En 1830/1 **1830** Hyde 3184

<< <untitled> >>

small 8vo

text n 5377, 5711, pp 11-12 <of *New Jerusalem Tract* no 4>; n 1667, 1668, pp 10-12 <of *New Jerusalem Tract* no 6>.

Reissue of X En 1829/1 and 2 published in *New Jerusalem Tracts* vol 1, by Adonis Howard Boston MA.

UK: SOC

X 49/01/En 1848/1 **1848** Hyde 3186

APPENDIX. | CONCERNING THE LAST JUDGMENT. | (From the A. C., 2117–2122.)

8vo

title and text <renumbered 1-6>, pp 29-31.

Edited by G Bush, published with separate pagination in *The Swedenborg Library: Selections from the memorabilia of Swedenborg* New York and London.

UK: NR

X 49/01/En 1865/1 **c 1865** Hyde 865

<<A Brief Exposition of the first three chapters of Genesis. being a combination of extracts. By An Adventurer. London: F. Pitman, 20, Paternoster Row, E.C.>>

small 8vo

title leaf, 2 pp; text n 1-120, pp 3-58.

Published about 1865.

Copy not seen; description recorded from Hyde 865.

X 49/01/En 1865/2 **1865** Hyde 865/a

<<**New Jerusalem Tracts.** | CONCERNING THE MEMORY OF MAN | REMAINING AFTER DEATH. | From the Arcana Coelestia of Emanuel Swedenborg. | Boston: T. Carter & Co., 21 Bromfield Street. | New York: J. P. Stuart, 20 Cooper Institute. | Cincinnati: Robert Clark & Co. | 1865.>>

small 8vo

title leaf, 2 pp; text unspecified.

Copy not seen; description deduced from Hyde 865/a and USA: ANC catalogue.

USA: ANC

X 49/01/En 1866/1 **1866** Hyde 866

<<The Doctrine of Charity and Faith. | From the *Arcana Coelestia* of Emanuel Swedenborg. | A new translation, | by Rev. T. B. Hayward. | Boston: | T. H. Carter and Son, 21, Bromfield Street. | Chicago: | E. B. Myers and Chandler. 1866.>>

16mo

title leaf, 2 pp; Contents, pp iii-iv; text n 1-338, pp 5-109.

Copy not seen; description deduced from Hyde 866.

USA: ANC, SHS

X 49/01/En 1866/2 **1866** Hyde 1677

CORRESPONDENCE. | 315

small 8vo

title leaf, pp 315-316; text n 4218-4227, 4403-4420, 4526-4533, 4622-4626, 4628-4633, 4652-4659, 4791-4805, 4932-4938, 4944-4949, 4951-4952, pp 317-390.

Translated by R N Foster, published in *The Divine Attributes* Philadelphia.

UK: SOC

X 49/01/En 1868/1 **1868** Hyde 867

THE DOCTRINE | OF | CHARITY AND FAITH. | <short rule> | FROM THE ARCANA CŒLESTIA | OF EMANUEL SWEDENBORG. | <short rule> | A NEW TRANSLATION: | BY REV. T. B. HAYWARD. | BOSTON: | T. H. CARTER AND SONS, | 25 BROMFIELD STREET. | 1868.
16mo
title leaf, 2 pp; Contents, pp iii-iv; text n 1-338, pp 5-109.
The same as X En 1866/1 = Hyde 866.
UK: soc; USA: anc, shs

X 49/01/En 1872/1 **1872** Hyde 868

SIGNS OF THE TIMES: | EXPLANATIONS APPLICABLE AND NECESSARY | FOR THE | PRESENT TIME. | EXTRACTED FROM THE WORKS OF THE | HONOURABLE EMANUEL SWEDENBORG. | TO WHICH IS ADDED A PAMPHLET | BY A MEMBER OF | "The Victorian Discussion Society." | <short rule> | "'Tis happiness to see a God employ'd | In all the good and ill that checker life! | Resolving all events, with their effects | And manifold results, into the will | And arbitration wise of the Supreme; | Whose eye rules all things, and intends | The least of our concerns; since from the least | The greatest oft originate." | <short wavy rule> | London: | SIMPKIN, MARSHALL, & CO., | STATIONERS' HALL COURT. | <short rule> | 1872. | ALL RIGHTS RESERVED.
verso: LONDON : | CLAYTON AND CO., TEMPLE PRINTING WORKS, | 17, BOUVERIE ST., FLEET ST.
half title: SIGNS OF THE TIMES
8vo
half title and title leaves, 4 pp; Contents, pp v-vi; Dedication, pp vii-x; Introductory chapter, pp 1-34 <see Hyde 1488>; text, pp 35-365; 'My Address to Christians', pp 366-400.
Prepared by Mrs E W Stafford. Some copies have a different imprint: London: Clayton and Co., 17, Bouverie Street, Fleet Street. 1872.
UK: soc; USA: anc

X 49/01/En nd/2 **no date** Hyde 868/a

New Jerusalem Tracts. | <short wavy rule> | CONCERNING | HEAVEN AND HEAVENLY JOY. | From the Arcana Celestia of Emanuel Swedenborg. <*stet* Celestia>
small 8vo
title and text n 449-459, 537-553, pp 1-14.
Published in *New Jerusalem Tracts* Boston ma. <UK: soc Archives S4/381>
UK: soc; USA: anc

X 49/01/En nd/3 **no date** Hyde 868/b

<<New Jerusalem Tracts. | <short wavy rule> | Concerning Man's Freedom ... From the Arcana Caelestia of Emanuel Swedenborg. Boston>>
small 8vo
title leaf, 2 pp; text unspecified.
Copy not seen; description deduced from catalogue of USA: anc.
USA: anc

X 49/01/En nd/4 **no date** Hyde 868/c

New Jerusalem Tracts. | <short wavy rule> | CONCERNING | THE STATE OF INFANTS IN THE OTHER LIFE. | From the Arcana Celestia of Emanuel Swedenborg. | Boston. <*stet* Celestia>
small 8vo
title and text n 2289-2309, 10 pp.
Published in *New Jerusalem Tracts* Boston ma. <UK: soc Archives S4/381>
UK: soc; USA: anc

X 49/01/En nd/5 **no date** Hyde 868/d
<<New Jerusalem Tracts. | ON THE RESURRECTION OF MAN FROM THE DEAD. | From the Arcana Coelestia of Emanuel Swedenborg. | Boston>>
small 8vo
title leaf, 2 pp; text unspecified.
Copy not seen; description deduced from catalogue of USA: ANC.
USA: ANC

X 49/01/En 1891/1 **1891** Hyde 868/–
<within an orn border 164 x 98 mm> THE | Spiritual Sense | OF | GENESIS IX–1 to 17. | EXTRACTED FROM | ✢ Arcana Cœlestia, ✢ | (SWEDENBORG,) | VOL. 1, NOS. 797, to 1056. <*stet* 797, TO 1056.>
small 8vo
title page, 1 p; text <extracted from n 971-1105>, 3 pp.
A leaflet containing n 980, 985, 993, 998, 1004, 1009, 1014, 1019, 1022, 1031, 1036, 1046, 1052, 1057. Issued with *New Church Home Reading* notes, published by The General Conference of the New Church, London.
UK: SOC

X 49/01/En 1910/1 **1910** Hyde 868/1
EXTRACTS FROM | ARCANA CŒLESTIA | ("HEAVENLY MYSTERIES") | TOGETHER WITH | THE EXPOSITIONS OF THE INTERNAL SENSE OF | GENESIS AND EXODUS | BY | EMANUEL SWEDENBORG | JAMES SPIERS | 1 BLOOMSBURY STREET, LONDON | 1910
half title: EXTRACTS FROM | ARCANA CŒLESTIA
8vo
half title and title leaves, 4 pp; Dedication, p v; Contents, pp vii; Introduction, pp ix-xi; text, pp 1-575.
Printed by Turnbull and Spears, Edinburgh.
UK: SOC; USA: ANC, SHS; AUS: SYD

X 49/01/En 1924/1 **1924** Hyde 868/1a
<within a double rule border 168 x 107 mm> *THE STORY OF CREATION* | <short rule> | THE EXPOSITION | OF | Genesis–Chapter I | EXTRACTED FROM THE WORK ENTITLED | THE ARCANA CŒLESTIA | (VOL. I) | BY | EMANUEL SWEDENBORG | LONDON | THE SWEDENBORG SOCIETY | 1 BLOOMSBURY STREET, W.C.1 | 1924
8vo
title leaf, 2 pp; text n 1-64, pp 1-31.
Printed by Turnbull & Spears, Edinburgh.
UK: SOC; SWE: ROY; USA: ANC, SHS

X 49/01/En 1931/1 **1931** Hyde 868/2
IV. | EXTRACTS FROM ARCANA COELESTIA | *Being the extracts concerning man's memory* | *which remains after death and the recollection of* | *what he had done in the life of the body.*
8vo
title and text, pp 22-36.
Published in A Roeder *Man's Two Memories* New York.
UK: SOC; USA: ANC

X 49/01/En 1940/1 **1940** Hyde 868/2a
THE END OF THE AGE | FORETOLD IN | THE GOSPEL OF MATTHEW | CHAPTERS XXIV AND

XXV | EXTRACTS | FROM THE WORK | ARCANA CŒLESTIA | BY | EMANUEL SWEDENBORG | SWEDENBORG SOCIETY (INCORPORATED) | SWEDENBORG HOUSE | 20/21 BLOOMSBURY WAY, LONDON, W.C.1 | 1940
verso: *Printed in Great Britain by* | *The Campfield Press, St. Albans*
foolscap 8vo
title leaf, 2 pp; Foreword, p 3; List of the paragraphs of *Arcana Caelestia* contained in this edition, p 4; text n 1-15, pp 5-90.
Edited by C E Newall.
The paragraphs extracted from *Arcana Caelestia* are n 3353-3356, 3486-3489, 3650-3655, 3751-3757, 3897-3901, 4056-4060, 4229-4231, 4332-4335, 4422-4424, 4535, 4635-4638, 4661-4663, 4807-4810, 4954-4959, 5063-5071.
UK: SOC, CHE, PUR; NET: GEN; SWE: ROY, UPP; USA: ANC, SHS

X 49/01/En 1942/1 **1942** Hyde 868/3
ON MIRACLES. | On Miracles, and that at this day, about the End | of the Age, none are to be expected. | BY EMANUEL SWEDENBORG.
8vo
title and text n 2870-2887, pp 400-411.
Translated from a photocopy of the MS of *Arcana Coelestia* by A Acton, published in *New Church Life* Bryn Athyn PA.
UK: SOC, NCC; NET: GEN; USA: ANC

X 49/01/En 1974/1 **1974** Hyde 868/3a
THE | INTERNAL SENSE | OF THE WORD | A translation of extracts | from | chapters fifteen to twenty-three of | ARCANA CÆLESTIA | by | EMANUEL | SWEDENBORG | THE SWEDENBORG SOCIETY | 20 BLOOMSBURY WAY, LONDON | 1974
verso: *Made and Printed in England* | *by The Campfield Press* | *St. Albans Herts*
half title: THE INTERNAL SENSE OF THE WORD
small 8vo
half title and title leaves, 4 pp; Contents, p 5; Translator's preface, p 7; text n 1984, 2135, 2310-2311, 2606-2609, 2760-2763, 2894-2900, 3004-3011, 1767-1776, 1869-1885, pp 9-49.
Translated by G T Hill, with D H Harley as Consultant; text also renumbered as 1-54.
UK: SOC, NR; NET: GEN; USA: ANC, SHS

X 49/01/En 1984/1, **D** En 1984/3 **1984** Hyde 868/3e, 3139/4
The Universal Human | PART 1 | REPRESENTATIONS AND | CORRESPONDENCES
The Universal Human | PART 2 | THE CORRESPONDENCE OF | ALL THE INNER AND OUTER | HUMAN ORGANS AND | MEMBERS WITH THE | UNIVERSAL HUMAN, WHICH | IS HEAVEN
8vo
Part 1: title leaf, pp 35-36; text n 3624-3648, 3742-3750, 3883-3895, pp 37-66.
Part 2: title leaf, pp 67-68; text n 4039-4054, 4218-4227, 4318-4330, 4403-4420, 4523-4533, 4622-4633, 4652-4659, 4791-4805, 4931-4952, 5050-5061, 5171-5189, 5377-5396, 5552-5573, 5711-5726, pp 69-223.
Edited and translated by G F Dole, published in *The Universal Human and Soul-Body Interaction* <**D** En 1984/3 = Hyde 3139/4>. The volume also contains 69/11/En 11/2 = Hyde 2577/10.
UK: SOC, CON, PUR, NR; NET: GEN, KB; USA: ANC, SHS

X 49/01/En 1992/1 **1992** Hyde 3233/43
Selections from Unknown Things About Heaven
A4 folded to A5
title and text n 2228, 3121, 8881, 10083, pp 22-23.

Translated by D F Gladish, published in *Seeing is Believing* <**D** X En 1992/2 = Hyde 3233/43> Bryn Athyn PA.

UK: SOC, NR; USA: ANC

X 49/01/En 2007/1 **2007** Hyde 868/3f

A Disclosure of | SECRETS OF HEAVEN | Contained in | SACRED SCRIPTURE | or | THE LORD'S WORD | Beginning Here with Those in | Genesis | *Together with Amazing Things seen | in the World of Spirits & in the Heaven of Angels* | by EMANUEL SWEDENBORG | Chapter 1 | Translated from the Latin by Lisa Hyatt Cooper | <rule> | <orn NR 327> | <rule> | SWEDENBORG FOUNDATION | *West Chester, Pennsylvania*

verso: Copyright 2007 by the Swedenborg Foundation, Inc. | This is the first chapter of the Swedenborg Foundation pub- | lication *Secrets of Heaven,* volume 1, ISBN 978-0-87785-486-9 | (hard cover), 978-0-87785-504-0 (paperback).

A4 folded to A5

title leaf, 2 pp; Introduction, p 3; quotation of Matthew 6:33, p 4; text of Genesis 1 and n 1-66, pp 5-61; Biographical note, p 63.

Translated by L H Cooper, an extract from En 8/1 = Hyde 618/14, West Chester PA; 6,000 copies were printed.

UK: SOC; USA: FOU

X 49/01/En 2008/1 **2008** Hyde 3233/–

A Disclosure of | SECRETS OF HEAVEN | Contained in | SACRED SCRIPTURE | or | THE LORD'S WORD | Beginning Here with Those in | Genesis | *Together with Amazing Things seen | in the World of Spirits & in the Heaven of Angels* | by EMANUEL SWEDENBORG | Chapter 1 | Translated from the Latin by Lisa Hyatt Cooper | <rule> | <orn NR 327> | <rule> | SWEDENBORG FOUNDATION | *West Chester, Pennsylvania*

verso: Copyright 2007 by the Swedenborg Foundation, Inc. | This is the first chapter of the Swedenborg Foundation pub- | lication *Secrets of Heaven,* volume 1, ISBN 978-0-87785-486-9 | (hard cover), 978-0-87785-504-0 (paperback).

A4 folded to A5

title leaf, 2 pp; Introduction, p 3; quotation of Matthew 6:33, p 4; text of Genesis 1 and n 1-66, pp 5-61; Biographical note, p 63.

A reprint of X En 2007/1.

USA: FOU

CZECH

49/01/Cz 1/1 **no date** Hyde —

<< <within a rule border 255 x 146 mm> ARCANA COELESTIA. | --- | NEBESKÁ TAJEMSTVÍ. | HHHHHHHHHHHHHHHHHHHH HHHHHHHHHH HHHHHHHHH | obsažená | v PÍSMU SVATÉM čili ve SLOVU PÁNĚ | mmmmmmmmmmmm mmmmmmmmmmmm | a nyní odhalená. | Zde, co jest v První knize Mojžíšově. | Zároveň podivuhodné věci, které byly | spatřeny a slyšeny ve světě duchovním | a v andělském nebi. | Od Immanuele Swedenborga. | mmmmmmmmmmmmmmmmmmmmmmmmm | Motto autorovo: | Hledejte nejprve | království Boží a | spravedlnost jeho | a všecko takové | Mat. 6, 33. bude vám přidáno. | PRAHA. | L. P. 1936.>>

4to

Typescript of a complete translation of *Arcana Coelestia* made by Ludmila Mařiá Magdalena Kubátová, from German versions. Copy not seen; description recorded from information provided by L Máchová, in whose care the MS was in 2008.

CZE: LM

CZECH EXTRACTS

X 49/01/Cz 1958/1 <1958> Hyde —

In 1991 J S Mařík reported in *Lifeline*, London, November p 4, that when he joined a group of New Church believers in Prague in 1958 they read and circulated typed extracts of *Arcana Caelestia*, translated from German by L M M Kubátová.

X 49/01/Cz 1999/1, **D** Cz 1999/1 **1999** Hyde —

Nebeská tajemství

8vo

title <with editorial notes>, p 15; text n 1, 10373, 17, 20, 231-232, 1594, 1799, 1834, 1949, 2694, 2535, 1990, 5321, 2034, 6716, 1999, 3318, 1690, 1812, 3212, 10152, 3854, 8717, 6574, pp 15-28.

Translated by L Máchová, published in *Tajemství víry* <**D** Cz 1999/1>. ISBN 0-945003-19-6.

UK: NR; CZE: LM; GER: WLB

DANISH

49/01/Da 1/1 **2006** Hyde 810/1a

ARCANA COELESTIA | HIMMELSKE HEMMELIGHEDER | indeholdt i | DEN HELLIGE SKRIFT ELLER HERRENS ORD | AFDÆKKET | SAMMEN MED FORUNDERIGE TING SET | ÅNDERNES | VERDEN OG | ENGLEHIMLEN. | Af | Emanuel Swedenborg | 1. Bind | Indeholdende | 1. MOSEBOG kap. 1-9, (n. 1 - 1113) | Oversat fra latin af Gudmund Boolsen | Forlag: Nykirkeligt Tidsskrift | København 2006

verso: [Forfattevens inskription] | Søg først Guds rige og hans retfærdighed, så skal alt det andet | gives jer i tilgift. Matt. 6:33.

half title: ARCANA COELESTIA | Forlag: NYKIRKELIGT TIDSSKRIFT

verso: NYKIRKELIGT TIDSSKRIFT TRYK | København 2006 | ISBN 87-91895-00-6 | Swedenborg Boglade, Valby Langgade 39, 1.th. | 2500 Valby. Tlf. 39 27 04 15

8vo

half title and title leaves, 4 pp; Forord, 1 p; [Indholdet af Første Mosebog] <Contents of the 1st volume>, p II; text of Genesis 1-9 and n 1-1113, pp 1-439.

UK: SOC; DEN: RLD; USA: ANC

49/01/Da 1/2 **2008** Hyde 810/1b

ARCANA COELESTIA | HIMMELSKE HEMMELIGHEDER | Indeholdt I | DEN HELLIGE SKRIFT ELLER HERRENS ORD | AFDÆKKET | SAMMEN MED FORUNDERLIGE TING SET I ÅNDERNES | VERDEN OG I ENGLEHIMLEN | Af | Emanuel Swedenborg | 2. Bind | Indeholdende | 1. MOSEBOG kap. 10-17, (1114-2134) | Oversat fra latin af Gudmund Boolsen | Forlag: Nykirkeligt Tidsskrift | København 2008

verso: [Forfatterens inskription] | Søg først Guds rige og hans retfærdighed, så skal alt det andet | gives jer i tilgift. Matt. 6:33.

half title: ARCANA COELESTIA | Forlag: NYKIRKELIGT TIDSSKRIFT

verso: NYKIRKELIGT TIDSSKRIFT TRYK | København 2008 | Swedenborg Boglade | www. Swedenborg-Boglade.dk | Tlf. 39-27 04 15

8vo

half title and title leaves, 4 pp; Indholdet af andet bind <Contents of the 2nd volume>, 1 p; text of Genesis 10-17 and n 1113-2134, pp 1-446; Væsentlige rettelser til første bind <Corrections to the 1st volume>, pp 447-448.

Translated by G Boolsen.

UK: SOC; DEN: RLD

49/01/Da 1/3 **2008** Hyde 810/1c

ARCANA COELESTIA | HIMMELSKE HEMMELIGHEDER | Indeholdt I | DEN HELLIGE SKRIFT ELLER HERRENS ORD | AFDÆKKET | SAMMEN MED FORUNDERLIGE TING SET I ÅNDERNES | VERDEN OG I ENGLEHIMLEN | Af | Emanuel Swedenborg | 3. Bind | Indeholdende | 1. MOSEBOG kap. 18-22, (2135 - 2893) | Oversat fra latin af Gudmund Boolsen | Forlag: Nykirkeligt Tidsskrift | København 2008
verso: [Forfatterens inskription] | Søg først Guds rige og hans retfærdighed, så skal alt det andet | gives jer i tilgift. Matt. 6:33.
half title: ARCANA COELESTIA | Forlag: NYKIRKELIGT TIDSKRIFT <*stet* TIDSKRIFT>
verso: NYKIRKELIGT TIDSSKRIFT TRYK | København 2008 | ISBN 87-91895-02-2 | Swedenborg Boglade | www.swedenborg-boglade.dk | Tlf. 39-27 04 15
8vo
half title and title leaves, 4 pp; Indholdet af Tredje Bind <Contents of the 3rd volume>, 1 p; text of Swedenborg's preface to Genesis 18, Genesis 18-22, Swedenborg's preface to Genesis 22, and n 2135-2893, pp 1-432; Rettelser til Andet Bind <Corrections to the 2nd volume>, pp 433-435.
Translated by G Boolsen.
UK: SOC; DEN: RLD

49/01/Da 1/4 **2009** Hyde 810/1d

ARCANA COELESTIA | HIMMELSKE HEMMELIGHEDER | Indeholdt i | DEN HELLIGE SKRIFT ELLER HERRENS ORD | AFDÆKKET | SAMMEN MED FORUNDERLIGE TING SET I ÅNDERNES | VERDEN OG I ENGLEHIMLEN | Af | Emanuel Swedenborg | 4. Bind | Indeholdende | 1. MOSEBOG kap. 23-27, (2894 - 3649) | Oversat fra latin af Gudmund Boolsen | Forlag: Nykirkeligt Tidsskrift | København 2009
verso: [Forfatterens inskription] | Søg først Guds rige og hans retfærdighed, så skal alt det andet | gives jer i tilgift. Matt. 6:33.
half title: ARCANA COELESTIA | Forlag: NYKIRKELIGT TIDSKRIFT <*stet* TIDSKRIFT>
verso: NYKIRKELIGT TIDSSKRIFT TRYK | København 2009 | Swedenborg Boglade | www.swedennborg-boglade.dk | Tlf. 39-27 04 15 <*stet* swedennborg-boglade>
8vo
half title and title leaves, 4 pp; Indholdet af Fjerje Bind <Contents of the 4th volume>, 1 p; text of Genesis 23-27 and n 2894-3649, pp 1-415; Rettelser til 3. bind <Corrections to volume 3>, pp 417-421.
Translated by G Boolsen.
UK: SOC; DEN: RLD

49/01/Da 1/5 **2010** Hyde 810/e

ARCANA COELESTIA | HIMMELSKE HEMMELIGHEDER | Indeholdt i | DEN HELLIGE SKRIFT ELLER HERRENS ORD | AFDÆKKET | SAMMEN MED FORUNDERLIGE TING SET I ÅNDERNES | VERDEN OG I ENGLEHIMLEN | Af | Emanuel Swedenborg | 5. Bind | Indeholdende | 1. MOSEBOG kap. 28-31, (3650 - 4228) | Oversat fra latin af Gudmund Boolsen | Forlag: Nykirkeligt Tidsskrift | København 2010
verso: [Forfatterens inskription] | Søg først Guds rige og hans retfærdighed, så skal alt det andet | gives jer i tilgift. Matt. 6:33.
half title: ARCANA COELESTIA | Forlag: NYKIRKELIGT TIDSSKRIFT
verso: NYKIRKELIGT TIDSSKRIFT TRYK | København 2010 | Swedenborg Boglade | www.swedenborg-boglade.dk | Tlf. 39-27 04 15
8vo

half title and title leaves, 4 pp; Indholdet af Femte Bind <Contents of the 5th volume>, 1 p; text of Genesis 28-31 and n 3650-4228, pp 1-378; Korrekturer til 4. bind <Corrections to volume 4>, pp 379-386.
Translated by G Boolsen.
UK: SOC; DEN: RLD

49/01/Da 1/6 **2010** Hyde 810/f
ARCANA COELESTIA | HIMMELSKE HEMMELIGHEDER | Indeholdt i | DEN HELLIGE SKRIFT ELLER HERRENS ORD | AFDÆKKET | SAMMEN MED FORUNDERLIGE TING SET I ÅNDERNES | VERDEN OG I ENGLEHIMLEN | Af | Emanuel Swedenborg | 6. Bind | Indeholdende | 1. MOSEBOG kap. 32-38, (4229- 4953) | Oversat fra latin af Gudmund Boolsen | Forlag: Nykirkeligt Tidsskrift | København 2010
verso: [Forfatterens inskription] | Søg først Guds rige og hans retfærdighed, så skal alt det andet | gives jer i tilgift. Matt. 6:33.
half title: ARCANA COELESTIA | Forlag: NYKIRKELIGT TIDSSKRIFT
verso: NYKIRKELIGT TIDSSKRIFT TRYK | København 2008 | ISBN 87-91895-05-7 | Swedenborg Boglade | www.swedenborg-boglade.dk | Tlf. 39-27 04 15 <*stet* 2008>
8vo
half title and title leaves, 4 pp; Indholdet af Sjette Bind <Contents of the 6th volume>, 1 p; text of Genesis 32-38 and n 4229-4953, pp 1-447; Korrekturen til 5. bind <Corrections to volume 5>, p 448.
Translated by G Boolsen.
The first copies received from the printer had errors on the half title verso <ISBN 87-91895-02-2>, the back cover <ISBN 87-91895-06-5>, and the spine of the volume <7 | 4954-5727 instead of 6 | 4229-4953>; and these were corrected before the issue was published.
UK: SOC; DEN: RLD

49/01/Da 1/7 **2011** Hyde 810/g
ARCANA COELESTIA | HIMMELSKE HEMMELIGHEDER | Indeholdt i | DEN HELLIGE SKRIFT ELLER HERRENS ORD | AFDÆKKET | SAMMEN MED FORUNDERLIGE TING SET I ÅNDERNES | VERDEN OG I ENGLEHIMLEN | Af | Emanuel Swedenborg | 7. Bind | Indeholdende | 1. MOSEBOG kap. 39-43, (4954-5727) | Oversat fra latin af Gudmund Boolsen | Forlag: Nykirkeligt Tidsskrift | København 2011
verso: [Forfatterens inskription] | Søg først Guds rige og hans retfærdighed, så skal alt det andet | gives jer i tilgift. Matt. 6:33.
half title: ARCANA COELESTIA | Forlag: NYKIRKELIGT TIDSSKRIFT
verso: NYKIRKELIGT TIDSSKRIFT TRYK | København 2008 | ISBN 87-91895-02-2 | Swedenborg Boglade | www.swedenborg-boglade.dk | Tlf. 39-27 04 15 <*stent* 2008 | ISBN 87-91895-02-2>
8vo
half title and title leaves, 4 pp; Indholdet af Syvende Bind <Contents of the 7th volume>, 1 p; text of Genesis 39-43 and n 4954-5727, pp 1-408; Rettelser til AC bind 6 <Corrections to volume 6>, p 408.
Translated by G Boolsen.
On the back cover the ISBN is correctly printed as 87-91895-06-5.
UK: SOC; DEN: RLD

DANISH EXTRACTS

X 49/01/Da 1906/1 **1906** Hyde 895/a
<<Hvorfor Herren vilde lade sig fode paa vor Jord og ikke paa nogen anden.>>
8vo
title and text n 9350-9361, pp 183-186.

Published in *Den Nye Tid* Copenhagen.
Copy not seen; description recorded from Hyde 895/a.
USA: ANC

DUTCH

49/01/Du 1/1 **1926** Hyde 810/1
HEMELSCHE VERBORGENHEDEN | (ARCANA COELESTIA) | IN DE HEILIGE SCHRIFT OF | HET WOORD DES HEEREN | ONTHULD | HIER VOOREERST DIE IN GENESIS | ALSMEDE DE WONDERLIJKE DINGEN, GEZIEN IN DE | WERELD DER GEESTEN EN IN DEN HEMEL DER ENGELEN | DOOR | EMANUEL SWEDENBORG | EERSTE NEDERLANDSCHE VERTALING DER ARCANA COELESTIA QUAE IN | SCRIPTURA SACRA SEU VERBO DOMINI SUNT, DETECTA. HIC PRIMUM | QUAE IN GENESI. UNA CUM MIRABILIBUS QUAE VISA SUNT IN MUNDO | SPIRITUUM ET IN COELO ANGELORUM. MDCCIL. | BAND I. | 's-GRAVENHAGE SWEDENBORG GENOOTSCHAP | LAAN VAN MEERDERVOORT 229 | 1926.
verso: MATTHEÜS 6: 33. | *Zoekt eerst hed Koninkrijk Gods en zijne Gerechtigheid,* | *en alle dingen zullen u toegeworpen worden.*
8vo
title leaf, 2 pp; Contents, pp 3-4; text of Genesis 1-9 and n 1-1113, pp 5-627.
Translated by A Zelling.
UK: SOC; NET: GEN, KB; SWE: ROY, UPP; USA: ANC

49/01/Du 1/2 **1927** Hyde 810/2
HEMELSCHE VERBORGENHEDEN | (ARCANA COELESTIA) | IN DE HEILIGE SCHRIFT OF | HET WOORD DES HEEREN | ONTHULD | HIER VOOREERST DIE IN GENESIS | ALSMEDE DE WONDERLIJKE DINGEN, GEZIEN IN DE | WERELD DER GEESTEN EN IN DEN HEMEL DER ENGELEN | DOOR | EMANUEL SWEDENBORG | EERSTE NEDERLANDSCHE VERTALING DER ARCANA COELESTIA QUAE IN | SCRIPTURA SACRA SEU VERBO DOMINI SUNT, DETECTA. UNA CUM MIRABI- | LIBUS QUAE VISA SUNT IN MUNDO SPIRITUUM ET IN COELO ANGELORUM. | BAND II | 's-GRAVENHAGE | SWEDENBORG GENOOTSCHAP | LAAN VAN MEERDERVOORT 229 | 1927
verso: MATTHEÜS 6: 33. | *Zoekt eerst het Koninkrijk Gods en zijne Gerechtigheid,* | *en alle dingen zullen u toegeworpen worden.*
8vo
title leaf, 2 pp; text of Genesis 10-17 and n 1114-2134, pp 3-640.
Translated by A Zelling.
UK: SOC; NET: GEN, KB; SWE: ROY, UPP; USA: ANC

49/01/Du 1/3 **1928** Hyde 810/3
HEMELSCHE VERBORGENHEDEN | (ARCANA COELESTIA) | IN DE HEILIGE SCHRIFT OF | HET WOORD DES HEEREN | ONTHULD | HIER VOOREERST DIE IN GENESIS | ALSMEDE DE WONDERLIJKE DINGEN, GEZIEN IN DE | WERELD DER GEESTEN EN IN DEN HEMEL DER ENGELEN | DOOR | EMANUEL SWEDENBORG | EERSTE NEDERLANDSE VERTALING DER ARCANA COELESTIA QUAE IN | SCRIPTURA SACRA SEU VERBO DOMINI SUNT, DETECTA. UNA CUM MIRABI- | LIBUS QUAE VISA SUNT IN MUNDO SPIRITUUM ET IN COELO ANGELORUM. | BAND III | 's-GRAVENHAGE | SWEDENBORG GENOOTSCHAP LAAN | VAN MEERDERVOORT 229 | 1928
verso: MATTHEÜS 6: 33 | *Zoekt eerst het Koninkrijk Gods en zijne Gerechtigheid,* | *en alle dingen zullen u toegeworpen worden.*
8vo
title leaf, 2 pp; text of Swedenborg's preface, Genesis 18-22, and n 2135-2893, pp 3-605.
Translated by A Zelling.
UK: SOC; NET: GEN, KB; SWE: ROY, UPP; USA: ANC

49/01/Du 1/4 **1929** Hyde 810/4

HEMELSCHE VERBORGENHEDEN | (ARCANA COELESTIA) | IN DE HEILIGE SCHRIFT OF | HET WOORD DES HEEREN | ONTHULD | HIER VOOREERST DIE IN GENESIS | ALSMEDE DE WONDERLIJKE DINGEN, GEZIEN IN DE | WERELD DER GEESTEN EN IN DEN HEMEL DER ENGELEN | DOOR | EMANUEL SWEDENBORG | EERSTE NEDERLANDSE VERTALING DER ARCANA COELESTIA QUAE IN | SCRIPTURA SACRA SEU VERBO DOMINI SUNT, DETECTA. UNA CUM MIRABI- | LIBUS QUAE VISA SUNT IN MUNDO SPIRITUUM ET IN COELO ANGELORUM. | BAND IV | 's-GRAVENHAGE | SWEDENBORG GENOOTSCHAP | LAAN VAN MEERDEVOORT 229 | 1929
verso: MATTHEÜS 6: 33 | *Zoekt eerst het Koninkrijk Gods en zijne Gerechtigheid,* | *en alle dingen zullen u toegeworpen worden.*
8vo
title leaf, 2 pp; text of Genesis 23-28 and n 2894-3750, pp 3-710.
Translated by A Zelling.
UK: SOC; NET: GEN, KB; SWE: ROY, UPP; USA: ANC

49/01/Du 1/5 **1941** Hyde 810/5

HEMELSCHE VERBORGENHEDEN | (ARCANA COELESTIA) | IN DE HEILIGE SCHRIFT OF | HET WOORD DES HEEREN | ONTHULD | HIER VOOREERST DIE IN GENESIS | ALSMEDE DE WONDERLIJKE DINGEN, GEZIEN IN DE | WERELD DER GEESTEN EN IN DEN HEMEL DER ENGELEN | DOOR | EMANUEL SWEDENBORG | EERSTE NEDERLANDSE VERTALING DER ARCANA COELESTIA QUAE IN | SCRIPTURA SACRA SEU VERBO DOMINI SUNT, DETECTA. UNA CUM MIRABI- | LIBUS QUAE VISA SUNT IN MUNDO SPIRITUUUM ET IN COELO ANGELORUM. | BAND V | 's-GRAVENHAGE | SWEDENBORG GENOOTSCHAP | 1941
verso: MATTHEÜS VI: 33 | *Zoekt eerst het Koninkrijk Gods en zijne Gerechtigheid,* | *en alle dingen zullen u toegeworpen worden.*
8vo
title leaf, 2 pp; text of Genesis 29-33 and n 3751-4421, pp 3-548.
Translated by A Zelling.
UK: SOC; NET: GEN, KB; SWE: ROY, UPP; USA: ANC

49/01/Du 1/6 **1950** Hyde 810/6

HEMELSCHE VERBORGENHEDEN | (ARCANA COELESTIA) | IN DE HEILIGE SCHRIFT OF | HET WOORD DES HEEREN | ONTHULD | HIER DIE IN GENESIS | ALSMEDE DE WONDERLIJKE DINGEN, GEZIEN IN DE | WERELD DER GEESTEN EN IN DEN HEMEL DER ENGELEN | DOOR | EMANUEL SWEDENBORG | EERSTE NEDERLANDSE VERTALING DER ARCANA COELESTIA QUAE IN | SCRIPTURA SACRA SEU VERBO DOMINI SUNT, DETECTA. UNA CUM MIRABI- | LIBUS QUAE VISA SUNT IN MUNDO SPIRITUUM ET IN COELO ANGELORUM | BAND VI | 's-GRAVENHAGE | SWEDENBORG GENOOTSCHAP | 1950
verso: MATTHEÜS VI: 33 | *Zoekt eerst het Koninkrijk Gods en zijn Gerechtigheid,* | *en alle dingen zullen u toegeworpen worden.*
8vo
title leaf, 2 pp; text of Genesis 34-40 and n 4422-5190, pp 3-626.
Translated by A Zelling.
UK: SOC; NET: GEN, KB; SWE: ROY, UPP; USA: ANC

49/01/Du 1/7 **1951** Hyde 810/7

HEMELSCHE VERBORGENHEDEN | (ARCANA COELESTIA) | IN DE HEILIGE SCHRIFT OF | HET WOORD DES HEREN | ONTHULD | HIER DIE IN GENESIS | ALSMEDE DE WONDERLIJKE DINGEN, GEZIEN IN DE | WERELD DER GEESTEN EN IN DEN HEMEL DER ENGELEN | DOOR | EMANUEL SWEDENBORG | EERSTE NEDERLANDSE VERTALING DER ARCANA COELESTIA QUAE

IN | SCRIPTURA SACRA SEU VERBO DOMINI SUNT, DETECTA. UNA CUM MIRABI- | LIBUS QUAE VISA SUNT IN MUNDO SPIRITUUM ET IN COELO ANGELORUM | BAND VII | 's-GRAVENHAGE | SWEDENBORG GENOOTSCHAP | 1951
verso: MATTHEÜS VI: 33 | *Zoekt eerst het Koninkrijk Gods en zijn Gerechtigheid,* | *en alle dingen zullen u toegeworpen worden.*
8vo
title leaf, 2 pp; text of Genesis 41-44 and n 5191-5866, pp 3-406.
Translated by A Zelling.
UK: soc; NET: gen, kb; SWE: roy, upp; USA: anc

49/01/Du 1/8 **1951** Hyde 810/8
HEMELSCHE VERBORGENHEDEN | (ARCANA COELESTIA) | IN DE HEILIGE SCHRIFT OF | HET WOORD DES HEREN | ONTHULD | HIER DIE IN GENESIS | ALSMEDE DE WONDERLIJKE DINGEN, GEZIEN IN DE | WERELD DER GEESTEN EN IN DEN HEMEL DER ENGELEN | DOOR | EMANUEL SWEDENBORG | EERSTE NEDERLANDSE VERTALING DER ARCANA COELESTIA QUAE IN | SCRIPTURA SACRA SEU VERBO DOMINI SUNT, DETECTA. UNA CUM MIRABI- | LIBUS QUAE VISA SUNT IN MUNDO SPIRITUUM ET IN COELO ANGELORUM | BAND VIII | 's-GRAVENHAGE | SWEDENBORG GENOOTSCHAP | 1951
verso: MATTHEÜS VI: 33 | *Zoekt eerst het Koninkrijk Gods en zijn Gerechtigheid,* | *en alle dingen zullen i toegeworpen wordon.*
8vo
title leaf, 2 pp; text of Genesis 45-50 and n 5867-6626, pp 3-460.
Translated by A Zelling.
UK: soc; NET: gen, kb; SWE: roy, upp; USA: anc

49/01/Du 1/9 **1960** Hyde 810/9
Hemelsche Verborgenheden | DIE IN | *DE HEILIGE SCHRIFT,* | OF | *HET WOORD DES HEREN* | ZIJN, ONTHULD: | Hier die in | *EXODUS,* | Tezamen met De Wonderlijke Dingen | Die gezien zijn | In de Wereld der Geesten, en in den Hemel der Engelen. | <2 spaced rules> | EERSTE DEEL. | Band I | <2 spaced rules> | *'S-GRAVENHAGE* | SWEDENBORG GENOOTSCHAP | 1960.
8vo
title leaf, 2 pp; facsimile of title page of La 1/6, p 1; text of Exodus 1-8 and n 6627-7487, pp 3-433.
Translated by A Zelling.
UK: soc; NET: gen, kb; SWE: roy, upp

49/01/Du 1/10 **1961** Hyde 810/10
Hemelsche Verborgenheden | DIE IN | *DE HEILIGE SCHRIFT,* | OF | *HET WOORD DES HEREN* | ZIJN, ONTHULD: | Hier die in | *EXODUS,* | Tezamen met De Wonderlijke Dingen | Die gezien zijn | In de Wereld der Geesten, en in den Hemel der Engelen. | <2 spaced rules> | EERSTE DEEL. | Band II | <2 spaced rules> | *'S-GRAVENHAGE* | SWEDENBORG GENOOTSCHAP | 1961.
8vo
title leaf, 2 pp; facsimile of title page of La 1/6, p 1; text of Exodus 9-15 and n 7488-8386, pp 3-429.
Translated by A Zelling.
UK: soc; NET: gen, kb; SWE: upp; USA: anc

49/01/Du 1/11 **1963** Hyde 810/11
Hemelsche Verborgenheden | DIE IN | *DE HEILIGE SCHRIFT,* | OF | *HET WOORD DES HEREN* | ZIJN, ONTHULD: | Hier die in | *EXODUS,* | Tezamen met de Wonderlijke Dingen | Die gezien zijn | In de Wereld der Geesten, en in den Hemel der Engelen. | <2 spaced rules> | TWEEDE DEEL, |

Band III | <two spaced rules> | *'S-GRAVENHAGE* | SWEDENBORG GENOOTSCHAP | 1963.
2nd title: <reproduced from La 1/8>
8vo
title leaves, 4 pp; text of Exodus 16-20 and n 8387- 8957, pp 3-318.
Translated by A Zelling.
UK: SOC; NET: GEN, KB; SWE: UPP; USA: ANC

49/01/Du 1/12 **1963** Hyde 810/12
Hemelsche Verborgenheden | DIE IN | *DE HEILIGE SCHRIFT,* | OF | *HET WOORD DES HEREN* | ZIJN, ONTHULD: | Hier die in | *EXODUS,* | Tezamen met de Wonderlijke Dingen | Die gezien zijn | In de Wereld der Geesten, en in den Hemel der Engelen. | <2 spaced rules> | TWEEDE DEEL, | Band IV | <2 spaced rules> | *'S-GRAVENHAGE* | SWEDENBORG GENOOTSCHAP 1963.
2nd title: <reproduced from La 1/8>
8vo
title leaves, 4 pp; text of Exodus 21-24 and n 8958-9442, pp 3-452.
Translated by A Zelling.
UK: SOC; NET: GEN, KB; SWE: UPP; USA: ANC

49/01/Du 1/13 **1964** Hyde 810/13
Hemelsche Verborgenheden | DIE IN | *DE HEILIGE SCHRIFT,* | OF | *HET WOORD DES HEREN* | ZIJN, ONTHULD: | Hier die in | *EXODUS,* | Tezamen met de Wonderlijke Dingen | Die gezien zijn | In de Wereld der Geesten, en in den Hemel der Engelen. | <2 spaced rules> | DERDE DEEL, | Band V | <2 spaced rules> | *'S-GRAVENHAGE* | SWEDENBORG GENOOTSCHAP 1964.
2nd title: <reproduced from La 1/9>
8vo
title leaves, 4 pp; text of Exodus 25-29 and n 9443-10166, pp 3-549.
Translated by A Zelling.
UK: SOC; NET: GEN, KB; SWE: UPP; USA: ANC

49/01/Du 1/14 **1964** Hyde 810/14
Hemelsche Verborgenheden | DIE IN | *DE HEILIGE SCHRIFT,* | OF | *HET WOORD DES HEREN* | ZIJN, ONTHULD: | Hier die in | *EXODUS,* | Tezamen met de Wonderlijke Dingen | Die gezien zijn | In de Wereld der Geesten, en in den Hemel der Engelen. | <2 spaced rules> | DERDE DEEL, | Band VI | <2 spaced rules> | *'S-GRAVENHAGE* | SWEDENBORG GENOOTSCHAP, 1964.
2nd title: <reproduced from La 1/9>
8vo
title leaves, 4 pp; text of Exodus 30-40 and n 10167-10837, pp 3-465.
Translated by A Zelling.
UK: SOC; NET: GEN, KB; SWE: UPP; USA: ANC

DUTCH EXTRACTS

X 49/01/Du 1913/1 **1913** Hyde —
<untitled>
small 8vo
text n 1311, 4056, 4057, 4060, pp 4, 5, 11-16.
Published in *Grondwaarheden der Christelijke Religie, de Wederkomst des Heeren* <Hyde 3249/1> 's-Gravenhage.
NET: GEN

X 49/01/Du 2006/1 **2006** Hyde —
Citaten uit Swedenborgs Hemelse Verborgenheded
A3 folded to A4
text n 1634, 1636, 1881, 5852, 1627, p 15.
Published in *Swedenborgiana* Editie 57, December 2006, Baarle Nassau, Netherlands.
The title quoted here is the running head on p 15.
UK: SOC, NR; NET: BOE, GEN, KB; USA: ANC

FRENCH

Translators:

- Fr 1 Jean Pierre Moët
- Fr 2 Jean Pierre Moët
- Fr 3 revision of Fr 1 or Fr 2 by J P Parraud and Daillant Delatouche
- Fr 4 not recorded
- Fr 5 Jean François Etienne Le Boys des Guays

49/01/Fr 1/1 **1782** Hyde 794x, 3442
Les | Arcanes Célestes. &c. | <short rule> | Ier. Partie. ch. Ier. - XVe. | <short rule> | 1782. <deleted>
small 8vo <210 x 162 mm>
2 loose leaves containing the text of Genesis 1; text of n 5-1885, pp 7-1009.
The binding of the MS has disintegrated, and the translator's title page and the text of n 1-4 are now missing, the details of the title page given above being reconstructed from later sections of the MS, which is in UK: SOC. <Archives B/2>. The version has not been printed.
The translator was Jean Pierre Moët; the MSS of Fr 1/1-9 and 2/1 were purchased from his widow by J A Tulk, and sent to J F E Le Boys des Guays.
UK: SOC

49/01/Fr 1/2 **1782** Hyde 794x, 3442
Les | Arcanes Célestes. &c. | <short rule> | IIem. Partie. ch. XVIe. - XXIe. | <short rule> | 1782. <deleted> | à die 20am. mensis Junii ad diem 4am. Septembram. <deleted> | <short rule>
small 8vo <212 x 165 mm>
3 blank leaves; title leaf, Swedenborg's preface, and text of n 1886-2759, 640 pp; 2 blank leaves.
The MS is in UK: SOC. <Archives B/2> The version has not been printed.
UK: SOC

49/01/Fr 1/3 **1783** Hyde 794x, 3442
Les | Arcanes Célestes. &c. | <short rule> | IIIe Partie. ch. XXIIe. - XXVIe. | <short rule> | 1783. <deleted> | a die ... mensis junii ad diem 26am mensis julii <deleted> | <short rule> | 1e Section. ch. 22e - 26e. <deleted>
small 8vo <210 x 165 mm>
1 blank leaf; title leaf, contents, Swedenborg's preface, and text of n 2760-3485, 635 pp; 1 blank leaf.
The MS is in UK: SOC. <Archives B/2> The version has not been printed.
UK: SOC

49/01/Fr 1/4 **1783** Hyde 794x, 3442
Les | Arcanes Célestes. &c. | IIIe. Partie, | 2e. Section, <deleted> ch 27e.-30e. | <short rule> | 1783. <deleted> | a die 1a mensis augusti ad diem 16em mensis Septembre. <deleted> | <short rule>

| 2e. Section, ch. 27e - 30e. <deleted>
small 8vo <210 x 165 mm>
1 blank leaf; title leaf and text of n 3486-4055, 536 pp.
The MS is in UK: soc. <Archives B/2> The version has not been printed.
UK: soc

49/01/Fr 1/5 **1783** Hyde 794x, 3442

Les | Arcanes Célestes. | <short rule> | IVe Partie. ch. XXXIe. - XLe. | <short rule> 1783. <deleted> | a die mensis octobri ad diem 22am. januarii 1784. <deleted> | <short rule>
small 8vo <210 x 165 mm>
1 blank leaf; title leaf, contents, and text of n 4056-5190, 1016 pp.
The MS is in UK: soc. <Archives B/2> The version has not been printed.
UK: soc

49/01/Fr 1/6 **1784** Hyde 794x, 3442

Les | Arcanes Célestes. | <short rule> | Ve Partie. ch. XLIe. - Le. | <short rule> | 1784. <deleted> | a die a mensis ... ad diem 7am Novembri. <deleted> | <short rule>
small 8vo <210 x 165 mm>
1 blank leaf; title leaf and contents list, 3 pp; text of n 5191-6626, 944 pp.
To the page facing the title page, the translator attached a note which speaks of illness preventing him from making a fair copy of his MS. <UK: soc Archives B/2> The version has not been printed.
UK: soc

49/01/Fr 1/7 **1785** Hyde 794x, 3442

Emmanuël Swedenborg. | <short rule> | Les | Arcanes Célestes, | qui sont dans l'Escriture Sainte, | ou dans la parole du Seigneur, | manifestés | (Ceux qui sont dans l'Exode): | avec | les merveilles qui ont été vues | dans le monde des Esprits | et dans le ciel des Anges. | <short rule> | 1785. | a die 1a. mensis martii ad diem 14am augusti. | <short rule> | 1e Partie, ch. 1er. de l'Exode jusqu'au XVe | Intra Sacrum et Saxum inveniuntur Regnum Dei | et Sanctitudo ejus. J. P. M... | imprimé in latin, (à Londres) 1753. in 4o.
4to <241 x 193 mm>
1 blank leaf; title leaf, 1 p; text of n 6627-8386, 662 pp; 1 blank leaf.
In place of translations of n 6695-6702, 6807-6817, 6921-6932, 7069-7079, 7170-7177, 7246-7254, 7358-7365, 7475-7487, 7620-7622, 7742-7751, 7799-7813, 8021-8032, 8111-8119, 8242-8251, 8371-8386, Moët refers the reader to the relevant passages in *Le traité des Terres dans l'Univers* <58/01> nos. 70-73.
The MS is in UK: soc. <Archives B/2> The version has not been printed.
UK: soc

49/01/Fr 1/8 **1785** Hyde 794x, 3442

Les | Arcanes Célestes. | <short rule> | 11e Partie de l'Exode, ch. XVIe - XXIVe. | <short rule> | 1785. 86. <deleted> | a die 1a Sbr. ad diem 6am. mensis April. <deleted> | <short rule>
4to <243 x 190 mm>
2 blank leaves; title leaf, 2 pp; text of n 8387-9442, 726 pp; 2 blank leaves.
In place of translations of n 8541-8547, 8627-8634, 8733-8741, 8846-8852, 8947-8957, 9104-9111, 9232-9238, 9350-9362, 9438-9442, Moët refers the reader to the relevant paragraphs in *Le Traité sur Terres dans l'Univers* <58/01>.
In the middle of this volume of the MS <UK: soc Archives B/2> is a leaf in Moët's handwriting with

two drafts of a title page for the whole work; the neater of the two (though crossed through) reads: Les Arcanes Célestes; | ou | Mysteres du Ciel | qui sont dans L'Ecriture Sainte | ou la Parole du Seigneur, | dévoilés: | Et | Merveilles qui ont été vues | dans le monde des Esprits | et | dans le ciel des Anges. | <rule> | Par Emmanuel Swedenborg | Serviteur du Seigneur Jesus Christ | <short rule> | Traduit du Latin sur l'Edition imprimée à | Londres de 1749 a 1758. Par J. P. Moët de | Versailles - et publiée par un Ami de la Vérité | Tome 1r. | comprenans 15. chap. de la Genése | a Paris | Chez Treuttel et Wurtz, rue Bourbon n. 17 | a Strasbourg, même Maison de Commerce | 1821 | <short rule>
Another leaf in Moët's handwriting gives instructions for the guidance of a compositor. The version has not been printed.
UK: SOC

49/01/Fr 1/9 **1786** Hyde 794x, 3442

Les | Arcanes Célestes. | <short rule> | IIIa Partie de l'Exode, ch. XXVe - XL. | <short rule> | 1786 <deleted> | a die 8a. aprilis ad diem 19am mensis Septembri. <deleted> | <short rule>
4to <240 x 194 mm>
2 blank leaves; title leaf, 2 pp; text of n 9443-10837, 905 pp;1 blank leaf.
In place of translations of n 9578-9584, 9693-9700, 9790-9795, 9967-9973, 10159-10166, 10311-10317, 10377-10385, 10513-10518, 10585-10590, 10708-10713, 10734-10739, 10751-10759, 10768-10772, 10783-10788, 10808-10814, 10833-10837, Moët refers the reader to the relevant paragraphs in *Le Traité sur les Terres dans l'Univers* <58/01>, though later he inserted translations of some of these sections. <UK: SOC Archives B/2> The version has not been printed.
UK: SOC

49/01/Fr 2/1 **no date** Hyde 3442

LES ARCANES CÉLESTES | ou | Mystères du Ciel, qui sont dans l'Ecriture sainte, | ou la Parole du SEIGNEUR, dévoilés; | avec | les Merveilles qui ont été vues dans le Monde des | Esprits, et dans le Ciel des Anges. | par Emmanuel Swedenborg, | Serviteur de Notre Seigneur Jesus-Christ. | <short rule> | Traduit du Latin dans l'Edition imprimée à Londres, de 1749 à 1758. | par J. P. Moët, de Versaille. | <short rule> | Tome Ier. | comprenant les 3 premiers Chapitres de la Génèse. | <short rule> | Paris.
small 4to <210 x 165 mm>
title leaf, 2 pp; text of n 1-313, 188 pp; 81 blank leaves.
The undated MS is in UK: SOC. <Archives B/2> The version has not been printed.
UK: SOC

49/01/Fr 3/1 **1820** Hyde —

The Intellectual Repository London 1821, pp 329-330, prints an extract from a letter written by J P Moët <though he is not named> from Geneva, dated 9 September 1820. In it he writes, 'At Lausanne ... they had heard of the printing at Bruxelles, and some having seen the Heaven and Hell <58/02/Fr 3/1>, and the Theology <71/02/Fr 2/1, 2/2>, in French, are interested for the appearance of the *Arcana*. This latter work is now under revisal at Paris, and will be put to the Press immediately on our arrival there, which will take place towards the commencement of the ensuing month.' It would appear that the writer's hopes were not realized. A similar statement is to be found in *The Intellectual Repository* London <1825 pp 515-516>: 'The next work that will be proceeded with is the Arcana Cœlestia: it is now under revisal by Messrs. P— and D—, but the printing will not be commenced till the whole of Genesis is corrected and ready. The sums already disbursed in this extensive undertaking amount to about 27,000 francs. The works are published by Messrs. Treuttel and Wurtz, at Paris, who have also a warehouse in Soho Square, London.'
'Messrs. P— and D—' were probably J P Parraud and Daillant Delatouche. In a letter to Edouard Richer (dated 20 October 1825) Dr Brunet wrote that Parraud was revising J P Moët's translations.

Delatouche was also a member of the group of Frenchmen who were active in translating and publishing French versions of Swedenborg's works at that time. <K-E Sjödén 'Swedenborg in France' *The New Philosophy* Bryn Athyn PA, 1996 pp 207-208>

49/01/Fr 4/1 <1836> Hyde —

Letter from L F de Tollenare printed in *The Precursor* Cincinnati OH, 1836, vol 1, no 1, p 18 <reprinted from *The New Jerusalem Magazine* Boston MA>, dated Nantes, July 25, 1836:
'.... I depart in a few days for England, where I shall remain a couple of months. I have the hope, and almost the certainty, of becoming possessed of the manuscript of a french translation of the Arcana Cœlestia of Swedenborg. One no longer meets with latin editions, and I am the only one here who possesses the english translation. My intention is to undertake the publication of the french translation, which I am going to procure for myself, if I find it faithful and a tolerable good copy....'

49/01/Fr 5/1 **1841** Hyde 795

ARCANES CÉLESTES | DE | L'ÉCRITURE SAINTE OU PAROLE DU SEIGNEUR | DÉVOILÉS, | AINSI QUE | LES MERVEILLES | QUI ONT ÉTÉ VUES DANS LE MONDE DES ESPRITS ET DANS LE CIEL DES ANGES. | <short rule> | OUVRAGE | D'EMMANUEL SWÉDENBORG | PUBLIÉ EN LATIN DE 1749 A 1756, | ET TRADUIT | PAR J. F. E. LE BOYS DES GUAYS. | <short rule> | TOME PREMIER. | GENÈSE, | CHAPITRES I - VII. | SAINT-AMAND (CHER). | A la Librairie de *LA NOUVELLE JÉRUSALEM*, chez Porte, libraire. | PARIS. | Chez <2 lines braced left> M. HARTEL, rue du Mail, 36. | TREUTTEL et WURTZ, libraires, rue de Lille, 17. | 1841 – 85
verso: MATHIEU, VI 33. | Cherchez premièrement le royaume de Dieu et sa justice, et toutes choses | vous seront données par surcroit. <*stet* MATHIEU>
half title: ARCANES CÉLESTES.
verso: <orn 2 x 8 mm> | PARIS. – IMPRIMERIE DE Mme Ve DONDEY-DUPRÉ, | Rue Saint-Louis, 46, au Marais. | <orn 2 x 8 mm>
large 8vo
half title and title leaves, 4 pp; <Contents,> 2 pp; text of Genesis 1-7 and n 1-823, pp 1-386; Table de Concordance, pp 387-390; Errata, p 391.
Originally published by instalments appended to *La Nouvelle-Jérusalem* vol 1, Saint-Amand (Cher), 1838, etc. Five volumes were published in this way. <Hyde>
The 'Table de Concordance' lists differences between the chapter and verse numbering in the Bible version used by Swedenborg and the numbering in Bibles in use in France.
UK: SOC, CON; DEN: RLD; NET: GEN; SWE: GSB, UPP; SWI: LAU; USA: SHS

49/01/Fr 5/2 **1843** Hyde 796

ARCANES CÉLESTES | DE | L'ÉCRITURE SAINTE OU PAROLE DU SEIGNEUR | DÉVOILÉS, | AINSI QUE | LES MERVEILLES | QUI ONT ÉTÉ VUES DANS LE MONDE DES ESPRITS ET DANS LE CIEL DES ANGES. | <short rule> | OUVRAGE | D'EMMANUEL SWÉDENBORG | PUBLIÉ EN LATIN DE 1749 A 1756, | ET TRADUIT | PAR J. F. E. LE BOYS DES GUAYS. | <short rule> | TOME SECOND. | GENÈSE, | CHAPITRES VIII–XII. | SAINT-AMAND (CHER). | A la Librairie de *LA NOUVELLE JÉRUSALEM*, chez Porte, libraire. | PARIS. | Chez <2 lines braced left> M. HARTEL, rue du Mail, 36. | TREUTTEL et WURTZ, libraires, rue de Lille, 17. | 1843 – 87.
verso: MATTHIEU, VI 33. | Cherchez premièrement le royaume de Dieu et sa justice, et toutes choses | vous seront données par surcroit
large 8vo
title leaf, 2 pp; text of Genesis 8-12 and n 824-1520, pp 1-417; Errata to vols 1 and 2, pp 417-418.
UK: SOC, CON; DEN: RLD; NET: GEN; SWE: GSB, UPP; SWI: LAU; USA: SHS

49/01/Fr 5/3 **1845** Hyde 797

ARCANES CÉLESTES | DE | L'ÉCRITURE SAINTE OU PAROLE DU SEIGNEUR | DÉVOILÉS, | AINSI QUE | LES MERVEILLES | QUI ONT ÉTÉ VUES DANS LE MONDE DES ESPRITS ET DANS LE CIEL DES ANGES. | <short rule> | OUVRAGE | D'EMMANUEL SWÉDENBORG | PUBLIÉ EN LATIN DE 1749 A 1756, | ET TRADUIT | PAR J. F. E. LE BOYS DES GUAYS. | <short rule> | TOME TROISIÈME. | GENÈSE, | CHAPITRES XIII–XVII. | SAINT-AMAND (CHER). | A la Librairie de *LA NOUVELLE JÉRUSALEM*, chez Porte, libraire. | PARIS. | Chez <2 lines braced left> M. HARTEL, rue du Mail, 36. | TREUTTEL et WURTZ, libraires, rue de Lille, 17. | 1845–89.

verso: MATTHIEU, VI 33. | Cherchez premièrement le royaume de Dieu et sa justice, et toutes choses vous | seront données par surcroit.

large 8vo

title leaf, 2 pp; text of Genesis 13-17 and n 1521-2134, pp 1-387; Errata to vol 3, p 388.

UK: SOC, CON; DEN: RLD; NET: GEN; SWE: GSB, UPP; SWI: LAU; USA: SHS

49/01/Fr 5/4 **1846** Hyde 798

ARCANES CÉLESTES | DE | L'ÉCRITURE SAINTE OU PAROLE DU SEIGNEUR | DÉVOILÉS, | AINSI QUE | LES MERVEILLES | QUI ONT ÉTÉ VUES DANS LE MONDE DES ESPRITS ET DANS LE CIEL DES ANGES. | <short rule> | OUVRAGE | D'EMMANUEL SWÉDENBORG | PUBLIÉ EN LATIN DE 1749 A 1756, | ET TRADUIT | PAR J. F. E. LE BOYS DES GUAYS. | <short rule> | TOME QUATRIÈME. | GENÈSE, | CHAPITRES XVIII–XXI. | SAINT-AMAND (CHER). | A la Librairie de *LA NOUVELLE JÉRUSALEM*, chez Porte, libraire. | PARIS. | Chez <2 lines braced left> M. HARTEL, rue du Mail, 36. | TREUTTEL et WURTZ, libraires, rue de Lille, 17. | 1846–90.

verso: MATTHIEU, VI 33. | Cherchez premièrement le royaume de Dieu et sa justice, et toutes choses vous | seront données par surcroit.

imprint: <rule> | Paris. –Imprimerie de A. APPERT, Passage du Caire, 54.

large 8vo

title leaf, 2 pp; text of Swedenborg's preface, Genesis 18-21, and n 2135-2759, pp 1-436; Errata, pp 437-438; catalogue, pp 439-440; imprint, p 440.

The errata include a note that the gatherings with signatures 8 and 9 bear the same pagination.

UK: SOC, CON; DEN: RLD; NET: GEN; SWE: GSB, UPP; SWI: LAU; USA: SHS

49/01/Fr 5/5 **1847** Hyde 799

ARCANES CÉLESTES | DE | L'ÉCRITURE SAINTE OU PAROLE DU SEIGNEUR | DÉVOILÉS, | AINSI QUE | LES MERVEILLES | QUI ONT ÉTÉ VUES DANS LE MONDE DES ESPRITS ET DANS LE CIEL DES ANGES. | OUVRAGE | D'EMMANUEL SWÉDENBORG | PUBLIÉ EN LATIN DE 1749 A 1756, | ET TRADUIT | PAR J. F. E. LE BOYS DES GUAYS. | TOME CINQUIÈME. | GENÈSE, | CHAPITRES XXII–XXVI. | SAINT-AMAND (CHER). | A la Librairie de *LA NOUVELLE JÉRUSALEM*, chez Porte, libraire. | PARIS. | Chez <2 lines braced left> M. HARTEL, rue du Mail, 36. | TREUTTEL et WURTZ, libraires, rue de Lille, 17. | 1847–91.

verso: MATTHIEU, VI 33. | Cherchez premièrement le royaume de Dieu et sa justice, et toutes choses vous | seront données par surcroit.

large 8vo

title leaf, 2 pp; text of Swedenborg's preface, Genesis 22-26, and n 2760-3485, pp 1-536; Errata, pp 537-538.

UK: SOC, CON; DEN: RLD; NET: GEN; SWE: GSB, UPP; SWI: LAU; USA: SHS

49/01/Fr 5/6 **1847** Hyde 805

ARCANES CÉLESTES | DE | L'ÉCRITURE SAINTE OU PAROLE DU SEIGNEUR | DÉVOILÉS, | AINSI QUE | LES MERVEILLES | QUI ONT ÉTÉ VUES DANS LE MONDE DES ESPRITS ET DANS

LE CIEL DES ANGES. | <short rule> | OUVRAGE | D'EMMANUEL SWÉDENBORG | PUBLIÉ EN LATIN DE 1749 A 1756, | ET TRADUIT | PAR J. F. E. LE BOYS DES GUAYS, | ET PUBLIÉ | PAR UN DISCIPLE (L. DE Z.) DES DOCTRINES DE LA VRAIE RELIGION CHRÉTIENNE. | <short rule> | TOME ONZIÈME. | EXODE, | CHAPITRES 1 – VIII. | SAINT-AMAND (CHER). | A la librairie de *LA NOUVELLE JÈRUSALEM*, chez Porte, libraire. | PARIS. | Chez <2 lines braced left> M. HARTEL, rue du Mail, 36. | TREUTTEL et WURTZ, libraires, rue de Lille, 17. | 1847– 91.
verso: MATTHIEU, VI, 33. | Cherchez premièrement le royaume de Dieu et sa justice, et toutes | choses vous seront données par surcroit. | <short rule> | Paris. – Imp. de J.-E. Gros, rue de Foin-St-Jacques, 18.
large 8vo
title leaf and advertisement, 3 pp; text of Exodus 1-8 and n 6627-7487, pp 1-443; Errata, p 444.
Published at the expense of Don Lino de Zaroa, a Spaniard who was formerly a priest in the Roman Catholic Church.
UK: soc, con; DEN: rld; NET: gen; SWE: gsb; SWI: lau; USA: shs

49/01/Fr 5/7 **1848** **Hyde 806**
ARCANES CÉLESTES | DE | L'ÉCRITURE SAINTE OU PAROLE DU SEIGNEUR | DÉVOILÉS, | AINSI QUE | LES MERVEILLES | QUI ONT ÉTÉ VUES DANS LE MONDE DES ESPRITS ET DANS LE CIEL DES ANGES. | <short rule> | OUVRAGE | D'EMMANUEL SWÉDENBORG | PUBLIÉ EN LATIN DE 1749 A 1756, | TRADUIT | PAR J. F. E. LE BOYS DES GUAYS, | ET PUBLIÉ | PAR UN DISCIPLE (L. DE Z.) DES DOCTRINES DE LA VRAIE RELIGION CHRÉTIENNE. | <short rule> | TOME DOUZIÈME. | EXODE, | CHAPITRES IX – XV. | SAINT-AMAND (CHER). | A la librairie de *LA NOUVELLE JÉRUSALEM*, chez Porte, libraire. | PARIS. | Chez <2 lines braced left> M. HARTEL, rue de Mail, 36. | TREUTTEL et WURTZ, libraires, rue de Lille, 17. | 1848– 91.
verso: MATTHIEU, VI 33. | Cherchez premièrement le royaume de Dieu et sa justice, et toutes choses | vous seront données par surcroit.
large 8vo
title leaf, 2 pp; text of Exodus 9-15 and n 7488-8386, pp 1-442; Errata, p 443.
Published at the expense of Don Lino de Zaroa.
UK: soc, con; DEN: rld; NET: gen; SWE: gsb; SWI: lau; USA: shs

49/01/Fr 5/8 **1850** **Hyde 800**
ARCANES CÉLESTES | QUI SONT DANS | L'ÉCRITURE SAINTE OU LA PAROLE DU SEIGNEUR | DÉVOILÉS, | Ici ceux qui sont dans la Genèse, | AVEC | LES MERVEILLES | QUI ONT ÉTÉ VUES DANS LE MONDE DES ESPRITS ET DANS LE CIEL DES ANGES. | <short rule> | OUVRAGE | D'EMMANUEL SWÉDENBORG | PUBLIÉ EN LATIN DE 1749 A 1756, | TRADUIT | PAR J. F. E. LE BOYS DES GUAYS. | <short rule> | TOME SIXIÈME. | GENÈSE, | CHAPITRES XXVII–XXX, | Nos 3486 à 4055. | SAINT-AMAND (CHER). | A la Librairie de *LA NOUVELLE JÉRUSALEM*, chez Porte, libraire. | PARIS. | Chez <2 lines braced left> M. MINOT, rue Guénégaud, 7. | TREUTTEL et WURTZ, libraires, rue de Lille, 17. | <short rule> | 1850.
verso: MATTHIEU, VI, 33. | Cherchez premièrement le royaume de Dieu et sa justice, et toutes choses | vous seront données par surcroit.
large 8vo
blank leaf, title leaf, and advertisement, pp i-vi; text of Genesis 27-30 and n 3486-4055, pp 1- 465; Errata, p 466.
UK: soc, con; DEN: rld; NET: gen; SWE: gsb; SWI: lau; USA: shs

49/01/Fr 5/9 **1851** **Hyde 807**
ARCANES CÉLESTES | QUI SONT DANS | L'ÉCRITURE SAINTE OU LA PAROLE DU SEIGNEUR

| DÉVOILÉS: | Ici ceux qui sont dans l'Exode, | AVEC | LES MERVEILLES | QUI ONT ÉTÉ VUES DANS LE MONDE DES ESPRITS ET DANS LE CIEL DES ANGES. | <short rule> | OUVRAGE | D'EMMANUEL SWÉDENBORG | PUBLIÉ EN LATIN DE 1749 A 1756, | TRADUIT | PAR J. F. E. LE BOYS DES GUAYS. | <short rule> | TOME TREIZIÈME. | EXODE. | CHAPITRES XVI – XXI. | Nos 8387 à 9111. | SAINT-AMAND (CHER). | A la librairie de *LA NOUVELLE JÉRUSALEM*, chez PORTE, libraire. | PARIS. | Chez <2 lines braced left> M. MINOT, rue Guénégaud, 7. | TREUTTEL et WURTZ, libraires, rue de Lille, 17. | <short rule> | 1851.
verso: MATTHIEU, VI, 33. | Cherchez premièrement le royaume de Dieu et sa justice, et toutes choses | vous seront données par surcroit.
large 8vo
title leaf, 2 pp; text of Exodus 16-21 and n 8387-9111, pp 1-470; Errata, p 470; avertissement, 1 p.
UK: SOC, CON; DEN: RLD; NET: GEN; SWE: GSB; SWI: LAU; USA: SHS

49/01/Fr 5/10 **1852** Hyde 808
ARCANES CÉLESTES | QUI SONT DANS | L'ÉCRITURE SAINTE OU LA PAROLE DU SEIGNEUR | DÉVOILÉS: | Ici ceux qui sont dans l'Exode, | AVEC | LES MERVEILLES | QUI ONT ÉTÉ VUES DANS LE MONDE DES ESPRITS ET DANS LE CIEL DES ANGES. | <short rule> | OUVRAGE | D'EMMANUEL SWÉDENBORG | PUBLIÉ EN LATIN DE 1749 A 1756, | ET TRADUIT | PAR J. F. E. LE BOYS DES GUAYS. | <short rule> | TOME QUATORZIÈME. | EXODE, | CHAPITRES XXII – XXV. | Nos 9112 à 9584. | SAINT-AMAND (CHER). | A la librairie de *LA NOUVELLE JÉRUSALEM,* chez PORTE, libraire. | PARIS. | Chez <2 lines braced left> M. MINOT, rue Guénégaud, 7. | TREUTTEL et WURTZ, libraires, rue de Lille, 17. | <short rule> | 1852.
verso: MATTHIEU, VI, 33. | Cherchez premièrement le royaume de Dieu et sa justice, et toutes choses | vous seront données par surcroit.
large 8vo
title leaf, 2 pp; text of Exodus 22-25 and n 9112-9584, pp 1-452; Errata, p 452.
UK: SOC, CON; DEN: RLD; NET: GEN; SWE: GSB; SWI: LAU; USA: SHS

49/01/Fr 5/11 **1852** Hyde 801
ARCANES CÉLESTES | QUI SONT DANS | L'ÉCRITURE SAINTE OU LA PAROLE DU SEIGNEUR | DÉVOILÉS, | Ici ceux qui sont dans la Genèse, | avec | LES MERVEILLES | QUI ONT ÉTÉ VUES DANS LE MONDE DES ESPRITS ET DANS LE CIEL DES ANGES. | <short rule> | OUVRAGE | D'EMMANUEL SWÉDENBORG | PUBLIÉ EN LATIN DE 1749 A 1756, | TRADUIT | PAR J. F. E. LE BOYS DES GUAYS. | <short rule> | TOME SEPTIÈME. | GENÈSE, | CHAPITRES XXXI–XXXV, | Nos 4056 à 4634. | SAINT-AMAND (CHER). | A la Librairie de *LA NOUVELLE JÉRUSALEM*, chez Porte, libraire. | PARIS. | Chez <2 lines braced left> M. MINOT, rue Guénégaud, 7. | TREUTTEL et WURTZ, libraires, rue de Lille, 17. | 1852.
verso: MATTHIEU, VI, 33. | Cherchez premièrement le royaume de Dieu et sa justice, et toutes choses | vous seront données par surcroit.
large 8vo
blank leaf and title leaf, 4 pp; text of Genesis 31-35 and n 4056-4634, pp 1-438; Errata, p 439.
UK: SOC, CON; DEN: RLD; NET: GEN; SWE: GSB; SWI: LAU

49/01/Fr 5/12 **1853** Hyde 802
ARCANES CÉLESTES | QUI SONT DANS | L'ÉCRITURE SAINTE OU LA PAROLE DU SEIGNEUR | DÉVOILÉS, | Ici ceux qui sont dans la Genèse, | AVEC | LES MERVEILLES | QUI ONT ÉTÉ VUES DANS LE MONDE DES ESPRITS ET DANS LE CIEL DES ANGES. | <short rule> | OUVRAGE | D'EMMANUEL SWÉDENBORG | PUBLIÉ EN LATIN DE 1749 A 1756, | TRADUIT | PAR J. F. E. LE BOYS DES GUAYS. | <short rule> | TOME HUITIÈME. | GENÈSE, | CHAPITRES XXXVI–XL, | Nos

4635 à 5190. | SAINT-AMAND (CHER). | A la Librairie de *LA NOUVELLE JÉRUSALEM*, chez Porte, libraire. | PARIS. | Chez <2 lines braced left> M. MINOT, rue Guénégaud, 7. | TREUTTEL et WURTZ, libraires, rue de Lille, 17. | 1853.
verso: MATTHIEU, VI. 33. | Cherchez premièrement le royaume de Dieu et sa justice, et toutes choses | vous seront données par surcroit.
large 8vo
blank leaf and title leaf, 4 pp; text of Genesis 36-40 and n 4635-5190, pp 1-432; Errata, p 433.
UK: soc, con; DEN: rld; NET: gen; SWE: gsb; SWI: lau

49/01/Fr 5/13 1853 Hyde 803
ARCANES CÉLESTES | QUI SONT DANS | L'ÉCRITURE SAINTE OU LA PAROLE DU SEIGNEUR | DÉVOILÉS: | Ici ceux qui sont dans la Genèse, | AVEC | LES MERVEILLES | QUI ONT ÉTÉ VUES DANS LE MONDE DES ESPRITS ET DANS LE CIEL DES ANGES. | <short rule> | OUVRAGE | D'EMMANUEL SWÉDENBORG | PUBLIÉ EN LATIN DE 1749 A 1756, | TRADUIT | PAR J. F. E. LE BOYS DES GUAYS. | <short rule> | TOME NEUVIÈME. | GENÈSE, | CHAPITRES XLI–XLIV. | Nos 5191 à 5866. | SAINT-AMAND (CHER). | A la Librairie de *LA NOUVELLE JÉRUSALEM*, chez Porte, libraire. | PARIS. | Chez <2 lines braced left> M. MINOT, rue Guénégaud, 7. | TREUTTEL et WURTZ, libraires, rue de Lille, 17. | <short rule> | 1853.
verso: MATTHIEU, VI. 33. | Cherchez premièrement le royaume de Dieu et sa justice, et toutes choses | vous seront données par surcroit.
large 8vo
blank leaf and title leaf, 4 pp; text of Genesis 41-44 and n 5191-5866, pp 1-392.
UK: soc, con; DEN: rld; NET: gen; SWE: gsb; SWI: lau

49/01/Fr 5/14 1853 Hyde 804
ARCANES CÉLESTES | QUI SONT DANS | L'ÉCRITURE SAINTE OU LA PAROLE DU SEIGNEUR | DÉVOILÉS: | Ici ceux qui sont dans la Genèse, | AVEC | LES MERVEILLES | QUI ONT ÉTÉ VUES DANS LE MONDE DES ESPRITS ET DANS LE CIEL DES ANGES. | <short rule> | OUVRAGE | D'EMMANUEL SWÉDENBORG | PUBLIÉ EN LATIN DE 1749 A 1756, | TRADUIT | PAR J. F. E. LE BOYS DES GUAYS. | <short rule> | TOME DIXIÈME. | GENÈSE, | CHAPITRES XLV–L. | Nos 5867 à 6626. | SAINT-AMAND (CHER). | A la Librairie de *LA NOUVELLE JÉRUSALEM*, chez Porte, libraire. | PARIS. | Chez <2 lines braced left> M. MINOT, rue Guénégaud, 7. | TREUTTEL et WURTZ, libraires, rue de Lille, 17. | LONDRES. | SWEDENBORG'S PRINTING SOCIETY, No 6, King Street, Holborn. | <short rule> | 1853.
verso: MATTHIEU, VI. 33. | Cherchez premièrement le royaume de Dieu et sa justice, et toutes choses | vous seront données par surcroit.
large 8vo
blank leaf and title leaf, 4 pp; text of Genesis 45-50 and n 5867-6626, pp 1-442; catalogue, 2 pp.
UK: soc, con; DEN: rld; NET: gen; SWE: gsb; SWI: lau

49/01/Fr 5/15 1853 Hyde 809
ARCANES CÉLESTES | QUI SONT DANS | L'ÉCRITURE SAINTE OU LA PAROLE DU SEIGNEUR | DÉVOILÉS: | Ici ceux qui sont dans l'Exode, | AVEC | LES MERVEILLES | QUI ONT ÉTÉ VUES DANS LE MONDE DES ESPRITS ET DANS LE CIEL DES ANGES. | <short rule> | OUVRAGE | D'EMMANUEL SWÉDENBORG | PUBLIÉ EN LATIN DE 1749 A 1756, | TRADUIT | PAR J. F. E. LE BOYS DES GUAYS. | <short rule> | TOME QUINZIÈME. | EXODE, | CHAPITRES XXVI – XXIX. | Nos 9585 à 10166. | SAINT-AMAND (CHER). | A la librairie de *LA NOUVELLE JÉRUSALEM*, chez PORTE, libraire. | PARIS. | Chez <2 lines braced left> M. MINOT, rue Guénégaud, 7. | TREUTTEL et WURTZ, libraires, rue de Lille, 17. | <short rule> | 1853.
verso: MATTHIEU, VI. 33. | Cherchez premièrement le royaume de Dieu et sa justice, et toutes choses | vous seront données par surcroit.

large 8vo
title leaf, 2 pp; text of Exodus 26-29 and n 9585-10166, pp 1-504; Errata, p 504.
UK: soc, con; DEN: rld; NET: gen; SWE: gsb; SWI: lau; USA: shs

49/01/Fr 5/16 1854 Hyde 810

ARCANES CÉLESTES | QUI SONT DANS | L'ÉCRITURE SAINTE OU LA PAROLE DU SEIGNEUR | DÉVOILÉS: | Ici ceux qui sont dans l'Exode, | AVEC | LES MERVEILLES | QUI ONT ÉTÉ VUES DANS LE MONDE DES ESPRITS ET DANS LE CIEL DES ANGES. | <short rule> | OUVRAGE | D'EMMANUEL SWÉDENBORG | PUBLIÉ EN LATIN DE 1749 A 1756, | TRADUIT | PAR J. F. E. LE BOYS DES GUAYS. | <short rule> | TOME SEIZIÈME. | EXODE, | CHAPITRES XXX – XL. | Nos 10167 à 10837. | SAINT-AMAND (CHER). | A la librairie de *LA NOUVELLE JÉRUSALEM,* chez PORTE, libraire. | PARIS. | Chez <2 lines braced left> M. MINOT, rue Guénégaud, 7. | TREUTTEL et WURTZ, libraires, rue de Lille, 17. | LONDRES. | SWEDENBORG'S PRINTING SOCIETY, No 6, King Street, Holborn. | <short rule> | 1854.
verso: MATTHIEU, VI, 33. | Cherchez premièrement le royaume de Dieu et sa justice, et toutes choses | vous seront données par surcroit.
half title: ARCANES CÉLESTES.
verso: <short rule> | SAINT-AMAND-MONT-ROND (CHER), | IMPRIMERIE DE DESTENAY ET LAMBERT, RUE LAFAYETTE, 55, | Place Mont-Rond. | <short rule>
large 8vo
half title and title leaves, 4 pp; text of Exodus 30-40 and n 10167-10837, pp 1-498; catalogue of Swedenborg's works, pp 499-500.
UK: soc, con; DEN: rld; NET: gen; SWE: gsb; SWI: lau; USA: shs

49/01/Fr 5/17 1986 Hyde 795/1

ARCANES CÉLESTES | DE | L'ÉCRITURE SAINTE OU PAROLE DU SEIGNEUR | DÉVOILÉS, | AINSI QUE | LES MERVEILLES | QUI ONT ÉTÉ VUES DANS LE MONDE DES ESPRITS ET DANS LE CIEL DES ANGES. | <short rule> | OUVRAGE | D'EMMANUEL SWÉDENBORG | PUBLIÉ EN LATIN DE 1749 A 1756, | ET TRADUIT | PAR J. F. E. LE BOYS DES GUAYS. | <short rule> | TOME PREMIER. | GENÈSE, | CHAPITRES I - VII. | SAINT-AMAND (CHER). | A la Librairie de *LA NOUVELLE JÉRUSALEM*, chez Porte, libraire. | PARIS. | Chez <2 lines braced left> M. HARTEL, rue du Mail, 36. | TREUTTEL et WURTZ, libraires, rue de Lille, 17. | 1841 – 85.
verso: MATHIEU, VI 33. | Cherchez premièrement le royaume de Dieu et sa justice, et toutes choses | vous seront données par surcroit. <*stet* MATHIEU>
large 8vo
title leaf, 2 pp; text of Genesis 1-7 and n 1-823, pp 1-386; Table de Concordance, pp 387-390; Errata, p 391.
Photographic replica reprint of Fr 5/1 = Hyde 795, published by the Swedenborg Foundation, New York, and Information Swedenborg Inc, Toronto.
UK: soc; SWI: lau; USA: anc

49/01/Fr 5/18 1994 Hyde 796/1

ARCANES CÉLESTES | DE | L'ÉCRITURE SAINTE OU PAROLE DU SEIGNEUR | DÉVOILÉS, | AINSI QUE | LES MERVEILLES | QUI ONT ÉTÉ VUES DANS LE MONDE DES ESPRITS ET DANS LE CIEL DES ANGES. | <short rule> | OUVRAGE | D'EMMANUEL SWÉDENBORG | PUBLIÉ EN LATIN DE 1749 A 1756, | ET TRADUIT | PAR J. F. E. LE BOYS DES GUAYS. | <short rule> | TOME SECOND. | GENÈSE, | CHAPITRES VIII-XII. | SAINT-AMAND (CHER). | A la Librairie de *LA NOUVELLE JÉRUSALEM*, chez Porte, libraire. | PARIS. | Chez <2 lines braced left> M. HARTEL, rue du Mail, 36. | TREUTTEL et WURTZ, libraires, rue de Lille, 17. | 1843 – 87.

half title: ARCANES CÉLESTES.
large 8vo
half title leaf, 2 pp; Avertissement aux lecteurs <Notice to the readers>, 2 pp; Biographie d'Emmanuel Swedenborg, 2 pp; title leaf, 2 pp; text of Genesis 8-12 and n 824-1520, pp 1-417; Errata to vols 1 and 2, 1 p; publishing details, 1 p.
Photographic replica reprint of Fr 5/2 = Hyde 7, with the addition of a brief introductory biography of Swedenborg, published by Cercle Swedenborg, Rouvray.
UK: SOC; USA: ANC

49/01/Fr 5/19 **1994** Hyde 798/–
ARCANES CÉLESTES | DE | L'ÉCRITURE SAINTE OU PAROLE DU SEIGNEUR | DÉVOILÉS, | AINSI QUE | LES MERVEILLES | QUI ONT ÉTÉ VUES DANS LE MONDE DES ESPRITS ET DANS LE CIEL DES ANGES. | <short rule> | OUVRAGE | D'EMMANUEL SWÉDENBORG | PUBLIÉ EN LATIN DE 1749 A 1756, | ET TRADUIT | PAR J. F. E. LE BOYS DES GUAYS. | <short rule> | TOME QUATRIÈME. | GENÈSE, | CHAPITRES XVIII-XXI. | SAINT-AMAND (CHER). | A la Librairie de LA NOUVELLE JÉRUSALEM, chez Porte, libraire. | PARIS. | Chez <2 lines braced left> M. HARTEL, rue du Mail, 36. | TREUTTEL et WURTZ, libraires, rue de Lille, 17. | 1846 – 90.
verso: MATTHIEU, VI 33. | Cherchez premièrement le royaume de Dieu et sa justice, et toutes choses | vous seront données par surcroit.
large 8vo
title leaf, 2 pp; text of Swedenborg's preface, Genesis 18-21, and n 2135-2759, pp 1-436; Errata, pp 437-438; catalogue, 2 pp.
Photographic replica reprint of Fr 5/4 = Hyde 798 published by Cercle Swedenborg, Rouvray.
USA: ANC

49/01/Fr 5/20 **1995** Hyde 797/1
ARCANES CÉLESTES | DE | L'ÉCRITURE SAINTE OU PAROLE DU SEIGNEUR| DÉVOILÉS, | AINSI QUE | LES MERVEILLES | QUI ONT ÉTÉ VUES DANS LE MONDE DES ESPRITS ET DANS LE CIEL DES ANGES. | <short rule> | OUVRAGE | D'EMMANUEL SWÉDENBORG | PUBLIÉ EN LATIN DE 1749 A 1756, | ET TRADUIT | PAR J. F. E. LE BOYS DES GUAYS. | de 1845 à 1889 | TOME TROISIÈME. | GENÈSE, | CHAPITRES XIII-XVII. | Cercle Swedenborg | 1995
verso: MATTHIEU, VI 33. | Cherchez premièrement le royaume de Dieu et sa justice, et toutes choses | vous seront données par surcroit.
large 8vo
title leaf, 2 pp; text of Genesis 13-16 and n 1521-2134, pp 1-387; Errata to vol 3, p 388; Avertissement aux lecteurs <Notice to readers>, 1 p; publishing details, 2 pp.
Photographic replica reprint of Fr 5/3 = Hyde 797 published by Cercle Swedenborg, Talant.
UK: SOC

49/01/Fr 5/21 **2005** Hyde 795/–
EMMANUEL SWEDENBORG | ARCANES CÉLESTES | DE | L'ÉCRITURE SAINTE | OU | PAROLE DU SEIGNEUR DÉVOILÉS | *ainsi que* | LES MERVEILLES | *qui ont été vues dans le monde des* | *esprits et dans le ciel des anges* | TOME I | Elibron Classics | www.elibron.com
verso: Elibron Classics series. | © 2005 Adamant Media Corporation. | ISBN 0-543-98856-2 (paperback) | ISBN 0-543-98855-4 (hardcover) | This Elibron Classics Replica Edition is an unabridged facsimile | of the edition published in 1885 by Porte, Saint-Amand; | M. Hartel; Treuttel et Wurtz, Paris. | Elibron and Elibron Classics are trademarks of | Adamant Media Corporation. All rights reserved. <*stet* 1885>
half title: ARCANES CÉLESTES.

verso: <orn 2 x 8 mm> | PARIS. – IMPRIMERIE DE Mme Ve DONDEY-DUPRÉ, | Rue Saint-Louis, 46, au Marais. | <orn 2 x 8 mm>
2nd title: ARCANES CÉLESTES | DE | L'ÉCRITURE SAINTE OU PAROLE DU SEIGNEUR | DÉVOILÉS, | AINSI QUE | LES MERVEILLES | QUI ONT ÉTÉ VUES DANS LE MONDE DES ESPRITS ET DANS LE CIEL DES ANGES. | <short rule> | OUVRAGE | D'EMMANUEL SWÉDENBORG | PUBLIÉ EN LATIN DE 1749 A 1756, | ET TRADUIT | PAR J. F. E. LE BOYS DES GUAYS. | <short rule> | TOME PREMIER. | GENÈSE, | CHAPITRES I - VII. | SAINT-AMAND (CHER). | A la Librairie de *LA NOUVELLE JÉRUSALEM*, chez Porte, libraire. | PARIS. | Chez <2 lines braced left> M. HARTEL, rue du Mail, 36. | TREUTTEL et WURTZ, libraires, rue de Lille, 17. | 1841 – 85
verso: MATHIEU, VI 33. | Cherchez premièrement le royaume de Dieu et sa justice, et toutes choses | vous seront données par surcroit. <*stet* MATHIEU>
large 8vo
title leaf, 2 pp; Publisher's note concerning the reproduction, 1 p; half title and 2nd title leaves, 4 pp; <Contents, untitled>, 2 pp; text of Genesis 1-7 and n 1-823, pp 1-386; Table de Concordance <with editorial notes>, pp 387-390; Errata, p 391; bar code and 'Made in the USA', p 394.
Photographic replica reprint of Fr 5/1 = Hyde 795, first published in 2001. The copy obtained 'print on demand' by Norman Ryder in 2007 has the copyright date '2005'. The date '1885' on the verso of the title leaf is a conflation of the publication date '1841 – 85' on the title page of Fr 5/1.
UK: NR

49/01/Fr 5/22 **2005** Hyde 796/–
<<EMMANUEL SWEDENBORG | ARCANES CÉLESTES | DE | L'ÉCRITURE SAINTE | OU | PAROLE DU SEIGNEUR DÉVOILÉS | *ainsi que* | LES MERVEILLES | *qui ont été vues dans le monde des* | *esprits et dans le ciel des anges* | TOME II | Elibron Classics | www.elibron.com>>
verso: <<Elibron Classics series. | © 2005 Adamant Media Corporation. | ISBN 0-543-98854-6 (paperback) | ISBN 0-543-98853-8 (hardcover) | This Elibron Classics Replica Edition is an unabridged facsimile | of the edition published in 1887 by Porte, Saint-Amand; | M. Hartel; Treuttel et Wurtz, Paris. | Elibron and Elibron Classics are trademarks of | Adamant Media Corporation. All rights reserved.>> <*stet* 1887>
half title: <<ARCANES CÉLESTES.>>
verso: << <orn 2 x 8 mm> | PARIS: – IMPRIMERIE DE Mme Ve DONDEY-DUPRÉ, | Rue Saint-Louis, 46, au Marais. | <orn 2 x 8 mm> >>
2nd title: <<ARCANES CÉLESTES | DE | L'ÉCRITURE SAINTE OU PAROLE DU SEIGNEUR | DÉVOILÉS, | AINSI QUE | LES MERVEILLES | QUI ONT ÉTÉ VUES DANS LE MONDE DES ESPRITS ET DANS LE CIEL DES ANGES. | <short rule> | OUVRAGE | D'EMMANUEL SWÉDENBORG | PUBLIÉ EN LATIN DE 1749 A 1756, | ET TRADUIT | PAR J. F. E. LE BOYS DES GUAYS. | <short rule> | TOME SECOND. | GENÈSE, | CHAPITRES VIII–XII. | SAINT-AMAND (CHER). | A la Librairie de *LA NOUVELLE JÉRUSALEM*, chez Porte, libraire. | PARIS. | Chez <2 lines braced left> M. HARTEL, rue du Mail, 36. | TREUTTEL et WURTZ, libraires, rue de Lille, 17. | 1843 – 87.>>
verso: <<MATTHIEU, VI 33. | Cherchez premièrement le royaume de Dieu et sa justice, et toutes choses | vous seront données par surcroit.>>
large 8vo
title leaf, 2 pp; Publisher's note concerning the reproduction, 1 p; half title and 2nd title leaf, 4 pp; text of Genesis 8-12 and n 824-1520, pp 1-417; Errata in vols 1 and 2, pp 417-418; bar code and 'Made in the USA', p 420.
Photographic replica reprint of Fr 5/2 = Hyde 796, first published in 2001. The date '1887' on the verso of the title leaf is a conflation of the publication date '1843 – 87' on the title page of Fr 5/2.
Copy not seen; description deduced from publisher's advertisement.

49/01/Fr 5/23 — 2005 — Hyde 797/–

<<EMMANUEL SWEDENBORG | ARCANES CÉLESTES | DE | L'ÉCRITURE SAINTE | OU | PAROLE DU SEIGNEUR DÉVOILÉS | *ainsi que* | LES MERVEILLES | *qui ont été vues dans le monde des* | *esprits et dans le ciel des anges* | TOME III | Elibron Classics | www.elibron.com>>
verso: <<Elibron Classics series. | © 2005 Adamant Media Corporation. | ISBN 0-543-98850-3 (paperback) | ISBN 0-543-98849 X (hardcover) | This Elibron Classics Replica Edition is an unabridged facsimile | of the edition published in 1889 by Porte, Saint-Amand; | M. Hartel; Treuttel et Wurtz, Paris. | Elibron and Elibron Classics are trademarks of | Adamant Media Corporation. All rights reserved.>> <*stet* 1889>
half title: <<ARCANES CÉLESTES.>>
verso: << <orn 2 x 8 mm> | PARIS. – IMPRIMERIE DE A. APPERT, | Passage du Caire, 54. | <orn 2 x 8 mm> >>
2nd title: <<ARCANES CÉLESTES | DE | L'ÉCRITURE SAINTE OU PAROLE DU SEIGNEUR | DÉVOILÉS, | AINSI QUE | LES MERVEILLES | QUI ONT ÉTÉ VUES DANS LE MONDE DES ESPRITS ET DANS LE CIEL DES ANGES. | <short rule> | OUVRAGE | D'EMMANUEL SWÉDENBORG | PUBLIÉ EN LATIN DE 1749 A 1756, | ET TRADUIT | PAR J. F. E. LE BOYS DES GUAYS. | <short rule> | TOME TROISIÈME. | GENÈSE, | CHAPITRES XIII–XVII. | SAINT-AMAND (CHER). | A la Librairie de *LA NOUVELLE JÉRUSALEM*, chez Porte, libraire. | PARIS. | Chez <2 lines braced left> M. HARTEL, rue du Mail, 36. | TREUTTEL et WURTZ, libraires, rue de Lille, 17. | 1845–89.>>
verso: <<MATTHIEU, VI 33. | Cherchez premièrement le royaume de Dieu et sa justice, et toutes choses vous | seront données par surcroit.>>
large 8vo
title leaf, 2pp; Publisher's note concerning the reproduction, 1 p; half title leaf and 2nd title leaf, 4 pp; text of Genesis 13-17 and n 1521-2134, pp 1-387; Errata in vol 3, p 388; bar code and 'Made in the USA', p 390.
Photographic replica reprint of Fr 5/3 = Hyde 797, first published in 2001. The date '1889' on the verso of the title leaf is a conflation of the publication date '1845 – 89' on the title page of Fr 5/3.
Copy not seen; description deduced from publisher's advertisement.

49/01/Fr 5/24 — 2005 — Hyde 798/–

<<EMMANUEL SWEDENBORG | ARCANES CÉLESTES | DE | L'ÉCRITURE SAINTE | OU | PAROLE DU SEIGNEUR DÉVOILÉS | *ainsi que* | LES MERVEILLES | *qui ont été vues dans le monde des* | *esprits et dans le ciel des anges* | TOME IV | Elibron Classics | www.elibron.com>>
verso: <<Elibron Classics series. | © 2001 Adamant Media Corporation. | ISBN 0-543-98848-1 (paperback) | ISBN 0-543-98847-3 (hardcover) | This Elibron Classics Replica Edition is an unabridged facsimile | of the edition published in 1890 by Porte, Saint-Amand; | M. Hartel; Treuttel et Wurtz, Paris. | Elibron and Elibron Classics are trademarks of | Adamant Media Corporation. All rights reserved.>> <*stet* 1890>
half title: <<ARCANES CÉLESTES.>>
verso: << <orn 2 x 8 mm> | Paris: – IMPRIMERIE DE A. APPERT, | Passage du Caire, 54. | <orn 2 x 8 mm> >>
2nd title: <<ARCANES CÉLESTES | DE | L'ÉCRITURE SAINTE OU PAROLE DU SEIGNEUR | DÉVOILÉS, | AINSI QUE | LES MERVEILLES | QUI ONT ÉTÉ VUES DANS LE MONDE DES ESPRITS ET DANS LE CIEL DES ANGES. | <short rule> | OUVRAGE | D'EMMANUEL SWÉDENBORG | PUBLIÉ EN LATIN DE 1749 A 1756, | ET TRADUIT | PAR J. F. E. LE BOYS DES GUAYS. | <short rule> | TOME QUATRIÈME. | GENÈSE, | CHAPITRES XVIII–XXI. | SAINT-AMAND (CHER). | A la Librairie de *LA NOUVELLE JÉRUSALEM*, chez Porte, libraire. | PARIS. | Chez <2 lines braced left> M. HARTEL, rue du Mail, 36. | TREUTTEL et WURTZ, libraires, rue de Lille, 17. | 1846–90.>>
verso: <<MATTHIEU, VI 33. | Cherchez premièrement le royaume de Dieu et sa justice, et toutes choses vous | seront données par surcroit.>>

imprint: <<Paris. –Imprimerie de A. APPERT, Passage du Caire, 54.>>
large 8vo
title leaf, 2 pp; Publisher's note concerning the reproduction, 1 p; half title leaf and 2nd title leaf, 4 pp; text of Swedenborg's preface, Genesis 18-21, and n 2135-2759, pp 1-436; Errata, pp 437-438; catalogue, pp 439-440; imprint, p 440; bar code and 'Made in the USA', p 442.
Photographic replica reprint of Fr 5/4 = Hyde 798. The date '1890' on the verso of the title leaf is a conflation of the publication date '1846 – 90' on the title page of Fr 5/4.
Copy not seen; description deduced from publisher's advertisement.

49/01/Fr 5/25 **2005** Hyde 799/–
<<EMMANUEL SWEDENBORG | ARCANES CÉLESTES | DE | L'ÉCRITURE SAINTE | OU | PAROLE DU SEIGNEUR DÉVOILÉS | *ainsi que* | LES MERVEILLES | *qui ont été vues dans le monde des* | *esprits et dans le ciel des anges* | TOME V | Elibron Classics | www.elibron.com>>
verso: <<Elibron Classics series. | © 2005 Adamant Media Corporation. | ISBN 1-4212-1034-7 (paperback) | ISBN 1-4212-1033-9 (hardcover) | This Elibron Classics Replica Edition is an unabridged facsimile | of the edition published in 1891 by Porte, Saint-Amand; | M. Hartel; Treuttel et Wurtz, Paris. | Elibron and Elibron Classics are trademarks of | Adamant Media Corporation. All rights reserved.>> <*stet* 1891>
half title: <<ARCANES CÉLESTES.>>
2nd title: <<ARCANES CÉLESTES | DE | L'ÉCRITURE SAINTE OU PAROLE DU SEIGNEUR | DÉVOILÉS, | AINSI QUE | LES MERVEILLES | QUI ONT ÉTÉ VUES DANS LE MONDE DES ESPRITS ET DANS LE CIEL DES ANGES. | OUVRAGE | D'EMMANUEL SWÉDENBORG | PUBLIÉ EN LATIN DE 1749 A 1756, | ET TRADUIT | PAR J. F. E. LE BOYS DES GUAYS. | TOME CINQUIÈME. | GENÈSE, | CHAPITRES XXII–XXVI. | SAINT-AMAND (CHER). | A la Librairie de *LA NOUVELLE JÉRUSALEM*, chez Porte, libraire. | PARIS. | Chez <2 lines braced left> M. HARTEL, rue du Mail, 36. | TREUTTEL et WURTZ, libraires, rue de Lille, 17. | 1847–91.>>
verso: <<MATTHIEU, VI 33. | Cherchez premièrement le royaume de Dieu et sa justice, et toutes choses vous | seront données par surcroit.>>
large 8vo
title leaf, 2 pp; Publisher's note concerning the reproduction, 1 p; half title leaf and 2nd title leaf, 4 pp; text of Swedenborg's preface, Genesis 22-26, and n 2760-3485, pp 1-536; Errata, pp 537-538; bar code and 'Made in the USA', p 540.
Photographic replica reprint of Fr 5/5 = Hyde 799. The date '1891' on the verso of the title leaf is a conflation of the publication date '1847 – 91' on the title page of Fr 5/5.
Copy not seen; description deduced from publisher's advertisement.

49/01/Fr 5/26 **2005** Hyde 800/–
<<EMMANUEL SWEDENBORG | ARCANES CÉLESTES | qui sont dans | L'ÉCRITURE SAINTE | OU | PAROLE DU SEIGNEUR DÉVOILÉS | Ici ceux qui sont dans la Genèse, | AVEC | LES MERVEILLES | *qui ont été vues dans le monde des* | *esprits et dans le ciel des anges* | TOME VI | Elibron Classics | www.elibron.com>>
verso: <<Elibron Classics series. | © 2005 Adamant Media Corporation. | ISBN 1-4212-2267-1 (paperback) | ISBN 1-4212-2286-3 (hardcover) | This Elibron Classics Replica Edition is an unabridged facsimile | of the edition published in 1850 by Porte, Saint-Amand; | M. Minot; Treuttel et Wurtz, Paris. | Elibron and Elibron Classics are trademarks of | Adamant Media Corporation. All rights reserved.>>
half title: <<ARCANES CÉLESTES.>>
2nd title: <<ARCANES CÉLESTES | QUI SONT DANS | L'ÉCRITURE SAINTE OU LA PAROLE DU SEIGNEUR | DÉVOILÉS, | Ici ceux qui sont dans la Genèse, | AVEC | LES MERVEILLES | QUI ONT ÉTÉ VUES DANS LE MONDE DES ESPRITS ET DANS LE CIEL DES ANGES. | <short rule> |

OUVRAGE | D'EMMANUEL SWÉDENBORG | PUBLIÉ EN LATIN DE 1749 A 1756, | TRADUIT | PAR J. F. E. LE BOYS DES GUAYS. | <short rule> | TOME SIXIÈME. | GENÈSE, | CHAPITRES XXVII–XXX, | Nos 3486 à 4055. | SAINT-AMAND (CHER). | A la Librairie de *LA NOUVELLE JÉRUSALEM*, chez Porte, libraire. | PARIS. | Chez <2 lines braced left> M. MINOT, rue Guénégaud, 7. | TREUTTEL et WURTZ, libraires, rue de Lille, 17. | <short rule> | 1850.>>
verso: <<MATTHIEU, VI, 33. | Cherchez premièrement le royaume de Dieu et sa justice, et toutes choses | vous seront données par surcroit.>>
large 8vo
title leaf, 2 pp; Publisher's note concerning the reproduction, 1 p; half title leaf and 2nd title leaf, 4 pp; text of Genesis 27-30 and n 3486-4055, pp 1- 465; Errata, p 466; bar code and 'Made in the USA', p 468.
Photographic replica reprint of Fr 5/8 = Hyde 800.
Copy not seen; description deduced from publisher's advertisement.

49/01/Fr 5/27 **2005** Hyde 801/–
<<EMMANUEL SWEDENBORG | ARCANES CÉLESTES | qui sont dans | L'ÉCRITURE SAINTE | OU | PAROLE DU SEIGNEUR DÉVOILÉS | Ici ceux qui sont dans la Genèse, | avec | LES MERVEILLES | *qui ont été vues dans le monde des* | *esprits et dans le ciel des anges* | TOME VII | Elibron Classics | www.elibron.com>>
verso: <<Elibron Classics series. | © 2005 Adamant Media Corporation. | ISBN 1-4212-3504-8 (paperback) | ISBN 1-4212-3503-X (hardcover) | This Elibron Classics Replica Edition is an unabridged facsimile | of the edition published in 1852 by Porte, Saint-Amand; | M. Minot; Treuttel et Wurtz, Paris. | Elibron and Elibron Classics are trademarks of | Adamant Media Corporation. All rights reserved.>>
half title: <<ARCANES CÉLESTES.>>
verso: << <short rule> | PARIS. – IMPRIMERIE DE J.-B. GROS, | Rue des Noyes, 74. | <short rule> >>
2nd title: <<ARCANES CÉLESTES | QUI SONT DANS | L'ÉCRITURE SAINTE OU LA PAROLE DU SEIGNEUR | DÉVOILÉS, | Ici ceux qui sont dans la Genèse, | avec | LES MERVEILLES | QUI ONT ÉTÉ VUES DANS LE MONDE DES ESPRITS ET DANS LE CIEL DES ANGES. | <short rule> | OUVRAGE | D'EMMANUEL SWÉDENBORG | PUBLIÉ EN LATIN DE 1749 A 1756, | TRADUIT | PAR J. F. E. LE BOYS DES GUAYS. | <short rule> | TOME SEPTIÈME. | GENÈSE, | CHAPITRES XXXI–XXXV, | Nos 4056 à 4634. | SAINT-AMAND (CHER). | A la Librairie de *LA NOUVELLE JÉRUSALEM*, chez Porte, libraire. | PARIS. | Chez <2 lines braced left> M. MINOT, rue Guénégaud, 7. | TREUTTEL et WURTZ, libraires, rue de Lille, 17. | 1852.>>
verso: <<MATTHIEU, VI, 33. | Cherchez premièrement le royaume de Dieu et sa justice, et toutes choses | vous seront données par surcroit.>>
large 8vo
title leaf, 2 pp; Publisher's note concerning the reproduction, 1 p; half title leaf and 2nd title leaf, 4 pp; text of Genesis 31-35 and n 4056-4634, pp 1-438; Errata, p 439; bar code and 'Made in the USA', p 442.
Photographic replica reprint of Fr 5/11 = Hyde 801.
Copy not seen; description deduced from publisher's advertisement.

49/01/Fr 5/28 **2005** Hyde 802/–
<<EMMANUEL SWEDENBORG | ARCANES CÉLESTES | qui sont dans | L'ÉCRITURE SAINTE | OU | PAROLE DU SEIGNEUR DÉVOILÉS | Ici ceux qui sont dans la Genèse, | avec | LES MERVEILLES | *qui ont été vues dans le monde des* | *esprits et dans le ciel des anges* | TOME VIII | Elibron Classics | www.elibron.com>>
verso: <<Elibron Classics series. | © 2005 Adamant Media Corporation. | ISBN 1-4212-2265-3 (paperback) | ISBN 1-4212-2264-6 (hardcover) | This Elibron Classics Replica Edition is an

unabridged facsimile | of the edition published in 1853 by Porte, Saint-Amand; | M. Minot; Treuttel et Wurtz, Paris. | Elibron and Elibron Classics are trademarks of | Adamant Media Corporation. All rights reserved.>>
half title: <<ARCANES CÉLESTES.>>
2nd title: <<ARCANES CÉLESTES | QUI SONT DANS | L'ÉCRITURE SAINTE OU LA PAROLE DU SEIGNEUR | DÉVOILÉS, | Ici ceux qui sont dans la Genèse, | AVEC | LES MERVEILLES | QUI ONT ÉTÉ VUES DANS LE MONDE DES ESPRITS ET DANS LE CIEL DES ANGES. | <short rule> | OUVRAGE | D'EMMANUEL SWEDENBORG | PUBLIÉ EN LATIN DE 1749 A 1756, | TRADUIT | PAR J. F. E. LE BOYS DES GUAYS. | <short rule> | TOME HUITIÈME. | GENÈSE, | CHAPITRES XXXVI–XL, | Nos 4635 à 5190. | SAINT-AMAND (CHER). | A la Librairie de *LA NOUVELLE JÉRUSALEM*, chez Porte, libraire. | PARIS. | Chez <2 lines braced left> M. MINOT, rue Guénégaud, 7. | TREUTTEL et WURTZ, libraires, rue de Lille, 17. | 1853.>>
verso: <<MATTHIEU, VI. 33. | Cherchez premièrement le royaume de Dieu et sa justice, et toutes choses vous | seront données par surcroit.>>
large 8vo
title leaf, 2 pp; Publisher's note concerning the reproduction, 1 p; half title and 2nd title leaf, 4 pp; text of Genesis 36-40 and n 4635-5190, pp 1-432; Errata, p 433; bar code and 'Made in the USA', p 436.
Photographic replica reprint of Fr 5/12 = Hyde 802, first published in 2001.
Copy not seen; description deduced from publisher's advertisement.

49/01/Fr 5/29 **2005** Hyde 803/–
<<EMMANUEL SWEDENBORG | ARCANES CÉLESTES | qui sont dans | L'ÉCRITURE SAINTE | OU | PAROLE DU SEIGNEUR DÉVOILÉS | Ici ceux qui sont dans la Genèse, | AVEC | LES MERVEILLES | *qui ont été vues dans le monde des* | *esprits et dans le ciel des anges* | TOME IX | Elibron Classics | www.elibron.com>>
verso: <<Elibron Classics series. | © 2005 Adamant Media Corporation. | ISBN 0-543-988-461 (paperback) | ISBN 0-543-988-454 (hardcover) | This Elibron Classics Replica Edition is an unabridged facsimile | of the edition published in 1853 by Porte, Saint-Amand; | M. Minot; Treuttel et Wurtz, Paris. | Elibron and Elibron Classics are trademarks of | Adamant Media Corporation. All rights reserved.>>
half title: <<ARCANES CÉLESTES.>>
2nd title: <<ARCANES CÉLESTES | QUI SONT DANS | L'ÉCRITURE SAINTE OU LA PAROLE DU SEIGNEUR | DÉVOILÉS: | Ici ceux qui sont dans la Genèse, | AVEC | LES MERVEILLES | QUI ONT ÉTÉ VUES DANS LE MONDE DES ESPRITS ET DANS LE CIEL DES ANGES. | <short rule> | OUVRAGE | D'EMMANUEL SWÉDENBORG | PUBLIÉ EN LATIN DE 1749 A 1756, | TRADUIT | PAR J. F. E. LE BOYS DES GUAYS. | <short rule> | TOME NEUVIÈME. | GENÈSE, | CHAPITRES XLI–XLIV. | Nos 5191 à 5866. | SAINT-AMAND (CHER). | A la Librairie de *LA NOUVELLE JÉRUSALEM*, chez Porte, libraire. | PARIS. | Chez <2 lines braced left> M. MINOT, rue Guénégaud, 7. | TREUTTEL et WURTZ, libraires, rue de Lille, 17. | <short rule> | 1853.>>
verso: <<MATTHIEU, VI. 33. | Cherchez premièrement le royaume de Dieu et sa justice, et toutes choses | vous seront données par surcroit.>>
large 8vo
title leaf, 2 pp; Publisher's note concerning the reproduction, 1 p; half title leaf and 2nd title leaf, 4 pp; text of Genesis 41-44 and n 5191-5866, pp 1-392; bar code and 'Made in the USA', p 394.
Photographic replica reprint of Fr 5/13 = Hyde 803.
Copy not seen; description deduced from publisher's advertisement.

49/01/Fr 5/30 **2005** Hyde 804/–
<<EMMANUEL SWEDENBORG | ARCANES CÉLESTES | qui sont dans | L'ÉCRITURE SAINTE | OU | PAROLE DU SEIGNEUR DÉVOILÉS | Ici ceux qui sont dans la Genèse, | AVEC | LES MERVEILLES |

qui ont été vues dans le monde des | esprits et dans le ciel des anges | TOME X | Elibron Classics | www.elibron.com>>
verso: <<Elibron Classics series. | © 2005 Adamant Media Corporation. | ISBN 1-4212-3502-1 (paperback) | ISBN 1-4212-3501-3 (hardcover) | This Elibron Classics Replica Edition is an unabridged facsimile | of the edition published in 1853 by Porte, Saint-Amand; | M. Minot; Treuttel et Wurtz, Paris. | Elibron and Elibron Classics are trademarks of | Adamant Media Corporation. All rights reserved.>>
half title: <<ARCANES CÉLESTES.>>
2nd title: <<ARCANES CÉLESTES | QUI SONT DANS | L'ÉCRITURE SAINTE OU LA PAROLE DU SEIGNEUR | DÉVOILÉS: | Ici ceux qui sont dans la Genèse, | AVEC | LES MERVEILLES | QUI ONT ÉTÉ VUES DANS LE MONDE DES ESPRITS ET DANS LE CIEL DES ANGES. | <short rule> | OUVRAGE | D'EMMANUEL SWÉDENBORG | PUBLIÉ EN LATIN DE 1749 A 1756, | TRADUIT | PAR J. F. E. LE BOYS DES GUAYS. | <short rule> | TOME DIXIÈME. | GENÈSE, | CHAPITRES XLV–L. | Nos 5867 à 6626. | SAINT-AMAND (CHER). | A la Librairie de *LA NOUVELLE JÉRUSALEM*, chez Porte, libraire. | PARIS. | Chez <2 lines braced left> M. MINOT, rue Guénégaud, 7. | TREUTTEL et WURTZ, libraires, rue de Lille, 17. | LONDRES. | SWEDENBORG'S PRINTING SOCIETY, No 6, King Street, Holborn. <short rule> | 1853.>>
verso: <<MATTHIEU, VI. 33. | Cherchez premièrement le royaume de Dieu et sa justice, et toutes choses | vous seront données par surcroit.>>
large 8vo
title leaf, 2 pp; Publisher's note concerning the reproduction, 1 p; half title leaf and 2nd title leaf, 4 pp; text of Genesis 45-50 and n 5867-6626, pp 1-442; catalogue, pp 443-444; bar code and 'Made in the USA', p 446.
Photographic replica reprint of Fr 5/14 = Hyde 804.
Copy not seen; description deduced from publisher's advertisement.

49/01/Fr 5/31 **2005** Hyde 805/–

<<EMMANUEL SWEDENBORG | ARCANES CÉLESTES | DE | L'ÉCRITURE SAINTE | OU | PAROLE DU SEIGNEUR DÉVOILÉS | *ainsi que* | LES MERVEILLES | *qui ont été vues dans le monde des | esprits et dans le ciel des anges* | TOME XI | Elibron Classics | www.elibron.com>>
verso: <<Elibron Classics series. | © 2005 Adamant Media Corporation. | ISBN 0-543-988-447 (paperback) | ISBN 0-543-988-430 (hardcover) | This Elibron Classics Replica Edition is an unabridged facsimile | of the edition published in 1891 by Porte, Saint-Amand; | M. Hartel; Treuttel et Wurtz, Paris. | Elibron and Elibron Classics are trademarks of | Adamant Media Corporation. All rights reserved.>> <*stet* 1891>
half title: <<ARCANES CÉLESTES.>>
2nd title: <<ARCANES CÉLESTES | DE | L'ÉCRITURE SAINTE OU PAROLE DU SEIGNEUR | DÉVOILÉS, | AINSI QUE | LES MERVEILLES | QUI ONT ÉTÉ VUES DANS LE MONDE DES ESPRITS ET DANS LE CIEL DES ANGES. | <short rule> | OUVRAGE | D'EMMANUEL SWÉDENBORG | PUBLIÉ EN LATIN DE 1749 A 1756, | ET TRADUIT | PAR J. F. E. LE BOYS DES GUAYS, | ET PUBLIÉ | PAR UN DISCIPLE (L. DE Z.) DES DOCTRINES DE LA VRAIE RELIGION CHRÉTIENNE. | <short rule> | TOME ONZIÈME. | EXODE, | CHAPITRES 1 – VIII. | SAINT-AMAND (CHER). | A la librairie de *LA NOUVELLE JÈRUSALEM*, chez Porte, libraire. | PARIS. | Chez <2 lines braced left> M. HARTEL, rue du Mail, 36. | TREUTTEL et WURTZ, libraires, rue de Lille, 17. | 1847 – 91.>>
verso: <<MATTHIEU, VI, 33. | Cherchez premièrement le royaume de Dieu et sa justice, et toutes | choses vous seront données par surcroit. | <short rule> | Paris. – Imp. de J.-E. Gros, rue de Foin-St.Jacques, 18.>>
large 8vo
title leaf, 2 pp; Publisher's note concerning the reproduction, 1 p; text of Exodus 1-8 and n 6627-7487, pp 1-443; Errata, p 444; bar code and 'Made in the USA', p 446.

Photographic replica reprint of Fr 5/6 = Hyde 805. The date '1891' on the verso of the title leaf is a conflation of the publication date '1847 – 91' on the title page of Fr 5/6.
Copy not seen; description deduced from publisher's advertisement.

49/01/Fr 5/32 **2005** Hyde 806/–
<<EMMANUEL SWEDENBORG | ARCANES CÉLESTES | DE | L'ÉCRITURE SAINTE | OU | PAROLE DU SEIGNEUR DÉVOILÉS | *ainsi que* | LES MERVEILLES | *qui ont été vues dans le monde des* | *esprits et dans le ciel des anges* | TOME XII | Elibron Classics | www.elibron.com>>
verso: <<Elibron Classics series. | © 2005 Adamant Media Corporation. | ISBN 0-543-988-423 (paperback) | ISBN 0-543-988-416 (hardcover) | This Elibron Classics Replica Edition is an unabridged facsimile | of the edition published in 1891 by Porte, Saint-Amand; | M. Hartel; Treuttel et Wurtz, Paris. | Elibron and Elibron Classics are trademarks of | Adamant Media Corporation. All rights reserved.>> <*stet* 1891>
half title: <<ARCANES CÉLESTES.>>
2nd title: <<ARCANES CÉLESTES | DE | L'ÉCRITURE SAINTE OU PAROLE DU SEIGNEUR | DÉVOILÉS, | AINSI QUE | LES MERVEILLES | QUI ONT ÉTÉ VUES DANS LE MONDE DES ESPRITS ET DANS LE CIEL DES ANGES. | <short rule> | OUVRAGE | D'EMMANUEL SWÉDENBORG | PUBLIÉ EN LATIN DE 1749 A 1756, | TRADUIT | PAR J. F. E. LE BOYS DES GUAYS, | ET PUBLIÉ | PAR UN DISCIPLE (L. DE Z.) DES DOCTRINES DE LA VRAIE RELIGION CHRÉTIENNE. | <short rule> | TOME DOUZIÈME. | EXODE, | CHAPITRES IX – XV. | SAINT-AMAND (CHER). | A la librairie de *LA NOUVELLE JÉRUSALEM*, chez Porte, libraire. | PARIS. | Chez <2 lines braced left> M. HARTEL, rue de Mail, 36. | TREUTTEL et WURTZ, libraires, rue de Lille, 17. | 1848– 91.>>
verso: <<MATTHIEU, VI 33. | Cherchez premièrement le royaume de Dieu et sa justice, et toutes choses | vous seront données par surcroit.>>
large 8vo
title leaf, 2 pp; Publisher's note concerning the reproduction, 1 p; half title leaf and 2nd title leaf, 4 pp; text of Exodus 9-15 and n 7488-8386, pp 1-442; Errata, p 443; bar code and 'Made in the USA', p 446.
Photographic replica reprint of Fr 5/7 = Hyde 806. The date '1891' on the verso of the title leaf is a conflation of the publication date '1848 – 91' on the title page of Fr 5/7.
Copy not seen; description deduced from publisher's advertisement.

49/01/Fr 5/33 **2005** Hyde 807/–
<<EMMANUEL SWEDENBORG | ARCANES CÉLESTES | qui sont dans | L'ÉCRITURE SAINTE | OU | PAROLE DU SEIGNEUR DÉVOILÉS | Ici ceux qui sont dans l'Exode, | AVEC | LES MERVEILLES | *qui ont été vues dans le monde des* | *esprits et dans le ciel des anges* | TOME XIII | Elibron Classics | www.elibron.com>>
verso: <<Elibron Classics series. | © 2005 Adamant Media Corporation. | ISBN 0-543-987-660 (paperback) | ISBN 0-543-987-594 (hardcover) | This Elibron Classics Replica Edition is an unabridged facsimile | of the edition published in 1851 by Porte, Saint-Amand; | M. Minot; Treuttel et Wurtz, Paris. | Elibron and Elibron Classics are trademarks of | Adamant Media Corporation. All rights reserved.>>
half title: <<ARCANES CÉLESTES.>>
2nd title: <<ARCANES CÉLESTES | QUI SONT DANS | L'ÉCRITURE SAINTE OU LA PAROLE DU SEIGNEUR | DÉVOILÉS: | Ici ceux qui sont dans l'Exode, | AVEC | LES MERVEILLES | QUI ONT ÉTÉ VUES DANS LE MONDE DES ESPRITS ET DANS LE CIEL DES ANGES. | <short rule> | OUVRAGE | D'EMMANUEL SWÉDENBORG | PUBLIÉ EN LATIN DE 1749 A 1756, | TRADUIT | PAR J. F. E. LE BOYS DES GUAYS. | <short rule> | TOME TREIZIÈME. | EXODE. | CHAPITRES XVI – XXI. | Nos 8387 à 9111. | SAINT-AMAND (CHER). | A la librairie de *LA NOUVELLE JÉRUSALEM*, chez PORTE, libraire. | PARIS. | Chez <2 lines braced left> M. MINOT, rue Guénégaud, 7. | TREUTTEL et WURTZ, libraires, rue de Lille, 17. | <short rule> | 1851.>>

verso: <<MATTHIEU, VI, 33. | Cherchez premièrement le royaume de Dieu et sa justice, et toutes choses | vous seront données par surcroit.>>
large 8vo
title leaf, 2 pp; Publisher's note concerning the reproduction, 1 p; half title leaf and 2nd title leaf, 4 pp; text of Exodus 16-21 and n 8387-9111, pp 1-470; Errata, p 470; avertissement, p 471; bar code and 'Made in the USA', p 474.
Photographic replica reprint of Fr 5/9 = Hyde 807.
Copy not seen; description deduced from publisher's advertisement.

49/01/Fr 5/34 **2005** Hyde 808/–

<<EMMANUEL SWEDENBORG | ARCANES CÉLESTES | qui sont dans | L'ÉCRITURE SAINTE | OU | PAROLE DU SEIGNEUR DÉVOILÉS | Ici ceux qui sont dans l'Exode, | AVEC | LES MERVEILLES | *qui ont été vues dans le monde des* | *esprits et dans le ciel des anges* | TOME XIV | Elibron Classics | www.elibron.com>>
verso: <<Elibron Classics series. | © 2005 Adamant Media Corporation. | ISBN 1-4212-3508-0 (paperback) | ISBN 1-4212-3507-2 (hardcover) | This Elibron Classics Replica Edition is an unabridged facsimile | of the edition published in 1852 by Porte, Saint-Amand; | M. Minot; Treuttel et Wurtz, Paris. | Elibron and Elibron Classics are trademarks of | Adamant Media Corporation. All rights reserved.>>
half title: <<ARCANES CÉLESTES.>>
verso: << <short rule> | SAINT-AMAND-MONT-ROND (CHER), | IMPRIMERIE DE DESTENAY ET LAMBERT, RUE LAFAYETTE, 55, | Place Mont-Rond. | <short rule> >>
2nd title: <<ARCANES CÉLESTES | QUI SONT DANS | L'ÉCRITURE SAINTE OU LA PAROLE DU SEIGNEUR | DÉVOILÉS: | Ici ceux qui sont dans l'Exode, | AVEC | LES MERVEILLES | QUI ONT ÉTÉ VUES DANS LE MONDE DES ESPRITS ET DANS LE CIEL DES ANGES. | <short rule> | OUVRAGE | D'EMMANUEL SWÉDENBORG | PUBLIÉ EN LATIN DE 1749 A 1756, | ET TRADUIT | PAR J. F. E. LE BOYS DES GUAYS. | <short rule> | TOME QUATORZIÈME. | EXODE, | CHAPITRES XXII – XXV. | Nos 9112 à 9584. | SAINT-AMAND (CHER). | A la librairie de *LA NOUVELLE JÉRUSALEM,* chez PORTE, libraire. | PARIS. | Chez <2 lines braced left> M. MINOT, rue Guénégaud, 7. | TREUTTEL et WURTZ, libraires, rue de Lille, 17. | <short rule> | 1852.>>
verso: <<MATTHIEU, VI, 33. | Cherchez premièrement le royaume de Dieu et sa justice, et toutes choses | vous seront données par surcroit.>>
large 8vo
title leaf, 2 pp; Publisher's note concerning the reproduction, 1 p; half title leaf and title leaf, 4 pp; text of Exodus 22-25 and n 9112-9584, pp 1-452; Errata, p 452; bar code and 'Made in the USA', p 454.
Photographic replica reprint of Fr 5/10 = Hyde 808.
Copy not seen; description deduced from publisher's advertisement.

49/01/Fr 5/35 **2005** Hyde 809/–

<<EMMANUEL SWEDENBORG | ARCANES CÉLESTES | qui sont dans | L'ÉCRITURE SAINTE | OU | PAROLE DU SEIGNEUR DÉVOILÉS | Ici ceux qui sont dans l'Exode, | AVEC | LES MERVEILLES | *qui ont été vues dans le monde des* | *esprits et dans le ciel des anges* | TOME XV | Elibron Classics | www.elibron.com>>
verso: <<Elibron Classics series. | © 2005 Adamant Media Corporation. | ISBN 0-543-988-409 (paperback) | ISBN 0-543-988-393 (hardcover) | This Elibron Classics Replica Edition is an unabridged facsimile | of the edition published in 1853 by Porte, Saint-Amand; | M. Minot; Treuttel et Wurtz, Paris. | Elibron and Elibron Classics are trademarks of | Adamant Media Corporation. All rights reserved.>>
half title: <<ARCANES CÉLESTES.>>

verso: << <short rule: SAINT-AMAND-MONT-ROND (CHER), | IMPRIMERIE DE DESTENAY ET LAMBERT, RUE LAFAYETTE, 55, | Place Mont-Rond. | <short rule> >>
2nd title: <<ARCANES CÉLESTES | QUI SONT DANS | L'ÉCRITURE SAINTE OU LA PAROLE DU SEIGNEUR | DÉVOILÉS: | Ici ceux qui sont dans l'Exode, | AVEC | LES MERVEILLES | QUI ONT ÉTÉ VUES DANS LE MONDE DES ESPRITS ET DANS LE CIEL DES ANGES. | <short rule> | OUVRAGE | D'EMMANUEL SWÉDENBORG | PUBLIÉ EN LATIN DE 1749 A 1756, | TRADUIT | PAR J. F. E. LE BOYS DES GUAYS. | <short rule> | TOME QUINZIÈME. | EXODE, | CHAPITRES XXVI – XXIX. | Nos 9585 à 10166. | SAINT-AMAND (CHER). | A la librairie de *LA NOUVELLE JÉRUSALEM*, chez PORTE, libraire. | PARIS. | Chez <2 lines braced left> M. MINOT, rue Guénégaud, 7. | TREUTTEL et WURTZ, libraires, rue de Lille, 17. | <short rule> | 1853.>>
verso: <<MATTHIEU, VI 33. | Cherchez premièrement le royaume de Dieu et sa justice, et toutes choses | vous seront données par surcroit.>>
large 8vo
title leaf, 2 pp; Publisher's note concerning the reproduction, 1 p; half title leaf and 2nd title leaf, 4 pp; text of Exodus 26-29 and n 9585-10166, pp 1-504; Errata, p 504; bar code and 'Made in the USA', p 506.
Photographic replica reprint of Fr 5/15 = Hyde 809.
Copy not seen; description deduced from publisher's advertisement.

49/01/Fr 5/36 **2005** Hyde 810/–
<<EMMANUEL SWEDENBORG | ARCANES CÉLESTES | qui sont dans | L'ÉCRITURE SAINTE | OU | PAROLE DU SEIGNEUR DÉVOILÉS | Ici ceux qui sont dans l'Exode, | AVEC | LES MERVEILLES | *qui ont été vues dans le monde des* | *esprits et dans le ciel des anges* | TOME XVI | Elibron Classics | www.elibron.com>>
verso: <<Elibron Classics series. | © 2005 Adamant Media Corporation. | ISBN 1-4212-2269-8 (paperback) | ISBN 1-4212-2268-X (hardcover) | This Elibron Classics Replica Edition is an unabridged facsimile | of the edition published in 1854 by Porte, Saint-Amand; | M. Minot; Treuttel et Wurtz, Paris. | Elibron and Elibron Classics are trademarks of | Adamant Media Corporation. All rights reserved.>>
half title: <<ARCANES CÉLESTES.>>
verso: << <short rule> | SAINT-AMAND-MONT-ROND (CHER), | IMPRIMERIE DE DESTENAY ET LAMBERT, RUE LAFAYETTE, 55, | Place Mont-Rond. | <short rule> >>
2nd title: <<ARCANES CÉLESTES | QUI SONT DANS | L'ÉCRITURE SAINTE OU LA PAROLE DU SEIGNEUR | DÉVOILÉS: | Ici ceux qui sont dans l'Exode, | AVEC | LES MERVEILLES | QUI ONT ÉTÉ VUES DANS LE MONDE DES ESPRITS ET DANS LE CIEL DES ANGES. | <short rule> | OUVRAGE | D'EMMANUEL SWÉDENBORG | PUBLIÉ EN LATIN DE 1749 A 1756, | TRADUIT | PAR J. F. E. LE BOYS DES GUAYS. | <short rule> | TOME SEIZIÈME. | EXODE, | CHAPITRES XXX – XL. | Nos 10167 à 10837. | SAINT-AMAND (CHER). | A la librairie de *LA NOUVELLE JÉRUSALEM,* chez PORTE, libraire. | PARIS. | Chez <2 lines braced left> M. MINOT, rue Guénégaud, 7. | TREUTTEL et WURTZ, libraires, rue de Lille, 17. | LONDRES. | SWEDENBORG'S PRINTING SOCIETY, No 6, King Street, Holborn. | <short rule> | 1854.>>
verso: <<MATTHIEU, VI 33. | Cherchez premièrement le royaume de Dieu et sa justice, et toutes choses | vous seront données par surcroit.>>
imprint: <<Saint-Amand (Cher). – Imprimerie de DESTENAY et LAMBERT.>>
large 8vo
title leaf, 2 pp; Publisher's note concerning the reproduction, 1 p; half title leaf and 2nd title leaf, 4 pp; text of Exodus 30-40 and n 10167-10837, pp 1-498; catalogue of Swedenborg's works, pp 499-500; imprint, p 500; bar code and 'Made in the USA', p 502.
Photographic replica reprint of Fr 5/16 = Hyde 810.
Copy not seen; description deduced from publisher's advertisement.

FRENCH EXTRACTS

X 49/01/Fr 1839/1 **1839** Hyde 869
Extrait des Arcanes Célestes.
8vo
title and text n 1079, 1080, 1088, pp 78-80.
Translated by J F E Le Boys des Guays, published in *La Nouvelle Jérusalem* Saint-Amand (Cher).
UK: SOC, CON

X 49/01/Fr 1841/1 **1841** Hyde —
<<L'Apocalypse dans son sens spirituel: d'après l'Apocalypse Révélée et l'Apocalypse Expliquée d'Emmanuel Swédenborg; suivie du sens spirituel du vint-quatrième chapitre de Matthieu, d'après les Arcana Célestes du même auteur / par J. F. E. Le Boys des Guays. Saint-Amand: Librairie de la Nouvelle Jérusalem; Chez Porte; Paris: M. Hartel; Treuttel et Wurtz. 1841. - 85.>>
8vo
title leaf, 2 pp; text <of *Arcana Caelestia*>, 382 pp.
The work is set out in two columns: on the left, the text of Matthew 24, 25; on the right, quotations. Copy not seen; description recorded from catalogue of GER: WLB.
GER: WLB

X 49/01/Fr 1846/1 **1846** Hyde 870
DOCTRINE | DE LA CHARITÉ, | PAR | EMMANUEL SWÉDENBORG, | extraite | DES ARCANES CÉLESTES, | TRADUITE DU LATIN | PAR J. F. E. LE BOYS DES GUAYS, | PUBLIÉE PAR UN DISCIPLE (L. DE Z.) DES DOCTRINES DE LA VRAIE RÉLIGION | CHRÉTIENNE, OU | LA NOUVELLE JÉRUSALEM, PRÉDITE PAR LE SEIGNEUR DANS DANIEL VII, | 13, 14, ET DANS L'APOCALYPSE XXI.1, 2. | <type orn 2 x 24 mm> | SAINT-AMAND (CHER), | A la librairie de la NOUVELLE JÉRUSALEM, chez PORTE, Libraire. | PARIS, | Chez M. HARTEL, rue du Mail, 36. | <short rule> | 1846–90.
half title: DOCTRINE DE LA CHARITÉ.
verso: IMPRIMERIE DE A. APPERT, | Passage du Caire, 54.
imprint: Paris. –Imprimerie de A. APPERT, Passage du Caire, 54.
small 8vo
half title and title leaves, 4 pp; Avertissement du traducteur <Translator's note>, pp 1-2; Préface de l'auteur <Swedenborg's preface>, pp 3-4; text n I-XL, pp 5-90; Table des matières <Table of contents>, pp 91-92; imprint, p 92.
Printed at the expense of L de Zaroa.
UK: SOC; FRA: BNF; NET: GEN; USA: SHS

X 49/01/Fr 1849/1 **1849-1850** Hyde 871/a
Extrait des Arcanes | Célestes de Swedenborg.
8vo <202 x 130 mm>
title and text, pp 1-15.
Bound manuscript volume containing a translation of n 10318, 10321, 10325, 9350-9362 in the handwriting of Lauren Paillard. The MS is in UK: SOC. <Archives A/118> This section is undated, though a preceding one is dated 1848 and a following one is dated 1851. The translation is almost word for word that which is to be found in J F E le Boys des Guays' version of these paragraphs <Fr 2/14, 2/16>. A later section of the volume contains a French version of 49/01, n 15, 2004, 2009, 1285, 29, 221, 936, 2498, 7696, 7697, 3425, 2768, 4299, 3425, 3605, 10219, 10228, 2904, 6344, 10019, 10248, 8864, 6476.
UK: SOC

X 49/01/Fr 1853/1 **1853** Hyde 871

<<DOCTRINE | DE LA CHARITÉ, | PAR | EMMANUEL SWEDENBORG, | extraite | DES ARCANES CÉLESTES, | TRADUITE DU LATIN | PAR J. F. E. LE BOYS DES GUAYS, | PUBLIÉE PAR UN DISCIPLE (L. DE Z.) DES DOCTRINES DE LA VRAIE RÉLIGION | CHRÉTIENNE, OU | LA NOUVELLE JÉRUSALEM, PRÉDITE PAR LE SEIGNEUR DANS DANIEL VII, | 13, 14, ET DANS L'APOCALYPSE XXI.1, 2. | Séconde Édition | PARIS>>
half title: <<DOCTRINE DE LA CHARITÉ.>>
16mo
half title and title leaves, 4 pp; Avertissement <Translator's note>, 2 pp; Préface de l'auteur <Swedenborg's preface>, pp 7-10; text, pp 11-170; Table générale <Contents>, pp 171-174; Table alphabétique et analytique <Subject index>, pp 1-30; Index des passages de la Parole <Index to Bible passages cited>, pp 31-34.
Reprinted from X Fr 1846/1.
Copy not seen; description recorded from X Fr 1846/1 and catalogues of FRA: BNF and SWE: GSB.
FRA: BNF; SWE: GSB; USA: SHS

X 49/01/Fr 1857/1 **1857** Hyde 872

TRAITÉ | DES | RÉPRESENTATIONS | et des | CORRESPONDANCES (*) | PAR | EMMANUEL SWEDENBORG. | traduit du latin | PAR J.-F.-E. LE BOYS DES GUAYS | ET PUBLIÉ | Par un Disciple (L. DE Z.) des Doctrines de la Vraie | Religion Chrétienne. | <short rule> | (*) Ce Traité est extrait du grand ouvrage de SWEDENBORG, | *Arcana Cœlestia*. | <short rule> | SAINT-AMAND (CHER), | A LA LIBRAIRIE DE LA *NOUVELLE JÉRUSALEM*, | Chez PORTE, Libraire, | Paris, | M. MINOT, RUE DU FOUR-SAINT-GERMAIN, 40, | TREUTTEL ET WURTZ, LIBRAIRES, RUE DE LILLE, 17. | LONDRES, Swedenborg society, 36 Bloomsbury street, Oxford street. | <short rule> | 1857. <*stet* society>
half title: DES | REPRÉSENTATIONS | et des | CORRESPONDANCES.
verso: SAINT–AMAND. — IMPRIMERIE DE DESTENAY, | Rue Lafayette, 70, place Mont-Rond. | <short rule>
16mo
half title and title leaves, 4 pp; text, pp 1-495; Table générale <Index>, pp 1-2; Table alphabétique et analytique <Subject index>, pp 3-109; Index des passages de la Parole <Index to Bible passages cited>, pp 110-111; Errata, 1 p; catalogue, 1 p.
Printed at the expense of L de Zaroa.
UK: SOC; NET: GEN; SWE: GSB, UPP; SWI: LAU

X 49/01/Fr 1875/1 **1875** Hyde 873

PETIT | ARCANA COELESTIA. | <short rule> | TRADUCTION ABRÉGÉE | DU | GRAND ARCANA COELESTIA. | <short rule> | ADAPTÉE A L'USAGE DE LA JEUNESSE. | <short rule> | VOLUME I. | <short orn rule> | BÂLE. | J. SCHWEIGHAUSER, LIBRAIRE-ÉDITEUR. | 1875.
8vo
title leaf, 2 pp; Editorial remarks, pp 3-4; Introduction, pp 5-14; text, pp 15-482.
UK: SOC; SWI: LAU; USA: ANC, SHS

X 49/01/Fr 1878/1 **1878** Hyde 874

PETIT | ARCANA COELESTIA. | <short rule> | TRADUCTION ABRÉGÉE | DU | GRAND ARCANA COELESTIA | ADAPTÉE A L'USAGE DE LA JEUNESSE. | <short rule> | Volume II. | <orn rule> | BÂLE. | J. SCHWEIGHAUSER, LIBRAIRE-ÉDITEUR. | 1878.
8vo
title leaf, 2 pp; Introduction, pp 3-6; text, pp 7-410; Sommaire du premier volume, pp 411-412; Sommaire du second volume, pp 413-414.
UK: SOC; SWI: LAU; USA: ANC, SHS

X 49/01/Fr 1885/1 **1885** Hyde 875

DOCTRINE | DE LA CHARITÉ | PAR | EMMANUEL SWEDENBORG | EXTRAITE | DES ARCANES CÉLESTES | TRADUIT DU LATIN | PAR J.-F.- E LE BOIS DES GUAYS | <short rule> | TROISIÈME ÉDITION | REVUE PAR C. H. | <type orn 2 x 20 mm> | PARIS | LIBRAIRIE DE LA NOUVELLE JÉRUSALEM | 12, RUE THOUIN, 12 | <short rule> | 1885 <*stet* BOIS>
half title: DOCTRINE DE LA CHARITÉ
verso: <short rule> | Imprimerie de DESTENAY à Saint-Amand (Cher). | <short rule>
12mo
half title and title leaves, 4 pp; Avertissement de la deuxième édition <Translator's note in the 2nd edition>, pp 1-2; Préface de l'auteur <Swedenborg's preface>, pp 3-5; text, pp 7-111; Table générale <Contents>, pp 113-114; Table alphabétique et analytique <Subject index>, pp 1-17; Index des passages de la Parole <Index to Bible passages cited>, pp 19-22.
Revised by C Humann.
UK: SOC; NET: GEN; SWI: LAU; USA: ANC

X 49/01/Fr 1985/1 **1985** Hyde 872/–

<<TRAITÉ | DES | RÉPRESENTATIONS | et des | CORRESPONDANCES (*) | PAR | EMMANUEL SWEDENBORG. | traduit du latin | PAR J.-F.-E. LE BOYS DES GUAYS | ET PUBLIÉ | (*) Ce Traité est extrait du grand ouvrage de SWEDENBORG, | *Arcana Cœlestia*. | <short rule> | PARIS | La Différence | 1985>>
16mo
title leaf, Préface by Jean-March Tisserant, and text, 198 pp.
A reprint of X Fr 1857/1 = Hyde 872. ISBN 2729 101624.
Copy not seen; description recorded from X Fr 1857/1 and catalogue of SWE: UPP.
SWE: UPP; SWI: LAU; USA: ANC

X 49/01/Fr 1995/1 **1995** Hyde —

<<Des Biens de la Charité | ou bonnes oeuvres et explication du Décalogue | par Emmanuel Swedenborg: | traduite du latin par J.-F.-E. Le Bois des Guays. 1885.>> <*stet* Bois>
half title: <<De la Charité>>
8vo
half title and title leaves, 4 pp; Préface de l'auteur <Swedenborg's preface>, pp 3-5; text, pp 7-111; Table générale <Contents>, pp 113-114; Table alphabétique et analytique <Subject index>, pp 1-17; Index des passages de la parole <Index to Bible passages cited>, pp 19-22.
Photographic replica reprint of X Fr 1885/1, published as *De la Charité* par Emmanuel Swedenborg with *Doctrine de la Nouvelle Jérusalem sur la Charité | ouvrage posthume d'Emmanuel Swedenborg ... extrait du grand ouvrage posthume de Swedenborg, Apocalypsis Explicata* 1853 <66/04/Fr 1/4> by Cercle Swedenborg (Reprographie par Les Éditions de Prieur), Talant.
Copy not seen; description recorded from X Fr 1885/1 and catalogue of USA: ANC.
USA: ANC

GERMAN

Translators:

Ge 1 J F I Tafel
Ge 2 J F F von Conring and J J Wurster, revised by W Pfirsch
Ge 3 F Horn and H Grob

49/01/Ge 1/1 **1845** Hyde 811

<<**Himmlische Geheimnisse, | welche in der | Heiligen Schrift | oder in dem | Worte des Herrn | enthalten, und nun enthüllt sind. | Hier zuerst, was in dem | Ersten Buche Mosis. | Zugleich die Wunder, | welche gesehen worden | in der Geisterwelt und im Himmel der Engel. | Von | Immanuel Swedenborg.** | <short rule> | **Aus der lateinischen Urschrift übersetzt | von** | Dr. **Joh. Fried. Immanuel Tafel, | Erster Band.** | <multiple rule> | **Tübingen, | in der Verlags=Expedition.** | 1845>>
verso: <<**Matth. 6, 33. | Trachtet am Gristen nach dem Reich Gottes, und nach seiner Ge- | rechtigkeit, so wird euch (solches) alles zufallen.**>>
8vo
title leaf, 2 pp; Vorrede des englischen Uebersetzers <Preface by the English translator, ie J Clowes>, pp iii-xxvii; text of Genesis 1-7 and n 1-823, pp 1-535.
The volume was first issued in 5 parts, 1837-1840.
Copy not seen; description deduced from Ge 1/2.
GER: WLB; SWE: ROY

49/01/Ge 1/2 **1850** Hyde 812

Himmlische Geheimnisse, | welche in der | Heiligen Schrift | oder in dem | Worte des Herrn | enthalten, und nun enthüllt sind. | Hier zuerst, was in dem | Ersten Buche Mosis. | Zugleich die Wunder, | welche gesehen worden | in der Geisterwelt und im Himmel der Engel. | Von | Immanuel Swedenborg. | <short rule> | **Aus der lateinischen Urschrift übersetzt | von** | Dr. **Joh. Fried. Immanuel Tafel, | Professor der Philosophie und Universitäts=Bibliothekar zu Tübingen. | Zweiter Band.** | <multiple rule> | **Tübingen, | in der Verlags=Expedition.** | 1850.
8vo
title leaf, 2 pp; catalogue, pp 1-6; text of Genesis 8-11 and n 824-1382, pp 1-487; Druckfehler <Errata>, p 488.
UK: SOC; GER: WLB; NET: GEN; SWE: ROY

49/01/Ge 1/3 **1855** Hyde 813

<<**Himmlische Geheimnisse, | welche in der | Heiligen Schrift | oder in dem | Worte des Herrn | enthalten, und nun enthüllt sind. | Hier zuerst, was in dem | Ersten Buche Mosis. | Zugleich die Wunder, | welche gesehen worden | in der Geisterwelt und im Himmel der Engel. | Von | Immanuel Swedenborg.** | <short rule> | **Aus der lateinischen Urschrift übersetzt | von** | Dr. **Joh. Fried. Immanuel Tafel, | Professor der Philosophie und Universitäts=Bibliothekar zu Tübingen. | Dritter Band | (oder ersten Theils letzter Band).** | <multiple rule> | **Tübingen, | in der Verlags-Expedition.** | 1855.>>
8vo
title leaf, 2 pp; text of Genesis 12-15 and n 1383-1885, pp 1-409.
Copy not seen; description deduced from Ge 1/2.
GER: WLB; SWE: ROY

49/01/Ge 1/4 **1856-1857** Hyde 814

<<**Himmlische Geheimnisse, | welche in der | Heiligen Schrift | oder in dem | Worte des Herrn | enthalten, und nun enthüllt sind. | Hier zuerst, was in dem | Ersten Buche Mosis. | Zugleich die Wunder, | welche gesehen worden | in der Geisterwelt und im Himmel der Engel. | Von | Immanuel Swedenborg.** | <short rule> | **Aus der lateinischen Urschrift übersetzt | von** | Dr. **Joh. Fried. Immanuel Tafel, | Professor der Philosophie und Universitäts=Bibliothekar zu Tübingen, | ordentlichem mitglied der historischtheologischen Gesellschaft zu Leipzig. | Vierten Bandes i und ii Abtheilung.** | <multiple rule> | **Tübingen, | in der Verlags-Expedition.** | 1857.>>

verso: << <Latin title> >>
8vo
title leaf, 2 pp; text of Vorrede <Swedenborg's preface>, pp 1-3; text of Genesis 16-17 and n 1886-2134, pp 4-237.
Part i, pp 4-95, was published separately in 1856 <Hyde 3443>.
Copy not seen; description deduced from Ge 1/2.
GER: WLB; SWE: ROY

49/01/Ge 1/5 **1861** Hyde 815
<<**Himmlische Geheimnisse, | welche in der | Heiligen Schrift | oder in dem | Worte des Herrn | enthalten, und nun enthüllt sind. | Hier zuerst, was in dem | Ersten Buche Mosis. | Zugleich die Wunder, | welche gesehen worden | in der Geisterwelt und im Himmel der Engel. | Von | Immanuel Swedenborg.** | <short rule> | **Aus der lateinischen Urschrift übersetzt | von |** Dr. **Joh. Fried. Immanuel Tafel, | Professor der Philosophie und Universitäts-Bibliothekar zu Tübingen, | ordentlichem Mitglied der historischtheologischen Gesellschaft zu Leipzig. | Vierten Bandes dritte und vierte Abtheilung. | Tübingen, | in der Verlags-Expedition.** | 1861.>>
verso: << <Latin title> >>
8vo
title leaf, 2 pp; catalogue, pp 1-6; text of Swedenborg's preface, Genesis 18-19, and n 2135-2494, pp 239-589.
Issued in two parts: Part iii, pp 239-403; Part iv, pp 404-589.
Copy not seen; description deduced from Ge 1/2.
GER: WLB; USA: ANC

49/01/Ge 1/6 **1863** Hyde 816
<<**Himmlische Geheimnisse, | welche in der | Heiligen Schrift | oder in dem Worte des Herrn | enthalten, und nun enthüllt sind. | Hier zuerst, was in dem | Ersten Buche Mosis. | Zugleich die Wunder, | welche gesehen worden | in der Geisterwelt und im Himmel der Engel. | Von | Immanuel Swedenborg.** | <short rule> | **Aus der lateinischen Urschrift übersetzt | von |** Dr. **Joh. Fried. Immanuel Tafel, | Professor der Philosophie und Universitäts=Bibliothekar zu Tübingen, | ordentlichem Mitglied der historischtheologischen Gesellschaft zu Leipzig. | Vierten Bandes fünfte Abtheilung.** | <multiple rule> | **Tübingen, | in der Verlags-Expedition.** | 1863.>>
8vo
title leaf, 2 pp; text of Genesis 20 and n 2495-2605, pp 593-721.
Copy not seen; description deduced from Ge 1/2.
GER: WLB; USA: ANC

49/01/Ge 2/1 **1866** Hyde 821
Himmlische Geheimnisse, | welche in der | Heiligen Schrift | oder in dem | Worte des Herrn | enthalten, und nun enthüllt sind. | Hier, was in dem | Ersten Buche Mosis. | Zugleich die Wunderdinge, | welche gesehen und gehört worden sind | in der Geisterwelt und im Himmel der Engel. | [Von | Immanuel Swedenborg.] | <short rule> | **Aus der lateinischen Urschrift übersetzt. | Fünfter Band.** | <double rule> | **Basel u. Ludwigsburg. | Druck und Verlag von Balmer u. Riehm.** | 1866.
small 8vo
title leaf, 2 pp; text of Genesis 21-25 and n 2606-3352, pp 1-670; catalogue, 2 pp.
Translated by J F F von Conring and J J Wurster, revised by W Pfirsch.
UK: SOC; GER: WLB; NET: GEN; SWE: UPP

49/01/Ge 2/2 **1866** Hyde 822

Himmlische Geheimnisse, | welche in der | Heiligen Schrift | oder in dem | Worte des Herrn | enthalten, und nun enthüllt sind. | Hier, was in dem | Ersten Buche Mosis. | Zugleich die Wunderdinge, | welche gesehen und gehört worden sind | in der Geisterwelt und im Himmel der Engel. | [Von | Immanuel Swedenborg.] | <short rule> | **Aus der lateinischen Urschrift übersetzt. | Sechster Band. | Enthaltend Kapitel 26 bis 30 mit Nro. 3353 bis 4055.** | <double rule> | **Basel u. Ludwigsburg. | Druck und Verlag von Ferd. Riehm.** | 1866.
small 8vo
title leaf, 2 pp; text of Genesis 26-30 and n 3353-4055, pp 1-712.
UK: soc; GER: wlb; NET: gen; SWE: upp

49/01/Ge 1/7 **1867** Hyde 817

Himmlische Geheimnisse, | welche in der | Heiligen Schrift | oder in dem | Worte des Herrn | enthalten, und nun enthüllt sind. | Hier, was in dem | Ersten Buche Mosis. | Zugleich die Wunderdinge, | welche gesehen und gehört worden sind | in der Geisterwelt und im Himmel der Engel. | [Von | Immanuel Swedenborg.] | <short rule> | **Aus der lateinischen Urschrift übersetzt. | Erster Band.** | <short double rule> | **Basel u. Ludwigsburg. | Druck und Verlag von Ferd. Riehm.** | 1867.
verso: **Matth. 6, 33. | Trachtet am Ersten nach dem Reich Gottes, und nach seiner Ge- | rechtigkeit, so wird euch (solches) alles zufallen.**
small 8vo
title leaf, 2 pp; Vorrede der englischen Vebersetzers <Preface by the English translator, ie J Clowes>, pp III-XXIV; Contents, pp 1-2; text of Genesis 1-7 and n 1-823, pp 3-481.
Reprinted from Ge 1/1 = Hyde 811.
UK: soc; SWE: upp; USA: anc, shs

49/01/Ge 1/8 **1867** Hyde 818

Himmlische Geheimnisse, | welche in der | Heiligen Schrift | oder in dem | Worte des Herrn | enthalten, und nun enthüllt sind. | Hier, was in dem | Ersten Buche Mosis. | Zugleich die Wunderdinge, | welche gesehen und gehört worden sind | in der Geisterwelt und im Himmel der Engel. | [Von | Immanuel Swedenborg.] | <short rule> | **Aus der lateinischen Urschrift übersetzt. | Zweiter Band. | Enthaltend 1. Buch Mosis Kap. 8 bis 11 mit Nro. 824 bis 1382.** | <double rule> | **Basel u. Ludwigsburg. In Commission bei Ferd. Riehm.** | <short rule>
small 8vo
title leaf, 2 pp; text of Genesis 8-11 and n 824-1382, pp 1-487; Druckfehler <Misprints>, 1 p.
Ge 1/2 = Hyde 812 with a fresh title page published in 1867.
UK: soc; SWE: upp; USA: anc, shs

49/01/Ge 1/9 **1867** Hyde 819

Himmlische Geheimnisse, | welche in der | Heiligen Schrift | oder in dem | Worte des Herrn | enthalten, und nun enthüllt sind. | Hier, was in dem | Ersten Buche Mosis. | Zugleich die Wunderdinge, | welche gesehen und gehört worden sind | in der Geisterwelt und im Himmel der Engel. | [Von | Immanuel Swedenborg.] | <short rule> | **Aus der lateinischen Urschrift übersetzt. | Dritter Band. | Enthaltend 1. Buch Mosis Kap. 12 bis 15 mit Nro. 1383 bis 1885.** | <double rule> | **Basel u. Ludwigsburg. In Commission bei Ferd. Riehm.** | <short rule>
small 8vo
title leaf, 2 pp; text of Genesis 12-15 and n 1383-1885, pp 1-409; catalogue, pp 1-5.
Ge 1/3 = Hyde 813 with a fresh title page published in 1867.
UK: soc; SWE: upp; USA: anc, shs

49/01/Ge 1/10 **1867** Hyde 820
Himmlische Geheimnisse, | welche in der | Heiligen Schrift | oder in dem | Worte des Herrn | enthalten, und nun enthüllt sind. | Hier, was in dem | Ersten Buche Mosis. | Zugleich die Wunderdinge, | welche gesehen und gehört worden sind | in der Geisterwelt und im Himmel der Engel. | [Von | Immanuel Swedenborg.] | <short rule> | **Aus der lateinischen Urschrift übersetzt. | Vierter Band. | Enthaltend 1. Buch Mosis Kap. 16 bis 20 mit Nro. 1886 bis 2605.** | <double rule> | **Basel u. Ludwigsburg. In Commission bei Ferd. Riehm.** | <short rule>
small 8vo
title leaf, 2 pp; Vorrede <Swedenborg's preface>, pp 1-3; text of Genesis 16-20 and n 1886-2605, pp 4-721.
Ge 1/4-1/6 = Hyde 814-816 with a fresh title page published in 1867.
UK: SOC; SWE: UPP; USA: SHS

49/01/Ge 2/3 **1867** Hyde 823
Himmlische Geheimnisse, | welche in der | Heiligen Schrift | oder in dem | Worte des Herrn | enthalten, und nun enthüllt sind. | Hier, was in dem | Ersten Buche Mosis. | Zugleich die Wunderdinge, | welche gesehen und gehört worden sind | in der Geisterwelt und im Himmel der Engel. | [Von | Immanuel Swedenborg.] | <short rule> | **Aus der lateinischen Urschrift übersetzt. | Siebenter Band.** | <double rule> | **Basel u. Ludwigsburg. Druck und Verlag von Balmer u. Riehm.** | 1867.
small 8vo
title leaf, 2 pp; text of Genesis 31-35 and n 4056-4634, pp 1-566.
UK: SOC; GER: WLB; NET: GEN; SWE: UPP; USA: ANC, SHS

49/01/Ge 2/4 **1867** Hyde 824
Himmlische Geheimnisse, | welche in der | Heiligen Schrift | oder in dem | Worte des Herrn | enthalten, und nun enthüllt sind. | Hier, was in dem | Ersten Buche Mosis. | Zugleich die Wunderdinge, | welche gesehen und gehört worden sind | in der Geisterwelt und im Himmel der Engel. | [Von | Immanuel Swedenborg.] | <short rule> | **Aus der lateinischen Urschrift übersetzt. | Achter Band.** | <double rule> | **Basel u. Ludwigsburg. Druck und Verlag von Ferd. Riehm.** | 1867.
small 8vo
title leaf, 2 pp; text of Genesis 36-40 and n 4635-5190, pp 1-558.
UK: SOC; GER: WLB; NET: GEN; USA: ANC, SHS

49/01/Ge 2/5 **1867** Hyde 825
Himmlische Geheimnisse, | welche in der | Heiligen Schrift | oder in dem | Worte des Herrn | enthalten, und nun enthüllt sind. | Hier, was in dem | Ersten Buche Mosis. | Zugleich die Wunderdinge, | welche gesehen und gehört worden sind | in der Geisterwelt und im Himmel der Engel. | [Von | Immanuel Swedenborg.] | <short rule> | **Aus der lateinischen Urschrift übersetzt. | Neunter Band. | Enthaltend Kapitel 41 bis 44 mit Nro. 5191 bis 5866.** | <double rule> | **Basel u. Ludwigsburg. | Druck und Verlag von Ferd. Riehm.** | 1867.
small 8vo
title leaf, 2 pp; text of Genesis 41-44 and n 5191-5866, pp 1-506.
UK: SOC; GER: WLB; NET: GEN; SWE: UPP; USA: ANC, SHS

49/01/Ge 2/6 **1867** Hyde 826
Himmlische Geheimnisse, | welche in der | Heiligen Schrift | oder in dem | Worte des Herrn | enthalten, und nun enthüllt sind. | Hier, was in dem | Ersten Buche Mosis. | Zugleich die

Wunderdinge, | welche gesehen und gehört worden sind | in der Geisterwelt und im Himmel der Engel. | [Von | Immanuel Swedenborg.] | <short rule> **| Aus der lateinischen Urschrift übersetzt. | Zehnter Band. | Enthaltend Kapitel 45 bis 50, mit Nro. 5867 bis 6626. |** <double rule> **| Basel u. Ludwigsburg. Druck und Verlag von Ferd. Riehm. |** 1867.
small 8vo
title leaf, 2 pp; text of Genesis 45-50 and n 5867-6626, pp 1-575.
UK: SOC; GER: WLB; NET: GEN; SWE: UPP; USA: ANC, SHS

49/01/Ge 2/7 **1868** Hyde 827
Himmlische Geheimnisse, | welche in der | Heiligen Schrift | oder in dem | Worte des Herrn | enthalten, und nun enthüllt sind. | Hier, was in dem | Zweiten Buche Mosis. | Zugleich die Wunderdinge, | welche gesehen und gehört worden sind | in der Geisterwelt und im Himmel der Engel. | [Von | Immanuel Swedenborg.] | <short rule> **| Aus der lateinischen Urschrift übersetzt. | Elfter Band. | Enthaltend 2. Buch Mosis Kapitel 1 bis 8 mit Nro. 6627 bis 7487. |** <double rule> **| Basel u. Ludwigsburg. | In Commission bei Ferd. Riehm. |** 1868.
small 8vo
title leaf, 2 pp; text of Exodus 1-8 and n 6627-7487, pp 1-586.
UK: SOC; GER: WLB; NET: GEN; SWE: UPP; USA: ANC, SHS

49/01/Ge 2/8 **1869** Hyde 828
Himmlische Geheimnisse, | welche in der | Heiligen Schrift | oder in dem | Worte des Herrn | enthalten, und nun enthüllt sind. | Hier, was in dem | Zweiten Buche Mosis. | Zugleich die Wunderdinge, | welche gesehen und gehört worden sind | in der Geisterwelt und im Himmel der Engel. | [Von | Immanuel Swedenborg.] | <short rule> **| Aus der lateinischen Urschrift übersetzt. | Zwölfter Band. | Enthaltend 2. Buch Mosis Kapitel 9 bis 15 mit Nro. 7488 bis 8386. |** <double rule> **| Basel u. Ludwigsburg. | In Commission bei Ferd. Riehm. |** 1868.
small 8vo
title leaf, 2 pp; text of Exodus 9-15 and n 7488-8386, pp 1-593.
UK: SOC; GER: WLB; NET: GEN; SWE: UPP; USA: ANC, SHS

49/01/Ge 2/9 **1869** Hyde 829
Himmlische Geheimnisse, | welche in der | Heiligen Schrift | oder in dem | Worte des Herrn | enthalten, und nun enthüllt sind. | Hier, was in dem | Zweiten Buche Mosis. | Zugleich die Wunderdinge, | welche gesehen und gehört worden sind | in der Geisterwelt und im Himmel der Engel. | [Von | Immanuel Swedenborg.] | <short rule> **| Aus der lateinischen Urschrift übersetzt. | Dreizehnter Band. | Enthaltend 2. Buch Mosis Kapitel 16 bis 21 mit Nro. 8337 bis 9111. |** <double rule> **| Basel u. Ludwigsburg. | In Commission bei Ferd. Riehm. |** 1869.
<*stet* 8337>
small 8vo
title leaf, 2 pp; text of Exodus 16-21 and n 8387-9111, pp 1-624.
UK: SOC; GER: WLB; NET: GEN; SWE: UPP; USA: ANC, SHS

49/01/Ge 2/10 **1869** Hyde 830
Himmlische Geheimnisse, | welche in der | Heiligen Schrift | oder in dem | Worte des Herrn | enthalten, und nun enthüllt sind. | Hier, was in dem | Zweiten Buche Mosis. | Zugleich die Wunderdinge, | welche gesehen und gehört worden sind | in der Geisterwelt und im Himmel der Engel. | [Von | Immanuel Swedenborg.] | <short rule> **| Aus der lateinischen Urschrift übersetzt. | Vierzehnter Band. | Enthaltend 2. Buch Mosis Kapitel 22 bis 25 mit Nro. 9112 bis 9584. |** <double rule> **| Basel u. Ludwigsburg. | In Commission bei Ferd. Riehm. |** 1869.

small 8vo
title leaf, 2 pp; text of Exodus 22-25 and n 9112-9584, pp 1-604.
UK: soc; GER: wlb; NET: gen; SWE: upp; USA: anc, shs

49/01/Ge 2/11 **1869** Hyde 831
Himmlische Geheimnisse, | welche in der | Heiligen Schrift | oder in dem | Worte des Herrn | enthalten, und nun enthüllt sind. | Hier, was in dem | Zweiten Buche Mosis. | Zugleich die Wunderdinge, | welche gesehen und gehört worden sind | in der Geisterwelt und im Himmel der Engel. | [Von | Immanuel Swedenborg.] | <short rule> | Aus der lateinischen Urschrift übersetzt. | Funfzehnter Band. | Enthaltend 2. Buch Mosis Kapitel 26 bis 29 mit Nro. 9585 bis 10166. | <double rule> | Basel u. Ludwigsburg. | In Commission bei Ferd. Riehm. | 1869.
small 8vo
title leaf, 2 pp; text of Exodus 26-29 and n 9585-10166, pp 1-693.
UK: soc; GER: wlb; NET: gen; SWE: upp; USA: anc, shs

49/01/Ge 2/12 **1869** Hyde 832
Himmlische Geheimnisse, | welche in der | Heiligen Schrift | oder in dem | Worte des Herrn | enthalten, und nun enthüllt sind. | Hier, was in dem | Zweiten Buche Mosis. | Zugleich die Wunderdinge, | welche gesehen und gehört worden sind | in der Geisterwelt und im Himmel der Engel. | [Von | Immanuel Swedenborg.] | <short rule> | Aus der lateinischen Urschrift übersetzt. | Sechszehnter Band. | Enthaltend 2. Buch Mosis Kapitel 30 bis 40 mit Nro. 10,167 bis 10,837. | <double rule> | Basel u. Ludwigsburg. | In Commission bei Ferd. Riehm. | 1869.
small 8vo
title leaf, 2 pp; text of Exodus 30-40 and n 10167-10837, pp 1-653.
UK: soc; GER: wlb; NET: gen; SWE: upp; USA: anc, shs

49/01/Ge 1/11 **1883** Hyde 833
Himmlische Geheimnisse, | welche in der | Heiligen Schrift | oder in dem | Worte des Herrn | enthalten, und nun enthüllt sind. | Hier, was in dem | Ersten Buche Mosis. | Zugleich die Wunderdinge, | welche gesehen und gehört worden sind | in der Geisterwelt und im Himmel der Engel. | [Von | Immanuel Swedenborg.] | <short rule> | Aus der lateinischen Urschrift übersetzt. | <short rule> | Zweiter Auflage. | <short rule> | Zweiter Band. | Enthaltend 1. Buch Mosis Kap. 8 bis 11 mit Nro. 824 bis 1382. | <double rule> | J. G. Mittnacht's Verlag | Frankfurt am Main. | 1883.
verso: Druck von Eduard Schauwecker in Reutlingen.
small 8vo
title leaf, 2 pp; text of Genesis 8-11 and n 824-1382, pp 3-413.
Reprinted from Ge 1/8 = Hyde 818.
UK: soc; NET: gen; USA: anc

49/01/Ge 1/12 **1893** Hyde 833/a
<<Himmlische Geheimnisse, | welche in der | Heiligen Schrift | oder in dem | Worte des Herrn | enthalten, und nun enthüllt sind. | Hier, was in dem | Ersten Buche Mosis. | Zugleich die Wunderdinge, | welche gesehen und gehört worden sind | in der Geisterwelt und im Himmel der Engel. | [Von | Immanuel Swedenborg.] | <short rule> | Aus der lateinischen Urschrift übersetzt. | Dritter Band. | Enthaltend 1. Buch Mosis, Kap. 12 bis 15 mit Nro. 1383 bis 1885. | Stuttgart. | Deutscher Swedenborg-Verein. | 1893.>>
small 8vo
title leaf, 2 pp; text of Genesis 12-15 and n 1383-1885, pp 1-358.

Reprinted from Ge 1/9 = Hyde 819.
Copy not seen; description deduced from Ge 1/9.
GER: WLB; NET: GEN; USA: ANC

49/01/Ge 1/13 **1911** Hyde 833/1
Himmlische Geheimnisse | welche in der | Heiligen Schrift | oder in dem | Worte des Herrn | enthalten, und nun enthüllt sind. | Hier, was in dem | Ersten Buche Mosis. | <short rule> | Zugleich die Wunderdinge, | welche gesehen und gehört worden sind | in der | Geisterwelt und im Himmel der Engel. | <short rule> | Von | Immanuel Swedenborg. | <short rule> | Aus der lateinischen Urschrift übersetzt. | <short rule> | Erster Band | Enthaltend 1. Buch Mosis, Kap. 1-7, mit Nr. 1- 823. | <short wavy rule> | <short double rule> | Dritte Auflage. | <short double rule> | <short wavy rule> | Stuttgart. Deutscher Swedenborg-Verein. 1911.
verso: Matth. 6, 33. | Trachtet am Ersten nach dem Reich Gottes, und nach seiner | Gerechtigkeit, so wird euch (solches) alles zufallen. | <short rule> | Druck von Karl Rohm in Lorch [Württemb.]
small 8vo
title leaf, 2 pp; Vorrede <Swedenborg's preface>, pp III-XXIV; Contents, pp 1-2; text of Genesis 1-7 and n 1-823, pp 3-481.
Reprinted from Ge 1/1 = Hyde 811.
NET: GEN; USA: ANC

49/01/Ge 1/14 **1913** Hyde 833/2
Himmlische Geheimnisse | welche in der | Heiligen Schrift oder in dem | Worte des Herrn | enthalten, und nun enthüllt sind. | <short rule> | Hier, was in dem | Ersten Buche Mosis. | <short rule> | Zugleich die Wunderdinge, | welche gesehen und gehört worden sind | in der Geisterwelt und im Himmel der Engel. | <short rule> | Von | Immanuel Swedenborg. | <short rule> | Aus der lateinischen Urschrift übersetzt. | <short rule> | Vierter Band. | Enthaltend 1, Buch Mosis Kap. 16 bis 20 mit. Nr. 1886 bis 2605. | <wavy rule> | <short double rule> | Zweiter Auflage. | <short double rule> | <wavy rule> | <type orn 2 x 47 mm> | Stuttgart. | Deutscher Swedenborg=Verein. | 1913.
small 8vo
title leaf, 2 pp; Vorrede <Swedenborg's preface>, pp 1-3; text of Genesis 16-20 and n 1886-2605, pp 4-696.
Reprinted from Ge 1/10 = Hyde 820.
NET: GEN; USA: ANC

49/01/Ge 1/15 **1966** Hyde —
EMANUEL SWEDENBORG | himmlische geheimnisse | DIE IN DER | HEILIGEN SCHRIFT, | DEM WORTE DES HERRN, | ENTHALTEN UND NUN ENTHÜLLT SIND | ERSTER BAND | (1. BUCH MOSE, KAP. 1 – 15, N. 1 – 1868) | STUDIENAUSGABE. | SWEDENBORG VERLAG / ZÜRICH
verso: *Arcana Cœlestia* | quæ in | *SCRIPTURA SACRA* | SEU | *VERBO DOMINI* | SUNT, DETECTA: | Hic, Primum quæ in | *GENESI.* | PARS PRIMA. | MDCCXLIX.
half title: EMANUEL SWEDENBORG: HIMMLISCHE GEHEIMNISSE IM WORTE GOTTES
4to
half title and title leaves, 4 pp; Vorwort und Hinweise <Foreword and introduction, by F Horn, editor> pp iii-xi; text of Genesis 1-15 and n 1-1868, pp 1-352.
ISBN 3-85927-001-X. Reprinted from Ge 1/7-1/9 = Hyde 817-819.
The inter-chapter sections of the text are omitted, but are printed in Ge 2/19.
GER: WLB; SWI: ZÜR; USA: ANC, SHS

49/01/Ge 1/16 **1966** Hyde —
EMANUEL SWEDENBORG | himmlische geheimnisse | DIE IN DER | HEILIGEN SCHRIFT, | DEM WORTE DES HERRN, | ENTHALTEN UND NUN ENTHÜLLT SIND | ZWEITER BAND | (1. BUCH MOSE, KAP. 16 – 21, N. 1886 – 2726) | STUDIENAUSGABE | SWEDENBORG VERLAG / ZÜRICH
half title: EMANUEL SWEDENBORG: HIMMLISCHE GEHEIMNISSE IM WORTE GOTTES
4to
half title and title leaves, 4 pp; text of Genesis 16-21 and n 1886-2726, pp 1-228.
ISBN 3-85927-002-8. n 1886-2605 reprinted from Ge 1/14 = Hyde 833/2; n 2605-2726 reprinted from Ge 2/1 = Hyde 821.
The inter-chapter sections of the text are omitted, but are printed in Ge 2/19.
GER: WLB; SWI: ZÜR; USA: ANC, SHS

49/01/Ge 2/13 **1967** Hyde —
EMANUEL SWEDENBORG | himmlische geheimnisse | DIE IN DER | HEILIGEN SCHRIFT, | DEM WORTE DES HERRN, | ENTHALTEN UND NUN ENTHÜLLT SIND | DRITTER BAND | (1. BUCH MOSE, KAP. 22 – 30, N. 2760 – 4038) | STUDIENAUSGABE | SWEDENBORG VERLAG / ZÜRICH
half title: EMANUEL SWEDENBORG: HIMMLISCHE GEHEIMNISSE IM WORTE GOTTES
4to
half title and title leaves, 4 pp; text of Genesis 22-30 and n 2760-4038, pp 1-359.
ISBN 3-85927-003-6. Reprinted from Ge 2/1, 2/2 = Hyde 821, 822.
The inter-chapter sections of the text are omitted, but are printed in Ge 2/19.
GER: WLB; SWI: ZÜR; USA: ANC

49/01/Ge 2/14 **1968** Hyde —
EMANUEL SWEDENBORG | himmlische geheimnisse | DIE IN DER | HEILIGEN SCHRIFT, | DEM WORTE DES HERRN, | ENTHALTEN UND NUN ENTHÜLLT SIND | VIERTER BAND | (1. BUCH MOSE, KAP. 31 – 40; Nr. 4056 – 5170) | STUDIENAUSGABE | SWEDENBORG VERLAG / ZÜRICH
half title: EMANUEL SWEDENBORG: HIMMLISCHE GEHEIMNISSE IM WORTE GOTTES
4to
half title and title leaves, 2 pp; text of Genesis 31-40 and n 4056-5170, pp 1-315.
ISBN 3-85927-004-4. Reprinted from Ge 2/3, 2/4 = Hyde 823, 824.
The inter-chapter sections of the text are omitted, but are printed in Ge 2/19.
GER: WLB; SWI: ZÜR; USA: ANC

49/01/Ge 2/15 **1969** Hyde —
EMANUEL SWEDENBORG | himmlische geheimnisse | DIE IN DER | HEILIGEN SCHRIFT, | DEM WORTE DES HERRN, | ENTHALTEN UND NUN ENTHÜLLT SIND | FÜNFTER BAND | (1. BUCH MOSE, KAP. 41 – 50; Nr. 5191 – 6597) | STUDIENAUSGABE | SWEDENBORG VERLAG / ZÜRICH
half title: EMANUEL SWEDENBORG: HIMMLISCHE GEHEIMNISSE IM WORTE GOTTES
4to
half title and title leaves, 4 pp; text of Genesis 41-50 and n 5191-6597, pp 1-297.
ISBN 3-85927-005-2. Reprinted from Ge 2/5, 2/6 = Hyde 825, 826.
The inter-chapter sections of the text are omitted, but are printed in Ge 2/19.
GER: WLB; SWI: ZÜR; USA: ANC

49/01/Ge 2/16 **1970** Hyde —
EMANUEL SWEDENBORG | himmlische geheimnisse | DIE IN DER | HEILIGEN SCHRIFT, | DEM WORTE DES HERRN, | ENTHALTEN UND NUN ENTHÜLLT SIND | SECHSTER BAND | (2. BUCH MOSE, KAP. 1 – 15, Nr. 6627 – 8370) | STUDIENAUSGABE | SWEDENBORG VERLAG | ZÜRICH

half title: EMANUEL SWEDENBORG: HIMMLISCHE GEHEIMNISSE IM WORTE GOTTES
4to
half title and title leaves, 4 pp; text of Exodus 1-15 and n 6627-8370, pp 1-353.
ISBN 3-85927-006-0. Reprinted from Ge 2/7, 2/8 = Hyde 827, 828.
The inter-chapter sections of the text are omitted, but are printed in Ge 2/19.
GER: WLB; SWI: ZÜR; USA: ANC

49/01/Ge 2/17 **1971** Hyde —
EMANUEL SWEDENBORG | himmlische geheimnisse | DIE IN DER | HEILIGEN SCHRIFT, | DEM WORTE DES HERRN, | ENTHALTEN UND NUN ENTHÜLLT SIND | SIEBENTER BAND | (2. BUCH MOSE, KAP. 16 – 25; Nr. 8395 – 9577) | STUDIENAUSGABE | SWEDENBORG VERLAG / ZÜRICH
half title: EMANUEL SWEDENBORG: HIMMLISCHE GEHEIMNISSE IM WORTE GOTTES
4to
half title and title leaves, 4 pp; text of Exodus 16-25 and n 8395-9577, pp 1-374.
ISBN 3-85927-007-9. Reprinted from Ge 2/9, 2/10 = Hyde 829, 830.
The inter-chapter sections of the text are omitted, but are printed in Ge 2/19.
GER: WLB; SWI: ZÜR; USA: ANC

49/01/Ge 2/18 **1972** Hyde —
EMANUEL SWEDENBORG | himmlische geheimnisse | DIE IN DER | HEILIGEN SCHRIFT, | DEM WORTE DES HERRN, | ENTHALTEN UND NUN ENTHÜLLT SIND | ACHTER BAND | (2. BUCH MOSE, KAP. 26 – 40; Nr. 9592 – 10831) | SWEDENBORG VERLAG | ZÜRICH
half title: EMANUEL SWEDENBORG: HIMMLISCHE GEHEIMNISSE IM WORTE GOTTES
4to
half title and title leaves, 4 pp; text of Exodus 26-40 and n 9592-10831, pp 1-404; advertisement, 1 p.
ISBN 3-85927-008-7. Reprinted from Ge 2/11, 2/12 = Hyde 831, 832.
The inter-chapter sections of the text are omitted, but are printed in Ge 2/19.
GER: WLB; SWI: ZÜR; USA: ANC

49/01/Ge 2/19 **1972** Hyde —
EMANUEL SWEDENBORG | Die himmlischen geheimnisse, | welche in der heiligen Schrift, | oder im Worte des Herrn usgedebt worden, | sind enthalten in der Auslegung, | welche der Innere Sinn des Wortes ist; | über die Beschaffenheit dieses Sinnes sehe man nach, | was von ihm aus der Erfahrung gezeigt worden ist, | n. 1767 bis 1777, n. 1869 bis 1879; | und überdies im zusammen hange | n.1 bis 5, 64, 65, 66, 167, 605, 920, 937, 1143, 1224, 1404, 1405, 1408, 1409, 1502 am Ende, 1540, 1659, 1783, 1807
half title: EMANUEL SWEDENBORG: HIMMLISCHE GEHEIMNISSE IM WORTE GOTTES
4to
half title and title leaves, 4 pp; text, pp 1-218; Index to Bible passages quoted in *Arcana Caelestia*, pp 219-267; Nachwort <Postscript>, p 268.
The text includes the passages omitted in Ge 1/15-16 and 2/13-18.
GER: WLB; SWI: ZÜR; USA: ANC

49/01/Ge 1/17 **1975** Hyde —
EMANUEL SWEDENBORG | himmlische geheimnisse | DIE IN DER | HEILIGEN SCHRIFT, | DEM WORTE DES HERRN, | ENTHALTEN UND NUN ENTHÜLLT SIND | ERSTER BAND | (1. BUCH MOSE, KAP. 1 – 15, N. 1 – 1868) | STUDIENAUSGABE. | SWEDENBORG VERLAG / ZÜRICH
verso: *Arcana Cœlestia* | quæ in | *SCRIPTURA SACRA* | SEU | *VERBO DOMINI* | SUNT, DETECTA: | Hic, Primum quæ in | *GENESI.* | PARS PRIMA. | MDCCXLIX.
half title: EMANUEL SWEDENBORG: HIMMLISCHE GEHEIMNISSE IM WORTE GOTTES

4to
half title and title leaves, 4 pp; Vorwort und Hinweise <Foreword and introduction, by F Horn, editor>, pp iii-xi; text of Genesis 1-15 and n 1-1868, pp 1-352.
ISBN 3-85927-001-X. Reprinted from Ge 1/15.
The inter-chapter sections of the text are omitted, but are printed in Ge 2/27.
SWI: ZÜR

49/01/Ge 1/18 **1976 or 1977** Hyde —
<<EMANUEL SWEDENBORG | himmlische geheimnisse | DIE IN DER | HEILIGEN SCHRIFT, | DEM WORTE DES HERRN, | ENTHALTEN UND NUN ENTHÜLLT SIND | ZWEITER BAND | (1. BUCH MOSE, KAP. 16 - 21, N. 1886 – 2605) | STUDIENAUSGABE. | SWEDENBORG VERLAG / ZÜRICH>>
half title: <<EMANUEL SWEDENBORG: HIMMLISCHE GEHEIMNISSE IM WORTE GOTTES>>
4to
half title and title leaves, 4 pp; text of Genesis 16-21 and n 1886-2605, pp 1-228.
Reprinted from Ge 1/16.
The inter-chapter sections of the text are omitted, but are printed in Ge 2/27.
Copy not seen; description deduced from Ge 1/16 and 1/19.

49/01/Ge 2/20 **1978** Hyde —
EMANUEL SWEDENBORG | himmlische geheimnisse | DIE IN DER | HEILIGEN SCHRIFT, | DEM WORTE DES HERRN, | ENTHALTEN UND NUN ENTHÜLLT SIND | DRITTER BAND | (1. BUCH MOSE, KAP. 22 – 30, N. 2760 – 4038) | STUDIENAUSGABE | SWEDENBORG VERLAG / ZÜRICH
half title: EMANUEL SWEDENBORG: HIMMLISCHE GEHEIMNISSE IM WORTE GOTTES
4to
half title and title leaves, 4 pp; text of Genesis 22-30 and n 2760-4038, pp 1-359.
ISBN 3-85927-003-6. Reprinted from Ge 2/13.
The inter-chapter sections of the text are omitted, but are printed in Ge 2/27.
SWI: ZÜR

49/01/Ge 2/21 **1979** Hyde —
EMANUEL SWEDENBORG | himmlische geheimnisse | DIE IN DER | HEILIGEN SCHRIFT, | DEM WORTE DES HERRN, | ENTHALTEN UND NUN ENTHÜLLT SIND | FÜNFTER BAND | (1. BUCH MOSE, KAP. 41 – 50; Nr. 5191 – 6597) | STUDIENAUSGABE | SWEDENBORG VERLAG / ZÜRICH
half title: EMANUEL SWEDENBORG: HIMMLISCHE GEHEIMNISSE IM WORTE GOTTES
4to
half title and title leaves, 4 pp; text of Genesis 41-50 and n 5191-6597, pp 1-297.
ISBN 3-85927-005-2. Reprinted from Ge 2/5, 2/6 = Hyde 825, 826.
The inter-chapter sections of the text are omitted, but are printed in Ge 2/27.
SWI: ZÜR

49/01/Ge 2/22 **1980** Hyde —
EMANUEL SWEDENBORG | himmlische geheimnisse | DIE IN DER | HEILIGEN SCHRIFT, | DEM WORTE DES HERRN, | ENTHALTEN UND NUN ENTHÜLLT SIND | VIERTER BAND | (1. BUCH MOSE, KAP. 31 – 40; Nr. 4056 – 5170) | STUDIENAUSGABE | SWEDENBORG VERLAG / ZÜRICH
half title: EMANUEL SWEDENBORG: HIMMLISCHE GEHEIMNISSE IM WORTE GOTTES
4to
half title and title leaves, 4 pp; text of Genesis 31-40 and n 4056-5170, pp 1-315.
ISBN 3-85927-004-4. Reprinted from Ge 2/14
The inter-chapter sections of the text are omitted, but are printed in Ge 2/27.
SWI: ZÜR

49/01/Ge 2/23 **1980** Hyde —

EMANUEL SWEDENBORG | himmlische geheimnisse | DIE IN DER | HEILIGEN SCHRIFT, | DEM WORTE DES HERRN, | ENTHALTEN UND NUN ENTHÜLLT SIND | ACHTER BAND | (2. BUCH MOSE, KAP. 26 – 40; Nr. 9592 – 10831) | SWEDENBORG VERLAG | ZÜRICH
half title: EMANUEL SWEDENBORG: HIMMLISCHE GEHEIMNISSE IM WORTE GOTTES
4to
half title and title leaves, 4 pp; text of Exodus 26-40 and n 9592-10831, pp 1-404; advertisement, 1 p.
ISBN 3-85927-008-7. Reprinted from Ge 2/18.
The inter-chapter sections of the text are omitted, but are printed in Ge 2/27.
SWI: ZÜR

49/01/Ge 2/24 **1981** Hyde —

EMANUEL SWEDENBORG | himmlische geheimnisse | DIE IN DER | HEILIGEN SCHRIFT, | DEM WORTE DES HERRN, | ENTHALTEN UND NUN ENTHÜLLT SIND | SECHSTER BAND | (2. BUCH MOSE, KAP. 1 – 15, Nr. 6627 – 8370) | STUDIENAUSGABE | SWEDENBORG VERLAG | ZÜRICH
half title: EMANUEL SWEDENBORG: HIMMLISCHE GEHEIMNISSE IM WORTE GOTTES
4to
half title and title leaves, 4 pp; text of Exodus 1-15 and n 6627-8370, pp 1-353.
ISBN 3-85927-006-0. Reprinted from Ge 2/7, 2/8 = Hyde 827, 828.
The inter-chapter sections of the text are omitted, but are printed in Ge 2/27.
SWI: ZÜR

49/01/Ge 2/25 **1981** Hyde —

EMANUEL SWEDENBORG | himmlische geheimnisse | DIE IN DER | HEILIGEN SCHRIFT, | DEM WORTE DES HERRN, | ENTHALTEN UND NUN ENTHÜLLT SIND | SIEBENTER BAND | (2. BUCH MOSE, KAP. 16 – 25; Nr. 8395 – 9577) | STUDIENAUSGABE | SWEDENBORG VERLAG / ZÜRICH
half title: EMANUEL SWEDENBORG: HIMMLISCHE GEHEIMNISSE IM WORTE GOTTES
4to
half title and title leaves, 4 pp; text of Exodus 16-25 and n 8395-9577, pp 1-374.
ISBN 3-85927-007-9. Reprinted from Ge 2/9, 2/10 = Hyde 829, 830.
The inter-chapter sections of the text are omitted, but are printed in Ge 2/27.
SWI: ZÜR

49/01/Ge 2/26 **1981** Hyde —

EMANUEL SWEDENBORG | himmlische geheimnisse | DIE IN DER | HEILIGEN SCHRIFT, | DEM WORTE DES HERRN, | ENTHALTEN UND NUN ENTHÜLLT SIND | ACHTER BAND | (2. BUCH MOSE, KAP. 26 – 40; Nr. 9592 – 10832) | STUDIENAUSGABE | SWEDENBORG VERLAG / ZÜRICH
half title: EMANUEL SWEDENBORG: HIMMLISCHE GEHEIMNISSE IM WORTE GOTTES
4to
half title and title leaves, 4 pp; text of Exodus 26-40 and n 9592-10832, pp 1-404.
The inter-chapter sections of the text are omitted, but are printed in Ge 2/27.
SWI: ZÜR

49/01/Ge 2/27 **1981** Hyde —

<no title page>
4to
text, pp 1-218; Index der zitienter Schriftstellen <Index to Bible passages quoted in *Arcana Caelestia*, translated from the Index in an English version>, pp 219-267; Nachwort <Postscript, by F Horn>, p 268.

The text includes the passages omitted in Ge 1/17-18 and 2/20-25. ISBN 3-85927-009-5.
SWI: ZÜR

49/01/Ge 1/19 **1985** Hyde —
EMANUEL SWEDENBORG | himmlische geheimnisse | DIE IN DER | HEILIGEN SCHRIFT, | DEM WORTE DES HERRN, | ENTHALTEN UND NUN ENTHÜLLT SIND | ERSTER BAND | (1. BUCH MOSE, KAP. 1 – 15, N. 1 – 1868) | STUDIENAUSGABE. | SWEDENBORG VERLAG / ZÜRICH
verso: *Arcana Cœlestia* | quæ in | *SCRIPTURA SACRA* | SEU | *VERBO DOMINI* | SUNT, DETECTA: | Hic, Primum quæ in | *GENESI.* | PARS PRIMA. | MDCCXLIX.
half title: EMANUEL SWEDENBORG: HIMMLISCHE GEHEIMNISSE IM WORTE GOTTES
4to
half title and title leaves, 4 pp; Vorwort und Hinweise <Foreword and introduction, by F Horn, editor>, pp iii-xi; text of Genesis 1-15 and n 1-1868, pp 1-352.
ISBN 3-85927-001-X. Reprinted from Ge 1/17.
The inter-chapter sections of the text are omitted, but are printed in Ge 2/34.
SWI: ZÜR

49/01/Ge 1/20 **1986** Hyde —
EMANUEL SWEDENBORG | himmlische geheimnisse | DIE IN DER | HEILIGEN SCHRIFT, | DEM WORTE DES HERRN, | ENTHALTEN UND NUN ENTHÜLLT SIND | ZWEITER BAND | (1. BUCH MOSE, KAP. 16 – 21, N. 1886 – 2726) | STUDIENAUSGABE | SWEDENBORG VERLAG / ZÜRICH
half title: EMANUEL SWEDENBORG: HIMMLISCHE GEHEIMNISSE IM WORTE GOTTES
4to
half title and title leaves, 4 pp; text of Genesis 16-21 and n 1886-2726, pp 1-228.
ISBN 3-85927-002-8. Reprinted from Ge 1/16.
The inter-chapter sections of the text are omitted, but are printed in Ge 2/34.
SWI: ZÜR

49/01/Ge 1/21 **1989** Hyde —
EMANUEL SWEDENBORG | himmlische geheimnisse | DIE IN DER | HEILIGEN SCHRIFT, | DEM WORTE DES HERRN, | ENTHALTEN UND NUN ENTHÜLLT SIND | ZWEITER BAND | (1. BUCH MOSE, KAP. 16 – 21, N. 1886 – 2726) | STUDIENAUSGABE | SWEDENBORG VERLAG / ZÜRICH
half title: EMANUEL SWEDENBORG: HIMMLISCHE GEHEIMNISSE IM WORTE GOTTES
4to
half title and title leaves, 4 pp; text of Genesis 16-21 and n 1886-2726, pp 1-228.
ISBN 3-85927-002-8. Reprinted from Ge 1/19.
The inter-chapter sections of the text are omitted, but are printed in Ge 2/34.
SWI: ZÜR

49/01/Ge 2/28 **1994** Hyde —
EMANUEL SWEDENBORG | himmlische geheimnisse | DIE IN DER | HEILIGEN SCHRIFT, | DEM WORTE DES HERRN, | ENTHALTEN UND NUN ENTHÜLLT SIND | DRITTER BAND | (1. BUCH MOSE, KAP. 22 – 30, N. 2760 – 4038) | STUDIENAUSGABE | SWEDENBORG VERLAG / ZÜRICH
half title: EMANUEL SWEDENBORG: HIMMLISCHE GEHEIMNISSE IM WORTE GOTTES
4to
half title and title leaves, 4 pp; text of Genesis 22-30 and n 2760-4038, pp 1-359.
ISBN 3-85927-003-6. Reprinted from Ge 2/20.
The inter-chapter sections of the text are omitted, but are printed in Ge 2/34.
SWI: ZÜR

49/01/Ge 1/22 **1994** Hyde —
EMANUEL SWEDENBORG | **himmlische geheimnisse** | DIE IN DER | HEILIGEN SCHRIFT, | DEM WORTE DES HERRN, | ENTHALTEN UND NUN ENTHÜLLT SIND | ERSTER BAND | (1. BUCH MOSE, KAP. 1 – 15, N. 1 – 1868) | STUDIENAUSGABE. | SWEDENBORG VERLAG / ZÜRICH
verso: *Arcana Cœlestia* | quæ in | *SCRIPTURA SACRA* | SEU | *VERBO DOMINI* | SUNT, DETECTA: | Hic, Primum quæ in | *GENESI.* | PARS PRIMA. | MDCCXLIX.
half title: EMANUEL SWEDENBORG: HIMMLISCHE GEHEIMNISSE IM WORTE GOTTES
4to
half title and title leaves, 4 pp; Vorwort und Hinweise <Foreword and introduction, by F Horn, editor>, pp iii-xi; text of Genesis 1-15 and n 1-1868, pp 1-352.
ISBN 3-85927-001-X. Reprinted from Ge 1/19.
The inter-chapter sections of the text are omitted, but are printed in Ge 2/34.
SWI: ZÜR

49/01/Ge 2/29 **1995** Hyde —
EMANUEL SWEDENBORG | **himmlische geheimnisse** | DIE IN DER | HEILIGEN SCHRIFT, | DEM WORTE DES HERRN, | ENTHALTEN UND NUN ENTHÜLLT SIND | VIERTER BAND | (1. BUCH MOSE, KAP. 31 – 40; Nr. 4056 – 5170) | STUDIENAUSGABE | SWEDENBORG VERLAG / ZÜRICH
half title: EMANUEL SWEDENBORG: HIMMLISCHE GEHEIMNISSE IM WORTE GOTTES
4to
half title and title leaves, 2 pp; text of Genesis 31-40 and n 4056-5170, pp 1-315.
ISBN 3-85927-004-4. Reprinted from Ge 2/22.
The inter-chapter sections of the text are omitted, but are printed in Ge 2/34.
SWI: ZÜR

49/01/Ge 2/30 **1995** Hyde —
EMANUEL SWEDENBORG | **himmlische geheimnisse** | DIE IN DER | HEILIGEN SCHRIFT, | DEM WORTE DES HERRN, | ENTHALTEN UND NUN ENTHÜLLT SIND | FÜNFTER BAND | (1. BUCH MOSE, KAP. 41 – 50; Nr. 5191 – 6597) | STUDIENAUSGABE | SWEDENBORG VERLAG / ZÜRICH
half title: EMANUEL SWEDENBORG: HIMMLISCHE GEHEIMNISSE IM WORTE GOTTES
4to
half title and title leaves, 4 pp; text of Genesis 41-50 and n 5191-6597, pp 1-297.
ISBN 3-85927-005-2. Reprinted from Ge 2/21.
The inter-chapter sections of the text are omitted, but are printed in Ge 2/34.
SWI: ZÜR

49/01/Ge 2/31 **1995** Hyde —
EMANUEL SWEDENBORG | **himmlische geheimnisse** | DIE IN DER | HEILIGEN SCHRIFT, | DEM WORTE DES HERRN, | ENTHALTEN UND NUN ENTHÜLLT SIND | SECHSTER BAND | (2. BUCH MOSE, KAP. 1 – 15, Nr. 6627 – 8370) | STUDIENAUSGABE | SWEDENBORG VERLAG | ZÜRICH
half title: EMANUEL SWEDENBORG: HIMMLISCHE GEHEIMNISSE IM WORTE GOTTES
4to
half title and title leaves, 4 pp; text of Exodus 1-15 and n 6627-8370, pp 1-353.
ISBN 3-85927-006-0. Reprinted from Ge 2/24.
The inter-chapter sections of the text are omitted, but are printed in Ge 2/34.
SWI: ZÜR

49/01/Ge 2/32 **1995** Hyde —
EMANUEL SWEDENBORG | **himmlische geheimnisse** | DIE IN DER | HEILIGEN SCHRIFT, | DEM WORTE DES HERRN, | ENTHALTEN UND NUN ENTHÜLLT SIND | SIEBENTER BAND | (2. BUCH

MOSE, KAP. 16 – 25; Nr. 8395 – 9577) | STUDIENAUSGABE | SWEDENBORG VERLAG / ZÜRICH
half title: EMANUEL SWEDENBORG: HIMMLISCHE GEHEIMNISSE IM WORTE GOTTES
4to
half title and title leaves, 4 pp; text of Exodus 16-25 and n 8395-9577, pp 1-374.
ISBN 3-85927-007-9. Reprinted from Ge 2/25.
The inter-chapter sections of the text are omitted, but are printed in Ge 2/34.
SWI: ZÜR

49/01/Ge 2/33 **1995** Hyde —
EMANUEL SWEDENBORG | himmlische geheimnisse | DIE IN DER | HEILIGEN SCHRIFT, | DEM WORTE DES HERRN, | ENTHALTEN UND NUN ENTHÜLLT SIND | ACHTER BAND | (2. BUCH MOSE, KAP. 26 – 40; Nr. 9592 – 10832) | STUDIENAUSGABE | SWEDENBORG VERLAG / ZÜRICH
half title: EMANUEL SWEDENBORG: HIMMLISCHE GEHEIMNISSE IM WORTE GOTTES
4to
half title and title leaves, 4 pp; text of Exodus 26-40 and n 9592-10832, pp 1-404.
ISBN 3-85927-008-7.
The inter-chapter sections of the text are omitted, but are printed in Ge 2/34.
SWI: ZÜR

49/01/Ge 2/34 **1995** Hyde —
EMANUEL SWEDENBORG | **Die himmlischen geheimnisse,** | welche in der heiligen Schrift, | oder im Worte des Herrn usgedebt worden, | sind enthalten in der Auslegung, | welche der Innere Sinn des Wortes ist; | über die Beschaffenheit dieses Sinnes sehe man nach, | was von ihm aus der Erfahrung gezeigt worden ist, | n. 1767 bis 1777, n. 1869 bis 1879; | und überdies im zusammen hange | n.1 bis 5, 64, 65, 66, 167, 605, 920, 937, 1143, 1224, 1404, 1405, 1408, 1409, 1502 am Ende, 1540, 1659, 1783, 1807
half title: EMANUEL SWEDENBORG: HIMMLISCHE GEHEIMNISSE IM WORTE GOTTES
4to
half title and title leaves, 4 pp; text, pp 1-218; Index to Bible passages quoted in *Arcana Caelestia*, pp 219-267; Nachwort <Postscript>, p 268.
The text includes the passages omitted in Ge 1/22 and 2/28-33. ISBN 3-85927-009-5.
SWI: ZÜR

49/01/Ge 3/1 **1997** Hyde —
EMANUEL SWEDENBORG | HIMMLISCHE | GEHEIMNISSE | IM WORTE GOTTES | DIE NUN ENTHÜLLT SIND | ERSTER BAND | (1. BUCH MOSE, KAP. 1-9, NR. 1 - 1105) | DEUTSCH VON IMMANUEL TAFEL UND ANDEREN | ÜBERARBEITET VON FRIEDEMANN HORN UND HEINZ GROB | SWEDENBORG- VERLAG ZÜRICH
verso: *Arcana Coelestia* | QUAE IN *SCRIPTURA SACRA,* | SEU | *VERBO DOMINI* | SUNT, DETECTA: | Hic Primum quae in | *GENESI.* | PARS PRIMA | MDCCXLIX. | © 1997 by Swedenborg-Verlag Zürich | Satz und Herstellung: Swedenborg-Verlag Zürich | Umschlaggestaltung: Johannes Horn | ISBN 3 - 85927 - 071-0
half title: HIMMLISCHE GEHEIMNISSE | IM WORTE GOTTES | nunc | <orn 2 x 12 mm> | licet
8vo
half title and title leaves; 4 pp; Einleitung und Vorwort <Preface and foreword>, pp 5-16; text of Genesis 1-9 and n 1-1105, pp 1-463.
Revision of Ge 1/15 in modern German edited by F Horn and Heinz Grob. The volumes of this edition are printed in roman, not fraktur, type.
The inter-chapter sections of the text are omitted, but are printed in Ge 3/10.
GER: WLB; SWE: ROY; SWI: ZÜR

49/01/Ge 3/2 **1997** Hyde —
EMANUEL SWEDENBORG | DIE HIMMLISCHEN | GEHEIMNISSE | *die in der Heiligen Schrift* | *oder im Worte des Herrn* | *enthalten und nun* | *enthüllt sind* | BAND 1 | 1. MOSE 1, 1-9, 29 / NR. 1-1105 | Orthographisch und typographisch revidierter Nachdruck | der Basler Ausgabe von 1867-69 | SWEDENBORG-VERLAG
verso: Titel der lateinischen Urfassung von 1749-56: | *ARCANA COELESTIA* | *quae in Scriptura Sacra* | *seu Verbo Domini sunt detecta:* | *nempe quae in Genesi et Exodo* | *una cum mirabilibus quae visa sunt in* | *Mundo Spirituum et in Caelo Angelorum* | © by Swedenborg-Verlag Zürich | Satz und Herstellung: Swedenborg-Verlag Zürich | Umschlaggestaltung: Johannes Horn | Einband: Ehe GmbH, Radolfzell | ISBN: 3-85927-250-0 <*stet* Caelo>
half title: DIE HIMMLISCHEN GEHEIMNISSE | nunc | <orn 2 x 12 mm> | licet
8vo
half title and title leaves, 4 pp; Inhaltsverzeichnis <List of contents>, p 5; Vorwort des Herausgebers <Editor's foreword>, pp 7-24; Vorbemerkungen der Verfassers <Swedenborg's preface>, pp 25-26; text of Genesis 1-9 and n 1-1105, pp 27-602.
Revision of Ge 1/15. The inter-chapter sections of the text are omitted, but are printed in Ge 3/10.
GER: VER

49/01/Ge 3/3 **1998** Hyde —
EMANUEL SWEDENBORG | DIE HIMMLISCHEN | GEHEIMNISSE | *die in der Heiligen Schrift* | *oder im Worte des Herrn* | *enthalten und nun* | *enthüllt sind.* | BAND 2 | 1. MOSE 10, 1-17, 27 / NR. 1130-2116 | Orthographisch und typographisch revidierter Nachdruck | der Basler Ausgabe von 1867-69 | SWEDENBORG-VERLAG
verso: Titel der lateinischen Urfassung von 1749-56: | *ARCANA CAELESTIA* | *quae in Scriptura Sacra* | *seu Verbo Domini sunt detecta:* | *nempe quae in Genesi et Exodo* | *una cum mirabilibus quae visa sunt in* | *Mundo Spirituum et in Caelo Angelorum* | © 1998 by Swedenborg-Verlag Zürich | Satz und Herstellung: Swedenborg-Verlag Zürich | Umschlaggestaltung: Johannes Horn | Einband: Ehe GmbH, Radolfzell | ISBN: 3-85927-251-9 <*stet* Caelo>
half title: DIE HIMMLISCHEN GEHEIMNISSE | nunc | <orn 2 x 12 mm> | licet
8vo
half title and title leaves, 4 pp; Inhaltsverzeichnis <List of contents>, p 5; text of Genesis 10-17 and n 1130-2116, pp 1-567.
Revision of Ge 1/8-10. The inter-chapter sections of the text are omitted, but are printed in Ge 3/17.
GER: VER, WLB; SWE: ROY; SWI: ZÜR

49/01/Ge 3/4 **1998** Hyde 819/–
EMANUEL SWEDENBORG | DIE HIMMLISCHEN | GEHEIMNISSE | *die in der Heiligen Schrift* | *oder im Worte des Herrn* | *enthalten und nun* | *enthüllt sind.* | BAND 3 | 1. Mose 18, 1-22, 24 / NR. 2135-2869 | Orthographisch und typographisch revidierter Nachdruck | der Basler Ausgabe von 1867-69 | SWEDENBORG-VERLAG
verso: Titel der lateinischen Urfassung von 1749-56: | *ARCANA COELESTIA* | *quae in Scriptura Sacra* | *seu Verbo Domini sunt detecta:* | *nempe quae in Genesi et Exodo* | *una cum mirabilibus quae visa sunt in* | *Mundo Spirituum et in Caelo Angelorum* | © 1998 by Swedenborg-Verlag Zürich | Satz und Herstellung: Swedenborg-Verlag Zürich | Umschlaggestaltung: Johannes Horn | Einband: Ehe GmbH, Radolfzell | ISBN: 3-85927-252-7 <*stet* Caelo>
half title: DIE HIMMLISCHEN GEHEIMNISSE | nunc | <orn 2 x 12 mm> | licet
4to
title leaf, 2 pp; text of Genesis 18-22 and n 2135-2869, pp 1-572.
Revision of Ge 1/10. The inter-chapter sections of the text are omitted, but are printed in Ge 3/10.
GER: VER, WLB; SWE: ROY; SWI: ZÜR

49/01/Ge 3/5 **1998** Hyde —
EMANUEL SWEDENBORG | DIE HIMMLISCHEN | GEHEIMNISSE | *die in der Heiligen Schrift* | *oder im Worte des Herrn* | *enthalten und nun* | *enthüllt* sind. | BAND 4 | 1. Mose 23, 1-27, 46 / NR. 2894-3623 | Orthographisch und typographisch revidierter Nachdruck | der Basler Ausgabe von 1867-69 | SWEDENBORG-VERLAG
verso: Titel der lateinischen Urfassung von 1749-56: | *ARCANA COELESTIA* | *quae in Scriptura Sacra* | *seu Verbo Domini sunt detecta:* | *nempe quae in Genesi et Exodo* | *una cum mirabilibus quae visa sunt in* | *Mundo Spirituum et in Caelo Angelorum* | © 1998 by Swedenborg-Verlag Zürich | Satz und Herstellung: Swedenborg-Verlag Zürich | Umschlaggestaltung: Johannes Horn | Einband: Ehe GmbH, Radolfzell | ISBN: 3-85927-253-5 <*stet* Caelo>
half title: DIE HIMMLISCHEN GEHEIMNISSE | nunc | <orn 2 x 12 mm> | licet
8vo
half title and title leaves, 4 pp; Inhaltsverzeichnis <List of contents>, p 5; text of Genesis 23-27 and n 2894-3623, pp 7-544.
Revision of Ge 1/10. The inter-chapter sections of the text are omitted, but are printed in Ge 3/10.
GER: VER, WLB; SWE: ROY; SWI: ZÜR

49/01/Ge 3/6 **1998** Hyde —
EMANUEL SWEDENBORG | DIE HIMMLISCHEN | GEHEIMNISSE | *die in der Heiligen Schrift* | *oder im Worte des Herrn* | *enthalten und nun* | *enthüllt sind.* | BAND 5 | 1. Mose 28, 1-32, 32 / NR. 3650-4317 | Orthographisch und typographisch revidierter Nachdruck | der Basler Ausgabe von 1867-69 | SWEDENBORG-VERLAG
verso: Titel der lateinischen Urfassung von 1749-56: | *ARCANA COELESTIA* | *quae in Scriptura Sacra* | *seu Verbo Domini sunt detecta:* | *nempe quae in Genesi et Exodo* | *una cum mirabilibus quae visa sunt in* | *Mundo Spirituum et in Caelo Angelorum* | © 1998 by Swedenborg-Verlag Zürich | Satz und Herstellung: Swedenborg-Verlag Zürich | Umschlaggestaltung: Johannes Horn | Einband: Ehe GmbH, Radolfzell | ISBN: 3-85927-254-3 <*stet* Caelo>
half title: DIE HIMMLISCHEN GEHEIMNISSE | nunc | <orn 2 x 12 mm> | licet
8vo
half title and title leaves, 4 pp; Inhaltsverzeichnis <List of contents>, p 5; text of Genesis 28-32 and n 3650-4317, pp 1-623.
Revision of Ge 2/2-3. The inter-chapter sections of the text are omitted, but are printed in Ge 3/10.
GER: VER, WLB; SWE: ROY; SWI: ZÜR

49/01/Ge 3/7 **1998** Hyde —
EMANUEL SWEDENBORG | DIE HIMMLISCHEN | GEHEIMNISSE | *die in der Heiligen Schrift* | *oder im Worte des Herrn* | *enthalten und nun* | *enthüllt sind.* | BAND 6 | 1. Mose 33, 1-39, 23 / NR. 4332-5071 Orthographisch und typographisch revidierter Nachdruck | der Basler Ausgabe von 1867-69 | SWEDENBORG-VERLAG
verso: Titel der lateinischen Urfassung von 1749-56: | *ARCANA COELESTIA* | *quae in Scriptura Sacra* | *seu Verbo Domini sunt detecta:* | *nempe quae in Genesi et Exodo* | *una cum mirabilibus quae visa sunt in* | *Mundo Spirituum et in Caelo Angelorum* | © 1998 by Swedenborg-Verlag Zürich | Satz und Herstellung: Swedenborg-Verlag Zürich | Umschlaggestaltung: Johannes Horn | Einband: Ehe GmbH, Radolfzell | ISBN: 3-85927-255-1 <*stet* Caelo>
half title: DIE HIMMLISCHEN GEHEIMNISSE | nunc | <orn 2 x 12 mm> | licet
8vo
half title and title leaves, 4 pp; Inhaltsverzeichnis <List of contents>, p 5; text of Genesis 33-39 and n 4332-5071, pp 1-563.
Revision of Ge 2/3-4. The inter-chapter sections of the text are omitted, but are printed in Ge 3/10.
GER: VER, WLB; SWE: ROY; SWI: ZÜR

49/01/Ge 3/8 **1998** Hyde —
EMANUEL SWEDENBORG | DIE HIMMLISCHEN | GEHEIMNISSE | *die in der Heiligen Schrift* | *oder im Worte des Herrn* | *enthalten und nun* | *enthüllt sind.* | BAND 7 | 1. Mose 40, 1-44, 34 / NR. 5072-5845 | Orthographisch und typographisch revidierter Nachdruck | der Basler Ausgabe von 1867-69 | SWEDENBORG-VERLAG
verso: Titel der lateinischen Urfassung von 1749-56: | *ARCANA COELESTIA* | *quae in Scriptura Sacra* | *seu Verbo Domini sunt detecta:* | *nempe quae in Genesi et Exodo* | *una cum mirabilibus quae visa sunt in* | *Mundo Spirituum et in Caelo Angelorum* | © 1998 by Swedenborg-Verlag Zürich | Satz und Herstellung: Swedenborg-Verlag Zürich | Umschlaggestaltung: Johannes Horn | Einband: Ehe GmbH, Radolfzell | ISBN: 3-85927-256-x <*stet* Caelo>
half title: DIE HIMMLISCHEN GEHEIMNISSE | nunc | <orn 2 x 12 mm> | licet
8vo
half title and title leaves, 4 pp; Inhaltsverzeichnis <List of contents>, p 5; text of Genesis 40-44 and n 5072-5845, pp 1-539.
Revision of Ge 2/4-5. The inter-chapter sections of the text are omitted, but are printed in Ge 3/10.
GER: VER, WLB; SWE: ROY; SWI: ZÜR

49/01/Ge 3/9 **1998** Hyde —
EMANUEL SWEDENBORG | DIE HIMMLISCHEN | GEHEIMNISSE | *die in der Heiligen Schrift* | *oder im Worte des Herrn* | *enthalten und nun* | *enthüllt sind.* | BAND 8 | 1. Mose 45, 1-50, 26 / NR. 5867-6597 | Orthographisch und typographisch revidierter Nachdruck | der Basler Ausgabe von 1867-69 | SWEDENBORG-VERLAG
verso: Titel der lateinischen Urfassung von 1749-56: | *ARCANA COELESTIA* | *quae in Scriptura Sacra* | *seu Verbo Domini sunt detecta:* | *nempe quae in Genesi et Exodo* | *una cum mirabilibus quae visa sunt in* | *Mundo Spirituum et in Caelo Angelorum* | © 1998 by Swedenborg-Verlag Zürich | Satz und Herstellung: Swedenborg-Verlag Zürich | Umschlaggestaltung: Johannes Horn | Einband: Ehe GmbH, Radolfzell | ISBN: 3-85927-258-6 <*stet* Caelo>
half title: DIE HIMMLISCHEN GEHEIMNISSE | nunc | <orn 2 x 12 mm> | licet
8vo
half title and title leaves, 4 pp; Inhaltsverzeichnis <List of contents>, p 5; text of Genesis 45-50 and n 5867-6597, pp 1-455.
Revision of Ge 2/6. The inter-chapter sections of the text are omitted, but are printed in Ge 3/10.
GER: VER, WLB; SWE: ROY; SWI: ZÜR

49/01/Ge 3/10 **1998** Hyde —
EMANUEL SWEDENBORG | DIE HIMMLISCHEN | GEHEIMNISSE | *die in der Heiligen Schrift* | *oder im Worte des Herrn* | *enthalten und nun* | *enthüllt sind* | BAND 15 | SUPPLEMENT | (NACHTRÄGE UND ERGÄNZUNGEN) | Orthographisch und typographisch revidierter Nachdruck | der Basler Ausgabe von 1867-69 | SWEDENBORG-VERLAG
verso: Titel der lateinischen Urfassung von 1749-56: | *ARCANA COELESTIA* | *quae in Scriptura Sacra,* | *seu Verbo Domini sunt, detecta:* | *hic quae in Exodo, una cum mirabilibus* | *quae visa sunt in Mundo Spirituum* | *et in Caelo Angelorum* | © 1998 by Swedenborg-Verlag Zürich | Satz und Herstellung: Swedenborg-Verlag Zürich | Umschlaggestaltung: Johannes Horn | Einband: Ehe GmbH, Radolfzell | ISBN: 3-85927-264-0 <*stet* Caelo>
half title: DIE HIMMLISCHEN GEHEIMNISSE | nunc | <orn 2 x 12 mm> | licet
8vo
half title and title leaves, 4 pp; Inhaltsverzeichnis <List of contents>, pp 5-6; Einleitung <Preface>, pp 7-8; text, pp 9-567.

Revision of Ge 2/19. This volume contains the text of the inter-chapter material omitted from volumes 1-14 in this edition.

GER: VER, WLB; SWE: ROY; SWI: ZÜR

49/01/Ge 3/11 1999 Hyde —

EMANUEL SWEDENBORG | DIE HIMMLISCHEN | GEHEIMNISSE | *die in der Heiligen Schrift* | *oder im Worte des Herrn* | *enthalten und nun* | *enthüllt sind* | BAND 9 | 2. Mose, 1,1-8,28 / NR. 6627-7474 | Orthographisch und typographisch revidierter Nachdruck | der Basler Ausgabe von 1867-69 | SWEDENBORG-VERLAG

verso: Titel der lateinischen Urfassung von 1749-56: | *ARCANA COELESTIA* | *quae in Scriptura Sacra* | *seu Verbo Domini sunt detecta:* | *hic quae in Exodo, una cum mirabilibus* | *quae visa sunt in* | *mundo spirituum* | *et in caelo angelorum* | © 1999 by Swedenborg-Verlag Zürich | Satz und Herstellung: Swedenborg-Verlag Zürich | Umschlaggestaltung: Johannes Horn | Einband: Ehe GmbH, Radolfzell | ISBN: 3-85927-258-6 <*stet* caelo>

half title: DIE HIMMLISCHEN GEHEIMNISSE | nunc | <orn 2 x 12 mm> | licet

8vo

half title and title leaves, 4 pp; Inhaltsverzeichnis <List of contents>, p 5; text of Exodus 1-8 and n 6627-7474, pp 7-480.

Revision of Ge 2/7. The inter-chapter sections of the text are omitted, but are printed in Ge 3/17.

GER: VER, WLB; SWE: ROY; SWI: ZÜR

49/01/Ge 3/12 1999 Hyde —

EMANUEL SWEDENBORG | Die himmlischen | Geheimnisse | *die in der Heiligen Schrift* | *oder im Worte des Herrn* | *enthalten und nun* | *enthüllt sind* | BAND 10 | 2. Mose, 9,1-15,27 / NR. 7496-8370 | Orthographisch und typographisch revidierter Nachdruck | der Basler Ausgabe von 1867-69 | SWEDENBORG-VERLAG

verso: Titel der lateinischen Urfassung von 1749-56: | *ARCANA COELESTIA* | *quae in Scriptura Sacra,* | *seu Verbo Domini sunt, detecta:* | *his quae in Exodo, una cum mirabilibus* | *quae visa sunt in Mundo Spirituum* | *et in Caelo Angelorum* | © 1999 by Swedenborg-Verlag Zürich | Satz und Herstellung: Swedenborg-Verlag Zürich | Umschlaggestaltung: Johannes Horn | Einband: Ehe GmbH, Radulfzell | ISBN: 3-85927-259-4 <*stet* Caelo>

half title: DIE HIMMLISCHEN GEHEIMNISSE | nunc | <orn 2 x 12 mm> | licet

8vo

half title and title leaves, 4 pp; Inhaltsverzeichnis <List of contents>, p 5; text of Exodus 9-15 and n 7496-8370, pp 1-492.

Revision of Ge 2/8. The inter-chapter sections of the text are omitted, but are printed in Ge 3/17.

GER: VER, WLB; SWE: ROY; SWI: ZÜR

49/01/Ge 3/13 1999 Hyde 827/—

EMANUEL SWEDENBORG | DIE HIMMLISCHEN | GEHEIMNISSE | *die in der Heiligen Schrift* | *oder im Worte des Herrn* | *enthalten und nun* | *enthüllt sind* | BAND 11 | 2. Mose, 16,1-21,37 / NR. 8395-9103 | Orthographisch und typographisch revidierter Nachdruck | der Basler Ausgabe von 1867-69 | SWEDENBORG-VERLAG

verso: Titel der lateinischen Urfassung von 1749-56: | *ARCANA COELESTIA* | *quae in Scriptura Sacra,* | *seu Verbo Domini sunt, detecta:* | *his quae in Exodo, una cum mirabilibus* | *quae visa sunt in Mundo Spirituum* | *et in Caelo Angelorum* | © 1999 by Swedenborg-Verlag Zürich | Satz und Herstellung: Swedenborg-Verlag Zürich | Umschlaggestaltung: Johannes Horn | Einband: Ehe GmbH, Radulfzell | ISBN: 3-85927-260-8 <*stet* Caelo>

half title: DIE HIMMLISCHEN GEHEIMNISSE | nunc | <orn 2 x 12 mm> | licet

8vo
half title and title leaves, 4 pp; Inhaltsverzeichnis <List of contents>, p 5; text of Exodus 16-21 and n 8395-9103, pp 1-524.
Revision of Ge 2/9. The inter-chapter sections of the text are omitted, but are printed in Ge 3/17.
GER: VER, WLB; SWE: ROY; SWI: ZÜR

49/01/Ge 3/14 **1999** Hyde 828/–
EMANUEL SWEDENBORG | DIE HIMMLISCHEN | GEHEIMNISSE | *die in der Heiligen Schrift* | *oder im Worte des Herrn* | *enthalten und nun* | *enthüllt sind* | BAND 12 | 2. Mose, 22,1-25,40 / NR. 9123-9577 | Orthographisch und typographisch revidierter Nachdruck | der Basler Ausgabe von 1867-69 | SWEDENBORG-VERLAG
verso: Titel der lateinischen Urfassung von 1749-56: | *ARCANA COELESTIA* | *quae in Scriptura Sacra,* | *seu Verbo Domini sunt, detecta:* | *his quae in Exodo, una cum mirabilibus* | *quae visa sunt in Mundo Spirituum* | *et in Caelo Angelorum* | © 1999 by Swedenborg-Verlag Zürich | Satz und Herstellung: Swedenborg-Verlag Zürich | Umschlaggestaltung: Johannes Horn | Einband: Ehe GmbH, Radulfzell | ISBN: 3-85927-261-6 <*stet* Caelo>
half title: DIE HIMMLISCHEN GEHEIMNISSE | nunc | <orn 2 x 12 mm> | licet
8vo
half title and title leaves, 4 pp; Inhaltsverzeichnis <List of contents>, p 5; text of Exodus 22-25 and n 9123-9577, pp 1-498.
Revision of Ge 2/10. The inter-chapter sections of the text are omitted, but are printed in Ge 3/17.
GER: VER, WLB; SWE: ROY; SWI: ZÜR

49/01/Ge 3/15 **1999** Hyde 829/–
EMANUEL SWEDENBORG | DIE HIMMLISCHEN | GEHEIMNISSE | *die in der Heiligen Schrift* | *oder im Worte des Herrn* | *enthalten und nun* | *enthüllt sind* | BAND 13 | 2. Mose, 26,1-29,46 / NR. 9592-10158 | Orthographisch und typographisch revidierter Nachdruck | der Basler Ausgabe von 1867-69 | SWEDENBORG-VERLAG
verso: Titel der lateinischen Urfassung von 1749-56: | *ARCANA COELESTIA* | *quae in Scriptura Sacra,* | *seu Verbo Domini sunt, detecta:* | *his quae in Exodo, una cum mirabilibus* | *quae visa sunt in Mundo Spirituum* | *et in Caelo Angelorum* | © 1999 by Swedenborg-Verlag Zürich | Satz und Herstellung: Swedenborg-Verlag Zürich | Umschlaggestaltung: Johannes Horn | Einband: Ehe GmbH, Radulfzell | ISBN: 3-85927-262-4 <*stet* Caelo>
half title: DIE HIMMLISCHEN GEHEIMNISSE | nunc | <orn 2 x 12 mm> | licet
8vo
half title and title leaves, 4 pp; Inhaltsverzeichnis <List of contents>, p 5; text of Exodus 26-29 and n 9592-10158, pp 1-585.
Revision of Ge 2/11. The inter-chapter sections of the text are omitted, but are printed in Ge 3/17.
GER: VER, WLB; SWE: ROY; SWI: ZÜR

49/01/Ge 3/16 **1999** Hyde 830/–
EMANUEL SWEDENBORG | DIE HIMMLISCHEN | GEHEIMNISSE | *die in der Heiligen Schrift* | *oder im Worte des Herrn* | *enthalten und nun* | *enthüllt sind* | BAND 14 | 2. Mose, 30-40 / NR. 10'175-10'832 | Orthographisch und typographisch revidierter Nachdruck | der Basler Ausgabe von 1867-69 | SWEDENBORG-VERLAG
verso: Titel der lateinischen Urfassung von 1749-56: | *ARCANA COELESTIA* | *quae in Scriptura Sacra,* | *seu Verbo Domini sunt, detecta:* | *hic quae in Exodo, una cum mirabilibus* | *quae visa sunt in Mundo Spirituum* | *et in caelo angelorum* | © 1999 by Swedenborg-Verlag Zürich |

Satz und Herstellung: Swedenborg-Verlag Zürich | Umschlaggestaltung: Johannes Horn | Einband: Ehe GmbH, Radulfzell | ISBN: 3-85927-260-8 <*stet* caelo>
half title: DIE HIMMLISCHEN GEHEIMNISSE | nunc | <orn 2 x 12 mm> | licet
4to
title leaf, 2 pp; text of Exodus 30-40 and n 10175-10832, pp 1-523.
Revision of Ge 2/12. The inter-chapter sections of the text are omitted, but are printed in Ge 3/17.
GER: VER, WLB; SWE: ROY; SWI: ZÜR

49/01/Ge 3/17 **2000** Hyde —
EMANUEL SWEDENBORG | DIE HIMMLISCHEN | GEHEIMNISSE | *die in der Heiligen* Schrift | oder im Worte des Herrn | enthalten und nun | enthüllt sind | BAND 15 | SUPPLEMENT | (NACHTRAGE UND ERGÄNZUNGEN) | Orthographisch und typographisch revidierter Nachdruck | der Basler Ausgabe von 1867-69 | SWEDENBORG-VERLAG
verso: Titel der lateinischen Urfassung von 1749-56: | *ARCANA COELESTIA* | *quae in Scriptura Sacra,* | *seu Verbo Domini sunt, detecta:* | *hic quae in Exodo, una cum mirabilibus* | *quae visa sunt in Mundo Spirituum* | *et in Caelo Angelorum* | Auflage 2000 | © by Swedenborg-Verlag, Zürich | Satz und Herstellung: Swedenborg-Verlag Zürich | Umschlaggestaltung: Johannes Horn | Einband: Ehe GmbH, Radolfzell | ISBN: 3-85927-264-0 <*stet* Caelo>
half title: DIE HIMMLISCHEN GEHEIMNISSE | nunc | <orn 2 x 12 mm> | licet
8vo
half title and title leaves, 4 pp; Inhaltsverzeichnis <List of contents>, pp 5-6; Einleitung <Preface>, pp 7-8; text, pp 9-567.
Reprint of Ge 3/10.
GER: VER, WLB; SWE: ROY; SWI: ZÜR

49/01/Ge 3/18 **2000** Hyde —
EMANUEL SWEDENBORG | DIE HIMMLISCHEN | GEHEIMNISSE | *die in der Heiligen Schrift* | *oder im Worte des Herrn* | *enthalten und nun* | *enthüllt sind* | BAND 1 | 1. MOSE 1, 1-9, 29 / NR. 1-1105 | Orthographisch und typographisch revidierter Nachdruck | der Basler Ausgabe von 1867-69 | SWEDENBORG-VERLAG
verso: Titel der lateinischen Urfassung von 1749-56: | *ARCANA COELESTIA* | *quae in Scriptura Sacra* | *seu Verbo Domini sunt detecta:* | *nempe quae in Genesi et Exodo* | *una cum mirabilibus quae visa sunt in* | *Mundo Spirituum et in Caelo Angelorum* | Auflage 2000 | © by Swedenborg-Verlag Zürich | Satz und Herstellung: Swedenborg-Verlag Zürich | Umschlaggestaltung: Johannes Horn | Einband: Ehe GmbH, Radolfzell | ISBN: 3-85927-250-0 <*stet* Caelo>
half title: DIE HIMMLISCHEN GEHEIMNISSE | nunc | <orn 2 x 12 mm> | licet
8vo
half title and title leaves, 4 pp; Inhaltsverzeichnis <Table of contents>, pp 5-6; Vorwort des Herausgebers <Editor's foreword>, pp 7-24; Vorbemerkungen der Verfassers <Swedenborg's preface>, pp 25-26; text of Genesis 1-9 and n 1-1105, pp 27-602.
Reprint of Ge 3/2. The inter-chapter sections of the text are omitted, but are printed in Ge 3/17.
GER: VER

49/01/Ge 3/19 **2000** Hyde —
EMANUEL SWEDENBORG | DIE HIMMLISCHEN | GEHEIMNISSE | *die in der Heiligen Schrift* | *oder im Worte des Herrn* | *enthalten und nun* | *enthüllt sind* | BAND 3 | 1. MOSE 18, 1-22, 24 / NR. 2135-2869 | Orthographisch und typographisch revidierter Nachdruck | der Basler Ausgabe von 1867-69 | SWEDENBORG-VERLAG
verso: Titel der lateinischen Urfassung von 1749-56: | *ARCANA COELESTIA* | *quae in Scriptura*

Sacra | *seu Verbo Domini sunt detecta:* | *nempe quae in Genesi et Exodo* | *una cum mirabilibus quae visa sunt in* | *Mundo Spirituum et in Caelo Angelorum* | Auflage 2000 | © by Swedenborg-Verlag Zürich | Satz und Herstellung: Swedenborg-Verlag Zürich | Umschlaggestaltung: Johannes Horn | Einband: Ehe GmbH, Radolfzell | ISBN: 3-85927-252-7 <*stet* Caelo>
half title: DIE HIMMLISCHEN GEHEIMNISSE | nunc | <orn 2 x 12 mm> | licet
8vo
half title and title leaves, 4 pp; Inhaltsverzeichnis <List of contents>, p 5; text of Genesis 18-22 and n 2135-2869, pp 7-572.
Reprint of Ge 3/4. The inter-chapter sections of the text are omitted, but are printed in Ge 3/17.
GER: VER

49/01/Ge 3/20 **2000** Hyde —
EMANUEL SWEDENBORG | DIE HIMMLISCHEN | GEHEIMNISSE | *die in der Heiligen Schrift* | *oder im Worte des Herrn* | *enthalten und nun* | *enthüllt sind.* | BAND 7 | 1. Mose 40, 1-44, 34 / NR. 5072-5845 | Orthographisch und typographisch revidierter Nachdruck | der Basler Ausgabe von 1867-69 | SWEDENBORG-VERLAG
verso: Titel der lateinischen Urfassung von 1749-56: | *ARCANA COELESTIA* | *quae in Scriptura Sacra* | *seu Verbo Domini sunt detecta:* | *nempe quae in Genesi et Exodo* | *una cum mirabilibus quae visa sunt in* | *Mundo Spirituum et in Caelo Angelorum* | Auflage 2000 | © by Swedenborg-Verlag Zürich | Satz und Herstellung: Swedenborg-Verlag Zürich | Umschlaggestaltung: Johannes Horn | Einband: Ehe GmbH, Radolfzell | ISBN: 3-85927-256-x <*stet* Caelo>
half title: DIE HIMMLISCHEN GEHEIMNISSE | nunc | <orn 2 x 12 mm> | licet
8vo
half title and title leaves, 4 pp; Inhaltsverzeichnis <List of contents>, p 5; text of Genesis 40-44 and n 5072-5845, pp 7-539.
Reprint of Ge 3/8. The inter-chapter sections of the text are omitted, but are printed in Ge 3/17.
GER: VER

GERMAN EXTRACTS

X 49/01/Ge 1765/1 1765 Hyde 876
Swedenborgs | **und anderer** | **Irrdische und himmlische** | PHILOSOPHIE, | **Zur Prüfung des Besten,** | **ans Licht gestellt** | **von** | **Friederich Christoph Oetinger,** | Special-Superintendent **en in Herrenberg,** | **Württemberger=Lands.** | <orn 31 x 43 mm> | <orn rule> | Franckfurt und Leipzig. 1765.
small 8vo
title leaf, 2 pp; Vorrede <Foreword>, 6 pp; text, pp 1-237; Innhalt <Contents>, pp 238-240; Register <Index>, pp 241-248.
The volume contains unspecified extracts from *Arcana Coelestia* vol 1.
NET: GEN

X 49/01/Ge nd/1 **no date** Hyde 878
Swedenborgs | **und anderer** | **Irrdische und Himmlische** | **Philosophie,** | **zur** | **Prüfung des Besten,** | **ans Licht gestellt** | **von** | **Friederich Christoph Oetinger,** | **Special=Superintendenten in Herrenberg,** | **Württemberger Lands.** | <orn 23 x 36 mm, foliage and tree stump> | <orn double rule> | **Franckfurt und Leipzig.**
small 8vo
title leaf, 2 pp; Vorrede <Foreword>, 6 pp; Innhalt <Contents>, 2 pp; text, pp 1-230.
Reprinted from X Ge 1765/1 = Hyde 876.
UK: SOC

X 49/01/Ge 1776/1 **1776** Hyde 880, 3149

<<**Swedenborgs und anderer irrdische und himmlische Philosophie, zur Prüfung des Besten, ans Licht gestellt von Friederich Christoph Oetinger, Special-Superintendenten in Herrenberg, Württemberger Lands.**>>

small 8vo

title leaf, 2 pp; text, pp 12-180.

Reprinted from X Ge nd/1 = Hyde 878, published in *Emanuel Swedenborg auserlesene Schrifter. Vierter Theil. Frankfurt am Mayn, zu finden bey dem Commercienrath Daniel Christian Hechtel*. <Hyde 3149>

Copy not seen; description recorded from Hyde 880, 3149.

X 49/01/Ge 1795/1 **1795** Hyde 882, 2813

<<**Zusatz der im ii Thiele, no. 757 (737) Seite 711, angeführten Stellen aus den *Himmlischen Geheimnissen*.**>>

8vo

title and text n 3353-3356, 3486-3489, 3650-3655, 3751-3755, 3757, 3897-3901, 4056-4060, 4230-4231, 4332-4335, 4422-4424, pp 857-904.

Translated by C A Donat, published in *Die ganze Theologie der Neuen Kirche* vol 2, Basel <71/02/Ge 2/2 = Hyde 2813>.

Copy not seen; description recorded from Hyde 882.

SWE: ROY

X 49/01/Ge 1806/1 **1806** Hyde 883

<<**Eine Auslegung, oder Erklärung des Vier und Zwanzigsten Kapitels im Evangelisten Matthäus, nach dem geistlichen und innern Sinne: woraus es sich ergiebt, dass die darin enthaltenen Weissagungen des Herrn eingetroffen und zu dieser zeit erfüllet sind. Durch Emanuel Swedenborg, einem Knecht des Herrn Jesu Christi. Nebst einem Katechismus zum Gebrauche für die Neue Kirche, und einem Briefe zur Ermahnung und Warnung, &c.** <Zech 14:8-9 quoted> **Gedruckt bei Wilhelm D. Lepper, zu Hannover.** 1806.>>

small 8vo

title leaf, 2 pp; Vorrede <Foreword>, pp iii-ix; text, pp 1-68; Katechismus, pp 70-79.

Copy not seen; description recorded from Hyde 883.

X 49/01/Ge 1833/1 **1833** Hyde 883/a

Grundzüge | des | christlichen Glaubens | nach dem Lehrbegriffe | der | Neuen Kirche. | Aus einem gröskern Werke Swedenborg's zusammen= | gestellt, und mit furzen Erklärungen begleitet. | <short orn rule> | **Herausgegeben | von | Dr. G. C. Seuffert.** | <orn wavy rule> | **Schweinfurt. | Christoph Webstein's Buchhandlung. | 1833.**

section title: **Grundzüge | des | christlichen Glaubens | nach dem Lehrbegriffe | der | Neuen Kirche.**

12mo

title leaf, 2 pp; Vorrede <Preface>, pp III-VI; Druckfehler <Corrections>, p VII; section title leaf, pp 1-2; text sections I-XXIII, pp 1-71.

UK: SOC; USA: ANC

X 49/01/Ge 1839/1 **1839** Hyde 883/–

Matthäi XXIV. und XXV; | erstmals aufgeschlossen, | mit dem | Schlüssel des HErrn; | Oder | Göttliche Vorverkündung | von dem | Entartungsverlaufe | der so noch benannten | Christen-Kirche. | <orn rule 3 x 28 mm> | **Uebersetzt aus den Himmelsgeheimnissen | Emanuel**

Swedenborg's | von | Ludwig Hofaker. | <orn rule 2 x 70 mm> **| Tübingen und Leipzig. | Verlag der Buchhandlung Zu-Guttenberg.** | 1839.
verso: <<**Die Ausführung, welche hier folgt, ist aus dem großen hermeneutischen Werk Emanuel Swedenborg's, betitelt Arcana coelestia (Himmelsgeheimnisse) genommen, und hier in's Teutsche wortgetreu übertragen. Die Stellen, worinn sie dort enthalten ist, sind die Ziffern:** 3353-3556, 3486-3489, 3650-3655, 3751-3757, 3897-3901, 4056-4060, 4229-4231, 4332-4335, 4422-4424, 4535, 4635-4638, 4661-4664, 4807, 4810, 4954-4959, 5063-5071.>>
large 8vo
title leaf, 2 pp; text, pp 1-20 <5 uncut sheets>.
Hofaker translated some of the paragraphs completely, with footnotes referring to other paragraphs throughout *Arcana Caelestia*. <Letter from E Zwink to N Ryder, 7-7-2004.>
Copy not seen; description deduced from notes provided by E Zwink and W R T Perizonius.
GER: WLB

X 49/01/Ge 1858/1 **1858** Hyde 883/b
<<**Swedenborgs und Anderer Irrdische und Himmlische Philosophie ... gestellt von F. C. Oetinger ... Neu herausgegeben von K. C. E. Ehmann ... Erster Theil. Reutlingen, Druck u. Verlag von Rupp u. Bauer.**>>
8vo
text: Unspecified material extracted from 49/01 etc, 375 pp.
Published as Part 2, vol 2, of Oetinger's *Collected Works*; wrongly dated by Hyde to 1855.
Copy not seen; description deduced from Hyde 883/b and catalogue of NET: GEN.
NET: GEN

X 49/01/Ge 1869/1 **1869** Hyde 884
<<**Grundzüge des christlichen Glaubens nach dem Lehrgegrisse der Neuen Kirche. Aus einem grössern Werke Swedenborg's zusammengestellt und mit kurzen Erklärungen begleitet. Zweite vom Verfasser revidirte Ausgabe. Basel: in Commission bei Ferd. Riehm.** 1869.>>
small 8vo
title leaf, 2 pp; Vorrede zur ersten Ausgabe <Foreword to the 1st edition, signed Dr G C Seiffert>, 1833, pp v-viii; Vorrede zur zweiten Ausgabe <Foreword to the 2nd edition>, pp ix-xii; text, pp 1-61.
Copy not seen; description recorded from Hyde 884.

X 49/01/Ge 1878/1 **1878** Hyde 885
Die | Kleine Arcana Cölestia | (Himmlische Geheimnisse) | enthaltend | die gedrängte Erklärung des ganzen | Ersten Buches Mose. | Nach Swedenborg's grösser Arcana Cölestia. | Herausgegeben von Anton Neumayer. | Korrigirt von H. Peisker, Prediger der Neuen Kirche. | Erster Band. | <type orn 2 x 41 mm> **| Wien. | Druck und Verlag von Melchior und Comp. | 1878.**
8vo
title leaf, 2 pp; Vorrede <Foreword>, 2 pp; Inhalt <Contents>, 1 p; text, pp 1-401; catalogue, 2 pp.
UK: SOC; USA: ANC

X 49/01/Ge 1878/2 **1878** Hyde 886
Swedenborg's | Himmlische Geheimnisse | im Auszuge | enthaltend die gedrängte Erklärung des ganzen | Ersten Buches Mose. | Erster Band | Kapitel 1 bis 25 umfassend. | Revidirt von H. Peisker, Prediger der Neuen Kirche. | <type orn 2 x 25 mm> **| Wien. | Verlag des Vereines der Neuen Kirche. | 1878.**
verso: <wavy rule> **| Druck von Melchior & Comp., Wien, IV, Mozartgasse 4. |** <wavy rule>
8vo

title leaf, 2 pp; Vorrede zum ersten Band <Editor's foreword to the 1st volume>, 1 p; Inhalt <Contents>, 2 pp; text, pp 1-401; catalogue, 2 pp.
The same as X Ge 1878/1, with a fresh title page.
UK: SOC

X 49/01/Ge 1882/1 **1882** Hyde 887
Swedenborg's | Himmlische Geheimnisse | im Auszuge | enthaltend die gedrängte Erklärung des ganzen | Ersten Buches Mose. | Zweiter Band | Kapitel 26 bis 50 umfassend. | <type orn 2 x 25 mm> | **Wien.** | **Verlag des Vereines der Neuen Kirche.** | **1882.**
verso: <wavy rule> | **Druck von Melchior & Comp., Wien, IV, Mozartgasse** 4. | <wavy rule>
8vo
title leaf, 2 pp; Vorrede zum zweiter Band <Editor's foreword to the 2nd volume>, 1 p; Inhalt <Contents>, 2 pp; text, pp 1-598; Druckfehler-Verzeichniss <List of misprints>, 2 pp.
These extracts were made by Frau A F Ehrenborg, and (after revision by H Peisker and J Zierhut) were printed at her expense.
UK: SOC; NET: GEN

X 49/01/Ge 1911/1 **1911** Hyde 887/1
Die Schöpfungsgeschichte Mosis. | <type orn 4 x 8 mm> | **Von Immanuel Swedenborg.** | <type orn 4 x 8 mm> | **Enthaltend | eine Erklärung der ersten zwei Kapitel | des ersten Buchs Mose | nach ihrem geistigen Sinn.** | <short rule> | **[Entnommen dem ersten Bande der Himmlischen Geheimnisse.]** | **Aus der lateinischen Urschrift übersetzt.** | <short rule> | **Stuttgart.** | **Deutscher Swedenborg=Verein** | 1911.
verso: **Druck von Karl Rohm in Lorch (Württbg.)**
8vo
title leaf, 2 pp; text, pp 3-101; Werbung <advertisement>, 3 pp.
GER: VER; USA: ANC

X 49/01/Ge 1950/1 **1950** Hyde 887/–
<<Die andere Welt. Mittelungen aus dem Werke "Himmlische Geheimnisse" die in der Heiligen Schrift oder im Worte des Herrn enthalten die Wunderdinge, welche gesehen und gehört worden sund in der Geisterwelt und im Himmel der Engel. Aus der lateinsichen Urschrift übersetzt.>>
8vo
title leaf, 2 pp; text, pp –.
Copy not seen; description recorded from catalogue of SWE: ROY.
SWE: ROY

X 49/01/Ge 1957/1 **1957** Hyde 887/2
Emanuel Swedenborg | UND ES WAR | ABEND | UND ES WAR | MORGEN | Die Stufen der Menschwerdung | Der innere Sinn der ersten zwei Kapitel des 1. Buches Mose | aus „Himmlische Geheimnisse" | *Mit einem Geleitwort von Wolfgang Kretschmer* | SWEDENBORG VERLAG | ZÜRICH
verso: *Diese Ausgabe enthält die ersten Kapitel des Werkes* Arcana | Coelestia, quae in Scriptura Sacra, seu Verbo Domini sunt, | detecta: hic quae in Genesi. Una cum mirabilibus, quae visa | sunt in Mundo Spirituum et Coelo Angelorum. Die Himmlischen | Geheimnisse, welche in der Heiligen Schrift oder dem Worte des | Herrn enthalten und nun enthüllt sind. Hier, was im ersten | Buch Mosis. Zugleich die Wunderdinge, welche in der Geister- | welt und im Himmel der Engel gesehen worden sind. London | 1747 bis 1758. 4557 Seiten. | *Die vorliegende Ausgabe wurde übertragen von Friedemann und* | *Hella Horn.* | Alle Rechte der deutschen Ausgabe | auch die

des auszugsweisen Nachdrucks | vorbehalten | Buchgestaltung Gerhard Gollwitzer | Gesetzt in der Weiss-Antiqua | Satz und Druck Karl Schahl Lörrach <*stet* 1747 bis 1758>
half title: <publisher's logo 12 x 12 mm> | DER SWEDENBORG BUCHEREI | BAND 2
small 8vo
half title and title leaves, 4 pp; Geleitwort <Introduction>, pp 5-8; Vorwort des Herausgebers <Editor's foreword>, pp 9-20; text, pp 21-118; Werbung <advertisement>, pp 119-120.
Extracted from *Arcana Caelestia* chapters 1 and 2, translated by Friedemann and Hella Horn. Foreword by Wolfgang Kretschmer. ISBN 3-85927-010-9.
UK: SOC; GER: VER, WLB; SWI: ZÜR; USA: SHS

X 49/01/Ge 1962/1 **1962** Hyde 887/3
EMANUEL SWEDENBORG | HOMO MAXIMUS | DER HIMMLISCHE UND DER LIEBLICHE MENSCH | EINFUHRUNG VON ERNST BENZ | <publisher's logo 13 x 7 mm> | OTTO WILHELM BARTH-VERLAG | WEILHEIM/OBERBAYERN
verso: Dieses Werk erscheint in der Sammlung | »ZEICHEN UND SYMBOLE« | *Den Umschlag gestalte Elisabeth Brüning / Baldham bei München unter Verwendung eines | Ausschnitts aus ihrem Gemälde* »Weltinsel« *(Originalformat 102.5 x 75 cm)* | 1962 | © 1962 by Otto Wilhelm Barth-Verlag GmbH · Weilheim/Oberbayern | Alle Recht - auch die des auszugsweisen Nachdrucks, der fotomechanischen Wiedergabe | und der Übersetzung - vorbehalten | Gesamtherstellung : Robert Koehler-Druck · München
half title: EMANUEL SWEDENBORG / HOMO MAXIMUS
verso: <introductory statement>
8vo
half title and title leaves, 4 pp; Vorwort <Foreword>, pp 5-8; text, pp 9-193; Hinweise des Verlages <publishing information>, p 194; Inhaltsverzeichnis <List of contents>, p 195; Werbung <advertisement>, pp 195-198.
GER: BAV, VER; SWI: ZÜR; USA: ANC, SHS

X 49/01/Ge 1975/1 **1975** Hyde 887/–
<<*Emanuel Swedenborg* | UND ES WAR | ABEND | UND ES WAR | MORGEN | Die Stufen der Menschwerdung | Der innere Sinn der ersten zwei Kapitel des 1. Buches Mose | aus „Himmlische Geheimnisse" | *Mit einem Geleitwort von Wolfgang Kretschmer* | SWEDENBORG VERLAG | ZÜRICH>>
small 8vo
half title and title leaves, 4 pp; Geleitwort <Introduction>, pp 5-8; Vorrede <Foreword>, pp 9-20; text, pp 21-118.
Reprint of X Ge 1957/1. ISSN 99-0493083-X.
Copy not seen; description deduced from catalogue of SWE: ROY and X Ge 1957/1.
SWE: ROY

X 49/01/Ge 1983/1 **1983** Hyde 887/–
<<EMANUEL SWEDENBORG | HOMO MAXIMUS | DER HIMMLISCHE UND DER LIEBLICHE MENSCH | *Auszüge aus »Himmlische Geheimnis im Worte Gottes«* | EINFÜHRUNG VON ERNST BENZ | Zweite, autorisierte Auflage. | SWEDENBORG VERLAG ZÜRICH>>
verso: <<© der ersten Auflage 1962 | by Otto Wilhelm Barth-Verlag GmbH | Auflage 1983 Swedenborg-Verlag Zürich>>
half title: <<EMANUEL SWEDENBORG/HOMO MAXIMUS | BAND 10 | DER SWEDENBORG BÜCHEREI | nunc | <type orn> | licet
8vo

half title leaf and title page, 3 pp; Inhaltsverzeichnis <List of contents>, p 4; Vorwort und Biographisches <Foreword and biographical statement>, pp 5-8; text, pp 1-193; Hinweise der verlages <Publishing information>, pp 194-195; Werbung <advertisement>, p 196.
Revised reprint of X Ge 1962/1. <Letter from E Zwink to N Ryder, 16-6-2004>
Copy not seen; description deduced from X Ge 1962/1 and catalogue of GER: WLB.
GER: WLB

X 49/01/Ge 1991/1 **1991** Hyde 887/–
<<Emanuel Swedenborg | Der himmlische und der natürliche Mensch>>
8vo
title and text, pp 309-317.
Published in *Lust an der Erkenntnis: Esoterik: von der Antike bis zur Gegenwart* ein Lesebuch herausgegeben von Michael Frensch. München; Zürich: Piper, 1991.
Extracted from X Ge 1962/1. <Letter from E Zwink to N Ryder, 16-6-2004>
Copy not seen; description deduced from X Ge 1962/1 and catalogue of GER: WLB.
GER: WLB

X 49/01/Ge 1995/1 **1995** Hyde 887/–
EMANUEL SWEDENBORG | HOMO MAXIMUS | DER HIMMLISCHE UND DER LEIBLICHE MENSCH | *Auszüge aus »Himmlische Geheimnisse im Worte Gottes«* | EINFÜHRUNG VON ERNST BENZ | SWEDENBORG VERLAG ZÜRICH
verso: Abänderungen gegenüber der 1. Auflage (Texte auf S. 2 und 5 f.) durch | Friedemann Horn | © der ersten Auflage 1962 | by Otto Wilhelm Barth-Verlag GmbH | Auflage 1995 Swedenborg-Verlag Zürich | Umschlag: Johannes Horn | Gesamtherstellung: Swedenborg-Verlag Zürich | ISBN: 3-85927-034-6
half title: EMANUEL SWEDENBORG / HOMO MAXIMUS | BAND 10 | DER SWEDENBORGBÜCHEREI | nunc | <orn 2 x 12 mm> | licet
verso: <Introductory statement>
small 8vo
half title and title leaves, 4 pp; Inhaltsverzeichnis <List of contents>, 1 p; Biographisches, pp 5-8; Einleitung: Auszüge aus Ernst Benz »Swedenborg« <Introduction: Extracts from Ernst Benz's 'Swedenborg'>, pp 9-24; text, pp 25-193; Hinweis des verlages <Publisher's note>, pp 194-195; Catalogue, 1 p.
Reprint of X Ge 1983/1. ISBN 3-85927-034-6.
GER: VER

X 49/01/Ge 1997/1 **1997** Hyde 887/–
Emanuel Swedenborg | UND ES WAR ABEND | UND | ES WAR MORGEN | *Die Stufen der Menschwerdung* | Der innere Sinn der ersten zwei Kapitel des | 1. Buches Mose aus „Himmlische Geheimnisse" | SWEDENBORG-VERLAG ZÜRICH
verso: Auflage 1997 | © by Swedenborg-Verlag Zürich | Gesamtherstellung: Swedenborg-Verlag Zürich | Printed in Germany | ISBN: 3-85927-010-9
half title: nunc | <orn 2 x 12 mm> | licet | BAND 2 | DER SWEDENBORGBÜCHEREI
small 8vo
half title and title leaves, 4 pp; Inhaltsverzeichnis <List of contents>, p 5; Geleitwort <Introduction>, pp 7-11; Vorwort des Herausgebers <Editor's foreword>, pp 11-24; text, pp 25-129; Werbung <advertisement>, pp 131-132.
Compiled and arranged by F Horn; revised by H Grob. Introduction by Wolfgang Kretschmer. Book design by J Horn; cover design by Horst Bergmann. Series title: Swedenborg Bücherei Band 2.
GER: VER; SWE: ROY

X 49/01/Ge 1998/1 **1998** Hyde 887/–

EMANUEL SWEDENBORG | HOMO MAXIMUS | DER HIMMLISCHE UND DER LEIBLICHE MENSCH | *Auszüge aus »Himmlische Geheimnisse im Worte Gottes«* | EINFÜHRUNG VON ERNST BENZ | SWEDENBORG VERLAG ZÜRICH

verso: Abänderungen gegenüber der 1. Auflage (Texte auf S. 2 und 5 f.) durch | Friedemann Horn | © der ersten Auflage 1962 | by Otto Wilhelm Barth-Verlag GmbH | Auflage 1998 Swedenborg-Verlag Zürich | Umschlag: Johannes Horn | Gesamtherstellung: Swedenborg-Verlag Zürich | ISBN: 3-85927-034-6

half title: EMANUEL SWEDENBORG / HOMO MAXIMUS | BAND 10 | DER SWEDENBORGBÜCHEREI | nunc | <orn 2 x 12 mm> | licet

verso: <Introductory statement>

small 8vo

half title and title leaves, 4 pp; Inhaltsverzeichnis <List of contents>, 1 p; Biographisches, pp 5-8; Einleitung: Auszüge aus Ernst Benz »Swedenborg« <Introduction: Extracts from Ernst Benz's 'Swedenborg'>, pp 9-24; text, pp 25-193; Hinweis des verlages <Publisher's note>, pp 194-195; Catalogue, 1 p.

Revised reprint of X Ge 1962/1.

GER: VER, WLB

X 49/01/Ge 2000/1 **2000** Hyde 887/–

Emanuel Swedenborg | UND ES WAR ABEND | UND | ES WAR MORGEN | *Die Stufen der Menschwerdung* | Der innere Sinn der ersten zwei Kapitel des | 1. Buches Mose aus „Himmlische Geheimnisse" | SWEDENBORG-VERLAG ZÜRICH

verso: Auflage 2000 | © by Swedenborg-Verlag Zürich | Gesamtherstellung: Swedenborg-Verlag Zürich | Printed in Germany | ISBN: 3-85927-010-9

half title: nunc | <orn 2 x 12 mm> | licet | BAND 2 | DER SWEDENBORGBÜCHEREI

small 8vo

half title and title leaves, 4 pp; Inhaltsverzeichnis <List of contents>, p 5; Geleitwort <Introduction>, pp 7-11; Vorwort der Herausgebers <Editor's foreword>, pp 11-24; text, pp 25-129; Werbung <advertisement>, pp 131-132.

Reprint of X Ge 1997/1.

GER: VER, WLB; USA: ANC

X 49/01/Ge 2006/1 **2006** Hyde 887/–

Emanuel Swedenborg | UND ES WAR ABEND | UND | ES WAR MORGEN | *Die Stufen der Menschwerdung* | Der innere Sinn der ersten zwei Kapitel des | 1. Buches Mose aus „Himmlische Geheimnisse" | SWEDENBORG-VERLAG ZÜRICH

verso: Auflage 2000 | © by Swedenborg-Verlag Zürich | Gesamtherstellung: Swedenborg-Verlag Zürich | Printed in Germany | ISBN: 3-85927-010-9

half title: nunc | <orn 2 x 12 mm> | licet | BAND 2 | DER SWEDENBORGBÜCHEREI

small 8vo

half title and title leaves, 4 pp; Inhaltsverzeichnis <List of contents>, p 5; Geleitwort <Introduction>, pp 7-11; Vorwort der Herausgebers <Editor's foreword>, pp 11-24; text, pp 25-129; Werbung <advertisement>, pp 131-132.

Reprint of X Ge 1997/1.

GER: VER

X 49/01/Ge 2006/2 **2006** Hyde 887/3a

EMANUEL SWEDENBORG | HOMO MAXIMUS | DER HIMMLISCHE UND DER LIEBLICHE MENSCH

| Auszüge aus »Himmlische Geheimnisse im Worte Gottes« | EINFÜHRUNG VON ERNST BENZ | SWEDENBORG-VERLAG ZÜRICH
verso: Abänderungen gegenüber der 1. Auflage | (Texte auf S.2 und 5 f.) durch Friedemann Horn | © der ersten Auflage 1962 | by Otto Wilhelm Barth-Verlag GmbH | Auflage 2006 Swedenborg-Verlag Zürich | Umschlag: Johannes Horn | Gesamtherstellung: Swedenborg-Verlag Zürich | ISBN: 3-85927-034-6
half title: EMANUEL SWEDENBORG • HOMO MAXIMUS | BAND 10 | DER SWEDENBORGBÜCHEREI | nunc | <orn 2 x 12 mm> | licet
small 8vo
half title and title leaves, 4 pp; Inhaltsverzeichnis <List of contents>, 1 p; Biographisches, pp 5-8; Einleitung: Auszüge aus Ernst Benz »Swedenborg« <Introduction: Extracts from Ernst Benz's 'Swedenborg'>, pp 9-24; text, pp 25-193; Hinweis des verlages <Publisher's note>, pp 194-195; Catalogue, 1 p.
UK: SOC; SWI: VER

GUJARATI

49/01/Gu 1/1 **1915** Hyde —
<beside an orn 109 x 91 mm, depicting a peacock and plant stems, 3 lines in Gujarati script>
સ્‌વર્‌ગીય મંત્‌રો | દ્રષ્ટા | ઇમેન્‌યુઅલ સ્‌વીડનબોર્‌ગ.
8vo
title leaf, 2 pp; text of n 1-5, Genesis 1, and n 6-51, pp <1-32>.
n 1-5 <pp 1-2> and headings on pp 1, 7 are printed in the Devanagari script.
Translated by M R Bhatt, published as a supplement to *The Heart of India* vol 1, no 1, for The Hindi Swedenborg Society, Bombay.
The Heart of India was a journal in which each of the four issues published had three parts: c 24 pp in English, 24 pp in Gujarati, and 32 pp with a Gujarati translation of *Arcana Caelestia* <see 49/01/Gu 1/1-4>. The page numbers of the two sections in Gujarati are in that language's script.
UK: SOC, CON; USA: SHS

49/01/Gu 1/2 **1915** Hyde —
<framed by an orn border above and to the left 86 x 99 mm, 2 lines in Gujarati script with an orn 4 x 30 mm between them>
સ્‌વર્‌ગીય મંત્‌રો. | ઇમેન્‌યુઅલ સ્‌વીડનબોર્‌ગ.
8vo
title leaf, 2 pp; text of n 52-72, Genesis 2:1-17, and n 73-120, pp <33-62>.
The inter-chapter material in n 64-72 <pp 38-42> and headings preceding n 67, 81 are printed in the Devanagari script.
Translated by M R Bhatt, published as a supplement to *The Heart of India* vol 1, no 2, for The Hindi Swedenborg Society, Bombay.
UK: SOC, CON; USA: SHS

49/01/Gu 1/3 **1915** Hyde —
<framed by an orn border above and to the left 86 x 99 mm, 2 lines in Gujarati script with an orn 4 x 30 mm between them, the same as in Gu 1/2>
સ્‌વર્‌ગીય મંત્‌રો. | ઇમેન્‌યુઅલ સ્‌વીડનબોર્‌ગ.
8vo
title leaf, 2 pp; text of n 121-130, Genesis 2:18-25, n 131-189, Genesis 3:1-13, and n 190-201, pp <63-92>.
The inter-chapter material in n 166-189 <pp 80-85> and headings preceding n 137, 168, 182 are printed in the Devanagari script.

Translated by M R Bhatt, published as a supplement to *The Heart of India* vol 1, no 3, for The Hindi Swedenborg Society, Bombay.

UK: SOC, CON; USA: SHS

49/01/Gu 1/4 **1915** Hyde —

<framed by an orn border above and to the left 86 x 99 mm, 2 lines in Gujarati script with an orn 4 x 30 mm between them, the same as in Gu 1/2>

સ્વર્ગીય મંત્રી. | ઇમેન્યુઅલ સ્વીડનબોર્ગ.

8vo

title leaf, 2 pp; text of n 202-233, Genesis 3:14-19, and n 234-272, pp <93-122>.

The heading preceding n 241 is printed in the Devanagari script.

Translated by M R Bhatt, published as a supplement to *The Heart of India* vol 1, no 4, for The Hindi Swedenborg Society, Bombay.

In an editorial note on p 97 of the English section of this issue of the journal the translator expressed his doubts as to being able to continue the work in the ensuing year. No further portions of this version are known.

UK: SOC, CON; USA: SHS

ITALIAN

49/01/It 1/1 **no date** Hyde —

In *The New Church Messenger* New York, 1880 p 10, the editor, C H Mann, records that at the Carmelite Monastery in Valletta, Malta, a MS translation of a portion of *Arcana Coelestia* had been made by Father Galia, Provincial of the Order, for his own use. Its current whereabouts were unknown.

49/01/It 2/1 **1895** Hyde —

In *The New Church Magazine* London, p 376, L Scocia reported, "I have for some time been engaged in translating 'The Arcana Caelestia'." No part of the work was published.

JAPANESE

Translators:

Ja 1 Yoshii Yanase
Ja 2 Tatsuya Nagashima

49/01/Ja 1/1 **1970** Hyde 859/7

<< <within a rule border 153 x 108 mm, divided into 3 panels by 2 rules 153 mm> <1:> イマヌエル・スエデンボルグ著　　柳瀬芳意　訳 <2:> 天界の秘義　第一巻 | ー創世記、出埃及記の内意ー | (附記　霊たちの世界と天使たちの天界に見聞された驚嘆すべき事柄) <3:> 静思社>>
verso: <<先づ神の国とその義とを求めなさい。そのときは、| この凡てのものはあなたたちに加えられるでしょう | (マタイ六・三三) | ー著者自身が記した聖言ー>>

8vo

title leaf, 2 pp; Preface, pp 1-4; text of Genesis 1-6 and n 1-691, pp 1-391; publishing information, under which is printed 0316—700102—4012, p 393.

Volume 1; translated by Yoshii Yanase, published by Seishi-sha, Tokyo; Shōwa 45-59.

In the catalogue of SWE: ROY title leaf information is transliterated as follows: Tenkai no higi / Emanueru Suedenborugu cho; Yanase Yoshii yaku; Tōkyō, Seishi-sha, Shōwa 45-59 [1970-84].

Copy not seen; description deduced from Ja 1/15 and catalogues of SWE: ROY and USA: ANC.

SWE: ROY; USA: ANC, SHS

49/01/Ja 1/2 **1970** Hyde 859/8

<< <within a rule border 153 x 108 mm, divided into 3 panels by 2 rules 153 mm> <1:> イマヌエル・スエデンボルグ著　柳瀬芳意　訳 <2:> 天界の秘義　第二巻 | 一創世記、出埃及記の内意一 | (附記　霊たちの世界と天使たちの天界に見聞された驚嘆すべき事柄) <3:> 静思社>>
verso: <<先づ神の国とその義とを求めなさい。そのときは、| この凡てのものはあなたたちに加えられるでしょう | (マタイ六・三三) | 一著者自身が記した聖言一>>

8vo

title leaf, 2 pp; Contents, pp 1-2; text of Genesis 7-9 and n 692-1113, pp 1-338; Commentary, pp 339-370; publishing information, under which is printed 0316—700202—4012, p 371.

Volume 2; translated by Y Yanase, published by Seishi-sha, Tokyo; Shōwa 45-59.

Copy not seen; description deduced from Ja 1/16 and catalogues of SWE: ROY and USA: ANC.

SWE: ROY; USA: ANC

49/01/Ja 1/3 **1971** Hyde 859/9

<within a rule border 153 x 108 mm, divided into 3 panels by 2 rules 153 mm> <1:> イマヌエル・スエデンボルグ著　柳瀬芳意　訳 <2:> 天界の秘義　第三巻 | 一創世記、出エジプト記の内意一 | (附記　霊たちの世界と天使たちの天界に見聞された驚嘆すべき事柄) <3:> 静思社
verso: 先づ神の国とその義とを求めなさい。そのとき | はこの凡てのものはあなたたちに加えられるで | しょう (マタイ六・三三) | 一著者自身が記した聖言一

8vo

title leaf, 2 pp; Preface, pp 1-2; Contents, p 3; text of Genesis 10-14 and n 1114-1764, pp 1-435; publishing information, p 437; advertisements, pp 439-443.

Volume 3; translated by Y Yanase, published by Seishi-sha, Tokyo; Shōwa 45-59.

UK: SOC; SWE: ROY; USA: ANC, SHS

49/01/Ja 1/4 **1971** Hyde 859/10

<within a rule border 153 x 108 mm, divided into 3 panels by 2 rules 153 mm> <1:> イマヌエル・スエデンボルグ著　柳瀬芳意　訳 <2:> 天界の秘義　第四巻 | 一創世記、出エジプト記の内意一 | (附記　霊たちの世界と天使たちの天界に見聞された驚嘆すべき事柄) <3:> 静思社
verso: 先づ神の国とその義とを求めなさい。そのとき | はこの凡てのものはあなたたちに加えられるで | しょう (マタイ六・三三) | 一著者自身が記した聖言一

8vo

title leaf, 2 pp; Contents, p 1; text of Genesis 15-17 and n 1767-2134, pp 1-318; Commentary, pp 319-348; publishing information, p 349.

Volume 4; translated by Y Yanase, published by Seishi-sha, Tokyo; Shōwa 45-59.

UK: SOC; SWE: ROY; USA: ANC, SHS

49/01/Ja 1/5 **1972** Hyde 859/11

<< <within a rule border 153 x 108 mm, divided into 3 panels by 2 rules 153 mm> <1:> イマヌエル・スエデンボルグ著　柳瀬芳意　訳 <2:> 天界の秘義　第五巻 | 一創世記、出エジプト記の内意一 | (附記　霊たちの世界と天使たちの天界に見聞された驚嘆すべき事柄) <3:> 静思社>>
verso: <<先づ神の国とその義とを求めなさい。そのとき | は、この凡てのものはあなたたちに加えられる | でしょう (マタイ六・三三) | 一著者自身が記した聖言一>>

8vo

title leaf, 2 pp; Contents, 1 p; Preface, 2 pp; text of Genesis 18-20 and n 2135-2605, pp 1-440; publishing information, under which is printed 3316—720102—4012, p 441.

Volume 5; translated by Y Yanase, published by Seishi-sha, Tokyo; Shōwa 45-59.

Copy not seen; description deduced from Ja 1/17 and catalogues of SWE: ROY and USA: ANC.

SWE: ROY; USA: ANC, SHS

49/01/Ja 1/6 **1972** Hyde 859/12

<within a rule border 153 x 108 mm, divided into 3 panels by 2 rules 153 mm> <1:> イマヌエル・スエデンボルグ著　柳瀬芳意　訳 <2:> 天界の秘義　第六巻 | ー創世記、出エジプト記の内意ー | (附記　霊たちの世界と天使たちの天界に見聞された驚嘆すべき事柄) <3:> 静思社
verso: 先づ神の国とその義とを求めなさい。そのとき | は、この凡てのものはあなたたちに加えられる | でしょう(マタイ六・三三) | ー著者自身が記した聖言ー
8vo
title leaf, 2 pp; Contents, 1 p; Preface, 1 p; text of Genesis 21-22 and n 2606-2893, pp 1-294; Commentary, pp 295-370; publishing information, p 371; advertisements, pp 373-378.
Volume 6; translated by Y Yanase, published by Seishi-sha, Tokyo; Shōwa 45-59.
UK: SOC; SWE: ROY; USA: ANC, SHS

49/01/Ja 1/7 **1972** Hyde 859/14

<< <within a rule border 153 x 108 mm, divided into 3 panels by 2 rules 153 mm> <1:> イマヌエル　スエデンボルグ著　柳瀬芳意　訳 <2:> 天界の秘義　第八巻 | ー創世記、出エジプト記の内意ー | (附記　霊たちの世界と天使たちの天界に見聞された驚嘆すべき事柄) <3:> 静思社>>
verso: <<先づ神の国とその義とを求めなさい。そのとき | は、この凡てのものはあなたたちに加えられるで | しょう(マタイ六・三三) | ー著者自身が記した聖言ー>>
8vo
title leaf, 2 pp; Contents, 1 p; Preface, 2 pp; text of Genesis 26-27 and n 3353-3649, pp 1-266; Commentary, pp 266-308; publishing information, p 309; advertisements, pp 311-318.
Volume 8; translated by Y Yanase, published by Seishi-sha, Tokyo; Shōwa 45-59.
Copy not seen; description deduced from Ja 1/18 and catalogues of SWE: ROY and USA: ANC.
SWE: ROY; USA: ANC, SHS

49/01/Ja 1/8 **1973** Hyde 859/13

<< <within a rule border 153 x 108 mm, divided into 3 panels by 2 rules 153 mm> <1:> イマヌエル・スエデンボルグ著　柳瀬芳意　訳 <2:> 天界の秘義　第七巻 | ー創世記、出エジプト記の内意ー | (附記　霊たちの世界と天使たちの天界に見聞された驚嘆すべき事柄) <3:> 静思社>>
verso: <<先づ神の国とその義とを求めなさい。そのと | きは、この凡てのものはあなたたちに加えられ | るでしょう(マタイ六・三三) | ー著者自身が記した聖言ー>>
8vo
title leaf, 2 pp; Contents, p 1; Preface, pp 2-3; text of Genesis 23-25 and n 2894-3353, pp 1-419; publishing information, p 421; advertisements, pp 423-428.
Volume 7; translated by Y Yanase, published by Seishi-sha, Tokyo; Shōwa 45-59.
Copy not seen; description deduced from Ja 1/19 and catalogues of SWE: ROY and USA: ANC.
SWE: ROY; USA: ANC, SHS

49/01/Ja 1/9 **1975** Hyde 859/15

<within a rule border 153 x 108 mm, divided into 3 panels by 2 rules 153 mm> <1:> イマヌエル・スエデンボルグ著　柳瀬芳意　訳 <2:> 天界の秘義　第九巻 | ー創世記、出エジプト記の内意ー | (附記　霊たちの世界と天使たちの天界に見聞された驚嘆すべき事柄) <3:> 静思社
verso: 先づ神の国とその義とを求めなさい。そのとき | はこの凡てのものはあなたたちに加えられるで | しょう(マタイ六・三三) | ー著者自身が記した聖言ー
8vo
title leaf, 2 pp; Contents, 1 p; Preface, 2 pp; text of Genesis 28-29 and n 3650-3896, pp 1-318; publishing information, p 319; advertisements, pp 320-324.
Volume 9; translated by Y Yanase, published by Seishi-sha, Tokyo; Shōwa 45-59.
UK: SOC; SWE: ROY; USA: ANC, SHS

49/01/Ja 1/10 **1975** Hyde 859/16

<within a rule border 153 x 108 mm, divided into 3 panels by 2 rules 153 mm> <1:> イマヌエル・スエデンボルグ著　柳瀬芳意　訳 <2:> 天界の秘義　第十巻 | ー創世記、出エジプト記の内意ー | (附記　霊たちの世界と天使たちの天界に見聞された驚嘆すべき事柄) <3:> 静思社
verso: 先づ神の国とその義とを求めなさい。そのとき | はこの凡てのものはあなたたちに加えられるで | しょう(マタイ六・三三) | ー著者自身が記した聖言ー
8vo
title leaf, 2 pp; Contents, 1 p; text of Genesis 30-31 and n 3897-4228, pp 1-320; Commentary, pp 321-340; publishing information, p 341; advertisements, pp 342-346.
Volume 10; translated by Y Yanase, published by Seishi-sha, Tokyo; Shōwa 45-59.
UK: soc; SWE: roy; USA: anc, shs

49/01/Ja 1/11 **1975** Hyde 859/17

<within a rule border 153 x 108 mm, divided into 3 panels by 2 rules 153 mm> <1:> イマヌエル・スエデンボルグ著　柳瀬芳意　訳 <2:> 天界の秘義　第十一巻 | ー創世記、出エジプト記の内意ー | (附記　霊たちの世界と天使たちの天界に見聞された驚嘆すべき事柄) <3:> 静思社
verso: 先づ神の国とその義とを求めなさい。そのとき | はこの凡てのものはあなたたちに加えられるで | しょう(マタイ六・三三) | ー著者自身が記した聖言ー
8vo
title leaf, 2 pp; Contents, p 1; Preface, p 3; text of Genesis 32-36 and n 4229-4660, pp 1-449; publishing information, p 451.
Volume 11; translated by Y Yanase, published by Seishi-sha, Tokyo; Shōwa 45-59.
UK: soc; SWE: roy; USA: anc, shs

49/01/Ja 1/12 **1976** Hyde 859/18

<within a rule border 153 x 108 mm, divided into 3 panels by 2 rules 153 mm> <1:> イマヌエル・スエデンボルグ著　柳瀬芳意　訳 <2:> 天界の秘義　第十二巻 | ー創世記、出エジプト記の内意ー | (附記　霊たちの世界と天使たちの天界に見聞された驚嘆すべき事柄) <3:> 静思社
verso: 先づ神の国とその義とを求めなさい。そのとき | はこの凡てのものはあなたたちに加えられるで | しょう(マタイ六・三三) | ー著者自身が記した聖言ー
8vo
title leaf, 2 pp; Contents, p 3; Preface, pp 4-5; text of Genesis 37-38 and n 4661-4953, pp 1-289; Commentary, pp 290-300; publishing information, p 301; advertisements, pp 302-307.
Volume 12; translated by Y Yanase, published by Seishi-sha, Tokyo; Shōwa 45-59.
UK: soc; SWE: roy; USA: anc, shs

49/01/Ja 1/13 **1977** Hyde 859/19

<within a rule border 153 x 108 mm, divided into 3 panels by 2 rules 153 mm> <1:> イマヌエルスエデンボルグ著　柳瀬芳意　訳 <2:> 天界の秘義　第十三巻 | ー創世記、出エジプト記の内意ー | (附記　霊たちの世界と天使たちの天界に見聞された驚嘆すべき事柄) <3:> 静思社
verso: 先づ神の国とその義とを求めなさい。そのときは、| この凡てのものはあなたたちに加えられるでしょう | (マタイ六・三三) | ー著者自身が記した聖言ー
8vo
title leaf, 2 pp; Contents, 1 p; Preface, 2 pp; text of Genesis 39-40 and n 4954-5190, pp 1-241; Commentary, pp 242-253; publishing information, p 255.
Volume 13; translated by Y Yanase, published by Seishi-sha, Tokyo; Shōwa 45-59.
UK: soc; SWE: roy; USA: anc, shs

49/01/Ja 1/14 **1977** Hyde 859/20

<within a rule border 153 x 108 mm, divided into 3 panels by 2 rules 153 mm> <1:> イマヌエル　スエデンボルグ著　柳瀬芳意　訳 <2:> 天界の秘義　第十四巻 | ー創世記、出エジプト記の内意ー | (附記　霊たちの世界と天使たちの天界に見聞された驚嘆すべき事柄) <3:> 静思社

verso: 先づ神の国とその義とを求めなさい。そのときは | この凡てのものはあなたたちに加えられるでしょ | う(マタイ六・三三) | ー著者自身が記した聖言ー

8vo

title leaf, 2 pp; Contents, 1 p; Preface, 2 pp; text of Genesis 41-43 and n 5191-5727, pp 1-429; publishing information, p 431.

Volume 14; translated by Y Yanase, published by Seishi-sha, Tokyo; Shōwa 45-59.

UK: SOC; SWE: ROY; USA: ANC, SHS

49/01/Ja 1/15 **1977** Hyde 859/7a

<within a rule border 153 x 108 mm, divided into 3 panels by 2 rules 153 mm> <1:> イマヌエル・スエデンボルグ著　柳瀬芳意　訳 <2:> 天界の秘義　第一巻 | ー創世記、出埃及記の内意ー | (附記　霊たちの世界と天使たちの天界に見聞された驚嘆すべき事柄) <3:> 静思社

verso: 先づ神の国とその義とを求めなさい。そのときは、| この凡てのものはあなたたちに加えられるでしょう | (マタイ六・三三) | ー著者自身が記した聖言ー

8vo

title leaf, 2 pp; Preface, pp 1-4; text of Genesis 1-6 and n 1-691, pp 1-391; publishing information, under which is printed 0316—700102—4012, p 393.

Volume 1; reprint of Ja 1/1 = Hyde 859/7, published by Seishi-sha, Tokyo; Shōwa 45-59.

UK: SOC

49/01/Ja 1/16 **1977** Hyde 859/8a

<within a rule border 153 x 108 mm, divided into 3 panels by 2 rules 153 mm> <1:> イマヌエル・スエデンボルグ著　柳瀬芳意　訳 <2:> 天界の秘義　第二巻 | ー創世記、出埃及記の内意ー | (附記　霊たちの世界と天使たちの天界に見聞された驚嘆すべき事柄) <3:> 静思社

verso: 先づ神の国とその義とを求めなさい。そのときは、| この凡てのものはあなたたちに加えられるでしょう | (マタイ六・三三) | ー著者自身が記した聖言ー

8vo

title leaf, 2 pp; Contents, pp 1-2; text of Genesis 7-9 and n 692-1113, pp 1-338; Commentary, pp 339-370; publishing information, under which is printed 0316—700202—4012, p 371.

Volume 2; reprint of Ja 1/2, published by Seishi-sha, Tokyo; Shōwa 45-59.

UK: SOC

49/01/Ja 1/17 **1977** Hyde 859/11a

<within a rule border 153 x 108 mm, divided into 3 panels by 2 rules 153 mm> <1:> イマヌエル・スエデンボルグ著　柳瀬芳意　訳 <2:> 天界の秘義　第五巻 | ー創世記、出エジプト記の内意ー | (附記　霊たちの世界と天使たちの天界に見聞された驚嘆すべき事柄) <3:> 静思社

verso: 先づ神の国とその義とを求めなさい。そのとき | は、この凡てのものはあなたたちに加えられる | でしょう(マタイ六・三三) | ー著者自身が記した聖言ー

8vo

title leaf, 2 pp; Contents, 1 p; Preface, 2 pp; text of Genesis 18-20 and n 2135-2605, pp 1-440; publishing information, under which is printed 3316—720102—4012, p 441.

Volume 5; reprint of Ja 1/5, published by Seishi-sha, Tokyo; Shōwa 45-59.

UK: SOC

49/01/Ja 1/18 **1977** Hyde 859/14a

<within a rule border 153 x 108 mm, divided into 3 panels by 2 rules 153 mm> <1:> イマヌエルスエデンボルグ著　柳瀬芳意　訳 <2:> 天界の秘義　第八巻 | 一創世記、出エジプト記の内意一 | (附記　霊たちの世界と天使たちの天界に見聞された驚嘆すべき事柄) <3:> 静思社
verso: 先づ神の国とその義とを求めなさい。そのとき | は、この凡てのものはあなたたちに加えられるで | しょう(マタイ六・三三) | 一著者自身が記した聖言一
8vo
title leaf, 2 pp; Contents, 1 p; Preface, 2 pp; text of Genesis 26-27 and n 3353-3649, pp 1-266; Commentary, pp 266-308; publishing information, p 309; advertisements, pp 311-318.
Volume 8; reprint of Ja 1/7, published by Seishi-sha, Tokyo; Shōwa 45-59.
UK: SOC

49/01/Ja 1/19 **1978** Hyde 859/13a

<within a rule border 153 x 108 mm, divided into 3 panels by 2 rules 153 mm> <1:> イマヌエル・スエデンボルグ著　柳瀬芳意　訳 <2:> 天界の秘義　第七巻 | 一創世記、出エジプト記の内意一 | (附記　霊たちの世界と天使たちの天界に見聞された驚嘆すべき事柄) <3:> 静思社
verso: 先づ神の国とその義とを求めなさい。そのと | きは、この凡てのものはあなたたちに加えられ | るでしょう(マタイ六・三三) | 一著者自身が記した聖言一
8vo
title leaf, 2 pp; Contents, p 1; Preface, pp 2-3; text of Genesis 23-25 and n 2894-3353, pp 1-419; publishing information, p 421; advertisements, pp 423-428.
Volume 7; reprint of Ja 1/8, published by Seishi-sha, Tokyo; Shōwa 45-59.
UK: SOC

49/01/Ja 1/20 **1979** Hyde 859/21

<within a rule border 153 x 108 mm, divided into 3 panels by 2 rules 153 mm> <1:> イマヌエル　スエデンボルグ著　柳瀬芳意　訳 <2:> 天界の秘義　第十五巻 | 一創世記、出エジプト記の内意一 | (附記　霊たちの世界と天使たちの天界に見聞された驚嘆すべき事柄) <3:> 静思社
verso: 先づ神の国とその義とを求めなさい。そのとき | はこの凡てのものはあなたたちに加えられるで | しょう(マタイ六・三三) | 一著者自身が記した聖言一
8vo
title leaf, 2 pp; Preface, 2 pp; Contents, 1 p; text of Genesis 44-47 and n 5728-6215, pp 1-357; publishing information, p 359.
Volume 15; translated by Y Yanase, published by Seishi-sha, Tokyo; Shōwa 45-59.
UK: SOC; SWE: ROY; USA: ANC, SHS

49/01/Ja 1/21 **1979** Hyde 859/22

<within a rule border 153 x 108 mm, divided into 3 panels by 2 rules 153 mm> <1:> イマヌエル　スエデンボルグ著　柳瀬芳意　訳 <2:> 天界の秘義　第十六巻 | 一創世記、出エジプト記の内意一 | (附記　霊たちの世界と天使たちの天界に見聞された驚嘆すべき事柄) <3:> 静思社
verso: 先づ神の国とその義とを求めなさい。そのとき | はこの凡てのものはあなたたちに加えられるで | しょう(マタイ六・三三) | 一著者自身が記した聖言一
8vo
title leaf, 2 pp; Preface, 2 pp; Contents, 1 p; text of Genesis 48-50 and n 6216-6626, pp 1-305; publishing information, p 306.
Volume 16; translated by Y Yanase, published by Seishi-sha, Tokyo; Shōwa 45-59.
UK: SOC; SWE: ROY; USA: ANC, SHS

49/01/Ja 1/22 **1979** Hyde 859/23

<within a rule border 153 x 108 mm, divided into 3 panels by 2 rules 153 mm> <1:> イマヌエル　スエデンボルグ著　柳瀬芳意　訳 <2:> 天界の秘義　第十七巻 | ー創世記、出エジプト記の内意ー | (附記　霊たちの世界と天使たちの天界に見聞された驚嘆すべき事柄) <3:> 静思社
verso: 先づ神の国とその義とを求めなさい。そのときは | この凡てのものはあなたたちに加えられるでしょ | う(マタイ六・三三) | ー著者自身が記した聖言ー

8vo

title leaf, 2 pp; Preface, 2 pp; Contents, 1 p; text of Exodus 1-4 and n 6627-7079, pp 3-327; publishing information, p 328.

Volume 17; translated by Y Yanase, published by Seishi-sha, Tokyo; Shōwa 45-59.

UK: SOC; SWE: ROY; USA: ANC, SHS

49/01/Ja 1/23 **1979** Hyde 859/24

<within a rule border 153 x 108 mm, divided into 3 panels by 2 rules 153 mm> <1:> イマヌエル　スエデンボルグ著　柳瀬芳意　訳 <2:> 天界の秘義　第十八巻 | ー創世記、出エジプト記の内意ー | (附記　霊たちの世界と天使たちの天界に見聞された驚嘆すべき事柄) <3:> 静思社
verso: 先づ神の国とその義とを求めなさい。そのときは | この凡てのものはあなたたちに加えられるでしょ | う(マタイ六・三三) | ー著者自身が記した聖言ー

8vo

title leaf, 2 pp; Preface, 1 p; Contents, 1 p; text of Exodus 5-8 and n 7080-7487, pp 1-254; publishing information, p 255.

Volume 18; translated by Y Yanase, published by Seishi-sha, Tokyo; Shōwa 45-59.

UK: SOC; SWE: ROY; USA: ANC, SHS

49/01/Ja 1/24 **1981** Hyde 859/25

<within a rule border 153 x 108 mm, divided into 3 panels by 2 rules 153 mm> <1:> イマヌエル　スエデンボルグ著　柳瀬芳意　訳 <2:> 天界の秘義　第十九巻 | ー創世記、出エジプト記の内意ー | (附記　霊たちの世界と天使たちの天界に見聞された驚嘆すべき事柄) <3:> 静思社
verso: 先づ神の国とその義とを求めなさい。そのときは | この凡てのものはあなたたちに加えられるでしょ | う(マタイ六・三三) | ー著者自身が記した聖言ー

8vo

title leaf, 2 pp; Preface, 1 p; Contents, 1 p; text of Exodus 9-12 and n 7488-8032, pp 1-330; publishing information, p 331.

Volume 19; translated by Y Yanase, published by Seishi-sha, Tokyo; Shōwa 45-59.

UK: SOC; SWE: ROY; USA: ANC, SHS

49/01/Ja 1/25 **1981** Hyde 859/26

<within a rule border 153 x 108 mm, divided into 3 panels by 2 rules 153 mm> <1:> イマヌエル・スエデンボルグ著　柳瀬芳意　訳 <2:> 天界の秘義　第二十巻 | ー創世記、出エジプト記の内意ー | (附記　霊たちの世界と天使たちの天界に見聞された驚嘆すべき事柄) <3:> 静思社
verso: 先づ神の国とその義とを求めなさい。そのとき | はこの凡てのものはあなたたちに加えられるで | しょう(マタイ六・三三) | ー著者自身が記した聖言ー

8vo

title leaf, 2 pp; Preface, pp 1-2; Contents, p 3; text of Exodus 13-15 and n 8033-8386, pp 1-242; publishing information, p 243.

Volume 20; translated by Y Yanase, published by Seishi-sha, Tokyo; Shōwa 45-59.

UK: SOC; SWE: ROY; USA: ANC, SHS

49/01/Ja 1/26 **1981** Hyde 859/27

<within a rule border 153 x 108 mm, divided into 3 panels by 2 rules 153 mm> <1:> イマヌエル・スエデンボルグ著　柳瀬芳意　訳 <2:> 天界の秘義　第二十一巻 | 一創世記、出エジプト記の内意一 | (附記　霊たちの世界と天使たちの天界に見聞された驚嘆すべき事柄) <3:> 静思社
verso: 先づ神の国とその義とを求めなさい。そのとき | はこの凡てのものはあなたたちに加えられるで | しょう(マタイ六・三三) | 一著者自身が記した聖言一
8vo
title leaf, 2 pp; Preface, pp 1-2; Contents, p 3; text of Exodus 16-19 and n 8387-8852, pp 1-308; publishing information, p 309.
Volume 21; translated by Y Yanase, published by Seishi-sha, Tokyo; Shōwa 45-59.
UK: SOC; SWE: ROY; USA: ANC, SHS

49/01/Ja 1/27 **1981** Hyde 859/28

<within a rule border 153 x 108 mm, divided into 3 panels by 2 rules 153 mm> <1:> イマヌエル・スエデンボルグ著　柳瀬芳意　訳 <2:> 天界の秘義　第二十二巻 | 一創世記、出エジプト記の内意一 | (附記　霊たちの世界と天使たちの天界に見聞された驚嘆すべき事柄) <3:> 静思社
verso: 先づ神の国とその義とを求めなさい。そのとき | はこの凡てのものはあなたたちに加えられるで | しょう(マタイ六・三三) | 一著者自身が記した聖言一
8vo
title leaf, 2 pp; Preface, p 1; Contents, p 2; text of Exodus 20-21 and n 8853-9111, pp 1-294; publishing information, p 295.
Volume 22; translated by Y Yanase, published by Seishi-sha, Tokyo; Shōwa 45-59.
UK: SOC; SWE: ROY; USA: ANC, SHS

49/01/Ja 1/28 **1982** Hyde 859/29

<within a rule border 153 x 108 mm, divided into 3 panels by 2 rules 153 mm> <1:> イマヌエル　スエデンボルグ著　柳瀬芳意　訳 <2:> 天界の秘義　第二三巻 | 一創世記、出エジプト記の内意一 | (附記　霊たちの世界と天使たちの天界に見聞された驚嘆すべき事柄) <3:> 静思社
verso: 先づ神の国とその義とを求めなさい。そのときは | この凡てのものはあなたたちに加えられるでしょ | う(マタイ六・三三) | 一著者自身が記した聖言一
8vo
title leaf, 2 pp; Preface, p 1; Contents, p 2; text of Exodus 22-23 and n 9112-9362, pp 1-335; publishing information, p 337.
Volume 23; translated by Y Yanase, published by Seishi-sha, Tokyo; Shōwa 45-59.
UK: SOC; SWE: ROY; USA: ANC, SHS

49/01/Ja 1/29 **1982** Hyde 859/30

<within a rule border 153 x 108 mm, divided into 3 panels by 2 rules 153 mm> <1:> イマヌエル　スエデンボルグ著　柳瀬芳意　訳 <2:> 天界の秘義　第二四巻 | 一創世記　出エジプト記の内意一 | (附記　霊たちの世界と天使たちの天界に見聞された驚嘆すべき事柄) <3:> 静思社
verso: 先づ神の国とその義とを求めなさい。そのときは | この凡てのものはあなたたちに加えられるでしょ | う(マタイ六・三三) | 一著者自身が記した聖言一
8vo
title leaf, 2 pp; Preface, p 1; Contents, p 2; text of Exodus 24-26 and n 9363-9700, pp 1-325; publishing information, p 327.
Volume 24; translated by Y Yanase, published by Seishi-sha, Tokyo; Shōwa 45-59.
UK: SOC; SWE: ROY; USA: ANC, SHS

49/01/Ja 1/30 **1982** Hyde 859/31

<within a rule border 153 x 108 mm, divided into 3 panels by 2 rules 153 mm> <1:> イマヌエル　スエデンボルグ著　柳瀬芳意　訳 <2:> 天界の秘義　第二五巻 | ー創世記、出エジプト記の内意ー | (附記　霊たちの世界と天使たちの天界に見聞された驚嘆すべき事柄) <3:> 静思社

verso: 先づ神の国とその義とを求めなさい。そのときは | この凡てのものはあなたたちに加えられるでしょ | う(マタイ六・三三) | ー著者自身が記した聖言ー

8vo

title leaf, 2 pp; Preface, p 3; Contents, p 5; text of Exodus 27-28 and n 9701-9973, pp 1-295; publishing information, p 297.

Volume 25; translated by Y Yanase, published by Seishi-sha, Tokyo; Shōwa 45-59.

UK: SOC; SWE: ROY; USA: ANC, SHS

49/01/Ja 1/31 **1983** Hyde 859/32

<within a rule border 153 x 108 mm, divided into 3 panels by 2 rules 153 mm> <1:> イマヌエル　スエデンボルグ著　柳瀬芳意　訳 <2:> 天界の秘義　第二六巻 | ー創世記、出エジプト記の内意ー | (附記　霊たちの世界と天使たちの天界に見聞された驚嘆すべき事柄) <3:> 静思社

verso: 先づ神の国とその義とを求めなさい。そのとき | はこの凡てのものはあなたたちに加えられるで | しょう(マタイ六・三三) | ー著者自身が記した聖言ー

8vo

title leaf, 2 pp; Preface, p 1; Contents, p 3; text of Exodus 29 and n 9974-10166, pp 1-257; publishing information, p 259.

Volume 26; translated by Y Yanase, published by Seishi-sha, Tokyo; Shōwa 45-59.

UK: SOC; SWE: ROY; USA: ANC, SHS

49/01/Ja 1/32 **1983** Hyde 859/33

<within a rule border 153 x 108 mm, divided into 3 panels by 2 rules 153 mm> <1:> イマヌエル　スエデンボルグ著　柳瀬芳意　訳 <2:> 天界の秘義　第二七巻 | ー創世記、出エジプト記の内意ー | (附記　霊たちの世界と天使たちの天界に見聞された驚嘆すべき事柄) <3:> 静思社

verso: 先づ神の国とその義とを求めなさい。そのとき | はこの凡てのものはあなたたちに加えられるで | しょう(マタイ六・三三) | ー著者自身が記した聖言ー

8vo

title leaf, 2 pp; Preface, p 1; Contents, p 3; text of Exodus 30-31 and n 10167-10385, pp 1-255; publishing information, p 257.

Volume 27; translated by Y Yanase, published by Seishi-sha, Tokyo; Shōwa 45-59.

UK: SOC; SWE: ROY; USA: ANC, SHS

49/01/Ja 1/33 **1983** Hyde 859/34

<within a rule border 153 x 108 mm, divided into 3 panels by 2 rules 153 mm> <1:> イマヌエルスエデンボルグ著　柳瀬芳意　訳 <2:> 天界の秘義　第二八巻(最終巻) | ー創世記、出エジプト記の内意ー | (附記　霊たちの世界と天使たちの天界に見聞された驚嘆すべき事柄) <3:> 静思社

verso: 先づ神の国とその義とを求めなさい。そのとき | はこの凡てのものはあなたたちに加えられるで | しょう(マタイ六・三三) | ー著者自身が記した聖言ー

8vo

title leaf, 2 pp; Preface, pp 1-3; Contents, pp 5-6; text of Exodus 32-40 and n 10386-10837, pp 1-380; publishing information, p 381.

Volume 28; translated by Y Yanase, published by Seishi-sha, Tokyo; Shōwa 45-59.

UK: SOC; SWE: ROY; USA: ANC, SHS

49/01/Ja 2/1 **2001** Hyde 859/36

エマヌエル・スヴェーデンボルイ著 | 天界の秘義　第一巻 | ラテン語原典訳 | 旧約聖書「創世記」、「出エジプト記」にある | ＜みことば＞に秘められた内的意味の開示 | 第一巻　「創世記」第１～９章 | アルカナ出版 | 徳島　２００１年　初版

verso: Ab Emanuele Swedenborgo detecta | "Arcana Caelestia" Tomus Primus | Continens Geneseos capita i-ix (n.1-1113) | Originale chirographum scriptum | A Emanuele Swedenborgo | In annis MDCCXLIX~MDCCLVI | Tertia Editio Latina prolata | A Societate Swedenborgiana in Anglia | In anno MCMXLIX | Primus Tomus translatus | E Latino in Japonicum | Editus ab Arcana Press in Japonia | Die 19mo, mensi Junii, anno MMI <*stent* Swedenborgo Caelestia A Emanuele Swedenborgo>

8vo

title leaf, 2 pp; Contents, 1 p; Translator's preface, pp i-vii; text: Swedenborg's introductory note, p 1; text of Genesis 1-9 and n 1-1113, pp 2-700; Epilogue <in Japanese characters>, pp 701-705; Epilogus <in Latin>, pp 706-711; Indexes, pp 712-725, 726-728; advertisements, pp 729-731; publishing information, p 732.

Volume 1, translated by Tatsuya Nagashima, published by Arcana Press, Tokushima-ken. ISBN 4-900449-24-5.

In each volume of this version, the Japanese text is printed horizontally from left to right on each page. The 'Translator's preface' begins on the verso of the 'Contents' leaf. The 'Epilogue/Epilogus' contain the translator's notes, including glossaries of doctrinal terms. The first Index is formatted in 5 columns as follows: <1> text references; <2 and 3> Japanese words; <4> Latin terms; <5> English equivalents. The 2nd Index is formatted in 3 columns as follows: <1> paragraph nos; <2> Japanese words; <3> comments in Japanese.

In **D** Ja 1999/1 the title is transliterated as follows: Tenkai no Higi.

UK: SOC; USA: ANC

49/01/Ja 2/2 **2002** Hyde 859/37

エマヌエル・スヴェーデンボルイ著　|　天界の秘義　第二巻　|　ラテン語原典訳　|　旧約聖書「創世記」、「出エジプト記」にある　|　＜みことば＞に秘められた内的意味の開示　|　第二巻「創世記」第１０～１７章　|　アルカナ出版　|　２００２年　初版

verso: Ab Emanuele Swedenborgo detecta | "Arcana Caelestia" Tomus Secundus | Continens Geneseos capita x-xvii (n.1114-2134) | Originale chirographum scriptum | A Emanuele Swedenborgo | In annis MDCCXLIX~MDCCLVI | Tertia Editio Latina prolata | A Societate Swedenborgiana in Anglia | In anno MCMXLIX | Secundus Tomus translatus | E Latino in Japonicum | Editus ab Arcana Press in Japonia | Die 19mo, mensi Junii, anno MMII <*stent* Swedenborgo Caelestia A Emanuele Swedenborgo>

8vo

title leaf, 2 pp; Contents, 1 p; Translator's preface, pp i-vii; text: Swedenborg's introductory note, p 1; text of Genesis 10-17 and n 1114-2134, pp 2-644; Epilogue, pp 645-656; Glossary of doctrinal terms, pp 657-664; Indexes, pp 665-672, 673-680; advertisements, pp 681-683; publishing information, p 684; 4 pages ruled for reader's notes.

Volume 2, translated by T Nagashima, published by Arcana Press, Tokushima-ken. ISBN 4-900449-25-3.

The 'Translator's preface' begins on the verso of the 'Contents' leaf. The 'Epilogue' contains the translator's notes. The Indexes are formatted in 3 columns as follows: <1> paragraph nos; <2> Japanese words; <3> comments in Japanese.

UK: SOC; USA: ANC

49/01/Ja 2/3 **2003** Hyde 859/38

エマヌエル・スヴェーデンボルイ著 | 天界の秘義　第三巻 | ラテン語原典訳 | 旧約聖書「創世記」、

「出エジプト記」にある｜<みことば>に秘められた内的意味の開示｜第三巻　「創世記」第１８～２２章｜アルカナ出版｜２００３年　初版
verso: Ab Emanuele Swedenborgo detecta | "Arcana Caelestia" Tomus Tertius | Continens Geneseos capita xviii-xxii (n.2135-2893) | Originale chirographum scriptum | A Emanuele Swedenborgo | In annis MDCCXLIX~MDCCLVI | Tertia Editio Latina prolata | A Societate Swedenborgiana in Anglia | In anno MCMXLIX | Tertius Tomus translatus | E Latino in Japonicum | Editus ab Arcana Press in Japonia | Die 19mo, mensi Junii, anno MMIII <*stent* Swedenborgo Caelestia A Emanuele Swedenborgo>
8vo
title leaf, 2 pp; Contents, 1 p; Translator's preface, pp i-iv; List of topics dealt with in inter-chapter sections, p v; Swedenborg's preface to chapter 18, pp 1-2; text of Genesis 18-22 and n 2135-2893, pp 2-627; Epilogue, pp 629-637; Glossary of doctrinal terms, pp 641-644; Indexes, pp 645-650, 651-656; advertisements, pp 657-659; publishing information, p 660; 6 pages ruled for reader's notes.
Volume 3, translated by T Nagashima, published by Arcana Press, Tokushima-ken. ISBN 4-90049-28-8.
The 'Translator's preface' begins on the verso of the 'Contents' leaf. The 'Epilogue' contains the translator's notes. The Indexes are formatted in 3 columns as follows: <1> paragraph nos; <2> Japanese words; <3> comments in Japanese.
UK: SOC; USA: ANC

49/01/Ja 2/4 **2004** Hyde 859/39
エマヌエル・スヴェーデンボルイ著｜天界の秘義　第四巻｜ラテン語原典訳｜旧約聖書「創世記」、「出エジプト記」に見る｜<みことば>に秘められた内的意味の開示｜第四巻　「創世記」第２３～２７章｜アルカナ出版｜２００４年　初版
verso: Ab Emanuele Swedenborgo detecta | "Arcana Caelestia" Tomus Quartus | Continens Geneseos capita xxiii-xvii (n.2894-3649) | Originale chirographum scriptum | A Emanuele Swedenborgo | In annis MDCCXLIX~MDCCLVI | Tertia Editio Latina prolata | A Societate Swedenborgiana in Anglia | In anno MCMXLIX | Quartus Tomus translatus | E Latino in Japonicum | Editus ab Arcana Press in Japonia | Die 19mo, mensi Junii, anno MMIV <*stent* Swedenborgo Caelestia A Emanuele Swedenborgo>
8vo
title leaf, 2 pp; Contents, 1 p; Translator's preface, pp i-iv; List of topics dealt with in inter-chapter sections, p v; text of Genesis 23-27 and n 2894-3649, pp 1-584; Epilogue, pp 585-598; Glossary of doctrinal terms <in Japanese, Latin, and English>, pp 599-604; Indexes, pp 605-609, 610-614; advertisements, pp 615-617; publishing information, p 618; 6 pages ruled for reader's notes.
Volume 4, translated by T Nagashima, published by Arcana Press, Tokushima-ken. ISBN 4-900449-30-X.
The 'Translator's preface' begins on the verso of the 'Contents' leaf. The 'Epilogue' contains the translator's notes. The Indexes are formatted in 3 columns as follows: <1> paragraph nos; <2> Japanese words; <3> comments in Japanese.
UK: SOC; USA: ANC

49/01/Ja 2/5 **2005** Hyde 859/40
エマヌエル・スヴェーデンボルイ著｜天界の秘義　第五巻｜ラテン語原典訳｜旧約聖書「創世記」、「出エジプト記」に見る｜<みことば>に秘められた内的意味の開示｜第五巻　「創世記」第２８～３１章｜アルカナ出版｜２００５年　初版
verso: Ab Emanuele Swedenborgo detecta | "Arcana Caelestia" Tomus Quintus | Continens Geneseos capita xxviii-xxxi (n.3650-4228) | Originale chirographum scriptum | A Emanuele Swedenborgo | In annis MDCCXLIX~MDCCLVI | Tertia Editio Latina prolata | A Societate Swedenborgiana in Anglia | In

anno MCMXLIX | Quintus Tomus translatus | E Latino in Japonicum | Editus ab Arcana Press in Japonia | Die 19mo, mensi Junii, anno MMV <*stent* Swedenborgo Caelestia A Emanuele Swedenborgo>
8vo
title leaf, 2 pp; Contents, 1 p; Translator's preface, pp i-iv; List of topics dealt with in inter-chapter sections, p v; text of Genesis 28-31 and n 3650-4228, pp 1-536; Epilogue, pp 537-554; Glossary of doctrinal terms <in Japanese, Latin, and English>, pp 555-563; illustration <76 x 61 mm, a flowering plant>, p 564; Indexes, pp 565-568, 569-572; advertisements, pp 573-575; publishing information, p 576; 10 pages ruled for reader's notes.
Volume 5, translated by T Nagashima, published by Arcana Press, Tokushima-ken. ISBN 40900449-32-6.
The 'Translator's preface' begins on the verso of the 'Contents' leaf. The 'Epilogue' contains the translator's notes. The Indexes are formatted in 3 columns as follows: <1> paragraph nos; <2> Japanese words; <3> comments in Japanese.
UK: SOC; USA: ANC

49/01/Ja 2/6 **2006** Hyde 859/41
エマヌエル・スヴェーデンボルイ著 | 天界の秘義　第六巻 | ラテン語原典訳 | 旧約聖書「創世記」、「出エジプト記」に見る　|　＜みことば＞に秘められた内的意味の開示　|　第六巻　「創世記」第３２～３８章 | アルカナ出版 | ２００６年　初版
verso: Ab Emanuele Swedenborgo detecta | "Arcana Caelestia" Tomus Sextus | Continens Geneseos capita xxxii-xxxviii (n.4229-4953) | Originale chirographum scriptum | A Emanuele Swedenborgo | In annis MDCCXLIX~MDCCLVI | Tertia Editio Latina prolata | A Societate Swedenborgiana in Anglia | In anno MCMXLIX | Sextus Tomus translatus | E Latino in Japonicum | Editus ab Arcana Press in Japonia | Die 19mo, mensi Junii, anno MMVI <*stent* Swedenborgo Caelestia A Emanuele Swedenborgo>
8vo
title leaf, 2 pp; Contents, 1 p; Translator's preface, pp i-iv; List of topics dealt with in inter-chapter sections, p v; text of Genesis 32-38 and n 4229-4953, pp 1- 640; Epilogue, pp 641-648; Glossary of doctrinal terms <in Japanese, Latin, and English>, pp 649-653; Indexes, pp 654-659, 660-665; advertisements, pp 666-668; illustration <98 x 6165 mm, a group of trees>, p 669; publishing information, p 670; 4 pages ruled for reader's notes.
Volume 6, translated by T Nagashima, published by Arcana press, Tokushima-ken. ISBN 4-900449-33-4.
The 'Translator's preface' begins on the verso of the 'Contents' leaf. The 'Epilogue' contains the translator's notes. The Indexes are formatted in 3 columns as follows: <1> paragraph nos; <2> Japanese words; <3> comments in Japanese.
UK: SOC; USA: ANC

49/01/Ja 2/7 **2008** Hyde 859/42
エマヌエル・スヴェーデンボルイ著 | 天界の秘義　第七巻 | ラテン語原典訳 | 旧約聖書「創世記」、「出エジプト記」に見る　|　＜みことば＞に秘められた内的意味の開示　|　第七巻　「創世記」第３９～４３章 | アルカナ出版 | ２００８年　初版
verso: Ab Emanuele Swedenborgo detecta | "Arcana Caelestia" Tomus Septimus | Continens Geneseos capita xxxix-xliii (n.4954-5727) | Originale chirographum scriptum | A Emanuele Swedenborgo | In annis MDCCXLIX~MDCCLVI | Tertia Editio Latina prolata | A Societate Swedenborgiana in Anglia | In anno MCMXLIX | Septimus Tomus translatus | E Latino in Japonicum | Editus ab Arcana Press in Japonia | Die 19mo, mensi Junii, anno MMVII <*stent* Swedenborgo Caelestia A Emanuele Swedenborgo>
8vo
title leaf, 2 pp; Contents, 1 p; Translator's preface, pp i-v; List of topics dealt with in inter-chapter

sections, p v; text of Genesis 39-43 and n 4954-5727, pp 1- 601; Epilogue, pp 603-614; Glossary of doctrinal terms <in Japanese, Latin, and English>, pp 615-624; Indexes, pp 625-630, 631-636; advertisements, pp 637-639; publishing information, p 640; 2 pages ruled for reader's notes.
Volume 7, translated by T Nagashima, published by Arcana Press, Tokushima-ken. ISBN 978-4-900449-34-3.
The 'Translator's preface' begins on the verso of the 'Contents' leaf. The 'Epilogue' contains the translator's notes. The Indexes are formatted in 3 columns as follows: <1> paragraph nos; <2> Japanese words; <3> comments in Japanese.
UK: soc

49/01/Ja 2/8 **2010** Hyde 859/43
エマヌエル・スヴェーデンボルイ著 | 天界の秘義　第八巻 | ラテン語原典訳 | 旧約聖書「創世記」、「出エジプト記」に見る | ＜みことば＞に秘められた内的意味の開示 | 第八巻 「創世記」第４４～５０章 | アルカナ出版 | ２０１０年　初版
verso: Ab Emanuele Swedenborgo detecta | "Arcana Caelestia" Tomus Octavus | Continens Geneseos capita xliv-l (n.5728-6626) | Originale chirographum scriptum | A Emanuele Swedenborgo | In annis MDCCXLIX~MDCCLVI | Tertia Editio Latina prolata | A Societate Swedenborgiana in Anglia | In anno MCMXLIX | Octavus Tomus translatus | E Latino in Japonicum | Editus ab Arcana Press in Japonia | Die 19mo, mensi Junii, anno MMIX <*stent* Swedenborgo Caelestia A Emanuele Swedenborgo>
8vo
title leaf, 2 pp; Contents, 1 p; Translator's preface, pp i-v; List of topics dealt with in inter-chapter sections, p v; text of Genesis 44-50 and n 5728-6626, pp 1-598; Epilogue, pp 599-612; Glossary of doctrinal terms <in Japanese, Latin, and English>, pp 613-620; Indexes, pp 621-624, 625-628; advertisements, pp 629-631; publishing information, p 632; 2 pages ruled for reader's notes.
Volume 8, translated by T Nagashima, published by Arcana Press, Tokushima-ken. ISBN 978-4-900449-35-0.
The 'Translator's preface' begins on the verso of the 'Contents' leaf. The 'Epilogue' contains the translator's notes. The Indexes are formatted in 3 columns as follows: <1> paragraph nos; <2> Japanese words; <3> comments in Japanese.
UK: soc

KOREAN

49/01/Ko 1/1 **<1996>** Hyde —
The online catalogue of USA: ANC records a 15-volume translation of *Arcana Coelestia*, published in 1996. The translator and publisher are not named; and the title is transliterated as 'Chun-gye bi-ui'.
Copy not seen; description recorded from catalogue of USA: ANC.
USA: ANC

49/01/Ko 2/1 **2003** Hyde —
<< <title page not recorded> >>
8vo
title leaf, 2 pp; text of Genesis 1-5 and n 1-546, pp –.
Translated by Dzin Pyung Kwak from La 5/1; published in an edition of 1,000 copies by Youl-Rin Malseum, New Church Publishing Company, Seoul.
In the catalogue of USA: ANC the title is transliterated as follows: Chun-gye bi-ui.
Copy not seen; description recorded from the Newsletter of Swedenborg Publishers International, Bryn Athyn PA, Fall 2003 and Spring 2004.

KOREAN EXTRACTS

X 49/01/Ko nd/1 — no date — Hyde —

<<Arcana Coelestia>>
title and text, n 3004-3352, pp –.
Translated by Yeong K Lee, published in <*The Representative Church*>.
Copy not seen; description recorded from the Newsletter of Swedenborg Publishers International, Bryn Athyn PA, Spring 2004, p 4.

X 49/01/Ko 1995/1, D Ko 1995/1 — 1995 — Hyde —

제3부 | 말세 (末世)의 올바른 이해 |—마태복음 24 • 25장 영해*— |*제3부는 스베덴보리가 저술한 천계비의 (天界秘義-Arcana) 제4-7권에 수 |록된 마태복음 24-25장의 해설을 옮긴 것이다. 참조난의 숫자는 본서에 수 |록된 관련 항수이다 (옮긴이).
8vo
title leaf, pp 193-194; text n 1-67, pp 195-301.
Translated by Yeong K Lee; extracted from 49/01, from the material preceding Genesis chapters 26-40 on the subject of the Last Judgment, renumbered by the translator. Published with 58/03/Ko 1/1 and 63/06/Ko 1/1.
USA: SHS

LATVIAN EXTRACTS

X 49/01/Lt 1927/1 — 1927 — Hyde 895/1

<<MOSIS RADĪŠANAS STĀHSTS, | Em. Swedenborga | isskaidrots. | Ar tulkotaja preeksch un pehzwahrdu. | Latwiski Parstrahdajis, R. GRAVA | ... | LIPĀJA: | JAUNĀ BAZNĪCA 1927>>
verso: <<ATSEGTI | *Debeškigi Noslēpumi* | KAS IR | *SVĒTAJOS RAKSTOS* | JEB | *KUNGA VĀRDA* | ŠE VISPIRMS, KAS | *RADĪŠANAS GRĀMATĀ* | Līdz ar Brīnumlietām, | Kas redzētas | Gasru Pasaulē un Enğeļu Debesī | <double rule> | PIRMĀ DAĻA | <double rule> | 1749.>>
2nd title : <<facsimile reproduction of title page of La 1/1>>
8vo
title leaves, 4 pp; text, 72 pp.
Translated and edited by R Grava.
Copy not seen; description deduced from X Lt 1960/1.
LAT: RIG; SWE: ROY; USA: ANC

X 49/01/Lt 1960/1 — 1960 — Hyde 895/1a

RADĪŠANAS | STĀSTS | EMANUELA SVEDENBORGA | IZSKAIDROTS | NO ORIĞINĀLA TULKOJIS | R. GRAVA | LATVJU JAUNĀS BAZNĪCA | IZDEVUMS | A.S.V. 1960.
verso: ATSEGTI | *Debeškigi Noslēpumi* | KAS IR | *SVĒTAJOS RAKSTOS* | JEB | *KUNGA VĀRDĀ* | Še vispirms, kas | *RADĪŠANAS GRĀMATĀ* | Līdz ar Brīnumlietām, | Kas redzētas | Garu Pasaulē un Enğeļu Debesī | <double rule> | PIRMĀ DAĻA | <double rule> | 1749. <This is a translation of the Latin title page reproduced on the facing page.>
2nd title: <facsimile reproduction of title page of La 1/1>
216 x 160 mm, perfect bound
blank leaf and title leaf, 4 pp; photographic reproduction of title page of 49/01/La 1/1, 1 p; Latvian translation of Matthew 6:33, 1 p; Priekšvārds <Preface>, pp I-IV; text n I-V, 6-181, pp 1-69.
Translated and edited by R Grava, with the translator's notes at the foot of each page. The Preface is dated September 1960 at Pikesville MD.
UK: SOC, NR; LAT: RIG; USA: ANC

NORWEGIAN EXTRACTS

X 49/01/No 1941/1 **1941** Hyde 895/2

VERDENS END | EN NY TID | Matt. 24–25 kap., tolket av | EM. SWEDENBORG | Førstegangs utgave på norsk | Eget Forlag. Post Box 881. | <short rule> | Oslo
verso: Centraltrykkiet – Drammen
half title: VERDENS ENDE | EN NY TID
8vo
half title and title leaves, 4 pp; Forord <Foreword>, pp 5-12; text unnumbered, pp 13-90; Innhold <Contents>, p 92.
An anonymous translation, privately published. No key is provided to indicate the paragraphs of 49/01 selected.
UK: SOC; USA: ANC

PORTUGUESE

Translators:
Pt 1 L C de La Fayette
Pt 2 C R Nobre

49/01/Pt 1/1 **1920-1924** Hyde —

<<Arcanos Celestes>>
A MS translation made by L C de La Fayette.
Copy not seen; description recorded from information supplied by A J Heilman.
BRA: RIO

49/01/Pt 2/1 **1987** Hyde —

A report by Eloah Castro and Patricia Santoro in *New Church Life* Bryn Athyn PA p 287, stated that portions of a translation by C R Nobre were in the course of being published in instalments in *A Nova Igreja* Rio de Janeiro.

49/01/Pt 2/2 **1999** Hyde 859/35

Arcanos Celestes | Que foram revelados na Escritura Santa | ou Palavra do SENHOR, a saber, | que estão no Gênesis e no Êxodo | juntamente com as | maravilhas que foram vistas | no Mundo dos Espíritos e no Céu dos Anjos | Por um servo do SENHOR | (Emanuel Swedenborg) | Tradução da | Editio Tertia, Londini, 1949 | pelo | Rev. Cristóvão Rabelo Nobre | Volume I - N°s. 1 - 691 | *Gênesis* Caps. I - VI | Sociedade Religiosa "A NOVA JERUSALÉM" | Rua das Graças, 45 - Fátima | CEP 20.240.030 - Rio de Janeiro. RJ | 1999
half title: Arcanos Celestes | Emanuel Swedenborg | Volume I
imprint: impressão e acabamento: | assai gráfica e editora ltda. | fone: (011) 458-0455
large 8vo
half title and title leaves, 4 pp; Nota do Editor <Editor's notes>, pp 5-9; text: Esquema da Obra, pelo Autor <Swedenborg's preface>, Genesis 1-6, and n 1-690, pp 11-238; Notas de referência, p 239; Índice Remissivo, pp 241-254; advertisements, pp 255-256; imprint, p 256.
In *Nota do Editor* the translator acknowledges the assistance given by Raymundo and Eloah de Araujo Castro Filho, Lygia Daalcin, and Patricia Santoro.
UK: SOC, NR; USA: ANC

RUSSIAN

Translators:
Ru 1 V A Klenovsky
Ru 2 H Y Vozovik

49/01/Ru 1/1 **1851** Hyde 839
Открытыя Неьесныя Тайны, | находящіяся | въ Священномъ Писаніи | йли | въ Словѣ Господа; | здѣсь говоритсяо томъ, что находится | въ Исходѣ, | вмѣстѣ съ достопамятностями, | видѣнными | въ Мірѣ духовъ и въ Небѣ Ангеловъ. | <short rule> | Твореніе | Эммануила Сведенборга. | <short rule> | Вторая часть или | xi Томъ всего сочиненія.
foolscap broad 4to <222 x 171 mm>
title leaf, 2 pp; text n 8387-9442, 1965 pp.
Translated by V A Klenovsky; the MS is dated 1851. <UK: soc Archives B/18>
UK: soc

49/01/Ru 1/2 **1852** Hyde 837
Открытыя Неьесныя Тайны, | которыя | находятся въ | Священномъ Писаніи | йли | въ Словѣ Господа, | здѣсь содержащіяся | въ Исходѣ, | въ Мірѣ духовъ и въ Небѣ Ангеловъ. | <short rule> | Твореніе | Эммануила Сведенборга. | Первй части | Томъ I, | или всего сочиненія Томъ IX. | <short rule> | <Cyrillic characters naming the translator as V Klenovsky, dated 1852>
foolscap broad 4to <219 x 175 mm>
title leaf, 2 pp; text n 6627-7487, 960 pp. <UK: soc Archives B/16>
UK: soc

49/01/Ru 1/3 **1853** Hyde 838
Открытыя Неьесныя Тайны, | находящіяся въ | Священномъ Писаніи | йли | въ Словѣ Господа: | здѣсь тѣ, которыя находится въ | Исходѣ, | вмѣстѣ съ достопамятностями, | видѣнными | въ Мірѣ духовъ, и въ Небѣ Ангеловъ. | <short rule> | Твореніе | Эммануила Сведенборга. | <short rule> | Первой части | Томъ II. | или всего творенія Томъ X.
foolscap broad 4to <222 x 178 mm>
title leaf, 2 pp; text n 7488-8386, 1077 pp.
Translated by V A Klenovsky. <UK: soc Archives B/7>
UK: soc

49/01/Ru 1/4 **1856** Hyde 840
Открытыя Неьесныя, | <short rule> | *Тайны, находящіяся* | *въ Священномъ Писаніи* | *йли* | *въ Словѣ Господа,* | *открытыя:* | *здѣсь находящіеся* | *въ Исходѣ,* | *вмѣстѣ съ достопамятностями,* | *видѣнными* | *въ Мірѣ духовъ, и въ Небѣ Ангеловъ.* | <short rule> | *Твореніе* | *Эммануила Сведенборга.* | <short rule> | I Томъ | третьей части, | или цѣлаго творенія | Томъ XII. | *Тnono 1856.*
foolscap broad 4to <225 x 175 mm>
title leaf, 2 pp; text n 9443-9973, 886 pp.
Translated by V A Klenovsky. <UK: soc Archives B/19>
UK: soc

49/01/Ru 1/5 **1856** Hyde 841
Открытыя | *Неьесныя Тайны,* | *содержащіяся* | *въ Священномъ Писаніи:* | *здѣсь находящіяся* | *въ Исходѣ,* | *вмѣстѣ съ достопамятностями,* | *видѣнным* | *въ Мірѣ духовъ, и въ Небѣ Ангеловъ.* |

<short rule> | *Сочиненіе* | *Эммануила Сведенборга.* | <short rule> | *Томъ II* | *третьей части* | *или цѣлаго сочиненія XIII* | *и послѣдній томъ.*
half title: *Неьесныя Тайны.* | <short rule> | *Томъ XIII.* | *В. К. 30*[по] *Тпопо 1856*
foolscap broad 4to <222 x 175 mm>
half title and title leaves, 4 pp; text n 9974-10837, 1795 pp.
Translated by V A Klenovsky. <UK: soc Archives B/20>
UK: soc

49/01/Ru 1/6 **1858** Hyde 836

Открытыя Неьесныя Тайны, | *находящіяся* | *Въ Священномъ Писаніи* | *или* | *Въ Словѣ Господа:* | *здѣсь же то, что находится* | *Въ Бытія.* | *Вмѣстѣ съ Достопамятностями,* | *Видѣнным* | *Въ Мірѣ Вуховъ и въ Небѣ Ангеловъ.* | <short rule> | *Сочиненіе* | *Эммануила Сведенборга.* | <short rule> | *Пятая Части* | *Или viii Томъ всего сочиненія.* | <short rule>
verso: *Матѳ: VI: 33.* | *И щите же прежде Царствя Божия и Нравды* | *Его, и ви сіе приложится вамы.*
half title: *29*[по] *Чпбо 1858*[по]
pott broad 4to <200 x 152 mm>
half title and title leaves, 4 pp; text n 5191-6626, 1605 pp.
Translated by V A Klenovsky. <UK: soc Archives B/15>.
UK: soc

49/01/Ru 1/7 **1862** Hyde 835

Открытыя Неьесныя Тайны, | *содержащіяся* | *въ Священномъ Писаніи* | *или* | *въ Словѣ Господнемъ:* | *здѣсь содержащіяся* | *въ Бытія,* | *вмѣстѣ съ достопамятностями,* | *видѣнными* | *въ Мірѣ духовъ и на Ангельскомъ Небѣ.* | <short rule> | *Сочиненіе* | *Эммануила Сведенборга.* | <short rule> | *Четвертая часть* | *II Тома.* | *или всего сочиненія VII Томъ.* | <quadruple rule> | *Москва.* | *1862.*
foolscap broad 4to <210 x 171 mm>
title leaf, 2 pp; text n 4635-5190, 619 pp.
Translated by V A Klenovsky. <UK: soc Archives B/14, which also contains a fair copy of n 4791-5190, on paper of the same size>
UK: soc

49/01/Ru 1/8 **1863** Hyde 834

Открытыя Неьесныя Тайны, | содержащіяся *въ Священномъ Писаніи* | *или* | *въ Словѣ Господнемъ*: | *здѣсь содержащіяся* | *въ Бытія,* | *вмѣстѣ съ достопамятностями,* | *видѣнным* | *въ Мірѣ духовъ и на Ангельскомъ Небѣ.* | <short rule> | *Сочиненіе* | *Эммануила Сведенборга.* | <short rule> | *I Томъ* | *четвертой части* | *или полнаго сочиненія vi Томъ.* | <quadruple rule> | *Москва* | *1863 г.*
section title: *Отвѣтъ Эммануила Сведенборга на письмо друга*
foolscap broad 4to <219 x 175 mm>
title leaf, 2 pp; title and text of *Отвѣтъ Эммануила Свегенборга на Письмо друга* <'Answer to a letter from a friend'> <69/12/Ru 1/1 = Hyde 2685>, pp 3-7; text n 4056-4280, 245 pp.
Translated by V A Klenovsky. <UK: soc Archives B/13>
UK: soc

49/01/Ru 2/1 **2003** Hyde —

<short rule> | PHILOSOPHY | <short rule> | <publisher's logo 8 x 8 mm> | Эманузль СВЕДЕНБОРГ | <rule> | ТАЙНЫ | НЕБЕСНЫЕ | <publisher's logo 9 x 10 mm> ЄРМАК | Москва | 2003

verso: УДК 23/28 | ББК 86.37 | С24 | *Серийное оормление А. А. Кудрябцеба* | *Перевод Е. Ю. Возовик* | Книга подговтовлена к печати при одействии | Крымского Общества Сведенборга | и Днерпетровского Общества Свеенборга | Подписано в печать 18.09.03. Формат 84х $108^1/_{32}$" | Усл. печ. л. 29,40. Тираж 5000 зкз. Заказ № 2035. | Сведенборг З. | С24 Тайны / З. СВЕДЕНБОРГ; Пер. Е. Ю. Возовик. – | М.: ООО «Издательство АСТ»; ЗАО НПП «Ермак», 2003.–555, | [5] с.–(Philosophy), | ISBN 5-17-020819-7 (ООО «Издательто АСТ») | ISBN 5-9577-0651-5 (ЗАО НПП «Ермак») | З. Сведенборг (1688–1772) – шведский ученый-естествоиспытатель и | философ-мистик, автор множства работ по математике, астрономии и тео- | софии. В знаменитом турде «Тайны небесные» З. Сведенборг изложил свои | мистнко-религиозные видеия и дал оригинальную трактовку сокровенного, | на его взгЛяд, смысла первых книг Ветхого Завета. | Религиозно-теософские теории Сведенборга всегда имели множество | стронников, а общества его поледоателей и по сей день существуют во | многих смиратранах. | УДК 23/28 | ББК 86.37 | © Перевод. Е.Ю. Возовик, 2003 | © Оформление. | ООО «Издательство АСТ», 2003
half title: <short rule> | PHILOSOPHY | <short rule> | <publisher's logo 8 x 8 mm>
8vo
half title and title leaves, 4 pp; Предисловие переводчика, pp 5-6; Пнятйный словарь <Word list>, pp 7-8; text n 1-1113, pp 9-556; Содержание <Contents>, pp 557-558; Information about Swedenborgian publishers, p 559; Information about the publisher, p 560.
Translated by Helen Y Vozovik, published by UKR: DNE.
UK: SOC, CON, NR; UKR: DNE; USA: ANC

49/01/Ru 2/2 **2005** Hyde —
<short rule> | PHILOSOPHY | <short rule> | <publisher's logo 8 x 8 mm> | Зманузль СВЕДЕНБОРГ | <rule> | ТАЙНЫ | НЕБЕСНЫЕ | <publisher's logo 9 x 10 mm> | ТРАНЗИТКНИГ | Москва | 2005
verso: УДК 23/28 | ББК 86.37 | С24 | Серия «Philosophy» | ARCANA COELESTIA | revealed through Emanuel Swedenborg | *Перевод Е. Ю. Возови* | *Серийное оормлние А. Кудрябцеба* | Компьюменый изайи В.А. Воронина | Книга подговтовлена к печати при одействии | Крымского Общества Сведенборга | и Днерпетровского Общества Свеенборга | Подписано в печать 25.07.05. Формат $84x108^1/_{32}$" | Усл. печ. л. 29,40. Тираж 3000 зкз. Заказ № 7770. | Сведенборг З. | С24 Тайны / Занузль СВЕДЕНБОРГ; Пер. Е.Ю.Возовик. — | М.: АСТ: АСТ МОСКВА: Транзиткнига, 2005. — 549, [11] с. — | (Philosophy). | ISBN 5-17-029097 -7 (ООО «Издательство АСТ») | ISBN 5-9713-0490-9 (ООО Издательство «АСТ МОСКВА») | ISBN 5-9578-2267-1 (ООО «Транзиткнига») | З. Сведенборг (1688—1772) — шведский ученый-естествоиспытатель и | философ-мистик, автор множства работ по математике, астрономии и тео- | софии. В знаменитом турде «Тайны небесные» З. Сведенборг изложил свои | мистнко-религиозные видеия и дал оригинальную трактовку сокровенного, | на его взгпяд, смысла 10 — 17 глав книги Бытия Втхого Завета. | Религиозно-теософские теории Сведенборга всегда имели множество | стронников, а общества его поледоателей и по сей день существуют во | многих смиратранах. | УДК 23/28 | ББК 86.37 | © Перевод. Е.Ю. Возовик, 2003 | © Оформление. | ООО «Издательство АСТ», 2005
half title: <short rule> | PHILOSOPHY | <short rule> | <publisher's logo 8 x 8 mm>
8vo
half title and title leaves, 4 pp; text of Genesis 10-17 and n 1114-2134, pp 5-550; Содержане <Contents>, pp 551-552; Information about Swedenborgian publishers, pp 553-554; Information about the publisher, pp 555-560.
Translated by Helen Y Vozovik, published by UKR: DNE.
UK: SOC, NCC, NR; NET: GEN; UKR: DNE; USA: ANC

49/01/Ru 2/3 **2007** Hyde —
<short rule> | PHILOSOPHY | <short rule> | <publisher's logo 8 x 8 mm> | Змануэль СВЕДЕНБОРГ | <rule> | ТАЙНЫ | НЕБЕСНЫЕ | ИСХОД | *Главы 1–8* | <publisher's logo 9 x 10 mm> | ХРАНИТЕЛь | Москва
verso: УДК 1(091) | ББК 87.3 | С24 | Серия «Philosophy» | ARCANA COELESTIA | Exodus (Chapters 1–8) | Revealed through Emanuel Swedenborg | *Перевод с английского Е.Ю. Возовик* | *Оформление А.А. Кудрявуева* | *Комньюмерныйй дизайн. Н.А. Хафизовой* | Подпнсано в печать 03.05.07. Формат 84x108¹/₃₂" | Усл. печ. л. 23,52. Тиражж 3000 зкз. Заказ № 6771. | Книга подготовлена к печаи при | Крымского Общества Сведенборга | и Днепропетровкого Общества Сведенборга | Сведенборг, З. | С24 Тайны небесные: Исход. Главы 1–8/Змануэль Сведенборг; пер. | с англ. Е.Ю. Возовик. – М.: АСТ: АСТ МОСКВА: ХРАНИТЕЛЬ, | 2007. – 444, [4] с. – (Philosophy). | ISBN 978-5-17-043620-0 (ООО «Издательство АСТ») | ISBN 978-59713-5785-8 (ООО Издательство «АСТ») | ISBN 978-5-9762-3280-8 (ООО «ХРАНИТЕЛЬ» | З. Сведенборг (1688–1772) – шведский ученый-естествоиспытатель и | философ-мистик, автор множества работ по математике, астрономии и | теософии. В знаменитом труде «Тайны небесные» З. Сведенборг изложил | свои мистик-религиозные видения и дал оригинальную трактовку сокровен- | ного, на его взгляд, смысла 1–8 глав книги Исход Ветхого Завета. | Религиозно-теософские теории Сведенборга всегда имели множество | сторонников, а общества его последователей и по сей день существуют во | многих странах мнра. | УДК 1(091) | ББК 87.3 | © Перевод. Е.Ю. Возовик, 2007 | © Оформление. | ООО «Издательство АСТ», 2007
half title: <short rule> | PHILOSOPHY | <short rule> | <publisher's logo 8 x 8 mm>
8vo
half title and title leaves, 4 pp; text of Exodus 1-8 and n 6627-7487, pp 5-443; Содержание <Contents>, pp 444-445; Information about Swedenborgian publishers, pp 446-447; Bibliographical information, p 448.
Translated by Helen Y Vozovik, published by UKR: DNE.
UK: SOC, NR; NET: GEN; UKR: DNE; USA: ANC

RUSSIAN EXTRACTS

X 49/01/Ru 1860/1 **c 1860** Hyde 888
Сочиненія Эм. Сведенборга. | <short rule> | *Ученіе Любви (*<illegible word of 3 Cyrillic characters> | <illegible word of 19 Cyrillic characters>*)* | *и Вѣры.* | *Изъ Небесныхъ Тайнъ.* | *Вынускъ II.* | *ч. I.* | *Лондонъ.* | *186.* <*stet* 186.>
foolscap broad 4to <219 x 171 mm>
title leaf, 2 pp; Preface, pp 3-18; text, pp 1-212.
This translation <UK: SOC Archives B/40> and that described as 58/04/Ru 1/1 = Hyde 1293 < UK: SOC Archives B/29> are in the same handwriting.
UK: SOC

X 49/01/Ru 1897/1 **1897** Hyde 889
УЧЕНІЕ | О | МИЛОЕРДІИ И ВѢРѢ | Эммануила СВЕДЕНБОРГА | <short wavy rule> | ПАРИЖЪ | ТИНОГРАФІЯ АДОЛЬФА РЕЙФФА | 3, Rue du Four, 3 | <short rule> | 1897
imprint: <rule> | ПАРИЖЪ. – Тин. Рейффа, 3, rue du Four.
small 8vo
title leaf, 2 pp; О Церкви <The Church>, pp 3-6; text, pp 7-70; Оглавленіе <Contents>, p 71; imprint, p 71.
UK: SOC

X 49/01/Ru 1906/1 **1906** Hyde 889/—

<<Зм. Сведенборгъ. | О ПОСЛѢДНМЪ | (страшномъ) СУМѢ. | С.-ПЕТЕБУРЪ. | Типографія Воейкова, Бассеиная, № 3. | 1906.>>

8vo

title leaf, 2 pp; text of Swedenborg's preface to chapter 22, n 3353-3356, 3486-3489, 3650-3655, 3751-3757, 3897-3901, 4056-4060, 4229-4231, 4332-4335, 4422-4424, 4535, pp 1- ??

Published in St Petersburg, the subject of these extracts is the Last Judgment.

Copy not seen; description deduced from information received from V A Vasiliev.

X 49/01/Ru 1908/1 **1908** Hyde 889/1

<<ТАИНЫ НебА (Extracts from Arcana Coelestia ...) Petrograd. 1908.>>

Copy not seen; description recorded from catalogue of USA: ANC.

USA: ANC

X 49/01/Ru 1997/1 **1997** Hyde 889/—

Эммануил Сбеднборг | лояснение первых уетырех глав | КНИГИ БЫТИЯ | Москва | 1997

verso: УДК 221 | ББК 86.37 | С 24 | С 24 *Эммануил Сбеднборг* | Порнене перых уетырех глав КНИГИ БЫТИЯ | — М.: ИЦА, 1997. - 164с. | <description of the contents of the book> | УДК 221 | ББК 86.37 | ISBN 5-89488-003-3 | © М.: ИЦА, | оформление, макет, 1997

8vo

title leaf, 2 pp; text n 1-63, 73-167, 190-313, 324-442, pp 1-162; Information about the publisher, p 163.

A revision of X Ru 1908/1, excluding terms which are not appropriate in contemporary language, published by the Research Centre of Astro-psychology; 2,000 copies printed.

In the text, paragraph number 323 is printed as 325.

UK: NCC

X 49/01/Ru 2000/1 **2000** Hyde 889/3

Эмануэль СВЕДЕНБОРГ | СОКРОВЕННЫ СМЫСЛ | СВЯЩЕННОГО ЛИСАНИЯ | Фрагменты иэ гпав 15-23 | «Небесных Та н» | Перевод с англи ского | ВИКТОРИИ СМИТ | Под редакцие | В. В. МАЛЯВИНА | Росси ское Сведенборгианское Общество | ИЛЦ «Диза н. Информация. Картография» | МОСКВА, 2000

verso: УДК 293 | ББК 86.376 | С24 | Росси ское Сведенборгианское общество бпагодарит | Международное Сведенборганское издатепьство, | Пондонское Сведенборгианское общество, | а также г-на Дункана Смита | за соде ствие в издании зто книги | Сведенборг З. | С24 Сокровенный смысл Свящнного Лисания / Лод ред. В.В. Малявина - М.; | Издательско-продюсерский центр «Дизай. Информаци. Картография», | 2000. - 36 с. | ISBN 5-287-00016-2 | Книга содержит разъяснения духовного мысла тектор Библи согласно учению | известного богослова и христианского лисателя Эмануэль Сведенборга (1688–1772.) | Зти разьяснения, влервые лубликумые на русском языке, апдресованы всем, кто ин- | тересуетср богословием и стремится познать смысп богооткровенных истин Ветхого | и Нового Заветов. | УДК 293 | ББК 86.376 | © Ройское Сведенборгианское | общество, 2000 | © Издательско-продюсерский центр | ISBN 0-287-00016-2 «Дизайн. Информация. Картография», 2000

half title: THE INTERNAL SENSE OF THE WORD | СОКРОВЕННЫ СМЫСЛ | СВЯЩЕННОГО ПСАНИЯИ

verso: Emanuel SWEDENBORG | THE | INTERNAL SENSE | OF THE WORD | A translation of extracts from | chapters fifteen to twenty-three of | ARCANA CAELESTIA | By | EMANUEL SWEDENBORG | THE SWEDENBORG SOCIETY | LONDON, 1974

A4 pages folded, paper covers

half title and title leaves, 4 pp; СОДЕРЖАНИЕ <Contents>, p 5; translation of English translator's preface, p 6; text n 1-54 <*Arcana Caelestia* n 1984, 2135, 2310-2311, 2606-2609, 2760-2763, 2894-2900, 3004-3011, 1767-1776, 1869-1885>, pp 7-34; Information about the publisher, p 36.
A translation of X 49/01/En 1974/1 by Victoria Smith <née Maliavina>, and edited by V V Maliavin. On p 8 '2135' is omitted before 2; and on p 12 '2608' and n 7 are omitted before the sentence beginning 'Пророчесие разделы содержат много описни веще и событи Царства Божьего –'.
UK: SOC, NR

X 49/01/Ru 2001/1 **2001** Hyde 889/–
<within an orn rule border 178 x 109 mm> УЧЕНИЕ | О МЛОСЕРДИИ | Из книги Тайны небесные | Леребод *Е. Возоьцк* <Doctrine of Charity from "Arcana Coelestia">
8vo
title and text n 1-158 <*Arcana Caelestia* n 6703-6712, 6818-6824, 6933-6938, 7080-7086, 7178-7182, 7255-7263, 7366-7377, 7488-7494, 7623-7627, 7752-7762, 7814-7821, 8033-8037, 8120-8124, 8252-8257, 8387-8394, 8548-8553, 8635-8640, 8742-8747, 8853-8858, 8958-8969, 9112-9122>, pp 7-36.
Translated by Helen Y Vozovik, published by UKR: DNE in ИЗБРАННЫЕ ПРОИЗВЕДЕНИЯ with X 49/01/Ru 2001/2, 58/04/Ru 2/1 = Hyde 1209/5, and 63/06/Ru 1/1 <ISBN 966-684-004-9>.
UK: SOC, CON, NR; USA: ANC

X 49/01/Ru 2001/2 **2001** Hyde 889/–
<within an orn rule border 178 x 109 mm> УЧЕНИЕ | О МЛОСЕРДИИ | И ВЕРЕ | Из книги Тайны небесные | Леребод *Е. Возоьцк* <Doctrine of Charity and Faith from "Arcana Coelestia">
8vo
title and text n 1-167 <*Arcana Caelestia* n 9239-9245, 9363-9369, 9443-9454, 9585-9591, 9701-9709, 9796-9803, 9974-9984, 10167-10175, 10318-10325, 10386-10392, 10519-10522, 10591-10597, 10714-10724, 10740-10749, 10760-10766, 10773-10781, 10789-10806, 10815-10831>, pp 37-66.
Translated by Helen Y Vozovik, published by UKR: DNE in ИЗБРАННЫЕ ПРОИЗВЕДЕНИЯ with X 49/01/Ru 2001/1, 58/04/Ru 2/1 = Hyde 1209/5, and 63/06/Ru 1/1 <ISBN 966-684-004-9>.
UK: SOC, CON, NR

X 49/01/Ru 2002/1 **2002** Hyde 889/–
Эмануэль СВЕДЕНБОРГ | СОКРОВЕННЫ СМЫСЛ | СВЯЩЕННОГО ЛИСАНИЯ | Фрагменты иэ гпав 15-23 | «Небесных Та н» | Перевод с англи ского | ВИКТОРИИ СМИТ | Под редакцие | В. В. МАЛЯВИНА | Росси ское Сведенборгианское Общество | ИЛЦ «Диза н. Информация. Картография» | МОСКВА, 2002
verso: УДК 293 | ББК 86.376 | С24 | Росси ское Сведенборгианское общество бпагодарит | Международное Сведенборганское издатепьство, | Пондонское Сведенборгианское общество, | а также г-на Дункана Смита | за соде ствие в издании зто книги | Сведенборг З. | С24 Сокровенный смысл Свящнного Лисания / Лод ред. В.В. Малявина - М.; | Издательско-продюсерский центр «Дизай. Информаци. Картография», | 2002. - 36 с. | ISBN 5-287-00016-2 | Книга содержит разъяснения духовного мысла текртор Библи согласно учению | известного богослова и христианского лисателя Эмануэль Сведенборга (1688–1772.) | Зти разьяснения, влервые лубликумые на русском языке, апдресованы всем, кто ин- |ココтересуетср богословием и стремится познать смысп богооткровенных истин Ветхого | и Нового Эаветов. | УДК 293 | ББК 86.376 | © Роийское Сведеборгианское | общество, 2000 | © Издательско-продюсеркий центр | ISBN 0-287-00016-2 «Дизай. Информация», 2000

half title: THE INTERNAL SENSE OF THE WORD | СОКРОВЕННЫ СМЫСЛ | СВЯЩЕННОГО ПСАНИЯИ
verso: Emanuel SWEDENBORG | THE | INTERNAL SENSE | OF THE WORD | A translation of extracts from | chapters fifteen to twenty-three of | ARCANA CAELESTIA | By | EMANUEL SWEDENBORG | THE SWEDENBORG SOCIETY | LONDON, 1974
A4 pages folded to A5, paper covers
half title and title leaves, 4 pp; СОДЕРЖАНИЕ <Contents>, p 5; translation of English translator's preface, p 6; text n 1-54 <*Arcana Caelestia* n 1984, 2135, 2310-2311, 2606-2609, 2760-2763, 2894-2900, 3004-3011, 1767-1776, 1869-1885>, pp 7-34; Information about the publisher, p 36.
A reprint of X Ru 2000/1.
UK: NR; GER: WLB

X 49/01/Ru 2003/1 **2003** Hyde 889/–
СОКРОВЕННЫ СМЫСЛ | СВЯЩЕННОГО ПСАНИЯИ
8vo
title leaf, pp 763-764; Preface, p 765; text, pp 766-802.
Reprint of X Ru 2000/1 = Hyde 889/3, published in the 2nd, enlarged edition of V V Maliavin's translation of *The Swedenborg Epic* <Hyde 3390/13, 3158/6>.
UK: SOC

X 49/01/Ru 2004/1 **2004** Hyde 889/–
Учение о млосердии | *(Из книди «Тайны небеные»)*
8vo
title and text n 1-158, pp 139-169.
Reprint of X 2001/1, published in Лророки и Псалмы Избранные Труды. ISBN 5-94355-095-X.
UK: SOC, CON, NR; USA: ANC

X 49/01/Ru 2004/2 **2004** Hyde 889/–
УЧЕНИЕ О МЛОСЕРДИИ И ВЕРЕ | *(Из книги «Тайны небесные"»)*
8vo
title and text n 1-168, pp 170-201.
Reprint of X 2001/2, published in Лророки и Псалмы Избранные Труды. ISBN 5-94355-095-X.
UK: NR

X 49/01/Ru 2004/3 **2004** Hyde 889/–
The report of the Projects Committee of Swedenborg Publishers International, 17-12-2003, referred to V V Maliavin's plan to translate G F Dole's translation *Emanuel Swedenborg: The Universal Human and Soul-Body Interaction* <X 49/01/ En 1984/1 = Hyde 868/3; 69/11/En 11/2 = Hyde 2577/10>. No publication of this version has been recorded.

X 49/01/Ru 2006/1 **2006** Hyde 889/3a
Эмануэль Сведенборг | СОКРОВЕННЫЙ СМЫСЛ | СВЯЩЕННОГО ЛИСАНИЯ | Фрагменты иэ гпав XV-XXIII | «Небесных Тайн» | *Перевод с английского* | *Виктории Смит* | *Под редакцией* | *В. В. Малявина* | Российское Сведенборгианское общество | Москва
verso: УДК 293 | ББК 86.376 | С24 | *Российское Сведенборгианское общество благодарит* | *Международное Сведенборганское издатепьство,* | *Пондонское Сведенборгианское общество,* | *а также г-на Дункана Смита* | *за содействие в издании зтой книги* | Сведенборг З. | Сокровенный смысл Свящнного Лисания [Текст]: ессе / Пер. с | англ. В. Смит / Под ред. В.В.

Малявина – М., 2002. – 36 с. | Книга содержит разъяснения духовного смысла текртор Библии | согласно учению известного богослова и христианского писателя | Эмануэлья Сведенборга (1688–1772). Зти разьяснения, влервые | лубликумые на русском языке, адресованы всем, кто интересуется | богословием и стремится познать смысл богооткровенных истин | Ветхого и Нового Эаветов. | © Российское Сведенборгианское | общество, 2002
A4 pages folded to A5, paper covers
title leaf, 2 pp; СОДЕРЖАНИЕ <Contents>, p 3; translation of English translator's preface, p 4; text n 1-54 <*Arcana Caelestia* n 1984, 2135, 2310-2311, 2606-2609, 2760-2763, 2894-2900, 3004-3011, 1767-1776, 1869-1885>, pp 5-35; Information about the publisher, p 36.
A reprint of X Ru 2002/1.
UK: SOC

X 49/01/Ru 2007/1, **D** Ru 2007/1 **2007** Hyde 889/–
Пророчества в Слове о последнем | (страшном) суде
8vo
title and text of quotations selected from 49/01 <reprinted from X 49/01/Ru 1906/1>, pp 20-54.
Edited by A V Vasiliev, published in О Последнем (страшном) Суде <D Ru 2007/1> Lvov.
UK: SOC, NR; UKR: DNE

SERBIAN EXTRACTS

X 49/01/Se 1986/1 **1986** Hyde —
О чудима / De Miraculis
A4 folded to A3
title and text n 5 and 18, p 18.
Translated by Ilana Milankova from X 49/01/LaEn 1943/1 = Hyde 868/4, published in *Knjizevna Rěc* Belgrade.
UK: SOC

SERBO-CROATIAN

49/01/SeCr 1/1 **<1991>** Hyde —
In April 1991 at the International Swedenborg Conference in Manchester Risto Rundo reported plans to publish volume 1 in a translation being made by Slobodan Beštić. In a letter to N Ryder dated 3 July 2004 he stated that the plans had not succeeded.

SPANISH EXTRACTS

X 49/01/Sp 1914/1, **D** X Sp 1914/1 **1914** Hyde 895/3, 2272/1
<short rule> | EXTRACTO DE ARCANA COELESTIA | <short rule>
verso: «El esperitu es el que da vida; la carne | nada aproveca; las palabras que yo os e | ablado son espiritu y son vida». | *(Juan, VI, 6, 3.)* | «La letra mata, mas et espiritu vivifica». | *(2 Corintios, III, 6.)*
8vo
title leaf, pp 1-2; text: *Extracto de Arcana Coelestia*, pp 5-44.
Published in *Extractos de Arcana Coelestia y Apocalipsis Revelata* <Hyde 2272/1>, translated by J H Andersen, Valencia, for La Sociedad Swedenborg Española para Establecer y Fomentar La Nueva Iglesia en España, Alameda, LL. Printed by Francisco Vives Mora.-Hernán Cortés, 6.
UK: SOC, CON, NR; SWE: ROY, UPP; USA: ANC, SHS

X 49/01/Sp 1915/1 **1915-1920** Hyde —
<Extractos de Arcana Coelestia>

4to
title and text: **1915** n 168-169, 314-319, pp 30-32; n 1114-1129, pp 39-40; n 4320-4322, p 43; n 2117-2122, pp 77-78; n 2123-2125, pp 84-85; **1916** n 607, p 104; n 2987-2994, pp 111-112; n 2995-3000, 3002, pp 119-120; n 3213-3220, pp 126-127; n 449-454, 457-459, pp 135-136; n 537-545, pp 143-144; n 1767, 1769-1771, pp 151-152; n 1776, 1869, 1871-1872, 1874-1875, pp 159-160; n 3475-3476, 3477-3478, 3482, pp 167-168; **1917** unnumbered, pp 206-207; n 8033-8037, 8120-8124, 8252-8257, pp 207-208; n 8387-8394, 8548-8551, 8553, 8635-8640, 8743-8747, pp 215-216; n 8853-8858, 8958-8969, pp 223-224; unnumbered, p 230; n 9112-9122, pp 231-232; n 9239-9245, 9363-9369, pp 239-240; unnumbered, p 240; unnumbered, p 246; n 9443-9454, 9585-9591, pp 247-248; n 5846, 5852, pp 254-255; n 5854-5859, pp 263-264; n 5860-5865, 5976-5979, pp 271-272; n 5980-5985, pp 279-280; unnumbered, pp 287-288; n 5986-5989, p 288; **1918** n 5990-5991, p 296; n 6053-6054, 5992-5993, pp 303-304; n 6055-6058, 6189-6191, pp 309-310; n 6192-6199, pp 319-320; n 6200-6203, pp 327-328; n 6204-6208, pp 335-336; n 6209-6213, pp 343-344; n 6214, 6307-6309, p 352; n 6310-6317, pp 359-360; n 6318-6322, pp 367-368; n 6323-6325, pp 375-376; n 6326, 6466-6471, pp 383-384; **1919** n 6472-6481, pp 391-392; n 6482-6485, pp 399-400; n 6486-6493, pp 407-408; n 6494-6495, 6598-6600, pp 415-416; n 6601-6607, pp 423-424; n 6608-6616, pp 431-432; n 6617-6624, pp 439-440; n 6625-6626, pp 447-448; n 6695-6700, pp 455-456; n 6701, 6807-6815, pp 463-464; n 6816, 6921-6929, pp 471-472; n 6930-6931, 7069-7078, pp 479-480; **1920** n 7170-7177, pp 485-486; n 7246-7253, 7358-7359, pp 494-495; n 7360-7364, 7475-7476, pp 503-504; n 7477-7483, pp 511-512.
Edited and translated by J H Andersen, published in *Heraldo de la Nueva Iglesia* 1, Valencia.
UK: SOC; SPA: MAD, SAL; SWE: ROY, UPP

X 49/01/Sp 1921/1 **1921** Hyde 895/4
Los habitantes de otras tierras | (Extracto de Arcana Coelestia)
4to
title and text: n 7620-7622, 7743-7750, pp 7-8; n 8021-8026, 8028-8031, 8111-8113, pp 23-24; n 8846-8851, 8947-8956, pp 63-64; n 9104-9110, 9232-9236, pp 71-72; n 9350-9361, p 79-80.
Edited and translated by J H Andersen, published in *Heraldo de la Nueva Iglesia* 2, Valencia.
UK: SOC; SPA: MAD, SAL; SWE: ROY, UPP

X 49/01/Sp 1921/2 **1921-1922** Hyde 895/5
Las tierras en el espacio sideral. | Sus habitantes, espíritus y ángeles | (Extracto de Arcana Coelestia)
4to
title and text: **1921** n 9438-9439, p 80; n 9440-9442, 9578, p 88; n 9579-9583, 9693-9698, pp 95-96; **1922** n 9790-9794, 9967-9972, pp 103-104; n 10159-10165, 10311-10316, 10377-10378, pp 111-112; n 10379-10380, 10382-10384, 10513-10517, pp 119-120; n 10585-10589, 10708-10712, pp 127-128; n 10734-10738, pp 135-136; n 10808-10812, pp 159-160; n 10813-10814, 10833-10837, pp 167-168.
Edited and translated by J H Andersen, published in *Heraldo de la Nueva Iglesia* 2, Valencia.
UK: SOC; SPA: MAD, SAL; SWE: ROY, UPP

X 49/01/Sp 1922/1 **1922-1923** Hyde 895/–
EL INFIERNO | (Extracto de Arcana Coelestia)
4to
title and text: **1922** n 692-700, 824-825, pp 175-176; n 826-831, pp 182-184; n 814-819, pp 191-192; **1923** n 820-823, 938-940, pp 199-200; n 941-948, pp 207-208; n 949-957, pp 214-216; n 958-969, pp 223-224; n 1106-1113, 1265-1270, pp 230-232.
Edited and translated by J H Andersen, published in *Heraldo de la Nueva Iglesia* 2, Valencia.
UK: SOC; SPA: MAD, SAL; SWE: ROY, UPP

X 49/01/Sp 1923/1 **1923-1926** Hyde 895/6

El Gran Hombre, que es el Cielo | (Extracto de Arcana Coelestia)
4to
title and text: **1923** n 3624-3631, pp 239-240; n 3632-3638, pp 247-248; n 3639-3646, pp 255-256; n 3647-3648, 3741-3743, pp 263-264; n 3744-3750, pp 270-272; n 3883-3887, pp 279-280; n 3888-3894, 3894, pp 287-288; **1924** n 3895, 4039-4046, pp 295-296; n 4047-4051, pp 303-304; n 4523, 4054, 4218-4222, pp 311-312; n 4223-4226, pp 319-320; n 4227, 4318-4319, pp 327-328; n 4320-4326, pp 335-336; n 4327-4329, pp 343-344; n 4430, 4403-4406, pp 351-352; n 4407-4414, pp 359-360; n 4415, 4523-4527, pp 366-368; n <4528>, 4529-4532, pp 375-376; n 4533, 4622, pp 383-384; **1925** n 4620, 4624-4627, pp 391-392; n 4628-4633, 4791-4793, pp 399-400; n 4794-4800, pp 407-408; n 4801-4803, p 416; n 4804-4805, 4931-4935, pp 423-424; n 4936-4943, pp 431-432; n 4944-4948, p 440; n 4949-4952, 5050-5051, pp 447-448; n 5052-5058, pp 455-456; n 5059-5061, 5171-5173, pp 463-464; n 5174-5181, pp 471-472; n 5182-5189, pp 479-480; **1926** n 5377-5380, pp 487-488; n 5381-5387, pp 495-496; n 5388-5393, pp 503-504; n 5394-5396, 5552-5557, pp 511-512; n 5558-5566, pp 519-520; n 5567-5573, pp 527-528.
Edited and translated by J H Andersen, published in *Heraldo de la Nueva Iglesia* 2, Valencia.
UK: SOC; SPA: MAD, SAL; SWE: ROY, UPP

X 49/01/Sp 1926/1 **1926** Hyde 895/7

Correspondencia de las enfermedades | con el mundo espiritual | (Extracto de Arcana Coelestia)
4to
title and text: n 5711-5717, pp 551-552; n 5718, p 560; n 5719-5722, p 568; n 5724-5726, p 576.
Edited and translated by J H Andersen, published in *Heraldo de la Nueva Iglesia* 2, Valencia.
UK: SOC; SPA: MAD, SAL; SWE: ROY, UPP

X 49/01/Sp 1927/1 **1927-1928** Hyde 895/8

La Doctrina de la Caridad | (Extracto de Arcana Coelestia)
4to
title and text: **1927** n 6703-6712, 6818-6824, pp 7-8; n 6933-6938, 7080-7086, pp 15-16; n 7178-7182, 7255-7261, pp 23-24; n 7262-7263, 7366-7377, pp 31-32; n 7488-7494, 7623-7627, 7752-7756, pp 39-40; n 7757-7762, 7814-7821, pp 47-48; n 8033-8037, 8120-8124, 8252-8257, 8387-8389, pp 55-56; n 8390-8393, 8548-8553, 8635-8638, pp 63-64; n 8639-8640, 8742-8747, 8853-8858, 8958-8962, pp 71-72; n 8963-8969, p 80; n 9112-9122, 9239-9240, pp 87-88; n 9241-9245, 9363-9369, pp 95-96; **1928** n 9443-9453, 9585-9591, pp 103-104; n 9701-9709, 9796-9803, 9974-9979, pp 111-112; n 9980-9981, <9982>-9984, 10167-10171, p 120; n 10172-10175, 10318-10325, 10386-10392, 10519-10522, 10591-10595, pp 127-128; n 10596-10597, 10714-10724, 10740-10749, 10760-10766, 10773-10774, pp 134-136; n 10775-10781, 10789-10795, 10797-10800, pp 143-144; n 10801-10806, 10815-10819, pp 151-152; n 10820-10831, pp 159-160.
Edited and translated by J H Andersen, published in *Heraldo de la Nueva Iglesia* 3, Valencia.
UK: SOC; SPA: MAD, SAL; SWE: ROY, UPP

X 49/01/Sp 1934/1 **1934** Hyde 895/9

REPRESENTATIVOS | Y CORRESPONDENCIAS | <short rule> | (Extracto de ARCANA COELESTIA)
4to
title and text: n 2987-2993, pp 7-8; n 2994-2998, pp 15-16; n 2999-3002, 3213-3214, pp 23-24; n 3216-3219, p 32; n 3220-3225, pp 39-40; n 3226, 3337-3340, pp 47-48; n 3341-3347, pp 55-56; n 3348-3349, pp 63-64; n 3350-3351, 3472-3476, pp 71-72; n 3476-3479, pp 79-80; n 3480-3483, pp 87-88; n 3484-3485, p 95.

Edited and translated by J H Andersen, published in *Heraldo de la Nueva Iglesia* 4, Valencia.
UK: soc

X 49/01/Sp 1934/2 **1934-1936** Hyde 895/10
Correspondencia del sér humano | con el Gran Hombre (Maximus | Homo) que es el Cielo. | <short rule> | (Extracto de ARCANA COELESTIA)
4to
title and text: **1934** n 3624-3629, pp 95-96; **1935** n 3630-3635, pp 103-104; n 3636-3640, pp 111-112; n 3642-3648, pp 119-120; n 3747-3749, pp 143-144; n 3750, 3883, p 152; n 3884-3887, pp 159-160; n 3887-3890, pp 167-168; n 3892-3895, 4039-4041, pp 175-176; n 4042-4046, pp 183-184; n 4047-4050, pp 191-192; **1936** n 4051-4054, pp 199-200; n 4219-4222, pp 207-208; n 4223-4226, pp 215-216; n 4227, 4325, pp 223-224; n 4326-4328, pp 231-232; n 4329-4330, pp 239-240.
Edited and translated by J H Andersen, published in *Heraldo de la Nueva Iglesia* 4, Valencia.
UK: soc

X 49/01/ Sp 1935/1 **1935** Hyde 895/–
Angeles y espiritus con el hombre | (De ARCANA COELESTIA)
4to
title and text: n 5847-5854, 5979, 5992, pp 127-128; n 3741-3747, pp 135-136.
Edited and translated by J H Andersen, published in *Heraldo de la Nueva Iglesia* 4, Valencia.
UK: soc

X 49/01 Sp 1936/1 **1936** Hyde 895/–
¿Por qué plugo al Señor nacer | en esta tierra y no enotra? | (Extracto de ARCANA COELESTIA)
4to
title and text: n 9350-9353, 9355-9360, pp 206-207.
Edited and translated by J H Andersen, published in *Heraldo de la Nueva Iglesia* 4, Valencia.
UK: soc

X 49/01/Sp 1984/1 **1984** Hyde —
<< <short rule> | EXTRACTO DE ARCANA COELESTIA | <short rule> >>
verso: <<«El esperitu es el que da vida; la carne | nada aproveca; las palabras que yo os e | ablado son espiritu y son vida». | *(Juan, VI, 6, 3.)* | «La letra mata, mas et espiritu vivifica». | *(2 Corintios, III, 6.)*>>
8vo
title leaf, pp 1-2; text: *Extracto de Arcana Coelestia*, pp 5-44.
Reprint of X Sp 1914/1, published by Ediciones del Peregrino, Buenos Aires.
Copy not seen. Reported in an article by J A Antón Pacheco, published in *The Annual Journal of the New Church Historical Society* Chester, 2006 p 69.

SWEDISH

Translators:

Sw 1 Johan Tybeck
Sw 2 Johan Adolf Sevén
Sw 3 Carl Johan Nilsson Manby
Sw 4 Eric Hjerpe
Sw 5 Ulf Fornander

49/01/Sw 1/1 **1817-1821** Hyde 842

<<ARCANA CŒLESTIA | D. Ä | HIMMELSKA LÖNLIGHETER, | SOM FINNAS I | **Den Heliga Skrift** | **eller HErrans Ord,** | UPPTÄCKTE. | <short rule> | *I. DELEN.* | *I. Stycket.* | <rule> | STOCKHOLM, | Tryckt Hos CARL DELEEN, 1821.>>
2nd title: ARCANA CŒLESTIA | D. Ä. | HIMMELSKA LÖNLIGHETER, | SOM FINNAS I | **Den Heliga Skrift** | **eller HErrans Ord,** | UPPTÄCKTE. | <short rule> | FÖRSTA MOSE-BOK. | <short rule> | JEMTE DET UNDRANSVÄRDA, | *som blifvit sedt* | I ANDARNES VERLD, OCH I ENGLARNES HIMMEL. | <short rule> | *I. DELEN.* | I. *Stycket.* | <short rule> | *ÖFVERSÄTTNING* | från Latinska Urskriften, som utkom 1749. | <rule> | STOCKHOLM, | Tryckt Hos CARL DELEEN, 1817.
verso: MATTH. 6: 33. | *Söker först Guds Rike, och dess Rätt- | färdighet, så skall allt falla eder till.*
12mo
title leaves, 4 pp; text of Genesis 1-9 and n 1-1113, pp 3-668.
Translated by J Tybeck, published by the Society *Pro Fide et Charitate*, Stockholm. The volume was issued in 9 sections between 1817 and 1821, the first of which bears the title described above as the 2nd title page. Copy of parts 2-8 not seen; description deduced from Sw 1/2 and Hyde 842. The copy in SWE: ROY has a 17-page MS index to the Bible passages quoted and cited.
UK: SOC <part 1>; SWE: ROY, GEN <parts 1 & 2>, GSB <parts 3 & 4>, UPP

49/01/Sw 1/2 **1822** Hyde 843

ARCANA CŒLESTIA | D. Ä | HIMMELSKA LÖNLIGHETER, | SOM FINNAS I | **Den Heliga Skrift** | **eller** | **HErrans Ord,** | UPTÄCKTE. | <short rule> | FÖRSTA MOSE-BOK. | <short rule> | JEMTE DET UNDRANSVÄRDA, | *som blifvit sedt* | I ANDARNES VERLD, OCH I ENGLARNES HIMMEL. | <short rule> | *II DELEN.* | *I. Stycket.* | <short rule> | ÖFVERSÄTTNING | från Latinska Urskriften, som utkom 1749. | <rule> | STOCKHOLM, | Tryckt Hos CARL DELEEN, 1822.
8vo
title leaf, 2 pp; text of Genesis 10-17 and n 1114-2134, pp 3-666; Rättelser <Corrections>, p 666.
Translated by J Tybeck. The volume was first issued in 8 sections between 1822 and 1826. No title page to the whole volume has been found; the one described above is the title page of the first section of this volume.
UK: SOC <parts 3 to 8>; SWE: ROY, GEN <part 2>, UPP; USA: FOU

49/01/Sw 1/3 **1827-1841, 1842** Hyde 844

ARCANA CŒLESTIA | D. Ä. | HIMMELSKA LÖNLIGHETER, | SOM FINNAS I | **Den Heliga Skrift** | **eller** | **HErrans Ord,** | UPTÄCKTE. | <short rule> | JEMTE DET UNDRANSVÄRDA, | *som blifvit sedt* | I ANDARNES VERLD, OCH I ENGLARNES HIMMEL. | <short rule> | *III. DELEN.* | <rule> | STOCKHOLM, 1842. | Tryckt Hos CARL DELEEN, R. W. O.
8vo
title leaf, 2 pp; Företal <Foreword>, 2 pp; text of Genesis 18-23 and n 2135-3003, pp 5-670.
Translated by J Tybeck, issued in 6 sections from 1827 to 1841 and then in one volume in 1842.
UK: SOC <parts 1 to 3>; SWE: ROY, GEN <part 3>; USA: FOU

49/01/Sw 1/4 **1838** Hyde 845

ARCANA CŒLESTIA | DET ÄR | HIMMELSKA LÖNNLIGHETER, | SOM FINNAS I | **Den Heliga Skrift** | **eller HErrans Ord,** | UPP TÄCKTE. | <short rule> | FÖRSTA MOSE-BOK. | <short rule> | JEMTE DET UNDRANSVÄRDA, | *som blifvit sedt* | I ANDARNES VERLD, OCH I ENGLARNES HIMMEL. | <short rule> | *I. DELEN.* | *I. Stycket.* | <short rule> | Andra Upplagan. | *ÖFVERSÄTTNING* | från Latinska Urskriften, som utkom 1749. | <rule> | STOCKHOLM, | Tryckt Hos CARL DELEEN, 1838.
verso: MATTH. 6:33. | *Söker först efter Guds Rike och Hans | rättfärdighet, och detta skall til falla eder.*

8vo
title leaf, 2 pp; text of Genesis 1 and n 1-66, pp 3-46.
Reprinted from the 1st section of Sw 1/1 = Hyde 842.
UK: soc; SWE: gsb, roy; USA: fou

49/01/Sw 2/1 **1859-1860** Hyde 846, 1615

ARCANA COELESTIA. | d. ä. | Himmelska Lönnligheter, | som finnas i | Den Heliga Skrift | eller | Herrans Ord, | Uptackte. | <short rule> | Jemte det undranswärda | som blifwit sedt | i andarnes werld, och i englarnes himmel. | <short rule> | Fjerde Delen. | <short rule> | WEXJÖ, | i C. G. Södergrens Bokhandel.
8vo
title leaf, 2 pp; text of Genesis 24:1 to 25:4 and n 3004-3242, pp 1-142.
Translated by J A Sevén. Published in bi-monthly parts in *Den Nye Budbäraren* Wexjö, June 1859 to March 1860. cp X 61/04/Sw 1859/1 = Hyde 1615.
UK: soc; SWE: roy, upp

49/01/Sw 2/2 **1860-1863** Hyde 846

ARCANA CAELESTIA. | d. ä. | Himmelska Lönnligheter, | som finnas i | Den Heliga Skrift | eller | Herrans Ord, | Uptackte. | <short rule> | Jemte det undranswärda | som blifwit sedt | i andarnes werld, och i englarnes himmel. | <short rule> | Fjerde Delen. | <short rule> | WEXJÖ, | i C. G. Södergrens Bokhandel.
imprint: Wexjö, | tryckt hos C. G. Södergren, 1863.
8vo
title leaf, 2 pp; text of Genesis 25:5 to 27 and n 3243-3649, pp 143-408; imprint, p 408.
Translated by J A Sevén. Published in parts.
UK: soc; SWE: roy, gen, upp

49/01/Sw 2/3 **1861** Hyde 847

ARCANA COELESTIA... | <short rule> | HIMMELSKA HEMLIGHETER, | SOM INNEHÅLLAS I | DEN HELIGA SKRIFT | ELLER | HERRANS ORD, | OCH NU BLIFVIT UPPTÄCKTA: | HÄR DE SOM FINNAS I | FÖRSTA MOSE BOK, | JEMTE DET UNDERBARA, | SOM BLIFVIT SEDT | I ANDARNAS VERLD OCH I ÄNGLARNAS HIMMEL. | <short rule> | ETT VERK AF | EMANUEL SWEDENBORG. | <short rule> | FÖRSTA BANDETS | FÖRRA AFDELNING | <short rule> | ÖFVERSÄTTNING FRÅN LATINSKA URSKRIFTEN. | <short rule> | CHRISTIANSTAD. | TRYCKT HOS HERMAN LANG, 1861.
verso: *Matth. 6: 33.* | *Söker först efter Guds Rike och Hans rättfärdighet,* | *och allt (detta) skall tillfalla eder.*
8vo
title leaf, 2 pp; Den engelska öfversättarens företal <Foreword to the English version>, pp iii-xix; Contents, pp 1-2; text of Genesis 1-3 and n 1-322 part, pp 3-144.
Translated by J A Sevén. The preface was translated from Ge 1/1 = Hyde 811. 1,000 copies were printed.
UK: soc; SWE: gen, gsb, upp; USA: anc

49/01/Sw 2/4 **1863** Hyde 847

ARCANA COELESTIA... | <short rule> | HIMMELSKA HEMLIGHETER, | SOM INNEHÅLLAS I | DEN HELIGA SKRIFT | ELLER | HERRANS ORD, | OCH NU BLIFVIT UPPTÄCKTA: | HÄR DE SOM FINNAS I | FÖRSTA MOSE BOK, | JEMTE DET UNDERBARA, | SOM BLIFVIT SEDT | I ANDARNAS VERLD OCH I ÄNGLARNAS HIMMEL. | <short rule> | ETT VERK AF | EMANUEL SWEDENBORG. | <short rule> | FÖRSTA BANDET. | <short rule> | ÖFVERSÄTTNING FRÅN LATINSKA URSKRIFTEN. |

<short rule> | CHRISTIANSTAD. | CENTERWALLSKA BOKHANDELN. | (HERMAN LANG).
verso: *Matth. 6: 33.* | *Söker först efter Guds Rike och Hans rättfärdighet,* | *och allt (detta) skall tillfalla eder.*
imprint: CHRISTIANSTAD. | TRYCKT HOS HERMAN LANG, 1863.
8vo
title leaf, 2 pp; text of Genesis 4-7 and n 322 part-823, pp 145-409; Tryckfel <Misprints>, p 409; imprint, p 410.
Translated by J A Sevén. Published by the Society for Publishing the Theological Works of Emanuel Swedenborg in Swedish, Christianstad. 1,000 copies were printed.
In the copy in UK: soc the title leaf is bound at the end of the volume.
UK: soc; SWE: roy, gsb, upp; USA: anc

49/01/Sw 2/5 **1864** Hyde 848
ARCANA COELESTIA... | <short rule> | HIMMELSKA HEMLIGHETER, | SOM INNEHÅLLAS I | DEN HELIGA SKRIFT | ELLER | HERRANS ORD, | OCH NU BLIFVIT UPPTÄCKTA: | HÄR DE SOM FINNAS I | FÖRSTA MOSE BOK, | JEMTE DET UNDERBARA, | SOM BLIFVIT SEDT | I ANDARNAS VERLD OCH I ÄNGLARNAS HIMMEL. | <short rule> | ETT VERK AF | EMANUEL SWEDENBORG. | <short rule> | ANDRA BANDET. | <short rule> | ÖFVERSÄTTNING FRÅN LATINSKA URSKRIFTEN. | <short rule> | CHRISTIANSTAD. | CENTERWALLSKA BOKHANDELN. | (HERMAN LANG.)
verso: *Matth. 6: 33.* | *Söker först efter Guds Rike och Hans rättfärdighet,* | *och allt (detta) skall tillfalla eder.* | CHRISTIANSTAD. | TRYCKT HOS HERMAN LANG, 1864.
8vo
title leaf, 2 pp; text of Genesis 8-11 and n 824-1382, pp 3-372; Tryckfel <Misprints>, p 372.
Translated by J A Sevén. Published by the Society for Publishing the Theological Works of Emanuel Swedenborg in Swedish, Christianstad. 1,000 copies were printed.
UK: soc; SWE: roy, gen, gsb, upp; USA: anc

49/01/Sw 2/6 **1866** Hyde 849
ARCANA COELESTIA... | <short rule> | HIMMELSKA HEMLIGHETER, | SOM INNEHÅLLAS I | DEN HELIGA SKRIFT | ELLER | HERRANS ORD, | OCH NU BLIFVIT UPPTÄCKTA: | HÄR DE SOM FINNAS I | FÖRSTA MOSE BOK, | JEMTE DET UNDERBARA, | SOM BLIFVIT SEDT | I ANDARNAS VERLD OCH I ÄNGLARNAS HIMMEL. | <short rule> | ETT VERK AF | EMANUEL SWEDENBORG. | <short rule> | TREDJE BANDET. | <short rule> | ÖFVERSÄTTNING FRÅN LATINSKA URSKRIFTEN. | <short rule> | CHRISTIANSTAD. | CENTERWALLSKA BOKHANDELN | (HERMAN LANG.)
verso: *Matth. 6: 33.* | *Söker först efter Guds Rike och Hans rättfärdighet,* | *och allt (detta) skall tillfalla eder.* | CHRISTIANSTAD. | TRYCKT HOS HERMAN LANG, 1866.
8vo
title leaf, 2 pp; text of Genesis 12-16 and n 1383-1885, pp 1-315; Anmärckningar till <Notes on> n 1713, 3 pp.
Translated by J A Sevén. Published by the Society for Publishing the Theological Works of Emanuel Swedenborg in Swedish, Christianstad. 1,000 copies were printed.
UK: soc, bl; SWE: roy, gen, gsb, upp; USA: anc

49/01/Sw 2/7 **1867** Hyde 850
ARCANA COELESTIA... | <short rule> | HIMMELSKA HEMLIGHETER, | SOM INNEHÅLLAS I | DEN HELIGA SKRIFT | ELLER | HERRANS ORD, | OCH NU BLIFVIT UPPTÄCKTA: | HÄR DE SOM FINNAS I | FÖRSTA MOSE BOK, | JEMTE DET UNDERBARA, | SOM BLIFVIT SEDT | I ANDARNAS VERLD OCH I ÄNGLARNAS HIMMEL. | <short rule> | ETT VERK AF | EMANUEL SWEDENBORG. | <short rule> | FJERDE BANDET. | <short rule> | ÖFVERSÄTTNING FRÅN LATINSKA URSKRIFTEN. | <short rule> | CHRISTIANSTAD. | CENTERWALLSKA BOKHANDELN. | (HERMAN LANG.)

verso: *Matth. 6: 33.* | *Söker först efter Guds Rike och Hans rättfärdighet,* | *och allt (detta) skall tillfalla eder.* | CHRISTIANSTAD. | TRYCKT HOS HERMAN LANG, 1867.
8vo
title leaf, 2 pp; text of Swedenborg's preface, Genesis 17-19, and n 1886-2494, pp 1-451.
Translated by J A Sevén. Published by the Society for Publishing the Theological Works of Emanuel Swedenborg in Swedish, Christianstad. 1,000 copies were printed.
UK: SOC, BL; SWE: ROY, GEN, GSB, UPP; USA: ANC

49/01/Sw 2/8 — 1868 — Hyde 851

ARCANA COELESTIA... | <short rule> | HIMMELSKA HEMLIGHETER, | SOM INNEHÅLLAS I | DEN HELIGA SKRIFT | ELLER | HERRANS ORD, | OCH NU BLIFVIT UPPTÄCKTA: | HÄR DE SOM FINNAS I | FÖRSTA MOSE BOK, | JEMTE DET UNDERBARA, | SOM BLIFVIT SEDT | I ANDARNAS VERLD OCH I ÄNGLARNAS HIMMEL. | <short rule> | ETT VERK AF | EMANUEL SWEDENBORG. | <short rule> | FEMTE BANDET. | <short rule> | ÖFVERSÄTTNING FRÅN LATINSKA URSKRIFTEN. | <short rule> | CHRISTIANSTAD. | CENTERWALLSKA BOKHANDELN. | (HERMAN LANG.)
verso: *Matth. 6: 33.* | *Söker först efter Guds Rike och Hans rättfärdighet,* | *och allt (della) skall tillfalla eder.* | CHRISTIANSTAD. | TRYCKT HOS HERMAN LANG, 1868.
8vo
title leaf, 2 pp; text of Genesis 20-23 and n 2495-3003, pp 1-421.
Translated by J A Sevén. Published by the Society for Publishing the Theological Works of Emanuel Swedenborg in Swedish, Christianstad. 1,000 copies were printed.
UK: SOC, BL; SWE: GEN, GSB, UPP; USA: ANC

49/01/Sw 2/9 — 1869 — Hyde 852

ARCANA COELESTIA... | <short rule> | HIMMELSKA HEMLIGHETER, | SOM INNEHÅLLAS I | DEN HELIGA SKRIFT | ELLER | HERRANS ORD, | OCH NU BLIFVIT UPPTÄCKTA: | HÄR DE SOM FINNAS I | FÖRSTA MOSE BOK, | JEMTE DET UNDERBARA, | SOM BLIFVIT SEDT | I ANDARNAS VERLD OCH I ÄNGLARNAS HIMMEL. | <short rule> | ETT VERK AF | EMANUEL SWEDENBORG. | <short rule> | SJETTE BANDET. | <short rule> | ÖFVERSÄTTNING FRÅN LATINSKA URSKRIFTEN. | <short rule> | CHRISTIANSTAD. | CENTERWALLSKA BOKHANDELN. | (HERMAN LANG.)
verso: *Matth. 6: 33.* | *Söker först efter Guds Rike och Hans rättfärdighet,* | *och allt (detta) skall tillfalle eder.* | CHRISTIANSTAD. | TRYCKT HOS HERMAN LANG, 1869.
8vo
title leaf, 2 pp; text of Genesis 24-26 and n 3004-3485, pp 1-396.
Reprinted from Sw 2/1, 2 = Hyde 846. Published by the Society for Publishing the Theological Works of Emanuel Swedenborg in Swedish, Christianstad. 1,000 copies were printed.
UK: SOC, BL; SWE: ROY, GEN, GSB, UPP; USA: ANC

49/01/Sw 2/10 — 1873 — Hyde 853

ARCANA COELESTIA... | <short rule> | HIMMELSKA HEMLIGHETER, | SOM INNEHÅLLAS I | DEN HELIGA SKRIFT | ELLER | HERRANS ORD, | OCH NU BLIFVIT UPPTÄCKTA: | HÄR DE SOM FINNAS I | FÖRSTA MOSE BOK, | JEMTE DET UNDERBARA, | SOM BLIFVIT SEDT | I ANDARNAS VERLD OCH I ÄNGLARNAS HIMMEL. | <short rule> | ETT VERK AF | EMANUEL SWEDENBORG. | <short rule> | SJUNDE BANDET. | <short rule> | ÖFVERSÄTTNING FRÅN LATINSKA URSKRIFTEN. | <short rule> | CHRISTIANSTAD. | HJALMAR MÖLLER. | DISTRIBUENT.
verso: *Matth. 6: 33.* | *Söker först efter Guds Rike och Hans rättfärdighet,* | *och allt (detta) skall tillfalle eder.* | CHRISTIANSTAD. | LANGSKA BOKTRYCKERIE, 1873.
8vo
title leaf, 2 pp; text of Genesis 27-30 and n 3486-4055, pp 1-527.

Translated by J A Sevén. Published by the Society for Publishing the Theological Works of Emanuel Swedenborg in Swedish, Christianstad. 1,000 copies were printed.
UK: SOC, BL; SWE: GEN, GSB, UPP; USA: ANC

49/01/Sw 3/1 **1882-1896** Hyde 854

ARCANA COELESTIA... | <short rule> | HIMMELSKA HEMLIGHETER, | SOM INNEHÅLLAS I | DEN HELIGA SKRIFT | ELLER | HERRENS ORD, | OCH NU BLIFVIT UPPTÄCKTA: | HÄR DE SOM FINNAS I | FÖRSTA MOSE BOK, | JEMTE DET UNDERBARA, | SOM BLIFVIT SEDT | I ANDARNAS VERLD OCH I ÄNGLARNAS HIMMEL. | FJERDE DELENS FÖRSTA BAND. | <short rule> | ETT VERK AF | EMANUEL SWEDENBORG. | <short rule> | FRÅN LATINSKA URSKRIFTEN ÖFVERSATT | AF | C. J. N. MANBY. | <short rule> | ÅTTONDE BANDET AF HELA VERKET. | <type orn 2 x 18 mm> | STOCKHOLM. | SWEDENBORGS-SAMFUNDETS FÖRLAG.
verso: *Matth. 6: 33.* | *Söker först efter Guds Rike och Hans rättfärdighet* | *och allt (detta) skall tillfalle eder.* | [Fjerde delen af latinska urskriften till verket "*Himmelska Hem-* | *ligheter i 1:sta Moses bok*" utkom år 1752.] | STOCKHOLM, | ISAAC MARCUS' BOKTRYCKERI-AKTIEBOLAG, 1882.
8vo
title leaf, 2 pp; text of Genesis 31-35 and n 4056-4634, pp 3-490; Rättelser <Corrections>, 1 p; catalogue, 1 p.
Printed in 6 parts, 1882-1896.
UK: SOC <1st of these 6 parts>; SWE: GEN, GSB, UPP; USA: ANC

49/01/Sw 3/2 **1898** Hyde 855

ARCANA COELESTIA... | <short rule> | HIMMELSKA HEMLIGHETER, | SOM INNEHÅLLAS I | DEN HELIGA SKRIFT | ELLER | HERRANS ORD, | OCH NU BLIFVIT UPPTÄCKTA: | HÄR DE SOM FINNAS I | FÖRSTA MOSE BOK, | JEMTE DET UNDERBARA, | SOM BLIFVIT SEDT | I ANDARNAS VERLD OCH I ÄNGLARNAS HIMMEL. | <short rule> | FJERDE ORIGINALDELENS ANDRA BAND. | ETT VERK AF | EMANUEL SWEDENBORG. | <short rule> | FRÅN LATINSKA URSKRIFTEN ÖFVERSATT | AF | C. J. N. MANBY, | PASTOR INOM NYA KYRKANS SVENSKA FÖRSAMLING. | <short rule> | NIONDE BANDET AF HELA VERKET. | <type orn 2 x 18 mm> | STOCKHOLM | NYKYRKLIGA BOKFÖRLAGET | 1898.
verso: *Matth. 6: 33.* | *Söker först efter Guds Rike och Hans rättfärdighet* | *och allt (detta) skall tillfalle eder.* | [Fjerde delen af latinska urskriften till verket »*Himmelska Hem-* | *ligheter i 1:sta Moses bok*» utkom år 1752.] | STOCKHOLM | K. L. BECKMANS BOKTRYCKERI | 1898.
8vo
title leaf, 2 pp; text of Genesis 36-40 and n 4635-5190, pp 1-464.
UK: SOC; SWE: GEN, GSB; USA: ANC

49/01/Sw 3/3 **1899** Hyde 856

ARCANA COELESTIA... | <short rule> | HIMMELSKA HEMLIGHETER, | SOM INNEHÅLLAS I | DEN HELIGA SKRIFT | ELLER | HERRANS ORD, | OCH NU BLIFVIT UPPTÄCKTA: | HÄR DE SOM FINNAS I | FÖRSTA MOSE BOK, | JEMTE DET UNDERBARA, | SOM BLIFVIT SEDT | I ANDARNAS VERLD OCH I ÄNGLARNAS HIMMEL. | <short rule> | FEMTE ORIGINALDELENS FÖRSTA BAND. | <short rule> | ETT VERK AF | EMANUEL SWEDENBORG. | <short rule> | FRÅN LATINSKA URSKRIFTEN ÖFVERSATT | AF | C. J. N. MANBY, | PASTOR INOM NYA KYRKANS SVENSKA FÖRSAMLING. | <short rule> | TIONDE BANDET AF HELA VERKET. | <type orn 2 x 18 mm> | STOCKHOLM, | NYKYRKLIGA BOKFÖRLAGET, | 1899.
verso: *Matth. 6: 33.* | *Söker först efter Guds Rike och Hans rättfärdighet,* | *och allt (detta) skall tillfalle eder.* | [Femte delen af latinska urskriften till verket »*Himmelska Hem-* | *ligheter i 1:sta Moses bok*» utkom år 1753.] | STOCKHOLM, | K. L. BECKMANS BOKTRYCKERI, | 1899.

8vo
title leaf, 2 pp; text of Genesis 41-44 and n 5191-5866, pp 1-421; Rättelser <Corrections>, p 421; catalogue, 1 p.
UK: SOC; SWE: GEN, GSB; USA: ANC

49/01/Sw 3/4 1900 Hyde 857

ARCANA COELESTIA... | <short rule> | HIMMELSKA HEMLIGHETER, | SOM INNEHÅLLAS I | DEN HELIGA SKRIFT | ELLER | HERRENS ORD, | OCH NU BLIFVIT UPPTÄCKTA: | HÄR DE SOM FINNAS I | FÖRSTA MOSE BOK, | JEMTE DET UNDERBARA, | SOM BLIFVIT SEDT | I ANDARNAS VERLD OCH I ÄNGLARNAS HIMMEL. | <short rule> | FEMTE ORIGINALDELENS ANDRA BAND. | <short rule> | ETT VERK AF | EMANUEL SWEDENBORG. | <short rule> | FRÅN LATINSKA URSKRIFTEN ÖFVERSATT | AF | C. J. N. MANBY, | PASTOR I NYA KYRKANS SVENSKA FÖRSAMLING. | <short rule> | ELFTE BANDET AF HELA VERKET. | <short orn rule> | STOCKHOLM, | NYKYRKLIGA BOKFÖRLAGET, | 1900.
verso: *Matt. 6: 33.* | *Söken först efter Guds rike och Hans rättfärdighet,* | *och allt (detta) skall tillfalla eder.* | [Femte delen af latinska urskriften till verket »*Himmelska Hem-* | *ligheter i 1:sta Mose bok*» utkom år 1753.] | STOCKHOLM, | K. L. BECKMANS BOKTRYCKERI, | 1900.
8vo
title leaf, 2 pp; text of Genesis 45-50 and n 5867-6626, pp 1-473; catalogue, 1 p.
UK: SOC; SWE: GEN, GSB; USA: ANC

49/01/Sw 3/5 1901 Hyde 858

ARCANA COELESTIA... | <short rule> | HIMMELSKA HEMLIGHETER, | SOM INNEHÅLLAS I | DEN HELIGA SKRIFT | ELLER | HERRENS ORD, | OCH NU BLIFVIT UPPTÄCKTA: | HÄR DE SOM FINNAS I | ANDRA MOSE BOK, | JEMTE DET UNDERBARA, | SOM BLIFVIT SEDT | I ANDARNAS VERLD OCH I ÄNGLARNAS HIMMEL. | <short rule> | FÖRSTA (SJETTE) ORIGINALDELENS FÖRSTA BAND. | <short rule> | ETT VERK AF | EMANUEL SWEDENBORG. | <short rule> | FRÅN LATINSKA URSKRIFTEN ÖFVERSATT | AF | C. J. N. MANBY, | PASTOR I NYA KYRKANS SVENSKA FÖRSAMLING. | <short rule> | TOLFTE BANDET AF HELA VERKET. | <short orn rule> | STOCKHOLM, | NYKYRKLIGA BOKFÖRLAGET, | 1901.
verso: [Första delen af latinska urskriften till verket »*Himmelska Hem-* | *ligheter i 2:dra Mose bok*» utkom år 1753.] | STOCKHOLM. | K. L. BECKMANS BOKTRYCKERI, | 1901.
8vo
title leaf, 2 pp; text of Exodus 1-8 and n 6627-7487, pp 1-478; Rättelser <Corrections>, p 478.
UK: SOC; SWE: GSB, UPP; USA: ANC

49/01/Sw 3/6 1902 Hyde 859

ARCANA COELESTIA... | <short rule> | HIMMELSKA HEMLIGHETER, | SOM INNEHÅLLAS I | DEN HELIGA SKRIFT | ELLER | HERRENS ORD, | OCH NU BLIFVIT UPPTÄCKTA: | HÄR DE SOM FINNAS I | ANDRA MOSE BOK, | JEMTE DET UNDERBARA, | SOM BLIFVIT SEDT | I ANDARNAS VERLD OCH I ÄNGLARNAS HIMMEL. | <short rule> | FÖRSTA (SJETTE) ORIGINALDELENS ANDRA BAND. | <short rule> | ETT VERK AF | EMANUEL SWEDENBORG. | <short rule> | FRÅN LATINSKA URSKRIFTEN ÖFVERSATT | AF | C. J. N. MANBY, | PASTOR I NYA KYRKANS SVENSKA FÖRSAMLING. | <short rule> | TRETTONDE BANDET AF HELA VERKET. | <short orn rule> | STOCKHOLM, | NYKYRKLIGA BOKFÖRLAGET, | 1902.
verso: [Första delen af latinska urskriften till verket »*Himmelska Hem-* | *ligheter i 2:dra Mose bok*» utkom år 1753.] | STOCKHOLM, | K. L. BECKMANS BOKTRYCKERI, | 1902.
8vo
title leaf, 2 pp; text of Exodus 9-15 and n 7488-8386, pp 1-484; Rättelser <Corrections>, p 484.
UK: SOC; SWE: GEN, GSB, UPP; USA: ANC

49/01/Sw 3/7 **1905** Hyde 859/1

ARCANA COELESTIA... | <short rule> | HIMMELSKA HEMLIGHETER, | SOM INNEHÅLLAS I | DEN HELIGA SKRIFT | ELLER | HERRENS ORD, | OCH NU BLIFVIT UPPTÄCKTA: | HÄR DE SOM FINNAS I | ANDRA MOSE BOK, | JEMTE DET UNDERBARA, | SOM BLIFVIT SEDT | I ANDARNAS VERLD OCH I ÄNGLARNAS HIMMEL. | <short rule> | ANDRA (SJUNDE) ORIGINALDELENS FÖRSTA BAND. | <short rule> | ETT VERK AF | EMANUEL SWEDENBORG. | <short rule> | FRÅN LATINSKA URSKRIFTEN ÖFVERSATT | AF | C. J. N. MANBY, | PASTOR I NYA KYRKANS SVENSKA FÖRSAMLING. | <short rule> | FJORTONDE BANDET AF HELA VERKET. | <short orn rule> | STOCKHOLM, | NYKYRKLIGA BOKFÖRLAGET. | 1905.

verso: [Andra delen af latinska urskriften till verket »*Himmelska Hem-* | *ligheter i 2:dra Mose bok*» utkom år 1754.] | STOCKHOLM, | K. L. BOSTRÖMS BOKTRYCKERI, | 1905.

8vo

title leaf, 2 pp; text of Exodus 16-21 and n 8387-9111, pp 1-491.

UK: SOC; SWE: GEN, GSB, UPP

49/01/Sw 3/8 **1907** Hyde 859/2

ARCANA COELESTIA... | <short rule> | HIMMELSKA HEMLIGHETER, | SOM INNEHÅLLAS I | DEN HELIGA SKRIFT | ELLER | HERRENS ORD, | OCH NU BLIFVIT UPPTÄCKTA: | HÄR DE SOM FINNAS I | ANDRA MOSE BOK, | JEMTE DET UNDERBARA, | SOM BLIFVIT SEDT | I ANDARNAS VERLD OCH I ÄNGLARNAS HIMMEL. | <short rule> | ANDRA (SJUNDE) ORIGINALDELENS ANDRA BAND. | <short rule> | ETT VERK AF | EMANUEL SWEDENBORG. | <short rule> | FRÅN LATINSKA URSKRIFTEN ÖFVERSATT | AF | C. J. N. MANBY, | PASTOR I NYA KYRKANS SVENSKA FÖRSAMLING. | <short rule> | FEMTONDE BANDET AF HELA VERKET. | <short orn rule> | STOCKHOLM, | NYKYRKLIGA BOKFÖRLAGET. | 1907.

verso: [Andra delen af latinska urskriften till verket »*Himmelska Hem-* | *ligheter i 2:dra Mose bok*» utkom år 1754.] | STOCKHOLM, | K. L. BOSTRÖMS BOKTRYCKERI, | 1907.

half title: ARCANA COELESTIA. | <short rule> | FEMTONDE BANDET. | <short rule>

8vo

half title and title leaves, 4 pp; Öfversättarens förord <Translator's foreword>, pp v-viii; text of Exodus 22-24 and n 9112-9442, pp 1-390; Nykyrklig Litteratur <advertisement>, p 391.

UK: SOC; SWE: GEN, GSB

49/01/Sw 3/9 **1909** Hyde 859/3

ARCANA COELESTIA... | <short rule> | HIMMELSKA HEMLIGHETER, | SOM INNEHÅLLAS I | DEN HELIGA SKRIFT | ELLER | HERRENS ORD, | OCH NU BLIFVIT UPPTÄCKTA: | HÄR DE SOM FINNAS I | ANDRA MOSE BOK, | JÄMTE DET UNDERBARA, | SOM BLIFVIT SEDT | I ANDARNAS VÄRLD OCH I ÄNGLARNAS HIMMEL. | <short rule> | TREDJE (ÅTTONDE) ORIGINALDELENS FÖRSTA BAND. | <short rule> | ETT VERK AF | EMANUEL SWEDENBORG. | <short rule> | FRÅN LATINSKA URSKRIFTEN ÖFVERSATT | AF | C. J. N. MANBY | PASTOR I NYA KYRKANS SVENSKA FÖRSAMLING. | <short rule> | SEXTONDE BANDET AF HELA VERKET. | <short orn rule> | STOCKHOLM, | NYKYRKLIGA BOKFÖRLAGET. | 1909.

verso: [Tredje delen af latinska urskriften till verket »*Himmelska Hem-* | *ligheter i 2:dra Mose bok*» utkom år 1756.] | <short rule> | Rättelser: | Sid. 65 rad. 20 *står:* (i följd) af; *läs:* (i följd af) | » 163 » 4 » hänemot; » hän emot. | <short rule> | STOCKHOLM | K. L. BOSTRÖMS BOKTRYCKERI | 1909.

8vo

title leaf, 2 pp; text of Exodus 25-28 and n 9443-9973, pp 1-423.

UK: SOC; SWE: ROY, GEN, GSB

49/01/Sw 3/10 1912 Hyde 859/4

ARCANA COELESTIA... | <short rule> | HIMMELSKA HEMLIGHETER, | SOM INNEHÅLLAS I | DEN HELIGA SKRIFT | ELLER | HERRENS ORD, | OCH NU BLIFVIT UPPTÄCKTA: | HÄR DE SOM FINNAS I | ANDRA MOSE BOK, | JÄMTE DET UNDERBARA, | SOM BLIFVIT SEDT | I ANDARNAS VÄRLD OCH I ÄNGLARNAS HIMMEL. | <short rule> | TREDJE (ÅTTONDE) ORIGINALDELENS ANDRA BAND. | <short rule> | ETT VERK AF | EMANUEL SWEDENBORG. | <short rule> | FRÅN LATINSKA URSKRIFTEN ÖFVERSATT | AF | C. J. N. MANBY | PASTOR I NYA KYRKANS SVENSKA FÖRSAMLING. | <short rule> | SJUTTONDE BANDET AF HELA VERKET. | <short orn rule> | STOCKHOLM, | NYKYRKLIGA BOKFÖRLAGET. | 1912.
verso: [Tredje delen af latinska urskriften till verket »*Himmelska Hem-* | *ligheter i 2:dra Mose bok*» utkom i London år 1756.] | <short rule> | Rättelser: | Sid. 448 rad. 12 *står:* dem *läs:* dem, | » 730 » 9 » [till] » (till) | <short rule> | STOCKHOLM | K. L. BOSTRÖMS BOKTRYCKERI | 1912.
8vo
title leaf, 2 pp; text of Exodus 29-40 and n 9974-10837, pp 1-760.
UK: SOC; SWE: GEN, GSB

49/01/Sw 3/11 1919 Hyde 859/5

ARCANA COELESTIA... | <short rule> | HIMMELSKA HEMLIGHETER, | SOM INNEHÅLLAS I | DEN HELIGA SKRIFT | ELLER | HERRENS ORD, | OCH NU BLIFVIT UPPTÄCKTA: | HÄR DE SOM FINNAS I | FÖRSTA MOSE BOK, | JÄMTE DET UNDERBARA, | SOM BLIFVIT SEDT | I ANDARNAS VÄRLD OCH I ÄNGLARNAS HIMMEL. | <short rule> | ETT VERK AF | EMANUEL SWEDENBORG. | <short rule> | FÖRSTA BANDETS | FÖRRA AFDELNING (SID. 1—144). | <short rule> | ÖFVERSÄTTNING FRÅN LATINSKA URSKRIFTEN | [AF D:R J. A. SEVÉN]. | 2:DRA UPPLAGAN, NÅGOT REVIDERAD AF | C. J. N. MANBY | PASTOR I NYA KYRKANS SVENSKA FÖRSAMLING. | <short rule> | STOCKHOLM, | NYKYRKLIGA BOKFÖRLAGET, | 1919.
verso: *Matt. 6: 33.* | *Söken först efter Guds Rike och Hans rättfärdighet,* | *och allt [detta] skall tillfalla eder.* | <short rule> | [*Anm.* För att lättare kunna finna de olika citerade | Bibelställena – då stundom paragraferna äro mycket | långa – ha i denna reviderade upplaga namnen på Bibelns | böcker utmärkts med svart stil, t. ex. Esaias.] | Rättelser. | Sid. 60, rad. 21, *står:* scharlakansröda *läs:* Scharlakansröda | » 127, sista raden *står: (fera) läs: (ferae)* | STOCKHOLM, | BOKFÖRL.-A.-B. TIDENS TRYCKERI, | 1919.
8vo
title leaf, 2 pp; text of Genesis 1-7 and n 1-823, pp 1-419.
Revised edition of Sw 2/3 = Hyde 847.
UK: SOC; SWE: GEN, UPP

49/01/Sw 4/1 1933 Hyde 859/6

ARCANA COELESTIA. | <short rule> | HIMMELSKA HEMLIGHETER, | SOM INNEHÅLLAS I | DEN HELIGA SKRIFT | ELLER | HERRENS ORD, | OCH NU BLIFVIT UPPTÄCKTA: | HÄR DE SOM FINNAS I | FÖRSTA MOSE BOK, | JÄMTE DET UNDERBARA, | SOM BLIFVIT SEDT | I ANDARNAS VÄRLD OCH I ÄNGLARNAS HIMMEL. | <short rule> | ETT VERK AV | EMANUEL SWEDENBORG. | <short rule> | FÖRSTA BANDETS | ANDRA AFDELNINGEN (SID 145—419). | <short rule> | ÖFVERSÄTTNING FRÅN LATINSKA URSKRIFTEN | [AF D:R J. A. SEVÉN.] | 2:DRA UPPLAGAN NÅGOT REVIDERAD AF | ERIK HJERPE | pastor i Nya kyrkans bekännares församling | <short rule> | STOCKHOLM, | NYKYRKLIGA BOKFÖRLAGET. | 1933.
8vo
title leaf, 2 pp; text of Genesis 4-7 and n 322-823, pp 145-419.
Revised edition of Sw 3/11 = Hyde 859/5, printed by Brobergs Boktryckeri, Frejjgatan 27, Stockholm.
UK: SOC; SWE: ROY, GEN, UPP

49/01/Sw 5/1 **1996** Hyde 842/1

EMANUEL SWEDENBORG | Arcana Caelestia | *(Den inre, andliga meningen | i Första och Andra Moseboken)* | Del 1 | *(1–1113)* | Första Moseboken 1–9 | Översatt från latinet | av | Ulf Fornander | PROPIUS FÖRLAG • STOCKHOLM 1995
verso: © 1996, Skandinaviska Swedenborgsällskapet, Stockholm, | samt Proprius förlag AB, Stockholm | Omslag: Bridget Swinton, Danmark | Tryckt hos Schmidts Tryckeri AB, Helsingborg 1996 | ISBN 91-7118-821-5
half title: Arcana Caelestia
section title: FÖRSTA | MOSEBOKEN
8vo
half title and title leaves, 4 pp; Förord <Foreword by O Hjern>, pp V-XI; Översättarens förord <Translator's foreword>, pp XII-XVIII; Table of the contents of each volume of the first Latin edition and of the projected volumes of this Swedish version, p XIX; Tack <Acknowledgement>, p XX; reduced replica of title page of La 1/1, p XXI; Företal av Em. Swedenborg <Preface by Swedenborg>, pp 1-2; section title leaf, pp 3-4; text of Genesis 1-9 and n 1-1113, pp 5-723.
Translated by Ulf Fornander.
UK: SOC; SWE: ROY, GEN; USA: ANC

49/01/Sw 5/2 **1998** Hyde 843/1

EMANUEL SWEDENBORG | Arcana Caelestia | *(Den inre, andliga meningen | i Första och Andra Moseboken)* | Del 2 | *(1114–2134)* | Första Moseboken 10–17 | Översatt från latinet | av | Ulf Fornander | PROPRIUS FÖRLAG • STOCKHOLM 1998
verso: © 1998, Skandinaviska Swededenborgsällskapet, Stockholm | samt Proprius förlag AB, Stockholm | Omslag: Bridget Swinton, Danmark | Tryckt hos Team Offset & Media AB, Malmö 1998 | ISBN 91-7118-852-5
half title: Arcana Caelestia
8vo
half title and title leaves, 4 pp; Förord <Foreword by O Hjern>, pp V-VII; Översättarens förord <Translator's foreword>, pp VIII-IX; Table of the contents of each volume of the first Latin edition and of the projected volumes of this Swedish version, p X; text of Genesis 10-17 and n 1114-2134, pp 1-715; Tack <Acknowledgement>, 1 p.
Translated by Ulf Fornander.
UK: SOC; SWE: ROY, GEN; USA: ANC

49/01/Sw 5/3 **2001** Hyde 844/1

EMANUEL SWEDENBORG | Arcana Caelestia | *(Den inre, andliga meningen | i Första och Andra Moseboken)* | Del 3 | *(2135–2893)* | Första Moseboken 18–22 | Översatt från latinet | av | Ulf Fornander | PROPRIUS FÖRLAG • STOCKHOLM 2001
verso: © 2001, Skandinaviska Swededenborgsällskapet, Stockholm | samt Proprius förlag AB, Stockholm | Omslag: Bridget Swinton, Danmark | Tryckt hos Prinfo/Team Offset & Media AB, Malmö 2001 | ISBN 91-7118-883-5
half title: Arcana Caelestia
8vo
half title and title leaves, 4 pp; Förord <Foreword by O Hjern>, pp V-VIII; Översättarens förord <Translator's foreword>, p IX; Table of the contents of each volume of the first Latin edition and of the projected volumes of this Swedish version, p X; text of Swedenborg's preface, Genesis 18-22, and n 2135-2893, pp 1-678; Tack <Acknowledgement>, p 679.
Translated by Ulf Fornander.
UK: SOC; SWE: ROY, GEN, GSB

SWEDISH EXTRACTS

X 49/01/Sw 1796/1 **c 1796** Hyde 890

<untitled>

pott broad 4to <197 x 152 mm>

title and text n 6-63, 73-110, 8476-8478, 8505, 8495, 8506-8516, 8643, 8648, 8658, 8685, 8694, 8725, 8690, 8700, 8722, 8724, 8539, 8859-8875, 8902, 8772, 9088-9089, 8995, 9135, pp 1-159.

MS translation by J P Odhner, bound in a volume labelled *Andel. Meningen af 1sta Moseb. m. m.*, formerly owned by C B Bragg, now in UK: CON. <Archives L/38 VII>

UK: CON

X 49/01/Sw nd/1 **no date** Hyde 891

Om Hellfwete

pott broad 4to <197 x 156 mm>

title and text n 692-700, 814-831, 938-969, 1106-1113, 5561, 2699, 2704, 5711-5726, 5846-5865, 5976-5993, 6189-6214, 6307-6326, 6466-6495, 6598-6626, 112 pp.

MS, formerly owned by the Exegetic and Philanthropic Society, Stockholm, in UK: SOC. <Archives B/44>

UK: SOC

X 49/01/Sw 1784/1 **1784** Hyde 892

<<Kärleks Läran.>>

4to

title and text n 6703-6712, 6818-6824, 6933-6938, 7080-7086, 7178-7182, 7255-7263, 7366-7377, 7488-7494, 7623-7626, 7752-7762, 7814-7821, 8033-8037, 8120-8124, pp 41-44, 49-52, 55-56, 59-60, 63-64.

Translated by J D Halldon, published in *Afton-Bladet, en vecko-skrift af ett Sällskap i Stockholm* Stockholm.

Copy not seen; description recorded from Hyde 892.

X 49/01/Sw 1864/1 **1864** Hyde 893

Om | Inflytelse, | samt om | Själens gemenskap med Kroppen. | Af. | Em. Swedenborg. | <short rule> | **Serskilt aftryckt ur** | Arcana Coelestia. | <short rule> | **Öfwersättning | från Latinska Urskriften, som utkom** 1749, | **af** | CARL DELEEN. | <short orn rule> | **WEXJÖ, | i C G Södergrens Bokhandel.**

8vo

title leaf, 2 pp; text, pp 3-50.

UK: SOC; SWE: GSB; USA: ANC

X 49/01/Sw 1864/2 **1864** Hyde 894

Nya Jerusalems | Lära om Kärleken. | Af | Em. Swedenborg. | <short rule> | **Serskilt aftryckt ur** | Arcana Coelestia. | <short rule> | **Öfwersättning | från Latinska Urskriften, som utkom** 1749. | **af** | CARL DELEEN. | <short orn rule> | **WEXJÖ, | i C G Södergrens Bokhandel.**

8vo

title leaf, 2 pp; text, pp 1-57.

UK: SOC; SWE: GSB; USA: ANC

X 49/01/Sw 1872/1 **1872** Hyde 895

Läran | om | Förebildningar | och | Motsvarigheter, | eller | om menniskans alla inre och yttre Organers | och Lemmars motsvarighet med den | Största Menniskan, | som är | Himmelen: | Grundad på mångårig erfarenhet genom um- | gänge med båda verldarnes invånare, | Af |

Eman. Swedenborg. | <short orn rule> | *Öfversättning* | från Latiniska Urskriften, som utkom | 1751–53. | <short orn rule> | WEXJÖ, | i C. G. Södergrens bokhandel.
8vo
title leaf, 2 pp; Förord <Foreword>, 2 pp; text, pp 1-189; Innehåll <Contents>, p 190; Rättelser <Corrections>, p 191.
UK: SOC; SWE: ROY, GSB; USA: ANC

X 49/01/Sw 1930/1 **1930** Hyde 895/–
<<Från paradiset till Babels torn. Förklaring av berättelse i det forngamla Ordet enligt Emanuel Swedenborg. Utgåva Eric von Born, Stockholm. 1930.>>
8vo
title leaf, 2 pp; text, pp 1-52.
Copy not seen; description recorded from catalogue of SWE: UPP.
SWE: GEN, UPP

X 49/01/Sw 1952/1 **1952** Hyde 895/a
DEN STORA MÄNNISKAN | *Ett verk innehållande framställningar* | I. Om förebildningar och motsvarigheter | II. Om motsvarigheten mellan människans alla organ | och lemmar, såväl de inre som de yttre, och | den Stora Människan, som är himlen | III. Om sjukdomars motsvarighet med den andliga världen | *och utgörande utdrag ur ARCANA COELESTIA* | *av* | *Emanuel Swedenborg* | Ny översättning från latinet | BOKFÖRLAGET NOVA ECCLESIA | BROMMA, STOCKHOLM
imprint: ANDRÉN & HOLMS BOKTRYCKERI, STOCKHOLM 1952
8vo
title leaf, 2 pp; Innehåll <Contents, listed by the translator>, p 3; Översättarens förord <Translator's foreword>, p 4; text n 1-321, pp 5-215; imprint, p 216.
Translated by E Sandström.
UK: SOC; SWE: ROY, UPP; USA: ANC

X 49/01/Sw 1999/1 **1999** Hyde 895/b
Om Underverk | *De Miraculis* | – ett efterlämnat verk av | Emanuel Swedenborg | Översättning och inledning | av Olle Hjern
verso: Omslag: Emanuel Swedenborg | Gravyr efter en teckning av J.W. Stör, 1734 | Originalets fullständiga titel: | De Miraculis et quod hodie circa finem sæculi nulla expectanda | © den svenska översättningen 1997, Olle Hjern, | Swedenborgs Minne och Skandinaviska Swedenborgssällskapet | Producktion: Björn Sahlin | Tryck: Mowys skrivbyrå, 1999 | ISSN 1102-1470
A4 folded to A5
title leaf, 2 pp; Förord <Translator's preface>, pp 3-6; text n 1-18, pp 7-20.
Translated by O Hjern.
UK: SOC; SWE: GEN

UKRAINIAN EXTRACTS

X 49/01/Ua 1993/1, D Ua 1993/1 **1993** Hyde 889/2
Пояснение первых четырех глав киги Бытия
8vo
title leaf, 2 pp; Foreword, pp 3-9; text n 1-442, pp 10-160.
A translation of *Arcana Coelestia* chapters 1-4, revised from X Ru 1908/1 = Hyde 889/1 and edited with a preface by V A Vasiliev, published in Тайны Неба <D Ua 1993/1 = Hyde 3158/3> with 62/03/Ua 1/1 and 63/01/Ua 1/1 by Presa Ukraine, Por-Royal, Kiev, 1993. ISBN 5-01-003665-4.
UK: SOC

49/02 Arcana Coelestia: Index of Words, Names, and Subjects Hyde CXLIII

The autograph MSS of the two Indices form Codices 112, 113, and 114 in the Library of the Royal Swedish Academy of Sciences, Stockholm.

Swedenborg drafted *Arcana Coelestia* vol 1 <n 1-1885> during 1748 and 1749, then published it in September 1749. On completion of his first draft of this volume, he appears to have compiled his first Index of it in Codex 112, and to have used this Codex in preparing a second Index, in Codices 113 and 114.

He drafted *Arcana Coelestia* vol 2 <n 1886-2759> and published it in 1750. He inserted references to it in his first Index, and then in his second Index.

It appears that he did not index *Arcana Coelestia* vols 3-8 <n 2760-10837> until he had completed the work; and he inserted references to these paragraphs only in his first Index.

His handwriting in the second Index is similar to that which he used in MSS sent to his printers and is therefore far easier to read than his 'first-draft' hand in the first Index. Entries in the first Index are generally in numerical sequence, whereas in the second Index Swedenborg rearranged many of them into a more rational order, though some such rearrangements also occur in parts of the first Index.

The items written on pp 453-462 of Codex 114 are described as 64/02 = Hyde CXLIIIa and 64/03 = Hyde CXLIIIb.

LATIN

Editions:

La 0 MSS
La 1 J A Tulk, editor
La 2 R L Tafel, editor
La 3 J Elliott, editor

49/02/La 0/1 **1749** Hyde 937

<< <untitled> >>

double foolscap long 4to <400 x 152 mm>

text: A to V, pp 3-48, 53-454; pp 49-52 and 455-466 are missing; pp 21, 91, 104, 134, 141, 310, 318-319, 321, 334, 389, 418, 447, 502, 504, 514, 516, 526, and 528 are blank; additions <not arranged alphabetically>, pp 467-530; table of references, p <531>; p <532> is blank.

Most of the references were crossed through by Swedenborg.
The MS forms Codex 112.
MS not seen; description deduced from La O/4.
SWE: KVA

49/02/La O/2 **1750** Hyde 938
<< <untitled> >>
pott long 4to <311 x 98 mm>
text: Memorandum on the inside of the front cover; p 1 is blank; A to O, pp 2-19, 23-271; pp 21-22 are missing; all pp bearing an even number <except pp 2, 16, 44 58, 68, 74, 104, 154, 170, 178, 210, 212> are blank.
The MS forms Codex 113.
An unpublished copy has been recorded as follows.

1 A copy of Codex 113 was in the possession of the Theosophical Society, London, in the charge of P B Chastanier, in 1784. From this the first Latin edition was printed, but its imperfect character made it necessary to prepare a new edition from the autograph MS at a later date. <Hyde 939>

MS not seen; description deduced from La O/4.
SWE: KVA

49/02/La O/3 **1750** Hyde 939, 955/a,b
<< <untitled> >>
foolscap long 4to <318 x 102 mm>
text: O to V and Z, pp 274-452; all pp bearing odd numbers <except pp 319, 341, 345, 365, 387, 411, 415, 429, 435> and pp 272, 336, 448, 450 are blank;
Summary of the internal sense of *Revelation* 1-4, p 453;
Summaria in Explicatione Apocalypseos <64/02 = Hyde CXLIIIa> cap. i-xx, pp 454-457;
Several memoranda, p 458; pp 459-461 are blank;
De Conjugio <64/03 = Hyde CXLIIIb>, p 462;
some pages at the end have been torn out.
The MS forms Codex 114.
An unpublished copy has been recorded as follows.

1 A copy of Codex 114 was in the possession of the Theosophical Society, London, in the charge of P B Chastanier, in 1784. From this the first Latin edition was printed, but its imperfect character made it necessary to prepare a new edition from the autograph MS at a later date. Neither of these printed editions contains what is on pp 453-462 of Codex 114. <Hyde 939>

MS not seen; description deduced from La O/4.
SWE: KVA

49/02/La 1/1 **1815** Hyde 940
INDEX | VERBORUM, NOMINUM ET RERUM | IN | ARCANIS CŒLESTIBUS. | <short orn rule> | EX OPERIBUS POSTHUMIS | EMANUELIS SWEDENBORGII. | <short orn rule> | LONDINI: | TYPIS T. BENSLEY, BOLT-COURT, FLEET-STREET, | IMPENSIS JOH. AUG. TULK. | <short rule> 1815.
4to
title leaf, 2 pp; text, in double columns, 177 pp; Corrigenda, 5 pp.
A conflation of the two Indices La O/2, 3 = Hyde 938, 939, with no introductory notes, by J A Tulk, and published at his expense.

A copy formerly owned by J Flaxman, with annotations in the margins of the entries 'Proprium' and 'Revelatio', is in the Library of UK: SOC. <Archives L/130>

UK: SOC, NR; GER: GSU, WLB; NET: GEN, THY; SWE: GSB, UPP; USA: FOU, SHS; AUS: SYD

49/02/La 2/1 **1890** Hyde 941

INDEX | VERBORUM, NOMINUM, ET RERUM | IN | ARCANIS CŒLESTIBUS | *OPUS POSTHUMUM* | EMANUELIS SWEDENBORGII | LONDINII | SWEDENBORG SOCIETY, BRITISH AND FOREIGN | (INSTITUTED 1810) | 36 BLOOMSBURY STREET | 1890

half title: INDEX VERBORUM, NOMINUM, ET RERUM | IN ARCANIS CŒLESTIBUS

verso: EDINBURGH | ROBERT R. SUTHERLAND, PRINTER, | HADDINGTON PLACE WORKS.

8vo

half title and title leaves, 4 pp; Praefatiuncula editoris, pp v-vii; Abbreviationes, 1 p; text, pp 1-368; Notae criticae editoris, pp 369-373.

Edited by R L Tafel from La 0/1 = Hyde 937; this edition has many printing errors.

UK: SOC, NCC; NET: GEN

49/02/La 0/4 **1916** Hyde 937/1, 938, 939/1, 955/1,4, 3038/14

EMANUELIS SWEDENBORGII | ARCANA COELESTIA | <short rule> | AD AUTOGRAPHI SIMILITUDINEM IN BIBLIOTHECA REGIAE ACADEMIAE SCIENTIARUM | SUECICAE ADSERVATI, OPE ARTIS PHOTOTYPOGRAPHICAE DELINEATI, EDITA JUSSU | CONVENTUS GENERALIS AMERICANI NOVAE HIEROSOLYMAE | SOCIETATIS AMERICANAE PRO SCRIPTIS EDENDIS SWEDENBORGII | ACADEMIAE NOVAE ECCLESIAE AMERICANAE | CONCILII GENERALIS NOVAE ECCLESIAE BRITANNICAE | CUSTODUM CURATELAE ROTCHIANAE AMERICANAE | ET | SOCIETATIS SWEDENBORGIANAE LONDINENSIS | <short orn rule> | VOL. V. | <orn 15 x 37 mm> | HOLMIAE | EX OFFICINA PHOTOTYPOGRAPHICA LAGRELIUS & WESTPHAL | MCMXVI.

half title: EMANUELIS SWEDENBORGII | AUTOGRAPHA | <short rule> | TOMUS XIV.

folio

half title and title leaves, 4 pp; Contenta, 1 p.

Codex 112: inside of front cover, p 2; text, pp 3-506; Calculations and Bible references, p 507; blank p and inside of back cover, pp 508-509; back and front covers of the Codex, pp 510-511.

Codex 113: inside of front cover and blank p, p 514; text, pp 515-643; blank p and inside of back cover, p 644; back and front covers of the Codex, pp 645-646.

Codex 114: inside of front cover and blank p, p 648; text, pp 649-739; Summaria in Explicatione Apocalypseos <64/02/La 0/2 = Hyde 955/1>, pp 739-741; blank pp, p 742-743; De Conjugio <64/03/La 0/2 = Hyde 955/4>, p 743; blank pp and inside of back cover, pp 744-745; back and front covers of the Codex, pp 746-747.

Reproduction of La 0/1-3, published in phototyped edition, vol 14, Stockholm.

Unpublished copies have been recorded as follows.

1 UK: SOC & USA: ANC, SHS A reproduction on microfilm 9, Bryn Athyn PA.

UK: SOC, BL, BOD, CAM, CON, LON, NCC, RYL, WIL; NET: GEN; SWE: ROY, KVA, UPP; USA: ANC, FOU, SHS; AUS: SYD; NZ: WEL

49/02/La 3/1 **2004** Hyde 3077/13, 937/2, 938/2, 939/2

EMANUEL SWEDENBORG | ARCANA | COELESTIA | INDEXES | <rule> | Compiled but not published | by the author himself | TRANSCRIBED AND EDITED | BY JOHN ELLIOTT | LONDON | THE SWEDENBORG SOCIETY | 2004

verso: Published by The Swedenborg Society | Swedenborg House, 20-21 Bloomsbury Way, London WC1A 2TH | © Swedenborg Society 2004 | Typeset in Palatino by | Cambridge Publishing

Management Ltd, Cambridge | Printed and bound in Great Britain | at the University Press, Cambridge | ISBN 0 85448 136 2 | British Library Cataloguing-in-Publication Data | A catalogue record for this book | is available from the British Library
half title: ARCANA COELESTIA: INDEXES
section title: INDEX 1 | <rule>
2nd section title: INDEX 2 | <rule>
8vo
half title and title leaves, 4 pp; Contents, p V; Editor's introduction, pp VII-XIV; Abbreviations, p XV; section title leaf, pp 1-2; text of Index 1, pp 3-441; 2nd section title leaf, p 443-444; text of Index 2, pp 445-551; Editor's notes, pp 553-560.
An initial printing was scrapped when it was found that compositor's misprints in the text had not been corrected on pp 405-441; see the 'running heads' on the odd-numbered pp and, for example, the heading on p 441.
Norman Ryder was the editor's consultant.
UK: SOC, NR; GER: GLB; NET: GEN; SWE: ROY; USA: ANC, SHS

ENGLISH

Translators:

En 1 J A Tulk
En 2 possibly Miss M G Cary
En 3 E Rich and H Larkin
En 4 E Rich
En 5 W Bruce
En 6 not stated; possibly J Worcester
En 7 J J G Hyde

49/02/En 1/1 **1810** Hyde 942
INDEX | TO THE | ARCANA CŒLESTIA; | OR | HEAVENLY MYSTERIES | CONTAINED IN | The Sacred Scriptures | <short orn rule> | TRANSLATED FROM THE ORIGINAL LATIN | OF | EMANUEL SWEDENBORG. | <short orn rule> | A POSTHUMOUS WORK OF THE AUTHOR. | <short double rule> | *LONDON:* | PRINTED BY THE PHILANTHROPIC SOCIETY, | AND SOLD FOR THE EDITOR BY THE SOCIETY FOR PRINTING AND | PUBLISHING THE WRITINGS OF THE HON. EMANUEL SWEDENBORG, | AND BY ALL OTHER BOOKSELLERS IN TOWN AND COUNTRY. | <short rule> | 1810.
half title: <double rule> | INDEX | TO THE | ARCANA CŒLESTIA, | &c. &c. | <double rule>
8vo
half title and title leaves, 4 pp; text, 459 unnumbered pp; Errata, 1 p.
Translated by J A Tulk and printed at his expense by the Philanthropic Society, St George's Fields, London.
UK: SOC, CON, NCC, NCH; USA: ANC, SHS

49/02/En 1/2 **1811** Hyde 943
INDEX | TO | THE PASSAGES | OF | SACRED SCRIPTURE | CONTAINED IN THE ARCANA CŒLESTIA. | <double rule> | *LONDON:* PRINTED BY THE PHILANTHROPIC SOCIETY, | *ST. GEORGE'S FIELDS;* | AND SOLD FOR THE EDITOR BY THE SOCIETY FOR PRINTING AND PUBLISHING | THE WRITINGS OF THE HONOURABLE EMANUEL SWEDENBORG, AT NO. 47, | DEVONSHIRE-STREET, QUEEN-SQUARE; AND BY ALL OTHER BOOKSELLERS | IN TOWN AND COUNTRY. | <short orn rule> | 1811.

8vo
title leaf, 2 pp; text, pp 1-120; Errata in the first Index <En 1/1 = Hyde 942>, 1 p.
Compiled from the MS by J A Tulk, and published at his own expense.
UK: SOC, CON, NCC; USA: SHS

49/02/En 1/3 **1833** Hyde 944
INDEX | TO THE | ARCANA CŒLESTIA; | OR | HEAVENLY MYSTERIES | CONTAINED IN | THE SACRED SCRIPTURES. | I. OF WORDS, NAMES, AND SUBJECTS. | II. OF PASSAGES OF SCRIPTURE. | <short wavy rule> | TRANSLATED FROM THE ORIGINAL LATIN OF | EMANUEL SWEDENBORG, | *Late Member of the House of Nobles in the Royal Diet of Sweden,* | *Assessor of the Royal Board of Mines,* | *Fellow of the Royal Society of Upsala, and of the Royal Academy of Sciences of Stockholm,* | *And Corresponding Member of the Academy of Sciences* | *of St. Petersburg.* | <short wavy rule> | A POSTHUMOUS WORK OF THE AUTHOR. | SECOND EDITION. | REVISED AND ENLARGED. | <short rule> | LONDON: | PUBLISHED BY J. S. HODSON, CROSS STREET, HATTON GARDEN, | SOLD ALSO BY W. SIMPKIN AND R. MARSHALL, STATIONERS HALL COURT, | LUDGATE STREET; AND W. CLARKE, MANCHESTER. | <short rule> | 1833.
verso: *This work is printed at the expense of, and published for,* "THE SOCIETY | FOR PRINTING AND PUBLISHING THE WRITINGS OF EMANUEL | SWEDENBORG, INSTITUTED IN LONDON IN THE YEAR 1810." | <short rule> | Printed by J. S. Hodson, Cross Street, Hatton Garden.
half title: INDEX | OF WORDS, NAMES, AND SUBJECTS | CONTAINED IN THE | ARCANA CŒLESTIA.
section title: INDEX | TO | THE PASSAGES OF SCRIPTURE | CONTAINED IN THE | ARCANA CŒLESTIA.
imprint: HODSON, PRINTER, CROSS STREET, HATTON GARDEN.
8vo
half title and title leaves, 4 pp; text of Words, etc, pp 1-451; section title leaf, 2 pp; text, pp 1-101; imprint, p 102.
Revised by J A Tulk; an edition of 500 copies was printed.
An unpublished compilation from En 1/1 or En 1/3 is recorded as follows.
1 UK: SOC A MS index prepared by J N Cossham of Bristol, written on 93 pp of 8vo paper. <Hyde 941/a>
UK: SOC, CON; USA: SHS

49/02/En 2/1 **1848** Hyde 945
INDEX | TO THE | HEAVENLY ARCANA | CONTAINED IN | THE SACRED SCRIPTURES. | I. OF WORDS, NAMES, AND SUBJECTS. | II. OF PASSAGES OF SCRIPTURE. | <short rule> | TRANSLATED FROM THE ORIGINAL LATIN OF | EMANUEL SWEDENBORG. | <short rule> | A POSTHUMOUS WORK OF THE AUTHOR. | BOSTON: | OTIS CLAPP, 12, SCHOOL STREET. | <short rule> | MDCCCXLVIII
verso: BOSTON: | PRINTED BY FREEMAN AND BULLES, | DEVONSHORE STREET.
section title: INDEX | OF WORDS, NAMES, AND SUBJECTS | CONTAINED IN THE | HEAVENLY ARCANA.
verso: <editorial note>
2nd section title: <short rule> | The following is the INDEX TO THE PASSAGES OF SCRIPTURE CONTAINED | IN THE HEAVENLY ARCANA. | <short rule>
8vo
half title, title, and section title leaves, 6 pp; text of Index of Words, etc, pp 1-447; 2nd section title, p 448; text of Index to Bible passages cited, pp 1-100.
Revised by a lady member of the Boston Society of the New Church <possibly Miss M G Cary>.
UK: SOC; USA: FOU

49/02/En 3/1 **1853** Hyde 946

INDEX | TO | SWEDENBORG'S | ARCANA CŒLESTIA, | OR | HEAVENLY MYSTERIES, | CONTAINED IN | THE SACRED SCRIPTURES. | VOLUME I.—A TO L. | LONDON: | WILLIAM NEWBERY, 6 KING STREET, HOLBORN. | 1853.
half title: INDEX | OF WORDS, NAMES, AND SUBJECTS | CONTAINED IN THE | ARCANA CŒLESTIA.
verso: This work is printed at the expense of, and published for | "THE SOCIETY FOR PRINTING AND PUBLISHING THE | WRITINGS OF EMANUEL SWEDENBORG, INSTITUTED IN | LONDON IN THE YEAR 1810." | <short rule> | LONDON: | PRINTED BY WALTON AND MITCHELL, WARDOUR STREET, OXFORD STREET.
8vo
half title and title leaves, 4 pp; Note, pp v-xiv; text, pp 1-638.
Prepared on the basis of La 1/1 = Hyde 940, by E Rich and H Larkin; an edition of 1,000 copies was printed.
UK: SOC; SWE: UPP; USA: ANC, SHS

49/02/En 3/2 **1855** Hyde 947

INDEX | TO | SWEDENBORG'S | ARCANA CŒLESTIA, | OR | HEAVENLY MYSTERIES, | CONTAINED | IN THE HOLY SCRIPTURE. | VOLUME I..—A TO L. | LONDON: | PUBLISHED BY THE SWEDENBORG SOCIETY, | (INSTITUTED 1810,) | 36, BLOOMSBURY STREET, OXFORD STREET. | EDIT. OF 1852.
half title: INDEX | OF WORDS, NAMES, AND SUBJECTS | CONTAINED IN THE | ARCANA CŒLESTIA.
verso: *This work is printed at the expense of, and published for,* | "THE SOCIETY FOR PRINTING AND PUBLISHING THE | WRITINGS OF EMANUEL SWEDENBORG, INSTITUTED IN | LONDON IN THE YEAR 1810." | <short rule> | PRINTED BY WALTON AND MITCHELL, WARDOUR STREET, OXFORD STREET.
half title and title leaves, 4 pp; Note, pp v-xiv; title page of En 3/1 = Hyde 946, 2 pp; text, pp 1-638.
En 3/1 = Hyde 946, with a fresh title page, issued in 1855.
UK: SOC; USA: SHS

49/02/En 4/1 **1860** Hyde 948

INDEX | TO | SWEDENBORG'S | ARCANA CŒLESTIA, | OR | HEAVENLY MYSTERIES, | CONTAINED | IN THE HOLY SCRIPTURE. | VOLUME II.—M TO Z. | LONDON: | PUBLISHED BY THE SWEDENBORG SOCIETY, | (INSTITUTED 1810,) | 36 BLOOMSBURY STREET, OXFORD STREET. | 1860.
half title: INDEX | OF WORDS, NAMES, AND SUBJECTS | CONTAINED IN THE | ARCANA CŒLESTIA.
verso: *This work is printed at the expense of, and published for,* | "THE SOCIETY FOR PRINTING AND PUBLISHING THE | WRITINGS OF EMANUEL SWEDENBORG, INSTITUTED IN | LONDON IN THE YEAR 1810." | <short rule> | LONDON: | MITCHELL AND SON, PRINTERS, WARDOUR STREET, W.
imprint: <short rule> | MITCHELL AND SON, PRINTERS, WARDOUR STREET, W.
8vo
half title and title leaves, 4 pp; Editor's note <signed E. R.>, pp v-vi; Main subdivisions of the text, pp vii-xxviii; Index of Words, etc, pp 639-1351; Supplement, pp 1352-1362; Index to Bible passages cited, pp 1363-1449; imprint, p. 1449.
Prepared on the basis of La 1/1 = Hyde 940 by E Rich, assisted at first by H Larkin. The Index to Bible passages had been formerly prepared by W Dodd. An edition of 1,005 copies was printed.
UK: SOC, NR; USA: SHS

49/02/En 3/3 **1865** Hyde 949

INDEX | TO | SWEDENBORG'S | ARCANA CŒLESTIA, | OR | HEAVENLY MYSTERIES, | CONTAINED IN THE | HOLY SCRIPTURE. | VOLUME I.—A TO M. | LONDON: | PUBLISHED BY THE SWEDENBORG SOCIETY, | (INSTITUTED 1810,) | 36 BLOOMSBURY STREET, W.C. | 1865.
verso: LONDON: MITCHELL AND HUGHES, PRINTERS, | WARDOUR STREET, W.
half title: INDEX | OF | WORDS, NAMES, AND SUBJECTS | CONTAINED IN THE | ARCANA CŒLESTIA.
imprint: LONDON: | MITCHELL AND HUGHES, PRINTERS, | WARDOUR STREET, W.
8vo
half title and title leaves, 4 pp; Main subdivisions of the text, pp v-xii; Index of Words, etc, pp 1-757; imprint, p 758.
A reprint of En 3/2 = Hyde 947, supervised by E E Bundy; an edition of 1,000 copies was printed. A new preface was prepared by E Rich and printed separately, to be inserted.
UK: SOC, BL, NR; USA: ANC; AUS: SYD

49/02/En 4/2 **1865** Hyde 950

INDEX | TO | SWEDENBORG'S | ARCANA CŒLESTIA, | OR | HEAVENLY MYSTERIES, | CONTAINED IN THE | HOLY SCRIPTURE. | VOLUME II.—N TO Z. | LONDON: | PUBLISHED BY THE SWEDENBORG SOCIETY, | (INSTITUTED 1810,) | 36 BLOOMSBURY STREET, W.C. | 1865.
verso: LONDON: MITCHELL AND HUGHES, PRINTERS, | WARDOUR STREET, W.
half title: INDEX | OF | WORDS, NAMES, AND SUBJECTS | CONTAINED IN THE | ARCANA CŒLESTIA.
8vo
half title and title leaves, 4 pp; Main subdivisions of the text, pp v-xxiv; Index of Words, etc, pp 1-599; Index to Bible passages, pp 601-687.
A reprint of En 4/1 = Hyde 948, supervised by E E Bundy; an edition of 1,000 copies was printed.
UK: SOC, BL; USA: ANC; AUS: SYD

49/02/En 5/1 **1880** Hyde 951

ARCANA CŒLESTIA | <short rule> | INDEX | TO THE | HEAVENLY MYSTERIES | CONTAINED IN | THE HOLY SCRIPTURE, OR WORD OF THE LORD | I. WORDS, NAMES, AND SUBJECTS | II. PASSAGES OF SCRIPTURE. | BY | EMANUEL SWEDENBORG | SWEDENBORG SOCIETY, BRITISH AND FOREIGN | (INSTITUTED 1810) | 36 BLOOMSBURY STREET, LONDON | 1880
section title: INDEX | TO | THE PASSAGES OF SACRED SCRIPTURE | CONTAINED IN THE | ARCANA CŒLESTIA
8vo
title leaf, 2 pp; Index of words, etc, pp 1-361; section title leaf, 2 pp; Index of Bible passages, pp 3-108.
Revised by W Bruce; an edition of 1,080 copies was printed by Muir and Paterson, Edinburgh.
UK: SOC; SWE: UPP; USA: ANC, SHS

49/02/En 6/1 **1907** Hyde 951/1

INDEX | TO | WORDS, NAMES, AND SUBJECTS | IN | THE HEAVENLY ARCANA | DISCLOSED | BY | EMANUEL SWEDENBORG | WITH REVISIONS AND ADDITIONS TO THE POSTHUMOUS | WORK OF THE AUTHOR | *First published in Latin, London,* 1815 | Rotch Edition | VOL. XX. | BOSTON | MASSACHUSETTS NEW-CHURCH UNION | 16 ARLINGTON STREET | 1907
small 8vo
title leaf, 2 pp; text, pp 3-316.
UK: SOC; NET: GEN; SWE: UPP; USA: ANC; SA: MMC

49/02/En 6/2 **1907** Hyde 951/2

INDEX | TO | WORDS, NAMES, AND SUBJECTS | IN | THE HEAVENLY ARCANA | DISCLOSED | BY | EMANUEL SWEDENBORG | WITH REVISIONS AND ADDITIONS TO THE POSTHUMOUS | WORK OF THE AUTHOR | *First published in Latin, London,* 1815 | Rotch Edition | VOL. XX. | BOSTON AND NEW YORK, | HOUGHTON, MIFFLIN & CO. | 1907.
small 8vo
title leaf, 2 pp; text, pp 3-316.
UK: soc; USA: anc; SA: mmc

49/02/En 7/1 **1909** Hyde 951/3

ARCANA CŒLESTIA | <short rule> | INDEX | OF | WORDS, NAMES, AND SUBJECTS | IN THE | HEAVENLY ARCANA | *FROM THE LATIN* | OF | EMANUEL SWEDENBORG | TO WHICH IS ADDED AN | INDEX TO THE SCRIPTURE PASSAGES | THE SWEDENBORG SOCIETY | (INSTITUTED 1810) | 1 BLOOMSBURY STREET, LONDON | 1909
half title: INDEX TO THE ARCANA CŒLESTIA
imprint: THE RIVERSIDE PRESS LIMITED, EDINBURGH.
8vo
half title and title leaves, 4 pp; Preface, pp v-vii; text, pp 1-547; imprint, p 547.
Translated by J J G Hyde.
UK: soc; NET: gen; SWE: roy, upp; USA: anc; AUS: syd

49/02/En 5/2 **1966** Hyde 951/–

ARCANA CŒLESTIA | <short rule> | INDEX | TO THE | HEAVENLY MYSTERIES | CONTAINED IN | THE HOLY SCRIPTURE, OR WORD OF THE LORD | I. WORDS, NAMES, AND SUBJECTS | II. PASSAGES OF SCRIPTURE. | BY | EMANUEL SWEDENBORG | SWEDENBORG SOCIETY, BRITISH AND FOREIGN | (INSTITUTED 1810) | 36 BLOOMSBURY STREET, LONDON | 1880
section title: INDEX | TO | THE PASSAGES OF SACRED SCRIPTURE | CONTAINED IN THE | ARCANA CŒLESTIA
8vo
title leaf, 2 pp; Index of words, etc, pp 1-361; section title leaf, 2 pp; Index of Bible passages, pp 3-108.
Photolithographic reprint of En 5/1 = Hyde 951, in an edition of 500 copies.
UK: soc

49/02/En 5/3 **1976** Hyde 951/–

ARCANA CŒLESTIA | <short rule> | INDEX | TO THE | HEAVENLY MYSTERIES | CONTAINED IN | THE HOLY SCRIPTURE, OR WORD OF THE LORD | I. WORDS, NAMES, AND SUBJECTS | II. PASSAGES OF SCRIPTURE. | BY | EMANUEL SWEDENBORG | SWEDENBORG SOCIETY, BRITISH AND FOREIGN | (INSTITUTED 1810) | 36 BLOOMSBURY STREET, LONDON | 1880
section title: INDEX | TO | THE PASSAGES OF SACRED SCRIPTURE | CONTAINED IN THE | ARCANA CŒLESTIA
8vo
title leaf, 2 pp; Index of words, etc, pp 1-361; section title leaf, 2 pp; Index of Bible passages, pp 3-108.
Photolithographic reprint of En 5/1 = Hyde 951, in an edition of 1,000 copies.
USA: shs

49/02/En 3/4 **2000** Hyde 949/–

<<INDEX | TO | SWEDENBORG'S | ARCANA CŒLESTIA, | OR | HEAVENLY MYSTERIES, |

CONTAINED IN THE | HOLY SCRIPTURE. | VOLUME I.—A TO M. | LONDON: | PUBLISHED BY THE SWEDENBORG SOCIETY, | (INSTITUTED 1810,) | 36 BLOOMSBURY STREET, W.C. | 1865.>>
verso: <<LONDON: MITCHELL AND HUGHES, PRINTERS, | WARDOUR STREET, W.>>
half title: <<INDEX | OF | WORDS, NAMES, AND SUBJECTS | CONTAINED IN THE | ARCANA CŒLESTIA.>>
8vo
half title and title leaves, 4 pp; Main subdivisions of the text, pp v-xii; Index of Words, etc, pp 1-757.
Photographic replica reprint of En 3/3 = Hyde 949, published by Adamant Media Corporation, New York. ISBN hard cover 978142188758; paperback 978142182921.
Copy not seen; description deduced from En 3/3 and publisher's advertisement.

49/02/En 4/3 **2000** Hyde 950/–
<<INDEX | TO | SWEDENBORG'S | ARCANA CŒLESTIA, | OR | HEAVENLY MYSTERIES, | CONTAINED IN THE | HOLY SCRIPTURE. | VOLUME II.—N TO Z. | LONDON: | PUBLISHED BY THE SWEDENBORG SOCIETY, | (INSTITUTED 1810,) | 36 BLOOMSBURY STREET, W.C. | 1865.>>
verso: <<LONDON: MITCHELL AND HUGHES, PRINTERS, | WARDOUR STREET, W.>>
half title: <<INDEX | OF | WORDS, NAMES, AND SUBJECTS | CONTAINED IN THE | ARCANA CŒLESTIA.>>
8vo
half title and title leaves, 4 pp; Main subdivisions of the text, pp v-xxiv; Index of Words, etc, pp 1-599; Index to Bible passages, pp 601-687.
Photographic replica reprint of En 4/2 = Hyde 950, published by Adamant Media Corporation, New York. ISBN hard cover 9781421204734; paperback 9781421204741.
Copy not seen; description deduced from En 4/2 and publisher's advertisement.

49/02/En 1/4 **2001** Hyde 944/–
<<INDEX | TO THE | ARCANA CŒLESTIA; | OR | HEAVENLY MYSTERIES | CONTAINED IN | THE SACRED SCRIPTURES. | I. OF WORDS, NAMES, AND SUBJECTS. | II. OF PASSAGES OF SCRIPTURE. | <short wavy rule> | TRANSLATED FROM THE ORIGINAL LATIN OF | EMANUEL SWEDENBORG, | *Late Member of the House of Nobles in the Royal Diet of Sweden,* | *Assessor of the Royal Board of Mines,* | *Fellow of the Royal Society of Upsala, and of the Royal Academy of Sciences of Stockholm,* | *And Corresponding Member of the Academy of Sciences* | *of St. Petersburg*. | <short wavy rule> | A POSTHUMOUS WORK OF THE AUTHOR. | SECOND EDITION. | REVISED AND ENLARGED. | <short rule> | LONDON: | PUBLISHED BY J. S. HODSON, CROSS STREET, HATTON GARDEN, | SOLD ALSO BY W. SIMPKIN AND R. MARSHALL, STATIONERS HALL COURT, | LUDGATE STREET; AND W. CLARKE, MANCHESTER. | <short rule> | 1833.>>
verso: <<*This work is printed at the expense of, and published for,* "THE SOCIETY | FOR PRINTING AND PUBLISHING THE WRITINGS OF EMANUEL | SWEDENBORG, INSTITUTED IN LONDON IN THE YEAR 1810." | <short rule> | Printed by J. S. Hodson, Cross Street, Hatton Garden.>>
half title: <<INDEX | OF WORDS, NAMES, AND SUBJECTS | CONTAINED IN THE | ARCANA CŒLESTIA.>>
section title: <<INDEX | TO | THE PASSAGES OF SCRIPTURE | CONTAINED IN THE | ARCANA CŒLESTIA.>>
8vo
half title and title leaves, 4 pp; text of Words, etc, pp 1-451; section title leaf, 2 pp; text, pp 1-101.
Photographic replica reprint of En 1/3 = Hyde 944, published by Adamant Media Corporation, New York. ISBN hard cover 9780543968128; paperback 9780543968135.
Copy not seen; description deduced from En 1/4 and publisher's advertisement.

49/02/En 3/5 **2004** Hyde 951/–
<<INDEX | TO | SWEDENBORG'S | ARCANA CŒLESTIA, | OR | HEAVENLY MYSTERIES, | CONTAINED IN THE | HOLY SCRIPTURE. | VOLUME I.—A TO M. | LONDON: | PUBLISHED BY THE SWEDENBORG SOCIETY, | (INSTITUTED 1810,) | 36 BLOOMSBURY STREET, W.C. | 1865.>>
verso: <<LONDON: MITCHELL AND HUGHES, PRINTERS, | WARDOUR STREET, W.>>
half title: <<INDEX | OF | WORDS, NAMES, AND SUBJECTS | CONTAINED IN THE | ARCANA CŒLESTIA.>>
8vo
half title and title leaves, 4 pp; Main subdivisions of the text, pp v-xii; Index of Words, etc, pp 1-757.
Photographic replica reprint of En 3/3, published by Kessinger Publishing, Whitefish MT.
Copy not seen; description deduced from En 3/3 and publisher's advertisement.

49/02/En 4/4 **2004** Hyde 951/–
<<INDEX | TO | SWEDENBORG'S | ARCANA CŒLESTIA, | OR | HEAVENLY MYSTERIES, | CONTAINED IN THE | HOLY SCRIPTURE. | VOLUME II.—N TO Z. | LONDON: | PUBLISHED BY THE SWEDENBORG SOCIETY, | (INSTITUTED 1810,) | 36 BLOOMSBURY STREET, W.C. | 1865.>>
verso: <<LONDON: MITCHELL AND HUGHES, PRINTERS, | WARDOUR STREET, W.>>
half title: <<INDEX | OF | WORDS, NAMES, AND SUBJECTS | CONTAINED IN THE | ARCANA CŒLESTIA.>>
8vo
half title and title leaves, 4 pp; Main subdivisions of the text, pp v-xxiv; Index of Words, etc, pp 1-599; Index to Bible passages, pp 601-687.
Photographic replica reprint of En 4/2, published by Kessinger Publishing, Whitefish MT.
Copy not seen; description deduced from En 4/2 and publisher's advertisement.

ENGLISH EXTRACTS

X 49/02/En 1816/1 **1816** Hyde 955, 1799
<<Article 'Word', from the Index to the ARCANA CŒLESTIA.>>
18mo
title and text, pp 1-19.
Appended to *The Doctrine of the New Jerusalem concerning the Sacred Scripture* <63/03/En 1/7 = Hyde 1799> Philadelphia.
Copy not seen; description recorded from Hyde 955.

FRENCH

49/02/Fr 1/1 **1858** Hyde 952
INDEX | DES MOTS, DES NOMS ET DES CHOSES | contenus dans les | ARCANES CÉLESTES | <short rule> | OUVRAGE POSTHUME | D'EMMANUEL SWEDENBORG | TRADUIT DU LATIN | PAR J.-F.-E. LE BOYS DES GUAYS | Sur l'Édition de Londres (1815). | <short rule> | SAINT-AMAND, (CHER), | A la librairie de *LA NOUVELLE JÉRUSALEM*, chez PORTE, Libraire. | PARIS, | M. MINOT, rue du Four-St-Germain, 40. | TREUTTEL et WURTZ, Libraires, rue de Lille, 17. | LONDRES, | SWEDENBORG SOCIETY, 36 Bloomsbury Street, Oxford Street. | <short rule> | 1858.
half title: INDEX | DES | ARCANES CÉLESTES
verso: <short rule> | SAINT-AMAND-MONT-ROND (CHER), | IMPRIMERIE DE DESTENAY, RUE LAFAYETTE, 70, | Place Mont-Rond. | <short rule>
8vo
half title and title leaves, 4 pp; Observations du Traducteur <Translator's remarks>, pp i-iv; text, pp 1-399; Errata, p 399; Tables des erreurs typographiques de l'édition latine <Table of

typographical errors in the Latin edition>, pp 400-406; Errata supplémentaire <Supplementary errata>, pp 406-408.
UK: SOC; NET: GEN; USA: SHS

49/02/Fr 1/2 **1863** Hyde 953
INDEX MÉTHODIQUE | OU | TABLE | ALPHABÉTIQUE ET ANALYTIQUE | DE CE QUI EST CONTENU DANS LES | ARCANES CÉLESTES D'EM. SWEDENBORG | PAR | J.-F.-E. LE BOYS DES GUAYS | <short rule> | TOME PREMIER | A—K. | <short rule> | SAINT-AMAND (CHER) | A la Librairie de LA NOUVELLE JÉRUSALEM, chez Porte, libraire. | PARIS | M. MINOT, rue Monsieur-le-Prince, 58. | E. JUNG-TREUTTEL, Libraire, rue de Lille, 19. | LONDRES | Swedenborg Society, 36, Bloomsbury street, Oxford street. | NEW-YORK | New Church Book-Room, 346, Broadway. | <short rule> | 1863
half title: INDEX MÈTHODIQUE | DES | ARCANES CÉLESTES
verso: <short rule> | SAINT-AMAND-MONT-ROND (CHER) | IMPRIMERIE DE DESTENAY, RUE LAFAYETTE, 70. | Place Mont-Rond. | <short rule>
8vo
half title and title leaves, 4 pp; Préface, pp i-iv; text, pp 1-519.
UK: SOC; NET: GEN; USA: SHS

49/02/Fr 1/3 **1864** Hyde 954
INDEX MÉTHODIQUE | OU | TABLE | ALPHABÉTIQUE ET ANALYTIQUE | DE CE QUI EST CONTENU DANS LES | ARCANES CÉLESTES D'EM. SWEDENBORG | PAR | J.-F.-E. LE BOYS DES GUAYS. | <short rule> | TOME DEUXIÈME. | L—Z. | <short rule> | SAINT-AMAND (CHER) | A la Librairie de LA NOUVELLE JÉRUSALEM, chez Porte, libraire. | PARIS | M. MINOT, rue Monsieur-le-Prince, 58. | E. JUNG-TREUTTEL, Libraire, rue de Lille, 19. | LONDRES | Swedenborg Society, 36, Bloomsbury street, Oxford street. | NEW-YORK | New Church Book-Room, 346, Broadway. | <short rule> | 1864
half title: INDEX MÈTHODIQUE | DES | ARCANES CÉLESTES
verso: <short rule> | SAINT-AMAND-MONT-ROND (CHER) | IMPRIMERIE DE DESTENAY, RUE LAFAYETTE, 70. | Place Mont-Rond. | <short rule>
8vo
half title and title leaves, 4 pp; text, pp 1-519; Errata, p 519; Note, 1 p.
UK: SOC; NET: GEN; USA: SHS

GERMAN

49/02/Ge 1/1 **1997** Hyde —
EMANUEL SWEDENBORG | HIMMLISCHE | GEHEIMNISSE | IM WORTE GOTTES | DIE NUN ENTHÜLLT SIND | STICHWORTREGISTER UND BIBELSTELLEN-INDEX | SWEDENBORG-VERLAG ZÜRICH
verso: *Arcana Coelestia* | QUAE IN | *SCRIPTURA SACRA,* | SEU | *VERBO DOMONI* | SUNT, DETECTA: | Hic Primum quae in | *GENESI.* | © 1997 by Swedenborg-Verlag Zürich | Satz und Herstellung: Swedenborg-Verlag Zürich | Umschlaggestaltung: Johannes Horn | ISBN: 3 - 85927 - 084 - 2 <*stet* DOMONI>
half title: HIMMLISCHE GEHEIMNISSE | nunc | <orn 2 x 12 mm> | licet
8vo
half title and title leaves, 4 pp; Vorwort <Foreword>, p 5; Stichwortregister <Keyword index>, pp 7-119; Bibelstellen-Index <Index to Bible passages cited>, pp 121-305.
Edited by F Horn.
GER: VER, WLB

49/02/Ge 1/2 **1998** Hyde —

EMANUEL SWEDENBORG | HIMMLISCHE | GEHEIMNISSE | IM WORTE GOTTES | DIE NUN ENTHÜLLT SIND | STICHWORTREGISTER UND BIBELSTELLEN-INDEX | SWEDENBORG-VERLAG ZÜRICH

verso: *Arcana Coelestia* | QUAE IN | *SCRIPTURA SACRA,* | SEU | *VERBO DOMINI* | SUNT, DETECTA: | Hic Primum quae in | *GENESI.* | © 1998 by Swedenborg-Verlag Zürich | Satz und Herstellung: Swedenborg-Verlag Zürich | Umschlaggestaltung: Johannes Horn | Einband: Ehe GmbH, Radolfzell | ISBN: 3 - 85927 - 265 - 9

half title: DIE HIMMLISCHE GEHEIMNISSE | nunc | <orn 2 x 12 mm> | licet

8vo

half title and title leaves, 4 pp; Vorwort <Foreword>, p 5; Stichwortregister <Keyword index>, pp 7-119; Bibelstellen-Index <Index to Bible passages cited>, pp 121-305.

Reprint of Ge 1/1.

GER: VER, WLB; SWE: ROY; SWI: ZÜR

50/01 On Influx Hyde CXXXIXa

The MS article is to be found on the flyleaf of Swedenborg's copy of J Swammerdam's *Biblia Naturae*. Though the text includes the statement 'anno 1750' <written in the year 1750>, it ends with references to *De Coelo et ejus Mirabilibus et de Inferno* published in 1758.

In a letter to A von Höpken dated 10 April 1760, Swedenborg stated that he was sending his copy of Swammerdam's book as a gift, 'Den boken tienar mig hädanefter intet mehra till nytta, emedan jag wendt mina tanckar ifrån Naturalia till Spiritualia.' <This book will be of no use to me hereafter for I have turned my thoughts from natural things to spiritual.>

LATIN

50/01/La O/1 **1750** Hyde —
<< <untitled> >>
folio
text, 1 p.
In 1877 R L Tafel recorded that the book containing this note was in the possession of Dr Lovén of the Carolinska Institut in Stockholm; it is now in the Library of SWE: KVA.
Unpublished copies have been recorded as follows.

1 UK: SOC A MS transcript made by J G Dufty c 1930. <Documents file 512>

2 USA: ANC A photolithographic reproduction, 1 p, and a typed transcript <which has many mistakes and does not contain all of Swedenborg's marginal additions>, 1 p. <ACSD n 758>.

3 UK: SOC & USA: ANC, SHS A reproduction of <2> on microfilm 32, Bryn Athyn PA

MS not seen; description quoted from R L Tafel *Documents* 2:2 p 750 <**E:b** En 1877/2> London.
SWE: KVA

ENGLISH

Translators:
En 1 R L Tafel
En 2 J Whitehead

50/01/En 1/1, **E:b** En 1877/2 **1877** Hyde 3276
SWEDENBORG'S THOUGHTS ON READING | SWAMMERDAM'S "BIBLIA NATURÆ."
royal 8vo
title and text, p 750.

Translated by R L Tafel, published in *Documents* 2:2 <**E:b** En 1877/2 = Hyde 3276> London.
An unpublished copy has been recorded as follows.

1 USA: ANC A typed transcript in ACSD n 758.

UK: SOC, CON, NCC, PUR, WIL, NR; GER: GSU; NET: GEN; SWE: SUB, UPP; USA: ANC, SHS; AUS: SYD

50/01/En 1/2, **E:b** En 1890/2 **1890** Hyde 3276/a
SWEDENBORG'S THOUGHTS ON READING | SWAMMERDAM'S "BIBLIA NATURÆ."
royal 8vo
title and text, p 750.
Reprint of En 1/1, published in *Documents* 3 <**E:b** En 1890/2 = Hyde 3276/a> London.
UK: SOC, BL; SWE: UPP; USA: SHS

50/01/En 2/1, **D** En 1914/1 **1914** Hyde 3118/2
INFLUX.
8vo
title and text, p 603.
Edited and translated by J Whitehead, published in *Posthumous Theological Works* 1 <**D** En 1914/1> New York.
UK: SOC, CON, PUR, NR; NET: GEN; USA: ANC, SHS

50/01/En 2/2, **D** En 1928/2 **1928** Hyde 3118/4
INFLUX.
8vo
title and text, p 603.
Reprinted from En 2/1, published in *Posthumous Theological Works* 1 <**D** En 1928/2> New York.
UK: SOC, NCC; NET: GEN, KB; SWE: ROY; USA: ANC, SHS

50/01/En 2/3, **D** En 1947/1 **1947** Hyde 3118/–
<<INFLUX.>>
8vo
title and text, p 603.
Reprinted from En 2/2 published in *Posthumous Theological Works* 1 <**D** En 1947/1> New York.
Copy not seen; description deduced from En 2/2 and catalogue of USA: SHS.
USA: SHS

50/01/En 2/4, **D** En 1951/1 **1951** Hyde 3118/–
INFLUX.
8vo
title and text, p 603.
The same as En 2/3, published in *Posthumous Theological Works* 1 <**D** En 1951/1> New York.
USA: ANC, SHS

50/01/En 2/5, **D** En 1954/1 **1954** Hyde 3118/–
INFLUX.
8vo
title and text, p 603.
The same as En 2/4, published in *Posthumous Theological Works* 1 <**D** En 1954/1> New York.
USA: ANC, SHS

50/01/En 2/6, **D** En 1956/1 **1956** Hyde 3118/–
INFLUX.
8vo
title and text, p 603.
The same as En 2/5, published in *Posthumous Theological Works* 1 <**D** En 1956/1> New York.
USA: ANC

50/01/En 2/7, **D** En 1961/1 **1961** Hyde 3118/–
INFLUX.
8vo
title and text, p 603.
The same as En 2/6, published in *Posthumous Theological Works* 1 <**D** En 1961/1> New York.
NET: GEN; SWE: UPP

50/01/En 2/8, **D** En 1969/1 **1969** Hyde 3118/–
INFLUX.
8vo
title and text, p 603.
The same as En 2/7, published in *Posthumous Theological Works* 1 <**D** En 1969/1> New York.
UK: PUR; USA: ANC; AUS: SYD; SA: MMC

50/01/En 2/9, **D** En 1972/1 **1972** Hyde 3118/–
INFLUX.
8vo
title and text, p 603.
The same as En 2/8, published in *Posthumous Theological Works* 1 <**D** En 1972/1> New York.
USA: ANC

50/01/En 2/10, **D** En 1978/1 **1978** Hyde 3118/–
INFLUX.
8vo
title and text, p 603.
The same as En 2/9, published in *Posthumous Theological Works* 1 <**D** En 1978/1> New York.
UK: NCC; USA: ANC, SHS

50/01/En 2/11, **D** En 1996/2 **1996** Hyde 3118/8
Influx
8vo
title and text, p 607.
Revision of En 2/1, edited by W R Woofenden, published in *Posthumous Theological Works* 2 <**D** En 1996/2 = Hyde 3118/8> West Chester PA.
UK: SOC, NR; SWE: ROY; USA: ANC, SHS

50/01/En 1/3, **E:b** En 2000/3 **2000** Hyde 3276/–
<<SWEDENBORG'S THOUGHTS ON READING | SWAMMERDAM'S "BIBLIA NATURÆ.">>
8vo
title and text, p 750.
Photographic replica reprint of En 1/1, published in *Documents* 2:2 <**E:b** En 2000/3> by

Adamant Media Corporation, New York.
Copy not seen; description deduced from En 1/1 and publisher's advertisement.

50/01/En 1/4, **E:b** En 2004/3 **2004** Hyde 3276/–
SWEDENBORG'S THOUGHTS ON READING | SWAMMERDAM'S "BIBLIA NATURÆ."
8vo
title and text, p 750.
Photographic replica reprint of En 1/1, published in *Documents* 2:2 <**E:b** En 2004/3> by Kessinger Publishing, Whitefish MT.
UK: NR

52/01 Almanac for 1752 Hyde CXLIa

The original printed Almanac, with interleaved blank pages on which Swedenborg wrote notes, is in the Royal Library, Stockholm. In *The Swedenborg Epic* <Hyde 3336/24, p 240> C O Sigstedt stated that the margins are filled with notes, most of which are Swedenborg's records of sending pages of the MS of *Arcana Caelestia* to the printer in London. Each time he noted the last few words on the page, for example:

> To John Lewis, p. 205, 206, 207, 208 in number 4700
> Ecclesia, non autem apud illos qui

On the verso of the interleaved pages Swedenborg made notes concerning what he planted in his garden on Hornsgatan.

On the inside of the front cover there is a note in the handwriting of G E Klemming which states that the Almanac was given to the Royal Library by N Wikström on 9 May 1881, and that he had bought it for 216 crowns from the heirs of M J Crusenstolpe.

SWEDISH

Editions:

Sw O MS
Sw 1 A H Stroh, editor

52/01/Sw O/1 **1752** Hyde —

<<**Almanach** | **För Skott-året,** | **Efter wår Fråſtares Jesu Christi** | **Födelſe,** | 1752, | **Til** STOCKHOLMS Horizont, | **Beſägen** 59 grad. 20 min. **Norr-om** Æquatoren | **och** 2 **tids** min. **Öster om** Upsala Observatorium: | **Utgifwen** | **Af Des Wetenskaps Academie.** | <orn 20 x 44 mm> | <rule> | Exemplaret **fåſjes håstat och skurit för 6 öre Kopp:mt.** | <rule> | **STOCKHOLM** | **Tryckt hos** LARS SALVIUS.>>

32mo

text: written on 24 interleaved pp and the insides of the front and back covers. <A H Stroh *Abridged Chronological List* Uppsala and Stockholm 1910, Hyde 3276/1>

Unpublished copies have been recorded as follows.

1 UK: SOC A MS transcript made by J G Dufty c 1930. <Documents file 519>

2 UK: SOC A photographic reproduction of the individual pp of Sw O/1; title and text, 22 pp. <Archives D/111>

Copy not seen; description deduced from <UK: SOC Archives D/111>.

SWE: ROY

52/01/Sw 1/1 **1903** Hyde —
<<Anteckningar i Swedenborgs Almanacka för 1752, förvarad å Kungl. Biblioteket i Stockholm>>
16mo
text: pp –.
Reproduction by A H Stroh in book form, published in Stockholm.
Copy not seen; description recorded from online catalogue of SWE: ROY. See also USA: ANC <S10/A L6>.
SWE: ROY, GSB; USA: ANC

SWEDISH EXTRACTS

X 52/01/Sw 1998/1 **1998** Hyde —
<untitled>
8vo
text: p 282.
Photographic reproduction of page of Sw 0/1, with text quoted in caption, edited by L Bergquist, published in *Swedenborgs Hemlighet* Stockholm.
UK: SOC; USA: ANC

SWEDISH/ENGLISH

52/01/SwEn 1/1 **no date** Hyde —
<<Swedenborg's Almanac for 1752 with annotations>>
32mo
Swedish: A photographic reproduction of the interleaved pages and the insides of the front and back covers, 39 sheets <USA: ANC L.II; 34>.
English: translation by Märta Perssons, 2 pp.
The Swedish portion appears to be a reproduction of all of Swedenborg's notes; the English text is entitled 'Translation of the Annotations concerning Swedenborg's Garden contained in the above-mentioned Almanac'.
Unpublished copies have been recorded as follows.
1 UK: SOC & USA: ANC, SHS A photographic reproduction on microfilm 32, Bryn Athyn PA.
Copy not seen; description recorded from ACSD, Bryn Athyn PA.
USA: ANC

ENGLISH EXTRACTS

X 52/01/En 1904 /1 **1904** Hyde —
<untitled>
8vo
text, p 683.
Translated by A Acton, quoted in *New Church Life* Bryn Athyn PA.
UK: SOC, NCC; USA: ANC

X 52/01/En 1/1 **1915** Hyde —
ANNOTATIONS CONCERNING SWEDENBORG'S GARDEN | CONTAINED IN HIS ALMANAC FOR THE YEAR 1752.
4to
title and text, pp 211-212.
Translated by C L Odhner <later Sigstedt>, published in *The New Church Weekly* London.
UK: SOC, CON

X 52/01/En 1923/1 **1923** Hyde —
Swedenborg's Hobby.
8vo
text: pp 65-72.
Quotations from Swedenborg's gardening notes in the *Almanac* with a quotation from the Introduction to *The Worship and Love of God,* in an article by C L Odhner <later Sigstedt>, published in *New Church Life* Bryn Athyn PA.
UK: SOC, NCC; USA: ANC

X 52/01/En 1952/1 **1952** Hyde 3336/24
<untitled>
8vo
text: pp 240-241.
Edited by C O Sigstedt, published in *The Swedenborg Epic* New York <Hyde 3336/24>.
UK: SOC, BOD, CON, NCC, NR; NET: GEN; USA: ANC, SHS

X 52/01/En 1981/1 **1981** Hyde 3336/–
<untitled>
8vo
text: pp 240-241.
Reprint of En 1952/1, London.
UK: SOC, NR; NET: GEN; USA: SHS

X 52/01/En 2005/1 **2005** Hyde —
<untitled>
8vo
text: p 240.
Photographic reproduction of page of Sw O/1, with English translation of text quoted in caption, edited by L Bergquist <X Sw 1998/1>, published in *Swedenborg's Secret* London.
UK: SOC, CON, NCC, NR; NET: GEN; SWE: ROY; USA: ANC

DUTCH EXTRACTS

X 52/01/Du 2005/1 **2005** Hyde —
<untitled>
A3 folded to A4
text, p 20.
Translation by G Janssens of X En 1952/1, published in *Swedenborgiana* editie 51, Baarle Nassau.
UK: SOC, NR; NET: BOE, GEN; USA: ANC

55/01 Memorandum on the Liquor Trade in Sweden Hyde CXLII

The autograph MS, a fragment of Swedenborg's original memorandum, is bound in the volume of *Riksdagsskrifter* which forms Codex 56 in the Library of the Royal Swedish Academy of Sciences, Stockholm. The fragment is signed 'Em. Swedenborg' and is dated Stockholm, 3 November 1755; it is not known whether the complete memorandum was presented to the Diet.

This very rough draft of part of the memorandum proposes that the distillation of alcoholic spirits should be rented out to the highest bidders in each town and judicial district. In *Documents* 1 p 493 <**E:b** En 1875/1 = Hyde 3274> R L Tafel stated that Swedenborg 'wrote on the fly-leaf of one of his theological MSS.: "The immoderate use of spirituous liquors will be the downfall of the Swedish people."' Tafel does not say which MS this is. See A Acton *Letters and Memorials* 2, pp 519-520 <**E:b** En 1955/1 = Hyde 3276/6> for information concerning the Swedish government's attempts to ban the distillation of alcoholic spirits.

See also 60/01 = Hyde CLII, in which Swedenborg returned to this subject in the final part of his memorandum to the Diet dated 17 November 1760.

SWEDISH

55/01/Sw 0/1 **1755** Hyde 935

<<Ödmjukt Memorial.>>

foolscap folio <343 x 194 mm>, folded lengthwise to form 4 pp

text, pp 7a-7b <the first 2 pp of the folded sheet>.

Unpublished copies have been recorded as follows.

1 USA: ANC A MS transcript made by R L Tafel in preparation for his publication of En 1/1 in *Documents* 1, London. <**E:b** En 1875/1 = Hyde 3274>

2 UK: SOC A MS transcript made c 1930 by J G Dufty. <Documents file 523>

3 UK: SOC & USA: ANC, SHS A reproduction of R L Tafel's transcript on microfilm 18 made in Bryn Athyn PA.

4 USA: ANC A typed copy of R L Tafel's transcript. <ACSD n 764>

Copy not seen; description deduced from Sw 0/2.

SWE: KVA

55/01/Sw 0/2 **1927** Hyde 935/1, 3038/29

Ödmjukt Memorial.

folio

title and text, pp 7a-7b.

Photographic reproduction of Sw 0/1, published in *Autographo Editio Photostata* vol 8 <Hyde 3038/29> Bryn Athyn PA.
Unpublished copies have been recorded as follows.
1 UK: soc & USA: ANC, SHS A reproduction on microfilm 22 made in 1962, Bryn Athyn PA.
UK: soc; USA: ANC

ENGLISH

Translators:
En 1 R L Tafel
En 2 A Acton

55/01/En 1/1, **E:b** En 1875/1 **1875** Hyde 936, 3274
FRAGMENT OF A MEMORIAL BY SWEDENBORG | TO THE HOUSES OF THE SWEDISH DIET IN | 1755, PRINCIPALLY RESPECTING THE | LIQUOR TRAFFIC.
royal 8vo
title, editorial notes, and text, pp 493-495.
Edited and translated by R L Tafel, published in *Documents* 1 <**E:b** En 1875/1 = Hyde 3274> London.
UK: soc, CON, NCC, PUR, WIL, NR; GER: GSU; NET: GEN; SWE: SUB, UPP; USA: ANC, SHS; AUS: SYD

55/01/En 2/1, **E:b** En 1955/1 **1955** Hyde 936/1, 3276/6
[MEMORIAL]
8vo
title and text, p 519.
Edited and translated by A Acton, published in *Letters and Memorials* 2 <**E:b** En 1955/1 = Hyde 3276/6> Bryn Athyn PA.
UK: soc, CON, NCC, PUR, NR; SWE: ROY, UPP; USA: ANC, SHS; AUS: SYD

55/01/En 1/2, **E:b** En 2000/1 **2000** Hyde 3276/–
<<FRAGMENT OF A MEMORIAL BY SWEDENBORG | TO THE HOUSES OF THE SWEDISH DIET IN | 1755, PRINCIPALLY RESPECTING THE | LIQUOR TRAFFIC.>>
8vo
title, editorial notes, and text, pp 493-495.
Photographic replica reprint of En 1/1, published in *Documents* 1 <**E:b** En 2000/1> by Adamant Media Corporation, New York.
Copy not seen; description deduced from En 1/1 and publisher's advertisement.

55/01/En 1/3, **E:b** En 2004/1 **2004** Hyde 3276/–
FRAGMENT OF A MEMORIAL BY SWEDENBORG | TO THE HOUSES OF THE SWEDISH DIET IN | 1755, PRINCIPALLY RESPECTING THE | LIQUOR TRAFFIC.
8vo
title, editorial notes, and text, pp 493-495.
Photographic replica reprint of En 1/1, published in *Documents* 1 <**E:b** En 2004/1> by Kessinger Publishing, Whitefish MT.
UK: NR

55/01/En 2/2, **E:b** En 2009/2 **2009** Hyde 3276/–
[MEMORIAL]

8vo
title and text, p 519.
Photographic replica reprint of En 2/1, published in *Letters and Memorials* 2 <**E:b** En 2009/2>
Bryn Athyn PA.
UK: SOC; USA: ANC